Writing and Reading Across the Curriculum

Tenth Edition

Laurence Behrens
University of California
Santa Barbara

Leonard J. Rosen
Bentley College

PEARSON
Longman

New York • San Francisco • Boston
London • Toronto • Sydney • Tokyo • Singapore • Madrid
Mexico City • Munich • Paris • Cape Town • Hong Kong • Montreal

Senior Sponsoring Editor: Virginia L. Blanford
Senior Supplements Editor: Donna Campion
Media Supplements Editor: Jenna Egan
Senior Marketing Manager: Sandra McGuire
Production Manager: Eric Jorgensen
Project Coordination, Text Design, and Electronic Page Makeup: Elm Street Publishing Services, Inc.
Cover Designer/Manager: Wendy Ann Fredricks
Designer: Nancy Sacks
Photo Researcher: Julie Tesser
Senior Manufacturing Buyer: Alfred C. Dorsey
Printer and Binder: Courier Corporation
Cover Printer: Courier Corporation

For permission to use copyrighted material, grateful acknowledgment is made to the copyright holders on pp. 835–839, which are hereby made part of this copyright page.

Library of Congress Cataloging-in-Publication Data

Behrens, Laurence.
    Writing and reading across the curriculum/Laurence Behrens, Leonard J. Rosen.—10th ed.
      p. cm.
    Includes bibliographical references and index.
    ISBN 0-321-48643-9
    ISBN 13 978-0-321-48643-1
      1. College readers. 2. Interdisciplinary approach in education—Problems, exercises, etc.
    3. English language—Rhetoric—Problems, exercises, etc. 4. Academic writing—Problems, exercises, etc. I. Rosen, Leonard J. II. Title.
PE1417.B396 2007b
808'.0427—dc22
                                        2006051528

Please visit us at www.ablongman.com/behrens

ISBN 0-321-48643-9
ISBN 13 978-0-321-48643-1

2 3 4 5 6 7 8 9 10—CRS—10 09 08 07

Detailed Contents

Chapter 5
Argument Synthesis   146

Chapter 6
Analysis   190

Chapter 7
Practicing Academic Writing   210

PART II
AN ANTHOLOGY OF READINGS   239

SOCIOLOGY
Chapter 8
Marriage and Family in America   241

PSYCHOLOGY
Chapter 9
Obedience to Authority   349

BIOLOGY
Chapter 11
To Sleep   **501**

Preface

With this tenth edition, *Writing and Reading Across the Curriculum* reaches a milestone: its twenty-fifth year in print. When *WRAC* was first published in 1982, it was—viewed from one angle—an experiment. We hoped to prove our hypothesis that both students and teachers would respond favorably to a composition reader organized by the kinds of specific topics that were typically studied in general education courses.

The response was both immediate and enthusiastic. Instructors found the topics in that first edition of *WRAC* both interesting and teachable, and students appreciated the links that such topics suggested to the courses they were taking concurrently in the humanities, the social sciences, and the sciences. Readers also told us how practical they found our "summary, synthesis, and critique" approach to writing college-level papers. Instructors, and students as well, welcomed the addition of "analysis" to our coverage in Part I of the ninth edition.

In the present edition, we add a new chapter, "Practicing Academic Writing," to Part I of the text, providing students the opportunity to use the skills they have learned in summary, critique, synthesis, and analysis to write a sequence of brief papers that lead to a fully developed, source-based argument.

In developing each edition of *WRAC*, we have been guided by the same principle: to retain the essential multidisciplinary character of the text while providing ample new topics and individual readings to keep it fresh and timely. Some topics have proven particularly enduring—our "Cinderella" and "Obedience" chapters have been fixtures of *WRAC* since the first edition. But we take care to make sure that at least a third of the book is completely new every time, both by extensively revising existing chapters and by creating new ones. Over ten editions, our discussion of rhetoric has expanded to seven chapters. While we have retained an emphasis on summary, critique, and synthesis—and now, analysis—we continue to develop content on such issues as the process of writing and argumentation that addresses the issues and interests of today's classrooms.

STRUCTURE

Like its predecessors, the tenth edition of *Writing and Reading Across the Curriculum* is divided into two parts. The first part introduces the strategies of summary, critique, synthesis, and analysis. We take students step-by-step through the process of writing papers based on source material, explaining and demonstrating how summaries, critiques, syntheses, and analyses can be generated from the kinds of readings students will encounter later in the book—and throughout their academic careers. The second part of the text consists of a series of subject chapters drawn from both academic and professional disciplines. Each subject is not only interesting in its own right but is also representative of the kinds of topics typically studied during the course of an undergraduate education. We also believe that students and teachers will discover connections among the thematic chapters of this edition that further enhance opportunities for writing, discussion, and inquiry.

CONTINUED FOCUS ON ARGUMENTATION

Part I of *Writing and Reading Across the Curriculum* is designed to prepare students for college-level assignments across the disciplines. The tenth edition continues the previous edition's strengthened emphasis on the writing process and on argument, in particular. In treating argument, we emphasize the following:

- **The Elements of Argument: Claim, Support, Assumption.** This section adapts the Toulmin approach to argument to the kinds of readings that students will encounter in Part II of the text.

- **The Three Appeals of Argument:** *Logos, Ethos, Pathos.* This discussion may be used to analyze and develop arguments in the readings that students will encounter in Part II of the book.

- **Developing and Organizing the Support for Your Arguments.** This section helps students to mine source materials for facts, expert opinions, and examples that will support their arguments.

- **Annotated Student Argument Paper.** A sample student paper highlights and discusses argumentative strategies that a student writer uses in drafting and developing a paper.

PART I: NEW APPARATUS, TOPICS, READINGS, AND STUDENT PAPERS

Chapter 1: Summary, Paraphrase, and Quotation

As in the previous edition, students are taken through the process of writing a summary of Barbara Graham's "The Future of Love: Kiss Romance Goodbye, It's Time for the Real Thing." We demonstrate how to annotate a source and divide it into sections, how to develop a thesis, and how to write and smoothly join section summaries. We also explain how to summarize narratives, illustrating our discussion with a summary of a new selection, Bruce Chatwin's "Dreams of Patagonia." And, as in previous editions, students learn how to

- summarize figures and tables;
- paraphrase sources;
- quote sources.

Chapter 2: Critical Reading and Critique

Chapter 2 offers a new model critique on "We Are Not Created Equal in Every Way" by Joan Ryan, an op-ed piece that takes a strong view of parents who push their children, at an early age, to become professional dancers and athletes. As in earlier editions, the critique section follows a set of guidelines for practicing critical reading.

Chapter 4: Explanatory Synthesis

Chapter 4 features a new model synthesis: Several brief selections on the topic of alternative energy vehicles precede discussion of the planning and writing of a student paper, "The Car of the Future?" The first draft is accompanied by detailed instructor comments and guides to revision.

Chapter 5: Argument Synthesis

Chapter 5 provides an argument synthesis, "Keeping Volunteerism Voluntary," along with summaries and excerpts of several source materials for that paper. The argument synthesizes opinion pieces by various advocates and opponents of national service. The chapter concludes with a new example comparison-contrast synthesis, framed as a response to an exam question on World War I and World War II.

Chapter 7: Practicing Academic Writing

In this new chapter, students are encouraged to practice the skills they have learned in writing summaries, critiques, syntheses, and analyses by working with a set of readings and a series of carefully sequenced assignments that build toward an argument on the controversial practice of "legacy" admissions—the granting of preferential treatment in the admissions process to the sons and daughters of college alumni. This practice chapter replaces the research chapter, the contents of which, as instructors have told us, are readily available in handbooks commonly assigned in tandem with *WRAC*. For quick reference, as an aid to helping students cite the sources they use in writing syntheses, we provide brief guides to basic MLA and APA citation formats. See the pages 846–849 of *WRAC* for these two, facing-page treatments.

PART II: NEW THEMATIC CHAPTERS

As in earlier editions, Part II of *Writing and Reading Across the Curriculum* provides students with opportunities to practice the skills of summary, synthesis, critique—and now analysis—that they have learned in Part I. We have prepared two new chapters for the tenth edition of *WRAC*.

Chapter 8: Marriage and Family in America

Definitions of marriage and family, husband and wife, mother and father are changing before our eyes. A once-stable (or so we thought) institution seems under attack—an unusually fertile context in which to offer a chapter on "Marriage and Family in America." The chapter pivots on the work of marriage scholars like historian Stephanie Coontz and sociologist David Popenoe. Other selections, such as those by Hope Edelman and Eric Bartels, offer personal, often charged accounts of marriage from the inside. Students will follow the debate over gay marriage; they will also examine two ongoing controversies concerning working mothers versus stay-at-home mothers (often referred to as "the Mommy Wars") and the so-called "stalled revolution"—the feminist complaint that, in an age of working women, men have not shouldered their share of household work. We've selected readings that will challenge student assumptions and produce writing informed not only by the provocative and sometimes emotionally raw views of chapter authors but also by their own personal experiences. For each of our students has direct experience with marriage and family—some positive, some not; and each, we believe, can bring the authority of that experience to bear in mature, college-level writing.

Chapter 11: To Sleep

Sleep is the most common and, until recently, one of the least understood of human behaviors. Annually, tens of millions of dollars fund basic research on sleep; but experts do not yet know precisely *why* we sleep. This chapter gathers the work of biologists, neurologists, psychologists, and journalists who specialize in science writing to investigate what one author in this chapter terms a "state so familiar yet so strange." Students will read an overview of sleep and an introduction to the physiology of sleep before moving on to the principal focus of the chapter: the sleep of adolescents—particularly, of college-age adolescents. Various researchers report on the state of adolescent sleep (generally insufficient) and the causes and consequences of and potential solutions to adolescent sleep debt. The chapter concludes with a cluster of readings on the medicalization of sleep, which provides an occasion to study differing interpretations of identical data. Quite aside from providing an insight into the science of sleep, this chapter serves a practical function: to educate college students on the mechanics and dangers of sleep debt. Even for those not intending a career in the sciences, learning what happens cognitively and physically when we deprive ourselves of sleep should make for fascinating reading—and create ample opportunities to practice college-level writing.

PART II: REVISED THEMATIC CHAPTERS

Five anthology chapters are carried over from the ninth edition; many of the reading selections for each are new to this edition.

Chapter 9: Obedience to Authority

The Obedience chapter continues to build on the profoundly disturbing Milgram experiments. Other selections in this chapter, such as Philip Zimbardo's account of his Stanford prison experiment and Solomon Asch's "Opinions and Social Pressure," have provided additional perspectives on the significance of the obedience phenomenon. This edition adds two new selections. In "Uncivil Disobedience," James J. Lopach and Jean A. Luckowski closely examine radical environmental groups and others who engage in planned disobedience. They find that such groups and individuals often fail to meet the standards of such former practitioners of civil disobedience as Socrates, Gandhi, and Martin Luther King, Jr. And making a return engagement from the first edition of *WRAC*, a key section from Jean Anouilh's play *Antigone* presents a classic confrontation between authority and individual conscience.

Chapter 10: What's Happening at the Mall?

In this chapter we gather the work of historians, an urban planner, a geographer, a sociologist, a theologian, an American studies scholar, and cultural critics to investigate a fixture on the American landscape: the shopping mall. Malls are not only ubiquitous (48,695 of them as of 2005); they stand at the confluence of streams in American myth, race, class, business, gender, law, and design. As James Farrell, one of the authors in this chapter, puts it: Malls are "a place where we answer important questions: What does it mean to be human? What are people for? What is the meaning of things? Why do we work? What do we work for?" What's happening at the mall, it turns out, is far from obvious. New to this edition: historian Kenneth Jackson's "A Brief History of Malls"; literary and cultural critic Richard K. Simon's "The Mall as Walled Garden"; theologian Jon Pahl's exploration of "The Mall as Sacred Space"; and cultural commentator Virginia Postrel's "The Mall as Setting for Authentic Life." The selections gathered here will challenge students' commonplace views of malls. With this chapter we have tried to make the ordinary a bit strange (malls as religious centers?) and in the process provide ample occasion for thoughtful writing.

Chapter 12: Fairy Tales: A Closer Look at Cinderella

This popular chapter includes variants of "Cinderella" along with the perspectives of a folklorist (Stith Thompson), a psychologist (Bruno Bettelheim), a historian (Bonnie Cullen), a novelist (Judith Rossner), and literary and cultural critics (Elisabeth Panttaja and Patricia J. Williams). New to this edition are two variants of the tale: "The Seven Foals," as rendered by Andrew Lang, which features a "Cinderlad," and an early Neapolitan variant, "The Cat Cinderella." Also new: "My Best White Friend: Cinderella Revisited" by law professor Patricia J. Williams, who explores the extent to which the story resonates for girls and women of color, and a selection by art historian Bonnie Cullen, who explains how Perrault's "Cinderella" came to be regarded as canonical. This chapter develops in students two basic skills: the ability to analyze by applying elements of a theoretical reading to one or more variants of "Cinderella"; and the ability to think and write comparatively by reading multiple versions of the story and by developing criteria by which to clarify similarities and differences.

Chapter 13: New and Improved: Six Decades of Advertising

The centerpiece of this chapter is a portfolio of 42 full-page advertisements for cigarettes, liquor and beer, automobiles, food, and beauty and cleaning products that have appeared in popular American magazines since the mid-1940s. Like genetic markers, advertisements are key indicators not only of our consumerism but also of our changing cultural values, as well as of our less variable human psychology. Students will find this material ideal for practicing their analysis skills. The chapter remains substantially the same as in the ninth edition, with the exception of a new ad for Camel cigarettes replacing the old Virginia Slims ad.

Chapter 14: Has the Jury Reached a Verdict?

This chapter places students in the role of jurors by asking that they apply points of law to facts of a case in order to arrive at a just verdict. Students must argue for their verdict (no prior legal education is necessary), principally by demonstrating the skill of analysis. More broadly, thinking and writing about legal issues are ideal approaches to the principles of effective argument: students must provide support (the facts of the case) for their claim (the verdict), based on relevant assumptions or warrants (the laws). This chapter (previously "You, the Jury") has been substantially revised: most of the cases included are new to this edition. They are arranged into five broad categories: emotional distress, freedom of speech, child custody, homicide, and parental responsibility for the destructive acts of their children. Each case type begins with an overview of the main issues, written for a nonlegal audience. Specific cases follow. Arriving at fair and reasonable verdicts will exercise students' powers of analysis—and appeal to their sense of drama.

ANCILLARIES

Student Supplements

- The *Writing and Reading Across the Curriculum* Companion Website (www.ablongman.com/behrens) includes additional exercises, links, model papers, and many more student resources.

Instructor Supplements

- The *Instructor's Manual* for the tenth edition of *Writing and Reading Across the Curriculum* provides sample syllabi and course calendars, chapter summaries, classroom ideas for writing assignments, introductions to each set of readings, case outcomes for the legal readings, and answers to review questions. Included as well are tips on how to incorporate the textbook's Companion Website into the course material. ISBN 0-321-48399-5.
- The Companion Website (www.ablongman.com/behrens) includes a link to the full *Instructor's Manual* in a password-protected instructor section. The site includes additional exercises, links, model papers, and many more student resources.

ACKNOWLEDGMENTS

We have benefited over the years from the suggestions and insights of many teachers—and students—across the country. We would especially like to thank these reviewers of the tenth edition: David Elias, Eastern Kentucky University; Kathy Ford, Lake Land College; Daven M. Kari, Vanguard University; Lindsay Lewan, Arapahoe Community College; Jolie Martin, San Francisco State Univerisity; Kathy Mendt, Front Range Community College–Larimer Campus; RoseAnn Morgan, Middlesex County College; David Moton, Bakersfield College; Thomas Pfau, Bellevue Community College; Amy Rybak, Bowling Green State University; Horacio Sierra, University of Florida; Deron Walker, California Baptist University.

We would also like to thank the following reviewers for their help in the preparation of past editions: James Allen, College of DuPage; Chris Anson, North Carolina State University; Phillip Arrington, Eastern Michigan University; Anne Bailey, Southeastern Louisiana University; Carolyn Baker, San Antonio College; Bob Brannan, Johnson County Community College; Joy Bashore, Central Virginia Community College; Nancy Blattner, Southeast Missouri State University; Mary Bly, University of California, Davis; Paul Buczkowski, Eastern Michigan University; Jennifer Bullis, Whatcom Community College; Paige Byam, Northern Kentucky University; Susan Callendar, Sinclair Community College; Anne Carr, Southeast Community College; Jeff Carroll, University of Hawaii; Joseph Rocky Colavito, Northwestern State University; Michael Colonnese, Methodist College; James A. Cornette, Christopher Newport University; Timothy Corrigan, Temple University; Kathryn J. Dawson, Ball State University; Cathy Powers Dice, University of Memphis; Kathleen Dooley, Tidewater Community College; Judith Eastman, Orange Coast College; David Elias, Eastern Kentucky University; Susan Boyd English, Kirkwood Community College; Kathy Evertz, University of Wyoming; Bill Gholson, Southern Oregon University; Karen Gordon, Elgin Community College; Deborah Gutschera, College of DuPage; Lila M. Harper, Central Washington University; M. Todd Harper, University of Louisville; Kip Harvigsen, Ricks College; Michael Hogan, Southeast Missouri State University; Sandra M. Jensen, Lane Community College; Anita Johnson, Whatcom Community College; Mark Jones, University of Florida; Jane Kaufman, University of Akron; Rodney Keller, Ricks College; Walt Klarner, Johnson County Community College; Jeffery Klausman, Whatcom Community College; Alison Kuehner, Ohlone College; William B. Lalicker, West Chester University; Dawn Leonard, Charleston Southern University; Clifford L. Lewis, U Mass Lowell; Signee Lynch, Whatcom Community College; Krista L. May, Texas A&M University; Stella Nesanovich, McNeese State University; Roark Mulligan, Christopher Newport University; Joan Mullin, University of Toledo; Susie Paul, Auburn University at Montgomery; Aaron Race, Southern Illinois University–Carbondale; Nancy Redmond, Long Beach City College; Deborah Reese, University of Texas at Arlington; Priscilla Riggle, Bowling Green State University; Jeanette Riley, University of New Mexico; Robert Rongner, Whatcom Community College; Sarah C. Ross, Southeastern Louisiana University; Raul Sanchez, University of Utah; Rebecca Shapiro, Westminster College; Mary Sheldon, Washburn University; Philip Sipiora, University of Southern Florida; Joyce Smoot, Virginia Tech; Bonnie A. Spears, Chaffey College; Bonnie Startt, Tidewater Community

College; R. E. Stratton, University of Alaska–Fairbanks; Katherine M. Thomas, Southeast Community College; Victor Villanueva, Washington State University; Jackie Wheeler, Arizona State University; Pat Stephens Williams, Southern Illinois University at Carbondale; and Kristin Woolever, Northeastern University.

We would also like to acknowledge the invaluable assistance freely rendered to us by many people during and after the preparation of the law-oriented chapter, "Has the Jury Reached a Verdict?" Amy Atchison, an attorney and law librarian at UCLA, provided numerous references, legal texts, and much-needed guidance through the legal research process. David Hricik, professor of law at Mercer University School of Law, also provided useful feedback. Leonard Tourney and Gina Genova, who teach legal writing courses at the University of California at Santa Barbara, provided valuable advice before and during the composition of this chapter. Our gratitude goes also to Lila Harper and her students at Central Washington University; Krista May and her students at Texas A&M University; Erik Peterson and his students at Central Washington University; and Sarah C. Ross and her students at Southeast Louisiana State University, all of whom helped us to field-test this chapter. The intelligent and perceptive comments of both instructors and students helped us make this chapter more focused and user-friendly than it was when they received it.

We gratefully acknowledge the work of Michael Behrens, who made significant contributions to the "Marriage and Family in America" chapter.

A special thanks to Ginny Blanford, Rebecca Gilpin, Beth Keister, and Martha Beyerlein for helping shepherd the manuscript through the editorial and production process. And our continued gratitude to Joe Opiela, longtime friend, supporter, and publisher.

LAURENCE BEHRENS
LEONARD J. ROSEN

A Note to the Student

Your sociology professor asks you to write a paper on attitudes toward the homeless population of an urban area near your campus. You are expected to consult books, articles, Web sites, and other online sources on the subject, and you are also encouraged to conduct surveys and interviews.

Your professor is making a number of assumptions about your capabilities. Among them:

- that you can research and assess the value of relevant sources;
- that you can comprehend college-level material, both print and electronic;
- that you can use theories and principles learned from one set of sources as tools to investigate other sources (or events, people, places, or things);
- that you can synthesize separate but related sources;
- that you can intelligently respond to such material.

In fact, these same assumptions underlie practically all college writing assignments. Your professors will expect you to demonstrate that you can read and understand not only textbooks but also critical articles and books, primary sources, Internet sources, online academic databases, CD-ROMs, and other material related to a particular subject of study. For example: For a paper on the progress of the Human Genome Project, you would probably look to articles and Internet sources for the most recent information. Using an online database, you would find articles on the subject in such print journals as *Nature, Journal of the American Medical Association,* and *Bioscience,* as well as leading newspapers and magazines. A Web search engine might lead you to a useful site called "A New Gene Map of the Human Genome" <http://www.ncbi.nlm.nih.gov/genemap99/> and the site of the "Human Genome Sequencing Department" at the Lawrence Berkeley National Laboratory <http://www-hgc.lbl.gov/>. You would be expected to assess the relevance of such sources to your topic and to draw from them the information and ideas you need. It's even possible that the final product of your research and reading may not be a conventional paper at all, but rather a Website you create that explains the science behind the Human Genome Project, explores a particular controversy about the project, or describes the future benefits geneticists hope to derive from the project.

You might, for a different class, be assigned a research paper on the films of director Martin Scorsese. To get started, you might consult your film studies textbook, biographical sources on Scorsese, and anthologies of criticism. Instructor and peer feedback on a first draft might lead you to articles in both popular magazines (such as *Time*) and scholarly journals (such as *Literature/Film Quarterly*), a CD-ROM database (such as *Film Index International*), and relevant Websites (such as the "Internet Movie Database" <http://us.imdb.com>).

These two example assignments are very different, of course; but the skills you need to work with them are the same. You must be able to research relevant sources. You must be able to read and comprehend these sources. You must be able to perceive the relationships among several pieces of source material. And you must be able to apply your own critical judgments to these various materials.

Writing and Reading Across the Curriculum provides you with the opportunity to practice the essential college-level skills we have just outlined and the forms of writing associated with them, namely:

- the *summary*
- the *critique*
- the *synthesis*
- the *analysis*

Each chapter of Part II of this text represents a subject from a particular area of the academic curriculum: Sociology, Psychology, American Studies, Biology, Folklore, Law, Marketing, and Advertising. These chapters, dealing with such topics as "Marriage and Family in America," "Obedience to Authority," and "What's Happening at the Mall?," illustrate the types of material you will study in your other courses.

Questions following the readings will allow you to practice typical college writing assignments. Review Questions help you recall key points of content. Discussion and Writing Suggestions ask you for personal, sometimes imaginative, responses to the readings. Synthesis Activities at the end of each chapter allow you to practice assignments of the type that are covered in detail in Part I of this book. For instance, you may be asked to *summarize* the Milgram experiment and the reactions to it, or to *compare and contrast* a controlled experiment with a real-life (or fictional) situation. Finally, Research Activities ask you to go beyond the readings in this text in order to conduct your own independent research on these subjects.

In this book, you'll find articles and essays written by physicians, literary critics, sociologists, psychologists, lawyers, folklorists, political scientists, journalists, and specialists from other fields. Our aim is that you become familiar with the various subjects and styles of academic writing and that you come to appreciate the interrelatedness of knowledge. Fairy tales can be studied by literary critics, folklorists, psychologists, and feminists. Human activity and human behavior are classified into separate subjects only for convenience. The novel you read in your literature course may be able to shed some light upon an assigned article for your economics course—and vice versa.

We hope, therefore, that your writing course will serve as a kind of bridge to your other courses and that as a result of this work you will become more skillful at perceiving relationships among diverse topics. Because it involves such critical and widely applicable skills, your writing course may well turn out to be one of the most valuable—and one of the most interesting—of your academic career.

LAURENCE BEHRENS
LEONARD J. ROSEN

How to Write Summaries, Critiques, Syntheses, and Analyses

Summary, Paraphrase, and Quotation

WHAT IS A SUMMARY?

The best way to demonstrate that you understand the information and the ideas in any piece of writing is to compose an accurate and clearly written summary of that piece. By a *summary* we mean a *brief restatement, in your own words, of the content of a passage* (a group of paragraphs, a chapter, an article, a book). This restatement should focus on the *central idea* of the passage. The briefest of summaries (one or two sentences) will do no more than this. A longer, more complete summary will indicate, in condensed form, the main points in the passage that support or explain the central idea. It will reflect the order in which these points are presented and the emphasis given to them. It may even include some important examples from the passage. But it will not include minor details. It will not repeat points simply for the purpose of emphasis. And it will not contain any of your own opinions or conclusions. A good summary, therefore, has three central qualities: *brevity, completeness,* and *objectivity.*

CAN A SUMMARY BE OBJECTIVE?

Of course, the last quality mentioned above, objectivity, might be difficult to achieve in a summary. By definition, writing a summary requires you to select some aspects of the original and leave out others. Since deciding what to select and what to leave out calls for your personal judgment, your summary really is a work of interpretation. And, certainly, your interpretation of a passage may differ from another person's. One factor affecting the nature and quality of your interpretation is your *prior knowledge* of the subject. For example, if you're attempting to summarize an anthropological article and you're a novice in that field, then your summary of the article will likely differ from that of your professor, who has spent 20 years studying this particular area and whose judgment about what is more or less significant is undoubtedly more reliable than your own. By the same token, your personal or professional *frame of reference* may also affect your interpretation. A union representative and a management representative attempting to summarize the latest management offer would probably come up with two very different accounts. Still, we believe that in most cases it's possible to produce a reasonably objective summary of a passage if you make a conscious, good-faith effort to be unbiased and to prevent your own feelings on the subject from distorting your account of the text.

USING THE SUMMARY

In some quarters, the summary has a bad reputation—and with reason. Summaries often are provided by writers as substitutes for analyses. As students, many of us have summarized books that we were supposed to *review critically*. All the same, the summary does have a place in respectable college work. First, writing a summary is an excellent way to understand what you read. This in itself is an important goal of academic study. If you don't understand your source material, chances are you won't be able to refer to it usefully in an essay or research paper. Summaries help you understand what you read because they force you to put the text into your own words. Practice with writing summaries also develops your general writing habits, since a good summary, like any other piece of good writing, is clear, coherent, and accurate.

WHERE DO WE FIND WRITTEN SUMMARIES?

Here are just a few of the types of writing that involve summary:

Academic Writing

- **Critique papers.** Summarize material in order to critique it.
- **Synthesis papers.** Summarize to show relationships between sources.
- **Analysis papers.** Summarize theoretical perspectives before applying them.
- **Research papers.** Note-taking and reporting research require summary.
- **Literature reviews.** Overviews of work presented in brief summaries.
- **Argument papers.** Summarize evidence and opposing arguments.
- **Essay exams.** Demonstrate understanding of course materials through summary.

Workplace Writing

- **Policy briefs.** Condense complex public policy.
- **Business plans.** Summarize costs, relevant environmental impacts, and other important matters.
- **Memos, letters, and reports.** Summarize procedures, meetings, product assessments, expenditures, and more.
- **Medical charts.** Record patient data in summarized form.
- **Legal briefs.** Summarize relevant facts of cases.

Second, summaries are useful to your readers. Let's say you're writing a paper about the McCarthy era in the United States, and in part of that paper you want to discuss Arthur Miller's *Crucible* as a dramatic treatment of the subject. A summary of the plot would be helpful to a reader who hasn't seen or read—or who doesn't remember—the play. Or perhaps you're writing a paper about the politics of recent American military interventions. If your reader isn't likely to be familiar with American actions in Kosovo and Afghanistan, it would be a good idea to summarize these events at some early point in the paper. In many cases (an exam, for instance), you can use a summary to demonstrate your knowledge of what your professor already knows; when writing a paper, you can use a summary to inform your professor about some relatively unfamiliar source.

Third, summaries are required frequently in college-level writing. For example, on a psychology midterm, you may be asked to explain Carl Jung's theory of the collective unconscious and to show how it differs from Sigmund Freud's theory of the personal unconscious. You may have read about this theory in your textbook or in a supplementary article, or your instructor may have outlined it in his or her lecture. You can best demonstrate your understanding of Jung's theory by summarizing it. Then you'll proceed to contrast it with Freud's theory—which, of course, you must also summarize.

THE READING PROCESS

It may seem to you that being able to tell (or retell) in summary form exactly what a passage says is a skill that ought to be taken for granted in anyone who can read at high school level. Unfortunately, this is not so: For all kinds of reasons, people don't always read carefully. In fact, it's probably safe to say that usually they don't. Either they read so inattentively that they skip over words, phrases, or even whole sentences, or, if they do see the words in front of them, they see them without registering their significance.

When a reader fails to pick up the meaning and implications of a sentence or two, usually there's no real harm done. (An exception: You could lose credit on an exam or paper because you failed to read or to realize the significance of a crucial direction by your instructor.) But over longer stretches— the paragraph, the section, the article, or the chapter—inattentive or haphazard reading interferes with your goals as a reader: to perceive the shape of the argument, to grasp the central idea, to determine the main points that compose it, to relate the parts of the whole, and to note key examples. This kind of reading takes a lot more energy and determination than casual reading. But, in the long run, it's an energy-saving method because it enables you to retain the content of the material and to use that content as a basis for your own responses. In other words, it allows you to develop an accurate and coherent written discussion that goes beyond summary.

CRITICAL READING FOR SUMMARY

- *Examine the context.* Note the credentials, occupation, and publications of the author. Identify the source in which the piece originally appeared. This information helps illuminate the author's perspective on the topic he or she is addressing.
- *Note the title and subtitle.* Some titles are straightforward, whereas the meanings of others become clearer as you read. In either case, titles typically identify the topic being addressed and often reveal the author's attitude toward that topic.
- *Identify the main point.* Whether a piece of writing contains a thesis statement in the first few paragraphs or builds its main point without stating it up front, look at the entire piece to arrive at an understanding of the overall point being made.
- *Identify the subordinate points.* Notice the smaller subpoints that make up the main point, and make sure you understand how they relate to the main point. If a particular subpoint doesn't clearly relate to the main point you've identified, you may need to modify your understanding of the main point.
- *Break the reading into sections.* Notice which paragraph(s) make up a piece's introduction, body, and conclusion. Break up the body paragraphs into sections that address the writer's various subpoints.
- *Distinguish between points, examples, and counterarguments.* Critical reading requires careful attention to what a writer is *doing* as well as what he or she is *saying.* When a writer quotes someone else, or relays an example of something, ask yourself why this is being done. What point is the example supporting? Is another source being quoted as support for a point, or as a counterargument that the writer sets out to address?
- *Watch for transitions within and between paragraphs.* In order to follow the logic of a piece of writing, as well as to distinguish between points, examples, and counterarguments, pay attention to the transitional words and phrases writers use. Transitions function like road signs, preparing the reader for what's next.
- *Read actively and recursively.* Don't treat reading as a passive, linear progression through a text. Instead, read as though you are engaged in a dialogue with the writer: Ask questions of the text as you read, make notes in the margin, underline key ideas in pencil, put question or exclamation marks next to passages that confuse or excite you. Go back to earlier points once you finish a reading, stop during your reading to recap what's come so far, and move back and forth through a text.

HOW TO WRITE SUMMARIES

Every article you read will present a unique challenge as you work to summarize it. As you'll discover, saying in a few words what has taken someone else a great many can be difficult. But like any other skill, the ability to summarize improves with practice. Here are a few pointers to get you started. They represent possible stages, or steps, in the process of writing a summary. These pointers are not meant to be ironclad rules; rather, they are designed to encourage habits of thinking that will allow you to vary your technique as the situation demands.

GUIDELINES FOR WRITING SUMMARIES

- *Read the passage carefully.* Determine its structure. Identify the author's purpose in writing. (This will help you distinguish between more important and less important information.) Make a note in the margin when you get confused or when you think something is important; highlight or underline points sparingly, if at all.
- *Reread.* This time divide the passage into sections or stages of thought. The author's use of paragraphing will often be a useful guide. *Label,* on the passage itself, each section or stage of thought. *Underline* key ideas and terms. Write notes in the margin.
- *Write one-sentence summaries,* on a separate sheet of paper, of each stage of thought.
- *Write a thesis—a one- or two-sentence summary of the entire passage.* The thesis should express the central idea of the passage, as you have determined it from the preceding steps. You may find it useful to follow the approach of most newspaper stories—naming the *what, who, why, where, when,* and *how* of the matter. For persuasive passages, summarize in a sentence the author's conclusion. For descriptive passages, indicate the subject of the description and its key feature(s). Note: In some cases, *a suitable thesis may already be in the original passage.* If so, you may want to quote it directly in your summary.
- *Write the first draft of your summary* by (1) combining the thesis with your list of one-sentence summaries or (2) combining the thesis with one-sentence summaries *plus* significant details from the passage. In either case, eliminate repetition and less important information. Disregard minor details or generalize them (e.g., George H. W. Bush and Bill Clinton might be generalized as "recent presidents"). Use as few words as possible to convey the main ideas.
- *Check your summary against the original passage* and make whatever adjustments are necessary for accuracy and completeness.

(continued)

- *Revise your summary,* inserting transitional words and phrases where necessary to ensure coherence. Check for style. *Avoid a series of short, choppy sentences.* Combine sentences for a smooth, logical flow of ideas. Check for grammatical correctness, punctuation, and spelling.

DEMONSTRATION: SUMMARY

To demonstrate these points at work, let's go through the process of summarizing a passage of expository material—that is, writing that is meant to inform and/or persuade. Read the following selection carefully. Try to identify its parts and understand how they work together to create an overall point.

The Future of Love: Kiss Romance Goodbye, It's Time for the Real Thing
Barbara Graham

Author of the satire Women Who Run with Poodles: Myths and Tips for Honoring Your Mood Swings *(Avon, 1994), Barbara Graham has written articles for* Vogue, Self, Common Boundary, *and other publications. She regularly contributes articles to the* Utne Reader, *from which this essay was taken.**

1   Freud and his psychoanalytic descendants are no doubt correct in their assessment that the search for ideal love—for that one perfect soulmate—is the futile wish of not fully developed selves. But it also seems true that the longing for a profound, all-consuming erotic connection (and the heightened state of awareness that goes with it) is in our very wiring. The yearning for fulfillment through love seems to be to our psychic structure what food and water are to our cells.

2   Just consider the stories and myths that have shaped our consciousness: Beauty and the Beast, Snow White and her handsome prince, Cinderella and Prince Charming, Fred and Ginger, Barbie and Ken. (Note that, with the exception of the last two couples, all of these lovers are said to have lived happily ever after—even though we never get details of their lives after the weddings, after children and gravity and loss have exacted their price.) Still, it's not just these

---

* Barbara Graham, "The Future of Love: Kiss Romance Goodbye, It's Time for the Real Thing," *Utne Reader* Jan.–Feb. 1997: 20–23.

lucky fairy tale characters who have captured our collective imagination. The tragic twosomes we cut our teeth on—Romeo and Juliet, Tristan and Iseult, Launcelot and Guinevere, Heathcliff and Cathy, Rhett and Scarlett—are even more compelling role models. Their love is simply too powerful and anarchic, too shattering and exquisite, to be bound by anything so conventional as marriage or a long-term domestic arrangement.

3   If recent divorce and remarriage statistics are any indication, we're not as astute as the doomed lovers. Instead of drinking poison and putting an end to our love affairs while the heat is still turned up full blast, we expect our marriages and relationships to be long-running fairy tales. When they're not, instead of examining our expectations, we switch partners and reinvent the fantasy, hoping that this time we'll get it right. It's easy to see why: Despite all the talk of family values, we're constantly bombarded by visions of perfect romance. All you have to do is turn on the radio or TV or open any magazine and check out the perfume and lingerie ads. "Our culture is deeply regressed," says Florence Falk, a New York City psychotherapist. "Everywhere we turn, we're faced with glamorized, idealized versions of love. It's as if the culture wants us to stay trapped in the fantasy and does everything possible to encourage and expand that fantasy." Trying to forge an authentic relationship amidst all the romantic hype, she adds, makes what is already a tough proposition even harder.

4   What's most unusual about our culture is our feverish devotion to the belief that romantic love and marriage should be synonymous. Starting with George and Martha, continuing through Ozzie and Harriet right up to the present day, we have tirelessly tried to formalize, rationalize, legalize, legitimize, politicize and sanitize rapture. This may have something to do with our puritanical roots, as well as our tendency toward oversimplification. In any event, this attempt to satisfy all of our contradictory desires under the marital umbrella must be put in historical context in order to be properly understood.

5   "Personal intimacy is actually quite a new idea in human history and was never part of the marriage ideal before the 20th century," says John Welwood, a Northern California–based psychologist and author, most recently, of *Love and Awakening*. "Most couples throughout history managed to live together their whole lives without ever having a conversation about what was going on within or between them. As long as family and society prescribed the rules of marriage, individuals never had to develop any consciousness in this area."

6   In short, marriage was designed to serve the economic and social needs of families, communities, and religious institutions, and had little or nothing to do with love. Nor was it expected to satisfy lust.

7   In *Myths to Live By*, Joseph Campbell explains how the sages of ancient India viewed the relationship between marriage and passion. They concluded that there are five degrees of love, he writes, "through which a worshiper is increased in the service and knowledge of his God." The first degree has to do with the relationship of the worshiper to the divine. The next three degrees of love, in order of importance, are friendship, the parent/child relationship, and marriage. The fifth and highest form is passionate, illicit love. "In marriage, it is declared, one is still possessed of reason," Campbell adds. "The seizure of passionate love

can be, in such a context, only illicit, breaking in upon the order of one's dutiful life in virtue as a devastating storm."

8   No wonder we're having problems. The pressures we place on our tender unions are unprecedented. Even our biochemistry seems to militate against long-term sexual relationships. Dr. Helen Fisher, an anthropologist at Rutgers University and author of *Anatomy of Love*, believes that human pair-bonds originally evolved according to "the ancient blueprint of serial monogamy and clandestine adultery" and are originally meant to last around four years—at least long enough to raise a single dependent child through toddlerhood. The so-called seven-year-itch may be the remains of a four-year reproductive cycle, Fisher suggests.

9   Increasingly, Fisher and other researchers are coming to view what we call love as a series of complex biochemical events governed by hormones and enzymes. "People cling to the idea that romantic love is a mystery, but it's also a chemical experience," Fisher says, explaining that there are three distinct mating emotions and each is supported in the brain by the release of different chemicals. Lust, an emotion triggered by changing levels of testosterone in men and women, is associated with our basic sexual drive. Infatuation depends on the changing levels of dopamine, norepinephrine, and phenylethylamine (PEA), also called the "chemicals of love." They are natural—addictive— amphetaminelike chemicals that stimulate euphoria and make us want to stay up all night sharing our secrets. After infatuation and the dizzying highs associated with it have peaked—usually within a year or two—this brain chemistry reduces, and a new chemical system made up of oxytocin, vasopressin, and maybe the endorphins kicks in and supports a steadier, quieter, more nurturing intimacy. In the end, regardless of whether biochemistry accounts for cause or effect in love, it may help to explain why some people—those most responsive to the release of the attachment chemicals—are able to sustain a long-term partnership, while thrillseekers who feel depressed without regular hits of dopamine and PEA are likely to jump from one liaison to the next in order to maintain a buzz.

10   But even if our biochemistry suggests that there should be term limits on love, the heart is a stubborn muscle and, for better or worse, most of us continue to yearn for a relationship that will endure. As a group, Generation Xers— many of whom are children of divorce—are more determined than any other demographic group to have a different kind of marriage than their parents and to avoid divorce, says Howard Markman, author of *Fighting for Your Marriage*. What's more, lesbians and gay men who once opposed marriage and all of its heterosexual, patriarchal implications now seek to reframe marriage as a more flexible, less repressive arrangement. And, according to the U.S. National Center for Health Statistics, in one out of an estimated seven weddings, either the bride or the groom—or both—are tying the knot for at least the third time—nearly twice as many as in 1970. There are many reasons for this, from the surge in the divorce rate that began in the '70s, to our ever-increasing life span. Even so, the fact that we're still trying to get love right—knowing all we know about the ephemeral nature of passion, in a time when the stigmas once

associated with being divorced or single have all but disappeared—says something about our powerful need to connect.

11   And, judging from the army of psychologists, therapists, clergy, and other experts who can be found dispensing guidance on the subject, the effort to save—or reinvent, depending on who's doing the talking—love and marriage has become a multimillion dollar industry. The advice spans the spectrum. There's everything from *Rules*, by Ellen Fein and Sherrie Schneider, a popular new book which gives 90's women 50's-style tips on how to catch and keep their man, to Harville Hendrix's *Getting the Love You Want*, and other guides to "conscious love." But regardless of perspective, this much is clear: Never before have our most intimate thoughts and actions been so thoroughly dissected, analyzed, scrutinized and medicalized. Now, people who fall madly in love over and over are called romance addicts. Their disease, modeled on alcoholism and other chemical dependencies, is considered "progressive and fatal."

12   Not everyone believes the attempt to deconstruct love is a good thing. The late philosopher Christopher Lasch wrote in his final (and newly released) book, *Women and the Common Life:* "The exposure of sexual life to scientific scrutiny contributed to the rationalization, not the liberation, of emotional life." His daughter, Elisabeth Lasch-Quinn, an historian at Syracuse University and the editor of the book, agrees. She contends that the progressive demystification of passionate life since Freud has promoted an asexual, dispassionate and utilitarian form of love. Moreover, like her father, she believes that the national malaise about romance can be attributed to insidious therapeutic modes of social control—a series of mechanisms that have reduced the citizen to a consumer of expertise. "We have fragmented life in such a way," she says, "as to take passion out of our experience."

13   Admittedly, it's a stretch to picture a lovesick 12th-century French troubadour in a 12-step program for romance addicts. Still, we can't overlook the fact that our society's past efforts to fuse together those historically odd bedfellows— passionate love and marriage—have failed miserably. And though it's impossible to know whether all the attention currently being showered on relationships is the last gasp of a dying social order—marriage—or the first glimmer of a new paradigm for relating to one another, it's obvious that something radically different is needed.

Read, Reread, Underline

Let's consider our recommended pointers for writing a summary.

As you reread the passage, note in the margins of the essay important points, shifts in thought, and questions you may have. Consider the essay's significance as a whole and its stages of thought. What does it say? How is it organized? How does each part of the passage fit into the whole? What do all these points add up to?

Here is how the first few paragraphs of Graham's article might look after you had marked the main ideas, by highlighting and by marginal notations.

Freud and his psychoanalytic descendants are no doubt correct in their assessment that the search for ideal love—for that one perfect soulmate—is the futile wish of not fully developed selves. But it also seems true that the longing for a profound, all-consuming erotic connection (and the heightened state of awareness that goes with it) is in our very wiring. The yearning for fulfillment through love seems to be to our psychic structure what food and water are to our cells.

psychic importance of love

Just consider the stories and myths that have shaped our consciousness: Beauty and the Beast, Snow White and her handsome prince, Cinderella and Prince Charming, Fred and Ginger, Barbie and Ken. (Note that, with the exception of the last two couples, all of these lovers are said to have lived happily ever after—even though we never get details of their lives after the weddings, after children and gravity and loss have exacted their price.) Still, it's not just these lucky fairy tale characters who have captured our collective imagination. The tragic twosomes we cut our teeth on—Romeo and Juliet, Tristan and Iseult, Launcelot and Guinevere, Heathcliff and Cathy, Rhett and Scarlett—are even more compelling role models. Their love is simply too powerful and anarchic, too shattering and exquisite, to be bound by anything so conventional as marriage or a long-term domestic arrangement.

fictional, sometimes tragic examples of ideal love

If recent divorce and remarriage statistics are any indication, we're not as astute as the doomed lovers. Instead of drinking poison and putting an end to our love affairs while the heat is still turned up full blast, we expect our marriages and relationships to be long-running fairy tales. When they're not, instead of examining our expectations, we switch partners and reinvent the fantasy, hoping that this time we'll get it right. It's easy to see why: Despite all the talk of family values, we're constantly bombarded by visions of perfect romance. All you have to do is turn on the radio or TV or open any magazine and check out the perfume and lingerie ads. "Our culture is deeply regressed," says Florence Falk, a New York City psychotherapist. "Everywhere we turn, we're faced with glamorized, idealized versions of love. It's as if the culture wants us to stay trapped in the fantasy and does everything possible to encourage and expand that fantasy." Trying to forge an authentic relationship amidst all the romantic hype, she adds, makes what is already a tough proposition even harder.

difficulty of having a real relationship in a culture that glamorizes ideal love

What's most unusual about our culture is our feverish devotion to the belief that romantic love and marriage should be synonymous. Starting with George and Martha, continuing through Ozzie and Harriet right up to the present day, we have tirelessly tried to formalize, rationalize, legalize, legitimize, politicize and sanitize rapture. This may have something to do with our puritanical roots, as well as our tendency toward oversimplification. In any event, this attempt to satisfy all of our contradictory

contradictions of ideal love and marriage

"personal intimacy" never considered part of marriage before 20th century

desires under the marital umbrella must be put in historical context in order to be properly understood.

"Personal intimacy is actually quite a new idea in human history and was never part of the marriage ideal before the 20th century," says John Welwood, a Northern California–based psychologist and author, most recently, of *Love and Awakening*. "Most couples throughout history managed to live together their whole lives without ever having a conversation about what was going on within or between them. As long as family and society prescribed the rules of marriage, individuals never had to develop any consciousness in this area."

In short, marriage was designed to serve the economic and social needs of families, communities, and religious institutions, and had little or nothing to do with love. Nor was it expected to satisfy lust.

Divide into Stages of Thought

When a selection doesn't contain sections with thematic headings, as is the case with "The Future of Love," how do you determine where one stage of thought ends and the next one begins? Assuming that what you have read is coherent and unified, this should not be difficult. (When a selection is unified, all of its parts pertain to the main subject; when a selection is coherent, the parts follow one another in logical order.) Look, particularly, for transitional sentences at the beginning of paragraphs. Such sentences generally work in one or both of the following ways: (1) they summarize what has come before; (2) they set the stage for what is to follow.

For example, look at the sentence that opens paragraph 10: "But even if our biochemistry suggests that there should be term limits on love, the heart is a stubborn muscle and, for better or worse, most of us continue to yearn for a relationship that will endure." Notice how the first part of this sentence restates the main idea of the preceding section. The second part of the transitional sentence announces the topic of the upcoming section: three paragraphs devoted to the efforts people make to attain, save, or reinvent romantic relationships.

Each section of an article generally takes several paragraphs to develop. Between paragraphs, and almost certainly between sections of an article, you will usually find transitions that help you understand what you have just read and what you are about to read. For articles that have no subheadings, try writing your own section headings in the margins as you take notes. Then proceed with your summary.

The sections of Graham's article may be described as follows:

```
Section 1: Introduction--a yearning for "fulfill-
ment through love" pervades our culture, and that
yearning is shaped by myths and romantic fan-
tasies (paragraphs 1-3).
```

> **Section 2:** *Marriage and love*--we expect pas-
> sionate love to lead to happy, lifelong mar-
> riage. This is a relatively new and unique
> practice in human history (paragraphs 4-7).
>
> **Section 3:** *Biochemistry and love*--love has a bio-
> chemical component, which complicates our abili-
> ties to sustain long-term relationships
> (paragraphs 8-9).
>
> **Section 4:** *Marriage and love revisited*--many
> people are currently trying to preserve and/or
> reinvent marriage and love (paragraphs 10-12).
>
> **Section 5:** *Conclusion*--the fusion of passionate
> love with the institution of marriage hasn't
> worked very well, and we need something "radical-
> ly different" to replace it (paragraph 13).

Write a One- or Two-Sentence Summary of Each Stage of Thought

The purpose of this step is to wean you from the language of the original passage, so that you are not tied to it when writing the summary. Here are one-
sentence summaries for each stage of thought in "The Future of Love"
article's five sections:

> *Section 1:* Introduction—a yearning for "fulfillment through love" per-
> vades our culture, and that yearning is shaped by myths and romantic fan-
> tasies (paragraphs 1–3).
>
> > Most members of American culture crave romantic
> > love, but we have unreal expectations based upon
> > idealized images of love we learn from fantasies
> > and fairy tales.
>
> *Section 2:* Marriage and love—we expect passionate love to lead to happy,
> lifelong marriage. This is a relatively new and unique practice in human
> history (paragraphs 4–7).
>
> > We expect the passionate love of fairy tales to
> > lead to "happily ever after" in the institution
> > of marriage, and when this fails, we move on and
> > try it again. Ironically, the idea that marriage
> > should be based on love--rather than upon social

```
and economic concerns-is a relatively recent
practice in Western history.
```

Section 3: Biochemistry and love—love has a biochemical component, which complicates our abilities to sustain long-term relationships (paragraphs 8–9).

```
Biochemists are discovering that love and lust
have hormonal causes, and their evidence suggests
that our biological makeup predisposes us to seek
the excitement of short-term relationships.
```

Section 4: Marriage and love revisited—many people are currently trying to preserve and/or reinvent marriage and love (paragraphs 10–12).

```
Despite all the difficulties, we spend a lot of
time analyzing the elements of relationships in
order to preserve or perhaps reinvent marriage.
We clearly want to make it work.
```

Section 5: Conclusion—the fusion of passionate love with the institution of marriage hasn't worked very well, and we need something "radically different" to replace it (paragraph 13).

```
Because confining passionate love to the institu-
tion of marriage hasn't worked very well, we need
to revise our model for human relationships.
```

Write a Thesis: A One- or Two-Sentence Summary of the Entire Passage

The thesis is the most general statement of a summary (or any other type of academic writing—see Chapter 3 for a more complete discussion of thesis statements). It is the statement that announces the paper's subject and the claim that you or—in the case of a summary—another author will be making about that subject. Every paragraph of a paper illuminates the thesis by providing supporting detail or explanation. The relationship of these paragraphs to the thesis is analogous to the relationship of the sentences within a paragraph to the topic sentence. Both the thesis and the topic sentences are general statements (the thesis being the more general) that are followed by systematically arranged details.

To ensure clarity for the reader, *the first sentence of your summary should begin with the author's thesis, regardless of where it appears in the article itself.* Authors may locate their thesis at the beginning of their work, in which case the thesis operates as a general principle from which details of the presentation follow. This is called a *deductive* organization: thesis first, supporting details second. Alternately, an author may locate his or her thesis at the end of the work, in which case the author begins with specific details and builds toward a more general conclusion, or thesis. This is called an *inductive* organization—an example of which you see in "The Future of Love."

A thesis consists of a subject and an assertion about that subject. How can we go about fashioning an adequate thesis for a summary of "The Future of Love"? Probably no two proposed thesis statements for this article would be worded identically, but it is fair to say that any reasonable thesis will indicate that the subject is the current state of love and marriage in American society. How does Graham view the topic? What *is* the current state of love and marriage, in her view? Looking back over our section summaries, Graham's focus on the illusions of fairy tales and myths, the difference between marriage in the present day and its earlier incarnations, and the problems of divorce and "romance addiction" suggests she does not view the current state of affairs in an altogether positive light. Does she make a statement anywhere that pulls all this together? Her conclusion, in paragraph 13, contains her main idea: "our society's past efforts to fuse together those historically odd bedfellows—passionate love and marriage—have failed miserably." Moreover, in the next sentence, she says, "it's obvious that something radically different is needed." Further evidence of Graham's main point can be found in the complete title of the essay: "The Future of Love: Kiss Romance Goodbye, It's Time for the Real Thing." Mindful of Graham's subject and the assertion she makes about it, we can write a thesis statement *in our own words* and arrive at the following:

> The contemporary institution of marriage is in trouble, and this may be due to our unrealistic expectations that passionate love leads to lasting union; it may be time to develop a new model for love and relationships.

To clarify for our readers the fact that this idea is Graham's and not ours, we'll qualify the thesis as follows:

> In her article "The Future of Love: Kiss Romance Goodbye, It's Time for the Real Thing," Barbara Graham describes how our unrealistic expectations that passionate love leads to lasting union may be partly causing the troubled state of marriage today; thus she suggests we develop a new model for love and relationships.

The first sentence of a summary is crucially important, for it orients readers by letting them know what to expect in the coming paragraphs. In the example above, the sentence refers directly to an article, its author, and the thesis for the upcoming summary. The author and title reference also could be indicated in the summary's title (if this were a freestanding summary), in which case their mention could be dropped from the thesis. And lest you become frustrated too quickly, keep in mind that writing an acceptable thesis for a summary takes time. In this case, it took three drafts, or roughly seven minutes to compose one sentence and another few minutes of fine-tuning after a draft of the entire summary was completed. The thesis needed revision because the first draft was too vague and incomplete; the second draft was more specific and complete, but left out the author's point about correcting the problem; the third draft was more complete, but was cumbersome.

> **Draft 1:** Barbara Graham argues that our attempts to confine passionate love to the institution of marriage have failed.
> *(Too vague—the problem isn't clear enough)*

> **Draft 2:** Barbara Graham ~~argues that our attempts to confine passionate love to the institution of marriage have failed.~~ describes how the contemporary institution of marriage is in trouble, and this may be due, she thinks, to our unrealistic expectations that passionate love will lead to lasting union.
> *(Incomplete—what about her call for a change?)*

> **Draft 3:** In her article "The Future of Love: Kiss Romance Goodbye, It's Time for the Real Thing," Barbara Graham describes how ~~the contemporary institution of marriage is in trouble, and this may be due, she thinks, to~~ our unrealistic expectations that passionate love will lead to lasting union may be causing the troubles in the contemporary institution of marriage today, so she argues that perhaps it's time to develop a new model for love and relationships.
> *(Wordy)*

> **Final:** In her article "The Future of Love: Kiss Romance Goodbye, It's Time for the Real Thing," Barbara Graham describes how our unrealistic expectations that passionate love leads to a lasting union may be partly causing the troubled state of ~~in the contemporary institution of~~ marriage today; thus she suggests we develop a new model for love and relationships.
> *(Add 'partly.' Cut out wordiness. Replace 'so' with 'thus')*

Write the First Draft of the Summary

Let's consider two possible summaries of the example passage: (1) a short summary, combining a thesis with one-sentence section summaries, and (2) a longer summary, combining thesis, one-sentence section summaries, and some carefully chosen details. Again, realize that you are reading final versions; each of the following summaries is the result of at least two full drafts.

Summary 1: Combine Thesis Sentence with One-Sentence Section Summaries

In her article "The Future of Love: Kiss Romance Goodbye, It's Time for the Real Thing," Barbara Graham describes how our unrealistic expectations that passionate love leads to lasting union may be partly causing the troubled state of marriage today; thus she suggests we develop a new model for love and relationships. The existing model, and our craving for romantic love, is based heavily upon idealized images of love we learn from fantasies and fairy tales.

We expect the passionate love of fairy tales to lead to "happily ever after" in the institution of marriage, and when this fails, we move on and try it again. Ironically, the idea that marriage should be based on love--rather than upon social and economic concerns--is a relatively recent practice in Western history. While the romantic marriage ideal doesn't fit with tradition, biological evidence is mounting against it as well. Biochemists are discovering that love and lust have hormonal causes, and their evidence suggests that our biological makeup predisposes us to seek the excitement of short-term relationships.

Nonetheless, despite all the difficulties, we spend a lot of time analyzing the elements of relationships in order to preserve or perhaps reinvent marriage. We clearly want to make it work. Because confining passionate love to the institution of marriage hasn't worked very well, Graham ends by suggesting that we ought to revise our model for human relationships.

Discussion

This summary consists essentially of a restatement of Graham's thesis plus the section summaries, altered or expanded a little for stylistic purposes. The first sentence encompasses the summary of Section 1 and is followed by the summaries of Sections 2, 3, 4, and 5. Notice the insertion of a transitional sentence (highlighted) between the summaries of Sections 2 and 3, helping to link the ideas more coherently.

Summary 2: Combine Thesis Sentence, Section Summaries, and Carefully Chosen Details

The thesis and one-sentence section summaries also can be used as the outline for a more detailed summary. However, most of the details in the passage won't be necessary in a summary. It isn't necessary even in a longer summary of this passage to discuss all of Graham's examples—specific romantic fairy tales, ancient Indian views of love and passion, the specific hormones involved with love and lust, or the examples of experts who examine and write about contemporary relationships. It would be appropriate, though, to mention one example of fairy tale romance, to refer to the historical information on marriage as an economic institution, and to explain some of the biological findings about love's chemical basis.

None of these details appeared in the first summary, but in a longer summary, a few carefully selected details might be desirable for clarity. How do you decide which details to include? First, since the idea that love and marriage are not necessarily compatible is the main point of the essay, it makes sense to cite some of the most persuasive evidence supporting this idea. For example, you could mention that for most of Western history, marriage was meant "to serve the economic and social needs of families, communities, and religious institutions," not the emotional and sexual needs of individuals. Further, you might explain the biochemists' argument that serial monogamy based on mutual interests and clandestine adultery—not lifelong, love-based marriage—are the forms of relationships best serving human evolution.

You won't always know which details to include and which to exclude. Developing good judgment in comprehending and summarizing texts is largely a matter of reading skill and prior knowledge (see page 3). Consider the analogy of the seasoned mechanic who can pinpoint an engine problem by simply listening to a characteristic sound that to a less experienced person is just noise. Or consider the chess player who can plot three separate winning strategies from a board position that to a novice looks like a hopeless jumble. In the same way, the more practiced a reader you are, the more knowledgeable you become about the subject, and the better able you will be to make critical distinctions between elements of greater and lesser importance. In the meantime, read as carefully as you can and use your own best judgment as to how to present your material.

Here's one version of a completed summary, with carefully chosen details. Note that we have highlighted phrases and sentences added to the original, briefer summary.

> In her article "The Future of Love: Kiss Romance
> Goodbye, It's Time for the Real Thing," Barbara
> Graham describes how our unrealistic expectations
> that passionate love leads to lasting union may

(Thesis)

be partly causing the troubled state of marriage today; thus she suggests we develop a new model for love and relationships.

Most members of American culture crave romantic love, but we have unreal expectations based upon idealized images of love we learn from fantasies and fairy tales such as "Beauty and the Beast" and "Cinderella." Tragedies such as Romeo and Juliet teach us about the all-consuming nature of "true love," and these stories are tragic precisely because the lovers never get to fulfill what we've been taught is the ideal: living happily ever after, in wedded bliss. The

(Section 1,
¶s 1–3)

idea that romantic love should be confined to marriage is perhaps the biggest fantasy to which we subscribe. When we are unable to make this fantasy real--and it seems that this is often the case--we end that marriage and move on to the next one. The twentieth century is actually the first century in Western history in which so much was asked of marriage. In earlier eras, marriage was designed to meet social and economic purposes,

(Section 2,
¶s 4–7)

rather than fulfill individual emotional and sexual desires.

Casting further doubt on the effectiveness of the current model of marriage, biochemists are discovering how hormones and enzymes influence feelings of love and lust. It turns out that the "chemistry" a person newly in love often feels for another has a basis in fact, as those early feelings of excitement and contentment are biochemical in nature. When people jump from one

(Section 3,
¶s 8–9)

relationship to the next, they may be seeking that chemical "rush." Further, these biochemical discoveries fit with principles of evolutionary survival, because short-term relationships--and even adulterous affairs--help to more quickly propagate the species.

Nonetheless, despite such historical and biological imperatives, we don't seem interested in abandoning the pursuit of love and marriage. In order to preserve or perhaps reinvent marriage, we spend a lot of time scrutinizing and dissecting

(Section 4,
¶s 10–12)

the dynamics of relationships. Self-help books on the subject of love and relationships fill bookstore shelves and top best-seller lists.

> While some argue that such scrutiny ruins rather than reinvigorates love, perhaps our efforts to understand relationships can help us to invent some kind of revised model for human relationships--since trying to confine passionate love to the institution of marriage clearly hasn't worked very well.

(Section 5, ¶ 13)

Discussion

The final two of our suggested steps for writing summaries are: (1) to check your summary against the original passage, making sure that you have included all the important ideas, and (2) to revise so that the summary reads smoothly and coherently.

The structure of this summary generally reflects the structure of the original—with one notable departure. As we noted earlier, Graham uses an inductive approach, stating her thesis at the end of the essay. The summary, however, states the thesis right away, then proceeds deductively to develop that thesis.

Compared to the first, briefer summary, this effort mentions fairy tales and tragedy, develops the point about traditional versus contemporary versions of marriage, explains the biochemical/evolutionary point, and refers specifically to self-help books and their role in the issue.

How long should a summary be? This depends on the length of the original passage. A good rule of thumb is that a summary should be no longer than one-fourth of the original passage. Of course, if you were summarizing an entire chapter or even an entire book, it would have to be much shorter than that. The summary above is about one-fourth the length of the original passage. Although it shouldn't be very much longer, you have seen (page 18) that it could be quite a bit shorter.

The length as well as the content of the summary also depends on its *purpose*. Let's suppose you decided to use Graham's piece in a paper that dealt with the biochemical processes of love and lust. In this case, you might summarize *only* Graham's discussion of Fisher's findings, and perhaps the point Graham makes about how biochemical discoveries complicate marriage. If, instead, you were writing a paper in which you argued against attempts to redefine marriage, you would likely give less attention to the material on biochemistry. To help support your view, you might summarize Graham's points in paragraph 10 about the persistent desire for lasting union found among members of Generation X and evidenced in the high numbers of marriages and remarriages. Thus, depending on your purpose, you would summarize either selected portions of a source or an entire source, as we will see more fully in the chapters on syntheses.

EXERCISE 1.1

Individual and Collaborative Summary Practice

For an exercise in writing summaries, see Chapter 7, a practice chapter that assembles several readings on the topic of legacy admissions in college. You will have an opportunity to write a summary that you then place into a larger argument.

SUMMARIZING A NARRATIVE OR PERSONAL ESSAY

Narratives and personal essays differ from expository essays in that they focus on personal experiences and/or views, they aren't structured around an explicitly stated thesis, and their ideas are developed more through the description of events or ideas than through factual evidence or logical explanation. A *narrative* is a story, a retelling of a person's experiences. That person and those experiences may be imaginary, as is the case with fiction, or they may be real, as in biography. In first-person narratives, you can't assume that the narrator represents the author of the piece, unless you know the narrative is a memoir or biography. In a *personal essay*, on the other hand, the narrator is the author. And while the writer of a personal essay may tell stories about his or her experiences, usually writers of such essays discuss thoughts and ideas as much as or more than telling stories. Personal essays also tend to contain more obvious points than do narratives. Summarizing personal essays or narratives presents certain challenges—challenges that are different from those presented by summarizing expository writing.

You have seen that an author of an *expository* piece (such as Graham's "The Future of Love") follows assertions with examples and statements of support. Narratives, however, usually are less direct. The author relates a story—event follows event—the point of which may never be stated directly. The charm, the force, and the very point of the narrative lie in the telling; generally, narratives do not exhibit the same logical development of expository writing. They do not, therefore, lend themselves to summary in quite the same way. Narratives do have a logic, but that logic may be emotional, imaginative, or plot-bound. The writer who summarizes a narrative is obliged to give an overview—a synopsis—of the story's events and an account of how these events affect the central character(s). The summary must explain the significance or *meaning* of the events.

Similarly, while personal essays sometimes present points more explicitly than do narratives, their focus and structure link them to narratives. Personal essays often contain inexplicit main points, or multiple points; they tend to *explore* ideas and issues, rather than make explicit *assertions* about those ideas. This exploratory character often means that personal essays exhibit a loose structure, and they often contain stories or narratives within them. While summarizing a personal essay may not involve a synopsis of events, an account of the progression of thoughts and ideas is necessary and, as with a narrative, summaries of personal essays must explain the significance of what goes on in the piece being summarized.

The following forms the first chapter of Bruce Chatwin's celebrated *In Patagonia* (1977), his narrative account of a journey to the remotest reaches of South America. Read the chapter, and as you do so consider how you might summarize it, possibly for a review of the book or for a paper on the literature of travel.

Dreams of Patagonia
Bruce Chatwin

Bruce Chatwin (1942–1989) began his career as a specialist in modern art at Sotheby's auction house. He later studied archeology and served as a journalist for the London Sunday Times Magazine, *which sent him on far-flung assignments, whetting his appetite for travel and honing his literary skills. After three years, he left the magazine to devote himself full time to travel writing, fiction, and essay writing.* In Patagonia *won the 1978 Hawthornden Prize and the 1979 E. M. Forster Award of the American Academy of Arts and Letters. Chatwin is equally well-known for his second literary travelogue,* The Songlines *(1987), an account of aboriginal "walkabouts" in Australia.**

1   In my grandmother's dining-room there was a glass-fronted cabinet and in the cabinet a piece of skin. It was a small piece only, but thick and leathery, with strands of coarse, reddish hair. It was stuck to a card with a rusty pin. On the card was some writing in faded black ink, but I was too young then to read.

2   "What's that?"

3   "A piece of brontosaurus."

4   My mother knew the names of two prehistoric animals, the brontosaurus and the mammoth. She knew it was not a mammoth. Mammoths came from Siberia.

5   The brontosaurus, I learned, was an animal that had drowned in the Flood, being too big for Noah to ship aboard the Ark. I pictured a shaggy lumbering creature with claws and fangs and a malicious green light in its eyes. Sometimes the brontosaurus would crash through the bedroom wall and wake me from my sleep.

6   This particular brontosaurus had lived in Patagonia, a country in South America, at the far end of the world. Thousands of years before, it had fallen into a glacier, travelled down a mountain in a prison of blue ice, and arrived in perfect condition at the bottom. Here my grandmother's cousin, Charley Milward the Sailor, found it.

7   Charley Milward was captain of a merchant ship that sank at the entrance to the Strait of Magellan. He survived the wreck and settled nearby, at Punta Arenas, where he ran a ship-repairing yard. The Charley Milward of my imagination was a god among men—tall, silent and strong, with black mutton-chop

---

* Bruce Chatwin, *In Patagonia* (New York: Penguin Books, 1977): 1–3.

whiskers and fierce blue eyes. He wore his sailor's cap at an angle and the tops of his sea-boots turned down.

8   Directly he saw the brontosaurus poking out of the ice, he knew what to do. He had it jointed, salted, packed in barrels, and shipped to the Natural History Museum in South Kensington. I pictured blood and ice, flesh and salt, gangs of Indian workmen and lines of barrels along a shore—a work of giants and all to no purpose; the brontosaurus went rotten on its voyage through the tropics and arrived in London a putrefied mess; which was why you saw brontosaurus bones in the museum, but no skin.

9   Fortunately cousin Charley had posted a scrap to my grandmother.

10   My grandmother lived in a red-brick house set behind a screen of yellow-spattered laurels. It had tall chimneys, pointed gables and a garden of blood-coloured roses. Inside it smelled of church.

11   I do not remember much about my grandmother except her size. I would clamber over her wide bosom or watch, slyly, to see if she'd be able to rise from her chair. Above her hung paintings of Dutch burghers, their fat buttery faces nesting in white ruffs. On the mantelpiece were two Japanese homunculi with red and white ivory eyes that popped out on stalks. I would play with these, or with a German articulated monkey, but always I pestered her: "Please can I have the piece of brontosaurus."

12   Never in my life have I wanted anything as I wanted that piece of skin. My grandmother said I should have it one day, perhaps. And when she died I said: "Now I can have the piece of brontosaurus," but my mother said: "Oh, that thing! I'm afraid we threw it away."

13   At school they laughed at the story of the brontosaurus. The science master said I'd mixed it up with the Siberian mammoth. He told the class how Russian scientists had dined off deep-frozen mammoth and told me not to tell lies. Besides, he said, brontosauruses were reptiles. They had no hair, but scaly armoured hide. And he showed us an artist's impression of the beast—so different from that of my imagination—grey-green, with a tiny head and gigantic switchback of vertebrae, placidly eating weed in a lake. I was ashamed of my hairy brontosaurus, but I knew it was not a mammoth.

14   It took some years to sort the story out. Charley Milward's animal was not a brontosaurus, but the mylodon or Giant Sloth. He never found a whole specimen, or even a whole skeleton, but some skin and bones, preserved by the cold, dryness and salt, in a cave on Last Hope Sound in Chilean Patagonia. He sent the collection to England and sold it to the British Museum. This version was less romantic but had the merit of being true.

15   My interest in Patagonia survived the loss of the skin; for the Cold War woke in me a passion for geography. In the late 1940s the Cannibal of the Kremlin shadowed our lives; you could mistake his moustaches for teeth. We listened to lectures about the war he was planning. We watched the civil defence lecturer ring the cities of Europe to show the zones of total and partial destruction. We saw the zones bump one against the other leaving no space in between. The instructor wore khaki shorts. His knees were white and knobbly, and we saw it was hopeless. The war was coming and there was nothing we could do.

16   Next, we read about the cobalt bomb, which was worse than the hydrogen bomb and could smother the planet in an endless chain reaction.

17   I knew the colour cobalt from my great-aunt's paintbox. She had lived on Capri at the time of Maxim Gorky and painted Capriot boys naked. Later her art became almost entirely religious. She did lots of St Sebastians, always against a cobalt-blue background, always the same beautiful young man, stuck through and through with arrows and still on his feet.

18   So I pictured the cobalt bomb as a dense blue cloudbank, spitting tongues of flame at the edges. And I saw myself, out alone on a green headland, scanning the horizon for the advance of the cloud.

19   And yet we hoped to survive the blast. We started an Emigration Committee and made plans to settle in some far corner of the earth. We pored over atlases. We learned the direction of prevailing winds and the likely patterns of fall-out. The war would come in the Northern Hemisphere, so we looked to the Southern. We ruled out Pacific Islands for islands are traps. We ruled out Australia and New Zealand, and we fixed on Patagonia as the safest place on earth.

20   I pictured a low timber house with a shingled roof, caulked against storms, with blazing log fires inside and the walls lined with the best books, somewhere to live when the rest of the world blew up.

21   Then Stalin died and we sang hymns of praise in chapel, but I continued to hold Patagonia in reserve.

If you have read the book *In Patagonia,* you may have done so because you were interested in the subject or because someone recommended it to you. Or you may have encountered this passage during the process of research or as an assigned reading for a course on the literature of travel, the

---

HOW TO SUMMARIZE PERSONAL ESSAYS AND NARRATIVES

- Your summary will not be a narrative, but rather the synopsis of a narrative or personal account. Your summary will likely be a paragraph at most.
- You will want to name and describe the principal character(s) of the narrative and describe the narrative's main actions or events; or, in the case of the personal essay, identify the narrator and his or her relationship to the discussion.
- You should seek to connect the narrative's character(s) and events: describe the significance of events for (or the impact of events on) the character(s), and/or the narrator.

culture and geography of South America, or social anthropology. In any case, you could draw on this passage for a number of purposes: to demonstrate the interplay of imagination and memory in motivating travel writers to set off on their journeys; to study narrative technique; to understand how an accomplished writer can, within a few pages—even within a few paragraphs—establish a voice; or to investigate how, in storytelling, facts can sometimes conflict with emotional truth. Having established your purpose, you decide to use the events recounted in this passage to support one or more points you intend to make.

When you summarize a narrative or personal essay, bear in mind the principles that follow, as well as those listed in the box on page 25.

To summarize events, reread the narrative and make a marginal note each time you see that an action advances the story from one moment to the next. (In Chatwin, the "actions" are two memories, separate but linked to the same remote, fascinating place: Patagonia.) The key here is to recall that narratives take place *in time*. In your summary, be sure to re-create for your reader a sense of time flowing. Name and describe the character(s) as well. (For our purposes, *character* refers to the person, real or fictional, about whom the narrative is written.) The trickiest part of the summary will be describing the connection between events and characters. Earlier (page 3) we made the point that summarizing any selection involves a degree of interpretation, and this is especially true of summarizing narratives and personal essays. What, in the case of Chatwin, is the significance of his narrative—or of any particular event he recounts? For example, what is the significance of the fact that the brontosaurus that figured so prominently in his childhood imagination turned out to be a remnant of a Giant Sloth? Or of his equally vivid, but mistaken, conviction that the world was going to end in a nuclear catastrophe and that he had better find the remotest region on earth if he hoped to survive? Such narrative moments—in Chatwin's case, recollections—may be used to illustrate a particular point. The events on which you choose to focus while summarizing a narrative will depend entirely on your purpose in using the narrative in the first place.

The general principles of summarizing narratives are similar to those of summarizing expository or persuasive passages. Make sure that you cover the major events, in the order in which they occurred (in line with your overall purpose, of course). Bring in details only to the extent that they support your purpose.

Here is a three-paragraph summary of the first chapter in Bruce Chatwin's *In Patagonia*. (The draft is the result of two prior drafts.)

> In the first chapter of In Patagonia, Bruce
> Chatwin recounts two childhood memories, one
> based on a misunderstanding and the other on an
> unrealized fear, that sparked his desire "to hold
> Patagonia in reserve" and one day travel there.
> First, Chatwin recalls a patch of brontosaurus
> skin (supposedly from Patagonia); later, he

recalls the fear of a Soviet-inspired nuclear holocaust and the realization that to survive he would need to travel to a safe, remote location (such as Patagonia).

Growing up, Chatwin coveted a flap of weathered skin his grandmother kept in a glass case and which he understood to be the partial remains of a brontosaurus. To account for the specimen, he constructed an elaborate story centered on an actual but mythologized distant relation, "Charley Milward the Sailor." When Captain Milward's ship sank at the tip of South America and he settled in Patagonia, he discovered, preserved, and shipped back to England a dinosaur that emerged whole from a glacier. The scrap of dinosaur skin found a place of honor in Grandmother's home, alongside "paintings of Dutch burghers . . . and Japanese homunculi." Patagonia later figured into young Chatwin's imagination when, growing up in England at the start of the Cold War, he feared an imminent nuclear holocaust. It was the Stalin era in the Soviet Union, and English school children like Chatwin believed that inhabitants of the Northern Hemisphere would soon be incinerated or die of radiation sickness. Chatwin and others therefore formed "an Emigration Committee [that] made plans to settle in some far corner of the earth" and survive the destruction. That "far corner" was Patagonia.

Both memories were proved unfounded. The brontosaurus skin that prompted in young Chatwin visions of "a shaggy lumbering creature with claws and fangs and a malicious green light in its eyes" turned out to be the remains of a Giant Sloth, part of which (not the whole animal) had been preserved in the dry, cold environment of Patagonia. Nor did Stalin launch the much-feared nuclear war that had prompted Chatwin to investigate a place so remote that the "likely patterns of fall-out" would not reach him. Both memories nonetheless prompted in young Chatwin a fascination with one of the most remote and, to his mind, one of the most exotic places on earth. His fascination would last into adulthood, eventually prompting the trip that would lead to his award-winning travelogue, In Patagonia.

Of course, depending upon how you use Chatwin's passage, you may not need as many details as are provided in the preceding summary. A briefer version would treat only the major events—the two childhood memories, one based on a misunderstanding and the other on a fear, but both contributing to a lifelong fascination. You might in this case preserve only a sentence or two of each of the original summary's three paragraphs, omitting such details as the description of the brontosaurus or of his grandmother's house. (The description of his grandmother and her home that "smelled of church" would be more relevant if you were writing a paper on the economy with which Chatwin describes people. The details you choose for a summary depend on the purpose to which you put the summary.)

Here is a briefer summary of the passage:

> In the first chapter of In Patagonia, Bruce
> Chatwin recounts two childhood memories, one based
> on a misunderstanding and the other on an unreal-
> ized fear, that sparked his interest in one day
> traveling to Patagonia. As a child, Chatwin was
> fascinated by a patch of what he thought was bron-
> tosaurus skin on display in his grandmother's
> home. That specimen was sent by distant relation
> "Charley Milward the Sailor" from Patagonia.
> Patagonia again figured into young Chatwin's imag-
> ination when, growing up in England at the start
> of the Cold War, he feared an imminent nuclear
> disaster and, in response, formed "an Emigration
> Committee" to scout remote locations that would
> escape nuclear destruction. Events later blurred
> these two memories. The brontosaurus skin turned
> out to be the remains of a Giant Sloth, and the
> much-feared war never materialized. Still,
> Chatwin's memories prompted in him a lifelong fas-
> cination with one of the most remote and, to his
> mind, one of the most exotic places on earth. As
> an adult, he would eventually make the trip that
> would end in his award-winning travelogue, In
> Patagonia.

The passage could be made briefer still: your purpose in your paper might be served by a one-sentence reference to Chatwin's narrative:

> In the first chapter of his award-winning travel-
> ogue, Bruce Chatwin recounts two childhood memo-
> ries that prompted his lifelong fascination with
> Patagonia.

Here, only the major purpose of Chatwin's opening chapter is treated, with no details offered about the two memories that prompted his later fascination with Patagonia. Brief as it is, this summary conveys how Chatwin traces his motivation to travel in and write about Patagonia to events in his childhood.

SUMMARIZING FIGURES AND TABLES

In your reading in the sciences and social sciences, often you will find data and concepts presented in nontext forms—as figures and tables. Such visual devices offer a snapshot, a pictorial overview of material that is more quickly and clearly communicated in graphic form than as a series of (often complicated) sentences. Note that in essence, figures and tables are themselves summaries. The writer uses a graph, which in an article or book is labeled as a numbered "figure," to present the quantitative results of research as points on a line or a bar, or as sections ("slices") of a pie. Pie charts show relative proportions, or percentages. Graphs, especially effective in showing patterns, relate one variable to another: for instance, income to years of education, or a college student's grade point average to hours of studying.

In the following sections, we present a number of figures and tables from two different sources, all related to romance and relationships. Figures 1.1, 1.2, and 1.3 and Table 1.1 come from a study (Hetsroni, 2000) of the criteria used by participants on television dating shows in the United States and Israel to pick dating partners.* The categories are self-explanatory, although we should note that the category "physical appearance" denotes features of height, weight, facial features, and hair, while "sexual anatomy and bedroom behavior" refers to specifically sexual features of physical appearance, as well as to "kissing

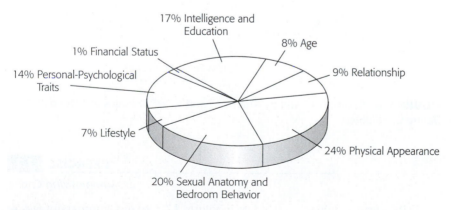

FIGURE 1.1   Categories Used by American and Israeli Males to Screen Dating Candidates

---

* Amir Hetsroni, "Choosing a Mate in Television Dating Games: The Influence of Setting, Culture, and Gender," *Sex Roles* 42.1–2 (2000): 90–97.

technique," "foreplay tactics," and the like. Figure 1.1 shows the criteria 266 American and Israeli men chose as most important in selecting a dating partner. Study this pie chart.

Here is a summary of the information presented:

> Males rated the categories of "physical appear-
> ance" and "sexual anatomy and bedroom behavior"
> as most important to them. Nearly half the males
> in the sample, or 44%, rated these two cate-
> gories, which both center on external rather than
> internal characteristics, as the most important
> ones for choosing a dating partner. Internal
> characteristics represented by the categories of
> "personal-psychological traits" and "intelligence
> and education" account for the next most impor-
> tant criteria, with a combined 31%. Males rated
> "relationship," "lifestyle," and "age" as nearly
> equal in their priorities; interestingly, a neg-
> ligible 1% rated "financial status" as an impor-
> tant criterion when selecting a dating candidate.

Figure 1.2 shows, in percentages, how women rate dating criteria.

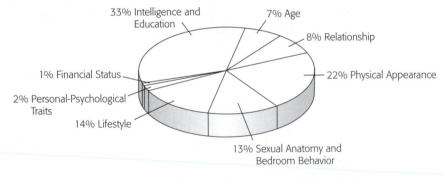

FIGURE 1.2   Categories Used by American and Israeli Females to Screen Dating Candidates

EXERCISE 1.2

Summarizing Charts

Write a brief summary of the data in Figure 1.2. Use our summary of Figure 1.1 as a model, but structure and word your own summary differently.

Bar graphs are useful for comparing two sets of data. Figure 1.3 illustrates this with a comparison of categories males and females use to select dating partners.

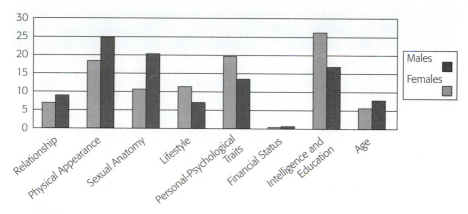

FIGURE 1.3　Comparison of Categories Used by American and Israeli Males and Females to Screen Dating Candidates

Here is a summary of the information in Figure 1.3:

> Males clearly differ from females in the criteria
> they use to select dating partners. Males in this
> sample focused on external characteristics such
> as "physical appearance" and especially "sexual
> anatomy and bedroom behavior" at significantly
> higher rates than did females. Conversely,
> females selected the internal characteristics of
> "lifestyle," "personal-psychological traits," and
> "intelligence and education" at much higher rates
> than did males. However, less significant differ-
> ences exist between males and females when rating
> the importance of "relationship," "financial
> status," and "age"; both male and female partici-
> pants rated these three criteria as of lesser
> importance when selecting a dating partner.

A table presents numerical data in rows and columns for quick reference. If the writer chooses, tabular information can be converted to graphic information. Charts and graphs are preferable when the writer wants to emphasize a pattern or relationship; tables are used when the writer wants to emphasize numbers. While the previous charts and graphs combined the Israeli with the American data collected in the TV dating show study, Table 1.1 breaks down the percentages by sex and nationality, revealing some significant differences between the nationality groups. (Note: *n* refers to the total number of respondents in each category.)

Sometimes a single graph presents information on two or more populations, or data sets, all of which are tracked with the same measurements. Figure 1.4 comes from a study of 261 college students—93 males and 168

	American Males (%) (n = 120)	Israeli Males (%) (n = 146)	American Females (%) (n = 156)	Israeli Females (%) (n = 244)
TABLE 1.1 Categories Used by American and Israeli Males and Females to Screen Dating Candidates				
Category				
Relationship	9.5	8.0	9.5	5.0
Physical appearance	18.5	30.0	12.0	22.0
Sexual anatomy and bedroom behavior	11.5	27.5	4.5	15.0
Lifestyle	9.0	6.0	11.0	11.5
Personal-psychological traits	20.0	8.0	27.0	15.0
Financial status	1.5	–	–	1.0
Intelligence and education	22.5	12.5	29.0	24.0
Age	7.5	8.0	7.0	6.0
TOTAL	100.0	100.0	100.0	100.0

females. The students were asked (among other things) to rate the acceptability of a hypothetical instance of sexual betrayal by both a male and a female heterosexual romantic partner who has agreed to be monogamous. The graph plots the ways in which gender of the transgressor played into the acceptability ratings given by male and female respondents. The researchers

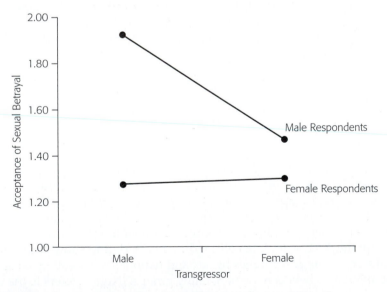

FIGURE 1.4   The Interaction of Sex of Respondent and Sex of Transgressor on the Acceptance of Sexual Betrayal

established mean values of 1 to 4 (indicating ratings of "totally unacceptable" to "totally acceptable"). A *mean* indicates the average of the ratings or scores given by a population or, in numerical terms, the sum of the scores divided by the number of scores. When respondents in the study were asked to assign a numerical rating of acceptability to instances of sexual betrayal, they chose numbers on a scale from 1 to 4, and these choices were averaged into mean acceptability ratings. None of the scores given by respondents in this study surpassed a mean acceptability rating of 2, but differences are evident between male and female ratings. The male respondents were more accepting of betrayal than the females, with an overall mean acceptability score of 1.63, whereas the females' mean score was 1.31.

A complete, scientific understanding of these findings would require more data, and statistical analysis of such data would yield precise information such as the exact amount of difference between male and female ratings. For example, in the original text of this study, the authors note that males were 11.6 times more accepting of sexual betrayal by male transgressors than were females. Even without such details, it is possible to arrive at a basic understanding of the data represented in the graph, and to summarize this information in simple terms. Here is a summary of the information reported in this graph:

> While males and females both rated sexual betrayal as unacceptable, males (with a mean rating of 1.63) were significantly more accepting overall than were females (with a mean rating of 1.31). Even more dramatic, however, is the difference between male and female ratings when the gender of the transgressor is factored in. Males rated male transgression as markedly more acceptable than female transgression, with approximate means of 1.90 for male transgressions and 1.43 for female transgressions. The males' ratings contrast sharply with those of females, who indicated a mean acceptability rating of approximately 1.25 for male transgressors, and 1.30 for female transgressors. Therefore, while both sexes found transgression by members of their own sex more acceptable than transgressions by the opposite sex, men were more accepting overall than women, and men believed male transgressors were significantly more acceptable than female transgressors. On the other hand, women found transgression overall less acceptable than males did, and women indicated far less difference in their ratings of male versus female transgressors than did the male respondents.

PARAPHRASE

In certain cases, you may want to *paraphrase* rather than summarize material. Writing a paraphrase is similar to writing a summary: It involves recasting a passage into your own words, so it requires your complete understanding of the material. The difference is that while a summary is a shortened version of the original, the paraphrase is approximately the same length as the original.

Why write a paraphrase when you can quote the original? You may decide to offer a paraphrase of material written in language that is dense, abstract, archaic, or possibly confusing.

The pointers below will help you write paraphrases.

HOW TO WRITE PARAPHRASES

- Make sure that you understand the source passage.
- Substitute your own words for those of the source passage; look for synonyms that carry the same meaning as the original words.
- Rearrange your own sentences so that they read smoothly. Sentence structure, even sentence order, in the paraphrase need not be based on that of the original. A good paraphrase, like a good summary, should stand by itself.

Let's consider an example. If you were investigating the ethical concerns relating to the practice of in vitro fertilization, you might conclude that you should read some medical literature. You might reasonably want to hear from the doctors who are themselves developing, performing, and questioning the procedures that you are researching. In professional journals and bulletins, physicians write to one another, not to the general public. They use specialized language. If you wanted to refer to a technically complex selection, you might need to write a paraphrase for the following selection.

In Vitro Fertilization: From Medical Reproduction to Genetic Diagnosis

Dietmar Mieth

[I]t is not only an improvement in the success-rate that participating research scientists hope for but, rather, developments in new fields of research in in-vitro gene diagnosis and in certain circumstances gene therapy. In view of this, the French expert J. F. Mattei has asked the following question: "Are we forced to accept that in vitro fertilization will become one of the most compelling methods of genetic diagnosis?" Evidently, by the introduction of a new law in France and Sweden (1994), this acceptance (albeit with certain restrictions) has already occurred prior to the application of in vitro fertilization reaching a technically mature and clinically applicable phase. This may seem astonishing in view of the question placed by the above-quoted French expert: the idea of embryo production so as to withhold one or two embryos before implantation presupposes a definite "attitude towards eugenics." And to destroy an embryo merely because of its genetic characteristics could signify the reduction of a human life to the sum of its genes. Mattei asks: "In face of a molecular judgment on our lives, is there no possibility for appeal? Will the diagnosis of inherited monogenetic illnesses soon be extended to genetic predisposition for multifactorial illnesses?"*

Like most literature intended for physicians, the language of this selection is somewhat forbidding to an audience of nonspecialists, who may have trouble with phrases such as "predisposition for multi-factorial illnesses." As a courtesy to your readers and in an effort to maintain a consistent tone and level in your essay, you could paraphrase this paragraph of the medical newsletter. First, of course, you must understand the meaning of the passage, perhaps no small task. But, having read the material carefully (and perhaps consulting a dictionary), you might eventually prepare a paraphrase like this one:

> Writing in the <u>Newsletter of the European Network for Biomedical Ethics,</u> Dietmar Mieth reports that fertility specialists today want not only to improve the success rates of their procedures but also to diagnose and repair genetic problems before they implant fertilized eggs. Since the result of the in vitro process is often more fertilized eggs than can be used in a procedure, doctors may examine test-tube embryos for genetic defects and "withhold one or two" before implanting them. The practice of selectively implanting embryos raises concerns about eugenics and the rights of rejected embryos. On what genetic grounds will specialists distinguish flawed from healthy embryos and make a decision whether or not to implant? The appearance of single genes linked directly to specific, or "monogenetic," illnesses could be grounds for destroying an embryo. More complicated would be genes that predispose people to an illness but in no way guarantee the onset of that illness. Would these genes, which are only one factor in "multi-factorial illnesses," also be labeled undesirable and lead to embryo destruction? Advances in fertility science raise difficult questions.

---

* Dietmar Mieth, "In Vitro Fertilization: From Medical Reproduction to Genetic Diagnosis," *Biomedical Ethics: Newsletter of the European Network for Biomedical Ethics* 1.1 (1996): 45.

> Already, even before techniques of genetic diag-
> nosis are fully developed, legislatures are writ-
> ing laws governing the practices of fertility
> clinics.

We begin our paraphrase with the same "not only/but also" logic of the original's first sentence, introducing the concepts of genetic diagnosis and therapy. The next four sentences in the original introduce concerns of a "French expert." Rather than quoting Mieth, quoting the expert, and immediately mentioning new laws in France and Sweden, we decided (first) to explain that in vitro fertilization procedures can give rise to more embryos than needed. We reasoned that nonmedical readers would appreciate our making explicit the background knowledge that the author assumes other physicians possess. Then we quote Mieth briefly ("withhold one or two" embryos) to provide some flavor of the original. We maintain focus on the ethical questions and wait until the end of the paraphrase before mentioning the laws to which Mieth refers. Our paraphrase is roughly the same length as the original, and it conveys the author's concerns about eugenics. As you can see, the paraphrase requires a writer to make some decisions about the presentation of material. In many, if not most, cases, you will need to do more than simply "translate" from the original, sentence by sentence, to write your paraphrase.

Paraphrases are generally about the same length as (sometimes shorter than) the passages on which they are based. But sometimes clarity requires that a paraphrase be longer than a tightly compacted source passage. For example, suppose you wanted to paraphrase this statement by Sigmund Freud:

> We have found out that the distortion in dreams which hinders our understanding of them is due to the activities of a censorship, directed against the unacceptable, unconscious wish-impulses.

If you were to paraphrase this statement (the first sentence in the Tenth Lecture of his *General Introduction to Psychoanalysis*), you might come up with something like this:

> It is difficult to understand dreams because they
> contain distortions. Freud believed that these
> distortions arise from our internal censor, which
> attempts to suppress unconscious and forbidden
> desires.

Essentially, this paraphrase does little more than break up one sentence into two and somewhat rearrange the sentence structure for clarity.

Like summaries, then, paraphrases are useful devices, both in helping you to understand source material and in enabling you to convey the essence of this source material to your readers. When would you choose to write a summary instead of a paraphrase (or vice versa)? The answer to this question depends on your purpose in presenting your source material. As we've said, summaries are generally based on articles (or sections of articles) or books. Paraphrases are generally based on particularly difficult (or important) paragraphs or sentences. You would seldom paraphrase a long passage, or summarize a short one, unless there were particularly good reasons for doing so. (For example, a lawyer might want to paraphrase several pages of legal language so that his or her client, who is not a lawyer, could understand it.) The purpose of a summary is generally to save your reader time by presenting him or her with a brief and quickly readable version of a lengthy source. The purpose of a paraphrase is generally to clarify a short passage that might otherwise be unclear. Whether you summarize or paraphrase may also depend on the importance of your source. A particularly important source—if it is not too long—may rate a paraphrase. If it is less important, or peripheral to your central argument, you may choose to write a summary instead. And, of course, you may choose to summarize only part of your source—the part that is most relevant to the point you are making.

EXERCISE **1.3**

Paraphrasing

Locate and photocopy three relatively complex, but brief, passages from readings currently assigned in your other courses. Paraphrase these passages, making the language more readable and understandable. Attach the photocopies to the paraphrases.

QUOTATION

A *quotation* records the exact language used by someone in speech or writing. A *summary*, in contrast, is a brief restatement in your own words of what someone else has said or written. And a *paraphrase* also is a restatement, although one that is often as long as the original source. Any paper in which you draw upon sources will rely heavily on quotation, summary, and paraphrase. How do you choose among the three?

Remember that the papers you write should be your own—for the most part: your own language and certainly your own thesis, your own inferences, and your own conclusion. It follows that references to your source materials should be written primarily as summaries and paraphrases, both of which are built on restatement, not quotation. You will use summaries when you need a *brief* restatement, and paraphrases, which provide more explicit detail than summaries, when you need to follow the development of a source closely. When you quote too much, you risk losing ownership of your work: More easily than you might think, your voice can be drowned out by the voices of those you've quoted. So *use quotation sparingly,* as you would a pungent spice.

Nevertheless, *quoting just the right source at the right time can significantly improve your papers.* The trick is to know when and how to use quotations.

Choosing Quotations

You'll find that using quotations can be particularly helpful in several situations.

WHEN TO QUOTE

- Use quotations when another writer's language is particularly memorable and will add interest and liveliness to your paper.
- Use quotations when another writer's language is so clear and economical that to make the same point in your own words would, by comparison, be ineffective.
- Use quotations when you want the solid reputation of a source to lend authority and credibility to your own writing.

Quoting Memorable Language

Frequently, we quote when the source material is worded so eloquently or powerfully that to summarize or paraphrase it would be to sacrifice much of the impact and significance of the meaning. Here, for example, is historian John Keegan describing how France, Germany, Austria, and Russia slid inexorably in 1914 into the cataclysm of World War I:

> In the event, the states of Europe proceeded, as if in a dead march and a dialogue of the deaf, to the destruction of their continent and its civilization.*

No paraphrase could do justice to the power of Keegan's words, as they appear in his 1998 book *The First World War*. You would certainly want to quote them in any paper dealing with the origins of this conflict.

Quotations can be direct or indirect. A *direct* quotation is one in which you record precisely the language of another. An *indirect* quotation is one in which you report what someone has said, although you are not obligated to repeat the words exactly as spoken (or written):

> **Direct quotation:** *Franklin D. Roosevelt said, "The only thing we have to fear is fear itself."*
>
> **Indirect quotation:** *Franklin D. Roosevelt said that we have nothing to fear but fear itself.*

The language in a direct quotation, which is indicated by a pair of quotation marks (" "), must be faithful to the language of the original passage. When using an indirect quotation, you have the liberty of changing words

---

* John Keegan, *The First World War* (New York: Vintage, 1998): 23.

(although not changing meaning). For both direct and indirect quotations, *you must credit your sources,* naming them either in (or close to) the sentence that includes the quotation or in a parenthetical citation. (Note: We haven't included parenthetical citations in our examples here; see pages 846–849 for guidance.)

Quoting Clear and Concise Language

You should quote a source when its language is particularly clear and economical—when your language, by contrast, would be wordy. Read this passage from a text by Patricia Curtis on biology:

> The honeybee colony, which usually has a population of 30,000 to 40,000 workers, differs from that of the bumblebee and many other social bees or wasps in that it survives the winter. This means that the bees must stay warm despite the cold. Like other bees, the isolated honeybee cannot fly if the temperature falls below 10°C (50°F) and cannot walk if the temperature is below 7°C (45°F). Within the wintering hive, bees maintain their temperature by clustering together in a dense ball; the lower the temperature, the denser the cluster. The clustered bees produce heat by constant muscular movements of their wings, legs, and abdomens. In very cold weather, the bees on the outside of the cluster keep moving toward the center, while those in the core of the cluster move to the colder outside periphery. The entire cluster moves slowly about on the combs, eating the stored honey from the combs as it moves.*

A summary of this paragraph might read as follows:

```
Honeybees, unlike many other varieties of bee,
are able to live through the winter by "cluster-
ing together in a dense ball" for body warmth.
```

A paraphrase of the same passage would be considerably more detailed:

```
Honeybees, unlike many other varieties of bee
(such as bumblebees), are able to live through
the winter. The 30,000 to 40,000 bees within a
honeybee hive could not, individually, move about
in cold winter temperatures. But when "clustering
together in a dense ball," the bees generate heat
by constantly moving their body parts. The clus-
ter also moves slowly about the hive, those on
the periphery of the cluster moving into the
center, those in the center moving to the periph-
ery, and all eating honey stored in the combs.
This nutrition, in addition to the heat generated
```

---

* Patricia Curtis, "Winter Organization," *Biology,* 2nd ed. (New York: Worth, 1976): 822–23.

```
by the cluster, enables the honeybee to survive
the cold winter months.
```

In both the summary and the paraphrase we've quoted Curtis's "clustering together in a dense ball," a phrase that lies at the heart of her description of wintering honeybees. For us to describe this clustering in any language other than Curtis's would be pointless since her description is admirably brief and precise.

Quoting Authoritative Language

You will also want to use quotations that lend authority to your work. When quoting an expert or some prominent political, artistic, or historical figure, you elevate your own work by placing it in esteemed company. Quote respected figures to establish background information in a paper, and your readers will tend to perceive that information as reliable. Quote the opinions of respected figures to endorse some statement that you've made, and your statement becomes more credible to your readers.

Consider this discussion of space flight. Author David Chandler refers to a physicist and a physicist-astronaut:

> A few scientists—notably James Van Allen, discoverer of the Earth's radiation belts—have decried the expense of the manned space program and called for an almost exclusive concentration on unmanned scientific exploration instead, saying this would be far more cost-effective.
>
> Other space scientists dispute that idea. Joseph Allen, physicist and former shuttle astronaut, says, "It seems to be argued that one takes away from the other. But before there was a manned space program, the funding on space science was zero. Now it's about $500 million a year."

Note that in the first paragraph Chandler has either summarized or used an indirect quotation to incorporate remarks made by James Van Allen into the discussion on space flight. In the second paragraph, Chandler directly quotes his next source, Joseph Allen. Both quotations, indirect and direct, lend authority and legitimacy to the article, for both James Van Allen and Joseph Allen are experts on the subject of space flight. Note also that Chandler provides brief but effective biographies of his sources, identifying both so that their qualifications to speak on the subject are known to all:

> James Van Allen, *discoverer of the Earth's radiation belts,* . . .

> Joseph Allen, *physicist and former shuttle astronaut,* . . .

The phrases in italics are called *appositives*. Their function is to rename the nouns they follow by providing explicit, identifying detail. Any information about a person that can be expressed in the following sentence pattern can be made into an appositive phrase:

> James Van Allen is the *discoverer of the Earth's radiation belts*. He has decried the expense of the manned space program.

Sentence with an appositive:

> James Van Allen, *discoverer of the Earth's radiation belts,* has decried the expense of the manned space program.

Appositives (in the example above, "discoverer of the Earth's radiation belts") efficiently incorporate identifying information about the authors you quote, while adding variety to the structure of your sentences.

Incorporating Quotations into Your Sentences

Quoting Only the Part of a Sentence or Paragraph That You Need

We've said that a writer selects passages for quotation that are especially *vivid and memorable, concise,* or *authoritative.* Now put these principles into practice. Suppose that while conducting research on college sports, you've come across the following, written by Robert Hutchins, former president of the University of Chicago:

> If athleticism is bad for students, players, alumni, and the public, it is even worse for the colleges and universities themselves. They want to be educational institutions, but they can't. The story of the famous half-back whose only regret, when he bade his coach farewell, was that he hadn't learned to read and write is probably exaggerated. But we must admit that pressure from trustees, graduates, "friends," presidents, and even professors has tended to relax academic standards. These gentry often overlook the fact that a college should not be interested in a full-back who is a half-wit. Recruiting, subsidizing, and the double educational standard cannot exist without the knowledge and the tacit approval, at least, of the colleges and universities themselves. Certain institutions encourage susceptible professors to be nice to athletes now admitted by paying them for serving as "faculty representatives" on the college athletic board.*

Suppose that in this entire paragraph you find a gem, a sentence with quotable words that will enliven your discussion. You may want to quote part of the following sentence:

---

* Robert Hutchins, "Gate Receipts and Glory," *The Saturday Evening Post* 3 Dec. 1983: 38.

These gentry often overlook the fact that a college should not be interested in a fullback who is a half-wit.

Incorporating the Quotation into the Flow of Your Own Sentence

Once you've selected the passage you want to quote, work the material into your paper in as natural and fluid a manner as possible. Here's how we would quote Hutchins:

> Robert Hutchins, former president of the University of Chicago, asserts that "a college should not be interested in a fullback who is a half-wit."

Note that we've used an appositive to identify Hutchins. And we've used only the part of the paragraph—a single clause—that we thought memorable enough to quote directly.

Avoiding Freestanding Quotations

A quoted sentence should never stand by itself—as in the following example:

> Various people associated with the university admit that the pressures of athleticism have caused a relaxation of standards. "These gentry often overlook the fact that a college should not be interested in a fullback who is a half-wit." But this kind of thinking is bad for the university and even worse for the athletes.

Even if it includes a parenthetical citation, a freestanding quotation would have the problem of being jarring to the reader. Introduce the quotation with a *signal phrase* that attributes the source not in a parenthetical citation, but in some other part of the sentence—beginning, middle, or end. Thus, you could write:

> As Robert Hutchins notes, "These gentry often overlook the fact that a college should not be interested in a fullback who is a half-wit."

Here's a variation with the signal phrase in the middle:

> "These gentry," asserts Robert Hutchins, "often overlook the fact that a college should not be interested in a fullback who is a half-wit."

Another alternative is to introduce a sentence-long quotation with a colon:

> But Robert Hutchins disagrees: "These gentry
> often overlook the fact that a college should not
> be interested in a fullback who is a half-wit."

Use colons also to introduce indented quotations (as in the cases when we introduce long quotations in this chapter).

When attributing sources in signal phrases, try to vary the standard *states, writes, says,* and so on. Other, stronger verbs you might consider: *asserts, argues, maintains, insists, asks,* and even *wonders.*

EXERCISE ▉ **1.4**

Incorporating Quotations

Return to the passage by Bruce Chatwin, "Dreams of Patagonia," pages 23–25, and find some sentences that you think make interesting points. Imagine you want to use these points in a paper you're writing on travel literature. Write five different sentences that use a variety of the techniques discussed thus far to incorporate whole sentences as well as phrases from the "Patagonia" passage.

Using Ellipses

Using quotations becomes somewhat complicated when you want to omit part of a quotation. Here's part of a paragraph from Henry David Thoreau's *Walden:*

> To read well, that is to read true books in a true spirit, is a noble exercise, and one that will task the reader more than any exercise which the customs of the day esteem. It requires a training such as the athletes underwent, the steady intention almost of the whole life to this object. Books must be read as deliberately and reservedly as they were written.*

Here is one way to quote the passage in part:

> Reading well is hard work, writes Henry David
> Thoreau in <u>Walden</u>, "that will task the reader
> more than any exercise which the customs of the
> day esteem. . . . Books must be read as deliber-
> ately and reservedly as they were written."

Whenever you quote a sentence but delete words from it, as we have done, indicate this deletion to the reader with three spaced periods—called an "ellipsis"—in the sentence at the point of deletion. The rationale for using an ellipsis mark is that a direct quotation must be reproduced *exactly* as it was written or spoken.

---

* Henry David Thoreau, *Walden* (New York: Signet Classic, 1960): 72.

When writers delete or change any part of the quoted material, readers must be alerted so they don't think the changes were part of the original. When deleting an entire sentence or sentences from a quoted paragraph, as in the example above, end the sentence you have quoted with a period, place the ellipsis, and continue the quotation.

If you are deleting the middle of a single sentence, use an ellipsis in place of the deleted words:

> "To read well . . . is a noble exercise, and one that will task the reader more than any exercise which the customs of the day esteem."

If you are deleting material from the end of one sentence through to the beginning of another sentence, add a sentence period before the ellipsis:

> "It requires a training such as the athletes underwent. . . . Books must be read as deliberately and reservedly as they were written."

If you begin your quotation of an author in the middle of his or her sentence, you need not indicate deleted words with an ellipsis. Be sure, however, that the syntax of the quotation fits smoothly with the syntax of your sentence:

> Reading "is a noble exercise," writes Henry David Thoreau.

Using Brackets to Add or Substitute Words

Use brackets whenever you need to add or substitute words in a quoted sentence. The brackets indicate to the reader a word or phrase that does not appear in the original passage but that you have inserted to avoid confusion. For example, when a pronoun's antecedent would be unclear to readers, delete the pronoun from the sentences and substitute an identifying word or phrase in brackets. When you make such a substitution, no ellipsis marks are needed. Assume that you wish to quote either of the underlined sentences in the following passage by Jane Yolen:

> Golden Press's *Walt Disney's Cinderella* set the new pattern for America's Cinderella. This book's text is coy and condescending. (Sample: "And her best friends of all were—guess who—the mice!") The illustrations are poor cartoons. And Cinderella herself is a disaster. She cowers as her sisters rip her homemade ball gown to shreds. (Not even homemade by Cinderella, but by the mice and birds.) She answers her stepmother with whines and pleadings. She is a sorry

excuse for a heroine, pitiable and useless. She cannot perform even a simple action to save herself, though she is warned by her friends, the mice. She does not hear them because she is "off in a world of dreams." Cinderella begs, she whimpers, and at last has to be rescued by—guess who—the mice!*

In quoting one of these sentences, you would need to identify to whom the pronoun *she* refers. You can do this inside the quotation by using brackets:

> Jane Yolen believes that "[Cinderella] is a sorry excuse for a heroine, pitiable and useless."

If the pronoun begins the sentence to be quoted, you can identify the pronoun outside the quotation and simply begin quoting your source one word later:

> Jane Yolen believes that in the Golden Press version, Cinderella "is a sorry excuse for a heroine, pitiable and useless."

Here's another example of a case where the pronoun needing identification occurs in the middle of the sentence to be quoted. Newspaper reporters must use brackets in these cases frequently when quoting sources, who in interviews might say something like this:

> After the fire they did not return to the station house for three hours.

If the reporter wants to use this sentence in an article, he or she needs to identify the pronoun:

> An official from City Hall, speaking on the condition that he not be identified, said, "After the fire [the officers] did not return to the station house for three hours."

You also will need to add bracketed information to a quoted sentence when a reference essential to the sentence's meaning is implied but not stated directly. An example:

> According to Robert Jastrow, a physicist and former official at NASA's Goddard Institute, "The proposition [that computers will emerge as a form of life] seems ridiculous because, for one thing, computers lack the drives and emotions of living creatures."

---

* Jane Yolen, "America's 'Cinderella,'" *Children's Literature in Education* 8 (1977): 22.

The bracketed phrase clarifying "proposition"—"that computers will emerge as a form of life"—is the writer's summary of Jastrow's proposition, discussed prior to the quoted passage.

INCORPORATING QUOTATIONS INTO YOUR SENTENCES

- **Quote only the part of a sentence or paragraph that you need.** Use no more of the writer's language than you need to make or reinforce your point.
- **Incorporate the quotation into the flow of your own sentence.** The quotation must fit, both syntactically and stylistically, into your surrounding language.
- **Avoid freestanding quotations.** A quoted sentence should never stand by itself. Use a *signal phrase*—at the beginning, the middle, or the end of the sentence—to attribute the source of the quotation.

- **Use ellipsis marks.** Indicate deleted language in the middle of a quoted sentence with ellipsis marks. Deleted language at the beginning or end of a sentence generally does not require ellipsis marks.

- **Use brackets to add or substitute words.** Use brackets to add or substitute words in a quoted sentence when the meaning of the quotation would otherwise be unclear—for example, when the antecedent of a quoted pronoun is ambiguous.

EXERCISE 1.5

Using Brackets

Write your own sentences incorporating the following quotations. Use brackets to clarify information that isn't clear outside of its original context—and refer to the original sources to remind yourself of this context.

From the Robert Hutchins passage on college sports:
(a) *They* want to be educational institutions, but they can't.
(b) *These gentry* often overlook the fact that a college should not be interested in a fullback who is a half-wit.

From the Jane Yolen excerpt on Cinderella:
(a) *This book's* text is coy and condescending.
(b) *She* cannot perform even a simple action to save herself, though she is warned by her friends, the mice.
(c) She does not hear *them* because she is "off in a world of dreams."

> ## WHEN TO SUMMARIZE, PARAPHRASE, AND QUOTE
>
> ### Summarize
> - To present main points of a lengthy passage (article or book)
> - To condense peripheral points necessary to discussion
>
> ### Paraphrase
> - To clarify a short passage
> - To emphasize main points
>
> ### Quote
> - To capture another writer's particularly memorable language
> - To capture another writer's clearly and economically stated language
> - To lend authority and credibility to your own writing

Remember that when you quote any work of another, you are obligated to credit—or cite—the author's work properly; otherwise, you may be guilty of plagiarism. See pages 846–849 for guidance on citing sources.

AVOIDING PLAGIARISM

Plagiarism is generally defined as the attempt to pass off the work of another as one's own. Whether born out of calculation or desperation, plagiarism is the least tolerated offense in the academic world. The fact that most plagiarism is unintentional—arising from ignorance of conventions rather than deceitfulness—makes no difference to many professors.

The ease of cutting and pasting whole blocks of text from Web sources into one's own paper makes it tempting for some to take the easy way out and avoid doing their own research and writing. But apart from the serious ethical issues involved, the same technology that makes such acts possible also makes it possible for instructors to detect them. Software marketed to instructors allows them to conduct Web searches, using suspicious phrases as keywords. The results often provide irrefutable evidence of plagiarism.

Of course, plagiarism is not confined to students. Recent years have seen a number of high-profile cases—some of them reaching the front pages of newspapers—of well-known scholars who were shown to have copied passages from sources into their own book manuscripts, without proper attribution. In some cases, the scholars maintained that these appropriations were simply a matter of carelessness, and that in the press and volume of work, they had lost track of which words were theirs and which were the words of their sources. But such excuses sounded hollow: These careless acts inevitably embarrassed the scholars professionally, disappointed their many admirers, and tarnished their otherwise fine work and reputations.

You can avoid plagiarism and charges of plagiarism by following the basic rules provided on page 49.

Following is a passage of text, along with several student versions of the ideas represented. (The passage is from Richard Rovere's article on Senator Joseph P. McCarthy, titled "The Most Gifted and Successful Demagogue This Country Has Ever Known.")

> McCarthy never seemed to believe in himself or in anything he had said. He knew that Communists were not in charge of American foreign policy. He knew that they weren't running the United States Army. He knew that he had spent five years looking for Communists in the government and that—although some must certainly have been there, since Communists had turned up in practically every other major government in the world—he hadn't come up with even one.*

One student wrote the following version of this passage:

```
McCarthy never believed in himself or in anything
he had said. He knew that Communists were not in
charge of American foreign policy and weren't run-
ning the United States Army. He knew that he had
spent five years looking for Communists in the
government, and although there must certainly have
been some there, since Communists were in practi-
cally every other major government in the world,
he hadn't come up with even one.
```

Clearly, this is intentional plagiarism. The student has copied the original passage almost word for word.

Here is another version of the same passage:

```
McCarthy knew that Communists were not running
foreign policy or the Army. He also knew that
although there must have been some Communists in
the government, he hadn't found a single one,
even though he had spent five years looking.
```

This student has attempted to put the ideas into her own words, but both the wording and the sentence structure still are so heavily dependent on the original passage that even if it *were* cited, most professors would consider it plagiarism.

---

* Richard Rovere, "The Most Gifted and Successful Demagogue This Country Has Ever Known," *New York Times Magazine* 30 Apr. 1967.

In the following version, the student has sufficiently changed the wording and sentence structure, and she uses a signal phrase (a phrase used to introduce a quotation or paraphrase, signaling to the reader that the words to follow come from someone else) to properly credit the information to Rovere, so that there is no question of plagiarism:

> According to Richard Rovere, McCarthy was fully aware that Communists were running neither the government nor the Army. He also knew that he hadn't found a single Communist in government, even after a lengthy search. (192)

And although this is not a matter of plagiarism, as noted above, it's essential to quote accurately. You are not permitted to change any part of a quotation or to omit any part of it without using brackets or ellipses (see pages 43–46).

RULES FOR AVOIDING PLAGIARISM

- Cite *all* quoted material and *all* summarized and paraphrased material, unless the information is common knowledge (e.g., the Civil War was fought from 1861 to 1865).
- Make sure that both the *wording* and the *sentence structure* of your summaries and paraphrases are substantially your own.

2 Critical Reading and Critique

CRITICAL READING

When writing papers in college, you are often called on to respond critically to source materials. Critical reading requires the abilities to both summarize and evaluate a presentation. As you have seen in Chapter 1, a *summary* is a brief restatement in your own words of the content of a passage. An *evaluation*, however, is a more difficult matter.

In your college work, you read to gain and *use* new information; but as sources are not equally valid or equally useful, you must learn to distinguish critically among them by evaluating them.

There is no ready-made formula for determining validity. Critical reading and its written equivalent—the *critique*—require discernment, sensitivity, imagination, knowledge of the subject, and above all, willingness to become involved in what you read. These skills cannot be taken for granted and are developed only through repeated practice. You must begin somewhere, though, and we recommend that you start by posing two broad categories of questions about passages, articles, and books that you read: (1) To what extent does the author succeed in his or her purpose? (2) To what extent do you agree with the author?

Question 1: To What Extent Does the Author Succeed in His or Her Purpose?

All critical reading *begins with an accurate summary.* Thus before attempting an evaluation, you must be able to locate an author's thesis and identify the selection's content and structure. You must understand the author's *purpose.* Authors write to inform, to persuade, and to entertain. A given piece may be primarily *informative* (a summary of the research on cloning), primarily *persuasive* (an argument on why the government must do something to alleviate homelessness), or primarily *entertaining* (a play about the frustrations of young lovers). Or it may be all three (as in John Steinbeck's novel *The Grapes of Wrath,* about migrant workers during the Great Depression). Sometimes, authors are not fully conscious of their purpose. Sometimes their purpose changes as they write. Also, more than one purpose can overlap: An essay may need to inform the reader about an issue in order to make a persuasive point. But if the finished piece is coherent, it will have a primary reason for having been written, and it should be apparent that the author is attempting primarily to inform, persuade, or entertain a particular audience. To identify this primary reason—this purpose—is your first job as a critical reader. Your next job is to deter-

---

WHERE DO WE FIND WRITTEN CRITIQUES?

Here are just a few types of writing that involve critique:

Academic Writing

- **Research papers.** Critique sources in order to establish their usefulness.
- **Position papers.** Stake out a position by critiquing other positions.
- **Book reviews.** Combine summary with critique.
- **Essay exams.** Demonstrate understanding of course material by critiquing it.

Workplace Writing

- **Legal briefs and legal arguments.** Critique previous rulings or arguments made by opposing counsel.
- **Business plans and proposals.** Critique other, less cost-effective approaches.
- **Policy briefs.** Communicate failings of policies and legislation through critique.

---

mine how successful the author has been. As a critical reader, you bring different criteria, or standards of judgment, to bear when you read pieces intended to inform, persuade, or entertain.

Writing to Inform

A piece intended to inform will provide definitions, describe or report on a process, recount a story, give historical background, and/or provide facts and figures. An informational piece responds to questions such as the following:

What (or who) is _____?

How does _____ work?

What is the controversy or problem about?

What happened?

How and why did it happen?

What were the results?

What are the arguments for and against _____?

To the extent that an author answers these and related questions and the answers are a matter of verifiable record (you could check for accuracy if you had the time and inclination), the selection is intended to inform. Having determined this, you can organize your response by considering three other criteria: accuracy, significance, and fair interpretation of information.

Evaluating Informative Writing

Accuracy of Information. If you are going to use any of the information presented, you must be satisfied that it is trustworthy. One of your responsibilities as a critical reader, then, is to find out if it is accurate. This means you should check facts against other sources. Government publications are often good resources for verifying facts about political legislation, population data, crime statistics, and the like. You can also search key terms in library databases and on the Web. Since material on the Web is essentially "self-published," however, you must be especially vigilant in assessing its legitimacy. A wealth of useful information is now available on the Internet—but there is also a tremendous amount of misinformation, distorted "facts," and unsupported opinion.

Significance of Information. One useful question that you can put to a reading is "So what?" In the case of selections that attempt to inform, you may reasonably wonder whether the information makes a difference. What can the person who is reading gain from this information? How is knowledge advanced by the publication of this material? Is the information of importance to you or to others in a particular audience? Why or why not?

Fair Interpretation of Information. At times you will read reports, the sole function of which is to relate raw data or information. In these cases, you will build your response on Question 1, introduced on page 50: To what extent does the author succeed in his or her purpose? More frequently, once an author has presented information, he or she will attempt to evaluate or interpret it— which is only reasonable, since information that has not been evaluated or interpreted is of little use. One of your tasks as a critical reader is to make a distinction between the author's presentation of facts and figures and his or her attempts to evaluate them. Watch for shifts from straightforward descriptions of factual information ("20 % of the population") to assertions about what this information means ("a *mere* 20 % of the population"), what its implications are, and so on. Pay attention to whether the logic with which the author connects interpretation with facts is sound. You may find that the information is valuable but the interpretation is not. Perhaps the author's conclusions are not justified. Could you offer a contrary explanation for the same facts? Does more information need to be gathered before firm conclusions can be drawn? Why?

Writing to Persuade

Writing is frequently intended to persuade—that is, to influence the reader's thinking. To make a persuasive case, the writer must begin with an assertion that is arguable, some statement about which reasonable people could disagree. Such an assertion, when it serves as the essential organizing principle of the article or book, is called a *thesis*. Here are two examples:

> Because they do not speak English, many children in this affluent land are being denied their fundamental right to equal educational opportunity.

> Bilingual education, which has been stridently promoted by a small group of activists with their own agenda, is detrimental to the very students it is supposed to serve.

Thesis statements such as these—and the subsequent assertions used to help support them—represent conclusions that authors have drawn as a result of researching and thinking about an issue. You go through the same process yourself when you write persuasive papers or critiques. And just as you are entitled to critically evaluate the assertions of authors you read, so your professors—and other students—are entitled to evaluate *your* assertions, whether they be encountered as written arguments or as comments made in class discussion.

Keep in mind that writers organize arguments by arranging evidence to support one conclusion and oppose (or dismiss) another. You can assess the validity of the argument and the conclusion by determining whether the author has (1) clearly defined key terms, (2) used information fairly, (3) argued logically and not fallaciously (see pages 57–61).

EXERCISE **2.1**

Informative and Persuasive Thesis Statements

With a partner from your class, identify at least one informative and one persuasive thesis statement from two passages of your own choosing. Photocopy these passages and highlight the statements you have selected.

As an alternative, and also working with a partner, write one informative and one persuasive thesis statement for *three* of the topics listed in the last paragraph of this exercise. For example, for the topic of prayer in schools, your informative thesis statement could read this way:

> Both advocates and opponents of school prayer frame their position as a matter of freedom.

Your persuasive thesis statement might be worded as follows:

> As long as schools don't dictate what kinds of prayers students should say, then school prayer should be allowed and even encouraged.

Don't worry about taking a position that you agree with or feel you could support. The exercise doesn't require that you write an essay at this point. The topics:

school prayer

gun control

sex education in schools

grammar instruction in English class

violent lyrics in music

teaching computer skills in primary schools

curfews in college dormitories

course registration procedures

Evaluating Persuasive Writing

Read the argument that follows on the nation's troubled "star" system for producing elite athletes and dancers. We will illustrate our discussion on defining terms, using information fairly, and arguing logically by referring to Joan Ryan's argument. The example critique that follows these illustrations will be based on this same argument.

We Are Not Created Equal in Every Way
Joan Ryan

In an opinion piece for The San Francisco Chronicle *(December 12, 2000), columnist and reporter Joan Ryan takes a stand on whether the San Francisco Ballet School did or did not discriminate against 8-year-old Fredrika Keefer when it declined to admit her on the grounds that she had the wrong body type to be a successful ballerina. Keefer's mother subsequently sued the ballet school for discrimination, claiming that the rejection had caused her daughter confusion and humiliation. Ryan examines the question of setting admissions standards and also the problems some parents create by pushing their young children to meet these standards.*

1   Fredrika Keefer is an 8-year-old girl who likes to dance, just like her mother and grandmother before her. She relishes playing the lead role of Clara in the Pacific Dance Theater's "Petite Nutcracker." So perhaps she is not as shy as many fourth-graders. But I wonder how she feels about her body being a topic of public discussion.

2   Fredrika and her mother filed suit because, as her mother puts it, she "did not have the right body type to be accepted" by the San Francisco Ballet School. "My daughter is very sophisticated, so she understands why we're doing this," Krissy Keefer said. "And the other kids think she's a celebrity."

3   There is no question Keefer raises a powerful point in her complaint. The values placed on an unnaturally thin body for female performers drives some

dancers to potentially fatal eating disorders. But that isn't exactly the issue here. This is: Does the San Francisco Ballet School have the right to give preference to leaner body types in selecting 300 students from this year's 1,400 applicants?

4   Yes, for the same reason UC Berkeley can reject students based on mental prowess and a fashion modeling school can reject students based on comeliness. Every institution has standards that weed out those who are less likely to succeed. I know this flies in the face of American ideals. But the reality is that all men and women are not created equal.

5   Like it or not, the ethereal, elongated body that can float on air is part of the look and feel of classical ballet. You and I might think ballet would be just as pleasing with larger bodies. But most of those who practice the art disagree, which is their right. This doesn't mean that women with different body types cannot become professional dancers. They just have to find a different type of dance—jazz, tap, modern— just as athletes have to find sports that fit certain body types. A tall, blocky man, for example, could not be a jockey but he could play baseball.

6   Having written extensively about the damaging pressures on young female gymnasts and figure skaters, I understand Keefer's concerns about body type. But for me, the more disturbing issue in this story isn't about weight but age.

7   The San Francisco Ballet School is very clear and open about the fact it is strictly a training ground for professional dancers. "We are not a recreation department," said a ballet spokeswoman.

8   In other words, children at age 8 are already training for adult careers. By age 12 or 13, the children are training so much that they either begin homeschooling or attend a school that accommodates the training schedule. The child has thrown all her eggs into this one little basket at an age when most kids can barely decide what to wear to school in the morning. And the child knows the parents are paying lots of money for this great opportunity.

9   The ballet school usually has a psychologist to counsel the students, but at the moment there is not one on staff. And the parents are given no training by the school on the pitfalls their daughters might encounter as they climb the ballet ladder: weight issues, physical ailments, social isolation, psychological pressure.

10   Just as in elite gymnastics and figure skating, these children are in the netherland of the law. They are neither hobbyists nor professionals. There is no safety net for them, no arm of government that makes sure that the adults in their lives watch out for their best interests.

11   Keefer said she would drop her lawsuit if the school accepted her daughter. The San Francisco Ballet School offers the best training in the Bay Area, she said. Fredrika, however, has said she is quite happy dancing where she is. Still, the mother gets to decide what's best for her daughter's dancing career. The child is clearly too young to make such a decision. Yet, in the skewed logic of elite athletics and dancing, she is not too young to pay the price for it.

Critical Reading Practice

Look back at the Critical Reading for Summary box on page 6 of Chapter 1. Use each of the guidelines listed there to examine the essay by Ryan. Note in the margins of the selection, or on a separate sheet of paper, the essay's main point, subpoints, and use of examples.

Persuasive Strategies

Clearly Defined Terms. The validity of an argument depends to some degree on how carefully an author has defined key terms. Take the assertion, for example, that American society must be grounded in "family values." Just what do people who use this phrase mean by it? The validity of their argument depends on whether they and their readers agree on a definition of "family values"—as well as what it means to be "grounded in" family values. If an author writes that in the recent past "America's elites accepted as a matter of course that a free society can sustain itself only through virtue and temperance in the people" (Charles Murray, "The Coming White Underclass," *Wall Street Journal,* October 20, 1993), readers need to know what, exactly, the author means by "elites" and by "virtue and temperance" before they can assess the validity of the argument. In such cases, the success of the argument—its ability to persuade—hinges on the definition of a term. So, in responding to an argument, be sure you (and the author) are clear on what exactly is being argued. Unless you are, no informed response is possible.

Ryan uses several terms important for understanding her argument. The primary one is the "body type" that the San Francisco Ballet School uses as an application standard. Ryan defines this type (paragraph 5) as "the elongated body that can float on air." Leaving other terms undefined, she writes that the ballet school's use of body type as a standard "flies in the face of American ideals" (paragraph 4). Exactly *which* ideals she leaves for the reader to define: These might include fair play, equality of access, or the belief that decisions ought to be based on talent, not appearance. The reader cannot be sure. When she reports that a spokeswoman for the school stated that "We are not a recreation department," Ryan assumes the reader will understand the reference. The mission of a recreation department is to give *all* participants equal access. In a youth recreation league, children of all abilities would get to play in a baseball game. In a league for elite athletes, in which winning was a priority, coaches would permit only the most talented children to play.

When writing a paper, you will need to decide, like Ryan, which terms to define and which you can assume the reader will define in the same way you do. As the writer of a critique, you should identify and discuss any undefined or ambiguous term that might give rise to confusion.

Fair Use of Information. Information is used as evidence in support of arguments. When you encounter such evidence, ask yourself two questions:
(1) "Is the information accurate and up-to-date?" At least a portion of an argument becomes invalid if the information used to support it is inaccurate or out-
of-date. (2) "Has the author cited *representative* information?" The evidence used
in an argument must be presented in a spirit of fair play. An author is less than
ethical when he presents only evidence favoring his views even though he is
well aware that contrary evidence exists. For instance, it would be dishonest to
argue that an economic recession is imminent and to cite only indicators of economic downturn while ignoring and failing to cite contrary (positive) evidence.

As you have seen, "We Are Not Created Equal in Every Way" is not an
information-heavy essay. The success of the piece turns on the author's use
of logic, not facts and figures. In this case, the reader has every reason to
trust that Ryan has presented the facts accurately: An 8-year-old girl has
been denied admission to a prestigious ballet school. The mother of the girl
has sued the school.

Logical Argumentation: Avoiding Logical Fallacies

At some point, you will need to respond to the logic of the argument itself. To
be convincing, an argument should be governed by principles of *logic*—clear
and orderly thinking. This does *not* mean that an argument should not be
biased. A biased argument—that is, an argument weighted toward one point
of view and against others, which is in fact the nature of argument—may be
valid as long as it is logically sound.

Several examples of faulty thinking and logical fallacies to watch for
follow.

Emotionally Loaded Terms. Writers sometimes attempt to sway readers by
using emotionally charged words—words with positive connotations to sway
readers to their own point of view (e.g., "family values") or words with negative connotations to sway readers away from the opposing point of view. The
fact that an author uses emotionally loaded terms does not necessarily invalidate the argument. Emotional appeals are perfectly legitimate and time-
honored modes of persuasion. But in academic writing, which is grounded in
logical argumentation, they should not be the *only* means of persuasion. You
should be sensitive to *how* emotionally loaded terms are being used. In particular, are they being used deceptively or to hide the essential facts?

Ryan appeals to our desire to protect children in "We Are Not Created
Equal in Every Way." She writes of "disturbing issue[s]," lack of a "safety net
for" young people on the star track to elite performance and an absence of
adults "watch[ing] out for [the children's] best interests." Ryan understands
that no reader wants to see a child abused; and while she does not use the
word *abuse* in her essay, she implies that parents who push young children
too hard to succeed commit abuse. That implication is enough to engage the
sympathies of the reader. As someone evaluating the essay, you should be

alert to this appeal to your emotions and then judge if the appeal is fair and convincing. Above all, you should not let an emotional appeal blind you to shortcomings of logic, ambiguously defined terms, or a misuse of facts.

Ad Hominem **Argument.** In an *ad hominem* argument, the writer rejects opposing views by attacking the person who holds them. By calling opponents names, an author avoids the issue. Consider this excerpt from a political speech:

> I could more easily accept my opponent's plan to increase revenues by collecting on delinquent tax bills if he had paid more than a hundred dollars in state taxes in each of the past three years. But the fact is, he's a millionaire with a millionaire's tax shelters. This man hasn't paid a wooden nickel for the state services he and his family depend on. So I ask you: Is *he* the one to be talking about taxes to *us?*

It could well be that the opponent has paid virtually no state taxes for three years; but this fact has nothing to do with, and is a ploy to divert attention from, the merits of a specific proposal for increasing revenues. The proposal is lost in the attack against the man himself, an attack that violates the principles of logic. Writers (and speakers) must make their points by citing evidence in support of their views and by challenging contrary evidence.

Does Ryan attack Fredrika Keefer's mother in this essay? You be the judge. Here are lines referring directly or indirectly to Krissy Keefer. Is Ryan attacking the mother, directly or indirectly? Point to specific words and phrases to support your conclusion:

> Fredrika and her mother filed suit because, as her mother puts it, she "did not have the right body type to be accepted" by the San Francisco Ballet School. "My daughter is very sophisticated, so she understands why we're doing this," Krissy Keefer said. "And the other kids think she's a celebrity."

> There is no question Keefer raises a powerful point in her complaint.

> Keefer said she would drop her lawsuit if the school accepted her daughter. The San Francisco Ballet School offers the best training in the Bay Area, she said. Fredrika, however, has said she is quite happy dancing where she is. Still, the mother gets to decide what's best for her daughter's dancing career. The child is clearly too young to make such a decision. Yet, in the skewed logic of elite athletics and dancing, she is not too young to pay the price for it.

Faulty Cause and Effect. The fact that one event precedes another in time does not mean that the first event has caused the second. An example: Fish begin dying by the thousands in a lake near your hometown. An environmental group immediately cites chemical dumping by several manufacturing plants as the cause. But other causes are possible: A disease might have affected the

---

TONE

Tone refers to the overall emotional effect produced by the writer's choice of language. Writers might use especially emphatic words to create a tone: A film reviewer might refer to a "magnificent performance" or a columnist might criticize "sleazeball politics."

These are extreme examples of tone; but tone can be more subtle, particularly if the writer makes a special effort *not* to inject emotion into the writing. As we've indicated above in the section on emotionally loaded terms, the fact that a writer's tone is highly emotional does not necessarily mean that the writer's argument is invalid. Conversely, a neutral tone does not ensure an argument's validity.

Note that many instructors discourage student writing that projects a highly emotional tone, considering it inappropriate for academic or preprofessional work. (One sure sign of emotion: the exclamation mark, which should be used sparingly.)

---

fish; the growth of algae might have contributed to the deaths; or acid rain might be a factor. The origins of an event are usually complex and are not always traceable to a single cause. So you must carefully examine cause-and-effect reasoning when you find a writer using it. In Latin, this fallacy is known as *post hoc, ergo propter hoc* ("after this, therefore because of this").

The debate over the San Francisco Ballet School's refusal to admit Fredrika Keefer involves a question of cause and effect. Is Fredrika Keefer's rejection by the ballet school caused by the school's insistence that its students have an "ethereal, elongated body"? Certainly if the school changes that standard, the outcome changes: Fredrika Keefer is admitted. Or is the cause of the rejection, as the school claims, Fredrika's body type? Change her body type (in a few years she may grow), and she may be admitted. The debate is at least partially about cause and effect. The ballet school and the mother are pointing to the same effect—Fredrika's rejection—but disagree, to the point of going to court, over the cause.

Ryan uses cause-and-effect logic in the essay to suggest that Fredrika Keefer's mother, and by extension all parent managers, can cause their children harm by pushing them too hard in their training. At the end of the essay, Ryan writes that Fredrika is too young "to decide what's best for her . . . dancing career" but that "she is not too young to pay the price for" the decisions her mother makes to promote that career. The "price" Fredrika pays will be "caused" by her mother's (poor) decisions.

Either/Or Reasoning. Either/or reasoning also results from an unwillingness to recognize complexity. If an author analyzes a problem and offers only two courses of action, one of which he or she refutes, then you are entitled to object that the other is not thereby true. Usually, several other options (at the very least) are possible. For whatever reason, the author has chosen to over-look them. As an example, suppose you are reading a selection on genetic engineering and the author builds an argument on the basis of the following:

> Research in gene splicing is at a crossroads: Either scientists will be carefully monitored by civil authorities and their efforts limited to acceptable applications, such as disease control; or, lacking regulato-ry guidelines, scientists will set their own ethical standards and begin programs in embryonic manipulation that, however well intended, exceed the proper limits of human knowledge.

Certainly, other possibilities for genetic engineering exist beyond the two mentioned here. But the author limits debate by establishing an either/or choice. Such limitation is artificial and does not allow for complexity. As a crit-ical reader, be on the alert for either/or reasoning.

Hasty Generalization. Writers are guilty of hasty generalization when they draw their conclusions from too little evidence or from unrepresentative evi-dence. To argue that scientists should not proceed with the human genome project because a recent editorial urged that the project be abandoned is to make a hasty generalization. This lone editorial may be unrepresentative of the views of most individuals—both scientists and laypeople—who have studied and written about the matter. To argue that one should never obey authority because Stanley Milgram's Yale University experiments in the 1960s show the dangers of obedience is to ignore the fact that Milgram's experi-ments were concerned primarily with obedience to *immoral* authority. Thus, the experimental situation was unrepresentative of most routine demands for obedience—for example, to obey a parental rule or to comply with a sum-mons for jury duty—and a conclusion about the malevolence of all authori-ty would be a hasty generalization.

False Analogy. Comparing one person, event, or issue to another may be illu-minating, but it may also be confusing or misleading. Differences between the two may be more significant than the similarities, and conclusions drawn from one may not necessarily apply to the other. A writer who argues that it is reasonable to quarantine people with AIDS because quarantine has been effective in preventing the spread of smallpox is assuming an analogy between AIDS and smallpox that is not valid (because of the differences between the two diseases).

Ryan compares the San Francisco Ballet School's setting an admissions standard to both a university's and a modeling school's setting standards. Are the analogies apt? Certainly one can draw a parallel between the stan-dards used by the ballet school and a modeling school: Both emphasize a candidate's appearance, among other qualities. Are the admissions standards to a university based on appearance? In principle, no. At least that's not a criterion any college admissions office would post on its Web site. A critical reader might therefore want to object that one of Ryan's analogies is faulty.

Ryan attempts to advance her argument by making another comparison:

> [The rejection of a candidate because she does not have a body suited to classical ballet] doesn't mean that women with different body types cannot become professional dancers. They just have to find a different type of dance—jazz, tap, modern—just as athletes have to find sports that fit certain body types. A tall, blocky man, for example, could not be a jockey but he could play baseball.

The words "just as" signal an attempt to advance the argument by making an analogy. What do you think? Is the analogy sufficiently similar to Fredrika Keefer's situation to persuade you?

Begging the Question. To beg the question is to assume as a proven fact the very thesis being argued. To assert, for example, that America is not in decline because it is as strong and prosperous as ever is not to prove anything: It is merely to repeat the claim in different words. This fallacy is also known as *circular reasoning.*

When Ryan writes that "There is no safety net for [children placed into elite training programs], no arm of government that makes sure that the adults in their lives watch out for their best interests," she assumes that there should be such a safety net. But, as you will read in the sample critique, this is a point that must be argued, not assumed. Is such intervention wise? Under what circumstances, for instance, would authorities intervene in a family? Would authorities have the legal standing to get involved if there were no clear evidence of physical abuse? Ryan is not necessarily wrong in desiring "safety nets" for young, elite athletes and dancers; but she assumes a point that she should be arguing.

Non Sequitur. *Non sequitur* is Latin for "it does not follow"; the term is used to describe a conclusion that does not logically follow from a premise. "Since minorities have made such great strides in the past few decades," a writer may argue, "we no longer need affirmative action programs." Aside from the fact that the premise itself is arguable (*have* minorities made such great strides?), it does not follow that because minorities *may* have made great strides, there is no further need for affirmative action programs.

Oversimplification. Be alert for writers who offer easy solutions to complicated problems. "America's economy will be strong again if we all 'buy American,'" a politician may argue. But the problems of America's economy are complex and cannot be solved by a slogan or a simple change in buying habits. Likewise, a writer who argues that we should ban genetic engineering assumes that simple solutions ("just say 'no'") will be sufficient to deal with the complex moral dilemmas raised by this new technology.

Understanding Logical Fallacies

Make a list of the nine logical fallacies discussed in the last section. Briefly define each one in your own words. Then, in a group of three or four classmates, review your definitions and the examples we've provided for each logical fallacy. Collaborate with your group to find or invent examples for each of the fallacies. Compare your examples with those generated by the other groups in your class.

Writing to Entertain

Authors write not only to inform and persuade but also to entertain. One response to entertainment is a hearty laugh, but it is possible to entertain without encouraging laughter: A good book or play or poem may prompt you to reflect, grow wistful, become elated, get angry. Laughter is only one of many possible reactions. As with a response to an informative piece or an argument, your response to an essay, poem, story, play, novel, or film should be precisely stated and carefully developed. Ask yourself some of the following questions (you won't have space to explore all of them, but try to consider some of the most important): Did I care for the portrayal of a certain character? Did that character (or a group of characters united by occupation, age, ethnicity, etc.) seem overly sentimental, for example, or heroic? Did his adversaries seem too villainous or stupid? Were the situations believable? Was the action interesting or merely formulaic? Was the theme developed subtly or powerfully, or did the work come across as preachy or shrill? Did the action at the end of the work follow plausibly from what had come before? Was the language fresh and incisive or stale and predictable? Explain as specifically as possible what elements of the work seemed effective or ineffective and why. Offer an overall assessment, elaborating on your views.

Question 2: To What Extent Do You Agree with the Author?

When formulating a critical response to a source, try to distinguish your evaluation of the author's purpose and success at achieving that purpose from your agreement or disagreement with the author's views. The distinction allows you to respond to a piece of writing on its merits. As an unbiased, evenhanded critic, you evaluate an author's clarity of presentation, use of evidence, and adherence to principles of logic. To what extent has the author succeeded in achieving his or her purpose? Still withholding judgment, offer your assessment and give the author (in effect) a grade. Significantly, your assessment of the presentation may not coincide with your views of the author's conclusions: You may agree with an author entirely but feel that the presentation is superficial; you may find the author's logic and use of evidence to be rock solid but at the same time may resist certain conclusions. A critical evaluation works well when it is conducted in two parts. After evaluating the author's purpose and design for achieving that purpose, respond to the author's main assertions. In doing so, you'll want to identify points of agreement and disagreement and also evaluate assumptions.

Identify Points of Agreement and Disagreement

Be precise in identifying points of agreement and disagreement with an author. You should state as clearly as possible what *you* believe, and an effective way of doing this is to define your position in relation to that presented in the piece. Whether you agree enthusiastically, disagree, or agree with reservations, you can organize your reactions in two parts: (1) summarize the author's position; and (2) state your own position and elaborate on your reasons for holding it. The elaboration, in effect, becomes an argument itself, and this is true regardless of the position you take. An opinion is effective when you support it by supplying evidence from your reading (which should be properly cited), your observation, or your personal experience. Without such evidence, opinions cannot be authoritative. "I thought the article on inflation was lousy." Or: "It was terrific." Why? "I just thought so, that's all." This opinion is worthless because the criticism is imprecise: The critic has taken neither the time to read the article carefully nor the time to explore his or her own reactions carefully.

EXERCISE 2.4

Exploring Your Viewpoints—in Three Paragraphs

Go to a Web site that presents short persuasive essays on current social issues, such as reason.com, opinion-pages.org, drudgereport.com, or Speakout.com. Or go to an Internet search engine and type in a social issue together with the word "articles," "editorials," or "opinion," and see what you find. Locate a selection on a topic of interest that takes a clear, argumentative position. Print out the selection on which you choose to focus. Write one paragraph summarizing the author's key argument. Write two paragraphs articulating your agreement or disagreement with the author. (Devote each paragraph to a *single* point of agreement or disagreement.) Be sure to explain why you think or feel the way you do and, wherever possible, cite relevant evidence—from your reading, experience, or observation.

Explore the Reasons for Agreement and Disagreement: Evaluate Assumptions

One way of elaborating your reactions to a reading is to explore the underlying *reasons* for agreement and disagreement. Your reactions are based largely on assumptions that you hold and how these assumptions compare with the author's. An *assumption* is a fundamental statement about the world and its operations that you take to be true. A writer's assumptions may be explicitly stated; but just as often, assumptions are implicit and you will have to "ferret them out"—that is, to infer them. Consider an example:

> *In vitro* fertilization and embryo transfer are brought about outside the bodies of the couple through actions of third parties whose competence and technical activity determine the success of the procedure. Such fertilization entrusts the life and identity of the embryo into the power of doctors and biologists and establishes the domination of technology over the origin and destiny of the human person. Such a relationship of domination is in itself contrary to the dignity and equality that must be common to parents and children.*

This paragraph is quoted from the February 1987 Vatican document on artificial procreation. Then Cardinal Joseph Ratzinger (and now Pope Benedict XVI), principal author of the document, makes an implicit assumption in this paragraph: No good can come of the domination of technology over conception. The use of technology to bring about conception is morally wrong. Yet thousands of childless couples, Roman Catholics included, have rejected this assumption in favor of its opposite: Conception technology is an aid to the barren couple; far from creating a relationship of unequals, the technology brings children into the world who will be welcomed with joy and love.

Assumptions provide the foundation on which entire presentations are built. If you find an author's assumptions invalid—that is, not supported by factual evidence—or if you disagree with value-based assumptions underlying an author's positions, you may well disagree with conclusions that follow from these assumptions. The author of a book on developing nations may include a section outlining the resources and time that will be required to industrialize a particular country and so upgrade its general welfare. Her assumption—that industrialization in that particular country will ensure or even affect the general welfare—may or may not be valid. If you do not share the assumption, in your eyes the rationale for the entire book may be undermined.

How do you determine the validity of assumptions once you have identified them? In the absence of more scientific criteria, you may determine validity by how well the author's assumptions stack up against your own experience, observations, reading, and values. A caution, however: The overall value of an article or book may depend only to a small degree on the validity of the author's assumptions. For instance, a sociologist may do a fine job of gathering statistical data about the incidence of crime in urban areas along the eastern seaboard. The sociologist also might be a Marxist, and you may disagree with the subsequent analysis of the data. Yet you may still find the data extremely valuable for your own work.

Readers will want to examine two assumptions at the heart of Ryan's essay on Fredrika Keefer and the San Francisco Ballet School's refusal to admit her. First, Ryan assumes that setting a standard for admission based on a candidate's appearance is equivalent to setting a standard based on a candi-

---

* From the Vatican document *Instruction on Respect for Human Life in Its Origin and on the Dignity of Procreation,* given at Rome, from the Congregation for the Doctrine of the Faith, 22 Feb. 1987, as presented in *Origins: N.C. Documentary Service* 16.40 (19 Mar. 1987): 707.

date's "mental prowess," the admissions standard (presumably) used by universities. An appearance-based standard, Ryan writes, will "weed out those who are less likely to succeed" in professional ballet. The writer of the critique that follows agrees with Ryan's assumption. But you may not. You may assume, by contrast, that standards based on appearance are arbitrary while those based on intellectual ability rest on documented talent (SAT scores or high school transcripts, for instance). Ryan makes a second assumption: that there is an appropriate and inappropriate way to raise children. She does not state these (appropriate) ways explicitly, but that does not keep Ryan from using them to judge Krissy Keefer harshly. You may disagree with Ryan and find a reason to cheer Krissy Keefer's defense of her daughter's rights. That's your decision. What you must do as a critical reader is recognize assumptions whether they are stated openly or not. You should spell them out and then accept or reject them. Ultimately, your agreement or disagreement with an author will rest on your agreement or disagreement with the author's assumptions.

CRITIQUE

In Chapter 1 we focused on summary—the condensed presentation of ideas from another source. Summary is key to much of academic writing because it relies so heavily on the works of others for support of claims. It's not going too far to say that summarizing is the critical thinking skill from which a majority of academic writing builds. However, most academic thinking and writing do not stop at summary; usually we use summary to restate our understanding of things we see or read. Then we put that summary to use. In academic writing, one typical use of summary is as a prelude to critique.

A *critique* is a *formalized, critical reading of a passage.* It also is a personal response, but writing a critique is considerably more rigorous than saying that a movie is "great," or a book is "fascinating," or "I didn't like it." These are all responses, and, as such, they're a valid, even essential, part of your understanding of what you see and read. But such responses don't illuminate the subject for anyone—even you—if you haven't explained how you arrived at your conclusions.

Your task in writing a critique is to turn your critical reading of a passage into a systematic evaluation in order to deepen your reader's (and your own) understanding of that passage. Among other things, you're interested in determining what an author says, how well the points are made, what assumptions underlie the argument, what issues are overlooked, and what implications can be drawn from such an analysis. Critiques, positive or negative, should include a fair and accurate summary of the passage; they may draw on and cite information and ideas from other sources (your reading or your personal experience and observations); and they should also include a statement of your own assumptions. It is important to remember that you bring to bear an entire set of assumptions about the world. Stated or not, these assumptions underlie every evaluative comment you make; you therefore

GUIDELINES FOR WRITING CRITIQUES

- *Introduce.* Introduce both the passage under analysis and the author. State the author's main argument and the point(s) you intend to make about it.

    Provide background material to help your readers understand the relevance or appeal of the passage. This background material might include one or more of the following: an explanation of why the subject is of current interest; a reference to a possible controversy surrounding the subject of the passage or the passage itself; biographical information about the author; an account of the circumstances under which the passage was written; or a reference to the intended audience of the passage.
- *Summarize.* Summarize the author's main points, making sure to state the author's purpose for writing.
- *Assess the presentation.* Evaluate the validity of the author's presentation, as distinct from your points of agreement or disagreement. Comment on the author's success in achieving his or her purpose by reviewing three or four specific points. You might base your review on one (or more) of the following criteria:

    Is the information accurate?

    Is the information significant?

    Has the author defined terms clearly?

    Has the author used and interpreted information fairly?

    Has the author argued logically?

- *Respond to the presentation.* Now it is your turn to respond to the author's views. With which views do you agree? With which do you disagree? Discuss your reasons for agreement and disagreement, when possible, tying these reasons to assumptions—both the author's and your own. Where necessary, draw upon outside sources to support your ideas.
- *Conclude.* State your conclusions about the overall validity of the piece—your assessment of the author's success at achieving his or her aims and your reactions to the author's views. Remind the reader of the weaknesses and strengths of the passage.

have an obligation, both to the reader and to yourself, to clarify your standards by making your assumptions explicit. Not only do your readers stand to gain by your forthrightness, but you do as well: In the process of writing a critical assessment, you are forced to examine your own knowledge, beliefs, and assumptions. Ultimately, the critique is a way of learning about yourself—yet another example of the ways in which writing is useful as a tool for critical thinking.

How to Write Critiques

You may find it useful to organize your critiques into five sections: introduction, summary, assessment of the presentation (on its own terms), your response to the presentation, and conclusion.

The box on page 66 offers some guidelines for writing critiques. Note that they are guidelines, not a rigid formula. Thousands of authors write critiques that do not follow the structure outlined here. Until you are more confident and practiced in writing critiques, however, we suggest you follow these guidelines. They are meant not to restrict you, but rather to provide a workable sequence for writing critiques.

DEMONSTRATION: CRITIQUE

The critique that follows is based on Joan Ryan's "We Are Not Created Equal in Every Way," which appeared in *The San Francisco Chronicle* as an op-ed piece on December 12, 2000 (see pages 54–55), and which we have to some extent already begun to examine. In this formal critique, you will see that it is possible to agree with an author's main point, at least provisionally, but disagree with other elements of the argument. Critiquing a different selection, you could just as easily accept the author's facts and figures but reject the conclusion he draws from them. As long as you carefully articulate the author's assumptions and your own, explaining in some detail your agreement and disagreement, the critique is yours to take in whatever direction you see fit.

Let's summarize the preceding sections by returning to the core questions that guide critical reading. You will see how, when applied to Joan Ryan's argument, they help to set up a critique.

To What Extent Does the Author Succeed in His or Her Purpose?

To answer this question, you will need to know the author's purpose. Joan Ryan's "We Are Not Created Equal in Every Way" is an argument—actually, *two* related arguments. She wants readers to accept her view that (1) a school of performing arts has the right to set admissions standards according to criteria it believes will ensure the professional success of its graduates; and (2) parents may damage their children by pushing them too hard to meet the standards set by these schools.

By supporting a ballet school's right to set admission standards based on appearance, Ryan supports the star system that produces our elite athletes and performers. At the same time, she disapproves of parents who risk their children's safety and welfare by pushing them through this system. Ryan both defends the system and attacks it. Her ambivalence on the issue keeps the argument from fully succeeding.

To What Extent Do You Agree with the Author? Evaluate Assumptions.

Ryan's views on the debate surrounding Fredrika Keefer's rejection from the San Francisco School of Ballet rest on the assumption that the school has the right to set its own admissions standards—even if we find those standards harsh. All institutions, she claims, have that right. The writer of the critique that follows agrees with Ryan, although you have seen previously how it is possible to disagree.

Ryan's second argument concerns the wisdom of subjecting an 8-year-old to the rigors of professional training. Ryan disapproves. The writer of the critique, while sympathetic to Ryan's concerns, states that as a practical and even as a legal matter it would be nearly impossible to prevent parents such as Krissy Keefer from doing exactly as they pleased in the name of helping their children. In our culture, parents have the right (short of outright abuse) to raise children however they see fit.

Finally, the writer of the critique notes a certain ambivalence in Ryan's essay: her support of the ballet school's admission standards on the one hand and her distaste of parent managers like Krissy Keefer on the other. The writer does not find evidence of a weak argument in Ryan's mixed message but rather a sign of confusion in the broader culture: We love our young stars but we condemn parents for pushing children to the breaking point in the name of stardom.

The selections you will be likely to critique are those, like Ryan's, that argue a specific position. Indeed, every argument you read is an invitation to agree or disagree. It remains only for you to speak up and justify your position.

MODEL CRITIQUE

Ralston 1

Eric Ralston
Professor Reilly
Writing 2
11 January 2007

A Critique of "We Are Not Created Equal
in Every Way" by Joan Ryan

1 Most freshmen know how it feels to apply to a school
and be rejected. Each year, college admissions offices
mail thousands of thin letters that begin: "Thank you
for your application. The competition this year was
unusually strong. . . ." We know that we will not get
into every college on our list or pass every test or

win the starring role after every audition, but we
believe that we deserve the chance to try. And we can
tolerate rejection if we know that we compete on a
level playing field. But when that field seems to
arbitrarily favor some candidates over others, we take
offense. At least that's when an ambitious mother took
offense, bringing to court a suit that claimed her
eight-year-old daughter, Fredrika Keefer, was denied
admission to the prestigious San Francisco Ballet
School because she had the wrong "body type" (A29).

2   In an opinion piece for the San Francisco
Chronicle (12 December 2000), Joan Ryan asks: "Does
[a ballet school] have the right to give preference
to leaner body types?" Her answer is a firm "yes."
Ryan argues that institutions have the right to set
whatever standards they want to ensure that those
they admit meet the physical or intellectual requirements for professional success. But she also believes
that some parents push their children too hard to
meet those standards. Ryan offers a questionable
approach to protecting children from the possible
abuses of such parents. Overall, however, she raises
timely issues in discussing the star system that produces our world-class athletes and performers. The
sometimes conflicting concerns she expresses reflect
contradictions and tensions in our larger culture.

3   The issue Ryan discusses is a particularly sensitive one because the child's mother charged the ballet
school with discrimination. As a society we have made
great strides over the past few decades in combating
some of the more blatant forms of discrimination--
racial, ethnic, and sexual. But is it possible, is it
desirable, to eliminate all efforts to distinguish
one person from another? When is a standard that permits some (but not all) people entry to an institution discriminatory and when is it a necessary part
of doing business? Ryan believes that schools discriminate all the time, and rightly so when candidates for admission fail to meet the stated criteria
for academic or professional success. That UC
Berkeley does not accept every applicant is discriminating, not discriminatory. Ryan recognizes the difference.

4   She maintains, correctly, that the San Francisco
Ballet School, like any other institution, has the
right to set standards by which it will accept or

reject applicants. Rejection is a part of life, she writes, expressing the view that gives her essay its title: "We Are Not Created Equal in Every Way." And because we are not created equal, not everyone will be admitted to his or her number one school or get a turn on stage. That's the inevitable consequence of setting standards: Some people will meet them and gain admission, others won't. Ryan quotes the spokesperson who explained that the San Francisco Ballet School is "'not a recreation department'" (A29). In other words, a professional ballet school, like a university, is within its rights to reject applicants with body types unsuited to its view of success in professional ballet. The standard may be cruel and to some even arbitrary, but it is understandable. To put the matter bluntly, candidates with unsuitable body types, however talented or otherwise attractive, are less likely to succeed in professional ballet than those with "classical" proportions. Female dancers, for example, must regularly be lifted and carried, as if effortlessly, by their male counterparts--a feat that is difficult enough even with "leaner body types." Ryan points out that candidates without the ideal body type for ballet are not barred from professional dance: "[t]hey just have to find a different type of dance . . . just as athletes have to find sports that fit certain body types" (A29).

5   The San Francisco Ballet School is <u>not</u> saying that people of a certain skin color or religious belief are not welcome. That <u>would</u> be discriminatory and wrong. But the standard concerning body type cuts across <u>all</u> people, rich or poor, black or white, Protestant or Jew, male or female. Such a broad standard could be termed an equal opportunity standard: If it can be used to distinguish among all people equally, it is discriminating, not discriminatory.

6   Ryan's parallel concern in this essay is the damage done to children by parents who push them at an early age to meet the high standards set by professional training programs. Children placed onto such star tracks attend special schools (or receive home schooling) in order to accommodate intense training schedules that sometimes lead to physical or psychological injuries. In healthy families, we might expect parents to protect children from such dangers. But

parents who manage what they view as their children's "careers" may be too single minded to realize that their actions may place Johnny and Susie at risk.

7   Ryan disapproves of a star track system that puts children into professional training at a young age. In pursuing a career in dance, for instance, a young "child has thrown all her eggs into this one little basket at an age when most kids can barely decide what to wear to school in the morning" (A29). The law makes no provision for protecting such elite performers in training, writes Ryan: "There is no safety net for them, no arm of government that makes sure that the adults in their lives watch out for their best interests" (A29).

8   Like the rest of us, Ryan assumes there are appropriate and inappropriate ways to raise children. While she does not explicitly share her preferred approach, she is very clear about what does not work: pushing children like Fredrika Keefer into professional ballet school. When Ryan points out that "no arm of government" looks out for children like Keefer, she implies the need for a Department of Youth Services to supervise parent managers. That is not a good idea.

9   There is no sure way to tell when a parent's managing of a child's dance or athletic schedule is abusive or constructive. Intense dedication is necessary for would-be elite athletes and performers to succeed, and such dedication often begins in childhood. Since young children are not equipped to organize their lives in pursuit of a single goal, parents step in to help. That's what the parents of Tiger Woods did on recognizing his talents:

> [H]is father . . . [started] him very early.
> . . . [Tiger] was on the Mike Douglas show hitting golf balls when he was three years old. I mean, this is a prodigy type thing. This is like Mozart writing his first symphony when he was six, that sort of thing, and he did show unique ability right from the beginning. And his life has been channeled into being a pro. His father has devoted his life to bringing him to this point. His father hasn't worked full-time since 1988. That's what it's been all about. (Feinstein)

10   Ryan would point out, correctly, that for every Tiger Woods or Michelle Kwan there are many child-athletes and performing artists who fall short of their goals. They may later regret the single-minded focus that robbed them of their childhood, but there is no way to know before committing a child to years of dedicated practice if he or she will become the next Tiger or an embittered also-ran. We simply do not have the wisdom to intervene in a parent manager's training program for her child. And Joan Ryan is not going to find an "arm of government" to intervene in the child rearing of Fredrika Keefer, however much she may "pay the price for" (A29) her mother's enthusiasm.

11   The tension in Ryan's essay over high standards and the intense preparation to meet them mirrors a tension in the larger culture. On the one hand, Ryan persuasively argues that elite institutions like the San Francisco Ballet School have the right to set standards for admission. At such institutions, high standards give us high levels of achievement-- dancers, for instance, who "can float on air" (A29). We cheer brilliant performers like Tiger Woods and Michelle Kwan who started on their roads to success while still children. The star system produces stars. On the other hand, Ryan condemns parents who buy into the star system by pushing their children into pro-fessional training programs that demand a single-minded focus. We are horrified to learn that Macaulay Culkin of the Home Alone movies never really had a childhood (Peterson). Of course Culkin and others like him didn't have childhoods: They were too busy practicing their lines or their jumps and spins. If Ryan defends high standards in one breath and criti-cizes parents in the next for pushing children to achieve these standards, she is only reflecting a confusion in the larger culture: We love our stars, but we cannot have our stars without a star system that demands total (and often damaging) dedication from our youngest and most vulnerable citizens. That parents can be the agent of this damage is especially troubling.

12   Joan Ryan is right to focus on the parents of would-be stars, and she is right to remind us that young children pressured to perform at the highest levels can suffer physically and psychologically. Perhaps it was better for Fredrika Keefer the child

Ralston 6

(as opposed to Fredrika Keefer the future professional dancer) that she was not admitted to the San
Francisco School of Ballet. For Keefer's sake and
that of other child performers, we should pay attention to the dangers of the star system and support
these children when we can. But without clear evidence of legally actionable neglect or abuse, we
cannot interfere with parent managers, however much
we may disagree with their decisions. We may be
legitimately concerned, as is Ryan, that such a
parent is driving her child to become not the next
Tiger Woods but the next admission to a psychiatric
ward. In a free society, for better or for worse,
parents have the right to guide (or misguide) the
lives of their children. All the rest of us can do is
watch--and hope for the best.

[New Page]

Ralston 7

Works Cited

Feinstein, John. "Year of the Tiger." Interview with Jim Lehrer.
    Online News Hour. 14 Apr. 1997. 28 Jan. 2006
    <http://www.pbs.org/newshour/bb/sports/tiger_4-14.html>.
Peterson, Paul. Interview with Gary James. 28 Jan. 2006
    <http://www.classicbands.com/PaulPetersonInterview.html>.
Ryan, Joan. "We Are Not Created Equal in Every Way." San Francisco
    Chronicle 12 Dec. 2000: A29.

EXERCISE 2.5

Informal Critique of Sample Essay

Before reading the discussion of this model critique, write your own informal
response to the critique. What are its strengths and weaknesses? To what
extent does the critique follow the general Guidelines for Writing Critiques
that we outlined on page 66? To the extent it varies from the guidelines, speculate on why. Jot down some ideas for a critique that takes a different
approach to Ryan's essay.

CRITICAL READING FOR CRITIQUE

- *Use the tips from Critical Reading for Summary on page 6.* Remember to examine the context; note the title and subtitle; identify the main point; identify the subpoints; break the reading into sections; distinguish between points, examples, and counterarguments; watch for transitions within and between paragraphs; and read actively.
- *Establish the writer's primary purpose in writing.* Is the piece primarily meant to inform, persuade, or entertain?
- *Evaluate informative writing. Use these criteria (among others):*

  Accuracy of information

  Significance of information

  Fair interpretation of information

- *Evaluate persuasive writing. Use these criteria (among others):*

  Clear definition of terms

  Fair use and interpretation of information

  Logical reasoning

- *Evaluate writing that entertains. Use these criteria (among others):*

  Interesting characters

  Believable action, plot, and situations

  Communication of theme

  Use of language

- *Decide whether you agree or disagree with the writer's ideas, position, or message.* Once you have determined the extent to which an author has achieved his or her purpose, clarify your position in relation to the writer's.

Discussion

- Paragraph 1 of the model critique introduces the issue to be reviewed. It provides brief background information and sets a general context that explains why the topic of fair (and unfair) competition is important.
- Paragraph 2 introduces the author and the essay and summarizes the author's main claims. The paragraph ends (see the final three sentences) with the writer's overall assessment of the essay.
- Paragraph 3 sets a specific context for evaluating Ryan's first claim concerning admissions standards. The writer summarizes Ryan's position by making a distinction between the terms *discriminating* and *discriminatory*.

- Paragraph 4 evaluates Ryan's first claim, that the ballet school has the right to set admission standards. The writer supports Ryan's position.

- Paragraph 5 continues the evaluation of Ryan's first claim. Again, the writer of the critique supports Ryan, returning to the distinction between *discriminating* and *discriminatory*.

- Paragraphs 6–7 summarize Ryan's second claim, that parents can damage their children by pushing them too hard through professional training programs at too early an age.

- Paragraphs 8–10 evaluate Ryan's second claim. In paragraph 8 the writer states that Ryan makes a mistake in implying that a government agency should safeguard the interests of children like Fredrika Keefer. Paragraphs 9–10 present a logic for disagreeing with Ryan on this point.

- Paragraph 11 evaluates the essay as a whole. Ryan defends the right of schools in the star system to set high standards but objects when parents push young children into this system. This "tension" in the essay reflects a confusion in the larger culture.

- Paragraph 12 concludes the critique. The writer offers qualified support of Ryan's position, agreeing that children caught in the star system can suffer. The writer also states that there is not much we can do about the problem, except watch and hope for the best.

3 Introductions, Theses, and Conclusions

WRITING INTRODUCTIONS

All writers, no matter how much they prepare, eventually have to face the question of writing an introduction. How to start? What's the best way to approach the subject? With high seriousness, a light touch, an anecdote? How best to engage the reader? Many writers avoid such agonizing choices by putting them off—productively. Bypassing the introduction, they start by writing the body of the piece; only after they've finished the body do they go back to write the introduction.

There's a lot to be said for this approach. Because you have presumably spent more time thinking and writing about the topic itself than about how you're going to introduce it, you are in a better position to begin directly with your presentation. And often, it's not until you've actually seen the piece on paper or screen and read it over once or twice that a natural way of introducing it becomes apparent. Even if there is no natural way to begin, you are generally in better psychological shape to write the introduction after the major task of writing is behind you and you know exactly what you're leading up to.

Perhaps, however, you can't operate this way. After all, you have to start writing *somewhere,* and if you have evaded the problem by skipping the introduction, that blank page may loom just as large whenever you do choose to begin. If this is the case, then go ahead and write an introduction, knowing full well that it's probably going to be flat and awful. Write whatever comes to mind, as long as you have a working thesis. Assure yourself that whatever you put down at this point (except for the thesis) "won't count" and that when the time is right, you'll go back and replace it with something that's fit for eyes other than yours. But in the meantime, you'll have gotten started.

The *purpose* of an introduction is to prepare the reader to enter the world of your paper. The introduction makes the connection between the more familiar world inhabited by the reader and the less familiar world of the writer's particular subject; it places a discussion in a context that the reader can understand.

You have many ways to provide such a context. We'll consider just a few of the most common.

Quotation

Here is an introduction to a paper on democracy:

"Two cheers for democracy" was E. M. Forster's not-quite-whole-hearted judgment. Most Americans would not agree. To them, our democracy is one of the glories of civilization. To one American in particular, E. B. White, democracy is "the hole in the stuffed shirt through which the sawdust slowly trickles . . . the dent in the high hat . . . the recurrent suspicion that more than half of the people are right more than half of the time" (915). American democracy is based on the oldest continuously operating written constitution in the world—a most impressive fact and a testament to the farsightedness of the founding fathers. But just how farsighted can mere humans be? In *Future Shock,* Alvin Toffler quotes economist Kenneth Boulding on the incredible acceleration of social change in our time: "The world of today . . . is as different from the world in which I was born as that world was from Julius Caesar's" (13). As we move into the twenty-first century, it seems legitimate to question the continued effectiveness of a governmental system that was devised in the eighteenth century; and it seems equally legitimate to consider alternatives.

The quotations by Forster and White help set the stage for the discussion of democracy by presenting the reader with some provocative and well-phrased remarks. Later in the paragraph, the quotation by Boulding more specifically prepares us for the theme of change that will be central to the paper as a whole.

Historical Review

In many cases, the reader will be unprepared to follow the issue you discuss unless you provide some historical background. Consider the following introduction to a paper on the film-rating system:

> Sex and violence on the screen are not new issues. In the Roaring Twenties there was increasing pressure from civic and religious groups to ban depictions of "immorality" from the screen. Faced with the threat of federal censorship, the film producers decided to clean their own house. In 1930, the Motion Picture Producers and Distributors of America established the Production Code. At first, adherence to the Code was voluntary; but in 1934 Joseph Breen, newly appointed head of the MPPDA, gave the Code teeth. Henceforth all newly produced films had to be submitted for approval to the Production Code Administration, which had the power to award or withhold the Code seal. Without a Code seal, it was virtually impossible for a film to be shown anywhere in the United States, since exhibitors would not accept it. At about the same time, the Catholic Legion of Decency was formed to advise the faithful which films were and were not objectionable. For several decades the Production Code Administration exercised powerful control over what was portrayed in American theatrical films. By the 1960s, however, changing standards of morality had considerably weakened the Code's grip. In 1968, the Production

> Code was replaced with a rating system designed to keep younger audiences away from films with high levels of sex or violence. Despite its imperfections, this rating system has proved more beneficial to American films than did the old censorship system.

The paper following this introduction concerns the relative benefits of the rating system. By providing some historical background on the rating system, the writer helps readers to understand his arguments. Notice the chronological development of details.

Review of a Controversy

A particular type of historical review is the review of a controversy or debate. Consider the following introduction:

> The *American Heritage Dictionary's* definition of civil disobedience is rather simple: "the refusal to obey civil laws that are regarded as unjust, usually by employing methods of passive resistance." However, despite such famous (and beloved) examples of civil disobedience as the movements of Mahatma Gandhi in India and the Reverend Martin Luther King, Jr., in the United States, the question of whether or not civil disobedience should be considered an asset to society is hardly clear cut. For instance, Hannah Arendt, in her article "Civil Disobedience," holds that "to think of disobedient minorities as rebels and truants is against the letter and spirit of a constitution whose framers were especially sensitive to the dangers of unbridled majority rule." On the other hand, a noted lawyer, Lewis Van Dusen, Jr., in his article "Civil Disobedience: Destroyer of Democracy," states that "civil disobedience, whatever the ethical rationalization, is still an assault on our democratic society, an affront to our legal order and an attack on our constitutional government." These two views are clearly incompatible. I believe, though, that Van Dusen's is the more convincing. On balance, civil disobedience is dangerous to society.*

The negative aspects of civil disobedience, rather than Van Dusen's article, are the topic of this paper. But to introduce this topic, the writer has provided quotations that represent opposing sides of the controversy over civil disobedience, as well as brief references to two controversial practitioners. By focusing at the outset on the particular rather than the abstract aspects of the subject, the writer hoped to secure the attention of her readers and to involve them in the controversy that forms the subject of her paper.

---

* Michelle Jacques, "Civil Disobedience: Van Dusen vs. Arendt," unpublished paper, 1993: 1. Used by permission.

From the General to the Specific

Another way of providing a transition from the reader's world to the less familiar world of the paper is to work from a general subject to a specific one. The following introduction begins a paper on improving our air quality by inducing people to trade the use of their cars for public transportation.

> While generalizations are risky, it seems pretty safe to say that most human beings are selfish. Self-interest may be part of our nature, and probably aids the survival of our species, since self-interested pursuits increase the likelihood of individual survival and genetic reproduction. Ironically, however, our selfishness has caused us to abuse the natural environment upon which we depend. We have polluted, deforested, depleted, deformed, and endangered our earth, water, and air to such an extent that now our species' survival is gravely threatened. In America, air pollution is one of our most pressing environmental problems, and it is our selfish use of the automobile that poses the greatest threat to clean air, as well as the greatest challenge to efforts to stop air pollution. Very few of us seem willing to give up our cars, let alone use them less. We are spoiled by the individual freedom afforded us when we can hop into our gas-guzzling vehicles and go where we want, when we want. Somehow, we as a nation will have to wean ourselves from this addiction to the automobile, and we can do this by designing alternative forms of transportation that serve our selfish interests.*

From the Specific to the General: Anecdote, Illustration

The following paragraph quotes an anecdote in order to move from the specific to a general topic:

> In an article on the changing American family, Ron French[†] tells the following story:
>
>> Six-year-old Sydney Papenheim has her future planned. "First I'm going to marry Jared," she told her mother. "Then I'm going to get divorced and marry Gabby." "No, honey," Lisa Boettcher says, "you don't plan it like that." That's news to Sydney. Her mother is divorced and remarried, as is her stepdad. Her grandparents are divorced and remarried, as are enough aunts and uncles to field a team for "Family Feud." She gets presents from her stepfather's ex-wife. Her stepfather's children sometimes play at the house of her father. "You never know what is going

---

* Travis Knight, "Reducing Air Pollution with Alternative Transportation," unpublished paper, 1998: 1. Used by permission.

† Ron French, "Family: The D-Word Loses Its Sting as Households Blend," *Detroit News* 1 Jan. 2000, 17 Aug. 2000 <http://detnews.com/specialreports/2000/journey/family/family.htm>.

> to happen from day to day," says Sydney's stepdad, Brian Boettcher. "It's an evolution." It's more like a revolution, from Norman Rockwell to Norman Lear.*
>
> French continues on to report that by the year 2007, blended families such as the Boettchers will outnumber traditional nuclear families. Yet most people continue to lament this change. We as a nation need to accept this new reality: The "till death do us part" version of marriage no longer works.†

The previous introduction went from the general (the statement that human beings are selfish) to the specific (how to decrease air pollution); this one goes from the specific (one little girl's understanding of marriage and divorce) to the general (the changing American family). The anecdote is one of the most effective means at your disposal for capturing and holding your reader's attention. Speakers have long begun their general remarks with a funny, touching, or otherwise appropriate story; in fact, there are plenty of books that are nothing but collections of such stories, arranged by subject.

Question

Frequently, you can provoke the reader's attention by posing a question or a series of questions:

> Are gender roles learned or inherited? Scientific research has established the existence of biological differences between the sexes, but the effect of biology's influence on gender roles cannot be distinguished from society's influence. According to Michael Lewis of the Institute for the Study of Exceptional Children, "As early as you can show me a sex difference, I can show you the culture at work." Social processes, as well as biological differences, are responsible for the separate roles of men and women.‡

Opening your paper with a question can be provocative, since it places readers in an active role: They begin by considering answers. *Are* gender roles learned? *Are* they inherited? In this active role, they are likely to continue reading with interest.

---

* Norman Lear (b. 1922): American television writer and producer noted for developing groundbreaking depictions of the American family in the 1970s, such as *All in the Family, Sanford and Son,* and *Maude.*

† Veronica Gonzalez, "New Family Formations," unpublished paper, 1999: 1. Used by permission.

‡ Tammy Smith, "Are Sex Roles Learned or Inherited?" unpublished paper, 1994: 1. Used by permission.

Statement of Thesis

Perhaps the most direct method of introduction is to begin immediately with the thesis:

> Every college generation is defined by the social events of its age. The momentous occurrences of an era—from war and economics to politics and inventions—give meaning to lives of the individuals who live through them. They also serve to knit those individuals together by creating a collective memory and a common historic or generational identity. In 1979, I went to 26 college and university campuses, selected to represent the diversity of American higher education, and asked students what social or political events most influenced their generation. I told them that the children who came of age in the decade after World War I might have answered the Great Depression. The bombing of Pearl Harbor, World War II, or perhaps the death of Franklin Roosevelt might have stood out for those born a few years later. For my generation, born after World War II, the key event was the assassination of John F. Kennedy. We remember where we were when we heard the news. The whole world seemingly changed in its aftermath.*

This paper begins with a general assertion: that large-scale social events shape generations of college students. The advantage of beginning with a general thesis like this is that it immediately establishes the broader context and the point illustrated by the paper's subsequent focus on contemporary college students.

Stating your thesis in the first sentence of an introduction also works when you make a controversial argument. Stating a provocative point right away, such as "Democracy is dead," for a paper examining the problems plaguing representative government in current society, forces the reader to sit up and take notice—perhaps even to begin protesting. This "hooks" a reader, who is likely to want to find out how your paper will support its strong thesis. In the example paragraph above, the general thesis is followed by specific examples of social events and their effects on college students, which prepares the reader to compare the experiences of current college students with those of earlier generations.

One final note about our model introductions: They may be longer than introductions you have been accustomed to writing. Many writers (and readers) prefer a shorter, snappier introduction. The length of an introduction can depend on the length of the paper it introduces, and it is also largely a matter of personal or corporate style: There is no rule concerning the correct length of an introduction. If you feel that a short introduction is appropriate, use one. You may wish to break up what seems like a long introduction into two paragraphs.

---

* Arthur Levine, "The Making of a Generation," *Change* Sept.–Oct. 1993: 8.

Drafting Introductions

Imagine that you are writing a paper using the topic, ideas, and thesis you developed in the earlier exercises in this book. Choose one of the seven types of introductions we've discussed—preferably one you have never used before—and draft an introduction that would work to open a paper on this topic. Use our examples as models to help you draft your practice introduction.

WRITING A THESIS

A thesis is a one-sentence (and sometimes a two-sentence) summary of a paper's content. It is similar, actually, to a paper's conclusion (see pages 91–98) but lacks the conclusion's concern for broad implications and significance. Your thesis will be the product of your thinking; it therefore represents *your* conclusion about the topic on which you're writing, and therefore you have to have spent some time thinking (inventing) in order to arrive at the thesis that begins your actual paper.

For a writer in the drafting stages, the thesis establishes a focus, a basis on which to include or exclude information. For the reader of a finished product, the thesis anticipates the author's discussion. *A thesis, therefore, is an essential tool for both writers and readers of academic material.*

The previous sentence is our thesis for this section. Based on this thesis, we, as the authors, have limited the content of the section; and you, as the reader, will be able to form certain expectations about the discussion that follows. You can expect a definition of a thesis; an enumeration of the uses of a thesis; and a discussion focused on academic material. As writers, we will have met our obligations to you only if in subsequent paragraphs we satisfy these expectations.

The Components of a Thesis

Like any other sentence, a thesis includes a subject and a predicate, which consists of an assertion about the subject. In the sentence "Lee and Grant were different kinds of generals," "Lee and Grant" is the subject and "were different kinds of generals" is the predicate. What distinguishes a thesis from any other sentence with a subject and predicate is that *the thesis presents the controlling idea of the paper.* The subject of a thesis must present the right balance between the general and the specific to allow for thorough discussion within the allotted length of the paper. The discussion might include definitions, details, comparisons, contrasts—whatever is needed to illuminate a subject and carry on an intelligent conversation. (If the sentence about Lee and Grant were a thesis, the reader would assume that the rest of the paper contained comparisons and contrasts between the two generals.)

Bear in mind when writing theses that the more general your subject and the more complex your assertion, the longer your paper will be. For instance, consider the following sentence as the thesis for a ten-page paper:

> Meaningful energy conservation requires a shrewd application of political, financial, and scientific will.

You could not write an effective ten-page paper based on this thesis. The topic alone would require pages merely to carefully define what is meant by "energy conservation" and then by "meaningful." Energy can be conserved in homes, vehicles, industries, appliances, and power plants, and each of these areas would need consideration. Having accomplished this task, you would then have to turn your attention to the claim, which entails a discussion of how politics, finance, and science individually and collectively influence energy conservation. Moreover, the thesis asks you to argue that "shrewd application" of politics, finance, and science is required. Although this thesis may very well be accurate and compelling, it promises entirely too much for a ten-page paper.

Limiting the Scope of the Thesis

To write an effective thesis and thus a controlled, effective paper, you need to limit your subject and your claims about it. There are two strategies for achieving a thesis of manageable proportions: (1) start with a working thesis (this strategy assumes that you are familiar with your topic) and (2) begin with a broad area of interest and narrow it (this strategy assumes that you are unfamiliar with your topic).

Starting with a Working Thesis

Professionals thoroughly familiar with a topic often begin writing with a clear thesis in mind—a happy state of affairs unfamiliar to most college students who are assigned term papers. But professionals usually have an important advantage over students: experience. Because professionals know their material, are familiar with the ways of approaching it, are aware of the questions important to practitioners, and have devoted considerable time to study of the topic, they are naturally in a strong position to begin writing a paper. In addition, many professionals are practiced at invention; the time they spend listing or outlining their ideas helps them work out their thesis statements. Not only do professionals have experience in their fields, but they also have a clear purpose in writing; they know their audience and are comfortable with the format of their papers.

Experience counts—there's no way around it. As a student, you are not yet an expert and therefore don't generally have the luxury of beginning your writing tasks with a definite thesis in mind. Once you choose and devote time to a major field of study, however, you will gain experience. In the meantime, you'll have to do more work than the professional to prepare yourself for writing a paper.

But let's assume that you *do* have an area of expertise, that you are in your own right a professional (albeit not in academic matters). We'll assume that you understand your nonacademic subject—say, backpacking—and have been given a clear purpose for writing: to discuss the relative merits of backpack designs. Your job is to write a recommendation for the owner of a sporting-goods chain, suggesting which line of backpacks the chain should carry. Because you already know a good deal about backpacks, you may already have some well-developed ideas on the topic before you start doing additional research.

Yet even as an expert in your field, you will find that beginning the writing task is a challenge, for at this point it is unlikely that you will be able to conceive a thesis perfectly suited to the contents of your paper. After all, a thesis is a summary, and it is difficult to summarize a presentation yet to be written—especially if you plan to discover what you want to say during the process of writing. Even if you know your material well, the best you can do at the early stages is to formulate a *working thesis*—a hypothesis of sorts, a well-informed hunch about your topic and the claim to be made about it. Once you have completed a draft, you can evaluate the degree to which your working thesis accurately summarizes the content of your paper. If the match is a good one, the working thesis becomes the thesis. If, however, sections of the paper drift from the focus set out in the working thesis, you'll need to revise the thesis and the paper itself to ensure that the presentation is unified. (You'll know that the match between the content and thesis is a good one when every paragraph directly refers to and develops some element of the thesis.)

This same model will work when you must venture into academic territory, such as government or medieval poetry. The difference is that when approaching topics that are less familiar to you than something like backpacking, you will have to spend more time gathering data and brainstorming. Such labor prepares you to make assertions about your subject.

Choosing and Narrowing a Topic

Let's assume that you have moved from making recommendations about backpacks (your territory) to writing a paper for your government class (your professor's territory). Whereas you were once the expert who knew enough about your subject to begin writing with a working thesis, you are now the student, inexperienced and in need of a great deal of information before you can begin to think of thesis statements. It may be a comfort to know that your government professor would likely be in the same predicament if asked to recommend backpack designs. She would need to spend at least a few weeks backpacking to become as experienced as you; and it is fair to say that you will need to spend several hours in the library before you are in a position to choose a topic suitable for an undergraduate paper.

Suppose you have been assigned an open-ended, ten-page paper in an introductory course on environmental science. Not only do you have to choose a subject, but you also have to narrow it sufficiently and formulate your thesis. Where will you begin? We take the unusual case of an essential-ly directionless assignment to demonstrate how you can use invention strate-gies to identify topics of interest and narrow the scope of your paper. Typically, your assignments will provide more guidance than "write a ten-page paper." In that case, you can still apply the techniques discussed here, though you will have less work to do.

So, how to begin thinking about your paper in environmental science? First, you need to select broad subject matter from the course and become knowledgeable about its general features. And if no broad area of interest occurs to you, you can approach your task from other angles:

- Work through the syllabus or your textbook(s). Identify topics that sparked your interest.
- Review course notes and pay especially close attention to lectures that held your interest.
- Scan recent headlines for news items that bear on your coursework.

Usually you can make use of material you've read in a text or heard in a lecture. The trick is to find a subject that is important to you, for whatever reason. (For a paper in sociology, you might write on the subject of bullying because of your own experience with school bullies. For an economics semi-nar, you might explore the factors that threaten banks with collapse because your great-great-grandparents lost their life savings during the Great Depression.) Whatever the academic discipline, try to discover a topic that you'll enjoy exploring; that way, you'll be writing for yourself as much as for your instructor.

Assume for your course in environmental science that you've settled on the broad topic of energy conservation. At this point, the goal of your research is to limit this subject to a manageable scope. A topic can be limited in at least two ways. First, you can seek out a general article (perhaps an encyclopedia entry, though these are not typically accepted as sources in a college-level paper). A general article may do the work for you by breaking the larger topic down into smaller subtopics that you can explore and, perhaps, limit even further. Second, you can limit a subject by asking several questions about it:

Who?
Which aspects?
Where?
When?
How?
Why?

These questions will occur to you as you conduct your research and see the ways in which various authors have focused their discussions. Having read several sources on energy conservation and having decided that you'd like to use them, you might limit the subject by asking *which aspects*, and deciding to focus on energy conservation as it relates to motor vehicles.

Certainly, "energy-efficient vehicles" offers a more specific focus than does "energy conservation." Still, the revised focus is too broad for a ten-page paper. (One can easily imagine several book-length works on the subject.) So again you try to limit your subject by posing additional questions, from the same list. In this case, you might ask which aspects of energy-efficient vehicles are possible and desirable and how auto manufacturers can be encouraged to develop them. In response to these questions, you may jot down such preliminary notes. For example:

- Types of energy-efficient vehicles

  All-electric vehicles

  Hybrid (combination of gasoline and electric) vehicles

  Fuel-cell vehicles

- Government action to encourage development of energy-efficient vehicles

  Mandates to automakers to build minimum quantities of energy-efficient vehicles by certain deadlines

  Additional taxes imposed on high-mileage vehicles

  Subsidies to developers of energy-efficient vehicles

Focusing on any *one* of these aspects as an approach to encouraging use of energy-efficient vehicles could provide the focus of a ten-page paper, and you do yourself an important service by choosing just one. To choose more would obligate you to too broad a discussion that would frustrate you: Either the paper would have to be longer than ten pages, or assuming you kept to the page limit, the paper would be superficial in its treatment. In both instances, the paper would fail, given the constraints of the assignment.

A certain level of judgment is involved in deciding whether a topic is too big or too small to generate the right number of pages. Judgment is a function of experience, of course, and in the absence of experience you will have to resort, at times, to trial and error. Still, the strategies offered above (locate an article that identifies parts of a topic or pose multiple questions and identify parts) can guide you. Ultimately, you will be able to tell if you've selected an appropriate topic as you reread your work and answer this question: *Have I developed all key elements of the thesis in depth, fully?* If you have skimmed the surface, narrow the topic and/or the claim of your thesis and redraft the paper. If you have added filler to meet the assignment's page requirements, broaden the topic and/or claim and redraft the paper. In general, you will do well to spend ample time gathering data, brainstorming, gathering more data, and then brainstorming again in order to limit your subject before attempting to write about it. Let's take an example. Assume that you settle on the following as an appropriately defined topic for a ten-page paper:

> Encouraging the development of fuel-cell vehicles

The process of choosing an initial subject (invention) depends heavily on the reading you do (data gathering). The more you read, the deeper your understanding. The deeper your understanding, the likelier it will be that you can divide a broad and complex subject into manageable—that is, researchable—topics. In the example above, your reading in the online and print literature may suggest that the development of fuel-cell technology is one of the most promising approaches to energy conservation on the highway. So reading allows you to narrow the subject "energy conservation" by answering the initial questions—those focusing on *which aspects* of the general subject. Once you narrow your focus to "energy-efficient vehicles," you may read further and quickly realize that this is a broad subject that also should be limited. In this way, reading stimulates you to identify an appropriate topic for your paper. Your process here is recursive—you move back and forth between stages of the process, each movement bringing you closer to establishing a clear focus *before* you attempt to write your paper.

EXERCISE 3.2

Practice Narrowing Topics

In groups of three or four classmates, choose one of the following and respond to the questions listed above for narrowing topics: Who? Which aspects? Where? When? How? Why? See if you can formulate a more narrow approach to the topic.

- Downloading music off the Internet
- College sports
- School violence
- Internet chat rooms
- America's public school system

Making an Assertion

A thesis statement is an assertion or claim you wish to make *about* your paper's topic. If you have spent enough time reading and gathering information, and brainstorming ideas about the assignment, you will be knowledgeable enough to have something to say about the subject, based on a combination of your own thinking and the thinking of your sources.

If you have trouble making an assertion, devote more time to invention strategies: Try writing your subject at the top of a page and then listing everything you now know and feel about it. Often from such a list you will discover an assertion that you then can use to fashion a working thesis. A good way to gauge the reasonableness of your claim is to see what other authors have asserted about the same topic. In fact, keep good notes on the views of others. These notes will prove a useful counterpoint to your own views as you write and think about your claim, and you may want to use them in your paper. Next, make several assertions about your topic, in order of increasing complexity, as in the following:

1. Fuel-cell technology has emerged as a promising approach to developing energy-efficient vehicles.
2. To reduce our dependence on nonrenewable fossil fuel, the federal government should encourage the development of fuel-cell vehicles.
3. The federal government should subsidize the development of fuel-cell vehicles as well as the hydrogen infrastructure needed to support them; otherwise, the United States will be increasingly vulnerable to recession and other economic dislocations resulting from our dependence on the continued flow of foreign oil.

Keep in mind that these are *working theses*. Because you haven't written a paper based on any of them, they remain *hypotheses* to be tested. You might choose one and use it to focus your initial draft. After completing a first draft, you would revise it by comparing the contents of the paper to the thesis and making adjustments as necessary for unity. The working thesis is an excellent tool for planning broad sections of the paper, but—again—don't let it prevent you from pursuing related discussions as they occur to you.

Using the Thesis to Plan a Structure

A working thesis will help you sketch the structure of your paper, since structure flows directly from the thesis. Consider, for example, the third thesis on fuel-cell technology:

> The federal government should subsidize the development of fuel-cell vehicles as well as the hydrogen infrastructure needed to support them; otherwise, the United States will be increasingly vulnerable to recession and other economic dislocations resulting from our dependence on the continued flow of foreign oil.

This thesis, compared to the mildly argumentative second statement and the explanatory first statement, is *strongly argumentative*, or *persuasive*. The economic catastrophes mentioned by the writer indicate a strong degree of urgency in the need for the solution recommended—federal subsidy of a national hydrogen infrastructure to support fuel-cell vehicles. If a paper based on this thesis is to be well developed, the writer must make a commitment to explaining (1) why fuel-cell vehicles are a preferred alternative to gasoline-powered vehicles; (2) why fuel-cell vehicles require a hydrogen infrastructure (i.e., the writer must explain that fuel cells produce power by mixing hydrogen and oxygen, generating both electricity and water in the process); (3) why the government needs to subsidize industry in developing fuel-cell vehicles; and (4) how continued reliance on fossil fuel technology could make the country vulnerable to economic dislocations. This thesis therefore helps the writer plan the paper, which should include a section on each of these four topics. Assuming that the paper follows the organizational plan we've proposed, the working thesis would become the final thesis, on the basis of which a reader could anticipate sections of the paper to come. In a finished product, the thesis becomes an essential tool for guiding readers.

Note, however, that this thesis is still provisional. It may turn out, as you research or begin drafting, that the paper to which this thesis commits you will be too long and complex. You may therefore decide to drop the second clause of the thesis dealing with the country's vulnerability to economic dislocations and focus almost exclusively on the need for the government to subsidize the development of fuel-cell vehicles and of a hydrogen infrastructure, relegating the economic concerns to your conclusion (if at all). If you make this change, your final thesis would read as follows:

> The federal government should subsidize the development of fuel-cell vehicles, as well as the hydrogen infrastructure needed to support them.

This revised thesis makes an assertive commitment to the subject, although the assertion is not as complex as the original. Still, it is more assertive than the second proposed thesis:

> To reduce our dependence on nonrenewable fossil fuel, the federal government should encourage the development of fuel-cell vehicles.

Here we have a *mildly argumentative* thesis that enables the writer to express an opinion. We infer from the use of the words "should encourage" that the writer endorses the idea of the government promoting fuel-cell development. But a government that "encourages" development is making a lesser commitment than one that "subsidizes," which means that it allocates funds for a specific policy. So a writer who argues for mere encouragement takes a milder position than one who argues for subsidies. Note also the contrast between this second thesis and the first one, in which the writer is committed to no involvement in the debate and no government involvement whatsoever.

> Fuel-cell technology has emerged as a promising approach to developing energy-efficient vehicles.

This first of the three thesis statements is *explanatory*, or *informative*. In developing a paper based on this thesis, the writer is committed only to explaining how fuel-cell technology works and why it is a promising approach to energy-efficient vehicles. Based on this particular thesis, then, a reader would *not* expect to find the author strongly recommending, for instance, that fuel-cell engines replace internal combustion engines at some point in the near future. Neither does the thesis require the writer to defend

---

HOW AMBITIOUS SHOULD YOUR THESIS BE?

Writing tasks vary according to the nature of the thesis.

- The *explanatory thesis* is often developed in response to short-answer exam questions that call for information, not analysis (e.g., "How does James Barber categorize the main types of presidential personality?").
- The *mildly argumentative thesis* is appropriate for organizing reports (even lengthy ones), as well as essay questions that call for some analysis (e.g., "Discuss the qualities of a good speech").
- The *strongly argumentative thesis* is used to organize papers and exam questions that call for information, analysis, *and* the writer's forcefully stated point of view (e.g., "Evaluate the proposed reforms of health maintenance organizations").

The strongly argumentative thesis, of course, is the riskiest of the three, since you must unequivocally state your position and make it appear reasonable—which requires that you offer evidence and defend against logical objections. But such intellectual risks pay dividends, and if you become involved enough in your work to make challenging assertions, you will provoke challenging responses that enliven classroom discussions and your own learning.

---

a personal opinion; he or she need only justify the use of the relatively mild term "promising."

As you can see, for any topic you might explore in a paper, you can make any number of assertions—some relatively simple, some complex. It is on the basis of these assertions that you set yourself an agenda for your writing—and readers set for themselves expectations for reading. The more ambitious the thesis, the more complex will be the paper and the greater will be your readers' expectations.

To Review: A thesis (a one-sentence summary of your paper) helps you organize your discussion, and it helps your reader anticipate it. Theses are distinguished by their carefully worded subjects and predicates, which should be just broad enough and complex enough to be developed within the length limitations of the assignment. Both novices and experts typically begin the initial draft of a paper with a working thesis—a statement that provides writers with structure enough to get started but with latitude enough to discover what they want to say as they write. Once you have completed a first draft, however, you test the "fit" of your thesis with the paper that follows. When you have a good fit, every element of the thesis is developed in the paper. Discussions that drift from your thesis should be deleted, or the thesis changed to accommodate the new discussions.

EXERCISE **3.3**

Drafting Thesis Statements

After completing the group exercise where you narrowed a topic (Exercise 3.2, page 87), work individually or in small groups to draft three possible theses in relation to your earlier ideas. Draft one *explanatory thesis,* one *explanatory but mildly argumentative thesis,* and one *strongly argumentative thesis.*

WRITING CONCLUSIONS

One way to view the conclusion of your paper is as an introduction worked in reverse, a bridge from the world of your paper back to the world of your reader. A conclusion is the part of your paper in which you restate and (if necessary) expand on your thesis. Essential to many conclusions is the summary, which is not merely a repetition of the thesis but a restatement that takes advantage of the material you've presented. The *simplest conclusion is a summary of the paper,* but you may want more than this for the end of your paper. Depending on your needs, you might offer a summary and then build onto it a discussion of the paper's significance or its implications for future study, for choices that individuals might make, for policy, and so on. You might also want to urge the reader to change an attitude or to modify behavior. Certainly, you are under no obligation to discuss the broader significance of your work (and a summary, alone, will satisfy the formal requirement that your paper have an ending); but the conclusions of better papers often reveal authors who are "thinking large" and want to connect the particular concerns of their papers with the broader concerns of society.

Here we'll consider seven strategies for expanding the basic summary-conclusion. But two words of advice are in order. First, no matter how clever or beautifully executed, a conclusion cannot salvage a poorly written paper. Second, by virtue of its placement, the conclusion carries rhetorical weight. It is the last statement a reader will encounter before turning from your work. Realizing this, writers who expand on the basic summary-conclusion often wish to give their final words a dramatic flourish, a heightened level of diction. Soaring rhetoric and drama in a conclusion are fine as long as they do not unbalance the paper and call attention to themselves. Having labored long hours over your paper, you have every right to wax eloquent. But keep a sense of proportion and timing. Make your points quickly and end crisply.

Statement of the Subject's Significance

One of the more effective ways to conclude a paper is to discuss the larger significance of what you have written, providing readers with one more reason to regard your work as a serious effort. When using this strategy, you move from the specific concern of your paper to the broader concerns of the reader's world. Often, you will need to choose among a range of significances: A paper on the Wright brothers might end with a discussion of air travel as it affects economies, politics, or families; a paper on contraception might end with a discussion of its effect on sexual mores, population, or the church. But don't overwhelm your reader with the importance of your remarks. Keep your discussion well focused.

The following paragraphs conclude a paper on George H. Shull, a pioneer in the inbreeding and crossbreeding of corn:

> . . . Thus, the hybrids developed and described by Shull 75 years ago have finally dominated U.S. corn production.
>
> The adoption of hybrid corn was steady and dramatic in the Corn Belt. From 1930 through 1979 the average yields of corn in the U.S. increased from 21.9 to 95.1 bushels per acre, and the additional value to the farmer is now several billion dollars per year.
>
> The success of hybrid corn has also stimulated the breeding of other crops, such as sorghum hybrids, a major feed grain crop in arid parts of the world. Sorghum yields have increased 300 percent since 1930. Approximately 20 percent of the land devoted to rice production in China is planted with hybrid seed, which is reported to yield 20 percent more than the best varieties. And many superior varieties of tomatoes, cucumbers, spinach, and other vegetables are hybrids. Today virtually all corn produced in the developed countries is from hybrid seed. From those blue bloods of the plant kingdom has come a model for feeding the world.*

The first sentence of this conclusion is a summary, and from it the reader can infer that the paper included a discussion of Shull's techniques for the hybrid breeding of corn. The summary is followed by a two-paragraph discussion on the significance of Shull's research for feeding the world.

Call for Further Research

In the scientific and social scientific communities, papers often end with a review of what has been presented (as, for instance, in an experiment) and the ways in which the subject under consideration needs to be further explored. If you raise questions that you call on others to answer, however, make sure you know that the research you are calling for hasn't already been conducted.

This next conclusion comes from a sociological report on the placement of the elderly in nursing homes.

> Our study shows a correlation between the placement of elderly citizens in nursing facilities and the significant decline of their motor and intellectual skills over the ten months following placement. What the research has not made clear is the extent to which this marked decline

---

* William L. Brown, "Hybrid Vim and Vigor," *Science* Nov. 1984: 77–78.

is due to physical as opposed to emotional causes. The elderly are referred to homes at that point in their lives when they grow less able to care for themselves—which suggests that the drop-off in skills may be due to physical causes. But the emotional stress of being placed in a home, away from family and in an environment that confirms the patient's view of himself as decrepit, may exacerbate—if not itself be a primary cause of—the patient's rapid loss of abilities. Further research is needed to clarify the relationship between depression and particular physical ailments as these affect the skills of the elderly in nursing facilities. There is little doubt that information yielded by such studies can enable health care professionals to deliver more effective services.

Notice how this call for further study locates the author in a large community of researchers on whom she depends for assistance in answering the questions that have come out of her own work. The author summarizes her findings (in the first sentence of the paragraph), states what the work has not shown, and then extends an invitation.

Solution/Recommendation

The purpose of your paper might be to review a problem or controversy and to discuss contributing factors. In such a case, it would be appropriate, after summarizing your discussion, to offer a solution based on the knowledge you've gained while conducting research. If your solution is to be taken seriously, your knowledge must be amply demonstrated in the body of the paper.

Here is a conclusion to a paper on problems in college sports:

(1) . . . The major problem in college sports today is not commercialism—it is the exploitation of athletes and the proliferation of illicit practices which dilute educational standards.

(2) Many universities are currently deriving substantial benefits from sports programs that depend on the labor of athletes drawn from the poorest sections of America's population. It is the responsibility of educators, civil rights leaders, and concerned citizens to see that these young people get a fair return for their labor both in terms of direct remuneration and in terms of career preparation for a life outside sports.

(3) Minimally, scholarships in revenue-producing sports should be designed to extend until graduation, rather than covering only four years of athletic eligibility, and should include guarantees of tutoring, counseling, and proper medical care. At institutions where the profits are particularly large (such as Texas A & M, which can afford to pay its football coach $280,000 a year), scholarships should also provide salaries that extend beyond room, board, and tuition. The important thing is that the athlete be remunerated fairly and have the opportunity to gain skills from a university environment without undue competition from a physically and psychologically demanding full-time job. This may well require that scholarships be extended over five or six years, including summers.

(4) Such a proposal, I suspect, will not be easy to implement. The current amateur system, despite its moral and educational flaws, enables universities to hire their athletic labor at minimal cost. But solving the fiscal crisis of the universities on the backs of America's poor and minorities is not, in the long run, a tenable solution. With the support of concerned educators, parents, and civil rights leaders, and with the help from organized labor, the college athlete, truly a sleeping giant, will someday speak out and demand what is rightly his—and hers—a fair share of the revenue created by their hard work.*

In this conclusion, the author summarizes his article in one sentence: "The major problem in college sports today is not commercialism—it is the exploitation of athletes and the proliferation of illicit practices which dilute educational standards." In paragraph 2, he continues with an analysis of the problem just stated and follows with a general recommendation—that "concerned educators, parents, and civil rights leaders" be responsible for the welfare of college athletes. In paragraph 3, he makes a specific proposal, and in the final paragraph, he anticipates resistance to the proposal. He concludes by discounting this resistance and returning to the general point, that college athletes should receive a fair deal.

Anecdote

An anecdote is a briefly told story or joke, the point of which in a conclusion is to shed light on your subject. The anecdote is more direct than an allusion. With an allusion, you merely refer to a story ("Too many people today live in Plato's cave . . . "); with the anecdote, you actually retell the story. The anecdote allows readers to discover for themselves the significance of a reference to another source—an effort most readers enjoy because they get to exercise their creativity.

The following anecdote concludes a political-philosophical paper. First, the author includes a paragraph summing up her argument, and she follows that with a brief story.

Ironically, our economy is fueled by the very thing that degrades our value system. But when politicians call for a return to "traditional family values," they seldom criticize the business interests that promote and benefit from our coarsened values. Consumer capitalism values things over people; it thrives on discontent and unhappiness since discontented people make excellent consumers, buying vast numbers of things that may somehow "fix" their inadequacies. We buy more than we need, the economy chugs along, but such materialism is the real culprit behind our warped value systems. Anthony de Mello tells the following story:

---

* Mark Naison, "Scenario for Scandal," *Commonweal* (2004).

> Socrates believed that the wise person would instinctively lead
> a frugal life, and he even went so far as to refuse to wear shoes.
> Yet he constantly fell under the spell of the marketplace and
> would go there often to look at the great variety and magnifi-
> cence of the wares on display.
>
> A friend once asked him why he was so intrigued with the
> allures of the market. "I love to go there," Socrates replied, "to
> discover how many things I am perfectly happy without."*

The writer chose to conclude the article with this anecdote. She could have
developed an interpretation, but this would have spoiled the dramatic value
for the reader. The purpose of using an anecdote is to make your point with
subtlety, so resist the temptation to interpret. Keep in mind three guidelines
when selecting an anecdote: It should be prepared for (readers should have
all the information they need to understand it), it should provoke the reader's
interest, and it should not be so obscure as to be unintelligible.

Quotation

A favorite concluding device is the quotation—the words of a famous person
or an authority in the field on which you are writing. The purpose of quoting another is to link your work to theirs, thereby gaining for your work
authority and credibility. The first criterion for selecting a quotation is its suitability to your thesis. But you should also carefully consider what your choice
of sources says about you. Suppose you are writing a paper on the American
work ethic. If you could use a line by comedian David Letterman or one by
the current secretary of labor to make the final point of your conclusion, which
would you choose and why? One source may not be inherently more effective
than the other, but the choice certainly sets a tone for the paper. The following
two paragraphs conclude a paper examining the popularity of vulgar and
insulting humor in television shows, movies, and other popular culture:

> But studies on the influence of popular culture suggest that cruel
> humor serves as more than a release in modern society. The ubiquitous
> media pick up on our baser nature, exaggerate it to entertain, and, by
> spitting it back at us, encourage us to push the boundaries even fur-
> ther. As a result, says Johns Hopkins' Miller, "We're gradually eroding
> the kinds of social forms and inhibitions that kept [aggressive] com-
> pulsions contained."
>
> Before the cycle escalates further, we might do well to consider the
> advice of Roman statesman and orator Cicero, who wrote at the peak
> of the Roman empire: "If we are forced, at every hour, to watch or
> listen to horrible events, this constant stream of ghastly impressions

---

* Frances Wageneck, *Family Values in the Marketplace*, unpublished paper, 2000: 6. Used by
permission.

will deprive even the most delicate among us of all respect for humanity."*

The two quotations used here serve different but equally effective ends. The first idea provides one last expert's viewpoint, then leads nicely into the cautionary note the writer introduces by quoting Cicero. The Roman's words, and the implied parallel being drawn between Rome and contemporary culture, are strong enough that the author ends there, without stepping in and making any statements of her own. In other cases, quotations can be used to set up one last statement by the author of a paper.

There is a potential problem with using quotations: If you end with the words of another, you may leave the impression that someone else can make your case more eloquently than you can. The language of the quotation will put your own prose into relief. If your own prose suffers by comparison—if the quotations are the best part of your paper—you'd be wise to spend some time revising. The way to avoid this kind of problem is to make your own presentation strong.

Question

Questions are useful for opening papers, and they are just as useful for closing them. Opening and closing questions function in different ways, however. The introductory question promises to be addressed in the paper that follows. But the concluding question leaves issues unresolved, calling on the readers to assume an active role by offering their own answers. Take a look at the following two paragraphs, written to conclude a paper on genetically modified (GM) food:

> Are GM foods any more of a risk than other agricultural innovations that have taken place over the years, like selective breeding? Do the existing and potential future benefits of GM foods outweigh any risks that do exist? And what standard should governments use when assessing the safety of transgenic crops? The "frankenfood" frenzy has given life to a policymaking standard known as the "precautionary principle," which has been long advocated by environmental groups. That principle essentially calls for governments to prohibit any activity that raises concerns about human health or the environment, even if some cause-and-effect relationships are not fully established scientifically. As Liberal Democrat MP [Member of Parliament] Norman Baker told the BBC: "We must always apply the precautionary principle. That says that unless you're sure of adequate control, unless you're sure the risk is minimal, unless you're sure nothing horrible can go wrong, you don't do it."
>
> But can any innovation ever meet such a standard of certainty— especially given the proliferation of "experts" that are motivated as

---

* Nina J. Easton, "The Meaning of America," *Los Angeles Times Magazine* 7 Feb. 1993: 21.

much by politics as they are by science? And what about those millions of malnourished people whose lives could be saved by trans-
genic foods?*

Perhaps you will choose to raise a question in your conclusion and then
answer it, based on the material you've provided in the paper. The answered
question challenges a reader to agree or disagree with your response and thus
also places the reader in an active role. The following brief conclusion ends
a student paper entitled "Is Feminism Dead?"

> So the answer to the question "Is the feminist movement dead?" is
> no, it's not. Even if most young women today don't consciously iden-
> tify themselves as "feminists"—due to the ways in which the term
> has become loaded with negative associations—the principles of
> gender equality that lie at feminism's core are enthusiastically
> embraced by the vast number of young women, and even a large per-
> centage of young men.

Speculation

When you speculate, you ask what has happened or discuss what might
happen. This kind of question stimulates the reader because its subject is the
unknown.

The following paragraph concludes "The New Generation Gap" by Neil
Howe and William Strauss. In this article, Howe and Strauss discuss the differences among Americans of various ages, including the "GI Generation"
(born between 1901 and 1924), the "Boomers" (born 1943–1961), the
"Thirteeners" (born 1961–1981), and the "Millennials" (born 1981–2000):

> If, slowly but surely, Millennials receive the kind of family protection
> and public generosity that GIs enjoyed as children, then they could
> come of age early in the next century as a group much like the GIs
> of the 1920s and 1930s—as a stellar (if bland) generation of rational-
> ists, team players, and can-do civic builders. Two decades from now
> Boomers entering old age may well see in their grown Millennial
> children an effective instrument for saving the world, while
> Thirteeners entering midlife will shower kindness on a younger gen-
> eration that is getting a better deal out of life (though maybe a bit less
> fun) than they ever got at a like age. Study after story after column
> will laud these "best damn kids in the world" as heralding a resur-
> gent American greatness. And, for a while at least, no one will talk
> about a generation gap.[†]

---

* "Frankenfoods Frenzy," *Reason* 13 Jan. 2000. 17 Aug. 2000 <http://reason.com/bi/bi-gmf.html>.

[†] Neil Howe and William Strauss, "The New Generation Gap," *Atlantic Monthly* Dec. 1992: 65.

Howe and Strauss thus conclude an article concerned largely with the apparently unbridgeable gaps of understanding between parents and children with a hopeful speculation that generational relationships will improve considerably in the next two decades.

EXERCISE 3.4

Drafting Conclusions

Imagine that you have written a paper using the topic, ideas, and thesis you developed in the earlier exercises in this chapter. Choose one of the seven types of conclusions we've discussed—preferably one you have never used before—and draft a conclusion that would work to end your paper. Use our examples as models to help you draft your practice conclusion.

Explanatory Synthesis

WHAT IS A SYNTHESIS?

A *synthesis* is a written discussion that draws on two or more sources. It follows that your ability to write syntheses depends on your ability to infer relationships among sources—essays, articles, fiction, and also nonwritten sources, such as lectures, interviews, and observations. This process is nothing new for you, since you infer relationships all the time—say, between something you've read in the newspaper and something you've seen for yourself, or between the teaching styles of your favorite and least favorite instructors. In fact, if you've written research papers, you've already written syntheses. In a *synthesis,* you make explicit the relationships that you have inferred among separate sources.

The skills you've already learned and practiced in the previous three chapters will be vital in writing syntheses. Clearly, before you're in a position to draw relationships between two or more sources, you must understand what those sources say; in other words, you must be able to *summarize* those sources. Readers will frequently benefit from at least partial summaries of sources in your synthesis essays. At the same time, you must go beyond summary to make judgments—judgments based, of course, on your *critical reading* of your sources: what conclusions you've drawn about the quality and validity of these sources, whether you agree or disagree with the points made in your sources, and why you agree or disagree.

Further, you must go beyond the critique of individual sources to determine the relationships among them. Is the information in source B, for example, an extended illustration of the generalizations in source A? Would it be useful to compare and contrast source C with source B? Having read and considered sources A, B, and C, can you infer something else— in other words, D (not a source, but your own idea)?

Because a synthesis is based on two or more sources, you will need to be selective when choosing information from each. It would be neither possible nor desirable, for instance, to discuss in a ten-page paper on the American Civil War every point that the authors of two books make about their subject. What you as a writer must do is select from each source the ideas and information that best allow you to achieve your purpose.

PURPOSE

Your purpose in reading source materials and then in drawing on them to write your own material is often reflected in the wording of an assignment. For instance, consider the following assignments on the Civil War:

WHERE DO WE FIND WRITTEN SYNTHESES?

Here are just a few of the types of writing that involve synthesis:

Academic Writing

- **Analysis papers.** Synthesize and apply several related theoretical approaches.
- **Research papers.** Synthesize multiple sources.
- **Argument papers.** Synthesize different points into a coherent claim or position.
- **Essay exams.** Demonstrate understanding of course material through comparing and contrasting theories, viewpoints, or approaches in a particular field.

Workplace Writing

- **Newspaper and magazine articles.** Synthesize primary and secondary sources.
- **Position papers and policy briefs.** Compare and contrast solutions for solving problems.
- **Business plans.** Synthesize ideas and proposals into one coherent plan.
- **Memos and letters.** Synthesize multiple ideas, events, and proposals into concise form.
- **Web sites.** Synthesize information from various sources to present in Web pages and related links.

American History: Evaluate the author's treatment of the origins of the Civil War.

Economics: Argue the following proposition, in light of your readings: "The Civil War was fought not for reasons of moral principle but for reasons of economic necessity."

Government: Prepare a report on the effects of the Civil War on Southern politics at the state level between 1870 and 1917.

Mass Communications: Discuss how the use of photography during the Civil War may have affected the perceptions of the war by Northerners living in industrial cities.

Literature: Select two twentieth-century Southern writers whose work you believe was influenced by the divisive effects of the Civil War. Discuss the ways this influence is apparent in a novel or a group of

short stories written by each author. The works
should not be *about* the Civil War.

Applied Technology: Compare and contrast the technology of warfare
available in the 1860s with the technology available
a century earlier.

Each of these assignments creates for you a particular purpose for writing. Having located sources relevant to your topic, you would select, for possible use in a paper, only those parts that helped you in fulfilling this purpose. And how you used those parts—how you related them to other material from other sources—would also depend on your purpose. For instance, if you were working on the government assignment, you might possibly draw on the same source as another student working on the literature assignment by referring to Robert Penn Warren's novel *All the King's Men*, about Louisiana politics in the early part of the twentieth century. But because the purposes of these assignments are different, you and the other student would make different uses of this source. Those same parts or aspects of the novel that you find worthy of detailed analysis might be mentioned only in passing—or not at all—by the other student.

USING YOUR SOURCES

Your purpose determines not only what parts of your sources you will use but also how you will relate them to one another. Since the very essence of synthesis is the combining of information and ideas, you must have some basis on which to combine them. *Some relationships among the material in your sources must make them worth synthesizing.* It follows that the better able you are to discover such relationships, the better able you will be to use your sources in writing syntheses. Notice that the mass communications assignment requires you to draw a *cause-and-effect* relationship between photographs of the war and Northerners' perceptions of the war. The applied technology assignment requires you to *compare and contrast* state-of-the-art weapons technology in the eighteenth and nineteenth centuries. The economics assignment requires you to *argue* a proposition. In each case, *your purpose will determine how you relate your source materials to one another.*

Consider some other examples. You may be asked on an exam question or in instructions for a paper to *describe* two or three approaches to prison reform during the past decade. You may be asked to *compare and contrast* one country's approach to imprisonment with another's. You may be asked to *develop an argument* of your own on this subject, based on your reading. Sometimes (when you are not given a specific assignment) you determine your own purpose: You are interested in exploring a particular subject; you are interested in making a case for one approach or another. In any event, your purpose shapes your essay. Your purpose determines which sources you research, which ones you use, which parts of them you use, at which points in your essay you use them, and in what manner you relate them to one another.

TYPES OF SYNTHESES: EXPLANATORY AND ARGUMENT

In this and the next chapter we categorize syntheses into two main types: *explanatory* and *argument.* The easiest way to recognize the difference between these two types may be to consider the difference between a newspaper article and an editorial on the same subject. Most likely, we'd say that the main purpose of the newspaper article is to convey *information,* and the main purpose of the editorial is to convey *opinion* or *interpretation.* Of course, this distinction is much too simplified: Newspaper articles often convey opinion or bias, sometimes subtly, sometimes openly; and editorials often convey unbiased information, along with opinion. But as a practical matter, we can generally agree on the distinction between a newspaper article that primarily conveys information and an editorial that primarily conveys opinion. You should be able to observe this distinction in the selections shown here as Explanation and Argument.

Explanation: *News Article from* The New York Times

Private Gets 3 Years for Iraq Prison Abuse
By David S. Cloud

September 28, 2005

1 Pfc. Lynndie R. England, a 22-year-old clerk in the Army who was photographed with naked Iraqi detainees at Abu Ghraib prison, was sentenced on Tuesday to three years in prison and a dishonorable discharge for her role in the scandal.

2 After the sentence was announced, Private England hung her head and cried briefly before hugging her mother, one of the few signs of emotion she showed in the six-day trial.

3 She had been found guilty on Monday of one count of conspiracy to maltreat prisoners, four counts of maltreatment and one count of committing an indecent act.

4 She made no comment on Tuesday as she was led out of the courthouse in handcuffs and leg shackles.

5 Earlier in the day, though, she took the stand and apologized for abusing the prisoners, saying her conduct was influenced by Specialist Charles A. Graner Jr., her boyfriend at the time.

6 She said she was "embarrassed" when photographs showing her posing next to naked detainees became public in 2004.

7 "I was used by Private Graner," she said. "I didn't realize it at the time."

8 Specialist Graner was reduced in rank after he was convicted in January as ringleader of the abuse.

9   Often groping for words and staring downward, Private England directed her apology to the detainees and to any American troops and their families who might have been injured or killed as a result of the insurgency in Iraq gaining strength.

10   Prosecutors argued on Tuesday that the anti-American feeling generated in Arab and Muslim countries by the Abu Ghraib scandal justified sentencing Private England to four to six years in prison and dishonorably discharging her from the Army. The charges the jury found her guilty of on Monday carried a maximum penalty of nine years. . . .

Argument: *Editorial from the* Boston Globe

Military Abuse

September 28, 2005

1   The court-martial conviction Monday of reservist Lynndie England for her role in the abuse of Iraqi prisoners at Abu Ghraib should fool no one that the Pentagon is taking seriously the mistreatment of Iraqis, especially after the release last Friday of a report on torture by members of the 82d Airborne Division stationed near Fallujah. . . .

2   If the [new] allegations are found credible, they further demolish the contention by officials that the abuse first reported at Abu Ghraib in 2004 was an isolated case of a few bad apples. Pentagon brass also tried to explain away the activities of England's unit as the actions of relatively untrained reservists. It is less easy to dismiss as a fluke such abuse when it occurs at the hands of the 82d Airborne, a thoroughly trained and highly decorated division.

3   The new charges, along with other accusations of abuse that have emerged since Abu Ghraib, including 28 suspicious detainee deaths, provide strong evidence that both reservist and active duty troops throughout Iraq were confused about their responsibility to treat detainees as prisoners of war under the terms of the Geneva Conventions. . . . Congress should have long since created a special commission, as proposed in a bill by Senator Carl Levin of Michigan, to investigate the issue of prisoner abuse. . . .

4   A truly independent inquiry, along the lines of the one done by the 9/11 commission, could trace accountability for prisoner abuse through statements and policies by ranking civilian and military officials in the Bush administration. Accountability for the shame of prisoner torture and abuse should not stop with Lynndie England and her cohort.

We'll say, for the sake of convenience, that the newspaper article provides an explanation and that the editorial provides an argument. This is essentially the distinction we make between explanatory and argument syntheses. As a further example of the distinction, read the following paragraph:

> Researchers now use recombinant DNA technology to analyze genetic changes. With this technology, they cut and splice DNA from different species, then insert the modified molecules into bacteria or other types of cells that engage in rapid replication and cell division. The cells copy the foreign DNA right along with their own. In short order, huge populations produce useful quantities of recombinant DNA molecules. The new technology also is the basis of genetic engineering, by which genes are isolated, modified, and inserted back into the same organism or into a different one.*

Now read this paragraph:

> Many in the life sciences field would have us believe that the new gene splicing technologies are irrepressible and irreversible and that any attempt to oppose their introduction is both futile and retrogressive. They never stop to even consider the possibility that the new genetic science might be used in a wholly different manner than is currently being proposed. The fact is, the corporate agenda is only one of two potential paths into the Biotech Century. It is possible that the growing number of anti-eugenic activists around the world might be able to ignite a global debate around alternative uses of the new science— approaches that are less invasive, more sustainable and humane and that conserve and protect the genetic rights of future generations.†

Both of these passages deal with the topic of biotechnology, but the two take quite different approaches. The first passage came from a biology textbook, while the second appeared in a magazine article. As we might expect from a textbook on the broad subject of biology, the first passage is explanatory and informative; it defines and explains some of the key concepts of biotechnology without taking a position or providing commentary about the implications of the technology. Magazine articles often present information in the same ways; however, many magazine articles take specific positions, as we see in the second passage. This passage is argumentative or persuasive. Its primary purpose is to convey a point of view regarding the topic of biotechnology.

While each of these excerpts presents a clear instance of writing that is either explanatory or argumentative, it is important to note that the sources for these excerpts—the textbook chapter and the magazine article—contain

---

* Cecie Starr and Ralph Taggart, "Recombinant DNA and Genetic Engineering," *Biology: The Unity and Diversity of Life* (New York: Wadsworth, 1998).

† Jeremy Rifkin, "The Ultimate Therapy: Commercial Eugenics on the Eve of the Biotech Century," *Tikkun* May–June 1998: 35.

elements of *both* explanation and argument. The textbook writers, while they refrain from taking a particular position, do note the controversies surrounding biotechnology and genetic engineering. They might even subtly reveal a certain bias in favor of one side of the issue, through their word choice and tone, and perhaps through devoting more space and attention to one point of view. Explanatory and argumentative writing are not mutually exclusive. The overlap in the categories of explanation and argument is also found in the magazine article: In order to make his case against genetic engineering, the writer has to explain certain elements of the issue. Yet, even while these categories overlap to a certain extent, the second passage clearly has argument as its primary purpose, whereas the first passage is primarily explanatory.

In Chapter 2 we noted that the primary purpose in a piece of writing may be informative, persuasive, or entertaining (or some combination of the three). Some scholars of writing argue that all writing is essentially persuasive, and even without entering into that complex argument, we've just seen how the varying purposes in writing do overlap. In order to persuade others of a particular position, we typically also must inform them about it; conversely, a primarily informative piece of writing also must work to persuade the reader that its claims are truthful. Both informative and persuasive writing often include entertaining elements, and writing intended primarily to entertain also typically contains information and persuasion. For practical purposes, however, it is possible—and useful—to identify the *primary* purpose in a piece of writing as informative/explanatory, persuasive/argumentative, or entertaining. Entertainment as a primary purpose is the one least often practiced in purely academic writing—perhaps to your disappointment!—but information and persuasion are ubiquitous. Thus, while recognizing the overlap between these categories, we distinguish in this and the following chapter between two types of synthesis writing: explanatory (or informative), and argument (or persuasive). Just as distinguishing the primary purpose in a piece of writing helps you to critically read and evaluate it, distinguishing the primary purpose in your own writing helps you to make the appropriate choices regarding your approach.

In this chapter we'll focus on explanatory syntheses. In the next chapter, we'll discuss the argument synthesis.

HOW TO WRITE SYNTHESES

Although writing syntheses can't be reduced to a lockstep method, it should help you to follow the guidelines listed in the box on pages 106–107.

THE EXPLANATORY SYNTHESIS

Many of the papers you write in college will be more or less explanatory in nature. An explanation helps readers understand a topic. Writers explain when they divide a subject into its component parts and present them to the

GUIDELINES FOR WRITING SYNTHESES

- *Consider your purpose in writing.* What are you trying to accomplish in your paper? How will this purpose shape the way you approach your sources?
- *Select and carefully read your sources,* according to your purpose. Then reread the passages, mentally summarizing each. Identify those aspects or parts of your sources that will help you fulfill your purpose. When rereading, *label* or *underline* the sources for main ideas, key terms, and any details you want to use in the synthesis.
- *Take notes on your reading.* In addition to labeling or underlining key points in the readings, you might write brief one- or two-sentence summaries of each source. This will help you in formulating your thesis statement, and in choosing and organizing your sources later.
- *Formulate a thesis.* Your thesis is the main idea that you want to present in your synthesis. It should be expressed as a complete sentence. You might do some predrafting about the ideas discussed in the readings in order to help you work out a thesis. If you've written one-sentence summaries of the readings, looking these over will help you to brainstorm connections between readings and to devise a thesis.

  When you write your essay drafts, you will need to consider where your thesis fits in your paper. Sometimes the thesis is the first sentence, but more often it is *the final sentence of the first paragraph.* If you are writing an *inductively arranged* synthesis (see page 162), the thesis sentence may not appear until the final paragraphs. (See Chapter 3 for more information on writing an effective thesis.)
- *Decide how you will use your source material.* How will the information and the ideas in the passages help you fulfill your purpose?
- *Develop an organizational plan,* according to your thesis. How will you arrange your material? It is not necessary to prepare a formal outline. But you should have some plan that will indicate the order

reader in a clear and orderly fashion. Explanations may entail descriptions that re-create in words some object, place, emotion, event, sequence of events, or state of affairs. As a student reporter, you may need to explain an event—to relate when, where, and how it took place. In a science lab, you would observe the conditions and results of an experiment and record them for review by others. In a political science course, you might review research on a particular subject—say, the complexities underlying the debate over gay in which you will present your material and that will indicate the relationships among your sources.

- *Draft the topic sentences for the main sections.* This is an optional step, but you may find it a helpful transition from organizational plan to first draft.
- *Write the first draft* of your synthesis, following your organizational plan. Be flexible with your plan, however. Frequently, you will use an outline to get started. As you write, you may discover new ideas and make room for them by adjusting the outline. When this happens, reread your work frequently, making sure that your thesis still accounts for what follows and that what follows still logically supports your thesis.
- *Document your sources.* You must do this by crediting them within the body of the synthesis—citing the author's last name and page number from which the point was taken and by providing full citation information in a list of "Works Cited" at the end. Don't open yourself to charges of plagiarism! (See pages 48–49; see also pages 846–849 for more information on documenting sources.)
- *Revise your synthesis,* inserting transitional words and phrases where necessary. Make sure that the synthesis reads smoothly, logically, and clearly from beginning to end. Check for grammatical correctness, punctuation, and spelling.

Note: The writing of syntheses is a recursive process, and you should accept a certain amount of backtracking and reformulating as inevitable. For instance, in developing an organizational plan (Step 6 of the procedure), you may discover a gap in your presentation that will send you scrambling for another source—back to Step 2. You may find that formulating a thesis and making inferences among sources occur simultaneously; indeed, inferences are often made before a thesis is formulated. Our recommendations for writing syntheses will give you a structure; they will get you started. But be flexible in your approach; expect discontinuity and, if possible, be comforted that through backtracking and reformulating you will eventually produce a coherent, well-crafted paper.

marriage—and then present the results of your research to your professor and the members of your class.

Your job in writing an explanatory paper—or in writing the explanatory portion of an argumentative paper—is not to argue a particular point, but rather *to present the facts in a reasonably objective manner.* Of course, explanatory papers, like other academic papers, should be based on a thesis (see pages 82–90). But the purpose of a thesis in an explanatory paper is less to advance a particular opinion than to focus the various facts contained in the paper.

DEMONSTRATION: EXPLANATORY SYNTHESIS— THE HYDROGEN-POWERED AUTOMOBILE

To illustrate how the process of synthesis works, we'll begin with a number of short extracts from several articles on the same subject.

Suppose you were writing a paper on a matter that auto manufacturers, along with many drivers who are upset with escalating gasoline prices, are discussing: efficient, environmentally sound alternatives to the internal combustion engine. Some writers and thinkers are excited about the possibility that one alternative energy source in particular, hydrogen fuel cells, could both free Americans of reliance on foreign oil and slow the degradation of the earth's atmosphere. Others, recognizing the need for new ways to power automobiles, cite difficulties with the current state-of-the-art fuel-cell technology and favor other approaches, including the hybrid (gasoline and electric) engine.

EXERCISE **4.1**

Exploring the Topic

Before reading what others have written on the subject of alternative energy vehicles, write a page or so exploring what you know and what you think about this topic. You might focus your first paragraph on your own experience with alternative energy sources—for instance, water power, steam, solar, wind, or hybrid. If you have no direct experience with the topic, recall what you have read, seen, or heard about levels of petroleum consumption in the United States, the controversies surrounding the search for oil in this country, or the advertising buzz surrounding hybrid cars. What do you imagine are some concerns people have about alternative energy vehicles? What do you think would be of the most interest to journalists, politicians, and businesspeople?

Because the topic of hydrogen fuel cells is technical and you may not have the expertise to write knowledgeably on it just yet, and also because you are aware that the hydrogen fuel cell is but one of several technologies being discussed as replacements to the internal combustion engine, you decide to investigate what has been written on the subject, both in print and electronic texts. In the following pages we present four passages from the kinds of articles your research might locate; the rest of the sources are listed in the "Works Cited" of the model synthesis on pages 135–143. In preparing your paper, of course you would draw upon the entire articles from which the excerpts were taken. (The discussion of how these passages can form the basis of an explanatory synthesis resumes on page 116.)

The Fuel Subsidy We Need
Ricardo Bayon

A fellow at the New America Foundation, Ricardo Bayon writes on the intersection of finance, public policy, and environmental studies. The following is excerpted from an article in Atlantic Monthly, *January/February 2003.*

1   The American economy is, after Canada's, the most energy-dependent in the advanced industrialized world, requiring the equivalent of a quarter ton of oil to produce $1,000 of gross domestic product. We require twice as much energy as Germany—and three times as much as Japan—to produce the same amount of GDP. Overall the United States consumes 25 percent of the oil produced in the world each year. This binds us to the Middle East, which still holds more than 65 percent of the world's proven oil reserves. Even if we were to buy all our oil from Venezuela, Canada, and Russia, or to find more oil here in the United States (which currently holds only 2.9 percent of proven reserves), Persian Gulf producers with excess capacity, such as Saudi Arabia and the United Arab Emirates, would still largely dictate the price we paid for it.

2   America's economic vulnerability to oil-price fluctuations has led Washington to strike a tacit bargain with Saudi Arabia and other Persian Gulf oil producers. In return for U.S. military protection and silence about the more unsavory aspects of their societies, these countries increase production when prices get too high and cut it when they get too low. In addition, they price their oil in dollars and recycle their petro-profits through U.S. financial institutions. But this has made the United States vulnerable not only to a sustained spike in oil prices but also to the possible fall of the dollar. In part because the dollar has been strong, we have been able to consume more than we produce and then to make up the difference by borrowing from abroad. As a result, our current net international debt has risen to $2.3 trillion, or 22.6 percent of GDP. What would happen if a war in Iraq went badly or if Islamic extremists gained ground in key oil-producing states? Oil prices could rise and the dollar could fall, inflicting a double blow to the U.S. economy from which it could not easily recover.

3   The way to escape this abiding insecurity is to wean the U.S. economy—and the world economy, too—off oil. And the way to do that is to encourage the commercial development of a technology called the hydrogen fuel cell. Solar power and windmills will surely be important parts of our energy future, but only the fuel cell can address our oil dependency by challenging the primacy of the internal-combustion engine.

4   Fuel cells are actually a relatively old technology (they were invented in 1839, Jules Verne wrote about them in the 1870s, and they were used by U.S. astronauts in the 1960s), and the concept underlying them is simple: by mixing hydrogen and oxygen, fuel cells generate both water and electricity. Not only do fuel cells turn two of nature's most abundant elements into enough energy to power a car, but they create no toxic emissions (drinkable water is their only by-product). And fuel cells are completely quiet, meaning that it is now realistic to imagine living in a world of silent cars and trucks.

5   The technology is not science fiction: fuel cells are on their way toward commercial viability. Fuel-cell-powered buses are running in Vancouver, Chicago, London, and parts of Germany. BMW has a prototype car powered solely by fuel cells. Honda, Toyota, and DaimlerChrysler announced recently that they would begin shipping fuel-cell cars to retail customers around the world; General Motors and Ford are not far behind. Honda's car was shipped to its first major customer—the city of Los Angeles—at the beginning of December.

6   Geoffrey Ballard, the founder of the Canadian manufacturer Ballard Power Systems, has said, "The internal-combustion engine will go the way of the horse. It will be a curiosity to my grandchildren." Even large oil companies believe that they must embrace hydrogen power.

Putting the Hindenburg to Rest
Jim Motavalli

Jim Motavalli is editor of the environmentally focused E Magazine *and writes extensively on environmental matters for newspapers and magazines nationally. This interview appeared in the* New York Times *on June 5, 2005.*

Some transportation experts are betting that hydrogen will eventually power most cars, while others see substantial, perhaps insurmountable, hurdles. Here is a primer on the benefits and disadvantages:

1   Q. What is hydrogen, and where does it come from?

2   A. It is the lightest gas and the simplest, most abundant element in the universe. Because it is present in so many compounds, including water, supplies cannot be exhausted. But hydrogen is not actually a fuel, and can be used in a vehicle only after it is separated from other elements. This process itself consumes energy.

3   Q. How is hydrogen used to power a car? And what's a fuel cell?

4   A. A fuel cell uses a chemical process, similar to that in a battery, to produce electricity—in this case, from hydrogen that flows into the cell from a storage tank. This electricity drives the fuel-cell car's electric motor; the only byproducts are heat and water.

5   Q. What are the potential advantages?

6   A. Because hydrogen is found everywhere, supplies are not only infinite, they pose no geographic challenges. It can be produced, albeit expensively, from emission-free sources like solar panels, wind turbines or even nuclear plants. Fuel cells can be easily scaled up or down in size, so they could replace small computer batteries or large power plants. A hydrogen car emits no pollution or global warming gases, aside from what might have resulted from producing the hydrogen itself.

7   Q. If it's so great, why aren't we driving hydrogen cars right now?

8   A. Widespread use of fuel-cell cars will have to wait until the cells become cheaper and more efficient, and until storage methods have evolved to give

vehicles a travel range of perhaps 300 miles. Hydrogen production will have to be scaled up and standardized, and pumping stations equipped for hydrogen refueling at an affordable price.

9 Q. I've heard about the Hindenburg—is hydrogen safe?

10 A. Hydrogen is very flammable, and poses special challenges: it burns without a visible flame, for instance. But it is arguably no more dangerous than gasoline, and fuel-cell cars are built with leak detectors and very strong crash-resistant tanks. As for the Hindenburg tragedy of 1937, a retired NASA engineer, Addison Bain, theorizes that the dirigible burned not because it contained hydrogen, but because its cloth skin was coated with highly flammable paint. Others disagree with his assessment.

11 Q. How will a car carry hydrogen?

12 A. Hydrogen can be stored as a gas, as a liquid or in metal hydrides, which are chemical sponges, but each form has advantages and disadvantages. Still, much of automakers' current research focuses on pressurized hydrogen gas.

13 Q. When will I have a hydrogen car in my driveway?

14 A. Joseph Romm, a former Department of Energy official and author of "The Hype About Hydrogen" (Island Press, 2004), says, "I doubt that in the next 20 years an affordable, durable and efficient vehicle will be delivered that will be attractive to the public." But a renewable energy advocate, Amory Lovins of the Rocky Mountain Institute, says the nation's car fleet could be converted to hydrogen in less than a decade, and a network of small hydrogen reformers (devices that produce hydrogen from natural gas or other sources) could be quickly installed in 10 to 20 percent of the nation's 180,000 gas stations for $2 billion to $4 billion.

15 Q. Is this just a lot of hype?

16 A. Some overblown claims have already been disproved. But there is also groundbreaking research backed by serious testing programs. Lawrence D. Burns, General Motors' vice president for research and planning, says G.M. aims to have a production-ready fuel-cell vehicle (built on an innovative "skateboard" platform that could support a variety of bodies) by 2010. DaimlerChrysler is running 30 fuel-cell buses in Europe and helping to seed a hydrogen infrastructure in Iceland.

Fuel-cell Toyota Highlanders are being tested at two California universities; both the City of Los Angeles and the State of New York are using Honda FCX's. Nissan will reportedly lease a few X-Trail fuel-cell S.U.V.'s to American businesses in 2007.

17 Q. Will fuel-cell cars be cheap to operate? Where will I fill up?

18 A. Hydrogen's current price is three to four times that of gasoline. The Department of Energy has issued optimistic cost estimates, but they assume widespread commercial acceptance of hydrogen fuel—which is at least a decade away. There are only a few hydrogen stations scattered around the country, though California envisions a 170-station "hydrogen highway" by 2010; Florida has announced a similar plan.

19 Q. How long will fuel cells last?

20 A. The journal of the American Institute of Chemical Engineers says the life of fuel cells may be only a fifth as long as that of a typical gasoline engine— about 30,000 miles versus 150,000. Ben Knight, vice president for automo-

tive engineering at Honda, agrees that the durability of fuel-cell stacks is "a work in progress," but promises "a significantly longer life" from newer designs.

21 Q. Can you run a regular engine with hydrogen, without fuel cells?

22 A. Yes. A hydrogen Cadillac was featured at President Jimmy Carter's inauguration in 1977. A Mini with a hydrogen-powered internal combustion engine was displayed at the Frankfurt auto show in 2001, and Ford has shown prototypes. BMW plans to offer a "dual fuel" 7 Series sedan, which could run on either gasoline or hydrogen, by 2008. That V-12 car would have a range of 125 miles on hydrogen and 185 on gasoline.

Using Fossil Fuels in Energy Process Gets Us Nowhere
Jeremy Rifkin

Jeremy Rifkin, a prolific author well known for his cautionary views on technology (especially genetic technologies), is the author of The Hydrogen Economy: The Creation of the World Wide Energy Web and the Redistribution of Power on Earth *(2002). This selection is excerpted from a longer piece in the* Los Angeles Times, *November 9, 2003.*

1 Hydrogen—the lightest and most abundant element of the universe—is the next great energy revolution. Scientists call it the "forever fuel" because it never runs out. And when hydrogen is used to produce power, the only byproducts are pure water and heat.

2 The shift to fuel cells and hydrogen energy—when it happens—will be as significant and far-reaching in its effect on the American and global economy as the steam engine and coal in the 19th century and the internal combustion engine and oil in the 20th century.

3 Hydrogen has the potential to end the world's reliance on oil from the Persian Gulf. It will dramatically cut down on carbon dioxide emissions and mitigate the effects of global warming. And because hydrogen is so plentiful, people who have never before had access to electricity will be able to generate it.

4 The environmental community is up in arms over the Bush hydrogen agenda. Why? Hydrogen has a Janus face. Though it is found everywhere on Earth, it rarely exists free-floating in nature. Hydrogen has to be extracted from fossil fuels or water or biomass.

5 In other words, there is "black" hydrogen and "green" hydrogen. And it is this critical difference that separates Bush's vision of a hydrogen future from the vision many of us hold in the environmental movement.

6 Bush and Secretary of Energy Spencer Abraham say hydrogen can free us from dependence on foreign oil. What they leave unsaid is that their plan calls for extracting hydrogen from all of the old energy sources—oil, natural gas and coal—and by harnessing nuclear power. Bush would like to take us into a hydrogen future without ever leaving the fossil fuels and nuclear past.

7 Today, most commercial hydrogen is extracted from natural gas via a steam reforming process. Although natural gas emits less carbon dioxide than other

fossil fuels in producing hydrogen, it is a finite resource and in relatively short supply.

8   Hydrogen can also be extracted from coal, and enthusiasts point out that the U.S. enjoys ample coal reserves. The problem is that coal produces twice as much carbon dioxide as natural gas, which means a dramatic increase in global warming.

9   The coal industry counters that it might be possible to safely store the carbon dioxide emissions underground or in the ocean depths for thousands of years and has convinced the White House to subsidize further research into this. For many environmentalists, the issue of storing carbon dioxide seems eerily reminiscent of the arguments used by the nuclear industry about nuclear waste.

10   The nuclear industry would like to produce hydrogen, but there are still unresolved issues surrounding the safe storage of nuclear waste, the skyrocketing costs of building new reactors and the vulnerability of nuclear power plants to terrorist attacks.

11   There is another way to produce hydrogen—the green way—that uses no fossil fuels or nuclear power. Renewable sources of energy—wind, hydro- and geothermal power and photovoltaic cells—are increasingly being used to produce electricity. That electricity, in turn, can be used, in a process called electrolysis, to split water into hydrogen and oxygen.

12   Hydrogen could also be extracted from sustainable energy crops and agricultural waste in a process called gasification. There would be no increase in carbon dioxide emissions because the carbon taken from the atmosphere by the plants is released back during hydrogen production.

13   The White House proposal calls for large subsidies to the coal and nuclear industries to extract hydrogen. The Secretary of Energy claims that the administration is equally committed to research and development of renewable sources of energy to extract hydrogen.

14   However, the White House and the Republican Party have systematically blocked efforts in Congress to establish target dates for the phasing in of renewable sources of energy in the generation of electricity and for transport.

15   If the U.S. is successful in steering the International Partnership for the Hydrogen Economy toward a black hydrogen future, it could lock the global economy into the old energy regime for much of the 21st century, with dire environmental and economic consequences.

16   The real benefits of a hydrogen future can be realized only if renewable sources of energy are phased in and eventually become the primary source for extracting hydrogen. In the interim, the U.S. government should be supporting much tougher automobile fuel standards, hybrid cars, the overhaul of the nation's power grid with emphasis on smart technology, the Kyoto Protocol on global warming and benchmarks for renewable energy adoption.

17   All of these other initiatives should be carried on concurrently with an ambitious national effort to subsidize and underwrite the research and development of renewable energy technology, hydrogen and fuel cells.

18   The goal should be a fully integrated green hydrogen economy by the end of the first half of the 21st century.

Lots of Hot Air About Hydrogen
Joseph J. Romm

Joseph Romm is a former acting assistant secretary of energy and author of the book The Hype About Hydrogen: Fact and Fiction in the Race to Save the Climate. *The selection origi- nally appeared in the* Los Angeles Times, *Opinion section, March 29, 2004.*

1   WASHINGTON—Earlier this month, the South Coast Air Quality Management District approved a $4-million program to put a mustache on the Mona Lisa— at least that's how it seems to me. What the agency actually did was approve spending millions to take 35 or so of the greenest, most energy-efficient sedans ever made—the hybrid gasoline-electric Toyota Prius—and turn them all into dirty energy guzzlers.

2   It is going to achieve this giant leap backward by converting the hybrids to run on hydrogen, the most overhyped alternative fuel since methyl tertiary-butyl ether, or MTBE.

3   Hybrids are already extremely efficient. The Prius, for example, generates only about 210 grams of carbon dioxide—the principal heat-trapping gas that causes global warming—per mile. The car is also a partial zero-emission vehi- cle, which means that when it uses California's low-sulfur gasoline, it produces very little of the smog-forming pollutants, like nitrogen oxides.

4   Hydrogen is not a primary fuel, like oil, that we can drill for. It is bound up tightly in molecules of water, or hydrocarbons like natural gas. A great deal of energy must be used to unbind it—something the AQMD plans to do by elec- trolyzing water into its constituents: hydrogen and oxygen. And because the resulting hydrogen is a gas, additional energy must be used to compress it to very high pressures to put it in the tank of your car.

5   With all the energy needed to create and compress that hydrogen—even with the relatively clean electric grid of California—a Prius running on hydrogen would result in twice as much greenhouse gas emissions per mile as an unmodi- fied car. It would result in more than four times as much nitrogen oxides per mile.

6   I own a Prius, so that's the hybrid I am most familiar with. But Honda also makes a hybrid vehicle, and thanks to California's leadership in vehicle emis- sions regulations, many other car companies plan to introduce them soon. These cars will get even greener over time as technology improves.

7   Sadly, two of the features I love most about my car would be wiped out by the AQMD's expensive "upgrade." First, the hybrid has cut my annual fuel bill by half. Hydrogen is so expensive to make that even with California's high gasoline prices, the hydrogen hybrid will have more than four times the annual fuel bill of a gasoline hybrid. Second, my car can go twice as far on a tank of gas as my old Saturn, so I have to make those unpleasant trips to the gas sta- tion only half as often. The hydrogen hybrid would have less than half the range of my car. With hydrogen fueling stations so scarce, hydrogen hybrid dri- vers will constantly be scampering back to the fueling stations before the tanks get too low.

8   Why is the AQMD spending millions of dollars to increase pollution and destroy all the desirable features of one of the greenest, most efficient cars ever made? It has bought into the hype about hydrogen, the myth that this miracle fuel will somehow solve all of our energy and environmental problems.

9   When I was helping to oversee clean-energy programs at the U.S. Department of Energy in the mid-1990s, I too was intrigued by hydrogen, mainly because of recent advances in fuel cells. Fuel cells are electrochemical devices that take in hydrogen and oxygen and generate electricity and heat with high efficiency. The only "emission" is water. They have been an elusive technological goal since the first fuel cell was invented in 1839. During the 1990s, we increased funding for hydrogen tenfold and for transportation fuel cells threefold.

10   I began to change my mind about hydrogen while researching a book over the last 12 months. After speaking to dozens of experts and reviewing the extensive literature, I came to realize that hydrogen cars still needed several major breakthroughs and a clean-energy revolution to be both practical and desirable.

11   A recent Energy Department report noted that transportation fuel cells were 100 times more expensive than internal combustion engines. Historically, even the most aggressively promoted energy technologies, such as wind and solar power, have taken 20 years just to see a tenfold decline in prices.

12   The most mature onboard hydrogen storage systems—using ultrahigh pressure—contain 10 times less energy per unit volume than gasoline, in addition to requiring a significant amount of compression energy. A National Academy of Sciences panel concluded in February that such storage had "little promise of long-term practicality for light-duty vehicles" and urged the Department of Energy to halt research in this area. Yet this kind of storage is precisely what the AQMD plans to put in its hydrogen hybrids.

13   Another problem with hydrogen is in how it is made. Although people seem to view hydrogen as a pollution-free elixir, hydrogen is just an energy carrier, like electricity. And, like electricity, it is no cleaner than the fuels used to make it. For the next several decades, the National Academy panel concluded, "it is highly likely that fossil fuels will be the principal sources of hydrogen." Making hydrogen from fossil fuels won't solve our major environmental problems.

14   It's possible, of course, to make hydrogen with renewable electricity, such as solar and wind power, but that is a lousy use for renewables, since they can directly displace more than four times as much carbon dioxide from coal power compared with using that renewable power to make hydrogen for vehicles. And these savings can all be achieved without spending hundreds of billions of dollars on a new hydrogen infrastructure and hydrogen vehicles.

15   As one 2002 British study concluded, "Until there is a surplus of renewable electricity, it is not beneficial in terms of carbon reduction to use renewable electricity to produce hydrogen—for use in vehicles, or elsewhere." That surplus is, sadly, a long way off, given that Congress hasn't been willing to pass legislation requiring that even 10% of U.S. electricity in 2020 be from renewables like wind and solar.

16   Finally, delivering renewable hydrogen to a car in usable form is prohibitively expensive today—equal to gasoline at $7 to $10 a gallon—and likely to remain so for decades in the absence of major technology advances.

17   For at least several decades, hydrogen cars are exceedingly unlikely to be a cost-effective solution for global warming. Until we achieve major breakthroughs in vehicle technology, hydrogen storage, hydrogen infrastructure and renewable hydrogen production, hydrogen cars will remain inferior to the best hybrids in cost, range, annual fueling bill, convenience, roominess, safety and greenhouse gas emissions.

18   While we wait, California should continue to lead the way in building renewable-power generation and in advancing the most environmentally responsible cars in the world—hybrid partial zero-emission vehicles.

Consider Your Purpose

The student writing the explanatory paper beginning on page 135 drew on more than these brief selections on hydrogen fuel-cell technology to write her paper. But these will do here for purposes of demonstration. How did she—how do you—go about synthesizing the sources?

First, remember that before considering the *how*, you must consider the *why*. In other words, what is your *purpose* in synthesizing these sources? You might use them for a paper dealing with a broader issue: "green," or environmentally friendly technologies, for instance. If this were your purpose, these sources would be used for perhaps two sections of your discussion, on the problems associated with petroleum-based technologies and on the eco-neutral potential of fuel cells. Because such a broader paper would consider power sources other than fuel cells (for instance, wind, solar, and geothermal), it would also need to draw on additional sources. For a marketing course, you might consider strategies for encouraging public acceptance of fuel cells, the challenge being that on first introduction they may be more expensive or less convenient than gasoline engines. The sources would clarify for you how fuel cells work, their potential, and the technical challenges that must be overcome in order for them to become a reasonable energy source. For a paper on the challenges of promoting acceptance of fuel cells, you would (again) need to consult more sources than we've gathered here in order to write an effective synthesis. Moving out of the academic world and into the commercial one, you might be an engineer preparing a brochure for your company's new fuel-cell design. In this brochure, you might want to address the challenges of conventional designs and the advantages that your company's product offers.

But for now let's keep it simple: You want to write a paper, or a section of a paper, that simply explains the potential of fuel-cell technology to alleviate our dependence on foreign oil and to provide a power source for cars that does not degrade the environment. Your job, then, is to write an *explanatory* synthesis—one that presents information but does not advance your own opinion on the *subject*.

Critical Reading for Synthesis

Look over the preceding readings and make a list of the ways they address the problems associated with petroleum-based technology and the potential of alternate technologies, especially fuel cells. Make your list as specific and detailed as you can. Assign a source to each item on the list.

We asked one of our students, Janice Hunte, to read these passages and to use them (and others) as sources in a paper on fuel-cell technology. We also asked her to write some additional comments describing the process of developing her ideas into a draft. We'll draw upon some of these comments in the following discussion.

Formulate a Thesis

The difference between a purpose and a thesis is a difference primarily of focus. Your purpose provides direction to your research and focus to your paper. Your thesis sharpens this focus by narrowing it and formulating it in the words of a single declarative statement. (Refer to Chapter 3 for additional discussion on formulating thesis statements.)

Since Hunte's purpose in this case was to synthesize source material with little or no comment, her thesis would be the most obvious statement she could make about the relationship among these passages. By "obvious" we mean a statement that is broad enough to encompass the main points of all these readings. Taken as a whole, what do they *mean?* Here Hunte describes the process she followed in coming up with a preliminary thesis for her explanatory synthesis:

> I began my writing process by looking over all the readings and noting the main point of each reading in a sentence on a piece of paper.
>
> Then I reviewed all of these points and identified the patterns in the readings. These I listed underneath my list of main points--All the readings focus on the energy needed to power cars and, more generally, the American economy. The readings explain America's dependence on foreign oil, the wisdom of that dependence, technologies that could free us of this dependence, and the plusses and minuses of two technologies in particular, hydrogen fuel cells and gasoline/electric hybrids.
>
> Looking over these points, I drafted a preliminary thesis. This thesis summed up the different issues in the sources and stated how these were interrelated.

> America's dependence on dwindling foreign oil
> reserves has spurred research into alternate
> technologies for powering cars.

This was a true statement, but it sounded too vague and too obvious. I didn't feel it adequately represented the readings' points, especially since several experts hotly debate the advantages of fuel cells vs. hybrids. I wanted my thesis to more fully reflect the complexity of people's concerns regarding how these technologies are evolving as auto manufacturers search for ever more efficient designs. My next version followed:

> Many people believe hybrids will solve our
> energy needs, but since hybrids still depend
> on gasoline, others insist that another technology will take its place: fuel cells.

This thesis reflected the disagreement among experts concerning the two technologies, but I didn't feel I said enough about what makes fuel cells so attractive--namely, that they are powered by hydrogen, which is a clean-burning fuel with a virtually inexhaustible supply (unlike petroleum). In my next attempt, I tried to be more specific and a little more emphatic:

> Although many see hybrids as merely transitional vehicles, since they require gasoline,
> others believe that fuel-cell vehicles powered
> by hydrogen, a clean-burning and abundant
> energy source, will become the norm for roadway and highway travel.

Although this sentence was too long and sounded awkward to me, I thought it could be a good working thesis because it would help to define important parts of my paper: for instance, what are hybrids, why would they be transitional, what are fuel cells, what are their advantages over hybrids? Now I proceeded to the next step in writing--organizing my material.

Decide How You Will Use Your Source Material

The easiest way to deal with sources is to summarize them. But because you are synthesizing *ideas* rather than sources, you will have to be more selective than if you were writing a simple summary. You don't have to treat *all* the ideas in your sources, only the ones related to your thesis. Some sources might be summarized in their entirety; others, only in part. Look over your earlier notes or sentences discussing the topics covered in the readings, and refer back to the readings themselves. Focusing on some of the more subtle elements of the issues addressed by the authors, expand your earlier summary sentences. Write brief phrases in the margin of the sources, underline key phrases or sentences, or take notes on a separate sheet of paper or in a word processing file or electronic data filing program. Decide how your sources can help you achieve your purpose and support your thesis. For example, how might you use a diagram explaining the basics of fuel-cell technology? How would you present disagreements over the perceived problems with and the potential of fuel-cell technology? How much would you discuss gasoline/electric hybrids?

Develop an Organizational Plan

An organizational plan is your map for presenting material to the reader. What material will you present? To find out, examine your thesis. Do the content and structure of the thesis (that is, the number and order of assertions) suggest an organizational plan for the paper? Expect to devote at least one paragraph of your paper to developing each section of this plan. Having identified likely sections, think through the possibilities of arrangement. Ask yourself: What information does the reader need to understand first? How do I build on this first section—what block of information will follow? Think of each section in relation to others until you have placed them all and have worked your way through to a plan for the whole paper.

Study your thesis, and let it help suggest an organization. Bear in mind that any one paper can be written—successfully—according to a variety of plans. Your job before beginning your first draft is to explore possibilities. Sketch a series of rough outlines: Arrange and rearrange your paper's likely sections until you develop a plan that both facilitates the reader's understanding and achieves your objectives as a writer. Think carefully about the logical order of your points: Does one idea or point lead to the next? If not, can you find a more logical place for the point, or are you just not clearly articulating the connections between the ideas?

Your final paper may well deviate from your final sketch, since in the act of writing you may discover the need to explore new material, to omit planned material, to refocus or to reorder your entire presentation. Just the same, a well-conceived organizational plan will encourage you to begin writing a draft.

Hunte describes the process of organizing the materials as follows.

Summary Statements

In these notes, Hunte refers to all the sources she used, not just to the four excerpted in this chapter.

In reviewing my sources and writing summary statements, I noted the most important aspects of problems associated with reliance on petroleum and the promise and problems of fuel cells and other alternative technologies:

- Saudi Arabia is running out of oil, and when it does the "Petroleum Age" will end with catastrophic results, unless economies prepare by changing their patterns of energy consumption (Klare).

- America is dangerously dependent on foreign oil. We can "wean" our economy off oil by developing hydrogen fuel-cell technology (Bayon).

- Hydrogen fuel cells work by combining hydrogen and oxygen. Because "free hydrogen" does not exist in nature, hydrogen must be separated from the substance to which it has bonded. This process requires energy (Ministry).

- There are eco-friendly (green) ways to isolate hydrogen and unfriendly (black) ways. Unless we focus on the green approaches, the environmental costs of producing hydrogen for fuel cells will be unacceptably high (Rifkin).

- The energy required to isolate hydrogen is "prohibitively expensive" and the much dreamed of "hydrogen economy" creates more problems than it solves (Anthrop).

- High gasoline prices have sparked interest in gasoline/electric hybrid cars such as Toyota's Prius. Though hybrids may not be the technology that ultimately replaces the gasoline engine, hybrids are selling "briskly" today (Mackinnon and Scott).

- Because of the energy needed to isolate hydrogen, the technical problems of storing hydrogen once it is isolated, and the cost of hydrogen to the consumer, hydrogen

>   fuel-cell technology should not replace
>   hybrid technology (Romm).

I tried to group some of these topics into categories that would have a logical order. The first thing that I wanted to communicate was the growing awareness that our dependence on petroleum is an increasing problem, both because of the dwindling reserves of the world's oil and because of the greenhouse emissions that result from burning oil.

Next, I thought I should explain what technologies are being developed to replace the gasoline engine: chiefly hybrids and fuel cells.

I also wanted to explain the problems people find with each of these technologies. Because the emphasis of my paper is on hydrogen fuel cells, this is the technology that should receive most of my attention. Still, because hybrid cars are gaining in popularity, I thought I should also devote some attention to them--both to their potential and to their limitations.

Finally, I intended to present the serious doubts people have about hydrogen as the fuel of the future. With all the optimism, there are still reasons to be cautious.

I returned to my thesis, converting it to two sentences to make it less awkward and adding a phrase or two:

>   Many see hybrids, which use gasoline, as merely
>   transitional vehicles. In the future, they
>   believe, fuel-cell vehicles powered by hydrogen, a
>   clean-burning and abundant energy source, will
>   become the norm for roadway and highway trans-
>   portation.

Based on her thesis, Hunte developed an outline for a 13-paragraph paper, including introduction and conclusion:

>   A. Set a context. Introduce the problem of
>   global warming.
>   B. Review the history of alternatives to
>   gasoline-powered internal combustion
>   engines, including compressed natural gas,
>   hybrids, and flexible-fuel hybrids.
>   C. Present hydrogen as an alternative fuel,
>   including its history. Explain how a
>   hydrogen fuel cell works.

D. Explain the problems that limit widespread
   use of hydrogen fuel at present. Provide
   examples of current (limited) use.

E. Report on U.S. government backing for
   hydrogen fuel-cell technology.

F. Conclude

Write the Topic Sentences

This is an optional step, but writing draft versions of topic sentences will get you started on each main idea of your synthesis and will help give you the sense of direction you need to proceed. Here are Hunte's draft topic sentences for sections based on the thesis and organizational plan she developed. Note that when read in sequence following the thesis, these sentences give an idea of the logical progression of the essay as a whole.

- In recent years, the major automakers have
  been exploring alternatives to the gasoline-powered internal combustion engine.
- Over the years, many alternative fuel
  technologies have been proposed, but all
  have shown limited practicality or appeal.
- The most popular alternative energy vehicle in this country is the hybrid, which
  combines an electric motor with a standard
  gasoline engine.

ORGANIZE A SYNTHESIS BY IDEA, *NOT* BY SOURCE

A synthesis is a blending of sources organized by *ideas*. The following rough sketches suggest how to organize and how *not* to organize a synthesis. The sketches assume you have read seven sources on a topic, sources A–G.

INCORRECT: *AVOID* ORGANIZING BY SOURCE + SUMMARY

The following is *not* a synthesis because it does not blend sources. Each source stands alone as an independent summary. No dialogue among sources is possible:

Thesis

Summary of source A in support of the thesis.

Summary of source B in support of the thesis.

Summary of source C in support of the thesis.

Etc.

Conclusion

- Hybrids may not be a long-term solution.
- A variation on the standard hybrid is the plug-in, flexible-fuel tank hybrid.
- There are two advantages that make hydrogen stand out from other alternative energy sources.
- The fuel cell was first proposed by a British physicist.
- At present, widespread use of hydrogen technology is not practical.
- Some major automakers recognize the inevitable end of the petroleum era. They have committed themselves to developing and producing fuel-cell vehicles.
- The federal government is supporting the new technology.
- Successful development of hydrogen fuel-cell vehicles faces significant roadblocks.
- There is also the problem of hydrogen leakage from large numbers of fuel-cell vehicles.
- Hydrogen fuel cells use platinum, which is a precious and expensive metal in limited supply.
- Taking these concerns into account, many experts believe that evolving technology will eventually solve the major problems and obstacles.

CORRECT: *DO* ORGANIZE BY IDEA

The following *is* a synthesis because the writer blends and creates a dialogue among sources in support of an idea. Each organizing idea, which can be a paragraph or group of related paragraphs, in turn supports the thesis:

Thesis

First idea: Refer to and discuss *parts* of sources (perhaps A, C, F) in support of the thesis.

Second idea: Refer to and discuss *parts* of sources (perhaps B, D) in support of the thesis.

Third idea: Refer to and discuss *parts* of sources (perhaps A, E, G) in support of the thesis.

Etc.

Conclusion

Write Your Synthesis

Here is the first draft of Hunte's explanatory synthesis. Thesis and topic sentences are highlighted. Modern Language Association (MLA) documentation style, summarized on pages 848–849, is used throughout.

Written as margin notes on the first draft, we have included comments and suggestions for revision from Hunte's instructor.

Discussion and Suggestions for Revision

In the following section, the notes in the margins summarize the key points and suggestions for revision made during the student's conference with her instructor. (For purposes of demonstration, these comments are likely to be more comprehensive than the selective comments provided by most instructors.)

Title and Paragraph 1

Your title could be more interesting and imaginative. The first paragraph gets off on the wrong foot because it provides a misleading impression of what the synthesis is going to be about. A reader might reasonably conclude from this paragraph that the paper was going to deal with global warming, rather than with alternative energy vehicles, and particularly with the hydrogen fuel-cell car. By the end of the first paragraph you do get to a thesis that more accurately reflects the actual subject of the paper, but this thesis seems awkwardly tacked on to the end of a paragraph about something else.

Suggestions for Revision

Make the title more interesting. Rewrite the first paragraph so that it provides a clear indication of the subject of the synthesis as a whole. You could begin with an anecdote that illustrates the subject, a provocative quotation, a set of questions, or a historical review of attempts to develop alternatives to the internal combustion engine.

Hunte 1

Janice Hunte
Professor Case
English 101
22 January 2007

The Hydrogen Fuel-Cell Car

1   One of the most serious problems facing the world today is global warming. According to Michael D. Mastrandrea and Stephen H. Schneider, in their article "Global Warming," "Global warming is an increase in the average temperature of the Earth's surface. Since the Industrial Revolution, that temperature has gone up by 0.7 to 1.4 °F." The authors point out that Americans are responsible for almost 25% of the greenhouse gas pollution that causes global warming, even though they make up only 5% of the world's population. The authors also note that global warming is caused primarily by the burning of fossil fuels, such as coal, natural gas, and oil, and that much of this burning occurs in the gasoline engines that power automobiles, as well as "in factories, and in electric power plants that provide energy for houses and office buildings" (47). It is clear, then, that gasoline-powered cars are a major cause of the greenhouse gas pollution that is responsible for global warming. In the

Hunte 2

future, some believe, this problem may be solved by vehicles powered by hydrogen, a clean-burning and abundant energy source, which will become the norm for roadway and highway transportation.

2   In recent years, the major automakers have been exploring alternatives to the gasoline-powered internal combustion engine. A few years ago, the electric car was widely seen as one viable alternative. Between 1996 and 2003, the Big Three U.S. automakers produced prototype electric vehicles, among them G.M.'s EVI, that were leased to a limited number of consumers. But these battery-powered, zero-emission cars proved problematic. Most had to be recharged every 100 miles or so, considerably limiting their range; and drivers found relatively few recharging stations. Manufacturers could never figure out how to reduce the batteries to manageable size or how to produce them at reasonable cost. In the end, the automakers reclaimed all but a few of the leased electric vehicles and destroyed them (Ortiz D1).

3   Over the years, many alternative fuel technologies have been proposed, but all have shown limited practicality or appeal. Compressed natural gas (CNG), which powers the Honda Civic GX, is a reliable, clean-burning, renewable (though fossil) fuel, in plentiful supply. But because of their limited range (about 200 miles) and the absence of a significant CNG infrastructure, natural gas vehicles are employed primarily in fleets that have relatively short routes and access to their own filling stations (Neil). A third alternative fuel vehicle, powered by compressed air, is being developed by a French company, Moteur Developpement International. A prototype car can

Paragraph 2

This paragraph does make the transition to the true subject of the synthesis: alternative energy vehicles, particularly the hydrogen fuel-cell car. But it could be more fully developed: consider discussing other reasons (besides the need to reduce greenhouse gas pollution) for the inevitable end of the internal combustion engine era. For example, we are rapidly exhausting our supplies of petroleum, a fact that may be more significant to automobile manufacturers—as well as to consumers—than the dangers of global warming.

Suggestions for Revision

Devise a clearer thesis and place it at the end of the first or second paragraph (depending upon how you introduce the synthesis). Expand your discussion of why gasoline will soon become impractical as the primary means of powering automobiles.

Paragraph 3

Since this paper is largely about the hydrogen fuel-cell car, you devote too much space to discussing vehicles powered by other energy sources. While you could mention natural gas, compressed air, and biodiesel vehicles in passing, your extensive discussion of them here tends to blur what should be a sharp focus on hydrogen fuel-cell vehicles.

Suggestions for Revision

Reduce the information in this paragraph to just two or three sentences. Consider appending these sentences to the paragraph discussing electric cars. This paragraph, then, would concern the least practical, appealing, or marketable alternative fuel technologies.

Paragraphs 4, 5, and 6

These paragraphs cover the subject of hybrids well, but this section is still too long, given that the real subject of the paper is the hydrogen fuel-cell car.

Suggestions for Revision

Consider combining these three paragraphs into one shorter paragraph, cutting the discussion by at least one-third. Perhaps reduce the block quotation from *Consumer Reports* to a summary sentence.

achieve a speed of 70 miles an hour and has a range of 120 miles. It takes about four hours to recharge the onboard air tanks, using a compressor that can be plugged into a wall outlet. So far, the company's U.S. representative has not sold any manufacturing franchises in this country and has had trouble attracting investment capital (Weikel B2). Another alternative energy source, biodiesel fuel, was promoted in mid-2005 by President Bush. Biodiesel fuel can be made from soybeans (which can be produced domestically). "Biodiesel burns more completely and produces less air pollution than gasoline or regular diesel," declared the president. "And every time we use homegrown diesel, we support American farmers, not foreign oil producers." Critics point out, however, that biodiesel fuel can be as much as 20 cents a gallon more expensive than gasoline (Chen 15). And diesel-powered cars have never caught on in the United States, as they have in Europe.

4   The most popular alternative energy vehicle in this country is the hybrid, which combines an electric motor with a standard gasoline engine. The battery is used to accelerate the car from a standing position to 30 to 35 miles an hour; then the gasoline engine takes over. Unlike all-electric vehicles, hybrid cars are self-charging; they don't need to be regularly plugged in (Mackinnon and Scott D1). Priuses have been so much in demand that there is an average waiting period of 6 months for new purchasers (McDonald 1). In 2004 Toyota announced that it would step up production of the vehicles and double the number for sale in the U.S. (Ohnsman E3). In 2006 the automaker

plans to introduce a hybrid version of its popular Camry. Other automakers have also been getting into the act: Honda is currently producing Civic, Insight, and Accord hybrids; Ford has introduced the hybrid Mercury Mariner and the Ford Escape (Mackinnon and Scott D1). Hybrids win praise from both consumers and critics. One satisfied customer, Wendy Brown of Akron, Ohio, said that she went "from Akron to Virginia Beach on one tank of gas. It was awesome" (qtd. in Mackinnon and Scott D1). In its April 2005 Auto Issue, Consumer Reports had this to say about the Prius:

> Toyota's second-generation Prius is unbeatable for its economy, acceleration and interior room. It couples a 1.5 liter gasoline engine with an electric motor, and it automatically switches between them or runs on both as needed. The car shuts the engine off at idle. We got an excellent 44 mpg overall in our tests. . . . Reliability has been outstanding. (77)

5   But hybrids may not be a long-term solution. Most Americans remain wary of the new technology, perhaps some thinking that with their gasoline engines, they may remain transitional vehicles. From 1999 to mid-2005, 340,000 hybrids have been sold worldwide. But in 2004 alone, Americans bought 900,000 gas-hungry SUVs (McDonald 1). Hybrids may use less gasoline than standard cars, but they still use gasoline, and therefore rely on a rapidly depleting resource. And hybrids aren't cheap: consumers pay a premium of about $3,000 over similarly sized cars: "The higher

initial purchase price, coupled with higher insurance premiums and related expenses, offset the gasoline savings, the recent Edmunds study concluded. Edmunds said a typical hybrid might actually cost its owner $5,283 more over five years than its nonhybrid counterpart" (qtd. in Mackinnon and Scott D1).

6   A variation of the standard hybrid is the plug-in, flexible-fuel tank hybrid. According to Newsweek columnist Fareed Zakaria, a standard hybrid that gets 50 miles to the gallon could get 75 if the electric motor could be recharged by plugging it into a 120-volt outlet. And "[r]eplace the conventional fuel tank with a flexible-fuel tank that can run on a combination of 15 percent petroleum and 85 percent ethanol or methanol, and you get between 400 and 500 miles per gallon of gasoline" (Zakaria 27). According to Max Boot, "[t]hat's not science fiction; that's achievable right now." Other advantages of plug-in, flexible-fuel hybrids: such technology would reduce U.S. dependence on foreign (i.e., Middle East) oil, reduce toxic emissions, and give a boost to U.S. carmakers, who could manufacture such vehicles, and sell them not only domestically, but also in Europe and Asia (Boot B5).

7   There are two advantages that make hydrogen stand out from other alternative energy sources. First, it is clean burning (the only by-products from the combining of hydrogen and oxygen are water and electricity), and secondly, it is an inexhaustible and widely available element. The principle behind the fuel-cell vehicle is simple. Essentially, an electric current is used to separate hydrogen from other elements with which it is bonded, such

Hunte 6

as oxygen. When the hydrogen is recombined with oxygen in a fuel cell, the
reverse process occurs and electricity
is generated. As reporter Elizabeth
Kolbert notes, "[t]he elegance of
hydrogen technology is hard to
resist"(40). She describes a visit to
the office of Bragi Aronson. Aronson is
a chemistry professor whose office is
in Reykjavik, Iceland, a country that
relies heavily on clean energy sources:

> On the counter was a device with a
> photovoltaic cell on one end and a
> little fan on the other. In between
> was a cylinder of water, some clear
> plastic tubes, and a fuel cell,
> which looked like two sheets of cel-
> lophane stretched over some wire
> mesh. When Aronson turned on a desk
> lamp, the photovoltaic cell began to
> produce electricity, which elec-
> trolyzed the water. Hydrogen and
> oxygen ran through the tubes to the
> fuel cell, where they recombined to
> produce more water, in the process
> turning the fan. It was an impres-
> sive display. (Kolbert 40)

The fuel cell was first proposed in
1839 by a British physicist (and justice of the high court), William Grove.
Jules Verne wrote about hydrogen fuel
cells in his 1875 novel The Mysterious
Island. And fuel cells have been used
by American astronauts since the 1960s
(Bayon 117). It is only in recent years
that hydrogen fuel-cells have been proposed and tested for use in automobiles
and other vehicles. The fuel-cell vehicle operates on the same principle as
the fan in Aronson's office. Pressurized or supercooled liquid hydrogen
from a storage cannister in the vehicle
flows into a stack of fuel cells, where
it is combined with oxygen. This chemical process generates electricity (and
water), which impels the electric

Paragraph 7

This paragraph provides a clear description of hydrogen fuel-cell technology, with good use of block quotation. (Providing a diagram of a fuel cell would enhance clarity, however.) But the transition from other alternative energy vehicles to hydrogen fuel-cell cars, by means of the topic (first) sentence, is overly abrupt. The writing is occasionally wordy and overly passive.

Suggestions for Revision

Develop an introductory sentence that more smoothly and effectively makes the transition between what has come before (a discussion of various alternative energy source vehicles) to what is to follow (a discussion of hydrogen fuel-cell vehicles). For emphasis, consider making this paragraph a short one and leaving the discussion of the mechanics of the fuel cell to the next paragraph. Rewrite the weak "There are" sentence opening ("There are two advantages . . ."), making the sentence more *active* ("Two advantages combine . . ."). Fix surface problems, like the inconsistency of "First" followed by "secondly." Toward the end of the paragraph, the repetition of "Aronson" is awkward. Rewrite, perhaps converting the sentence beginning "Aronson is a chemistry professor" into an appositive phrase ("a chemistry professor") and combining this phrase with the previous sentence. You could also create a stronger transition, after the block quotation, to the historical development of the hydrogen fuel cell. Finally, try to find a diagram of a fuel cell to help readers understand the process.

motor, which turns the vehicle's wheels (Kolbert 38; Motavalli 12.1). The process is clean, cool, and virtually silent (Kolbert 39—40).

8   At present, widespread use of hydrogen technology (corresponding to widespread use of hybrid cars) is not practical. For one thing, fuel cells are expensive. It costs more to generate a kilowatt of electricity from a fuel cell than it does to generate a corresponding quantity of power from an internal combustion engine. Second, the nation has no hydrogen infrastructure through which hydrogen can be extracted from water or natural gas and then delivered to customers through a network of hydrogen stations (Bayon 118). But this situation is likely to change, if not over the next few years, then over the next few decades. Hydrogen fuel cells are more promising than that of other alternative fuel technologies, such as electric cars or natural gas or compressed air vehicles. This is because some of the major automakers recognize the inevitable end of the petroleum era. Accordingly, they have to a significant degree committed themselves to developing and producing fuel-cell vehicles. In 2003 General Motors developed an early fuel-cell prototype vehicle, the Hy-Wire, which it proudly showed off to reporters and National Highway Traffic Safety Administration officials (Kolbert 38). GM's vice president for research and planning, Lawrence D. Burns, says that the company "aims to have a production-ready fuel-cell vehicle . . . by 2010" (Motavalli 12.1). In January 2005, GM introduced its hydrogen fuel-cell prototype, the Sequel. This is the first hydrogen fuel-cell vehicle with a range of 300 miles, the minimum necessary to render it marketable. The Ford Motor

Paragraph 8

This paragraph does a nice job of presenting some of the advantages of hydrogen fuel-cell vehicles, but it gets off on the wrong foot by focusing initially on the problems with the technology. Since you deal at some length with these problems later in the synthesis, it would be better to move the opening sentences of the paragraph to a later point. And while the examples of hydrogen prototype vehicles are fine, they may be more than you need to establish the fact that auto manufacturers are interested in developing the new technology.

Suggestions for Revision

Move the first few sentences of this paragraph to a later paragraph where you begin focusing on the problems with and drawbacks of hydrogen fuel technology. Cut some of the repetitive examples of prototype hydrogen fuel-cell vehicles in operation around the world. Fix occasionally awkward phrases ("are more promising than that of other alternative fuel technologies"), choppy sentence structure ("This is because . . ."), and illogical series.

Hunte 8

Company will provide hydrogen-powered buses for passengers at Dallas-Fort Worth International Airport (Schneider A.01). BMW, Honda, Toyota, and DaimlerChrysler are all developing vehicles using the new technology. As Bayon reports, "[f]uel cell-powered buses are running in Vancouver, Chicago, London, and parts of Germany" (117). Hydrogen fuel-cell buses are also undergoing trials in other cities, including Perth, Stockholm, Barcelona, Amsterdam, and Madrid ("Buses" 12). Nissan plans to lease fuel-cell SUVs to selected American businesses in 2007 (Motavalli 12.1). And in November 2004, "a Shell station in Washington, D.C. became the first in the nation to provide a hydrogen-fuel dispenser alongside its gasoline pumps" to service the six HydroGen3 minivans that GM uses to demonstrate hydrogen technology to members of Congress (Solheim).

9   The federal government is also supporting the new technology. In 2003 President Bush, who has long been identified with the oil industry, proposed, in his State of the Union address, a $1.2 billion research program for the development of hydrogen cars (Kolbert 36). The following year he recommended spending $227 million for fuel-cell research and development in 2005. The ultimate goal is to make hydrogen fuel-cell vehicles "road ready by 2020" (Durbin).

10   In spite of these promising steps, successful development of hydrogen fuel-cell vehicles faces significant roadblocks. As indicated above, hydrogen fuel cells are expensive to produce and the nation has no hydrogen infrastructure. But there may be more fundamental problems. According to Peter Eisenberger, chairman of the American Physical Society, "major scientific

Paragraph 9
This paragraph is fine as a means of illustrating federal government support of hydrogen fuel-cell technology.

Suggestions for Revision
Only minor tinkering needed here: perhaps combine the first two and the last two sentences.

Paragraph 10
Since, in this generally well-developed paragraph, you begin discussing the drawbacks of hydrogen fuel-cell technology, you can move some of the material in the opening sentences of paragraph 8 here (as discussed in the comments above) and combine them with the opening sentences of the present paragraph. Otherwise, fix wordy sentences and awkward constructions.

Suggestions for Revision
Combine opening sentences of paragraph 8 and paragraph 10 here. Fix wordiness later in the paragraph by replacing "who is" constructions with appositive phrases. Make "a proven vehicle technology" into another appositive.

Paragraph 11
This paragraph works well to establish the potential environmental drawbacks of hydrogen fuel-cell technology. It begins awkwardly, however, with a "There is" topic sentence.

Suggestions for Revision
Make the first sentence more active and perhaps combine it with the second sentence. Eliminate the "who is" construction after "Jeremy Rifkin"; create an appositive phrase here.

breakthroughs are needed for the hydrogen economy to succeed" (qtd. in Durbin). Though hydrogen is the most abundant element in the universe (Motavalli 12.1), it rarely occurs in free form in nature: it is typically bound up with other elements, such as oxygen or carbon. Significant quantities of energy must be employed to unbind it. Donald F. Anthrop, who is a professor of environmental science at San Jose State University, points out that the energy required to operate fuel cells will exceed the energy that they produce. He further argues that "[t]he cost of this energy will be prohibitively expensive" (Anthrop 10). Joseph Romm, who is a former acting assistant secretary of energy, believes that hybrids are a proven vehicle technology, and that they are preferable to hydrogen fuel-cell vehicles. He argues that fossil fuels such as coal and natural gas are likely to be our major sources of hydrogen, and that the process of extracting hydrogen from these sources and then compressing the gas for storage in tanks will not only consume large quantities of energy, it will also generate significant quantities of carbon dioxide. Thus, "[m]aking hydrogen . . . won't solve our major environmental problems" (Romm M3).

11   There is also the problem of hydrogen leakage from large numbers of fuel-cell vehicles. Over time this process could increase the level of greenhouse gases and affect the world's climate. "Hydrogen is not necessarily more benign," maintains Werner Zittel, a German energy consultant. "It depends on how you produce it" (qtd. in Ananthaswamy 6). Jeremy Rifkin, who is a supporter of hydrogen fuel-cell development, cautions that we should

Hunte 11

focus on the development of "green hydrogen," rather than "black hydrogen." The latter, extracted from such fossil fuels as oil, coal, and natural gas, or derived from nuclear power, generates large quantities of carbon dioxide and other toxic emissions. "Green hydrogen," on the other hand, derives from renewable energy sources such as wind, water, geothermal power, energy crops, and agricultural waste (Rifkin M5).

12   Plus, hydrogen fuel cells use platinum, which is a precious and expensive metal in limited supply. There is not enough platinum in the world to replace all the existing internal combustion engines with fuel cells--at least not with fuel cells built on existing technology (Mackintosh and Morrison 22). Some people are concerned about the safety of hydrogen. These people remember the Hindenburg disaster in 1937 in which the hydrogen-filled transatlantic German airship burst into flames shortly before landing in Lakehurst, New Jersey, killing 36 persons (Motavalli 12.1). But others downplay both concerns. Alternatives to platinum may be found and future hydrogen fuel cells will use considerably less of the metal (Mackintosh and Morrison 22). Safety measures can prevent another Hindenburg-type disaster (Motavalli 12.1).

13   Taking these concerns into account, many experts believe that evolving technology will eventually solve the major problems and obstacles. But whether the car of the future is powered by hydrogen fuel cells or by some other form of energy, it is clear that gasoline-powered cars are going the way of the dinosaurs. We must take steps, as soon as possible, to reduce our

Paragraph 12
This paragraph needs a better topic sentence to introduce a paragraph that deals both with shortage and safety issues.

Suggestions for Revision
Write a topic sentence that covers both the platinum supply and safety concerns. Eliminate the awkward repetition of "people" ("Some people . . . These people") later in the paragraph. Provide a transitional word or term before the final sentence of the paragraph.

Paragraph 13
The conclusion is overgeneralized. While the first sentence provides the beginning of an effective transition to the closing, what follows merely summarizes what has come before ("We must take steps . . . to reduce our dependence upon the internal combustion engine"). The final sentence is vague and anticlimactic.

Suggestions for Revision
Develop a conclusion more rooted in specific facts and quotations by those who believe the problems described in the preceding paragraphs will be overcome. Appeal to reader interest in the subject as a way of closing strongly.

> dependence upon the internal combustion engine. Hopefully, human ingenuity will prevail in solving this critical problem.

Revise Your Synthesis: Global, Local, and Surface Revisions

Many writers find it helpful to plan for three types of revision: global, local, and surface. *Global revisions* affect the entire paper: the thesis, the type and pattern of evidence employed, the overall organization, the tone. A global revision may also emerge from a change in purpose. For example, the writer of this paper might decide to rewrite, focusing not on a broad introduction to and explanation of fuel-cell technology but on plans to create a national hydrogen infrastructure, similar to the existing network of gas stations, that would enable drivers to refuel their hydrogen-powered vehicles at their convenience.

Local revisions affect paragraphs: topic and transitional sentences; the type of evidence presented within a paragraph; evidence added, modified, or dropped within a paragraph; logical connections from one sentence or set of sentences within a paragraph to another.

Surface revisions deal with sentence style and construction, word choice, and errors of grammar, mechanics, spelling, and citation form.

Revising the First Draft: Highlights

Global

- Refocus the paper so that it emphasizes hydrogen fuel-cell vehicles and de-emphasizes (while still briefly covering) such other alternative energy vehicles as hybrids and electrics.
- Sharpen the *thesis* so that it focuses on hydrogen fuel-cell vehicles.
- In the body of the paper (e.g., paragraphs 3–6), cut back on references to alternative energy vehicles other than hydrogen fuel-cell cars.

Local

- More fully develop paragraph 2, providing additional reasons for the inevitable end of the internal combustion engine era.
- Combine information in paragraphs 4, 5, and 6 into one shorter paragraph, cutting the discussion by at least one-third.
- Improve topic and transitional sentences in paragraphs 7, 8, and 12.

- Move the opening sentences of paragraph 8 to a corresponding position in paragraph 10 to improve coherence and logic.

- In paragraph 8, cut some of the repetitive examples of prototype hydrogen fuel-cell vehicles around the world.

- Improve the conclusion, making it more specific and appealing more strongly to reader interest.

Surface

- Avoid passive phrases, such as "is used."

- Avoid phrases such as "there is" and "there are."

- Fix mechanics errors, such as placing titles of articles within quotation marks, rather than italicizing or underlining them.

- Follow the principle of parallelism for items in series: "First" should be followed by "Second," not "Secondly."

- Reduce wordiness throughout.

- Fix awkward phrases (e.g., "are more promising than that of other alternative fuel technologies").

EXERCISE 4.3

Revising the Sample Synthesis

Try your hand at creating a final draft of the paper on pages 124–134 by following the revision suggestions above, together with using your own best judgment about how to improve the first draft. Make global, local, and surface changes. After trying to create your own version of the paper, compare it to the revised version of our student-produced paper below.

REVISED MODEL SYNTHESIS

(Thesis and topic sentences are highlighted.)

Hunte 1

Janice Hunte
Professor Case
English 101
31 January 2007

The Car of the Future?

1   In July 2005 a California family, the Spallinos, took proud possession of a new silver and blue Honda FCX. Never heard of the FCX? That's because this particular model is not a part of Honda's standard product

line. It's a prototype powered by hydrogen fuel cells. Although companies like Honda, Toyota, GM, and DaimlerChrysler have been experimenting with hydrogen-powered vehicles for some years, the Spallinos' car is the first to be placed in private hands for road testing. The family was selected by Honda because they already own a Civic powered by natural gas and so are used to the inconveniences of driving a vehicle that needs the kind of fuel available only in a limited number of commercial outlets. Mr. Spallino is excited at the prospect of test driving the FCX: "Maybe this is the technology of the future. Maybe it isn't," says Spallino, who commutes 77 miles a day. "But if I can be part of the evolution of this technology, that would be a lot of fun" (Molloy 18).

2   Are hydrogen fuel-cell cars the wave of the future? In recent years, the major automakers, with some financial incentives from the federal government, have been exploring alternatives to the gasoline-powered internal combustion engine. We've seen vehicles powered by electricity, natural gas, even compressed air. Diesel engines have been popular in Europe for decades, though they have a much smaller customer base in the United States. Currently, the most popular alternative energy vehicles are the hybrids, such as the Toyota Prius, vehicles that run on both gasoline engines and electric motors. But many see hybrids, which use gasoline, as merely transitional vehicles. In the future, they believe, fuel-cell vehicles powered by hydrogen, a clean-burning and abundant energy source, will become the norm for roadway and highway transportation.

3   But why not continue to rely indefinitely on gasoline? The answer is that the days of the gasoline-powered internal combustion engine are numbered. First, gasoline is an environmentally dirty fuel that, when burned, creates the toxic greenhouse gas pollution that contributes to global warming. Second, oil is a rapidly depleting resource. As energy expert Paul Roberts points out, "the more you produce, the less remains in the ground, and the harder it is to bring up that remainder"(M1). Today, we import most of our oil from Saudi Arabia, a country previously thought to have virtually inexhaustible supplies of

oil. But many experts believe that the Saudi fields are in decline, or have at least "matured," with most of their easily extractable petroleum already gone. In the near future, the Saudis may no longer be able to meet world demand (Klare B9). Roberts notes that the demand for oil today stands at 29 billion barrels of oil a year. Currently, the supply matches the demand; but by 2020, with increasing demands for oil by emerging industrial countries like India and China, the demand will far outstrip the supply, and prices, currently around $60 a barrel, may soar to $100. If the U.S. does not reduce its demand for oil, a future shortage could mean that "the global economy is likely to slip into a recession so severe that the Great Depression will look like a dress rehearsal" (Roberts M1).

4   Over the years, many alternative fuel technologies have been proposed, but all have shown limited practicality or appeal. Fifteen to twenty years ago, electric cars looked attractive. But these battery-powered, zero-emission cars proved problematic: most had to be recharged every 100 miles or so, considerably limiting their range. Manufacturers could never figure out how to reduce the batteries to manageable size or how to produce them at reasonable cost. Other alternative fuel sources include compressed natural gas (CNG), compressed air, and biodiesel fuel. While prototype vehicles using these various technologies have been built, none appears likely to succeed in the American mass market.

5   Currently, the most popular alternative energy vehicle in this country is the hybrid, which combines an electric motor with a standard gasoline engine. The battery is used to accelerate the car from a standing position to 30 to 35 miles an hour; then the gasoline engine takes over. Unlike all-electric vehicles, hybrid cars are self-charging; they don't need to be regularly plugged in (Mackinnon and Scott D1). The most popular hybrid, the Toyota Prius, is in so much demand that new purchasers must typically wait six months to get one. Other manufacturers, including Honda, Ford, and General Motors, also sell or soon plan to offer hybrid vehicles. Consumer Reports called the Prius "unbeatable for its economy, accel-

eration and interior room" and in 2005 declared the Honda Accord hybrid its highest scoring family sedan ("Best" 76–77). Despite their advantages, however, hybrids may still be transitional vehicles. They may use less gasoline than standard cars, but they still use gasoline and therefore rely on a rapidly depleting resource. And hybrids aren't cheap: consumers pay a premium of about $3,000 over similarly sized cars, an amount that could easily offset for years any savings in gasoline expenses. A variation of the standard hybrid, the plug-in, flexible-fuel tank hybrid, offers greatly improved fuel economy. In these vehicles, gasoline could be mixed with cheaper fuels like ethanol or methanol. Of course, consumers may find plugging in their cars inconvenient or (if they are on the road) impractical; and flexible-fuel hybrids would be reliant on a national ethanol/methanol infrastructure, which doesn't yet exist.

6   With these alternatives to the standard gasoline-powered internal combustion engine, what is the special appeal of the hydrogen fuel-cell vehicle? Two advantages combine to make hydrogen stand out from the rest: it is clean burning (the only by-products from the combining of hydrogen and oxygen are water and electricity), and it is an inexhaustible and widely available element.

7   The principle behind the fuel-cell vehicle is simplicity itself. Essentially, an electric current is used to separate hydrogen from other elements with which it is bonded, such as oxygen. When the hydrogen is recombined with oxygen in a fuel cell, the reverse process occurs and electricity is generated. As reporter Elizabeth Kolbert notes, "[t]he elegance of hydrogen technology is hard to resist"(40). She describes a visit to the office of Bragi Aronson, a chemistry professor, in his office in Reykjavik, Iceland, a country that relies heavily on clean energy sources:

> On the counter was a device with a photovoltaic cell on one end and a little fan on the other. In between was a cylinder of water, some clear plastic tubes, and a fuel cell, which looked like two sheets of cellophane stretched over some wire mesh. When Aronson turned on a desk lamp, the photovoltaic cell began to

Hunte 5

produce electricity, which electrolyzed the water.
Hydrogen and oxygen ran through the tubes to the fuel
cell, where they recombined to produce more water, in
the process turning the fan. It was an impressive
display. (40)

8   The fuel cell is not exactly cutting-edge technology: the concept itself was first proposed in 1839
by British physicist (and justice of the high court)
William Grove. Jules Verne wrote about hydrogen fuel
cells in his 1875 novel The Mysterious Island. And
fuel cells have been used by American astronauts
since the 1960s (Bayon 117). It is only in recent
years, however, that hydrogen fuel cells have been
proposed and tested for use in automobiles and other
vehicles. The fuel-cell vehicle operates on the same
principle as the fan in Aronson's office. Pressurized
or supercooled liquid hydrogen from a storage cannister in the vehicle flows into a stack of fuel cells,
where it is combined with oxygen. This chemical
process generates electricity (and water), which
impels the electric motor, which turns the vehicle's
wheels (Kolbert 38; Motavalli 12.1). (See Figure 1.)
The process is clean, cool, and virtually silent
(Kolbert 39—40).

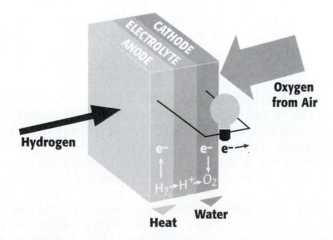

FIGURE 1   How a hydrogen fuel cell works*
*Source: The World Fuel Cell Council e.V.

9   What makes the successful development of hydrogen fuel cells more promising than that of other alternative fuel technologies, such as electric cars or natural gas or compressed air vehicles, is that a number of major automakers, recognizing the inevitable end of the petroleum era, have to a significant degree committed themselves to developing and producing fuel-cell vehicles. In 2003 General Motors developed an early fuel-cell prototype vehicle, the Hy-Wire (Kolbert 38). In January 2005, GM introduced the Sequel, a hydrogen vehicle with a range of 300 miles --the minimum necessary to render it marketable. The company "aims to have a production-ready fuel-cell vehicle . . . by 2010" (Motavalli 12.1). The Ford Motor Company plans to provide hydrogen-powered buses for passengers at Dallas-Fort Worth International Airport (Schneider). BMW, Honda, Toyota, and DaimlerChrysler are all developing vehicles using the new technology. As Bayon reports, "[f]uel cell-powered buses are running in Vancouver, Chicago, London, and parts of Germany" (118), and they are undergoing trials elsewhere. Nissan plans to lease fuel-cell SUVs to selected American businesses in 2007 (Motavalli 12.1).

10   The federal government is also supporting the new technology: in 2003 President Bush, long identified with the oil industry, proposed in his State of the Union address a $1.2 billion research program for the development of hydrogen cars (Kolbert 36). The following year he recommended spending $227 million for fuel-cell research and development in 2005, with the ultimate goal of making hydrogen fuel-cell vehicles "road ready by 2020" (Durbin).

11   At present, widespread use of hydrogen technology (corresponding to widespread use of hybrid cars) is not practical (Committee 116—17). For one thing, fuel cells are expensive. It costs more to generate a kilowatt of electricity from a fuel cell than it does to generate a corresponding quantity of power from an internal combustion engine. For another, the nation has no hydrogen infrastructure through which hydrogen can be extracted from water or natural gas and then delivered to customers through a network of hydrogen stations (Bayon 118). This situation is likely to change, however, if not over the next few years, then over the next few decades. But there may be more fundamental problems

with hydrogen fuel-cell technology. According to Peter Eisenberger, chairman of the American Physical Society, "major scientific breakthroughs are needed for the hydrogen economy to succeed" (qtd. in Durbin). Though hydrogen is the most abundant element in the universe (Motavalli 12.1), it rarely occurs in free form in nature: it is typically bound up with other elements, such as oxygen or carbon. Significant quantities of energy must be employed to unbind it. Donald F. Anthrop, a professor of environmental science at San Jose State University, points out that the energy required to operate fuel cells will exceed the energy that they produce. He further argues that "[t]he cost of this energy will be prohibitively expensive" (10). Joseph Romm, a former acting assistant secretary of energy, believes that hybrids, a proven vehicle tech-nology, are preferable to hydrogen fuel-cell vehicles. He argues fossil fuels such as coal and natural gas are likely to be our major sources of hydrogen and that the process of extracting hydrogen from these sources and then compressing the gas for storage in tanks will not only consume large quantities of energy but will also generate significant quantities of carbon dioxide. Thus, "[m]aking hydrogen . . . won't solve our major environmental problems" (Romm M3).

12   Others worry about hydrogen leakage from large numbers of fuel-cell vehicles, which could, over time, increase the level of greenhouse gases and affect the world's climate. "Hydrogen is not neces sarily more benign," maintains Werner Zittel, a German energy consultant. "[Its ecological impact] depends on how you produce it" (qtd. in Ananthaswamy 6). Jeremy Rifkin, a supporter of hydrogen fuel-cell development, cautions that we should focus on the development of "green hydrogen," rather than "black hydrogen." The latter, extracted from such fossil fuels as oil, coal, and natural gas, or derived from nuclear power, generates large quantities of carbon dioxide and other toxic emissions. "Green hydrogen," on the other hand, derives from renewable energy sources such as wind, water, geothermal power, energy crops, and agricultural waste (Rifkin M5).

13   Other problems confront hydrogen advocates. Hydrogen fuel cells use platinum, a precious and expensive metal in limited supply. There is not enough platinum in the world to replace all the

Hunte 8

existing internal combustion engines with fuel cells
--at least not with fuel cells built on existing technology (Mackintosh and Morrison 22). Some are concerned about the safety of hydrogen--mindful of the
Hindenburg disaster in 1937 in which the hydrogen-
filled transatlantic German airship burst into flames
shortly before landing in Lakehurst, New Jersey,
killing 36 persons (Motavalli 12.1). But others downplay both concerns: alternatives to platinum may be
found and future hydrogen fuel cells will use considerably less of the metal (Mackintosh and Morrison
22). And safety measures can prevent another
Hindenburg-type disaster (Motavalli 12.1).

14   Taking these concerns into account, many experts
believe that evolving technology will eventually solve
the major problems and obstacles. To critics like Max
Boot, widespread use of hydrogen fuel-cell cars is
"science fiction" (B5). But it's worth remembering
that in 1870 the telephone was science fiction, as was
the airplane in 1900, home television in 1920, the
desktop computer in 1970, and the World Wide Web in
1990. In none of those years was the know-how and
technology yet available for the corresponding scientific development. Such developments were made possi-
ble--and, in later years, both affordable and
indispensable to modern life--because of the commitment and hard work of one or more individuals. One
reader of Joseph Romm's article ("Lots of Hot Air
About Hydrogen") responded, "Had bureaucrats like
Romm discouraged James Watt in the eighteenth century
regarding the harnessing of steam energy, our economic engines would still be powered by horses" (Hoffman
B4). It may indeed turn out that the problems of
developing affordable and practical hydrogen vehicles
on a large scale prove insurmountable. But many
believe that the promise of hydrogen fuel cells as a
provider of clean and virtually inexhaustible energy
makes further research and development vital for the
transportation needs of the twenty-first century. As
for the internal combustion engine--according to
Geoffrey Ballard, founder of Ballard Power Systems,
it "will go the way of the horse. It will be a
curiosity to my grandchildren" (qtd. in Bayon 118).

[new page]

Works Cited

Ananthaswamy, Anil. "Reality Bites for the Dream of a Hydrogen Economy." New Scientist 15 Nov. 2003: 6+.

Anthrop, Donald F. Letter. "Renewable Energy and Fuel Cells." Oil and Gas Journal 10 Oct. 2004: 10.

Bayon, Ricardo. "The Fuel Subsidy We Need." Atlantic Monthly Jan.-Feb. 2003: 117-18.

"Best 2005 Cars." Consumer Reports Apr. 2005: 76 (Toyota Prius); 77 (Honda Accord).

Boot, Max. "The 500-Mile-Per-Gallon Solution." Los Angeles Times 24 Mar. 2005: B5.

Committee on Alternatives and Strategies for Future Hydrogen Production and Use, Board on Energy and Environmental Systems. The Hydrogen Economy: Opportunities, Costs, Barriers, and RD Needs. Washington: National Academies Press, 2004.

Durbin, Dee-Ann. "Official Defends Fuel Cell Study Funds." Associated Press 8 Mar. 2004.

Hoffman, Robert D. Letter. Los Angeles Times 3 Apr. 2004: B4.

"How a Hydrogen Fuel Cell Works." Creating a Sustainable Energy System for New Zealand. Ministry of Economic Development, New Zealand. Oct. 2004. 18 Jan. 2006 <http://www.med.govt.nz/templates/MultipageDocumentPage_10138.aspx>.

Klare, Michael T. "The Vanishing Mirage of Saudi Oil: Dwindling Reserves May End the Petroleum Age." Los Angeles Times 27 June 2005: B9.

Kolbert, Elizabeth. "The Car of Tomorrow." The New Yorker 11 Aug. 2003: 36-40.

Mackinnon, Jim, and Dave Scott. "Prices Fueling Hybrid Interest." Akron Beacon Journal 24 July 2005: D1+.

Mackintosh, James, and Kevin Morrison. "Car Makers Gear Up for the Next Shortage--Platinum." Financial Times [London] 6 July 2005: 22.

Molloy, Tim. "Tomorrow's Car: It's a Gas to Drive." The Courier Mail [Queensland, Australia] 2 July 2005: 18.

Motavalli, Jim. "Putting the Hindenburg to Rest." New York Times 5 June 2005: 12.1.

Rifkin, Jeremy. "Using Fossil Fuels in Energy Process Gets Us Nowhere." Los Angeles Times 9 Nov. 2003: M5.

Roberts, Paul. "Running Out of Oil--and Time." Los Angeles Times 7 Mar. 2004: M1.

Romm, Joseph J. "Lots of Hot Air About Hydrogen." Los Angeles Times 28 Mar. 2004: M3.

Schneider, Greg. "Automakers Put Hydrogen Power on the Fast Track." Washington Post 9 Jan. 2005: A.01.

CRITICAL READING FOR SYNTHESIS

- *Use the tips from Critical Reading for Summary on page 6.* Remember to examine the context; note the title and subtitle; identify the main point; identify the subpoints; break the reading into sections; distinguish between points, examples, and counterarguments; watch for transitions within and between paragraphs; and read actively and recursively.
- *Establish the writer's primary purpose.* Use some of the guidelines discussed in Chapter 2; is the piece primarily informative, persuasive, or entertaining? Assess whether the piece achieves its purpose.
- *Read to identify a key idea.* If you begin reading your source materials with a key idea or topic already in mind, read to identify what your sources have to say about the idea.
- *Read to discover a key idea.* If you begin the reading process without a key idea in mind yet, read to discover a key idea that your sources address.
- *Read for relationships.* Regardless of whether you already have a key idea, or whether you are attempting to discover one, your emphasis in reading should be on noting the ways in which the readings relate to each other, to a key idea, and to your purpose in writing the synthesis.

Writing Assignment: The "Legacy" Question in College Admissions

Now we'll give you an opportunity to practice your skills in planning and writing an explanatory synthesis. See Chapter 7, page 216, where we provide multiple sources on the controversial issue of "legacy" status in the college admissions process. At certain schools, the admissions staff gives preferential consideration to the sons and daughters of alumni. Should they? In the synthesis, your task will be to understand and present to others less knowledgeable than you the practice, history, and extent of legacy admissions. You will also explain the debate sparked by legacy admissions.

Note that your instructor may assign related assignments for summary and paraphrase in Chapter 7 to help you prepare for writing an explanatory synthesis.

EXERCISE 4.4

Exploring Online Sources

The electronic databases to which you have access through your school's library, as well as Internet search engines such as Google.com, will yield many sources beyond the ones gathered on the topic of "legacy admissions" in Chapter 7. Read the articles on pages 217–235. Then use one or more of your library's databases or conduct an Internet search to locate articles and discussions on the influence of legacy status in college admissions. You may find more recent pieces than those we've collected here.

5 Argument Synthesis

WHAT IS AN ARGUMENT SYNTHESIS?

An argument is an attempt to persuade a reader or listener that a particular and debatable claim is true. Writers argue in order to establish facts, to make statements of value, and to recommend policies. For instance, answering the question *Why do soldiers sometimes commit atrocities in wartime?* would involve making an argument. To develop this argument, researchers might conduct experiments, collect historical evidence, and examine and interpret data. The researchers might then present their findings at professional conferences and in journals and books. The extent to which readers (or listeners) accept these findings depends upon the quality of the supporting evidence and upon the care with which the researchers have argued their case. What we are calling an argument *synthesis* draws upon evidence from a variety of sources in an attempt to persuade others of the truth or validity of a debatable claim.

By contrast, the explanatory synthesis, as we have seen, is fairly modest in purpose. It emphasizes the sources themselves, not the writer's use of sources to persuade others. The writer of an explanatory synthesis aims to inform, not persuade. Here, for example, is a thesis devised for an explanatory synthesis on the subject computer-mediated communication (or CMC)—the use of the computer (e-mail, instant messaging, etc.) to form serious online relationships:

> While many praise CMC's potential to bridge barriers
> and promote meaningful dialogue, others caution that
> CMC is fraught with dangers.

This thesis summarizes the viewpoints people espouse in regard to CMC, neither arguing for or against any one viewpoint.

In contrast, an argumentative thesis is *persuasive* in purpose. Writers working with the same source material might conceive of and support opposing theses. An example:

> CMC threatens to undermine human intimacy, connection,
> and ultimately community.

So the thesis for an argument synthesis is a claim about which reasonable people could disagree. It is a claim with which—given the right arguments—your audience might be persuaded to agree. The strategy of your argument synthesis is therefore to find and use convincing *support* for your *claim*.

The Elements of Argument: Claim, Support, and Assumption

Let's consider the terminology we've just used. One way of looking at an argument is to see it as an interplay of three essential elements: claim, support, and assumption. A *claim* is a proposition or conclusion that you are trying to prove. You prove this claim by using *support* in the form of fact or expert opinion. Linking your supporting evidence to your claim is your *assumption* about the subject. This assumption, also called a *warrant*, is—as we've discussed in Chapter 2—an underlying belief or principle about some aspect of the world and how it operates. By nature, assumptions (which are often unstated) tend to be more general than either claims or supporting evidence.

For example, here are the essential elements of an argument advocating parental restriction of television viewing for their high school children:

> *Claim*
> High school students should be restricted to no more than two hours of TV viewing per day.

> *Support*
> An important new study and the testimony of educational specialists reveal that students who watch more than two hours of TV a night have, on average, lower grades than those who watch less TV.

> *Assumption*
> Excessive TV viewing adversely affects academic performance.

As another example, let's consider our argumentative claim on the topic of CMC:

> CMC threatens to undermine human intimacy, connection, and ultimately community.

Here are the elements of this argument:

> *Support*
> * While the Internet presents us with increased opportunities to meet people, these meetings are limited by geographical distance.

- People are spending increasing amounts of time in cyberspace: In 1998, the average Internet user spent over four hours per week online, a figure that has nearly doubled recently.
- College health officials report that excessive Internet usage threatens many college students' academic and psychological well-being.
- New kinds of relationships fostered on the Internet often pose challenges to pre-existing relationships.

Assumptions

- The communication skills used and the connections formed during Internet contact fundamentally differ from those used and formed during face-to-face contact.
- "Real" connection and a sense of community are sustained by face-to-face contact, not by Internet interactions.

For the most part, arguments should be constructed logically so that assumptions link evidence (supporting facts and expert opinions) to claims. As we'll see, however, logic is only one component of effective arguments.

EXERCISE **5.1**

Practicing Claim, Support, and Assumption

Devise two sets of claims with support and assumptions for each. First, in response to the example immediately above on computer-mediated communication and relationships, devise a one-sentence claim addressing the positive impact (or potentially positive impact) of CMC on relationships—whether you personally agree with the claim or not. Then list the support on which such a claim might rest, and the assumption that underlies these. Second, write a claim that states your own position on any debatable topic you choose. Again, devise statements of support and relevant assumptions.

The Three Appeals of Argument: *Logos, Ethos*, and *Pathos*

Speakers and writers have never relied on logic alone in advancing and supporting their claims. More than 2,000 years ago, the Athenian philosopher and rhetorician Aristotle explained how speakers attempting to persuade others to their point of view could achieve their purpose by relying on one or more *appeals*, which he called *logos, ethos*, and *pathos*.

Since we frequently find these three appeals employed in political argument, we'll use political examples in the following discussion. But keep in mind that these appeals are also used extensively in advertising, legal cases, business documents, and many other types of argument.

Logos

Logos is the rational appeal, the appeal to reason. If speakers expect to persuade their audiences, they must argue logically and must supply appropriate evidence to support their case. Logical arguments are commonly of two types (often combined): deductive and inductive. The *deductive* argument begins with a generalization, then cites a specific case related to that generalization, from which follows a conclusion. A familiar example of deductive reasoning, used by Aristotle himself, is the following:

All men are mortal. (*generalization*)

Socrates is a man. (*specific case*)

Socrates is mortal. (*conclusion about the specific case*)

In the terms we've just been discussing, this deduction may be restated as follows:

Socrates is mortal. (*claim*)

Socrates is a man. (*support*)

All men are mortal. (*assumption*)

An example of a deductive argument may be seen in President John F. Kennedy's address to the nation in June 1963 on the need for sweeping civil rights legislation. Kennedy begins with the generalizations that it "ought to be possible . . . for American students of any color to attend any public institution they select without having to be backed up by troops" and that "it ought to be possible for American citizens of any color to register and vote in a free election without interference or fear of reprisal." Kennedy then provides several specific examples (primarily recent events in Birmingham, Alabama) and statistics to show that this was not the case. He concludes:

> We face, therefore, a moral crisis as a country and a people. It cannot be met by repressive police action. It cannot be left to increased demonstrations in the streets. It cannot be quieted by token moves or talk. It is time to act in the Congress, in your state and local legislative body, and, above all, in all of our daily lives.

Underlying Kennedy's argument is the following reasoning:

> All Americans should enjoy certain rights. (*assumption*)
>
> Some Americans do not enjoy these rights. (*support*)
>
> We must take action to ensure that all Americans enjoy these rights. (*claim*)

Another form of logical argumentation is *inductive* reasoning. A speaker or writer who argues inductively begins not with a generalization, but with several pieces of specific evidence. The speaker then draws a conclusion from this evidence. For example, in a 1990 debate on gun control, Senator Robert C. Byrd (D-WV) cites specific examples of rampant crime involving guns: "I read of young men being viciously murdered for a pair of sneakers, a leather jacket, or $20." He also offers statistical evidence of the increasing crime rate: "in 1951, there were 3.2 policemen for every felony committed in the United States; this year [1990] nearly 3.2 felonies will be committed per every police officer." He concludes, "Something has to change. We have to stop the crimes that are distorting and disrupting the way of life for so many innocent, law-respecting Americans. The bill that we are debating today attempts to do just that."

Senator Edward M. Kennedy (D-MA) also used statistical evidence in arguing for passage of the Racial Justice Act of 1990, designed to ensure that minorities were not disproportionately singled out for the death penalty. Kennedy points out that between 1973 and 1980, 17 defendants in Fulton County, Georgia, were charged with killing police officers, but the only defendant who received the death sentence was a black man. Kennedy also cites statistics to show that "those who killed whites were 4.3 times more likely to receive the death penalty than were killers of blacks," and that "in Georgia, blacks who killed whites received the death penalty 16.7 percent of the time, while whites who killed received the death penalty only 4.2 percent of the time."

Of course, the mere piling up of evidence does not in itself make the speaker's case. As Donna Cross explains in "Politics: The Art of Bamboozling,"* politicians are very adept at "card-stacking." And statistics can be selected and manipulated to prove anything, as demonstrated in Darrell Huff's landmark book *How to Lie with Statistics* (1954). Moreover, what appears to be a logical argument may, in fact, be fundamentally flawed. (See Chapter 2 for a discussion of logical fallacies and faulty reasoning strategies.) On the other hand, the fact that evidence can be distorted, statistics misused, and logic fractured does not mean that these tools of reason can be dispensed with or should be dismissed. It means only that audiences have to listen and read critically—perceptively, knowledgeably, and skeptically (though not necessarily cynically).

---

* Donna Cross, *Word Abuse: How the Words We Use Use Us* (New York: Coward, 1979).

Sometimes, politicians can turn their opponents' false logic against them. Major R. Owens (D-NY) attempted to counter what he took to be the reasoning on welfare adopted by his opponents:

> Welfare programs create dependency and so should be reformed or abolished. (*assumption*)

> Aid to Families with Dependent Children (AFDC) is a welfare program. (*support*)

> AFDC should be reformed or abolished. (*claim*)

In his speech opposing the Republican welfare reform measure of 1995, Owens simply changes the specific (middle) term, pointing out that federal subsidies for electric power in the West and Midwest and farmers' low-rate home loan mortgages are, in effect, welfare programs. ("We are spoiling America's farmers by smothering them with socialism.") The logical conclusion—that we should reform or eliminate farmers' home loan mortgages—would clearly be unacceptable to many of those pushing for reform of AFDC. Owens thus suggests that opposition to AFDC is based less on reason than on lack of sympathy for its recipients.

EXERCISE 5.2

Using Deductive and Inductive Logic

Choose an issue currently being debated at your school or, a college-related issue about which you are concerned. Write down a claim about this issue. Then write two paragraphs addressing your claim—one in which you organize your points deductively, and one in which you organize them inductively. Some sample issues might include college admissions policies, classroom crowding, or grade inflation. Alternatively, you could base your paragraphs on a claim generated in Exercise 5.1.

Ethos

Ethos, or the ethical appeal, is based not on the ethical rationale for the subject under discussion, but rather on the ethical nature of the person making the appeal. A person making an argument must have a certain degree of credibility: That person must be of good character, have sound sense, and be qualified to hold the office or recommend policy.

For example, Elizabeth Cervantes Barrón, running for senator as the peace and freedom candidate, begins her statement with "I was born and raised in central Los Angeles. I grew up in a multiethnic, multicultural environment where I learned to respect those who were different from me. . . . I am a teacher and am aware of how cutbacks in education have affected our children and our communities."

On the other end of the political spectrum, American Independent gubernatorial candidate Jerry McCready also begins with an ethical appeal: "As a self-employed businessman, I have learned firsthand what it is like to try to make ends meet in an unstable economy being manipulated by out-of-touch politicians." Both candidates are making an appeal to *ethos*, based on the strength of their personal qualities for the office they seek.

L. A. Kauffman is not running for office but rather writing an article arguing against socialism as a viable ideology for the future ("Socialism: No." *Progressive*, 1 Apr. 1993). To defuse objections that he is simply a tool of capitalism, Kauffman begins with an appeal to *ethos*: "Until recently, I was executive editor of the journal *Socialist Review*. Before that I worked for the Marxist magazine, *Monthly Review*. My bookshelves are filled with books of Marxist theory, and I even have a picture of Karl Marx up on my wall." Thus, Kauffman establishes his credentials to argue knowledgeably about Marxist ideology.

Conservative commentator Rush Limbaugh frequently makes use of the ethical appeal by linking himself with the kind of Americans he assumes his audiences to be (what author Donna Cross calls "glory by association"):

> In their attacks [on me], my critics misjudge and insult the American people. If I were really what liberals claim—racist, hatemonger, blowhard—I would years ago have deservedly gone into oblivion. The truth is, I provide information and analysis the media refuses to disseminate, information and analysis the public craves. People listen to me for one reason: I am effective. And my credibility is judged in the marketplace every day. . . . I represent America's rejection of liberal elites. . . . I validate the convictions of ordinary people.*

EXERCISE   5.3

Using Ethos

Return to the claim you used for Exercise 5.2, and write a paragraph in which you use an appeal to *ethos* to make a case for that claim.

Pathos

Finally, speakers and writers appeal to their audiences by use of *pathos*, the appeal to the emotions. Nothing is inherently wrong with using an emotional appeal. Indeed, since emotions often move people far more powerfully than reason alone, speakers and writers would be foolish not to use emotion. And it would be a drab, humorless world if human beings were not subject to the sway of feeling, as well as reason. The emotional appeal becomes problematic only if it is the *sole* or *primary* basis of the argument. This imbalance of emotion over logic is the kind of situation that led, for example, to the internment of Japanese Americans during World War II or that leads to periodic political spasms to enact anti-flag-burning legislation.

---

* Rush Limbaugh, "Why I Am a Threat to the Left,"*Los Angeles Times* 9 Oct. 1994: B5.

President Reagan was a master of emotional appeal. He closed his first inaugural address with a reference to the view from the Capitol to the Arlington National Cemetery, where lie thousands of markers of "heroes":

> Under one such marker lies a young man, Martin Treptow, who left his job in a small-town barbershop in 1917 to go to France with the famed Rainbow Division. There, on the western front, he was killed trying to carry a message between battalions under heavy artillery fire. We're told that on his body was found a diary. On the flyleaf under the heading, "My Pledge," he had written these words: "America must win this war. Therefore, I will work, I will save, I will sacrifice, I will endure, I will fight cheerfully and do my utmost, as if the issue of the whole struggle depended on me alone." The crisis we are facing today does not require of us the kind of sacrifice that Martin Treptow and so many thousands of others were called upon to make. It does require, however, our best effort and our willingness to believe in ourselves and to believe in our capacity to perform great deeds, to believe that together with God's help we can and will resolve the problems which now confront us.

Surely, Reagan implies, if Martin Treptow can act so courageously and so selflessly, we can do the same. The logic is somewhat unclear, since the connection between Martin Treptow and ordinary Americans of 1981 is rather tenuous (as Reagan concedes); but the emotional power of Martin Treptow, whom reporters were sent scurrying to research, carries the argument.

A more recent president, Bill Clinton, also used *pathos*. Addressing an audience of the nation's governors about his welfare plan, Clinton closed his remarks by referring to a conversation he had held with a welfare mother who had gone through the kind of training program Clinton was advocating. Asked by Clinton whether she thought that such training programs should be mandatory, the mother said, "I sure do." Clinton in his remarks explained what she said when he asked her why:

> "Well, because if it wasn't, there would be a lot of people like me home watching the soaps because we don't believe we can make anything of ourselves anymore. So you've got to make it mandatory." And I said, "What's the best thing about having a job?" She said, "When my boy goes to school, and they say, 'What does your mama do for a living?' he can give an answer."

Clinton uses the emotional power he counts on in that anecdote to set up his conclusion: "We must end poverty for Americans who want to work. And we must do it on terms that dignify all of the rest of us, as well as help our country to work better. I need your help, and I think we can do it."

EXERCISE 5.4

Using Pathos

Return to the claim you used for Exercises 5.2 and 5.3, and write a paragraph in which you use an appeal to *pathos* to argue for that claim.

DEMONSTRATION: DEVELOPING AN ARGUMENT SYNTHESIS—VOLUNTEERING IN AMERICA

To demonstrate how to plan and draft an argument synthesis, let's consider another subject. If you were taking an economics or sociology course, you might at some point consider the phenomenon of volunteerism, the extent to which Americans volunteer—that is, give away their time freely—for causes they deem worthy. In a market economy, why would people agree to forgo wages in exchange for their labor? Are there other kinds of compensation for people who volunteer? Is peer pressure involved? Can a spirit of volunteerism be taught or encouraged? And, in light of the articles that follow and the example argument based on them, can the government—which has the constitutional right to compel military service—*compel* citizens to serve their communities (rendering their service something other than an act of volunteering)?

Suppose, in preparing to write a short paper on volunteering, you located the following sources:

- "A New Start for National Service," John McCain and Evan Bayh
- "Calls for National Service," Landrum, Eberly, and Sherraden
- "Politics and National Service: A Virus Attacks the Volunteer Sector," Bruce Chapman

Read these sources (which follow) carefully, noting as you do the kinds of information and ideas you could draw upon to develop an *argument synthesis*. Note: To save space and for the purpose of demonstration, two of the three passages are excerpts only. In preparing your paper, naturally you would draw upon entire articles and book chapters from which the extracts were taken. And you would draw upon more articles than these in your search for materials in support of your argument (as the writer of the example paper has done on pages 164–172). But these three sources set the poles of the debate. The discussion of how these passages can form the basis of an argument synthesis resumes on page 159.

A New Start for National Service
John McCain and Evan Bayh

John McCain (R-AZ) and Evan Bayh (D-IN) are U.S. senators. This op-ed piece appeared in the New York Times *on November 6, 2001, a few weeks after the terrorist attacks of September 11.**

1 Since Sept. 11, Americans have found a new spirit of national unity and purpose. Forty years ago, at the height of the cold war, President John F. Kennedy

---

challenged Americans to enter into public service. Today, confronted with a challenge no less daunting than the cold war, Americans again are eager for ways to serve at home and abroad. Government should make it easier for them to do so.

2   That is why we are introducing legislation to revamp national service programs and dramatically expand opportunities for public service.

3   Many tasks lie ahead, both new and old. On the home front, there are new security and civil defense requirements, like increased police and border patrol needs. We will charge the Corporation for National Service, the federal office that oversees national volunteer programs, with the task of assembling a plan that would put civilians to work to assist the Office of Homeland Security. The military will need new recruits to confront the challenges abroad, so our bill will also improve benefits for our servicemembers.

4   At the same time, because the society we defend needs increased services, from promoting literacy to caring for the elderly, we expand AmeriCorps and senior service programs to enlarge our national army of volunteers.

5   AmeriCorps' achievements have been impressive: thousands of homes have been built, hundreds of thousands of seniors given the care they need to live independently and millions of children tutored.

6   Since its inception in 1993, nearly 250,000 Americans have served stints of one or two years in AmeriCorps. But for all its concrete achievements, AmeriCorps has been too small to rouse the nation's imagination. Under our bill, 250,000 volunteers each year would be able to answer the call—with half of them assisting in civil defense needs and half continuing the good work of AmeriCorps.

7   We must also ask our nation's colleges to promote service more aggressively. Currently, many colleges devote only a small fraction of federal work-study funds to community service, while the majority of federal resources are used to fill low-skill positions. This was not Congress's vision when it passed the Higher Education Act of 1965. Under our bill, universities will be required to promote student involvement in community activities more vigorously.

8   And for those who might consider serving their country in the armed forces, the benefits must keep pace with the times. While the volunteer military has been successful, our armed forces continue to suffer from significant recruitment challenges.

9   Our legislation encourages more young Americans to serve in the military by allowing the Defense Department to create a new, shorter-term enlistment option. This "18-18-18" plan would offer an $18,000 bonus—in addition to regular pay—for 18 months of active duty and 18 months of reserve duty. And we would significantly improve education payments made to service members under current law.

10 Public service is a virtue, and national service should one day be a rite of passage for young Americans. This is the right moment to issue a new call to service and give a new generation a way to claim the rewards and responsibilities of active citizenship.

Calls for National Service
Roger Landrum, Donald J. Eberly, and Michael W. Sherraden

The passage that follows introduces the work of William James, a Harvard philosopher whose speech "The Moral Equivalent of War" (1906) helped set an agenda for the national service movement. The essay appears in a collection of scholarly commentaries on national service, edited by Sherraden and Eberly.

1   The first major call for a national service in the United States was by the social philosopher and psychologist William James. James' seminal essay "The Moral Equivalent of War" was given as a major address at Stanford University in 1906 and first published in 1910. The essay proposed national service as a pragmatic means by which a democratic nation could maintain social cohesiveness apart from the external threat of war. In his extraordinarily vivid language, James attacked a view he considered ingrained in Western civilization from Alexander the Great through Theodore Roosevelt: that war's "dreadful hammer is the welder of men into cohesive states, and nowhere but in such states can human nature adequately develop its capacity." James wasn't any easier on pacifists, suggesting that the "duties, penalties, and sanctions pictured in the utopias they paint are all too weak and tame to substitute for war's disciplinary function." The most promising line of conciliation between militarists and pacifists, James thought, was some "moral equivalent of war."

> Men now are proud of belonging to a conquering nation, and without a murmur they lay down their persons and their wealth, if by so doing they may fight off subjugation. But who can be sure that other aspects of one's country may not, with time and education and suggestion enough, come to be regarded with similarly effective feelings of pride and shame? Why should men not someday feel that it is worth a blood-tax to belong to a collectivity superior in any ideal respect? Why should they not blush with indignant shame if the community that owns them is vile in any way whatsoever?
>
> Individuals, daily more numerous, now feel this civic passion. It is only a question of blowing on the spark till the whole population gets incandescent, and on the ruins of the old morals of military honor, until a stable system of morals of civic honor builds itself up. What the whole community comes to believe in grasps the individual as in a vise. The war function has grasped us so far; but constructive interests may someday seem no less imperative, and impose on the individual a hardly lighter burden.
>
> If now—and this is my idea—there were, instead of military conscription, a conscription of the whole youthful population to form for a certain number of years a part of the army enlisted against *Nature*, the injustice would tend to be evened out, and numerous other goods to the commonwealth would follow. . . .
>
> Such a conscription, with the state of public opinion that would have required it, and the many moral fruits it would bear, would preserve in the midst of a pacific civilization the manly virtues which the military party is so afraid of seeing disappear in peace.[1]

James argued that a permanently successful peace economy cannot be a simple pleasure economy. He proposed a conscription of the youthful population of the United States into national service to provide a new sense of "civic discipline" outside the context of war. James also believed that national service would benefit young people. They would experience "self-forgetfulness" rather than "self-seeking." No one would be "flung out of employment to degenerate because there is no immediate work for them to do." None would "remain blind, as the luxurious classes now are blind, to man's relations to the globe he lives on." The childishness would be "knocked out of them." The moral equivalent of war would cultivate in youth "toughness without callousness, healthier sympathies and soberer ideas, ideals of hardihood and discipline, and civic temper."

2   The logic and rhetoric of James' call for national service have an antique ring today. James was clearly thinking only of young men and the image of Ivy League undergraduates seemed to be at the center of his thinking. He didn't consider the issue of constitutional limits on involuntary servitude. His recommendation of conscription was softened only by the concepts of collectivity and social sanctions: "What the whole community comes to believe in grasps the individual as in a vise." He said nothing of cost and organization. Of course, there were half as many young people in those days, only 15 percent of them in high school, and a vastly different organization of the work force. Still, James succeeded in embedding a phrase, "the moral equivalent of war," in the national consciousness; he raised the fundamental issue of proper socialization of youth in the context of a democracy at peace; and he planted the idea of national service.

Note

1. William James, "The Moral Equivalent of War," *International Conciliation*, no. 27 (Washington, D.C.: Carnegie Endowment for International Peace, 1910), pp. 8–20.

Politics and National Service: A Virus Attacks the Volunteer Sector
Bruce Chapman

Bruce Chapman, former U.S. Ambassador to the UN organizations in Vienna and former senior fellow at the Hudson Institute, currently serves as president of the Discovery Institute of Seattle, Washington, a public policy center for studying national and international affairs. An early proponent of the all-volunteer army who dedicated many years to public service (as secretary of state for the State of Washington, former director of the U.S. Census Bureau, and as aide to President Reagan), Chapman argues that volunteerism, "true service," is "corrupted" when it is in any way coerced or induced—through government programs, for instance, that pay stipends. The excerpted selection that follows appears in a collection of essays, National Service: Pro & Con *(1990).*

1   Proposals for government-operated national service, like influenza, flare up from time to time, depress the resistance of the body politic, run their course, and seem to disappear, only to mutate and afflict public life anew. Unfortunately, another epidemic may be on the way. The disease metaphor comes to mind not as an aspersion on the advocates of national service because, with good-natured patience, persistence, and seemingly relentless political invention, they mean well, but from the frustration of constantly combating the changing strains of a statist idea that one thought had been eliminated in the early 1970s, along with smallpox.

2   Why does the national service virus keep coming back? Perhaps because its romance is so easy to catch, commanding a nostalgic imagination and evoking times when Americans were eager to sacrifice for their country. Claiming to derive inspiration from both military experience and the social gospel—if we could only get America's wastrel youth into at least a psychic uniform we might be able to teach self-discipline again and revive the spirit of giving—it hearkens back to William James's call for a "moral equivalent of war." But at the end of the twentieth century should we be looking to war for moral guidance?

3   True service is one of the glories of our civilization in the West, especially in the great independent (or volunteer) sector of American society. Inspiration for service in the West comes from the Bible in parable and admonition and is constantly restated in the long historical tradition of Judeo-Christian faith. Personal service is a freewill offering to God. This is very different from performance of an obligation to government, which is a tax on time or money.

4   True service, then, has a spiritual basis, even for some outside the Judeo-Christian tradition per se. Fulfillment of an obligation to government, in contrast, has a contractual basis unless it is founded on an outright commitment to a coercive utopianism. Either way, it is not true service. Nor can enrollment in a government-funded self-improvement project or acceptance of a government job be called true service. Indeed, when coercion or inducements are provided, as in the various national service schemes, the spirit of service is to that degree corrupted.

5   In practice the service in a federal program of national service would be contaminated by governmental determination of goals, bureaucratization of procedures, and, inevitably, government insistence on further regulating the independent sector with which it contracted. National service would tend to demoralize those citizens who volunteer without expectation of financial reward and stigmatize the honest labor of people whose fields were invaded by stipened and vouchered volunteers.

6   Government intervention is always a potential threat to the voluntary sector. When totalitarians have come to power in other Western countries, they have sought to absorb this sector, conferring official sponsorship on certain organizations and scorning others, thereby inculcating in the citizenry the government's valuation even on use of free time. Although in the United States totalitarianism is not a current danger to our liberal democracy, coercive utopianism is always a legitimate concern.

7   Alexis de Tocqueville saw in our own early history that the genius of voluntary association was America's superior answer to the leadership energy provided in other societies by aristocracies. But government, he warned, may seek

to direct the voluntary sector in the same way it erroneously seeks to control industrial undertakings:

> Once it leaves the sphere of politics to launch out on this new task, it will, even without intending this, exercise an intolerable tyranny. For a government can only dictate precise rules. It imposes the sentiments and ideas which it favors, and it is never easy to tell the difference between its advice and its commands.[1]

Note

1. Alexis de Tocqueville, *Democracy in America*, vol. 2, book 2, chap. 5, J. P. Mayer (New York: Doubleday, 1969).

Consider Your Purpose

As with the explanatory synthesis, your specific purpose in writing an argument synthesis is crucial. What, exactly, you want to do will affect your claim, the evidence you select to support your claim, and the way you organize the evidence. Your purpose may be clear to you before you begin research, may emerge during the course of research, or may not emerge until after you have completed your research. Of course, the sooner your purpose is clear to you, the fewer wasted motions you will make. On the other hand, the more you approach research as an exploratory process, the likelier that your conclusions will emerge from the sources themselves, rather than from preconceived ideas.

Let's say that while reading these sources, your own encounters with a service organization (perhaps you help schoolchildren improve their literacy skills) have influenced your thinking on the subject. You find yourself impressed that so many people at the literacy center volunteer without being compelled to do so. You observe that giving time freely adds to the pleasures of volunteering, and to its significance as well. Meanwhile, perhaps your school is considering a service "requirement"—that is, a mandate that all students perform a given number of community service hours in order to graduate. The juxtaposition of "compelled" service with freely given service sparks in you an idea for a source-based paper.

On the one hand, you can understand and even sympathize with the viewpoints of educators who believe that while they have students in their clutches (so to speak), they have an opportunity to pass on an ethic of service. To students who would not volunteer time on their own, setting a graduation requirement makes sense. On the other hand, it seems to you that forced volunteerism, a contradiction in terms if ever there was one, defeats the essential quality of volunteering: that it is time given freely. The donation of time to meet the needs of others is an act of selflessness that brings you profound satisfaction. Your purpose in writing, then, emerges from these kinds of responses to the source material.

Making a Claim: Formulate a Thesis

As we indicated in the introduction to this chapter, one useful way of approaching an argument is to see it as making a *claim*. A claim is a proposition, a conclusion that you are trying to prove or demonstrate. If your purpose is to demonstrate that the state should not compel people to serve their communities, then that is the claim at the heart of your argument. The claim is generally expressed in one-sentence form as a *thesis*. You draw *support* from your sources as you argue logically for your claim. At times, you may also argue by making appeals to *ethos* and *pathos* (see pages 151–153).

Of course, not every piece of information in a source is useful for supporting a claim. By the same token, you may draw support for your claim from sources that make entirely different claims. You may use as support for your own claim, for example, a sentiment expressed in William James's "On the Moral Equivalent of War," that values such as selfless concern for the common good, learned through service, are desirable. Yet while James called for "a conscription of the whole youthful population" to nonmilitary service projects, you may believe that service should be voluntary. Still, you could cite James and comment, where you think appropriate, on where you and he diverge.

Similarly, you might use one source as part of a *counterargument*—an argument opposite to your own—so that you can demonstrate its weaknesses and, in the process, strengthen your own claim. On the other hand, the author of one of your sources may be so convincing in supporting a claim that you adopt it yourself, either partially or entirely. The point is that *the argument is in your hands*: You must devise it yourself and use your sources in ways that will support the claim expressed in your thesis.

You may not want to divulge your thesis until the end of the paper, to draw the reader along toward your conclusion, allowing the thesis to flow naturally out of the argument and the evidence on which it is based. If you do this, you are working *inductively*. Or you may wish to be more direct and *begin* with your thesis, following the thesis statement with evidence to support it. If you do this, you are working *deductively*. In academic papers, deductive arguments are far more common than inductive arguments.

Based on your own experience and reactions to reading sources, you may find yourself agreeing with Bruce Chapman's argument that compelled or monetarily induced service "corrupts" the experience of service. At the same time, you may find yourself unwilling to take Chapman's extreme stance that even modest stipends such as the ones earned while working for AmeriCorps and other government programs constitute "corruption." While you believe that government programs encouraging service are beneficial, you certainly don't want to see the federal government create a non-military version of compulsory national service. After a few tries, you develop the following thesis:

> The impulse to expand service through volunteer
> programs like AmeriCorps, VISTA, and the Peace
> Corps is understandable, even praiseworthy. But

```
        as volunteerism grows and gains public support,
        we should resist letting its successes become an
        argument for compulsory national service.
```

Decide How You Will Use Your Source Material

Your claim commits you to (1) discussing the benefits of service in government-sponsored programs like AmeriCorps and VISTA, and (2) arguing
that, benefits notwithstanding, there are compelling reasons not to make
national service compulsory. The sources (some provided here, some located elsewhere) offer information and ideas—that is, evidence—that will
allow you to support your claim. (You might draw on one universally available source, the U.S. Constitution, not included in the materials here.) The
selection by Senators McCain and Bayh provides pro-service arguments,
while the essay by Bruce Chapman provides a negative one. Roger
Landrum, Donald Eberly, and Michael Sherraden provide a philosophical
and historical foundation for the synthesis. (Note that other sources not
included in this chapter will be cited in the example paper.)

Develop an Organizational Plan

Having established your overall purpose and your claim, having developed
a thesis (which may change as you write and revise the paper), and having
decided how to use your source materials, how do you logically organize
your essay? In many cases, including this one, a well-written thesis will suggest an overall organization. Thus, the first part of your argument synthesis
will define volunteerism and set a broad context regarding its pervasiveness
and history, along with mention of a possible early attempt to make national
service compulsory. The second part will argue that national service should
not be made compulsory. Sorting through your material and categorizing it
by topic and subtopic, you might arrive at the following outline:

```
    I. Introduction. Pervasiveness of volunteerism
       in America. Use Bureau of Labor Statistics
       data.
   II. The desire to "make more of a good thing."
       The McCain/Bayh "Call to Service Act."
       Thesis.
  III. Intellectual history of service:
       A. Recent history. Refer to William James.
          State that service need not be military.
       B. Ancient history. Refer to Plato. State
          that citizens owe the State an obligation.
```

    IV. Can the U.S. government compel citizens to service?

        A. Military service: Yes. Right granted by U.S. Constitution.

        B. Transition: military vs. civilian.

        C. Civilian service: No.

          1. Logical reason: public service is not analogous to military service.

          2. Legal reason: U.S. Constitution (Amendment XIII) forbids involuntary servitude.

          3. Moral reason: compelled or induced service (that is, with money) "corrupts" spirit of service.

            a. Concede point that "less pure" forms of service that pay stipends, such as AmeriCorps and VISTA, are beneficial.

            b. But state forcefully that compulsory (as opposed to minimally compensated) service does corrupt the spirit of service.

    V. Conclusion:

        A. Government should expand opportunities to serve <u>voluntarily</u> (even with pay).

        B. It should resist the impulse to compel young people to serve.

Argument Strategy

The argument represented by this outline will build not only on evidence drawn from sources but also on the writer's assumptions. Consider the bare-bones logic of the argument:

Voluntary service, paid or unpaid, promotes good citizenship and benefits the community. (*assumption*)

People who have worked in volunteer programs have made significant contributions to community and public life. (*support*)

We should support programs that foster volunteerism. (*claim*)

The crucial point about which reasonable people will disagree is the *assumption* that unpaid *and* paid volunteer service promotes good citizenship.

One source author, Bruce Chapman, makes a partial and extreme form of this assumption when he writes that financially rewarded service is "corrupted" (see page 158). A less extreme assumption—the one guiding the model paper—is possible: Citizenship can be learned in a minimally paid environment such as AmeriCorps. The writer of the model paper agrees with Chapman, however, about another assumption: that service should never be compelled.

Writers can accept or partially accept an opposing assumption by making a *concession*, in the process establishing themselves as reasonable and willing to compromise (see page 179). In our example, the writer does exactly this (see paragraph 10 in the sample synthesis that follows) and then uses as *supporting evidence* facts from a report that many paid veterans of government-sponsored teaching programs learn about citizenship and continue to teach after their contracted time is up. By raising potential objections and making concessions, the writer blunts the effectiveness of *counterarguments*.

The *claim* of the example argument about service is primarily a claim about *policy*, about actions that should (or should not) be taken. An argument can also concern a claim about *facts* (Does X exist? Does X lead to Y? How can we define X?) or a claim about *value* (What is X worth?). You have seen that the present argument rests on an assumed definition of "service." Depending on how you define the term, you will agree—or not—with the writer. Among the source authors, Bruce Chapman defines service one way (it is neither rewarded with money nor compelled), while Senators McCain and Bayh define it another (as work done with or without minimal pay to help others and reinforce core values). As you read the following paper, watch how these opposing views are woven into the argument.

A well-reasoned argument will involve a claim primarily about fact, value, *or* policy. Secondary arguments are sometimes needed, as in the present example, to help make a case.

Draft and Revise Your Synthesis

The final draft of a completed synthesis, based on the above outline, follows. Thesis, transitions, and topic sentences are highlighted; Modern Language Association (MLA) documentation style is used throughout.

A cautionary note: When writing syntheses, it is all too easy to become careless in properly crediting your sources. Before drafting your paper, please review the section on "Avoiding Plagiarism" in Chapter 1 (pages 48–49) as well as the materials on "Documentation Basics" on pages 846–849.

MODEL SYNTHESIS

(Thesis and topic sentences are highlighted.)

Michael Kikuchi
Professor Carcich
English 3
31 January 2007

Keeping Volunteerism Voluntary

1 The spirit of volunteerism flourishes in America. In
2002-2003, 28.8 percent of Americans, 16 and older,
some 63.8 million, freely gave time to their communities (Bureau, "Volunteering"). Prompted by a desire
to serve others without thought of personal gain,
more than one-quarter of us donate 52 hours a year,
more than one full work-week, to building shelters,
coaching Little League, caring for the elderly,
teaching literacy, and countless other community
minded pursuits (Bureau, "Volunteering"; "Table 1").
Not included in these numbers are the many tens of
thousands who donate time through less "pure" volunteer programs run by the government, such as
AmeriCorps, VISTA (Volunteers in Service to America),
and the Peace Corps, all of which pay recruits a small
stipend. Volunteerism is so pervasive that it seems
bred into the American character. A former director of
the U.S. Census Bureau observes that "Alexis de
Tocqueville saw in [America's] early history that the
genius of voluntary association was [the country's]
superior answer to the leadership energy provided in
other societies by aristocracies" (Chapman 134).

2 Advocates claim that volunteerism builds character, teaches citizenship, and addresses unfulfilled
national needs (Gorham 22). But if only one American
in four volunteers, a percentage that surely could be
improved, and if volunteerism is such a boon to communities, it is little wonder that from time to time
politicians propose to make more of a good thing. In
this spirit, in November 2001 Senators John McCain (R-
AZ) and Evan Bayh (D-IN) introduced Bill S1274, the
"Call to Service Act," which would dramatically
increase the opportunities to serve in government-
sponsored volunteer programs. "Public service is a
virtue," write the senators in a New York Times op-ed
piece not quite two months after the horrors of

September 11, 2001. "[N]ational service should one day be a rite of passage for young Americans." The senators believe that this "is the right moment to issue a new call to service and give a new generation a way to claim the rewards and responsibilities of active citizenship" (A31). The impulse to expand service through volunteer programs like AmeriCorps, VISTA, and the Peace Corps is understandable, even praiseworthy. But as volunteerism grows and gains public support, we should resist letting its successes become an argument for compulsory national service.

3   Senators McCain and Bayh do not call for compulsory service. Nonetheless, one can hear an echo of the word "compulsory" in their claim that "national service should one day be a rite of passage for young Americans." The word "should" suggests nothing if not obligation, and the word "all" is clearly implied. It's not a stretch to imagine the senators and others at some point endorsing a program of compulsory service, an idea that has been around for nearly a century. In 1906, the philosopher William James called for "a conscription of the whole youthful population" to non-military projects that would improve character (14). James, whom many consider the intellectual father of national service, admired the discipline and sacrifice of soldiers but thought it absurd that such "[m]artial virtues" as "intrepidity, contempt of softness, surrender of private interest, [and] obedience to command" should be developed only in the service of war. He imagined a "reign of peace" in which these qualities would "remain the rock upon which" peaceful states might be built (16). In a famous passage of his talk at Stanford University, which he titled "The Moral Equivalent of War," James urges on youth a hard (but non-military) service:

> To coal and iron mines, to freight trains, to fishing fleets in December, to dishwashing, clothes-washing, and window washing, to road-building and tunnel-making, to foundries and stoke-holes, and to the frames of skyscrapers, would our gilded youths be drafted off, according to their choice, to get the childishness knocked out of them, and to come back into society with healthier sympathies and soberer ideas. They would have paid their blood-tax, done their own part in the immemorial human warfare

> against nature; they would tread the earth more
> proudly, the women would value them more highly,
> they would be better fathers and teachers of the
> following generation. (17)

James's "gilded youths" were the (male) students of
elite colleges. In the early twentieth century,
there were not nearly as many young people as today,
both in absolute terms and in college (Landrum,
Eberly, and Sherraden 23-25), and so the logistics
of compulsory national service may have seemed manageable. A century later we might regard his proposal as impractical or even illegal, but at the time
he struck an important chord. His vision of learning
the virtues and disciplines of citizenship through a
non-military regimen in peace time (a "moral equivalent of war") entered our national vocabulary and
remains a part of it today (Landrum, Eberly, and
Sherraden 27).

4   The question of what sort of service, or obligation, citizens owe a country is as old as the first
gathering of peoples into a collective for mutual
safety and comfort. In one of his famous dialogues,
Plato records a conversation between Socrates, whom
Athens had imprisoned and condemned to death for corrupting the city's youth with his teachings, and a
friend who urges that he escape and save himself.
Socrates argues that if he has accepted and enjoyed
the privileges of citizenship, then he must also
accept the judgment of the State, even if that judgment calls for his execution:

> [A]fter having brought you into the world, and nur-
> tured and educated you, and given you and every
> other citizen a share in every good that we [that
> is, the State] had to give, we further proclaim and
> give the right to every Athenian, that if he does
> not like us when he has come of age and has seen the
> ways of the city, and made our acquaintance, he may
> go where he pleases and take his goods with him; and
> none of us laws will forbid him or interfere with
> him. Any of you who does not like us and the city,
> and who wants to go to a colony or to any other
> city, may go where he likes, and take his goods with
> him. But he who has experience of the manner in
> which we order justice and administer the State, and
> still remains, has entered into an implied contract
> that he will do as we command him. (qtd. in Plato)

Kikuchi 4

Citizens obligate themselves to the State when they accept its bounties and protections. But how is that obligation to be paid? Some twenty-four hundred years after Socrates accepted his fate and drank his cup of hemlock, Americans pay their obligations to the government through taxes, jury duty, and obedience to laws passed by elected representatives.

5   Can the government compel us to do more? Can it compel us, for instance, to military or non-military service? The U.S. Constitution grants Congress the right to raise armies (Article 1, Section 8, Clause 14). The way Congress chooses to do this, however, reflects the needs of a particular time. During World War II and the Vietnam War, the government implemented a military draft. Today, for reasons of professionalism and morale, the Department of Defense prefers an all-volunteer army to an army of conscripts. The Chairman of the Joint Chiefs of Staff was recently reported to have said that the "country doesn't need a draft because the all-volunteer force works--in fact, the United States has the most effective military in the world precisely because it is all-volunteer" (Rhem 150). Defense Secretary Rumsfeld sees distinct disadvantages to the draft: "[P]eople are involuntarily forced to serve, some for less than they could earn on the outside. . . . Troops are 'churned' through training, serve the minimum amount of time and leave--thus causing more money to be spent to churn more draftees through the system" (qtd. in Rhem).

6   Clearly the State has a constitutional right to compel young people into military service in times of military need, whether it chooses to exercise that right through an all-volunteer or a conscripted army. Does the State have an equivalent right to press citizens into non-military service? For example, because our libraries are understaffed, our parks ill-kept, and our youth reading below grade level, should the State compel citizens into service for the common good? No--for logical, legal, and moral reasons.

7   Military need is not logically equivalent to non-military need, primarily because non-military needs are typically met through the normal operations of representative government and the market economy. When the State identifies work to be done for the common good, it taxes citizens and directs its employees to perform that work. Alternately, it

may put out bids and pay contractors to perform the work. This is how highways and libraries get built. If the State does not adequately perform these basic functions, it fails in its responsibilities. The remedy to this failure should not be the drafting of America's youth into national service for one or two years. The State could not honestly or reasonably call for universal service as a means of upgrading the moral character of youth when its real need is to plug holes in its own leaky ship. Such disingenuous arguments would only call attention to the State's failures. If the State lacks the money or competence to do its work, then citizens should overhaul the system by electing a new, more efficient administration. If necessary, the legislature could raise taxes. But it should not make a bogus public "need" into an occasion to compel public service.

8   Nor does the State have a legal basis on which to press its citizens into national service. While the Constitution grants Congress the authority to raise armies, it expressly forbids forced service: "Neither slavery nor involuntary servitude, except as a punishment for crime whereof the party shall have been duly convicted, shall exist within the United States, or any place subject to their jurisdiction" (Amendment XIII). A program for compulsory national service, however noble its aims, would never withstand a legal challenge.

9   But even if advocates could circumvent the logical and legal obstacles to compulsory national service, they could not on moral grounds compel youth to serve against their will. Advocates argue, persuasively, that volunteerism builds character and promotes citizenship (Gorham 18). And, in fact, volunteer service does foster selflessness, a concern for community, and an appreciation of country (McCain and Bayh; Gergen; James; Patterson). Still, the essential quality of volunteerism is that it is time given freely. "True service," writes Bruce Chapman, "has a spiritual basis [rooted in the Judeo-Christian tradition]. . . . Fulfillment of an obligation to government, in contrast, has a contractual basis." Chapman argues that "performance of an obligation to government . . . is a

tax on time and money." The spirit of service is "corrupted" when it is compelled or encouraged with
stipends (140-141).

10   One need not agree, however, that volunteer programs that pay youth in room and board, health care,
and tuition vouchers "corrupt" the spirit of giving.
Chapman makes an extreme argument that ignores the
financial realities of many young people. Were they to
get no compensation, many would forgo volunteering and
the possibility of learning from programs that encourage civic participation and patriotism. That would be
a shame, for the members of AmeriCorps, the Peace
Corps, and VISTA, all of whom are paid a small
stipend, grow as individuals and as citizens, learning
life-long lessons. David Gergen vividly makes this
point:

> Voluntary service when young often changes people
> for life. They learn to give their fair share. Some
> 60 percent of alumni from Teach for America, a mar-
> velous program, now work full time in education, and
> many others remain deeply involved in social change.
> Mark Levine, for example, has started two community-
> owned credit unions in Washington Heights, NY, for
> recent immigrants. Alumni of City Year, another ter-
> rific program, vote at twice the rates of their
> peers. Or think of the Peace Corps alumni. Six now
> serve in the House of Representatives, one
> (Christopher Dodd) in the Senate. (60)

Unquestionably, national programs for volunteers can
benefit both the individuals serving and the communities served. For example, AmeriCorps sets goals lofty
enough to ensure that all involved will benefit. The
Corps helps communities when it places members in projects designed to have a positive educational, social,
and environmental impact. Communities are also
strengthened when culturally and racially diverse
people work side by side to achieve project goals.
Additionally, AmeriCorps seeks through its programming
and its job and educational benefits to improve the
lives of members (Corporation). Both communities and
individuals gain from AmeriCorps' efforts.

11   Still, as Chapman points out, volunteerism that
is compelled in any way, that turns the impulse to

serve into an obligation, would be a corruption. If
the State instituted obligatory non-military service
for the "good" of the individual (and recall that it
could not reasonably or honestly do so for the social
"needs" of the State), the act of service would no
longer be rooted in generosity. And it is the spirit
of generosity, of one person's freely giving to another, that underlies all the good that volunteering
achieves. Convert the essential generous impulse to an
obligation, and the very logic for compelling service-
-to teach civic values--disappears. The State could no
more expect the veterans of obligatory service to have
learned the values of good citizenship or to feel special affection for the country than we could expect a
child whose parents order him to "make friends with
Johnny" to have learned anything useful about friendship or to feel a special kinship with Johnny.
Affection, citizenship, and patriotism don't work that
way. They are freely given, or they are coerced. And
if coerced, they are corrupt. Compelled allegiance is
a form of bullying that teaches nothing so much as
resentment.

12   Without any inducement other than the good it
would do their communities and their own hearts, 63.8
million Americans--more than one quarter of the coun-
try--volunteer. Could more people volunteer, specifically more young people? Yes, especially in light of
the finding that young people in their early twenties
volunteer the least, relative to all other age groups
(Bureau, "Table 1"). The McCain/Bayh "Call to Service
Act" deserves enthusiastic support, as does any government effort to encourage service by people younger
than 25. Those who learn to serve while young turn
out to be more involved with their communities over
the course of their lives (Gergen; Corporation), and
such involvement can only benefit us all. Reasonable
inducements such as tuition vouchers, minimal pay,
health care, and room and board can give young people
the safety net they need to experiment with serving
others and in that way discover their own wellsprings
of generosity.

13   So let's support McCain/Bayh and every such effort
to encourage service. Ideally, enough programs will be

Kikuchi 8

in place one day to offer all high school and college graduates the option of serving their communities. "[T]oo often," writes Richard North Patterson, "we offer young people a vision of community which extends to the nearest shopping mall." Government-sponsored programs for service can make us better than that, and we should promote volunteerism wherever and whenever we can. But we must guard against using the success of these programs as a pre-text for establishing mandatory national or community service. Such a mandate would fail legal and logical tests and, most importantly, a moral test: Volunteerism is built on choice. To command someone to do good works, to make good works obligatory, is to poison the very essence of service.

[new page]

Kikuchi 9

Works Cited

Bureau of Labor Statistics. "Table 1: Volunteers by Selected Characteristics, September 2003." 17 Dec. 2003. 17 Jan. 2004 <http://www.bls.gov/ news.release/volun.t01.htm>.

---. "Volunteering in the United States, 2003." 18 Dec. 2003. 17 Jan. 2004 <http://www.bls.gov/news.release/volun.nr0.htm>.

Chapman, Bruce. "Politics and National Service: A Virus Attacks the Volunteer Sector." National Service: Pro & Con. Ed. Williamson M. Evers. Stanford, CA: Hoover Institution P, 1990. 133-44.

"Constitution of the United States of America." The New York Public Library Desk Reference. New York: Webster's New World, 1989.

Corporation for National and Community Service. "AmeriCorps Mission." Americorps: Getting Things Done. Program Directory, Spring/Summer 1995. Microfiche Y2N.21/29 10AM3. Washington, DC: GPO, 1995.

Gergen, David. "A Time to Heed the Call." U.S. News & World Report 24 Dec. 2001: 60.

Gorham, Eric B. "National Service, Political Socialization, and Citizenship." National Service, Citizenship, and Political Education. Albany: SUNY P, 1992. 5-30.

James, William. "The Moral Equivalent of War." International Conciliation 27 (Washington, DC: Carnegie Endowment for International Peace, 1910): 8-20.

Landrum, Roger, Donald J. Eberly, and Michael W. Sherraden. "Calls for National Service." National Service, Social, Economic and Military Impacts. Ed. Michael W. Sherraden and Donald J. Eberly. New York: Pergamon, 1982. 21–38.

McCain, John, and Evan Bayh. "A New Start for National Service." New York Times 6 Nov. 2001: A31.

Patterson, Richard North. "Keeping Alive the Spirit of National Service." Boston Globe 1 Aug. 1999: A27.

Plato. "Crito." Classic Literature Online Library. Trans. Benjamin Jowett. 17 July 2004 <http://www.greece.com/library/plato/crito_04.html>.

Rhem, Kathleen T. "Rumsfeld: No Need for Draft." American Forces Information Service 7 Jan. 2004. 17 July 2004 <http://www.dod.gov/news/Jan2003/n01072003_200301074.html>.

Discussion

The writer of this argument synthesis on compulsory national service attempts to support a *claim*—one that favors national service but insists on keeping it voluntary—by offering *support* in the form of facts (rates of volunteerism from the Bureau of Labor Statistics) and opinions (testimony of experts). However, since the writer's claim rests on a definition of "true service," its effectiveness depends partially upon the extent to which we, as readers, agree with the *assumptions* underlying that definition. (See our discussion of assumptions in Chapter 2, pages 63–65.) An assumption (sometimes called a *warrant*) is a generalization or principle about how the world works or should work—a fundamental statement of belief about facts or values. In this particular case, the underlying assumption is that "true service" to a community must be voluntary, never required. The writer makes this assumption explicit. Though you are under no obligation to do so, stating assumptions explicitly will clarify your arguments to readers.

Assumptions often are deeply rooted in people's psyches, sometimes deriving from lifelong experiences and observations and not easily changed, even by the most logical of arguments. People who learned the spirit of volunteerism early in life, perhaps through "required" activities in religious or public school, might not accept the support offered for the claim that required service would be illogical, illegal, and "corrupted." But others might well be persuaded and might agree that programs to expand opportunities for national service should be supported, though service itself should never be compelled. A discussion of the model argument's paragraphs, along with the argument strategy for each, follows. Note that the paper devotes one paragraph to developing every section of the outline on pages 161–162. Note also that the writer avoids plagiarism by careful attribution and quotation of sources.

- **Paragraph 1:** The writer uses statistics to establish that a culture of volunteerism is alive and well in America.

  Argument strategy: In this opening paragraph, the writer sets up the general topic—volunteerism in America—and establishes that Americans volunteer in impressive numbers. The writer uses information from the Bureau of Labor Statistics, as well as the reference to volunteerism in early America, to anticipate and deflect possible criticism from those who might say: "So few of us volunteer that we should require national service in order to promote citizenship and to build character."

- **Paragraph 2:** Here the writer sets a context for and introduces the McCain/Bayh proposal to expand national service. The writer then presents the thesis.

  Argument strategy: This paragraph moves in one direction with an inspiring call to service by Senators McCain and Bayh and then takes a sharp, contrasting turn to the thesis. The first part of the thesis, "as volunteerism grows and gains public support," clearly follows from (and summarizes) the first part of paragraph 2. The transition "But" signals the contrast, which sets up the warning. A contrast generates interest by creating tension, in this case prompting readers to wonder: "Why *should* we resist compulsory service?"

- **Paragraphs 3 and 4:** In these paragraphs, the writer discusses the intellectual history of service: first, the writing of William James in the early years of the past century, and next, Plato's account of a dialogue between Socrates and a student. The writer quotes both authors at length and then discusses their relevance to the issue at the center of this essay: service to the greater community.

  Argument strategy: At this point, the writer is *preparing* to offer reasons for accepting the claim that we must resist compulsory service. The goal of paragraphs 3 and 4 is to set a deep historical context for the essay by establishing service as a significant cultural norm in America and, more broadly, by showing that the notion of obligation to the State is fundamental to civil societies. The end of paragraph 4 makes a transition to modern-day America and begins to move from the preparation for argument to argument.

- **Paragraph 5:** This paragraph opens with a question and sets up a key distinction in the essay between military and non-military service. After raising the distinction, the writer devotes the paragraph to establishing the right of the American government to draft citizens into the army. High-ranking military administrators are quoted to the effect that the all-volunteer army is a better fighting force than earlier, conscripted armies.

Argument strategy: This paragraph begins moving the reader into the argument by introducing and discussing the first part of the distinction just presented: military service. The writer establishes that compelled military service is constitutional and in keeping with the historical obligations that citizens owe the State. But even here, in a case in which the State has the clear authority to conscript people, the writer quotes military officials to the effect that voluntary service is superior to compulsory service. The reader will find this strong preference for volunteerism continued in the second part of the essay devoted to non-military service.

- **Paragraph 6:** This transitional paragraph raises the core question on which the argument hangs: Does the State have the right, as it does in military matters, to press citizens into non-military, national service? The writer answers the question in the final sentence of this paragraph and, in so doing, forecasts the discussion to follow.

    Argument strategy: Here the writer sets up the second part of the essay, where reasons for accepting the claim will be presented. Up to this point, the writer has established that (1) volunteers can build character through service, (2) citizens owe a debt to the State, and (3) the State can legally collect on that debt by drafting citizens into the army in time of war. In this transition paragraph, the writer poses the question that will take the rest of the paper to answer. The question becomes an invitation to read.

- **Paragraphs 7–9:** In each of these three paragraphs, the writer answers—in the negative—the question posed in paragraph 6. The State does *not* have the right to press citizens into national service. Paragraph 7 offers a logical reason: that military and non-military service are not equivalent. Paragraph 8 offers a legal reason: that the Constitution prohibits "involuntary servitude." Paragraph 9 offers a moral reason: that coerced or compelled service is "corrupted."

    Argument strategy: These paragraphs lay out the main reasons for accepting the claim that we should resist letting the successes of volunteerism become an argument for compulsory national service. The writer argues on multiple grounds—logical, legal, and moral—in an effort to build a strong case.

- **Paragraph 10:** Here the writer concedes a problem with the view (expressed by Chapman) in paragraph 9 that service that is either compelled or financially rewarded is corrupted. Allowing that this extreme position does not take into account the financial needs of young people, the writer endorses an alternate view, that minimal payment for service is legitimate. To support this more moderate position, the writer quotes David Gergen at length and also refers to the AmeriCorps mission statement.

    Argument strategy: With this concession, the writer backs off an extreme view. The tactic makes the writer look both reasonable and realistic just prior to arguing very firmly, in the next paragraph, against compulsory service.

- **Paragraph 11:** Here the writer endorses one of Chapman's strongly held positions: Forced service is not service at all and corrupts the spirit of volunteerism.

    Argument strategy: Here is the emotional core of the argument. The writer has previously argued that for logical (paragraph 7) and legal (paragraph 8) reasons, compulsory service must be rejected. The writer devotes three paragraphs to developing moral reasons. In paragraph 11, the writer uses an analogy for the first time: Compelling service is equivalent to compelling a child to like someone. Neither works. The value of service rests on the offering of oneself freely to those in need.

- **Paragraphs 12–13:** The writer concludes by restating the claim—in two paragraphs.

    Argument strategy: These concluding paragraphs parallel the two-part structure of the thesis: Part 1 (paragraph 12), that volunteerism has many benefits and deserves support; Part 2 (paragraph 13), that we must resist any effort to make service compulsory.

Other approaches to an argument synthesis would be possible, based on the available sources. One could agree with Bruce Chapman and adopt the extreme view against both compulsory and paid service. Such an argument would make no concessions of the sort found in paragraph 10 of the model synthesis. Another approach would be to argue that young people must be taught the value of service before they take these values on themselves, and that the best way to teach an ethic of service is to require a year or two of "compulsory volunteering." That which is required, goes the logic of this argument, eventually becomes second nature. We might make a parallel case about teaching kids to read. Kids may not enjoy practicing 30 minutes every night, but eventually they come to realize the joys and benefits of reading, which last a lifetime. Still another argument might be to focus on the extent to which Americans meet (or fail to meet) their obligations to the larger community. This would be a glass-half-full/half-empty argument, beginning with the statistic that one-quarter of Americans regularly volunteer. The half-full argument would praise current efforts and, perhaps, suggest policies for ensuring continued success. The half-empty argument would cite the statistic with alarm, claim that we have a problem of shockingly low volunteer rates, and then propose a solution. Whatever your approach to the subject, in first *critically examining* the various sources and then *synthesizing* them to support a position about which you feel strongly, you are engaging in the kind of critical thinking that is essential to success in a good deal of academic and professional work.

DEVELOPING AND ORGANIZING SUPPORT FOR YOUR ARGUMENTS

- *Summarize, paraphrase, and quote supporting evidence.* Draw upon the facts, ideas, and language in your sources.
- *Provide various types of evidence and motivational appeal.* Appeal to *logos*, *ethos*, and *pathos*. The appeal to *logos* is based on evidence from facts, statistics, and expert testimony.
- *Use climactic order.* Save the most important evidence in support of your argument for the *end* where it will have the most impact. Use the next most important evidence *first*.
- *Use logical or conventional order.* Use a form of organization appropriate to the topic, such as problem/solution; sides of a controversy; comparison/contrast; or a form of organization appropriate to the academic or professional discipline, such as a report of an experiment or a business plan.
- *Present and respond to counterarguments.* Anticipate and respond to arguments against your position.
- *Use concession.* Concede that one or more arguments against your position have some validity; re-assert, nonetheless, that your argument is the stronger one.

DEVELOPING AND ORGANIZING THE SUPPORT FOR YOUR ARGUMENTS

Experienced writers seem to have an intuitive sense of how to develop and present supporting evidence for their claims; this sense is developed through much hard work and practice. Less experienced writers wonder what to say first, and having decided on that, wonder what to say next. There is no single method of presentation. But the techniques of even the most experienced writers often boil down to a few tried and tested arrangements.

As we've seen in the model synthesis in this chapter, the key to devising effective arguments is to find and use those kinds of support that most persuasively strengthen your claim. Some writers categorize support into two broad types: *evidence* and *motivational appeals*. Evidence, in the form of facts, statistics, and expert testimony, helps make the appeal to *logos* or reason. Motivational appeals—appeals to *pathos* and *ethos*—are employed to get people to change their minds, to agree with the writer or speaker, or to decide upon a plan of activity.

Following are some of the most common principles for using and organizing support for your claims.

Summarize, Paraphrase, and Quote Supporting Evidence

In most of the papers and reports you will write in college and the professional world, evidence and motivational appeals derive from summarizing, paraphrasing, and quoting material in the sources that either have been provided to you or that you have independently researched. (See Chapter 1 on when to summarize, paraphrase, and quote material from sources.) For example, in paragraph 10 of the model argument synthesis, you will find a block quotation from David Gergen used to make the point that minimally paid volunteer programs can provide lifelong lessons. You will also find two other block quotations in the argument and a number of brief quotations woven into sentences throughout. In addition, you will find summaries and a paraphrase. In each case, the writer is careful to cite sources.

Provide Various Types of Evidence and Motivational Appeals

Keep in mind the appeals to both *logos* and *pathos*. As we've discussed, the appeal to *logos* is based on evidence that consists of a combination of *facts, statistics,* and *expert testimony*. In the model synthesis, the writer uses all of these varieties of evidence: facts (from David Gergen's article on how "[v]oluntary service . . . often changes people for life"); statistics (the incidence of volunteering in the United States); and testimony (from Eric Gorham, Bruce Chapman, David Gergen, Roger Landrum, Donald Rumsfeld, and William James). The model synthesis makes an appeal to *pathos* by engaging the reader's self-interest: Certainly if the federal government were to institute compulsory national service, the lives of readers would be touched. More explicitly, paragraph 11 makes a moral argument against compulsory service. Through analogy (compelling citizens to service is equivalent to ordering a child to like someone), the writer attempts to claim the reader's sympathy and respect for common sense. In effect, the writer says, responsible parents would never do such a thing; responsible governments shouldn't either. (Of course, readers could reject the analogy and the assumption about good parenting on which it rests. Some parents might very well push their children into friendships and believe themselves justified for doing so.)

Use Climactic Order

Climactic order is an arrangement of examples or evidence in order of anticipated impact on the reader, least to greatest. Organize by climactic order when you plan to offer a number of categories or elements of support for your claim. Recognize that some elements will be more important—and likely more persuasive—than others. The basic principle here is that you should *save the most important evidence for the end,* since whatever you have said last is what readers are likely to most remember. A secondary principle is that whatever you say first is what they are *next* most likely to remember. Therefore, when you have several reasons in support of your claim, an effective argument strategy is to present the second most important, then one or more additional reasons, and finally, the most important reason. Paragraphs 7–11 of the model synthesis do exactly this.

Use Logical or Conventional Order

Using logical or conventional order means that you use as a template a pre-established pattern or plan for arguing your case.

- One common pattern is describing or arguing a *problem/solution*. Using this pattern, you begin with an introduction in which you typically define the problem, then perhaps explain its origins, then offer one or more solutions, then conclude.

- Another common pattern is presenting *two sides of a controversy*. Using this pattern, you introduce the controversy and (if an argument synthesis) your own point of view or claim, then explain the other side's arguments, providing reasons why your point of view should prevail.

- A third common pattern is *comparison-contrast*. In fact, this pattern is so important that we will discuss it separately in the next section.

- The order in which you present elements of an argument is sometimes dictated by the conventions of the discipline in which you are writing. For example, lab reports and experiments in the sciences and social sciences often follow this pattern: *Opening* or *Introduction, Methods and Materials* [of the experiment or study], *Results, Discussion*. Legal arguments often follow the so-called IRAC format: *Issue, Rule, Application, Conclusion*.

Present and Respond to Counterarguments

When developing arguments on a controversial topic, you can effectively use *counterargument* to help support your claims. When you use counterargument, you present an argument *against* your claim, but then show that this argument is weak or flawed. The advantage of this technique is that you demonstrate that you are aware of the other side of the argument and that you are prepared to answer it.

Here is how a counterargument typically is developed:

   I. Introduction and claim
   II. Main opposing argument
   III. Refutation of opposing argument
   IV. Main positive argument

Use Concession

Concession is a variation of counterargument. As in counterargument, you present the opposing (or otherwise objectionable) viewpoint, but instead of demolishing that argument, you *concede* that it does have some validity and even some appeal, although your own argument is the stronger one. This concession bolsters your own standing—your own *ethos*—as a fair-minded person who is not blind to the virtues of the other side. See paragraphs 9 and 10 of the model synthesis for one version of the concession argument. You'll find that instead of making an opposing argument, the writer produces a supporting argument but views one part of it as flawed. The writer rejects that section (the extreme position that *any* form of compensation corrupts the spirit of volunteerism) and endorses the remaining sections. In terms of overall argument strategy, the result—the reader sees the writer as being reasonable—is the same as it would be if the writer had used the more standard concession in which an opposing argument is viewed as having some merit. Here is an outline for a more typical concession argument:

I. Introduction and claim

II. Important opposing argument

III. Concession that this argument has some validity

IV. Positive argument(s)

Sometimes, when you are developing a counterargument or concession argument, you may become convinced of the validity of the opposing point of view and change your own views. Don't be afraid of this happening. Writing is a tool for learning. To change your mind because of new evidence is a sign of flexibility and maturity, and your writing can only be the better for it.

Avoid Common Fallacies in Developing and Using Support

In Chapter 2, in the section on Critical Reading, we considered some of the criteria that, as a reader, you may use for evaluating informative and persuasive writing (see pages 56–61). We discussed how you can assess the accuracy, the significance, and the author's interpretation of the information presented. We also considered the importance in good argument of clearly defined key terms and the pitfalls of emotionally loaded language. Finally, we saw how to recognize such logical fallacies as either/or reasoning, faulty cause-and-effect reasoning, hasty generalization, and false analogy. As a writer, no less than as a critical reader, be aware of these common problems and try to avoid them.

Be aware, also, of your responsibility to cite source materials appropriately. When you quote a source, double- and triple-check that you have done so accurately. When you summarize or paraphrase, take care to use your own language and sentence structures (though you can, of course, also quote within these forms). When you refer to someone else's idea—even if you are not quoting, summarizing, or paraphrasing—give the source credit. By maintaining an ethical stance with regard to the use of sources, you take your place in and perpetuate the highest traditions of the academic community.

EXERCISE **5.5**

Practicing Arguments

Read the articles in Chapter 7 on legacy admissions in the college application process. To practice your skills in writing arguments, you will argue for or against the practice of giving sons and daughters of alumni an advantage in the college application process; or you will argue that the practice should or should not be made public. Chapter 7 provides a series of sequenced assignments that will help to prepare you for writing your argument. As you read the selections on pages 217–235, you will need to decide what types of evidence—facts, statistics, and expert opinions—would best support your claim. What motivational appeals would be appropriate? Which counterarguments would you address, and how would you address them? Finally, what concessions would you make (if any)?

THE COMPARISON-AND-CONTRAST SYNTHESIS

A particularly important type of argument synthesis is built on patterns of comparison and contrast. Techniques of comparison and contrast enable you to examine two subjects (or sources) in terms of one another. When you compare, you consider *similarities*. When you contrast, you consider *differences*. By comparing and contrasting, you perform a multifaceted analysis that often suggests subtleties that otherwise might not have come to your (or your reader's) attention.

To organize a comparison-and-contrast argument, you must carefully read sources in order to discover *significant criteria for analysis*. A *criterion* is a specific point to which both of your authors refer and about which they may agree or disagree. (For example, in a comparative report on compact cars, criteria for *comparison and contrast* might be road handling, fuel economy, and comfort of ride.) The best criteria are those that allow you not only to account for obvious similarities and differences—those concerning the main aspects of your sources or subjects—but also to plumb deeper, exploring subtle yet significant comparisons and contrasts among details or subcomponents, which you can then relate to your overall thesis.

Note that comparison-contrast is frequently not an end in itself, but serves some larger purpose. Thus, a comparison-contrast synthesis may be a component of a longer paper that is essentially a critique, an explanatory synthesis, an argument synthesis, or an analysis.

Organizing Comparison-and-Contrast Syntheses

Two basic approaches to organizing a comparison-and-contrast synthesis are available: organization by *source* and organization by *criteria*.

Organizing by Source or Subject

You can organize a comparative synthesis by first summarizing each of your sources or subjects, and then discussing significant similarities and differences between them. Having read the summaries and become familiar with the distinguishing features of each source, your readers will most likely be able to appreciate the more obvious similarities and differences. In the discussion, your task is to focus on both the obvious and subtle comparisons and contrasts, focusing on the most significant—that is, on those that most clearly support your thesis.

Organization by source or subject is best saved for passages that can be briefly summarized. If the summary of your source or subject becomes too long, your readers might forget the points you made in the first summary as they are reading the second. A comparison-and-contrast synthesis organized by source or subject might proceed like this:

I. Introduce the paper; lead to thesis.

II. Summarize source/subject A by discussing its significant features.

III. Summarize source/subject B by discussing its significant features.

IV. Write a paragraph (or two) in which you discuss the significant points of comparison and contrast between sources or subjects A and B. Alternatively, begin comparison-contrast in Section III upon introducing source or subject B.

End with a conclusion in which you summarize your points and, perhaps, raise and respond to pertinent questions.

Organizing by Criteria

Instead of summarizing entire sources one at a time with the intention of comparing them later, you could discuss two sources simultaneously, examining the views of each author point by point (criterion by criterion), comparing and contrasting these views in the process. The criterion approach is best used when you have a number of points to discuss or when passages or subjects are long and/or complex. A comparison-and-contrast synthesis organized by criteria might look like this:

I. Introduce the paper; lead to thesis.

II. Criterion 1

A. Discuss what author #1 says about this point. Or present situation #1 in light of this point.

B. Discuss what author #2 says about this point, comparing and contrasting #2's treatment of the point with #1's. Or present situation #2 in light of this point and explain its differences from situation #1.

III. Criterion 2

A. Discuss what author #1 says about this point. Or present situation #1 in light of this point.

B. Discuss what author #2 says about this point, comparing and contrasting #2's treatment of the point with #1's. Or present situation #2 in light of this point and explain its differences from situation #1.

And so on. Proceed criterion by criterion until you have completed your discussion. Be sure to arrange criteria with a clear method; knowing how the discussion of one criterion leads to the next will ensure smooth transitions throughout your paper. End by summarizing your key points and, perhaps, raising and responding to pertinent questions.

However you organize your comparison-and-contrast synthesis, keep in mind that comparing and contrasting are not ends in themselves. Your discussion should point somewhere: to a conclusion, an answer to "So what—why bother to compare and contrast in the first place?" If your discussion is part of a larger synthesis, point to and support the larger claim. If you write a stand-alone comparison-and-contrast, though, you must by the final paragraph answer the "Why bother?" question. The model comparison-and-contrast synthesis that follows does exactly this.

EXERCISE 5.6

Comparing and Contrasting

Refer back to two of the readings on the compulsory national service controversy: Bruce Chapman's "Politics and National Service: A Virus Attacks the Volunteer Sector" (page 157) and Senators McCain and Bayh's "A New Start For National Service" (page 154). Identify at least two significant criteria that you can use for a comparative analysis—two specific points to which both readings refer and about which they agree or disagree. Then imagine you are preparing to write a short comparison-and-contrast paper and devise two outlines: the first organized by source, and the second organized by criteria.

A Case for Comparison-Contrast: World War I and World War II

We'll see how these principles can be applied to a response to a final examination question in a course on modern history. Imagine that having attended classes involving lecture and discussion, and having read excerpts from such texts as John Keegan's *The First World War* and Tony Judt's *Postwar: A History of Europe Since 1945*, students were presented with the following examination question:

Based on your reading to date, compare and contrast the two World Wars in light of any four or five criteria you think significant. Once you have called careful attention to both similarities and differences, conclude with an observation. What have you learned? What can your comparative analysis teach us?

Comparison-Contrast (Organized by Criteria)

Here is a plan for a response, essentially a comparison-contrast synthesis, organized by *criteria*. The thesis—and the *claim*—follows:

> <u>Thesis</u>: In terms of the impact on cities and civil-
> ian populations, the military aspects of the two
> wars in Europe, and their aftermaths, the differ-
> ences between World War I and World War II consider-
> ably outweigh the similarities.
>
>   I. Introduction. World Wars I and II were the
>   most devastating conflicts in history. <u>Thesis</u>
>   II. Summary of main similarities: causes, coun-
>   tries involved, battlegrounds, global scope.
> III. First major difference: Physical impact of
>   war.
>   A. WWI was fought mainly in rural
>   battlegrounds.
>   B. In WWII cities were destroyed.
>   IV. Second major difference: Effect on civilians.
>   A. WWI fighting primarily involved soldiers.
>   B. WWII involved not only military but also
>   massive non-combatant casualties: civilian
>   populations were displaced, forced into
>   slave labor, and exterminated.
>   V. Third major difference: Combat operations.
>   A. World War I, in its long middle phase, was
>   characterized by trench warfare.
>   B. During the middle phase of World War II,
>   there was no major military action in
>   Nazi-occupied Western Europe.
> VI. Fourth major difference: Aftermath.
>   A. Harsh war terms imposed on defeated
>   Germany contributed significantly to the
>   rise of Hitler and World War II.
>   B. Victorious allies helped rebuild West
>   Germany after World War II, but allowed
>   Soviets to take over Eastern Europe.
> VII. Conclusion. Since the end of World War II,
>   wars have been far smaller in scope and
>   destructiveness, and warfare has expanded to
>   involve stateless combatants committed to
>   acts of terror.

Following is a comparison-contrast synthesis by criteria, written according to the preceding plan. (Thesis and topic sentences are highlighted.)

MODEL EXAM RESPONSE
(Thesis and topic sentences are highlighted.)

1   World War I (1914-18) and World War II (1939-45) were the most catastrophic and destructive conflicts in human history. For those who believed in the steady but inevitable progress of civilization, it was impossible to imagine that two wars in the first half of the twentieth century could reach levels of barbarity and horror that would outstrip those of any previous era. Historians estimate that more than 22 million people, soldiers and civilians, died in World War I; they estimate that between 40 and 50 million died in World War II. In many ways, these two conflicts were similar: they were fought on many of the same European and Russian battlegrounds, with more or less the same countries on opposing sides. Even many of the same people were involved: Winston Churchill and Adolf Hitler figured in both wars. And the main outcome in each case was the same: total defeat for Germany. However, in terms of the impact on cities and civilian populations, the military aspects of the two wars in Europe, and their aftermaths, the differences between World Wars I and II considerably outweigh the similarities.

2   The similarities are clear enough. In fact, many historians regard World War II as a continuation--after an intermission of about twenty years--of World War I. One of the main causes of each war was Germany's dissatisfaction and frustration with what it perceived as its diminished place in the world. Hitler launched World War II partly out of revenge for Germany's humiliating defeat in World War I. In each conflict Germany and its allies (the Central Powers in WWI, the Axis in WWII) went to war against France, Great Britain, Russia (the Soviet Union in WWII), and eventually, the United States. Though neither conflict literally included the entire world, the participation of countries not only in Europe, but also in the Middle East, the Far East, and the Western hemisphere made both of these conflicts global in scope. And as indicated earlier, the number

of casualties in each war was unprecedented in history, partly because modern technology had enabled the creation of deadlier weapons--including tanks, heavy artillery, and aircraft--than had ever been used in warfare.

3   Despite these similarities, the differences between the two world wars are considerably more significant. One of the most noticeable differences was the physical impact of each war in Europe and Russia --the western and eastern fronts. The physical destruc-tion of World War I was confined largely to the battlefield. The combat took place almost entirely in the rural areas of Europe and Russia. No major cities were destroyed in the first war; cathedrals, museums, government buildings, urban houses and apartments were left untouched. During the second war, in contrast, almost no city or town of any size emerged unscathed. Rotterdam, Warsaw, London, Minsk, and--when the Allies began their counterattack-- almost every major city in Germany and Japan, including Berlin and Tokyo, were flattened. Of course, the physical devastation of the cities created millions of refugees, a phenomenon never experienced in World War I.

4   The fact that World War II was fought in the cities as well as on the battlefields meant that the second war had a much greater impact on civilians than did the first war. With few exceptions, the civilians in Europe during WWI were not driven from their homes, forced into slave labor, starved, tortured, or systematically exterminated. But all of these crimes happened routinely during WWII. The Nazi occupation of Europe meant that the civilian population of France, Belgium, Norway, the Netherlands and other conquered lands, along with the industries, railroads, and farms of these countries, were put into the service of the Third Reich. Millions of people from conquered Europe--those who were not sent directly to the death camps--were forcibly transported to Germany and put to work in support of the war effort.

5   During both wars, the Germans were fighting on two fronts--the western front in Europe and the eastern front in Russia. But while both wars were characterized by intense military activity during their initial and final phases, the middle and longest phases--at least in Europe--differed considerably. The middle phase of the First World War was charac-

terized by trench warfare, a relatively static form of military activity in which fronts seldom moved, or moved only a few hundred yards at a time, even after major battles. By contrast, in the years between the German conquest of most of Europe by early 1941 and the Allied invasion of Normandy in mid-1944, there was no major fighting in Nazi-occupied Western Europe. (The land battles then shifted to North Africa and the Soviet Union.)

6   And of course, the two world wars differed in their aftermaths. The most significant consequence of World War I was that the humiliating and costly war reparations imposed on the defeated Germany by the terms of the 1919 Treaty of Versailles made possible the rise of Hitler and thus led directly to World War II. In contrast, after the end of the Second World War in 1945, the Allies helped rebuild West Germany (the portion of a divided Germany which it controlled), transformed the new country into a democracy, and helped make it into one of the most thriving economies of the world. But perhaps the most significant difference in the aftermath of each war involved Russia. That country, in a considerably weakened state, pulled out of World War I a year before hostilities ended so that it could consolidate its 1917 Revolution. Russia then withdrew into itself and took no significant part in European affairs until the Nazi invasion of the Soviet Union in 1941. In contrast, it was the Red Army in World War II that was most responsible for the crushing defeat of Germany. In recognition of its efforts and of its enormous sacrifices, the Allies allowed the Soviet Union to take control of the countries of Eastern Europe after the war, leading to fifty years of totalitarian rule --and the Cold War.

7   While the two world wars that devastated much of Europe were similar in that, at least according to some historians, they were the same war interrupted by two decades, and similar in that combatants killed more efficiently than armies throughout history ever had, the differences between the wars were significant. In terms of the physical impact of the fighting, the impact on civilians, the action on the battlefield at mid-war, and the aftermaths, World Wars I and II differed in ways that matter to us decades later. Recently, the wars in Iraq, Afghanistan, and Bosnia have involved an alliance of nations pitted against single nations; but we have

not seen, since the two world wars, grand alliances
moving vast armies across continents. The destruction
implied by such action is almost unthinkable today.
Warfare is changing, and "stateless" combatants like
Hamas and Al Qaeda wreak destruction of their own.
But we may never see, one hopes, the devastation that
follows when multiple nations on opposing sides of a
conflict throw millions of soldiers--and civilians--
into harm's way.

Discussion

The general strategy of this argument is an organization by *criteria*. The writer argues that although the two world wars of the first part of the twentieth century evinced some similarities, the differences between the two conflicts were more significant. Note that the writer's thesis doesn't merely establish these significant differences; it enumerates them in a way that anticipates both the content and the structure of the response to follow.

In argument terms, the *claim* the writer makes is the conclusion that the two global conflicts were significantly different, if superficially similar. The *assumption* is that careful attention to the impact of the wars upon cities and civilian populations and to the consequences of the Allied victories are keys to understanding the differences between them. The *support* comes in the form of particular historical facts regarding the level of casualties, the scope of destruction, the theaters of conflict, the events following the conclusions of the wars, and so on.

- **Paragraph 1:** The writer begins by commenting on the unprecedented level of destruction of World Wars I and II and concludes with the thesis summarizing the key similarities and differences.
- **Paragraph 2:** The writer summarizes the key similarities in the two wars: the wars' causes, their combatants, their global scope, the level of destructiveness made possible by modern weaponry.
- **Paragraph 3:** The writer discusses the first of the key differences: the fact that the battlegrounds of World War I were largely rural, but in World War II cities were targeted and destroyed.
- **Paragraph 4:** The writer discusses the second of the key differences: the impact on civilians. In World War I, civilians were generally spared from the direct effects of combat; in World War II, civilians were targeted by the Nazis for systematic displacement and destruction.
- **Paragraph 5:** The writer discusses the third key difference: Combat operations during the middle phase of World War I were characterized by static trench warfare. During World War II, in contrast, there

were no major combat operations in Nazi-occupied Western Europe during the middle phase of the conflict.

- **Paragraph 6:** The writer focuses on the fourth key difference: the aftermath of the two wars. After World War I, the victors imposed harsh conditions on defeated Germany, leading to the rise of Hitler and the Second World War. After World War II, the Allies helped Germany rebuild and thrive. However, the Soviet victory in 1945 led to its postwar domination of Eastern Europe.

- **Paragraph 7:** In the conclusion, the writer sums up the key similarities and differences just covered, but makes some additional comments about the course of more recent wars since World War II. In this way, the writer responds to the question posed in the latter part of the assignment: "What have you learned? What can your comparative analysis teach us?"

SUMMARY OF SYNTHESIS CHAPTERS

In this chapter and Chapter 4 preceding it, we've considered three main types of synthesis: the *explanatory synthesis*, the *argument synthesis*, and the *comparison-contrast synthesis*. Although for ease of comprehension we've placed them into separate categories, these types are not, of course, mutually exclusive. Both explanatory syntheses and argument syntheses often involve elements of one another, and comparison-contrast syntheses can fall into either of the previous categories. Which approach you choose will depend upon your *purpose* and the method that you decide is best suited to achieve this purpose.

If your main purpose is to help your audience understand a particular subject, and in particular to help them understand the essential elements or significance of this subject, then you will be composing an explanatory synthesis. If your main purpose, on the other hand, is to persuade your audience to agree with your viewpoint on a subject, or to change their minds, or to decide upon a particular course of action, then you will be composing an argument synthesis. If one effective technique of making your case is to establish similarities or differences between your subject and another one, then you will compose a comparison-contrast synthesis—which may well be just *part* of a larger synthesis.

In planning and drafting these syntheses, you can draw on a variety of strategies: supporting your claims by summarizing, paraphrasing, and quoting from your sources; using appeals to *logos*, *pathos*, and *ethos*; and choosing from among strategies such as climactic or conventional order, counterargument, and concession that will best help you to achieve your purpose.

The strategies of synthesis you've practiced in these last two chapters form the basis of your work in that category of synthesis commonly known as the research paper. The research paper involves all of the skills in summary, critique, and synthesis that we've discussed so far, the main difference being, of course, that you'll have to find your own sources.

We turn, now, to analysis, which is another important strategy for academic thinking and writing. Chapter 6, on Analysis, will introduce you to a strategy that, like synthesis, draws upon all the strategies you've been practicing as you move through *Writing and Reading Across the Curriculum*.

WRITING ASSIGNMENT: THE "LEGACY" QUESTION IN COLLEGE ADMISSIONS

Now we'll give you an opportunity to practice your skills in planning and writing an argument synthesis. See Chapter 7, pages 217–235, where we provide nine sources on the controversial issue of "legacy" status in the college admissions process. At certain schools, the admissions staff gives preferential consideration to the sons and daughters of alumni. Should they? In the synthesis, you will take a stand in response to this question and then defend your response to readers.

6 Analysis

WHAT IS AN ANALYSIS?

An *analysis* is an argument in which you study the parts of something to understand how it works, what it means, or why it might be significant. The writer of an analysis uses an analytical tool: a *principle* or *definition* on the basis of which an object, an event, or a behavior can be divided into parts and examined. Here are excerpts from two analyses of L. Frank Baum's *The Wizard of Oz:*

> At the dawn of adolescence, the very time she should start to distance herself from Aunt Em and Uncle Henry, the surrogate parents who raised her on their Kansas farm, Dorothy Gale experiences a hurtful reawakening of her fear that these loved ones will be rudely ripped from her, especially her Aunt (Em—M for Mother!).[Harvey Greenberg, *The Movies on Your Mind* (New York: Dutton, 1975).]

> [*The Wizard of Oz*] was originally written as a political allegory about grassroots protest. It may seem harder to believe than Emerald City, but the Tin Woodsman is the industrial worker, the Scarecrow [is] the struggling farmer, and the Wizard is the president, who is powerful only as long as he succeeds in deceiving the people.[Peter Dreier, "Oz Was Almost Reality," *Cleveland Plain Dealer* 3 Sept. 1989.]

As these paragraphs suggest, what you discover through an analysis depends entirely on the principle or definition you use to make your insights. Is *The Wizard of Oz* the story of a girl's psychological development, or is it a story about politics? The answer is *both*. In the first example, psychiatrist Harvey Greenberg applies the principles of his profession and, not surprisingly, sees *The Wizard of Oz* in psychological terms. In the second example, a newspaper reporter applies the political theories of Karl Marx and, again not surprisingly, discovers a story about politics.

Different as they are, these analyses share an important quality: Each is the result of a specific principle or definition used as a tool to divide an object into parts to see what it means and how it works. The writer's choice of analytical tool simultaneously creates and limits the possibilities for analysis. Thus, working with the principles of Freud, Harvey Greenberg sees *The Wizard of Oz* in psychological, not political, terms; working with the theories of Karl Marx, Peter Dreier understands the movie in terms of the economic relationships among characters. It's as if the writer of an analysis who adopts one analytical tool puts on a pair of glasses and sees an object in a specific way. Another writer, using a different tool (and a different pair of glasses), sees the object differently.

WHERE DO WE FIND WRITTEN ANALYSES?

Here are just a few types of writing that involve analysis:

Academic Writing

- **Experimental and lab reports.** Analyze the meaning or implications of the study results in the Discussion section.
- **Research papers.** Analyze information in sources; apply theories to material being reported.
- **Process analysis.** Break down the steps or stages involved in completing a process.
- **Literary analysis.** Analyze characterization, plot, imagery, or other elements in works of literature.
- **Essay exams.** Demonstrate understanding of course material by analyzing data using course concepts.

Workplace Writing

- **Grant proposals.** Analyze the issues you seek funding for in order to address them.
- **Reviews of the arts.** Employ dramatic or literary analysis to assess artistic works.
- **Business plans.** Break down and analyze capital outlays, expenditures, profits, materials, and the like.
- **Medical charts.** Perform analytical thinking and writing in relation to patient symptoms and possible options.
- **Legal briefs.** Break down and analyze facts of cases and elements of legal precedents; apply legal rulings and precedents to new situations.
- **Case studies.** Describe and analyze the particulars of a specific medical, social service, advertising, or business case.

You might protest: Are there as many analyses of *The Wizard of Oz* as there are people to read it? Yes, or at least as many analyses as there are analytical tools. This does not mean that all analyses are equally valid or useful. The writer must convince the reader. In creating an essay of analysis, the writer must organize a series of related insights, using the analytical tool to examine first one part and then another of the object being studied. To read Harvey Greenberg's essay on *The Wizard of Oz* is to find paragraph after paragraph of related insights—first about Aunt Em, then the Wicked Witch, then Toto, and then the Wizard. All these insights point to Greenberg's single conclusion: that "Dorothy's 'trip' is a marvelous metaphor for the psychological journey every adolescent must make." Without Greenberg's analysis, we probably would not have thought about the movie as a psychological journey. This is precisely the power of an analysis: its ability to reveal objects or events in ways we would not otherwise have considered.

The writer's challenge is to convince readers that (1) the analytical tool being applied is legitimate and well matched to the object being studied; and (2) the analytical tool is being used systematically to divide the object into parts and to make a coherent, meaningful statement about these parts and the object as a whole.

DEMONSTRATION: ANALYSIS

Two examples of analyses follow. The first was written by a professional writer. The second was written by a student, in response to an assignment in his sociology class. Each analysis illustrates the two defining features of analysis just discussed: a statement of an analytical principle or definition, and the use of that principle or definition in closely examining an object, behavior, or event. As you read, try to identify these features. An exercise with questions for discussion follows each example.

The Plug-In Drug
Marie Winn

The following analysis of television viewing as an addictive behavior appeared originally in Marie Winn's 2002 book, The Plug-In Drug: Television, Computers, and Family Life. *A writer and media critic, Winn has been interested in the effect of television on both individuals and the larger culture. In this passage, she carefully defines the term* addiction *and then applies it systematically to the behavior under study.*

1   The word "addiction" is often used loosely and wryly in conversation. People will refer to themselves as "mystery-book addicts" or "cookie addicts." E. B. White wrote of his annual surge of interest in gardening: "We are hooked and are making an attempt to kick the habit." Yet nobody really believes that reading mysteries or ordering seeds by catalogue is serious enough to be compared with addictions to heroin or alcohol. In these cases the word "addiction" is used jokingly to denote a tendency to overindulge in some pleasurable activity.

2   People often refer to being "hooked on TV." Does this, too, fall into the lighthearted category of cookie eating and other pleasures that people pursue with unusual intensity? Or is there a kind of television viewing that falls into the more serious category of destructive addiction?

3   Not unlike drugs or alcohol, the television experience allows the participant to blot out the real world and enter into a pleasurable and passive mental state. To be sure, other experiences, notably reading, also provide a temporary respite from reality. But it's much easier to stop reading and return to reality than to

stop watching television. The entry into another world offered by reading includes an easily accessible return ticket. The entry via television does not. In this way television viewing, for those vulnerable to addiction, is more like drinking or taking drugs—once you start it's hard to stop.

4   Just as alcoholics are only vaguely aware of their addiction, feeling that they control their drinking more than they really do ("I can cut it out any time I want—I just like to have three or four drinks before dinner"), many people over-estimate their control over television watching. Even as they put off other activ-ities to spend hour after hour watching television, they feel they could easily resume living in a different, less passive style. But somehow or other while the television set is present in their homes, it just stays on. With television's easy gratifications available, those other activities seem to take too much effort.

5   A heavy viewer (a college English instructor) observes:

> I find television almost irresistible. When the set is on, I cannot ignore it.
> I can't turn it off. I feel sapped, will-less, enervated. As I reach out to turn
> off the set, the strength goes out of my arms. So I sit there for hours and
> hours.

6   Self-confessed television addicts often feel they "ought" to do other things—but the fact that they don't read and don't plant their garden or sew or crochet or play games or have conversations means that those activities are no longer as desirable as television viewing. In a way, the lives of heavy viewers are as unbal-anced by their television "habit" as drug addicts' or alcoholics' lives. They are living in a holding pattern, as it were, passing up the activities that lead to growth or development or a sense of accomplishment. This is one reason people talk about their television viewing so ruefully, so apologetically. They are aware that it is an unproductive experience, that by any human measure almost any other endeavor is more worthwhile.

7   It is the adverse effect of television viewing on the lives of so many people that makes it feel like a serious addiction. The television habit distorts the sense of time. It renders other experiences vague and curiously unreal while taking on a greater reality for itself. It weakens relationships by reducing and sometimes eliminating normal opportunities for talking, for communicating.

8   And yet television does not satisfy, else why would the viewer continue to watch hour after hour, day after day? "The measure of health," wrote the psy-chiatrist Lawrence Kubie, "is flexibility . . . and especially the freedom to cease when sated." But heavy television viewers can never be sated with their tele-vision experiences. These do not provide the true nourishment that satiation requires, and thus they find that they cannot stop watching.

EXERCISE 6.1

Reading Critically: Winn

In analyses, an author first presents the analytical principle in full and then systematically applies parts of the principle to the object or phenomenon under study. In her brief analysis of television viewing, Marie Winn pursues an alternate, though equally effective, strategy by *distributing* parts of her analytical principle across the essay. Locate where Winn defines key elements of addiction. Locate where she uses each element as an analytical lens to examine television viewing as a form of addiction.

What function does paragraph 4 play in the analysis?

In the first two paragraphs, how does Winn create a funnel-like effect that draws readers into the heart of her analysis?

Recall a few television programs that genuinely moved you, educated you, humored you, or stirred you to worthwhile reflection or action. To what extent does Winn's analysis describe your positive experiences as a television viewer? (Consider how Winn might argue that from within an addicted state, a person may feel "humored, moved or educated" but is in fact—from a sober outsider's point of view—deluded.) If Winn's analysis of television viewing as an addiction does *not* account for your experience, does it follow that her analysis is flawed? Explain.

Edward Peselman wrote the following paper as a first-semester sophomore, in response to the following assignment from his sociology professor:

> Read Chapter 3, "The Paradoxes of Power," in Randall Collins's Sociological Insight: An Introduction to Non-Obvious Sociology *(2nd ed., 1992).* Use any of Collins's observations to examine the sociology of power in a group with which you are familiar. Write for readers much like yourself: freshmen or sophomores who have taken one course in sociology. Your object in this paper is to use Collins as a way of learning something "nonobvious" about a group to which you belong or have belonged.

Note: The citations are in APA format. (See pages 846–847.)

MODEL ANALYSIS

Coming Apart 1

The Coming Apart of a Dorm Society
Edward Peselman
Sociology of Everyday Life
Murray State University
Murray, Kentucky
23 March 2007

Center information horizontally and vertically on the page.

The Coming Apart of a Dorm Society

1 During my first year of college, I lived in a dormitory, like most freshmen on campus. We inhabitants of
the dorm came from different cultural and economic
backgrounds. Not surprisingly, we brought with us
many of the traits found in people outside of college. Like many on the outside, we in the dorm sought
personal power at the expense of others. The gaining
and maintaining of power can be an ugly business, and
I saw people hurt and in turn hurt others all for the
sake of securing a place in the dorm's prized social
order. Not until one of us challenged that order did
I realize how fragile it was.

2   Randall Collins, a sociologist at the University
of California, Riverside, defines the exercise of
power as the attempt "to make something happen in
society" (1992, p. 61). A society can be understood
as something as large and complex as "American society"; something more sharply defined—such as a corporate or organizational society; or something smaller
still—a dorm society like my own, consisting of six
18-year-old men who lived at one end of a dormitory
floor in an all male dorm.

3   In my freshman year, my society was a tiny but
distinctive social group in which people exercised
power. I lived with two roommates, Dozer and Reggie.
Dozer was an emotionally unstable, excitable individual who vented his energy through anger. His insecurity and moodiness contributed to his difficulty in
making friends. Reggie was a friendly, happy-go-lucky
sort who seldom displayed emotions other than con-
tentedness. He was shy when encountering new people,
but when placed in a socially comfortable situation
he would talk for hours.

4   Eric and Marc lived across the hall from us and
therefore spent a considerable amount of time in our
room. Eric could be cynical and was often blunt: He
seldom hesitated when sharing his frank and sometimes
unflattering opinions. He commanded a grudging
respect in the dorm. Marc could be very moody and,
sometimes, was violent. His temper and stubborn
streak made him particularly susceptible to conflict.
The final member of our miniature society was
Benjamin, cheerful yet insecure. Benjamin had certain

characteristics which many considered effeminate, and
he was often teased about his sexuality—which in turn
made him insecure. He was naturally friendly but,
because of the abuse he took, he largely kept to him
self. He would join us occasionally for a pizza or
late-night television.

5   Together, we formed an independent social structure. Going out to parties together, playing cards,
watching television, playing ball: These were the
activities through which we got to know each other
and through which we established the basic pecking
order of our community. Much like a colony of
baboons, we established a hierarchy based on power
relationships. According to Collins, what a powerful
person wishes to happen must be achieved by controlling others. Collins's observation can help to define
who had how much power in our social group. In the
dorm, Marc and Eric clearly had the most power.
Everyone feared them and agreed to do pretty much
what they wanted. Through violent words or threats of
violence, they got their way. I was next in line: I
wouldn't dare to manipulate Marc or Eric, but the
others I could manage through occasional quips.
Reggie, then Dozer, and finally Benjamin.

6   Up and down the pecking order, we exercised control
through macho taunts and challenges. Collins writes
that "individuals who manage to be powerful and get
their own way must do so by going along with the laws
of social organization, not by contradicting them" (p.
61). Until mid-year, our dorm motto could have read:
"You win through rudeness and intimidation." Eric
gained power with his frequent and brutal assessments
of everyone's behavior. Marc gained power with his
temper—which, when lost, made everyone run for cover.
Those who were not rude and intimidating drifted to the
bottom of our social world. Reggie was quiet and unemo-
tional, which allowed us to take advantage of him
because we knew he would back down if pressed in an
argument. Yet Reggie understood that on a "power scale"
he stood above Dozer and often shared in the group's
tactics to get Dozer's food (his parents were forever
sending him care packages). Dozer, in turn, seldom
missed opportunities to take swipes at Benjamin, with
references to his sexuality. From the very first week
of school, Benjamin could never—and never wanted to—
compete against Eric's bluntness or Marc's temper.

Coming Apart 4

Still, Benjamin hung out with us. He lived in our corner of the dorm, and he wanted to be friendly. But everyone, including Benjamin, understood that he occupied the lowest spot in the order.

7   That is, until he left mid-semester. According to Collins, "any social arrangement works because people avoid questioning it most of the time" (p. 74). The inverse of this principle is as follows: When a social arrangement is questioned, that arrangement can fall apart. The more fragile the arrangement (the flimsier the values on which it is based), the more quickly it will crumble. For the entire first semester, no one questioned our rude, macho rules and because of them we pigeon-holed Benjamin as a wimp. In our dorm society, gentle men had no power. To say the least, ours was not a compassionate community. From a distance of one year, I am shocked to have been a member of it. Nonetheless, we had created a mini-society that somehow served our needs.

8   At the beginning of the second semester, we found Benjamin packing up his room. Marc, who was walking down the hall, stopped by and said something like: "Hey buddy, the kitchen get too hot for you?" I was there, and I saw Benjamin turn around and say: "Do you practice at being such a _____, or does it come naturally? I've never met anybody who felt so good about making other people feel lousy. You'd better get yourself a job in the army or in the prison system, because no one else is going to put up with your _____." Marc said something in a raised voice. I stepped between them, and Benjamin said: "Get out." I was cheering.

9   Benjamin moved into an off-campus apartment with his girlfriend. This astonished us, first because of his effeminate manner (we didn't know he had a girl-friend) and second because none of the rest of us had been seeing girls much (though we talked about it constantly). Here was Benjamin, the gentlest among us, and he blew a hole in our macho society. Our social order never really recovered, which suggests its flimsy values. People in the dorm mostly went their own ways during the second semester. I'm not surprised, and I was more than a little grateful. Like most people in the dorm, save for Eric and Marc, I both got my lumps and I gave them, and I never felt good about either. Like Benjamin, I wanted to fit in with my new social

surroundings. Unlike him, I didn't have the courage to challenge the unfairness of what I saw.

10   By chance, six of us were thrown together into a dorm and were expected, on the basis of proximity alone, to develop a friendship. What we did was sink to the lowest possible denominator. Lacking any real basis for friendship, we allowed the forceful, macho personalities of Marc and Eric to set the rules, which for one semester we all subscribed to—even those who suffered.

11   The macho rudeness couldn't last, and I'm glad it was Benjamin who brought us down. By leaving, he showed a different and a superior kind of power. I doubt he was reading Randall Collins at the time, but he somehow had come to Collins's same insight: As long as he played by the rules of our group, he suffered because those rules placed him far down in the dorm's pecking order. Even by participating in pleasant activities, like going out for pizza, Benjamin supported a social system that ridiculed him. Some systems are so oppressive and small minded that they can't be changed from the inside. They've got to be torn down. Benjamin had to move, and in moving he made me (at least) question the basis of my dorm friendships.

[new page]

Reference

Collins, R. (1992). *Sociological insight: An introduction to non-obvious sociology* (2nd ed.). New York: Oxford University Press.

EXERCISE 6.2

Reading Critically: Peselman

What is the function of paragraph 1? Though Peselman does not use the word *sociology,* what signals does he give that this will be a paper that examines the social interactions of a group? Peselman introduces Collins in paragraph 2. Why? What does Peselman accomplish in paragraphs 3–4? How does his use of Collins in paragraph 5 logically follow the presentation in paragraphs 3–4?

> The actual analysis in this paper takes place in paragraphs 5–11. Point to where Peselman draws on the work of Randall Collins, and explain how he uses Collins to gain insight into dorm life.

HOW TO WRITE ANALYSES

Consider Your Purpose

Whether you are assigned a topic to write on or are left to your own devices, you inevitably face this question: What is my idea? Like every paper, an analysis has at its heart an idea you want to convey. For Edward Peselman, it was the idea that a social order based on flimsy values is not strong enough to sustain a direct challenge to its power, and thus will fall apart eventually. From beginning to end, Peselman advances this one idea: first, by introducing readers to the dorm society he will analyze; next, by introducing principles of analysis (from Randall Collins); and finally, by examining his dorm relationships in light of these principles. The entire set of analytical insights coheres as a paper because the insights are *related* and point to Peselman's single idea.

Peselman's paper offers a good example of the personal uses to which analysis can be put. Notice that he gravitated toward events in his life that confused him and about which he wanted some clarity. Such topics can be especially fruitful for analysis because you know the particulars well and can provide readers with details; you view the topic with some puzzlement; and, through the application of your analytical tool, you may come to understand it. When you select topics to analyze from your experience, you provide yourself with a motivation to write and learn. When you are motivated in this way, you spark the interest of readers.

Using Randall Collins as a guide, Edward Peselman returns again and again to the events of his freshman year in the dormitory. We sense that Peselman himself wants to know what happened in that dorm. He writes, "I saw people hurt and in turn hurt others all for the sake of securing a place in the dorm's prized social order." Peselman does not approve of what happened, and the analysis he launches is meant to help him understand.

Locate an Analytical Principle

When you are given an assignment that asks for analysis, use two specific reading strategies to identify principles and definitions in source materials.

- **Look for a sentence that makes a general statement about the way something works.** The statement may strike you as a rule or a law. The line that Edward Peselman quotes from Randall Collins has this quality: "[A]ny social arrangement works because people avoid questioning it most of the time." Such statements are generalizations—

conclusions to sometimes complicated and extensive arguments. You can use these conclusions to guide your own analyses as long as you are aware that for some audiences, you will need to re-create and defend the arguments that resulted in these conclusions.

- **Look for statements that take this form: "X" can be defined as (or "X" consists of) the following: A, B, and C.** The specific elements of the definition—A, B, and C—are what you use to identify and analyze parts of the object being studied. You've seen an example of this approach in Marie Winn's multipart definition of addiction, which she uses to analyze television viewing. As a reader looking for definitions suitable for conducting an analysis, you might come across Winn's definition of addiction and then use it for your own purposes, perhaps to analyze the playing of video games as an addiction.

Essential to any analysis is the validity of the principle or definition being applied, the analytical tool. Make yourself aware, both as writer and reader, of a tool's strengths and limitations. Pose these questions of the analytical principles and definitions you use: Are they accurate? Are they well accepted? Do *you* accept them? What are the arguments against them? What are their limitations? Since every principle or definition used in an analysis is the end product of an argument, you are entitled—even obligated—to challenge it. If the analytical tool is flawed, then the analysis that follows from it will be flawed also.

Following is a page from Collins's *Sociological Insight*; Edward Peselman uses a key sentence from this extract as an analytical tool in his essay on power relations in his dorm (see page 197). Notice that Peselman underlines the sentence he will use in his analysis.

1 Try this experiment some time. When you are talking to someone, make them explain everything they say that isn't completely clear. The result, you will discover, is a series of uninterrupted interruptions:

A: Hi, how are you doing?
B: What do you mean when you say "how"?
A: You know. What's happening with you?
B: What do you mean, "happening"?
A: Happening, you know, what's going on.
B: I'm sorry. Could you explain what you mean by "what"?
A: What do you mean, what do I mean? Do you want to talk to me or not?

2   It is obvious that this sort of questioning could go on endlessly, at any rate if the listener doesn't get very angry and punch you in the mouth. But it illustrates two important points. First, virtually everything can be called into question. We are able to get along with other people not because everything is clearly spelled out, but because we are willing to take most things people say without explanation. Harold Garfinkel, who actually performed this sort of experiment,

points out that there is an infinite regress of assumptions that go into any act of social communication. Moreover, some expressions are simply not explainable in words at all. A word like "you," or "here," or "now" is what Garfinkel calls "indexical." You have to know what it means already; it can't be explained.

3   "What do you mean by 'you'?"

4   "I mean *you, you!*" About all that can be done here is point your finger.

5   The second point is that people get mad when they are pressed to explain things that they ordinarily take for granted. This is because they very quickly see that explanations could go on forever and the questions will never be answered. If you really demanded a full explanation of everything you hear, you could stop the conversation from ever getting past its first sentence. The real significance of this for a sociological understanding of the way the world is put together is not the anger, however. It is the fact that people try to avoid these sorts of situations. They tacitly recognize that we have to avoid these endless lines of questioning. Sometimes small children will start asking an endless series of "whys," but adults discourage this.

6   <u>In sum, any social arrangement works because people avoid questioning it most of the time</u>. That does not mean that people do not get into arguments or disputes about just what ought to be done from time to time. But to have a dispute already implies there is a considerable area of agreement. An office manager may dispute with a clerk over just how to take care of some business letter, but they at any rate know more or less what they are disputing about. They do not get off into a . . . series of questions over just what is meant by everything that is said. You could very quickly dissolve the organization into nothingness if you followed that route: there would be no communication at all, even about what the disagreement is over.

7   Social organization is possible because people maintain a certain level of focus. If they focus on one thing, even if only to disagree about it, they are taking many other things for granted, thereby reinforcing their social reality.

The statement that Peselman has underlined—"any social arrangement works because people avoid questioning it most of the time"—is the end result of an argument that takes Collins several paragraphs to develop. Peselman agrees with the conclusion and uses it in paragraph 7 of his essay. Observe that for his own purposes Peselman does *not* reconstruct Collins's argument. He selects *only* Collins's conclusion and then imports that into his essay. Once he identifies in Collins a principle he can use in his analysis, he converts the principle into questions that he then directs to his topic: life in his freshman dorm. Two questions follow directly from Collins's insight:

1. What was the social arrangement in the dorm?
2. How was this social arrangement questioned?

Peselman clearly defines his dormitory's social arrangement in paragraphs 3–6 (with the help of another principle borrowed from Collins). Beginning with paragraph 7, he explores how one member of his dorm questioned that arrangement:

```
That is, until he left mid-semester. According to
Collins, "any social arrangement works because
people avoid questioning it most of the time" (p.
74). The inverse of this principle is as follows:
When a social arrangement is questioned, that
arrangement can fall apart. The more fragile the
arrangement (the flimsier the values on which it
is based), the more quickly it will crumble. For
the entire first semester, no one questioned our
rude, macho rules and because of them we pigeon-
holed Benjamin as a wimp. In our dorm society,
gentle men had no power. To say the least, ours
was not a compassionate community. From a dis-
tance of one year, I am shocked to have been a
member of it. Nonetheless, we had created a mini-
society that somehow served our needs.
```

Formulate a Thesis

An analysis is a two-part argument. The first part states and establishes the writer's agreement with a certain principle or definition.

Part One of the Argument

This first argument essentially takes this form:

> **Claim #1:** Principle "X" (or definition "X") is valuable.

Principle "X" can be a theory as encompassing and abstract as the statement that *myths are the enemy of truth*. Principle "X" can be as modest as the definition of a term—for instance, *addiction* or *comfort*. As you move from one subject area to another, the principles and definitions you use for analysis will change, as these assignments illustrate:

Sociology: *Write a paper in which you place yourself in American society by locating both your absolute position and relative rank on each single criterion of social stratification used by Lenski & Lenski. For each criterion, state whether you have attained your social position by yourself or if you have "inherited" that status from your parents.*

Literature: *Apply principles of Jungian psychology to Hawthorne's "Young Goodman Brown." In your reading of the story, apply Jung's principles of the shadow, persona, and anima.*

Physics: *Use Newton's second law* (F = ma) *to analyze the acceleration of a fixed pulley, from which two weights hang:* m_1 *(.45 kg) and* m_2 *(.90 kg). Explain in a paragraph the principle of Newton's law and your method of applying it to solve the problem. Assume your reader is not comfortable with mathematical explanations: do not use equations in your paragraph.*

Finance: *Using Guidford C. Babcock's "Concept of Sustainable Growth"* [Financial Analysis 26 *(May–June 1970): 108–14], analyze the stock price appreciation of the XYZ Corporation, figures for which are attached.*

The analytical tools to be applied in these assignments change from discipline to discipline. Writing in response to the sociology assignment, you would use sociological principles developed by Lenski and Lenski. In your

---

GUIDELINES FOR WRITING ANALYSIS

Unless you are asked to follow a specialized format, especially in the sciences or the social sciences, you can present your analysis as a paper by following the guidelines below. As you move from one class to another, from discipline to discipline, the principles and definitions you use as the basis for your analyses will change, but the following basic components of analysis will remain the same:

- *Create a context for your analysis.* Introduce and summarize for readers the object, event, or behavior to be analyzed. Present a strong case about why an analysis is needed: Give yourself a motivation to write, and give readers a motivation to read. Consider setting out a problem, puzzle, or question to be investigated.
- *Introduce and summarize the key definition or principle* that will form the basis of your analysis. Plan to devote the first part of your analysis to arguing for the validity of this principle or definition *if* your audience is not likely to understand it or if they are likely to think that the principle or definition is *not* valuable.
- *Analyze your topic.* Systematically apply elements of this definition or principle to parts of the activity or object under study. You can do this by posing specific questions, based on your analytic principle or definition, about the object. Discuss what you find part by part (organized perhaps by question), in clearly defined sections of the essay.
- *Conclude by stating clearly what is significant about your analysis.* When considering your essay as a whole, what new or interesting insights have you made concerning the object under study? To what extent has your application of the definition or principle helped you to explain how the object works, what it might mean, or why it is significant?

literature class, you would use principles of Jungian psychology; in physics, Newton's second law; and in finance, a particular writer's concept of "sustainable growth." But whatever discipline you are working in, the first part of your analysis will clearly state which (and whose) principles and definitions you are applying. For audiences unfamiliar with these principles, you will need to explain them; if you anticipate objections, you will need to argue that they are legitimate principles capable of helping you as you conduct an analysis.

Part Two of the Argument

In the second part of an analysis, you *apply* specific parts of your principle or definition to the topic at hand. Regardless of how it is worded, this second argument in an analysis can be rephrased to take this form:.

> **Claim #2:** By applying Principle (or definition) "X," we can understand
> *(topic)* as *(conclusion based on analysis)*.

This is your thesis, the main idea of your analytical essay. Fill in the first blank with the specific object, event, or behavior you are examining. Fill in the second blank with your conclusion about the meaning or significance of this object, based on the insights made during your analysis. Mary Winn completes the second claim of her analysis this way:

> By applying my multipart definition, we can understand *television viewing* as *an addiction*.

Develop an Organizational Plan

You will benefit enormously in the writing of a first draft if you plan out the logic of your analysis. You will want to turn key elements of your analytical principle or definition into questions and then develop the paragraph-by-paragraph logic of the paper.

Turning Key Elements of a Principle or Definition into Questions

Prepare for an analysis by developing questions based on the definition or principle you are going to apply, and then by directing these questions to the activity or object to be studied. The method is straightforward: State as clearly as possible the principle or definition to be applied. Divide the principle or definition into its parts and, using each part, develop a question. For example, Marie Winn develops a multipart definition of addiction, each part of which is readily turned into a question that she directs at a specific behavior: television viewing. Her analysis of television viewing can be understood as *responses* to each of her analytical questions. Note that in her brief analysis, Winn does not first define addiction and then analyze television viewing. Rather, *as* she defines aspects of addiction, she analyzes television viewing.

Developing the Paragraph-by-Paragraph Logic of Your Paper

The following paragraph from Edward Peselman's essay illustrates the typical logic of a paragraph in an analytical essay:

> Up and down the pecking order, we exercised control through macho taunts and challenges. Collins writes that "individuals who manage to be powerful and get their own way must do so by going along with the laws of social organization, not by contradicting them" (p. 61). Until mid-year, our dorm motto could have read: "You win through rudeness and intimidation." Eric gained power with his frequent and brutal assessments of everyone's behavior. Marc gained power with his temper—which, when lost, made everyone run for cover. Those who were not rude and intimidating drifted to the bottom of our social world. Reggie was quiet and unemotional, which allowed us to take advantage of him because we knew he would back down if pressed in an argument. Yet Reggie understood that on a "power scale" he stood above Dozer and often shared in the group's tactics to get Dozer's food (his parents were forever sending him care packages). Dozer, in turn, seldom missed opportunities to take swipes at Benjamin, with references to his sexuality. From the very first week of school, Benjamin could never—and never wanted to—compete against Eric's bluntness or Marc's temper. Still, Benjamin hung out with us. He lived in our corner of the dorm, and he wanted to be friendly. But everyone, including Benjamin, understood that he occupied the lowest spot in the order.

We see in this example paragraph the typical logic of analysis:

- ***The writer introduces a specific analytical tool.*** Peselman quotes a line from Randall Collins:

  > "[I]ndividuals who manage to be powerful and get their own way must do so by going along with the laws of social organization, not by contradicting them."

- ***The writer applies this analytical tool to the object being examined.*** Peselman states his dorm's law of social organization:

> ```
> Until mid-year, our dorm motto could have read:
> "You win through rudeness and intimidation."
> ```

- *The writer uses the tool to identify and then examine the meaning of parts of the object.* Peselman shows how each member (the "parts") of his dorm society conforms to the laws of "social organization":

> ```
> Eric gained power with his frequent and brutal
> assessments of everyone's behavior. Marc gained
> power with his temper—which, when lost, made
> everyone run for cover. Those who were not rude
> and intimidating drifted to the bottom of our
> social world. . . .
> ```

An analytical paper takes shape when a writer creates a series of such paragraphs and then links them with an overall logic. Here is the logical organization of Edward Peselman's paper:

- Paragraph 1: Introduction states a problem—provides a motivation to write and to read.

- Paragraph 2: Randall Collins is introduced—the author whose work will provide principles for analysis.

- Paragraphs 3–4: Background information is provided—the cast of characters in the dorm.

- Paragraphs 5–9: The analysis proceeds—specific parts of dorm life are identified and found significant, using principles from Collins.

- Paragraphs 10–11: Summary and conclusion are provided—the freshman dorm society disintegrated for reasons set out in the analysis. A larger point is made: Some oppressive systems must be torn down.

Draft and Revise Your Analysis

You will usually need at least two drafts to produce a paper that presents your idea clearly. The biggest changes in your paper will typically come between your first and second drafts. No paper that you write, including an analysis, will be complete until you revise and refine your single compelling idea: your analytical conclusion about what the object, event, or behavior being examined means or how it is significant. You revise and refine by evaluating your first draft, bringing to it many of the same questions you pose when evaluating any piece of writing, including these:

- Are the facts accurate?
- Are my opinions supported by evidence?
- Are the opinions of others authoritative?
- Are my assumptions clearly stated?

- Are key terms clearly defined?
- Is the presentation logical?
- Are all parts of the presentation well developed?
- Are dissenting points of view presented?

Address these same questions on the first draft of your analysis, and you will have solid information to guide your revision.

Write an Analysis, Not a Summary

The most common error made in writing analyses—which is *fatal* to the form—is to present readers with a summary only. For analyses to succeed, you must *apply* a principle or definition and reach a conclusion about the object, event, or behavior you are examining. By definition, a summary (see Chapter 1) includes none of your own conclusions. Summary is naturally a part of analysis; you will need to summarize the object or activity being examined and, depending on the audience's needs, summarize the principle or definition being applied. But in an analysis, you must take the next step and share insights that suggest the meaning or significance of some object, event, or behavior.

Make Your Analysis Systematic

Analyses should give the reader the sense of a systematic, purposeful examination. Marie Winn's analysis illustrates the point: She sets out specific elements of addictive behavior in separate paragraphs and then uses each, within its paragraph, to analyze television viewing. Winn is systematic in her method, and we are never in doubt about her purpose.

Imagine another analysis in which a writer lays out four elements of a definition but then applies only two, without explaining the logic for omitting the others. Or imagine an analysis in which the writer offers a principle for analysis but directs it to only a half or a third of the object being discussed, without providing a rationale for doing so. In both cases, the writer would be failing to deliver on a promise basic to analyses: Once a principle or definition is presented, it should be thoroughly and systematically applied.

Answer the "So What?" Question

An analysis should make readers *want* to read. It should give readers a sense of getting to the heart of the matter, that what is important in the object or activity under analysis is being laid bare and discussed in revealing ways. If when rereading the first draft of your essay, you cannot imagine readers saying, "I never thought of _____ this way," then something may be seriously wrong. Reread closely to determine why the paper might leave readers flat and exhausted, as opposed to feeling that they have gained new and important insights. Closely reexamine your own motivations for writing. Have *you* learned anything significant through the analysis? If not, neither will readers, and they will turn away. If you have gained important insights through your analysis, communicate them clearly. At some point, pull together your related insights and say, in effect: "Here's how it all adds up."

Attribute Sources Appropriately

By nature of the form, in an analysis you work with one or two sources and apply insights from those to some object or phenomenon you want to understand more thoroughly. Because you are not synthesizing a great many sources, and because the strength of an analysis derives mostly from *your* application of a principle or definition, the opportunities for not appropriately citing sources are diminished. Take special care to cite and quote, as necessary, the one or two sources you use throughout the analysis.

For an additional opportunity to hone your skills in writing analyses, see Chapter 7, pages 217–235. Using principles of ethical decision making, you will analyze the ethics of "legacy admissions," the practice of granting special consideration to the sons and daughters of alumni in the college application process.

CRITICAL READING FOR ANALYSIS

- *Read to get a sense of the whole in relation to its parts.* Whether you are clarifying for yourself a principle or definition to be used in an analysis, or are reading a text that you will analyze, understand how parts function to create the whole. If a definition or principle consists of parts, use these to organize sections of your analysis. If your goal is to analyze a text, be aware of its structure: Note the title and subtitle; identify the main point and subordinate points and where they are located; break the material into sections.

- *Read to discover relationships within the object being analyzed.* Watch for patterns. When you find them, be alert—for you create an occasion to analyze, to use a principle or definition as a guide in discussing what the pattern may mean.

  In fiction, a pattern might involve responses of characters to events or to each other, recurrence of certain words or phrasings, images, themes, or turns of plot, to name a few.

  In poetry, a pattern might involve rhyme schemes, rhythm, imagery, figurative or literal language, and more.

  Your challenge as a reader is first to see a pattern (perhaps using a guiding principle or definition to do so) and then to locate other instances of that pattern. By reading carefully in this way, you prepare yourself to conduct an analysis.

WRITING ASSIGNMENT: ANALYSIS

Now we'll give you an opportunity to practice your skills in planning and writing an analysis. See Chapter 7, pages 217–235, where we provide nine sources on the controversial issue of "legacy" status in the college admissions process. At certain schools, the admissions staff gives preferential consideration to the sons and daughters of alumni. Is such a practice ethical? In your analysis, you will use one or more definitions of ethics to answer this question.

ANALYSIS: A TOOL FOR UNDERSTANDING

As this chapter has demonstrated, analysis involves applying principles as a way to probe and understand. With incisive principles guiding your analysis, you will be able to pose questions, observe patterns and relationships, and derive meaning. Do not forget that this meaning will be one of several possible meanings. Someone else, possibly you, using different analytical tools could observe the same phenomena and arrive at very different conclusions regarding meaning or significance. We end the chapter, therefore, as we began it: with the two brief analyses of *The Wizard of Oz*. The conclusions expressed in one look nothing like the conclusions expressed in the other, save for the fact that both seek to interpret the same movie. And yet we can say that both are useful, both reveal meaning:

> At the dawn of adolescence, the very time she should start to distance herself from Aunt Em and Uncle Henry, the surrogate parents who raised her on their Kansas farm, Dorothy Gale experiences a hurtful reawakening of her fear that these loved ones will be rudely ripped from her, especially her Aunt (Em—M for Mother!). [Harvey Greenberg, *The Movies on Your Mind* (New York: Dutton, 1975).]

> [*The Wizard of Oz*] was originally written as a political allegory about grass-roots protest. It may seem harder to believe than Emerald City, but the Tin Woodsman is the industrial worker, the Scarecrow [is] the struggling farmer, and the Wizard is the president, who is powerful only as long as he succeeds in deceiving the people. [Peter Dreier, "Oz Was Almost Reality," *Cleveland Plain Dealer* 3 Sept. 1989.]

You have seen in this chapter how it is possible for two writers, analyzing the same object or phenomenon but applying different analytical principles, to reach vastly different conclusions about what the object or phenomenon may mean or why it is significant. *The Wizard of Oz* is both an inquiry into the psychology of adolescence and a political allegory. What else the classic film may be awaits revealing with the systematic application of other analytical tools. The insights you gain as a writer of analyses depend entirely on your choice of tool and the subtlety with which you apply it.

7 Practicing Academic Writing

MERIT VS. PRIVILEGE IN COLLEGE ADMISSIONS

This chapter will give you the chance to apply the skills you have learned in summary, critique, synthesis, and analysis. You will read nine brief selections on the competing roles of merit (hard work and talent) versus privilege (birth and connections) in personal advancement. You will then write several responses, drawing on the source materials provided.

The specific issue for your writing is "legacy" admissions: the controversial policy of giving special consideration to the sons and daughters of alumni during the admissions process at certain colleges. Through legacy programs, alumni children are sometimes admitted to a freshman class over applicants with higher test scores and higher grades. Is this fair? Is it necessary, from the school's point of view? Whether or not you attend a college with a legacy program, the broader questions involved are central to your present and future success.

Here's why: Americans are a people who regard merit—that is, talent—as the fundamental measure of a person's worth. (At least this is what we're taught in school.) In a meritocracy, hard work and talent supposedly trump the privileges of family name, money, and connections. Privileging family over merit was the old, European way of doing business. Americans broke with that tradition when we founded a republic.

For most students, especially those who may be the first of their families to attend college, the conviction that one rises through merit, not birth, is the foundation upon which all dreams of the future rest. Why else would anyone work two jobs while attending school or study until 3 A.M. to get an A on an exam? The assumption, the bargain we make, is that hard work pays off. You put in the effort, get the grades, and gain access to all America offers: a good job or a first-rate education if you have truly shined in your studies.

What you will discover in the following readings is a more complicated reality. College admissions staffs routinely allow privilege to trump merit in selecting candidates for a freshman class. You will read about this issue and will explore it through writing. As you do so, remember that the question at hand is broader than college admissions. Imagine for a moment that on completing your degree you apply for a job and lose out because the company decides instead to hire the son or daughter of an existing employee—someone clearly less qualified than you. How would you feel? Most likely, angry and betrayed, as if someone had changed the rules mid-game. The issues with legacy admissions are identical.

Your main assignment in this practice chapter will be to write an argument that synthesizes what various authors have written on the topic with your own insights. To prepare, you will complete several briefer assignments that require you to work closely with your sources. In this progression of assignments, you will write a combination of summaries, paraphrases, critiques, and explanations that will prepare you for—and that will actually produce sections of—your more ambitious argument synthesis. In this respect, the assignment at hand is typical of other writing you will do in college: While, at times, you will be called on to write a stand-alone critique or a purely explanatory paper, you will also write papers that blend the basic forms of college writing that you have studied in this text.

The set of readings on legacy admissions amounts to controlled research. We have provided the topic; and through a search of books, journals, magazines, and newspapers, we have gathered selections that can provide the basis of an informed discussion that you will present as an academic paper. When an instructor asks you to write a research paper, the end point of your research will be exactly what you will encounter below: a series of readings that await your synthesis.

THE ASSIGNMENTS

Summary

Summary Assignment #1: Summarizing Text

Summarize the *USA Today* editorial that supports the practice of legacy admissions (pages 232–233) and the article by DeKoven (pages 224–225), which opposes the practice. Make careful notes on the selections as you prepare your summary. Follow the guidelines covered in Chapter 1, particularly the Guidelines for Writing Summaries box on pages 7–8.

As for the selections you are *not* summarizing, read carefully and highlight the text *as if* you were preparing to write a summary.

Summary Assignment #2: Summarizing Tables

Study the two tables (pages 230 and 231) in Mark Megalli's article "So Your Dad Went to Harvard." In a paragraph, summarize the key information contained in these tables.

Paraphrase

Write a paraphrase of the second paragraph in Howell and Turner's article "The History of Legacy Admissions" (pages 226–228). Read the paragraph with care, using a dictionary as necessary, to understand

difficult passages. Then follow the suggestions for writing a paraphrase on pages 34–37.

Critique

Choose the *USA Today* editorial favoring legacy admissions (pages
232–233) or the DeKoven article (pages 224–225), which opposes the
practice, and write a critique. If you want to save yourself some work later
when writing your argument synthesis, critique the selection that *opposes*
the position you will be taking in your argument. (In an academic argument, you raise and then respond to objections to your own position.
Thus, if in this assignment you critique the article that opposes your position, you will be able to use your work in the larger argument.) To select
which of the passages to critique, read the Argument Synthesis assignment (pages 213–214), read the selections, and then choose a position.

Since the writing you do for this assignment will be incorporated into
a larger argument with its own introduction and conclusion, you need
not write an introduction or conclusion for this critique. Instead, write
an *abbreviated* critique, consisting of the following parts:

1. a summary of the selection, (your response to Summary Assignment #1);

2. an evaluation of the presentation for accuracy, clarity, logic,
   and/or fairness; and

3. a statement of your agreement and/or disagreement with the author.

For parts 2 and 3, be sure to support your evaluation with reasons.
Refer to the selection, summarizing or quoting key elements, as
needed. See pages 65–66 for advice on writing critiques, particularly
the Guidelines for Writing Critiques box on page 66 along with the
hints on incorporating quoted material into your own writing, pages
41–47.

Explanatory Synthesis

Based on the reading selections in this chapter, write three explanations that might follow one another in a larger paper. The explanations should each be one or two well-developed paragraphs. The topics are as follows: (1) Explain the practice of legacy admissions,
making sure to explain how widespread the practice is, why it exists,
and whom it affects. (2) Explain the arguments *in favor* of legacy admissions. (3) Explain the arguments *opposing* legacy admissions.

Key requirements for each explanation:

- Each paragraph of explanation should begin with a clear topic
  sentence.

- Each paragraph of explanation should refer to *at least two* different
  sources. Be sure to set up the reference (which can be a summary,
  paraphrase, or quotation) with care. Use appropriate citation format, likely MLA (see pages 846–849).

- To help you explain, use facts, examples, statistics, and expert opinions from your sources, as needed.

Argument Synthesis

Develop an argument in which you adopt *one* of four claims regarding the controversy over legacy admissions in college. You will complete your chosen claim by providing reasons to be developed in your paper:

1. Giving legacy applicants preferred treatment in the admissions process is defensible because . . .

2. Giving legacy applicants preferred treatment in the admissions process is indefensible because . . .

3. Admissions Offices should keep private their policies concerning legacy applicants because . . .

4. Admissions Offices should openly discuss their policies concerning legacy applicants because . . .

In developing reasons to support your claim, draw on the sources that follow. You don't have to use *all* of the passages; as you plan your synthesis, you may want to research additional sources (for instance, the legacy policies of your own school or a school that rejected you). Your response to this assignment, like many of the arguments you will write in college, will combine elements of summary, evaluation, and explanation. Specifically, you will be using your responses to the earlier writing assignments, above, in preparing your argument synthesis. Your paper should consist of these parts:

- An introductory paragraph that sets a context for the topic and presents the claim you are going to support in the argument that follows. Your claim (your thesis) may appear at the end of this paragraph (or introductory section).

- A paragraph defining the practice and extent of legacy admissions. See the Explanatory Synthesis assignment and the second Summary assignment.

- A paragraph that paraphrases the history of legacy admissions. See the Paraphrase assignment.

- A paragraph or two explaining the objections to legacy admissions. See the Explanatory Synthesis assignment and the first Summary assignment.

- A paragraph or two explaining the support for legacy admissions. See the Explanatory Synthesis assignment and the first Summary assignment.

- Reasons for supporting or rejecting legacy admissions, if you choose to write on claim #1 or #2; OR reasons for supporting or rejecting the current, largely hidden practice in considering legacy admissions, if you choose to write on claim #3 or #4. *This is the main section of the argument.* It should consist of several paragraphs—at least three or four, each focused on a specific reason to support your claim. Use source materials to help present these reasons.

- Counterargument: A paragraph explaining the merits of the argument opposing yours. See the first Summary assignment. (Use your summary of the reading selection that *opposes* the position you take in this argument.)

- Rebuttal to counterargument: A paragraph or two evaluating and ultimately rejecting the argument opposing yours. See the Critique assignment. (If you chose to critique a reading that opposes your position in this argument, use that critique here.)

- A conclusion.

Where you place the various elements of this argument synthesis will be your decision, as writer. Which sources to use and what logic to present in defense of your claim are also yours to decide. See pages 176–182 for help in thinking about structuring and supporting your argument.

A Note on Incorporating Quotations.   Identify the sources you intend to use for your synthesis. Working with a phrase, sentence, or brief passage from each, use a variety of the techniques discussed in the section Incorporating Quotations into Your Sentences (pages 41–47) to write sentences that you can use to advance your argument. Some of these sentences should demonstrate the use of ellipsis marks and brackets. See pages 43–47 in Chapter 1.

Analysis

As an alternative to the Argument Synthesis assignment above, complete *one* of the following Analysis assignments:

Analysis Assignment #1

In preparation for writing an analysis, read "Making Ethical Decisions" by Gerald F. Cavanagh (pages 235–237). In this piece you will find three principles for analysis—*utilitarianism, justice,* and *individual rights*—that you can use to answer the following question: Is the college admissions practice of giving legacy applicants preferential treatment ethical?

To answer this question, select one—or, if you are feeling ambitious, more than one—principle from Cavanagh's article and use it as a lens to analyze the controversy over legacy admissions. In using different principles for analysis, you may reach different conclusions, an outcome consistent with what you read at the outset of the discussion of analysis in Chapter 6. As you write, be sure to focus on answering the question posed above. Your answer will be an argument, guided by one of two claims:

1. The college admissions practice of giving legacy applicants preferential treatment is ethical because . . .

2. The college admissions practice of giving legacy applicants preferential treatment is unethical because . . .

Complete your chosen claim by providing reasons to be developed through your analysis.

In writing your analysis, follow the Guidelines for Writing Analysis on page 203, in Chapter 6. Use the fruits of your earlier assignments involving summary, paraphrase, and explanation. Certainly, before you analyze a phenomenon, you must define or explain it, and your earlier work should help you to do this. Consider using the following structure for your analysis:

- A paragraph of introduction that sets a context for the topic and presents the claim you are going to support in the analysis that follows. Your claim (your thesis) may appear at the end of this paragraph (or introductory section).

- A paragraph defining the practice and extent of legacy admissions. See the Explanatory Synthesis assignment and the second Summary assignment.

- A paragraph that paraphrases the history of legacy admissions. See the Paraphrase assignment.

- A paragraph or two explaining the objections to legacy admissions. See the Explanatory Synthesis assignment and the first Summary assignment.

- A paragraph or two explaining the support for legacy admissions. See the Explanatory Synthesis assignment and the first Summary assignment.

- An analysis of legacy admissions using one (or more) of Cavanagh's principles for reaching ethical decisions. *This is the key part of your paper.* If you use one of Cavanagh's principles, your analysis should be three or four paragraphs. If you use more than one of Cavanagh's principles, limit yourself to two paragraphs of development for each. Remember that your analysis provides your reasons for judging the practice of legacy admissions to be ethical or unethical.

- A conclusion in which you argue that, based on the insights gained through your analysis, the practice of legacy admissions is ethical or unethical.

Analysis Assignment #2

Write an analysis of the legacy admissions phenomenon. Follow the advice presented in Chapter 6. See especially the Guidelines for Writing Analysis box on page 203. In preparing your paper, use, as needed, the fruits of your earlier assignments involving summary, paraphrase, and explanation. Certainly, before you analyze a phenomenon, you must define or explain it, and your earlier work should help you to do this.

You might follow the suggestions above, in Analysis Assignment #1, for structuring your analysis. However, instead of basing your analysis on a principle from Cavanagh's article, use one of the following statements—or another of your own choosing—some drawn from the sources that follow. Plan to write three or four well-developed paragraphs of analysis, based on the principle you select:

The more you look at modern America, the more you are struck by how frequently it departs from the meritocratic ideal.

—The Economist, "The Curse of Nepotism"

While people may argue that everyone should be treated exactly the same, the truth is that we all favor some sorts of criteria. The ethical trick is to make those criteria morally relevant.

—Miriam Schulman, "May the Best Man or Woman Win"

[T]here is no defense—moral, practical, or financial—for [elite colleges'] hereditary spoils system.

—Jesse Shapiro, "A Second Look: Attacking Legacy Preference"

Simply put, legacy admissions are defensible and, in any event, affect such a tiny portion of the nation's college applicants as to be negligible.

—Debra Thomas and Terry Shepard, "Legacy Admissions Are Defensible Because the Process Can't Be 'Fair'"

Elite schools, like any luxury brand, are an aesthetic experience—an exquisitely constructed fantasy of what it means to belong to an elite—and they have always been mindful of what must be done to maintain that experience.

—Malcolm Gladwell, "Getting In: The Social Logic of Ivy League Admissions"

[T]he legacy preferential system perpetuates elitism by conferring considerable advantage upon privileged white children and, as a result, disfavoring blacks and others whose parents were less likely to have gone to college.

—Mark Megalli, "So Your Dad Went to Harvard"

At the end of the day, this isn't about money. It's about right and wrong.

—John Edwards, "End Special Privilege"

Choosing a diverse student body that contributes to a stimulating campus environment is a freedom worth preserving.

—USA Today, "Preserve Universities' Right to Shape Student Community"

THE READINGS

Read the following passages, then complete the writing assignments, above. In summarizing, quoting, paraphrasing, evaluating, analyzing, and synthesizing these sources, you practice the skills fundamental to all college-level writing.

A cautionary note: When writing syntheses, it is all too easy to become careless in properly crediting your sources. Before drafting your paper, please review the section on Avoiding Plagiarism in Chapter 1 (pages 48–49) as well as the quick reference guides to citing sources on pages 846–849).

The Curse of Nepotism
The Economist

Nepotism is the favoring of friends, family, or others closely associated with decision makers. The term suggests a lack of fairness and, at its worst, corruption. This piece first appeared in The Economist *(January 10, 2004).*

1   America likes to think of itself as the very embodiment of the spirit of meritocracy: a country where all people are judged on their individual abilities rather than their family connections. The American Revolution swept away the flummery of feudal titles. Thomas Jefferson dreamed of creating a "natural aristocracy." Benjamin Franklin sniped that "a man who makes boast of his ancestors doth but advertise his own insignificance."

2   The Founding Fathers had a rather narrow view of who should be admitted to their meritocratic republic, to be sure. But today most Americans believe that their country has done a reasonable job of getting rid of the most blatant forms of discrimination towards blacks and women and building a ladder of educational opportunity. Americans are far more confident than Europeans that people deserve what they get in life.

3   But are they right? The more you look at modern America, the more you are struck by how frequently it departs from the meritocratic ideal. George Bush's Washington is a study in family influence: Look at the Powells, the Chao/McConnells, the Scalias and the Cheneys, not to mention the Shrub himself.*

4   The biggest insult to meritocracy, however, is found in the country's top universities. These institutions, which control access to the country's most impressive jobs, consider themselves far above Washington and its grubby spoils system. Yet they continue to operate a system of "legacy preferences"—affirmative action for the children of alumni.

5   These preferences are surprisingly widespread. In most Ivy League institutions, "legacies" make up between 10% and 15% of every freshman class. At Notre Dame they make up 23%. They are also common in good public univer-

---

* President George W. Bush.

sities such as the University of Virginia. Legatees are two to four times more likely to be admitted to the best universities than non-legatees.

6   America's universities are probably the most politically correct places on the planet. So what are they doing pandering to the (overwhelmingly white) children of the overclass? University administrators offer two justifications. The first may be crudely characterised as fund-raising. Universities are always asking their alumni for a helping hand and for money. The least the alumni can expect in return is that the universities will take a careful look at their college-age offspring.

7   But is it reasonable for universities to use their admissions systems as tools of alumni management—let alone fund-raising? Universities are supposed to be guardians of objective standards. They are also the recipients of huge amounts of public money as well as private donations. In short, there is no need to.

8   The second justification is that alumni preferences aren't really preferences at all. William Fitzsimmons, dean of admissions at Harvard College, considers them simply an "ever so slight tip." He admits that 40% of the children of alumni get into Harvard compared with only 11% of ordinary applicants, but says that is mainly because of self-selection. Successful legatees have almost the same test scores as successful non-legatees.

9   Given the secrecy of the admissions process, this argument is hard to verify. It is worrying that a Department of Education report in 1990 concluded that the average Harvard legacy student is "significantly less qualified" than the average non-legacy student in every area except sports. But even if you give Harvard the benefit of the doubt, the system is still a disgrace. This is a university that has to turn down more than 2,000 high-school valedictorians every year. If you are going to offer a "slight tip" to anyone, why offer it to people who are already on the inside track—who not only come from privileged homes, but also have an insider's knowledge of how the admissions system works?

May the Best Man or Woman Win
Miriam Schulman

According to Miriam Schulman, those who pin their hopes on meritocracy for a "fair" outcome in college admissions might find, on closer examination, that "[e]qual is not necessarily fair." Schulman is director of communications at the Markkula Center for Applied Ethics (Santa Clara University). The center publishes Issues in Ethics, *in which this selection first appeared (Fall 1996).*

1   An old teacher of mine used to claim he graded our papers by throwing them all up the stairs and giving A's to the ones that landed on the top step. Now, there was a case of someone treating every student equally.

2   Although this example is obvious *reductio ad absurdum*, it serves to demonstrate an important point: Equal is not necessarily fair. That principle is worth reiterating in any discussion of affirmative action in college admissions, which often boils down to a controversy over fairness. While people may argue that everyone should be treated exactly the same, the truth is that we all favor some sorts of criteria. The ethical trick is to make those criteria morally relevant.

3   If you think this is an easy matter, consider legacy admissions: young people who get into a school because their parents are alums. According to a report from U.C.-Berkeley's Institute for the Study of Social Change issued in 1991, more legacy students were admitted to 10 of the country's most elite institutions than the combined number of all African Americans and Chicanos admitted under affirmative action programs.

4   Many people defend legacy admissions as acceptable because they help to ensure the financial continuity of the institution, without which no one would be able to enter the university. But such a rationale can be a slippery slope. Indeed, the hypocrisy tweakers had a field day recently when the *Los Angeles Times* reported that several of the U.C. regents who had voted to abolish affirmative action had themselves pulled strings to get relatives, friends, and the children of business associates into UCLA.

Morally Relevant Criteria

5   My point here is not so much to challenge the moral relevance of this particular preference, but to point out that race is only one among many possible attributes we might take into account in admission decisions. If, ultimately, we want to disallow it as a basis for preference, we should be prepared to justify why it is any less worthy than other characteristics we do consider.

6   One justifiable criterion might be ability: May the best man or woman win. While there may be general agreement on the relevance of this determinant, there is much less agreement on a fair way to measure it. On the surface, it might seem logical that the people with the best grades and scores should get the college slots. Indeed, this argument is at the heart of several cases, such as *Bakke vs. Regents of the University of California*, which have challenged affirmative action in the courts.

7   Although we might conclude that grades and scores are the most objective criteria we can come up with to assess ability, there are more than a few reasons to question our moral certainty about the justice of this system. First, standards of grading vary enormously from school to school; an A from one might be a C from another. Such variability was behind the creation of standardized tests like the SATs, which were supposed to provide a single measure for students across the country.

8   But these tests have been accused repeatedly of bias against minorities. In 1990, a national commission sponsored by the Ford Foundation found that the differences in test scores between minority and majority test takers were typically larger than the differences in their grades or job ratings. "We must stop pretending that any single standard test can illuminate equally well the talents and help promote the learning of people from dramatically different backgrounds," their report concluded.

Flutists and Football Players

9   While academic ability is hard to measure fairly, most people still want to include that factor in college admissions. But it is not, by far, the only characteristic that might be considered. A long-established criterion has been diversity. By this, I don't mean only the relatively new argument that student bodies should reflect the multiethnic society from which they are drawn; I mean the old practice of creating a freshman class that has a much-needed linebacker, a new first flute for the university orchestra, and a high-school senior-class president who may go on to a leadership position in college student government.

10   Athletic prowess, musical talent, and unusual community service have all been defended as morally acceptable considerations for college admissions because they add to the well-roundedness of the student body. If these attributes can be considered relevant to admissions, why not race?

11   Of course, there is nothing inherently edifying about attending school with people who have different physical attributes. Introducing more redheads into a student population would bring about no discernible benefit. But, in this country, having a different skin color means having a different life experience. Bringing that difference into the mix at our universities can greatly enhance the quality of the dialogue that goes on there.

12   On the larger stage, our society is enriched by the many different backgrounds and traditions of its members. For example, as a woman, I know I benefit from the increasing numbers of female health practitioners, who have brought women's health issues such as breast cancer to the fore-front of national consciousness. It does not surprise or even anger me that male doctors did not pursue these issues more forcefully—they lie outside men's personal experience—but I do want my experience to be represented.

13   Similarly, I have to confront the needs and perspectives of other members of my community, which I might ignore, however unwittingly, were they not represented in our universities and in the larger public discussion.

Legacy Admissions Are Defensible Because the Process Can't Be 'Fair'
Debra Thomas and Terry Shepard

In an article that generated heated reader feedback, Debra Thomas and Terry Shepard defend the practice of legacy admissions. Thomas is a public relations director at Rice University. Shepard is vice president for public affairs at Rice. This selection first appeared in The Chronicle of Higher Education *(March 14, 2003).*

1   It was inevitable that the U.S. Supreme Court's decision to hear two lawsuits involving affirmative action in admissions at the University of Michigan would prompt discussion of other types of admissions preferences. The policies of most

colleges to grant preference to children of alumni—so-called legacies—have suddenly become a hot topic.

2   Meanwhile, who is discussing issues with far greater impact and importance—like the sorry state of government support for elementary and secondary education? In his book *Savage Inequalities* (Crown, 1991), Jonathan Kozol described the horrors of districts so poor that they could do no more than cover gaping holes in roofs with canvas; schools with no working restrooms; and a classroom consisting of an abandoned swimming pool. That was a decade ago, and, if anything, support for public schools in areas outside prosperous suburbs has deteriorated.

3   But instead of focusing on that crucial issue, politicians like Senator John Edwards, a Democrat from North Carolina, along with newspapers and magazines like *The Wall Street Journal, The New York Times,* and *Time,* are talking about how legacy admissions should be impermissible. State universities in Georgia and California already have eliminated legacy consideration in the face of such challenges.

4   Let's clear the smoke screen that obscures the real issues. Simply put, legacy admissions are defensible and, in any event, affect such a tiny portion of the nation's college applicants as to be negligible.

5   That view results from our decades of collective experience at many different kinds of institutions—including a large public university and four highly selective private colleges—and our evaluations, as outside consultants, of the admissions programs of more than 20 other institutions. We have seen firsthand numerous admissions staffs agonize over choosing from an excess of highly qualified applicants.

6   What we have learned is that objective merit and fairness are attractive concepts with no basis in reality. Admissions decisions cannot be "fair" when there are fewer spots in a class than qualified applicants. Moreover, there exists no single standard of "merit" that can be objectively applied. Rather, admission to any institution that has more qualified applicants than it has spaces is based on an array of attributes that lead an institution to prefer the students it selects.

7   It may be useful, therefore, to ask: Is there a preference that most people would agree is permissible?

8   Should a state university give preference to in-state students? We would suggest yes, since the taxes paid by state residents support the institution. If one agrees, then that establishes that preference is permissible for those who financially support the university—especially if their support contributes to a better education for all of the students enrolled.

9   Alumni support their colleges and universities, public and private alike, in many ways, including financially. In 2001, alumni provided 28 percent of the private donations to higher education, or almost $7 billion. The major donors contribute far more than the cost of their children's education. Thus, having agreed that state universities may give preference to students whose families support them through their tax dollars, should we not agree that institutions also may give preference to those whose families voluntarily support them and all other students as well? (And it is all other students: Since even full tuition at

most private institutions pays for only about 60 percent of the cost of an undergraduate education, the only reason any student gets a high-quality education is the generosity of donors.)

10   Moreover, any development professional will testify that a family's financial commitment is likely to grow with additional members' and generations' common affiliation. Witness the multimillion-dollar gifts that the Packard family has given Stanford.

11   In the most practical terms, honoring alumni commitment is a way to maintain quality. If states fully supported their public universities, they would have at least some justification to consider barring any preference for the children of alumni or, indeed, anyone from out of state. However, many "state" universities receive far less than half the support they need from their state—and the portion is declining. With inadequate government support, public universities face a choice: Allow the quality of education to drop to the level of support; raise tuition to levels that the public would reject; or cultivate supporters among their alumni. Which makes the most sense?

12   Because the tuition at private institutions, too, covers only a portion of the cost of instruction, they face a similar choice: Drop the quality of education to the level that net tuition income can support; virtually double tuition and cut back on financial aid; or cultivate alumni support. Again, which makes the most sense for all of the students of an institution?

13   Apart from those logical rationales, legacy preference is simply not the major issue that the news media, through dominant play and dire tone, suggest. Let's review a few facts:

- Legacy preference is a nonissue for the vast majority of college applicants. At no more than 100 of the nation's 3,500 colleges and universities are admissions competitive enough for such a status to matter. At that handful of institutions, legacies are only a small fraction of the applicants. And only a portion of those legacy applicants are admitted. Many of those admitted are top students who would have been accepted in any event. (For example, *The New York Times* reported in February that the average SAT of 30 legacies in the current freshman class at Middlebury College was 1389—33 points higher than that of the class as a whole.) Thus, the legacy issue involves a fraction of a portion of a fraction of applicants at 3 percent of all institutions.

- Legacy status does not guarantee admission. Many legacies are turned down. There is one universally relevant standard for admission: Does the student have the ability to complete the course of study at the institution? A college would be foolish to admit a legacy who could not meet that standard, for the student would fail and the family would be alienated.

- Upward mobility does not depend on admission to the handful of institutions where admission is competitive enough for legacy status to matter. On the contrary, a study of Fortune 500 CEO's showed a vast array of alma maters— liberal-arts colleges and nonflagship state universities greatly outnumbering Ivy League institutions or big-name publics. One can get a top education, and a great start in life, at hundreds of institutions. Alas, that seemed better understood when high-school counselors, a good education, and a good fit—not status and magazine rankings—guided college decisions.

- Legacy preference will increasingly include minority students. It was only one generation ago that most colleges began enrolling and graduating significant numbers of minority students. In coming years, those graduates' children will increasingly show up as second-generation applicants.

Those who call for admissions to be based only on "merit" have yet to provide a rational definition. Which shows more merit—an A in an easy course or a B in a much tougher course? Does a brilliant student who suffers from test anxiety have less merit than a student with a natural aptitude for multiple-choice questions? Besides grades and test scores, are other attributes nonmeritorious? A university with a school of music lacks a bassoon in its student orchestra. Who has more merit for admission: a talented bassoonist or a nonmusician with slightly higher grades and test scores?

14   We have been led to believe that merit can be defined and measured, and that prospective students can be ranked by it. All an institution must do is start at the top of such a list and work its way down. But can the value and potential of human beings be strictly ranked? Could any of us rank our friends by merit? Yes, our best friends might be fairly easy to name; likewise, admissions offices have little trouble identifying the students they most desire. But how would we distinguish between our No. 7 friend and our No. 8 friend? How do we compare their different kinds of merit—one is more thoughtful, another has a better sense of humor, a third is particularly generous, a fourth a great conversationalist? And how could one possibly, as some expect of an admissions office, distinguish between the 649th and 650th friends, or the 5,296th and 5,297th?

15   Colleges and universities have done themselves a disservice by trying to portray their admissions decisions as "fair." Those decisions, like most other conclusions about the potential of human beings, involve experience, judgment, perception, and intuition. In other words, they are an art. And "fair" has no meaning in art.

16   We should strive to describe our admissions processes as what they are: not fair, but rational. Rational because they seek a rounded class of students who can learn from each other. Rational because they contribute to our institutions' specific and clearly stated goals and missions. Rational because they exercise the First Amendment rights that Justice Felix Frankfurter referred to as the "four essential freedoms" of a university to determine for itself, on academic grounds, who may teach, what may be taught, how it shall be taught, and who may be admitted to study.

17   Let us be rational in another way. Let us not allow the negligible matter of legacies to obscure issues that have vastly greater impact on vastly greater numbers of students. Let's start with the need for government support of primary and secondary public education, especially in poor school districts. Let's see some headlines about preparing all of America's children for access to, and success in, college.

Time to Bury the Legacy
Robert DeKoven

The following article opposing legacy admissions first appeared in the San Diego Union-Tribune *on February 12, 2003. Robert DeKoven teaches at California Western School of Law.*

1   As the Supreme Court considers admissions standards in college admissions, perhaps the court should review how college admissions treat not just the disadvantaged, but also the advantaged, a group that public and private college officials have long recruited and favored over the less affluent.

2   Parents and students are not aware that many students on college campuses today are not there based entirely upon merit, but because a parent attended the university, or the family contributed money in the past or made a pledge to the school.

3   Private universities depend upon tuition and endowment income. So it's no secret that, in achieving a "diverse" student body, some schools accept students whose entering credentials are less than glowing.

4   One practice that benefits the affluent is preferring legacies, or children of alumni, almost always contributors.

5   At Notre Dame, for example, 57 percent of students admitted were children of alumni, with 23 percent of these students actually enrolled at the university.

6   Overall, 10 percent to 15 percent of students at many Ivy League schools are children of graduates and are also admitted in much higher rates than other students. It's not as if the legacies have to meet the same standards as other prospective students.

7   In 1964, George W. Bush applied to Yale University with a C average from high school and a 566 SAT verbal score. However, George W. was a legacy—a third-generation legacy—and Yale University accepted him and rejected others with far more impressive credentials.

8   Private schools defend the legacy practice because it builds school loyalty and generates alumni contributions. Prospective students have an incentive to apply and attend, knowing that their kids will have an edge when they apply.

9   Public colleges, which receive most of their support from public tax dollars, also prefer legacies. According to *The Badger Herald*, while a "minor" factor, the University of Wisconsin considers "being the child of an alumni" a "plus factor," among many indicators.

10   But other elite public schools, such as the University of Virginia and University of Pennsylvania, also prefer legacies. Penn admitted 41 percent of legacies and enrolled 14 percent of them.*

---

* *Union-Tribune* Editors: the University of Pennsylvania is [not] a public institution. In fact, it is private, although it is chartered by the state of Pennsylvania and the governor is president of the Board of Trustees. [February 14, 2003.]

11   Giving an edge based upon being a legacy is, in reality, an advantage based largely upon race. Keep in mind that many private universities routinely discriminated against persons of color (and women) in admissions. Even public universities engaged in segregation until 1954.

12   The reality is that getting that playing field even for persons of color and women wasn't even started until passage of federal laws in the 1960s and 1970s denying funds (and tax-exempt status) to schools engaged in race or gender bias.

13   Even so, under-represented minorities, in addition to other obstacles, have had to contend with the legacy factor as they tried to get admitted into schools based upon merit, while others, like George W., have had lesser credentials, but benefited from the legacy factor.

14   Legacies are a form of positive bias based upon one's lineage. It's bad when done privately, but antithetical to the Constitution and our notions of fairness when the state gives credit for being born to affluent parents. It's a mark of achievement to overcome poverty and adversity, it's luck of the gene pool to be the son of George H.W. and Barbara Bush.

15   For a state university to give weight for having been born into a home of college-educated folks violates the Equal Protection Clause of the Constitution. Another practice that is even more controversial is the practice of preferring students whose parents are major donors to the university or who have made a pledge.

16   The practice received attention in "The Sopranos," where Tony Soprano, whose trade is extortion, discovered that he could really improve his daughter's chances of getting admitted to a prestigious school if he simply pledged money for a building fund. Though he didn't like the shakedown, he realized it was a cost of doing business, and he did it.

17   Data about this practice are difficult to get, especially from private colleges, which can claim student privacy to defeat access to data to show how pledges and admissions correlate.

18   One case from Illinois, involving the admission of 83 entering medical students in the 1970s, showed that 64 had pledges made in their behalf, totaling $2 million. Apparently the medical school seats went from between $3,000 to $100,000, presumably based upon the applicant's entering credentials.

19   How widespread the practice continues to be is difficult to know. It's not like university admissions files are audited to see that the data that schools present in their reports to college guides is truly accurate.

20   If we learned anything from last summer's episode involving admissions officers at one Ivy League school getting caught tampering with the computer files of students at another Ivy League school, some schools are not above unethical behavior and espionage.

21   California law prohibits the use of race as a factor in admissions for public colleges. But the law should extend to legacies and admissions based on whether the applicant or his or her family has donated or pledged funds to secure admission.

22   Affirmative action for the affluent is a practice that shouldn't need a Supreme Court edict to end this inequality.

The History of Legacy Admissions
Cameron Howell and Sarah E. Turner

You may be surprised to learn that the history of legacy admissions in America is tied to an unpleasant history of race and ethnicity. The brief overview that follows first appeared in Research in Higher Education *(June 2004). Cameron Howell wrote his doctoral dissertation on legacy admissions, with a focus on that practice at the University of Virginia. Sarah Turner works at the National Bureau of Economic Research, also at the University of Virginia. (Note: For the sake of brevity, the authors' list of references has been deleted.)*

leg·a·cy (lĕg'E-sē) *n., pl.* **–cies.** 1. Money or property bequeathed to someone by will. 2. Something handed on from those who have come before. [< Lat. *legare,* to bequeath as a legacy.]

—American Heritage Dictionary, Second College Edition

1   In the world of college and university admissions, the word "legacy" has a peculiar definition that cannot be found in most standard dictionaries. It means "the son or daughter of an alumnus or alumna," but the practical application of the word, in the admissions community, reveals how it has been derived from its original meaning of inheritance. Graduates of many of America's most elite institutions of higher education bequeath to their sons and daughters a sizable advantage in the admissions process. Known as legacies, these children are admitted at twice the rate of other applicants at some universities (Bowen and Bok, 1998; Lamb, 1993), and average SAT scores for legacies are, in some cases, lower than the average scores of their peers (U.S. Department of Education's Office for Civil Rights, 1990). On the surface, these facts raise serious questions for the admissions enterprise, which heralds the ideals of merit and equity.

• • •

2   Institutions of higher education have promoted intergenerational attachments since the earliest days of Harvard College. Henry Adams (1907), who graduated from Harvard in 1858, described the familial ties among Harvard alumni in his autobiography:

> For generation after generation, Adamses and Brookses and Boylstons and Gorhams had gone to Harvard College, and although none of them, as far as known, had ever done any good there, or thought himself the better for it, custom, social ties, convenience, and, above all, economy, kept each generation in the track. (1907, p. 55)

In the era before increased competition in college admissions, "all alumni children who could demonstrate a minimum level of ability were admitted" to U.S. institutions of higher education (Duffy and Goldberg, 1998, p. 47). This policy attracted no attention until it was threatened. The threat materialized early in the twentieth century, when a series of dynamics increased the quantity and quality of applicants vying for admission to elite colleges. Among these applicants were a growing number of highly qualified Jewish students. In the 1920s, Ivy League institutions such as Harvard, Yale, and Princeton formalized their admissions policies that favored children of alumni in order to appease graduate fathers and in order to limit the number of Jewish matriculants (Lamb, 1993; Synnott, 1979).

3   Later in the twentieth century, a boom in the number of college-age students coincided with improved access to institutions of higher education. Increasingly, students began to apply to and attend colleges and universities outside of their home states (Hoxby, 2002). Geographic integration of selective institutions began in earnest after World War II, when a combination of factors including reduced transportation costs and increased reliance on standardized testing enabled the recruitment of highly talented students from across the nation. Then, beginning in the late 1960s, many institutions entered the era of coeducation, admitting women to undergraduate degree programs. (Coeducation at selective institutions had the dual effects of increasing the number of qualified applicants while also increasing the size of the legacy pool.) During the same decade, colleges and universities responded to the Civil Rights movement by actively seeking to increase minority enrollment. In some Southern states, this era brought an end to segregation in higher education. These changes in the gender, race, and geographic representation of applicants increased the overall level of competition for admission to these institutions, thereby infringing on the traditional advantages of legacy applicants while also making legacy preferences more valuable to their potential recipients. Alumni fathers feared that more and better applicants would surely displace their children in the admissions process.

4   These fears became especially frenzied at Yale University, when R. Inslee Clark was named the Dean of Admissions in 1965 (Lemann, 1999). The share of alumni sons admitted to the university plummeted from 20% to 12% in Clark's first year as dean, and "open warfare" commenced (p. 149). "An apocrypha of Clark horror stories" circulated among the alumni, who felt insulted and threatened (p. 150). William F. Buckley Jr. lobbied for a position on the Yale Corporation, the university's overseeing board, on the premise that Yale's favoritism of alumni sons should be restored. Kingman Brewster Jr., the President of Yale, managed to ease tensions among the alumni after he published an apologetic piece in the university's alumni magazine and leaked an internal letter stating that "[t]he only preference by inheritance which seems to deserve recognition is the Yale son" (p. 151).

5   To this day, a preference by inheritance persists at Yale and other selective colleges. Three national surveys—conducted by the American Association of Collegiate Registrars and Admissions Officers, American College Testing, the College Board, Educational Testing Service, and the National Association of College Admission Counselors—track the use of legacy policies among college and universities across time (Breland et al., 1995). The survey results show that both public and private institutions of higher education commonly provide some preference for children of alumni.

6   The prevalence of legacy admissions preferences at selective colleges and universities is also evident in the share of legacies that comprise some under-

graduate student bodies. At Notre Dame, 23% of enrolled students are children of alumni (Golden, 2003). The percentage of legacies among enrolled students reaches 14% at the University of Pennsylvania, 13% at Harvard, 11% at Princeton, and 11% at the University of Virginia. Thus, at many institutions, the share of legacies enrolled is far from trivial and often exceeds the percentage of black students within the student body.

Getting In: The Social Logic of Ivy League Admissions
Malcolm Gladwell

The following selection is an excerpt from the final section of a review of Jerome Karabel's The Chosen: The Hidden History of Exclusion at Harvard, Yale, and Princeton *(2005), which first appeared in the* New Yorker *on October 10, 2005. Well-known lecturer and writer Malcolm Gladwell, a staff writer at the* New Yorker, *earned rave reviews for* The Tipping Point *(2000), an exploration of how ideas and products "tip" from relative obscurity to becoming cultural phenomena. He is the author most recently of* Blink *(2005), an exploration of instinct-based decision making.*

1   I once had a conversation with someone who worked for an advertising agency that represented one of the big luxury automobile brands. He said that he was worried that his client's new lower-priced line was being bought disproportionately by black women. He insisted that he did not mean this in a racist way. It was just a fact, he said. Black women would destroy the brand's cachet. It was his job to protect his client from the attentions of the socially undesirable.

2   This is, in no small part, what Ivy League admissions directors do. They are in the luxury-brand-management business, and [Jerome Karabel's] *The Chosen,* in the end, is a testament to just how well the brand managers in Cambridge, New Haven, and Princeton have done their job in the past seventy-five years. In the nineteen twenties, when Harvard tried to figure out how many Jews they had on campus, the admissions office scoured student records and assigned each suspected Jew the designation j1 (for someone who was "conclusively Jewish"), j2 (where the "preponderance of evidence" pointed to Jewishness), or j3 (where Jewishness was a "possibility"). In the branding world, this is called customer segmentation. In the Second World War, as Yale faced plummeting enrollment and revenues, it continued to turn down qualified Jewish applicants. As Karabel writes, "In the language of sociology, Yale judged its symbolic capital to be even more precious than its economic capital." No good brand manager would sacrifice reputation for short-term gain. The admissions directors at Harvard have always, similarly, been diligent about rewarding the children of graduates, or, as they are

quaintly called, "legacies." In the 1985-92 period, for instance, Harvard admitted children of alumni at a rate more than twice that of non-athlete, non-legacy applicants, despite the fact that, on virtually every one of the school's magical ratings scales, legacies significantly lagged behind their peers. Karabel calls the practice "unmeritocratic at best and profoundly corrupt at worst," but rewarding customer loyalty is what luxury brands do. Harvard wants good graduates, and part of their definition of a good graduate is someone who is a generous and loyal alumnus. And if you want generous and loyal alumni you have to reward them. Aren't the tremendous resources provided to Harvard by its alumni part of the reason so many people want to go to Harvard in the first place? The endless battle over admissions in the United States proceeds on the assumption that some great moral principle is at stake in the matter of whom schools like Harvard choose to let in—that those who are denied admission by the whims of the admissions office have somehow been harmed. If you are sick and a hospital shuts its doors to you, you are harmed. But a selective school is not a hospital, and those it turns away are not sick. Elite schools, like any luxury brand, are an aesthetic experience—an exquisitely constructed fantasy of what it means to belong to an elite—and they have always been mindful of what must be done to maintain that experience.

So Your Dad Went to Harvard
Mark Megalli

In the following selection, Mark Megalli examines the pro-white racial bias inherent in legacy admissions. He argues that conservatives who criticize affirmative action, an admissions practice favoring candidates of color, should be willing, in the name of consistency, to criticize legacy programs. Both programs "subvert meritocracy," he claims. This article first appeared in the Journal of Blacks in Higher Education *(Spring, 1995).*

1   Legacy preference is limited neither to the Ivy League nor to the elite northeastern higher education establishment. According to data provided by The College Board, well over 600 universities and colleges across the nation use or accept the "common application form" (CAF) in the admissions process. The CAF, meant to cut down on the sheer volume of paperwork that must be completed by applicants to several schools, asks the "legacy question" and thus ensures that legacy preference at least will be made possible, if not actually put into practice, at the hundreds of schools that use the form. Colleges that use the form, besides Harvard, include Wesleyan, Johns Hopkins, Williams, New York University, Duke, Swarthmore, Rice, and Vassar. Of course, many schools, including Yale, Princeton, Stanford, and Amherst, that do not use the CAF in the application process still ask on their own forms where an applicant's parents were educated.

2   The U.S. Department of Education's Office for Civil Rights (OCR) report on Harvard found that preference for legacies disproportionately helps white applicants—hardly shocking, because 96 percent of all living Ivy League alumni are white. However, the commission did not charge Harvard with violating Title VI of the Civil Rights Act of 1964, which states in part, "No person in the United States shall on the ground of race, color, or national origin be excluded from participation in, be denied the benefits of, or be otherwise subjected to discrimination under any program to which this part applies." Instead, OCR held that Harvard's preferences for children of alumni is a "legitimate institutional goal" necessary to "1) encourage alumni volunteer services; 2) encourage alumni financial contributions; and, 3) maintain community relations."

At Many of the Nation's Most Prestigious Universities, Legacy Applicants Are Accepted Far More Frequently Than Applicants in General

Institution	% of All Applicants Accepted	% of Legacy Applicants Accepted
Harvard	16%	35%
Yale	22	45
Princeton	15	43
Dartmouth	27	57
Columbia	32	51
Univ. of Penn.	40	66
Cornell	37	43
MIT	30	55

Sources: *The Washington Monthly,* June 1991, p. 10; Lamb, pp. 503 and 505; *Daily Princetonian,* November 19, 1993; and JBHE telephone interviews conducted in February 1994 and April 1995.

3   Critics have faulted OCR for applying a rational basis test rather than a disparate impact analysis in exculpating Harvard from charges of discrimination against its minority applicants. In other words, some say OCR should have found the legacy policy at Harvard to be discriminatory against minorities because the actual effect is that minorities are disproportionately disadvantaged by such a policy. Instead OCR dismissed such charges due to a lack of de jure discrimination. Simply put, OCR bought Harvard's "economics" argument.

4   But many do not accept the idea that in order to maintain their financial strength, elite universities must open the floodgates to the often less-qualified children of alumni. According to the OCR report, alumni in 1989 gave $36 million to the Harvard College Fund, "much of which is used to provide financial aid and scholarship to needy students." Let us conservatively assume "much" to mean "all," and let us further consider that based on the fact that there were 63,088 living Harvard College alumni that year, the average alumni contribution to the Harvard College Fund was $571. If legacies were admitted at the rate of nonlegacies, as estimated above, there would be about 200 fewer accepted legacy applicants in a given year. Assuming the alumni parents of every one of these rejected candidates for admission never gave another penny to Harvard,

the total lost by the institution per year would be expected to amount to $114,200 based on the average $571 alumni contribution. Even under these extremely conservative conditions, this sum is indeed paltry considering the fact that Harvard *earns* an equivalent sum on its $6.2 billion endowment in a little over two hours.* The calculation does not include added revenue from donations given by the families of nonlegacy students who would end up taking the places of the 200 rejected legacies in this scenario. So we see that, even by this incredibly conservative estimate, the "financial necessity" argument holds little water.

Alumni Children Have Lower SAT Scores

Mean Scores of Admitted Students at Harvard University on Selected Admissions Criteria 1983 to 1992

	Children of Alumni	Nonalumni/Nonathlete
SAT math	695.0	717.7
SAT verbal	674.1	686.7
Athletic rating	3.08	3.11
Academic rating	2.40	2.19
Extracurricular rating	2.52	2.43
Personal rating	2.53	2.44
Teacher rating	2.32	2.08
Counselor rating	2.34	2.14
Alumni rating	2.25	2.06
Class rank	92.47	96.73

Note: SAT scores range from 200 to 800. For other ratings, lower numbers indicate superior performance. Class rank ranges from 0 (worst) to 100 (best).

5   Furthermore, one might wonder why applicants of wealthy families in general are not given preference based on the financial-needs argument. Certainly Harvard would be able to raise more money if its entire student body consisted of millionaires, yet few would give credence to a policy that based admission primarily on family wealth. The practice of legacy preferences amounts to a toned-down version of this absurd scenario.

6   Conservatives who are quick to point out the unfairness of preferential admissions for racial minorities on the grounds that these preferences "subvert meritocracy" would do well to reexamine their views on the legacy systems currently in place at the nation's leading universities. In addition to the racial impact, the legacy preferential system perpetuates elitism by conferring considerable advantage upon privileged white children and, as a result, disfavoring blacks and others whose parents were less likely to have gone to college.

---

* Assuming an 8 percent annual return on Harvard's endowment, the university earns $496 million per year or $56,621 per hour. [Editors: As of 2006, Harvard's endowment was $29.2 billion.]

Preserve Universities' Right to Shape Student Community
USA Today

USA Today's editorial page editors argue against interfering in a university's admissions poli-cies. The editors hold that universities should be free to shape their freshman class as they see fit—a prerogative that extends to legacy admissions. This editorial ran on January 26, 2004, in tandem with an editorial opposing legacy admissions by Senator John Edwards, the Democratic candidate for Vice President in 2004.

1 Each year, Dickinson College admits about half of the students who apply to the Pennsylvania liberal arts school. But if applicants' parents or siblings graduat-ed from Dickinson, their chance of admission shoots up to 75%. Overall, 12% of Dickinson's incoming freshmen have family connections that give them a leg up over other applicants that has nothing to do with grades or SAT scores.

2 Universities long have favored legacy admissions as a way to boost support from alumni, who are more likely to stay active and make donations if their chil-dren are enrolled. But now the practice is coming under fire. Critics claim legacy preference programs are most likely to give affluent white students a boost. That's particularly unfair, they say, now that minorities increasingly are being excluded from admission preference plans because some colleges are dropping their affirmative action programs.

3 Sen. John Edwards of North Carolina, who is seeking the Democratic presi-dential nomination, says legacies undermine the principle that college admis-sions should be based on a student's academic accomplishments. Sen. Ted Kennedy, D-Mass., himself a Harvard legacy, is pushing legislation that would require colleges to disclose how many legacy students they accept.

4 Critics rightly point out that legacy applicants get at least a degree of special treatment that isn't based on academics. But they aren't unique. To attract stu-dents with a range of talents and interests, colleges commonly show preferences for attributes that go beyond academics. Hence, special provisions are made to attract gifted athletes, ensure broad geographic diversity or even maintain a renowned a capella group. While any preference program can be taken too far, such admissions acknowledge that a vibrant college is more than the sum of stu-dents' grades and standardized test scores.

5 By pressuring colleges to drop legacy admissions, the federal government would interfere with the right of universities to manage their own affairs as long as they aren't violating anti-discrimination laws.

6 Some universities are ending legacy admissions on their own. Texas A&M stopped the practice last month in the face of criticism that it kept legacy pref-erences even after dropping affirmative action.

7 Pressuring all universities to follow Texas A&M's example, however, sends the federal government down a slippery slope. Using the same logic, the gov-ernment could question colleges' freedom to:

- Reflect their unique character. The University of Notre Dame's freshman class is 85% Roman Catholic. Federal attempts to dictate admissions policies could infringe on a college's ability to shape its student body.
- Control their financing. Many colleges rely on private giving, often from alumni. At Dickinson, alumni provide 25% of its budget, allowing the school to keep tuition to $28,380 and offer aid to families that can't afford the cost. College officials say eliminating legacy admissions would reduce donations and drive up tuition.

8   Donations aren't the sole reason colleges have legacy policies. Many say students of alumni fortify school traditions and have more active parents. They also say legacy students have stronger academic records on average than other students admitted.

9   Critics say admissions should be based solely on merit. But that argument assumes an objective standard can assess merit across the nation's wide range of college-bound students. In the subjective world of admissions, pure merit does not exist. Nor should it.

10   Choosing a diverse student body that contributes to a stimulating campus environment is a freedom worth preserving.

Admissions Confidential: An Insider's Account of the Elite College Selection Process
Rachel Toor

Rachel Toor spent three years as an admissions officer at Duke University. In this passage, excerpted from her book Admissions Confidential: An Insider's Account of the Elite College Selection Process *(2001), she describes the manner in which children of Duke alumni and of major donors to the university ("development" applicants) are treated during the stages (rounds) of the admission process. During this process, admissions officers assign applicants numerical points for their scores in such areas as GPA, College Board tests, and AP classes. The Admissions Office sets threshold scores. Anyone exceeding the threshold is automatically admitted; anyone below the threshold is automatically denied admission—unless special numerical codes assigned for other, nonacademic qualifications are added to the score during subsequent rounds of the admissions process.*

1   Then there was the preparation for alum and development rounds. . . . The director [of admissions] never wanted to admit these kids and had to fight to be able to keep them out. He usually lost. He wanted to make sure that the admissions officer gave him as much ammunition as possible to use against them. He'd make sure we looked for midterm grades and new testing. He was not much interested in our personal opinions of the applicant and didn't give an opportunity to express them. That rarely stopped us.

2   Alum and development rounds consisted of the director, the head of the university's development [fund-raising] office, and the Alumni liaison to admissions. Alumni were coded as either A or B. An A meant that they had been active and involved with the school since graduation; often this meant that they had a history of consistent giving, but also rewarded were the good soldiers who showed up for reunions and were involved in their local alumni clubs. The alum B category got less of a boost—it simply meant that these people kept their records and whereabouts up-to-date with the alumni office. And then there were the alum Xs. The alumni office had lost track of them, so even if a kid had written on her application that her parent had gone to Duke, it didn't help. Development codes were high, for those who had not only the potential to give loads of money, but who had a history of giving it to Duke; medium, [for] those who also had loads of money, had never given it to Duke but had given to similar kinds of places; and low, which could mean that the family was rich but not philanthropic, or that someone somewhere (usually fairly high up, could be a trustee, could be the basketball coach) had some kind of personal interest in the application. These kids were always discussed, but the director often triumphed in keeping them out.

3   Alum and development rounds were usually an all-day affair. We were allowed to sit in and speak only if spoken to. It was hard to remain silent and sometimes I failed. But the process gave a good overview of long-term institutional goals and the directions of the university, a big picture focus that we the foot soldiers in admissions were rarely privy to. Here we would learn about plans for a new Center for Jewish Life, a Genomics Institute, an addition to the gym. These planning goals were being made possible by large gifts, and although there was never a quid pro quo for donors with children applying, the development office wanted to be sure that everything possible was done for them. So they arranged special tours and VIP interviews for these applicants (didn't help them, but it made them feel special), and then they came into rounds to plead their case.

4   The kids who went to these special rounds had already been denied, either as auto denies [automatic denials, based on numerical codes corresponding to applicants' academic qualifications] or in committee. They were, without a doubt, the weakest portion of our applicant pool. Sitting in on the rounds could be highly amusing—the director of development was a smart, very funny man. It could also be tense. The director had to reserve a number of places in the class for these kids, places that could easily have been filled by regular kids whom we then had to deny in rounds. Our target numbers for our regions were deflated; even though I was only able to admit forty kids from Massachusetts, once you took into account the athletes and the alum and development admits, the final number would be much greater.

5   Most admissions officers hated to see these kids get in. I know I did. Occasionally you'd find a kid you liked whom you knew wasn't going to make it on her own. Those you hoped might be coded [provided additional points for nonacademic reasons]. That happened rarely. More often they were arrogant, entitled, or just plain not smart enough for you to want to have them admitted and take a place from a more deserving kid. The biggest problem with admitting

so many of these truly mediocre kids—they made the BWRK's [bright, well-rounded kids] look like fascinating geniuses—was that when they were admitted they usually matriculated. Though the top tier of our applicant pool generally turned us down for other schools, the alum and development kids were lucky to get in and came. The Duke student body was disproportionately heavy with them.

For Analysis Assignment #1 Only

Making Ethical Decisions
Gerald F. Cavanagh

Gerald Cavanagh is professor of management, associate dean, and director of graduate programs in the University of Detroit's College of Business Administration. Cavanagh holds degrees in engineering, philosophy, theology, and management. He was ordained as a Jesuit priest in 1964. This selection appeared originally in his book American Business Values *(1990).*

1 The basic method of making ethical judgments involves just three steps: (1) gathering relevant factual information, (2) determining the moral norm that is most applicable, and (3) making the ethical judgment on the rightness or wrongness of the act or policy.

2   Nevertheless, ethical judgments are not always easy to make. The facts of the case are often not clear-cut, and the ethical criteria or principles to be used are not always agreed on, even by the experts themselves.

• • •

Ethical Norms for . . . [Decision Making]

3 Ethical criteria and ethical models have been the subject of much reflection over the centuries. Of all ethical theories, utilitarianism is the one business-people feel most at home with. This is not surprising, as the theory traces its origins to Adam Smith, the father of modern economics. The main proponents of utilitarianism, however, were Jeremy Bentham and John Stuart Mill, both of whom helped to formulate the theory more precisely. Utilitarianism evaluates actions in terms of their consequences. In any given situation, the one action which would result in the greatest net gain for all concerned parties is considered to be the right, or morally obligatory, action. The theory of rights focuses on the entitlements of individual persons. Immanuel Kant (personal rights) and John Locke (property rights) were the first to fully develop the theory of rights. The theory of justice has a longer tradition, going back to Plato and Aristotle in the fourth century B.C. . . .

The Norm of Utilitarianism

4 Utilitarianism judges that an action is right if it produces the greatest utility, "the greatest good for the greatest number." The decision process is very much like a cost-benefit analysis applied to all parties who would be touched by the decision. That action is right which produces the greatest net benefit when all the costs and benefits to all the affected parties are taken into account. Although it would be convenient if these costs and benefits could be measured in some comparable unit, this is rarely possible. Many important values (e.g., human life and liberty) cannot be quantified. Thus, the best that can be done is to enumerate the effects and the magnitude of their costs and benefits as clearly and accurately as possible.

5 The utilitarian principle says that the right action is that which produces the greatest net benefit over any other possible action. This does not mean that the right action produces the greatest good for the person performing the action. Rather, it is the action that produces the greatest net good for all those who are affected by the action. Utilitarianism can handle some ethical cases quite well, especially those that are complex and affect many parties. Although the model and the methodology are clear in theory, carrying out the calculations is often difficult. Taking into account so many affected parties, along with the extent to which the action touches them, can be a tallying nightmare.

6 Hence several shortcuts have been proposed that can reduce the complexity of utilitarian calculations. Each shortcut involves a sacrifice of accuracy for ease of calculation. Among these shortcuts are (1) adherence to a simplified rule (e.g., the Golden Rule, "Do unto others as you would have them do unto you"); (2) calculation of costs and benefits in dollar terms for ease of comparison; (3) restriction of consideration to those directly affected by the action, putting aside indirect effects. In using these shortcuts, an individual should be aware that they result in simplification and that some interests may not be sufficiently taken into consideration.

7 In the popular mind, the term *utilitarianism* sometimes suggests selfishness and exploitation. For our purposes, the term should be considered not to have these connotations. However, a noteworthy weakness of utilitarianism as an ethical norm is that it can advocate, for example, abridging an individual's right to a job or even life for the sake of the greater good of a larger number of people. . . . One additional caution in using utilitarian rules is in order: It is considered unethical to opt for narrower benefits (e.g., personal goals, career, or money) at the expense of the good of a larger number, such as a nation or a society. Utilitarian norms emphasize the good of the group; it is a large-scale ethical model. As a result, an individual and what is due that individual may be overlooked. The theory of rights has been developed to emphasize the individual and the standing of that individual with peers and within society.

The Norm of Individual Rights

8 A right is a person's entitlement to something. Rights may flow from the legal system, such as our constitutional rights of freedom of conscience or freedom of

speech. The U.S. Bill of Rights and the United Nations Universal Declaration of Human Rights are examples of documents that spell out individual rights in detail. Legal rights, as well as others which may not be written into law, stem from the human dignity of persons. Moral rights have these characteristics: (1) They enable individuals to pursue their own interests, and (2) they impose correlative prohibitions or requirements on others.

9   Hence, every right has a corresponding duty. My right to freedom of conscience is supported by the prohibition of other individuals from unnecessarily limiting that freedom of conscience. From another perspective, my right to be paid for my work corresponds to a duty of mine to perform "a fair day's work for a fair day's pay." In the latter case, both the right and duty stem from the right to private property, which is a traditional pillar of American life and law. However, the right to private property is not absolute. A factory owner may be forced by law, as well as by morality, to spend money on pollution control or safety equipment. . . .

10   People also have the right not to be lied to or deceived, especially on matters which they have a right to know about. A supervisor has the duty to be truthful in giving feedback on work performance even if it is difficult for the supervisor to do so. Each of us has the right not to be lied to by salespeople or advertisements. Perjury under oath is a serious crime; lying on matters where another has a right to accurate information is also seriously unethical. Truthfulness and honesty are basic ethical norms.

• • •

The Norm of Justice

11 Justice requires all persons, and thus managers too, to be guided by fairness, equity, and impartiality. Justice calls for evenhanded treatment of groups and individuals (1) in the distribution of the benefits and burdens of society, (2) in the administration of laws and regulations, and (3) in the imposition of sanctions and the rewarding of compensation for wrongs suffered. An action or policy is just if it is comparable to the treatment accorded to others.

12   Standards of justice are generally considered to be more important than the utilitarian consideration of consequences. If a society is unjust to a minority group (e.g., apartheid treatment of blacks in South Africa), we generally consider that society to be unjust and we condemn it, even if the results of the injustices bring about greater economic productivity. On the other hand, we seem willing to trade off some equity if the results will bring about greater benefits for all. For example, income and wealth differences are justified only if they bring greater benefits for all.

13   Standards of justice are not as often in conflict with individual rights as are utilitarian norms. This is not surprising, since justice is largely based on the moral rights of individuals. The moral right to be treated as a free and equal person, for example, undergirds the notion that benefits and burdens should be distributed equitably. . . .

An Anthology
of Readings

Marriage and Family in America

8

Between 40 and 50% of all American marriages will fail. An even higher percentage of second marriages will end in divorce. Failed marriages of young couples have become cynically known as "Starter Marriages." Cohabitation is on the rise, and more people than ever before are choosing to stay single. A survey released by the U.S. Census Bureau in October 2006 found that domiciles led by married couples were now in the minority—just 49.7% of all households. Yet marriage continues to fascinate and inspire us—as it has every known culture throughout human history. The wedding industry generates over $60 billion a year in expenses ranging from embossed invitations to rented tuxedos to $10,000 video shoots. Newsstands are choked with bridal magazines. Tabloids splash celebrity weddings across their covers; and most Hollywood comedies still end with the prospect of a wedding. Everybody, it seems, plans on getting married. According to one set of statistics, 85% of Americans will marry at some point in their lives, and 99% say they plan to do so.

Why? What is it about the marital state that is so universally appealing? Why do we continue to wed, despite the fact that most of us, through personal experience, have experienced or witnessed divorce? For some young people, marriage is simply another fact of life—perhaps part of a dimly glimpsed future, along with 401(k) plans, 9-to-5 jobs, and other pillars of adulthood. Others may see the institution in more specific terms—for instance, a teenage girl obsessing over the color of her future bridesmaids' dresses and the merits of white versus pink roses for the centerpieces.

Whether marriage fuels our childhood fantasies or fulfills (or frustrates) our expectations as adults, very few of us can describe what it means to be married—if it ever occurred to us to do so. Doesn't this seem odd? After all, most people have no trouble describing "friendship" as a form of human relationship or "employment" or "citizenship." Yet marriage, an institution to which nearly all of us aspire, and a condition in which most of us will spend many years of our lives, resists easy interpretation. If pressed, most of us would probably characterize the marriage relationship as primarily romantic. The most idealistic and starry-eyed of us, who see marriage as a way for soul mates to pledge unending devotion to one another, dwell at one end of this spectrum. Others, aware that love can be fickle and ephemeral, sense that marriage must be about other things: maturity and commitment, an indication that one has "settled down," perhaps even a rite of passage to adulthood. (Yes, you are marrying someone you love, but you loved at 20 and didn't marry. What changed? *You* did.)

Sociologists Maria Kefalas and Kathryn Edin have demonstrated how, among poorer Americans, marriage has become a luxury item, to be purchased only when a couple has "arrived" financially, last on a "to-do" list, behind a home mortgage and new furniture. And at least some of us suspect that marriage involves pragmatic considerations of a social, political, or even avaricious nature. As they say, it's just as easy to fall in love with and marry a rich girl (or guy) as a poor one.

As the selections in this chapter will show, these conflicting and tangled motives for marrying are no accident. The very meaning of marriage has been changing over the centuries, an evolution that can be traced to broad cultural, intellectual, and economic trends. If anything, these changes seem to be accelerating. (To borrow from Hemingway—the changes seem to be happening slowly, and all at once.) But what significance can we draw from this evolution? Conservative cultural commentators point to the muddled state of contemporary marriage as proof that our society has taken a wrong turn. Yet a wrong turn from what—some historical, universally acclaimed ideal of marriage? As marriage historian Stephanie Coontz notes:

> Everyone agrees that marriage isn't what it used to be, and everyone is quite right. But most of what "everyone knows" about what matrimony used to be and just how it has changed is wrong.

With Coontz's observation as our starting point, this chapter examines the state of marriage and family in contemporary America. Historians, sociologists, anthropologists, political scientists, legal scholars, political activists, and journalists have studied marriage from their various perspectives; and they have offered observations about its impact on our culture, our lives, and indeed our very sense of who we are. Some call marriage a vital public institution that must be safeguarded for the civic good (we allude, here, to the debate over gay marriage). Others view marriage as a private concern between two consenting adults. Some venerate marriage as the ultimate partnership between the sexes. Others charge that marriage forces men and women into rigid—and unequal—gender roles.

The selections in this chapter reveal an institution in flux, the mutable nature of which forces Americans to create their own definitions—not just of marriage and family, but also of what it means to be a wife, a husband, a mother, and a father. The viewpoint in these selections ranges from the scholarly to the personal. A common theme, as you will notice, revolves around the female half of the marriage equation. Debates over the role of women, both in families and in society as a whole, underlie the most contentious debates regarding modern marriages and families. We will examine two of these disputes—working versus stay-at-home mothers, and the continued gender divide between women and men over the subject of child care and housework. As you read the selections, think about your own experiences with marriage and family. You may not be married yourself, or have even thought much about marriage; but certainly you have witnessed the marriages of family members and of friends. Ask yourself whether the viewpoint being expressed in the selections squares with your own observations and your own beliefs on the subject.

The chapter opens with two opposing perspectives, written 29 years apart by one woman, Terry Martin Hekker, on the subject of stay-at-home mothers.

Taken together, these two essays paint a stark portrait of marital disillusionment and personal despair that you are unlikely to forget any time soon. The next group of selections provides historical, sociological, and anthropological views of marriage throughout history and different cultures. In the first, historian Stephanie Coontz describes the horror with which many societies treated the "Radical Idea of Marrying for Love"—an idea most of us now take for granted. In the next selection, "The State of Our Unions," marriage researchers David Popenoe and Barbara Dafoe Whitehead use national marriage statistics to argue that the institution of marriage now faces its gravest crisis. In contrast, sociologists Mary Ann Schwartz and BarBara Marliene Scott debunk five common "myths" about marriage, asking: "Were the 'good old days' really that good for all marriages and families?"

The next two selections take on the contentious topic of gay marriage, as debated by two prominent cultural commentators. First, Andrew Sullivan argues why conservatives ought to support gay marriage. Then, conservative commentator William Bennett charges that opening marriage to homosexuals would destroy the institution itself.

The chapter next turns to an extended examination of two ongoing debates regarding marriage: working mothers versus stay-at-home mothers (often referred to as the "Mommy Wars" or "the opt-out debate") and the "stalled revolution"—the feminist complaint that, in an age of working women, men still refuse to shoulder their share of the housework or child care. In the first of these perspectives, *New York Times* writer Louise Story reports that an increasing number of women at elite Ivy League colleges say they plan to stop working—at least for a number of years—when they have children. Story's article prompted a number of heated responses, including the next selection, Karen Stabiner's "What Yale Women Want, and Why It Is Misguided." Stabiner accuses the Ivy Leaguers of a "startling combination of naiveté and privilege." In contrast to both Story's and Stabiner's viewpoints, Lynette Clemetson finds that African-American professional women are "opting out of the opt-out debate." As one of the women she reports on says, "We don't generally have the time or luxury for the guilt and competition that some white mothers engage in."

Following these are two selections detailing another skirmish on the marital front: housework. According to recent research, the amount of time men spend on housework has not changed in 40 years. While an increasing number of women have joined the workforce, often earning more than their husbands, women still do the bulk of the cooking, laundry, and childrearing. Naturally, this state of affairs has occasioned anger and bitterness among wives. Is this a private issue among spouses or a more systemic, feminist one? In "A Marriage Agreement," written in 1970, feminist Alix Kates Shulman proposes a dramatic solution to hold men to their side of the equal-housework bargain. Next, Caitlin Flanagan, in "How Serfdom Saved the Women's Movement," dismisses the idea that there ever was a bargain, and charges that modern feminists have found another way out of the conundrum of housework: hiring illegal nannies and maids.

The next two selections, by Hope Edelman and Eric Bartels, offer personal perspectives on married life that range across several of the issues raised by previous selections. Their writings provide a raw, honest look at the daily reality of married life. As a tongue-in-cheek solution to the kinds of problems described by Edelman and Bartels, Michelle Cottle makes a modest proposal: Married couples should acquire an extra wife.

If, after reading these selections, you're wondering why anybody in his or her right mind would want to get married at all, you're not alone. In the final selection, *Boston Globe* writer Keith O'Brien chronicles the growing phenomenon of people who are single—and have every intention of staying that way.

These selections on marriage are intended to be provocative—to cause you to think about what marriage and family mean to you. After all, if you are like 85% of Americans, one day you too will be married.

The Satisfactions of Housewifery and Motherhood/Paradise Lost (Domestic Division)
Terry Martin Hekker

We begin with a matched set of op-ed columns written nearly 30 years apart for the New York Times *by the same author. At the time her December 20, 1977, column "The Satisfactions of Housewifery and Motherhood" was published, Terry Martin Hekker was a housewife living in South Nyack, New York, who had been married 22 years to her husband, John Hekker, a lawyer and South Nyack village judge. The column deals with Hekker's experiences as a "stay-at-home" mom at a time—the late 1970s—when many women were opting to enter the workforce rather than stay home to raise their children. As a result of the extraordinary response to Hekker's column—some of which she describes in her follow-up 2006 piece, "Paradise Lost"—she expanded the essay into a book,* Ever Since Adam and Eve, *published by William Morrow in 1979. "Paradise Lost" was published on January 1, 2006. Like her first column, it aroused much comment in op-ed pieces and blogs around the nation.*

(1977)

regrets the shame

1   My son lied about it on his college application. My husband mutters it under his breath when asked. And I had grown reluctant to mention it myself.

2   *regrets mini*   The problem is my occupation. But the statistics on women that have come out since the Houston conference have given me a new outlook. I have ceased thinking of myself as obsolete and begun to see myself as I really am—an endangered species. Like the whooping crane and the snow leopard, I deserve attentive nurturing and perhaps a distinctive metal tag on my foot. Because I'm one of the last of the dying breed of human females designated, "Occupation: Housewife."

3   I know it's nothing to crow about. I realize that when people discuss their professions at parties I am more of a pariah than a hooker or a loan shark is. I have been castigated, humiliated and scorned. In an age of do-your-own-thing, it's clear no one meant me. I've been told (patiently and a little louder than nec-

essary, as one does with a small child) that I am an anachronism (except that they avoid such a big word). I have been made to feel so outmoded that I wouldn't be surprised to discover that, like a carton of yogurt, I have an expiration date stamped on my bottom.

[handwritten margin note: people view her as lazy and old-fashioned]

4   I once treasured a small hope that history might vindicate me. After all, nursing was once just such a shameful occupation, suitable for only the lowest women. But I abandoned any thought that my occupation would ever become fashionable again, just as I had to stop counting on full-figured women coming back into style. I'm a hundred years too late on both counts.

5   Now, however, thanks to all these new statistics, I see a brighter future for myself. Today, fewer than 16 percent of American families have a full-time housewife-mother. Comparing that with previous figures, at the rate it's going I calculate I am less than eight years away from being the last housewife in the country. And then I intend to be impossible.

[handwritten margin note: back to uniqueness]

6   I shall demand enormous fees to go on talk shows, and will charge for my autograph. Anthropologists will study my feeding and nesting habits through field glasses and keep notebooks detailing my every move. That is, if no one gets the bright idea that I'm so unique that I must be put behind sealed glass like the Book of Kells. In any event, I can expect to be a celebrity and to be pampered. I cannot, though, expect to get even.

7   There's no getting even for years of being regarded as stupid or lazy, or both. For years of being considered unproductive (unless you count five children, which no one does). For years of being viewed as a parasite, living off a man (except by my husband whose opinion doesn't seem to matter). For years of fetching other women's children after they'd thrown up in the lunchroom, because I have nothing better to do, or probably there is nothing I do better, while their mothers have "careers." (Is clerking in a drug store a bona fide career?) For years of caring for five children and a big house and constantly being asked when I'm going to work.

[handwritten margin note: anger for the scorn]

8   I come from a long line of women, most of them more Edith Bunker* than Betty Friedan,† who never knew they were unfulfilled. I can't testify that they were happy, but they *were* cheerful. And if they lacked "meaningful relationships," they cherished relations who meant something. They took pride in a clean, comfortable home and satisfaction in serving a good meal because no one had explained to them that the only work worth doing is that for which you get paid.

[handwritten margin note: it's in her family]

9   They enjoyed rearing their children because no one ever told them that little children belonged in church basements and their mothers belonged somewhere else. They lived, very frugally, on their husbands' paychecks because they didn't realize that it's more important to have a bigger house and a second car than it is to rear your own children. And they were so incredibly ignorant that they died never suspecting they'd been failures.

[handwritten margin note: irony]

---

* Edith Bunker (wife of Archie Bunker) was a character in the 1970s sitcom *All in the Family*; in the first few years of the series, she was a traditional stay-at-home housewife.

† Betty Friedan (1921–2006) was an author and activist; her 1963 book *The Feminine Mystique*, documenting the stifling and vaguely dissatisfied lot of the mid-20th century traditional housewife, launched the "second wave" feminist revolution.

10   That won't hold true for me. I don't yet perceive myself as a failure, but it's not for want of being told I am.

11   The other day, years of condescension prompted me to fib in order to test a theory. At a party where most of the guests were business associates of my husband, a Ms. Putdown asked me who I was. I told her I was Jack Hekker's wife. That had a galvanizing effect on her. She took my hand and asked if that was all I thought of myself—just someone's wife? I wasn't going to let her in on the five children but when she persisted I mentioned them but told her that they weren't mine, that they belonged to my dead sister. And then I basked in the glow of her warm approval.

12   It's an absolute truth that whereas you are considered ignorant to stay home to rear *your* children, it is quite heroic to do so for someone else's children. Being a housekeeper is acceptable (even to the Social Security office) as long as it's not *your* house you're keeping. And treating a husband with attentive devotion is altogether correct as long as he's not *your* husband.

13   Sometimes I feel like Alice in Wonderland. But lately, mostly, I feel like an endangered species.

Paradise Lost (Domestic Division)

(2006)

1   A while back, at a baby shower for a niece, I overheard the expectant mother being asked if she intended to return to work after the baby was born. The answer, which rocked me, was, "Yes, because I don't want to end up like Aunt Terry."

2   That would be me.

3   In the continuing case of Full-Time Homemaker vs. Working Mother, I offer myself as Exhibit A. Because more than a quarter-century ago I wrote an Op-Ed article for *The New York Times* on the satisfaction of being a full-time housewife in the new age of the liberated woman. I wrote it from my heart, thoroughly convinced that homemaking and raising my children was the most challenging and rewarding job I could ever want.

4   "I come from a long line of women," I wrote, "most of them more Edith Bunker than Betty Friedan, who never knew they were unfulfilled. I can't testify that they were happy, but they were cheerful. They took pride in a clean, comfortable home and satisfaction in serving a good meal because no one had explained that the only work worth doing is that for which you get paid."

5   I wasn't advocating that mothers forgo careers to stay home with their children; I was simply defending my choice as a valid one. The mantra of the age may have been "Do your own thing," but as a full-time homemaker, that didn't seem to mean me.

6   The column morphed into a book titled *Ever Since Adam and Eve,* followed by a national tour on which I, however briefly, became the authority on homemaking as a viable choice for women. I ultimately told my story on *Today* and

to Dinah Shore, Charlie Rose and even to Oprah, when she was the host of a local TV show in Baltimore.

7   In subsequent years I lectured on the rewards of homemaking and house-wifery. While others tried to make the case that women like me were parasites and little more than legalized prostitutes, I spoke to rapt audiences about the importance of being there for your children as they grew up, of the satisfactions of "making a home," preparing family meals and supporting your hard-working husband.

8   So I was predictably stunned and devastated when, on our 40th wedding anniversary, my husband presented me with a divorce. I knew our first anniversary would be paper, but never expected the 40th would be papers, 16 of them meticulously detailing my faults and flaws, the reason our marriage, according to him, was over.

9   We had been married by a bishop with a blessing from the pope in a country church filled with honeysuckle and hope. Five children and six grandchildren later we were divorced by a third-rate judge in a suburban courthouse reeking of dust and despair.

10   Our long marriage had its full share of love, complications, illnesses, joy and stress. Near the end we were in a dismal period, with my husband in treatment for alcoholism. And although I had made more than my share of mistakes, I never expected to be served with divorce papers. I was stunned to find myself, at this stage of life, marooned. And it was small comfort that I wasn't alone. There were many other confused women of my age and circumstance who'd been married just as long, sharing my situation.

11   I was in my teens when I first read Dickens's *Great Expectations*, with the tale of Miss Haversham, who, stood up by her groom-to-be, spent decades in her yellowing wedding gown, sitting at her cobweb-covered bridal banquet table, consumed with plotting revenge. I felt then that to be left waiting at the altar with a church full of people must be the most crushing thing that could happen to a woman.

12   I was wrong. No jilted bride could feel as embarrassed and humiliated as a woman in her 60's discarded by her husband. I was confused and scared, and the pain of being tossed aside by the love of my life made bitterness unavoidable. In those first few bewildering months, as I staggered and wailed through my life, I made Miss Haversham look like a good sport.

13   Sitting around my kitchen with two friends who had also been dumped by their husbands, I figured out that among the three of us we'd been married 110 years. We'd been faithful wives, good mothers, cooks and housekeepers who'd married in the 50's, when "dress for success" meant a wedding gown and "wife" was a tenured position.

14   Turns out we had a lot in common with our outdated kitchen appliances. Like them we were serviceable, low maintenance, front loading, self-cleaning and (relatively) frost free. Also like them we had warranties that had run out. Our husbands sought sleeker models with features we lacked who could execute tasks we'd either never learned or couldn't perform without laughing.

15   Like most loyal wives of our generation, we'd contemplated eventual widowhood but never thought we'd end up divorced. And "divorced" doesn't begin

to describe the pain of this process. "Canceled" is more like it. It began with my credit cards, then my health insurance and checkbook, until, finally, like a used postage stamp, I felt canceled too.

16   I faced frightening losses and was overwhelmed by the injustice of it all. He got to take his girlfriend to Cancun, while I got to sell my engagement ring to pay the roofer. When I filed my first nonjoint tax return, it triggered the shocking notification that I had become eligible for food stamps.

yet more pity

17   The judge had awarded me alimony that was less than I was used to getting for household expenses, and now I had to use that money to pay bills I'd never seen before: mortgage, taxes, insurance and car payments. And that princely sum was awarded for only four years, the judge suggesting that I go for job training when I turned 67. Not only was I unprepared for divorce itself, I was utterly lacking in skills to deal with the brutal aftermath.

18   I read about the young mothers of today—educated, employed, self-sufficient—who drop out of the work force when they have children, and I worry and wonder. Perhaps it is the right choice for them. Maybe they'll be fine. But the fragility of modern marriage suggests that at least half of them may not be.

advice

19   Regrettably, women whose husbands are devoted to their families and are good providers must nevertheless face the specter of future abandonment. Surely the seeds of this wariness must have been planted, even if they can't believe it could ever happen to them. Many have witnessed their own mothers jettisoned by their own fathers and seen divorced friends trying to rear children with marginal financial and emotional support.

20   These young mothers are often torn between wanting to be home with their children and the statistical possibility of future calamity, aware that one of the most poverty-stricken groups in today's society are divorced older women. The feminine and sexual revolutions of the last few decades have had their shining victories, but have they, in the end, made things any easier for mothers?

regretting previous article

21   I cringe when I think of that line from my Op-Ed article about the long line of women I'd come from and belonged to who were able to find fulfillment as homemakers "because no one had explained" to us "that the only work worth doing is that for which you get paid." For a divorced mother, the harsh reality is that the work for which you do get paid is the only work that will keep you afloat.

22   These days couples face complex negotiations over work, family, child care and housekeeping. I see my children dealing with these issues in their marriages, and I understand the stresses and frustrations. It becomes evident that where traditional marriage through the centuries had been a partnership based on mutual dependency, modern marriage demands greater self-sufficiency.

23   While today's young women know from the start they'll face thorny decisions regarding careers, marriage and children, those of us who married in the 50's anticipated lives similar to our mothers' and grandmothers'. Then we watched with bewilderment as all the rules changed, and the goal posts were moved.

24   If I had it to do over again, I'd still marry the man I married and have my children: they are my treasure and a powerful support system for me and for one another. But I would have used the years after my youngest started school to further my education. I could have amassed two doctorates using the time and

energy I gave to charitable and community causes and been better able to support myself.

25   But in a lucky twist, my community involvement had resulted in my being appointed to fill a vacancy on our Village Board. I had been serving as titular deputy mayor of my hometown (Nyack, N.Y.) when my husband left me. Several weeks later the mayor chose not to run again because of failing health, and I was elected to succeed him, becoming the first female mayor.

26   I held office for six years, a challenging, full-time job that paid a whopping annual salary of $8,000. But it consumed me and gave me someplace to go every day and most nights, and as such it saved my sanity. Now, mostly retired except for some part-time work, I am kept on my toes by 12 amazing grandchildren.

27   My anachronistic book was written while I was in a successful marriage that I expected would go on forever. Sadly, it now has little relevance for modern women, except perhaps as a cautionary tale: never its intended purpose. So I couldn't imagine writing a sequel. But my friend Elaine did come up with a perfect title: "Disregard First Book."

Discussion and Writing Suggestions

1. Hekker discovered that events have a way of reversing our most cherished beliefs. To what extent, based on your own life and on your observations of others, does Hekker's sadder-but-wiser experience appear to be universal? Can one—should one—prepare for such reversals in life? What is gained, and what is lost, by such preparation?

2. In her 1977 column, Hekker writes that traditional mothers "lived, very frugally, on their husbands' paychecks because they didn't realize that it's more important to have a bigger house and a second car than it is to rear your own children." Based on your own observations of working mothers, to what extent do you feel that Hekker's suggestion that most mothers choose to work in order to maintain an affluent lifestyle is fair and/or accurate?

3. In her 2006 column, Hekker writes, "It becomes evident that where traditional marriage through the centuries had been a partnership based on mutual dependency, modern marriage demands greater self-sufficiency." Assuming the truth of this statement, which type of marriage would you prefer—traditional or modern? Why?

4. In 2006, notwithstanding her divorce and the bitter lessons learned, Hekker maintained that she would still have stayed at home with her children until the youngest was school-age. Presumably that choice in 2006, as in the 1970s, would have involved some sacrifice of money and/or career goals. Assume that you faced this same choice. That is, assume that you are married, have a career you care about, yet also want to raise a family. Based on your values regarding childrearing,

would you stay at home until the youngest is school-age? What financial and career sacrifices would you be willing to make in order to maintain this arrangement? Describe your ideal child-care arrangement.

5. In her 2006 column, Hekker writes, "Women whose husbands are devoted to their families and are good providers must nevertheless face the specter of future abandonment." To what extent do you agree with this statement? Assuming it is true, would you want to live in this way— either being a suspicious woman or an implicitly distrusted man?

6. To what extent do you feel that the self-confident Hekker of the 1977 column got her comeuppance? To what extent do you feel that she deserves your sympathy and support? On a blog site in response to the 2006 column, one poster criticized Hekker as self-pitying and bitter. Do you agree with this assessment? Describe your own reaction upon read- ing the paragraphs beginning, "So I was predictably stunned and devas- tated when, on our 40th wedding anniversary, my husband presented me with a divorce."

The Radical Idea of Marrying for Love
Stephanie Coontz

One of the bedrock assumptions of modern marriage is the once-radical idea that newly- weds must be in love. Marriage and love have existed through the ages, of course. But according to historian Stephanie Coontz, only in the relatively recent past, beginning in the eighteenth century, did the political and economic institution of marriage take on romantic associations. Reminding us through historical and cultural examples that many people were (and still are) horrified by the idea of marrying for love, and loving the one we marry, Coontz traces the intellectual development of this subversive notion back to the Enlightenment. She then hints at the long-term consequences it held for the institution of marriage.

Stephanie Coontz teaches history and family studies at Evergreen State College in Olympia, Washington, and has written numerous books on marriage and family in America, including The Way We Never Were: American Families and the Nostalgia Trap *(1992) and* The Way We Really Are: Coming to Terms with America's Changing Families *(1998). The following selec- tion first appeared in* Marriage: A History: From Obedience to Intimacy, or How Love Conquered Marriage *(2005).*

1 George Bernard Shaw described marriage as an institution that brings together two people "under the influence of the most violent, most insane, most delu- sive, and most transient of passions. They are required to swear that they will remain in that excited, abnormal, and exhausting condition continuously until death do them part."

2   Shaw's comment was amusing when he wrote it at the beginning of the twen- tieth century, and it still makes us smile today, because it pokes fun at the unre-

alistic expectations that spring from a dearly held cultural ideal—that marriage should be based on intense, profound love and a couple should maintain their ardor until death do them part. But for thousands of years the joke would have fallen flat.

3   For most of history it was inconceivable that people would choose their mates on the basis of something as fragile and irrational as love and then focus all their sexual, intimate, and altruistic desires on the resulting marriage. In fact, many historians, sociologists, and anthropologists used to think romantic love was a recent Western invention. This is not true. People have always fallen in love, and throughout the ages many couples have loved each other deeply.

4   But only rarely in history has love been seen as the main reason for getting married. When someone did advocate such a strange belief, it was no laughing matter. Instead, it was considered a serious threat to social order.

5   In some cultures and times, true love was actually thought to be incompatible with marriage. Plato believed love was a wonderful emotion that led men to behave honorably. But the Greek philosopher was referring not to the love of women, "such as the meaner men feel," but to the love of one man for another.

6   Other societies considered it good if love developed after marriage or thought love should be factored in along with the more serious considerations involved in choosing a mate. But even when past societies did welcome or encourage married love, they kept it on a short leash. Couples were not to put their feelings for each other above more important commitments, such as their ties to parents, siblings, cousins, neighbors, or God.

7   In ancient India, falling in love before marriage was seen as a disruptive, almost antisocial act. The Greeks thought lovesickness was a type of insanity, a view that was adopted by medieval commentators in Europe. In the Middle Ages the French defined love as a "derangement of the mind" that could be cured by sexual intercourse, either with the loved one or with a different partner. This cure assumed, as Oscar Wilde once put it, that the quickest way to conquer yearning and temptation was to yield immediately and move on to more important matters.

8   In China, excessive love between husband and wife was seen as a threat to the solidarity of the extended family. Parents could force a son to divorce his wife if her behavior or work habits didn't please them, whether or not he loved her. They could also require him to take a concubine if his wife did not produce a son. If a son's romantic attachment to his wife rivaled his parents' claims on the couple's time and labor, the parents might even send her back to her parents. In the Chinese language the term *love* did not traditionally apply to feelings between husband and wife. It was used to describe an illicit, socially disapproved relationship. In the 1920s a group of intellectuals invented a new word for love between spouses because they thought such a radical new idea required its own special label.

9   In Europe, during the twelfth and thirteenth centuries, adultery became idealized as the highest form of love among the aristocracy. According to the Countess of Champagne, it was impossible for true love to "exert its powers between two people who are married to each other."

10   In twelfth-century France, Andreas Capellanus, chaplain to Countess Marie of Troyes, wrote a treatise on the principles of courtly love. The first rule was that "marriage is no real excuse for not loving." But he meant loving someone outside the marriage. As late as the eighteenth century the French essayist Montaigne wrote that any man who was in love with his wife was a man so dull that no one else could love him.

11   Courtly love probably loomed larger in literature than in real life. But for centuries, noblemen and kings fell in love with courtesans rather than the wives they married for political reasons. Queens and noblewomen had to be more discreet than their husbands, but they too looked beyond marriage for love and intimacy.

12   This sharp distinction between love and marriage was common among the lower and middle classes as well. Many of the songs and stories popular among peasants in medieval Europe mocked married love.

13   The most famous love affair of the Middle Ages was that of Peter Abelard, a well-known theologian in France, and Héloïse, the brilliant niece of a fellow churchman at Notre Dame. The two eloped without marrying, and she bore him a child. In an attempt to save his career but still placate Héloïse's furious uncle, Abelard proposed they marry in secret. This would mean that Héloïse would not be living in sin, while Abelard could still pursue his church ambitions. But Héloïse resisted the idea, arguing that marriage would not only harm his career but also undermine their love.

"Nothing Is More Impure Than to Love One's Wife as if She Were a Mistress"

14 Even in societies that esteemed married love, couples were expected to keep it under strict control. In many cultures, public displays of love between husband and wife were considered unseemly. A Roman was expelled from the Senate because he had kissed his wife in front of his daughter. Plutarch conceded that the punishment was somewhat extreme but pointed out that everyone knew that it was "disgraceful" to kiss one's wife in front of others.

15   Some Greek and Roman philosophers even said that a man who loved his wife with "excessive" ardor was "an adulterer." Many centuries later Catholic and Protestant theologians argued that husbands and wives who loved each other too much were committing the sin of idolatry. Theologians chided wives who used endearing nicknames for their husbands, because such familiarity on a wife's part undermined the husband's authority and the awe that his wife should feel for him. Although medieval Muslim thinkers were more approving of sexual passion between husband and wife than were Christian theologians, they also insisted that too much intimacy between husband and wife weakened a believer's devotion to God. And, like their European counterparts, secular writers in the Islamic world believed that love thrived best outside marriage.

16   Many cultures still frown on placing love at the center of marriage. In Africa, the Fulbe people of northern Cameroon do not see love as a legitimate emotion, especially within marriage. One observer reports that in conversations with their neighbors, Fulbe women "vehemently deny emotional attachment to a husband." In many peasant and working-class communities, too much love

between husband and wife is seen as disruptive because it encourages the couple to withdraw from the wider web of dependence that makes the society work.

17   As a result, men and women often relate to each other in public, even after marriage, through the conventions of a war between the sexes, disguising the fondness they may really feel. They describe their marital behavior, no matter how exemplary it may actually be, in terms of convenience, compulsion, or self-interest rather than love or sentiment. In Cockney rhyming slang, the term for *wife* is *trouble and strife*.

18   Whether it is valued or not, love is rarely seen as the main ingredient for marital success. Among the Taita of Kenya, recognition and approval of married love are widespread. An eighty-year-old man recalled that his fourth wife "was the wife of my heart. . . . I could look at her and no words would pass, just a smile." In this society, where men often take several wives, women speak wistfully about how wonderful it is to be a "love wife." But only a small percentage of Taita women experience this luxury, because a Taita man normally marries a love wife only after he has accumulated a few more practical wives.

19   In many cultures, love has been seen as a desirable outcome of marriage but not as a good reason for getting married in the first place. The Hindu tradition celebrates love and sexuality in marriage, but love and sexual attraction are not considered valid reasons for marriage. "First we marry, then we'll fall in love" is the formula. As recently as 1975, a survey of college students in the Indian state of Karnataka found that only 18 percent "strongly" approved of marriages made on the basis of love, while 32 percent completely disapproved.

20   Similarly, in early modern Europe most people believed that love developed after marriage. Moralists of the sixteenth and seventeenth centuries argued that if a husband and wife each had a good character, they would probably come to love each other. But they insisted that youths be guided by their families in choosing spouses who were worth learning to love. It was up to parents and other relatives to make sure that the woman had a dowry or the man had a good yearly income. Such capital, it was thought, would certainly help love flower.

"[I]t Made Me Really Sick, Just as I Have Formerly Been When in Love with My Wife"

21 I don't believe that people of the past had more control over their hearts than we do today or that they were incapable of the deep love so many individuals now hope to achieve in marriage. But love in marriage was seen as a bonus, not as a necessity. The great Roman statesman Cicero exchanged many loving letters with his wife, Terentia, during their thirty-year marriage. But that didn't stop him from divorcing her when she was no longer able to support him in the style to which he had become accustomed.

22   Sometimes people didn't have to make such hard choices. In seventeenth-century America, Anne Bradstreet was the favorite child of an indulgent father who gave her the kind of education usually reserved for elite boys. He later arranged her marriage to a cherished childhood friend who eventually became the governor of Massachusetts. Combining love, duty, material security, and marriage was not the strain for her that it was for many men and women of that era. Anne wrote love poems to her husband that completely ignored the injunc-

tion of Puritan ministers not to place one's spouse too high in one's affections. "If ever two were one," she wrote him, "then surely we; if ever man were loved by wife, then thee. . . . I prize thy love more than whole mines of gold, or all the riches that the East doth hold; my love is such that rivers cannot quench, nor ought but love from thee, give recompense."

23 The famous seventeenth-century English diarist Samuel Pepys chose to marry for love rather than profit. But he was not as lucky as Anne. After hearing a particularly stirring piece of music, Pepys recorded that it "did wrap up my soul so that it made me really sick, just as I have formerly been when in love with my wife." Pepys would later disinherit a nephew for marrying under the influence of so strong yet transient an emotion.

24 There were always youngsters who resisted the pressures of parents, kin, and neighbors to marry for practical reasons rather than love, but most accepted or even welcomed the interference of parents and others in arranging their marriages. A common saying in early modern Europe was "He who marries for love has good nights and bad days." Nowadays a bitter wife or husband might ask, "Whatever possessed me to think I loved you enough to marry you?" Through most of the past, he or she was more likely to have asked, "Whatever possessed me to marry you just because I loved you?"

"Happily Ever After"

25 Through most of the past, individuals hoped to find love, or at least "tranquil affection," in marriage. But nowhere did they have the same recipe for marital happiness that prevails in most contemporary Western countries. Today there is general agreement on what it takes for a couple to live "happily ever after." First, they must love each other deeply and choose each other unswayed by outside pressure. From then on, each must make the partner the top priority in life, putting that relationship above any and all competing ties. A husband and wife, we believe, owe their highest obligations and deepest loyalties to each other and the children they raise. Parents and in-laws should not be allowed to interfere in the marriage. Married couples should be best friends, sharing their most intimate feelings and secrets. They should express affection openly but also talk candidly about problems. And of course they should be sexually faithful to each other.

26 This package of expectations about love, marriage, and sex, however, is extremely rare. When we look at the historical record around the world, the customs of modern America and Western Europe appear exotic and exceptional.

27 Leo Tolstoy once remarked that all happy families are alike, while every unhappy family is unhappy in its own way. But the more I study the history of marriage, the more I think the opposite is true. Most unhappy marriages in history share common patterns, leaving their tear-stained—and sometimes blood-stained—records across the ages. But each happy, successful marriage seems to be happy in its own way. And for most of human history, successful marriages have not been happy in *our* way.

28 A woman in ancient China might bring one or more of her sisters to her husband's home as backup wives. Eskimo couples often had cospousal arrangements, in which each partner had sexual relations with the other's spouse. In Tibet and

parts of India, Kashmir, and Nepal, a woman may be married to two or more brothers, all of whom share sexual access to her.

29   In modern America, such practices are the stuff of trash TV: "I caught my sister in bed with my husband"; "My parents brought their lovers into our home"; "My wife slept with my brother"; "It broke my heart to share my husband with another woman." In other cultures, individuals often find such practices normal and comforting. The children of Eskimo cospouses felt that they shared a special bond, and society viewed them as siblings. Among Tibetan brothers who share the same wife, sexual jealousy is rare.

30   In some cultures, cowives see one another as allies rather than rivals. In Botswana, women add an interesting wrinkle to the old European saying "Woman's work is never done." There they say: "Without cowives, a woman's work is never done." A researcher who worked with the Cheyenne Indians of the United States in the 1930s and 1940s told of a chief who tried to get rid of two of his three wives. All three women defied him, saying that if he sent two of them away, he would have to give away the third as well.

31   Even when societies celebrated the love between husband and wife as a pleasant by-product of marriage, people rarely had a high regard for marital intimacy. Chinese commentators on marriage discouraged a wife from confiding in her husband or telling him about her day. A good wife did not bother her husband with news of her own activities and feelings but treated him "like a guest," no matter how long they had been married. A husband who demonstrated open affection for his wife, even at home, was seen as having a weak character.

32   In the early eighteenth century, American lovers often said they looked for "candor" in each other. But they were not talking about the soul-baring intimacy idealized by modern Americans, and they certainly did not believe that couples should talk frankly about their grievances. Instead candor meant fairness, kindliness, and good temper. People wanted a spouse who did *not* pry too deeply. The ideal mate, wrote U.S. President John Adams in his diary, was willing "to palliate faults and Mistakes, to put the best Construction upon Words and Action, and to forgive Injuries."

33   Modern marital advice books invariably tell husbands and wives to put each other first. But in many societies, marriage ranks very low in the hierarchy of meaningful relationships. People's strongest loyalties and emotional connections may be reserved for members of their birth families. On the North American plains in the 1930s, a Kiowa Indian woman commented to a researcher that "a woman can always get another husband, but she has only one brother." In China it was said that "you have only one family, but you can always get another wife." In Christian texts prior to the seventeenth century, the word *love* usually referred to feelings toward God or neighbors rather than toward a spouse.

34   In Confucian philosophy, the two strongest relationships in family life are between father and son and between elder brother and younger brother, not between husband and wife. In thirteenth-century China the bond between father and son was so much stronger than the bond between husband and wife that legal commentators insisted a couple do nothing if the patriarch of the household raped his son's wife. In one case, although the judge was sure that a woman's rape accusation against her father-in-law was true, he ordered the

young man to give up his sentimental desire "to grow old together" with his wife. Loyalty to parents was paramount, and therefore the son should send his wife back to her own father, who could then marry her to someone else. Sons were sometimes ordered beaten for siding with their wives against their father. No wonder that for 1,700 years women in one Chinese province guarded a secret language that they used to commiserate with each other about the griefs of marriage.

35   In many societies of the past, sexual loyalty was not a high priority. The expectation of mutual fidelity is a rather recent invention. Numerous cultures have allowed husbands to seek sexual gratification outside marriage. Less frequently, but often enough to challenge common preconceptions, wives have also been allowed to do this without threatening the marriage. In a study of 109 societies, anthropologists found that only 48 forbade extramarital sex to both husbands and wives.

36   When a woman has sex with someone other than her husband and he doesn't object, anthropologists have traditionally called it wife loaning. When a man does it, they call it male privilege. But in some societies the choice to switch partners rests with the woman. Among the Dogon of West Africa, young married women publicly pursued extramarital relationships with the encouragement of their mothers. Among the Rukuba of Nigeria, a wife can take a lover at the time of her first marriage. This relationship is so embedded in accepted custom that the lover has the right, later in life, to ask his former mistress to marry her daughter to his son.

37   Among the Eskimo of northern Alaska, as I noted earlier, husbands and wives, with mutual consent, established comarriages with other couples. Some anthropologists believe cospouse relationships were a more socially acceptable outlet for sexual attraction than was marriage itself. Expressing open jealousy about the sexual relationships involved was considered boorish.

38   Such different notions of marital rights and obligations made divorce and remarriage less emotionally volatile for the Eskimo than it is for most modern Americans. In fact, the Eskimo believed that a remarried person's partner had an obligation to allow the former spouse, as well as any children of that union, the right to fish, hunt, and gather in the new spouse's territory.

39   Several small-scale societies in South America have sexual and marital norms that are especially startling for Europeans and North Americans. In these groups, people believe that any man who has sex with a woman during her pregnancy contributes part of his biological substance to the child. The husband is recognized as the primary father, but the woman's lover or lovers also have paternal responsibilities, including the obligation to share food with the woman and her child in the future. During the 1990s researchers taking life histories of elderly Bari women in Venezuela found that most had taken lovers during at least one of their pregnancies. Their husbands were usually aware and did not object. When a woman gave birth, she would name all the men she had slept with since learning she was pregnant, and a woman attending the birth would tell each of these men: "You have a child."

40   In Europe and the United States today such an arrangement would be a sure-fire recipe for jealousy, bitter breakups, and very mixed-up kids. But among the

Bari people this practice was in the best interests of the child. The secondary fathers were expected to provide the child with fish and game, with the result that a child with a secondary father was twice as likely to live to the age of fifteen as a brother or sister without such a father.

41   Few other societies have incorporated extramarital relationships so successfully into marriage and child rearing. But all these examples of differing marital and sexual norms make it difficult to claim there is some universal model for the success or happiness of a marriage.

42   About two centuries ago Western Europe and North America developed a whole set of new values about the way to organize marriage and sexuality, and many of these values are now spreading across the globe. In this Western model, people expect marriage to satisfy more of their psychological and social needs than ever before. Marriage is supposed to be free of the coercion, violence, and gender inequalities that were tolerated in the past. Individuals want marriage to meet most of their needs for intimacy and affection and all their needs for sex.

43   Never before in history had societies thought that such a set of high expectations about marriage was either realistic or desirable. Although many Europeans and Americans found tremendous joy in building their relationships around these values, the adoption of these unprecedented goals for marriage had unanticipated and revolutionary consequences that have since come to threaten the stability of the entire institution.

. . .

44   [B]y the beginning of the seventeenth century a distinctive marriage system had taken root in Western Europe, with a combination of features that together not only made it different from marriage anywhere else in the world but also made it capable of very rapid transformation. Strict divorce laws made it difficult to end a marriage, but this was coupled with more individual freedom to choose or refuse a partner. Concubinage had no legal status. Couples tended to marry later and to be closer to each other in age. And upon marriage a couple typically established an independent household.

45   During the eighteenth century the spread of the market economy and the advent of the Enlightenment wrought profound changes in record time. By the end of the 1700s personal choice of partners had replaced arranged marriage as a social ideal, and individuals were encouraged to marry for love. For the first time in five thousand years, marriage came to be seen as a private relationship between two individuals rather than one link in a larger system of political and economic alliances. The measure of a successful marriage was no longer how big a financial settlement was involved, how many useful in-laws were acquired, or how many children were produced, but how well a family met the emotional needs of its individual members. Where once marriage had been seen as the fundamental unit of work and politics, it was now viewed as a place of refuge from work, politics, and community obligations.

46   The image of husbands and wives was also transformed during the eighteenth century. The husband, once the supervisor of the family labor force, came to be seen as the person who, by himself, provided for the family. The wife's role was redefined to focus on her emotional and moral contributions to family life

rather than her economic inputs. The husband was the family's economic motor, and the wife its sentimental core.

47   Two seismic social changes spurred these changes in marriage norms. First, the spread of wage labor made young people less dependent on their parents for a start in life. A man didn't have to delay marriage until he inherited land or took over a business from his father. A woman could more readily earn her own dowry. As day labor replaced apprenticeships and provided alternatives to domestic service, young workers were no longer obliged to live in a master's home for several years. They could marry as soon as they were able to earn sufficient wages.

48   Second, the freedoms afforded by the market economy had their parallel in new political and philosophical ideas. Starting in the mid-seventeenth century, some political theorists began to challenge the ideas of absolutism. Such ideas gained more adherents during the eighteenth-century Enlightenment, when influential thinkers across Europe championed individual rights and insisted that social relationships, including those between men and women, be organized on the basis of reason and justice rather than force. Believing the pursuit of happiness to be a legitimate goal, they advocated marrying for love rather than wealth or status. Historian Jeffrey Watts writes that although the sixteenth-century Reformation had already "enhanced the dignity of married life by denying the superiority of celibacy," the eighteenth-century Enlightenment "exalted marriage even further by making love the most important criterion in choosing a spouse."

49   The Enlightenment also fostered a more secular view of social institutions than had prevailed in the sixteenth and seventeenth centuries. Marriage came to be seen as a private contract that ought not be too closely regulated by church or state. After the late eighteenth century, according to one U.S. legal historian, marriage was increasingly defined as a private agreement with public consequences, rather than as a public institution whose roles and duties were rigidly determined by the family's place in the social hierarchy.

50   The new norms of the love-based, intimate marriage did not fall into place all at once but were adopted at different rates in various regions and social groups. In England, the celebration of the love match reached a fever pitch as early as the 1760s and 1770s, while the French were still commenting on the novelty of "marriage by fascination" in the mid-1800s. Many working-class families did not adopt the new norms of marital intimacy until the twentieth century.

51   But there was a clear tipping point during the eighteenth century. In England, a new sentimentalization of wives and mothers pushed older anti-female diatribes to the margins of polite society. Idealization of marriage reached such heights that the meaning of the word *spinster* began to change. Originally an honorable term reserved for a woman who spun yarn, by the 1600s it had come to mean any woman who was not married. In the 1700s the word took on a negative connotation for the first time, the flip side of the new reverence accorded to wives.

52   In France, the propertied classes might still view marriage as "a kind of joint-stock affair," in the words of one disapproving Englishwoman, but the common

people more and more frequently talked about marriage as the route to "happiness" and "peace." One study found that before the 1760s fewer than 10 percent of French couples seeking annulments argued that a marriage should be based on emotional attachment to be fully valid, but by the 1770s more than 40 percent thought so.

53   Romantic ideals spread in America too. In the two decades after the American Revolution, New Englanders began to change their description of an ideal mate, adding companionship and cooperation to their traditional expectations of thrift and industriousness.

54   These innovations spread even to Russia, where Tsar Peter the Great undertook westernizing the country's army, navy, bureaucracy, and marriage customs all at once. In 1724 he outlawed forced marriages, requiring bride and groom to swear that each had consented freely to the match. Russian authors extolled "the bewitchment and sweet tyranny of love."

55   The court records of Neuchâtel, in what is now Switzerland, reveal the sea change that occurred in the legal norms of marriage. In the sixteenth and seventeenth centuries, judges had followed medieval custom in forcing individuals to honor betrothals and marriage contracts that had been properly made, even if one or both parties no longer wanted the match. In the eighteenth century, by contrast, judges routinely released people from unwanted marriage contracts and engagements, so long as the couple had no children. It was no longer possible for a man to force a woman to keep a marriage promise.

56   In contrast to the stories of knightly chivalry that had dominated secular literature in the Middle Ages, late eighteenth-century and early nineteenth-century novels depicted ordinary lives. Authors and audiences alike were fascinated by domestic scenes and family relations that had held no interest for medieval writers. Many popular works about love and marriage were syrupy love stories or melodramatic tales of betrayals. But in the hands of more sophisticated writers, such as Jane Austen, clever satires of arranged marriages and the financial aspects of courtship were transformed into great literature.

57   One result of these changes was a growing rejection of the legitimacy of domestic violence. By the nineteenth century, male wife-beaters rather than female "scolds" had become the main target of village shaming rituals in much of Europe. Meanwhile, middle- and upper-class writers condemned wife beating as a "lower-class" vice in which no "respectable" man would indulge.

58   Especially momentous for relations between husband and wife was the weakening of the political model upon which marriage had long been based. Until the late seventeenth century the family was thought of as a miniature monarchy, with the husband king over his dependents. As long as political absolutism remained unchallenged in society as a whole, so did the hierarchy of traditional marriage. But the new political ideals fostered by the Glorious Revolution in England in 1688 and the even more far-reaching revolutions in America and France in the last quarter of the eighteenth century dealt a series of cataclysmic blows to the traditional justification of patriarchal authority.

59   In the late seventeenth century John Locke argued that governmental authority was simply a contract between ruler and ruled and that if a ruler

exceeded the authority his subjects granted him, he could be replaced. In 1698 he suggested that marriage too could be seen as a contract between equals. Locke still believed that men would normally rule their families because of their greater strength and ability, but another English writer, Mary Astell, pushed Locke's theories to what she thought was their logical conclusion, "If Absolute Sovereignty be not necessary in a State," Astell asked, "how comes it to be so in a Family?" She answered that not only was absolutism unnecessary within marriage, but it was actually "more mischievous in Families than in kingdomes," by exactly the same amount as "100,000 tyrants are worse than one."

60   During the eighteenth century people began to focus more on the mutual obligations required in marriage. Rejecting analogies between the absolute rights of a husband and the absolute rights of a king, they argued that marital order should be based on love and reason, not on a husband's arbitrary will. The French writer the Marquis de Condorcet and the British author Mary Wollstonecraft went so far as to call for complete equality within marriage.

61   Only a small minority of thinkers, even in "enlightened" circles, endorsed equality between the sexes. Jean Jacques Rousseau, one of the most enthusiastic proponents of romantic love and harmonious marriage, also wrote that a woman should be trained to "docility . . . for she will always be in subjection to a man, or to man's judgment, and she will never be free to set her own opinion above his." The German philosopher J. G. Fichte argued in 1795 that a woman could be "free and independent only as long as she had no husband." Perhaps, he opined, a woman might be eligible to run for office if she promised not to marry. "But no rational woman can give such a promise, nor can the state rationally accept it. For woman is destined to love, and . . . when she loves, it is her duty to marry."

62   In the heady atmosphere of the American and French revolutions of 1776 and 1789, however, many individuals dared draw conclusions that anticipated feminist demands for marital reform and women's rights of the early twentieth century. And even before that, skeptics warned that making love and companionship the core of marriage would open a Pandora's box.

The Revolutionary Implications of the Love Match

63 The people who pioneered the new ideas about love and marriage were not, by and large, trying to create anything like the egalitarian partnerships that modern Westerners associate with companionship, intimacy, and "true love." Their aim was to make marriage more secure by getting rid of the cynicism that accompanied mercenary marriage and encouraging couples to place each other first in their affections and loyalties.

64   But basing marriage on love and companionship represented a break with thousands of years of tradition. Many contemporaries immediately recognized the dangers this entailed. They worried that the unprecedented idea of basing marriage on love would produce rampant individualism.

65   Critics of the love match argued—prematurely, as it turns out, but correctly—that the values of free choice and egalitarianism could easily spin out of control. If the choice of a marriage partner was a personal decision, conservatives asked, what would prevent young people, especially women, from choos-

ing unwisely? If people were encouraged to expect marriage to be the best and happiest experience of their lives, what would hold a marriage together if things went "for worse" rather than "for better"?

66   If wives and husbands were intimates, wouldn't women demand to share decisions equally? If women possessed the same faculties of reason as men, why would they confine themselves to domesticity? Would men still financially support women and children if they lost control over their wives' and children's labor and could not even discipline them properly? If parents, church, and state no longer dictated people's private lives, how could society make sure the right people married and had children or stop the wrong ones from doing so?

67   Conservatives warned that "the pursuit of happiness," claimed as a right in the American Declaration of Independence, would undermine the social and moral order. Preachers declared that parishioners who placed their husbands or wives before God in their hierarchy of loyalty and emotion were running the risk of becoming "idolaters." In 1774 a writer in England's *Lady Magazine* commented tartly that "the idea of matrimony" was not "for men and women to be always taken up with each other" or to seek personal self-fulfillment in their love. The purpose of marriage was to get people "to discharge the duties of civil society, to govern their families with prudence and to educate their children with discretion."

68   There was a widespread fear that the pursuit of personal happiness could undermine self-discipline. One scholar argues that this fear explains the extraordinary panic about masturbation that swept the United States and Europe at the end of the eighteenth century and produced thousands of tracts against "the solitary vice" in the nineteenth. The threat of female masturbation particularly repelled and fascinated eighteenth-century social critics. To some it seemed a short step from two people neglecting their social duties because they were "taken up with each other" to one person pleasuring herself without fulfilling a duty to anyone else at all.

69   As it turned out, it took another hundred years for the contradictions that gave rise to these fears to pose a serious threat to the stability of the new system of marriage.

Review Questions

1. What are the two main reasons, according to Coontz, that the norms about the relationship between love and marriage began to change in the eighteenth century?

2. According to Coontz, what was the aim of people who championed the "love match" model of marriage in the eighteenth century?

3. What did a conservative writer in a 1774 issue of England's *Lady Magazine* claim was the purpose of marriage?

4. Describe the two values that critics of the "love match" feared could lead to widespread individualism. Cite at least one feared consequence of each value.

Discussion and Writing Suggestions

1. Reread the excerpt from Barbara Graham's "The Future of Love: Kiss Romance Goodbye, It's Time for the Real Thing" (presented as a basis for summary practice) in Chapter 1, pages 8–11. Compare and contrast Graham's history of the intertwining of love and marriage with Stephanie Coontz's in "The Radical Idea of Marrying for Love."

2. Coontz begins the selection with a cynical observation of marriage by George Bernard Shaw: that marriage brings together two people "under the influence of the most violent, most insane, most delusive, and most transient of passions. They are required to swear that they will remain in that excited, abnormal, and exhausting condition until death do them part." To what extent—before your reading of this selection—would you (or others you know) have subscribed to the assumptions about marriage that are the object of Shaw's scorn? To what extent do you think that Shaw is overstating the case? Explain.

3. Coontz notes that only a "small minority" of the Enlightenment thinkers who called for greater equality within marriage actually endorsed equality between the sexes. Is there a difference between equality within marriage and equality between the sexes? Is it contradictory to believe in one but not the other? Explain your answer.

4. Coontz writes that with the advent of the love-based marriage, "The measure of a successful marriage was no longer how big a financial settlement was involved, how many useful in-laws were acquired, or how many children were produced, but how well a family met the emotional needs of its individual members." To what degree would you agree that this statement describes the reality of modern marriages? Do you feel that issues such as money, number of offspring, and in-laws can or should be separated from the "emotional needs" of husband and wife? If possible, when stating your opinion, cite specific examples of marriages you have known about or witnessed.

5. Critics of the love match argued that allowing people to choose their mates would also allow them to choose badly. But presumably some arranged marriages also resulted in bad matches. Do you feel that one sort of bad match is worse than the other? And what does a "bad match" mean, exactly?

6. In her historical and cultural survey of attitudes toward love in marriage, Coontz notes that many cultures have believed that married people should "love" one another. But these cultures have also differentiated married love from romantic love, which they felt was transitory and fleeting. Do you see any distinction(s) between married love and romantic love?

The State of Our Unions
David Popenoe and Barbara Dafoe Whitehead

At the end of the previous selection, Stephanie Coontz hinted at the consequences that the rise of the "love match" would have for the institution of marriage. So how is marriage faring? In the following selection, the codirectors of the National Marriage Project at Rutgers State University warn that the institutions of marriage and family are in a state of crisis. David Popenoe is a professor of sociology at Rutgers University in New Brunswick, New Jersey. An expert in the study of marriage and family life, he has written or edited ten books, most recently War Over the Family *(2005). Barbara Dafoe Whitehead lectures and writes on the well-being of families and children for scholarly and popular audiences. She is the author of* The Divorce Culture: Rethinking Our Commitment to Marriage and Family *(1997). The following selection combines sections of Popenoe and Whitehead's 2002 and 2005 reports on marriage, presented here in three parts: Marriage, Divorce, and Unmarried Cohabitation. The earlier report appeared in* USA Today Magazine *in July 2002. The later report appears on the National Marriage Project Web site at <http://marriage.rutgers.edu/Publications/SOOO/TEXTSOOU2005.htm>.*

1   Each year, the National Marriage Project at Rutgers University publishes an assessment of the health of marriage and marital relationships in America entitled "The State of Our Unions." It is based on a thorough review and evaluation of the latest statistics and research findings about marriage, family, and courtship trends, plus our own special surveys.

2   Americans haven't given up on marriage as a cherished ideal. Indeed, most continue to prize and value it as an important life goal, and the vast majority (an estimated 85%) will marry at least once in a lifetime. Almost all couples enter marriage with a strong desire and determination for a life-long, loving partnership, and this desire may even be increasing among the young. Since the 1980s, the percentage of high school seniors who say that having a good marriage is extremely important to them as a life goal has gone up, though only slightly.

· · ·

Marriage

3   Key Finding: Marriage trends in recent decades indicate that Americans have become less likely to marry, and the most recent data show that the marriage rate in the United States continues to decline. Of those who do marry, there has been a moderate drop since the 1970s in the percentage of couples who consider their marriages to be "very happy," but in the past decade this trend has swung in a positive direction.

4   Americans have become less likely to marry. This is reflected in a decline of nearly 50 percent, from 1970 to 2004, in the annual number of marriages per 1,000 unmarried adult women (Figure 1). Some of this decline—it is not clear just how much—results from the delaying of first marriages until older ages: the median age at first marriage went from 20 for females and 23 for males in 1960 to about 26 and 27, respectively, in 2004. Other factors accounting for the decline are the growth of unmarried cohabitation and a small decrease in the tendency of divorced persons to remarry.

FIGURE 1   Number of Marriages per 1,000 Unmarried Women Age 15 and Older, by Year, United States[a]

Year	Number[b]
1960	73.5
1970	76.5
1975	66.9
1980	61.4
1985	56.2
1990	54.5
1995	50.8
2000	46.5
2004	39.9

a. We have used the number of marriages per 1,000 unmarried women age 15 and older, rather than the Crude Marriage Rate of marriages per 1,000 population to help avoid the problem of compositional changes in the population, that is, changes which stem merely from there being more or less people in the marriageable ages. Even this more refined measure is somewhat susceptible to compositional changes.
b. Per 1,000 unmarried women age 14 and older.
Source: U.S. Department of the Census, Statistical Abstract of the United States, 2001, Page 87, Table 117; and Statistical Abstract of the United States, 1986, Page 79, Table 124. Figure for 2004 was obtained using data from the Current Population Surveys, March 2004 Supplement, as well as Births, Marriages, Divorces, and Deaths: Provisional Data for 2004, National Vital Statistics Report 53:21, June 26, 2005, Table 3.
(http://www.cdc.gov/nchs/data/nvsr/nvsr53/nvsr53_21.pdf) The CPS, March Supplement, is based on a sample of the U.S. population, rather than an actual count such as those available from the decennial census. See sampling and weighting notes at http://www.bis.census.gov:80/cps/ads/2002/ssampwgt.htm

5   The decline also reflects some increase in lifelong singlehood, though the actual amount cannot be known until current young and middle-aged adults pass through the life course.

6   The percentage of adults in the population who are currently married has also diminished. Since 1960, the decline of those married among all persons age 15 and older has been 14 percentage points—and over 29 points among black females (Figure 2). It should be noted that these data include both people who have never married and those who have married and then divorced. (For some economic implications of the decline of marriage, see the accompanying box: "The Surprising Economic Benefits of Marriage.")

7   In order partially to control for a decline in married adults simply due to delayed first marriages, we have looked at changes in the percentage of persons age 35 through 44 who were married (Figure 3). Since 1960, there has been a drop of 22 percentage points for married men and 20 points for married women.

8   Marriage trends in the age range of 35 to 44 are suggestive of lifelong singlehood. In times past and still today, virtually all persons who were going to marry during their lifetimes had married by age 45. More than 90 percent of women have married eventually in every generation for which records exist, going back to the mid-1800s. By 1960, 94 percent of women then alive had been married at least once by age 45—probably an historical high point.[1] For the generation of 1995, assuming a continuation of then current marriage rates,

---

[1] Andrew J. *Cherlin, Marriage, Divorce, and Remarriage* (Cambridge, MA: Harvard University Press, 1992): 10; Michael R. Haines, "Long-Term Marriage Patterns in the United States from Colonial Times to the Present," *The History of the Family* 1-1 (1996): 15–39.

FIGURE 2   Percentage of All Persons Age 15 and Older Who Were Married, by Sex and Race, 1960–2004 United States[a]

Year	Total Males	Black Males	White Males
1960	69.3	60.9	70.2
1970	66.7	56.9	68
1980	63.2	48.8	65
1990	60.7	45.1	62.8
2000	57.9	42.8	60
2004[b]	55.1	38.1	57.4

a. Includes races other than Black and White.
b. In 2003, the U.S. Census Bureau expanded its racial categories to permit respondents to identify themselves as belonging to more than one race. This means that racial data computations beginning in 2004 may not be strictly comparable to those in prior years.
Source: U.S. Bureau of the Census, Current Population Reports, Series P20-506; America's Families and Living Arrangements: March 2000 and earlier reports; and data calculated from the Current Population Surveys, March 2004 Supplement.

several demographers projected that 88 percent of women and 82 percent of men would ever marry.[2] If and when these figures are recalculated for the early years of the 21st century, the percentage of women and men ever marrying will almost certainly be lower.

9   It is important to note that the decline in marriage does not mean that people are giving up on living together with a sexual partner. On the contrary, with the incidence of unmarried cohabitation increasing rapidly, marriage is

FIGURE 3   Percentage of Persons Age 35 through 44 Who Were Married, by Sex, 1960–2004, United States

Year	Males	Females
1960	88.0	87.4
1970	89.3	86.9
1980	84.2	81.4
1990	74.1	73.0
2000	69.0	71.6
2004	65.7	67.3

Source: U.S. Bureau of the Census, Statistical Abstract of the United States, 1961, Page 34, Table 27; Statistical Abstract of the United States, 1971, Page 32, Table 38; Statistical Abstract of the United States, 1981, Page 38, Table 49; and U.S. Bureau of the Census, General Population Characteristics, 1990, Page 45, Table 34; and Statistical Abstract of the United States, 2001, Page 48, Table 51; internet tables (http://www.census.gov/population/socdemo/hh-fam/cps2003/tabA1-all.pdf) and data calculated from the Current Population Surveys, March 2004 Supplement. Figure for 2004 was obtained using data from the Current Population Surveys rather than data from the census. The CPS, March Supplement, is based on a sample of the U.S. population, rather than an actual count such as those available from the decennial census. See sampling and weighting notes at http://www.bls.census.gov:80/cps/ads/2002/ssampwgt.htm

---

[2] Robert Schoen and Nicola Standish, "The Retrenchment of Marriage: Results from Marital Status Life Tables for the United States, 1995." *Population and Development Review* 27-3 (2001): 553–563.

FIGURE 4 Percentage of Married Persons Age 18 and Older Who Said Their Marriages Were "Very Happy," by Period, United States

Period	Men	Women
1973–1976	69.6	68.6
1977–1981	68.3	64.2
1982–1986	62.9	61.7
1987–1991	66.4	59.6
1993–1996	63.2	59.7
1998–2002	64.6	60.3

Source: The General Social Survey, conducted by the National Opinion Research Center of the University of Chicago. The trend for both men and women is statistically significant ($p < .01$ on a two-tailed test).

giving ground to unwed unions. Most people now live together before they marry for the first time. An even higher percentage of those divorced who subsequently remarry live together first. And a growing number of persons, both young and old, are living together with no plans for eventual marriage.

10   There is a common belief that, although a smaller percentage of Americans are now marrying than was the case a few decades ago, those who marry have marriages of higher quality. It seems reasonable that if divorce removes poor marriages from the pool of married couples and cohabitation "trial marriages" deter some bad marriages from forming, the remaining marriages on average should be happier. The best available evidence on the topic, however, does not support these assumptions. Since 1973, the General Social Survey periodically has asked representative samples of married Americans to rate their marriages

THE SURPRISING ECONOMIC BENEFITS OF MARRIAGE

When thinking of the many benefits of marriage, the economic aspects are often overlooked. Yet the economic benefits of marriage are substantial, both for individuals and for society as a whole. Marriage is a wealth generating institution. Married couples create more economic assets on average than do otherwise similar singles or cohabiting couples. A 1992 study of retirement data concluded that "individuals who are not continuously married have significantly lower wealth than those who remain married throughout their lives." Compared to those continuously married, those who never married have a reduction in wealth of 75% and those who divorced and didn't remarry have a reduction of 73%.[a]

One might think that the explanation for why marriage generates economic assets is because those people who are more likely to be wealth creators are also more likely to marry and stay married. And this is certainly true, but only in part. The institution of marriage itself provides a wealth-generation bonus. It does this through providing economies of scale (two can live more cheaply than one), and as implicitly a long-term personal contract it encourages economic specialization. Working as a couple, individuals can develop those skills in which they excel, leaving others to their partner.

Also, married couples save and invest more for the future, and they can act as a small insurance pool against life uncertainties such as illness and job loss.[b] Probably because of marital social norms that encourage healthy, productive behavior, men tend to become more economically productive after marriage; they earn between 10 and 40% more than do single men with similar education and job histories.[c] All of these benefits are independent of the fact that married couples receive more work-related and government-provided support, and also more help and support from their extended families (two sets of in-laws) and friends.[d]

Beyond the economic advantages of marriage for the married couples themselves, marriage has a tremendous economic impact on society. It is a major contributor to family income levels and inequality. After more than doubling between 1947 and 1977, the growth of median family income has slowed over the past 20 years, increasing by just 9.6%. A big reason is that married couples, who fare better economically than their single counterparts, have been a rapidly decreasing proportion of total families. In this same 20 year period, and largely because of changes in family structure, family income inequality has increased significantly.[e]

Research has shown consistently that both divorce and unmarried childbearing increase child poverty. In recent years the majority of children who grow up outside of married families have experienced at least one year of dire poverty.[f] According to one study, if family structure had not changed between 1960 and 1998, the black child poverty rate in 1998 would have been 28.4% rather than 45.6%, and the white child poverty rate would have been 11.4% rather than 15.4%.[g] The rise in child poverty, of course, generates significant public costs in health and welfare programs.

Marriages that end in divorce also are very costly to the public. One researcher determined that a single divorce costs state and federal governments about $30,000, based on such things as the higher use of food stamps and public housing as well as increased bankruptcies and juvenile delinquency. The nation's 1.4 million divorces in 2002 are estimated to have cost the taxpayers more than $30 billion.[h]

Notes

a. Janet Wilmoth and Gregor Koso, "Does Marital History Matter? Marital Status and Wealth Outcomes Among Preretirement Adults," *Journal of Marriage and the Family* 64:254–68, 2002.

(continued)

b. Thomas A. Hirschl, Joyce Altobelli, and Mark R. Rank, "Does Marriage Increase the Odds of Affluence? Exploring the Life Course Probabilities," *Journal of Marriage and the Family* 65-4 (2003): 927–938; Joseph Lupton and James P. Smith, "Marriage, Assets and Savings," in Shoshana A. Grossbard-Schectman (ed.) *Marriage and the Economy* (Cambridge: Cambridge University Press, 2003): 129–152.

c. Jeffrey S. Gray and Michael J. Vanderhart, "The Determination of Wages: Does Marriage Matter?," in Linda Waite, et al. (eds.) *The Ties that Bind: Perspectives on Marriage and Cohabitation* (New York: Aldine de Gruyter, 2000): 356–367; S. Korenman and D. Neumark, "Does Marriage Really Make Men More Productive?" *Journal of Human Resources* 26-2 (1991): 282–307; K. Daniel, "The Marriage Premium," in M. Tomassi and K. Ierulli (eds.) *The New Economics of Human Behavior* (Cambridge: Cambridge University Press, 1995) 113–125.

d. Lingxin Hao, "Family Structure, Private Transfers, and the Economic Well-Being of Families with Children," *Social Forces* 75 (1996): 269–292.

e. U.S. Bureau of the Census, Current Population Reports, P60-203, *Measuring 50 Years of Economic Change Using the March Current Population Survey*, U.S. Government Printing Office, Washington, DC, 1998; John Iceland, "Why Poverty Remains High: The Role of Income Growth, Economic Inequality, and Changes in Family Structure, 1949–1999," *Demography* 40-3:499–519, 2003.

f. Mark R. Rank and Thomas A. Hirschl, "The Economic Risk of Childhood in America: Estimating the Probability of Poverty Across the Formative Years," *Journal of Marriage and the Family* 61:1058–1067, 1999.

g. Adam Thomas and Isabel Sawhill, "For Richer or For Poorer: Marriage as an Antipoverty Strategy," *Journal of Policy Analysis and Management* 21:4, 2002.

h. David Schramm, "The Costly Consequences of Divorce in Utah: The Impact on Couples, Community, and Government," Logan, UT: Utah State University, 2003. Unpublished preliminary report.

as either "very happy," "pretty happy," or "not too happy."[3] As Figure 4 indicates, the percentage of both men and women saying "very happy" has declined moderately over the past 25 years.[4] This trend, however, is now heading in a positive direction.

Divorce

11 Key Finding: The American divorce rate today is nearly twice that of 1960, but has declined slightly since hitting the highest point in our history in the early 1980s. For the average couple marrying in recent years, the lifetime probability of divorce or separation remains between 40 and 50 percent.

---

[3] Conducted by the National Opinion Research Center of the University of Chicago, this is a nationally representative study of the English-speaking, non-institutionalized population of the United States age 18 and over.

[4] Using a different data set that compared marriages in 1980 with marriages in 1992, equated in terms of marital duration, Stacy J. Rogers and Paul Amato found similarly that the 1992 marriages had less marital interaction, more marital conflict, and more marital problems. "Is Marital Quality Declining? The Evidence from Two Generations," *Social Forces* 75 (1997): 1089.

FIGURE 5   Number of Divorces per 1,000 Married Women Age 15 and Older, by Year, United States[a]

Year	Divorces
1960	9.2
1965	10.6
1970	14.9
1975	20.3
1980	22.6
1985	21.7
1990	20.9
1995	19.8
2000	18.8
2004	17.7

a. We have used the number of divorces per 1,000 married women age 15 and older, rather than the Crude Divorce Rate of divorces per 1,000 population to help avoid the problem of compositional changes in the population. Even this more refined measure is somewhat susceptible to compositional changes.
Source: Statistical Abstract of the United States, 2001, Page 87, Table 117; National Vital Statistics Reports, August 22, 2001; California Current Population Survey Report: 2000, Table 3, March 2001; Births, Marriages, Divorces, and Deaths: Provisional Data for 2004, National Vital Statistics Report 53:21, June 26, 2005, Table 3, (http://www.cdc.gov/nchs/data/nvsr/nvsr53/nvsr53_21.pdf) and calculations by the National Marriage Project for the U.S. [not including] California, Georgia, Hawaii, Indiana, Louisiana and Oklahoma using the Current Population Surveys, 2004.

12   The increase in divorce, shown by the trend reported in Figure 5, probably has elicited more concern and discussion than any other family-related trend in the United States. Although the long-term trend in divorce has been upward since colonial times, the divorce rate was level for about two decades after World War II during the period of high fertility known as the baby boom. By the middle of the 1960s, however, the incidence of divorce started to increase and it more than doubled over the next fifteen years to reach an historical high point in the early 1980s. Since then the divorce rate has modestly declined, a trend described by many experts as "leveling off at a high level." The decline apparently represents a slight increase in marital stability.[5] Two probable reasons for this are an increase in the age at which people marry for the first time, and a higher educational level of those marrying, both of which are associated with greater marital stability.[6]

13   Although a majority of divorced persons eventually remarry, the growth of divorce has led to a steep increase in the percentage of all adults who are currently divorced (Figure 6). This percentage, which was only 1.8 percent for males and 2.6 percent for females in 1960, quadrupled by the year 2000. The percentage of divorce is higher for females than for males primarily because divorced men are more likely to remarry than divorced women. Also, among those who do remarry, men generally do so sooner than women.

---

[5] Joshua R. Goldstein, "The Leveling of Divorce in the United States," *Demography* 36 (1999): 409–414.

[6] Tim B. Heaton, "Factors Contributing to Increased Marital Stability in the United States," *Journal of Family Issues* 23 (2002): 392–409.

FIGURE 6   Percentage of All Persons Age 15 and Older Who Were Divorced, by Sex and Race, 1960–2004, United States

Year	Total	Males Blacks	Males Whites	Total	Females Blacks	Females Whites
1960	1.8	2	1.8	2.6	4.3	2.5
1970	2.2	3.1	2.1	3.5	4.4	3.4
1980	4.8	6.3	4.7	6.6	8.7	6.4
1990	6.8	8.1	6.8	8.9	11.2	8.6
2000	8.3	9.5	8.4	10.2	11.8	10.2
2004[a]	8.2	9.1	8.3	10.9	12.9	10.9

a. In 2003, the U.S. Census Bureau expanded its racial categories to permit respondents to identify themselves as belonging to more than one race. This means that racial data computations beginning in 2004 may not be strictly comparable to those of prior years.
Source: U.S. Bureau of the Census, Current Population Reports, Series P20-537; America's Families and Living Arrangements: March 2000 and earlier reports; and Current Population Surveys, March 2004 supplement, raw data.

14   Overall, the chances remain very high—estimated between 40 and 50 percent—that a marriage started in recent years will end in either divorce or separation before one partner dies.[7] (But see the accompanying box: "Your Chances of Divorce May Be Much Lower Than You Think.") The likelihood of divorce has varied considerably among different segments of the American population, being higher for Blacks than for Whites, for instance, and higher in the West than in other parts of the country. But these variations have been diminishing. The trend toward a greater similarity of divorce rates between Whites and Blacks is largely attributable to the fact that fewer blacks are marrying.[8] Divorce rates in the South and Midwest have come to resemble those in the West, for reasons that are not well understood, leaving only the Eastern Seaboard and the Central Plains with significantly lower divorce.

15   At the same time, there has been little change in such traditionally large divorce rate differences as between those who marry when they are teenagers compared to those who marry after age 21, high-school drop outs versus college graduates, and the non-religious compared to the religiously committed. Teenagers, high-school drop outs, and the non-religious who marry have considerably higher divorce rates.[9]

Unmarried Cohabitation

16 Key Finding: The number of unmarried couples has increased dramatically over the past four decades, and the increase is continuing. Most younger Americans

---

[7] Robert Schoen and Nicola Standish, "The Retrenchment of Marriage: Results from Marital Status Life Tables for the United States, 1995," *Population and Development Review* 27-3 (2001): 553–563; R. Kelly Raley and Larry Bumpass, "The Topography of the Divorce Plateau: Levels and Trends in Union Stability in the United States after 1980," *Demographic Research* 8-8 (2003): 245–259.

[8] Jay D. Teachman, "Stability across Cohorts in Divorce Risk Factors," *Demography* 39-2 (2002): 331–351.

[9] Raley and Bumpass, 2003.

YOUR CHANCES OF DIVORCE MAY BE MUCH LOWER THAN YOU THINK

By now almost everyone has heard that the national divorce rate is close to 50% of all marriages. This is true, but the rate must be interpreted with caution and several important caveats. For many people, the actual chances of divorce are far below 50/50.

The background characteristics of people entering a marriage have major implications for their risk of divorce. Here are some percentage point decreases in the risk of divorce or separation *during the first ten years of marriage*, according to various personal and social factors:[a]

Factors	Percent Decrease in Risk of Divorce
Annual income over $50,000 (vs. under $25,000)	−30
Having a baby seven months or more after marriage (vs. before marriage)	−24
Marrying over 25 years of age (vs. under 18)	−24
Own family of origin intact (vs. divorced parents)	−14
Religious affiliation (vs. none)	−14
Some college (vs. high-school dropout)	−13

So if you are a reasonably well-educated person with a decent income, come from an intact family and are religious, and marry after age twenty-five without having a baby first, your chances of divorce are very low indeed.

Also, it should be realized that the "close to 50%" divorce rate refers to the percentage of marriages entered into during a particular year that are projected to end in divorce or separation before one spouse dies. Such projections assume that the divorce and death rates occurring that year will continue indefinitely into the future—an assumption that is useful more as an indicator of the instability of marriages in the recent past than as a predictor of future events. In fact, the divorce rate has been dropping, slowly, since reaching a peak around 1980, and the rate could be lower (or higher) in the future than it is today.[b]

Notes
a. Matthew D. Bramlett and William D. Mosher, *Cohabitation, Marriage, Divorce and Remarriage in the United States*, National Center for Health Statistics, Vital and Health Statistics, 23 (22), 2002. The risks are calculated for women only.
b. Rose M. Kreider and Jason M. Fields, "Number, Timing and Duration of Marriages and Divorces, 1996," *Current Population Reports*, P70-80, Washington, DC: U.S. Census Bureau, 2002.

FIGURE 7   Number, in Thousands, of Cohabiting, Unmarried, Adult Couples of the Opposite Sex, by Year, United States

Year	Number
1960	439
1970	523
1980	1,589
1990	2,856
2000	4,736
2004	5,080

Source: U.S. Bureau of the Census, Current Population Reports, Series P20-537; America's Families and Living Arrangements: March 2000; and U.S. Bureau of the Census, Population Division, Current Population Survey, 2004 Annual Social and Economic Supplement (http://www.census.gov/population/socdemo/hh-fam/cps2004).

now spend some time living together outside of marriage, and unmarried cohabitation commonly precedes marriage.

17   Between 1960 and 2004, as indicated in Figure 7, the number of unmarried couples in America increased by nearly 1200 percent. Unmarried cohabitation—the status of couples who are sexual partners, not married to each other, and sharing a household—is particularly common among the young. It is estimated that about a quarter of unmarried women age 25 to 39 are currently living with a partner and an additional quarter have lived with a partner at some time in the past. Over half of all first marriages are now preceded by living together, compared to virtually none 50 years ago.[10]

18   For many, cohabitation is a prelude to marriage, for others, simply an alternative to living alone, and for a small but growing number, it is considered an alternative to marriage. Cohabitation is more common among those of lower educational and income levels. Recent data show that among women in the 19 to 44 age range, 60 percent of high-school dropouts have cohabited compared to 37 percent of college graduates.[11] Cohabitation is also more common among those who are less religious than their peers, those who have been divorced, and those who have experienced parental divorce, fatherlessness, or high levels of marital discord during childhood. A growing percentage of cohabiting couple households, now over 40 percent, contain children.

19   The belief that living together before marriage is a useful way "to find out whether you really get along," and thus avoid a bad marriage and an eventual divorce, is now widespread among young people. But the available data on the effects of cohabitation fail to confirm this belief. In fact, a substantial body of evidence indicates that those who live together before marriage are more likely to break up after marriage. This evidence is controversial, however, because it is dif-

---

[10] Larry Bumpass and Hsien-Hen Lu, "Trends in Cohabitation and Implications for Children's Family Contexts in the U. S.," *Population Studies* 54 (2000) 29–41.

[11] Bumpass and Lu, 2000.

ficult to distinguish the "selection effect" from the "experience of cohabitation effect." The selection effect refers to the fact that people who cohabit before marriage have different characteristics from those who do not, and it may be these characteristics, and not the experience of cohabitation, that leads to marital instability. There is some empirical support for both positions. Also, a recent study based on a nationally representative sample of women concluded that premarital cohabitation (and premarital sex), when limited to a woman's future husband, is not associated with an elevated risk of marital disruption.[12] What can be said for certain is that no evidence has yet been found that those who cohabit before marriage have stronger marriages than those who do not.[13]

Conclusions

20 As a **stage in the life course of adults,** marriage is shrinking. Americans are living longer, marrying later, exiting marriages more quickly, and choosing to live together before marriage, after marriage, in between marriages, and as an alternative to marriage. A small but growing percentage, an estimated 15% [as of 2002], will never marry, compared to about five percent during the 1950s. As a consequence, marriage gradually is giving way to partnered and unpartnered singlehood, with or without children. Since 1960, the percentage of persons age 35 through 44 who were married has dropped from 88% to 66% for men and 87% to 67% for women.

21   As an **institution,** marriage has lost much of its legal, social, economic, and religious meaning and authority. The marital relationship once consisted of an economic bond of mutual dependency, a social bond supported by the extended family and larger community, and a spiritual bond upheld by religious doctrine, observance, and faith. Today, there are many marriages that have none of these elements. The older ideal of marriage as a permanent contractual union, strongly supported by society and designed for procreation and childrearing, is giving way to a new reality of it as a purely individual contract between two adults. Moreover, marriage is also quietly losing its place in the language and in popular culture. Unmarried people now tend to speak inclusively about "relationships" and "intimate partners." In the entertainment industry—including films, television, and music—marriage is often neglected or discredited.

22   If these have been the main changes, what, then, has marriage become in 21st-century America? First, let us not forget that many of the marriage-related trends of recent decades have been positive. The legal, sexual, and financial emancipation of women has become a reality as never before in history. With few restrictions on divorce, a married woman who is seriously abused by her hus-

---

[12] Jay Teachman, "Premarital Sex, Premarital Cohabitation, and the Risk of Subsequent Marital Disruption among Women," *Journal of Marriage and the Family* 65 (2003): 444–455.

[13] For a full review of the research on cohabitation see: Pamela J. Smock, "Cohabitation in the United States," *Annual Review of Sociology* 26 (2000); and David Popenoe and Barbara Dafoe Whitehead, *Should We Live Together? What Young Adults Need to Know About Cohabitation Before Marriage—A Comprehensive Review of Recent Research,* 2nd Edition (New Brunswick, NJ: The National Marriage Project, Rutgers University, 2002).

band can get out of the relationship, which she previously might have been stuck in for life. Due to great tolerance of family diversity, adults and children who through no fault of their own end up in nontraditional families are not marked for life by social stigma. Moreover, based on a companionship of equals, many marriages today may be more emotionally satisfying than ever before.

23   We have described the new marriage system as "emotionally deep, but socially shallow." For most Americans, marriage is a "couples relationship" designed primarily to meet the sexual and emotional needs of the spouses. Increasingly, happiness in marriage is measured by each partner's sense of psychological well-being, rather than the more-traditional measures of getting ahead economically, boosting children up to a higher rung on the educational ladder than the parents, or following religious teachings on marriage. People tend to be puzzled or put off by the idea that marriage has purposes or benefits that extend beyond fulfilling individual adult needs for intimacy and satisfaction. Eight out of 10 of the young adults in our survey agreed that "marriage is nobody's business, but that of the two people involved."

24   It is a sign of the times that the overwhelming majority (94%) of never-married singles in our survey agreed that "when you marry, you want your spouse to be your soul mate, first and foremost." This perspective, surely encouraged not only by the changing nature of marriage, but by the concern about divorce and therefore the seeming necessity of finding the one right person, is something that most people in the older generation would probably consider surprising. In times past, people married to start a new family, and therefore they looked for a competent and reliable mate to share life's tasks. To the degree that a soul mate was even considered, it was more likely to have been thought of as the end result of a lifetime of effort put into making a marriage work, not something you start out with.

25   Of course, having a soul mate as a marriage partner would be wonderful. In many ways, it is reassuring that today's young people are looking for a marriage that is both meaningful and lasting. Yet, there is a danger that the soul mate expectation sets a standard so high it will be hard to live up to. Also, if people believe that there is just one soul mate waiting somewhere out there for them, as most of today's youths in fact do according to our survey, doesn't it seem more likely that a marriage partner will be dropped when the going gets rough? Isn't it easier to say, "I must have picked the wrong person"? In other words, perhaps we have developed a standard for marriage that tends to destabilize the institution.

26   There are some hopeful signs in the recent statistics that may bode well for the future of marriage. The divorce rate has slowly been dropping since the early 1980s. Since the early 1990s, the teen birthrate has decreased by about 20%, with some indications that teenagers have become sexually more conservative. Overall, the percentage of unwed births has remained at its current level for the past five years. Indeed, due to fewer divorces and stabilized unwed births, the percentage of children living in single-parent families dropped slightly in the past few years, after having increased rapidly and continuously since 1960.

27   Moreover, one can see glimmers of hope here and there on the cultural scene. There are stirrings of a grassroots "marriage movement." Churches in several

hundred communities have joined together to establish a common set of pre-marital counseling standards and practices for engaged couples. Marriage education has emerged as a prominent theme among some family therapists, family life educators, schoolteachers, and clergy. In several states, legislatures have passed bills promoting marriage education in the schools and even seeking ways to cut the divorce rate, mainly through educational means. More books are being published with the theme of how to have a good marriage, and seemingly fewer with the theme of divorcing to achieve personal liberation. Questions are being raised more forcefully by members of Congress, on both sides of the aisle, about the "family values" of the entertainment industry. These positive trends bear watching and are encouraging, but it is too soon to tell whether they will persist or result in the revitalization of this critical social institution.

Review Questions

1. What factors significantly reduce the incidence of divorce, according to Popenoe and Whitehead?

2. According to Popenoe and Whitehead, which two factors are most likely responsible for the slight increase in marital stability (i.e., a decline in the divorce rate) since the early 1980s?

3. The data show that the percentage of divorced females is higher than that of males. Why?

4. Popenoe and Whitehead suggest that it might it be erroneous to claim that, based on recent data, people who live together before marriage are more likely to experience marital instability. Explain.

Discussion and Writing Suggestions

1. Popenoe and Whitehead's key finding is that "Marriage trends in recent decades indicate that Americans have become less likely to marry, and . . . that the marriage rate in the United States continues to decline." To what extent does this finding square with your own observations and impressions of contemporary marriage? How do you account for the declining marriage rate?

2. Popenoe and Whitehead assert that, despite the conventional wisdom among many young people that living together before marriage is a useful way to discover whether a couple is really compatible, and therefore to avoid a bad marriage and eventual divorce, "No evidence has yet been found that those who cohabit before marriage have stronger marriages than those who do not." In light of this assertion, have your opinions about whether or not people should live together before marriage changed? Explain your answer.

3. Noting that 94% of never-married singles agreed with the statement that "when you marry, you want your spouse to be your soul mate, first and foremost," Popenoe and Whitehead worry that this "soul mate expectation" sets up an unrealistically high standard for marriage. How do you define "soul mate"? Do you agree that expecting a spouse to be a soul mate can destabilize the institution of marriage?

4. Popenoe and Whitehead claim that, as an institution, marriage has lost much of its "legal, social, economic, and religious meaning and authority," and that marriage is becoming devalued in popular culture. Contrast these statements with the multitudes of bridal magazines on sale at every newsstand and the breathless attention with which tabloids follow celebrity marriages. To what extent does such evidence of our culture's fascination with marriage contradict Popenoe and Whitehead's thesis? Explain your answer.

Debunking Myths about Marriages and Families
Mary Ann Schwartz and BarBara Marliene Scott

While the previous selection relied on data to gauge the current state of the institutions of marriage and family, many people use a simpler method—their sense of what a family should be, and how current families measure up to that ideal. For example, many people assume that the nuclear family—defined as a family consisting of a father, mother, and their children—is the most basic and traditional form of family. But are such assumptions valid? In the following selection, two sociologists deconstruct five common myths about marriages and families. Mary Ann Schwartz is professor of sociology and women's studies and former chair of the sociology department at Northeastern Illinois University, where she cofounded the Women's Studies Program. BarBara Marliene Scott is professor of sociology and women's studies and coordinator of African and African American studies at Northeastern Illinois University. This selection is excerpted from their book Marriages and Families: Diversity and Change *(2000).*

1   Take a few minutes to think about the "traditional family." If you are like most people, your vision of the traditional family is similar to or the same as your more general view of families. Therefore, you probably describe the traditional family in terms of some combination of the following traits:

- Members loved and respected one another and worked together for the good of the family.
- Grandparents were an integral and respected part of the family.
- Mothers stayed home and were happy, nurturant, and always available to their children.
- Fathers worked and brought home the paycheck.
- Children were seen and not heard, mischievous but not "bad," and were responsible and learned a work ethic.

2   These images of past family life are still widely held and have a powerful influence on people's perceptions and evaluations of today's families. The problem, however, is that these are mostly mythical images of the past based on many different kinds of marriages and families that never coexisted in the same time and place. A leading authority on U.S. family history, Stephanie Coontz (1992), argues in her book *The Way We Never Were* that much of today's political and social debate about family values and the "real" family is based on an idealized vision of a past that never actually existed. Coontz further argues that this idealized and selective set of remembrances of families of yesteryear in turn determines much of our contemporary view of traditional family life.

— we were never as traditional as we thought

. . .

3   Our memory of past family life is often clouded by myths. A **myth** is a false, fictitious, imaginary, or exaggerated belief about someone or something. Myths are generally assumed to be true and often provide the justification or rationale for social behaviors, beliefs, and institutions. And, in fact, most myths do contain some elements of truth. As we will see, however, different myths contain different degrees of truth.

4   Some family myths have a positive effect in the sense that they often bond individual family members together in familial solidarity. When they create unrealistic expectations about what families can or should be and do, however, myths can be dangerous. Many of the myths that most Americans hold today about traditional families or families of the past are white middle-class myths. This is true because the mass media, controlled primarily by white middle-class men, tend to project a primarily white middle-class experience as a universal trend or fact. Such myths, then, distort the diverse experiences of other familial groups in this country, both presently and in the past, and they do not even describe most white middle-class families accurately. We now take a closer look at five of the most popular myths and stereotypes about the family that are directly applicable to current debates about family life and gender roles: (1) the universal nuclear family, (2) the self-reliant traditional family, (3) the naturalness of different spheres for wives and husbands, (4) the unstable African American family, and (5) the idealized nuclear family of the 1950s.

Myth 1: The Universal Nuclear Family

5   While some form of marriage and family is found in all human societies, the idea that there is a universal, or single, marriage and family pattern blinds us to the historical reality and legitimacy of diverse marriage and family arrangements. The reality is that marriages and families vary in organization, membership, life cycles, emotional environments, ideologies, social and kinship networks, and economic and other functions. Although it is certainly true that a woman and man (egg and sperm) must unite to produce a child, social kinship ties or living arrangements, however, do not automatically flow from such biological unions. For example, although some cultures have weddings and cultural notions about monogamy and permanence, other cultures lack one or more of these characteristics. In some cultures, mating and childbirth occur outside of legal marriage and sometimes without couples living together. In other cultures, wives, husbands, and children live in separate residences.

Myth 2: The Self-Reliant Traditional Family

6 The myth of the self-reliant family assumes that, in the past, families were held together by hard work, family loyalty, and a fierce determination not to be beholden to anyone, especially the state. It is popularly believed that such families never asked for handouts; rather, they stood on their own feet even in times of crisis. Unlike some families today, who watch the mail for their government checks, families of yesteryear did not accept or expect "charity." Any help they may have received came from other family members.

7 This tendency to overestimate the self-reliance of earlier families ignores the fact that external support for families has been the rule, and not the exception, in U.S. family history. Although public assistance has become less local and more impersonal over the past two centuries, U.S. families have always depended to some degree on other institutions. For example, colonial families made extensive use of the collective work of others, such as African American slaves and Native Americans, whose husbandry and collective land use provided for the abundant game, plants, and berries colonial families consumed to survive. Early families were also dependent on a large network of neighbors, churches, courts, government officials, and legislative bodies for their sustenance. For example, the elderly, ill, and orphaned dependents were often taken care of by people who were not family members, and public officials often gave money to facilitate such care. Immigrant, African American, and native-born white workers could not have survived in the past without sharing and receiving assistance beyond family networks. Moreover, middle-class as well as working-class families were dependent on fraternal and mutual aid organizations to assist them in times of need.

Myth 3: The Naturalness of Different Spheres for Wives and Husbands

8 This myth dates to the mid-nineteenth century, when economic changes led to the development of separate spheres for women and men. Prior to this, men shared in child rearing. They were expected to be at least as involved in child rearing as mothers. Fatherhood meant much more than simply inseminating. It was understood as a well-defined set of domestic skills, including provisioning, hospitality, and child rearing (Gillis, 1999). With industrialization, wives and mothers became the caregivers and moral guardians of the family, while husbands and fathers provided economic support and protection and represented their families to the outside world. Thereafter, this arrangement was viewed as natural, and alternative forms were believed to be destructive to family harmony. Thus, today's family problems are seen as stemming from a self-defeating attempt to equalize women's and men's roles in the family. It is assumed that the move away from a traditional gendered division of labor to a more egalitarian ideal denies women's and men's differing needs and abilities and thus destabilizes family relations. Those who hold to this myth advocate a return to traditional gender roles in the family and a clear and firm boundary between the family and the outside world. As we shall see later on, however, the notions of separate spheres and ideal family form are far from natural and have not always existed.

Myth 4: The Unstable African American Family

9   Although many critics of today's families believe that the collapse of the family affects all racial and ethnic groups, they frequently single out African American families as the least stable and functional. According to sociologist Ronald Taylor (1994), myths and misconceptions about the nature and quality of African American family life are pervasive and deeply entrenched in American popular thought. Although there are far fewer systematic studies of black families than of white families, African American families have been the subject of far more sweeping generalizations and myths. The most pervasive myth, the myth of the collapse of the African American family, is fueled by racist stereotypes and media exaggerations and distortions that overlook the diversity of African American family life. No more is there one black family type than there is one white family type.

10   Nonetheless, this myth draws on some very real trends that affect a segment of the African American community. . . . Early in this decade, almost two-thirds of African American babies were born to unmarried couples, a trend especially evident among lower-income and less educated African Americans. In addition, there has been a major increase in the number of African American one-parent families. Although these trends have occurred among white families as well, their impact on black families has been much more substantial, resulting in increasingly different marital and family experiences for these two groups (Taylor, 1994).

11   Based on middle-class standards, these trends seem to support the myth of an unstable, disorganized family structure in part of the African American community. And, indeed, among some individuals and families, long-term and concentrated poverty and despair, racism, social contempt, police brutality, and political and governmental neglect have taken their toll and are often manifested in the behaviors just described. To generalize these behaviors to the entire African American community, however, is inaccurate and misleading. Moreover, to attribute these behaviors, when they do occur, to a deteriorating, immoral family life-style and a lack of middle-class family values ignores historical, social, and political factors, such as a history of servitude, legal discrimination, enforced segregation and exclusion, **institutional racism**—the systematic discrimination against a racial group by the institutions within society—and structural shifts in the economy and related trends that have created new and deeper disparities in the structure and quality of family life between blacks and whites in this society. In addition, such claims serve to perpetuate the myth that one particular family arrangement is a workable model for all families in modern society.

· · ·

Myth 5: The Idealized Nuclear Family of the 1950s

12   During the 1950s, millions of Americans came to accept an image of the family as a middle-class institution consisting of a wise father who worked outside the home; a mother whose major responsibility was to take care of her husband, children, and home; and children who were well behaved and obedient. This

image, depicted in a number of 1950s family sitcoms, such as "Leave It to Beaver," "Father Knows Best," "The Donna Reed Show," and "The Adventures of Ozzie and Harriet," is said to represent the epitome of traditional family structure and values. Many critics today see the movement away from this model as evidence of the decline in the viability of the family, as well as a source of many family problems.

13   It is true that, compared with the 1990s, the 1950s were characterized by younger ages at marriage, higher birthrates, and lower divorce and premarital pregnancy rates. To present the 1950s as representing "typical" or "normal" family patterns, however, is misleading. Indeed, the divorce rates have increased since the 1950s, but this trend started in the nineteenth century, with more marital breakups in each succeeding generation. Today's trends of low marriage, high divorce, and low fertility are actually consistent with long-term historical trends in marriage and family life. Recent changes in marriage and family life are considered deviant only because the marriage rates for the postwar generation represented an all-time high for the United States. This generation married young, moved to the suburbs, and had three or more children. The fact is that this pattern was deviant in that it departed significantly from earlier twentieth-century trends in marriage and family life. According to some, if the 1940s and 1950s had not happened, marriage and family life today would appear normal (Skolnick and Skolnick, 1999). Although some people worry that young people today are delaying marriage to unusually late ages, . . . the median age at first marriage in the late 1990s [was] 24.8 for women and 27.1 for men, the highest levels since these data were first recorded in 1890, [which] more closely approximates the 1890 average than it does the 1950s average of 20.3 for women and 22.8 for men. The earlier age at marriage in the 1950s was a reaction to the hardships and sacrifices brought about by the depression and World War II. Thus, marriage and family life became synonymous with the "good life." Furthermore, images of the good life were now broadcast into living rooms across the country via the powerful new medium of television. Even then, however, there were signs that all was not well. Public opinion polls taken during the 1950s suggested that approximately 20 percent of all couples considered themselves unhappy in marriage, and another 20 percent reported only "medium happiness" (quoted in Mintz and Kellogg, 1988:194).

14   Connected to the myth of the idealized nuclear family is the myth that families have been essentially the same over the centuries, until recently when they began to disintegrate. The fact is that families have never been static, they have always changed: When the world around them changes, families change in response. The idea of the traditional family of old is itself relative. According to John Gillis (1999), we are in the habit of updating our notion of the traditional family so that the location of the golden age of the family constantly changes. For example, for the Victorians, the traditional family was rooted in a time period prior to industrialization and urbanization; for those who came of age during World War I, the traditional family was associated with the Victorians themselves; and today, most people think of the 1950s and 1960s as the epitome of traditional marriage and family life.

15   This discussion of mythical versus real families underscores the fact that not all families are the same; there is not now and never has been a single model of the family. Families and their experiences are indeed different; however, difference does not connote better or worse. The experiences of a poor family are certainly not the same as those of a rich family; the experiences of a young family with young children are little like those of either a child-free family or an older family whose children have "left the nest." Even within families the experiences of older members are different from those of younger members, and the experiences of females and males are different. Certainly the experiences of Latina/o, Native American, Asian American, and black families are not the same as those of white families, regardless of class. Nor are lesbian and gay family experiences the same as heterosexual family experiences. Families are products of their historical context, and at any given historical period families occupy different territories and have varied experiences, given the differential influence of the society's race, class, and gender systems.

Review Questions

1. Based on your reading of Schwartz and Scott, offer an example of the way in which U.S. families have historically relied on institutions outside of marriage.

2. What economic change led to wives and mothers becoming the primary caregivers of children?

3. According to Schwartz and Scott, those who believe that family gender roles should return to a more traditional standard are basing their views on a myth. What is that myth?

4. Why did people marry at younger ages in the 1950s, according to Schwartz and Scott?

Discussion and Writing Suggestions

1. Schwartz and Scott's "Myth 2" concerns the "self-reliant traditional family" (see page 278). To what extent do you see evidence that American politicians use this myth to advance a political agenda, attack the positions of opponents, or argue for or against changes in the law? (Consider, for example, the extent to which politicians invoke the "self-reliant traditional family" in debates over health care, welfare, or relief from natural disasters.)

2. Politicians and conservative commentators often blame a "breakdown of the family" for many of the ills facing society. Schwartz and Scott claim that the universal nuclear family is a myth—and, thus, logically speaking, no "breakdown" could have occurred. How might the public's general acceptance that the traditional family is a myth be used to shape public policy intended to help American families?

3. Schwartz and Scott argue that the marriage patterns of the 1950s were an anomaly, not the norm, in American marriage trends. Does this observation invalidate for you the 1950s family model of "a wise father who worked outside the home; a mother whose major responsibility was to take care of her husband, children, and home; and children who were well behaved and obedient"? If you were designing your own ideal family model, which elements of the 1950s family would you keep, and which would you jettison?

4. In the section dealing with African-American families, Schwartz and Scott label as a myth the belief that "one particular family arrangement is a workable model for all families in modern society." From your experience of your own family, or families you have known, describe a non-nuclear family arrangement that you have witnessed—for example, a family in which a grandparent lived with the family. Did you feel this arrangement was successful? Explain why or why not.

A DEBATE ON GAY MARRIAGE

There are few more hot-button topics in American politics today than gay marriage. In the Defense of Marriage Act of 1996, the federal government defined marriage as the legal union of a man as husband and a woman as wife. Similar legislation has been passed in 38 states. In November 2003, however, the Massachusetts Supreme Court ruled that denying marriage licenses to gay couples violated the state's Equal Protection Clause. The following year, the city of San Francisco began issuing marriage licenses to gay couples. Hundreds of same-sex couples were legally married in the aftermath of these rulings. Responding in outrage, many conservative state legislatures rushed to pass or reaffirm laws banning gay marriage. In July 2006, court rulings in New York, Nebraska, and Washington limited marriage to unions between a man and a woman.

For Gay Marriage
Andrew Sullivan

The debate over gay marriage highlights a vast cultural divide that typically hinges on core beliefs regarding the nature of marriage itself. In the following selection from Andrew Sullivan's book Virtually Normal: An Argument about Homosexuality *(1995), Sullivan articulates a vision of marriage as a public contract that should be available to any two citizens. Andrew Sullivan is a former editor of the* New Republic *magazine who writes on a wide range of political and social topics, including gay and lesbian issues. He lives in Washington, D.C.*

1 Marriage is not simply a private contract; it is a social and public recognition of a private commitment. As such, it is the highest public recognition of person-

al integrity. Denying it to homosexuals is the most public affront possible to their public equality.

2   This point may be the hardest for many heterosexuals to accept. Even those tolerant of homosexuals may find this institution so wedded to the notion of heterosexual commitment that to extend it would be to undo its very essence. And there may be religious reasons for resisting this that, within certain traditions, are unanswerable. But I am not here discussing what churches do in their private affairs. I am discussing what the allegedly neutral liberal state should do in public matters. For liberals, the case for homosexual marriage is overwhelming. As a classic public institution, it should be available to any two citizens.

3   Some might argue that marriage is by definition between a man and a woman; and it is difficult to argue with a definition. But if marriage is articulated beyond this circular fiat, then the argument for its exclusivity to one man and one woman disappears. The center of the public contract is an emotional, financial, and psychological bond between two people; in this respect, heterosexuals and homosexuals are identical. The heterosexuality of marriage is intrinsic only if it is understood to be intrinsically procreative; but that definition has long been abandoned in Western society. No civil marriage license is granted on the condition that the couple bear children; and the marriage is no less legal and no less defensible if it remains childless. In the contemporary West, marriage has become a way in which the state recognizes an emotional commitment by two people to each other for life. And within that definition, there is no public way, if one believes in equal rights under the law, in which it should legally be denied homosexuals.

4   Of course, no public sanctioning of a contract should be given to people who cannot actually fulfill it. The state rightly, for example, withholds marriage from minors, or from one adult and a minor, since at least one party is unable to understand or live up to the contract. And the state has also rightly barred close family relatives from marriage because familial emotional ties are too strong and powerful to enable a marriage contract to be entered into freely by two autonomous, independent individuals, and because incest poses a uniquely dangerous threat to the trust and responsibility that the family needs to survive. But do homosexuals fall into a similar category? History and experience strongly suggest they don't. Of course, marriage is characterized by a kind of commitment that is rare—and perhaps declining—even among heterosexuals. But it isn't necessary to prove that homosexuals or lesbians are less—or more—able to form long-term relationships than straights for it to be clear that at least *some* are. Moreover, giving these people an equal right to affirm their commitment doesn't reduce the incentive for heterosexuals to do the same.

5   In some ways, the marriage issue is exactly parallel to the issue of the military. Few people deny that many homosexuals are capable of the sacrifice, the commitment, and the responsibilities of marriage. And indeed, for many homosexuals and lesbians, these responsibilities are already enjoined—as they have been enjoined for centuries. The issue is whether these identical relationships should be denied equal legal standing, not by virtue of anything to do with the relationships themselves but by virtue of the internal, involuntary nature of the homosexuals involved. Clearly, for liberals, the answer to this is clear. Such a denial is a classic case of unequal protection of the laws.

6   But perhaps surprisingly, . . . one of the strongest arguments for gay marriage is perhaps best illustrated by a comparison with the alternative often offered by liberals and liberationists to legal gay marriage, the concept of "domestic partnership." Several cities in the United States have domestic partnership laws, which allow relationships that do not fit into the category of heterosexual marriage to be registered with the city and qualify for benefits that had previously been reserved for heterosexual married couples. In these cities, a variety of interpersonal arrangements qualify for health insurance, bereavement leave, insurance, annuity and pension rights, housing rights (such as rent-control apartments), adoption, and inheritance rights. Eventually, the aim is to include federal income tax and veterans' benefits as well. Homosexuals are not the only beneficiaries; heterosexual "live-togethers" also qualify.

7   The conservative's worries start with the ease of the relationship. To be sure, potential domestic partners have to prove financial interdependence, shared living arrangements, and a commitment to mutual caring. But they don't need to have a sexual relationship or even closely mirror old-style marriage. In principle, an elderly woman and her live-in nurse could qualify, or a pair of frat buddies. Left as it is, the concept of domestic partnership could open a Pandora's box of litigation and subjective judicial decision making about who qualifies. You either are or you're not married; it's not a complex question. Whether you are in a domestic partnership is not so clear.

8   More important for conservatives, the concept of domestic partnership chips away at the prestige of traditional relationships and undermines the priority we give them. Society, after all, has good reasons to extend legal advantages to heterosexuals who choose the formal sanction of marriage over simply living together. They make a deeper commitment to one another and to society; in exchange, society extends certain benefits to them. Marriage provides an anchor, if an arbitrary and often weak one, in the maelstrom of sex and relationships to which we are all prone. It provides a mechanism for emotional stability and economic security. We rig the law in its favor not because we disparage all forms of relationship other than the nuclear family, but because we recognize that not to promote marriage would be to ask too much of human virtue.

9   For conservatives, these are vital concerns. There are virtually no conservative arguments either for preferring no social incentives for gay relationships or for preferring a second-class relationship, such as domestic partnership, which really does provide an incentive for the decline of traditional marriage. Nor, if conservatives are concerned by the collapse of stable family life, should they be dismayed by the possibility of gay parents. There is no evidence that shows any deleterious impact on a child brought up by two homosexual parents, and considerable evidence that such a parental structure is clearly preferable to single parents (gay or straight) or no effective parents at all, which, alas, is the choice many children now face. Conservatives should not balk at the apparent radicalism of the change involved, either. The introduction of gay marriage would not be some sort of leap in the dark, a massive societal risk. Homosexual marriages have always existed, in a variety of forms; they have just been euphemized. Increasingly they exist in every sense but the legal one. As it has

become more acceptable for homosexuals to acknowledge their loves and commitments publicly, more and more have committed themselves to one another for life in full view of their families and friends. A law institutionalizing gay marriage would merely reinforce a healthy trend. Burkean conservatives should warm to the idea.

10   It would also be an unqualified social good for homosexuals. It provides role models for young gay people, who, after the exhilaration of coming out can easily lapse into short-term relationships and insecurity with no tangible goal in sight. My own guess is that most homosexuals would embrace such a goal with as much (if not more) commitment as heterosexuals. Even in our society as it is, many lesbian and gay male relationships are virtual textbooks of monogamous commitment; and for many, "in sickness and in health" has become a vocation rather than a vow. Legal gay marriage could also help bridge the gulf often found between homosexuals and their parents. It could bring the essence of gay life— a gay couple—into the heart of the traditional family in a way the family can most understand and the gay offspring can most easily acknowledge. It could do more to heal the gay-straight rift than any amount of gay rights legislation.

11   More important, perhaps, as gay marriage sank into the subtle background consciousness of a culture, its influence would be felt quietly but deeply among gay children. For them, at last, there would be some kind of future; some older faces to apply to their unfolding lives, some language in which their identity could be properly discussed, some rubric by which it could be explained—not in terms of sex, or sexual practices, or bars, or subterranean activity, but in terms of their future life stories, their potential loves, their eventual chance at some kind of constructive happiness. They would be able to feel by the intimation of myriad examples that in this respect their emotional orientation was not merely about pleasure, or sin, or shame, or otherness (although it might always be involved in many of those things), but about the ability to love and be loved as complete, imperfect human beings. Until gay marriage is legalized, this fundamental element of personal dignity will be denied a whole segment of humanity. No other change can achieve it.

12   Any heterosexual man who takes a few moments to consider what his life would be like if he were never allowed a formal institution to cement his relationships will see the truth of what I am saying. Imagine life without a recognized family; imagine dating without even the possibility of marriage. Any heterosexual woman who can imagine being told at a young age that her attraction to men was wrong, that her loves and crushes were illicit, that her destiny was singlehood and shame, will also appreciate the point. Gay marriage is not a radical step; it is a profoundly humanizing, traditionalizing step. It is the first step in any resolution of the homosexual question—more important than any other institution, since it is the most central institution to the nature of the problem, which is to say, the emotional and sexual bond between one human being and another. If nothing else were done at all, and gay marriage were legalized, 90 percent of the political work necessary to achieve gay and lesbian equality would have been achieved. It is ultimately the only reform that truly matters.

13   So long as conservatives recognize, as they do, that homosexuals exist and that they have equivalent emotional needs and temptations as heterosexuals,

then there is no conservative reason to oppose homosexual marriage and many conservative reasons to support it. So long as liberals recognize, as they do, that citizens deserve equal treatment under the law, then there is no liberal reason to oppose it and many liberal reasons to be in favor of it. So long as intelligent people understand that homosexuals are emotionally and sexually attracted to the same sex as heterosexuals are to the other sex, then there is no human reason on earth why it should be granted to one group and not the other.

Review Questions

1. According to Sullivan, what definition of marriage prohibits any public way for marriage to be legally denied to homosexuals "if one believes in equal rights under the law"?

2. Which two classes of people, according to Sullivan, does the state believe cannot fulfill the contract of marriage?

3. Summarize Sullivan's "conservative" arguments preferring gay marriage to "domestic partnership."

4. How does Sullivan believe that gay marriage will "bridge the gulf" that is often found between homosexuals and their parents?

Discussion and Writing Suggestions

1. Write a critique of Sullivan's argument in favor of gay marriage. To what extent do you agree, for example, that "the marriage issue [for gays] is exactly parallel to the issue of the military"? Or that "[l]egal gay marriage could . . . help bridge the gulf often found between homosexuals and their parents"? Follow the principles discussed in Chapter 2.

2. Sullivan makes the surprising case that conservatives should support, rather than oppose, gay marriage because marriage is a fundamentally conservative institution (more conservative, for instance, than domestic partnership). To what extent do you agree with his reasoning?

3. Imagine for a moment, as Sullivan suggests, that you belong to a class of people that has been denied the right to marry or have a recognized family. To what extent do you feel that this restriction would affect your approach to life? For example, do you feel that you would be drawn more to short-term relationships—as Sullivan suggests is true of some young gays? To what extent do you feel that the lack of these rights would adversely affect your life?

4. Sullivan writes: "[G]iving [homosexuals] an equal right to affirm their commitment doesn't reduce the incentive for heterosexuals to do the same." However, many antigay marriage activists make precisely that argument—that gay marriage "devalues" heterosexual marriage, by implication making it less attractive to men and women. To what degree

does the value you place on marriage depend on its being an institution reserved for a heterosexual man and woman?

5. Sullivan writes that marriage provides a bulwark against the "maelstrom of sex and relationships to which we are all prone." Do you agree that people who have undertaken the public commitment of marriage are less likely to yield to temptation than, say, people who have made a private commitment that has not been publicly recognized? If so, describe what it is about the public nature of the commitment that would tend to encourage fidelity.

6. Noting that "it is difficult to argue with a definition," Sullivan bypasses the argument that marriage is by definition between a man and a woman. Instead, he insists on articulating for the sake of his argument a broader and more complex definition of the nature of marriage: as a public contract that has, at its center, an "emotional, financial, and psychological bond between two people." However, since other relationships—such as that between a father and son—are often characterized by emotional, financial, and psychological bonds, clearly more is needed before this definition could be called comprehensive. In a sentence beginning "Marriage is . . . ," craft your own comprehensive definition of marriage, one that reflects your own beliefs.

Against Gay Marriage
William J. Bennett

In the following selection, William J. Bennett, a prominent cultural conservative, explains why he thinks that allowing gays to marry would damage the institution of marriage. Note that Bennett attempts to rebut Andrew Sullivan's pro-gay marriage arguments. Bennett served as chairman of the National Endowment for the Humanities (1981–85) and secretary of education (1985–88) under President Ronald Reagan, and as President George H. W. Bush's "drug czar" (1989–90). His writings on cultural issues in America include The Book of Virtues *(1997) and* The Broken Hearth: Reversing the Moral Collapse of the American Family *(2001). He has served as senior editor of the conservative journal* National Review *and is codirector of Empower America, a conservative advocacy organization. This piece first appeared as an op-ed column in the* Washington Post *on May 21, 1996.*

1 We are engaged in a debate which, in a less confused time, would be considered pointless and even oxymoronic: the question of same-sex marriage.

2   But we are where we are. The Hawaii Supreme Court has discovered a new state constitutional "right"—the legal union of same-sex couples. Unless a "compelling state interest" can be shown against them, Hawaii will become the first state to sanction such unions. And if Hawaii legalizes same-sex marriages, other states might well have to recognize them because of the Constitution's Full Faith and Credit Clause. Some in Congress recently introduced legislation to prevent this from happening.

3   Now, anyone who has known someone who has struggled with his homo-sexuality can appreciate the poignancy, human pain and sense of exclusion that are often involved. One can therefore understand the effort to achieve for homosexual unions both legal recognition and social acceptance. Advocates of homosexual marriages even make what appears to be a sound conservative argument: Allow marriage in order to promote faithfulness and monogamy. This is an intelligent and politically shrewd argument. One can even concede that it might benefit some people. But I believe that overall, allowing same-sex mar-riages would do significant, long-term social damage.

4   Recognizing the legal union of gay and lesbian couples would represent a pro-found change in the meaning and definition of marriage. Indeed, it would be the most radical step ever taken in the deconstruction of society's most impor-tant institution. It is not a step we ought to take.

5   The function of marriage is not elastic; the institution is already fragile enough. Broadening its definition to include same-sex marriages would stretch it almost beyond recognition—and new attempts to broaden the definition still further would surely follow. On what principled grounds could the advocates of same-sex marriage oppose the marriage of two consenting brothers? How could they explain why we ought to deny a marriage license to a bisexual who wants to marry two people? After all, doing so would be a denial of that person's sexuality. In our time, there are more (not fewer) reasons than ever to preserve the essence of marriage.

6   Marriage is not an arbitrary construct; it is an "honorable estate" based on the different, complementary nature of men and women—and how they refine, support, encourage and complete one another. To insist that we maintain this traditional understanding of marriage is not an attempt to put others down. It is simply an acknowledgment and celebration of our most precious and impor-tant social act.

7   Nor is this view arbitrary or idiosyncratic. It mirrors the accumulated wisdom of millennia and the teaching of every major religion. Among worldwide cul-tures, where there are so few common threads, it is not a coincidence that mar-riage is almost universally recognized as an act meant to unite a man and a woman.

8   To say that same-sex unions are not comparable to heterosexual marriages is not an argument for intolerance, bigotry or lack of compassion (although I am fully aware that it will be considered so by some). But it is an argument for making distinctions in law about relationships that are themselves distinct. Even Andrew Sullivan, among the most intelligent advocates of same-sex mar-riage, has admitted that a homosexual marriage contract will entail a greater understanding of the need for "extramarital outlets." He argues that gay male relationships are served by the "openness of the contract," and he has written that homosexuals should resist allowing their "varied and complicated lives" to be flattened into a "single, moralistic model."

9   But this "single, moralistic model" is precisely the point. The marriage com-mitment between a man and a woman does not—it cannot—countenance extramarital outlets. By definition it is not an open contract; its essential idea is fidelity. Obviously that is not always honored in practice. But it is normative, the ideal to which we aspire precisely because we believe some things are right

(faithfulness in marriage) and others are wrong (adultery). In insisting that marriage accommodate the less restrained sexual practices of homosexuals, Sullivan and his allies destroy the very thing that supposedly has drawn them to marriage in the first place.

10   There are other arguments to consider against same-sex marriage—for example, the signals it would send, and the impact of such signals on the shaping of human sexuality, particularly among the young. Former Harvard professor E. L. Pattullo has written that "a very substantial number of people are born with the potential to live either straight or gay lives." Societal indifference about heterosexuality and homosexuality would cause a lot of confusion. A remarkable 1993 article in *The Post* supports this point. Fifty teenagers and dozens of school counselors and parents from the local area were interviewed. According to the article, teenagers said it has become "cool" for students to proclaim they are gay or bisexual—even for some who are not. Not surprisingly, the caseload of teenagers in "sexual identity crisis" doubled in one year. "Everything is front page, gay and homosexual," according to one psychologist who works with the schools. "Kids are jumping on it . . . [counselors] are saying, 'What are we going to do with all these kids proclaiming they are bisexual or homosexual when we know they are not?' "

11   If the law recognizes homosexual marriages as the legal equivalent of heterosexual marriages, it will have enormous repercussions in many areas. Consider just two: sex education in the schools and adoption. The sex education curriculum of public schools would have to teach that heterosexual and homosexual marriage are equivalent. "Heather Has Two Mommies" would no longer be regarded as an anomaly; it would more likely become a staple of a sex education curriculum. Parents who want their children to be taught (for both moral and utilitarian reasons) the privileged status of heterosexual marriage will be portrayed as intolerant bigots; they will necessarily be at odds with the new law of matrimony and its derivative curriculum.

12   Homosexual couples will also have equal claim with heterosexual couples in adopting children, forcing us (in law at least) to deny what we know to be true: that it is far better for a child to be raised by a mother and a father than by, say, two male homosexuals.

13   The institution of marriage is already reeling because of the effects of the sexual revolution, no-fault divorce and out-of-wedlock births. We have reaped the consequences of its devaluation. It is exceedingly imprudent to conduct a radical, untested and inherently flawed social experiment on an institution that is the keystone in the arch of civilization. That we have to debate this issue at all tells us that the arch has slipped. Getting it firmly back in place is, as the lawyers say, a "compelling state interest."

Review Questions

1. What is the "intelligent and politically shrewd" conservative argument for marriage, according to Bennett?

2. What "enormous repercussion" does Bennett predict in the area of sex education, if the law recognizes homosexual marriage?

3. Summarize two of Bennett's arguments against broadening "the meaning and definition" of marriage to include same-sex marriages.

4. According to Bennett, what distinguishes the sexual behavior of heterosexuals from that of homosexuals?

Discussion and Writing Suggestions

1. Write a critique of Bennett's arguments against gay marriage. Follow the principles discussed in Chapter 2. For example, to what extent do you agree with Bennett's assertion that one argument against same-sex marriage is that it sends "the wrong signals"? Or his assertion that "it is far better for a child to be raised by a mother and a father than by, say, two male homosexuals"? You may wish to include some of Andrew Sullivan's points in your discussion.

2. Contending that homosexual relationships involve "less restrained sexual practices" than heterosexual ones, Bennett quotes Andrew Sullivan, who admits that a homosexual marriage contract will need to feature an acknowledgment of the need for "extramarital outlets." Propose a definition of marriage that allows for such outlets.

3. Imagine that you are one of the advocates of same-sex marriage to whom Bennett refers in the fifth paragraph of his op-ed column. In a brief paragraph, argue why same-sex marriages should be allowed, but not the marriage of two consenting brothers.

Many Women at Elite Colleges Set Career Path to Motherhood
Louise Story

Should young mothers stay home to raise their children? Should they be encouraged to pursue their careers—putting the kids in day care, or (for those who can afford them) in the care of nannies? Since World War II, women have been entering the workforce in steadily greater numbers. In 1940, less than 10% of mothers with children under 18 worked outside the home; by 1948, that ratio had risen to about 25%. By 2003, 71% of mothers with children under 18 worked outside the home. In recent years, however, newspaper and magazine writers have coined such phrases as "the opt-out revolution" (i.e., women opting out of work) to suggest that more and more women are abandoning careers in favor of full-time motherhood. Feminists and other liberal cultural commentators often decry such reports and books on the subject, charging that the "Mommy Wars" these publications purport to describe are largely a media creation, whipped up to sell books and magazines, and perhaps to advance an antifeminist, reactionary agenda.

Louise Story's article "Many Women at Elite Colleges Set Career Path to Motherhood," pub-lished on the front page of the New York Times *on September 20, 2005, landed squarely in the middle of this dispute. The response, both in the "blogosphere" and in op-ed pieces in publications such as the online magazine* Slate *and the* Los Angeles Times, *was immediate and heated—so much so that three days later, the* New York Times *published a follow-up article by Story outlining the methodology of her survey. Louise Story was a student at the Columbia School of Journalism and an intern at the* New York Times *when she wrote the article, based on a questionnaire e-mailed to 138 Yale undergraduate women as well as interviews with undergraduate women at Yale and other universities.*

1   Cynthia Liu is precisely the kind of high achiever Yale wants: smart (1510 SAT), disciplined (4.0 grade point average), competitive (finalist in Texas ora-tory competition), musical (pianist), athletic (runner) and altruistic (hospital volunteer). And at the start of her sophomore year at Yale, Ms. Liu is full of ambition, planning to go to law school. So will she join the long tradition of famous Ivy League graduates? Not likely. By the time she is 30, this accom-plished 19-year-old expects to be a stay-at-home mom. "My mother's always told me you can't be the best career woman and the best mother at the same time," Ms. Liu said matter-of-factly. "You always have to choose one over the other."

2   At Yale and other top colleges, women are being groomed to take their place in an ever more diverse professional elite. It is almost taken for granted that, just as they make up half the students at these institutions, they will move into lead-ership roles on an equal basis with their male classmates. There is just one prob-lem with this scenario: many of these women say that is not what they want.

3   Many women at the nation's most elite colleges say they have already decid-ed that they will put aside their careers in favor of raising children. Though some of these students are not planning to have children and some hope to have a family and work full time, many others, like Ms. Liu, say they will happily play a traditional female role, with motherhood their main commitment.

4   Much attention has been focused on career women who leave the work force to rear children. What seems to be changing is that while many women in col-lege two or three decades ago expected to have full-time careers, their daugh-ters, while still in college, say they have already decided to suspend or end their careers when they have children.

5   "At the height of the women's movement and shortly thereafter, women were much more firm in their expectation that they could somehow combine full-time work with child rearing," said Cynthia E. Russett, a professor of American history who has taught at Yale since 1967. "The women today are, in effect, turning realistic." Dr. Russett is among more than a dozen faculty members and administrators at the most exclusive institutions who have been on campus for decades and who said in interviews that they had noticed the changing attitude.

6   Many students say staying home is not a shocking idea among their friends. Shannon Flynn, an 18-year-old from Guilford, Conn., who is a freshman at Harvard, says many of her girlfriends do not want to work full time. "Most prob-ably do feel like me, maybe even tending toward wanting to not work at all," said Ms. Flynn, who plans to work part time after having children, though she

is torn because she has worked so hard in school. "Men really aren't put in that position," she said.

7   Uzezi Abugo, a freshman at the University of Pennsylvania who hopes to become a lawyer, says she, too, wants to be home with her children at least until they are in school. "I've seen the difference between kids who did have their mother stay at home and kids who didn't, and it's kind of like an obvious difference when you look at it," said Ms. Abugo, whose mother, a nurse, stayed home until Ms. Abugo was in first grade.

8   While the changing attitudes are difficult to quantify, the shift emerges repeatedly in interviews with Ivy League students, including 138 freshman and senior females at Yale who replied to e-mail questions sent to members of two residential colleges over the last school year. The interviews found that 85 of the students, or roughly 60 percent, said that when they had children, they planned to cut back on work or stop working entirely. About half of those women said they planned to work part time, and about half wanted to stop work for at least a few years. Two of the women interviewed said they expected their husbands to stay home with the children while they pursued their careers. Two others said either they or their husbands would stay home, depending on whose career was furthest along. The women said that pursuing a rigorous college education was worth the time and money because it would help position them to work in meaningful part-time jobs when their children are young or to attain good jobs when their children leave home.

9   In recent years, elite colleges have emphasized the important roles they expect their alumni—both men and women—to play in society. For example, earlier this month, Shirley M. Tilghman, the president of Princeton University, welcomed new freshmen, saying: "The goal of a Princeton education is to prepare young men and women to take up positions of leadership in the 21st century. Of course, the word 'leadership' conjures up images of presidents and C.E.O.'s, but I want to stress that my idea of a leader is much broader than that." She listed education, medicine and engineering as other areas where students could become leaders. In an e-mail response to a question, Dr. Tilghman added: "There is nothing inconsistent with being a leader and a stay-at-home parent. Some women (and a handful of men) whom I have known who have done this have had a powerful impact on their communities."

10   Yet the likelihood that so many young women plan to opt out of high-powered careers presents a conundrum. "It really does raise this question for all of us and for the country: when we work so hard to open academics and other opportunities for women, what kind of return do we expect to get for that?" said Marlyn McGrath Lewis, director of undergraduate admissions at Harvard, who served as dean for coeducation in the late 1970's and early 1980's. It is a complicated issue and one that most schools have not addressed. The women they are counting on to lead society are likely to marry men who will make enough money to give them a real choice about whether to be full-time mothers, unlike those women who must work out of economic necessity.

11   It is less than clear what universities should, or could, do about it. For one, a person's expectations at age 18 are less than perfect predictors of their life choices 10 years later. And in any case, admissions officers are not likely to ask applicants whether they plan to become stay-at-home moms. University offi-

cials said that success meant different things to different people and that universities were trying to broaden students' minds, not simply prepare them for jobs. "What does concern me," said Peter Salovey, the dean of Yale College, "is that so few students seem to be able to think outside the box; so few students seem to be able to imagine a life for themselves that isn't constructed along traditional gender roles."

12   There is, of course, nothing new about women being more likely than men to stay home to rear children. According to a 2000 survey of Yale alumni from the classes of 1979, 1984, 1989 and 1994, conducted by the Yale Office of Institutional Research, more men from each of those classes than women said that work was their primary activity—a gap that was small among alumni in their 20's but widened as women moved into their prime child-rearing years. Among the alumni surveyed who had reached their 40's, only 56 percent of the women still worked, compared with 90 percent of the men. A 2005 study of comparable Yale alumni classes found that the pattern had not changed. Among the alumnae who had reached their early 40's, just over half said work was their primary activity, compared with 90 percent of the men. Among the women who had reached their late 40's, some said they had returned to work, but the percentage of women working was still far behind the percentage of men. A 2001 survey of Harvard Business School graduates found that 31 percent of the women from the classes of 1981, 1985 and 1991 who answered the survey worked only part time or on contract, and another 31 percent did not work at all, levels strikingly similar to the percentages of the Yale students interviewed who predicted they would stay at home or work part time in their 30's and 40's.

13   What seems new is that while many of their mothers expected to have hardcharging careers, then scaled back their professional plans only after having children, the women of this generation expect their careers to take second place to child rearing. "It never occurred to me," Rebecca W. Bushnell, dean of the School of Arts and Sciences at the University of Pennsylvania, said about working versus raising children. "Thirty years ago when I was heading out, I guess I was just taking it one step at a time." Dr. Bushnell said young women today, in contrast, are thinking and talking about part-time or flexible work options for when they have children. "People have a heightened awareness of trying to get the right balance between work and family." Sarah Currie, a senior at Harvard, said many of the men in her American Family class last fall approved of women's plans to stay home with their children. "A lot of the guys were like, 'I think that's really great,'" Ms. Currie said. "One of the guys was like, 'I think that's sexy.' Staying at home with your children isn't as polarizing of an issue as I envision it is for women who are in their 30's now."

14   For most of the young women who responded to e-mail questions, a major factor shaping their attitudes seemed to be their experience with their own mothers, about three out of five of whom did not work at all, took several years off or worked only part time. "My stepmom's very proud of my choice because it makes her feel more valuable," said Kellie Zesch, a Texan who graduated from the University of North Carolina two years ago and who said that once she had children, she intended to stay home for at least five years and then consider working part time. "It justified it to her, that I don't look down on her for not having a career." Similarly, students who are committed to full-time careers,

without breaks, also cited their mothers as influences. Laura Sullivan, a sophomore at Yale who wants to be a lawyer, called her mother's choice to work full time the "greatest gift." "She showed me what it meant to be an amazing mother and maintain a career," Ms. Sullivan said.

15   Some of these women's mothers, who said they did not think about these issues so early in their lives, said they were surprised to hear that their college-age daughters had already formed their plans. Emily Lechner, one of Ms. Liu's roommates, hopes to stay home a few years, then work part time as a lawyer once her children are in school. Her mother, Carol, who once thought she would have a full-time career but gave it up when her children were born, was pleasantly surprised to hear that. "I do have this bias that the parents can do it best," she said. "I see a lot of women in their 30's who have full-time nannies, and I just question if their kids are getting the best." For many feminists, it may come as a shock to hear how unbothered many young women at the nation's top schools are by the strictures of traditional roles. "They are still thinking of this as a private issue; they're accepting it," said Laura Wexler, a professor of American studies and women's and gender studies at Yale. "Women have been given full-time working career opportunities and encouragement with no social changes to support it. "I really believed 25 years ago," Dr. Wexler added, "that this would be solved by now."

16   Angie Ku, another of Ms. Liu's roommates who had a stay-at-home mom, talks nonchalantly about attending law or business school, having perhaps a 10-year career and then staying home with her children. "Parents have such an influence on their children," Ms. Ku said. "I want to have that influence. Me!" She said she did not mind if that limited her career potential. "I'll have a career until I have two kids," she said. "It doesn't necessarily matter how far you get. It's kind of like the experience: I have tried what I wanted to do." Ms. Ku added that she did not think it was a problem that women usually do most of the work raising kids. "I accept things how they are," she said. "I don't mind the status quo. I don't see why I have to go against it." After all, she added, those roles got her where she is. "It worked so well for me," she said, "and I don't see in my life why it wouldn't work."

Review Questions

1. Of the 138 freshman and senior females at Yale who replied to the e-mail questions sent by the *New York Times,* how many indicated that when they had children, they planned to work less or stop working entirely?

2. How many of these female students said that they expected their husbands to stay home? How many said they or their husbands would stay home, "depending on whose career was furthest along"?

3. According to the 2000 survey of Yale alumnae from the classes of 1979, 1984, 1989, and 1994, what percentage of female alumnae in their

forties still worked? What percentage of male alumnae in their forties still worked?

Discussion and Writing Questions

1. Are you surprised by the results of Story's survey? Talk to some of your female classmates (in other courses, as well as in your writing course) about their marriage and career plans. To what extent does your informal survey bear out Story's conclusions?

2. Story quotes a female University of Pennsylvania student as follows: "I've seen the difference between kids who did have their mothers stay at home and kids who didn't, and it's kind of like an obvious difference when you look at it." What do you think the student means by "an obvious difference"? Have you noticed any such differences—obvious or not?

3. According to Story, "many" women at the nation's elite universities say they are not planning to work after they have children. According to the article, this conclusion is based on the responses of 138 women to an e-mailed questionnaire. In your opinion, does the number of women interviewed justify the article's use of the word "many" in that context? Explain why or why not.

4. A majority of the women interviewed for the article said that, after they had children, they planned to work less or stop working entirely. If you are a female student, briefly describe your plan for working once you have children. If you are a male student, briefly describe what kind of plan you would like your wife to have.

5. Story quotes Shirley M. Tilghman, the president of Princeton University, as follows: "The goal of a Princeton education is to prepare young men and women to take up positions of leadership in the 21st century." Imagine that you are an admissions official at Princeton, and your duty is to admit the students who you believe are best qualified to become leaders in the twenty-first century. You are trying to decide between two students, both of whom are equally qualified in all ways, except for the fact that one student has stated that she intends to pursue a full-time career, and the other has stated that she intends to work for ten years, then give up her career to raise her children. In light of the second student's stated plan, would you be more likely to admit the first student? Or would this knowledge of their goals have no bearing on your decision? Explain your reasoning.

6. According to Story, the example set by their mothers' choices regarding career versus motherhood affected many female students' values and beliefs on the subject. Describe your own mother's choices in this area. How did you feel about her choices when you were growing up, and how do you feel about them now? How likely is it that when you have

children, your mother's example will affect your own eventual decision (if you are woman) about whether or not to work, or (if you are a man) whether or not you will want your wife to work?

What Yale Women Want, and Why It Is Misguided
Karen Stabiner

Four days after Louise Story's article appeared in the New York Times, *writer Karen Stabiner published the following response as an op-ed in the* Los Angeles Times. *Stabiner has written about health, women's and family issues for such publications as the* New Yorker, *the* New York Times *and the* Los Angeles Times. *She is the author of six books, including* My Girl: Adventures with a Teen in Training *(2005) and* The Empty Nest: 31 Writers Tell the Truth about Relationships, Love and Freedom after the Kids Fly the Coop *(2007). Stabiner lives in Santa Monica, California.*

1   If the last generation of women obsessed about cracking the glass ceiling, a new crop of college undergrads seems less interested in the professional stratosphere than in a soft—a cushy—landing.

2   The *New York Times* recently got its hands on a Yale University questionnaire in which 60 percent of the 138 female respondents said that they intend to stop working when they have children, and then to work part time, if at all, once the kids are in school. A reporter talked to students at other elite East Coast colleges who echoed the same back-to-the-future sentiment: Work is but a way-station; a woman's place is in the home.

3   The young women think they're doing the right thing for their eventual children, having watched too many of their moms' generation try to juggle career and family. And at least one male student at Harvard finds the whole lord-and-master idea "sexy." This, from excellent students who have clambered over the backs of other, merely good students to gain entry into schools that traditionally have incubated tomorrow's leaders.

4   These future moms betray a startling combination of naivete and privilege. To plot this kind of future, a woman has to have access to a pool of wealthy potential husbands, she has to stay married at a time when half of marriages end in divorce, and she has to ignore the history of the women's movement. (Homework assignment: research Betty Friedan's motivation for writing "The Feminine Mystique.") It's also helpful if she ignores the following: The number of dual-working couples is on the rise. Ditto, the number of women in the work force.

5   The one number that's dwindling? Households supported by one adult, who in the current fantasy would be the extremely well-paid husband. Fewer than 25 percent of American households survive on one paycheck, and in a few years that number will decline to fewer than 20 percent.

6   If the undergrads still believe they can beat the odds, they must've slept through statistics. Or worse, they think they're above the fray. They seem to

have learned one lesson—I'm in it for me—far too well, confusing personal comfort with social progress.

7   Laura Wexler, a Yale professor of American studies and women's and gender studies, confessed surprise that women still consider this a "private" issue, and she wondered how 25 years could pass without more social change to make women's decisions easier.

8   Her colleague, Yale College Dean Peter Salovey, expressed concern that so few students were able to think "outside the box," gender-wise.

9   And a Tiffany's box it is; every step of this retro scenario requires capital, from law school—a popular goal for most of these aspiring if temporary professionals—to the husband with bucks. The choice of law is a little chilling in its practicality: You can't take 10 years off from biomedical research or orthopedic surgery and fit right in when you choose to go back to work, but the law is more of an evergreen profession.

10   As a working mother, I have nothing but empathy for the desire to avoid what author Arlie Hochschild rightly calls the second shift—in her book of that name—the double workday that most employed mothers put in. I have nothing but anger at the proposed solution. Do we grab a private solution or address the public issue? Is a hedge-fund husband the answer, or should women smart enough to be tomorrow's leaders seek new ideas that pay more than lip-service to family values?

11   There are only two possibilities here: If these young women are right that staying home means better children, we have to come up with a way to give more parents—moms and dads—the chance to be at home more frequently during their kids' formative years. The women's movement is about choice and responsibility, not just choice, and the math here should be simple for girls who get over 700 on their math SAT: Opportunity for one coed does not equal choice for all.

12   Or they're wrong, and in their smugness have managed to insult every mother in this country who needs to work. Surely some of the mothers of these 138 young women had jobs. Are their daughters worse off than those whose mothers stayed at home? If all of the undergrads agree that some among them turned out better than others—and that's where their stay-home logic inevitably leads them—then they should step forward.

13   No consensus?

14   Class dismissed.

Discussion and Writing Questions

1. Comment on Stabiner's contention that what Yale women want (as indicated in Story's survey) is "misguided." To what extent do you agree?

2. Stabiner writes: "If the last generation of women obsessed about cracking the glass ceiling, a new crop of college undergrads seems less interested in the professional stratosphere than in a soft—and a cushy— landing." To what extent do you believe that this description fairly

characterizes the viewpoints of the Yale and other undergrads quoted and summarized in Story's article? In your answer, refer to specific parts of Story's article.

3. Stabiner faults the Yale students for, among other things, "confusing personal comfort with social progress." She cites approvingly a Yale professor quoted by Story who expresses surprise that students still consider this a "private" issue. To what extent do you believe that people who support social progress have a duty to factor this support into their own personal choices?

4. As a solution to the issues raised by the Story article, Stabiner proposes the kind of social change that would allow parents to stay at home regularly during their children's formative years. In a brief paragraph, propose how such changes might come about. Your solution may take any form—from legislative initiatives to consciousness raising—but be specific.

5. Stabiner implies that the viewpoint about suspending their careers articulated by the Yale women collapses if children of working mothers turn out to be not "worse off" than children of stay-at-home mothers. For what other reasons (besides taking care of the children) do you think a woman—or a man, for that matter—might want or need to take a break from her or his career? List some of these reasons, and explain whether or not you find each reason valid.

6. Stabiner accuses some of the students in Story's survey of managing "to insult every mother in this country who needs to work." What do you think she means by this? Is she right?

Work vs. Family, Complicated by Race
Lynette Clemetson

Some critics have charged that the "Mommy Wars" amount to little more than mudslinging between two groups of upper-middle-class women: those who choose to pursue or continue their careers after having children and those who don't. The problem, the critics assert, is that the members of this highly educated elite (the types of people who graduate from Yale, or write for the New York Times*), no matter what their personal lifestyle choices, lead privileged lives far removed from those of average Americans, yet they also comprise the "tastemakers" (authors, academics, journalists) whose concerns dominate the media and, therefore, the cultural discourse. To what extent is this criticism valid? In the following selection, published in the* New York Times *on February 9, 2006, an African-American professional woman offers a different perspective on the "opt-out" debate.*

1   The subject, yet again, was motherhood and work. Over tea and hors d'oeuvres in this affluent Washington suburb, a cluster of well-educated women gathered to discuss the work-life debate. Most in the roomful of lawyers, technology experts, corporate managers and entrepreneurs had read dispatches from the so-

called "mommy wars," the books and articles grounded in the gulch between working and stay-at-home mothers.

2   But for the women in attendance—all of them black—those discussions inevitably fell short. "They don't speak to my reality," said Robin Rucker Gaillard, 41, a lawyer and mother of two. "We don't generally have the time or luxury for the guilt and competition that some white mothers engage in."

3   Around the country black women are opting out of the "opt-out" debate, the often-heated exchange about the compatibility of motherhood and work. Steeped in issues like working versus staying at home, nannies versus day care, and the benefits or garish excess of $800 strollers, the discussion has become a hot topic online, in newspapers and in book publishing.

4   It is not that black mothers do not wrestle with some of the same considerations as white mothers. But interviews with more than two dozen women suggest that the discussions as portrayed in books and the news media often lack the nuances and complexities particular to their experience.

5   For professional black women, debates about self-fulfillment can seem incomprehensibly narrow against the need to build sustainable wealth and security for their families. The discussions also pale in comparison to worries about shielding sons and daughters from the perils that black children face growing up, and overlook the practical pull of extended families in need of financial support.

6   Ms. Gaillard and others had gathered to broaden the working-mother debate by discussing a new book, *I'm Every Woman: Remixed Stories of Marriage, Motherhood and Work*.

7   Equal parts memoir, history lesson and cultural critique, the book, by Lonnae O'Neal Parker, a reporter for *The Washington Post* and a mother of three, celebrates the balancing act practiced by black women. Published in November by Amistad, an imprint of HarperCollins, it takes a sometimes wrenching, sometimes joyful look at black motherhood from slavery and the great migration to suburbia, the corporate workplace and the ascendancy of hip-hop. And since it came out, Ms. O'Neal Parker has been invited to gatherings around the country by black women eager to talk about motherhood on their own terms.

8   "It was a breath of fresh air to have a conversation that resonated with me," said Pamela Walker, 41, a professor at Northwestern Business College in Chicago. A married mother of six, she attended a reading of *I'm Every Woman* at Sensual Steps, a shoe boutique in the predominantly black Bronzeville section on the South Side of Chicago. "My family can afford expensive things, but why would I think about spending hundreds on a stroller when I could help a cousin buy textbooks for college? That is not my world."

9   Black mothers have traditionally worked in higher percentages than white women. And educated black mothers are still more likely to work than their white counterparts. According to census data from March 2005, 83.7 percent of college-educated black women with children under 18 are in the labor force, compared to 74 percent of college-educated white mothers.

10   Census figures from 2005 also show that college-educated black women earn slightly more than their white counterparts, largely because they are more likely to stay in the work force and work longer hours than white women after having children.

11   The commitment of black women to work is in large part economically driven. They have lower marriage rates than white women, meaning they are more likely to be single parents. Those who are married are more likely than their white counterparts to earn more than their husbands, census figures show.

12   But for black middle-class women from Mary Church Terrell, a charter member of the N.A.A.C.P., to Coretta Scott King, working has also been a matter of choice. For generations black women have viewed work as a means for elevating not only their own status as women, but also as a crucial force in elevating their family, extended family and their entire race.

13   Black women are not the only women feeling airbrushed out of today's images of motherhood as represented in the literature of the opt-out debate, which includes articles like one in *The New York Times* last year reporting that many women at Ivy League colleges plan to drop their careers, at least temporarily, once they start having children.

14   Another article, by Linda R. Hirshman in the December issue of *The American Prospect*, a magazine devoted to liberal ideas, provoked sharp debate by arguing that women who stay home with children are in for a letdown, and that the workplace is the only realm where women find true fulfillment. This is, Ms. Hirshman acknowledged, not a new idea. It was the theme of *The Feminine Mystique*, written more than 40 years ago by Betty Friedan.

15   Some white working-class and middleclass women have complained that both sides of the opt-out debate have an elitist tone. Recently members of a group called Latina Mami in Austin, Tex., vented about the lack of perspective in many of the motherhood books in bookstores.

16   Some insiders in the battles have acknowledged the narrowness of public discourse. "The conflict seems to be pretty much driven by white upper-middle-class angst, and the debate has been taken over by that," said Leslie Morgan Steiner, a white mother of three and the editor of *Mommy Wars*, an anthology of essays to be published by Random House next month.

17   Ms. Steiner's book includes essays from Ms. O'Neal Parker and two other black writers, as well as a Pakistani mother who writes of her struggles with child care, and a Latina who was introduced to stay-at-home mothering through a bout with cancer.

18   Tension between working and stay-at-home black mothers—friction that seems less prevalent and intense than among their white peers, many women said—is often driven by a pressure for persistent racial striving. Smiling at the circle of friends gathered in her Mitchellville living room, Frances Luckett, the principal at a private, predominantly black elementary school, welcomed her guests with an exhortation. "Your journey is not just about you," Ms. Luckett said to the two dozen women, aged 19 to 85. "It's about adding to the journey of those who came before you and paving a way for the journeys after yours."

19   There were knowing groans as Ms. O'Neal Parker read aloud from *I'm Every Woman* about "bone memory" and the specter of a weary but resolute slave woman, who "sticks a knee in my back and squares up my shoulders" when life feels unfair.

20   There was empathetic laughter when she lovingly discussed the "kink coefficient," a term she coined to describe the extra hours black mothers build into

their packed schedules to groom daughters whose kinky hair "grows out instead of down."

21   The personal motherhood struggles that black women face are often complicated variations on more broadly voiced themes. Some professional women have mixed emotions about hiring nannies when they can recall women in their own families who cared for other women's children and cleaned their homes.

22   Some of those who consider leaving jobs to raise children worry that it will be more difficult for them to resume their careers than for white peers. "As black women who still have a hard time moving up, there is a fear that opting out will be one more strike against you," said Linda Burke, the owner of an executive search firm and a founder of a Washington group called Sistermoms that invited Ms. O'Neal Parker for a book reading last month.

23   Linda McGhee, a lawyer and member of Sistermoms, got her son into a private elementary school in Northwest Washington but decided against sending him, in part because she wanted to help her parents, who raised 12 children on meager resources, with health care.

24   Her neighborhood public school did not meet her standards, so Ms. McGhee and her husband, a computer specialist for the federal government, pushed to get him into a high-performing public school in the same neighborhood as the private school they turned down.

25   "I grew up in a housing project, and without my parents always pushing I wouldn't have three degrees," said Ms. McGhee, 44, who just completed a Ph.D. in clinical psychology. "We just decided that, in the scheme of things, we didn't want to spend $20,000 on kindergarten."

26   Some concerns are more social than personal. Cheryl Roberts, a college administrator in Seattle, was the host at a private reading featuring Ms. O'Neal Parker on Martin Luther King Day. The guests at the catered affair included several federal judges and banking and aerospace executives whose successes eased worries about outcomes for their children. But as the discussion opened up, the women engaged in a passionate exchange on the lingering effects of a ballot initiative that ended the state's affirmative action programs.

27   "Our discussions have to move to a socially conscious place," said Ms. Roberts, 48. "It is part of the ethos of being an African-American woman. We understand there but for the grace of God go I."

28   Like their white counterparts, black mothers who leave careers to raise their children do sometimes face disapproval from working mothers. But even that judgment is driven less by gender politics than racial sensibilities, some women say.

29   Tracie Miller-Mitchell, the daughter of Frances Luckett, was the only stay-at-home mother at her mother's afternoon function. Ms. Miller-Mitchell, who belongs to Mocha Moms, a national support group for black at-home mothers, said her mother was the person who most disapproved of her choice.

30   "A lot of financial sacrifice went into helping her get two degrees," said Ms. Luckett, recalling her struggles as a divorced single parent. "There are no guarantees in life, and I worry that if she just gives up her career, is just a wife and a mother, she will have nothing to fall back on."

31   Ms. Miller-Mitchell, 39, replied: "I have my degrees to fall back on. Isn't what all that sacrifice was for? So I could have a choice?"

32   Differences aside, the women gathered at Ms. Luckett's home said they felt refreshed by the discussion.

33   "I understand and respect the issues of white mothers, I truly do," Ms. Gaillard said. "But I also need for them to understand and respect mine."

Review Questions

1. Summarize the reaction to the "opt-out" debate of the women quoted and depicted in the article.

2. According to U.S. Census data, what percentage of college-educated black women with children under 18 work?

3. Summarize some of the issues that professional black women say concern them regarding the ongoing debate over the "compatibility of motherhood and work."

Discussion and Writing Suggestions

1. According to Clemetson, some black working mothers feel that the "opt-out" dilemmas of their white counterparts are largely irrelevant to their own concerns. Based on your experience or observations, in what areas other than motherhood and work do you believe that racial perspectives in this country significantly differ? Identify some specific points of difference. Cite anecdotes to support your observations.

2. The article quotes one African-American mother as saying that she does not have the "time or luxury for the guilt and competition that some white mothers engage in." To what extent do you agree with her suggestion that the "opt-out" debate is fueled by such factors as "guilt" and "competition"?

3. After reading this selection, has your perspective changed on the reasons a mother of young children might go to work? Explain your answer.

4. Clemetson quotes an African-American school principal telling other African-American women: "Your journey is not just about you. It's about adding to the journey of those who came before you and paving a way for the journeys after yours." To what extent do you agree that "your journey is not just about you"? Is there a person, or are there persons—your family, perhaps, or your community—to whom you feel a particular responsibility as you conduct your life? Explain.

A Marriage Agreement
Alix Kates Shulman

The subject may seem mundane, but housework remains a highly contentious issue between spouses. According to the National Healthy Marriage Resource Center, the issue of "housework and childcare" was among the top five sources of conflict between couples with new babies. A recent study found that married women continued to spend more than twice as much time on household chores as their husbands. Overall, married American women perform 70–80% of the total domestic work—regardless of their employment status. This gender gap persists even in the face of a professed willingness among husbands to share the burden. One study showed that men who claimed to support feminist ideals performed an average of only four minutes more housework per day than those who professed traditional beliefs. Nor does a wife's relatively high income motivate her husband to increase his level of household support. Recent research indicates that in cases where women contribute more than half of the family's income, the more money she makes, the more housework she does—an average of five to six hours more each week. Many married women cite a willingness to help out more around the house as the main thing they would change about their husbands. Perhaps this explains why marital researchers have found that married men who perform more housework and child-care duties have better sex lives and happier marriages than those who don't.

Alix Kates Shulman's "A Marriage Agreement" is a famous document in the history of intra-marital labor negotiations. The piece was first published in 1970 in a feminist journal and subsequently reprinted as a cover story in Life *magazine, appearing as well in* Ms., New York Magazine, *and* Redbook. *In the "Agreement," Shulman argues that men and women should share housework equally and then proposes a novel (some would say drastic) measure to ensure that they do. When first published, the "Agreement" provoked heated responses from such writers as Norman Mailer and Joan Didion. It is now featured in the standard Harvard textbook on contract law.*

1   When my husband and I were first married, a decade ago, keeping house was less a burden than a game. We both worked full-time in New York City, so our small apartment stayed empty most of the day and taking care of it was very little trouble. Twice a month we'd spend Saturday cleaning and doing our laundry at the laundromat. We shopped for food together after work, and though I usually did the cooking, my husband was happy to help. Since our meals were simple and casual, there were few dishes to wash. We occasionally had dinner out and usually ate breakfast at a diner near our offices. We spent most of our free time doing things we enjoyed together, such as taking long walks in the evenings and spending weekends in Central Park. Our domestic life was beautifully uncomplicated.

2   When our son was born, our domestic life suddenly became *quite* complicated; and two years later, when our daughter was born, it became impossible. We automatically accepted the traditional sex roles that society assigns. My husband worked all day in an office; I left my job and stayed at home, taking on almost all the burdens of housekeeping and child raising.

3   When I was working I had grown used to seeing people during the day, to having a life outside the home. But now I was restricted to the company of two demanding preschoolers and to the four walls of an apartment. It seemed unfair that while my husband's life had changed little when the children were born, domestic life had become the only life I had.

4   I tried to cope with the demands of my new situation, assuming that other women were able to handle even larger families with ease and still find time for themselves. I couldn't seem to do that.

5   We had to move to another apartment to accommodate our larger family, and because of the children, keeping it reasonably neat took several hours a day. I prepared half a dozen meals every day for from one to four people at a time— and everyone ate different food. Shopping for this brood—or even just running out for a quart of milk—meant putting on snowsuits, boots and mittens; getting strollers or carriages up and down the stairs; and scheduling the trip so it would not interfere with one of the children's feeding or nap or illness or some other domestic job. Laundry was now a daily chore. I seemed to be working every minute of the day—and still there were dishes in the sink; still there wasn't time enough to do everything.

6   Even more burdensome than the physical work of housekeeping was the relentless responsibility I had for my children. I loved them, but they seemed to be taking over my life. There was nothing I could do, or even contemplate, without first considering how they would be affected. As they grew older, just answering their constant questions ruled out even a private mental life. I had once enjoyed reading, but now if there was a moment free, instead of reading for myself, I read to them. I wanted to work on my own writing, but there simply weren't enough hours in the day. I had no time for myself; the children were always *there*.

7   As my husband's job began keeping him at work later and later—and some-times taking him out of town—I missed his help and companionship. I wished he would come home at six o'clock and spend time with the children so they could know him better. I continued to buy food with him in mind and dutiful-ly set his place at the table. Yet sometimes whole weeks would go by without his having dinner with us. When he did get home the children often were asleep, and we both were too tired ourselves to do anything but sleep.

8   We accepted the demands of his work as unavoidable. Like most couples, we assumed that the wife must accommodate to the husband's schedule, since it is his work that brings in the money.

9   As the children grew older I began free-lance editing at home. I felt I had to squeeze it into my "free" time and not allow it to interfere with my domestic duties or the time I owed my husband—just as he felt he had to squeeze in time for the children during weekends. We were both chronically dissatisfied, but we knew no solutions.

10   After I had been home with the children for six years I began to attend meet-ings of the newly formed Women's Liberation Movement in New York City. At these meetings I began to see that my situation was not uncommon; other women too felt drained and frustrated as housewives and mothers. When we started to talk about how we would have chosen to arrange our lives, most of us

agreed that even though we might have preferred something different, we had never felt we had a choice in the matter. We realized that we had slipped into full domestic responsibility simply as a matter of course, and it seemed unfair.

11   When I added them up, the chores I was responsible for amounted to a hectic 6 A.M.–9 P.M. (often later) job, without salary, breaks or vacation. No employer would be able to demand these hours legally, but most mothers take them for granted—as I did until I became a feminist.

12   For years mothers like me have acquiesced to the strain of the preschool years and endless household maintenance without any real choice. Why, I asked myself, should a couple's decision to have a family mean that the woman must immerse years of her life in their children? And why should men like my husband miss caring for and knowing their children?

13   Eventually, after an arduous examination of our situation, my husband and I decided that we no longer had to accept the sex roles that had turned us into a lame family. Out of equal parts love for each other and desperation at our situation, we decided to re-examine the patterns we had been living by, and starting again from scratch, to define our roles for ourselves.

14 We began by agreeing to share completely all responsibility for raising our children (by then aged five and seven) and caring for our household. If this new arrangement meant that my husband would have to change his job or that I would have to do more free-lance work or that we would have to live on a different scale, then we would. It would be worth it if it could make us once again equal, independent and loving as we had been when we were first married.

15   Simply agreeing verbally to share domestic duties didn't work, despite our best intentions. And when we tried to divide them "spontaneously," we ended up following the traditional patterns. Our old habits were too deep-rooted. So we sat down and drew up a formal agreement, acceptable to both of us, that clearly defined the responsibilities we each had.

16   It may sound a bit formal, but it has worked for us. Here it is:

Marriage Agreement

I. Principles

17 We reject the notion that the work which brings in more money is more valuable. The ability to earn more money is a privilege which must not be compounded by enabling the larger earner to buy out of his/her duties and put the burden either on the partner who earns less or on another person hired from outside.

18   We believe that each partner has an equal right to his/her own time, work, value, choices. As long as all duties are performed, each of us may use his/her extra time any way he/she chooses. If he/she wants to use it making money, fine. If he/she wants to spend it with spouse, fine. If not, fine.

19   As parents we believe we must share all responsibility for taking care of our children and home—not only the work but also the responsibility. At least during the first year of this agreement, *sharing responsibility* shall mean dividing the *jobs* and dividing the *time*.

20   In principle, jobs should be shared equally, 50-50, but deals may be made by mutual agreement. If jobs and schedule are divided on any other than a 50-50 basis, then at any time either party may call for a re-examination and redistribution of jobs or a revision of the schedule. Any deviation from 50-50 must be for the convenience of both parties. If one party works overtime in any domestic job, he/she must be compensated by equal extra work by the other. The schedule may be flexible, but changes must be formally agreed upon. The terms of this agreement are rights and duties, not privileges and favors.

II. Job Breakdown and Schedule

(A) Children

(1) Mornings: Waking children; getting their clothes out; making their lunches; seeing that they have notes, homework, money, bus passes, books; brushing their hair; giving them breakfast (making coffee for us). Every other week each parent does all.

(2) Transportation: Getting children to and from lessons, doctors, dentists (including making appointments), friends' houses, park, parties, movies, libraries. Parts occurring between 3 and 6 P.M. fall to wife. She must be compensated by extra work from husband (see 10 below). Husband does all weekend transportation and pick-ups after 6.

(3) Help: Helping with homework, personal problems, projects like cooking, making gifts, experiments, planting; answering questions; explaining things. Parts occurring between 3 and 6 P.M. fall to wife. After 6 P.M. husband does Tuesday, Thursday and Sunday; wife does Monday, Wednesday and Saturday. Friday is free for whoever has done extra work during the week.

(4) Nighttime (after 6 P.M.): Getting children to take baths, brush their teeth, put away their toys and clothes, go to bed; reading with them; tucking them in and having nighttime talks; handling if they wake or call in the night. Husband does Tuesday, Thursday and Sunday. Wife does Monday, Wednesday and Saturday. Friday is split according to who has done extra work during the week.

(5) Baby sitters: Getting baby sitters (which sometimes takes an hour of phoning). Baby sitters must be called by the parent the sitter is to replace. If no sitter turns up, that parent must stay home.

(6) Sick care: Calling doctors; checking symptoms; getting prescriptions filled; remembering to give medicine; taking days off to stay home with sick child; providing special activities. This must still be worked out equally, since now wife seems to do it all. (The same goes for the now frequently declared school closings for so-called political protests, whereby the mayor gets credit at the expense of the mothers of young children. The mayor closes only the schools, not the places of business or the government offices.) In any case, wife must be compensated (see 10 below).

(7) Weekends: All usual child care, plus special activities (beach, park, zoo). Split equally. Husband is free all Saturday, wife is free all Sunday.

(B) Housework

(8) Cooking: Breakfast; dinner (children, parents, guests). Breakfasts during the week are divided equally; husband does all weekend breakfasts (including shopping for them and dishes). Wife does all dinners except Sunday nights. Husband does Sunday dinner and any other dinners on his nights of responsibility if wife isn't home. Whoever invites guests does shopping, cooking and dishes; if both invite them, split work.

(9) Shopping: Food for all meals, housewares, clothing and supplies for children. Divide by convenience. Generally, wife does local daily food shopping; husband does special shopping for supplies and children's things.

(10) Cleaning: Dishes daily; apartment weekly, biweekly or monthly. Husband does dishes Tuesday, Thursday and Sunday. Wife does Monday, Wednesday and Saturday. Friday is split according to who has done extra work during week. Husband does all the house cleaning in exchange for wife's extra child care (3 to 6 daily) and sick care.

(11) Laundry: Home laundry, making beds, dry cleaning (take and pick up). Wife does home laundry. Husband does dry-cleaning delivery and pickup. Wife strips beds, husband remakes them.

21   Our agreement changed our lives. Surprisingly, once we had written it down, we had to refer to it only two or three times. But we still had to work to keep the old habits from intruding. If it was my husband's night to take care of the children, I had to be careful not to check up on how he was managing. And if the baby sitter didn't show up for him, I would have to remember it was *his* problem.

22   Eventually the agreement entered our heads, and now, after two successful years of following it, we find that our new roles come to us as readily as the old ones had. I willingly help my husband clean the apartment (knowing it is his responsibility) and he often helps me with the laundry or the meals. We work together and trade off duties with ease now that the responsibilities are truly shared. We each have less work, more hours together and less resentment.

23   Before we made our agreement I had never been able to find the time to finish even one book. Over the past two years I've written three children's books, a biography and a novel and edited a collection of writings (all will have been published by spring of 1972). Without our agreement I would never have been able to do this.

24   At present my husband works a regular 40-hour week, and I write at home during the six hours the children are in school. He earns more money now than I do, so his salary covers more of our expenses than the money I make with my free-lance work. But if either of us should change jobs, working hours or income, we would probably adjust our agreement.

25   Perhaps the best testimonial of all to our marriage agreement is the change that has taken place in our family life. One day after it had been in effect for only four months our daughter said to my husband, "You know, Daddy, I used to love Mommy more than you, but now I love you both the same."

Review Questions

1. What "notion" does the "Agreement," in its first paragraph, explicitly reject? What does the "Agreement" call the "ability to earn more money"?

2. According to the "Agreement," what does shared responsibility mean, in terms of taking care of the children and the home?

3. If one party works overtime in any domestic job, according to the "Agreement," what must the other party do?

4. Who is responsible for all of the housecleaning, according to the "Agreement"? What reason is given for this provision?

Discussion and Writing Suggestions

1. In the next article, Caitlin Flanagan writes that Shulman's "marriage agreement virtually demanded to be ridiculed." Do you agree? For example, is the agreement itself a ridiculous idea, or are some of its specific provisions ridiculous? Explain your responses.

2. Describe your own reaction upon reading the paragraph beginning, "Even more burdensome than the physical work of housekeeping was the relentless responsibility I had for my children."

3. The "Agreement" states that the larger earner in a family is not entitled to "buy out" of the housework duties. Describe your reaction to the priorities implied by this statement. To what extent do you believe that earning money can or should be separated from household duties?

4. Describing how she and her husband had to "keep the old habits from intruding," Shulman writes that she had to be careful not to check up on him to see how he was managing, and to remember that if the sitter didn't show up, it was his problem. To what "old habit" do you think she is referring? Why do you think Shulman uses the word "habit," rather than, for example, *trait?*

5. In the following selection, Caitlin Flanagan describes the circumstances surrounding "A Marriage Agreement": Shulman's marriage was troubled and eventually ended in divorce. To what extent does this knowledge change your perception of "A Marriage Agreement"?

6. Write an "Agreement" that explicitly regulates your relationship with another person (or persons) in your life. This may be a personal, business, or educational relationship. What would be the advantages and disadvantages of having such an agreement govern the relationship?

7. Note that the "Agreement" provides for the husband and wife to alternate days on which each is responsible for helping their children with "personal problems." Try the following creative writing exercise: In a brief paragraph, write from the point of view of a 7-year-old child living in

such a family. Describe what it is like to have parents who have made such an arrangement and your feelings about the "Agreement."

How Serfdom Saved the Women's Movement
Caitlin Flanagan

"Why not just get a maid?" In the following article, Caitlin Flanagan agrees with this simple solution to the problem of housework (as outlined by Alix Kates Shulman in the previous selection)—but accuses feminists who employ "household help" of hypocrisy. Note her extended discussion of Shulman's marriage agreement. Flanagan writes for The Atlantic *and the* New Yorker. *She is the author of the book* To Hell with All That *(2006), based on her collected writings, in which a revised version of the following selection appears.*

1   I didn't know a single child who had a nanny when I was growing up. Nannies existed in English nursery rhymes and children's stories, in *Mary Poppins* and *Peter Pan*. The Brady Bunch, of course, had Alice, but she seemed to be part and parcel of the double family tragedy, never even alluded to, that had brought them all together. *The Courtship of Eddie's Father* had Mrs. Livingston, but again: tragedy. My father was always very proud of a scar on his right elbow, which he had received at the hands of an incompetent nurse who scalded him in the bath when he was an infant, and whom my grandfather had sent packing that very day. The scar proved to my father that his family had once been a tiny bit grand; it proved to me that he had been born a long, long time ago: a nurse? When I was growing up, in Berkeley in the 1960s, faculty wives—which is what my mother was—stayed home, kept house, and raised children. When my mother died, I gave a maudlin eulogy about all the days we spent together when I was small, shopping at Hink's department store and eating peeled apricots and lying down for naps in the big bed under the gable window of her bedroom. I probably should have found something more estimable to say about her, but in the days after her death all I could think about was what a wonderful thing it had been to be raised at home, by a mother who loved me. But by the 1970s, of course, the idyll was coming to an end; many of the younger wives had begun to want out. I remember being sent in 1977, at age fifteen, to my very first psychotherapist, a young wife and mother with a capacious office on Bancroft Avenue. I can't remember a thing I talked about on all those darkening afternoons, but I do remember very clearly a day on which she suddenly sat up straight in her chair and began discussing, for reasons I could not fathom and in the most heated terms imaginable, not the vagaries of my sullen adolescence but, rather, marriage—specifically, her own. "I mean, who's going to do the shit work?" she asked angrily. "Who's going to make the pancakes?"

2   I stared at her uncomprehendingly. The only wife I knew intimately was my mother, who certainly had her discontents, but whom I couldn't even imagine using the term "shit work," let alone using it to characterize the making of pan-

cakes—something she did regularly, competently, and, as far as I could tell, happily (she liked pancakes; so did the rest of us). But in 1978 shit work was becoming a real problem. Shit work, in fact, was threatening to put the brakes on the women's movement. Joan Didion's unparalleled 1972 essay on the movement ("To make an omelette," the essay begins, "you need not only those broken eggs but someone 'oppressed' to break them") described the attempts women of the era made to arrive at an equitable division of household labor:

> They totted up the pans scoured, the towels picked off the bathroom floor, the loads of laundry done in a lifetime. Cooking a meal could only be "dog-work," and to claim any pleasure from it was evidence of craven acquiescence in one's own forced labor. Small children could only be odious mechanisms for the spilling and digesting of food, for robbing women of their "freedom." It was a long way from Simone de Beauvoir's grave and awesome recognition of woman's role as "the Other" to the notion that the first step in changing that role was Alix Kates Shulman's marriage contract ("wife strips beds, husband remakes them").

3   Alix Kates Shulman's marriage contract, which I have read, is so perfectly a document of its time that it might stand alone, a kind of synecdoche for twenty years' worth of arguing and slamming doors and fuming over the notorious inability of husbands to fold a fitted sheet or get the children's breakfast on the table without leaving behind a scrim of crumbs and jelly on every flat surface in the room. Originally published in 1970, in a feminist magazine called *Up From Under,* the contract—like the women's-liberation movement itself—quickly moved from the radical margins of society to its very center: it was reprinted in the debut issue of *Ms.,* no surprise, but also in *Redbook* and *New York* and *Life,* in which it was part of a cover story on the subject of experimental marriages. (That a marriage in which the husband helped out with housework qualified as "experimental" tells you how much things have changed in the past three decades.) It was also taken seriously in some very high quarters, including the standard Harvard textbook on contract law, in which it was reprinted.

4   The document, which I first encountered when I read the Didion essay as a girl, struck me as odd; I could see how a bride on the eve of her wedding could think ahead to the making and unmaking of beds (although it was only once I was deep into marriage that it occurred to me this task might be a chore, as opposed to yet another delightful aspect of married sexuality, which I could imagine only in the most thrilling terms), but there was other language in it that seemed born of actual and bitter experience. Shulman and her husband, for example, were going to divide "the week into hours during which the children were to address their 'personal questions' to either one parent or another." It was difficult for me to conceive of a bride's coming up with such a disillusioned view of the thing, even a bride fully alerted to the oppression of motherhood, but it turns out that Shulman was no bride when she wrote it. I have since learned that her marriage agreement—talk about a doomed cause—was of the post-nuptial variety.

5   Alix Kates Shulman's marriage—under way a full decade before she sat down at her typewriter, aglow with "feminist irony, idealism, audacity, and glee," and

punched out the notorious contract—had been buffeted by many of the forces at play in American cultural life of the late sixties and early seventies, but she and her husband evinced an impressive ability to up the ante. He worked; she stayed home with the kids and wrote "subversive" essays, short stories, and position papers, all of which centered on her growing desire to come Up From Under. He retaliated by starting a new business venture in another state and taking up with a UC Berkeley student. She double-retaliated by taking a young lover of her own and publishing an essay about her husband's inability to bring her to orgasm, an essay that ended with the half jaunty, half exasperated imperative "Think clitoris!" At this point Alix and her husband were apparently seized by the one patently sensible idea of their entire marriage; they needed to get divorced.

6   Now the story begins to get complicated. In the early seventies there was no such thing as joint custody in the state of New York, and Alix realized that a divorce was not going to be much of a boon to her, since it would leave her with the kids full time, which would mean a heck of a lot of breakfasts to prepare and lunch boxes to pack—activities that would sorely cut into the time available for her to make pronouncements on behalf of the voiceless clitoris. When friends heard about her rotten marriage and asked her when she was going to divorce the bum, she would snappily reply, "Not until you're ready to help me take care of my kids." Thus the marriage agreement—which Shulman originally, and more accurately, wanted to title "A Divorce Dilemma and a Marriage Agreement"—was born, a way to husk the marriage of any pretense of emotional fulfillment and reduce it to a purely labor-sharing arrangement. (Her husband signed it, ran off with his coed, and then—proving himself to be one of the great masochists of the twentieth century—returned to Shulman for another full decade of punishment before they finally switched off the lights.)

7   The marriage agreement virtually demanded to be ridiculed, and ridiculed it was: not only by Joan Didion but also by Russell Baker and Norman Mailer. (In his 1971 anti-feminist manifesto *The Prisoner of Sex*, Mailer considered the agreement at some length, concluding that he "would not be married to such a woman." The potential of the agreement to serve as a lifetime protection policy against marriage to Norman Mailer makes me half want to hold onto my own copy, just to be on the safe side.) Certainly Shulman has earned herself a spot on almost any short list of very silly people. Yet I am reluctant to make too much sport of her document, or of the countless similar ones that it inspired. I am a wife and mother of young children in a very different time from Shulman's, a time that is in many respects more brutal and more brutalizing, a time that has been morally coarsening for many of us, a time that has made hypocrites of many contemporary feminists in ways that Shulman and her sisters in arms were not hypocrites. I have never once argued with my husband about which of us was going to change the sheets of the marriage bed, but then—to my certain knowledge—neither one of us ever has changed the sheets. Or scrubbed the bathtubs, or dusted the cobwebs off the top of the living-room bookcase, or used the special mop and the special noncorrosive cleanser on the hardwood floors. Two years ago our little boys got stomach flu, one right after the other, and there were ever so many loads of wash to do, but we did not do them. The nanny did.

8   To get at the larger point here, let us look, for a moment, at a product not of Shulman's time but of our own. Let us look at a most unremarkable comment in a most unremarkable essay, a comment that, at first blush, does not demand to be made fun of, or even really to be noticed at all, a comment that would not cause the least consternation in the most progressive households, among the most liberated and most liberating women.

9   Anita Diamant is the author of several novels and works of nonfiction, most notably a runaway best seller called *The Red Tent*, which *The Boston Globe* described as being "what the Bible would be like if it had been written by women." This past fall she published a collection of personal essays, *Pitching My Tent: On Marriage, Motherhood, Friendship, and Other Leaps of Faith*. In one of them, "Airing It Out," she describes a marital rough patch that she and her husband struck not long after their only child was born: "Things between us were bad. We weren't talking. We weren't kissing. We weren't, well, you know." They went to a marriage counselor, who gave them advice so standard it might have been torn from the pages of one of the family magazines Diamant once wrote for.

> By way of "homework" the therapist suggested several commonsense gimmicks. We were to spend ten minutes each evening debriefing about our respective days. We were to take turns and not interrupt each other. He also suggested regular sex dates. Sounds mechanical, but it sure takes the pressure off the rest of the week. And for heaven's sake, said the therapist, if you're fighting about who cleans the bathroom, why not just pay someone else to do it for you?

10   For heaven's sake. It's a no-brainer. Hiring someone to clean the toilets will certainly put an immediate end to fights about that unpleasant topic. Hiring someone to strip the beds and remake them might have rendered Alix Kates Shulman's marriage agreement entirely unnecessary; it might even have saved her marriage. But it wasn't perversity or thick-headedness or even economic hardship that precluded her from turning to this easy and efficient solution, which Diamant's marriage counselor found so obvious—*for heaven's sake!*—that he seems to have issued it in a fit of pique at his clients' obtuseness. Shulman's marital crisis occurred in the 1970s, a very bad time to be in need of domestic help. Black women, who had held a centuries-old unhappy lock on the work, were abandoning it in huge numbers, taking advantage of the civil-rights movement to get the kind of jobs that had historically been out of their reach. Tainted by the stigma of slave days, poorly paid and culturally resented, "living in" (the most hated of domestic-work arrangements) was becoming increasingly rare, even in much of the Deep South. Day work, its slightly less loathed companion, was becoming the sole employment option of fewer and fewer black women. The availability of domestic workers was reaching a dramatic low point at the very moment when the need for them (with millions of middle-class women voluntarily entering the work force) was approaching an all-time high. The two phenomena were on a crash course, set to destroy much of what Betty Friedan and her compatriots had begun.

11   A second factor intensified the dilemma. Give those old libbers their due: they spent a lot of time thinking about the unpleasantness of housework and the unfairness of its age-old tendency to fall upon women. (They could hardly have imagined that in twenty years' time Martha Stewart would build an empire on the notion that ironing and polishing silver and sweeping a kitchen floor might offer an almost sacred communion with what is most essentially and attractively feminine.) They were loath, they claimed, to foist such demeaning work on other human beings (well, not all of them were loath: Betty Friedan had a crack cleaning woman on staff when she was busy writing about the oppression of domestic work). Indeed, Shulman's contract specifies that the "burden" of the cleaning work should not be placed on "someone hired from outside." Members of the women's movement believed that it was of great importance, politically and psychologically, for men to share equally in the care of households and children. Further, feminists of the period had also thought deeply about race, and about the tendency of white women to shape comfortable lives around the toil and suffering of black women. The members of a thousand consciousness-raising groups drove themselves into a thousand tizzies trying to think up a solution to this homely yet vexing problem. The notorious Wages for Housework campaign ("WE WANT IT IN CASH, RETROACTIVE AND IMMEDIATELY. AND WE WANT ALL OF IT") came to naught. Pat Mainardi's much read *The Politics of Housework* included many strategies for cajoling a reluctant male into taking on some washing and cooking, from the deeply Marxist ("Arm yourself with some knowledge of the psychology of oppressed peoples") to the stubbornly practical ("Use timesheets"), but you can know chapter and verse about the psychology of oppressed peoples and still not get a man to turn out a nice meal—the rice ready at the same time as the meat—come the end of a long day. Communes, which had offered the promise of a collective approach to domestic work, turned out to be yet another bust. As Vivian Estellachild wrote in 1971, the typical hippie commune's recruitment ad could have read, "Wanted: groovy, well-built chick to share apartment and do the cooking and cleaning."

12   Certainly there was a bit of hope in the abandonment of bourgeois housekeeping standards, something that the most radical factions were demanding and that even the less political groups saw as promising. *The Feminine Mystique* has its roots in a questionnaire that Betty Friedan sent to her Smith College classmates on the occasion of their fifteenth reunion. Included on it were questions one might expect: "Did you have career ambitions?" "Who manages the family finances, you or your husband?" But there were also these two telling questions: "Do you put the milk bottle on the table? Use paper napkins?" Milk decanted into a pitcher, and a linen napkin beside the breakfast plate—the physical embodiment of an approach to daily life that included moments of grace and loveliness, that showed (to use the old phrase) a woman's touch—suddenly seemed the very stuff of oppression. But even with the fillips abandoned, with the milk plunked down on the table and the kids wiping at grotty faces with paper napkins, there was still a heck of a lot of housework and child care that simply couldn't be streamlined.

13   And so, because of these petty, almost laughably low concerns—the unmade beds, the children with their endless questions, the crumbs and jelly on the

counter, the tendency of a good fight over housework to stop the talking and the kissing and the, well, you know—one of the most profound cultural revolutions in American history came perilously close to running aground. And then, like magic, as though the fairy godmother of women's liberation had waved a starry wand, the whole problem got solved. You must take a deus ex machina where you find one, and in the case of the crumbs and jelly on the counter tops, the deus ex machina turned out to be the forces of global capitalism. With the arrival of a cheap, easily exploited army of poor and luckless women—fleeing famine, war, the worst kind of poverty, leaving behind their children to do it, facing the possibility of rape or death on the expensive and secret journey—one of the noblest tenets of second-wave feminism collapsed like a house of cards. The new immigrants were met at the docks not by a highly organized and politically powerful group of American women intent on bettering the lot of their sex but, rather, by an equally large army of educated professional-class women with booming careers who needed their children looked after and their houses cleaned. Any supposed equivocations about the moral justness of white women's employing dark-skinned women to do their shit work simply evaporated.

. . .

14   How these workers became available to middle-class women is well known and amply reported, both in the press and in dozens of fine books, including Rhacel Salazar Parreñas's *Servants of Globalization* and Grace Chang's *Disposable Domestics*. But how so many middle-class American women went from not wanting to oppress other women to viewing that oppression as a central part of their own liberation—that is a complicated and sorry story. In it you will find the seeds of things we don't like to discuss much, including the elitism and hypocrisy of the contemporary feminist movement, the tendency of working and nonworking mothers to pit themselves against one another, and the way that adult middle-class life has become so intensely, laughably child-centered that in the past month I have chaperoned my children to eight birthday parties, yet not attended a single cocktail party (do they even exist anymore?).

15   To begin, let us turn to the best book ever written on American working mothers, a book that ought to be required reading in any women's-studies course: *The Equality Trap*, by Mary Ann Mason, who is a law and social-welfare professor at Berkeley. In it she reveals that there were in fact two distinct groups of mothers who entered the work force in the 1970s, for two distinct sets of reasons. There were middle-class women, fed up with housework and eager for the challenge, the respite, the intellectual engagement, of work. (Imagine my mother: it is 1976, and a casserole is defrosting on her kitchen counter, but she is far away from that counter; she is on a BART train, rocketing along to her new office at Equitable Life Insurance, pleased as punch.) It is these women, and now their daughters (imagine me, with an advanced degree and a book contract, sitting down at the computer, pleased as punch), who have driven a tremendous amount of the public debate and policy on the subject of working mothers.

16   But there was a second group of women, a quieter and more invisible group, who were not at all pleased as punch. Mason writes,

The dramatic shift from a manufacturing to a service economy, which occurred in the seventies, rendered the concept of a "family wage," earned by a relatively well-paid union member father, an anachronism. Their husbands' lower wages were driving mothers into the labor market in unprecedented numbers.

The number of women in each group continued to grow, but as Mason chillingly and accurately notes,

The great majority of American women workers were . . . striving to make ends meet in women's occupations and were not entering high-paying male-dominated occupations such as law, medicine, and corporate management. But it was the relatively small class of women who were trying to push into the high-stakes male professions . . . [that] drove the feminist movement . . . [These women] were not greatly concerned with secretaries or poor single parents.

Moreover, "Clusters of women rally around hot button issues like abortion rights, domestic violence, and gay parenting while academic women fret on queer theory, but there is no longer a compelling activist vision." And the pure, ugly truth of the thing: "Ironically, perhaps the only impact the feminist drive for equal rights in the workplace has had on this poorest, fastest growing segment of women is as a cheerleader for women's participation in the workplace, no matter how mean her job or how difficult her family burden."

17   The feminist movement, from its earliest days, has always proceeded from the assumption that all women—rich and poor—constitute a single class, and that all members of the class are, by virtue simply of being female, oppressed. In many regards this was once entirely true: all women were denied the vote; employment law discriminated against all women; and all women lacked the right to legal abortion. But this paradigm has led to a new assumption: that all working mothers—rich and poor—constitute a single class, that they are all similarly oppressed, and that they are united in a struggle against common difficulties. At its best this is vaguely well-intentioned but sloppy thinking. At its worst it is brutal and self-serving and shameful thinking.

18   The professional-class working mother—grateful inheritor of Betty Friedan's realizations about domestic imprisonment and the happiness and autonomy offered by work—is oppressed by guilt about her decision to keep working, by a society that often questions her commitment to and even her love for her children, by the labor-intensive type of parenting currently in vogue, by children's stalwart habit of falling deeply and unwaveringly in love with the person who provides their physical care, and by her uneasy knowledge that at-home mothers are giving their children much more time and personal attention than she is giving hers. She feels more than oppressed—she feels outraged! she wants something done about this!—by a corporate culture that refuses to let a working mother postpone an important meeting if it happens to coincide with the fourth-grade Spring Sing.

19   On the other hand, the nonprofessional-class working mother—unhappy inheritor of changes in the American economy that have thrust her unenthu-

siastically into the labor market—is oppressed by very different forces. She is oppressed by the fact that her work is oftentimes physically exhausting, ill-paid, and devoid of benefits such as health insurance and paid sick leave. She is oppressed by the fact that it is impossible to put a small child in licensed day care if you make minimum wage, and she is oppressed by the harrowing child-care options that are available on an unlicensed, inexpensive basis. She is oppressed by the fact that she has no safety net: if she falls out of work and her child needs a visit to the doctor and antibiotics, she may not be able to afford those things and will have to treat her sick child with over-the-counter med-ications, which themselves are far from cheap. She is oppressed by the fact that—another feminist gain—single motherhood has been so championed in our culture, along with the sexual liberation of women and the notion that a woman doesn't really need a man. In this climate she is often left shouldering the immense burden of parenthood alone.

. . .

20   Perhaps if enough women held power and authority and economic clout they would work to improve the economic lot of women without power and clout; perhaps a high tide of female power would raise all boats. Unfortunately, this has proved not to be true. The most educated and powerful women are the ones most likely to employ nannies, and when they do so, it is very often on the most undesirable terms.

21   We have come, of course, to the case of Zoe Baird, who had done her time at a lucrative big firm, who didn't blink when motherhood came along but kept on charging blindly forward, and who found herself in due time a candidate for one of the high government appointments—Attorney General—for which such firms groom lawyers. But it all went bust, as you will recall, in Nannygate.

. . .

22   Baird's nomination hearings came to an abrupt halt when it was revealed that she employed two Peruvian illegal immigrants as domestic workers, one of them as her child's nanny, and had failed to pay the required Social Security taxes on their wages. (The two, by the way, earned around $6.00 an hour, whereas their employers' household income was well in excess of half a million dollars a year.)

. . .

23   To the contemporary feminist, Zoe Baird was a victim principally of the national antagonism toward working mothers, and specifically of a problem common to all such women: there simply isn't enough affordable, high-quality child care in this country. (To the extent that the feminist thinks at all about the Peruvian couple in Baird's employ, it is usually to characterize them as sub-victims of the same problem.) It is a problem, feminists argue, that the govern-ment ought to address posthaste. In a new book called *The Mommy Myth*, Susan J. Douglas and Meredith W. Michaels report that "for most mothers, work is an absolute necessity, and so, hello, Earth to Congress, some reliable form of childcare is also an absolute necessity." Because most of their readers don't have time to review everything that "those half-wits in the District" have to say on the subject of universal day care, the authors provide a fairly accurate overview of how the program has died a thousand deaths in Congress. They conclude, "A

clear villain emerges—the far right wing in the United States." They're mostly right about that, and they're definitely right that millions of working-poor families are desperately in need of child care.

24   But guess what? We're told a single mother with a waitressing job is in exactly the same boat as a wealthy woman with a partnership in a major law firm and a similarly well employed husband. Joan K. Peters is the author of a highly regarded book called *When Mothers Work: Loving Our Children Without Sacrificing Our Selves*. It proceeds from an assumption dear to many women's hearts: "I argue that mothers should work outside the home," she tells us at the outset. "If they do not, they cannot preserve their identities or raise children to have both independent and family lives." (Good news for sweatshop workers and their children everywhere—Mom's identity as an underpaid seamstress is vital to healthy family functioning.) To Peters, as to so many of her philosophical sisters, all working mothers are united in a common struggle.

> Whether they are applying for the post of attorney general like Zoe Baird, or moving from welfare to work, child care is a visible issue in their lives. As more employed women balk at trading their jobs for full-time motherhood, subsidized quality child care will become one of their primary political demands.

No, it won't. The chances that someone like Zoe Baird—a woman who, at the time of her predicament, was working a huge number of hours at a highly remunerative job—would make use of subsidized child care are close to zilch. *Getting It Right*, by Laraine T. Zappert, is based on a "landmark study" of "more than three hundred women who have graduated from Stanford's Graduate School of Business," and who are "successfully taking up the challenge of life, family and career." The book is organized like a B[usiness]-school PowerPoint presentation, with chapters divided into heavily bullet-pointed sections such as "Experience," "Lessons Learned," and "Action Plan." The chapter on child care unequivocally advises readers to eschew day care in favor of employing nannies, because they are clearly the best option for professional women; in the first place, such employees "obviate the need for time-consuming pickups and deliveries." (Even the nomenclature suggests why a woman anxious about her choices in life wouldn't like day care: a good mother doesn't want to admit to having to make "deliveries" and "pickups" of her children, as though they were so many dirty shirts being sent to the laundry.) As one professional woman said, "Good help and lots of it is key to making the whole thing possible." Any moral equivocations about the larger ramifications of hiring a woman for such a job can be dispensed with quickly. Zappert points out, "The premiums offered to find and retain an excellent child-care provider are often more beneficent than any of the workplace perks that most professional women themselves enjoy." (Good thing Zoe's Peruvians didn't hear about those perks; they might have demanded access to an on-site gym and an annual executive physical.) True, such arrangements "can have a downside for the care provider." But there is always a silver lining where working mothers are involved: "Princeton sociologist Marta Tienda points out that 'because we rely on other women to take care of our children, two women can enter the labor force for every one that takes on a new job . . . all of [whom] are driving economic growth in a profound way.' " Granted, one of these two women has taken a job in which she may be paid under the table and denied Social Security set-asides, and is very probably (more good news for our booming, child-care-based economy) leaving her own children with yet a third woman in an arrangement in which cash changes hands and Social Security is never mentioned. But the professional-class working mother need not dwell on such unpleasantness: "Political economics aside," Zappert says, "it is clear from our survey that if you can do it, and particularly if you are working full time and/or have more than one child, having in-home child care can greatly decrease the stress of balancing work and life priorities."

25   So here we have the crux of the problem: ask an upper-middle-class woman why she is exploiting another woman for child care, and she will cry that she has to do it because there's no universal day care. But get a bunch of professional-class mothers together, and they will freely admit that day care sucks; get a nanny. This was a truth that Naomi Wolf—feminist, Yalie, Rhodes scholar, big thinker—learned the hard way after giving birth to her first child. In *Misconceptions*, Wolf reports,

> I never thought I would become one of those women who took up a fore-ordained place in a hierarchy of class and gender. Yet here we were, to my horror and complicity, shaping our new family structure along class and gender lines—daddy at work, mommy and caregiver from two different economic classes, sharing the baby work during the day.

Her dreams of parenthood, apparently formed while tripping across green New Haven quadrangles on her way to feminist-theory classes, were starkly different: "I had wanted us to be a mother and a father raising children side by side, the man moving into the world of children, the woman into the world of work, in equitable balance, maybe each working flexibly from home, the two making the same world and sharing the same experiences and values." She had wanted a revolution; what she got was a Venezuelan.

. . .

26   What few will admit—because it is painful, because it reveals the unpleasant truth that life presents a series of choices, each of which precludes a host of other attractive possibilities—is that when a mother works, something is lost. Children crave their mothers. They always have and they always will. And women fortunate enough to live in a society where they have access to that greatest of levelers, education, will always have the burning dream of doing something more exciting and important than tidying Lego blocks and running loads of laundry. If you want to make an upper-middle-class woman squeal in indignation, tell her she can't have something. If she works she can't have as deep and connected a relationship with her child as she would if she stayed home and raised him. She can't have the glamour and respect conferred on career women if she chooses instead to spend her days at "Mommy and Me" classes. She can't have both things. I have read numerous accounts of the anguish women have felt leaving small babies with caregivers so that they could

go to work, and I don't discount those stories for a moment. That the separation of a woman from her child produces agony for both is one of the most enduring and impressive features of the human experience, and it probably accounts for why we've made it as far as we have. I've read just as many accounts of the despair that descends on some women when their world is abruptly narrowed to the tedium and exhaustion of the nursery; neither do I discount these stories: I've felt that self-same despair.

27   In my case, the despair was lessened—greatly—by a nanny. Without her I could never have launched a second career as a writer. Her kindness, her patience, and her many (and oftentimes extreme) acts of generosity have shaped my family as much as any other force. But the implications of this solution to my domestic problems are grave, and ever since I read *Doméstica*, two years ago, I have been turning over in my mind the high moral cost of my decision. Even if one pays a fair wage, hires a legal resident of the United States, and pays both one's own share of the required taxes and the employee's, so as not to short her take-home pay (all of which I do), one is still part of a system that exposes women to the brutalities of illegal immigration, only to reward their suffering with the jobs that ease our already comfortable lives.

28   It's easy enough to dismiss the dilemma of the professional-class working mother as the whining of the elite. But people are entitled to their lives, and within the context of privilege there are certainly hard choices, disappointments, sorrows. Upper-middle-class working mothers may never have calm hearts regarding their choices about work and motherhood, but there are certain things they can all do. They can acknowledge that many of the gains of professional-class working women have been leveraged on the backs of poor women. They can legitimize those women's work and compensate it fairly, which means—at the very least—paying Social Security taxes on it. They can demand that feminists abandon their current fixation on "work-life balance" and on "ending the mommy wars" and instead devote themselves entirely to the real and heartrending struggle of poor women and children in this country. And they can stop using the hardships of the poor as justification for their own choices. About this much, at least, there ought to be agreement.

Review Questions

1. Summarize in one paragraph Flanagan's argument.

2. In one or two sentences, sum up the particulars of the Zoe Baird case, as Flanagan presents them.

3. Explain why Flanagan thinks that even those who pay a "fair wage," hire legal U.S. residents, and pay the appropriate taxes bear moral responsibility for the decision to hire household help.

4. Why does Flanagan find it inappropriate for people who demand universal child care to support their argument by referring to the Zoe Baird scandal?

Discussion and Writing Suggestions

1. Flanagan charges that privileged white working mothers are able to achieve self-fulfillment in their careers and home life only by exploiting and oppressing less fortunate minority women. To what extent do you think that she makes a valid point? Base your response upon your own experience, observations, or reading.

2. Do you interpret Flanagan as arguing that upper-middle-class white women should stop hiring nannies or sending their kids to day care and instead stay home and look after their own children? If not, what do you think she *is* recommending?

3. Describe your reaction to Flanagan's statement that "when a mother works, something is lost." Based on what you have experienced, observed, or read, to what extent do you agree with this assertion?

4. Flanagan uses words such as "tizzies" and "squeal" to describe the reactions of privileged white women to perceived dilemmas and problems they face. What connotations do such words carry? Why do you think Flanagan chose to use them? Taking into account your response to Flanagan's main point, to what extent do you think this kind of loaded language helps or hurts her arguments?

5. To what extent do you agree with Flanagan's assertion that those who hire household help bear a moral responsibility for that decision—regardless of the wages and taxes they pay—because they are participating in a system that exploits women?

6. In response to Flanagan, some critics might argue that paying for household help—assuming the terms are fair and legal—is no different from paying for any other kind of service—for example, paying a hair stylist to cut your hair. Write a brief paragraph either in support of or against this argument.

The Myth of Co-Parenting: How It Was Supposed to Be. How It Was.
Hope Edelman

The previous selections in the chapter (Hekker excepted) have dealt with issues of modern marriage from a journalistic, scholarly, or activist viewpoint. In the following two essays, two professional writers—a woman and a man—offer personal perspectives on their own marriages. You are already familiar with some of the issues they will discuss. What is distinctive about these selections is their tone: The writing is by turns raw, wounded, angry, and defensive and offers an unflinchingly honest, if brutal, assessment of each writer's marriage. These essays strikingly reveal the miscommunication and resentment that can afflict even mature, thoughtful, dedicated couples. In the first, Hope Edelman describes the disillusionment and anger she felt when, after the birth of their child, her husband immersed himself in his career, leaving her to run their household alone.

Hope Edelman has written three nonfiction books, including Motherless Daughters *(1995). Her essays and articles have appeared in the* New York Times, *the* Chicago Tribune, *the* San Francisco Chronicle, *and* Seventeen *magazine. She lives with her husband and two children in Los Angeles. This essay was written for the anthology* The Bitch in the House *(2002).*

1 Throughout much of 1999 and 2000, my husband spent quite a lot of time at work. By "quite a lot" I mean the kind of time Fermilab scientists spent trying to split the atom, which is to say, every waking moment. The unofficial count one week came in at ninety-two hours, which didn't include cell phone calls answered on grocery checkout lines or middle-of-the-night brainstorms that had to be e-mailed before dawn. Often I would wake at 3:00 A.M. and find him editing a business plan down in the living room, drinking herbal tea in front of his laptop's ethereal glow. If he had been a lawyer tallying billable hours, he would have made some firm stinking rich.

2 He was launching an Internet company back then, and these were the kind of hours most people in his industry were putting in. Phrases like "window of opportunity" and "ensuring our long-term security" were bandied about our house a lot, usually during the kind of exasperating late-night conversations that began with "The red-eye to New York? *Again?*" and included "I mean, it's not like you're trying to find a cure for cancer," somewhere within. I was working nearly full-time myself, though it soon became clear this would have to end. Our daughter was a year and a half old, and the phrase "functionally orphaned" was also getting thrown around our house a lot, usually by me.

3 So as my husband's work hours exponentially increased, I started cutting back on mine. First a drop from thirty-five per week to twenty-five, and then a dwindle down to about eighteen. At first I didn't really mind. With the exception of six weeks postpartum, this was the first time since high school that I had a good excuse not to work like a maniac, and I was grateful for the break. Still, there was something more than vaguely unsettling about feeling that my choice hadn't been much of an actual choice. When one parent works ninety-two hours a week, the other one, by necessity, has to start picking up the slack. Otherwise, some fairly important things—like keeping the refrigerator stocked, or filing income taxes, or finding a reliable baby-sitter, not to mention giving a child some semblance of security and consistency around this place, for God's sake—won't get done. A lot of slack was starting to pile up around our house. And because I was the only parent spending any real time there, the primary de-slacker was me.

4 How did I feel about this? I don't mind saying. I was extremely pissed off.

5 Like virtually every woman friend I have, I entered marriage with the belief that co-parenting was an attainable goal. In truth, it was more of a vague assumption, a kind of imagined parity I had superimposed on the idea of marriage without ever really thinking it through. *If I'm going to contribute half of the income, then he'll contribute half of the housework and child care.* Like that. If you'd asked me to elaborate, I would have said something impassioned and emphatic, using terms like "shared responsibility" and "equal division of labor." The watered-down version of feminism I identified with espoused those catchphrases, and in lieu of a

more sophisticated blueprint for domestic life, I co-opted the talk as my own. But really, I didn't know what I was talking about beyond the fact that I didn't want to be the dominant parent in the house.

6   When I was growing up in suburban New York, my mother seemed to do everything. *Everything.* Carpooling, haircuts, vet appointments, ice cream cakes, dinners in the Crock-Pot, book-report dioramas—the whole roll call for a housewife of the 1960s and 1970s. My father, from my child's point of view, did three things. He came home from work in time for dinner. He sat at the kitchen table once a month and paid the bills. And, on weekend trips, he drove the car. Certainly he did much more than that, including earn all of our family's income, but my mother's omnipresence in our household meant that anyone else felt, well, incidental in comparison. The morning after she died, of breast cancer at forty-two, my younger siblings and I sat at the kitchen table with our father as dawn filtered through the yellow window shades. I looked at him sitting there, in a polo shirt and baseball cap, suddenly so small beneath his collapsed shoulders. I was barely seventeen. He was fifty-one. *Huh,* I thought. *Who are you?*

7   There were no chore charts taped to the refrigerator, no family powwows, no enthusiastic TV nannies suddenly materializing outside our front door. My father taught himself to use a microwave and I started driving my siblings for their haircuts and that, as they say, was that.

8   My cousin Lorraine, a devout Baha'i, once told me it doesn't matter how many orgasms a potential husband gives you; what really matters is the kind of father he'll be. At first I thought she said this because Baha'is disavow premarital sex, but the more men I dated, the more I realized Lorraine was right. Loyalty and devotion are undoubtedly better traits to have in a spouse than those fleeting moments of passion, though I can't deny the importance of the latter. When I met John, it was like winning the boyfriend jackpot. He was beautiful and sexy, and devoted and smart, *so* smart, and he had the kindest green eyes. The first time I saw those eyes, when I was negotiating an office sublease from him in New York, he smiled right at me and it happened, just the way you dream about when you're twelve: I knew this was someone I would love. *And* he wanted children, which immediately separated him from a cool three-quarters of the men I'd dated before. I was thirty-two when we started dating, and just becoming acutely aware that I didn't have unlimited time to wait.

9   What happened next happened fast. Within two years, John and I were parents and homeowners in a canyon outside Los Angeles. By then he was deep into the process of starting his own company, which left us with barely an hour to spend together at the end of each day. And even though I so badly wanted him to succeed, to get the acclaim a smart, hardworking, honest person deserves—and even though I was grateful that his hard, honest work earned enough to support us both—well, let me put it bluntly. Back there when I was single and imagining the perfect partnership? This wasn't what I had in mind.

10   When John became so scarce around our house, I had to compensate by being utterly present in every way: as a kisser of boo-boos; a dispenser of discipline; an employer of baby-sitters; an assembler of child furniture; a scary-monster slayer, mortgage refinancer, reseeder of dying backyards. And that's before I even opened my office door for the day. Balancing act? I was the whole damn circus, all three rings.

11   It began to make me spitting mad, the way the daily duties of parenting and home ownership started to rest entirely on me. It wasn't even the additional work I minded as much as the total responsibility for every decision made. The frustration I felt after researching and visiting six preschools during my so-called work hours, trying to do a thorough job for both of us, and then having John offhandedly say, "Just pick the one you like best." Or the irritation I felt when, after three weeks of weighing the options, I finally made the choice, and then he raised his eyebrows at the cost. *I didn't sign up for this!* I began shouting at my sister over the phone.

12   How does it happen, I wondered both then and now, that even today, in this post–second wave, post-superwoman, dual-income society we're supposed to live in, the mother nearly always becomes the primary parent, even when she, too, works full-time—the one who meets most or all of the children's and the household's minute-by-minute needs? We start out with such grand intentions for sharing the job, yet ultimately how many fathers handle the dental appointments, shop for school clothes, or shuttle pets to and from the vet? Nine times out of ten, it's still the mother who plans and emcees the birthday parties, the mother who cuts the meeting short when the school nurse calls. Women have known about this Second Shift for years, the way the workday so often starts up again for women when they walk through the door at the end of the *other* workday—a time mandated perhaps by the baby-sitter's deadline, but also by their own guilt, sense of responsibility, tendency to prioritize their husband's job first, or a combination of all three. Still, I—like many other enlightened, equality-oriented women having babies in this era—had naïvely thought that a pro-feminist partner, plus my own sheer willpower, would prevent this from happening to me. I hadn't bargained for how deeply the gender roles of "nurturer" and "provider" are ingrained in us all, or—no matter how much I love being a mother to my daughter—how much I would grow to resent them.

13   When it became clear that my husband and I were not achieving the kind of co-parenting I'd so badly wanted us to achieve, I felt duped and infuriated and frustrated and, beneath it all, terribly, impossibly sad. Sad for myself, and sad for my daughter, who—just like me as a child—had so little one-on-one time with her father. No matter how sincerely John and I tried to buck convention, no matter how often I was the one who sat down at the kitchen table to pay the bills, there we were: he absorbed in his own world of work, me consumed by mine at home. My parents all over again.

14 The intensity of John's workplace was, originally, supposed to last for six months, then for another six months, then for only about three months more. But there was always some obstacle on the horizon: first-round funding, second-round funding, hirings, firings, had to train a sales force, had to meet a new goal. And meetings, all those meetings. Seven in the morning, nine at night. How were all those other dot-com wives managing?

15   There was no time together for anything other than the most pragmatic exchanges. When he walked through the door at 10:00 P.M., I'd lunge at him with paint chips to approve, or insurance forms to sign, or leaks to examine before I called the plumber first thing in the morning. Fourteen hours of con-

versation compressed into twenty highly utilitarian minutes before we fell, exhausted, into bed. A healthy domestic situation, it was not.

16   I was angry with the kind of anger that had nothing to do with rationality. A lot of the time, I was mad at Gloria Steinem for having raised women's expectations when I was just a toddler—but at least she lived by her principles, marrying late and never trying to raise kids; so then I got mad at Betty Friedan for having started it all with *The Feminine Mystique*, and when that wasn't satisfying enough, I got mad at all the women in my feminist criticism class in graduate school, the ones who'd sat there and so smugly claimed it was impossible for a strong-willed woman to ever have an equal partnership with a man. Because it was starting to look as if they'd been right.

17   But mostly I was mad at John, because he'd never actually sat down with me to say, "This is what starting a dot-com company will involve," or even, "I'd like to do this—what do you think?"—the way I imagine I would have with him before taking on such a demanding project (which, of course, we'd then have realized together was not feasible unless he quit his job or cut back dramatically, which—of course—was out of the question). Legitimate or not, I felt that at least partly because he was "the husband" and his earning power currently eclipsed mine, his career took precedence, and I had to pick up the household slack, to the detriment of my own waning career—or in addition to it. Before our marriage, I had never expected that. I don't remember the conversation where I asked him to support me financially in exchange for me doing everything else. In fact, I'd never wanted that and still decidedly didn't. I was not only happy to put in my portion of the income (though it would inevitably be less than usual during any year I birthed and breast-fed an infant), I expected to and *wanted* to contribute as much as I could: Part of who I was—what defined me and constituted a main source of my happiness and vitality—was my longtime writing and teaching career. I didn't want to give it up, but I also didn't want hired professionals running my household and raising my child. It felt like an impossible catch-22.

18 Face-to-face, John and I didn't give ultimatums. At first, we didn't even argue much out loud. Instead we engaged in a kind of low-level quibbling where the stakes were comfortably low. Little digs that didn't mean much in isolation but eventually started to add up. Like bickering about whose fault it was we never took vacations. (He said mine, I said his.) And whether we should buy our daughter a swing set. (I said yes, he said not now.) And about who forgot to roll the trash cans to the bottom of the driveway, again. (Usually him.)

19   I'd been through therapy. I knew the spiel. How you were supposed to say, "When you're gone all the time, it makes me feel angry and resentful and lonely," instead of, "How much longer do you realistically think I'm going to put up with this crap?" I tried that first approach, and there was something to it, I admit. John listened respectfully. He asked what he could do to improve. Then it was his turn. He told me how he'd begun to feel like a punching bag in our home. How my moods ruled our household, how sometimes he felt like wilting when he heard that sharp edge in my voice. Then he said he was sorry and I said I was sorry, and he said he'd try to be home more and I said I'd try to lighten up. And this would work, for a while. Until the night John would say he'd be home

at eight to put Maya to bed but would forget to call about the last-minute staff meeting that started at six, and when he'd walk through the door at ten I'd be too pissed off to even say hello. Instead, I'd snap, "How much longer do you realistically think I'm going to put up with this crap?" And the night would devolve from there.

20   Neither of us was "wrong." Neither was completely right. The culpability was shared. Both of us were stuck together on that crazy carousel, where the more time John spent away from home, the more pissed off I got, and the more pissed off I got, the less he wanted to be around.

21 One day I said fuck it, and I took John's credit card and bought a swing set. Not one of those fancy redwood kinds that look like a piece of the Alamo, but a sturdy wood one nonetheless with a tree house at the top of the slide, and I paid for delivery and assembly, too. On the way home I stopped at one of those places that sell the fancy redwood kind and ordered a playground-quality bucket swing for another seventy bucks.

22   Fuck it.

23   There were other purchases I'd made like this, without John's involvement—the silk bedroom curtains, the Kate Spade wallet I didn't really need—each one thrilling me with a momentary, devilish glee. But the swing set: the swing set was my gutsiest act of rebellion thus far. Still, when it was fully installed on our side lawn, the cloth roof of the tree house gently flapping in the breeze, I felt oddly unfulfilled. Because, after all, what had I really achieved? My daughter had a swing set, but I was still standing on the grass by myself, furiously poking at gopher holes with my foot, thinking about whether I'd have time on Thursday to reseed the lawn alone. When what I really wanted was for my husband to say, "Honey, let me help you with that reseeding, and then we'll all three go out for dinner together." I just wanted him to come home, to share with me—and Maya—all the joys and frustrations and responsibilities of domestic life.

24   On bad days, when the baby-sitter canceled or another short-notice business trip had just been announced, he would plead with me to hire a full-time nanny—we'd cut corners elsewhere, we'd go into savings, whatever it took, he said. I didn't want to hear it. "I don't need a nanny, I need a husband!" I shouted. Didn't he understand? My plan hadn't been to hire someone to raise our child. My plan had been to do it together: two responsible parents with two fulfilling jobs, in an egalitarian marriage with a well-adjusted kid who was equally bonded to us both.

25 In writing class I tell my students there are just two basic human motivators: desire and fear. Every decision we make, every action we take, springs from this divided well. Some characters are ruled by desire. Others are ruled by fear. So what was my story during the year and a half that John spent so much time at work? He claimed that I was fear-driven, that I was threatened by the loss of control, which may in fact have been true. When I try to dissect my behavior then, reaching beneath all the months of anger and complaints, I do find fear: the fear that I'd never find a way to balance work and family life without constantly compromising one, the other, or both. But mostly what I find is desire.

For my daughter to have a close relationship with her father, for my husband to have more time to spend with me, for me to find a way to have some control over my time, even with a husband and a child factored into the mix. And then there was the big one: for my husband to fulfill the promise I felt he made to me on our wedding day, which was to be my partner at home and in life. Somewhere along the way, we'd stopped feeling like a team, and I wanted that fellowship back.

26   I wish, if only to inject a flashy turning point into this story right about now, that I could say some climactic event occurred from which we emerged dazed yet transformed, or that one of us delivered an ultimatum the other couldn't ignore and our commitment to each other was then renewed. But in reality, the way we resolved all this was gradual, and—in retrospect—surprisingly simple. John got the company stabilized and, as he'd promised, finally started working fewer hours. And I, knowing he would be home that much more, slowly started adding hours to my workday. With the additional income, we hired a live-in nanny, who took over much of the housework as well. And then, a few months after Francis arrived, Maya started preschool two mornings a week. Those became blessed writing hours for me, time when I was fully released of the guilt of paying others to watch my child. Between 9:00 A.M. and 12:30 P.M. Maya was exactly where she was supposed to be and, within that time frame, so was I.

27   With Francis came an additional benefit: a baby-sitter on Friday nights. For the first time since Maya's birth, John and I had a set night each week to devote to each other, and as we split combination sushi plates and did side-by-side chatarangas in a 6:00 P.M. yoga class, we began to slowly build upon the foundation we'd laid with our marriage—and, thankfully, even in the darkest months, we'd always trusted hadn't disappeared. Yes, there were still some Friday nights when I watched TV alone because John was flying back from New York, and other Fridays when I had to sit late in front of the computer to meet a deadline. And there were some weekend days when John still had to take meetings, though they became fewer and fewer over time.

28 It has taken real effort for me to release the dream of completely equal co-parenting, or at least to accept that we may not be the family to make it real. We're still quite a distance from that goal, and even further when you factor in the amount of household support we now have. Does John do 50 percent of the remaining child care? No. But neither do I contribute 50 percent of the income, as I once did. Ours is still an imbalanced relationship in some ways, but imbalance I've learned to live with—especially after the extreme inequity we once had.

29   What really matters now—more than everything being absolutely equal, more than either my husband or me "striking it rich"—is that John is home before Maya's bedtime almost every night now to join the pileup on her bed, and that we took our first real family vacation last December. This is the essence of what I longed for during those bleak, angry months of my daughter's first two years. It was a desire almost embarrassing in its simplicity, yet one so strong that, in one of the greatest paradoxes of my marriage, it might have torn my husband and me apart: the desire to love and be loved, with reciprocity and conviction,

with fairness and respect; the desire to capture that elusive animal we all grow up believing marriage is, and never stop wanting it to be.

Discussion and Writing Questions

1. Reread paragraph 5, which begins, "Like virtually every woman friend I have." To what extent does this paragraph describe your own expectations regarding coparenting with your (eventual) spouse? To what extent has reading about an experience such as Edelman's caused you to adjust these expectations? Explain.

2. In a brief paragraph, describe the parenting roles played by your own parents when you were growing up. How much of the parenting did your mother perform? Your father? What were your feelings about this parenting arrangement then, and what are your feelings now? How likely is it that your parents' example will affect your own expectations of your husband or wife, when you are married and attempting to divide household responsibilities between yourself and your spouse?

3. Edelman writes that even though she wanted her husband to succeed and was glad for the money he was making, she couldn't escape the feeling that the life she was living "wasn't what [she] had in mind" when she had been single and "imagining the perfect partnership." In a brief paragraph, describe your own "perfect partnership" with a spouse. Be sure to take into account the "reality check" that essays such as Edelman's (and Shulman's) provide—that is, it's probably unrealistic to imagine a high-earning spouse who is also able to perform at least half of the housework and child-raising duties.

4. Edelman writes, "I hadn't bargained for how deeply the gender roles of 'nurturer' and 'provider' are ingrained in us all." To what extent do you agree that the kinds of division-of-household-labor problems Edelman describes stem from ingrained gender roles? In responding, draw upon your own experiences and observations.

5. Edelman writes: "Neither of us was 'wrong.' Neither was completely right." Do you agree? Explain your response.

6. Edelman explains that her problem was eventually solved when, among other things, she and her husband hired a nanny. However, elsewhere in the essay Edelman describes her resistance to the idea of hiring professional help. Describe your reaction to her (presumed) compromise. To what extent do you feel it was a betrayal of her ideals? To what extent do you feel it was the right thing to do in her situation?

7. *For men only:* Write a response to Edelman's essay, as if you were her husband.

My Problem with Her Anger
Eric Bartels

In the previous selection, Hope Edelman describes how her husband's absence made her feel "angry and resentful and lonely." In the following essay, Eric Bartels writes about what it is like to be on the receiving end of such spousal anger. Eric Bartels is a feature writer for the Portland Tribune *in Portland, Oregon, where he lives with his wife and two children. This is a revised version of the essay by this title that appeared in* The Bastard on the Couch: 27 Men Try Really Hard to Explain Their Feelings About Love, Loss, Fatherhood, and Freedom (2004), *an anthology edited by Daniel Jones.*

1   My wife and kids were sleeping when I finished the dishes the other night, shook the water off my hands and smudged them dry with one of the grimy towels hanging on the door to the oven. I gave the kitchen floor a quick sweep, clearing it of all but the gossamer tufts of cat hair that always jet away from the broom as if under power.

2   I turned to shut the lights, but then I noticed the two metal grills I had left to soak in the basin. They're the detachable, (cast iron type) (stove-top kind) that we occasionally use to affect a kind of indoor, open-flame cooking experience. Submerging them in water for awhile makes it easier to remove the carbonized juices and bits of flesh that get welded on during use. It's a good, sensible way to save labor.

3   The problem was that they'd been in the sink for several days now. And then it occurred to me: What I was staring at was the dark heart of the divide between men and women.

4   It's unlikely I was any less harried or less tired the previous few nights as I went about my kitchen duties, a responsibility that has fallen to me more or less exclusively of late. No, my energy level is fairly constant—that is to say depleted—at that particular point of just about any day. I could, and probably should have finished the grill-cleaning project sooner. Just as I should make the bed every morning instead of occasionally. Just as I should always throw my underwear into the hamper before showering, rather than leaving them on top of it, or on the floor next to it.

5   These are the things men do that quietly annoy the living shit out of a woman. Until she becomes a mother. Then they inspire a level of fury unlike anything she has ever experienced. And that fury won't be kept secret. On the receiving end, the husband will be left to wonder why the punishment is so wildly out of line with the crime. This is the kind of vitriol that should be reserved for lying politicians, corporate greed and hitters who don't take a pitch when their team trails in the late innings—not a dedicated marriage partner with garden-variety human foibles.

6   .Yet here we are, my wife and me. We're both good people. We have lots of friends. We make a decent living at relatively satisfying professional jobs: She, half-time at a small advertising firm; I, as a newspaper writer. And we're dedicated, attentive parents to a six-year old daughter and a two-year old son.

7   We don't use profanity in front of the children, unless we're arguing angrily. We don't talk to each other disrespectfully, except when arguing angrily. And we don't say bad things about each other to the kids, unless, of course, we just finished arguing angrily.

8   I know my wife's life is hard. She spends more time with the kids than I do and is almost completely responsible for running them around to day care and school. I contribute regularly and earnestly to the shopping, cooking and cleaning, but a fair amount of it still falls to her. And her job, although part-time for the last six years, presents her with Hell's own revolving door of guilt over neglecting her work for kids and vice versa.

9   I work hard to take pressure off her and have given up some freedoms myself since our first child was born: time with friends, regular pickup basketball games, beer. And I honestly don't mind living without these things. What gets me, though, is how little credit I get for the effort. My wife gets tired. She gets frustrated. She gets angry. And she seems to want to take it out on me.

10   Then logic starts moving backward in an ugly zigzag pattern. If, in her mind, my shortcomings provide the justification for her anger, then the perception of my behavior must be groomed like the playing field of a game I can't seem to win. The things I do that don't conform to my new loser image—and to think this woman once thought I was cooler than sliced bread—don't even show up on the scoreboard. Until, finally, nothing I do is right.

11   My efforts to organize the contents of the armoire one day—a project she had suggested—led to a screaming fight. The clutter I was planning to move to the basement would just create more junk down there, she said. But we hardly use the basement, I thought, and besides, why couldn't we just make another, separate project of sorting out the basement later? Doesn't it solve the more pressing armoire problem in the meantime? Isn't that logical?

12   Evidently not.

13   One night she stomped into the kitchen as I was cleaning up after a dinner that I may well have cooked and served and announced in angry tones that she needed more help getting the kids ready for bed than I had been providing, as if she had just found me drinking beer and playing video games. Isn't that something we could discuss rationally, I asked her, when we're not both right in the middle of our respective (unpleasant) (demanding) nightly routines?

14   It didn't occur to her, I guess.

15   And a few nights later, after bathing the kids in succession, putting them in their pajamas and feeding them their vitamins, I was rocking our son to sleep when I heard my wife approach. I think she had been downstairs doing laundry. She walks into the bathroom and scornfully asks no one in particular "Why is there still water in the bathtub?"

16   I missed it.

17   I make a nice dinner after a long day at work, broiled pork chops with steamed zuccini, perhaps, and she asks why I made rice instead of pasta. At the grocery store, I try to buy food that's somewhere between not entirely toxic and prohibitively expensive, but I often disappoint her. I wash clothes the wrong way, not separating them properly by color. I spend too much time rinsing off dishes before loading them into the dishwasher.

18   If this is my castle, it is under siege. From within.

19   At times, the negativity threatens to grind my spirit into dust. I make it through an arduous week, gleeful to have it behind me, only to come home to the sound of her loudly and impatiently scolding our son for standing on a chair or turning on the TV or dumping his cheese puffs on the floor, exactly the stuff two-year old boys are supposed to do. Okay, children need to learn "no," and my wife does a lot of the teaching, but I'm certain there's a gentler way to pronounce the word.

20   I try to make this point calmly, and when that doesn't work, I make it more forcefully. Then we fight, until the (shame and) futility of that leaves me feeling deflated and distant, in a place where passion of any kind has slipped into a coma. And then it's time to start all over.

21   At times I watch my wife's mercury rise steadily, predictably to that point where she lashes out, almost as if she wanted to get there. I tell her, in the quietest, most reasonable tone I can manage, to please relax. Choose: "(You, Your Daughter, Your Son) did/did not do (this, that, the other)," she replies, her ire mounting. But, I think to myself, I didn't ask her what she's angry about, I asked her to stay calm. Aren't those different things?

22   I think it's fairly well established by now that marriage is a challenge, a creaky, old institution that may not have fully adapted itself to modern life, one that now fails in this country more often than not. Put children in the picture and you have an exponentially higher degree of difficulty.

23   Motherhood asks the modern woman, who has grown up seeing professional success as hers for the taking, to add the loss of a linear career path to an already considerable burden: child rearing, body issues, a shifting self-image and a husband who fell off his white horse long, long ago. I suppose this would make anyone angry.

24   Perhaps for women of recent generations, anger has replaced the quiet desperation of the past. That seems like a healthy development to me. But that doesn't mean there aren't several good reasons why, having seen the frustrated, angry, resentful place that the demands of modern motherhood will almost certainly take them, women shouldn't take the next logical, evolutionary step.

25   It seems to me that a woman should now focus only secondarily on what the world, and more specifically, her partner can do for her during the challenging early years of child rearing. She must now truly empower herself by turning to the more important issue: Controlling the monstrous effects that motherhood can have on her own emotional landscape.

26   In other words, buck up.

27   For better or worse, men don't experience life the way women do. Absent the degree of intuition and empathy that seem an integral (natural) part of a woman's nurturing instinct, men grow up in a simpler milieu in which challenges are to be quickly surmounted, without a great deal of fanfare. Something breaks, you fix it and move on. (But don't throw it out, it could come in handy at some point.)

28   It's not a mindset that lends itself to a great deal of introspection and deep thought. That's not to say that women can't fix things or that men are shallow-minded. These (just seem like) are philosophical tendencies propelled by disparate biological imperatives. The result in men is an inclination not to worry

about things before they happen. This imbues them with a confidence that, however vexing a problem might seem, it can and will be resolved.

29   I don't think most women share this confidence. A friend of mine says that everything in a woman's world starts with fear. Everything becomes tied in some way to fears of disapproval and abandonment and loss of control and God knows what else. To make matters worse, a man's more measured response to (in) certain situations is likely to suggest to his wife that he is not sufficiently engaged. Indifferent. Oblivious.

30   Am I the only guy who feels like he forever stands accused of not understanding the pressures my wife is under? That I can't possibly fathom her frustrations? After all, what would a man know about controlling his impulses?

31   What would he know? I like that one. Remember, we're talking about men here, the people with the built-in testosterone factory. The ones whose favorite childhood entertainments run to breaking windows, starting fires and dismembering small animals. The ones who instantly want to know if their first car will do 100 mph. The ones who attend beery high school parties with the goal of getting laid, but who'll settle for a good fistfight. Women should be eager to learn what most men know about managing anger.

32   For many years, I made a living as a bartender. I was good at it and loved the challenge of having to nimbly beat back the surging, immediate gallery of tasks that a big crowd and a busy night present. But it's a job where things go wrong pretty much constantly and I would occasionally lose my cool, kicking a cooler door closed or angrily sending an empty bottle smashing into a bin with an ear-splitting explosion. I imagined I was just blowing off a little steam.

33   I didn't know what I was really doing until I was a patron at someone else's bar one night. I watched a bartender momentarily capture everyone's attention with a loud fit of pique and realized quickly that witnesses saw the whole thing as landing somewhere between laughable and pathetic. We didn't care what was bothering him. We were having drinks and a good time. Too bad he wasn't enjoying the evening himself.

34   Was the guy under a lot of pressure? Yes. Was he being vexed by all manner of impediments to his ability to do his job? Almost certainly. Did anybody care? No.

35   I did a lot less kicking doors and throwing things after that.

36   Of course I care about my wife's happiness. Whether we're bothered by the same things or react to challenges the same way is irrelevant. She is my partner and I love her. We have important things to do together. The life we've built depends heavily on her ability to find contentment.

37   But she's not the only one in the family who has tough days. I have my own stuff to deal with and so do our kids, young as they are. When my wife decides it's okay to look darkly at her self or the day she's having, she's giving herself permission to ignore what's going on in other's lives. However little she regards the obligations and pressures of my existence, the fact is that I have some less than radiant days myself.

38   Women could try to accept that it is theoretically possible for a man to be tired, feel stress and even need a bit of emotional support himself. The children can certainly provide a lift, but they are also notoriously inconsistent about refraining from imperfect, untimely behaviors: talking in loud, excited voices,

soiling themselves and moving at high speed in close proximity to valued objects and unforgiving hardwood furniture.

39 An overworked wife is certainly within her rights, as ever, to express her concerns and wishes at these moments. But that is not the same as a bilious, ill-timed attack that suggests her husband, through arrogance and selfishness, knows absolutely nothing of the realities of her world. In fact, he probably has a pretty good idea. He's probably even willing to meet any reasonable request to help. He'd just like it if someone would ask him nicely.

40 I'm amazed at how willing my wife is to push my buttons sometimes. And it's not like she's unfamiliar with the instrument panel. She evidently hasn't noticed that I occasionally ignite like dry kindling.

41 I should probably admit about now that I'm not always a model of decorum. I'm a personable, intelligent guy, but I'm not one of those wise, super-evolved aliens with the massive cranium from science fiction. I've said unkind things to people. I've thrown elbows on the basketball court. Gripped by paroxysmic anger, I've sent any number of small appliances to the promised land. And I do like to win. But this is about not fighting.

42 Anyone who's ever watched a young child's face crumple in fear and bewilderment as parents unleash their anger, in any direction, knows instantly what's the stakes are. Parents do not need the toxic stew of anger coursing through them while in charge of small, impressionable children. And partners who are struggling to remember what particular disease of the brain led to their union won't be helped back to the right path by the rotating wheel of frustration, resentment and blame.

43 I fear that when anger is allowed to manifest itself regularly, it becomes less and less necessary to question its origins. No need to examine it, no need to work backward in the hope of identifying and defusing the triggers to the fast-replicating chain of events. And what is the hope of altering a behavior if you don't know where it came from and never see it coming?

44 It baffles me that someone of my wife's intelligence would shout at our son to stop yelling or demand in a voice twisted with exasperation that our daughter stop whining. Can't she see what she's doing? It's like hitting someone to curb his or her violent tendencies. Of course I understand her frustration. But to let the expression of that frustration take any form, however inappropriate or unproductive, is indefensible.

45 Anger can spread quickly and I don't want us to poison the house where our kids are growing up. I don't know for a fact that whiney, self-centered children are always the product of undisciplined, self-indulgent parents, but what reasonable person would want to take that chance? Isn't a bit of restraint a rather small price to pay?

46 Anger is not power. Managing anger is power. A good friend of many years, with whom I've had many passionate debates on all manner of issues, used to tell me how his father would sit impassively during their own lively exchanges. His father, a university department head, would never lose his temper, never so much as raise his voice. I think I dismissed it as humanly impossible. My friend said it drove him crazy. But he is now an eloquent, engaging orator who runs a weekly literary discussion group out of his home. Then again, he also has two young sons and is divorced.

47   The level of discipline my friend learned from his father doesn't generally reside where my wife grew up. Individually, my in-laws are charming, intelligent, accomplished people. But together, they struggle mightily to break old habits. You can get one or another of them to acknowledge the familiar cycle of intolerance, blame and recrimination that often cripples their dealings with each other, but no one seems to have the will to fix it. As if the patience it would require would be seen as weakness.

48   My wife is the black sheep of that family. She has a quick mind, both analytical and imaginative. She has no love for convention and looks easily through hypocrisy of all kinds. She also has big-time Type A tendencies, character traits that make her the choice for many of the organizational and administrative duties in our shared life like paying bills and scheduling the kids' activities.

49   But these proclivities also work against her. The chaotic, unpredictable reality of having two small children threatens and at times overwhelms her compulsion for order. She breaks down. Traveling, with the on-the-fly time-management it requires, makes her crazy. I watched her walk face-first into a glass door at the airport. Another time, near the baggage carousel, she distractedly pushed our son's stroller into another child. The child was seated at the time. A pointless quarrel over a trip to the Home Depot led to her backing out of the driveway and into a parked mail truck one morning.

50   My wife and I need to fix this anger thing. We knew, or should have known, what we were getting into. We signed the contract. Shook on it. Kissed, actually. But I think we missed some of the small print. We wanted kids and had a vague idea that it would involve some work. Well, I have a news flash: It can be really, really hard.

51   And that goes for guys, too. I don't recall being told about spending more money each year than I actually earn, with no exotic vacations, nice cars or fancy anything else to show for it. I wasn't informed that I would give up golf altogether, just as I was pushing my handicap down toward single digits. And I'm certain I was not warned that sex would become a rarer commodity than at any time in the thirty years since I learned to participate in it.

52   But I've gotten used to all that. I do what most men do. I take a deep breath and push ahead, fairly confident that if I can just soldier on, the things I've sacrificed and more will be my reward down the road.

53   I suppose the anger issues in our household loom as large as they do, in part, because of my fervor to confront (defeat) them. It's been a battlefield at times. My wife and I have been mean and fought dirty and we've hurt each other. We need to recognize that and make up our minds to change, no matter how much work it requires.

54   But hey, we're still here. Our children, who we love so dearly, are growing up and every day we can count on the reassuring rhythms of life: the sun rises in the morning, a weather system slips over the Oregon Cascades and blots it out, cats barf up hairballs on the carpet. I'm optimistic. I don't think we've done any permanent damage. I don't think it's anything we can't fix.

55   But that's just me.

Discussion and Writing Questions

1. Reflecting on his wife and other working mothers, Bartels concludes: "To truly empower herself, she will need to find a way to get beyond— on her own, with help, or however—the destructive impulses that the frustrations of modern motherhood can bring out in her." Your response?

2. Bartels suggests that women "of his generation" seem more comfortable expressing anger than women of previous generations did, and he attributes this, in part, to the fact that they have been in the workforce. To what extent do you find this explanation plausible? Explain your answer.

3. Bartels describes his failure to promptly clean the indoor grill, as well as a propensity for leaving dirty underwear on the floor, as typical "domestic lapses" common to men. To what extent does this square with your own observations of male behavior? To what extent do you feel, as Bartels implies, that such behavior cannot be modified?

4. Write a critique of Bartels's argument that, for the sake of their marriage and family, his wife needs to move past her "destructive impulses." Pay particular attention to the persuasive strategies he employs to support his thesis (for example, his use of *ethos*—pp. 151–152). Now respond to his argument. With which of his points do you agree, and with which do you disagree? State your overall conclusion as to the validity of the piece. Follow the principles in Chapter 2.

5. With the goal of suggesting a possible solution to the challenges Bartels and his wife face, evaluate his marriage according to one or more of the principles you have read about in previous selections. If Bartels's grievances are to be assuaged, to what extent do he and his wife need to fundamentally reexamine their assumptions regarding, say, the household division of labor? How much of that change should be Bartels's? How much his wife's?

6. *For women only:* Write a response to Bartels, as if you were his wife.

Two-Timing: Life Lessons from "Big Love"
Michelle Cottle

What most marriages need, observes writer Michelle Cottle in this tongue-in-cheek essay, is someone to fill the void when women work and men won't do the dishes. Someone subservient, and serenely unconcerned with self-fulfillment. Someone like—well, another wife. Michelle Cottle is a senior editor at the New Republic *magazine. Before that, she was an editor of the* Washington Monthly, *and is a regular panelist for the PBS political affairs show* Tucker Carlson Unfiltered. *This essay first appeared in the* New Republic *on May 22, 2006.*

1   As both my husband and I scrambled to meet work deadlines last week—while simultaneously juggling multiple doctors' appointments and assuring our daughter's day care teachers that, yes, one of us would still be able to watch the class for an hour during the monthly staff meeting—it once again struck me: What most modern marriages really need is an extra wife.

2   I've been thinking about this a lot lately in response to all the buzz surrounding HBO's new polygamy-themed hit, "Big Love." Conservatives have taken to brandishing the show as Exhibit A in the fight against gay marriage. That is, once we breach that hard, bright line delineating marriage as the union of one man and one woman, the next thing you know, we'll all be living in multi-spouse chaos, with too many kids, credit card bills, pool toys, cat fights, complex copulation schedules, and Viagra prescriptions for any sane person to keep track of.

3   To a certain extent, I agree (with the criticism of polygamy, not of gay marriage), but largely because "Big Love"'s Henrickson clan has approached this whole multi-spouse business from exactly the wrong angle. As in real life, the show's polygamy—or, more specifically, its polygyny—is wrapped up in the biblical mandate to be fruitful and multiply. As soon as one wife gets too old and run down to breed efficiently, you bring in a new model. But let's face it: No matter how devoutly Pat Robertson wishes it were so, none of us is living in Old Testament times. And the major problem facing the American family today is not a shortage of children.

4   In far too many modern families, however, there is a corrosive shortage of support—of the physical, logistical, and, perhaps most importantly, emotional kinds—once consistently provided by your garden variety housewife. Just look at the ever-growing pile of articles, books, and polls pointing to how much stress and friction couples are suffering in their eternal struggle to balance conflicting work and family duties. Typically, the gist of these discussions is that, if only women could find a way to lighten the domestic load that still tends to fall disproportionately on their shoulders, marital bliss would follow.

5   Maybe. But probably not. Certainly, there's no question that having good child care and a husband who knows his way around the kitchen can make a gal's life easier. And, for those with the financial means, an army of highly competent domestic help can remove most of the sting of housekeeping. Still, no matter how many nannies or housekeepers or personal assistants the more affluent among us employ, at the end of a long day, most of us still won't come home to someone whose primary mission in life is to see to the well-being of our households. Even if the government began issuing every family its own Mary Poppins and men suddenly decided that they desperately wanted to spend their evenings folding laundry and frosting cupcakes for preschool, this still wouldn't address the emotional and spiritual void left by the disappearance of the traditional housewife about which Caitlin Flanagan writes so nostalgically in her recent book *To Hell with All That.*

6   With her unflinching focus on what we lost with the women's movement, Flanagan has drawn heavy fire from many working mommies and their ilk. But the book is so inflammatory in part because of its uncomfortable-but-tough-to-dispute observations. For instance, at the end of a chapter examining our tendency to farm out domestic chores once handled by housewives, Flanagan notes:

"What's missing from so many affluent American households is the one thing you can't buy: the presence of someone who cares deeply and principally about that home and the people who live in it."

7   Of course, it's not only affluent households missing this nurturing figure. Moving down the income ladder, the issue of moms working may be more about economic need than personal fulfillment, but the result is the same. And, before we blame this entire mess on mom's selfish insistence on a career, keep in mind that even today's full-time mommies bear little resemblance to the housewives of yore. As Flanagan points out, just note the difference in nomenclature. A huge chunk of today's "stay-at-home moms" are home because they are utterly devoted to raising perfect, perfectly adjusted children; but, with all the music lessons, soccer practices, and tumbling camps for the kids, they often have as little (maybe even less) time to devote to their houses and marriages as do their working counterparts. In these households, as surely as in those of hard-charging careerist mommies, gone is the kind of woman who greeted her husband at the door each evening with a kiss and a cold martini, assured him that the homefront was under control, and insisted that he tell her all about his day in the trenches.

8   It is into this breach that an extra wife could step. Better still, since the kind of multi-spouse arrangement I'm envisioning isn't about maximizing the number of offspring, one could just as easily have a household with two husbands. Indeed, the key to this brand of polygamy would be to make clear up front that the second-spouse slot was for a woman or man specifically *not* interested in procreating. After all, how could you save labor with two full families' worth of kids but not two full families' worth of parents?

9   Obviously, this kind of life wouldn't be for everyone. The search for a less self-abnegating existence is, after all, what destroyed the institution of housewifery to begin with. But maybe with a bit of clever marketing, you could appeal to men and women looking to indulge their inner domestic goddess—or simply to find stable companionship—without the strain of bearing all the responsibilities of spousehood alone.

10   Despite the obvious advantages of an extra spouse, some couples might be a tad skittish about jumping into anything so permanent as a second marriage. Never fear: For them, I have an alternative solution proffered by a Georgetown student responding to a blog item I recently wrote on this subject. What I seemed to be advocating, noted the student, wasn't a full-fledged second spouse so much as a marital intern—unpaid, naturally, as all good interns are. Now that is *exactly* the kind of outside-the-box thinking my husband and I could use at our house. Just give us a call, kid. We've got a pile of laundry and a defrosted pork roast awaiting your tender ministrations. And we both like our martinis made with gin, not vodka. We're traditional that way.

Discussion and Writing Suggestions

1. Cottle humorously proposes what many would consider a somewhat impractical solution to a pressing domestic problem. In this, she follows

the satirical lead of eighteenth-century satirist Jonathan Swift, who suggested in his "Modest Proposal" that poor Irishwomen unable to support their children could sell them to be cooked as meals for people of quality. Develop your own "modest proposal" to solve another troublesome modern problem.

2. To what extent do you agree with Cottle that the vanishing of the "traditional housewife" left a "spiritual and emotional void" in American households? Explain your answer.

3. Compose a "personal ad" in which you and an imagined spouse advertise for an "extra wife" (or an "extra husband"). Describe the attributes and qualifications you are looking for in an extra mate, what her (or his) expected duties will be, and what compensation you will be prepared to offer her (or him) for the performance of these duties.

Single Minded
Keith O'Brien

In view of the many challenges that attend modern marriage, you may, by this point, be wondering why anyone would want to get married at all! You wouldn't be alone. An increasing number of single Americans are electing to remain that way—single. This phenomenon is nothing new in other countries, such as Italy, where professional men often live with their mothers well into their thirties. (The Italians even have a name for them: "mammoni"— mama's boys.) But in the United States, where marriage remains such an integral part of the American dream, satisfied singles still find themselves in a distinct minority. This article, published in the Boston Globe *on June 4, 2006, describes some of the ways in which unattached Americans cope with their marginalized status in a society of "Couplists" and "Perkytogethers."*

1   They have names for themselves now: Quirkyalone, Modern Spinsters, Marriagefree, and Spinsterellas. Couplists depress them, and even worse are the Perkytogethers, the sort who feed each other in public or make out in movie theaters or hold hands while riding bicycles. "Yes," wrote one Quirkyalone in an online chat room after recently spotting such a four-wheeled spectacle, "I wanted to see the Tyranny of Coupledom take a tumble."

2   This message launched dozens of responses. "I had to vent," wrote the woman who started it all. And who can blame her? Singles can feel subjected to an endless stream of Couplists riding bicycles while holding hands and asking as they pedal by: "So, when are you going to get married?"

3   It is the question that has dogged single people—perhaps more than any other—ever since the invention of the prying mother. But now, tired of being marginalized and scrutinized by a wedded society, unattached Americans are throwing a cultural curveball. They're announcing they're happy just as they are. They're buying houses on their own, having children on their own, and

even planning to retire on their own. Single folks today have what one advertising executive calls a feeling of "growing militancy." And they've got numbers. More than ever before, men and women are living single well into their 30s, 40s, and beyond. It's been estimated that, as early as 2008, a majority of U.S. households will be headed by an unmarried person—a shift that has already taken hold in Massachusetts, Rhode Island, and 15 other states. People continue to marry later in life, especially in this state, and some are opting out altogether, posing Couplists a question of their own: "Why bother?"

4   In 1970, only 7.8 percent of Americans aged 30 to 34 had never married, and 65.4 percent of all men were hitched, as were 59.7 percent of all women. By 2003, the number of never-marrieds aged 30 to 34 had exploded to 27.9 percent. The number of all men who were married had dropped to 55.4 percent, and barely half of all women were wed.

5   Few places are as single-minded as Boston. According to the U.S. Census, a stunning 53.6 percent of all men here have never married, tops in the nation. And the city's women are close behind; more than 45 percent have never walked down the aisle, a figure that trails only Newark and Washington, D.C. In other words, Boston isn't a city that never sleeps; it's a city that sleeps alone or sleeps around, depending on how you look at it.

6   How we got here is the result of countless cultural shifts: the feminist movement, the jump in the divorce rate, the decline of the loveless marriage, and the rise of a soulmate society born of a quaint, high-minded ideal called love. One recent poll found that almost all young adults believe there is someone special out there for them, and they will not settle just to be married. They will wait. And that decision is changing how we define happiness and the need for partners, and it's transforming the look of our neighborhoods. Less than 50 years removed from *Leave It to Beaver*, everyone wants to know what will happen if the tyranny of coupledom finally tumbles.

7   This story, like all good stories about the single life, begins in a cafe, three days before Valentine's Day on the night of the biggest snowstorm of last winter. Nancy Howell couldn't have counted on the blizzard, which by morning would bury Boston in snow. But everything else she could have predicted. Here she was, once again, alone and soon to be without a date on the Couplists' favorite holiday.

8   Howell, a textbook proofreader and Brighton resident, had not planned her life this way. "Thirty," she tells me, "kind of meant I should be settling down. Maybe buying a house, buying a condo." But that milestone birthday came and went in June 2005, and Howell was still unattached and renting. She thought about how, when she was a kid, 30 seemed so old. And how, when her mother was 30, she wasn't only married, she was pregnant. Then Howell thought about her parents' divorce just a few years ago, and she remembered something else about herself: "I have never felt like I needed to be with someone."

9   Howell is not alone in this regard. Hollywood would have us believe that single people are falling over themselves to find a mate, yet the Pew Internet & American Life Project reported in February that 55 percent of single people nationwide have no active interest in seeking a partner. While Pew found that

26 percent of singles are in committed relationships, it also discovered that just 16 percent are actively looking for love—a number that would seem to contradict everything we've ever been told about being single. Happy, uncommitted singles were suddenly everywhere, and not just in the survey. Boston has them. The suburbs have them. Even rural Pittsfield has them. They are men and women, gay and straight.

10   The Pew researchers set out to ask 3,200 people about the significance of Internet dating—not the idea of not dating at all. But in the course of their research they uncovered what Philip Morgan calls "a very interesting phenomenon." Morgan, a Duke University sociology professor who helped prepare the survey, says today, months later, he's still not sure what the answers mean. And he acknowledges that survey subjects may have misinterpreted the questions or fudged the truth. Nonetheless, after years of believing that single people must want to be married, Americans should now consider the possibility that this simply isn't true, Morgan says. The single life, once a way station, is becoming a movement.

11   "This is the future," says Bella DePaulo, an unwed author in Santa Barbara, California, whose book, *Singled Out,* will be published this fall. "People have the option now to stay single and live full lives and be just as, to put it directly, morally significant as married couples." Lobbying groups argue as much. The Alternatives to Marriage Project, founded in Boston and now based in Brooklyn, New York, fought the nomination of Samuel Alito Jr. to the U.S. Supreme Court, saying he has discriminated on the basis of marital status. Unmarried America, formerly known as the American Association for Single People, has opposed tax breaks that favor the married and insurance rates that punish the single. And then there is the group where Nancy Howell finds kinship. She is a Quirkyalone.

12   The word, taken from Sasha Cagen's 2004 book, *Quirkyalone,* is defined as "a person who enjoys being single (but is not opposed to being in a relationship) and generally prefers to be alone rather than date for the sake of being in a couple." Cagen, a 32-year-old writer in San Francisco, came up with the definition to describe herself and later wrote an essay about it in *Utne Reader.* "I thought maybe five people would write me a letter," she says. Instead, Cagen received thousands. "I got letters from prisoners. Mix tapes. Marriage proposals. Everything." An agent called. A book deal followed. A website went up, and thousands of people gathered in virtual reality to vent about Perkytogethers and plan Quirkyalone parties.

13   "Glad to be here among 'kindred spirits,' " Nancy Howell wrote in the Quirkyalone chat room in October 2004, not long after reading Cagen's book. She had found a community, one that even has its own holiday, International Quirkyalone Day, its answer to Valentine's Day.

14   Howell suggested an IQD party for Boston on the website last January. Her message got 400 hits and several replies, and she began planning. They would meet at the Otherside Cafe on Newbury Street the Saturday before Valentine's Day. They would have drinks and make valentines for friends on construction paper, and it would be perfect. Then the blizzard started rolling in, and only three people showed up: Howell, her roommate, and one of their friends.

15   "It bombed," says Howell.

16   *Forbes* magazine consistently ranks Boston as one of the best cities in the country for singles. We have night life. We have culture. We have "coolness," according to the *Forbes* rankings, and smarts, according to the U.S. Census. Boston is ranked in the top 10 most educated cities, and the state is number one when it comes to people with higher degrees. And so, the thinking goes, young educated singles should be able to find plenty of mates or dates, leading to a life of happiness and joy. The end.

17   But this life can be elusive. Many singles who are satisfied now didn't start out that way. They were miserable, depressed, even desperate—everything society told them they should be. Rankings and "coolness" aside, Boston is as hard a place to be single and looking as any other city. Diane Darling, a 47-year-old Cambridge woman, says that in her 30s, finding a man was like holding mercury in her hand: "The tighter I squeezed, the more it slipped through my fingers."

18   Darling had always planned on being married and being a mother. Throughout her 20s and 30s, she bought children's clothes as she traveled overseas. One day, she knew, she would be glad she had that toddler's dress from Italy and the striped jacket from Thailand. But as she approached 40, Darling began to panic.

19   "You're almost out there sperm shopping," she says. "You feel such pressure, and you hate feeling like you're going out there, trying to shop and force something. We all watch the movies, *Sleepless in Seattle,* whatever it may be. We have this idea that it should all fall into place." But it didn't happen that way for Darling. She turned 40 without a husband. She worked for a dot-com that went bust. She had reasons to feel sorry for herself—and then she found success. Darling started a company called Effective Networking Inc. and wrote one book about business networking, then another. She now speaks regularly to executives and young professionals. The woman who spent years gathering kids' clothes now has made peace with not being a mother. "I feel like I'm happier single in my 40s than I was in my 20s and 30s," she says from her Copley Place office. "I think in my 20s and 30s there was a lot of pressure to pair up, and I just never met that person."

20   In another era not so long ago, Darling might have settled. Found a man, any man. Historically, there was nothing wrong with a loveless partnership, wrote Stephanie Coontz in her 2005 book, *Marriage, a History.* Love took a back seat to economics, politics, and, for women, survival. "They needed a man," says Coontz. "They didn't have the luxury of waiting until it was absolutely, perfectly right. They either convinced themselves that the man was absolutely, perfectly right, or they suffered."

21   Today, by and large, that's not the case. Darling can wait, concentrating on her career, and Ayana Meade can do the same. A 30-year-old Brighton resident, Meade recently organized the Boston chapter of the Lunch Club, a group focused on connecting people—mostly singles—with the idea that "eating alone is boring." Meade now works part time planning events for some 800 people, but she says her goal is to start her own online business. And while she does want to get married, she'd like to get the business going first. "My whole philosophy may be a little bit different than others. I think my getting married will depend

on my achieving my goals," she says. But whether she ever achieves those goals or not, one thing is clear for Meade: "I'm certainly not willing to settle. And I think that's what a lot of people do—they settle."

22   More educated, economically self-sufficient, and socially independent, women can afford to be choosy. They can wait for a soul mate, even turn down prospects—and men can, too. But soul mates are harder to find than just any old mates. Love slips through fingers like mercury and leaves many singles searching late into life.

23   Steve Doucette, for example, hasn't given up on marrying. "But it would take one hell of a girl," says the 40-year-old IT professional living in Mansfield. After all, Doucette likes his life. This summer, he plans to finish getting his pilot's license, a dream he's not sure he would have realized with a wife and kids. One day, he says, he may even buy a share of a small plane to fly on weekends to Cape Cod and beyond. Maybe with a woman. Maybe not.

24 Historically, advertisers have ignored people like Darling and Doucette. At best, executives pushing products saw older singles as insignificant and unable to influence others with their purchases. At worst, they were perceived as losers. Even the word "single" suggests that something is missing, says Chip Walker, executive vice president and director of account planning at the Chicago office of BBDO Worldwide. There, working for one of the largest advertising agencies in the world, he has tried over the years to get companies to focus on what he calls "the midlife single." "I have not been successful," admits Walker, who's single himself. The demographic, he explains, was not regarded as "aspirational."

25   Now, ever so slowly, this is beginning to change. As more and more people choose to be single, more and more companies are trying to capture their disposable income. Tom Collinger, a marketing professor at Northwestern University, home of one of the country's top advertising education programs, goes so far as to call today's singles "an absolute zeitgeist." There's De Beers telling women to buy their own diamond rings—the right-hand diamond—and Conde Nast coming out with *Men's Vogue* for guys who pick out their own clothes. In Boston, New York, and other major cities, lifestyle consultants help men do everything from buying shoes to home appliances—things their wives used to do—and single people, especially single women, are buying property in droves.

26   Married couples still account for more than half of recent home buyers nationally. But single women make up the second largest group, at 21 percent nationally and 15 percent across the state, almost triple and double the rate of single men, respectively. Women aren't just buying rings for themselves; they're buying it all.

27   Take Mary Gniadek. Now 46, Gniadek wanted to marry her boyfriend of eight years in 2002, but the timing wasn't right for him. Soon thereafter, in between jobs, she left Malden, where she had lived for 14 years, and moved to Pittsfield, into her parents' house. Gniadek slept in the den of the house for a while, wondering why she wasn't married. "You know how you set goals for yourself?" she asks. "Well, I didn't meet my goal." Here she was, a former Pittsfield High School cheerleader, alone, in her 40s, and living with her parents again.

"You might as well put yourself in a grave," she says. "Bury yourself. . . . It's the truth." But she rebounded. Gniadek, who works in accounts payable, bought a mobile home in a cute middle-class neighborhood in Pittsfield and soon began to worry more about home projects than men.

28   "I'm just having too much fun now. And you know what? I don't have the energy" for the mating game, Gniadek said inside her immaculate home last April. "Somewhere down the road, I don't know when, it'd be nice to find that soul mate and get married to them. But I'm not searching for them like I was when I was younger. I know I can take care of things by myself."

29   While Gniadek plans for retirement, other single homeowners are planning families. Scott Ullrich, 47, a self-employed headhunter who lives in Jamaica Plain, adopted his 12-year-old son, Joey, in January 2005. Ullrich, who is gay, made the decision only after he and his partner split up. He is now planning to adopt a second child.

30   Jennifer Waddell, a publishing company archivist, already has two. Waddell, 43, gave birth to Ralphie and Violet last August after years of fruitless dating. She made a habit, she says, of dating "not nice men" and eventually became "absolutely desperate to be pregnant." She did get pregnant—with the help of doctors, a fertility clinic, and a sperm bank—but then worried if she would really be able to raise twins on her own. She gave birth, held her babies for the first time, and felt what she called "instant love," a love she had never found in a man. "Now every misstep I took, every yucky guy I dated, got me here to these babies," Waddell says, inside the Boston home she bought before the children were born. "Now I don't have any more regrets. No regrets. . . . It's like my life started at 40."

31 In a room this spring in Western Massachusetts, a dozen single people sit on couches in a circle to talk about being alone. Niela Miller, a 71-year-old Acton woman, has led this workshop at the Rowe Camp and Conference Center for some 20 years. In the past, it's been part of an Easter weekend for singles where the goal was meeting a mate. But recently Miller changed the title of her three-day workshop. This year, it's "Being Alive! How to Be Single and Happy."

32   Some in the group are divorced, some widowed, some have never been married, and all of them, to varying extents, are struggling with their singleness. Miller tries to help them find contentment within themselves. "No one's saying it's easy," she tells them. "But it is a choice, and there are skills you can learn if you want to go in that direction." One man, 58 and never married, begins to compare it to *The Wizard of Oz*. Maybe, he says, happiness has been right there with him all along, like Scarecrow's brain or the Lion's courage. Still, he says, "I don't want to live out my life alone."

33   Despite all the changes, single folks still have much to overcome in what they see as a Couplists society. Researchers have found that married people are happier than single people, live longer, and make more money. Meanwhile, cultural critics tell singles they are ruining America with their choices and say a successful society needs men and women to partner up and procreate. George Gilder, the author of 1992's *Men and Marriage* who lives in Western Massachusetts, calls this abandonment of tradition "a great mistake."

34   Yet every indicator suggests the marriage rate will continue to fall. Committed singles will never cause coupledom to tumble—but they surely will earn more acceptance as their numbers grow.

35   On a recent Sunday afternoon, Nancy Howell, the Quirkyalone member, sits in her Brighton apartment with another single friend, Tracy Strauss. The plan: dye a blue streak into Howell's hair. This isn't some moment of youthful angst or punk expression. It is simply something Howell has included on a list of things she must do before turning 31 this month.

36   She came up with the idea for the list last year before she turned 30. She wanted to distract herself from the milestone by forcing herself to do things she had never done before—an idea that worked so well, she decided to do it again this year. On the list: "Read *The Color Purple*. . . . Go to a Chippendales show." And then, number 22: "Put blue streak in my hair."

37   The other tasks have gone well. This one does not. By the time Howell is done with the bottle of dye, there is no blue streak. It's more like her whole head is bluish black, and she and Strauss stand in the bathroom discussing the problem. Howell laughs. She is not troubled. The dye job will fade, other tasks are on her list, she will be all right, and soon she will be on vacation.

38   This weekend, she is in Aruba celebrating her 31st birthday on a beach in the sun. By herself.

Review Questions

1. Cite some of the reasons, according to the article, for the rising number of unmarried Americans.

2. According to the Pew Internet & American Life Project, what percent of unmarried people have no active interest in seeking a partner?

3. What is the second largest group of home buyers nationally, behind married couples?

Discussion and Writing Questions

1. Based on your own observations, how representative are the many satisfied singles that O'Brien interviewed for this article? Do you agree that singlehood is becoming a significant social trend?

2. The article quotes a young woman as saying: "I have never felt like I needed to be with someone." How important it is to you to "be with someone"? (Answer as honestly as you can.) To what extent can you imagine going through life single? What do you imagine would be the disadvantages of such a life? What would be the advantages?

3. The article quotes another person as declaring that she is not willing to "settle" for a spouse that is less than perfectly compatible with her, and that she thinks "that's what a lot of people do—they settle." Based on marriages and relationships you have witnessed, to what extent does

this sentiment square with your own observations? To what extent do you feel that the concept of "settling" reflects an ideal—the soul mate—that may be unrealistic?

4. Many singles, according to O'Brien, see the United States as a "Couplists society." To what extent do you agree—do you see evidence that the social and economic advantages are stacked in favor of couples and against singles? For example, can you recall places, or situations, where singles are made to feel—even if subtly so—unwelcome?

5. Do you know any older singles—perhaps in your own extended family, perhaps among your circle of acquaintances? Assuming that you are reasonably familiar with their circumstances, why are they single? Do you know if they wish to remain single? To what extent do they appear contented with their lives? What conclusions, if any, can you draw from their examples?

SYNTHESIS ACTIVITIES

1. Write an explanatory synthesis focused on the development of the "love match" model of marriage. Why did it emerge? When? How does it differ from previous models? Explain the effect of the rise of the "love match" model on the institution of marriage as a whole. Focus particularly on the effect this model has had on people's expectations of marriage and on who should get married. For your sources, draw upon Graham (in Chapter 1, pages 8–11), Coontz, Popenoe and Whitehead, Schwartz and Scott, Sullivan, Edelman, Bartels, Cottle, and O'Brien. *An option:* As part of an extended conclusion that might be as long as a third of the final paper, explore the role you expect (hope?) love to play in your own marriage. So that your conclusion remains a part of the overall synthesis, let your exploration emerge from your awareness of the historical determinants of the love match. You now know that there have been other models for marriage—the "economic" match, for instance, or the "compatibility" match. As you contemplate your own (prospective) marriage, to what extent will you insist on a love match?

2. Explain the working mother versus stay-at-home mother debate. Focus in particular on the struggles women face as they try to balance the concerns of work versus family. You may also wish to touch upon the issue of housework, as the two issues sometimes overlap. Because this is an *explanatory* synthesis, make sure that your explanation of the varying viewpoints remains objective. Draw primarily upon the selections by Hekker, Story, Stabiner, Clemetson, Shulman, Flanagan, Cottle, and Edelman (as well as Bartels, if you find it relevant).

3. Argue that one parent should—or should not—stop working (at least for a time) when children are born. In formulating your argument, be sure to acknowledge the various arguments on all sides of the issue. Then assert which course of action, overall, would best benefit American families. Draw upon as many of the articles in this chapter as will support your case.

4. In "Work vs. Family, Complicated by Race," Lynette Clemetson argues that the "work-life debate" for professional white women often does not reflect the reality faced by many of their black counterparts. To what extent do you find that some of the problems discussed by the authors in this chapter do not reflect the reality that you have observed or experienced about married couples? Draw, for example, on the selections by Story, Stabiner, Clemetson, Flanagan, Edelman, and Bartels.

5. Devise a blueprint for contemporary wives and husbands to avoid (or at least effectively address) common marital conflicts. First explain elements of your blueprint and then argue for its viability. For example, first explain how best to take care of the children when both parents must work or prefer to work. Then argue that your plan is reasonable. You could do the same for devising a fair division of household labor. In developing this combination explanatory/argument synthesis, consult such sources as Coontz, Popenoe and Whitehead, Story, Stabiner, Clemetson, Shulman, Flanagan, Edelman, Bartels, and Cottle.

6. To what extent is it a good idea for young people to delay getting married until their late twenties or beyond? In supporting your argument for earlier or later marriage, draw upon such sources as Popenoe and Whitehead, Story, Stabiner, Flanagan, Edelman, and Bartels.

7. Compare and contrast Terry Martin Hekker's first essay, on the satisfactions of being a stay-at-home mother, with the Edelman and Shulman selections. How does each of these women feel about her married and family lives? As points of comparison and contrast, consider their attitudes toward housework, their children, their husbands, and their desire for self-fulfillment. In writing your conclusion, consider what factors might have been responsible for these women's differing views on these matters.

8. Analyze a marital relationship—real or fictional—using one or more of the principles in articles from the chapter. (If you have read any Jane Austen novels or Leo Tolstoy's *Anna Karenina* or Gustave Flaubert's *Madame Bovary,* you may wish to use the marriages of characters in those books.) Focus on how the principle you have chosen allows one to better understand the relationship in question. Follow the general format for writing analyses discussed in Chapter 6.

9. Compare and contrast Sullivan's and Bennett's arguments on gay marriage. In particular, focus on the assumptions regarding the nature of marriage that each brings to his argument. (You may want to consider how Sullivan's argument follows from a principle found in the selection by Coontz.)

10. Discuss whether or not, as Eric Bartels writes, "marriage is a creaky, old institution that may not have fully adapted itself to modern life." In supporting your argument, draw upon Hekker, Coontz, Popenoe and Whitehead, Schwartz and Scott, Edelman, Bartels, Cottle, O'Brien, and any of the other selections you think relevant. Follow the general format for writing argument syntheses in Chapter 5.

11. Conduct an analysis of a bridal or newlywed magazine, movie, or television show, guided by a principle you select from one or more selections in this chapter. Use this analytical principle to understand more clearly how popular culture, as expressed in the magazine, movie, or television show you have selected, helps to form, reinforce, or (perhaps) undermine our expectations of marriage. Follow the guidelines in Chapter 6 for writing your analysis.

12. Alix Kates Shulman's "A Marriage Agreement" applies legal language to an intimate domestic issue, creating a juxtaposition that some readers find jarring. Argue that it is appropriate—or inappropriate (perhaps even wildly so)—to expect that a marriage could/should be governed by such a document. For your sources, draw upon Hekker, Flanagan, Edelman, and Bartels.

13. Offer—and explain—the one piece of advice that you would give to someone who is about to get married. In supporting your argument that this is the single most important advice that anybody who is getting married should follow, draw from among the following selections: Hekker, Coontz, Popenoe and Whitehead, Schwartz and Scott, Story, Stabiner, Clemetson, Edelman, Bartels, Cottle, and O'Brien.

RESEARCH ACTIVITIES

1. The *New York Times* article "Many Women at Elite Colleges Set Career Path to Motherhood" inspired the response "Homeward Bound," by Linda Hirshman in *American Prospect* (December 2005). Hirshman argues that, for the good of all women and society in general, every mother should work. Compare and contrast Hirshman's article with the Story, Stabiner, and Flanagan selections.

2. Do an Internet search, using Google or another search engine, for reaction to the Terry Martin Hekker 2006 essay "Paradise Lost (Domestic Division)." Locate mentions of the piece on blogs (try sites dealing with the "Mommy Wars," working mothers, or stay-at-home mothers), in letters to the editor of the *New York Times*, and

in op-ed pieces; then synthesize some of the responses that
Hekker's essay inspired.

3. Find and report on additional articles dealing with the "Mommy
Wars"—the dispute over whether mothers should stay at home to
take care of the children or whether they should pursue careers,
leaving their children with other caregivers. To what extent has the
controversy evolved over the past few years? To what extent does a
critical consensus appear to be forming—perhaps by feminists, perhaps by traditionalists—over what young mothers should do?
Write a synthesis explaining your findings, and, perhaps, arguing
your own position.

4. What is the state of gay marriage in the United States today? How
many states, for example, allow gay marriage? Prohibit gay marriage? How many recognize civil unions? What has been the position of the federal government over the past 15 years? What kinds of
state and federal legislation have been passed (or debated) in recent
years, and what kinds of decisions have been made by state and federal courts in response? What do recent polls about the subject
reveal? Based on your findings, do you believe that the social and
political climate for gay marriage is improving or deteriorating?

5. Research arranged marriages—either in an ethnic subculture in the
United States or in a foreign country. On the whole, how happy do
people report being in these marriages? Provide statistical and/or
anecdotal evidence concerning this rate of satisfaction. Compare
this rate to that of people in nonarranged marriages, preferably in
that same culture—or, if that information is not available, compare
it to the rate of marital satisfaction in our country, as reported by
sources such as the National Marriage Project (<http://marriage
.rutgers.edu/>). If you know people who have been in an arranged
marriage, ask for their views on the subject.

6. While marriage agreements such as Alix Kates Shulman's never
took hold, another sort of contract regarding marriage has become
commonplace—the prenuptial agreement. Research and write an
overview of prenuptial contracts (including, if possible, some of the
more notorious lawsuits they have engendered). Search, in particular, for pieces that express an opinion regarding their use (op-ed
pieces, magazine articles, letters to the editor). You may also wish
to conduct an informal poll among your friends as to whether or
not they approve of their use, whether or not they might insist,
before their own marriage, on a prenuptial contract, etc. Report on
your findings.

7. Investigate the effect that no-fault divorce laws have had on marriage in this country. Write a synthesis summarizing the circumstances under which the states passed such laws, the effect of these
laws on the national divorce rate, and a brief overview of the controversy over the laws and their effect on the institution of marriage.

8. President John Adams and First Lady Abigail Adams had one of the more famous marriages in the history of the presidency. Abigail Adams's letters to her husband, in which she counseled him on matters public and private and in which she was an early advocate for women's issues, are still widely read, and in part form the lyrics for the Broadway musical *1776*. Research John and Abigail Adams's marriage. In which ways was it typical of its time and place? In which ways was it atypical—i.e., in which ways did it seem more like a modern marriage?

9. The 1950s are often considered the "Golden Age" of marriage. When conservative commentators evoke the "good old days" of marriage, it is almost always the 1950s model they have in mind—a father with a good job, a mother who stays home and raises the children, a house in the suburbs, and an extended family that is usually located in another town or even state. Such marriages were the basis of popular contemporary 1950s sitcoms like *Father Knows Best* and *Ozzie and Harriet,* and they were also satirized in the 1998 film *Pleasantville.*

   Research the realities of marriage in the 1950s. (Stephanie Coontz has written extensively on this subject.) To what extent is the stereotype accurate? Was there a "dark side" to marriage in the 1950s? Consider the political, economic, and cultural climate of the 1950s. What effect did these factors have on marriages of the day?

10. Research the issue of day care in this country. Locate studies that have shown positive or negative consequences to putting kids in day care. Draw also upon op-ed pieces, articles, sections in books, or personal opinions you have discovered (for example, on blogs concerning motherhood, working mothers, or stay-at-home mothers), and write a synthesis reporting on your findings.

11. Marriage researcher Andrew Cherlin has noted how weddings, once events controlled by kinship groups or parents, are now increasingly controlled by the couples themselves. One result is that the wedding has become a status symbol—"an important symbol of the partners' personal achievements and a stage in their self-development." Research the wedding industry in this country, which generates over $60 billion annually. On what is all this money being spent? What kinds of services are most popular among clients—and why? Where are people getting married? Examine a bridal magazine. What do you think the industry is *really* selling? Try to find quotations from wedding industry professionals on this topic.

Obedience to Authority

9

Would you obey an order to inflict pain on another person? Most of us, if confronted with this question, would probably be quick to answer: "Never!" Yet if the conclusions of researchers are to be trusted, it is not psychopaths who kill noncombatant civilians in wartime and torture victims in prisons around the world but rather ordinary people following orders. People obey. This is a basic, necessary fact of human society. As psychologist Stanley Milgram has written, "Obedience is as basic an element in the structure of social life as one can point to. Some system of authority is a requirement of all communal living."

The question, then, is not, "Should we obey the orders of an authority figure?" but rather, "To what *extent* should we obey?" Each generation seems to give new meaning to these questions. During the Vietnam War, a number of American soldiers followed a commander's orders and murdered civilians in the hamlet of My Lai. In 1987 former White House military aide Oliver North was prosecuted for illegally diverting money raised by selling arms to Iran—considered by the U.S. government to be a terrorist state—to fund the anticommunist Contra (resistance) fighters in Nicaragua. North's attorneys claimed that he was following the orders of his superiors. And, although North was found guilty,* the judge who sentenced him to perform community service (there was no prison sentence) largely agreed with this defense when he called North a pawn in a larger game played by senior officials in the Reagan administration. In the 1990s the world was horrified by genocidal violence in Rwanda and in the former nation of Yugoslavia. These were civil wars, in which people who had been living for generations as neighbors suddenly, upon the instigation and orders of their leaders, turned upon and slaughtered one another.

Finally, in April 2004, the world (particularly, the Muslim world) was horrified by accounts—and graphic photographs—of the degrading torture and humiliation of Iraqi prisoners at the hands of American soldiers in a Baghdad prison. Among the questions raised by this incident: Were these soldiers obeying orders to "soften up" the prisoners for interrogation? Were they fulfilling the roles of prison guards they thought were expected of them? Were they abusing others because, given the circumstances, they could? President Bush asserted that this kind of abuse "does not reflect the nature of the American people." But as the Milgram and Zimbardo experiments in this chapter demonstrate, we are likely to be unpleasantly surprised by revelations of just what our "nature" really is—not only as Americans but, more fundamentally, as human beings.

---

* In July 1990, North's conviction was overturned on appeal.

In less dramatic ways, conflicts over the extent to which we obey orders surface in everyday life. At one point or another, you may face a moral dilemma at work. Perhaps it will take this form: The boss tells you to overlook File X in preparing a report for a certain client. But you're sure that File X pertains directly to the report and contains information that will alarm the client. What should you do? The dilemmas of obedience also emerge on some campuses with the rite of fraternity or sports-related hazing. Psychologists Janice Gibson and Mika Haritos-Fatouros have made the startling observation that whether the obedience in question involves a pledge's joining a fraternity or a torturer's joining an elite military corps, the *process* by which one acquiesces to a superior's order (and thereby becomes a member of the group) is remarkably the same:

> There are several ways to teach people to do the unthinkable, and we have developed a model to explain how they are used. We have also found that college fraternities, although they are far removed from the grim world of torture and violent combat, use similar methods for initiating new members, to ensure their faithfulness to the fraternity's rules and values. However, this unthinking loyalty can sometimes lead to dangerous actions: Over the past 10 years, there have been countless injuries during fraternity initiations and 39 deaths. These training techniques are designed to instill obedience in people, but they can easily be a guide for an intensive course in torture.

1. *Screening to find the best prospects:*
   - Normal, well-adjusted people with the physical, intellectual, and, in some cases, political attributes necessary for the task.
2. *Techniques to increase binding among these prospects:*
   - Initiation rites to isolate people from society and introduce them to a new social order, with different rules and values.
   - Elitist attitudes and "in-group" language, which highlight the differences between the group and the rest of society.
3. *Techniques to reduce the strain of obedience:*
   - Blaming and dehumanizing the victims, so it is less disturbing to harm them.
   - Harassment, the constant physical and psychological intimidation that prevents logical thinking and promotes the instinctive responses needed for acts of inhuman cruelty.
   - Rewards for obedience and punishments for not cooperating.
   - Social modeling by watching other group members commit violent acts and then receive rewards.
   - Systematic desensitization to repugnant acts by gradual exposure to them, so they appear routine and normal despite conflicts with previous moral standards.*

---

* Janice T. Gibson and Mika Haritos-Fatouros, "The Education of a Torturer," *Psychology Today* November 1986. Reprinted with permission from *Psychology Today Magazine.* Copyright 1986 Sussex Publishers, Inc.

Many of these processes appear to have been at work in the Iraqi prison scandal.

In this chapter, you will explore the dilemmas inherent in obeying the orders of an authority. First, psychologist Solomon Asch describes an experiment he devised to demonstrate the powerful influence of group pressure upon individual judgment. Psychologist Stanley Milgram then reports on his own landmark study in which he set out to determine the extent to which ordinary individuals would obey the clearly immoral orders of an authority figure. The results were shocking, not only to the psychiatrists who predicted that few people would follow such orders but also to many other social scientists—some of whom applauded Milgram for his fiendishly ingenious design, some of whom bitterly attacked him for unethical procedures. We include one of these attacks, a scathing review by psychologist Diana Baumrind. Another, and later, perspective on the reaction to Milgram's experiment, and on the effect of this experiment on Milgram's own career, is provided by British writer Ian Parker in his essay "Obedience."

Next, Philip Zimbardo reports on his famous—and equally controversial— Stanford Prison Experiment, in which volunteers exhibited astonishingly convincing authoritarian and obedient attitudes as they playacted at being prisoners and guards. Psychoanalyst and philosopher Erich Fromm then discusses the comforts of obedient behavior in "Disobedience as a Psychological and Moral Problem." In "Uncivil Disobedience: Violating the Rules for Breaking the Law," James J. Lopach and Jean A. Luckowski apply the standards of such famous civil disobedience practitioners as Mohandas Gandhi and Martin Luther King, Jr., to more contemporary acts of protest, including environmental activism. They conclude that many such activities fail to qualify as true civil disobedience. Finally, in his modern version of the Greek tragedy *Antigone,* the French playwright Jean Anouilh explores the recurring conflict between individual conscience and the authority of the state.

Opinions and Social Pressure
Solomon E. Asch

In the early 1950s, Solomon Asch (1907–1996), a social psychologist at Rutgers University, conducted a series of simple but ingenious experiments on the influence of group pressure upon the individual. Essentially, he discovered, individuals can be influenced by groups to deny the evidence of their own senses. Together with the Milgram experiments of the next decade (see the selections that follow here), these studies provide powerful evidence of the degree to which individuals can surrender their own judgment to others, even when those others are clearly in the wrong. The results of these experiments have implications far beyond the laboratory: They can explain a good deal of the normal human behavior we see every day—at school, at work, at home.

1   That social influences shape every person's practices, judgments, and beliefs is a truism to which anyone will readily assent. A child masters his "native" dialect down to the finest nuances; a member of a tribe of cannibals accepts cannibalism as altogether fitting and proper. All the social sciences take their departure from the observation of the profound effects that groups exert on their members. For psychologists, group pressure upon the mind of the individual raises a host of questions they would like to investigate in detail.

2   How, and to what extent, do social forces constrain people's opinions and attitudes? This question is especially pertinent in our day. The same epoch that has witnessed the unprecedented technical extension of communication has also brought into existence the deliberate manipulation of opinion and the "engineering of consent." There are many good reasons why, as citizens and as scientists, we should be concerned with studying the ways in which human beings form their opinions and the role that social conditions play.

3   Studies of these questions began with the interest in hypnosis aroused by the French physician Jean Martin Charcot (a teacher of Sigmund Freud) toward the end of the 19th century. Charcot believed that only hysterical patients could be fully hypnotized, but this view was soon challenged by two other physicians, Hyppolyte Bernheim and A. A. Liébault, who demonstrated that they could put most people under hypnotic spell. Bernheim proposed that hypnosis was but an extreme form of a normal psychological process which became known as "suggestibility." It was shown that monotonous reiteration of instructions could induce in normal persons in the waking state involuntary bodily changes such as swaying or rigidity of the arms, and sensations such as warmth and odor.

4   It was not long before social thinkers seized upon these discoveries as a basis for explaining numerous social phenomena, from the spread of opinion to the formation of crowds and the following of leaders. The sociologist Gabriel Tarde summed it all up in the aphorism: "Social man is a somnambulist."

5   When the new discipline of social psychology was born at the beginning of this century, its first experiments were essentially adaptations of the suggestion demonstration. The technique generally followed a simple plan. The subjects, usually college students, were asked to give their opinions or preferences concerning various matters; some time later they were again asked to state their choices, but now they were also informed of the opinions held by authorities or large groups of their peers on the same matters. (Often the alleged consensus was fictitious.) Most of these studies had substantially the same result: confronted with opinions contrary to their own, many subjects apparently shifted their judgments in the direction of the views of the majorities or the experts. The late psychologist Edward L. Thorndike reported that he had succeeded in modifying the esthetic preferences of adults by this procedure. Other psychologists reported that people's evaluations of the merit of a literary passage could be raised or lowered by ascribing the passage to different authors. Apparently the sheer weight of numbers or authority sufficed to change opinions, even when no arguments for the opinions themselves were provided.

6   Now the very ease of success in these experiments arouses suspicion. Did the subjects actually change their opinions, or were the experimental victories

scored only on paper? On grounds of common sense, one must question whether opinions are generally as watery as these studies indicate. There is some reason to wonder whether it was not the investigators who, in their enthusiasm for a theory, were suggestible, and whether the ostensibly gullible subjects were not providing answers which they thought good subjects were expected to give.

7 The investigations were guided by certain underlying assumptions, which today are common currency and account for much that is thought and said about the operations of propaganda and public opinion. The assumptions are that people submit uncritically and painlessly to external manipulation by suggestion or prestige, and that any given idea or value can be "sold" or "unsold" without reference to its merits. We should be skeptical, however, of the supposition that the power of social pressure necessarily implies uncritical submission to it: independence and the capacity to rise above group passion are also open to human beings. Further, one may question on psychological grounds whether it is possible as a rule to change a person's judgment of a situation or an object without first changing his knowledge or assumptions about it.

8 In what follows I shall describe some experiments in an investigation of the effects of group pressure which was carried out recently with the help of a number of my associates. The tests not only demonstrate the operations of group pressure upon individuals but also illustrate a new kind of attack on the problem and some of the more subtle questions that it raises.

9 A group of seven to nine young men, all college students, are assembled in a classroom for a "psychological experiment" in visual judgment. The experimenter informs them that they will be comparing the lengths of lines. He shows two large white cards [see Figure 1]. On one is a single vertical black line—the standard whose length is to be matched. On the other card are three vertical lines of various lengths. The subjects are to choose the one that is of the same length as the line on the other card. One of the three actually is of the same length; the other two are substantially different, the difference ranging from three quarters of an inch to an inch and three quarters.

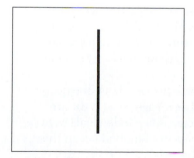
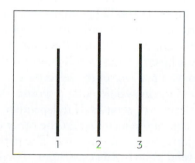

FIGURE 1   Subjects were shown two cards. One bore a standard line. The other bore three lines, one of which was the same length as the standard. The subjects were asked to choose this line.

10   The experiment opens uneventfully. The subjects announce their answers in the order in which they have been seated in the room, and on the first round every person chooses the same matching line. Then a second set of cards is exposed; again the group is unanimous. The members appear ready to endure politely another boring experiment. On the third trial there is an unexpected disturbance. One person near the end of the group disagrees with all the others in his selection of the matching line. He looks surprised, indeed incredulous, about the disagreement. On the following trial he disagrees again, while the others remain unanimous in their choice. The dissenter becomes more and more worried and hesitant as the disagreement continues in succeeding trials; he may pause before announcing his answer and speak in a low voice, or he may smile in an embarrassed way.

11   What the dissenter does not know is that all the other members of the group were instructed by the experimenter beforehand to give incorrect answers in unanimity at certain points. The single individual who is not a party to this pre-arrangement is the focal subject of our experiment. He is placed in a position in which, while he is actually giving the correct answers, he finds himself unexpectedly in a minority of one, opposed by a unanimous and arbitrary majority with respect to a clear and simple fact. Upon him we have brought to bear two opposed forces: the evidence of his senses and the unanimous opinion of a group of his peers. Also, he must declare his judgments in public, before a majority which has also stated its position publicly.

12   The instructed majority occasionally reports correctly in order to reduce the possibility that the naive subject will suspect collusion against him. (In only a few cases did the subject actually show suspicion; when this happened, the experiment was stopped and the results were not counted.) There are 18 trials in each series, and on 12 of these the majority responds erroneously.

13   How do people respond to group pressure in this situation? I shall report first the statistical results of a series in which a total of 123 subjects from three institutions of higher learning (not including my own Swarthmore College) were placed in the minority situation described above.

14   Two alternatives were open to the subject: he could act independently, repudiating the majority, or he could go along with the majority, repudiating the evidence of his senses. Of the 123 put to the test, a considerable percentage yielded to the majority. Whereas in ordinary circumstances individuals matching the lines will make mistakes less than 1 per cent of the time, under group pressure the minority subjects swung to acceptance of the misleading majority's wrong judgments in 36.8 per cent of the selections.

15   Of course individuals differed in response. At one extreme, about one quarter of the subjects were completely independent and never agreed with the erroneous judgments of the majority. At the other extreme, some individuals went with the majority nearly all the time. The performances of individuals in this experiment tend to be highly consistent. Those who strike out on the path of independence do not, as a rule, succumb to the majority even over an extended series of trials, while those who choose the path of compliance are unable to free themselves as the ordeal is prolonged.

16   The reasons for the startling individual differences have not yet been investigated in detail. At this point we can only report some tentative generalizations from talks with the subjects, each of whom was interviewed at the end of the experiment. Among the independent individuals were many who held fast because of staunch confidence in their own judgment. The most significant fact about them was not absence of responsiveness to the majority but a capacity to recover from doubt and to reestablish their equilibrium. Others who acted independently came to believe that the majority was correct in its answers, but they continued their dissent on the simple ground that it was their obligation to call the play as they saw it.

17   Among the extremely yielding persons we found a group who quickly reached the conclusion: "I am wrong, they are right." Others yielded in order "not to spoil your results." Many of the individuals who went along suspected that the majority were "sheep" following the first responder, or that the majority were victims of an optical illusion; nevertheless, these suspicions failed to free them at the moment of decision. More disquieting were the reactions of subjects who construed their difference from the majority as a sign of some general deficiency in themselves, which at all costs they must hide. On this basis they desperately tried to merge with the majority, not realizing the longer-range consequences to themselves. All the yielding subjects underestimated the frequency with which they conformed.

18   Which aspect of the influence of a majority is more important—the size of the majority or its unanimity? The experiment was modified to examine this question. In one series the size of the opposition was varied from one to 15 persons. The results showed a clear trend. When a subject was confronted with only a single individual who contradicted his answers, he was swayed little: he continued to answer independently and correctly in nearly all trials. When the opposition was increased to two, the pressure became substantial: minority subjects now accepted the wrong answer 13.6 per cent of the time. Under the pressure of a majority of three, the subjects' errors jumped to 31.8 per cent. But further increases in the size of the majority apparently did not increase the weight of the pressure substantially. Clearly the size of the opposition is important only up to a point.

19   Disturbance of the majority's unanimity had a striking effect. In this experiment the subject was given the support of a truthful partner—either another individual who did not know of the prearranged agreement among the rest of the group, or a person who was instructed to give correct answers throughout.

20   The presence of a supporting partner depleted the majority of much of its power. Its pressure on the dissenting individual was reduced to one fourth: that is, subjects answered incorrectly only one fourth as often as under the pressure of a unanimous majority. The weakest persons did not yield as readily. Most interesting were the reactions to the partner. Generally the feeling toward him was one of warmth and closeness; he was credited with inspiring confidence. However, the subjects repudiated the suggestion that the partner decided them to be independent.

21   Was the partner's effect a consequence of his dissent, or was it related to his accuracy? We now introduced into the experimental group a person who was instructed to dissent from the majority but also to disagree with the subject. In some experiments the majority was always to choose the worst of the comparison lines and the instructed dissenter to pick the line that was closer to the length of the standard one; in others the majority was consistently intermediate and the dissenter most in error. In this manner we were able to study the relative influence of "compromising" and "extremist" dissenters.

22   Again the results are clear. When a moderate dissenter is present the effect of the majority on the subject decreases by approximately one third, and extremes of yielding disappear. Moreover, most of the errors the subjects do make are moderate, rather than flagrant. In short, the dissenter largely controls the choice of errors. To this extent the subjects broke away from the majority even while bending to it.

23   On the other hand, when the dissenter always chose the line that was more flagrantly different from the standard, the results were of quite a different kind. The extremist dissenter produced a remarkable freeing of the subjects; their errors dropped to only 9 percent. Furthermore, all the errors were of the moderate variety. We were able to conclude that dissents *per se* increased independence and moderated the errors that occurred, and that the direction of dissent exerted consistent effects.

24   In all the foregoing experiments each subject was observed only in a single setting. We now turned to studying the effects upon a given individual of a change in the situation to which he was exposed. The first experiment examined the consequences of losing or gaining a partner. The instructed partner began by answering correctly on the first six trials. With his support the subject usually resisted pressure from the majority: 18 of 27 subjects were completely independent. But after six trials the partner joined the majority. As soon as he did so, there was an abrupt rise in the subjects' errors. Their submission to the majority was just about as frequent as when the minority subject was opposed by a unanimous majority throughout.

25   It was surprising to find that the experience of having had a partner and of having braved the majority opposition with him had failed to strengthen the individuals' independence. Questioning at the conclusion of the experiment suggested that we had overlooked an important circumstance; namely, the strong specific effect of "desertion" by the partner to the other side. We therefore changed the conditions so that the partner would simply leave the group at the proper point. (To allay suspicion it was announced in advance that he had an appointment with the dean.) In this form of the experiment, the partner's effect outlasted his presence. The errors increased after his departure, but less markedly than after a partner switched to the majority.

26   In a variant of this procedure the trials began with the majority unanimously giving correct answers. Then they gradually broke away until on the sixth trial the naive subject was alone and the group unanimously against him. As long as the subject had anyone on his side, he was almost invariably independent,

but as soon as he found himself alone, the tendency to conform to the majority rose abruptly.

27   As might be expected, an individual's resistance to group pressure in these experiments depends to a considerable degree on how wrong the majority was. We varied the discrepancy between the standard line and the other lines systematically, with the hope of reaching a point where the error of the majority would be so glaring that every subject would repudiate it and choose independently. In this we regretfully did not succeed. Even when the difference between the lines was seven inches, there were still some who yielded to the error of the majority.

28   The study provides clear answers to a few relatively simple questions, and it raises many others that await investigation. We would like to know the degree of consistency of persons in situations which differ in content and structure. If consistency of independence or conformity in behavior is shown to be a fact, how is it functionally related to qualities of character and personality? In what ways is independence related to sociological or cultural conditions? Are leaders more independent than other people, or are they adept at following their followers? These and many other questions may perhaps be answerable by investigations of the type described here.

29   Life in society requires consensus as an indispensable condition. But consensus, to be productive, requires that each individual contribute independently out of his experience and insight. When consensus comes under the dominance of conformity, the social process is polluted and the individual at the same time surrenders the powers on which his functioning as a feeling and thinking being depends. That we have found the tendency to conformity in our society so strong that reasonably intelligent and well-meaning young people are willing to call white black is a matter of concern. It raises questions about our ways of education and about the values that guide our conduct.

30   Yet anyone inclined to draw too pessimistic conclusions from this report would do well to remind himself that the capacities for independence are not to be underestimated. He may also draw some consolation from a further observation: those who participated in this challenging experiment agreed nearly without exception that independence was preferable to conformity.

Review Questions

1. What is "suggestibility"? How is this phenomenon related to social pressure?

2. Summarize the procedure and results of the Asch experiment. What conclusions does Asch draw from these results?

3. To what extent did varying the size of the majority and its unanimity affect the experimental results?

4. What distinction does Asch draw between consensus and conformity?

Discussion and Writing Suggestions

1. Before discussing the experiment, Asch considers how easily people's opinions or attitudes may be shaped by social pressure. To what extent do you agree with this conclusion? Write a short paper on this subject, drawing upon examples from your own experience or observation or from your reading.

2. Do the results of this experiment surprise you? Or do they confirm facts about human behavior that you had already suspected, observed, or experienced? Explain, in two or three paragraphs. Provide examples, relating these examples to features of the Asch experiment.

3. Frequently, the conclusions drawn from a researcher's experimental results are challenged on the basis that laboratory conditions do not accurately reflect the complexity of human behavior. Asch draws certain conclusions about the degree to which individuals are affected by group pressures based on an experiment involving subjects choosing matching line lengths. To what extent, if any, do you believe that these conclusions lack validity because the behavior at the heart of the experiment is too dissimilar to real-life situations of group pressure on the individual? Support your opinions with examples.

4. We are all familiar with the phenomenon of "peer pressure." To what extent do Asch's experiments demonstrate the power of peer pressure? To what extent do you think that other factors may be at work? Explain, providing examples.

5. Asch's experiments, conducted in the early 1950s, involved groups of "seven to nine young men, all college students." To what extent do you believe that the results of a similar experiment would be different today? To what extent might they be different if the subjects had included women, as well, and subjects of various ages, from children, to middle-aged people, to older people? To what extent do you believe that the social class or culture of the subjects might have an impact upon the experimental results? Support your opinions with examples and logical reasoning. (Beware, however, of overgeneralizing, based upon insufficient evidence.)

The Perils of Obedience
Stanley Milgram

In 1963, a Yale psychologist conducted one of the classic studies on obedience. Stanley Milgram designed an experiment that forced participants either to violate their conscience by obeying the immoral demands of an authority figure or to refuse those demands.

Surprisingly, Milgram found that few participants could resist the authority's orders, even when the participants knew that following these orders would result in another person's pain. Were the participants in these experiments incipient mass murderers? No, said Milgram. They were "ordinary people, simply doing their jobs." The implications of Milgram's conclusions are immense.

Consider these questions: Where does evil reside? What sort of people were responsible for the Holocaust, and for the long list of other atrocities that seem to blight the human record in every generation? Is it a lunatic fringe, a few sick but powerful people who are responsible for atrocities? If so, then we decent folk needn't ever look inside ourselves to understand evil since (by our definition) evil lurks out there, in "those sick ones." Milgram's study suggested otherwise: that under a special set of circumstances the obedience we naturally show authority figures can transform us into agents of terror.

The article that follows is one of the longest in this book, and it may help you to know in advance the author's organization. In paragraphs 1–11, Milgram discusses the larger significance and the history of dilemmas involving obedience to authority; he then summarizes his basic experimental design and follows with a report of one experiment. Milgram organizes the remainder of his article into sections, which he has subtitled "An Unexpected Outcome," "Peculiar Reactions," "The Etiquette of Submission," and "Duty Without Conflict." He begins his conclusion in paragraph 108. If you find the article too long or complex to complete in a single sitting, then plan to read sections at a time, taking notes on each until you're done. Anticipate the article that immediately follows this one: It reviews Milgram's work and largely concerns the ethics of his experimental design. Consider these ethics as you read so that you, in turn, can respond to Milgram's critics.

Stanley Milgram (1933–1984) taught and conducted research at Yale and Harvard Universities and at the Graduate Center, City University of New York. He was named Guggenheim Fellow in 1972–1973 and a year later was nominated for the National Book Award for Obedience to Authority. *His other books include* Television and Antisocial Behavior *(1973),* The City and the Self *(1974),* Human Aggression *(1976), and* The Individual in the Social World *(1977).*

1   Obedience is as basic an element in the structure of social life as one can point to. Some system of authority is a requirement of all communal living, and it is only the person dwelling in isolation who is not forced to respond, with defiance or submission, to the commands of others. For many people, obedience is a deeply ingrained behavior tendency, indeed a potent impulse overriding training in ethics, sympathy, and moral conduct.

2   The dilemma inherent in submission to authority is ancient, as old as the story of Abraham, and the question of whether one should obey when commands conflict with conscience has been argued by Plato, dramatized in *Antigone*, and treated to philosophic analysis in almost every historical epoch. Conservative philosophers argue that the very fabric of society is threatened by disobedience, while humanists stress the primacy of the individual conscience.

3   The legal and philosophic aspects of obedience are of enormous import, but they say very little about how most people behave in concrete situations. I set up a simple experiment at Yale University to test how much pain an ordinary citizen would inflict on another person simply because he was ordered to by an experimental sci-

entist. Stark authority was pitted against the subjects' strongest moral imperatives against hurting others, and with the subjects' ears ringing with the screams of the victims, authority won more often than not. The extreme willingness of adults to go to almost any lengths on the command of an authority constitutes the chief finding of the study and the fact most urgently demanding explanation.

4   In the basic experimental design, two people come to a psychology laboratory to take part in a study of memory and learning. One of them is designated as a "teacher" and the other a "learner." The experimenter explains that the study is concerned with the effects of punishment on learning. The learner is conducted into a room, seated in a kind of miniature electric chair; his arms are strapped to prevent excessive movement, and an electrode is attached to his wrist. He is told that he will be read lists of simple word pairs, and that he will then be tested on his ability to remember the second word of a pair when he hears the first one again. Whenever he makes an error, he will receive electric shocks of increasing intensity.

5   The real focus of the experiment is the teacher. After watching the learner being strapped into place, he is seated before an impressive shock generator. The instrument panel consists of thirty level switches set in a horizontal line. Each switch is clearly labeled with a voltage designation ranging from 15 to 450 volts. The following designations are clearly indicated for groups of four switches, going from left to right: Slight Shock, Moderate Shock, Strong Shock, Very Strong Shock, Intense Shock, Extreme Intensity Shock, Danger: Severe Shock. (Two switches after this last designation are simply marked XXX.)

6   When a switch is depressed, a pilot light corresponding to each switch is illuminated in bright red; an electric buzzing is heard; a blue light, labeled "voltage energizer," flashes; the dial on the voltage meter swings to the right; and various relay clicks sound off.

7   The upper left-hand corner of the generator is labeled SHOCK GENERATOR, TYPE ZLB, DYSON INSTRUMENT COMPANY, WALTHAM, MASS. OUTPUT 15 VOLTS— 450 VOLTS.

8   Each subject is given a sample 45-volt shock from the generator before his run as teacher, and the jolt strengthens his belief in the authenticity of the machine.

9   The teacher is a genuinely naive subject who has come to the laboratory for the experiment. The learner, or victim, is actually an actor who receives no shock at all. The point of the experiment is to see how far a person will proceed in a concrete and measurable situation in which he is ordered to inflict increasing pain on a protesting victim.

10   Conflict arises when the man receiving the shock begins to show that he is experiencing discomfort. At 75 volts, he grunts; at 120 volts, he complains loudly; at 150, he demands to be released from the experiment. As the voltage increases, his protests become more vehement and emotional. At 285 volts, his response can be described only as an agonized scream. Soon thereafter, he makes no sound at all.

11   For the teacher, the situation quickly becomes one of gripping tension. It is not a game for him; conflict is intense and obvious. The manifest suffering of the learner presses him to quit; but each time he hesitates to administer a shock,

the experimenter orders him to continue. To extricate himself from this plight, the subject must make a clear break with authority.*

12   The subject, Gretchen Brandt,† is an attractive thirty-one-year-old medical technician who works at the Yale Medical School. She had emigrated from Germany five years before.

13   On several occasions when the learner complains, she turns to the experimenter coolly and inquires, "Shall I continue?" She promptly returns to her task when the experimenter asks her to do so. At the administration of 210 volts, she turns to the experimenter, remarking firmly, "Well, I'm sorry, I don't think we should continue."

14   EXPERIMENTER: The experiment requires that you go on until he has learned all the word pairs correctly.

15   BRANDT: He has a heart condition. I'm sorry. He told you that before.

16   EXPERIMENTER: The shocks may be painful but they are not dangerous.

17   BRANDT: Well, I'm sorry, I think when shocks continue like this, they *are* dangerous. You ask him if he wants to get out. It's his free will.

18   EXPERIMENTER: It is absolutely essential that we continue. . . .

19   BRANDT: I'd like you to ask him. We came here of our free will. If he wants to continue I'll go ahead. He told you he had a heart condition. I'm sorry. I don't want to be responsible for anything happening to him. I wouldn't like it for me either.

20   EXPERIMENTER: You have no other choice.

21   BRANDT: I think we are here on our own free will. I don't want to be responsible if anything happens to him. Please understand that.

22   She refuses to go further and the experiment is terminated.

23   The woman is firm and resolute throughout. She indicates in the interview that she was in no way tense or nervous, and this corresponds to her controlled appearance during the experiment. She feels that the last shock she administered to the learner was extremely painful and reiterates that she "did not want to be responsible for any harm to him."

24   The woman's straightforward, courteous behavior in the experiment, lack of tension, and total control of her own action seem to make disobedience a simple and rational deed. Her behavior is the very embodiment of what I envisioned would be true for almost all subjects.

An Unexpected Outcome

25 Before the experiments, I sought predictions about the outcome from various kinds of people—psychiatrists, college sophomores, middle-class adults, graduate students, and faculty in the behavioral sciences. With remarkable similarity, they predicted that virtually all subjects would refuse to obey the

---

* The ethical problems of carrying out an experiment of this sort are too complex to be dealt with here, but they receive extended treatment in the book from which this article is adapted.

† Names of subjects described in this piece have been changed.

experimenter. The psychiatrists, specifically, predicted that most subjects would not go beyond 150 volts, when the victim makes his first explicit demand to be freed. They expected that only 4 percent would reach 300 volts, and that only a pathological fringe of about one in a thousand would administer the highest shock on the board.

26   These predictions were unequivocally wrong. Of the forty subjects in the first experiment, twenty-five obeyed the orders of the experimenter to the end, punishing the victim until they reached the most potent shock available on the generator. After 450 volts were administered three times, the experimenter called a halt to the session. Many obedient subjects then heaved sighs of relief, mopped their brows, rubbed their fingers over their eyes, or nervously fumbled cigarettes. Others displayed only minimal signs of tension from beginning to end.

27   When the very first experiments were carried out, Yale undergraduates were used as subjects, and about 60 percent of them were fully obedient. A colleague of mine immediately dismissed these findings as having no relevance to "ordinary" people, asserting that Yale undergraduates are a highly aggressive, competitive bunch who step on each other's necks on the slightest provocation. He assured me that when "ordinary" people were tested, the results would be quite different. As we moved from the pilot studies to the regular experimental series, people drawn from every stratum of New Haven life came to be employed in the experiment: professionals, white-collar workers, unemployed persons, and industrial workers. *The experiment's total outcome was the same as we had observed among the students.*

28   Moreover, when the experiments were repeated in Princeton, Munich, Rome, South Africa, and Australia, the level of obedience was invariably somewhat *higher* than found in the investigation reported in this article. Thus one scientist in Munich found 85 percent of his subjects to be obedient.

29   Fred Prozi's reactions, if more dramatic than most, illuminate the conflicts experienced by others in less visible form. About fifty years old and unemployed at the time of the experiment, he has a good-natured, if slightly dissolute, appearance, and he strikes people as a rather ordinary fellow. He begins the session calmly but becomes tense as it proceeds. After delivering the 180-volt shock, he pivots around in his chair and, shaking his head, addresses the experimenter in agitated tones:

30   PROZI: I can't stand it. I'm not going to kill that man in there. You hear him hollering?

31   EXPERIMENTER: As I told you before, the shocks may be painful, but . . .

32   PROZI: But he's hollering. He can't stand it. What's going to happen to him?

33   EXPERIMENTER (*his voice patient, matter-of-fact*): The experiment requires that you continue, Teacher.

34   PROZI: Aaah, but unh, I'm not going to get that man sick in there—know what I mean?

35   EXPERIMENTER: Whether the learner likes it or not, we must go on, through all the word pairs.

36   PROZI: I refuse to take the responsibility. He's in there hollering!

37 EXPERIMENTER: It's absolutely essential that you continue, Prozi.

38 PROZI (*indicating the unused questions*): There's too many left here. I mean, Jeez, if he gets them wrong, there's too many of them left. I mean, who's going to take the responsibility if anything happens to that gentleman?

39 EXPERIMENTER: I'm responsible for anything that happens to him. Continue, please.

40 PROZI: All right. (*Consults list of words.*) The next one's "Slow—walk, truck, dance, music." Answer, please (*A buzzing sound indicates the learner has signaled his answer.*) Wrong. A hundred and ninety-five volts. "Dance." (*Zzumph!*)

41 LEARNER (*yelling*): Let me out of here! My heart's bothering me! (*Teacher looks at experimenter.*)

42 EXPERIMENTER: Continue, please.

43 LEARNER (*screaming*): Let me out of here! You have no right to keep me here! Let me out of here, my heart's bothering me, let me out!

44 PROZI (*shakes head, pats the table nervously*): You see, he's hollering. Hear that? Gee, I don't know.

45 EXPERIMENTER: The experiment requires . . .

46 PROZI (*interrupting*): I know it does, sir, but I mean—hunh! He don't know what he's getting in for. He's up to 195 volts! (*Experiment continues, through 210 volts, 225 volts, 240 volts, 255 volts, 270 volts, at which point Prozi, with evident relief, runs out of word-pair questions.*)

47 EXPERIMENTER: You'll have to go back to the beginning of that page and go through them again until he's learned them all correctly.

48 PROZI: Aw, no. I'm not going to kill that man. You mean I've got to keep going up with the scale? No sir. He's hollering in there. I'm not going to give him 450 volts.

49 EXPERIMENTER: The experiment requires that you go on.

50 LEARNER: Ohhh. I absolutely refuse to answer anymore. (*Shouting urgently now.*) Let me out of here! You can't hold me here! Get me out. Get-me-out-of-here!

51 EXPERIMENTER: Continue. The next word is "Green," please.

52 PROZI: "Green—grass, hat, ink, apple." (*Nothing happens. No answering buzz. Just gloomy silence.*)

53 PROZI: I don't think he is going to answer.

54 EXPERIMENTER: If the learner doesn't answer in a reasonable time, about four or five seconds, consider the answer wrong. And follow the same procedures you have been doing for wrong answers. Say, "Wrong," tell him the number of volts, give him the punishment, read him the correct answer. Continue, please.

55 PROZI: "Green—grass, hat, ink, apple." Answer, please. (*More silence. Subject just sits there.*)

56 EXPERIMENTER: Go on with the procedure, please.

57 PROZI: Three hundred and fifteen volts. The answer is "ink." (*Zzumph!*)

58 LEARNER: Ohh. Ooohh.

59 PROZI (*relieved to hear response*): Next one . . .

60 LEARNER: I absolutely refuse to answer.

61   PROZI: You got to. You get a shock if you don't answer. (*Experiment continues with learner refusing to answer, and finally, failing even to grunt or groan. At 375 volts, the subject stands up.*)

62   PROZI: I think something's happened to that fellow in there. I don't get no answer. He was hollering at less voltage. Can't you check in and see if he's all right, please?

63   EXPERIMENTER (*with same detached calm*): Not once we've started. Please continue, Teacher.

64   PROZI (*sits down, sighs deeply*): "Cool—day, shade, water, paint." Answer, please. Are you all right in there? Are you all right?

65   EXPERIMENTER: Please continue, Teacher. Continue, please. (*Subject pushes lever. Zzumph!*)

66   PROZI (*swiveling around in his chair*): Something's happened to that man in there. (*Swiveling back.*) Next one. "Low—dollar, necklace, moon, paint." (*Turning around again.*) Something's happened to that man in there. You better check on him, sir. He won't answer or nothing.

67   EXPERIMENTER: Continue. Go on, please.

68   PROZI: You accept all responsibility?

69   EXPERIMENTER: The responsibility is mine. Correct. Please go on. (*Subject returns to his list, starts running through words as rapidly as he can read them, works through to 450 volts.*)

70   PROZI: That's that.

71   EXPERIMENTER: Continue using the 450 switch for each wrong answer. Continue, please.

72   PROZI: But I don't get anything!

73   EXPERIMENTER: Please continue. The next word is "white."

74   PROZI: Don't you think you should look in on him, please?

75   EXPERIMENTER: Not once we've started the experiment.

76   PROZI: What if he's dead in there? (*Gestures toward the room with the electric chair.*) I mean, he told me he can't stand the shock, sir. I don't mean to be rude, but I think you should look in on him. All you have to do is look in on him. All you have to do is look in the door. I don't get no answer, no noise. Something might have happened to the gentleman in there, sir.

77   EXPERIMENTER: We must continue. Go on, please.

78   PROZI: You mean keep giving him what? Four-hundred-fifty volts, what he's got now?

79   EXPERIMENTER: That's correct. Continue. The next word is "white."

80   PROZI (*now at a furious pace*): "White—cloud, horse, rock, house." Answer, please. The answer is "horse." Four hundred and fifty volts. (*Zzumph!*) Next word, "Bag—paint, music, clown, girl." The answer is "paint." Four hundred and fifty volts. (*Zzumph!*) Next word is "Short—sentence, movie . . . "

81   EXPERIMENTER: Excuse me, Teacher. We'll have to discontinue the experiment.

Peculiar Reactions

82 Morris Braverman, another subject, is a thirty-nine-year-old social worker. He looks older than his years because of his bald head and serious demeanor. His

brow is furrowed, as if all the world's burdens were carried on his face. He appears intelligent and concerned.

83   When the learner refuses to answer and the experimenter instructs Braverman to treat the absence of an answer as equivalent to a wrong answer, he takes his instruction to heart. Before administering 300 volts he asserts officiously to the victim, "Mr. Wallace, your silence has to be considered as a wrong answer." Then he administers the shock. He offers half-heartedly to change places with the learner, then asks the experimenter, "Do I have to follow these instructions literally?" He is satisfied with the experimenter's answer that he does. His very refined and authoritative manner of speaking is increasingly broken up by wheezing laughter.

84   The experimenter's notes on Mr. Braverman at the last few shocks are:

> Almost breaking up now each time gives shock. Rubbing face to hide laughter. Squinting, trying to hide face with hand, still laughing. Cannot control his laughter at this point no matter what he does. Clenching fist, pushing it onto table.

85   In an interview after the session, Mr. Braverman summarizes the experiment with impressive fluency and intelligence. He feels the experiment may have been designed also to "test the effects on the teacher of being in an essentially sadistic role, as well as the reactions of a student to a learning situation that was authoritative and punitive." When asked how painful the last few shocks administered to the learner were, he indicates that the most extreme category on the scale is not adequate (it read EXTREMELY PAINFUL) and places his mark at the edge of the scale with an arrow carrying it beyond the scale.

86   It is almost impossible to convey the greatly relaxed, sedate quality of his conversation in the interview. In the most relaxed terms, he speaks about his severe inner tension.

87   EXPERIMENTER: At what point were you most tense or nervous?

88   MR. BRAVERMAN: Well, when he first began to cry out in pain, and I realized this was hurting him. This got worse when he just blocked and refused to answer. There was I. I'm a nice person, I think, hurting somebody, and caught up in what seemed a mad situation . . . and in the interest of science, one goes through with it.

89   When the interviewer pursues the general question of tension, Mr. Braverman spontaneously mentions his laughter.

90   "My reactions were awfully peculiar. I don't know if you were watching me, but my reactions were giggly, and trying to stifle laughter. This isn't the way I usually am. This was a sheer reaction to a totally impossible situation. And my reaction was to the situation of having to hurt somebody. And being totally helpless and caught up in a set of circumstances where I just couldn't deviate and I couldn't try to help. This is what got me."

91   Mr. Braverman, like all subjects, was told the actual nature and purpose of the experiment, and a year later he affirmed in a questionnaire that he had learned something of personal importance: "What appalled me was that I could possess this capacity for obedience and compliance to a central idea, i.e., the

value of a memory experiment, even after it became clear that continued adherence to this value was at the expense of violation of another value, i.e., don't hurt someone who is helpless and not hurting you. As my wife said, 'You can call yourself Eichmann.'* I hope I deal more effectively with any future conflicts of values I encounter."

The Etiquette of Submission

92 One theoretical interpretation of this behavior holds that all people harbor deeply aggressive instincts continually pressing for expression, and that the experiment provides institutional justification for the release of these impulses. According to this view, if a person is placed in a situation in which he has complete power over another individual, whom he may punish as much as he likes, all that is sadistic and bestial in man comes to the fore. The impulse to shock the victim is seen to flow from the potent aggressive tendencies, which are part of the motivational life of the individual, and the experiment, because it provides social legitimacy, simply opens the door to their expression.

93   It becomes vital, therefore, to compare the subject's performance when he is under orders and when he is allowed to choose the shock level.

94   The procedure was identical to our standard experiment, except that the teacher was told that he was free to select any shock level on any of the trials. (The experimenter took pains to point out that the teacher could use the highest levels on the generator, the lowest, any in between, or any combination of levels.) Each subject proceeded for thirty critical trials. The learner's protests were coordinated to standard shock levels, his first grunt coming at 75 volts, his first vehement protest at 150 volts.

95   The average shock used during the thirty critical trials was less than 60 volts—lower than the point at which the victim showed the first signs of discomfort. Three of the forty subjects did not go beyond the very lowest level on the board, twenty-eight went no higher than 75 volts, and thirty-eight did not go beyond the first loud protest at 150 volts. Two subjects provided the exception, administering up to 325 and 450 volts, but the overall result was that the great majority of people delivered very low, usually painless, shocks when the choice was explicitly up to them.

96   This condition of the experiment undermines another commonly offered explanation of the subjects' behavior—that those who shocked the victim at the most severe levels came only from the sadistic fringe of society. If one considers that almost two-thirds of the participants fall into the category of "obedient" subjects, and that they represented ordinary people drawn from working, managerial, and professional classes, the argument becomes very shaky. Indeed, it is highly reminiscent of the issue that arose in connection with Hannah Arendt's 1963 book, *Eichmann in Jerusalem*. Arendt contended that the prosecution's efforts to depict Eichmann as a sadistic monster was fundamentally wrong, that he came

---

* *Adolf Eichmann* (1906–1962), the Nazi official responsible for implementing Hitler's "Final Solution" to exterminate the Jews, escaped to Argentina after World War II. In 1960, Israeli agents captured him and brought him to Israel, where he was tried as a war criminal and sentenced to death. At his trial, Eichmann maintained that he was merely following orders in arranging murders of his victims.

closer to being an uninspired bureaucrat who simply sat at his desk and did his job. For asserting her views, Arendt became the object of considerable scorn, even calumny. Somehow, it was felt that the monstrous deeds carried out by Eichmann required a brutal, twisted personality, evil incarnate. After witnessing hundreds of ordinary persons submit to the authority in our own experiments, I must conclude that Arendt's conception of the banality of evil comes closer to the truth than one might dare imagine. The ordinary person who shocked the victim did so out of a sense of obligation—an impression of his duties as a sub-ject—and not from any peculiarly aggressive tendencies.

97   This is, perhaps, the most fundamental lesson of our study: ordinary people, simply doing their jobs, and without any particular hostility on their part, can become agents in a terrible destructive process. Moreover, even when the destructive effects of their work become patently clear, and they are asked to carry out actions incompatible with fundamental standards of morality, rela-tively few people have the resources needed to resist authority.

98   Many of the people were in some sense against what they did to the learner, and many protested even while they obeyed. Some were totally convinced of the wrongness of their actions but could not bring themselves to make an open break with authority. They often derived satisfaction from their thoughts and felt that—within themselves, at least—they had been on the side of the angels. They tried to reduce strain by obeying the experimenter but "only slightly," encouraging the learner, touching the generator switches gingerly. When inter-viewed, such a subject would stress that he had "asserted my humanity" by administering the briefest shock possible. Handling the conflict in this manner was easier than defiance.

99   The situation is constructed so that there is no way the subject can stop shocking the learner without violating the experimenter's definitions of his own competence. The subject fears that he will appear arrogant, untoward, and rude if he breaks off. Although these inhibiting emotions appear small in scope alongside the violence being done to the learner, they suffuse the mind and feel-ings of the subject, who is miserable at the prospect of having to repudiate the authority to his face. (When the experiment was altered so that the experi-menter gave his instructions by telephone instead of in person, only a third as many people were fully obedient through 450 volts.) It is a curious thing that a measure of compassion on the part of the subject—an unwillingness to "hurt" the experimenter's feelings—is part of those binding forces inhibiting his dis-obedience. The withdrawal of such deference may be as painful to the subject as to the authority he defies.

Duty Without Conflict

100 The subjects do not derive satisfaction from inflicting pain, but they often like the feeling they get from pleasing the experimenter. They are proud of doing a good job, obeying the experimenter under difficult circumstances. While the subjects administered only mild shocks on their own initiative, one experi-mental variation showed that, under orders, 30 percent of them were willing to deliver 450 volts even when they had to forcibly push the learner's hand down on the electrode.

101   Bruno Batta is a thirty-seven-year-old welder who took part in the variation requiring the use of force. He was born in New Haven, his parents in Italy. He has a rough-hewn face that conveys a conspicuous lack of alertness. He has some difficulty in mastering the experimental procedure and needs to be corrected by the experimenter several times. He shows appreciation for the help and willingness to do what is required. After the 150-volt level, Batta has to force the learner's hand down on the shock plate, since the learner himself refuses to touch it.

102   When the learner first complains, Mr. Batta pays no attention to him. His face remains impassive, as if to dissociate himself from the learner's disruptive behavior. When the experimenter instructs him to force the learner's hand down, he adopts a rigid, mechanical procedure. He tests the generator switch. When it fails to function, he immediately forces the learner's hand onto the shock plate. All the while he maintains the same rigid mask. The learner, seated alongside him, begs him to stop, but with robotic impassivity he continues the procedure.

103   What is extraordinary is his apparent total indifference to the learner; he hardly takes cognizance of him as a human being. Meanwhile, he relates to the experimenter in a submissive and courteous fashion.

104   At the 330-volt level, the learner refuses not only to touch the shock plate but also to provide any answers. Annoyed, Batta turns to him, and chastises him: "You better answer and get it over with. We can't stay here all night." These are the only words he directs to the learner in the course of an hour. Never again does he speak to him. The scene is brutal and depressing, his hard, impassive face showing total indifference as he subdues the screaming learner and gives him shocks. He seems to derive no pleasure from the act itself, only quiet satisfaction at doing his job properly.

105   When he administers 450 volts, he turns to the experimenter and asks, "Where do we go from here, Professor?" His tone is deferential and expresses his willingness to be a cooperative subject, in contrast to the learner's obstinacy.

106   At the end of the session he tells the experimenter how honored he has been to help him, and in a moment of contrition, remarks, "Sir, sorry it couldn't have been a full experiment."

107   He has done his honest best. It is only the deficient behavior of the learner that has denied the experimenter full satisfaction.

108   The essence of obedience is that a person comes to view himself as the instrument for carrying out another person's wishes, and he therefore no longer regards himself as responsible for his actions. Once this critical shift of viewpoint has occurred, all of the essential features of obedience follow. The most far-reaching consequence is that the person feels responsible *to* the authority directing him but feels no responsibility *for* the content of the actions that the authority prescribes. Morality does not disappear—it acquires a radically different focus: the subordinate person feels shame or pride depending on how adequately he has performed the actions called for by authority.

109   Language provides numerous terms to pinpoint this type of morality: *loyalty, duty, discipline* all are terms heavily saturated with moral meaning and refer to the degree to which a person fulfills his obligations to authority. They refer not to the "goodness" of the person per se but to the adequacy with which a subordinate fulfills his socially defined role. The most frequent defense of the individual who has performed a heinous act under command of authority is that

he has simply done his duty. In asserting this defense, the individual is not introducing an alibi concocted for the moment but is reporting honestly on the psychological attitude induced by submission to authority.

110   For a person to feel responsible for his actions, he must sense that the behavior has flowed from "the self." In the situation we have studied, subjects have precisely the opposite view of their actions—namely, they see them as originating in the motives of some other person. Subjects in the experiment frequently said, "If it were up to me, I would not have administered shocks to the learner."

111   Once authority has been isolated as the cause of the subject's behavior, it is legitimate to inquire into the necessary elements of authority and how it must be perceived in order to gain compliance. We conducted some investigations into the kinds of changes that would cause the experimenter to lose his power and to be disobeyed by the subject. Some of the variations revealed that:

- *The experimenter's physical presence has a marked impact on his authority.* As cited earlier, obedience dropped off sharply when orders were given by telephone. The experimenter could often induce a disobedient subject to go on by returning to the laboratory.
- *Conflicting authority severely paralyzes action.* When two experimenters of equal status, both seated at the command desk, gave incompatible orders, no shocks were delivered past the point of their disagreement.
- *The rebellious action of others severely undermines authority.* In one variation, three teachers (two actors and a real subject) administered a test and shocks. When the two actors disobeyed the experimenter and refused to go beyond a certain shock level, thirty-six of the forty subjects joined their disobedient peers and refused as well.

112   Although the experimenter's authority was fragile in some respects, it is also true that he had almost none of the tools used in ordinary command structures. For example, the experimenter did not threaten the subjects with punishment— such as loss of income, community ostracism, or jail—for failure to obey. Neither could he offer incentives. Indeed, we should expect the experimenter's authority to be much less than that of someone like a general, since the experimenter has no power to enforce his imperatives, and since participation in a psychological experiment scarcely evokes the sense of urgency and dedication found in warfare. Despite these limitations, he still managed to command a dismaying degree of obedience.

113   I will cite one final variation of the experiment that depicts a dilemma that is more common in everyday life. The subject was not ordered to pull the lever that shocked the victim, but merely to perform a subsidiary task (administering the word-pair test) while another person administered the shock. In this situation, thirty-seven of forty adults continued to the highest level on the shock generator. Predictably, they excused their behavior by saying that the responsibility belonged to the man who actually pulled the switch. This may illustrate a dangerously typical arrangement in a complex society: it is easy to ignore responsibility when one is only an intermediate link in a chain of action.

114   The problem of obedience is not wholly psychological. The form and shape of society and the way it is developing have much to do with it. There was a

time, perhaps, when people were able to give a fully human response to any situation because they were fully absorbed in it as human beings. But as soon as there was a division of labor things changed. Beyond a certain point, the breaking up of society into people carrying out narrow and very special jobs takes away from the human quality of work and life. A person does not get to see the whole situation but only a small part of it, and is thus unable to act without some kind of overall direction. He yields to authority but in doing so is alienated from his own actions.

115   Even Eichmann was sickened when he toured the concentration camps, but he had only to sit at a desk and shuffle papers. At the same time the man in the camp who actually dropped Cyclon-b into the gas chambers was able to justify *his* behavior on the ground that he was only following orders from above. Thus there is a fragmentation of the total human act; no one is confronted with the consequences of his decision to carry out the evil act. The person who assumes responsibility has evaporated. Perhaps this is the most common characteristic of socially organized evil in modern society.

Review Questions

1. Milgram states that obedience is a basic element in the structure of social life. How so?

2. What is the dilemma inherent in obedience to authority?

3. Summarize the obedience experiments.

4. What predictions did experts and laypeople make about the experiments before they were conducted? How did these predictions compare with the experimental results?

5. What are Milgram's views regarding the two assumptions bearing on his experiment that (1) people are naturally aggressive and (2) a lunatic, sadistic fringe is responsible for shocking learners to the maximum limit?

6. How do Milgram's findings corroborate Hannah Arendt's thesis about the "banality of evil"?

7. What, according to Milgram, is the "essence of obedience"?

8. How did being an intermediate link in a chain of action affect a subject's willingness to continue with the experiment?

9. In the article's final two paragraphs, Milgram speaks of a "fragmentation of the total human act." To what is he referring?

Discussion and Writing Suggestions

1. Milgram writes (paragraph 2): "Conservative philosophers argue that the very fabric of society is threatened by disobedience, while human-

ists stress the primacy of the individual conscience." Develop the arguments of both the conservative and the humanist regarding obedience to authority. Be prepared to debate the ethics of obedience by defending one position or the other.

2. Would you have been glad to have participated in the Milgram experiments? Why or why not?

3. The ethics of Milgram's experimental design came under sharp attack. Diana Baumrind's review of the experiment typifies the criticism; but before you read her work, try to anticipate the objections she raises.

4. Given the general outcome of the experiments, why do you suppose Milgram gives as his first example of a subject's response the German émigré's refusal to continue the electrical shocks?

5. Does the outcome of the experiment upset you in any way? Do you feel the experiment teaches us anything new about human nature?

6. Comment on Milgram's skill as a writer of description. How effectively does he portray his subjects when introducing them? When re-creating their tension in the experiment?

7. Mrs. Braverman said to her husband: "You can call yourself Eichmann." Do you agree with her? Explain.

8. Reread paragraphs 29 through 81, the transcript of the experiment in which Mr. Prozi participated. Appreciating that Prozi was debriefed—that is, was assured that no harm came to the learner—imagine what Prozi might have been thinking as he drove home after the experiment. Develop your thoughts into a monologue, written in the first person, with Prozi at the wheel of his car.

Review of Stanley Milgram's Experiments on Obedience
Diana Baumrind

Many of Milgram's colleagues saluted him for providing that "hard information" about human nature. Others attacked him for violating the rights of his subjects. Still others faulted his experimental design and claimed he could not, with any validity, speculate on life outside the laboratory based on the behavior of his subjects within.

In the following excerpted review, psychologist Diana Baumrind excoriates Milgram for "entrapping" his subjects and potentially harming their "self-image or ability to trust adult authorities in the future." In a footnote at the end of this selection (page 376), we summarize Milgram's response to Baumrind's critique.

Diana Baumrind is a psychologist who, when writing this review, worked at the Institute of Human Development, University of California, Berkeley. The review appeared in American Psychologist *shortly after Milgram published the results of his first experiments in 1963.*

1   . . . The dependent, obedient attitude assumed by most subjects in the experimental setting is appropriate to that situation. The "game" is defined by the experimenter and he makes the rules. By volunteering, the subject agrees implicitly to assume a posture of trust and obedience. While the experimental conditions leave him exposed, the subject has the right to assume that his security and self-esteem will be protected.

2   There are other professional situations in which one member—the patient or client—expects help and protection from the other—the physician or psychologist. But the interpersonal relationship between experimenter and subject additionally has unique features which are likely to provoke initial anxiety in the subject. The laboratory is unfamiliar as a setting and the rules of behavior ambiguous compared to a clinician's office. Because of the anxiety and passivity generated by the setting, the subject is more prone to behave in an obedient, suggestible manner in the laboratory than elsewhere. Therefore, the laboratory is not the place to study degree of obedience or suggestibility, as a function of a particular experimental condition, since the base line for these phenomena as found in the laboratory is probably much higher than in most other settings. Thus experiments in which the relationship to the experimenter as an authority is used as an independent condition are imperfectly designed for the same reason that they are prone to injure the subjects involved. They disregard the special quality of trust and obedience with which the subject appropriately regards the experimenter.

3   Other phenomena which present ethical decisions, unlike those mentioned above, *can* be reproduced successfully in the laboratory. Failure experience, conformity to peer judgment, and isolation are among such phenomena. In these cases we can expect the experimenter to take whatever measures are necessary to prevent the subject from leaving the laboratory more humiliated, insecure, alienated, or hostile than when he arrived. To guarantee that an especially sensitive subject leaves a stressful experimental experience in the proper state sometimes requires special clinical training. But usually an attitude of compassion, respect, gratitude, and common sense will suffice, and no amount of clinical training will substitute. The subject has the right to expect that the psychologist with whom he is interacting has some concern for his welfare, and the personal attributes and professional skill to express his good will effectively.

4   Unfortunately, the subject is not always treated with the respect he deserves. It has become more commonplace in sociopsychological laboratory studies to manipulate, embarrass, and discomfort subjects. At times the insult to the subject's sensibilities extends to the journal reader when the results are reported. Milgram's (1963) study is a case in point. The following is Milgram's abstract of his experiment:

> This article describes a procedure for the study of destructive obedience in the laboratory. It consists of ordering a naive S to administer increasingly

more severe punishment to a victim in the context of a learning experiment.* Punishment is administered by means of a shock generator with 30 graded switches ranging from Slight Shock to Danger: Severe Shock. The victim is a confederate of E. The primary dependent variable is the maximum shock the S is willing to administer before he refuses to continue further.† 26 Ss obeyed the experimental commands fully, and administered the highest shock on the generator. 14 Ss broke off the experiment at some point after the victim protested and refused to provide further answers. The procedure created extreme levels of nervous tension in some Ss. Profuse sweating, trembling, and stuttering were typical expressions of this emotional disturbance. One unexpected sign of tension—yet to be explained—was the regular occurrence of nervous laughter, which in some Ss developed into uncontrollable seizures. The variety of interesting behavioral dynamics observed in the experiment, the reality of the situation for the S, and the possibility of parametric variations† within the framework of the procedure point to the fruitfulness of further study [p. 371].

5   The detached, objective manner in which Milgram reports the emotional disturbance suffered by his subjects contrasts sharply with his graphic account of that disturbance. Following are two other quotes describing the effects on his subjects of the experimental conditions:

> I observed a mature and initially poised businessman enter the laboratory smiling and confident. Within 20 minutes he was reduced to a twitching, stuttering wreck, who was rapidly approaching a point of nervous collapse. He constantly pulled on his earlobe, and twisted his hands. At one point he pushed his fist into his forehead and muttered: "Oh God, let's stop it." And yet he continued to respond to every word of the experimenter, and obeyed to the end [p. 377].

> In a large number of cases the degree of tension reached extremes that are rarely seen in sociopsychological laboratory studies. Subjects were observed to sweat, tremble, stutter, bite their lips, groan, and dig their fingernails into their flesh. These were characteristic rather than exceptional responses to the experiment.
>
>   One sign of tension was the regular occurrence of nervous laughing fits. Fourteen of the 40 subjects showed definite signs of nervous laughter and smiling. The laughter seemed entirely out of place, even bizarre. Full-blown, uncontrollable seizures were observed for 3 subjects. On one occasion we observed a seizure so violently convulsive that it was necessary to call a halt to the experiment. . . [p. 375].

---

* In psychological experiments, *S* is an abbreviation for *subject; E* is an abbreviation for *experimenter*.

† In the context of a psychological experiment, a *dependent variable* is a behavior that is expected to change as a result of changes in the experimental procedure.

‡ *Parametric variation* is a statistical term that describes the degree to which information based on data for one experiment can be applied to data for a slightly different experiment.

Milgram does state that,

> After the interview, procedures were undertaken to assure that the subject
> would leave the laboratory in a state of well being. A friendly reconciliation
> was arranged between the subject and the victim, and an effort was made to
> reduce any tensions that arose as a result of the experiment [p. 374].

It would be interesting to know what sort of procedures could dissipate the type
of emotional disturbance just described. In view of the effects on subjects, traumatic to a degree which Milgram himself considers nearly unprecedented in
sociopsychological experiments, his casual assurance that these tensions were
dissipated before the subject left the laboratory is unconvincing.

6   What could be the rational basis for such a posture of indifference? Perhaps
Milgram supplies the answer himself when he partially explains the subject's
destructive obedience as follows, "Thus they assume that the discomfort caused
the victim is momentary, while the scientific gains resulting from the experiment are enduring" [p. 378]. Indeed such a rationale might suffice to justify the
means used to achieve his end if that end were of inestimable value to humanity or were not itself transformed by the means by which it was attained.

7   The behavioral psychologist is not in as good a position to objectify his faith
in the significance of his work as medical colleagues at points of breakthrough.
His experimental situations are not sufficiently accurate models of real-life experience; his sampling techniques are seldom of a scope which would justify the
meaning with which he would like to endow his results; and these results are
hard to reproduce by colleagues with opposing theoretical views. Unlike the
Sabin vaccine,* for example, the concrete benefit to humanity of his particular
piece of work, no matter how competently handled, cannot justify the risk that
real harm will be done to the subject. I am not speaking of physical discomfort,
inconvenience, or experimental deception per se, but of permanent harm, however slight. I do regard the emotional disturbance described by Milgram as
potentially harmful because it could easily effect an alteration in the subject's
self-image or ability to trust adult authorities in the future. It is potentially harmful to a subject to commit, in the course of an experiment, acts which he himself considers unworthy, particularly when he has been entrapped into
committing such acts by an individual he has reason to trust. The subject's personal responsibility for his actions is not erased because the experimenter reveals
to him the means which he used to stimulate these actions. The subject realizes
that he would have hurt the victim if the current were on. The realization that
he also made a fool of himself by accepting the experimental set results in additional loss of self-esteem. Moreover, the subject finds it difficult to express his
anger outwardly after the experimenter in a self-acceptant but friendly manner
reveals the hoax.

8   A fairly intense corrective interpersonal experience is indicated wherein the
subject admits and accepts his responsibility for his own actions, and at the same
time gives vent to his hurt and anger at being fooled. Perhaps an experience as

---

* The Sabin vaccine provides immunization against polio.

distressing as the one described by Milgram can be integrated by the subject, provided that careful thought is given to the matter. The propriety of such experimentation is still in question even if such a reparational experience were forthcoming. Without it I would expect a naive, sensitive subject to remain deeply hurt and anxious for some time, and a sophisticated, cynical subject to become even more alienated and distrustful.

9   In addition the experimental procedure used by Milgram does not appear suited to the objectives of the study because it does not take into account the special quality of the set which the subject has in the experimental situation. Milgram is concerned with a very important problem, namely, the social consequences of destructive obedience. He says,

> Gas chambers were built, death camps were guarded, daily quotas of corpses were produced with the same efficiency as the manufacture of appliances. These inhumane policies may have originated in the mind of a single person, but they could only be carried out on a massive scale if a very large number of persons obeyed orders [p. 371].

But the parallel between authority-subordinate relationships in Hitler's Germany and in Milgram's laboratory is unclear. In the former situation the SS man or member of the German Officer Corps, when obeying orders to slaughter, had no reason to think of his superior officer as benignly disposed towards himself or their victims. The victims were perceived as subhuman and not worthy of consideration. The subordinate officer was an agent in a great cause. He did not need to feel guilt or conflict because within his frame of reference he was acting rightly.

10   It is obvious from Milgram's own description that most of his subjects were concerned about their victims and did trust the experimenter, and that their distressful conflict was generated in part by the consequences of these two disparate but appropriate attitudes. Their distress may have resulted from shock at what the experimenter was doing to them as well as from what they thought they were doing to their victims. In any case there is not a convincing parallel between the phenomena studied by Milgram and destructive obedience as the concept would apply to the subordinate-authority relationship demonstrated in Hitler's Germany. If the experiments were conducted "outside of New Haven and without any visible ties to the university," I would still question their validity on similar although not identical grounds. In addition, I would question the representativeness of a sample of subjects who would voluntarily participate within a noninstitutional setting.

11   In summary, the experimental objectives of the psychologist are seldom incompatible with the subject's ongoing state of well being, provided that the experimenter is willing to take the subject's motives and interests into consideration when planning his methods and correctives. Section 4b in *Ethical Standards of Psychologists* (APA, undated) reads in part:

> Only when a problem is significant and can be investigated in no other way is the psychologist justified in exposing human subjects to emotional stress or other possible harm. In conducting such research, the psychologist must

seriously consider the possibility of harmful aftereffects, and should be prepared to remove them as soon as permitted by the design of the experiment.
Where the danger of serious aftereffects exists, research should be conducted only when the subjects or their responsible agents are fully informed
of this possibility and volunteer nevertheless [p. 12].

From the subject's point of view procedures which involve loss of dignity, self-
esteem and trust in rational authority are probably most harmful in the long run
and require the most thoughtfully planned reparations, if engaged in at all. The
public image of psychology as a profession is highly related to our own actions,
and some of these actions are changeworthy. It is important that as research psychologists we protect our ethical sensibilities rather than adapt our personal
standards to include as appropriate the kind of indignities to which Milgram's
subjects were exposed. I would not like to see experiments such as Milgram's
proceed unless the subjects were fully informed of the dangers of serious aftereffects and his correctives were clearly shown to be effective in restoring their
state of well being.*

References

American Psychological Association (n.d.). *Ethical standards of psychologists: A summary of ethical principles.* Washington, DC: APA.

Milgram, S. (1963). Behavioral study of obedience. *Journal of Abnormal and Social
Psychology. 67,* 371–378.

---

* Stanley Milgram replied to Baumrind's critique in a lengthy critique of his own [From Stanley
Milgram, "Issues in the Study of Obedience: A Reply to Baumrind," *American Psychologist* 19, 1964, pp.
848–851]. Following are his principal points:

• Milgram believed that the experimental findings were in large part responsible for Baumrind's criticism. He writes:

Is not Baumrind's criticism based as much on the unanticipated findings as on the method? The findings were that some subjects performed in what appeared to be a shockingly immoral way. If, instead,
every one of the subjects had broken off at "slight shock," or at the first sign of the learner's discomfort, the results would have been pleasant, and reassuring, and who would protest?

• Milgram objected to Baumrind's assertion that those who participated in the experiment would have
trouble justifying their behavior. Milgram conducted follow-up questionnaires. The results, summarized in Table 1, indicate that 84 percent of the subjects claimed they were pleased to have been a
part of the experiment.

• Baumrind objected that studies of obedience cannot meaningfully be carried out in a laboratory setting, since the obedience occurred in a context where it was appropriate. Milgram's response: "I reject
Baumrind's argument that the observed obedience does not count because it occurred where it is
appropriate. That is precisely why it *does* count. A soldier's obedience is no less meaningful because
it occurs in a pertinent military context." (Footnote continued on next page.)

Review Questions

1. Why might a subject volunteer for an experiment? Why do subjects typically assume a dependent, obedient attitude?

2. Why is a laboratory not a suitable setting for a study of obedience?

3. For what reasons does Baumrind feel that the Milgram experiment was potentially harmful?

4. For what reasons does Baumrind question the relationship between Milgram's findings and the obedient behavior of subordinates in Nazi Germany?

Discussion and Writing Suggestions

1. Baumrind contends that the Milgram experiment is imperfectly designed for two reasons: (1) The laboratory is not the place to test obedience; (2) Milgram disregarded the trust that subjects usually show an experimenter. To what extent do you agree with Baumrind's objections? Do you find them all equally valid?

2. Baumrind states that the ethical procedures of the experiment keep it from having significant value. Do you agree?

3. Do you agree with Baumrind that the subjects were "entrapped" into committing unworthy acts?

4. Assume the identity of a participant in Milgram's experiment who obeyed the experimenter by shocking the learner with the maximum voltage. You have just returned from the lab, and your spouse asks you about your day. Compose the conversation that follows.

• Milgram concludes his critique in this way: "If there is a moral to be learned from the obedience study, it is that every man must be responsible for his own actions. This author accepts full responsibility for the design and execution of the study. Some people may feel it should not have been done. I disagree and accept the burden of their judgment."

TABLE 1   Excerpt from Questionnaire Used in a Follow-up Study of the Obedience Research

Now That I Have Read the Report, and All Things Considered . . .	Defiant	Obedient	All
1. I am very glad to have been in the experiment	40.0%	47.8%	43.5%
2. I am glad to have been in the experiment	43.8%	35.7%	40.2%
3. I am neither sorry nor glad to have been in the experiment	15.3%	14.8%	15.1%
4. I am sorry to have been in the experiment	0.8%	0.7%	0.8%
5. I am very sorry to have been in the experiment	0.0%	1.0%	0.5%

Note—Ninety-two percent of the subjects returned the questionnaire. The characteristics of the nonrespondents were checked against the respondents. They differed from the respondents only with regard to age; younger people were overrepresented in the nonresponding group.

Obedience
Ian Parker

As Ian Parker points out, Milgram's experiment became "the most cited, celebrated—and reviled—experiment in the history of social psychology." Parker also explains, however, that for Milgram himself the experiment was a mixed blessing: it would both "make his name and destroy his reputation."

Milgram was fascinated by the Asch experiment, but when all was said and done, this experiment was only about lines. He wondered if it were possible "to make Asch's conformity experiment more humanely significant." Milgram's breakthrough, his "incandescent moment," came when he asked himself, "Just how far would a person go under the experimenter's orders?" We have seen the results in the experiment he describes and discusses in an earlier selection.

In the following selection, Ian Parker, a British writer who lives in New York, focuses on both the immediate and the long-term reaction to Milgram's experiments among both the general public and Milgram's professional colleagues and also of the effect of the experiment upon the experimenter himself. This selection is excerpted from an article that Parker wrote for the Autumn 2000 issue of Granta. *Parker writes regularly for the* New Yorker *and has also written for* Human Sciences, History of the Human Sciences, Political Studies, *and* Human Relations.

1   Milgram had a world exclusive. He had caught evil on film. He had invented a kind of torture machine. But it was not immediately clear what he should do with his discovery. When he began the study, he had no theory, nor was he planning to test another man's theory. His idea had sprung from contemplation of Solomon Asch, but the "incandescent" moment at Princeton was a shift away from theory into experimental practice. He had had an idea for an experiment. Now, he was in an odd situation: he had caused something extraordinary to happen, but, technically, his central observation counted for nothing. With no provocation, a New Haven man had hit a fellow citizen with 450 volts. To the general observer, this will come as a surprise, but it is not a social scientific discovery, as Edward E. Jones, the distinguished editor of the *Journal of Personality*, made clear to Milgram when he declined the invitation to publish Milgram's first paper. "The major problem," Jones wrote to Milgram, "is that this is really the report of some pilot research on a method for inducing stress or conflict . . . your data indicate a kind of triumph of social engineering . . . we are led to no conclusions about obedience, really, but rather are exhorted to be impressed with the power of your situation as an influence context." The *Journal of Abnormal and Social Psychology* also rejected the paper on its first submission, calling it a "demonstration" rather than an experiment.

2   Milgram had described only one experimental situation. When he resubmitted the paper to the same journal, he now included experimental variables, and it was publishable. In the rewrite, Milgram put the emphasis on the way in which differences in situation had caused differences in degrees of obedience:

the closer the learner to the teacher, the greater the disobedience, and so on. These details were later lost as the experiment moved out of social psychology into the larger world. But it could hardly have happened otherwise. The thought that people were zapping each other in a Yale laboratory is bound to be more striking than the thought that zapping occurs a little less often when one is looking one's victim in the eye. The unscientific truth, perhaps, is that the central comparison in Milgram's study is not between any two experimental variables: it is between what happened in the laboratory, and what we thought would happen. The experimental control in Milgram's model is our hopelessly flawed intuition.

3   "Somehow," Milgram told a friend in 1962, "I don't write as fast or as easily as I run experiments. I have done about all the experiments I plan to do on Obedience, am duly impressed with the results, and now find myself acutely constipated." Milgram found it hard to knock the experiment into social scientific shape. It would be another decade before he incorporated his findings into a serious theory of the sources of human obedience. When he did so, in the otherwise absorbing and beautifully written book *Obedience to Authority* (1974), his thoughts about an "agentic state"—a psychological zone of abandoned autonomy—were not widely admired or developed by his peers, not least because they were so evidently retrospective. Most readers of *Obedience to Authority* are more likely to take interest in the nods of acknowledgment made to Arthur Koestler's *The Ghost in the Machine*, and to Alex Comfort, the English anarchist poet, novelist, and author of *The Joy of Sex*. Most readers will take more pleasure—and feel Milgram took more pleasure—in the novelistic and strikingly unscientific descriptions of his experimental subjects. ("Mrs Dontz," he wrote, "has an unusually casual, slow-paced way of speaking, and her tone expresses constant humility; it is as if every assertion carries the emotional message: 'I'm just a very ordinary person, don't expect a lot from me.' Physically, she resembles Shirley Booth in the film *Come Back, Little Sheba*.")

4   But while Milgram was struggling to place his findings in a proper scientific context, they seemed to have found a natural home elsewhere. Stanley Milgram—a young social psychology professor at the start of his career—appeared to be in a position to contribute to one of the late twentieth century's most pressing intellectual activities: making sense of the Holocaust. Milgram always placed the experiments in this context, and the figure of Adolf Eichmann, who was seized in Buenos Aires in the spring of 1960, and whose trial in Jerusalem began a year later, loomed over his proceedings. (In a letter that urged Alan Elms to keep up the supply of experimental volunteers, Milgram noted that this role bore "some resemblance to Mr. Eichmann's position.") The trial, as Peter Novick has recently written in *The Holocaust in American Life*, marked "the first time that what we now call the Holocaust was presented to the American public as an entity in its own right, distinct from Nazi barbarism in general." When Milgram published his first paper on the obedience studies in 1963, Hannah Arendt's articles about the trial had just appeared in the *New Yorker*, and in her book, *Eichmann in Jerusalem*, and they had given widespread currency to her perception about "the banality of evil." Milgram put Eichmann's name in the first paragraph of his first obedience paper, and so claimed a place

in a pivotal contemporary debate. His argument was this: his study showed how ordinary people are surprisingly prone to destructive obedience; the crimes of the Holocaust had been committed by people obeying orders; those people, therefore, could now be thought ordinary. The argument had its terrifying element and its consoling element: according to Milgram, Americans had to see themselves as potential murderers; at the same time we could understand Nazis to be no more unusual than any New Haven guy in a check shirt.

5   It may seem bizarre now: Milgram returned to ordinary Nazis their Nuremberg defense, nicely polished in an American laboratory. But the idea struck a chord, and news quickly spread of Milgram's well-meaning, all-American torturers. "Once the [Holocaust] connection was in place," said Arthur G. Miller, a leading Milgram scholar, "then the experiments took on a kind of a larger-than-life quality." Milgram's work was reported in the *New York Times* (65% IN TEST BLINDLY OBEY ORDER TO INFLICT PAIN), and the story was quickly picked up by *Life, Esquire,* ABC television, UPI, and the British press. The fame of the experiments spread, and as the Sixties acquired their defining spirit, Holocaust references were joined by thoughts of My Lai; this was a good moment in history to have things to say about taking orders. By the time Milgram had published his book and released a short film of the experiment, his findings had spread into popular culture, and into theological, medical, and legal discussions. Thomas Blass, a social psychologist at the University of Maryland, Baltimore County, who is preparing a Milgram biography, has a large collection of academic references, including a paper in the context of accountancy ethics. (Is it unthinking obedience that causes accountants to act unlawfully on behalf of clients?) Outside the academy, Dannie Abse published an anti-Milgram play, *The Dogs of Pavlov,* in 1973, and two years later, in America, CBS broadcast a television movie, *The Tenth Level,* that made awkward melodrama out of the obedience experiments, and starred William Shatner as a spookily obsessed and romantically disengaged version of Professor Milgram. ("You may know your social psychology, Professor, but you have a lot to learn about the varieties of massage.") Peter Gabriel sang "We Do What We're Told (Milgram's 37)" in 1986. And there would be more than a whiff of Milgram in the 1990 episode of *The Simpsons,* "There's No Disgrace Like Home," in which the family members repeatedly electrocute one another until the lights across Springfield flicker and dim. Last year, "The Stanley Milgram Experiment"—a comedy sketch duo—made its off-off-Broadway debut in New York. Robbie Chafitz, one of the pair, had been startled and amused by the Milgram film as a teenager, and had always vowed to use the name one way or another. Besides, as he told me, "anything with electricity and people is funny."

6   But however celebrated the experiments became, there was a question they could never shake off. It was an ethical issue: had Stanley Milgram mistreated his subjects? Milgram must have seen the storm coming, at least from the moment when Herbert Winer marched into his office, talking of heart attacks. In the summer of 1962, other subjects recorded their feelings about the experiment in response to a questionnaire sent out by Milgram along with a report explaining the true purpose of the experiment. Replies were transferred on to

index cards and are now held—unpublished and anonymous—at Yale. "Since taking part in the experiment," reads one card, "I have suffered a mild heart attack. The one thing my doctor tells me that I must avoid is any form of tension." Another card: "Right now I'm in group therapy. Would it be OK if I showed this report to [the] group and the doctors at the clinic?"

7   Since then, the experiment has been widely attacked from within the profession and from outside. To many, Milgram became a social psychological demon; Alan Elms has met people at parties who have recoiled at the news that he was a Milgram lieutenant. The psychologist Bruno Bettelheim described Milgram's work as "vile" and "in line with the human experiments of the Nazis." In his defense, Milgram would always highlight the results of post-experimental psychological studies—which had reported "no evidence of any traumatic reactions"—and the fact of the debriefings in Linsly-Chittenden Hall, in which care had been taken to give obedient subjects reasons not to feel bad about themselves. They were told to remember, for example, that doctors routinely hurt people in a thoroughly good cause. (Alan Elms wonders if this debriefing was *too* effective, and that subjects should have been obliged to confront their actions more fully.)

8   But Milgram never quite won the ethical argument. And the controversy was immediately damaging to his career. Someone—perhaps a Yale colleague, according to Thomas Blass—quickly brought the experiment to the attention of the American Psychological Association, and Milgram's application for APA membership was delayed while the case against him was considered. Today, although the APA is happy to include Milgram's shock generator in a traveling psychology exhibition, it is careful to describe the experiments as "controversial" in its accompanying literature. As the APA points out, modern ethical guidelines (in part inspired by Milgram) would prevent the obedience studies from being repeated today.

9   The controversy followed him. In 1963 Milgram left Yale for Harvard. He was happy there. This is where his two children were born. And when a tenured job came up, he applied. But he needed the unanimous support of his colleagues, and could not secure it. He was blackballed by enemies of the obedience work. (According to Alexandra Milgram, her husband once devised a board game based on the tenure of university professors.) The late Roger Brown, a prominent Harvard psychologist, told Thomas Blass that there had been those in the department who thought of Milgram as "sort of manipulative, or the mad doctor. They felt uneasy about him."

10   So in 1967 Stanley Milgram left Harvard to become head of the social psychology programme in the psychology department in the Graduate Center of the City University of New York (CUNY). In one sense, it was a promotion; he was a full professor at thirty-three. "But after Yale and Harvard, it was the pits," said Milgram's friend and fellow social psychologist, Philip Zimbardo. "Most people I know who didn't get tenure, it had a permanent effect on their lives. You don't get to Yale or Harvard unless you've been number one from kindergarten on, you've been on top—so there's this discontinuity. It's the first time in your life you've failed. You're Stanley Milgram, and people all over the world are

talking about your research, and you've failed." Milgram was the most cited man in social psychology—Roger Brown, for example, considered his research to be of "profound importance and originality"—yet in later life, he was able to tell Zimbardo that he felt under-appreciated.

11   The ethical furor preyed on Milgram's mind—in the opinion of Arthur G. Miller, it may have contributed to his premature death—but one of its curious side effects was to reinforce the authenticity of his studies in the world outside psychology departments. Among those with a glancing knowledge of Milgram, mistreatment of experimental subjects became the only Milgram controversy. The studies remained intellectually sound, a minor building block of Western thought, a smart conversational gambit at cocktail parties. "People identified the problem with Milgram as just a question of ethics," says Henderikus Stam, of the University of Calgary in Canada, who trained as a social psychologist, but who lost faith and is now a psychological theoretician and historian. "So in a way people never got beyond that. Whereas there's a deeper epistemological question, which is: what can we actually know when we've done an experiment like that, what are we left with? What have we learned about obedience?"

12   Within the academy, there was another, quieter, line of criticism against Milgram: this was methodological. In a paper in 1968 the social psychologists Martin Orne and Charles Holland raised the issue of incongruity, pointing out that Milgram's subjects had been given two key pieces of information: a man in apparent danger, and another man—a man in a lab coat—whose lack of evident concern suggested there was no danger. It seemed possible that obedient subjects had believed in the more plausible piece of information (no danger), and thus concluded, at some conscious or semi-conscious level, that the experiment was a fake, and—in a "pact of ignorance"—been generous enough to role-play for the sake of science. In other words, they were only obeying the demands of amateur dramatics.

13   Perhaps forgetting that people weep in the theatre, Milgram's response was to argue that the subjects' signs of distress or tension—the twitching and stuttering and racing heartbeats—could be taken as evidence that they had accepted the experiment's reality. He also drew upon the questionnaire he had sent out in 1962, in which his volunteers—now entirely in the know—had been asked to agree with one of five propositions, running from, "I fully believed the learner was getting painful shocks" to "I was certain the learner was not getting the shocks." Milgram was pleased to note that three-quarters of the subjects said they believed the learner was definitely or probably getting the shocks. (He added, reasonably, "It would have been an easy out at this point to deny that the hoax had been accepted.")

14   Herbert Winer reports that he was fully duped, and Alan Elms told me that, watching through the mirror during the summer of 1961, he saw very little evidence of widespread disbelief. But it is worth pointing out that Milgram could have reported his questionnaire statistics rather differently. He could have said that only fifty-six per cent accepted his first proposition: "I fully believed the learner was getting painful shocks." Forty-four per cent of Milgram's subjects claimed to be at least partially unpersuaded. (Indeed, on

his own questionnaire, Winer said he had some doubts.) These people do not have much of a presence in Milgram's writings, but you catch a glimpse of them in the Yale Library index cards. One reads: "I was quite sure 'grunts and screams' were electrically reproduced from a speaker mounted in [the] students' room." (They were.) "If [the learner] was making the sounds I should have heard the screams from under the door—which was a poorly fit [*sic*] thin door. I'm sorry that I didn't have enough something to get up and open this door. Which was not locked. To see if student was still there." On another card: "I think that one of the main reasons I continued to the end was that . . . I just couldn't believe that Yale would concoct anything that would be [as] dangerous as the shocks were supposed to be." Another subject had noticed how the experimenter was watching him rather than the learner. Another hadn't understood why he was not allowed to volunteer to be the learner. And another wrote, "I had difficulty describing the experiment to my wife as I was so overcome with laughter—haven't had such a good laugh since the first time I saw the 4 Marx Bros—some 25 years ago."

15   For an experiment supposed to involve the undeserved torture of an innocent Irish-American man, there was a lot of laughter in Yale's Interaction Laboratory. Frequently, Milgram's subjects could barely contain themselves as they moved up the shock board. ("On one occasion," Milgram later wrote, "we observed a seizure so violently convulsive that it was necessary to call a halt to the experiment.") Behind their one-way mirror, Milgram and Elms were at times highly amused. And when students are shown the Milgram film today, there tends to be loud laughter in the room. People laugh, and—despite the alleged revelation of a universal heart of darkness—they go home having lost little faith in their friends and their families.

16   According to Henderikus Stam, the laughter of the students, and perhaps that of the subjects, is a reasonable response to an absurd situation. It's a reaction to the notion that serious and complex moral issues, and the subtleties of human behaviour, can reasonably be illuminated through play-acting in a university laboratory. The experiment does nothing but illuminate itself. "What it does is it says, 'Aren't we clever?' If you wanted to demonstrate obedience to authority wouldn't you be better showing a film about the Holocaust, or news clips about Kosovo? Why do you need an experiment, that's the question? What does the experiment do? The experiment says that if we really want to know about obedience to authority we need an abstract representation of that obedience, removed from all real forms of the abuse of authority. But what we then do is to use that representation to refer back to the real historical examples."

17   What happens when we refer back to historical examples? Readers of *Hitler's Willing Executioners*, Daniel Jonah Goldhagen's study of the complicity of ordinary German citizens in the Holocaust, will learn within one paragraph of a German policeman, Captain Wolfgang Hoffmann, a "zealous executioner of Jews," who "once stridently disobeyed a superior order that he deemed morally objectionable." The order was that he and members of his company should sign a declaration agreeing not to steal from Poles. Hoffmann was affronted that anyone would think the declaration necessary, that anyone would imagine his

men capable of stealing. "I feel injured," he wrote to his superiors, "in my sense of honour." The genocidal killing of thousands of Jews was one thing, but plundering from Poles was another. Here was an order to which he was opposed, and which he felt able to disobey.

18   Goldhagen is impatient with what he calls "the paradigm of external compulsion," which sets the actions of the Holocaust's perpetrators in the context of social-psychological or totalitarian state forces. His book aims to show how the crimes of the Holocaust were carried out by people obeying their own consciences, not blindly or fearfully obeying orders. "If you think that certain people are evil," he told me, "and that it's necessary to do away with them—if you hate them—and then someone orders you to kill them, you're not carrying out the deed only because of the order. You're carrying it out because you think it's right. So in all those instances where people are killing people they hate—their enemies or their perceived enemies—then Milgram is just completely inapplicable."

19   Goldhagen wonders if the Milgram take on the Holocaust met a particular need, during the Cold War, for America's new German allies "to be thought well of." He also wonders if, by robbing people of their agency, "of the fact that they're moral beings," the experiment tapped into the kind of reductive universalism by which, he says, Americans are easily seduced—the belief that all men are created equal, and in this case equally obedient. Goldhagen has no confidence in the idea that Milgram was measuring obedience at all. The experimental conditions did not properly control for other variables, such as trust, nor did they allow for the way decisions are made in the real world—over time, after consultation. Besides, said Goldhagen, in a tone close to exasperation, "people disobey all the time! Look around the world. Do people always pay all their taxes? Do what their bosses tell them? Or quietly accept what any government decides? Even with all kinds of sanctions available, one of the greatest problems that institutions face is to get their members to comply with rules and orders." Milgram's findings, he says, "are roundly, repeatedly and glaringly falsified by life."

20   In the opinion of Professor Stam, this comes close to defining the problems of social psychology itself. It is a discipline, he says, that makes the peculiar claim that "if you want to ask questions about the social world, you have to turn them into abstract technical questions." The Milgram experiment, he says, "has the air of scientificity about it. But it's not scientific, it's . . . *scientistic.*"

21   And there is Milgram's problem: he devised an intensely powerful piece of tragicomic laboratory theatre, and then had to smuggle it into the faculty of social science. His most famous work—which had something to say about trust, embarrassment, low-level sadism, willingness to please, exaggerated post-war respect for scientific research, the sleepy, heavy-lidded pleasure of being asked to *take part*, and, perhaps, too, the desire of a rather awkward young academic to secure attention and respect—had to pass itself off as an event with a single, steady meaning. And that disguise has not always been convincing. It's odd to hear Arthur G. Miller—one of the world's leading Milgram scholars—acknowledge that there have been times when he has wondered, just for a moment, if the experiments perhaps mean nothing at all.

22   But the faculty of social psychology is not ready to let Milgram go. And there may be a new way to rescue the experiments from their ungainly ambiguity. This is the route taken by Professors Lee Ross and Richard E. Nisbett (at Stanford and the University of Michigan respectively), whose recent synthesis of social psychological thinking aims to give the subject new power. According to Professor Ross, the experiments may be "performance," but they still have social psychological news to deliver. If that is true, then we can do something that the late professor was not always able to do himself: we can make a kind of reconciliation between the artist and the scientist in Stanley Milgram.

23   Ross and Nisbett find a seat for Stanley Milgram at social psychology's high table. They do this slyly, by taking the idea of obedience—Milgram's big idea—and putting it quietly to one side. When Ross teaches Milgram at Stanford, he makes a point of giving his students detailed instructions on how to prepare for the classes—instructions that he knows will be thoroughly ignored. He is then able to stand in front of his students and examine their disobedience. "I asked you to do something that's good for you rather than bad for you," he tells them. "And I'm a legitimate authority rather than an illegitimate one, and I actually have power that the Milgram experimenter doesn't have. And yet you didn't obey. So the study can't just be about obedience." What it is primarily about, Ross tells his students—and it may be about other things too—is the extreme power of a situation that has been built without obvious escape routes. (As Herbert Winer said: "At no time was there a pause or a break when anything could be raised. . . . ") "There was really no exit," Ross told me, "there was no channel for disobedience. People who were discomforted, who wanted to disobey, didn't quite know how to do it. They made some timid attempts, and it got them nowhere. In order to disobey they have to step out of the whole situation, and say to the experimenter, 'Go to hell! You can't tell me what to do!' As long as they continue to function within that relationship, they're asking the experimenter for permission not to give shocks, and as long as the experimenter denies them that permission, they're stuck. They don't know how to get out of it." Ross suspects that things would have turned out very differently given one change to the situation. It's a fairly big change: the addition of a prominent red button in the middle of the table, combined with a clearly displayed notice signed by the "Human Subjects' Committee" explaining that the button could be pressed "by any subject in any experiment at any time if he or she absolutely refuses to continue."

24   According to Ross and Nisbett (who are saying something that Milgram surely knew, but something he allowed to become obscured), the Obedience Experiments point us towards a great social psychological truth, perhaps *the* great truth, which is this: people tend to do things because of where they are, not who they are, and we are slow to see it. We look for character traits to explain a person's actions—he is clever, shy, generous, arrogant—and we stubbornly underestimate the influence of the situation, the way things *happened to be* at that moment. So, if circumstances had been even only subtly different (if she hadn't been running late; if he'd been *told* the film was a comedy), the behaviour might have been radically different. Under certain controlled circumstances, then, people can be induced to behave unkindly: to that extent,

Milgram may have something to say about a kind of destructive obedience. But under other circumstances, Professor Ross promised me, the same people would be nice. Given the correct situation, he said, we could be led to do "terrifically altruistic and self-sacrificing things that we would never have agreed to before we started."

25   So the experiment that has troubled us for nearly forty years (that buzzing and howling), and which caused Milgram to have dark thoughts about America's vulnerability to fascism, suddenly has a new complexion. Now, it is about the influence of *any* situation on behaviour, good or bad: "You stop on the highway to help someone," Professor Ross said, "and then the help you try to give doesn't prove to be enough, so you give the person a ride, and then you end up lending them money or letting them stay in your house. It wasn't because that was the person in the world you cared about the most, it was just one thing led to another. Step by step."

26   That's the Milgram situation. "We can take ordinary people," Ross said, "and make them show a degree of obedience or conformity—or for that matter altruism or bravery, whatever—to a degree that we would normally assume you would only see in the rare few. And that's relevant to telling us what we're capable of making people do, but it also tells us that when we observe the world, we are often going to be making an attribution error, because lots of times, the situational factors have been opaque to us, and therefore we are making erroneous inferences about people. The South African government says, 'Can we deal with this fellow Mandela?' and the answer is, 'No, he's a terrorist.' But a social psychologist would say, 'Mandela, in *one* context, given *one* set of situations, was a terrorist.'" According to Ross, that's the key lesson of social psychology; that's how the discipline can be useful in education, the work place, and law. "Our emphasis," he says, "should be on creating situations that promote what we want to promote, rather than searching endlessly for the right person. Don't assume that people who commit atrocities are atrocious people, or people who do heroic things are heroic. Don't get overly carried away; don't think, because you observed someone under one set of discrete situational factors, that you know *what they're like*, and therefore can predict what they would do in a very different set of circumstances."

27   It's hard not to think of Stanley Milgram in another set of circumstances— to imagine the careers he did not have in films or in the theatre, and to wonder how things would have turned out if his work had appeared at another time, or had been read a little differently. It may now be possible to place the Obedience Experiments somewhere near the center of the social psychological project, but that's not how it felt in the last years of Milgram's life. He had failed to secure tenure at Harvard. Disappointed, he moved to New York, assuming he would soon be leaving again, to take up a post at a more glamorous institution. But he was still at CUNY seventeen years later, at the time of his premature death. "He had hoped it would be just for five years," Alexandra Milgram told me, "but things got much more difficult to move on to other places. You were glad to have what you had. And he was happy to do the work that he did. I don't think he was as happy at the university as he was at, say, Harvard, but he was a very independent person: he had his ideas, he had his research."

28   The research pushed Milgram into a kind of internal exile. Confirming his reputation as social psychology's renegade, he pursued work that, although often brilliantly conceived and elegantly reported, could look eccentric and old-fashioned to colleagues, and that ran the risk of appearing to place method ahead of meaning. "It would flash and then burn out," says Professor Miller, "and then he'd go on to something else." He sent his (young, able-bodied) students on to the New York subway to ask people to give up their seats. He co-wrote a paper about *Candid Camera's* virtues as an archive for students of human behaviour. Pre-empting the play *Six Degrees of Separation*, he studied the "small world" phenomenon, investigating the chains of acquaintance that link two strangers. He took photographs of rail commuters and showed them to those who travelled on the same route, to explore the notion of the "familiar stranger." In an expensive, elaborate, and ultimately inconclusive experiment in 1971, he explored the links between antisocial acts seen on television and similar acts in real life by getting CBS to produce and air two versions of a hit hospital drama, *Medical Center*. He asked students to try to give away money on the street. He tested how easy it was for people to walk between a pavement photographer and his subject. And when he was recuperating from one of a series of heart attacks, he made an informal study of the social psychology of being a hospital patient. He was only fifty-one when he died.

29   Once, shortly before the Obedience Experiments had begun, Milgram had written from Yale about his fear of having made the wrong career move. "Of course," he told a friend, "I am glad that the present job sometimes engages my genuine interests, or at least, a part of my interests, but there is another part that remains submerged and somehow, perhaps because it is not expressed, seems most important." He described his routine: pulling himself out of bed, dragging himself to the lecture room "where I misrepresent myself for two hours as an efficient and persevering man of science . . . I should not be here, but in Greece shooting films under a Mediterranean sun, hopping about in a small boat from one Aegean isle to the next." He added, in a spirit of comic self-laceration, "Fool!"

Review Questions

1. Why was Milgram's article rejected when it was first submitted for publication? What did Milgram do to ensure its professional acceptability?

2. What does Parker mean when he says (paragraph 5) that "Milgram returned to ordinary Nazis their Nuremberg defense, nicely polished in an American laboratory"?

3. In what sense did his obedience experiments ruin Milgram's career?

4. Based on what you have read about Daniel Jonah Goldhagen, explain the meaning of the title of his book, *Hitler's Willing Executioners*.

5. What does Henderikus Stam mean when he charges that Milgram's experiment is "not scientific, it's . . . scientistic"?

Discussion and Writing Suggestions

1. Parker charts the course of the Milgram experiments working their way into popular consciousness—from magazine articles to TV dramas, to episodes of *The Simpsons*. Why do you think that the obedience experiments, more than thousands of other social science experiments performed during the 1960s, made such an indelible impact, even outside the profession of social psychology?

2. Parker focuses in part upon the ethical problems with Milgram's experiments. To what extent do you believe that these experiments were unethical? To what extent does Milgram's chief rejoinder—that his surveys taken after the fact show that the vast majority of his subjects suffered no permanent ill effects—effectively rebut the ethical objections?

3. One theory about why many of Milgram's subjects behaved as they did—going all the way to the top of the shock register—is that they did not really believe that the subjects were being shocked; they simply went along with the experimenter because they did not think it possible that a prestigious institution like Yale would be a party to inflicting harm on people. To what extent do you find this theory plausible?

4. Parker notes that not only did many of Milgram's subjects laugh during the experiments and later, in recounting it to others, but many students also laugh when they watch Milgram's film ("Obedience") in class. If you saw the film, did you laugh when you saw it? Did others? Attempt to account for this apparently incongruous reaction.

5. How necessary was Milgram's experiment? Parker notes that many have argued that if we want to learn about the power of authority to compel obedience, all we need do is study the numerous historical examples (the Holocaust being the one most often cited) of obedience to malign authority. To what extent do the results of Milgram's experiments add anything to what we already know about obedience from actual historical events?

6. Parker includes the following quotation from Daniel Jonah Goldhagen, author of *Hitler's Willing Executioners:* "If you think that certain people are evil . . . and that it's necessary to do away with them—if you hate them—and then someone orders you to kill them, you're not carrying out the deed only because of the order. You're carrying it out because you think it's right" (paragraph 18). In other words, people who commit evil acts do so less because they feel compelled to obey external authority figures than because they are following their own consciences, their own sense of who is the enemy. To what extent do you find that this theory accounts for many of the evil acts in the world?

7. Parker cites Ross's theory that an important reason that so many of Milgram's subjects were fully obedient is that they had no "escape route"—the experimenter never gave them time or opportunity to call a

halt to the experimental procedure. To what extent do you find this theory plausible? Would a "red button" to stop the experiment likely have led to a different set of results?

8. Lee Ross and Richard E. Nisbett believe that the main factor determining the obedience of Milgram's subjects was not the *character* of the subjects, but rather the *situation*—that given a different situation (i.e., a situation not involving a carefully controlled laboratory experiment), the same subjects who were so obedient might have behaved very differently. To what extent do you find this theory plausible? Can you think of examples in which people will behave in different ways in different situations?

The Stanford Prison Experiment
Philip G. Zimbardo

As well known—and as controversial—as the Milgram obedience experiments, the Stanford Prison Experiment (1973) raises troubling questions about the ability of individuals to resist authoritarian or obedient roles, if the social setting requires these roles. Philip G. Zimbardo, professor of psychology at Stanford University, set out to study the process by which prisoners and guards "learn" to become compliant and authoritarian, respectively. To find subjects for the experiment, Zimbardo placed an advertisement in a local newspaper:

> Male college students needed for psychological study of prison life. $15 per day for 1–2 weeks beginning Aug. 14. For further information & applications, come to Room 248, Jordan Hall, Stanford U.

The ad drew 75 responses. From these Zimbardo and his colleagues selected 21 college-age men, half of whom would become "prisoners" in the experiment, the other half "guards." The elaborate role-playing scenario, planned for two weeks, had to be cut short due to the intensity of subjects' responses. This article first appeared in the New York Times Magazine *on April 8, 1973.*

> *In prison, those things withheld from and denied to the prisoner become precisely what he wants most of all.*
> —Eldridge Cleaver, "Soul on Ice"

> *Our sense of power is more vivid when we break a man's spirit than when we win his heart.*
> —Eric Hoffer, "The Passionate State of Mind"

> *Every prison that men build / Is built with bricks of shame, / And bound with bars lest Christ should see / How men their brothers maim.*
> —Oscar Wilde, "The Ballad of Reading Gaol"

Wherever anyone is against his will that is to him a prison.
—Epictetus, "Discourses"

1   The quiet of a summer morning in Palo Alto, Calif., was shattered by a screech-
ing squad car siren as police swept through the city picking up college students
in a surprise mass arrest. Each suspect was charged with a felony, warned of his
constitutional rights, spread-eagled against the car, searched, handcuffed, and
carted off in the back seat of the squad car to the police station for booking.

2   After fingerprinting and the preparation of identification forms for his
"jacket" (central information file), each prisoner was left isolated in a detention
cell to wonder what he had done to get himself into this mess. After a while, he
was blindfolded and transported to the "Stanford County Prison." Here he
began the process of becoming a prisoner—stripped naked, skin-searched,
deloused, and issued a uniform, bedding, soap, and towel.

3   The warden offered an impromptu welcome:

4   "As you probably know, I'm your warden. All of you have shown that you are
unable to function outside in the real world for one reason or another—that
somehow you lack the responsibility of good citizens of this great country. We
of this prison, your correctional staff, are going to help you learn what your
responsibilities as citizens of this country are. Here are the rules. Sometime in
the near future there will be a copy of the rules posted in each of the cells. We
expect you to know them and to be able to recite them by number. If you follow
all of these rules and keep your hands clean, repent for your misdeeds, and show
a proper attitude of penitence, you and I will get along just fine."

5   There followed a reading of the 16 basic rules of prisoner conduct, "Rule
Number One: Prisoners must remain silent during rest periods, after lights are out,
during meals, and whenever they are outside the prison yard. Two: Prisoners must
eat at mealtimes and only at mealtimes. Three: Prisoners must not move, tamper,
deface, or damage walls, ceilings, windows, doors, or other prison property. . . .
Seven: Prisoners must address each other by their ID number only. Eight: Prisoners
must address the guards as 'Mr. Correctional Officer.' . . . Sixteen: Failure to obey
any of the above rules may result in punishment."

6   By late afternoon these youthful "first offenders" sat in dazed silence on the
cots in their barren cells trying to make sense of the events that had transformed
their lives so dramatically.

7   If the police arrests and processing were executed with customary detach-
ment, however, there were some things that didn't fit. For these men were now
part of a very unusual kind of prison, an experimental mock prison, created by
social psychologists to study the effects of imprisonment upon volunteer
research subjects. When we planned our two-week-long simulation of prison
life, we sought to understand more about the process by which people called
"prisoners" lose their liberty, civil rights, independence, and privacy, while those
called "guards" gain social power by accepting the responsibility for controlling and managing the lives of their dependent charges.

8   Why didn't we pursue this research in a real prison? First, prison systems are
fortresses of secrecy, closed to impartial observation, and thereby immune to

critical analysis from anyone not already part of the correctional authority. Second, in any real prison, it is impossible to separate what each individual brings into the prison from what the prison brings out in each person.

9   We populated our mock prison with a homogeneous group of people who could be considered "normal-average" on the basis of clinical interviews and personality tests. Our participants (10 prisoners and 11 guards) were selected from more than 75 volunteers recruited through ads in the city and campus newspapers. The applicants were mostly college students from all over the United States and Canada who happened to be in the Stanford area during the summer and were attracted by the lure of earning $15 a day for participating in a study of prison life. We selected only those judged to be emotionally stable, physically healthy, mature, law-abiding citizens.

10   The sample of average, middle-class, Caucasian, college-age males (plus one Oriental student) was arbitrarily divided by the flip of a coin. Half were randomly assigned to play the role of guards, the others of prisoners. There were no measurable differences between the guards and the prisoners at the start of the experiment. Although initially warned that as prisoners their privacy and other civil rights would be violated and that they might be subjected to harassment, every subject was completely confident of his ability to endure whatever the prison had to offer for the full two-week experimental period. Each subject unhesitatingly agreed to give his "informed consent" to participate.

11   The prison was constructed in the basement of Stanford University's psychology building, which was deserted after the end of the summer-school session. A long corridor was converted into the prison "yard" by partitioning off both ends. Three small laboratory rooms opening onto this corridor were made into cells by installing metal barred doors and replacing existing furniture with cots, three to a cell. Adjacent offices were refurnished as guards' quarters, interview-testing rooms, and bedrooms for the "warden" (Jaffe) and the "superintendent" (Zimbardo). A concealed video camera and hidden microphones recorded much of the activity and conversation of guards and prisoners. The physical environment was one in which prisoners could always be observed by the staff, the only exception being when they were secluded in solitary confinement (a small, dark storage closet, labeled "The Hole").

12   Our mock prison represented an attempt to simulate the psychological state of imprisonment in certain ways. We based our experiment on an in-depth analysis of the prison situation, developed after hundreds of hours of discussion with Carlo Prescott (our ex-con consultant), parole officers, and correctional personnel, and after reviewing much of the existing literature on prisons and concentration camps.

13   "Real" prisoners typically report feeling powerless, arbitrarily controlled, dependent, frustrated, hopeless, anonymous, dehumanized, and emasculated. It was not possible, pragmatically or ethically, to create such chronic states in volunteer subjects who realize that they are in an experiment for only a short time. Racism, physical brutality, indefinite confinement, and enforced homosexuality were not features of our mock prison. But we did try to reproduce those elements of the prison experience that seemed most fundamental.

14   We promoted anonymity by seeking to minimize each prisoner's sense of uniqueness and prior identity. The prisoners wore smocks and nylon stocking caps; they had to use their ID numbers; their personal effects were removed and they were housed in barren cells. All of this made them appear similar to each other and indistinguishable to observers. Their smocks, which were like dresses, were worn without undergarments, causing the prisoners to be restrained in their physical actions and to move in ways that were more feminine than masculine. The prisoners were forced to obtain permission from the guard for routine and simple activities such as writing letters, smoking a cigarette, or even going to the toilet; this elicited from them a childlike dependency.

15   Their quarters, though clean and neat, were small, stark, and without esthetic appeal. The lack of windows resulted in poor air circulation, and persistent odors arose from the unwashed bodies of the prisoners. After 10 P.M. lockup, toilet privileges were denied, so prisoners who had to relieve themselves would have to urinate and defecate in buckets provided by the guards. Sometimes the guards refused permission to have them cleaned out, and this made the prison smell.

16   Above all, "real" prisons are machines for playing tricks with the human conception of time. In our windowless prison, the prisoners often did not even know whether it was day or night. A few hours after falling asleep, they were roused by shrill whistles for their "count." The ostensible purpose of the count was to provide a public test of the prisoners' knowledge of the rules and of their ID numbers. But more important, the count, which occurred at least once on each of the three different guard shifts, provided a regular occasion for the guards to relate to the prisoners. Over the course of the study, the duration of the counts was spontaneously increased by the guards from their initial perfunctory 10 minutes to a seemingly interminable several hours. During these confrontations, guards who were bored could find ways to amuse themselves, ridiculing recalcitrant prisoners, enforcing arbitrary rules, and openly exaggerating any dissension among the prisoners.

17   The guards were also "deindividualized": They wore identical khaki uniforms and silver reflector sunglasses that made eye contact with them impossible. Their symbols of power were billy clubs, whistles, handcuffs, and the keys to the cells and the "main gate." Although our guards received no formal training from us in how to be guards, for the most part they moved with apparent ease into their roles. The media had already provided them with ample models of prison guards to emulate.

18   Because we were as interested in the guards' behavior as in the prisoners', they were given considerable latitude to improvise and to develop strategies and tactics of prisoner management. Our guards were told that they must maintain "law and order" in this prison, that they were responsible for handling any trouble that might break out, and they were cautioned about the seriousness and potential dangers of the situation they were about to enter. Surprisingly, in most prison systems, "real" guards are not given much more psychological preparation or adequate training than this for what is one of the most complex, demanding, and dangerous jobs our society has to offer. They are expected to learn how to adjust to their new employment mostly from on-the-job experience, and from

contacts with the "old bulls" during a survival-of-the-fittest orientation period. According to an orientation manual for correctional officers at San Quentin, "the only way you really get to know San Quentin is through experience and time. Some of us take more time and must go through more experiences than others to accomplish this; some really never do get there."

19   You cannot be a prisoner if no one will be your guard, and you cannot be a prison guard if no one takes you or your prison seriously. Therefore, over time a perverted symbiotic relationship developed. As the guards became more aggressive, prisoners became more passive; assertion by the guards led to dependency in the prisoners; self-aggrandizement was met with self-deprecation, authority with helplessness, and the counterpart of the guards' sense of mastery and control was the depression and hopelessness witnessed in the prisoners. As these differences in behavior, mood, and perception became more evident to all, the need for the now "righteously" powerful guards to rule the obviously inferior and powerless inmates became a sufficient reason to support almost any further indignity of man against man:

20   Guard K: "During the inspection, I went to cell 2 to mess up a bed which the prisoner had made and he grabbed me, screaming that he had just made it, and he wasn't going to let me mess it up. He grabbed my throat, and although he was laughing I was pretty scared. . . . I lashed out with my stick and hit him in the chin (although not very hard), and when I freed myself I became angry. I wanted to get back in the cell and have a go with him, since he attacked me when I was not ready."

21   Guard M: "I was surprised at myself . . . I made them call each other names and clean the toilets out with their bare hands. I practically considered the prisoners cattle, and I kept thinking: 'I have to watch out for them in case they try something.'"

22   Guard A: "I was tired of seeing the prisoners in their rags and smelling the strong odors of their bodies that filled the cells. I watched them tear at each other on orders given by us. They didn't see it as an experiment. It was real and they were fighting to keep their identity. But we were always there to show them who was boss."

23   Because the first day passed without incident, we were surprised and totally unprepared for the rebellion that broke out on the morning of the second day. The prisoners removed their stocking caps, ripped off their numbers, and barricaded themselves inside the cells by putting their beds against the doors. What should we do? The guards were very much upset because the prisoners also began to taunt and curse them to their faces. When the morning shift of guards came on, they were upset at the night shift who, they felt, must have been too permissive and too lenient. The guards had to handle the rebellion themselves, and what they did was startling to behold.

24   At first they insisted that reinforcements be called in. The two guards who were waiting on stand-by call at home came in, and the night shift of guards voluntarily remained on duty (without extra pay) to bolster the morning shift. The guards met and decided to treat force with force. They got a fire extinguisher that shot a stream of skin-chilling carbon dioxide and forced the prisoners away

from the doors; they broke into each cell, stripped the prisoners naked, took the beds out, forced the prisoners who were the ringleaders into solitary confinement, and generally began to harass and intimidate the prisoners.

25 After crushing the riot, the guards decided to head off further unrest by creating a privileged cell for those who were "good prisoners" and then, without explanation, switching some of the troublemakers into it and some of the good prisoners out into the other cells. The prisoner ringleaders could not trust these new cellmates because they had not joined in the riot and might even be "snitches." The prisoners never again acted in unity against the system. One of the leaders of the prisoner revolt later confided:

26 "If we had gotten together then, I think we could have taken over the place. But when I saw the revolt wasn't working, I decided to toe the line. Everyone settled into the same pattern. From then on, we were really controlled by the guards."

27 It was after this episode that the guards really began to demonstrate their inventiveness in the application of arbitrary power. They made the prisoners obey petty, meaningless, and often inconsistent rules, forced them to engage in tedious, useless work, such as moving cartons back and forth between closets and picking thorns out of their blankets for hours on end. (The guards had previously dragged the blankets through thorny bushes to create this disagreeable task.) Not only did the prisoners have to sing songs or laugh or refrain from smiling on command; they were also encouraged to curse and vilify each other publicly during some of the counts. They sounded off their numbers endlessly and were repeatedly made to do pushups, on occasion with a guard stepping on them or a prisoner sitting on them.

28 Slowly the prisoners became resigned to their fate and even behaved in ways that actually helped to justify their dehumanizing treatment at the hands of the guards. Analysis of the tape-recorded private conversations between prisoners and of remarks made by them to interviewers revealed that fully half could be classified as nonsupportive of other prisoners. More dramatic, 85 percent of the evaluative statements by prisoners about their fellow prisoners were uncomplimentary and deprecating.

29 This should be taken in the context of an even more surprising result. What do you imagine the prisoners talked about when they were alone in their cells with each other, given a temporary respite from the continual harassment and surveillance by the guards? Girl friends, career plans, hobbies or politics?

30 No, their concerns were almost exclusively riveted to prison topics. Their monitored conversations revealed that only 10 percent of the time was devoted to "outside" topics, while 90 percent of the time they discussed escape plans, the awful food, grievances or ingratiating tactics to use with specific guards in order to get a cigarette, permission to go to the toilet, or some other favor. Their obsession with these immediate survival concerns made talk about the past and future an idle luxury.

31 And this was not a minor point. So long as the prisoners did not get to know each other as people, they only extended the oppressiveness and reality of their life as prisoners. For the most part, each prisoner observed his fellow prisoners allowing the guards to humiliate them, acting like compliant sheep, carrying out

mindless orders with total obedience, and even being cursed by fellow prisoners (at a guard's command). Under such circumstances, how could a prisoner have respect for his fellows, or any self-respect for what *he* obviously was becoming in the eyes of all those evaluating him?

32   The combination of realism and symbolism in this experiment had fused to create a vivid illusion of imprisonment. The illusion merged inextricably with reality for at least some of the time for every individual in the situation. It was remarkable how readily we all slipped into our roles, temporarily gave up our identities, and allowed these assigned roles and the social forces in the situation to guide, shape, and eventually to control our freedom of thought and action.

33   But precisely where does one's "identity" end and one's "role" begin? When the private self and the public role behavior clash, what direction will attempts to impose consistency take? Consider the reactions of the parents, relatives, and friends of the prisoners who visited their forlorn sons, brothers, and lovers during two scheduled visitors' hours. They were taught in short order that they were our guests, allowed the privilege of visiting only by complying with the regulations of the institution. They had to register, were made to wait half an hour, were told that only two visitors could see any one prisoner; the total visiting time was cut from an hour to only 10 minutes, they had to be under the surveillance of a guard, and before any parents could enter the visiting area, they had to discuss their son's case with the warden. Of course they complained about these arbitrary rules, but their conditioned, middle-class reaction was to work within the system to appeal privately to the superintendent to make conditions better for their prisoners.

34   In less than 36 hours, we were forced to release prisoner 8612 because of extreme depression, disorganized thinking, uncontrollable crying, and fits of rage. We did so reluctantly because we believed he was trying to "con" us—it was unimaginable that a volunteer prisoner in a mock prison could legitimately be suffering and disturbed to that extent. But then on each of the next three days another prisoner reacted with similar anxiety symptoms, and we were forced to terminate them, too. In a fifth case, a prisoner was released after developing a psychosomatic rash over his entire body (triggered by rejection of his parole appeal by the mock parole board). These men were simply unable to make an adequate adjustment to prison life. Those who endured the prison experience to the end could be distinguished from those who broke down and were released early in only one dimension—authoritarianism. On a psychological test designed to reveal a person's authoritarianism, those prisoners who had the highest scores were best able to function in this authoritarian prison environment.

35   If the authoritarian situation became a serious matter for the prisoners, it became even more serious—and sinister—for the guards. Typically, the guards insulted the prisoners, threatened them, were physically aggressive, used instruments (night sticks, fire extinguishers, etc.) to keep the prisoners in line, and referred to them in impersonal, anonymous, deprecating ways: "Hey, you," or "You [obscenity], 5401, come here." From the first to the last day, there was a significant increase in the guards' use of most of these domineering, abusive tactics.

36   Everyone and everything in the prison was defined by power. To be a guard who did not take advantage of this institutionally sanctioned use of power was to appear "weak," "out of it," "wired up by the prisoners," or simply a deviant

from the established norms of appropriate guard behavior. Using Erich Fromm's definition of sadism, as "the wish for absolute control over another living being," all of the mock guards at one time or another during this study behaved sadistically toward the prisoners. Many of them reported—in their diaries, on critical-incident report forms, and during post-experimental interviews—being delighted in the new-found power and control they exercised and sorry to see it relinquished at the end of the study.

37   Some of the guards reacted to the situation in the extreme and behaved with great hostility and cruelty in the forms of degradation they invented for the prisoners. But others were kinder; they occasionally did little favors for the prisoners, were reluctant to punish them, and avoided situations where prisoners were being harassed. The torment experienced by one of these good guards is obvious in his perceptive analysis of what it felt like to be responded to as a "guard":

38   "What made the experience most depressing for me was the fact that we were continually called upon to act in a way that just was contrary to what I really feel inside. I don't feel like I'm the type of person that would be a guard, just constantly giving out [orders] . . . and forcing people to do things, and pushing and lying—it just didn't seem like me, and to continually keep up and put on a face like that is just really one of the most oppressive things you can do. It's almost like a prison that you create yourself—you get into it, and it becomes almost the definition you make of yourself, it almost becomes like walls, and you want to break out and you want just to be able to tell everyone that 'this isn't really me at all, and I'm not the person that's confined in there—I'm a person who wants to get out and show you that I am free, and I do have my own will, and I'm not the sadistic type of person that enjoys this kind of thing.'"

39   Still, the behavior of these good guards seemed more motivated by a desire to be liked by everyone in the system than by a concern for the inmates' welfare. No guard ever intervened in any direct way on behalf of the prisoners, ever interfered with the orders of the cruelest guards, or ever openly complained about the subhuman quality of life that characterized this prison.

40   Perhaps the most devastating impact of the more hostile guards was their creation of a capricious, arbitrary environment. Over time the prisoners began to react passively. When our mock prisoners asked questions, they got answers about half the time, but the rest of the time they were insulted and punished—and it was not possible for them to predict which would be the outcome. As they began to "toe the line," they stopped resisting, questioning and, indeed, almost ceased responding altogether. There was a general decrease in all categories of response as they learned the safest strategy to use in an unpredictable, threatening environment from which there is no physical escape—do nothing, except what is required. Act not, want not, feel not, and you will not get into trouble in prisonlike situations.

41   Can it really be, you wonder, that intelligent, educated volunteers could have lost sight of the reality that they were merely acting a part in an elaborate game that would eventually end? There are many indications not only that they did, but that, in addition, so did we and so did other apparently sensible, responsible adults.

42   Prisoner 819, who had gone into an uncontrollable crying fit, was about to be prematurely released from the prison when a guard lined up the prisoners and had them chant in unison, "819 is a bad prisoner. Because of what 819 did to prison property we all must suffer. 819 is a bad prisoner." Over and over again. When we realized 819 might be overhearing this, we rushed into the room where 819 was supposed to be resting, only to find him in tears, prepared to go back into the prison because he could not leave as long as the others thought he was a "bad prisoner." Sick as he felt, he had to prove to them he was not a "bad" prisoner. He had to be persuaded that he was not a prisoner at all, that the others were also just students, that this was just an experiment and not a prison and the prison staff were only research psychologists. A report from the warden notes, "While I believe that it was necessary for *staff* [me] to enact the warden role, at least some of the time, I am startled by the ease with which I could turn off my sensitivity and concern for others for 'a good cause.'"

43   Consider our overreaction to the rumor of a mass escape plot that one of the guards claimed to have overheard. It went as follows: Prisoner 8612, previously released for emotional disturbance, was only faking. He was going to round up a bunch of his friends, and they would storm the prison right after visiting hours. Instead of collecting data on the pattern of rumor transmission, we made plans to maintain the security of our institution. After putting a confederate informer into the cell 8612 had occupied to get specific information about the escape plans, the superintendent went back to the Palo Alto Police Department to request transfer of our prisoners to the old city jail. His impassioned plea was only turned down at the last minute when the problem of insurance and city liability for our prisoners was raised by a city official. Angered at this lack of cooperation, the staff formulated another plan. Our jail was dismantled, the prisoners, chained and blindfolded, were carted off to a remote storage room. When the conspirators arrived, they would be told the study was over, their friends had been sent home, there was nothing left to liberate. After they left, we would redouble the security features of our prison making any future escape attempts futile. We even planned to lure ex-prisoner 8612 back on some pretext and imprison him again, because he had been released on false pretenses! The rumor turned out to be just that—a full day had passed in which we collected little or no data, worked incredibly hard to tear down and then rebuild our prison. Our reaction, however, was as much one of relief and joy as of exhaustion and frustration.

44   When a former prison chaplain was invited to talk with the prisoners (the grievance committee had requested church services), he puzzled everyone by disparaging each inmate for not having taken any constructive action in order to get released. "Don't you know you must have a lawyer in order to get bail, or to appeal the charges against you?" Several of them accepted his invitation to contact their parents in order to secure the services of an attorney. The next night one of the parents stopped at the superintendent's office before visiting time and handed him the name and phone number of her cousin who was a public defender. She said that a priest had called her and suggested the need for

a lawyer's services! We called the lawyer. He came, interviewed the prisoners, discussed sources of bail money, and promised to return again after the weekend.

45   But perhaps the most telling account of the insidious development of this new reality, of the gradual Kafkaesque metamorphosis of good into evil, appears in excerpts from the diary of one of the guards, Guard A:

46   *Prior to start of experiment:* "As I am a pacifist and nonaggressive individual. I cannot see a time when I might guard and/or maltreat other living things."

47   *After an orientation meeting:* "Buying uniforms at the end of the meeting confirms the gamelike atmosphere of this thing. I doubt whether many of us share the expectations of 'seriousness' that the experimenters seem to have."

48   *First Day:* "Feel sure that the prisoners will make fun of my appearance and I evolve my first basic strategy—mainly not to smile at anything they say or do which would be admitting it's all only a game. . . . At cell 3 I stop and setting my voice hard and low say to 5486, 'What are you smiling at?' 'Nothing, Mr. Correctional Officer.' 'Well, see that you don't.' (As I walk off I feel stupid.)"

49   *Second Day:* "5704 asked for a cigarette and I ignored him—because I am a non-smoker and could not empathize. . . . Meanwhile since I was feeling empathetic towards 1037, I determined not to talk with him. . . . After we had count and lights out [Guard D] and I held a loud conversation about going home to our girl friends and what we were going to do to them."

50   *Third Day (preparing for the first visitors' night):* "After warning the prisoners not to make any complaints unless they wanted the visit terminated fast, we finally brought in the first parents. I made sure I was one of the guards on the yard, because this was my first chance for the type of manipulative power that I really like—being a very noticed figure with almost complete control over what is said or not. While the parents and prisoners sat in chairs, I sat on the end of the table dangling my feet and contradicting anything I felt like. This was the first part of the experiment I was really enjoying. . . . 817 is being obnoxious and bears watching."

51   *Fourth Day:* ". . . The psychologist rebukes me for handcuffing and blindfolding a prisoner before leaving the [counseling] office, and I resentfully reply that it is both necessary security and my business anyway."

52   *Fifth Day:* "I harass 'Sarge' who continues to stubbornly overrespond to all commands. I have singled him out for the special abuse both because he begs for it and because I simply don't like him. The real trouble starts at dinner. The new prisoner (416) refuses to eat his sausage . . . we throw him into the Hole ordering him to hold sausages in each hand. We have a crisis of authority; this rebellious conduct potentially undermines the complete control we have over the others. We decide to play upon prisoner solidarity and tell the new one that all the others will be deprived of visitors if he does not eat his dinner. . . . I walk by and slam my stick into the Hole door. . . . I am very angry at this prisoner for causing discomfort and trouble for the others. I decided to force-feed him, but he wouldn't eat. I let the food slide down his face. I didn't believe it was me doing it. I hated myself for making him eat but I hated him more for not eating."

53   *Sixth Day:* "The experiment is over. I feel elated but am shocked to find some other guards disappointed somewhat because of the loss of money and some because they are enjoying themselves."

54   We were no longer dealing with an intellectual exercise in which a hypothesis was being evaluated in the dispassionate manner dictated by the canons of the scientific method. We were caught up in the passion of the present, the suffering, the need to control people, not variables, the escalation of power, and all the unexpected things that were erupting around and within us. We had to end this experiment: So our planned two-week simulation was aborted after only six (was it only six?) days and nights.

55   Was it worth all the suffering just to prove what everybody knows—that some people are sadistic, others weak, and prisons are not beds of roses? If that is all we demonstrated in this research, then it was certainly not worth the anguish. We believe there are many significant implications to be derived from this experience, only a few of which can be suggested here.

56   The potential social value of this study derives precisely from the fact that normal, healthy, educated young men could be so radically transformed under the institutional pressures of a "prison environment." If this could happen in so short a time, without the excesses that are possible in real prisons, and if it could happen to the "cream-of-the-crop of American youth," then one can only shudder to imagine what society is doing both to the actual guards and prisoners who are at this very moment participating in that unnatural "social experiment."

57   The pathology observed in this study cannot be reasonably attributed in pre-existing personality differences of the subjects, that option being eliminated by our selection procedures and random assignment. Rather, the subjects' abnormal social and personal reactions are best seen as a product of their transaction with an environment that supported the behavior that would be pathological in other settings, but was "appropriate" in this prison. Had we observed comparable reactions in a real prison, the psychiatrist undoubtedly would have been able to attribute any prisoner's behavior to character defects or personality maladjustment, while critics of the prison system would have been quick to label the guards as "psychopathic." This tendency to locate the source of behavior disorders inside a particular person or group underestimates the power of situational forces.

58   Our colleague, David Rosenhan, has very convincingly shown that once a sane person (pretending to be insane) gets labeled as insane and committed to a mental hospital, it is the label that is the reality which is treated and not the person. This dehumanizing tendency to respond to other people according to socially determined labels and often arbitrarily assigned roles is also apparent in a recent "mock hospital" study designed by Norma Jean Orlando to extend the ideas in our research.

59   Personnel from the staff of Elgin State Hospital in Illinois role-played either mental patients or staff in a weekend simulation on a ward in the hospital. The mock mental patients soon displayed behavior indistinguishable from that we usually associate with the chronic pathological syndromes of acute mental patients: Incessant pacing, uncontrollable weeping, depression, hostility, fights, stealing from each other, complaining. Many of the "mock staff" took advantage of their power to act in ways comparable to our mock guards by dehumanizing their powerless victims.

60   During a series of encounter debriefing sessions immediately after our experiment, we all had an opportunity to vent our strong feelings and to reflect upon the moral and ethical issues each of us faced, and we considered how we might react more morally in future "real-life" analogues to this situation. Year-long follow-ups with our subjects via questionnaires, personal interviews, and group reunions indicate that their mental anguish was transient and situationally specific, but the self-knowledge gained has persisted.

61   By far the most disturbing implication of our research comes from the parallels between what occurred in that basement mock prison and daily experiences in our own lives—and we presume yours. The physical institution of prison is but a concrete and steel metaphor for the existence of more pervasive, albeit less obvious, prisons of the mind that all of us daily create, populate, and perpetuate. We speak here of the prisons of racism, sexism, despair, shyness, "neurotic hang-ups," and the like. The social convention of marriage, as one example, becomes for many couples a state of imprisonment in which one partner agrees to be prisoner or guard, forcing or allowing the other to play the reciprocal role—invariably without making the contract explicit.

62   To what extent do we allow ourselves to become imprisoned by docilely accepting the roles others assign us or, indeed, choose to remain prisoners because being passive and dependent frees us from the need to act and be responsible for our actions? The prison of fear constructed in the delusions of the paranoid is no less confining or less real than the cell that every shy person erects to limit his own freedom in anxious anticipation of being ridiculed and rejected by his guards—often guards of his own making.

Review Questions

1. What was Zimbardo's primary goal in undertaking the prison experiment?

2. What was the profile of the subjects in the experiment? Why is this profile significant?

3. Zimbardo claims that there is a "process" (paragraphs 2, 7) of becoming a prisoner. What is this process?

4. What inverse psychological relationships developed between prisoners and guards?

5. What was the result of the prison "riot"?

6. Why did prisoners have no respect for each other or for themselves?

7. How does the journal of Guard A illustrate what Zimbardo calls the "gradual Kafkaesque metamorphosis of good into evil"? (See paragraphs 45–54.)

8. What are the reasons people would voluntarily become prisoners?

9. How can the mind keep people in jail?

Discussion and Writing Suggestions

1. Reread the four epigraphs to this article. Write a paragraph of response to any one of them, in light of Zimbardo's discussion of the prison experiment.

2. You may have thought, before reading this article, that being a prisoner is a physical fact, not a psychological state. What are the differences between these two views?

3. In paragraph 8, Zimbardo explains his reasons for not pursuing his research in a real prison. He writes that "it is impossible to separate what each individual brings into the prison from what the prison brings out in each person." What does he mean? And how does this distinction prove important later in the article? (See paragraph 58.)

4. Zimbardo reports that at the beginning of the experiment each of the "prisoner" subjects "was completely confident of his ability to endure whatever the prison had to offer for the full two-week experimental period" (paragraph 10). Had you been a subject, would you have been so confident, prior to the experiment? Given what you've learned of the experiment, do you think you would have psychologically "become" a prisoner or guard if you had been selected for these roles? (And if not, what makes you so sure?)

5. Identify two passages in this article: one that surprised you relating to the prisoners and one that surprised you relating to the guards. Write a paragraph explaining your response to each. Now read the two passages in light of each other. Do you see any patterns underlying your responses?

6. Zimbardo claims that the implications of his research matter deeply—that the mock prison he created is a metaphor for prisons of the mind "that all of us daily create, populate, and perpetuate" (paragraph 61). Zimbardo mentions the prisons of "racism, sexism, despair, [and] shyness." Choose any one of these and discuss how it might be viewed as a mental prison.

7. Reread paragraphs 61 and 62. Zimbardo makes a metaphorical jump from his experiment to the psychological realities of your daily life. Prisons—the artificial one he created and actual prisons—stand for something: social systems in which there are those who give orders and those who obey. All metaphors break down at some point. Where does this one break down?

8. Zimbardo suggests that we might "choose to remain prisoners because being passive and dependent frees us from the need to act and be responsible for our actions" (paragraph 62). Do you agree? What are the burdens of being disobedient?

Disobedience as a Psychological and Moral Problem
Erich Fromm

Erich Fromm (1900–1980) was one of the twentieth century's distinguished writers and thinkers. Psychoanalyst and philosopher, historian and sociologist, he ranged widely in his interests and defied easy characterization. Fromm studied the works of Freud and Marx closely, and published on them both, but he was not aligned strictly with either. In much of his voluminous writing, he struggled to articulate a view that could help bridge ideological and personal conflicts and bring dignity to those who struggled with isolation in the industrial world. Author of more than 30 books and contributor to numerous edited collections and journals, Fromm is best known for Escape from Freedom *(1941),* The Art of Loving *(1956), and* To Have or To Be? *(1976).*

In the essay that follows, first published in 1963, Fromm discusses the seductive comforts of obedience, and he makes distinctions among varieties of obedience, some of which he believes are destructive, and others, life affirming. His thoughts on nuclear annihilation may seem dated in these days of post–Cold War cooperation, but it is worth remembering that Fromm wrote his essay just after the Cuban missile crisis, when fears of a third world war ran high. (We might note that despite the welcome reductions of nuclear stockpiles, the United States and Russia still possess, and retain battle plans for, thousands of warheads.) And in the wake of the 9/11 attacks, the threat of terrorists acquiring and using nuclear weapons against the United States seems very real. On the major points of his essay, concerning the psychological and moral problems of obedience, Fromm remains as pertinent today as when he wrote more than 40 years ago.

1   For centuries kings, priests, feudal lords, industrial bosses, and parents have insisted that *obedience is a virtue* and that *disobedience is a vice*. In order to introduce another point of view, let us set against this position the following statement: *human history began with an act of disobedience, and it is not unlikely that it will be terminated by an act of obedience.*

2   Human history was ushered in by an act of disobedience according to the Hebrew and Greek myths. Adam and Eve, living in the Garden of Eden, were part of nature; they were in harmony with it, yet did not transcend it. They were in nature as the fetus is in the womb of the mother. They were human, and at the same time not yet human. All this changed when they disobeyed an order. By breaking the ties with earth and mother, by cutting the umbilical cord, man emerged from a prehuman harmony and was able to take the first step into independence and freedom. The act of disobedience set Adam and Eve free and opened their eyes. They recognized each other as strangers and the world outside them as strange and even hostile. Their act of disobedience broke the primary bond with nature and made them individuals. "Original sin," far from corrupting man, set him free; it was the beginning of history. Man had to leave the Garden of Eden in order to learn to rely on his own powers and to become fully human.

3   The prophets, in their messianic concept, confirmed the idea that man had been right in disobeying; that he had not been corrupted by his "sin," but freed

from the fetters of pre-human harmony. For the prophets, *history* is the place where man becomes human; during its unfolding he develops his powers of reason and of love until he creates a new harmony between himself, his fellow man, and nature. This new harmony is described as "the end of days," that period of history in which there is peace between man and man, between man and nature. It is a "new" paradise created by man himself, and one which he alone could create because he was forced to leave the "old" paradise as a result of his disobedience.

4   Just as the Hebrew myth of Adam and Eve, so the Greek myth of Prometheus sees all human civilization based on an act of disobedience. Prometheus, in stealing the fire from the gods, lays the foundation for the evolution of man. There would be no human history were it not for Prometheus' "crime." He, like Adam and Eve, is punished for his disobedience. But he does not repent and ask for forgiveness. On the contrary, he proudly says: "I would rather be chained to this rock than be the obedient servant of the gods."

5   Man has continued to evolve by acts of disobedience. Not only was his spiritual development possible only because there were men who dared to say no to the powers that be in the name of their conscience or their faith, but also his intellectual development was dependent on the capacity for being disobedient—disobedient to authorities who tried to muzzle new thoughts and to the authority of long-established opinions which declared a change to be nonsense.

6   If the capacity for disobedience constituted the beginning of human history, obedience might very well, as I have said, cause the end of human history. I am not speaking symbolically or poetically. There is the possibility, or even the probability, that the human race will destroy civilization and even all life upon earth within the next five to ten years. There is no rationality or sense in it. But the fact is that, while we are living technically in the Atomic Age, the majority of men—including most of those who are in power—still live emotionally in the Stone Age; that while our mathematics, astronomy, and the natural sciences are of the twentieth century, most of our ideas about politics, the state, and society lag far behind the age of science. If mankind commits suicide it will be because people will obey those who command them to push the deadly buttons; because they will obey the archaic passions of fear, hate, and greed; because they will obey obsolete clichés of State sovereignty and national honor. The Soviet leaders talk much about revolutions, and we in the "free world" talk much about freedom. Yet they and we discourage disobedience—in the Soviet Union explicitly and by force, in the free world implicitly and by the more subtle methods of persuasion.

7   But I do not mean to say that all disobedience is a virtue and all obedience is a vice. Such a view would ignore the dialectical relationship between obedience and disobedience. Whenever the principles which are obeyed and those which are disobeyed are irreconcilable, an act of obedience to one principle is necessarily an act of disobedience to its counterpart and vice versa. Antigone is the classic example of this dichotomy. By obeying the inhuman laws of the State, Antigone necessarily would disobey the laws of humanity. By obeying the latter, she must disobey the former. All martyrs of religious faiths, of freedom, and of science have had to disobey those who wanted to muzzle them in order

to obey their own consciences, the laws of humanity, and of reason. If a man can only obey and not disobey, he is a slave; if he can only disobey and not obey, he is a rebel (not a revolutionary); he acts out of anger, disappointment, resentment, yet not in the name of a conviction or a principle.

8   However, in order to prevent a confusion of terms an important qualification must be made. Obedience to a person, institution, or power (heteronomous obedience) is submission; it implies the abdication of my autonomy and the acceptance of a foreign will or judgment in place of my own. Obedience to my own reason or conviction (autonomous obedience) is not an act of submission but one of affirmation. My conviction and my judgment, if authentically mine, are part of me. If I follow them rather than the judgment of others, I am being myself; hence the word *obey* can be applied only in a metaphorical sense and with a meaning which is fundamentally different from the one in the case of "heteronomous obedience."

9   But this distinction still needs two further qualifications, one with regard to the concept of conscience and the other with regard to the concept of authority.

10   The word *conscience* is used to express two phenomena which are quite distinct from each other. One is the "authoritarian conscience" which is the internalized voice of an authority whom we are eager to please and afraid of displeasing. This authoritarian conscience is what most people experience when they obey their conscience. It is also the conscience which Freud speaks of, and which he called "Super-Ego." This Super-Ego represents the internalized commands and prohibitions of father, accepted by the son out of fear. Different from the authoritarian conscience is the "humanistic conscience"; this is the voice present in every human being and independent from external sanctions and rewards. Humanistic conscience is based on the fact that as human beings we have an intuitive knowledge of what is human and inhuman, what is conducive of life and what is destructive of life. This conscience serves our functioning as human beings. It is the voice which calls us back to ourselves, to our humanity.

11   Authoritarian conscience (Super-Ego) is still obedience to a power outside of myself, even though this power has been internalized. Consciously I believe that I am following *my* conscience; in effect, however, I have swallowed the principles of *power*; just because of the illusion that humanistic conscience and Super-Ego are identical, internalized authority is so much more effective than the authority which is clearly experienced as not being part of me. Obedience to the "authoritarian conscience," like all obedience to outside thoughts and power, tends to debilitate "humanistic conscience," the ability to be and to judge oneself.

12   The statement, on the other hand, that obedience to another person is *ipso facto* submission needs also to be qualified by distinguishing "irrational" from "rational" authority. An example of rational authority is to be found in the relationship between student and teacher; one of irrational authority in the relationship between slave and master. Both relationships are based on the fact that the authority of the person in command is accepted. Dynamically, however, they are of a different nature. The interests of the teacher and the student, in the ideal case, lie in the same direction. The teacher is satisfied if he succeeds in furthering the student; if he has failed to do so, the failure is his and the student's. The slave owner, on the other hand, wants to exploit the slave as much as pos-

sible. The more he gets out of him the more satisfied he is. At the same time, the slave tries to defend as best he can his claims for a minimum of happiness. The interests of slave and master are antagonistic, because what is advantageous to the one is detrimental to the other. The superiority of the one over the other has a different function in each case; in the first it is the condition for the furtherance of the person subjected to the authority, and in the second it is the condition for his exploitation. Another distinction runs parallel to this: rational authority is rational because the authority, whether it is held by a teacher or a captain of a ship giving orders in an emergency, acts in the name of reason which, being universal, I can accept without submitting. Irrational authority has to use force or suggestion, because no one would let himself be exploited if he were free to prevent it.

13   Why is man so prone to obey and why is it so difficult for him to disobey? As long as I am obedient to the power of the State, the Church, or public opinion, I feel safe and protected. In fact it makes little difference what power it is that I am obedient to. It is always an institution, or men, who use force in one form or another and who fraudulently claim omniscience and omnipotence. My obedience makes me part of the power I worship, and hence I feel strong. I can make no error, since it decides for me; I cannot be alone, because it watches over me; I cannot commit a sin, because it does not let me do so, and even if I do sin, the punishment is only the way of returning to the almighty power.

14   In order to disobey, one must have the courage to be alone, to err, and to sin. But courage is not enough. The capacity for courage depends on a person's state of development. Only if a person has emerged from mother's lap and father's commands, only if he has emerged as a fully developed individual and thus has acquired the capacity to think and feel for himself, only then can he have the courage to say "no" to power, to disobey.

15   A person can become free through acts of disobedience by learning to say no to power. But not only is the capacity for disobedience the condition for freedom; freedom is also the condition for disobedience. If I am afraid of freedom, I cannot dare to say "no," I cannot have the courage to be disobedient. Indeed, freedom and the capacity for disobedience are inseparable; hence any social, political, and religious system which proclaims freedom, yet stamps out disobedience, cannot speak the truth.

16   There is another reason why it is so difficult to dare to disobey, to say "no" to power. During most of human history obedience has been identified with virtue and disobedience with sin. The reason is simple: thus far throughout most of history a minority has ruled over the majority. This rule was made necessary by the fact that there was only enough of the good things of life for the few, and only the crumbs remained for the many. If the few wanted to enjoy the good things and, beyond that, to have the many serve them and work for them, one condition was necessary: the many had to learn obedience. To be sure, obedience can be established by sheer force. But this method has many disadvantages. It constitutes a constant threat that one day the many might have the means to overthrow the few by force; furthermore there are many kinds of work which cannot be done properly if nothing but fear is behind the obedience. Hence the obedience which is only rooted in the fear of force must

be transformed into one rooted in man's heart. Man must want and even need to obey, instead of only fearing to disobey. If this is to be achieved, power must assume the qualities of the All Good, of the All Wise; it must become All Knowing. If this happens, power can proclaim that disobedience is sin and obedience virtue; and once this has been proclaimed, the many can accept obedience because it is good and detest disobedience because it is bad, rather than to detest themselves for being cowards. From Luther to the nineteenth century one was concerned with overt and explicit authorities. Luther, the pope, the princes, wanted to uphold it; the middle class, the workers, the philosophers, tried to uproot it. The fight against authority in the State as well as in the family was often the very basis for the development of an independent and daring person. The fight against authority was inseparable from the intellectual mood which characterized the philosophers of the enlightenment and the scientists. This "critical mood" was one of faith in reason, and at the same time of doubt in everything which is said or thought, inasmuch as it is based on tradition, superstition, custom, power. The principles *sapere aude* and *de omnibus est dubitandum*—"dare to be wise" and "of all one must doubt"— were characteristic of the attitude which permitted and furthered the capacity to say "no."

17   The case of Adolf Eichmann [see note, page 366] is symbolic of our situation and has a significance far beyond the one in which his accusers in the courtroom in Jerusalem were concerned with. Eichmann is a symbol of the organization man, of the alienated bureaucrat for whom men, women and children have become numbers. He is a symbol of all of us. We can see ourselves in Eichmann. But the most frightening thing about him is that after the entire story was told in terms of his own admissions, he was able in perfect good faith to plead his innocence. It is clear that if he were once more in the same situation he would do it again. And so would we—and so do we.

18   The organization man has lost the capacity to disobey, he is not even aware of the fact that he obeys. At this point in history the capacity to doubt, to criticize, and to disobey may be all that stands between a future for mankind and the end of civilization.

Review Questions

1. What does Fromm mean when he writes that disobedience is "the first step into independence and freedom"?

2. Fromm writes that history began with an act of disobedience and will likely end with an act of obedience. What does he mean?

3. What is the difference between "heteronomous obedience" and "autonomous obedience"?

4. How does Fromm distinguish between "authoritarian conscience" and "humanistic conscience"?

5. When is obedience to another person *not* submission?

6. What are the psychological comforts of obedience, and why would authorities rather have people obey out of love than out of fear?

Discussion and Writing Suggestions

1. Fromm suggests that scientifically we live in the modern world but that politically and emotionally we live in the Stone Age. As you observe events in the world, both near and far, would you agree? Why?

2. Fromm writes: "If a man can only obey and not disobey, he is a slave; if he can only disobey and not obey, he is a rebel (not a revolutionary)" (paragraph 7). Explain Fromm's meaning here. Explain, as well, the implication that to be fully human one must have the freedom to both obey and disobey.

3. Fromm writes that "obedience makes me part of the power I worship, and hence I feel strong" (paragraph 13). Does this statement ring true for you? Discuss, in writing, an occasion in which you felt powerful because you obeyed a group norm.

4. In paragraphs 15 and 16, Fromm equates obedience with cowardice. Can you identify a situation in which you were obedient but, now that you reflect on it, were also cowardly? That is, can you recall a time when you caved in to a group but now wish you hadn't? Explain.

5. Fromm says that we can see ourselves in Adolf Eichmann—that as an organization man he "has lost the capacity to disobey, he is not even aware of the fact that he obeys." To what extent do you recognize yourself in this portrait?

Uncivil Disobedience: Violating the Rules for Breaking the Law
James J. Lopach and Jean A. Luckowski

Most of the readings in this chapter have illustrated the dangers of unthinking obedience to either individual or group authority. But we don't mean to suggest that disobedience is always the best, the wisest, the most moral, or the most logical choice. As even Stanley Milgram acknowledged at the beginning of his article, "Some system of authority is a requirement of all communal living, and it is only the person dwelling in isolation who is not forced to respond, with defiance or submission, to the commands of others" (page 359). Many believe that even in cases of civil disobedience, when people break laws they consider to be unjust, they should base their actions on respect for fundamental principles, rather than on personal preferences.

In the following article, James J. Lopach and Jean A. Luckowski consider the circumstances under which acts of civil disobedience are justified—and, particularly, whether or not they follow the precepts of such honored practitioners as Socrates, Mohandas Gandhi, and Martin Luther King, Jr. The authors urge teachers and students to find a reasonable balance between the two poles of authority and anarchy.

James J. Lopach is a professor in the department of political science at the University of Montana, where he teaches American government and public law. Jean A. Luckowski is a professor in the department of curriculum and instruction at the University of Montana, where she teaches social studies methods and professional ethics. This article was originally published in Education Next, *Spring 2005.*

1   A new kind of civil disobedience came to Missoula, Montana, recently. On a bridge over the Clark Fork River, a group from Wild Rockies Earth First! blocked a truck carrying logs from the Bitterroot Forest. Two of the protesters tied ropes to the rig, lowered themselves and their sign, "Globalization Kills Our Forests," to within a few feet of the torrent below, and refused to cooperate with rescuers who were dispatched from local fire stations to "rescue" them. The Earth Firsters were eventually coaxed to safety and charged with felony criminal endangerment. At their arraignment they denied that they had put the firefighters at risk, demanded to be set free, and ridiculed the conditions of their release on bail. One defendant brandished what a local newspaper called her "flame-and-monkey-wrench tattoos," an emblem, apparently, of her willingness to wreck rather than to respect government.

2   Earth First's brand of civil disobedience—frequently ill-tempered, not always nonviolent, and often coolly self-righteous—seems to be increasingly popular these days. Groups as diverse as ACT UP (gay rights), Critical Mass (environmental bicyclists), even the archconservative Catholic League are getting on the civil disobedience bandwagon. After the Ninth Circuit Court upheld a ban on "under God" in the Pledge of Allegiance in 2003, the League's president wrote, "It is up to the teachers in the nine western states affected by this decision to break the law. They should instruct their students on the meaning of civil disobedience and then practice it." Some of the new breed of lawbreakers lay claim to the traditions of civil disobedience. ACT UP, for instance, says its "fusion of organized mass struggle and nonviolence . . . originated largely with Mohandas Gandhi." Appreciation of that past seems to be shockingly selective, however. Indeed, as even the Catholic League president insinuated, our schools, incubators of civic culture, play a significant role in instructing students about civil disobedience. But are American schools teaching the fundamentals of the social contract? Do our teachers appreciate that there is more to civil disobedience than mere self-expression or simple claims on conscience?

Not Your Father's Disobedience

3   Traditional civil disobedience has usually combined deep spiritual beliefs with intense political ones. And while appreciating the differences in the two worlds—render unto Caesar what is Caesar's and to God what is God's—practitioners respected both. Gandhi, for instance, while leading a massive populist movement against British occupation of India (in the 1930s and 1940s), grew distrustful of mass demonstrations because participants were unwilling to

go through the difficult process of purifying their actions; that is, grounding their activism in religious faith and human dignity. Martin Luther King, who warned that civil disobedience risked anarchy, went to jail "openly, lovingly, and with a willingness to accept the penalty."

4   While sometimes willful and defiant and sometimes passive to the point of self-extinction (Socrates did not protest his punishment), the heroes of civil disobedience believed in the need to obey a higher authority and to be cleansed of self-interestedness. For instance, King's words from an Alabama jail cell in 1963 (where he was being punished for marching in defiance of a court order): "A just law is a man-made code that squares with the moral law or the law of God. . . . An unjust law is a human law that is not rooted in eternal law and natural law." Compare those sentiments with the words written 40 years later by Craig Marshall, an Earth Liberation Front activist, from his Oregon jail cell (where he was serving a five-year term for setting fire to logging trucks): "There are necessary evils if we want to be effective in our struggles, such as the use of petro-fuels in igniting huge bonfires in which we can watch corporations go bankrupt. . . . I hope I don't sound as if I'm condemning these activities—by all means, burn the [expletive deleted] to the ground."

5   Compare the reasoning of Gandhi and King, who presume harmony between a moral order and a rightly formed conscience, to the rationalizing of Earth First! and its political cousin the Earth Liberation Front (ELF). For Earth First! an ethic of "Deep Ecology" justifies "using all the tools in the tool box—ranging from grassroots organizing [to] monkey wrenching [which includes] ecotage, ecodefense, billboard bandits, desurveying, road reclamation, tree spiking."

6   Similarly, the Earth Liberation Front argues that "dependence on the substances in the natural environment" justifies "more and more step[ping] outside of this societal law to enforce natural law" and boasts that since late 1997 "there have been over two dozen major actions performed by the ELF in North America alone resulting in nearly $40 million in damage."

7   In many respects Martin Luther King would seem to have more in common with the Supreme Court, which dismissed his Birmingham appeal, than with modern protesters. "In fair administration of justice no man can be judge in his own case," the Court wrote in 1967, "however exalted his station, however righteous his motives, and irrespective of his race, color, politics, or religion. . . . Respect for judicial process is a small price to pay for the civilizing hand of law, which alone can give abiding meaning to constitutional freedom."

Then and Now—and Then Again

8   In 1972, when the United States was experiencing race riots, war protests, and campus violence, Harvard political scientist Edward C. Banfield penned an essay, "How Many, and Who, Should Be Set at Liberty?" describing an American society spinning out of control. Banfield sounded an alarm that should resonate for teachers, administrators, and curriculum committees today as they consider their civic education duties. Banfield quoted John Locke grouching about youth's innate "inability to control impulses and to take the future into account." He went on to warn that society would only prolong this adolescent predisposition if it instructed the individual "that he must be his own

ultimate judge of what is right and wrong and that the 'moral censure' of anyone claiming authority over him is mere opinion." Quoting another political philosopher, John Stuart Mill, Banfield notes that no society can reasonably expect a liberated individual to naturally "accept and act upon certain indispensable social rules," and so society must transmit the wisdom and authority of "received opinion" to its young lest they remain mere children.

9   Unfortunately, contemporary social studies practice runs the risk of increasing, more than decreasing, the likelihood that students leave schools as mere children. Even aside from the question of whether schools are adequately exposing students to ideas of political theorists like Locke and Mill (much less to those of Plato, Jean-Jacques Rousseau, or Thomas Jefferson), the learning theory known as "constructivism"* has encouraged the ahistorical trend. Now widely accepted among educators, constructivism has, inadvertently perhaps, undermined a sense of responsibility to the larger community by, as Diane Ravitch has observed, encouraging students to "construct . . . their own knowledge through their own discoveries."

10   When viewed simply as a student-centered methodology and poorly applied, constructivism can—and does—lead to inadequate teacher-led explanations of complex ideas like that of the "unjust law." And by emphasizing that children are their own measure of things, teachers shirk their responsibility as subject-matter experts. Students with a faulty moral compass and nothing but half-baked opinions come away from the classroom thinking that laws are simply inconvenient obstacles to achieving personal goals.

What's Taught—What's Not

11 In fact, there are civil disobedience lesson plans, but most are based on poorly applied constructivist theory. One developed by Gallaudet University, for instance, invites high school students to compare the Underground Railroad with some other act of civil disobedience in U.S. history, but offers no basic definition of the concept and instead simplistically asks students "when they might consider breaking the law because it is unjust." Typical of these lesson plans, it is thin on substance, leaves the students to teach themselves about civil dis-

---

* **Constructivism:** According to the Southwest Educational Development Laboratory (a nonprofit educational development corporation based in Austin, Texas, <http://www.sedl.org/scimath/compass/v0ln03/>), constructivism is a method for "constructing knowledge in the classroom." The child learns

> by gathering information and experiencing the world around her. Such learning exemplifies constructivism—an idea that has caused much excitement and interest among educators. Constructivism emphasizes the importance of the knowledge, beliefs, and skills an individual brings to the experience of learning. It recognizes the construction of new understanding as a combination of prior learning, new information, and readiness to learn. Individuals make choices about what new ideas to accept and how to fit them into their established views of the world.
>
> —*Classroom Compass*, Winter 1994 (1:3)

obedience, and does not help teachers whose own knowledge of civil disobedience is weak.

12   Even the best of social studies materials can set students on the wrong track. A PBS lesson plan on civil disobedience, packaged with the video, "A Force More Powerful: A Century of Nonviolent Conflict," says that Gandhi's method of nonviolence had three parts: "identify an unjust law . . . , refuse to obey it, and accept the consequences." While more substantive than many such materials, the PBS lesson still leaves out the critical Gandhian step of self-purification. According to Gandhi, who was also known as Mahatma, or "Great Soul," this is the time when practitioners must make a "total moral commitment," that is, commit themselves to "a living faith in a living God" and not to a "useful political strategy in a specific situation." This is no small matter in the civil disobedience tradition—and it could be considered a major omission from the PBS lesson. King, too, urged his followers to steel themselves to passive nonviolence in the manner of Jesus Christ. For Gandhi and King, law-breaking is justified only when it respects authority and recognizes the opponent's human dignity.

13   Another PBS lesson plan on civil disobedience asks students to identify "issues of concern" (such as school uniforms or a tax exemption for a business that pollutes), "brainstorm different ways people make their opinions known about issues of concern," "discuss which of these methods are 'acceptable' means of protest to them," and "identify possible negative consequences of activism to individuals engaged in these activities." Missing from the plan is a definition of civil disobedience or mention of the four essential components of civil disobedience—or even the three components that they had identified in the earlier lesson. Nor does the lesson discuss the difference between a fundamental principle and a personal desire or between legal protest, civil disobedience, and purely criminal activity, much less the threats that each poses to a democratic society. In these and other lessons, the teacher is directed to place the burden on the student to "construct" his or her own understanding of civil disobedience—a notion that contradicts the beliefs of the most profound protesters.

14   In matters of civil disobedience such constructivism only pushes students toward a naive belief in the primacy of conscience (which can easily become a synonym for self-centeredness). Even the Center for Civic Education, a 40-year-old nonprofit organization whose National Advisory Committee reads like a Who's Who of democratic values and traditions (including a dozen current and former members of Congress and a couple of Supreme Court justices), does not explain in its curriculum standards that civil disobedience is rooted in fundamental principles as opposed to personal preferences.

A Defective Canon

15 It is not surprising, then, that history and government textbooks, increasingly shaped by loose standards, incomplete assessments, and a generation of constructivist pedagogy, poorly serve the teacher's critical need for solid information about civil disobedience. Many U.S. history textbooks make only superficial mention of civil disobedience, generally in relation to the modern civil-rights movement. One widely used 8th-grade text, *American Odyssey*, by Gary Nash,

contends that King followed the "Gandhian strategy of nonviolence . . . investigation, negotiation, publicity, and demonstration," but omits mention of self-purification and the need to accept the consequences of one's actions.

16   Twelfth-grade American government texts, where a political theory perspective is expected, routinely say almost nothing about civil disobedience. The Center for Civic Education's secondary-level *We the People* ignores the acceptance of consequences in its answer to the question, "Must you obey bad rules?" Another senior government text (*American Government*, by Steven Kelman) implies that all peaceful protest is legal protest and describes King's nonviolent activities without explaining civil disobedience. Though these texts do not specifically condone civil disobedience, neither do they encourage students to consider the wisdom of the past while making their own judgments.

17   To provide some perspective on the question of what is not taught in most civics texts, we look at *American Civics* by William Hartley and William Vincent. They provide one of the more succinct definitions of civil disobedience offered to high schoolers: "The right of all Americans to express their dissent against laws in these and many other ways is protected by the Constitution. People do not have the right, however, to break the laws while expressing their dissent. . . . During the civil-rights movement, and at other times in the past, some Americans have shown their dissent by intentionally disobeying laws they believed to be wrong. This practice is called civil disobedience. As you know, people who disobey a law must face the consequences." This kind of treatment is needed for students who should be wrestling with fundamental concepts of government rather than their personal feelings about it.

Do as I Say—Or as I Do?

18 A student's inclination to cross the line of legality under the guise of self-expression can also be abetted by imprudent teachers. According to a 2003 report in a Maryland newspaper, a local high school English teacher, as part of a lesson on Henry David Thoreau, urged his students to perform a "nonconformist act." Two young women were suspended from school after they stood on top of a cafeteria table, staged a long kiss, and shouted "End homophobia now!" What lessons the teacher drew from this event we do not know. But such pedagogy merely trivializes civil disobedience and panders to students' desires to be outrageous and to make adults uncomfortable.

19   A Kentucky high school teacher took negative role modeling further, getting convicted for trespassing on the U.S. government's Western Hemisphere Institute for Security Cooperation at Fort Benning, Georgia, and then fired for missing class while serving her 90-day jail sentence. While she complained, according to *Education Week*, that the school district should have granted her a leave of absence, a letter writer to the newspaper reminded the teacher of her history: "While civil disobedience and legal protest have long been used as ways of attracting attention to a cause, civil disobedience is unique because it has always carried with it the obvious risk of arrest and possible imprisonment."

20   Though the trespassing teacher is surely an anomaly, her apparent failure to appreciate the important nuances in balancing liberty and authority is an all-too-common failing of the new civil disobedience. Coming to the correct bal-

ance means neither empowering political majorities to regulate liberty in new ways nor excusing individuals from the consequences of their actions. Getting the balance right means thwarting the present trend toward teaching the tenets of personal autonomy and ignoring the history that has already taught us much about the need for—and limits of—legitimate government. The forces that shape civics education—teachers, standards, methods, and materials—have important roles to play. But they must state clearly that civil disobedience differs from peaceful and legal protest; that civil disobedience involves violating a law that a rightly formed conscience determines to be in conflict with a fundamental principle of human dignity; and that civil disobedience is circumscribed by the practitioner's obligation to honor legitimate government by accepting punishment openly and respectfully. Without this tilt toward authority and away from anarchy, individual liberty will be endangered.

Review Questions

1. In what ways do the tactics of organizations like Earth First! and the Earth Liberation Front violate the central tenets of civil disobedience, as practiced by Mohandas Gandhi and Martin Luther King, according to Lopach and Luckowski?

2. What are the "four essential components of civil disobedience," according to the authors?

3. How has the teaching of civil disobedience been "defective," according to the authors?

Discussion and Writing Suggestions

1. The authors begin with an example of civil disobedience practiced by the environmental group Earth First! What do you think of the goals and tactics of such environmental groups? Before responding, you may want to conduct a preliminary Web search for information about Earth First!

2. Lopach and Luckowski draw a distinction between the kinds of civil disobedience practiced by Socrates, Gandhi, and King and the kind practiced by contemporary groups such as Earth First! and other practioners of "constructivisim." They also draw a distinction between disobedience "rooted in fundamental principles as opposed to [disobedience rooted in] personal preferences." To what extent do you understand and accept these differences? Who should be the arbiter of such distinctions? To what extent might members of Earth First! or the Earth Liberation Front accept or reject these distinctions or argue that they are indeed acting in support of "fundamental principles"?

3. The authors blame many social science and civics textbooks of the last 30 years, as well as teachers, for presenting inaccurate or incomplete accounts of civil disobedience. In some cases, "such pedagogy merely

trivializes civil disobedience and panders to students' desires to be out-rageous and to make adults uncomfortable." They also assert (provoca-tively) that "[s]tudents with a faulty moral compass and nothing but half-baked opinions come away from the classroom thinking that laws are simply inconvenient obstacles to achieving personal goals." Consider your own education in civil disobedience, both from textbooks and from teachers. To what extent do Lopach and Luckowski appear justified in their critique? For example, does your understanding of civil disobedi-ence include the willingness to go to jail, or to face other legal penalties, as a consequence of disobeying what you consider unjust laws?

4. Lopach and Luckowski argue that teachers should emphasize that "civil disobedience involves violating a law that a rightly formed conscience determines to be in conflict with a fundamental principle of human dig-nity. . . . " (See also paragraph 5.) What do they mean by a "rightly formed conscience"? What do *you* think a "rightly formed conscience" means? For example, does it mean a state of mind that impels you to do whatever you would prefer to do (and what duly constituted authori-ty—whether parents, teachers, or government—prohibits you from doing), consistent with your own general principles of morality? To what extent could the standard of a "rightly formed conscience" be used to justify *any* behavior?

Antigone
Jean Anouilh

Jean Anouilh (1910–1987) is a French dramatist whose first play, L'Hermine, was produced when he was 22 years old. The recurring theme in much of Anouilh's work is the loss of inno-cence involved in struggling for survival in a decadent world. Antigone was first produced in German-occupied Paris during World War II. With its theme of individual conscience versus the authority of the state, the play was both timely and controversial. It was often produced—in modern dress—during the revolutionary 1960s when the Vietnam War had provoked wide-spread rebelliousness against government (and other) authority. Anouilh's Antigone (1942) follows the plot of its predecessor, written by Sophocles in 400 B.C. Antigone is the spirited daughter of the dead King Oedipus. Her two brothers, Polynices and Eteocles, die in combat, having led armies against each other before the gates of Thebes. Creon, king of Thebes and Antigone's uncle, orders the body of Eteocles to be buried with full funeral rites. But Polynices must be left to rot in the sun because he attacked the city. Anyone who violates Creon's decree by attempting to bury Polynices is to be punished by death. Antigone, who cannot abide by her uncle's edict, buries her brother to ensure the peace of his soul and is arrest-ed. Enraged upon learning of Antigone's disobedience, Creon confronts his niece.

The following excerpt from Antigone is from Lewis Galantière's 1946 translation.

CREON: Why did you try to bury your brother?
ANTIGONE: I owed it to him.

CREON: I had forbidden it.

ANTIGONE: I owed it to him. Those who are not buried wander eternally and find no rest. If my brother were alive, and he came home weary after a long day's hunting, I should kneel down and unlace his boots, I should fetch him food and drink, I should see that his bed was ready for him. Polynices is home from the hunt. I owe it to him to unlock the house of the dead in which my father and my mother are waiting to welcome him. Polynices has earned his rest.

5 CREON: Polynices was a rebel and a traitor, and you know it.

ANTIGONE: He was my brother.

CREON: You heard my edict. It was proclaimed throughout Thebes. You read my edict. It was posted up on the city walls.

ANTIGONE: Of course I did.

CREON: You knew the punishment I decreed for any person who attempted to give him burial.

10 ANTIGONE: Yes, I knew the punishment.

CREON: Did you by any chance act on the assumption that a daughter of Oedipus, a daughter of Oedipus' stubborn pride, was above the law?

ANTIGONE: No, I did not act on that assumption.

CREON: Because if you had acted on that assumption, Antigone, you would have been deeply wrong. Nobody has a more sacred obligation to obey the law than those who make the law. You are a daughter of lawmakers, a daughter of kings, Antigone. You must observe the law.

ANTIGONE: Had I been a scullery maid washing my dishes when that law was read aloud to me, I should have scrubbed the greasy water from my arms and gone out in my apron to bury my brother.

15 CREON: What nonsense! If you had been a scullery maid, there would have been no doubt in your mind about the seriousness of that edict. You would have known that it meant death; and you would have been satisfied to weep for your brother in your kitchen. But you! You thought that because you come of the royal line, because you were my niece and were going to marry my son, I shouldn't dare have you killed.

ANTIGONE: You are mistaken. Quite the contrary. I never doubted for an instant that you would have me put to death.

A pause, as CREON *stares fixedly at her.*

CREON: The pride of Oedipus! Oedipus and his headstrong pride all over again. I can see your father in you—and I believe you. Of course you thought that I should have you killed! Proud as you are, it seemed to you a natural climax in your existence. Your father was like that. For him as for you human happiness was meaningless; and mere human misery was not enough to satisfy his passion for torment. [*He sits on stool behind the table.*] You come of people for whom the human vestment is a kind of straitjacket: it cracks at the seams. You spend your lives wriggling to get out of it. Nothing less than a cosy tea party with death and destiny will quench your thirst. The happiest hour of your father's life came when he listened greedily to the story of how, unknown to himself, he had killed his own father and dishonored the bed of his own mother. Drop by drop, word by word, he drank in the dark story that the gods had destined him first to live and then to hear. How avidly men and women drink the brew of such a tale when their names are Oedipus—and Antigone! And it is so simple, afterwards, to do what your father did, to put out one's eyes and take one's daughter begging on the highways.

Let me tell you, Antigone: those days are over for Thebes. Thebes has a right to a king without a past. My name, thank God, is only Creon. I stand here with both feet firm on the ground; with both hands in my pockets; and I have decided that so long as I am king—being less ambitious than your father was—I shall merely devote myself to introducing a little order into this absurd kingdom; if that is possible.

Don't think that being a king seems to me romantic. It is my trade; a trade a man has to work at every day; and like every other trade, it isn't all beer and skittles. But since it is my trade, I take it seriously. And if, tomorrow, some wild and bearded messenger walks in from some wild and distant valley—which is what happened to your dad—and tells me that he's not quite sure who my parents were, but thinks that my wife Eurydice is actually my mother, I shall ask him to do me the kindness to go back where he came from; and I shan't let a little matter like that persuade me to order my wife to take a blood test and the police to let me know whether or not my birth certificate was forged. Kings, my girl, have other things to do than to surrender themselves to their private feelings. [*He looks at her and smiles.*] Hand *you* over to be killed! [*He rises, moves to end of table and sits on the top of table.*] I have other plans for you. You're going to marry Haemon; and I want you to fatten up a bit so that you can give him a sturdy boy. Let me assure you that Thebes needs that boy a good deal more than it needs your death. You will go to your room, now, and do as you have been told; and you won't say a word about this to anybody. Don't fret about the guards: I'll see that their mouths are shut. And don't annihilate me with those eyes. I know that you think I am a brute, and I'm sure you must consider me very prosaic. But the fact is, I have always been fond of you, stubborn though you always were. Don't forget that the first doll you ever had came from me. [*A pause.* ANTIGONE *says nothing, rises, and crosses slowly below the table toward the arch.* CREON *turns and watches her; then*] Where are you going?

ANTIGONE [*stops downstage. Without any show of rebellion*]: You know very well where I am going.

CREON [*after a pause*]: What sort of game are you playing?

20 ANTIGONE: I am not playing games.

CREON: Antigone, do you realize that if, apart from those three guards, a single soul finds out what you have tried to do, it will be impossible for me to avoid putting you to death? There is still a chance that I can save you; but only if you keep this to yourself and give up your crazy purpose. Five minutes more, and it will be too late. You understand that?

ANTIGONE: I must go and bury my brother. Those men uncovered him.

CREON: What good will it do? You know that there are other men standing guard over Polynices. And even if you did cover him over with earth again, the earth would again be removed.

ANTIGONE: I know all that. I know it. But that much, at least, I can do. And what a person can do, a person ought to do.

Pause.

25 CREON: Tell me, Antigone, do you believe all that flummery about religious burial? Do you really believe that a so-called shade of your brother is condemned to wander for ever homeless if a little earth is not flung on his corpse to the accompaniment of some priestly abracadabra? Have you ever listened to the priests of Thebes when they were mumbling their formula? Have you ever watched those dreary bureaucrats while they were preparing the dead for burial—skipping half the gestures required by the ritual, swallowing half their words, hustling the dead into their graves out of fear that they might be late for lunch?

ANTIGONE: Yes, I have seen all that.

CREON: And did you never say to yourself as you watched them, that if someone you really loved lay dead under the shuffling, mumbling ministrations of the priests, you would scream aloud and beg the priests to leave the dead in peace?

ANTIGONE: Yes, I've thought all that.

CREON: And you still insist upon being put to death—merely because I refuse to let your brother go out with that grotesque passport; because I refuse his body the wretched consolation of that mass-production jibber-jabber, which you would have been the first to be embarrassed by if I had allowed it. The whole thing is absurd!

30 ANTIGONE: Yes, it's absurd.

CREON: Then why, Antigone, why? For whose sake? For the sake of them that believe in it? To raise them against me?

ANTIGONE: No.

CREON: For whom then if not for them and not for Polynices either?

ANTIGONE: For nobody. For myself.

A pause as they stand looking at one another.

35 CREON: You must want very much to die. You look like a trapped animal.

ANTIGONE: Stop feeling sorry for me. Do as I do. Do your job. But if you are a human being, do it quickly. That is all I ask of you. I'm not going to be able to hold out for ever.

CREON [*takes a step toward her*]: I want to save you, Antigone.

ANTIGONE: You are the king, and you are all-powerful. But that you cannot do.

CREON: You think not?

40 ANTIGONE: Neither save me nor stop me.

CREON: Prideful Antigone! Little Oedipus!

ANTIGONE: Only this can you do: have me put to death.

CREON: Have you tortured, perhaps?

ANTIGONE: Why would you do that? To see me cry? To hear me beg for mercy? Or swear whatever you wish, and then begin over again?

A pause.

45 CREON: You listen to me. You have cast me for the villain in this little play of yours, and yourself for the heroine. And you know it, you damned little mischief-maker! But don't you drive me too far! If I were one of your preposterous little tyrants that Greece is full of, you would be lying in a ditch this minute with your tongue pulled out and your body drawn and quartered. But you can see something in my face that makes me hesitate to send for the guards and turn you over to them. Instead, I let you go on arguing; and you taunt me, you take the offensive. [*He grasps her left wrist.*] What are you driving at, you she devil?

ANTIGONE: Let me go. You are hurting my arm.

CREON [*gripping her tighter*]: I will not let you go.

ANTIGONE [*moans*]: Oh!

CREON: I was a fool to waste words. I should have done this from the beginning. [*He looks at her.*] I may be your uncle—but we are not a particularly affectionate family. Are we, eh? [*Through his teeth, as he twists.*] Are we? [CREON *propels* ANTIGONE *round below him to his side.*] What fun for you, eh? To be able to spit in the face of a king who has all the power in the world; a man who has done his own killing in his day; who has killed people just as pitiable as you are—and who is still soft enough to go to all this trouble in order to keep you from being killed.

A pause.

50 ANTIGONE: Now you are squeezing my arm too tightly. It doesn't hurt any more.

CREON *stares at her, then drops her arm.*

CREON: I shall save you yet. [*He goes below the table to the chair at end of table, takes off his coat, and places it on the chair.*] God knows, I have things enough to do today without wasting my time on an insect like you. There's plenty to do, I assure you, when you've just put down a revolution. But urgent things can wait. I am not going to let politics be the cause of your death. For it is a fact that this whole business is nothing but politics: the mournful shade of Polynices, the decomposing corpse, the sentimental weeping, and the hysteria that you mistake for heroism—nothing but politics.

Look here. I may not be soft, but I'm fastidious. I like things clean, ship-shape, well scrubbed. Don't think that I am not just as offended as you are by the thought of that meat rotting in the sun. In the evening, when the breeze comes in off the sea, you can smell it in the palace, and it nauseates me. But I refuse even to shut my window. It's vile; and I can tell you what I wouldn't tell anybody else: it's stupid, monstrously stupid. But the people of Thebes have got to have their noses rubbed into it a little longer. My God! If it was up to me, I should have had them bury your brother long ago as a mere matter of public hygiene. I admit that what I am doing is childish. But if the featherheaded rabble I govern are to understand what's what, that stench has got to fill the town for a month!

ANTIGONE [*turns to him*]: You are a loathsome man!

CREON: I agree. My trade forces me to be. We could argue whether I ought or ought not to follow my trade; but once I take on the job, I must do it properly.

ANTIGONE: Why do you do it at all?

55 CREON: My dear, I woke up one morning and found myself King of Thebes. God knows, there were other things I loved in life more than power.

ANTIGONE: Then you should have said no.

CREON: Yes, I could have done that. Only, I felt that it would have been cowardly. I should have been like a workman who turns down a job that has to be done. So I said yes.

ANTIGONE: So much the worse for you, then. I didn't say yes. I can say no to anything I think vile, and I don't have to count the cost. But because you said yes, all that you can do, for all your crown and your trappings, and your guards—all that you can do is to have me killed.

CREON: Listen to me.

60 ANTIGONE: If I want to. I don't have to listen to you if I don't want to. You've said your *yes*. There is nothing more you can tell me that I don't know. You stand there, drinking in my words. [*She moves behind chair.*] Why is it that you don't call your guards? I'll tell you why. You want to hear me out to the end; that's why.

CREON: You amuse me.

ANTIGONE: Oh, no, I don't. I frighten you. That is why you talk about saving me. Everything would be so much easier if you had a docile, tongue-tied little Antigone living in the palace. I'll tell you something, Uncle Creon: I'll give you back one of your own words. You are too fastidious to make a good tyrant. But you are going to have to put me to death today, and you know it. And that's what frightens you. God! Is there anything uglier than a frightened man!

CREON: Very well. I am afraid, then. Does that satisfy you? I am afraid that if you insist upon it, I shall have to have you killed. And I don't want to.

ANTIGONE: I don't have to do things that I think are wrong. If it comes to that, you didn't really want to leave my brother's body unburied, did you? Say it! Admit that you didn't.

65 CREON: I have said it already.

ANTIGONE: But you did it just the same. And now, though you don't want to do it, you are going to have me killed. And you call that being a king!

CREON: Yes, I call that being a king.

ANTIGONE: Poor Creon! My nails are broken, my fingers are bleeding, my arms are covered with the welts left by the paws of your guards—but I am a queen!

CREON: Then why not have pity on me, and live? Isn't your brother's corpse, rotting there under my windows, payment enough for peace and order in Thebes? My son loves you. Don't make me add your life to the payment. I've paid enough.

70 ANTIGONE: No, Creon! You said yes, and made yourself king. Now you will never stop paying.

CREON: But God in heaven! Won't you try to understand me! I'm trying hard enough to understand you! There had to be one man who said yes. Somebody had to agree to captain the ship. She had sprung a hundred leaks; she was loaded to the water line with crime, ignorance, poverty. The wheel was swinging with the wind. The crew refused to work and were looting the cargo. The officers were building a raft, ready to slip overboard and desert the ship. The mast was splitting, the wind was howling, the sails were beginning to rip. Every man jack on board was about to drown—and only because the only thing they thought of was their own skins and their cheap little day-to-day traffic. Was that a time, do you think, for playing with words like yes and no? Was that a time for a man to be weighing the pros and cons, wondering if he wasn't going to pay too dearly later on; if he wasn't going to lose his life, or his family, or his touch with other men? You grab the wheel, you right the ship in the face of a mountain of water. You shout an order, and if one man refuses to obey, you shoot straight into the mob. Into the mob, I say! The beast as nameless as the wave that crashes down upon your deck; as nameless as the whipping wind. The thing that drops when you shoot may be someone who poured you a drink the night before; but it has no name. And you, braced at the wheel, you have no name, either. Nothing has a name—except the ship, and the storm. [*A pause as he looks at her.*] Now do you understand?

ANTIGONE: I am not here to understand. That's all very well for you. I am here to say no to you, and die.

CREON: It is easy to say no.

ANTIGONE: Not always.

75 CREON: It is easy to say no. To say yes, you have to sweat and roll up your sleeves and plunge both hands into life up to the elbows. It is easy to say no, even if saying no means death. All you have to do is to sit still and wait. Wait to go on living; wait to be killed. That is the coward's part. *No* is one of your man-made words. Can you imagine a world in which trees say *no* to the sap? In which beasts say *no* to hunger or to propagation? Animals are good, simple, tough. They move in droves, nudging one another onwards, all traveling the same road. Some of them keel over, but the rest go on; and no matter how many may fall by the wayside, there are always those few left that go on bringing their young into the world, traveling the same road with the same obstinate will, unchanged from those who went before.

ANTIGONE: Animals, eh, Creon! What a king you could be if only men were animals! . . .

Review Questions

1. How does Antigone force Creon to obey his own laws?
2. Why does Creon wish to save Antigone?
3. Under what conditions did Creon decide to become king of Thebes?
4. What does politics have to do with Creon's decision not to bury Polynices?
5. Creon and Antigone agree that "the whole thing is absurd." *What* is absurd?

Discussion and Writing Suggestions

1. Is Antigone being responsible (in the sense that she is adhering to a code of morality that supersedes the law of Thebes); irresponsible (in the sense that it is selfish to be a martyr who need not compromise her beliefs in order to live in a community); or both, in insisting on burying her brother and defying Creon's will?

2. Creon puts the needs of the state above all private concerns. ("Kings, my girl, have other things to do than to surrender themselves to their private feelings.") Explain Creon's commitment to the law and his conviction that laws make civilization possible. (Pay particular attention to his speech about the sinking ship.)

3. Why does Creon argue that it is "easy" to say no? For whom is the predicament of the play more troubling? Why?

4. "Grotesque passport." "Wretched consolation." What makes these expressions poetic? Locate other such expressions and explain their effectiveness.

5. Discuss Creon's metaphor of the sinking ship. Why is it appropriate for this situation? What do you learn of Creon's character from this speech?

6. CREON: . . . I admit that what I am doing is childish. But if the feather-headed rabble I govern are to understand what's what, that stench [of Polynices's rotting body] has got to fill the town for a month!
   ANTIGONE: You are a loathsome man!
   CREON: I agree. My trade forces me to be. We could argue whether I ought or ought not to follow my trade; but once I take on the job, I must do it properly.

   Must the trade of lawmaker force one to be loathsome? Do you think that the "featherheaded rabble" could have understood the need for submission to the law without having to endure the stench of Polynices's decomposing body? Develop your answers, and your defense of them, into an argument.

7. "A world populated only by Antigones could never exist." In an essay, discuss why or why not.

8. Read the original *Antigone* by Sophocles and a complete version of Anouilh's play. Compare and contrast the two plays. You might want to particularly consider the effect of Anouilh's modernization. Is it odd to read characters created over 2,000 years ago speaking of blood tests? There are many other modernisms. Can such an old play dressed in new clothes be successful?

SYNTHESIS ACTIVITIES

1. Compare and contrast the Asch and the Milgram experiments, considering their separate (1) objectives, (2) experimental designs and

procedures, (3) results, and (4) conclusions. To what extent do the findings of these two experiments reinforce one another? To what extent do they highlight different, if related, social phenomena? To what extent do their results reinforce those of Zimbardo's prison experiment?

2. Milgram writes that "perhaps the most fundamental lesson of our study [is that] ordinary people, simply doing their jobs, and without any particular hostility on their part, can become agents in a terrible destructive process." Using this statement as a principle, analyze several situations recounted in this chapter, and perhaps some outside this chapter, of which you are aware because of your studies, your reading, and possibly even your own experience. Draw upon not only Milgram himself, but also Asch, Zimbardo, and Fromm.

3. The writer Doris Lessing has argued that children need to be taught how to disobey so they can recognize and avoid situations that give rise to harmful obedience. If you were the curriculum coordinator for your local school system, how would you teach children to disobey responsibly? What would be your curriculum? What homework would you assign? What class projects? What field trips? One complicated part of your job would be to train children to understand the difference between *responsible* disobedience and anarchy. What is the difference?

    Take up these questions in a paper that draws on both your experiences as a student and your understanding of the selections in this chapter. Points that you might want to consider in developing the paper: defining overly obedient children; appropriate classroom behavior for responsibly disobedient children (as opposed to inappropriate behavior); reading lists; homework assignments; field trips; class projects.

4. A certain amount of obedience is a given in society. Stanley Milgram and others observe that social order, civilization itself, would not be possible unless individuals were willing to surrender a portion of their autonomy to the state. Allowing that we all are obedient (we must be), define the point at which obedience to a figure of authority becomes dangerous.

    As you develop your definition, consider the ways you might use the work of authors in this chapter and their definitions of acceptable and unacceptable levels of obedience. Do you agree with the ways in which others have drawn the line between reasonable and dangerous obedience? What examples from current stories in the news or from your own experience can you draw on to test various definitions?

5. Describe a situation in which you were faced with a moral dilemma of whether or not to obey a figure of authority. After describing the situation and the action you took (or didn't take),

analyze your behavior in light of any two readings in this chapter. You might consider a straightforward, four-part structure for your paper: (1) your description; (2) your discussion, in light of source A; (3) your discussion, in light of source B; and (4) your conclusion—an overall appraisal of your behavior.

6. Erich Fromm equates disobedience with courage: "In order to disobey, one must have the courage to be alone, to err, and to sin." Novelist Doris Lessing makes much the same statement by equating obedience with shame: "among our most shameful memories is this, how often we said black was white because other people were saying it." Using such statements as principles for analysis, examine an act of obedience or disobedience in your own life and determine the extent to which, following Fromm or Lessing, you now consider it courageous or shameful. Having completed this part of your analysis, conclude by reassessing your behavior. Write one or more paragraphs on whether or not you would behave similarly if given a second chance in the same situation.

7. Discuss the critical reaction to the Milgram experiments. Draw upon Baumrind and Parker, as well as Milgram himself, in summarizing both the ethical and procedural objections to the experiments. Following these summaries, develop your own critique, positive or negative, bringing in Milgram himself, where appropriate.

8. In his response to Diana Baumrind, Stanley Milgram makes a point of insisting that follow-up interviews with subjects in his experiments show that a large majority were pleased, in the long run, to have participated. (See Table 1 in the footnote to Baumrind, page 377.) Writing on his own postexperiment surveys and interviews, Philip Zimbardo writes that his subjects believed their "mental anguish was transient and situationally specific, but the self-knowledge gained has persisted" (paragraph 60). Why might they *and* the experimenters nonetheless have been eager to accept a positive, final judgment of the experiments? Develop a paper in response to this question, drawing on the selections by Milgram, Zimbardo, and Baumrind.

9. Develop a synthesis in which you extend Baumrind's critique of Milgram (and possibly, the critiques of others, as discussed by Parker) to the Stanford Prison Experiment. This assignment requires that you understand the core elements of Baumrind's critique; that you have a clear understanding of Zimbardo's experiment; and that you systematically apply elements of the critique(s), as you see fit, to Zimbardo's work. In your conclusion, offer your overall assessment of the Stanford Prison Experiment. To do this, you might answer Zimbardo's own question in paragraph 55: "Was [the experiment] worth all the suffering?" Or you might respond to another question: Do you agree that Zimbardo is warranted in

extending the conclusions of his experiment to the general population?

10. In response to the question "Why is man so prone to obey and why is it so difficult for him to disobey?" Erich Fromm suggests that obedience lets people identify with the powerful and invites feelings of safety. Disobedience is psychologically more difficult and requires an act of courage (see paragraphs 13 and 14). Solomon Asch notes that the tendency to conformity is generally stronger than the tendency to independence. And in his final paragraph, Philip Zimbardo writes that a "prison of fear" keeps people compliant and frees them of the need to take responsibility for their own actions. In a synthesis that draws on these three sources, explore the interplay of *fear* and its opposite, *courage,* in relation to obedience. To prevent the paper from becoming too abstract, direct your attention repeatedly to a single case, the details of which will help to keep your focus. This case may be based upon a particular event from your own life or the life of someone you know.

11. For purposes of evaluating the moral aspects of acts of obedience and disobedience, Erich Fromm posits two kinds of obedience: "heteronomous" and "autonomous." The first, which is an act of submission, is obedience "to a person, institution, or power." The second is obedience "to my own reason or conviction," and so is not submission, but rather affirmation. Fromm makes further distinctions, such as that between the "authoritarian conscience" and the "humanistic conscience" and between submission to "rational authority" and submission to "irrational authority." Compare and contrast some of Lopach and Luckowski's distinctions (such as the distinction between "fundamental principles" and "personal preferences") with Fromm's distinctions. Evaluate some of the acts of obedience (for example, by radical environmental groups) discussed by Lopach and Luckowski in light of some of Fromm's categories.

12. Evaluate Antigone's acts of obedience and disobedience in light of some of Fromm's categories, as outlined in the previous question. Cite particular lines to support your conclusions. How might Creon, as the enforcer of the laws, evaluate Fromm's distinctions? How might he evaluate Lopach and Luckowski's?

RESEARCH ACTIVITIES

1. When Milgram's results were first published in book form in 1974, they generated heated controversy. The reactions reprinted here (by Baumrind and Parker) represent only a very small portion of that controversy. Research other reactions to the Milgram experiments and discuss your findings. Begin with the reviews listed and

excerpted in the *Book Review Digest;* also use the *Social Science Index,* the *Readers' Guide to Periodical Literature,* and newspaper indexes to locate articles, editorials, and letters to the editor on the experiments. (Note that editorials and letters are not always indexed. Letters appear within two to four weeks of the weekly magazine articles to which they refer, and within one to two weeks of newspaper articles.) What were the chief types of reactions? To what extent were the reactions favorable?

2. Milgram begins his book *Obedience to Authority* with a reference to Nazi Germany. The purpose of his experiment, in fact, was to help throw light on how the Nazi atrocities could have happened. Research the Nuremberg war crimes tribunals following World War II. Drawing specifically on the statements of those who testified at Nuremberg, as well as those who have written about it, show how Milgram's experiments do help explain the Holocaust and other Nazi crimes. In addition to relevant articles, see Telford Taylor, *Nuremberg and Vietnam: An American Tragedy* (1970); Hannah Arendt, *Eichmann in Jerusalem: A Report on the Banality of Evil* (1963); Richard A. Falk, Gabriel Kolko, and Robert J. Lifton (eds.), *Crimes of War* (1971).

3. Obtain a copy of the transcript of the trial of Adolf Eichmann—the Nazi official who carried out Hitler's "final solution" for the extermination of the Jews. Read also Hannah Arendt's *Eichmann in Jerusalem: A Report on the Banality of Evil,* along with the reviews of this book. Write a critique both of Arendt's book and of the reviews it received.

4. The My Lai massacre in Vietnam in 1969 was a particularly egregious case of overobedience to military authority in wartime. Show the connections between this event and Milgram's experiments. Note that Milgram himself treated the My Lai massacre in the epilogue to his *Obedience to Authority: An Experimental View* (1974).

5. Investigate the court-martial of Lt. William Calley, convicted for his role in the My Lai massacre. Discuss whether President Nixon was justified in commuting his sentence. Examine in detail the dilemmas the jury must have faced when presented with Calley's defense that he was only following orders.

6. Research the Watergate break-in of 1972 and the subsequent cover-up by Richard Nixon and members of his administration, as an example of overobedience to authority. Focus on one particular aspect of Watergate (e.g., the role of the counsel to the president, John Dean, or why the crisis was allowed to proceed to the point where it actually toppled a presidency). In addition to relevant articles, see Robert Woodward and Carl Bernstein, *All the President's Men* (1974); Leon Jaworski, *The Right and the Power: The Prosecution of Watergate* (1976); *RN: The Memoirs of Richard Nixon* (1978); John Dean, *Blind Ambition* (1976); John Sirica, *To Set the Record Straight:*

The Break-in, the Tapes, the Conspirators, the Pardon (1979); Sam Ervin, *The Whole Truth: The Watergate Conspiracy* (1980); John Ehrlichman, *Witness to Power: The Nixon Years* (1982).

7. In April 2004, news broke of the systematic abuse, including beatings and sexual humiliation, by American military police, of Iraqi "detainees" at Baghdad's Abu Ghraib prison. The scandal was intensified—as was outrage in the Muslim world—by graphic photographs that the soldiers had taken of these activities. A high-level American inquiry uncovered some of the following abuses:

> Punching, slapping, and kicking detainees; jumping on their naked feet . . . positioning a naked detainee on a MRE Box, with a sandbag on his head, and attaching wires to his fingers, toes, and penis to simulate electric torture . . . having sex with a female detainee. . . . Using military working dogs (without muzzles) to intimidate and frighten detainees, and in at least one case biting and severely injuring a detainee. . . . Breaking chemical lights and pouring the phosphoric liquid on detainees. . . . Beating detainees with a broom handle and a chair. . . . Sodomizing a detainee with a chemical light and perhaps a broom stick.

In the days following, many commentators noted the similarities between the Abu Ghraib guards' behavior and the behavior of some of the subjects in the Milgram and Zimbardo experiments. Zimbardo himself, in an op-ed piece in the *Boston Globe,* wrote:

> The terrible things my guards [at Stanford] did to their prisoners were comparable to the horrors inflicted on the Iraqi detainees. My guards repeatedly stripped their prisoners naked, hooded them, chained them, denied them food or bedding privileges, put them into solitary confinement, and made them clean toilet bowls with their bare hands. . . . Over time, these amusements took a sexual turn, such as having the prisoners simulate sodomy on each other. . . . Human behavior is much more under the control of situational forces than most of us recognize or want to acknowledge. In a situation that implicitly gives permission for suspending moral values, many of us can be morphed into creatures alien to our usual natures.

Research the Abu Ghraib scandal; then write a paper comparing and contrasting what happened in the Baghdad prison with what happened in Zimbardo's Stanford Prison Experiment—and possibly also in Milgram's electric shock experiments. Focus not only on what happened, but also on *why* it may have happened.

8. Examine conformity as a social phenomenon (and a particular manifestation of obedience to group authority) in some particular area. For example, you may choose to study conformity as it exists among schoolchildren, adolescent peer groups, social clubs or associations, or businesspeople. You may want to draw upon your sociology or social psychology textbooks and such classic studies as William H. Whyte's *The Organization Man* (1956) or David

Riesman's *The Lonely Crowd* (1950), or focus upon more recent books and articles, such as Rosabeth Moss Kantor's *A Tale of "O": On Being Different in an Organization* (1980) and John Goldhammer's 1996 book *Under the Influence: The Destructive Effects of Group Dynamics* (1996). You may also find enlightening some fictional treatments of conformity, such as Sinclair Lewis's *Babbitt* (1922), Sloan Wilson's *The Man in the Gray Flannel Suit* (1950), and Herman Wouk's *The Caine Mutiny: A Novel of World War II* (1951). What are the main factors creating the urge to conform among the particular group you are examining? What kinds of forces may be able to counteract conformity?

9. At the outset of his article, Stanley Milgram refers to imaginative works revolving around the issue of obedience to authority: the story of Abraham and Isaac; three of Plato's dialogues, "Apology," "Crito," and "Phaedo"; and the story of Antigone (dramatized by both the fifth-century B.C. Athenian Sophocles and the twentieth-century Frenchman Jean Anouilh). Many other fictional works deal with obedience to authority—for example, George Orwell's *1984* (1949), Herman Wouk's novel *The Caine Mutiny* (and his subsequent play *The Caine Mutiny Court Martial*), and Shirley Jackson's "The Lottery." Check with your instructor, with a librarian, and with such sources as the *Short Story Index* to locate other imaginative works on this theme. Write a paper discussing the various ways in which the subject has been treated in fiction and drama. To ensure coherence, draw comparisons and contrasts among works showing the connections and the variations on the theme of obedience to authority.

10 What's Happening at the Mall?

Perhaps you think the answer to this chapter's opening question is obvious. After all, we Americans frequent shopping centers more than we do houses of worship. Each month, nearly 200 million of us shop at a mall and buy fully one-half of the nation's consumer goods (excluding cars and car parts), some $1.8 trillion worth. So what's happening at the mall? We shop, which is hardly news. Yet if leading scholars and cultural critics can be believed, we do much, much more, often unaware of a larger drama being staged in which we play a significant part. As the historian and American studies scholar James J. Farrell observes:

> Shopping centers are constructed of steel and concrete, bricks and mortar, but they are also made of culture. Indeed, culture is about the only thing they *can* be made of. . . . They're a place where we answer important questions: What does it mean to be human? What are people for? What is the meaning of things? Why do we work? What do we work for? And what, in fact, are we shopping for? Like colleges and churches, malls provide answers to these critical questions.

So we may go to malls to buy designer jeans or the latest electronic gear. But because malls are where we also go to see and be seen, to judge, to learn, and to buy both what we want as well as what we need, in visiting the mall we are participating in a larger cultural phenomenon—likely without realizing it.

Geographers describe shopping centers as "built environments" in which the engine of mass production capitalism meets you, the end-consumer. Consider the matchup: On entering the mall, you come face-to-face with billions of dollars invested in product design, manufacturing, advertising, and distribution—not to mention additional millions devoted to making the mall itself an appealing space in which to shop. Management knows that, on average, you will spend $71.04 on your 3.2 visits per month and devotes considerable effort to liberating you from your money. From employing broad strategies like corridor designs that direct pedestrian flow past the maximum number of stores, to narrow ones like selecting background music to create just the right ambience for your visit, mall owners strive to provide a satisfying, stimulating experience—and they employ retail science to aid the process: Have you ever considered why the metal chairs in most food courts lack padding? Management has. Comfortable chairs encourage leisurely meals and discourage shopping. Make chairs *un*comfortable and customers will return to the stores more quickly. Whether or not you recognize these strate-gies, they exist and management employs them.

The shopping mall has become so commonplace a fixture on the retail landscape that we overlook its relatively new arrival as a building type. In the post–World War II years, the Eisenhower administration initiated the con-struction of thousands of miles of highways to promote interstate commerce just as automobiles became widely available. By the millions, Americans fol-lowed the highways out of town, abandoning the city and its problems for homes in the safer, cleaner, less expensive suburbs. Visionary architect Victor Gruen understood that the rapidly expanding suburbs lacked not only oppor-tunities for shopping but also spaces that fostered the spirited give and take of community life. A carefully designed structure might achieve both, Gruen reasoned, a place in which to meet, stroll, and talk—as people had in markets for thousands of years—as well as a place in which to shop. Gruen set to work. Mindful of the way that automobiles choked traditional shopping dis-tricts, he relegated cars to parking lots, away from the stores, thereby creating inside his shopping centers pedestrian promenades reminiscent of the grand arcades of nineteenth-century Europe. He also improved the shopping expe-rience by carefully controlling the mix of retail tenants. Because the center was (and continues to be) private property, management could exclude bars and pool halls and other businesses that, in its view, detracted from its image of upbeat consumerism. Gone, too, were vagrants and political protesters, who may have enjoyed constitutional protections on Main Street but who were considered trespassers at the mall. And finally, implementing a technical solu-tion that had been impractical before the 1950s, Gruen enclosed his centers to protect shoppers from the elements. His centrally heated and cooled build-ings created a spring-like shopping environment, year-round.

One-half of Gruen's vision proved prophetic. In the 50 years following the debut of his innovative Southdale Center in Edina, Minnesota, developers opened 45,000 other centers across the country (the number includes open-air, enclosed, and strip malls). However, developers eventually abandoned Gruen's call to merge community and commercial functions in a single, town-like shopping environment. If the appearance of community could enhance sales, mall management would offer community services. But if the noisy and sometimes rude exercise of community threatened business, management would protect its profits by barring, for example, picketers. Court cases fol-lowed that raised questions of how free free-speech ought to be in America's new public (though legally private) gathering places. Thus the mall emerged on the American scene with a mixed identity as both a commercial and a com-munity space, an identity that remains fractured to this day. Victor Gruen lived long enough to see the profit motive overtake the needs of community in the design and management of shopping centers, and he left America for Europe deeply disappointed.

Meanwhile malls have grown ever larger and more extravagant, with espe-cially ambitious ones offering lavish entertainment. Restaurants, movie the-aters, amusement parks, and water parks attract and *keep* crowds for extended periods. As a building type, the mall became so dominant that public venues began to incorporate mall-like features. Attend a special exhibit at your local museum and the exit will likely funnel you into a gift shop. Catch a plane to visit a friend, and you will find the airport looking every bit like a mall, with wide pedestrian boulevards opening onto storefronts. Malls, and elements of mall design, are everywhere.

Historians, geographers, religious studies experts, architects, psychologists, anthropologists, sociologists, and cultural critics all study what goes on (and does not go on) in shopping centers, and all have something to say about their significance in our lives. In reading the 11 selections that follow, you will learn more about these perspectives. And because you have almost certainly shopped in malls, you will bring direct experience to your reading and writing on the topic. The chapter opens with a selection from *One Nation Under Goods*, in which American studies scholar James J. Farrell asks, "Why should we think about malls?" The next three selections set the emergence of shopping centers in a broad context. Kenneth T. Jackson provides a brief history of shopping malls from ancient times to the present. Victor Gruen, one of the most influential shopping mall developers of the twentieth century, offers his vision for shopping centers that would provide "in modern community life [what] the ancient Greek Agora, the Medieval Market Place and our own Town Squares provided in the past."Geographer Richard Francaviglia then suggests the ways in which Walt Disney's Main Street USA, his idealized re-creation of late nineteenth- and early twentieth-century small-town Main Streets, became a prototype for modern mall design.

Writing on the opening of the Mall of America, the nation's largest, David Guterson suggests that malls offer "only a desolate substitute for the rich, communal lifeblood of the traditional marketplace." Richard Keller Simon argues that malls have much in common with formal gardens of the past. Theologian Jon Pahl regards malls as "sacred spaces," and libertarian commentator Virginia Postrel finds reason to be heartened that actual, authentic life can be found at malls.

The chapter ends with sociological, historical, and psychological analyses. Sociologist George Lewis, writing in the *Journal of Popular Culture,* claims that management may publicly promote the *idea* of the mall as a community space but privately discourages the emergence of real communities. Even so, authentic communities of elders and teens manage to form at the mall, their priority being to socialize, not shop. Historian Lizabeth Cohen explores the ways in which mall development has perpetuated America's class and racial divisions. In recounting the battles of developers to exclude undesirable elements (for example, political protesters and the homeless) from malls, Cohen finds a threat to the "shared public sphere upon which our democracy depends." Finally, in a chapter from his classic book *The Malling of America,* William Kowinski writes humorously but pointedly on "mallaise," a zombie-like mental state that can overtake unwary shoppers.

Some authors in this chapter indict mall culture; others celebrate it. Your goal in reading and writing on this topic will be to challenge and clarify your own thinking. And you may, after working with this material, come to regard the most ordinary of activities, shopping at the mall, in a strange, new light.

Shopping for American Culture
James J. Farrell

Our discussion of malls and their place in American culture opens with "Shopping for American Culture," the introduction to James J. Farrell's One Nation Under Goods: Malls and the Seductions of American Shopping *(Smithsonian Books, 2003). Farrell, a historian, directs the American Studies program at St. Olaf College. Unapologetic in his enjoyment of malls (unlike several others in the chapter), he writes: "I love malls. I love them for all the obvious reasons. I love the color and the crowds. . . . I love people watching: seeing the wonder of children's eyes and the animated conversations of teenagers." If we want to understand American culture, says Farrell, we must study life at America's shopping malls, for malls express our consumer culture, revealing us to ourselves.*

1 Malls are an American cultural phenomenon. The United States now has more shopping centers than high schools, and in the last forty years, shopping center space has increased by a factor of twelve. By 2000, there were more than forty-five thousand shopping malls with 5.47 billion square feet of gross leasable space in the United States. Currently, America's shopping centers (most of which are strip malls) generate more than a trillion dollars in annual sales. Not counting sales of cars and gasoline, that's slightly more than half of the nation's retail activity. The International Council of Shopping Centers (ICSC) reported that in 2000, America's shopping centers served 196 million Americans a month and employed more than 10.6 million workers, about 8 percent of the nonfarm workforce in the country. We go to malls 3.2 times a month and spend an average of $71.04 each time (a one-third increase in spending from 1995 to 2000). Shopping centers also support our state and city governments, generating $46.6 billion in sales taxes, almost half of all state tax revenue (see Table 10.1).[1]

2 Shopping is such a common part of America's pursuit of happiness that we usually take shopping centers for granted. But although malls are usually places of consumer forgetfulness, they can inspire a sense of thoughtfulness. It's no particular problem if we come back from the mall empty-handed, but it should be a deep disappointment if we come back empty-headed.[2]

3 But why should we think about malls?

4 Quite simply, because Americans go to malls. We may not like the malling of America, but if we want to understand Americans, we have to look for them where they are, not where we think they ought to be. We need to follow

TABLE 10.1	Shopping Centers in the United States			
	1970	1980	1990	2000
Number of shopping centers	11,000	22,100	36,500	45,000
Total leasable sales area (billions of square feet)	1.49	2.96	4.39	5.57
Retail sales in shopping centers (billions of dollars)	82.0	305.4	681.4	1,136.0
Employment in shopping centers (millions of people)	2.49	5.28	8.60	10.69

Source: Data from ICSC, *Scope.* (*Scope* is a publication of the International Council of Shopping Centers, Inc., New York, N.Y.; reprinted by permission.)

Americans to the mall and see what they're doing because shopping centers can reveal cultural patterns that we don't usually see. In some ways, culture is what happens when we are not paying attention. When we are fully conscious of our choices, they are likely to express our individual values and preferences, but when we're going about our daily business with little thought about what we're doing, we act according to the habits of our hearts, and those habits are shaped as much by culture as by character.[3]

5   Malls are a great place for the pleasures of shopping, but they're an even better place for the pleasures of thinking, in part because they help us think about the cultural contours of shopping. Shopping is, etymologically, the process of going to shops to purchase goods and services. According to Webster, a shop is a small retail store; the word comes from a root that denoted the booths or stalls of the marketplace. The verb *to shop* appeared in the late eighteenth century; by the late twentieth century, shopping had become a way of life. Measured in constant dollars, the average American of today consumes twice as many goods and services as the average American of 1950 and ten times as much as a counterpart from 1928. On average, we each consume more than one hundred pounds of materials a day. Shopping, it seems, might be more American than apple pie.[4]

6   Sometimes shopping is a utilitarian act. We need a shirt or a suitcase, and we go to the mall to get it. Sometimes, though, shopping is intrinsically pleasurable, and we go to the mall to just do it. Shopping itself can be therapeutic, even fun, whether or not anything ends up in the shopping bag. So an exploration of malls can help us think about what we have in mind—as well as what we don't have in mind—when we are shopping.[5]

7   When we get home from the mall, we tell the family, "I was shopping." It sounds simple. Yet shopping is a complex act, or, more precisely, a complex interaction. It's not just a matter of choosing items and paying for them, it's an act of desire that is shaped individually and culturally, an interaction with shops and with a complex infrastructure of production and distribution. It's an act of conscience in which our own values interact with commercial and cultural values. Shopping requires a biological being to enter an architectural space outfitted with commercial art and designed to sell artifacts manufactured and dis-

tributed in a market economy. Shopping centers are built of solid materials, but the spaces are also socially constructed and regulated by political entities. Our malls reflect and affect personal perceptions, social norms, religious beliefs, ethical values, cultural geography, domestic architecture, foreign policy, and social psychology. And the artifacts within shopping centers are equally complex, synthesizing material form and symbolic meaning. Shopping is no simple task.

8   Malls are a good place to think about retailing and retail culture, an important subset of American commercial culture. Because we are consumers, we think we know how consumption works, but we don't usually pay attention to how consumption is *produced*. In malls of America, consumption is not just happenstance. It's carefully planned and programmed. To be informed consumers, therefore, we need information not just about the products we buy but also about the spaces—architectural and social—where we buy them.

9   Malls are America's public architecture, a primary form of public space, the town halls of the twentieth and twenty-first centuries. Sociologist Mark Gottdiener contends that the mall "has become the most successful form of environmental design in contemporary settlement space." The late nineteenth century was known for its train stations and department stores. In the early twentieth century it was skyscrapers and subways. Mid-twentieth-century Americans created suburban forms, including subdivisions, malls, and office parks. The late twentieth century was an era of malls and airports, and the airports increasingly looked like malls.[6]

10   Malls are also art galleries, carefully crafted collections of commercial art. To the connoisseur, they offer an unending display of artful design, including product design, package design, retail design, visual merchandising, sculpture, and architecture. The artists we find in museums often challenge our conceptions of ourselves and unsettle our sense of society. The artists who exhibit their skills in the museums we call malls, on the other hand, tend to reinforce our sense of ourselves, producing a commercial art that makes malls more popular than museums in American culture. But even people who have taken courses in art appreciation don't always take time to appreciate the creativity of commercial art.

11   Malls are also outstanding museums of contemporary American material culture. In them, we find a huge collection of the artifacts that help us make sense of our world. And as in most museums, reading these artifacts can help us read the culture.

12   Indeed, as cultural institutions, malls perform what Paul Lauter calls "cultural work," a term that describes "the ways in which a book or other kind of 'text'—a movie, a Supreme Court decision, an advertisement, an anthology, an international treaty, a material object—helps construct the frameworks, fashion the metaphors, create the very language by which people comprehend their experience and think about their world." In short, malls help teach us the common sense of our culture. If we look closely at malls, we will soon be looking inside our own heads. So it is partly the purpose of this book to explain this social construction of common sense—the way we teach each other, both explicitly and implicitly, the common sense of our culture.[7]

13   Understanding a single act of shopping means understanding the culture in which it occurs. When we go to the mall looking for jeans, we find ourselves

embedded in a cultural fabric that fits us like a pair of jeans. Shopping centers are constructed of steel and concrete, bricks and mortar, but they are also made of culture. Indeed, culture is about the only thing they *can* be made of. Retailers routinely use our cultural values to stimulate sales. Shopping centers reinforce these values even as they distract us from other American values—justice, equality, democracy, and spirituality—that might also animate our lives.[8]

14   As this suggests, malls are a manifestation of popular philosophy. They're a place where we answer important questions: What does it mean to be human? What are people for? What is the meaning of things? Why do we work? What do we work for? And what, in fact, are we shopping for? Like colleges and churches, malls provide answers to these critical questions. Like colleges, malls are places where we make statements about the good, the true, and the beautiful. Like churches, they are places where we decide what is ultimately valuable and how we will value it. And malls are places where we act out, and institutionalize, our values.[9]

15   As the local outlet of the new world order, malls can teach us a great deal about the central institutions of our American lives. Malls are the intersection of manufacturing and merchandising, nature and culture, home and away, love and money. At the mall, we can see the market at work, and we can contemplate what it means to live in a society shaped by the powerful institutions of commercial capitalism. American individualism often makes it hard for Americans to understand institutions and the prescriptions and patterns that structure our lives. We forget that when we walk into a mall, we walk into a market full of *cultural* questions and controversies. Anthropologists Mary Douglas and Baron Isherwood contend that "consumption is the very arena in which culture is fought over and licked into shape." Malls, therefore, are one place where we make significant decisions both as individuals and as a society.[10]

16   Yet if we want to understand malls, we must examine them within a broader framework. The mall makes sense in the flow of our whole lives, as we compare and contrast it to what we experience every day. The mall, for example, tells us immediately that it's not home and it's not work. It's an architecture of pleasure, not of comfort or efficiency. Shopping is what academics would call an "intertextual experience," an activity that only makes sense if we know how to read many different cultural "texts": ads, stores, mannequins, clothes, logos, race, class, gender, and sexuality. And the mall's complexities are multiplied by its customers.

17   There are many malls in America, and each mall is many things to many people. Architecturally, a mall is singular, but sociologically, psychologically, and culturally, it's plural. Each store is a variety store, not just because it sells a variety of products but because it evokes different responses from a variety of people. Each of us brings our own cognitive map to the mall, so it's a different place to a mother and her child, to a mall worker and a mall walker. It's different if we're different in any way—and we all are. Malls mean different things to women and men, to blacks and whites, to gay people and their heterosexual friends, to teenagers and senior citizens. The mall looks and feels different to poor people than it does to the affluent. Although the mall may try to be all things to all people, it succeeds mainly by being different things to different people. It's possible to speak truthfully about an American consumer culture, but if we look

closely, we'll see that we are a consumption society with many different and interconnected consumer cultures.[11]

. . .

18   . . . We often go to malls to buy things we don't have—a pair of pants, a toaster, a new lamp, a book, or a CD. Yet we also go to buy more important things—an identity, a secure sense of self, a set of social relationships, a deeper sense of community, an expression of who we are and who we would like to be. We go to shopping centers with the unfulfilled needs of our American lives, so the mall's attractions are one way of studying the deficiencies of American life. We can use the things we carry *at* the mall to help us understand the things we carry *to* the mall. We can use the mall to make sense of our everyday life.

19   This book is the story of the stories we tell at the mall. Whatever else they may be, shopping centers are places where we tell stories about ourselves— about who we are and what we value. In the plot to separate us from our money, malls are also plotted. They tell stories—about business, about shoppers, about work and leisure, about good and evil, about American culture(s). Stores, and not just bookstores, are full of stories. Victoria's Secret is a romance novel about sex, seduction, and desire, about bodies and beauty, about femininity and masculinity. Sportsmart is the sports page of the mall, telling stories about striving and success. Abercrombie & Fitch combines adventure stories with coming-of-age stories. The Gap started by telling stories about the generation gap, but now their stories are about "cool" characters and their "casual" lives. The stories of progress at Radio Shack are often futuristic fantasies, and Hot Topic tells stories about individualism and conformity, dissent and deviance. The Rainforest Café spins adventure yarns and nature stories. The department stores tell stories about abundance and choice. All of the retailers tell stories about "the good life" and about America. All of the *things* in the mall also have a story. Each artifact is a story of nature becoming culture, of raw material (com)modified to make it meaningful to Americans. At the mall, it's always story time, and, at least according to the publicity, there's almost always a happy ending.

20   This book is the story of all those stories. It's a storybook.

21   It's also my story. It's a story by me, of course, but it's also a story about me, because I'm one of the people I'm writing about. I'm not a power shopper, but I love malls. I love them for all the obvious reasons. I love the color and the crowds. I love looking at commercial art, because it is, in fact, beautiful. I love people watching: seeing the wonder of children's eyes and the animated conversations of teenagers. I like the oasis of pedestrianism in a car culture: I like walking, and I like to walk in malls. But I also love malls because in them, as geographer Jon Goss says, "I have learned a great deal about myself: about my humanity, the values and beliefs of 'my' culture, and my intimate desires."[12]

22   I appreciate malls more now than I did at the beginning of my research. When you look closely at their complexity, especially the intricate coordination needed to produce each day's consumption, it's a miracle that they work as well as they do. I have come to understand that shopping centers are part of a huge

conspiracy, a conspiracy of customer satisfaction. The people who work in malls genuinely want to please the people who shop in malls. So I appreciate the ways that shopping center professionals study Americans to see just what, in fact, will please us, and I appreciate the many pleasures that are to be found at the mall, whether or not we ever buy anything.

23   But I also appreciate the ways that a shopping center can be a "social trap," an institution in which the sum total of perfectly good behavior is not so good. Still, my main complaint is not primarily with malls but with a larger commercial culture that characterizes us mainly as consumers. My main argument is with an America that sells itself short by buying into the cluster of values expressed so powerfully in our malls.[13]

Notes

1. International Council of Shopping Centers (ICSC), "Scope USA," at the ICSC web site, www.icsc.org; John Fetto, "Mall Rats," *American Demographics* 24 (March 2002): 10; Judith Ann Coady, "The Concrete Dream: A Sociological Look at the Shopping Mall" (Ph.D. diss., Boston University, 1987), 720; Ira G. Zepp Jr., *The New Religious Image of Urban America: The Shopping Mall as Ceremonial Center*, 2d ed. (Niwot: University Press of Colorado, 1997), 10.

2. As my colleague Eric Nelson says, malls "are the last place anyone would go to think seriously. There is nothing, however, that demands more serious thought." Eric Nelson, *Mall of America: Reflections of a Virtual Community* (Lakeville, Minn.: Galde Press, 1998), 152.

3. Zepp, *New Religious Image*, 10.

4. John C. Ryan and Alan Durning, *Stuff: The Secret Lives of Everyday Things* (Seattle: Northwest Environment Watch, 1997), 4–5.

5. Barry J. Babin, William R. Darden, and Mitch Griffin, "Work and/or Fun: Measuring Hedonic and Utilitarian Shopping Value," *Journal of Consumer Research* 20 (March 1994): 646–47.

6. Mark Gottdiener, "Recapturing the Center: A Semiotic Analysis of Shopping Malls," in *The City and the Sign: An Introduction to Urban Semiotics*, ed. Mark Gottdiener and Alexandros Ph. Lagopoulos (New York: Columbia University Press, 1986), 291.

7. Paul Lauter, *From Walden Pond to Jurassic Park: Activism, Culture, and American Studies* (Durham N.C.: Duke University Press, 2001), 11.

8. Leon G. Schiffman and Leslie Lazar Kanuk, *Consumer Behavior*, 5th ed. (Englewood Cliffs, N.J.: Prentice Hall, 1994), 437.

9. Jon Goss, "Once-upon-a-Time in the Commodity World: An Unofficial Guide to Mall of America," *Annals of the Association of American Geographers* 89 (March 1999): 47.

10. Mary Douglas and Baron Isherwood, *The World of Goods* (New York: Basic Books, 1979), 57.

11. Elizabeth Chin, *Purchasing Power: Black Kids and American Consumer Culture* (Minneapolis: University of Minnesota Press, 2001), 12–13.

12. Goss, "Once-upon-a-Time," 49.

13. David Orr, *Ecological Literacy: Education and the Transition to a Postmodern World* (Albany: State University of New York Press, 1992), 5.

Review Questions

1. According to Farrell, why should anyone think seriously about shopping centers?

2. In what ways can malls be understood as "cultural institutions"?

3. Farrell claims that the mall is "a place where we answer important questions." What are these questions?

4. How do shopping malls "tell stories"?

5. Why does Farrell appreciate malls?

Discussion and Writing Suggestions

1. Of the statistics concerning shopping centers that Farrell cites in paragraph 1 and Table 10.1, which do you find most striking? Why?

2. In paragraph 7 Farrell makes a series of provocative claims in developing the assertion that "shopping is a complex act, or, more precisely, a complex interaction." Choose any of the sentences in paragraph 7 that follow this assertion and then write for five minutes in response. Share your insights with others who have read the selection.

3. Reread paragraph 14 and select one of the questions that Farrell claims is raised by mall culture. Write two paragraphs in response: First, explain what you think Farrell means in posing the question. (For example, explain how malls help us to investigate "What does it mean to be human?") Second, discuss the validity of the question in relation to malls. (For instance, discuss how reasonable it seems to contemplate what it means to be human in a shopping mall.)

4. Farrell writes (paragraph 14): "Like churches, [malls] are places where we decide what is ultimately valuable and how we will value it." Your comments?

5. Farrell suggests (in paragraph 16) that elements of shopping malls can be "read" like a "text" for meaning. How can one find clues to understanding American culture in advertisements? Store layouts? Mannequins? Clothes? Logos?

6. Do you agree with Farrell (paragraph 18) that we go to malls in search of "an identity, a secure sense of self, a set of social relationships, a deeper sense of community, an expression of who we are and who we would like to be"? How can these things be bought?

A Brief History of Malls
Kenneth T. Jackson

Plato may not have shopped at "The Mall of Ancient Greece," but enclosed shopping areas have been around longer than you might imagine. This first section of a longer article in the American Historical Review *(October 1996) provides a brief history of shopping malls. Kenneth T. Jackson is Jacques Barzun Professor of History and the Social Sciences at Columbia University. He is widely noted for his work in American social and urban history. His publications include* Cities in American History *(1972) and* Crabgrass Frontier: The Suburbanization of the United States *(1985). He serves as editor of* The Encyclopedia of New York City *(1995).*

1   The Egyptians have pyramids, the Chinese have a great wall, the British have immaculate lawns, the Germans have castles, the Dutch have canals, the Italians have grand churches. And Americans have shopping centers. They are the common denominator of our national life, the best symbols of our abundance. By 1992, there were 38,966 operating shopping centers in the United States, 1,835 of them large, regional malls, and increasingly they were featuring the same products, the same stores, and the same antiseptic environment. They have been called "the perfect fusion of the profit motive and the egalitarian ideal," and one wag has remarked, only partially in jest, that either America is a shopping center or the one shopping center in existence is moving about the country at the speed of light.[1]

2   To be sure, the shopping center and even the shopping mall are not entirely American innovations. Merchandising outside city walls began in the Middle Ages, when traders often established markets or "fairs" beyond the gates to avoid the taxes and congestion of the urban core. For this privilege, they typically paid a fee to the lord or feudal authority who commanded the walls above the field. Similarly, enclosed shopping spaces have also existed for centuries, from the agora of ancient Greece to the Palais Royal of prerevolutionary Paris. The Jerusalem bazaar has been providing a covered shopping experience for 2,000 years, while Istanbul's Grand Bazaar was doing the same when sultans ruled the Ottoman Empire from the nearby Topkapi Palace. In England, Chester has been famous for centuries for interconnected second-story shops, protected wonderfully from the wind and the rain, which stretch for blocks at the center of town. London's Burlington Arcade, completed in 1819, was one of the world's earliest retail shopping arcades, while the Crystal Palace Exhibition of 1851, which featured a nineteen-acre building that was entirely walled and roofed in panels of

---

[1] On the number of shopping centers, see Witold Rybczynski, "The New Downtowns," *Atlantic Monthly* 271 (May 1993): 98. See also William Severini Kowinski, *The Malling of America: An Inside Look at the Great Consumer Paradise* (New York, 1985); Howard Gillette, Jr., "The Evolution of the Planned Shopping Center in Suburb and City," *Journal of the American Planning Association* 51 (Autumn 1985): 449–60; George Sternlieb and James W. Hughes, eds., *Shopping Centers, USA* (Piscataway, N.J., 1981); William H. Whyte, *The City: Rediscovering the Center* (New York, 1988); and William Glaberson, "The Heart of the City Now Beats in the Mall," *New York Times* (March 27, 1992): A1, B4.

dazzling "crystal" glass, had many characteristics of the modern mall. Its designers brought the outdoors inside and made the "palace" into a giant garden, complete with an elaborate fountain and several full-grown trees. Within the
mammoth structure, crowds from many nations and social classes jostled
through long aisles, entertained as much by the passing parade and the spectacle as by the official displays.

3   The most famous pre-twentieth-century enclosed retail space is the Galleria
Vittorio Emanuele II in Milan, which was built to commemorate the 1859 victory of the French and Sardinians (led by King Victor Emmanuel) over Austria
at the Battle of Magenta. Located near the Duomo and opened to the public
in 1867, it is really a prolongation of the public street. It houses scores of separate merchants, with a glass vault on top rather than a single, enclosed building
(there are no doors). Cruciform in shape, it has a four-story interior façade that
stretches 645 feet in one direction and 345 feet in the other, bordered by shops,
cafés, and restaurants at the ground level and mezzanine. Despite its age, the
Galleria looks and feels like a modern mall, and it remains at the center of political and commercial life in Milan.[2]

4   At the end of the twentieth century, the shopping mall has become a global
phenomenon. Hong Kong has as many modern malls as any metropolitan region
in the United States, and tourists in Kowloon might easily imagine that they are
in Orlando or Spokane. In France, the Parly II Center opened outside Paris and
near Versailles in 1968. It includes all-weather air-conditioning, fountains,
marble floors, sculptured plaster ceilings, and scores of shops on two floors.
Singapore, Taipei, Sydney, Melbourne, Hamburg, and a hundred other cities
have similarly elaborate edifices; the Kaisergalerie in Berlin and GUM in
Moscow are particularly notable. Even England, ever protective of its countryside, is falling victim to regional malls and the acres of parking lots that surround
them. For example, seventeen miles east of central London, set among the
rolling hills of Essex, is the Lakeside Centre, a 1.35 million square-foot clone of
suburban America, complete with two McDonalds, a Sam Goody, and a Gap.
Since the mid-1980s, a half-dozen other regional malls, as well as 250 smaller
regional clusters, have gone up among the shires and sleepy hamlets of
Shakespeare's scepter'd isle. By 1993, these new shopping and exurban centers
were claiming more than 17 percent of the British retail market, a three-fold
increase in less than fifteen years.[3]

5   Below-ground shopping malls have also proliferated. Since 1962, for example, Montrealers have been able to survive their harsh winters by working, shopping, and living, often for months at a time, underground—or at least inside
glass and concrete. Large parts of the core city are now linked by miles of subterranean walkways, all lined with shops, restaurants, snack bars, and theaters.
In posh Westmount Square, tenants in high-rise apartment buildings have only

---

[2] A good overview of the early development of the arcade idea is Alexander Garvin, *The American City:
What Works, What Doesn't* (New York, 1996), 101–20. See also Johann Friedrich Geist, *Arcades: The
History of a Building Type* (Cambridge, Mass., 1982).

[3] *New York Times* (May 9, 1993): E16.

to take an elevator to find a supermarket, a bookstore, a bank, a movie theater, a bar and restaurant, or such expensive specialty shops as Givenchy and Pierre Cardin.[4] Similarly, in Osaka, the buried-mall concept is now almost a third of a century old. There, more than a million people per day file over the lighted signs in the floor or past the giant wall maps of the connecting Umeda and Hankyu malls to buy food, clothes, toys, and even lizards and seaweed, or to pay for overseas trips. Hawkers banging tambourines urge passers-by to sample their restaurants. Even pornography shops flourish.

6   But, as was the case with the automobile, which also was invented in Europe, it is in the United States that the shopping center and the shopping mall have found especially fertile ground. In the North American republic, large-scale retailing, once associated almost exclusively with central business districts, began moving away from the urban cores between the world wars. Baltimore's Roland Park Shopping Center (1896) is often cited as the first of the modern genus, but Country Club Plaza in Kansas City, begun in 1923, was more influential and was the first automobile-oriented shopping center. Featuring extensive parking lots behind ornamented, Old California–style brick walls, it was the effort of a single entrepreneur, Jesse Clyde Nichols, who put together a concentration of retail stores and used leasing policy to determine the composition of stores in the concentration. By doing that, Nichols created the idea of the planned regional shopping center. At the same time, he understood, as no one had before him, that customers for the 100 shops would arrive by car. Free parking was not an afterthought; it was part of the original conception. And as Country Club Plaza expanded over the decades to encompass 978,000 square feet of retail space, the number of parking spaces multiplied as well, until by 1990 there were more than 5,000 spaces for the ubiquitous motorcar.[5]

7   By the mid-1930s, the concept of the planned shopping center, as a collection of businesses under one management and with convenient parking facilities, was well known and was recognized as the best method of serving the growing market of drive-in customers. But the Great Depression and World War II had a chilling effect on private construction, and as late as 1946 there were only eight shopping centers in the United States. They included Upper Darby Center in West Philadelphia (1927), Suburban Square in Ardmore, Pennsylvania (1928), Highland Park Shopping Village outside Dallas (1931), River Oaks in Houston (1937), Hampton Village in St. Louis (1941), Colony in Toledo (1944), Shirlington in Arlington, Virginia (1944), and Belleview Square in Seattle (1946).[6]

---

[4] The Montreal complex was designed by Vincent Ponte, a native of Boston, as a way of reducing congestion on downtown streets. *New York Times*, December 17, 1976.

[5] This paragraph summarizes material in Kenneth T. Jackson, *Crabgrass Frontier: The Suburbanization of the United States* (New York, 1985), 257–61. See also William S. Worley, *J. C. Nichols and the Shaping of Kansas City* (Columbia, Mo., 1990), 10–28; Rybczynski, "New Downtowns," 98–100; S. R. De Boer, *Shopping Districts* (Washington, D.C., 1937); and Yehoshua S. Cohen, *Diffusion of an Innovation in an Urban System: The Spread of Planned Regional Shopping Centers in the United States, 1949–1968* (Chicago, 1972).

[6] John B. Rae, *The Road and the Car in American Life* (Cambridge, Mass., 1971), 230. New York City department stores began to decentralize rather early, beginning in the late 1920s. Regional Plan Association, *Suburban Branch Stores in the New York Metropolitan Region* (New York, 1951).

8   The first major planned retail shopping center in the world went up in Raleigh, North Carolina, in 1949, the brainchild of Homer Hoyt, a well-known author and demographer best remembered for his sector model of urban growth. Another early prototype was Northgate, which opened on the outskirts of Seattle in 1950. Designed by architect John Graham, Jr., it featured a long, open-air pedestrian way lined with a number of small specialty shops and ending with a department store. The idea was that the "anchor" facility would attract people, who would then shop their way to their destination. Predictably, it went up next to a highway and provided a free 4,000-space parking lot.

9   The enclosed, climate-controlled indoor mall was introduced by Victor Gruen (see following selection), an Austrian refugee from the Nazis, at the Southdale Shopping Center in Edina, Minnesota, a suburb of Minneapolis, in 1956. From the beginning, the 679,000 square-foot complex (later expanded to 1.35 million square feet) included two department stores, 139 shops, parking for 5,200 cars, and a two-story, sky-lit pedestrian walkway. Gruen had been inspired by Milan's Galleria and also by the markets of the Austrian and Swiss towns he had visited on bicycle as a young man. In America, ironically, he wanted to stop suburban sprawl, and he thought the shopping mall would do the trick. Because Minneapolis was so often cold, Gruen advertised that "in Southdale Center every day will be a perfect shopping day." The concept proved wildly popular, and it demonstrated that climate-controlled shopping arcades were likely to be more profitable than open-air shopping centers. Indoor malls proliferated, slowly at first but with increasing frequency, and within fifteen years anything that was not enclosed came to be considered second-rate.[7]

10   A few of the indoor behemoths, such as Midtown Plaza in Rochester and Chapel Square Mall in New Haven, were located downtown, but more typical were Paramus Park and Bergen Mall in New Jersey, Woodfield Mall in Schaumburg outside Chicago, King's Plaza outside Manhattan, Tyson's Corner outside Washington, and Raleigh Mall in Memphis—all of which were located on outlying highways and all of which attracted shoppers from trading areas of a hundred square miles and more. Within a mere quarter-century, they transformed the way Americans lived and worked. Indeed, reports were commonplace by the 1970s that the typical American was spending more time at the mall than at any other place other than home or work. And the shopping mall had become, along with the tract house, the freeway, and the backyard barbecue, the most distinctive product of the American postwar years.[8]

---

[7] T. R. Reid, "The Magic of Malls," *Washington Post*, September 16, 1985. Late in life, after thirty years in the United States, Gruen argued that the shopping-center idea that he pioneered had been subverted and that the country was mindlessly subsidizing suburban sprawl. He retired in frustration to Vienna, Austria. Among his many writings on the subject, see especially Victor Gruen, *The Heart of Our Cities: Diagnosis and Cure* (New York, 1964).

[8] William Severini Kowinski, "The Malling of America," *New Times* 10 (May 1, 1978); 31–55.

Review Questions

1. What were some of the precursors of the modern shopping mall?

2. In what ways was Country Club Plaza of Kansas City a prototype, in 1923, of the modern regional shopping center?

3. What was the Crystal Palace of 1851, and what was its significance?

4. Shopping malls have gone global. How so?

5. What was distinctive about the Southdale Shopping Center of Edina, Minnesota? Why do histories of shopping centers, like Jackson's, reference it today?

Discussion and Writing Suggestions

1. By "the 1970s . . . the typical American was spending more time at the mall than at any other place other than home or work." Based on personal observations, do you think this continues to be the case? What is your reaction to this news?

2. The Crystal Palace of 1851 afforded the opportunity for "crowds from many . . . social classes . . . [to be] entertained as much by the passing parade and the spectacle as by the official displays." In what ways does this report of the Crystal Palace remind you of the modern shopping mall? (Note that Jackson's reference to "the passing parade" is not to a formal parade but to a steady stream of people.)

3. Have you ever visited a mall outside the United States? In what ways was that mall similar to those in this country? Different? To what extent, when you were in a foreign mall, did you continue to feel as though you were in a foreign country? For that matter, how different is the experience of a mall in Chicago from the experience of a mall in Atlanta or Portland? Do you expect differences, even in a foreign country, or is this not a factor when visiting a mall?

4. What does Jackson mean when he refers to shopping malls as "the perfect fusion of the profit motive and the egalitarian ideal"? What has egalitarianism to do with shopping and, particularly, with malls?

5. "[A]s was the case with the automobile, which also was invented in Europe, it is in the United States that the shopping center and the shopping mall have found especially fertile ground." Why do you think this might be?

The Mall as Civic/Cultural Center
Victor Gruen and Larry Smith

Victor Gruen (born Viktor Grüenbaum, 1903–1980) is the American architect credited with creating the modern shopping mall. Born and trained in Vienna, he fled the Nazi occupation and moved to New York in 1938, where he worked as an architect before opening his own firm in 1951 in Los Angeles. Gruen believed that shopping centers would promote the interests not only of businesses but also of suburbanites, who lived in vast, culturally isolated developments that lacked the community focus of urban neighborhoods. Shopping centers could become community centers, argued Gruen, and in the process promote American values. Gruen is credited with building the first fully enclosed, air-conditioned shopping mall in Edina, Minnesota, in 1956. Ultimately, he returned to Europe, disappointed that other mall developers pursued profits more than they did community development. The following selection, in which Gruen articulates his vision for shopping centers, appears as part of the "Prologue" in Shopping Towns USA *(Reinhold Publishing, 1960).*

1   No democratic society can flourish without law and order which, when applied to the physical environment, necessitates planning. In a complex and highly mechanized society environmental planning safeguards the basic human rights. By providing the best conditions for physical and mental health, it protects *life*. By establishing barriers against anarchy and the infringements of hostile natural and man-made forces, it protects *liberty*. By the creation of a humane environment it invites and encourages the *pursuit of happiness*.

2   When environmental planning is applied to the designing of new commercial facilities, many conditions must be analyzed, criteria weighed, requirements met, and problems solved. These all involve in various ways and to varying degrees the needs and desires of the shopper. It is deeply significant that the term is "shopping center," not "selling center." This indicates clearly that the wishes and desires of the shopper take priority over those of the seller. (An earlier term, "parking center," failed to catch on.)

3   The basic need of the suburban shopper is for a conveniently accessible, amply stocked shopping area with plentiful and free parking. This is the purely practical need for which the shopping center was originally conceived and which many centers most adequately fulfill. Good planning, however, will create additional attractions for shoppers by meeting other needs which are inherent in the psychological climate peculiar to suburbia. By affording opportunities for social life and recreation in a protected pedestrian environment, by incorporating civic and educational facilities, shopping centers can fill an existing void. They can provide the needed place and opportunity for participation in modern community life that the ancient Greek *Agora*, the Medieval Market Place and our own Town Squares provided in the past.

4   That the shopping center can fulfill this perhaps subconscious but nonetheless urgent need of suburbanites for the amenities of urban living, is convincingly proved in a large number of centers. In such centers, pedestrian areas are filled with teeming life not only during normal shopping hours, but on Sundays

and holidays when people windowshop, promenade, relax in the garden courts, view exhibits and patronize the restaurants.

5   All age groups are provided for. Auditoriums are booked to capacity. Meeting rooms are busy with civic and cultural affairs. Dance schools, music schools, and ice skating rinks attract teen-agers; amusement centers are popular with children.

6   Such a planning concept also results in an upgrading of the residential area surrounding the center. It not only protects surrounding communities from blight but actually raises their desirability and consequently their property values.

7   If the shopping center becomes a place that not only provides suburbanites with their physical living requirements, but simultaneously serves their civic, cultural and social community needs, it will make a most significant contribution to the enrichment of our lives.

Discussion and Writing Suggestions

1. In paragraph 1, Gruen offers a vigorous defense of centrally planned shopping centers, arguing that retail development, just like democracy, demands law and order. We gain the free exercise of life, liberty, and happiness, he suggests, through maintaining order. How convinced are you by Gruen's defense of centralized shopping center design?

2. Gruen states (in paragraph 4) that "the shopping center can fulfill [a] subconscious but nonetheless urgent need of suburbanites for the amenities of urban living." What are these needs? To what extent do you believe that people living in the suburbs have them?

3. Reread the final paragraph of this selection. Gruen was a visionary who believed that shopping centers could meet "civic, cultural, and social community needs," as well as the commercial needs of suburbanites. Are you sympathetic to this vision? In your experience, to what extent do shopping centers today meet his standards?

The Mall as Disneyland
Richard Francaviglia

What models did developers turn to when creating the modern American shopping mall? In this next selection, Richard Francaviglia argues that Walt Disney played a key role. His romanticized "Main Street USA," a re-creation of small-town America's shopping district for his new theme park, Disneyland, set the standard for carefully designed and managed shopping environments. Main Street USA, moved indoors to a climate-controlled environment, became the modern shopping mall. A geographer and historian, Francaviglia directs the Center for Greater Southwestern Studies and the History of Cartography at the University of Texas, Arlington. This selection appeared in his book Main Street Revisited: Time, Space, and Image-Building in Small-Town America *(University of Iowa Press, 1996), which won the J. B. Jackson*

Prize for conveying "the insights of professional geography in language that is interesting and attractive to a lay audience."

1 Main Street USA . . . fits into the genre of intensely designed and orchestrated space/place. On every inch of Disney's Main Street USA, from the public square to the Plaza, architecture, street furniture, and all aspects of the streetscape are historically themed and carefully engineered. It is this sense of "history" that nearly overwhelms the visitor. All of the street lights are patterned after the "whiteway" lights that lined Main Streets in the early twentieth century. The park benches, wrought iron railings, plantings—everything on Main Street is carefully designed to convey a feeling of the late Victorian period. Even the trees and bushes are carefully sculpted and tended. On Main Street USA, most visitors imbibe the ambience of the past, but they are in fact participating in something far more elementary; their attitudes and perceptions are being shaped through a type of social engineering. This leads to the fourteenth axiom of Main Street development.* *Main Street is essentially a stage upon which several types of human dramas are performed simultaneously, each character or actor in the drama having a designated role that is dependent on his or her relationship to the "set."* Whether one stands behind the counter or in front of a store window brings with it different expectations. Disney was the ultimate merchant on Main Street, and visitors to Main Street USA are the ultimate customers.

2 In Disney's Main Street USA, architecture becomes the façade that creates the impression that all was right with the world in the small town at the turn of the century; it implies that commerce (and merchants) thrive along Main Street, and that society and a community are working together in harmony. Of course, Disney's Main Street does not feature those inevitable services that indicate the other, or darker, side of life. There are no funeral parlors, pool halls, or bars. It should come as no surprise that Disney created small-town America as it *should* have been. His Main Street mirrors a pre-adolescent period free from the change and turmoil that characterizes much of life. . . .

3 What concerns, even infuriates, historians and scholars most about Walt Disney is that he created an abstracted image that it is so tempting to confuse with reality. Disney masterfully abstracted his experiences in [one of his hometowns] *Marceline* and worked with his designers to capture the essences of other towns to produce a small-town image that has nearly universal appeal. In so doing, Disney intuitively knew that *all* planned townscapes—including those Main Streets created in the eighteenth and nineteenth centuries—were in a sense engineered to create effects. Even the vistas down Main Street USA were carefully designed to have significant features (the Railroad Station and Sleeping Beauty's Castle), or, as Disney himself is reported to have said, there should be a "wienie at the end of every street.". . .

---

* Throughout the book from which this selection was taken, Francaviglia draws broad lessons, what he sees as fundamental truths, about the evolution of Main Streets across America during the nineteenth and twentieth centuries. Main Street's being a "stage upon which . . . human dramas are performed" is one such axiom. You will notice that James Farrell, earlier in the chapter, uses much the same language to discuss what goes on in shopping malls.

4   At symbolic levels, Disney's engineering of the small-town environment in Main Street USA is revealing because he so beautifully captured the essence of the romanticism of the small town. Disney himself was moved by the originals, and shaped them into an icon that affects the way we will view its "real" counterparts. To the general public, Main Street USA in Disneyland was very credible in that it featured towers and architectural turrets where they seemed logical, and even though the trim was fairly lavish, it was subdued enough to remind one of Main Streets in the relatively prosperous period during the "McKinley Era"* at about the turn of the century.

5   Students of urban design know that Disney possessed an element of genius in that he carefully designed this Main Street to have an intersection about halfway between the public square and the plaza. That intersection provides a node of activity where merchants have materials on display outside and where towers can form visual exclamation points for the architecture. Looking down one of these side streets, one sees trees that convey the feeling that the commercial streetscape is yielding to a residential area. But in reality, the trees seen behind that intersection on Main Street are the trees of Jungleland, so close is the juxtaposition between one "world" of Disneyland and another. The entire Disneyland theme park is magnificently engineered into only about ninety-six acres of space, which is smaller than the area encompassed within the city limits of most American towns! In world history, few places this small have had such a powerful effect on so many people.

6   In keeping with his ability to create magic through place, Disney used night to his advantage. Because Main Street USA is experienced at night as well as during the daytime, Disney provided marvelous rim-lighting on the buildings. Incandescent bulbs were strung along all of the cornices to convey a very stylized and ornate appearance, enabling the architecture and the streetscape to "shine" at night as well as in the daytime. The Main Street electrical parade runs through the area at night, and Main Street at night provides a kind of visual excitement that was rarely, perhaps never, actually seen in the small towns of America. Rim-lighting of this kind was, however, common in pavilions and the grand buildings of expositions. Like many of Disney's creations, rim-lighting in this context brings a touch of the exotic or even whimsical to Main Street, rather reminding one more of the festive environments of parks and fairs than the Main Street of the typical American small town. Historian and social critic Jon Weiner recently noted that "Disneyland's Main Street is a fiction; the real Main Streets of real small towns at the turn of the century were not so nice"[1]—an understatement borne out by architectural historians and historical geographers. And yet, as architect Paul Goldberger accurately noted, Disney produced "a kind of universally true Main Street—it's better than the real Main Street of the turn of the century ever could be."[2] That Disney's Main Street seems so universally beautiful comes as less of a surprise when one realizes that Walt Disney was rather sophisticated and widely travelled: in fact, Tivoli Gardens in Copenhagen, Denmark, was said to have

---

* William McKinley (1843–1901), the twenty-fifth President of the United States (1897–1901), was assassinated while in office.

greatly impressed Walt Disney in 1952—a seminal year in the early designs of Disneyland.[3] Disney and his designers reportedly were impressed by an exhibit called "Yesteryear's Main Street" at the Museum of Science and Industry in Chicago, which was sponsored by General Motors.[4] Disney's Main Street, which, according to WED (which stands for Walter Elias Disney) imagineering historian David Mumford, "is actually a typical representation of a Walt Disney imagineering project, since it represents a collaborative effort by many creative people,"[5] was thus inspired by many places. . . .

7   If this description of [Main Street USA] sounds familiar, and it should indeed, that is because it has in fact become the model of the typical American shopping mall, where the visitor or shopper leaves the car in the parking lot and enters an environment that is climatically controlled, and where the real world is left outside. In malls, as in Disney's Main Streets, every aspect of design and circulation is carefully orchestrated (Fig. 10.1). This should come as no surprise,

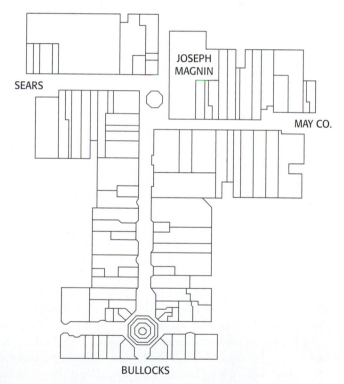

FIGURE 10.1   The Mall as Main Street. This diagram of the South Coast Plaza Shopping Center, a mall in Costa Mesa, California, reveals many of the same design elements seen in Disneyland's Main Street USA—notably an important intersection of four radiating axes (bottom) and a linear thoroughfare running into another point of decision-making where a carousel is positioned (upper center). The similarities are more than coincidental, as many shopping center designers have studied Disney's Main Street. Computer graphic based on a 1975 map in a kiosk at the mall.

for many of the designers of shopping centers and malls in the United States have visited Disney's parks in order to develop a much better understanding of how people move through, appreciate, and patronize a retail environment.[6]

8   It is ironic that Walt Disney, who was politically conservative and espoused rugged individualism, actually produced an environment that embodies such nearly total social engineering and control. According to architectural critic Jane Holtz Kay, Disney's Main Street and shopping malls embody both "public persona" and "private autocracy."[7] The autocratic control of theme parks, of course, is linked to safety and security, and is perhaps one reason why shopping centers are highly successful, and highly criticized by those who feel that such places are "contrived." Malls, too, are able to control behavior using their "private" status. As William Kowinski succinctly stated in his classic article entitled "The Malling of America":

> Malls are designed for Disney's children. Stores are pressed close together; they have small low façades. In fact, everything about malls is minimized . . . the mall is laid out with few corners and no unused space along store rows so that there are no decisions to make—you just flow on.[8] *

9   Few can deny the attractiveness of mall environments to a generation of retail shoppers drawn to the relative serenity and the climate control of the shopping center. That such malls are a current incarnation of Main Street is borne out by the flourishing social life and the persistence of marketing and craft fairs within today's shopping centers. The relative visual uniformity of shopping centers from coast to coast should not be particularly surprising; they, like Disney's Main Street, are archetypal environments of popular culture. This has caused architectural critics to blast the lack of "imagination" of their creators while, ironically, reflecting nostalgically on the days of the *real* American town in, perhaps, the 1880s when, critics contend, there was far greater "individuality."

10   In reality, of course, this was not the case; as we have seen, by the 1880s Victorian-era Main Streets had developed into highly standardized forms. Their major architectural components could—like McDonald's—be found from coast to coast. That scholars lament the standardization of the mall while praising the architectural integrity of historic Main Streets reveals the power of nostalgia in affecting even the most educated of our citizens. Whatever else one may say about the typical shopping center, it is an abstracted reincarnation of Main Street, where pedestrians have the right of way over vehicular traffic, where *all* store façades are attractive and where all of the merchants agree to maintain regular hours and carefully control their signage and sales pitches—techniques which avoid the appearance of haphazard or eccentric individualism.

11   Sociologists have long known that people visit shopping centers for far more than commercial reasons. More than twenty years ago, when Edward Tauber insightfully stated that "not all shopping motives, by any means, are even related to the product,"[9] he introduced the concept of "sociorecreational shopping." Several very revealing articles over the last dozen or more years have shown that

---

* A selection from Kowinski's *Malling of America* appears later in this chapter.

shopping centers are important places of social interaction where people may wind up meeting future spouses and friends; where families go simply to stroll, to see people and to be seen by them; where young people go to "hang out" and socialize. Whereas academicians may condemn this type of behavior as manipulated or inauthentic, it is in fact one of the major reasons why commercial and marketing towns have existed for centuries. This may be stated as the fifteenth axiom of Main Street development: *Despite its market-driven businesses, Main Street is primarily a social environment.* Main Street is an integral element in the "collective consciousness," as geographer Alan Baker used the term, to refer to landscape creation and perception that is linked to a national identity.[10]

Notes

1. Jon Weiner, "Tall Tales and True," *Nation* 258, no. 4: 134.
2. Paul Goldberger, in Judith Adams, *The American Amusement Park Industry:* 98.
3. Arline Chambers, "The Architecture of Reassurance: Designing the Disney Theme Parks," "Disney Chronology" (unpublished paper), p. 5.
4. Andrew Lainsbury, personal communication with author, July 13, 1995.
5. Letter from David Mumford to Jack and Leon Janzen, November 13, 1992, reproduced in Jack E. Janzen, "MAIN STREET . . . Walt's Perfect Introduction to Disneyland": 30.
6. Richard Francaviglia, "Main Street Revisited."
7. Jane Holtz Kay, "When You Stimulate a Star," *Landscape Architecture*, June 1990: 54.
8. *New Times*, May 1, 1978: 33.
9. Edward Tauber, "Sociorecreational Shopping," *Human Behavior* 2, no. 4; reproduced in *Intellectual Digest* 4, no. 3 (November 1973): 38.
10. Alan R. H. Baker, "Collective Consciousness and the Last Landscape: National Ideology and the Commune Council of Mesland (Loir-et-Cher) as Landscape Architect during the 19th Century," chapter 12 in *Ideology and Landscape in Historical Perspective*, edited by Alan Baker and Gideon Biger: 255–88.

Review Questions

1. Describe the ways in which Disney's Main Street USA is a carefully controlled environment.
2. What impression does Disney's street create for the visitor, according to Francaviglia?
3. What is the critics' chief complaint about this street?
4. In what ways does mall design borrow from Disney's Main Street USA?
5. Why is the placement of an intersection important to the success of Main Street USA as well as to the typical shopping mall?

Discussion and Writing Suggestions

1. If you have visited Disneyland or Disneyworld, describe your experiences on Main Street USA. Did the street impress you as it did Francaviglia? To what extent do you find shopping mall design similar in key respects to the design of Main Street USA?

2. "Whatever else one may say about the typical shopping center, it is an abstracted reincarnation of Main Street, where pedestrians have the right of way over vehicular traffic, where *all* store facades are attractive and where all of the merchants agree to maintain regular hours and carefully control their signage and sales pitches—techniques which avoid the appearance of haphazard or eccentric individualism" (paragraph 10). To what extent do you agree that these aims are desirable?

3. In paragraph 11, quoting another author, Francaviglia introduces the term "sociorecreational shopping." Define the term and relate it to your own experiences as a mall shopper.

4. This selection is excerpted from a book-length study of America's Main Streets. Throughout the longer work, Francaviglia offers a number of "axioms" regarding his subject. You find two of these axioms in this selection. See paragraph 1: "Main Street is essentially a stage upon which several types of human dramas are performed simultaneously." An *axiom* is a statement that is universally recognized as true. Do you agree that Francaviglia's statement is beyond dispute?

5. Following question 4, Francaviglia offers a second axiom in this selection. See paragraph 11: "Despite its market-driven businesses, Main Street is primarily a social environment." Do you agree that Francaviglia's statement is beyond dispute?

The Mall as Prison
David Guterson

In 1993 journalist and novelist David Guterson, on assignment for Harper's *magazine, spent a week in the recently opened Mall of America. As you will discover, Guterson approached the mall with a skeptical eye, both fascinated with and wary of its massive scale. Guterson agrees with James Farrell that one can take the pulse of American culture by spending time in malls. But what Guterson sees is cause for alarm. A contributing editor to* Harper's, *Guterson has most notably written a collection of short stories,* The Country Ahead of Us, the Country Behind *(Vintage, 1996) and the novel* Snow Falling on Cedars, *which won the 1995 PEN/Faulkner Award.*

1   Last April, on a visit to the new Mall of America near Minneapolis, I carried with me the public-relations press kit provided for the benefit of reporters. It included an assortment of "fun facts" about the mall: 140,000 hot dogs sold each

week, 10,000 permanent jobs, 44 escalators and 17 elevators, 12,750 parking places, 13,300 short tons of steel, $1 million in cash disbursed weekly from 8 automatic-teller machines. Opened in the summer of 1992, the mall was built on the 78-acre site of the former Metropolitan Stadium, a five-minute drive from the Minneapolis–St. Paul International Airport. With 4.2 million square feet of floor space—including twenty-two times the retail footage of the average American shopping center—the Mall of America was "the largest fully enclosed combination retail and family entertainment complex in the United States."

2   Eleven thousand articles, the press kit warned me, had already been written on the mall. Four hundred trees had been planted in its gardens, $625 million had been spent to build it, 350 stores had been leased. Three thousand bus tours were anticipated each year along with a half-million Canadian visitors and 200,000 Japanese tourists. Sales were projected at $650 million for 1993 and at $1 billion for 1996. Donny and Marie Osmond had visited the mall, as had Janet Jackson and Sally Jesse Raphael, Arnold Schwarzenegger, and the 1994 Winter Olympic Committee.* The mall was five times larger than Red Square† and twenty times larger than St. Peter's Basilica;‡ it incorporated 2.3 miles of hallways and almost twice as much steel as the Eiffel Tower. It was also home to the nation's largest indoor theme park, a place called Knott's Camp Snoopy.

3   On the night I arrived, a Saturday, the mall was spotlit dramatically in the manner of a Las Vegas casino. It resembled, from the outside, a castle or fort, the Emerald City or Never-Never Land,§ impossibly large and vaguely unreal, an unbroken, windowless multi-storied edifice the size of an airport terminal. Surrounded by parking lots and new freeway ramps, monolithic and imposing in the manner of a walled city, it loomed brightly against the Minnesota night sky with the disturbing magnetism of a mirage.

4   I knew already that the Mall of America had been imagined by its creators not merely as a marketplace but as a national tourist attraction, an immense zone of entertainments. Such a conceit raised provocative questions, for our architecture testifies to our view of ourselves and to the condition of our souls. Large buildings stand as markers in the lives of nations and in the stream of a people's history. Thus I could only ask myself: Here was a new structure that had cost more than half a billion dollars to erect—what might it tell us about ourselves? If the Mall of America was part of America, what was that going to mean?

---

* Celebrities Donnie and Marie Osmond, part of a Salt Lake City–based family entertainment team, were best known for three television variety shows that aired on prime time between 1976 and 1981. Sally Jesse Raphael is a talk show host whose programs aired between 1985 and 2002. Arnold Schwarzenegger needs no introduction.

† Red Square is the central square in the ancient center of Moscow, near the Kremlin, where during the Communist Soviet era military parades were held on May 1st.

‡ Built in the sixteenth century in the Italian Renaissance style, St. Peter's Basilica is the great church of Vatican City.

§ The Emerald City and Never-Never Land are the exotic, imaginary destinations featured in *The Wizard of Oz* and *Peter Pan*, respectively.

5 I passed through one of the mall's enormous entranceways and took myself inside. Although from a distance the Mall of America had appeared menacing—exuding the ambience of a monstrous hallucination—within it turned out to be simply a shopping mall, certainly more vast than other malls but in tone and aspect, design and feel, not readily distinguishable from them. Its nuances were instantly familiar as the generic features of the American shopping mall at the tail end of the twentieth century: polished stone, polished tile, shiny chrome and brass, terrazzo floors, gazebos. From third-floor vistas, across vaulted spaces, the Mall of America felt endlessly textured—glass-enclosed elevators, neon-tube lighting, bridges, balconies, gas lamps, vaulted skylights—and densely crowded with hordes of people circumambulating in an endless promenade. Yet despite the mall's expansiveness, it elicited claustrophobia, sensory deprivation, and an unnerving disorientation. Everywhere I went I spied other pilgrims who had found, like me, that the straight way was lost and that the YOU ARE HERE landmarks on the map kiosks referred to nothing in particular.

6 Getting lost, feeling lost, being lost—these states of mind are intentional features of the mall's psychological terrain. There are, one notices, no clocks or windows, nothing to distract the shopper's psyche from the alternate reality the mall conjures. Here we are free to wander endlessly and to furtively watch our fellow wanderers, thousands upon thousands of milling strangers who have come with the intent of losing themselves in the mall's grand, stimulating design. For a few hours we share some common ground—a fantasy of infinite commodities and comforts—and then we drift apart forever. The mall exploits our acquisitive instincts without honoring our communal requirements, our eternal desire for discourse and intimacy, needs that until the twentieth century were traditionally met in our marketplaces but that are not met at all in giant shopping malls.

7 On this evening a few thousand young people had descended on the mall in pursuit of alcohol and entertainment. They had come to Gators, Hooters, and Knuckleheads, Puzzles, Fat Tuesday, and Ltl Ditty's. At Players, a sports bar, the woman beside me introduced herself as "the pregnant wife of an Iowa pig farmer" and explained that she had driven five hours with friends to "do the mall party scene together." She left and was replaced by Kathleen from Minnetonka, who claimed to have "a real shopping thing—I can't go a week without buying new clothes. I'm not fulfilled until I buy something."

8 Later a woman named Laura arrived, with whom Kathleen was acquainted. "I *am* the mall," she announced ecstatically upon discovering I was a reporter. "I'd move in here if I could bring my dog," she added. "This place is heaven, it's a *mecca*."

9 "We egg each other on," explained Kathleen, calmly puffing on a cigarette. "It's like, sort of, an addiction."

10 "You want the truth?" Laura asked. "I'm constantly suffering from megamall withdrawal. I come here all the time."

11 Kathleen: "It's a sickness. It's like cocaine or something; it's a drug."

12 Laura: "Kathleen's got this thing about buying, but I just need to *be* here. If I buy something it's an added bonus."

13   Kathleen: "She buys stuff all the time; don't listen."

14   Laura: "Seriously, I feel sorry for other malls. They're so small and *boring*."

15   Kathleen seemed to think about this: "Richdale Mall," she blurted finally. She rolled her eyes and gestured with her cigarette. "Oh, my God, Laura. Why did we even *go* there?"

16 There is, of course, nothing naturally abhorrent in the human impulse to dwell in marketplaces or the urge to buy, sell, and trade. Rural Americans traditionally looked forward to the excitement and sensuality of market day; Native Americans traveled long distances to barter and trade at sprawling, festive encampments. In Persian bazaars and in the ancient Greek agoras the very soul of the community was preserved and could be seen, felt, heard, and smelled as it might be nowhere else. All over the planet the humblest of people have always gone to market with hope in their hearts and in expectation of something beyond mere goods—seeking a place where humanity is temporarily in ascendance, a palette for the senses, one another.

17   But the illicit possibilities of the marketplace also have long been acknowledged. The Persian bazaar was closed at sundown; the Greek agora was off-limits to those who had been charged with certain crimes. One myth of the Old West we still carry with us is that market day presupposes danger; the faithful were advised to make purchases quickly and repair without delay to the farm, lest their attraction to the pleasures of the marketplace erode their purity of spirit.

18   In our collective discourse the shopping mall appears with the tract house, the freeway, and the backyard barbecue as a product of the American postwar years, a testament to contemporary necessities and desires and an invention not only peculiarly American but peculiarly of our own era too. Yet the mall's varied and far-flung predecessors—the covered bazaars of the Middle East, the stately arcades of Victorian England, Italy's vaulted and skylit gallerias, Asia's monsoon-protected urban markets—all suggest that the rituals of indoor shopping, although in their nuances not often like our own, are nevertheless broadly known. The late twentieth-century American contribution has been to transform the enclosed bazaar into an economic institution that is vastly profitable yet socially enervated, one that redefines in fundamental ways the human relationship to the marketplace. At the Mall of America—an extreme example— we discover ourselves thoroughly lost among strangers in a marketplace intentionally designed to serve no community needs.

19   In the strict sense the Mall of America is not a marketplace at all—the soul of a community expressed as a *place*—but rather a tourist attraction. Its promoters have peddled it to the world at large as something more profound than a local marketplace and as a destination with deep implications. "I believe we can make Mall of America stand for all of America," asserted the mall's general manager, John Wheeler, in a promotional video entitled *There's a Place for Fun in Your Life*. "I believe there's a shopper in all of us," added the director of marketing, Maureen Hooley. The mall has memorialized its opening-day proceedings by producing a celebratory videotape: Ray Charles singing "America the Beautiful," a laser show followed by fireworks, "The Star-Spangled Banner" and "The Stars and Stripes Forever," the Gatlin Brothers, and Peter Graves.

"Mall of America . . . ," its narrator intoned. "The name alone conjures up images of greatness, of a retail complex so magnificent it could only happen in America."

20   Indeed, on the day the mall opened, Miss America visited. The mall's logo—a red, white, and blue star bisected by a red, white, and blue ribbon—decorated everything from the mall itself to coffee mugs and the flanks of buses. The idea, director of tourism Colleen Hayes told me, was to position America's largest mall as an institution on the scale of Disneyland or the Grand Canyon, a place simultaneously iconic and totemic, a revered symbol of the United States and a mecca to which the faithful would flock in pursuit of all things purchasable.

21   On Sunday I wandered the hallways of the pleasure dome with the sensation that I had entered an M.C. Escher drawing*—there was no such thing as up or down, and the escalators all ran backward. A 1993 Ford Probe GT was displayed as if popping out of a giant packing box; a full-size home, complete with artificial lawn, had been built in the mall's rotunda. At the Michael Ricker Pewter Gallery I came across a miniature tableau of a pewter dog peeing on a pewter man's leg; at Hologram Land I pondered 3-D hallucinations of the Medusa and Marilyn Monroe. I passed a kiosk called The Sportsman's Wife; I stood beside a life-size statue of the Hamm's Bear, carved out of pine and available for $1,395 at a store called Minnesot-ah! At Pueblo Spirit I examined a "dream catcher"—a small hoop made from deer sinew and willow twigs and designed to be hung over its owner's bed as a tactic for filtering bad dreams. For a while I sat in front of Glamour Shots and watched while women were groomed and brushed for photo sessions yielding high-fashion self-portraits at $34.95 each. There was no stopping, no slowing down. I passed Mug Me, Queen for a Day, and Barnyard Buddies, and stood in the Brookstone store examining a catalogue: a gopher "eliminator" for $40 (it's a vibrating, anodized-aluminum stake), a "no-stoop" shoehorn for $10, a nose-hair trimmer for $18. At the arcade inside Knott's Camp Snoopy I watched while teenagers played Guardians of the 'Hood, Total Carnage, Final Fight, and Varth Operation Thunderstorm; a small crowd of them had gathered around a lean, cool character who stood calmly shooting video cowpokes in a game called Mad Dog McCree. Left thumb on his silver belt buckle, biceps pulsing, he banged away without remorse while dozens of his enemies crumpled and died in alleyways and dusty streets.

22   At Amazing Pictures a teenage boy had his photograph taken as a body-builder—his face smoothly grafted onto a rippling body—then proceeded to purchase this pleasing image on a poster, a sweatshirt, and a coffee mug. At Painted Tipi there was wild rice for sale, hand-harvested from Leech Lake, Minnesota. At Animalia I came across a polyresin figurine of a turtle retailing for $3,200. At Bloomingdale's I pondered a denim shirt with its sleeves ripped away, the sort of thing available at used-clothing stores (the "grunge look," a

---

* M.C. Escher (1898–1972) was a printmaker famous for images that confused viewers' perceptions of geometric space, making (for instance) finite walkways into infinite loops from which people could never exit. For examples of his work, go to <http://www.mcescher.com/> and select "Gallery."

Bloomingdale's employee explained), on sale for $125. Finally, at a gift shop in Knott's Camp Snoopy, I came across a game called Electronic Mall Madness, put out by Milton Bradley. On the box, three twelve-year-old girls with good features happily vied to beat one another to the game-board mall's best sales.

23 At last I achieved an enforced self-arrest, anchoring myself against a bench while the mall tilted on its axis. Two pubescent girls in retainers and braces sat beside me sipping coffees topped with whipped cream and chocolate sprinkles, their shopping bags gathered tightly around their legs, their eyes fixed on the passing crowds. They came, they said, from Shakopee—"It's nowhere," one of them explained. The megamall, she added, was "a buzz at first, but now it seems pretty normal. 'Cept my parents are like Twenty Questions every time I want to come here. 'Specially since the shooting."

24 On a Sunday night, she elaborated, three people had been wounded when shots were fired in a dispute over a San Jose Sharks jacket. "In the *mall*," her friend reminded me. "Right here at megamall. A shooting."

25 "It's like nowhere's safe," the first added.

26 They sipped their coffees and explicated for me the plot of a film they saw as relevant, a horror movie called *Dawn of the Dead,* which they had each viewed a half-dozen times. In the film, they explained, apocalypse had come, and the survivors had repaired to a shopping mall as the most likely place to make their last stand in a poisoned, impossible world. And this would have been perfectly all right, they insisted, except that the place had also attracted hordes of the infamous living dead—sentient corpses who had not relinquished their attraction to indoor shopping.

27 I moved on and contemplated a computerized cash register in the infant's section of the Nordstrom store: "The Answer Is Yes!!!" its monitor reminded clerks. "Customer Service Is Our Number One Priority!" Then back at Bloomingdale's I contemplated a bank of televisions playing incessantly an advertisement for Egoïste, a men's cologne from Chanel. In the ad a woman on a wrought-iron balcony tossed her black hair about and screamed long and passionately; then there were many women screaming passionately, too, and throwing balcony shutters open and closed, and this was all followed by a bottle of the cologne displayed where I could get a good look at it. The brief, strange drama repeated itself until I could no longer stand it.

. . .

28 On Valentine's Day last February—cashing in on the promotional scheme of a local radio station—ninety-two couples were married en masse in a ceremony at the Mall of America. They rode the roller coaster and the Screaming Yellow Eagle and were photographed beside a frolicking Snoopy, who wore an immaculate tuxedo. "As we stand here together at the Mall of America," presiding district judge Richard Spicer declared, "we are reminded that there is a place for fun in your life and you have found it in each other." Six months earlier, the Reverend Leith Anderson of the Wooddale Church in Eden Prairie conducted services in the mall's rotunda. Six thousand people had congregated by 10:00 A.M., and Reverend Anderson delivered a sermon entitled "The Unknown God of the Mall." Characterizing the mall as a "direct descendant" of the ancient Greek agoras, the reverend pointed out that, like the Greeks before us, we Americans have many gods. Afterward, of course, the flock went

shopping, much to the chagrin of Reverend Delton Krueger, president of the Mall Area Religious Council, who told the *Minneapolis Star Tribune* that as a site for church services, the mall may trivialize religion. "A good many people in the churches," said Krueger, "feel a lot of the trouble in the world is because of materialism."

29 But a good many people in the mall business today apparently think the trouble lies elsewhere. They are moving forward aggressively on the premise that the dawning era of electronic shopping does not preclude the building of shopping-and-pleasure palaces all around the globe. Japanese developers, in a joint venture with the [developers of Canada's West Edmonton Mall], are planning a $400 million Mall of Japan, with an ice rink, a water park, a fantasy-theme hotel, three breweries, waterfalls, and a sports center. We might shortly predict, too, a Mall of Europe, a Mall of New England, a Mall of California, and perhaps even a Mall of the World. The concept of shopping in a frivolous atmosphere, concocted to loosen consumers' wallets, is poised to proliferate globally. We will soon see monster malls everywhere, rooted in the soil of every nation and offering a preposterous, impossible variety of commodities and entertainments.

30   The new malls will be planets unto themselves, closed off from this world in the manner of space stations or of science fiction's underground cities. Like the Mall of America and West Edmonton Mall—prototypes for a new generation of shopping centers—they will project a separate and distinct reality in which an "outdoor café" is not outdoors, a "bubbling brook" is a concrete watercourse, and a "serpentine street" is a hallway. Safe, surreal, and outside of time and space, they will offer the mind a potent dreamscape from which there is no present waking. This carefully controlled fantasy—now operable in Minnesota—is so powerful as to inspire psychological addiction or to elicit in visitors a catatonic obsession with the mall's various hallucinations. The new malls will be theatrical, high-tech illusions capable of attracting enormous crowds from distant points and foreign ports. Their psychology has not yet been tried pervasively on the scale of the Mall of America, nor has it been perfected. But in time our marketplaces, all over the world, will be in essential ways interchangeable, so thoroughly divorced from the communities in which they sit that they will appear to rest like permanently docked spaceships against the landscape, windowless and turned in upon their own affairs. The affluent will travel as tourists to each, visiting the holy sites and taking photographs in the catacombs of far-flung temples.

31   Just as Victorian England is acutely revealed beneath the grandiose domes of its overwrought train stations, so is contemporary America well understood from the upper vistas of its shopping malls, places without either windows or clocks where the temperature is forever seventy degrees. It is facile to believe, from this vantage point, that the endless circumambulations of tens of thousands of strangers—all loaded down with the detritus of commerce—resemble anything akin to community. The shopping mall is not, as the architecture critic Witold Rybczynski has concluded, "poised to become a real urban place" with "a variety of commercial and noncommercial functions." On the contrary, it is poised to multiply around the world as an institution offering only a desolate substitute

for the rich, communal lifeblood of the traditional marketplace, which will not survive its onslaught.

32   Standing on the Mall of America's roof, where I had ventured to inspect its massive ventilation units, I finally achieved a full sense of its vastness, of how it overwhelmed the surrounding terrain—the last sheep farm in sight, the Mississippi River incidental in the distance. Then I peered through the skylights down into Camp Snoopy, where throngs of my fellow citizens caroused happily in the vast entrails of the beast.

Review Questions

1. According to Guterson, what is one key difference between shopping places of old and modern malls?

2. What is the difference between a marketplace and a tourist attraction?

3. What has been America's "contribution" to the closed bazaar, according to Guterson?

4. Reread paragraphs 7–15, in which Guterson reports on an interview he conducted with several mall patrons. Characterize these interviewees. Why does Guterson include these conversations in the article? What point is he making (indirectly)?

5. Reread paragraphs 21–22, in which Guterson relates his experiences wandering "the hallways of the pleasure dome." By the end of paragraph 22, what impression has he created?

6. What predictions does Guterson make concerning modern megamalls?

Discussion and Writing Suggestions

1. Guterson opens this article by citing some of the Mall of America's vital statistics. What effect do these statistics have on you?

2. Guterson makes a judgment in this selection about the Mall of America and, more broadly, about American culture. What is this judgment? As evidence for your answer, cite three or four sentences.

3. In paragraph 4, Guterson writes that the building of the Mall of America as a tourist attraction "raise[s] provocative questions, for our architecture testifies to our view of ourselves and to the condition of our souls." In paragraph 31 he makes a similar point, referring to Victorian England's nineteenth-century train stations. Explain the connection Guterson makes between architecture and the broader culture.

4. In paragraph 5, Guterson refers to fellow shoppers at the Mall of America as "other pilgrims." Speculate on his use of "pilgrims." Why does he not simply refer to these people as "shoppers"?

5. In paragraph 16, Guterson writes: "All over the planet the humblest of people have always gone to market with hope in their hearts and in expectation of something beyond mere goods—seeking a place where humanity is temporarily in ascendance." What does he mean? Is this your hope in going to the mall?

6. Guterson devotes paragraph 26 to a summary of the movie *Dawn of the Dead*. Speculate on his reasons for including the summary in this article.

The Mall as Walled Garden
Richard Keller Simon

Classical gardens controlled the visitor's experience through carefully planned vistas and walkways. According to Richard Keller Simon, shopping malls do the same—and the comparisons don't end there. Simon's exploration of the mall as garden reflects his interest in the connections between modern mass culture and the artworks, literary and visual, of the past. Simon is a professor of English and director of the humanities program at California Polytechnic State University. The following essay first appeared in the collection Mapping American Culture *(eds. Wayne Franklin and Michael Steiner, 1992) and later as a chapter in Simon's* Trash Culture: Popular Culture and the Great Tradition *(1999).*

1   The contemporary American shopping mall is the formal garden of late twentieth century culture, a commodified version of the great garden styles of Western history with which it shares fundamental characteristics. Set apart from the rest of the world as a place of earthly delight like the medieval walled garden; filled with fountains, statuary, and ingeniously devised machinery like the Italian Renaissance garden; designed on grandiose and symmetrical principles like the seventeenth-century French garden; made up of the fragments of cultural and architectural history like the eighteenth-century irregular English garden; and set aside for the public like the nineteenth-century American park, the mall is the next phase of this garden history, a synthesis of all these styles that have come before. But it is now joined with the shopping street, or at least a sanitized and standardized version of one, something that never before has been allowed within the garden.

. . .

2   Visitors learn the meanings of a consumer society at the mall, not only in the choices they make in their purchases, but also in the symbol systems they walk through, just as visitors to those earlier gardens were invited to learn about the meanings of their own times from their experiences of the space and from the pastoral adventures presented to them. "Remember ever the garden and the

groves within," the Earl of Shaftesbury wrote in *The Moralists* in the eighteenth century: "There build, there erect what statues, what virtues, what ornament or orders of architecture thou thinkest noblest. There walk at leisure and in peace; contemplate, regulate, dispose. . . ."[1] In his reading of "The Poetic Garden" of the eighteenth century, Ronald Paulson explains that "the visitor, sometimes supplied with a bench to sit on, saw a carefully-arranged scene, something between a stage set and a landscape painting, with statues, temples, and other objects of a high degree of denotation arranged to express a topos* on which he could meditate or converse." The visitor to the contemporary shopping mall reads an updated version of this cultural space, and while it appears to be less "poetic" than its predecessor, it is just as rich with meanings. The garden Paulson describes, which is "devoted to the pleasures and temptations of retirement,"[2] has been replaced by the mall, devoted to the pleasures and temptations of consumption, but the objects remain. Jean Baudrillard argues, "Through objects each individual and each group searches out his-her place in an order,"[3] and what the mall presents to us is a great surfeit of objects. "In buying products with certain 'images' we create ourselves, our personality, our qualities, even our past and our future," Judith Williamson argues in her reading of consumer life.[4]

3   Like the gardens before it, the mall is a construct of promenades, walls, vistas, mounts, labyrinths, fountains, statues, archways, trees, grottoes, theaters, flowering plants and shrubs, trellises, and assorted reproductions from architectural history, all artfully arranged. Some of these features have undergone technological or economic modification, to be sure, such as the mount, which was a standard part of garden design from the Middle Ages to the eighteenth century, the earthworks designed to present a vista of the garden to the visitor and typically reached by path or staircase. This has now been replaced by the escalator, which rises at key points in the enclosed central parts of the mall, where it presents a similar vista of the space to the visitor, who is now lifted dramatically from the floor below by unseen forces without any effort on his or her part. And this, in its turn, is only a modification of a standard feature from Italian Renaissance gardens, the elaborate hydraulic machinery or automata that engineers had devised to move statues about in striking dramatic tableaux. Now, in the mall, it is the visitors who are moved about by the escalators, becoming themselves the actors in the tableau "modern shopping."

4   Combining the mount with the automata, the mall then encloses this machinery in two or three stories of space, topped with skylights. And this result, something like Houston's Galleria Mall, a massive three-story enclosed mall topped with skylights, is only an updated version of Henry VIII's garden at Hampton Court, where "on top of the mount was the South or Great Round Arbour, three storeys in height, almost all of glass, with a leaden cupola surmounted by the inevitable king's beasts and a great gilded crown."[5] What was once set aside for the king and his guests is now available to everyone willing to embrace the consumer ethic. We have dispensed, therefore, with the beasts and the gilded crown; joggers run on the roof of the Galleria. But, of course, the

---

* *Topos:* Greek for "topic" or "theme."

mount allowed the visitor to look both inside and outside the garden. The escalator within the enclosed mall only allows the visitor to look at the inside space.

5   Similarly, the labyrinth, the maze of pathways or hedges which confounded the visitor's attempts to find an easy way out and was a favorite device of Renaissance gardens, is now the cleverly laid out pattern of aisles within some department stores which are designed quite successfully to discourage the visitor's easy exit. Shoppers simply cannot find a way out. Bloomingdale's in the Willow Grove Mall in suburban Philadelphia received so many complaints from irate shoppers lost in its mazes that finally small, discrete exit signs were posted. What "may have had . . . [its] origins in the penitential mazes of the Christian Church" on the model of the paths "laid out in stone or tiles" on which "the penitent performed the journey on his knees, saying particular prayers at particular points," and was then moved out into the garden where it was secularized, has now become thoroughly commodified, a journey in which purchases have replaced prayers. Buy enough and we will let you out. Played against the maze and labyrinth in the Renaissance garden were the axial and radial avenues, which began as extensions of the hallways of the palace and ended in suitably grand natural vistas, a structuring device which allowed house and garden to become "a single unit."[6] Played against the department store maze in the mall are the axial and radial avenues, which begin as extensions of hallways of one anchor department store and end in the grand vistas of the entrances to others.

6   The kitchen garden, that area of the formal garden closest to the house and set aside for the production of food, has become the food court, that area of the mall set aside for the consumption of food. The statues, assorted imitations of Greek and Roman models, portraits of contemporary royalty, or stylized representations of the ancient virtues, now decked out in fashionable clothing, have become the mannequins, the generalized imitations of consumers in their most beautiful, heroic, and changeable poses, portraits of contemporary anonymous life that we should see as stylized representations of the modern virtues: poise, flexibility, nubility, interchangeability, emotional absence. The generalized faces on the statues are now the empty faces of the mannequins.

7   And the various architectural antiquities which became a feature of eighteenth-century English irregular gardens—the miscellaneous copies of Greek temples, Gothic ruins, Japanese pagodas, Roman triumphal arches, and Italian grottoes—are now represented not so much by the miscellaneous architectural reproductions that appear seasonally in the mall, as in the Easter Bunny's cottage or Santa's Workshop, but much more profoundly by many of the stores themselves, which present idealized versions of architectural and cultural history to the consumer: the Victorian lingerie shop, the high modernist fur salon, the nineteenth-century western goods store, the adobe Mexican restaurant, the barnlike country store, the dark grottolike bar. Also present in smaller details such as the grand staircase, the wall of mirrors, the plush carpeting, and the man playing the white grand piano are echoes of the 1930s movie set; in the merry-go-round, the popcorn cart, and the clown with balloons, the echoes of funland. The eighteenth-century garden included such historical reproductions in an effort to make sense of its past and to accommodate its cultural inheritances to

new situations. One can say the same about the mall's inclusion of historical recollections.

. . .

8   The Stanford Shopping Center in Palo Alto presents such [an assemblage] of cultural and architectural history: Crabtree and Evelyn with its images of eighteenth-century life, Laura Ashley with its images of romantic and early Victorian life, Victoria's Secret (the late Victorian bordello with overtones of French fashion), Banana Republic (the late Victorian colonial outfitter), the Disney Store with its images of 1940s art, and nearby the Nature Company, closest to the sixteenth century and the rise of science, since it is full of simple instruments and simple observations of nature. (Not present at this mall, but at others are stores like the Sharper Image, with its images of the twenty-first century.) One walks through history, then, or, to be more precise, through the images of history, just as one did in the formal garden, but now it can be appropriated by the act of consuming. One buys images, but learns "history." It is a clean, neat, and middle-class version of history without the homeless of downtown San Francisco and thus a retreat from the frenzy of contemporary urban life, which is exactly what the formal garden was also designed to be. To one side is an alley devoted to food, a lavishly idealized greengrocer, a pseudo-Italian coffee bar, and Max's Opera Cafe, a reproduction of a grand nineteenth-century cafe in Vienna—but what one finds when one wanders inside is not real or ersatz Vienna, but a glorified deli. Here the history of central Europe is rewritten as it might have been.

. . .

9   In the formal gardens of the past, where nature was rearranged to fit the aesthetic taste of the period, one walked through the landscape contemplating the vistas and approaching the beautiful. In the mall, where nature is similarly rearranged to fit the commercial needs of the period, one walks through the landscape, now contemplating not the vistas of nature, which have been completely blocked out, but the vistas represented by the entrances to the anchor department stores, and now not approaching the beautiful, but contemplating the commodities by which one can become the beautiful. These are practical times. The earlier aristocratic citizen who walked down the path of the garden admired the flowers and smelled their scents; the twentieth-century middle-class citizen who walks down the path of the shopping mall buys the flower scents in bottles and then smells like the flower or the musk ox. The focus has shifted, from the individual in reverie facing an artificial version of nature, to the individual in excitement facing a garden of consumer products.

Notes

1. James Turner, *The Politics of Landscape: Rural Scenery and Society in English Poetry, 1630–1660* (Cambridge, Mass.: Harvard University Press, 1979), 247.

2. Ronald Paulson, *Emblem and Expression: Meaning in English Art of the Eighteenth Century* (Cambridge, Mass.: Harvard University Press, 1975), 20, 23.

3. Jean Baudrillard, *For a Critique of the Political Economy of the Sign* (St. Louis: Telos Press, 1981), 38.

4. Judith Williamson, *Decoding Advertisements: Ideology and Meaning in Advertising* (London: Marion Boyars, 1978), 70.

5. Strong, *Renaissance Garden*, 28.

6. Ibid., 10.

Review Questions

1. How does the tradition of labyrinths in formal gardens find expression in contemporary malls?

2. How and why did formal gardens present versions of history to its visitors? How do shopping malls do the same?

3. In what ways do our visits to the mall teach us about the meaning of our place and time, just as visitors to formal gardens learned of their place and time?

Discussion and Writing Suggestions

1. Simon argues that the shopping mall operates in much the same way as formal gardens of the past. Does Simon's argument persuade you? What is the most compelling part of the argument? The least compelling?

2. Simon develops his argument as an extended comparison-and-contrast. Choose any two paragraphs in the selection and take notes on how he develops the main point of each. Be prepared to present your findings to a group or to your entire class.

3. Critics have knocked malls for their "unreality." They fault, for instance, the malls' policy of refusing entry to vagrants or political protesters. Malls may be cleaner, safer, and less hectic than real city streets, but they also lack the vitality of real, lived-in spaces. Yet Simon observes that if malls provide "a retreat from the frenzy of contemporary urban life, [this] is exactly what the formal garden was also designed to be." With this observation, how effectively does Simon blunt the criticism of malls as "unreal" places? Explain.

4. Formal gardens were packaged "cultural space[s]," says Simon, designed for effect. Do you agree that the experience of shoppers at malls is similarly packaged? Cite evidence from your recent trips to the mall indicating that your experience is being managed by the mall's designers.

5. In earlier times, visitors to gardens found beauty and an occasion for contemplation and relaxation. To what extent do you find similar occasions for reflection and relaxation at the mall?

The Mall as Sacred Space
Jon Pahl

The American shopping mall as "sacred" space? A number of serious theologians consider the idea quite plausible. Jon Pahl (who received his PhD from the University of Chicago Divinity School) is professor of the history of Christianity in North America at the Lutheran Theological Seminary at Philadelphia. At the seminary, Pahl's teaching interests include "History of Christian Thought," "Religions in North America," and "American Sacred Places," the course description for which reads as follows: "From the Mall of America to Walt Disney World, Niagara Falls to the Alamo, Americans have made pilgrimages to some interesting places. At the same time, more traditional sanctuaries or shrines dot the historical landscape of the U.S. What does this fascination with making places sacred mean, and what do places (both built and culturally-constructed) reveal about particular historical communities and individuals?" Such questions inform the following selection, which first appeared in Pahl's Shopping Malls and Other Sacred Spaces: Putting God in Place *(2003).*

1   Thankfully, I'm not the only one to see shopping malls as sacred places. Ira G. Zepp, a professor of religious studies at Western Maryland College, has suggested in a brief book, *The New Religious Image of Urban America*, that any large shopping center functions "interchangeably and simultaneously [as] a ceremonial center, an alternative community, a carnival, and a secular cathedral."[1] More specifically, Zepp contends that malls "as we experience them cannot be reduced to commercial and financial enterprises. They are far more than places of business." It is this "more" about malls that Zepp finds particularly interesting. People don't just visit malls to shop, he points out. Pilgrims go to malls to hang out, to exercise, to pray, even to get married. This latter function should not be surprising, since malls are designed to be like temples. Zepp quotes approvingly James Rouse, an architect responsible for over sixty malls, including many of the earliest and most famous in the United States. According to Rouse, "it is in the marketplace that all people come together—rich and poor, old and young, black and white. It is the democratic, unifying, universal place which gives spirit and personality to the city."[2] Such faith in the "spirit" and "unifying" potential of the marketplace led Rouse to design malls in ways that drew upon common symbols from the Protestant faith he practiced his entire life. According to Rouse, businesspeople were the clergy of a new religion that transcended the parochial boundaries of creed and cult. The shopping mall, then, was to be the cathedral in this new religion, the sacred space for a "universal" faith with a distinct spirit.[3]

2   Just how successful Rouse was in realizing his dream can be verified easily enough. Visit a mall, as I did at Southlake Mall in Merrillville, Indiana, one afternoon with a group of students, and observe and ask questions. Expect resistance. You'll be trampling on some folks' sacred compulsions, sort of like violating the taboo against swearing in church or talking about religion at a private party. If you want to be legitimate, make your first stop the management offices. You will probably not get any further. My students, typically not concerned with either ritual or legitimacy, simply started interviewing people with my video

camera: "So," they asked, "do you think the mall is a sacred place?" They made it through about a dozen interviews with bewildered or amused shopper/pilgrims before the security guards found them and shut them down. "You can't ask people questions in here," the guards said. Indeed, questions might make people think about why they are there, thereby disrupting the process of disorientation and reorientation by means of which the place induces us to buy. People expect a mall to be a public place. Of course, it's not. It's a privately owned enterprise that can establish its own rules about who is in, who is not, and on what terms.

3   Malls communicate the "spirit" of the market through a common formula. They *disorient* us, by using natural and religious symbols and spatial patterns in an enclosed indoor setting, and then *reorient* us toward one or another of the purveyors of goods. During my young adulthood, I would get a headache after more than a half-hour in a mall. Without some critical distance from the place, my brain couldn't take the constant stimuli that sought to persuade me that my salvation depended upon this or that acquisition. Surely, the mall is a sensual feast, if not an assault. For within the labyrinth of the typical mall, we experience water, light, trees, words, food, music, and bodies, the combined effect of which is to make us feel entranced, dazed, disoriented, and, finally, lacking something. Thus vulnerable, the soul can sell itself to the nearest, if not always the lowest, bidder. To feel lost is the customary, indeed intended, feeling. Fully 40 percent of visitors to the mall do not intend to purchase anything. Only 10 percent get out without lighter purses or wallets.[4]

4   Water, for instance, is used in almost every mall to prepare one to "go with the flow" of shopping. Water dissolves boundaries and is a widespread religious symbol. . . . Among the religious meanings of water, of course, is purification: malls use fountains, waterfalls, and reflecting pools symbolically to cleanse shoppers of any filthiness all the lucre involved in the place might suggest. Zepp points out that at many malls you might bathe symbolically in a fountain, be refreshed by the sound of a mock waterfall, or even be baptized symbolically beside mini-flowers of water—as I pointed out to my students at Southlake Mall. In short, water initiates the visitor into an experience that is designed to be "more" than a shopping trip. As Zepp argues, "mall developers have attempted ingeniously to satisfy [the] human longing to be near water. . . . We consider water a gift."[5] But of course, this "gift" is one we will, ordinarily, feel compelled to pay for. Furthermore, we will be happy to do so, for the water in malls is "safe" water, controlled water. There is never a need for an ark in a mall. Water in malls has no utilitarian purpose—it's not necessary. It does have a poetic, and a political, function, and more than one pilgrim has gotten soaked in the process.

5   Just as malls use water to appear to be something "more" than an ordinary place, so too do malls abound with light, yet another vital religious symbol. . . . Light of many kinds is featured in shopping malls, but each light is strategically placed to draw the senses in and toward one attraction or another. Neon light is used to beckon with its peculiar glow, especially in the signs above the entries to mall attractions, casting an aura that entices with its soft yet vibrant colors. Natural light is also a prominent feature of most mall designs. At the center of most malls, as Zepp notes: "You can usually find . . . a huge skylight or a colorful and often circular series of lamps shedding such bright light . . . that you

know you are in a space set apart."[6] Light, of course, is our primary experience of energy. Thus, Zepp concludes, "malls, at their centers, strive to be places of vitality and energy."[7] That they succeed admirably in drawing visitors like moths to a candle is evident in the fact that the largest one, the "Mall of America," welcomes 35 to 40 million guests annually. That's some serious energy.

6   Along with water and light, the powerful symbols of the tree and vegetation are commonly employed in mall design. Growing things are held sacred in almost every religion, and many traditions have stories or myths about trees of life or gardens of human delight. . . . The inclusion of growing things in shopping malls is, again, more than a utilitarian decision by mall developers to help keep interior air clean. For, significantly, none of the trees in the mall ever die. The trees in malls are all evergreens, even if they are deciduous. Life—abundant, even eternal—is the message. Malls thus play upon the human desire to experience growth and new life, even while juxtaposing such symbolism with profit-making that clearly tries to sap (sorry) as much life from visitors as possible. Still, the symbolism is powerful and effective: life is growth, offers this gospel, in exactly the terms that we want it. This is the Garden of Eden without the fall; the resurrection without the cross; spring and summer without fall or winter. That this growth in fact comes at a price is constantly masked or obscured by the clever design that entices us to imagine that we're inhabiting a garden of free delight. The constantly green trees whisper to us just that message, if we only have ears to hear: "Don't count the cost."

7   More directly, malls advertise themselves in words that promise us unity, devotion, love, happiness, and other phenomena that were once the benefits of traditional religious practices. Zepp catalogs dozens of advertising slogans and catchphrases that clarify the point. He admits being surprised by the use of religious language in advertising, and in fact, most of us rarely pay attention to the words used in malls. We're too busy being disoriented or distracted by the water, light, trees, or music. Yet the words are there, with unmistakable religious meanings when we start to think about them. Thus the mall offers community: "You're a part of us," one intimates. And the mall promises us devotion. It's a place "devoted to eating, shopping, and the pursuit of happiness," offers another. The words cascade together in a barrage of religious meanings: "You are going to *love* the experience." "We want to touch your life!" "We can identify with all your needs!"[8] Really? Of course not. There is no "we" there. But clothed in such promises, and covered up by soothing music, the naked reality of the mall as a place to turn a profit is concealed, and we are enticed to partake in the sacred rites. The mall cloaks its profit-driven purpose in a poetics of promise.

8   Now, I move here into an area that risks offending some readers, but it seems obvious to me that until very recently malls primarily targeted women, and their bodies, with their messages of salvation. Like other images that encourage consumption—notably those on television—malls are filled with mannequins, posters, and other props that promote an image of an ideal female body—always young, always slim, and always "beautiful," in a stereotypical kind of way. Such images, of course, seek to reduce the identity of women to their desires for the commodities that can help them "match" the ideal. As the poster in one shop window put it, "When French women want it, they put it on The Card." This

is a fascinating assertion. Of course women, and not only French ones, "want it." But if what they want can be put "on the card," or charged on a piece of plastic, then the body becomes nothing more than a naked place on which to hang commodities, or "it." In the mall, the body then becomes nothing more than a whirl of atoms: a place without soul, consciousness, or orientation. All places are equal; desire has no bounds, as long as "it" can be put on "the card." Thus vacated, the body can be possessed—so to speak—by any number of spirits of the place, attached to any number of illusions that guarantee the body some "it"—something "new" or "improved" or "bigger" or "better" or "more." People have often been possessed by such promises.

9   Men, of course, experience the consequences of this system differently—but in no less damaging ways. "Real" men, for instance, are supposed to disdain the mall. Many have confided in me, after reading drafts of this chapter or hearing me speak about it: "I hate the mall, too. I guess it's a guy thing." As I've reflected on this comment, it amuses me and makes me sad. As it happens, I don't hate malls, and in fact I have learned to enjoy them quite a bit—while simply recognizing them for what they are. As I've put it before, malls have lots of cool stuff, and the best ones have manifold delights for the senses. We can smell perfumes and colognes, eat lunch, a snack, or an entire dinner, listen to music or scan books for hours on end, and revel in displays of human craftsmanship, ingenuity, and diversity. My sons, and many young people, have taught me to appreciate my experience of the mall without having to buy into the sacred promises. When guys tell me, then, that they "hate the mall, too," it suggests that men can't take pleasure in the carnivalesque atmosphere of the mall or in the sensual or aesthetic pleasures the places convey. And the fact is that most men in America aren't terribly attuned to this level of experience. By being unable to appreciate the obvious delights of such a place, men ironically "buy into" the flip side of the gender stereotypes that oppress women, although men's bodies, too, increasingly are subject to pressures to conform to stereotypical ideals of beauty.

10   I'm glad, then, that my children and other young people have taught me how to appreciate malls without getting a headache in them. In fact, I can even admire inveterate mall pilgrims, especially the numerous senior citizens who exercise in them, or who otherwise find malls sanctuaries of civility in an otherwise uncivil society.[9] I've come to understand, in fact, that malls may be functioning better as "churches" than are many buildings bearing the name. As Ira Zepp concludes: "The shopping mall, open almost every day from 10 A.M. to 9 P.M. . . . is a more inclusive and egalitarian center [than] most churches."[10] That he is right is a sign of just how disoriented believers in God have become in America. If churches aren't connecting people to true happiness, how can we blame people for seeking happiness in a place that promises it to them accompanied by powerful experiences of water, light, trees, and bodies? Zepp again: "Malls are contemporary versions of that age-old combination of commerce and community. They will continue to fill the void created by our social institutions' failure in providing centers of ritual and meaning."[11] Malls have become sacred places because traditional churches, synagogues, temples, and mosques have failed.

11   Finally, however, even though traditional religious communities often fail to fulfill their own promises, I also have to say a gentle but clear "no" to the promises of the mall. For the success of the mall's offer of salvation depends upon my coming to feel a fabricated sense that somehow I lack something that only the mall, as a cathedral of the market, can provide. And, frankly, the most serious absences in my life have not been due to my failure to acquire a particular commodity, but can be traced directly to my own poor choices or uncertain will. Sin, to use an old-fashioned word for that lack, is a little deeper than my failure to acquire a wide-screen TV, and surely human suffering is more serious than not having the latest style of tennis shoes. Still, we all can get trapped in the false logic, because we do not want to have to confront our deepest personal, moral, or political failings. It's much easier to have to "confront" only the absences that the images of the mall make us feel. Indeed, malls exist to mask true absences, deny them, or make us forget them. All the mall can give us are very finite experiences of consuming whatever commodity happens to strike our current fancy, in exchange for our cash. The promises of "unity" and "happiness" and "love" are lies. This stairway to heaven is, then, really nothing new in history; it's as old as humanity. It's the same system rejected in the *Bhagavad Gita,* the same system that the Buddha saw through as he sat under the Bo tree, and the same system that Luther protested in the Reformation, in which people were offered salvation for dropping a few coins in an indulgence coffer. But today the system is packaged in such a way that souls continue to climb this stairway to heaven, when it is really an escalator, leading nowhere.

Notes

1. Ira G. Zepp, *The New Religious Image of Urban America: The Shopping Mall as Ceremonial Center* (Westminster, Md.: Christian Classics: 1986), 15.

2. James Rouse, "The Regional Shopping Center: Its Role in the Community It Serves," unpublished lecture at Harvard Graduate School of Design, April 26, 1963, as cited in Zepp, *New Religious Image,* 31.

3. Scholars have recently turned from disdain for malls to appreciation for their "hip" character or at least have tried to present a more balanced account of the commodification of the world. See, for a relatively tame example, Leigh Eric Schmidt, *Consumer Rites: The Buying and Selling of American Holidays* (Princeton, N.J.: Princeton University Press, 1995). As a historian, Schmidt tries to "put balance before judgment" (p. 7). That this is, in effect, a judgment itself seems to elude Schmidt, although he offers belated "confessions" of his own "slippery positioning" on "ongoing cultural contests" at the end of the work.

4. Zepp, *New Religious Image,* 15.

5. Ibid., 58–9.

6. Ibid., 56.

7. Ibid., 37.

8. Ibid., 6–8, 12–13.

9. See on this theme Witold Rybczynski, *City Life: Urban Expectations in a New World* (New York: Scribner, 1996).

10. Zepp, *New Religious Image*, 80.

11. Ibid., 150.

Review Questions

1. How are shoppers like pilgrims? What do they seek at the mall?

2. In what ways do shopping malls purposefully disorient and reorient us?

3. What is the significance of water, light, and vegetation in shopping malls, according to Pahl?

4. In what ways can women be "possessed" at shopping malls?

5. Pahl ultimately says "a gentle but clear 'no' to the promises of the mall." Why?

Discussions and Writing Suggestions

1. A famous designer of malls, James Rouse, writes, "It is in the marketplace that all people come together—rich and poor, old and young, black and white. It is the democratic, unifying, universal place which gives spirit and personality to the city." Your response?

2. Evaluate the logic of *one* of Pahl's paragraphs (4–6) in which he argues for the sacred significance of light, water, and vegetation in shopping malls. Do you accept his argument? Follow the guidelines for writing critiques on page 66.

3. In paragraph 3 Pahl writes that as a young man he would get headaches at shopping malls before he was able to gain "some critical distance from the place." What is this "critical distance"? Distance from what? In responding to the question, see paragraph 9, where Pahl writes: "I don't hate malls, and in fact I have learned to enjoy them quite a bit—while simply recognizing them for what they are." How does "critical distance" play a role in Pahl's "recognizing" meaning in malls?

4. Following up on Discussion and Writing Suggestion #3 above, what do you suppose are the dangers of entering a mall without "critical distance"?

5. Pahl argues that malls incorporate the symbols of sacred spaces into their design through the use of lighting, water, vegetation, and dramatic architecture. Does the use of such symbols, alone, make a place sacred? In your view, what requirements of a space, aside from the appearance of certain symbols, make it sacred?

6. Pahl concludes that the mall's "promises of 'unity' and 'happiness' and 'love' are lies." Does his rejection of the mall as a place that can address "our deepest personal, moral, or political failings" invalidate his thesis that the shopping mall can be viewed as a sacred space?

The Mall as Setting for Authentic Life
Virginia Postrel

Critics like David Guterson slam shopping malls for being cookie-cutter replications, a national embarrassment, and a symbol of all that is basely profit driven and inauthentic in American life. Cultural commentator Virginia Postrel takes a different view: The mall, "exuberantly fake" by design, provides a comfortable, safe place for people to meet and interact. Postrel has served as editor of Reason *magazine, writes for several news outlets as well as a column for* The Atlantic, *and has authored two books:* The Future and Its Enemies *(1998) and* The Substance of Style *(2003), the opening pages of which appear below.*

1   As soon as the Taliban fell, Afghan men lined up at barbershops to have their beards shaved off. Women painted their nails with once-forbidden polish. Formerly clandestine beauty salons opened in prominent locations. Men traded postcards of beautiful Indian movie stars, and thronged to buy imported TVs, VCRs, and videotapes. Even burka merchants diversified their wares, adding colors like brown, peach, and green to the blue and off-white dictated by the Taliban's whip-wielding virtue police. Freed to travel to city markets, village women demanded better fabric, finer embroidery, and more variety in their traditional garments.

2   When a Michigan hairdresser went to Kabul with a group of doctors, nurses, dentists, and social workers, she intended to serve as an all-purpose assistant to the relief mission's professionals. Instead, she found her own services every bit as popular as the serious business of health and welfare. "When word got out there was a hairdresser in the country, it just got crazy," she said. "I was doing haircuts every fifteen minutes."

3   Liberation is supposed to be about grave matters: elections, education, a free press. But Afghans acted as though superficial things were just as important. As a political commentator noted, "The right to shave may be found in no international treaty or covenant, but it has, in Afghanistan, become one of the first freedoms to which claim is being laid."

4   That reaction challenged many widely held assumptions about the nature of aesthetic value. While they cherish artworks like the giant Bamiyan Buddhas leveled by the Taliban, social critics generally take a different view of the frivolous, consumerist impulses expressed in more mundane aesthetic pleasures. "How depressing was it to see Afghan citizens celebrating the end of tyranny by buying consumer electronics?" wrote Anna Quindlen in a 2001 Christmas column berating Americans for "uncontrollable consumerism."

5   Respectable opinion holds that our persistent interest in variety, adornment, and new sensory pleasures is created by advertising, which generates "the desire for products consumers [don't] need at all," as Quindlen put it, declaring that "I do not need an alpaca swing coat, a tourmaline brooch, a mixer with a dough hook, a CD player that works in the shower, another pair of boot-cut black pants, lavender bath salts, vanilla candles or a KateSpadeGucciPradaCoach bag."

6   What's true for New Yorkers should be true for Afghans as well. Why buy a green burka when you're a poor peasant and already have two blue ones? Why paint your nails red if you're a destitute widow begging on the streets? These indulgences seem wasteful and irrational, just the sort of false needs encouraged by commercial manipulation. Yet liberated Kabul had no ubiquitous advertising or elaborate marketing campaigns. Maybe our desires for impractical decoration and meaningless fashion don't come from Madison Avenue after all. Maybe our relation to aesthetic value is too fundamental to be explained by commercial mind control.

7   Human beings know the world, and each other, through our senses. From our earliest moments, the look and feel of our surroundings tell us who and where we are. But as we grow, we imbibe a different lesson: that appearances are not just potentially deceiving but frivolous and unimportant—that aesthetic value is not real except in those rare instances when it transcends the quotidian to become high art. We learn to contrast surface to substance, to believe that our real selves and the real world exist beyond the superficiality of sensation.

8   We have good cause, of course, to doubt the simple evidence of our senses. The sun does not go around the earth. Lines of the same length can look longer or shorter depending on how you place arrows on their ends. Beautiful people are not necessarily good, nor are good people necessarily beautiful. We're wise to maintain reasonable doubts.

9   But rejecting our sensory natures has problems of its own. When we declare that mere surface cannot possibly have legitimate value, we deny human experience and ignore human behavior. We set ourselves up to be fooled again and again, and we make ourselves a little crazy. We veer madly between overvaluing and undervaluing the importance of aesthetics. Instead of upholding rationality against mere sensuality, we tangle ourselves in contradictions.

10   This book [*The Substance of Style*] seeks to untangle those confusions, by examining afresh the nature of aesthetic value and its relation to our personal, economic, and social lives. It's important to do so now, because sensory appeals are becoming ever more prominent in our culture. To maintain a healthy balance between substance and surface, we can no longer simply pretend that surfaces don't matter. Experience suggests that the comfortable old slogans, and the theories behind them, are wrong.

11   Afghanistan is not the only place where human behavior confounds conventional assumptions, raising questions about the sources of aesthetic value. Consider "authenticity," which aesthetic authorities consider a prime measure of worth. Here, too, experience suggests a more complex standard, or perhaps a more subjective definition of what's authentic, than intellectual discourse usually provides.

12   Built atop one of the hills that divide the San Fernando Valley from the core of Los Angeles, Universal CityWalk is deliberately fake. Its architect calls the open-air shopping mall "a great simulacrum of what L.A. should do. This isn't the L.A. we did get, but it's the L.A. we could have gotten—the quintessential, idealized L.A."

13   Like the rest of Los Angeles, CityWalk's buildings are mostly stucco boxes. Their aesthetic energy comes from their façades, which are adorned with bright

signs, colorful tiles, video screens, murals, and such playful accessories as a giant King Kong. Unlike the typical shopping center, CityWalk has encouraged its tenants to let their decorative imaginations run wild. The place has a tiny artificial beach and, of course, palm trees. A fountain shoots water up through the sidewalk. A fictional radio station sells hamburgers, and a real museum displays vintage neon signs. The three blocks of city "street" are off-limits to vehicles.

14   When City Walk opened in 1993, it was roundly condemned as an inauthentic facsimile of real city life. Intellectuals saw only a fortress, a phony refuge from the diversity and conflict of a city recently torn by riots. A conservative journalist called it "Exhibit A in a hot new trend among the beleaguered middle classes: bunkering," while a liberal social critic said CityWalk "has something of the relationship to the real city that a petting zoo has to nature."

15   The public reacted differently. Almost immediately, CityWalk became not a bunker but a grand mixing zone. "Suddenly CityWalk was full of people. And they were all grinning," wrote a delighted veteran of European cafés shortly after the new mall opened. He predicted that the artificial city street would soon become a beloved hangout, that locals would never want to leave. He was right. A decade later, CityWalk may be "the most vital public space in Los Angeles," declares a magazine report. On a Saturday night,

> People from all across L.A. have gathered here in one great undifferentiated mass, as they rarely do in the city itself. Toddlers are tearing across CityWalk's sidewalk fountain. Salvadoran, Armenian, Korean, black, and white, they squeal as the hidden water jets erupt, soaking their overalls. Hundreds of teenagers who have made CityWalk their hangout are picking each other up and sucking down frozen mochas. Families from Encino to East L.A. are laughing, stuffing their faces, gawking at the bright spires of light.

16   So much for the assumption that artifice and interaction are contradictory, that the only experience a "simulacrum" can produce is inauthentic. By offering a place of shared aesthetic pleasures, CityWalk has created not an isolated enclave but a space where people from many different backgrounds can enjoy themselves together.

17   Half a world away is an even more artificial environment, where not only the street but the sky itself is fake. The social results are similar. "It's a very special building, very different, very beautiful," says a black South African of Johannesburg's Montecasino, a casino that replicates a Tuscan village, right down to imported cobblestones and an old Fiat accumulating parking tickets by the side of the make-believe road. Unlike many places in Johannesburg, Montecasino attracts a racially mixed crowd, including unemployed black men who chat beneath its artificial trees and watch the gamblers at play. Like CityWalk, the casino offers its aesthetic pleasures to all comers. Its deracinated design is central to its appeal.

18   "Montecasino imposes nothing on anyone. It is completely, exuberantly fake," writes a Togo-based critic. "And, as in Las Vegas, it is this fakeness that ensures its egalitarian popularity. Blacks and whites feel equally at home in this reassuringly bogus Tuscany. The price of democracy, it would seem, is inau-

thenticity." Or maybe something is wrong with aesthetic standards that would deny people pleasures that don't conform to their particular era or ethnicity. Maybe we've misunderstood the meaning and value of authenticity.

Review Questions

1. How does Postrel characterize Anna Quindlan's reaction to Afghans rushing to purchase consumer electronics after being liberated?

2. What distinction do people sometimes make between "substance" and "surface"? How does Postrel object to this distinction? (In answering, you may want to use the statement quoted for Discussion and Writing Suggestion #3.)

3. Postrel says that CityWalk and other "exuberantly fake" places like Las Vegas surprise critics. How so? What have the similarities of such places to do with Postrel's exploration of substance and surface?

Discussion and Writing Suggestions

1. "Liberation is supposed to be about grave matters: elections, education, a free press. But Afghans acted as though superficial things [like shaving or getting nails polished] were just as important." Your comments?

2. Have you ever been to a place like CityWalk or Las Vegas, so obvious in its fakeness, its *in*authenticity, that you find yourself relaxing and having a good time? In what ways does the very inauthenticity of the setting lend itself to a kind of intimacy? Perhaps this was not your experience, and the fakeness of the setting offended (or amused) you—as the Mall of America offended David Guterson (see pages 450–457). If so, explain that reaction.

3. "The price of democracy, it would seem, is inauthenticity." Postrel quotes a Togo-based critic here (see paragraph 18) who is referring to the success of a Johannesburg casino fashioned after a Tuscan village. What is the special appeal of such a purposely fake place? What is it about a place like Las Vegas that "ensures its egalitarian popularity"?

The Mall as Refuge
George Lewis

In this article, which first appeared in the Journal of Popular Culture *(Fall 1990), George Lewis investigates the extent to which shopping malls "really act as [a] social magnet, bringing people together in a true sense of community." Through public service programs and promotions, mall management would have us believe that its facilities function as town centers in the spirit that Victor Gruen had envisioned. But Lewis, a sociologist at the University of the*

Pacific, challenges that view, concluding that the groups that congregate in malls "seldom share the common ties and engage in the sort of social interactions necessary to forge a sense of 'we-ness.'" Lewis bases his insights on a study of two groups—elders and teenagers—at a New England shopping center.

1 Everyday life in America, in the past three decades, has been critically affected by the evolution and spread of the shopping mall as the central concept in American retailing. These economic monoliths, evolving from the earlier retail form of the suburban shopping center, are now about far more than just shopping. People go to the modern mall for professional services, such as legal, medical or optical aid. There are fashion shows, art shows and musical performances in these climate controlled, air conditioned spaces. Restaurants, video arcades, movie theatres and even ice skating rinks and sand beaches with tanning lights focused upon them are found in the contemporary enclosed mall. In a word, the regional shopping mall has become a kind of civic center, a point of attraction for millions of Americans, whether they choose to buy something there regularly or not.

. . .

Community in the Mall: Manufactured Illusion or Social Reality?

2 With all its promotions and public service programs, does the mall really act as this sort of social magnet, bringing people together in a true sense of community? The answer, if one is to define community as more than just the bringing together of demographically similar persons in one locale, is more apt to be negative than it is positive. Malls can, and do, lure and assemble *collectivities* and *crowds* of shoppers, but these groups seldom share the common ties and engage in the sort of social interactions necessary to forge a sense of "we-ness"—of community—from the raw social material of a crowd.

3 Jessie Bernard makes a crucial conceptual distinction here between "the community," which emphasizes *locale* as its most important and fundamental criterion, and "community," which emphasizes *common ties* and *interaction* as significant criteria in its conceptualization. "Community," then, is characterized not by locale, but by the *gemeinschaften* spirit of communal and primary relationships in which intimacy, sentiment, and a sense of belonging exist among individuals.[1]

4 Thomas Bender agrees, further defining community as characterized by close, usually face to face relationships. "Individuals are bound together by affective or emotional ties rather than by a perception of individual self-interest. There is a 'we-ness' in a community; one is a member."[2]

5 If this is the sort of social relationship one means by community, then it is difficult to find among customers at most shopping malls. Physically, malls are geared for high turnover. Chairs and benches in rest areas and food courts are unpadded in the seat—designed to be uncomfortable if sat in too long. The architecture of the mall itself, behind the colorful neon store logos and displays, is anonymous, uniform, predictable and plain. The corridors are wide and filled with hurrying customers. Security guards discourage loiterers and help to move foot traffic along. The muzak, if it exists, reinforces the image of the mall as a public space—a place where strangers encounter one another en route to their desired locations.

6   Most shoppers who frequent the mall, even if lured there by some promotional scheme, come alone or in small groups of two or three.[3] They are intent upon their business, focusing upon shopping and not upon interaction with other mall customers. For the most part, they do not know each other and they don't come to the mall on any regular, day-to-day basis. In short, the high turnover, volume of persons, and transiency that is a designed part of most malls works *against* the development and emergence of community within their walls.

7   This is understood by mall managers and developers. As one put it: "Having the *perception* of a community feeling does not mean that it actually exists. It is not the same thing. Perception is not necessarily reality."[4] So the important thing, from a marketing perspective, is to create the warm *illusion* of community, while at the same time quietly stacking the deck against its actual development. "We don't want the mall to be a community in any real sense, because we'll attract people we don't want to. People who are not here to shop but are coming for some other purpose. It would upset our tenants who want to make money. We don't want anything to upset our tenants."

8   And yet, within this illusion, this false setting of community, the seeds of community have been planted. Ironically, among the very sorts of persons the managers and developers do not want to see attracted to the mall—the non-shoppers—have arisen fledgling forms of community, characterized by primary ties, face to face interaction, daily meeting and the development of social networks. These developing communities, or social worlds—one comprised mainly of retired persons and others over 65, and the other of teenagers—are the empirical focus of this paper. The data presented here were collected in June and July of 1988 in a series of unstructured interviews conducted in a large shopping center in New England. The interviews, which total over 200 hours of material, are one portion of a research effort undertaken by the Salt Center For Cultural Studies, in examining various facets of the impact of popular and mass culture on regional cultural forms.[5]

. . .

The Elderly

9   The mall is a central life setting for many elderly persons who frequent it on a regular basis. They walk back and forth, up and down the common area of the older wing of the mall (the "old mall"), greeting friends and acquaintances and sitting with them, visiting, in the sunken circular seating areas they have named the "north hole," "south hole," or "center hole." Some visit the mall every day, arriving when the doors are opened in the morning. Many stay all day, leaving in mid to late afternoon. A few will have a light dinner at one of the mall eateries before going home for the evening.

10   Many of these persons are retired, many widowed. They feel they have little else to fill their days. Their time in the mall usually conforms to set routines. They will be found in a specific seating area at a regular time, have coffee at the same restaurant at the same time, and leave the mall each day within 15 or 20 minutes of their leaving time the day before. This patterning of behavior is pervasive among the elderly and characterizes the nature of their social interaction at the mall.

11   Bert, for example, a 78-year-old retiree, comes to the mall every day of the week. "I come here at quarter of eleven and I leave at twenty minutes past one," he says matter-of-factly, as he sneaks a glance at his watch. "I do this every day. Every day except. . . ."

12   His two companions finish for him; "Five days a week. He's missed one day this year."

13   Bert resumes his own account. "And I have my lunch here at noontime." This is Bert's eleven o'clock stop, outside of Porteous, one of the large department-style anchor stores of the mall. He won't be here at eleven-thirty.

14   "I move every half hour. I go from here down to where the clock is. Then where the clock is, I go down in front of Woolworth's, then I come back again and go up there and take my bus by the front of JC Penney."

15   Linda, a mall custodian, noted that the elderly "would rather be at the mall than anywhere else. They probably know more about the place than I do. Probably know more than security does, too. I know 'cause my father-in-law is one of 'em. He comes in twice a day, every day. Ya, he sets over in the old mall, then he comes down and sets by Porteous for a while, then over by McDonalds."

16   The controlled environment of the mall offers another benefit to the elderly—it is a safe and comfortable place to walk for exercise. As Jacobs has pointed[6] out, many malls have instituted some form of walking program for the elderly—though the impetus for these programs usually comes from outside the mall itself, as the elderly are most often perceived by mall management as a group who does very little, if any, buying and thus contributes quite minimally in proportion to their presence, to the economic life of the mall.

17   "We really don't want them to come here if they're not going to shop," a mall manager remarked. "They take up seats we would like to have available for shoppers." However, from a public relations standpoint, it is difficult for mall management to overtly discourage the elderly from using the mall for their own purposes. Conversely, management can sometimes be talked into the minimal support of programs such as walking-for-health, in hopes it shows off to the community of shoppers they do want to attract, the degree of social consciousness and responsibility they supposedly feel.

18   The mall studied here is no exception to this pattern. A local doctor and the YMCA spearheaded the senior walking program, which opened in the spring of 1987 and which is now jointly sponsored by the doctor, the Y and the mall. The program encourages the elderly to walk laps and to record their own progress. To date, there are over 300 walkers signed into this program.

19   For those participating, entrance to the mall can be as early as 6:00 a.m., when security unlocks the doors—a full 3 or 4 hours prior to the opening of most commercial establishments inside the mall.

20   Pat, a regular "miler" in the program, usually arrives by car a few minutes before six and waits until the glass doors are unlocked.

21   "Age first," Pat insists as he holds a door for his two companions. Inside the mall, silent mannequins observe the three men begin their daily laps. Pat, now eighty years old, decides to take a short cut.

22   "You cheated," accuses the security guard.

23   "No, *you're* cheatin'," Pat accuses. "You're supposed to unlock all these doors and you're talkin' instead. I gotta bum hip, and when you get to my age, you won't be walkin'!" He smiles and disappears down the corridor. Two women call out to him in disbelief.

24   "You were here before us!"

25   "That's right," Pat laughs. "You're gettin' lazy."

26   After his five miles of walking laps, Pat sits down at his favorite restaurant, just now opening for business. Coming to the mall, he says, "gets me out of the house. I wish they opened at five. Pretty soon I'll be meeting six or seven fellas I know. We talk, shoot the breeze. I just come out here to kill a little time, that's all. What am I going to do at home?"

27   He leans back to prop his elbow on the back of his chair. His eyes follow a woman in red high heels taking choppy steps past a boutique. "I was in business 65 years. Was in the meat business. Gave it to my son, my son gave it to his son. I don't know whether you ever heard of it—Pat's Meat Mart?"

28   Two elderly ladies in cotton skirts and sneakers walk past and wave to Pat. "Morning," he answers. These women he identifies as past customers of his, as he jokes with them. "I have a lot of customers, really I do . . . people know us, ya know."

29   He looks down and then away, as if he doesn't want to talk anymore. Then: "I was going to show you my darlin's picture." He pulls out his wallet and unfolds a fragile, yellowed newspaper clipping. "She was the nicest. Everybody loved her. They only make one like her. . . . I miss this one, I tell ya. I do, I really do. Oh, we were inseparable. I had her for 34 years. She died when she was 51, so— God wanted her. There's nothing I could do, ya know. That's the story of my life." A tight little smile.

30   "Where do ya want me to send the bill?" he asks, snapping back to the present.

31   Retired and living alone, many of these elderly seek the mall as a safe and neutral ground to keep up old job contacts—not just the more surface relationships with old customers, but more primary ties with workmates themselves. George, who worked for a large electrical plant until they "closed out" in 1983 and forced him into retirement, meets his work buddies every Friday in the mall for lunch. Over the five years he has done this, he notes, fewer and fewer are alive to attend. "Every month," he says, "the faces we used to see, they're thinnin' out, . . . thinnin' out. . . ."

32   Charlie comes to the mall to meet people and to avoid heat in the summer and cold in the winter. "Some people I meet here," he says, "I've known for forty years." The elderly congregate in knots and clusters, laughing and joking among themselves. Charlie flags down Bob and Irene in the crowd and gives them two coupons from the previous day's paper, good for money off at a mall fast food stand.

33   Connie complains of telephone sales people to the group—especially a seller of cemetery plots. "I told him I have my plot all picked out. I'm just sitting here waiting to go. He didn't call back." She continues, "Here (in the mall) we sit and talk about our illnesses, medications, diets. We have a lot of fun."

34   More than most social worlds, the world of the elderly in the mall takes its shape and character from the face to face relationships of the people who regu-

larly are a part of it. For these elderly—most of whom are retired, who live alone, and are most probably widowed—there is now little or no need to expend energy, concern and time in the areas of career, job development, self-improvement, spousal relations, or even in family and community activities. Cut off from these concerns and ties, their status and power position in the larger society lowered, they find meaning in the construction and maintenance of networks of personal relationships with others like themselves.[7] These "personal communities," then, are not defined by a bounded area so much as they are a web-like network of personal relationships in which each person is selectively attached to a definite number of discrete persons. At the edges of this network are those persons, such as the servers in the restaurants, the custodians, and the security personnel, with whom relationships are affectively neutral, of a surface level, and usually joking in nature.

35   Harry sums it up. "It's hard being a senior citizen. Very hard. It's a monotonous life. You know, when you're constructive for a good many years and then you have to relax and do nothing—and you're alone—that's worse."

36   Tom, sitting beside Harry, points out that he has some pretty good friends at the mall. He continues; "Girls down in the food court. They all look for us. We don't come in, they ask everybody where we are. They think we're sick, or something."

37   Harry and Bert tip their heads in agreement. "They look out for us. We kid a lot with them and everything."

38   Harry takes it from there. "Well, you're seeing a face, you know. If you stayed at home and you're alone, you see nothing. No matter where you'd live, you'd see a car go by. But people, you don't see." Silence. Then, "So you come out here to see the living, more or less." He looks to his friends for reinforcement. "Am I right? I think so."

39   Tom jumps in. "But you make everything sound so *sad*, Harry. My Lord, it's not *that* bad. I come out here to see my friends. To get out of the house. That's all."

The Teens

40   Teenagers visit the mall on an almost daily basis. They arrive in groups or individually to meet their friends. A number work in the mall, usually at minimum wage, in the fast food establishments located, for the most part, in the "new wing" of the mall, built just three years ago. When they are off work, they "hang out" with other youths, who use the mall as a place for social gathering.

41   The mall is one of the few places teenagers can go in this society where they are—albeit reluctantly—allowed to stay without being asked to leave.[8] Many who frequent the mall don't go to school. Some also try to stay away from their homes, but they really don't have anywhere else they can be on their own. As Millison concluded, malls are much the suburban equivalent to the urban street corners where inner city kids congregate.[9] Suburban kids come to malls to look around, meet and make friends, stay away from home, and hang out—because there is nowhere else to go.

42   Paul, a security guard, explains. "We aren't allowed to harass the kids, and I know they gotta hang out somewhere. But we tell them to keep moving, especially around the seats and tables in the food service area. They know they have

to keep moving. If they get too loud, or talk back, or are creating any kind of disturbance like that, then we clear them out. Troublemakers we identify, and we don't let them back in."

43   Calling themselves "mall rats" (males) and "mall bunnies" (females), the teens congregate in the new wing of the mall, the largest number of them arriving in the late afternoon. They wander around the different shops, playing video games in the arcade, smoking cigarettes, showing off their latest hair, makeup and clothing styles, and waiting for something, anything, to happen. Most of them will stay until nine-thirty or ten, when the stores close and the mall shuts down.

44   Derick, 15, his hands jammed into the pockets of his frayed cutoff jean shorts, admits that the mall is "a place to go before I have to go to work. I only work right across the street. I have nowhere else to hang out. Most of my friends hang out here."

45   Looking at the arcade in the adjacent wing of the mall, he gestures towards it with a quick nod of his head. "Go over there to play video games. Spend all my money. I don't like spending all my money, but it's there." He shrugs. "Fuck it."

46   Standing near Derick in the small knot of teenagers, Ed, 16, takes a long, slow drag off his cigarette and exhales out the corner of his mouth. "I just started coming on almost a daily basis last year, because it was something to do," he says. "You can come here anytime. It's pretty good, but if we didn't have anything, you'd probably get in more trouble than we would if we came here, so it kinda works out, you know. It's something to do and it kinda keeps you outa trouble."

47   As he says this, he scans the familiar row of neon lit food stalls. Shoppers rush by, but he appears calm and undisturbed, like his four friends standing nearby. They chatter noisily among themselves, making jokes, and playfully pushing each other around, only half aware, seemingly, of the bustle and motion of other people.

48   Nodding toward his friends, Ed goes on to explain the social networking that takes place in the mall. "I met all these people here. I've met lots of other people, too. One place where you can always find someone. If you know somebody, they know somebody else, they'll probably see 'em here, and you'll know them, then they'll know someone who is walking around and you know that person. So when you come here, you kinda build on people."

49   Some teens spend a great deal of time networking in the mall. For them, it is practically a second home. Tammy, age 14, says, "I used to come here every Saturday from eleven o'clock to nine-thirty, and just walk around with my friends, like Gina here, just walk around and check out the guys."

50   When roaming from shop to shop, playing video games, or cruising the strip becomes tiresome, teens usually migrate to the food court. Here they sit, talk, bum change, smoke cigarettes and try to avoid the attention of the security people, even as most of the activities they are engaged in will inevitably attract it.

51   The group gathers around a table, some standing, others sitting and talking. One of the girls breaks from her conversation to announce that Bob is coming. Bob has been kicked out of the mall for boisterous behavior and is not allowed in for another two months.

52   "Just about all of us have gotten kicked out at one time or another," Tony says in a matter of fact manner. "I was sitting down without anything to eat once, and like I didn't know the policy and he said, 'Move,' and I go, 'Why?' I ran my mouth a little too much. What I basically did was stand up for myself, but he didn't like that, so he just booted me for a couple months."

53   "Actually, I'm not supposed to even be in here. He said he's kicked me out forever, but I mean like I changed my hair style so he doesn't recognize me anymore."

54   Ed nods. "I changed mine and I changed my jacket. I used to wear a big leather jacket. I used to wear that all the time. That gave me away. But I've started wearing this jacket now with all my KISS pins on. And as long as I don't act up or do anything, they don't really care. See, I like it here so much I hafta come back."

55   Liz, 15, discusses relationships with the security guards in general. "Some days they can really get on us and other days they just won't come and like we'll be sitting down at the table and on busy days or on days they're not in a really good mood, they'll come over and tell us to move."

56   "They have no respect for mall rats," a boy standing on the edge of the group adds. "It's just days like that they can be real dinks."

57   And yet the mild harassment of the security guards is easily borne, especially when changing one's costume or haircut can many times be enough to erase identity in their eyes. Indeed, such treatment is better, for most, than the treatment they can expect elsewhere. And this relatively light scrutiny given them by the security guards also allows some teens to get away with minor interpersonal drug transactions, especially when the mall is crowded and busy.

58   "Other than The Beach, which is just like, 'deal it out on the streets,' I mean ya can get just about anything out here—pot, acid, hash, right here on Saturdays, when it is crowded."

59   "If you know the right people, you can pick up anything."

60   "And we pretty much know everybody here."

61   For some teens, the mall—with or without drugs—is an escape from home or school. Heather, 16, explains that she comes here "to get away from home, get away from problems 'cause I can't stay at home. Because of my nephew and my sister. They bother me. So I come to the mall." Slouching in her seat, she flips open the top of her red Marlboro box and counts her cigarettes. "School is no better. I go through a year of school, and they still put me through the next grade even if I'm failing. I like it, but it's not gonna get me through college if I do that. I don't care about partying. I just wanna get through school."

62   For Tiffany the mall has become a second home of sorts. At the age of thirteen she lives with Tony, another of the mall rats, and one other mall friend. "My mom kicked me out when I was eleven," she says with an edge of anger in her voice. "She's a bitch. I call her every day and she's just. . . ." Tiffany stops short as she shakes her head and rolls her eyes.

63   "I started going to foster homes and everything and I just quit. Now, I'm in State custody and I just. . . ." She stops again and laughs nervously and blushes. "Sorry about that," she says, apologizing to her friends, seeming to imply that

she has become too personal, too emotional. Abruptly, she continues, "I don't do anything that they want me to do." She lets out a quick triumphant laugh.

64   "I swear to God if they came up to me and dragged me where I didn't want to go, I'd beat the crap right out of them. I would kill 'em. I got 'em twisted around my little finger. They don't mess with me." She growls, as she clenches her teeth and curls her small fist, pounding it lightly on the table.

65   Tony leans back and shakes his head slightly to part his long hair from his face. "I left home and I quit school and moved from, like, hotel to hotel for awhile with a Navy buddy and that wasn't a really good situation, 'cause we were getting kicked outta hotels and motels. We didn't have anywhere to go. So we went up to The Beach and when I went up there it's like there's a Burger King and an auto parts store and a Shop and Save and it's like . . . there was no mall. I was real glad to get back down here, 'cause it was, like, up there, it was boring the hell out of me."

66   The social world of these teens revolves around their contacts and time at the mall. Indeed, this world of the teenager is, in its larger sense, one of segregation from adults and the assumption of adult sexual, economic, and social roles. This segregation, and the relative lack of any clearly defined and socially supported roles for youth, help define the mall community of "rats and bunnies," especially those who have opted out, or been driven from, socially acceptable school and family settings.

67   These youths, disallowed entrance into the social world of adulthood, are attempting to forge meaning and community from their shifting networks of face to face peer relationships in the mall. And yet, unlike the elderly, theirs is a relatively unstable social system. Teens come and go and, more importantly, they do grow up. As a consequence, relationships rest almost entirely in present time and revolve around present circumstances. The past is seldom spoken of, or shared. "Best friends" at the mall may part ways next month, and not see each other again. This fluidity and change in social relationships is a socially uncertain part of the teen years which, for mall rats and bunnies, is also characterized by a lingering malaise concerning the world outside their fragile community—a malaise in which jealousy, mistrust and despair are prominent features. As Tony says:

68   "We are the mall rats. We are the mall. What the fuck else can I say?"

Conclusion: Community in the Mall

69 The American shopping mall has been bemoaned by critics for its impersonality, its uniformity, its total focus on meaningful interaction as rational and economic in nature. Where are the primary relations, the face to face interactions, the social networks that exist along with the economic transactions of the traditional marketplace, the local community, or even the urban village? This case study of one American mall suggests that, for shoppers in the mall, one does indeed need to look elsewhere for the primary interactive ties of community, no matter how cleverly mall management creates the *illusion* of community at the mall. In the end, it seems, this is a shared illusion—neither management nor shoppers are fooled by it, but both can *pretend* that they are creating or engaging in the meaningful and socially necessary relations of community.

70   Ironically, then, the real community ties that do exist in the mall have little to do with its economic function. The elder and the teen spend very little money there and do not frequent the mall for economic reasons. They are there, each day, to greet friends, to create and strengthen their meaningful, face to face primary relationships, to define themselves as a social world, whether it be one of "milers" or of "mall rats"—a community of kind to which they can give emotional support and from which they can draw a sense of self and group identity.

71   Mall management does not like to see such groups develop. They use mall space for other than economic purposes. These warm knots of community can and do disrupt the cool smooth flow of economic transaction. Group members take seats designed for shoppers. They create a focus in the mall that is not economic in nature.

72   Politically, however, it is hard—especially with the elderly—to ban, or even to overtly discourage their presence. But it can be contained and monitored by security personnel. And, especially with the teens, if it becomes too socially visible and disruptive, some members of the group can be ejected.

73   Why, then, under these less than ideal circumstances, do the elderly and teenagers use the mall as their locus of community? It seems likely there are at least five general social reasons for this choice. First, and probably most important, elders and teens both represent social groupings for whom our society provides little social space. The elderly, once they are retired especially, are cut off from the familiar and fulfilling world of work. Their income drops sharply. They are likely to be treated more and more as children by both their families and their non-elderly acquaintances. If they are widowed and live at home, they have lost most of the primary face to face support they have relied on for most of their adult lives.[10]

74   Consequently, they have a need to seek out others in similar situations. The mall is a central, safe place to get to, and there is usually regularly scheduled mass transportation available for the benefit of the shoppers (when it most likely would *not* be available on any regular basis for, say, transport to a non-economically oriented center or meeting place, such as a park or activities center).

75   For the teens, caught as they are between the statuses of childhood and adulthood, there are few social spaces or physical places open where they can congregate and develop their own contacts and social networks.[11] Most often, their activity is too closely defined, monitored, and circumscribed for them to see it as their own (in institutions such as the family and the school). Or, if they do find a niche of their own—such as cruising Main Street or hanging out in a park or fast food parking lot—they are usually dispersed by the authorities, or caught in curfews, or both.

76   And when school and family settings become nonviable alternatives, teens really have very few places to go. Once again, the mall offers its lure. It is centrally located, easy to get to for those with or without their own transportation, seen as a "safe" place by parents, and may, for some, also be the location of their full- or part-time job (usually for minimum wage—but that is another bit of discrimination teens have to bear).

77   Second, the elderly and teens are, to a great extent, faceless persons to adult American society. They are categorized as "old people" or "kids," and, because of the unimportance of their marginal status, they tend to be overlooked as indi-

viduals, though they are stereotypically reacted to as members of groups. For both of these groups, this social reaction increases their need to affirm identity and to create meaningful community for themselves.[12]

78   It also means that, in the mall setting, the elderly are usually overlooked, are nearly invisible to the shoppers hurrying on their way. Being socially invisible, the elderly cannot get much in the way of shoppers and thus their presence, as disruption, is less likely to be an issue requiring action on the part of mall management.

79   For the teens, even the security guards who keep them under surveillance can easily be fooled by a simple change of hair style or jacket. The boisterous teen who is ejected from the mall easily "slips out" of his or her public identity and is back the next day or week, a unique *person* returning to his or her community, invisible in return even to the watching security guards.

80   Third, as alluded to in point one above, the mall is centrally located, easy to get to, safe and climate controlled. The amenities that exist there for the shoppers—restaurants, rest rooms, benches and seats—can also be used by the non-shopper, as long as mall management does not actively discourage such usage.

81   Fourth, for the elderly, discouragement could be dangerous, in a public relations sense. Conversely, the elderly can be used to advantage to further the mall's illusion of community by publicizing their support of community programs such as that of walking-for-health. For the teens, many of them work in the fast food stores and do leave money in the video arcade and the record stores. Therefore they do have some economic links to some of the businesses operating in the mall. The mall rats and bunnies also provide a visually exciting and socially validating backdrop for these youth oriented businesses, for other youths and young adults who come to shop.

82   Finally, these communities seem, in general, to police themselves quite well. They are aware of their status in the eyes of mall management and attempt, each in their own distinctive way, to keep a low enough profile so their presence is tolerated.[13]

83   Ironically, then, and for these reasons, deep within the impersonal and concrete structure of the mall, cultural chains of belonging seem to have been forged. The sense of community, to such an extent denied these groupings of the elderly and the young, in the larger society, is being created and shared in the mall, while shoppers rush blindly past under lights of cold neon, across the polished sheen of endless tiled floors.

Notes

1. Jessie Bernard, *The Sociology of Community* (Glenview, Ill: Scott, Foresman, 1973), p. 3.

2. Thomas Bender, *Community and Social Change in America* (Baltimore: Johns Hopkins University Press, 1978), p. 7.

3. Chain Store Age Executive, "Why They Shop Some Centers," 1987, 54, 33.

4. Interview with mall marketing director, 1986.

5. The author served as Director of Research for this study. Interviews quoted in this paper were conducted by himself, SALT staff members Pamela Wood and Hugh French, and students Brett Jenks, Edite Pedrosa, Amy Rowe, Julie Maurer, Peter Lancia, Harry Brown, Amy Schnerr and Lou Brown. Original tapes and transcripts are on file at SALT CENTER, Kennebunkport, ME 04609.

6. Jerry Jacobs, *The Mall: An Attempted Escape From Every Day Life* (Prospect Heights, Ill: Waveland Press, 1984), pp. 27–32.

7. Robert Atchley, *Social Forces and Aging* (Belmont, CA: Wadsworth, 1985), pp. 56–58.

8. Bob Greene, "Fifteen: Young Men Cruising Shopping Malls," *Esquire*, 1982, 98, pp. 17–18; Kowinski, *op. cit.*, pp. 68–73.

9. Martin Millison, *Teenage Behavior In Shopping Centers*, International Council of Shopping Centers, 1976, p. 11.

10. Peggy Eastman, "Elders Under Siege," *Psychology Today*, 1984, January, p. 30.

11. Richard Flacks, *Youth and Social Change* (Chicago: Markham, 1971), p. 17.

12. *Loc. cit.*, p. 223.

13. This includes relations between the two groups. The elderly mainly frequent the old wing of the mall, while the teens frequent the new wing. The elderly arrive very early and usually leave by late afternoon. The teens usually arrive in mid to late afternoon and stay until the mall closes.

Review Questions

1. In what sense have modern malls become "civic centers"?

2. What are the differences between "the community" and "community," according to Lewis? Why does he introduce this distinction early in the article?

3. What conditions at malls inhibit the growth of community?

4. For what reasons do elders come to the mall? How does mall management react to their presence?

5. Why do teenagers visit the mall?

6. What characteristics do the teenage community and the elderly community share when at the mall?

7. In what sense is the world of the mall a "shared illusion," according to Lewis?

8. What five reasons does Lewis give for teens and elders seeking out the mall as a place to build their communities?

Discussion and Writing Suggestions

1. Lewis quotes a mall manager saying: "Having the *perception* of a community feeling does not mean that it actually exists. It is not the same thing." Why would mall managers take the trouble to create an illusion that malls encourage community ties?

2. Why is it "ironic," according the Lewis, that malls have become the meeting place for actual communities?

3. In shopping malls you have visited, what evidence do you find of an elders' community similar to the one Lewis describes?

4. Read the account of Pat, a mall regular (paragraphs 20–29). What is your response to Pat's story?

5. Reread paragraphs 43–57. Based on your experience, how accurate is Lewis's description of what teenagers do at the mall?

6. One of the key investigative tools for a sociologist like Lewis is the personal interview. Reread those portions of the article devoted to interviews of the elderly and teenagers. How important are these interviews to the success of Lewis's argument? What, in your view, do they add to the selection?

7. Write several paragraphs describing one of your experiences as a "mall rat" or "mall bunny." Include an account of the teenagers who gather at the mall as well as a description of the mall itself (for example, discuss its location, its appearance, the type of customers it attracts). In a final paragraph describe the extent to which you think the people you have described form a community.

The Mall as Threat to Democratic Values
Lizabeth Cohen

In the following article, which appeared in the American Historical Review *(October 1996), Lizabeth Cohen traces the "restructuring of the consumer marketplace" that followed America's population shift to the suburbs after World War II. Millions of people who had lived in the cities, walking to the corner store, faced an entirely new experience as shoppers once they moved to the suburbs. In their new homes, a trip to the store meant a ride in the car, likely to a shopping center where relations between store owner and customer had fundamentally changed. Cohen, a professor of history at New York University, studies the effects that the new mass-consumption society had on America. You will see that she identifies two developments, relating to segregation and free speech, that threaten our general welfare.*

1   Whereas, at first, developers had sought to legitimize the new shopping centers by arguing for their centrality to both commerce and community, over time they discovered that those two commitments could be in conflict. The rights of free speech and assembly traditionally safeguarded in the public forums of democratic communities were not always good for business, and they could conflict with the rights of private property owners—the shopping centers—to control entry to their land. Beginning in the 1960s, American courts all the way up to the Supreme Court struggled with the political consequences of having moved public life off the street and into the privately owned shopping center. Shopping centers,

in turn, began to reconsider the desirable balance between commerce and community in what had become the major sites where suburbanites congregated.[1]

2   Once regional shopping centers like the Paramus malls had opened in the 1950s, people began to recognize them as public spaces and to use them to reach out to the community. When the Red Cross held blood drives, when labor unions picketed stores in organizing campaigns, when political candidates campaigned for office, when anti-war and anti-nuclear activists gathered signatures for petitions, they all viewed the shopping center as the obvious place to reach masses of people. Although shopping centers varied in their responses—from tolerating political activists to monitoring their actions to prohibiting them outright—in general, they were wary of any activity that might offend customers. A long, complex series of court tests resulted, culminating in several key Supreme Court decisions that sought to sort out the conflict between two basic rights in a free society: free speech and private property. Not surprisingly, the cases hinged on arguments about the extent to which the shopping center had displaced the traditional "town square" as a legitimate public forum.[2]

3   The first ruling by the Supreme Court was *Amalgamated Food Employees Union Local 590 vs. Logan Valley Plaza, Inc.* (1968), in which Justice Thurgood Marshall, writing for the majority, argued that refusing to let union members picket the Weis Markets in the Logan Valley Plaza in Altoona, Pennsylvania, violated the workers' First Amendment rights, since shopping centers had become the "functional equivalent" of a sidewalk in a public business district. Because peaceful picketing and leaflet distribution on "streets, sidewalks, parks, and other similar public places are so historically associated with the exercise of First Amendment rights," he wrote, it should also be protected in the public thoroughfare of a shopping center, even if privately owned. The Logan Valley Plaza decision likened the shopping center to a company town, which had been the subject of an important Supreme Court decision in *Marsh vs. Alabama* (1946), upholding the First Amendment rights of a Jehovah's Witness to proselytize in the company town of Chickasaw, Alabama, despite the fact that the Gulf Shipbuilding Corporation owned all the property in town. The "Marsh Doctrine" affirmed First Amendment rights over private property rights when an owner opened up his or her property for use by the public.[3] The stance taken in Logan Valley began to unravel, however, as the Supreme Court became more conservative under President Richard Nixon's appointees. In *Lloyd Corp. vs. Tanner* (1972), Justice Lewis F. Powell, Jr., wrote for the majority that allowing anti-war advocates to pass out leaflets at the Lloyd Center in Portland, Oregon, would be an unwarranted infringement of property rights "without significantly enhancing the asserted right of free speech." Anti-war leaflets, he argued, could be effectively distributed elsewhere, without undermining the shopping center's appeal to customers with litter and distraction.[4]

4   The reigning Supreme Court decision today is *PruneYard Shopping Center vs. Robbins* (1980). The Supreme Court upheld a California State Supreme Court ruling that the state constitution granted a group of high school students the right to gather petitions against the U.N. resolution "Zionism Is Racism." The court decided that this action did not violate the San Jose mall owner's rights under the U.S. Constitution. But, at the same time, the court reaffirmed its earlier decisions in *Lloyd vs. Tanner* and *Scott Hudgens vs. National Labor Relations*

Board (1976) that the First Amendment did not guarantee access to shopping malls, and it left it to the states to decide for themselves whether their own constitutions protected such access.

5   Since *PruneYard*, state appellate courts have been struggling with the issue, and mall owners have been winning in many more states than they have lost. Only in six states, California, Oregon, Massachusetts, Colorado, Washington, and most recently New Jersey, have state supreme courts protected citizens' right of free speech in privately owned shopping centers. In New Jersey, the courts have been involved for some time in adjudicating free speech in shopping centers. In 1983, the Bergen Mall was the setting of a suit between its owners and a political candidate who wanted to distribute campaign materials there. When a Paramus Municipal Court judge ruled in favor of the mall, the candidate's attorney successfully appealed on the familiar grounds that "there is no real downtown Paramus. Areas of the mall outside the stores are the town's public sidewalks." He further noted that the mall hosted community events and contained a meeting hall, post office, and Roman Catholic chapel. In this case, and in another one the following year over the right of nuclear-freeze advocates to distribute literature at the Bergen Mall, free speech was protected on the grounds that the mall was equivalent to a town center.[5]

6   Such suits should be unnecessary (at least for a while) in New Jersey, because in a historic decision in December 1994 the New Jersey Supreme Court affirmed that the state constitution guaranteed free speech to opponents of the Persian Gulf War who wanted to distribute leaflets at ten regional malls throughout the state. Writing for the majority, Chief Justice Robert N. Wilentz confirmed how extensively public space has been transformed in postwar New Jersey:

> The economic lifeblood once found downtown has moved to suburban shopping centers, which have substantially displaced the downtown business districts as the centers of commercial and social activity. . . . Found at these malls are most of the uses and activities citizens engage in outside their homes. . . . This is the new, the improved, the more attractive downtown business district—the new community—and no use is more closely associated with the old downtown than leafletting. Defendants have taken that old downtown away from its former home and moved all of it, except free speech, to the suburbs.

Despite the New Jersey Supreme Court's commitment to free speech, it nonetheless put limits on it, reaffirming the regional mall owners' property rights. Its ruling allowed only the distribution of leaflets—no speeches, bullhorns, pickets, parades, demonstrations, or solicitation of funds. Moreover, the court granted owners broad powers to regulate leaflet distribution by specifying days, hours, and areas in or outside the mall permissible for political activity. Thus, although shopping centers in New Jersey and five other states have been forced to accommodate some political activity, they have retained authority to regulate it and are even finding ways of preventing legal leafletters from exercising their constitutional rights, such as by requiring them to have million-dollar liability policies, which are often unobtainable or prohibitively expensive. In many other states, shopping centers have been able to prohibit political action outright, much as they control the economic and social behavior of shoppers and store owners.[6]

7   An unintended consequence of the American shift in orientation from public town center to private shopping center, then, has been the narrowing of the ground where constitutionally protected free speech and free assembly can legally take place.

. . .

8   Mass consumption in postwar America created a new landscape, where public space was more commercialized [and] more privatized within the regional shopping center than it had been in the traditional downtown center. This is not to romanticize the city and its central business district. Certainly, urban commercial property owners pursued their own economic interests, [and] political activity in public spaces was sometimes limited. . . . Nonetheless, the legal distinction between public and private space remained significant; urban loitering and vagrancy laws directed against undesirables in public places have repeatedly been struck down by the courts, while privately owned shopping centers have been able to enforce trespassing laws.[7] Overall, an important shift from one kind of social order to another took place between 1950 and 1980, with major consequences for Americans. A free commercial market attached to a relatively free public sphere (for whites) underwent a transformation to a more regulated commercial marketplace (where mall management controlled access, favoring chains over local independents, for example) and a more circumscribed public sphere of limited rights. Economic and social liberalism went hand in hand and declined together.

9   Not by accident, public space was restructured and segmented by class and race in New Jersey, as in the nation, just as African Americans gained new protections for their right of equal access to public accommodations. Although civil rights laws had been on the books in New Jersey since the late nineteenth century, comprehensive legislation with mechanisms for enforcement did not pass until the 1940s. With the "Freeman Bill" of 1949, African Americans were finally guaranteed equal access to schools, restaurants, taverns, retail stores, hotels, public transportation, and facilities of commercial leisure such as movie theaters, skating rinks, amusement parks, swimming pools, and beaches, with violators subject to fines and jail terms. Throughout the 1940s and 1950s, African-American citizens of New Jersey—and other northern states—vigilantly challenged discrimination by private property owners. Yet larger structural changes in community marketplaces were under way, financed by private commercial interests committed to socioeconomic and racial segmentation. While African Americans and their supporters were prodding courts and legislatures to eliminate legal segregation in public places, real-estate developers, retailers, and consumers were collaborating to shift economic resources to new kinds of segregated spaces.[8]

10   The landscape of mass consumption created a metropolitan society in which people were no longer brought together in central marketplaces and the parks, streets, and public buildings that surrounded them but, rather, were separated by class and race in differentiated commercial sub-centers. Moreover, all commercial sub-centers were not created equal. Over time, shopping centers became increasingly class stratified, with some like the Bergen Mall marketing themselves to the lower middle class, while others like the Garden State Plaza went upscale to attract upper middle-class consumers. If tied to international capital,

some central business districts—such as New York and San Francisco—have prospered, although they have not been left unscarred from recent retail mergers and leveraged buy-outs. Other downtowns, such as Hackensack and Elizabeth, New Jersey, have become "Cheap John Bargain Centers" serving customers too poor and deprived of transportation to shop at malls. Even in larger American cities, poor urban populations shop downtown on weekends while the white-collar workers who commute in to offices during the week patronize the suburban malls closer to where they live. Some commercial districts have been taken over by enterprising, often newly arrived, ethnic groups, who have breathed new life into what would otherwise have been in decay, but they nonetheless serve a segmented market. Worst off are cities like Newark, once the largest shopping district in the state, which saw every one of its major department stores close between 1964 and 1992 and much of its retail space remain abandoned, leaving residents such as Raymond Mungin to wonder, "I don't have a car to drive out to the malls. What can I do?" Mass consumption was supposed to bring standardization in merchandise and consumption patterns. Instead, diverse social groups are no longer integrated into central consumer marketplaces but rather are consigned to differentiated retail institutions, segmented markets, and new hierarchies.[9]

11   Finally, the dependence on private spaces for public activity and the more recent privatization of public space gravely threaten the government's constitutional obligations to its citizens. Not only freedom of speech and public assembly in shopping centers are at issue. Just recently, Amtrak's Pennsylvania Station in New York City tried to stave off two suits requiring it to respect constitutional rights guaranteed in public places: an effort by artist Michael Lebron to display a political message on the gigantic curved and lighted billboard that he had rented for two months, and a case brought by the Center for Constitutional Rights to force Amtrak to stop ejecting people from the station because they are homeless. When Jürgen Habermas theorized about the rise and fall of a rational public sphere, he recognized the centrality in the eighteenth and nineteenth centuries of accessible urban places—cafés, taverns, coffeehouses, clubs, meeting houses, concert and lecture halls, theaters, and museums—to the emergence and maintenance of a democratic political culture. Over the last half-century, transformations in America's economy and metropolitan landscape have expanded the ability of many people to participate in the mass market. But the commercializing, privatizing, and segmenting of physical gathering places that has accompanied mass consumption has made more precarious the shared public sphere upon which our democracy depends.[10]

Notes

1. Shopping centers retreated from promoting themselves as central squares and street corners not only because of the free speech issue but also to limit the loitering of young people. *New York Times:* "Supermarkets Hub of Suburbs," February 7, 1971: 58; "Coping with Shopping-Center Crises, Dilemma: How Tough to Get If Young Are Unruly," March 7, 1971: sect. 3, p. 1; "Shopping Centers Change and Grow," May 23, 1971: sect. 7, p. 1.

2. For a useful summary of the relevant court cases and legal issues involved, see Curtis J. Berger, "*PruneYard* Revisited: Political Activity on Private Lands," *New York University Law Review* 66 (June 1991): 633–94; also "Shopping Centers Change and Grow," *New York Times* (May 23, 1971): sect. 7, p. 1. The corporate shopping center's antagonism to free political expression and social action is discussed in Herbert I. Schiller, *Culture Inc.: The Corporate Takeover of Public Expression* (New York, 1989), 98–101.

3. On *Amalgamated vs. Logan Valley Plaza*, see "Property Rights vs. Free Speech," *New York Times* (July 9, 1972): sect. 7, p. 9; "Amalgamated Food Employees Union Local 590 v. Logan Valley Plaza," 88 S.Ct. 1601 (1968), *Supreme Court Reporter*, 1601–20; 391 US 308, U.S. Supreme Court Recording Briefs 1967, No. 478, microfiche; "Free Speech: Peaceful Picketing on Quasi-Public Property," *Minnesota Law Review* 53 (March 1969): 873–82. On *Marsh vs. State of Alabama*, see 66 S.Ct. 276, *Supreme Court Reporter*, 276–84. Other relevant cases between *Marsh vs. Alabama* and *Amalgamated vs. Logan Valley Plaza* are *Nahas vs. Local 905, Retail Clerks International Assoc.* (1956), *Amalgamated Clothing Workers of America vs. Wonderland Shopping Center, Inc.* (1963), *Schwartz-Torrance Investment Corp. vs. Bakery and Confectionary Workers' Union, Local No. 31* (1964); with each case, the Warren court was moving closer to a recognition that the shopping center was becoming a new kind of public forum.

4. "4 Nixon Appointees End Court's School Unanimity, Shopping Centers' Right to Ban Pamphleteering Is Upheld, 5 to 4," *New York Times* (June 23, 1972): 1; "Shopping-Center Industry Hails Court," *New York Times* (July 2, 1972): sect. 3, p. 7; "Lloyd Corporation, Ltd. v. Donald M. Tanner (1972)," 92 S.Ct. 2219 (1972), *Supreme Court Reporter*, 2219–37. The American Civil Liberties Union brief went to great lengths to document the extent to which shopping centers have replaced traditional business districts; see "Brief for Respondents," U.S. Supreme Court Record, microfiche, 20–29. See also People's Lobby Brief, U.S. Supreme Court Record, microfiche, 5.

   The Supreme Court majority wanted to make it clear that in finding in favor of the Lloyd Center, it was not reversing the Logan Valley decision, arguing for a distinction based on the fact that anti-war leafletting was "unrelated" to the shopping center, while the labor union was picketing an employer. The four dissenting justices, however, were less sure that the distinction was valid and that the Logan Valley decision was not seriously weakened by Lloyd. The important court cases between *Amalgamated vs. Logan Valley Plaza* and *Lloyd vs. Tanner* included *Blue Ridge Shopping Center vs. Schleininger* (1968), *Sutherland vs. Southcenter Shopping Center* (1971), and *Diamond vs. Bland* (1970, 1974).

5. Berger, "*PruneYard* Revisited"; Kowinski, *Malling of America*, 196–202, 355–59; "Shopping Malls Protest Intrusion by Protesters," *New York Times* (July 19, 1983): B1; "Opening of Malls Fought," *New York Times* (May 13, 1984): sect. 11 (New Jersey), 7; "Michael Robins v. PruneYard Shopping Center (1979)," 592 P. 2nd 341, *Pacific Reporter*, 341–51; "PruneYard Shopping Center v. Michael Robins," 100 S.Ct. 2035 (1980), *Supreme Court Reporter*, 2035–51; U.S. Supreme Court Record, *PruneYard Shopping Center vs. Robins* (1980), microfiche. The most important Supreme Court case between *Lloyd vs. Tanner* and *PruneYard* was *Scott Hudgens vs. National Labor Relations Board* (1976), where the majority decision backed further away from Logan Valley Plaza and refused to see the mall as the functional equivalent of downtown. "Scott Hudgens v. National Labor Relations Board," 96 S.Ct. 1029 (1976), *Supreme Court Reporter*, 1029–47.

6. "Court Protects Speech in Malls," *New York Times* (December 21, 1994): A1; "Big Malls Ordered to Allow Leafletting," *Star-Ledger* (December 21, 1994): 1; "Now, Public

Rights in Private Domains," *New York Times* (December 25, 1994): E3; "Free Speech in the Mall," *New York Times* (December 26, 1994): 38; Frank Askin, "Shopping for Free Speech at the Malls," 1995, unpublished ms. in possession of the author.

7. "Amtrak Is Ordered Not to Eject the Homeless from Penn Station," *New York Times* (February 22, 1995): A1.

8. Article on passage of New Jersey Civil Rights Bill, *New York Times*, March 24, 1949; Marion Thompson Wright, "Extending Civil Rights in New Jersey through the Division Against Discrimination," *Journal of Negro History* 38 (1953): 96–107; State of New Jersey, Governor's Committee on Civil Liberties, "Memorandum on Behalf of Joint Council for Civil Rights in Support of a Proposed Comprehensive Civil Rights Act for New Jersey," 1948, II, B 8, Folder "Civil Rights, New Jersey, 1941–48," NAACP Papers, Library of Congress, Washington, D.C.; "Report of Legislative Committee, NJ State Conference of NAACP Branches," March 26, 1949, II, B 8, Folder "Civil Rights, New Jersey, 1941–48," NAACP Papers. Other NAACP files on discrimination document the actual experiences of African Americans in New Jersey during the 1940s and 1950s.

9. "Closing of 'Last' Department Store Stirs Debate on Downtown Trenton," *Star-Ledger*, June 5, 1983; "Urban Areas Crave Return of Big Markets," *Star-Ledger*, July 17, 1984; "Elizabeth Clothier Mourns Demise of Century-Old Customized Service," *Sunday Star-Ledger*, January 10, 1988; "President's Report to the Annual Meeting Passaic Valley Citizens Planning Association." Box A, Folder 3.

10. Jürgen Habermas, *The Structural Transformation of the Public Sphere: An Inquiry into a Category of Bourgeois Society*, Thomas Burger trans., with Frederick Lawrence (Cambridge, Mass., 1989); Geoff Eley, "Nations, Publics, and Political Cultures: Placing Habermas in the Nineteenth Century," in Nicholas B. Dirks, Geoff Eley, and Sherry B. Ortner, eds., *Culture/Power/History: A Reader in Contemporary Social Theory* (Princeton, N.J., 1994), 297–335.

Review Questions

1. In what sense was suburbanization a new form of racial segregation, according to Cohen?

2. Explain the legal battles that arose in connection with shopping centers.

3. The rise of the shopping center over the last 50 years has given many people access to the mass market, says Cohen. But this access has come at a price. What is that price?

Discussion and Writing Suggestions

1. Cohen argues that shopping centers gave rise to a new form of racial segregation in this country. In your own experience, have you observed or experienced segregation at a shopping center?

2. Reread paragraph 9 and comment on this passage: "While African Americans and their supporters were prodding courts and legislatures to eliminate legal segregation in public places, real-estate developers, retail-

ers, and consumers were collaborating to shift economic resources to new kinds of segregated spaces." To what extent do you agree that suburban shopping malls constitute "segregated spaces"?

3. What evidence do you find from your own experience that shopping centers are "class stratified"—that is, some centers cater to the upper-middle class, some to the lower-middle class?

4. Have you seen any evidence that political activity (for instance, protesting or gathering of signatures for petitions) is any less welcome in a shopping center than it is on a city street? Write a descriptive paragraph or two describing the experience.

5. Interview an older acquaintance or relative, perhaps a grandparent, on how shopping has changed over the years. Does this person recall a time before the rise of shopping centers? What was better about shopping in the middle of the twentieth century versus shopping at the beginning of the twenty-first? What was worse?

Mallaise: How to Know If You Have It
William Kowinski

William Kowinski's The Malling of America: An Inside Look at the Great Consumer Paradise *(William Morrow, 1985) has become a classic in the literature on the cultural impact of shopping centers. The following selection, which forms a chapter in* Malling, *is representative of Kowinski's tone throughout: ironic, playful, and pointed in its critique of malls and their effects. "Mallaise" is his attempt to name the disease that some people feel on being absorbed by the totality of the mall's environment. Perhaps you will recognize one or more of the symptoms.*

1 Malls make some people sick. Literally, sometimes. They feel feverish, their eyes glaze, their stomachs tumble, they fall down, they throw up.

2   Some people are just annoyed by one or another aspect of a mall, or a non-specific quality of a particular mall, or malls in general. "That mall makes me *sick!*" they say. Or "I don't like malls—I *hate* them." Malls make people angry. Some of these people are shoppers, but some are people who work in malls or even own mall stores.

3   Malls affect people. They're designed to. But in some ways, either by their nature or by a side effect caused by their main ingredients, they do things to people that people are unaware of or don't understand, but if they knew or understood, they probably wouldn't like it.

4   There are other more obvious things that happen to people in malls that they don't or wouldn't like. Crime, for instance.

5   This section of *The Malling of America* is about some of the negative aspects of malls that affect people and that people perceive. Does the mall make you

tired? Set your nerves on edge? Do you find it difficult to concentrate? Do you feel the absence of certain phenomena—weather, for example, or civil liberties? Do you sometimes wonder if you are really as safe as mall management would like you to believe?

6   If you're a parent, do you fear for your children's ability to survive outside comfort control because they spend so much time in the mall? And if you're an adolescent, do you feel your horizons becoming limited to a hundred chain store-outlets and three anchor department stores? Or are you worried that this is precisely the world your parents do live in, and where they want you always to remain?

7   These are some of the symptoms of mallaise. Perhaps you have one or two, or know someone who does, or perhaps you want to be prepared, just in case. Then perhaps you should read on.

8   I had my first attack of *mal de mall* in Columbia, Maryland. I was in a restaurant in the Columbia Mall having coffee. The attack was characterized by feverishness, sudden fatigue, and high anxiety, all recurring whenever I glanced out at the mall itself. The thought of going out there again made me sweat and swoon, and I had to fight the hallucinatory certainty that when I left the restaurant I would be in Greengate mall, or maybe Woodfield, or Tysons Corner. Or *all* of them.

9   *Mal de mall*, or mall sickness, is one of the classifications of mallaise, the general term for physical and psychological disturbances caused by mall contact. I know because I made them all up. Among the symptoms I have personally observed or heard about from their victims are these:

10   *Dismallcumbobulation:* "I don't like to go to malls because I always get lost," a woman told me, "and that's embarrassing. I feel stupid. It makes me mad." The hyped-up overabundance of similar products plus the bland sameness of many mall environments make people feel lost even when they aren't. Even familiar malls relocate stores and reconfigure themselves, which adds to the feeling of a continuous featureless space. And the similarity of one mall to another is disorienting. You walk out of the Stuft Potato and you not only don't remember which way your car is, you might not remember what mall this is. There are other kinds of dismallcumbobulation: the loss of a sense of time as well as place, and forgetting one's purpose in coming to the mall—all of which can lead to apathy and hopelessness, loss of consciousness, or fainting. Some victims recommend deep-breathing exercises every fifteen minutes while at the mall.

11   *Inability to Relate to Others:* "It's impossible to talk to someone when you're shopping at the mall," a friend told me, explaining why she prefers to shop alone. "I notice it at the mall all the time—you see two people together but they aren't really talking to each other. They're talking, but they're staring off in different directions, and pretty soon they just wander away from each other." Among the possible effects of this symptom are disenchantment and divorce.

12   *Plastiphobia,* or the fear of being enclosed in a cocoon of blandness. "Suddenly I just stood still and looked around," a young man said. "I saw all the people and what we were all doing there, what we were spending our day doing, and I suddenly just couldn't wait to get out. I was in a plastic place with plastic people buying plastic products with plastic charge cards. I had to escape." Sometimes

this reaction is accompanied by severe anxiety, alienation from the human race, and in at least one very severe case I know of, by all the usual manifestations of a drug overdose.

13   All of these, and their variations, are unfortunate side effects (or perhaps just extreme cases) of the main psychological effects that the mall intends. Excitement may become overstimulation; relaxation may drift into confusion and torpor. The combination is what I call the Zombie Effect.

14   There is, in fact, a fine line between the ideal mall shopper and the dismayed mall shopper, between mall bliss and mallaise, between the captivated shopper and the Zombie Effect. The best description of the Zombie Effect I've heard was Barbara Lambert's, which she imparted while we toured the malls of Chicagoland.

15   It hits you, Barbara said, when you're standing there naked, looking in the mirror of the dressing room. Your clothes are in a pile on the floor or draped over a chair. Maybe it's just a little cubicle with a curtain, and you can still hear the hum and buzz of the mall and the tiny timbres of Muzak. You're about to try something on, in an effortless repetition of what you've been doing since you came to the mall. And suddenly you realize *you've been here all day*. Time has in fact been passing while you've been gliding through store after store in a tender fuzz of soft lights and soft music. The plash of fountains, the glow of people, but almost no intrusive sound has broken your floating—no telephone, no demands, nothing to dodge or particularly watch out for. Just a gentle visual parade of clothes, fabric tags, and washing instructions. Racks, displays, cosmetics, brisk signs, flowing greenery, and spasms of color in the dream light. An ice-cream cone, a cup of coffee. Other figures have glided by: walking models of the mall's products, or walking models of the weird. An old man who reminds you of your grandfather, sitting on a blond-wood bench under a potted palm. A woman who may or may not have been your best friend's other best friend in high school, striding by on strange shoes—or maybe that's a new style and yours are strange? You're looking at your naked image in a bare little room, and a little breeze touches you. Whatever you actually came here for is in the distant past. You've been floating here . . . for hours.

16   But that's the whole idea of this psychological structure: to turn off your mind and let you float; to create a direct and unfettered connection between eyeing and buying; and the more you do, the easier it becomes. Malls make for great eye/hand-on-credit-card co-ordination.

17   The way it's done is with a combination of peacefulness and stimulation. The environment bathes you in sweet neutrality with soft light, candied music, and all the amenities that reassure and please without grabbing too much individual attention. At the same time, the stores and products dance for you with friendly smiles and colorful costumes. The sheer number of products and experiences you pay for and their apparent variety are in themselves factors that excite and focus.

18   Once again, it's all a lot like television. TV lulls and stimulates simultaneously. The medium itself is familiar and comfortable and friendly; the programs can be interesting but it is not really by accident that they are not as compact, colorful, dramatic, or insistent as the commercials. Watching television we are everywhere and nowhere in particular, just as at the mall. Suddenly you might realize that you've been watching it all day, just floating for hours. And if you

look at people watching television—especially their eyes—they look pretty much like mall shoppers: the Zombie Effect.

19   But these effects are all supposed to be pleasant and unconscious. When either the lulling or stimulating quality—or especially the combination and conflict between them—is strongly felt, then it's no longer pleasant. Overstimulation causes anxiety, and sometimes an intense focus on heavy-duty, no-nonsense, get-out-of-my-way shopping, or else a frenzied need to get out of there, fast and forever. The lulling and sense deprivation cause listlessness and confusion, and occasionally rebellion at being Muzaked into implacable mushy madness. The conflict of both going on at the same time can cause the sense of dislocation and exhaustion that is the clearest indicator of the Zombie Effect. The victim shuffles and mumbles, is distant or unduly preoccupied, doesn't listen, acts automatically, and not only can't remember where the car is parked but often doesn't care.

20   There are ancilliary symptoms and causes as well: headaches caused by guilt at buying too much; depression at not being able to buy everything; the walking emptiness caused by consistently emphasized, endless greed.

21   The cure for all forms of mallaise is theoretically simple: The victim leaves the mall. There are no laws requiring people to stay in the mall, or even to go there in the first place. It isn't anyone's civic, moral, spiritual, or intellectual duty. The mall may be the best place—or even the only place—to shop for certain products, but that doesn't mean the shopper has to stay there for hours. Nevertheless, it isn't always easy to leave.

22   For that is another aspect of the Zombie Effect: Victims stay for no good or apparent reason, and even beyond their conscious desire to be there. Shoppers mallinger partly because of the mall's psychological apparatus, its implicit promise of safety, sanctuary, and salvation. Of Nirvana! The Crystal City! A New Heaven on a New Earth! The mall hasn't become the most successful artificial environment in America for nothing.

23   With its real walls and psychological illusions, the mall protects against so many hazards and uncertainties that the mallaise sufferer may well mallinger a little longer to ponder the consequences of walking out. Such a person may fear trading the malladies of the Zombie Effect for the perils of mall withdrawal, which is characterized by shaking in downtown areas, fear of crossing streets, inordinate terror in the presence of rain or sunshine, confusion when actual travel is required between purchases, and the feeling of estrangement when wearing a coat.

24   I wish I could say that medical science is on top of this new set of malladies, but the truth is that it is scandalously behind the times. Right now, there may be many thousands of Zombie Effect sufferers, untreated and undiagnosed. If you find this hard to believe—well, have you been to the mall lately?

25   There is one more form of mallaise that is especially frustrating because it is not so simply cured, even theoretically. It is the state of being malcontented with what the mall offers and how it offers it. Sufferers will rail on about the same limited clothing styles reproduced in a hundred mall shops, or the same five movies shown in two dozen mall theaters—the only cinemas around. They will complain endlessly about fast-print outlets masquerading as bookstores, where clerks don't know anything more about books than what appears on the

computer stock list. They will raise angry fists against the screening boxes calling themselves cinemas, with their dark and blurry unwatchable images on the screen, and cold and tinny sound.

26   These unfortunate mallcontents really have a problem, because in many places they don't have any alternative: If they want to shop for clothes, see a first-run movie, buy a new book or record, it's the mall or nothing.

27   They flail away at the promises the mall implies but does not keep. They are in a sense prisoners of the mall, if only because the mall's predominance has destroyed the alternatives they miss, even the imaginary ones.

Discussion and Writing Suggestions

1. At what point in this selection did you realize that Kowinski has a sense of humor? Work through the piece and mark what in your view are the funniest lines.

2. Through humor, Kowinski makes a number of penetrating observations about mall culture. Of the various maladies he catalogs (with tongue in cheek), which one seems the most insightful? Why?

3. Have you observed in yourself, a friend, or family member any symptoms of *mal de mall?* Describe your experience.

4. Kowinski compares mall shopping to television watching (see paragraph 18). Is the comparison apt, in your view?

5. In paragraph 16, Kowinski writes that the "whole idea of [the mall's] psychological structure [is] to turn off your mind and let you float; to create a direct and unfettered connection between eyeing and buying." Have you ever noticed that malls are designed to have a "psychological structure"? Explain.

6. In introducing the Zombie Effect (see paragraph 18), Kowinski writes: "Watching television we are everywhere and nowhere in particular, just as at the mall." Do you agree?

7. Kowinski gives the feeling of being lost in a mall a funny name: *dismallcumbobulation.* But he is making a serious point in noting the essential sameness of malls. Have you noticed how one mall often looks like others—with the same chain stores and repeating architectural features? One could shop at a mall in Louisville or in Buffalo and not be able to tell them apart. How do you respond to these similarities? Have you ever been dismallcumbobulated?

8. In paragraph 25, Kowinski may come closest to expressing his underlying view of malls than at any other point in the selection. Reread the paragraph and summarize what you take to be his general attitude toward malls.

SYNTHESIS ACTIVITIES

1. In an explanatory paper that draws on several selections in this chapter, explain to a time traveler from the sixteenth century, or a visitor from the remotest regions on present-day Earth, the phenomenon of shopping malls. Answer basic questions, such as: What is a mall? When did malls appear? Why? How are malls organized and managed? Discuss important factors that gave rise to malls: weather; transportation (development of cars and highways); and the growth of suburbs. Finally, without taking sides, explain the controversies sparked by malls.

2. In an exploratory paper, one in which you speculate more than argue, attempt to define the deep-seated appeal that shopping centers hold for many people. The selections by Pahl, Postrel, and Francaviglia should be helpful. Working with these and one or two other authors in this chapter, explore the psychological (and if Pahl is to be believed, even spiritual) changes that can come over shoppers as they enter a mall.

3. James Farrell (paragraph 14) writes: "Like churches, [malls] are places where we decide what is ultimately valuable and how we will value it." Jon Pahl devotes considerable effort to understanding malls as sacred spaces. Richard Keller Simon suggests that malls, like formal gardens, present packaged views of what a culture values. Working with these authors and any others in the chapter who can contribute to the discussion, write an argument on the spiritual or religious dimensions of shopping malls. In this argument, you could discount the connection entirely, accept it, or accept it in part.

4. Lizabeth Cohen argues that malls built in the suburbs effectively shut out people who lived in the city and who could not afford a car—a development Cohen regards as a new expression of an old problem: racial and economic segregation. In your experience with shopping malls, what evidence do you find of either or both types of segregation? In developing a response, draw on the selection by Farrell (and his notion that malls tell "stories"). Descriptions of your own experiences in malls could figure heavily into your paper.

5. Richard Francaviglia writes that "Sociologists have long known that people visit shopping centers for far more than commercial reasons" (paragraph 11). In a paper that draws on the work of Francaviglia, Gruen, Pahl, Postrel, and Lewis as well as on your own experience, explain these noncommercial reasons for going to the mall.

6. Francaviglia characterizes mall management as "autocratic." In a paper that draws on Francaviglia and also on Cohen and Guterson, answer this question: For customers, store owners, and mall man-

agement, what is gained and what is lost in rigorously controlling activities at the mall?

7. Several authors in this chapter write on the layout of malls. Simon and Kowinski relate the experience of getting lost. Francaviglia writes on the importance of intersections. For Guterson, the mall feels like a giant prison. Given the work of these authors and your experience at malls, write a paper examining the importance of mall design.

8. Use William Kowinski's concept of "mallaise" to analyze one or more of your visits to a mall. As independent evidence for mallaise, you might refer to the selections by Guterson (especially paragraph 5) and Pahl (especially paragraph 3). The test of your analysis will be how successfully Kowinski's vocabulary helps you to see your shopping experience(s) in new and interesting ways.

9. Jackson (paragraph 2) and Guterson (paragraphs 6, 16–18) recall the bazaars and marketplaces of old in which people came not only to buy but also to engage in the give and take of community life. Guterson (see especially paragraph 31) and Lewis (see paragraphs 1–7), particularly, claim that authentic community is difficult to find in modern shopping centers. Postrel, by contrast, argues that authentic communication is possible in malls. What is your sense of shopping malls as a center of community life? Drawing on the views of authors in this chapter, develop your answer into an argument.

10. Guterson, Kowinski, Cohen, Lewis, and Pahl have criticized shopping malls. By contrast, Farrell, Postrel, Francaviglia, and Gruen find much to recommend in malls. Given your experiences in malls, with which set of authors do you tend to agree? Do malls please you more than they disturb you, or vice versa? Draw on the authors in this chapter as you develop your answer in an argument.

11. In *Shopping Towns USA,* Victor Gruen envisioned shopping centers becoming the hub of suburban life. Centers would combine commercial space with public, civic space into "crystallization points" that would free suburbanites from traveling to the city to make major purchases. Moreover, shopping centers with their tightly controlled programs for design and management would make rational the previously haphazard method of locating stores in suburbia. Gruen did not live to see his vision fulfilled. Was his plan naive? Do you think the community function of shopping centers could coexist with the commercial function? Is there still hope for such a combination, or is the mall's effort best left to making money?

12. In the introduction to this chapter you will find a block quotation from James J. Farrell's book *One Nation Under Goods.* Farrell claims that shopping centers are places where the culture answers fundamental questions about itself, such as: "What does it mean to be

human? What are people for?" Reread the full list of questions, select *one*, and write a synthesis in which you argue that it is possible, or impossible, to answer such a question by studying shopping centers. In addition to using Farrell's selection, you might draw on the work of Francaviglia, Gruen, Lewis, Pahl, and Cohen.

13. Relate an experience you've had in a shopping center and analyze it in light of any of the reading selections in this chapter. How can the insights of one (or more) of the chapter's authors help you to understand your experience?

RESEARCH ACTIVITIES

1. Devote some time to viewing movies that are set, at least partially, in malls: You might consider the horror classic George Romero's *Dawn of the Dead* (a sequel to *Night of the Living Dead*), *Mall Rats, Scenes from a Mall*, and *Fast Times at Ridgemont High*. Watch one or more of the movies several times, and then write a paper in which you "read" the director's vision of modern American life as it is expressed in shopping malls. As part of your research, you might draw on movie reviews. More ambitious projects will involve a comparative treatment of two or more movies.

2. Investigate and report on the types of data that social scientists collect in their efforts to help store owners boost sales. You might begin with a book like *Why We Buy: The Science of Shopping*, in which Paco Underhill (an anthropologist) relates how he conducts field studies of shoppers in the act of shopping. Others who investigate the purchasing habits of shoppers include sociologists, psychologists, and economists. The general topic, the "science of shopping," is very broad, and you will want to narrow the focus. Some possibilities: the design of store displays, the training of sales staff, the choice of background music, or the routing of customers through a retail space. This assignment stresses information, so you will be writing an explanatory synthesis.

3. Read William Kowinski's *Malling of America*, from which one selection in this chapter ("Mallaise") was excerpted. *Malling* has become something of a classic. After you read it, gather book reviews from around the country (check the *Book Review Digest*) and report on the book's reception.

4. Identify one shopping mall project about which you would like to learn more. The project may be a national destination mall, like the Mall of America, or a regional mall near your home. Based on newspaper and magazine articles, trace for readers the mall's progress from the permit process to the opening. How involved was the community in the process? Were there protests? Did the town or city government provide incentives for mall development? Did the developers rely on union labor? These are just of a few of the many

questions you might explore in your research. Your goal is to tell the mall's story, from conception to design to building to occupancy.

5. Research the phenomenon of "dead" or "ghost" malls: facilities that are 20 years or older that have been left vacant. What are the forces that drive malls to failure? (Possibilities: population trends; an anchor store's not renewing its lease; competition from new or neighboring malls.) How great a problem are vacant malls? How have communities repurposed them? In writing your paper, gather enough research to point out broad, industrywide trends and then, as a case study, illustrate these trends by relating the demise of a *particular* shopping mall.

6. Choose a shopping mall to visit three or four times over the course of several weeks. On your first visit, spend one hour watching people shop, and take notes. Later, review your notes and decide on a particular question you would like to explore on return visits. Pose that question as precisely as possible: It may concern a partic- ular population at the mall (seniors, mothers with kids, fathers with kids, couples, teens, etc.); a particular aspect of mall management (perhaps security, janitorial, or food services); mall architecture; traffic flow. Any of the readings in this chapter will help you to identify a particular question to pursue. Having framed the ques- tion, return to the mall for a series of one-hour visits in which you make and record observations. (Avoid shopping! Your focus is on gathering information.) Write a paper in which you report on your research. Include a description of the mall studied, a context for your question (a discussion of why the question is interesting), data that you recorded (albeit informally), and a discussion of what you discovered.

7. Research one of the predecessors of the modern mall. You might research the Greek stoa, the Roman Forum, the Middle Eastern bazaar or souk, the Grand Bazaar of Constantinople, the Royal Exchange (London), the Palais Royal (Paris), or the arcades of London or Milan. The research paper that you write will be explanatory in nature. Assume that your audience is familiar with shopping malls but unfamiliar with the shopping venues through- out history that preceded the mall.

8. Reread paragraphs 1–7 in Lizabeth Cohen's article "The Mall as Threat to Democratic Values," and select for further research one of the Supreme Court cases she discusses concerning the limits to free speech in privately owned shopping centers. Locate the Supreme Court opinion and summarize it. Re-create for readers the conflict that led to the court case, and discuss (after your summary) the implications of the Court's decision on future protests at shopping centers. You might try conducting your research on the Internet, particularly if you have access to the LexisNexis database. Select "Federal Case Law" and, within this area, "Supreme Court" cases. Choose "Guided Search," as opposed to "Basic Search," so that you

can use more keywords and combinations of keywords. Try such keywords as "free speech" OR "freedom of speech" AND "mall" OR "privately owned shopping center" and other such terms; and search for "all available dates." If you have the citation number for a case (like "485 U.S. 112"), you can directly input the citation (without the need for keywords) to retrieve the case.

9. Research differences in shopping patterns between men and women. You might focus on one or more of the following questions: Do men and women shop with different expectations about the speed of making purchases? Do either tend to shop for the sake of (that is, the pleasure of) shopping? Do women "look" more than men? Do either tend to regard shopping more as a social as opposed to functional, or necessary, activity? Do men more than women tend to be impulse shoppers? Locate carefully controlled studies when conducting your research.

To Sleep

> Every night nearly every person on the planet undergoes an astounding meta-
> morphosis. As the sun sets, a delicate timing device at the base of our brain
> sends a chemical signal throughout our body, and the gradual slide toward
> sleep begins. Our body becomes inert, and our lidded eyes roll slowly from
> side to side. Later, the eyes begin the rapid eye movements that accompany
> dreams, and our mind enters a highly active state where vivid dreams trace
> our deepest emotions. Throughout the night we traverse a broad landscape of
> dreaming and nondreaming realms, wholly unaware of the world outside.
> Hours later, as the sun rises, we are transported back to our bodies and to
> waking consciousness.
>
> And we remember almost nothing.

So begins *The Promise of Sleep* by researcher and sleep pioneer William Dement, who
for 50 years has investigated what happens each night after we close our eyes. Later
in this chapter you will hear more from Dement; but for the moment, let his sense of
wonder about what another author in this chapter calls that "state so familiar yet
so strange" spark your own interest in sleep, a behavior that will occupy one-third
of your life.

Not until 1929 did Johannes Berger use a new device called the electroencephalogram (EEG) to confirm that far from shutting down while asleep, our brains
remain highly active. With the insight that sleep is not merely the absence of wakefulness, and the subsequent discovery that each night's sleep unfolds in five classi-
fiable stages, sleep research accelerated in the twentieth century. Yet for thousands
of years sleep (and its frustrating absence) has sparked the inquiries of physicians,
scientists, and philosophers. As early as 1300 BCE, the Egyptians used opium as a
medication to treat insomnia. Nearly a thousand years later, Aristotle framed his
inquiry into sleep with questions that occupy us still:

> With regard to sleep and waking, we must consider what they are: whether
> they are peculiar to soul or to body, or common to both; and if common, to what
> part of soul or body they appertain: further, from what cause it arises that they
> are attributes of animals, and whether all animals share in them both. . . .
> —*"On Sleep and Sleeplessness"*

Allowing for the fact that modern sleep researchers do not investigate the "soul," per
se, they nevertheless retain a high level of interest in the nature of consciousness and
what happens to it when we sleep. The ancients thought of sleep as a daily,
metaphorical death. If sleep is not a death, then what precisely *is* it? Does sleep
repair the body? Does it consolidate the day's learning? Is it a strategy for keeping
the sleeper safe? Does it aid in development and maintenance of the central nervous
system? Researchers have investigated each of these questions but have found no

definitive answers. Theoretical explanations of sleep aside, at the clinical level specialists cannot yet remedy all 84 known sleep disorders, which rob sufferers of needed rest and keep them, according to the famous insomniac poet and critic Samuel Taylor Coleridge, in "anguish and in agony." The investigations, therefore, continue.

Up to 40 million Americans suffer from sleep disruptions that for some trigger serious health risks, including cardiovascular disease, obesity, and depression. Sleep loss leads to measurable cognitive and physical deficits comparable to those observed in people impaired by alcohol. The sleep that *we don't* get each day adds up to a cumulative debt that we must "repay" in order to function at full capacity, say sleep specialists. Failure to sleep enough (eight hours is the norm, though individual requirements vary) leads to quantifiable costs:

- Americans spend $15 billion per year in direct health care costs related to problems with sleeping.
- The U.S. economy loses $50 billion per year in diminished productivity due to problems with sleeping.
- The National Highway Traffic and Safety Administration estimates that sleep-deprived drivers cause 100,000 accidents each year, resulting in 1,500 fatalities and 71,000 injuries.

The literature of sleep research is vast. Investigators study the sleep of insects, fish, amphibians, birds, and mammals (including humans) with the tools of biology, neurology, chemistry, psychology, and a host of other disciplines. This chapter brings the study of sleep to a focus very close to home for readers of this book: the sleep of adolescents, one of the many subspecialties of sleep medicine. You may know that the sleep of infants and toddlers merits special attention from specialists since, when children don't sleep well, few others in the home do, either. And you may be aware that the sleep of older people, which can grow troubled due to both physiological and psychological changes, has been the subject of intense study. An equally active area among researchers is the sleep of 10- to 19-year-olds, who require one hour more of sleep each night (due to rapidly maturing bodies) than do adults or children who no longer nap—and this at a time in life when the scheduling demands of school and work tend to decrease the amount of sleep available to adolescents.

If you find yourself at the threshold of late adolescence and early adulthood, or are otherwise connected to an adolescent who is a sibling or friend, you will discover much of interest in this chapter on the "strange state" of sleep. We begin with an overview of the subject, "A Third of Life" by Paul Martin, in which you will learn (among other things) that certain dolphins put one-half of their brains to sleep at a time so that the other half can keep then swimming—and surfacing for air. In "The Science of Sleep," Susan Ince reviews the fundamentals of sleep medicine, including REM (rapid eye movement) and non-REM sleep. We move next to a news release on the troubled state of adolescent sleep, based on a poll conducted by the National Sleep Foundation. Researcher Mary A. Carskadon then explains how the biological, behavioral, and social worlds converge to make sleeping so difficult for many adolescents. William C. Dement and Christopher Vaughan follow with "Sleep Debt and the Mortgaged Mind," an inquiry into what happens to a body deprived of sleep.

So that you can assess the current state of your own sleep, we offer the Pittsburgh Sleep Quality Index, a self-scoring assessment used in many sleep studies. Use the PSQI to rate your sleep along seven dimensions and determine your overall sleep score. In "How Sleep Debt Hurts College Students," June J. Pilcher and Amy S. Walters deprive students of a night's sleep and test their cognitive functioning the next day. (The news is not good for those who pull "all-nighters.") "Starting Time and School Life" reports on the progress of the first major experiment in the United States to align the starting time of high school with the sleep/wake cycles of adolescents. The chapter concludes with a cluster of readings on the rise in the use of prescription sleep aids among adolescents. "The Medicalization of Sleep" presents four readings that open with a news release about new sleep data, followed by differing interpretations of the data in *USA Today* and the *New York Times,* and concludes with a critique of these competing interpretations by a watchdog group from George Mason University.

The National Institutes of Health distributes $200 million a year for sleep research, with some of that money reserved for new curricula that alert science students to the importance of good sleep hygiene. In effect, this chapter offers such a curriculum. In reading the selections that follow, not only will you gain an opportunity to practice the skills of summary, synthesis, critique, and analysis; you will also gain information that can help you feel and function better in your daily life.

A Third of Life
Paul Martin

In our chapter opening, Paul Martin, who holds a PhD in behavioral biology from Cambridge University, provides an overview of sleep and its place in both human and animal evolution. Martin introduces the concept of sleep debt and its consequences—a principal focus of this chapter—and then reviews the behavioral characteristics of sleep. The present selection forms the first chapter of Martin's Counting Sheep: The Science and Pleasures of Sleep and Dreams *(2002).*

> Man . . . consumes more than one third of his life in this his irrational situation.
> Erasmus Darwin, *Zoonomia* (1801)

1 Sleep: a state so familiar yet so strange. It is the single most common form of human behaviour and you will spend a third of your life doing it—25 years or

more, all being well. When you die, a bigger slice of your existence will have passed in that state than in making love, raising children, eating, playing games, listening to music, or any of those other activities that humanity values so highly.

2   Sleep *is* a form of behaviour, just as eating or socialising or fighting or copulating are forms of behaviour, even if it is not the most gripping to observe. Most of the action goes on inside the brain. It is also a uniquely private experience, even when sharing a bed. When we are awake we all inhabit a common world, but when we sleep each of us occupies a world of our own. Most of us, however, have precious little awareness of what we experience in that state. Our memories of sleeping and dreaming mostly evaporate when we awake, erasing the record every morning.

3   Many of us do not get enough sleep and we suffer the consequences, often without realising what we are doing to ourselves. The demands of the 24-hour society are marginalising sleep, yet it is not an optional activity. Nature imposes it upon us. We can survive for longer without food. When our sleep falls short in quantity or quality we pay a heavy price in depressed mood, impaired performance, damaged social relationships and poorer health. But we usually blame something else.

4   Sleep is an active state, generated within the brain, not a mere absence of consciousness. You are physiologically capable of sleeping with your eyelids held open by sticking plaster, bright lights flashing in your eyes and loud music playing in your ears. We shall later see how science has revealed the ferment of electrical and chemical activity that goes on inside the brain during sleep, and how the sleeping brain operates in a quite different mode from waking consciousness. We shall see too how lack of sleep erodes our quality of life and performance while simultaneously making us more vulnerable to injuries and illness. Science amply supports William Shakespeare's view that sleep is the 'chief nourisher in life's feast'.

5   What is sleep and what is it for? Why do so many people have such problems with it? Why do we dream? Although sleep forms a central strand of human and animal life it is still poorly understood and widely neglected. It is an inglorious example of familiarity breeding contempt. Sleep is so much a part of our everyday existence that we take it for granted. We are ignorant even of our ignorance. In 1758, Doctor Samuel Johnson summed it up like this:

> Among the innumerable mortifications that waylay human arrogance on every side may well be reckoned our ignorance of the most common objects and effects . . . Vulgar and inactive minds confound familiarity with knowledge, and conceive themselves informed of the whole nature of things when they are shown their form or told their use . . . Sleep is a state in which a great part of every life is passed. No animal has been yet discovered whose existence is not varied with intervals of insensibility. Yet of this change so frequent, so great, so general, and so necessary, no searcher has yet found either the efficient or final cause; or can tell by what power the mind and body are thus chained down in irresistible stupefaction; or what benefits the animal receives from this alternate suspension of its active powers.

The scientists who do know something about sleep often bemoan society's ignorance of it. They point to the vast gap between current scientific understanding of sleep, patchy though it is, and the practical benefits it could bring if that knowledge were absorbed and acted upon by society. Our collective indifference towards sleep has enormous and largely avoidable costs.

A sleep-sick society?

> The mere presence of an alarm clock implies sleep deprivation, and what bedroom lacks an alarm clock?
>
> James Gleick, *Faster* (1999)

6   All is not well with the state of sleep. Many of us depend on an alarm clock to prise us out of bed each morning, and children's bedrooms increasingly resemble places of entertainment rather than places of sleep. When given the opportunity, we sleep in at the weekends and feel only half awake when we do get up. On that long-awaited holiday we find the change of scenery (or is it the air?) makes us even sleepier. We are told that lying around and sleeping too much will only make us sleepier. But in truth we feel sleepy at weekends and on holidays not because we are sleeping too much, but because we have slept too little the rest of the time.

7   A century ago the majority toiled long hours while the affluent few idled away their time. Today, however, the more conventionally successful you are, the less free time you will probably have. Having nothing to do is seen as a sign of worthlessness, while ceaseless activity signifies status and success. Supposedly unproductive activities are deprioritised or delegated. And according to prevailing cultural attitudes, sleeping is one of the least productive of all human activities. . . . In their ceaseless pursuit of work and pleasure the cash-rich buy time from others, hiring them to clean their houses, look after their children and cook their food. But one of the activities you simply cannot delegate to anyone else is sleeping.

8   Evolution equipped humans, in common with all other animals, with biological mechanisms to make us sleep at roughly the same time every day. However, those mechanisms evolved to cope with a pre-industrial world that was vastly different from the one we now inhabit.

9   Our daily cycles of sleep and activity are no longer driven by dawn and dusk, but by clocks, electric lighting and work schedules. Sleep has become increasingly devalued in the 24-hour society. Many regard sleep as wasted time and would prefer to sacrifice less of their busy lives to it. We live in a world where there are too many tired, sleep-deprived people. Think of those pinched, yawning faces you can see every day on the trains and in buses and in cars crawling through jams. They look as if they have been brainwashed, but they are just tired.

10   We pay a steep price for neglecting sleep, in our ignorance and indifference. The scientific evidence tells us that far too many people in industrialised societies are chronically sleep-deprived, with damaging consequences for their

mental and physical health, performance at work, quality of life and personal relationships. William Dement, a pioneering scientist in the field, believes that we now live in a 'sleep-sick society'. Scientists have not yet reached a consensus about the precise extent of sleep deprivation in society, but they do all agree that sleepiness is a major cause of accidents and injuries. In fact, sleepiness is responsible for far more deaths on the roads than alcohol or drugs.

11   Everyone has heard about the need for a balanced diet and physical exercise, even if many of us fail to follow the advice. But sleep is lost in a deep well of ignorance and apathy. Even the medical profession pays it scant regard. Sleep and its disorders barely feature in the teaching of medicine, and few physicians are fully equipped to deal with the sleep problems they regularly encounter. When researchers from Oxford University investigated British medical education in the late 1990s, they discovered that the average amount of time devoted to sleep and sleep disorders in undergraduate teaching was five minutes, rising to a princely peak of 15 minutes in preclinical training. Your doctor is therefore unlikely to be an expert on the subject.

12   The general public and the medical profession are not the only ones to display a remarkable indifference to sleep. So too do most contemporary writers. Considering that sleep accounts for a third of human existence, it features remarkably rarely in novels, biographies, social histories or learned texts on neurobiology, psychology and medicine. And the few accounts that have made it into print are mostly concerned with what happens when it goes wrong. Insomnia and nightmares loom large in the tiny literature of sleep.

13   Few biographies mention the sleep behaviour or dreams of their subjects. That part of their story is almost invariably missing, as if somehow we all cease to exist at night. And most of those scholarly books that set out to explain how the human mind works say little or nothing about what goes on during the several hours of every day when the mind is sleeping and dreaming. They are really just books about how the brain works when it is awake. Our neglect of sleep is underlined by its absence from our literature.

14   Vladimir Nabokov once said that all the great writers have good eyes. What has happened to the eyes of writers as far as sleep and dreams are concerned? It was not always so. Older literature is distinctly richer in references to sleeping and dreaming, perhaps because darkness and sleep and dreams were much more prominent aspects of everyday life before the invention of the electric light bulb and the advent of the 24-hour society. Shakespeare's works are thick with allusions to sleep and dreams, as are Dickens's. We shall encounter some of them later. Meanwhile, to set the right tone, here is Sancho Panza's eulogy to sleep from *Don Quixote*:

> God bless the inventor of sleep, the cloak that covers all man's thoughts, the food that cures all hunger, the water that quenches all thirst, the fire that warms the cold, the cold that cools the heat; the common coin, in short, that can purchase all things, the balancing weight that levels the shepherd with the king and the simple with the wise.

The universal imperative

> Almost all other animals are observed to partake of sleep, aquatic, winged, and terrestrial creatures alike. For every kind of fish and the soft-shelled species have been seen sleeping, as has every other creature that has eyes.
>
> Aristotle (384–322 B.C.), *On Sleep and Waking*

15 Sleep is a universal human characteristic, like eating and drinking. Absolutely everybody does it. Sleep occupies about one third of each human life, and up to two thirds of a baby's time. (According to Groucho Marx, the proportion rises to three thirds if you live in Peoria.) It is a common bond that ties us all together. We have no choice: the longer we go without sleep, the stronger our desire for it grows. Tiredness, like hunger and thirst, will eventually force us to do the right thing whether we want to or not.

16   The dreams that accompany sleep are equally ubiquitous features of human life, even if many of us retain little memory of them after we awake. Dreaming is a classless activity that unites monarchs and paupers, a thought that Charles Dickens mused upon in one of his essays:

> Here, for example, is her Majesty Queen Victoria in her palace, this present blessed night, and here is Winking Charley, a sturdy vagrant, in one of her Majesty's jails . . . It is probable that we have all three committed murders and hidden bodies. It is pretty certain that we have all desperately wanted to cry out, and have had no voice; that we have all gone to the play and not been able to get in; that we have all dreamed much more of our youth than of our later lives.

Sleep is not a specifically human trait, of course. On the contrary, it is a universal characteristic of complex living organisms, as Aristotle deduced more than 23 centuries ago. Sleep is observed in animals of every sort, including insects, molluscs, fish, amphibians, birds and mammals. Within the animal world, sleep does vary enormously in quantity, quality and timing, accounting for anything up to 80 per cent of some animals' lifespans. But they all do it, one way or another. Some species, especially predators, spend more of their lives asleep than they do awake, a fact that TV documentaries and natural-history books seldom mention.

17   How do we know that an animal is sleeping? It is hard enough sometimes to be sure that a human is asleep, let alone a fish or a fly. The ultimate indicator of whether an animal or person is asleep is the distinctive pattern of electrical activity in its brain. During deep sleep the billions of individual nerve cells in the brain synchronise their electrical activity to some extent, generating characteristic waves of tiny voltage changes that can be detected by electrodes placed on the scalp. We shall be exploring the nature and internal structure of sleep later. The easiest way to recognise sleep, however, is from overt behaviour.

18   Sleep has several rather obvious distinguishing characteristics. A sleeping person or animal will generally remain in the same place for a prolonged period, perhaps several hours. There will be a certain amount of twitching, shifting of

posture and fidgeting. Young animals will suckle while they sleep and ruminants will carry on chewing the cud. But sleepers normally do not get up and change their location. (When they do, we recognise it as a curious phenomenon and call it sleepwalking.)

19   Sleeping organisms also adopt a characteristic posture. Sloths and bats, for example, sleep hanging upside down from a branch. The Mediterranean flour moth sleeps with its antennae swivelled backwards and the tips tucked under its wings. If you are careful, you can gently lift the sleeping moth's wing without disturbing it—a trick that will definitely not work when it is awake. A lizard will settle on a branch during the hours before sunset, curl up its tail, close its eyelids, retract its eyeballs and remain in that distinctly sleep-like posture all night unless it is disturbed. A partridge, like many birds, will rest its weight on one leg while it sleeps. It is said that some gourmets can tell *which* leg, from its taste.

20   Monkeys and apes, including humans, usually sleep lying down. Indeed, we are built in such a way that we find it difficult to sleep properly unless we are lying down. People can and sometimes do sleep after a fashion while sitting, notably in aeroplanes, business meetings and school classrooms. If you are really exhausted, you might even manage to snatch some sleep standing up. But sleep taken while standing or sitting upright is generally fitful, shallow and unrefreshing. The non-horizontal sleeper may repeatedly nod off, but as soon as they descend beyond the shallowest stages of sleep their muscles relax, they begin to sway and their brain wakes them up again. That is why we 'nod off'. If you travel frequently on trains or buses, you might have had the dubious pleasure of sitting next to a weary commuter who has nodded off all over your shoulder. Recordings of brain-wave patterns show that people sleeping in an upright sitting position achieve only the initial stages of light sleep, not the sustained, deep sleep we require to wake up feeling truly refreshed. The reason is simple. Our muscles relax when we are fully asleep and we would fall over if we were not already lying down. Our brains therefore do not permit us to enter sustained, deep sleep unless we are in a physically stable, horizontal (or near-horizontal) posture.

21   Despite the virtual impossibility of sleeping deeply while sitting upright, we are sometimes forced to try. In *Down and Out in Paris and London*, George Orwell describes a particularly unwelcoming form of overnight accommodation that was known to the homeless of prewar London as the Twopenny Hangover. At the Twopenny Hangover the night's residents would sit in a row along a bench. In front of them was a rope, and the would-be sleepers would lean on this rope as though leaning over a fence. In that posture they were supposed to sleep. At five o'clock the next morning an official, wittily known as the valet, would cut the rope so that the residents could begin another day of wandering the streets.

22   Nowadays, tourist-class airline passengers travelling long distances can enjoy an experience similar to the Twopenny Hangover, albeit at vastly greater expense. George Orwell's autobiographical account of grinding poverty in the late 1920s is also a sharp reminder that lack of money is often accompanied by lack of decent sleep. Rough sleepers rarely get a good night's sleep.

23   Sleep has several other distinctive characteristics besides immobility and posture. In many species, including humans, individuals return to the same place each night (or each day, if they are nocturnal) in order to sleep. More generally, all members of a given species will tend to choose the same sorts of sleeping places. The distinctive feature of those places is often their security. Birds usually sleep on inaccessible branches or ledges. Many small mammals sleep in underground burrows where they are safer from predators. Fishes lie on the bottom, or wedge themselves into a crevice or against the underside of a rock. We humans prefer to sleep in relatively private and secure places. Given the choice, we rarely opt to sleep on busy streets or in crowded restaurants.

24   One obvious feature of sleep is a marked reduction in responsiveness to sights, sounds and other sensory stimuli. To provoke a response from a sleeping organism, stimuli have to be more intense or more relevant to the individual. For example, the reef fish known as the slippery dick sleeps during the hours of darkness, partly buried in the sand. While it is in this state, the sleeping slippery dick can be gently lifted to the surface by hand without it waking up and swimming off.

25   A sort of perceptual wall is erected during sleep, insulating the mind from the outside world. You would still be able to sleep if you had no eyelids, because your sleeping brain would not register what your eyes could see. This sensory isolation is highly selective, however. You can sleep through relatively loud noises from traffic or a radio, but a quiet mention of your name can rouse you immediately. Your brain is not simply blocked off during sleep. Moreover, this reduced responsiveness is rapidly reversible—a characteristic that distinguishes sleep from states such as unconsciousness, coma, anaesthesia and hibernation. A suitable stimulus, particularly one signifying immediate danger, can snap a sleeping person into staring-eyed alertness in an instant.

26   Another diagnostic feature of sleep is its regular cycle of waxing and waning. Living organisms sleep and wake according to a regular 24-hour cycle, or circadian rhythm. All members of a given species tend to sleep during the same part of the 24-hour cycle, when their environment is least favourable for other activities such as looking for food. For most species this means sleeping during the hours of darkness, but some species do the reverse. Many small mammals, which would be more vulnerable to predators during daylight, sleep by day and forage at night. Aside from a few nocturnal specialists such as owls, birds cannot easily fly in the dark, and most reptiles find it hard to maintain a sufficiently high body temperature to be active during the cool of night. Most birds and reptiles therefore sleep at night. Predators tend to sleep when their prey are asleep and hunt when their prey are up and about.

27   Sleep, then, is characterised by a special sleeping place and posture, prolonged immobility, a selective and rapidly reversible reduction in responsiveness to stimuli, and a 24-hour cycle. According to these and other criteria, all mammals, birds, fish, amphibians, reptiles and insects that have been inspected have been found to sleep.

. . .

Half asleep

> And the small fowl are making melody
> That sleep away the night with open eye
>
>   Geoffrey Chaucer, A *Prologue to* The Canterbury Tales (c. 1387)

28 Sleep is such an overriding biological imperative that evolution has found ingenious ways of enabling animals to do it in the face of formidable obstacles. Nature, it seems, will do almost anything to ensure that animals sleep.

29 Consider dolphins, for example. They are air-breathing mammals like us, so they must swim to the surface each time they want to take a breath. They would drown if they fell into deep sleep while deep underwater. One possible solution to this biological design conundrum would be to wake up each time a breath of air was required. However, evolution has produced a more elegant solution: only one half of the dolphin's brain goes to sleep at a time.

30 Dolphins are capable of what is known as unihemispheric sleep, in which one hemisphere of the brain submerges into deep sleep while the other hemisphere remains awake. The two halves of the brain take it in turns to sleep, swapping at intervals of between one and three hours. This cerebral juggling trick enables dolphins to sleep underwater without drowning, which is just as well considering that they spend a good third of their lives asleep. Unihemispheric sleep has been recorded in several species of dolphins, porpoises and whales, including bottlenosed and Amazonian dolphins, Black Sea porpoises and white whales.

31 Despite the apparent convenience of being able to sleep and stay awake simultaneously, very few mammals are capable of unihemispheric sleep. The biological benefits of sleeping with only half of the brain at a time presumably outweigh the disadvantages only under unusual conditions, such as those encountered by air-breathing mammals living in the deep oceans.

32 Unihemispheric sleep is widespread in birds, however. They do it for a different biological reason. Sleeping with half the brain awake and one eye open allows them to sleep while simultaneously remaining vigilant for predators. In birds, each eye exclusively feeds the visual processing areas in the opposite half of the brain: thus, all the nerve fibres coming from the right eye connect to the left hemisphere of the brain and vice versa. When a bird is in unihemispheric sleep its open eye is the one corresponding to the waking half of the brain, while the closed eye is connected to the sleeping half. If a bird feels relatively safe, it closes both eyes, and both sides of its brain go to sleep.

33 An experiment with mallard ducks demonstrated how unihemispheric sleep helps birds to stay safe from predators. Four ducks were placed in a row along a perch, the idea being that the ducks at either end of the row would feel more vulnerable to predators than the two in the middle. In the natural world it is generally a bad idea to be on the edge of a group if you might end up as some other animal's dinner. As predicted, video recordings showed that the outer two birds were much more likely to sleep with one eye open than the two on the inside; their unihemispheric sleep increased by 150 per cent. The amount of unihemispheric sleep rose further when the ducks were shown frightening video images of an approaching predator.

34　　The relationship between unihemispheric sleep and vigilance was finely controlled. The exposed birds on the ends of the row preferentially opened their outward-facing eye—the one directed towards potential danger. From time to time, a bird would turn round and switch eyes, so that the open eye was still the one facing out. Simultaneous recordings of brain activity confirmed that the brain hemisphere corresponding to the open eye was always awake, while the hemisphere corresponding to the closed eye was the one in deep sleep.

35　　The one-eyed tactic was effective: when an attacking predator was simulated on a video screen, the birds sleeping with one eye open were able to react in a fraction of a second—far faster than if they had been in deep sleep with both eyes shut.

36　　Humans are not capable of unihemispheric sleep, although at least one writer has played with the fantasy. Damon Runyon wrote of how he once played cards with a fading champion card player who now lacked the stamina to stay awake during marathon games of gin rummy lasting eight or ten hours. When the man lost a game after making a bad play, the punters betting on him to win clamoured to remove their bets from the next game, on the grounds that he was asleep. Then someone pointed out that the allegedly sleeping player's eyes were open, so he must be awake. 'The one on your side is', retorted one of the backers, 'but the one on the other side is closed. He is sleeping one-eye.'

Review Questions

1. What are some of the qualities of sleep that make it "so strange," in Martin's view?

2. Cite some signs of sleep deprivation, and indicate some aspects of modern life that lead to lack of sleep.

3. What are the distinguishing characteristics of sleep, and which species have been observed to sleep?

4. What is unihemispheric sleep, and why is it a characteristic of some marine mammals and birds?

Discussion and Writing Suggestions

1. Before reading Martin's article, to what extent did you consider sleep a "behavior"? How did you think of it, if not as a behavior? Explain.

2. What accounts for the relatively scant attention sleep has received in popular culture? In developing your answer, read what Samuel Johnson said on the matter in 1758 (see paragraph 5). To what extent does his response answer this question today?

3. What single observation about sleep stands out for you from this article? Explain your fascination.

4. Martin writes that "[e]volution equipped humans . . . to . . . sleep at roughly the same time every day . . . to cope with a pre-industrial world

that was vastly different from the one we now inhabit" (paragraph 8). Imagine the world before the invention of electric or gas lighting. (If you go camping, you have direct experience with this world.) In what ways do you think that modern life is working at odds with bodily rhythms that evolved over tens of thousands of years?

5. Do you consider yourself sleep deprived? Several other authors in this chapter will address the issue; but based on the signs of sleep deprivation that Martin reviews, how serious is your sleep debt? Write about one incident that prompted you to consider getting more sleep.

The Science of Sleep
Susan Ince

Of the hundreds of introductions to the physiology of sleep, this selection by science writer Susan Ince, appearing in the Harvard Health Letter, *is among the clearest for audiences without a formal background in medicine. We excerpt the opening sections of the larger report: overviews of sleep mechanics, sleep control, and sleeping throughout life.*

1   Thanks to technology, with the push of a button you can summon a movie on your television, speed-dial a friend's cell phone, or ensure fresh coffee awaits you in the morning. Unfortunately, there's no button to push that instantly puts you to sleep and wakes you up feeling refreshed. Instead, just like your primitive ancestors, you must lie down and wait for nature to take its course. Sleep may come quickly, slowly, or not at all.

2   If you have trouble sleeping, you're not alone. Recent surveys by the National Sleep Foundation found that more than half of American adults experience one or more symptoms of *insomnia* a few nights a week, and two-thirds of older adults report frequent sleep problems. An estimated 40 million Americans have chronic sleep disorders such as *sleep apnea, narcolepsy,* and *restless legs syndrome*. We pay a high price for all the sleep deprivation caused by sleep problems. For example:

- Insufficient sleep is directly linked to poor health, with new research suggesting it increases the risk of diabetes, heart disease, and obesity. Even a few nights of bad sleep can be detrimental.
- The combination of sleep deprivation and driving can have deadly consequences. Nearly one in five drivers admits to having fallen asleep at the wheel, and the National Highway Traffic Safety Administration conservatively estimates that drowsy drivers cause 100,000 police-reported crashes each year.
- Sleep deprivation has played a role in catastrophes such as the Exxon Valdez oil spill off the coast of Alaska, the space shuttle Challenger disaster, and the nuclear accident at Three Mile Island.

3   Sleep problems affect virtually every aspect of day-to-day living, including mood, mental alertness, work performance, and energy level. Yet fewer than 3% of Americans are treated for their sleep problems.

. . .

Sleep Mechanics

4 For centuries, scientists scrutinized minute aspects of human activity, but showed little interest in the time that people spent in sleep. Sleep seemed inaccessible to medical probing and was perceived as an unvarying period of inactivity—a subject best suited to poets and dream interpreters who could conjure meaning out of the void. All that changed in the 1930s, when scientists learned to place sensitive electrodes on the scalp and record the signals produced by electrical activity in the brain. These brain waves can be seen on an *electroencephalogram*, or EEG (see Figure 1), which today is captured on a computer screen.

5   After a few years of brain wave study, it became clear that sleep was a highly complex activity. Using electrodes to monitor sleepers' eye movements, muscle tone, and brain wave patterns, scientists now have identified several discrete stages of sleep. Researchers are continually learning more about the roles certain stages of sleep play in maintaining health, growth, and daytime functioning.

6   Scientists divide sleep into two major types: *rapid eye movement (REM) sleep* or dreaming sleep, and non-REM or *quiet sleep*. Surprisingly, they are as different from one another as sleeping is from waking.

Quiet Sleep

7 Sleep specialists have called non-REM or quiet sleep "an idling brain in a movable body." During this phase, thinking and most physiological activities slow down, but movement can still occur, and a person often shifts position while sinking into progressively deeper stages of sleep.

8   To an extent, the convention of describing people "descending" or "dropping" into sleep actually parallels changes in brain wave patterns at the onset of non-REM sleep. When you are awake, billions of brain cells receive and analyze sensory information, coordinate behavior, and maintain bodily functions by sending electrical impulses to one another. If you're fully awake, the EEG will record a messy, irregular scribble of activity. Once your eyes are closed and your nerve cells no longer receive visual input, brain waves settle into a steady and rhythmic pattern of about 10 cycles per second. This is the alpha-wave pattern, characteristic of calm, relaxed wakefulness. Unless something disturbs the process, you will soon proceed smoothly through the four stages of quiet sleep.

Four Stages of Quiet Sleep

9 **Stage 1.** In making the transition from wakefulness into light sleep, you spend about five minutes in Stage 1 sleep. On the EEG, the predominant brain waves slow to 4–7 cycles per second, a pattern called theta waves. Body temperature begins to drop, muscles become relaxed, and eyes often move slowly from side to side. People in Stage 1 sleep lose awareness of their surroundings, but they are easily jarred awake. However, not everyone experiences Stage 1 sleep in the

same way: If awakened, one person might recall being drowsy, while another might describe having been asleep.

10   **Stage 2.** This first stage of true sleep lasts 10–25 minutes. Your eyes are still, and your heart rate and breathing are slower than when awake. Your brain's electrical activity is irregular. Large, slow waves intermingle with brief bursts of activity called sleep spindles, when brain waves speed up for roughly half a second or longer. About every two minutes, EEG tracings show a pattern called a K-complex, which scientists think represents a sort of built-in vigilance system that keeps you poised to be awakened if necessary. K-complexes can also be provoked by certain sounds or other external or internal stimuli. Whisper someone's name during Stage 2 sleep, and a K-complex will appear on the EEG. You spend about half the night in Stage 2 sleep, which leaves you moderately refreshed.

11   **Stages 3 and 4.** Eventually, large slow brain waves called delta waves become a major feature on the EEG. Together, Stages 3 and 4 are known as *deep sleep* or

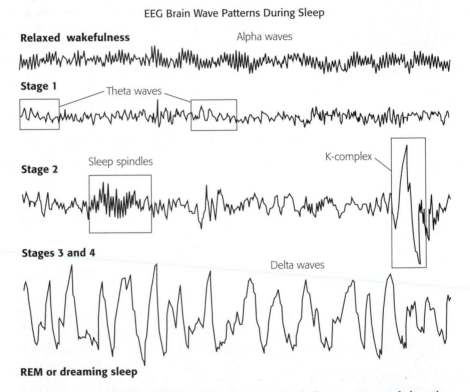

EEG Brain Wave Patterns During Sleep

Relaxed wakefulness   Alpha waves

Stage 1   Theta waves

Stage 2   Sleep spindles   K-complex

Stages 3 and 4   Delta waves

REM or dreaming sleep

FIGURE 1 Clinicians distinguish between several discrete stages of sleep by using electrodes to monitor brain wave patterns on an *electroencephalogram (EEG)*. *Alpha waves* occur when the eyes are closed and are characteristic of a calm, relaxed wakefulness. *Theta waves* indicate Stage 1 sleep. *Sleep spindles* and *K-complexes* represent brief bursts of activity during Stage 2 sleep. *Delta waves* represent deep or slow-wave sleep.

slow-wave sleep. Stage 3 becomes Stage 4 when at least half of the brain waves are delta waves. During deep sleep, breathing becomes more regular. Blood pressure falls and pulse rate slows to about 20%–30% below the waking rate. The brain becomes less responsive to external stimuli, making it difficult to wake the sleeper.

12   Deep, slow-wave sleep seems to be a time for your body to renew and repair itself. Blood flow is directed less toward your brain, which cools measurably. At the beginning of this stage, the pituitary gland releases a pulse of growth hormone that stimulates tissue growth and muscle repair. Researchers have also detected increased blood levels of interleukin and other substances that activate your immune system, raising the possibility that deep sleep helps the body defend itself against infection.

13   Normally, young people spend about 20% of their sleep time in stretches of slow-wave sleep lasting up to half an hour, but slow-wave sleep is nearly absent in most people over age 65 (see "The later years," page [519]). Someone whose deep sleep is restricted will wake up feeling unrefreshed, no matter how long he or she has been in bed. When a sleep-deprived person gets some sleep, he or she will pass quickly through the lighter sleep stages into the deeper stages and spend a greater proportion of sleep time there, suggesting that slow-wave sleep fills an essential need.

Dreaming (REM) Sleep

14 Dreaming occurs during REM sleep, which has been described as an "active brain in a paralyzed body." Your brain races, thinking and dreaming, as your eyes dart back and forth rapidly behind closed lids. Your body temperature rises. Unless you have circulatory or other physical problems, the penis or clitoris becomes erect. Your blood pressure increases, and your heart rate and breathing speed up to daytime levels. The sympathetic nervous system, which creates the fight-or-flight response, is twice as active as when you're awake. Despite all this activity, your body hardly moves, except for intermittent twitches; muscles not needed for breathing or eye movement are quiet.

15   Just as deep sleep restores your body, scientists believe that REM or dreaming sleep restores your mind, perhaps in part by helping clear out irrelevant information. Studies show, for example, that REM sleep facilitates learning and memory. People tested to measure how well they had learned a new task improved their scores after a night's sleep. If roused from REM sleep, however, the improvements were lost. On the other hand, if they were awakened an equal number of times from slow-wave sleep, the improvements in the scores were unaffected. These findings may help explain why students who stay up all night cramming for an examination generally retain less information than classmates who get some sleep.

16   About three to five times a night, or about every 90 minutes, a sleeper enters REM sleep. The first such episode usually lasts only for a few minutes, but REM time increases progressively over the course of the night. The final period of REM sleep may last a half-hour. Altogether, REM sleep makes up about 25% of total sleep in young adults. If someone who has been deprived of REM sleep is left undisturbed for a night, he or she enters this stage earlier and spends a higher proportion of sleep time in it—a phenomenon called REM rebound.

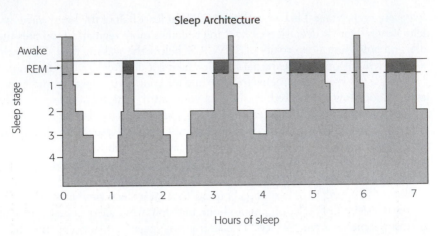

Sleep Architecture

Hours of sleep

FIGURE 2 When sleep stages are charted on a hypnogram, the different levels resemble a drawing of the city skyline. Sleep experts call this pattern sleep architecture. This hypnogram shows a typical night's sleep of a healthy young adult.

Sleep Architecture

17 During the night, a normal sleeper moves between different sleep stages in a fairly predictable pattern, alternating between REM and non-REM sleep. When these stages are charted on a diagram, called a *hypnogram* (see Figure 2), the different levels resemble a drawing of a city skyline. Sleep experts call this pattern *sleep architecture*.

18   In a young adult, normal sleep architecture usually consists of four or five alternating non-REM and REM periods. Most deep sleep occurs in the first half of the night; as the night progresses, periods of REM sleep get longer and alternate with Stage 2 sleep. Later in life, the sleep skyline will change, with less deep sleep, more Stage 1 sleep and more awakenings.

Circadian Rhythm: Understanding Your Internal Clock

19 Scientists have discovered that certain brain structures and chemicals produce the states of sleeping and waking. Understanding these control mechanisms helps doctors pinpoint what can go wrong and plan effective treatments.

20   A pacemaker-like mechanism in the brain regulates the *circadian rhythm* of sleeping and waking. ("Circadian" means "about a day.") This internal clock, which gradually becomes established during the first months of life, controls the daily ups and downs of biological patterns, including body temperature, blood pressure, and the release of hormones.

21   The circadian rhythm makes people's desire for sleep strongest between midnight and dawn, and to a lesser extent in midafternoon. In one study, researchers instructed a group of people to try to stay awake for 24 hours. Not surprisingly, many slipped into naps despite their best efforts not to. When the investigators plotted the times when the unplanned naps occurred, they found peaks between 2 a.m. and 4 a.m. and between 2 p.m. and 3 p.m.

22   Most Americans sleep during the night as dictated by their circadian rhythms, although many nap in the afternoon on the weekends. In societies where taking a siesta is the norm, people can respond to their bodies' daily dips in alertness with a one- to two-hour afternoon nap during the workday and a correspondingly shorter sleep at night.

Mechanisms of Your "Sleep Clock"

23 In the 1970s, the location of the internal clock in rodents was found to be the suprachiasmatic nucleus. This cluster of cells is part of the hypothalamus, the brain center that regulates appetite and other biological states. When this tiny area was damaged, the sleep/wake rhythm disappeared and the rats no longer slept on a normal schedule. Although the clock is largely self-regulating, its location allows it to respond to several types of external cues to keep it set at 24 hours. Scientists call these cues "zeitgebers," a German word meaning "time givers." These are as follows:

24   **Light.** Light striking your eyes is the most influential zeitgeber. When researchers invited volunteers into the laboratory and exposed them to light at intervals that were at odds with the outside world, the participants unconsciously reset their biological clocks to match the new light input. The circadian rhythm disturbances and sleep problems that affect up to 90% of blind people demonstrate the importance of light to sleep/wake patterns.

25   **Time cues.** As a person reads clocks, follows work and train schedules, and demands that the body remain alert for certain tasks and social events, there is cognitive pressure to stay on schedule.

26   **Melatonin.** Cells in the suprachiasmatic nucleus contain receptors for *melatonin*, a hormone produced in a predictable daily rhythm by the pineal gland, which is located deep in the brain between the two hemispheres. Levels of melatonin begin climbing after dark and ebb after dawn. The hormone induces drowsiness in some people, and scientists believe its daily light-sensitive cycles help keep the sleep/wake cycle on track.

Your Clock's Hour Hand

27 As the circadian rhythm counts off the days, another part of the brain acts like the hour hand on a watch. This clock is located in a cluster of nerve cells within the brain stem, the area that controls breathing, blood pressure, and heartbeat. Fluctuating activity in the nerve cells and the chemical messengers they produce seem to coordinate the timing of wakefulness, arousal, and the 90-minute changeover between REM and non-REM sleep.

28   Several neurotransmitters (natural brain chemicals that neurons release to communicate with adjacent cells) play a role in arousal. Their actions help explain why medications that mimic or counteract their effects can influence sleep. Adenosine and gamma-aminobutyric acid (GABA) are believed to promote sleep. Acetylcholine regulates REM sleep. Norepinephrine, epinephrine, dopamine, and the newly discovered hypocretin peptides—also known as orexins—stimulate wakefulness. Individuals vary greatly in their natural levels of neurotransmitters and in their sensitivity to these chemicals.

Sleep throughout Life

29 To a certain extent, heredity determines how people sleep throughout their lives. Identical twins, for example, have much more similar sleep patterns than nonidentical twins or other siblings. Differences in sleeping and waking seem to be inborn. There are night owls and early-morning larks, sound sleepers and light ones, people who are perky after five hours of sleep and others who are groggy if they log less than nine hours. Nevertheless, many factors can affect how a person sleeps. Aging is the most important influence on basic sleep rhythms, because it affects how much sleep you get in a typical night as well as your sleep architecture.

Childhood

30 For an adult to sleep like a baby is not only unrealistic but also undesirable. A newborn may sleep eight times a day, accumulating 18 hours of sleep and spending about half of it in REM sleep. The REM to non-REM cycle is shorter, usually lasting less than an hour.

31   At about the age of four weeks, a newborn's sleep periods get longer. By six months, infants spend longer and more regular periods in non-REM sleep; most begin sleeping through the night and taking naps in the morning and afternoon. During the pre-school years, daytime naps gradually shorten, until by age six most children are awake all day and sleep for about 10 hours a night.

32   Between age seven and puberty, nocturnal melatonin production is at its lifetime peak, and sleep at this age is deep and restorative. At this age, if a child is sleepy during the day, it's cause for concern.

Adolescence

33 In contrast, adolescents are noted for their daytime drowsiness. Except for infancy, adolescence is the most rapid period of body growth and development. Although teenagers need about an hour more sleep than they did as young children, most of them actually sleep an hour or so less. Parents usually blame teenagers' busy schedule of activities for their grogginess and difficulty awakening in the morning. However, the problem may also be biological. One study indicated that some adolescents might have *delayed sleep phase syndrome*, where they are not sleepy until well after the usual bedtime and cannot wake at the time required for school, producing conflicts between parents and sleepy teenagers as well as with secondary schools, which usually open earlier than elementary schools. It is unknown whether this phase shift occurs primarily as a physiological event or as a response to abnormal light exposure.

Adulthood

34 During young adulthood, sleep patterns usually seem stable but in fact are slowly evolving. Between age 20 and age 30, the amount of deep sleep drops by about half, and nighttime awakenings double. By age 40, Stage 4 sleep has almost disappeared.

35   Women's reproductive cycles can greatly influence sleep. During the first trimester of pregnancy, many women are sleepy all the time and may log an extra two hours a night if their schedules permit. As pregnancy continues, hormonal and anatomical changes reduce sleep efficiency so that less of a woman's

time in bed is actually spent sleeping. As a result, fatigue increases. . . . The post-partum period usually brings dramatic sleepiness and fatigue—because the mother's ability to sleep efficiently has not returned to normal, because she is at the mercy of her newborn's rapidly cycling shifts between sleeping and waking, and because breast-feeding promotes sleepiness. Researchers are beginning to probe whether sleep disturbances during pregnancy may contribute to postpar-tum depression and compromise the general physical and mental well-being of new mothers.

36   Women who aren't pregnant may experience monthly shifts in sleep habits. During the second phase of the menstrual cycle, between ovulation and the next menses, some women fall asleep and enter REM sleep more quickly than usual. A few experience extreme sleepiness. Investigators are probing the rela-tionship between such sleep alterations, cyclic changes in body temperature, and levels of the hormone progesterone to see whether these physiologic patterns also correlate with premenstrual mood changes.

Middle Age

37 When men and women enter middle age, Stage 3 sleep begins to diminish. Nighttime awakenings become more frequent and last longer. It's particularly common for people to wake up after about three hours of sleep. During menopause, many women experience hot flashes that can interrupt sleep, some-times leading to chronic insomnia. Obese people are more prone to nocturnal breathing problems, which often start during middle age. Here's where it pays to be physically active. Men and women who are physically fit sleep more soundly as they grow older, compared with their sedentary peers.

The Later Years

38 Like younger people, older adults still spend about 20% of sleep time in REM sleep, but other than that, they sleep differently. Deep sleep accounts for less than 5% of sleep time, and in some people it is completely absent. Falling asleep takes longer, and the shallow quality of sleep results in dozens of awakenings during the night. Over a 24-hour period, however, older adults manage to accu-mulate the same amount of total sleep as younger people, thanks to napping. Doctors used to reassure older people that they needed less sleep than younger ones to function well, but sleep experts now know that isn't true: It was a mis-take scientists made when they failed to account for daytime naps logged by older folks. Generally, most sleep experts discourage napping . . . , but if you find that you need a nap, it's best to take one midday nap, rather than several brief ones scattered throughout the day and evening.

39   Sleep disturbances in elderly people, particularly in those who have Alzheimer's disease or other forms of dementia, are very disruptive for caregivers. In one study, 70% of caregivers cited these problems as the decisive factor in seeking nursing home placement for a loved one. When caregivers of partici-pants in adult day programs were interviewed, more than a third reported being distressed and sleep-deprived because they were looking after someone with dis-ruptive nocturnal behaviors—such as insomnia, nightmares, wandering, phys-ical aggression, loud screaming and talking, or calling for help. In a five-year test project in New York, adult day program participants are being treated for sleep

disorders to see if therapy can increase the amount of time that they are able to remain at home.

40   Although sleep patterns inevitably change with age, older people need not lose alertness and pleasure in life because they can't sleep. No matter how old you are, treatment of sleep disorders and do-it-yourself techniques to maximize sleep quality can bring improvement.

Review Questions

1. What are the costs of disturbed sleep?

2. Explain why sleep is an active, not a passive, state. In your answer, refer to REM and non-REM sleep.

3. Studies suggest that "students who stay up all night cramming for an examination generally retain less information than classmates who get some sleep." Why?

4. To what does the term "sleep architecture" refer? What pattern does a normal sleeper's sleep architecture follow?

5. What is "circadian rhythm"? For what is it responsible and what part of the body controls it?

6. What habits affect sleep quality? How so?

7. How does sleep architecture change throughout a person's life?

Discussion and Writing Suggestions

1. Based on personal observation, what direct evidence do you have that people in different stages of life, from infants to elders, have different sleep patterns?

2. Study Figure 2, "Sleep Architecture." In a paragraph, describe the hypnogram's presentation of a "a typical night's sleep of a healthy young adult." Describe transitions through stages of sleep, and REM and non-REM sleep. In a second paragraph, discuss your reactions upon learning of the complex architecture of sleep.

3. "Parents usually blame teenagers' activities for their grogginess and difficulty awakening in the morning. However, the problem may well be biological," writes Ince. Recall any battles you had in your adolescent past over your "grogginess." Would it have changed anyone's reactions to know that your developing body (as opposed to your work, party, or TV schedule) was to blame?

4. Have you ever suffered through a period of disrupted sleep? Describe the experience in two paragraphs—the first written in the first person (the "I" perspective), the second written in the third person (the "he" or "she" perspective). Compare paragraphs. Which do you prefer? Why?

America's Sleep-Deprived Teens
Nodding Off at School, Behind the Wheel
National Sleep Foundation

The National Sleep Foundation (NSF), according to its Web site, "is an independent nonprofit organization dedicated to improving public health and safety by achieving understanding of sleep and sleep disorders, and by supporting sleep-related education, research, and advocacy." (See <http://www.sleepfoundation.org/>.) The NSF periodically issues news releases on studies its member physicians conduct. The following release, dated March 28, 2006, helped focus national attention on the dangers of adolescent sleep debt.

1 Many of the nation's adolescents are falling asleep in class, arriving late to school, feeling down and driving drowsy because of a lack of sleep that gets worse as they get older, according to a new poll released today by the National Sleep Foundation (NSF).

2   In a national survey on the sleep patterns of U.S. adolescents (ages 11–17), NSF's 2006 *Sleep in America* poll finds that only 20% of adolescents get the recommended nine hours of sleep on school nights, and nearly one-half (45%) sleep less than eight hours on school nights.

3   What's more, the poll finds that parents are mostly in the dark about their adolescents' sleep. While most students know they're not getting the sleep they need, 90% of parents polled believe that their adolescent is getting enough sleep at least a few nights during the school week.

4   The poll indicates that the consequences of insufficient sleep affect nearly every aspect of teenage life. Among the most important findings:

- At least once a week, more than one-quarter (28%) of high school students fall asleep in school, 22% fall asleep doing homework, and 14% arrive late or miss school because they oversleep.
- Adolescents who get insufficient amounts of sleep are more likely than their peers to get lower grades, while 80% of adolescents who get an optimal amount of sleep say they're achieving As and Bs in school.
- More than one-half (51%) of adolescent drivers have driven drowsy during the past year. In fact, 15% of drivers in 10th to 12th grades drive drowsy at least once a week.
- Among those adolescents who report being unhappy, tense and nervous, 73% feel they don't get enough sleep at night and 59% are excessively sleepy during the day.
- More than one-quarter (28%) of adolescents say they're too tired to exercise.

5   The poll also finds that the amount of sleep declines as adolescents get older. The survey classifies nine or more hours a night as an optimal amount of sleep in line with sleep experts' recommendations for this age group, with less than eight hours classified as insufficient. Sixth-graders report they sleep an average of 8.4 hours on school nights, while 12th-graders sleep just 6.9 hours—1.5 hours less than their younger peers and two hours less than recommended. In fact,

by the time adolescents become high school seniors, they're missing out on nearly 12 hours (11.7) of needed sleep each week.

6   "This poll identifies a serious reduction in adolescents' sleep as students transition from middle school to high school. This is particularly troubling as adolescence is a critical period of development and growth—academically, emotionally and physically," says Richard L. Gelula, NSF's chief executive officer. "At a time of heightened concerns about the quality of this next generation's health and education, our nation is ignoring a basic necessity for success in these areas: adequate sleep. We call on parents, educators and teenagers themselves to take an active role in making sleep a priority."

Awareness gap between parents and teens about sleep

7   While nine out of ten parents state their adolescent is getting enough sleep at least a few nights during the school week, more than one-half (56%) of adolescents say they get less sleep than they think they need to feel their best. And, 51% say they feel too tired or sleepy during the day.

8   Also at issue is the quality of sleep once an adolescent goes to bed. Only 41% of adolescents say they get a good night's sleep every night or most nights. One in 10 teens reports that he/she rarely or never gets a good night's sleep.

9   Overall, 7% of parents think their adolescent may have a sleep problem, whereas 16% of adolescents think they have or may have one. Many adolescents (31%) who think they have a sleep problem have not told anyone about it.

Everyday pressures + nature = less sleep

10 As children reach adolescence, their circadian rhythms—or internal clocks— tend to shift, causing teens to naturally feel more alert later at night and wake up later in the morning. A trick of nature, this "phase delay" can make it difficult for them to fall asleep before 11:00 p.m.; more than one-half (54%) of high school seniors go to bed at 11:00 p.m. or later on school nights. However, the survey finds that on a typical school day, adolescents wake up around 6:30 a.m. in order to go to school, leaving many without the sleep they need.

11   "In the competition between the natural tendency to stay up late and early school start times, a teen's sleep is what loses out," notes Jodi A. Mindell, PhD, co-chair of the poll task force and an NSF vice chair. "Sending students to school without enough sleep is like sending them to school without breakfast. Sleep serves not only a restorative function for adolescents' bodies and brains, but it is also a key time when they process what they've learned during the day." Dr. Mindell is the director of the Graduate Program in Psychology at Saint Joseph's University and associate director of the Sleep Center at The Children's Hospital of Philadelphia.

12   It is also important for teens, like all people, to maintain a consistent sleep schedule across the entire week. Poll respondents overwhelmingly go to bed and get up later and sleep longer on non-school nights. However, teens rarely make up for the sleep that they lose during the school week. Overall, adolescents get an average of 8.9 hours of sleep on a non-school night, about equal to the opti-

mal amount recommended per night. Again, the poll finds this amount trends downward as adolescents get older.

13   Survey results also show that sleepy adolescents are more likely to rely on naps, which sleep experts point out should not be a substitute for, but rather complement, a good night's sleep. About one-third (31%) of adolescents take naps regularly, and these nappers are more likely than non-nappers to say they feel cranky or irritable, too tired during the day, and fall asleep in school—all signs of insufficient sleep. And, their naps average 1.2 hours, well beyond the 45-minute maximum recommended by sleep experts so that naps do not interfere with nighttime sleep.

14   "Irregular sleep patterns that include long naps and sleeping in on the weekend negatively impact adolescents' biological clocks and sleep quality—which in turn affects their abilities and mood," says Mary Carskadon, PhD, who chairs the 2006 poll task force. "This rollercoaster system should be minimized. When students' schedules are more consistent and provide for plenty of sleep, they are better prepared to take on their busy days." Dr. Carskadon is the director of the E.P. Bradley Hospital Sleep and Chronobiology Research Lab at Brown University.

15   In terms of overall demographics, there are more similarities than differences among adolescents' responses to sleep-related questions. Boys and girls have similar sleep patterns. In terms of racial/ethnic comparisons, African-American adolescents report getting 7.2 hours of sleep on school nights, as compared to 7.6 hours reported by Hispanic adolescents, 7.4 hours by other minorities and 7.7 hours by White adolescents.

Other factors affecting adolescent sleep

16 Caffeine plays a prominent role in the life of today's adolescent. Three-quarters of those polled drink at least one caffeinated beverage every day, and nearly one-third (31%) consume two or more such drinks each day. Adolescents who drink two or more caffeinated beverages daily are more likely to get an insufficient amount of sleep on school nights and think they have a sleep problem.

17   Technology may also be encroaching on a good night's sleep. The poll finds that adolescents aren't heeding expert advice to engage in relaxing activities in the hour before bedtime or to keep the bedroom free from sleep distractions:

- Watching television is the most popular activity (76%) for adolescents in the hour before bedtime, while surfing the internet/instant-messaging (44%) and talking on the phone (40%) are close behind.
- Boys are more likely than girls to play electronic video games (40% vs. 12%) and/or exercise (37% vs. 27%) in the hour prior to bedtime; girls are more likely than boys to talk on the phone (51% vs. 29%) and/or do homework/study (70% vs. 60%) in that time.
- Nearly all adolescents (97%) have at least one electronic item—such as a television, computer, phone or music device—in their bedroom. On average, 6th-graders have more than two of these items in their bedroom, while 12th-graders have about four.

TIPS FOR TEENS

1. Sleep is food for the brain. Lack of sleep can make you look tired and feel depressed, irritable or angry. Even mild sleepiness can hurt your performance—from taking school exams to playing sports or video games. Learn how much sleep you need to function at your best—most adolescents need between 8.5 and 9.25 hours of sleep each night—and strive to get it every night. You should awaken refreshed, not tired.
2. Keep consistency in mind: establish a regular bedtime and waketime schedule, and maintain this schedule during weekends and school (or work) vacations. Don't stray from your schedule frequently, and never do so for two or more consecutive nights. If you must go off schedule, avoid delaying your bedtime by more than one hour. Awaken the next day within two hours of your regular schedule, and, if you are sleepy during the day, take an early afternoon nap.
3. Get into bright light as soon as possible in the morning, but avoid it in the evening. The light helps to signal to the brain when it should wake up and when it should prepare to sleep.
4. Understand your circadian rhythms. Then you can try to maximize your schedule throughout the day according to your internal clock. For example, to compensate for your "slump (sleepy) times," participate in stimulating activities or classes that are interactive. Try to avoid lecture classes and potentially unsafe activities, including driving.
5. After lunch (or after noon), stay away from caffeinated coffee and colas as well as nicotine, which are all stimulants. Also avoid alcohol, which disrupts sleep.
6. Relax before going to bed. Avoid heavy reading, studying and computer games within one hour of going to bed. Don't fall asleep with the television on—flickering light and stimulating content can inhibit restful sleep.

- Adolescents with four or more such items in their bedrooms are much more likely than their peers to get an insufficient amount of sleep at night and almost twice as likely to fall asleep in school and while doing homework.

18   "Many teens have a technological playground in their bedrooms that offers a variety of ways to stay stimulated and delay sleep. Ramping down from the day's activities with a warm bath and a good book are much better ways to transition to bedtime," notes Dr. Carskadon. "The brain learns when it's time to sleep from the lessons it receives. Teens need to give the brain better signals about when nighttime starts . . . turning off the lights—computer screens and TV, too—is the very best signal."

- **Be a bed head, not a dead head.** Understand the dangers of insufficient sleep—and avoid them! Encourage your friends to do the same. Ask others how much sleep they've had lately before you let them drive you somewhere. Remember: friends don't let friends drive drowsy.
- **Brag about your bedtime.** Tell your friends how good you feel after getting more than 8 hours of sleep!
- **Do you study with a buddy?** If you're getting together after school, tell your pal you need to catch a nap first, or take a nap break if needed. (Taking a nap in the evening may make it harder for you to sleep at night, however.)
- **Steer clear of raves and say no to all-nighters.** Staying up late can cause chaos in your sleep patterns and your ability to be alert the next day . . . and beyond. Remember, the best thing you can do to prepare for a test is to get plenty of sleep. All-nighters or late-night study sessions might seem to give you more time to cram for your exam, but they are also likely to drain your brainpower.

How parents can help teens get more sleep

19 Dr. Mindell notes that "the poll data suggest that parents may be missing red flags that their teenager is not getting the sleep that he or she desperately needs. Simply asking teens if they get enough sleep to feel their best is a good way for parents to begin a valuable conversation about sleep's importance."

20   Some warning signs that your child may not be getting the sleep he/she needs:

- Do you have to wake your child for school? And, is it difficult to do so?
- Has a teacher mentioned that your child is sleepy or tired during the day?
- Do you find your child falling asleep while doing homework?
- Is your child sleeping two hours later or more on weekends than on school nights?
- Is your child's behavior different on days that he/she gets a good night's sleep vs. days that he/she doesn't?
- Does he/she rely on a caffeinated drink in the morning to wake up? And/or drink two or more caffeinated drinks a day?
- Does he/she routinely nap for more than 45 minutes?

21   Parents can play a key role in helping their adolescents develop and maintain healthy sleep habits. In general, it is important for parents and adolescents to talk about sleep—including the natural phase delay—and learn more about good sleep habits in order to manage teens' busy schedules. What's more, teens often mirror their parents' habits, so adults are encouraged to be good role models by getting a full night's sleep themselves.

22   And, there are ways to make it easier for an adolescent to get more sleep and a better night's sleep:

- Set a consistent bedtime and waketime (even on weekends) that allows for the recommended nine or more hours of sleep every night.
- Have a relaxing bedtime routine, such as reading for fun or taking a warm bath or shower.
- Keep the bedroom comfortable, dark, cool and quiet.
- Get into bright light as soon as possible in the morning, but avoid it in the evening.
- Create a sleep-friendly environment by removing TVs and other distractions from the bedroom and setting limits on usage before bedtime.
- Avoid caffeine after lunchtime.

23   NSF released the poll findings as part of its 9th annual National Sleep Awareness Week® campaign, held March 27–April 2, 2006. For more sleep tips for parents and adolescents, as well as the Summary of Findings for the 2006 *Sleep in America* poll, visit NSF's website at <www.sleepfoundation.org>.

Methodology

24 The 2006 *Sleep in America* poll was conducted for the National Sleep Foundation by WB&A Market Research. Telephone interviews were conducted between September 19 and November 29, 2005, with a targeted random sample of 1,602 caregivers and, separately, their adolescent children ages 11–17 in grades 6–12. Using the targeted random sample, quotas were established by grade and race/ethnicity, with minority respondents being oversampled to reflect equal proportions of respondents by grade, as well as the actual distribution of race/ethnicity based on the U.S. census. The poll's margin of error is plus or minus 2.4%; the response rate for the survey was 27%.

Review Questions

1. What is the recommended amount of sleep for a teenager? What percentage of American teenagers get this much sleep? How knowledgeable are their parents about their sleep?

2. How much sleep debt do high school seniors typically accumulate in a week? Cite some of the consequences of getting insufficient sleep as a teenager, according to the poll results.

3. Why is a lack of sleep in the teenage years particularly harmful, according to experts?

4. What is a "phase delay" and how does it contribute to an adolescent's sleep debt?

5. What percentage of adolescents take regular naps? Optimally, how should naps be used? What is the recommended amount of daytime napping? What is the danger of especially long naps?

6. What is "rollercoaster" sleep and why is it not healthy?

7. How do consumer electronics affect adolescent sleep?

Discussion and Writing Suggestions

1. According to the survey results, once a week roughly one-quarter of high school students fall asleep in class, 22% fall asleep doing homework, and 14% are late to or miss school because of insufficient sleep. Are/were you one of these students? Do you know these students? Why are America's teenagers not getting sufficient sleep, in your view?

2. How does the amount and quality of your sleep compare to that of teenagers who responded to the National Sleep Foundation survey?

3. To what extent do you believe that consumer electronics in your bedroom (or dorm room) affect the quality of your sleep? How do you respond to the finding that with four or more such items, you are more likely to suffer a sleep deficit? Can you explain the correlation?

4. At the end of this article, the NSF offers several recommendations for helping adolescents get more sleep. How realistic do you find these recommendations? Cite some factors in the lives of active adolescents that make it problematic to get the recommended nine hours of sleep each night.

When Worlds Collide: Adolescent Need for Sleep Versus Societal Demands
Mary A. Carskadon

Consult the reference list of any scientific article on adolescent sleep, or type the words "adolescent" and "sleep" into any search engine, and the name "Mary Carskadon" will stand out, as if in relief. A professor of psychiatry and human behavior at Brown University School of Medicine and director of sleep and chronobiology research at E.P. Bradley Hospital in Rhode Island, Carskadon has authored widely cited, foundational studies on the sleep of adolescents. In the present selection, which first appeared as a chapter in Adolescent Sleep Needs and School Starting Times *(1999), Carskadon reviews the biological, behavioral, and social forces that converge to make getting an adequate night's sleep such a challenge for so many teenagers.*

1   Our understanding of the development of sleep patterns in adolescents has advanced considerably in the last 20 years. Along the way, theoretical models of the processes underlying the biological regulation of sleep have improved, and certain assumptions and dogmas have been examined and found wanting. Although the full characterization of teen sleep regulation remains to be accomplished, our current understanding poses a number of challenges for the education system.

2   The early 1970s found us with a growing awareness that sleep patterns change fundamentally at the transition to adolescence—a phenomenon that is widely acknowledged today. Survey studies clearly showed then and contin-

ue to show that the reported timing of sleep begins to shift in early adolescence, with bedtime and rising time both occurring at later hours. This delayed sleep pattern is particularly evident on nonschool nights and days, though the evening delay is obvious on school nights as well. Associated with the delay of sleep is a decline in the amount of sleep obtained and an increase in the discrepancy between school nights and weekend nights. Although the nonschool-night "oversleeping" was acknowledged as recovery from insufficient sleep during the school week, we initially assumed that the amount of sleep required declines with age. This was axiomatic: the older you are, the less sleep you need.

Assessing the Need for Sleep in the Second Decade

3   A longitudinal study begun in 1976 at the Stanford University summer sleep camp attempted to examine this axiom.[1] Boys and girls enrolled in this research project at ages 10, 11, or 12 and came to the lab for a 72-hour assessment each year for five or six years. They were asked to keep a fixed schedule, sleeping 10 hours a night for the week before the study, and their sleep was recorded on three consecutive nights from 10 p.m. to 8 a.m. Our hypothesis was that the reduced need for sleep in older children would manifest itself through less sleep within this 10-hour nocturnal window. This hypothesis was *not* confirmed. In fact, regardless of age or developmental stage, the children all slept about 9¼ of the 10 hours. Furthermore, delays in sleep resulted in a reduced likelihood of spontaneous waking before 8 a.m. for all but the youngest participants. One conclusion, therefore, was that the need for sleep does not change across adolescent development.

4   This study also showed an interesting pattern with respect to waking alertness, which was assessed using a technique called the Multiple Sleep Latency Test (MSLT). The MSLT measures the speed of falling asleep across repeated 20-minute trials in standard conditions. Thus a child who stays awake 20 minutes can be considered alert, faster sleep onsets are a sign of reduced alertness, and a child who falls asleep in five minutes or less is excessively sleepy.[2] The longitudinal study demonstrated that—even though the total amount of sleep was unchanged—alertness declined in association with pubertal development.[3] Figure 1 illustrates the MSLT patterns: under these experimental conditions, more mature adolescents showed signs of reduced alertness even though they slept an equivalent amount at night. One interpretation of these data is that older teenagers may need *more* sleep than when they were younger. On the other hand, the pattern of sleep tendency showing a midafternoon dip may reflect maturation of a regulated behavioral pattern favoring an afternoon nap or siesta.

Behavioral Factors

5   The principle that adolescents sleep later and less because of a panoply of psychosocial factors was also axiomatic during the 1970s and the 1980s. The evidence for this included a change in parental involvement in youngsters' sleep schedules as the children age. Thus, until about ages 11 or 12, more children than not reported that they woke spontaneously in the morning and that parents set their bedtimes. Fewer children in their early teens reported that parents

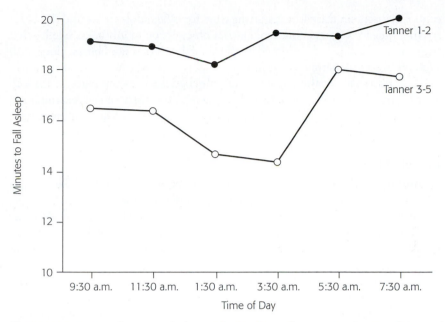

FIGURE 1   Developmetnal Change in Daytime Alertness Under Conditions of 'Optimal' Sleep*

The upper line, labeled Tanner 1-2, shows that pre- and early-pubescent boys and girls with a 10-hour sleep opportunity are not at all sleepy. The lower line, labeled Tanner 3-5, shows that more physically mature youngsters are sleepier, even though they have the same sleep opportunity.

still set their bedtimes, and most said that they required an alarm clock or a parent to assist them in waking up.[4]

6   Other behavioral factors contributing to the changing sleep patterns with age include increased social opportunities and growing academic demands. Another major contributor to changing adolescent sleep patterns is employment. One survey of youngsters in New England in the late 1980s found that two-thirds of high school students had jobs and that nearly 30% worked 20 or more hours in a typical school week.[5] Those high school students who worked 20 hours or more reported later bedtimes, shorter sleep times, more frequent episodes of falling asleep in school, and more frequent oversleeping and arriving late at school.

7   In addition to changing parental involvement, increasing school and social obligations, and greater participation in the work force, there are a myriad of other phenomena that have not been well explored. Access in the bedroom to computers, televisions, telephones, and so forth probably contributes to the delay of and reduction in sleep.

8   Another factor that has a major influence on adolescent sleep is the school schedule. The starting time of school puts limits on the time available for sleep. This is a nonnegotiable limit established largely without concern for sleep. Most

---

* The "Tanner Scale" measures sexual maturity. The higher the scale number, the more sexually mature the person.

school districts set the earliest starting time for older adolescents and the latest starting time for younger children. District officials commonly acknowledge that the school schedule is determined by the availability of school buses, along with such other factors as time of local sunrise, sports teams' schedules, and so forth. . . . [C]oncerns about the impact of school schedules on sleep patterns (as well as concerns about after-school teen delinquency) have sparked a reexamination in a number of districts. Our studies indicate that such a reexamination is merited by the difficulties many teenagers experience.

Biological Factors

9 As findings of the tendency for adolescent sleep patterns to be delayed were reported not only in North America but also in South America, Asia, Australia, and Europe, a sense arose that intrinsic developmental changes may also play a role in this phenomenon.[6] At the same time, conceptual models of the underlying internal mechanisms that control the length and timing of sleep began to take shape.

10 Current models posit three factors that control human sleep patterns. One of these factors is behavior and includes external factors such as those discussed above. The intrinsic factors have been called "sleep/wake homeostasis" and the "circadian timing system," or "process S" and "process C" in one model.[7] Sleep/wake homeostasis more simply stated is that sleep favors wake and wake favors sleep. All other things being equal, therefore, the longer one is awake, the greater the pressure for sleep to occur. Conversely, the closer one is to having slept, the less pressure there is to sleep. This process accounts for the increased need for sleep after staying awake all night and the difficulty of staying awake in general when faced with a chronic pattern of insufficient sleep. Process S can be examined using measures of sleep tendency, such as the MSLT, or measures of EEG (electroencephalogram) slow wave activity (SWA) during sleep. Sleep tendency and SWA increase with insufficient sleep. Both factors also show changes across adolescent development that may be related to the timing of sleep.

11 Under conditions of optimal sleep, such as those described in the longitudinal study of sleep, slow wave sleep declines by 40% from early to late adolescence. This decline may indicate a reduced pressure for sleep with greater maturation. One interpretation of this finding is that the reduced pressure for sleep makes staying up late an easier task for older adolescents. Others have interpreted this finding as marking a structural change in the brain (thinning of cortical synaptic density) that is unrelated to sleep/wake homeostasis. The change in sleep tendency—that is, the appearance of a midday trough at midpuberty (Figure 1)—may indicate a reorganization of the sleep/wake homeostatic mechanism to favor daytime napping and an extended late-day waking period, again favoring a later bedtime. These hypotheses are speculative and require additional study.

12 Much of the contemporary excitement about adolescent sleep comes from studies of the circadian timing mechanism, which independently and interactively exerts influences on sleep through processes that favor or inhibit sleep according to the dictates of an internal biological "clock." Several features of

the human circadian timing system and its interactions with sleep and wake-fulness are relevant here.

- Circadian rhythms are biological oscillations with periods of about 24 hours.
- Circadian rhythms are synchronized to the 24-hour day chiefly by light signals.
- The chief circadian oscillator in mammals is located deep within the brain in the suprachiasmatic nuclei (SCN) of the hypothalamus.
- Circadian rhythms can be assessed by measuring the timing of biological events. . . .
- Circadian rhythms control the timing of REM (rapid eye movement) sleep within the sleep period.

13   A first attempt to examine whether the circadian timing system undergoes developmental changes during adolescent maturation involved a survey of sixth-grade girls. In this survey, one series of questions allowed us to estimate physical development and another series gave a measure of circadian phase preference. Phase preference refers to an individual's tendency to favor activities in the morning or evening, i.e., morningness/eveningness. In these 275 sixth-grade girls, the puberty score and circadian phase preference score showed a significant relationship: less mature girls favored earlier hours, and more mature girls favored later hours.[8] These data were the first to implicate a biological process in the later timing of adolescent sleep.

· · ·

14   One other important finding from our studies is that the circadian timing system can be reset if light exposure is carefully controlled. In many of our studies, we require adolescents to keep a specific sleep schedule (for example, 10 p.m. to 8 a.m.) and to wear eyeshades to exclude light during these hours. In fact, we pay adolescents to keep this schedule! When we measure melatonin secretion* before the students go on the new schedule (when they are still on their self-selected routine) and again after 10 or 11 nights on the new schedule, we find that the melatonin secretion has moved significantly toward a common time: those who were early melatonin secretors move to a later time, and those who were late secretors move to a later time, and those who were late secretors move earlier.[9] Thus we know that the system is not immutable; with time, effort, *and* money, we can get adolescents to realign their rhythms!

15   Let us summarize what we now know about the developmental trends in adolescent sleep behavior and adolescents' sleep/wake and circadian systems.

- As they mature, adolescents tend to go to bed later and to wake up later (given the opportunity).
- Adolescents also tend to sleep less as they mature.

---

* [O]ne of the best ways to identify time in the intrinsic biological clock in humans is to examine melatonin secretion. Melatonin is a hormone that is produced by the pineal gland and regulated by the circadian timing system. Melatonin secretion occurs during nocturnal hours in both day-active species, like humans, and night-active species. Melatonin can be measured from saliva samples collected in dim lighting conditions.

- The difference between the amount and timing of sleep on weekend nights versus school nights grows during adolescence.
- These trends are apparent in adolescents both in North America and in industrialized countries on other continents.
- Sleep requirements do not decline during adolescent development.
- Daytime sleep tendency is augmented during puberty.
- The timing of events controlled by the circadian timing system is delayed during puberty.

16   We propose that the delay of sleep during adolescent development is favored by behavioral and intrinsic processes and that the reduction of sleep experienced by adolescents is largely driven by a collision between the intrinsic processes and the expectations and demands of the adult world. The study described in the following section illustrates this point.

School Transition Project

17   Our school transition project took a look at what happened to sleep and circadian rhythms in a group of youngsters for whom the transition from junior high school to senior high school required a change in the starting time for school from 8:25 a.m. to 7:20 a.m. Twenty-five youngsters completed our study at two time points, in the spring of the ninth grade and in the autumn of the 10th grade.[10] These boys and girls were all well beyond the beginning changes of puberty; some were physically mature. They were enrolled in the study with instructions simply to keep their usual schedules, to wear small activity monitors on their wrists, and to keep diaries of their activities and sleep schedule for two consecutive weeks. At the end of the two weeks, participants came to the sleep laboratory for assessment of the onset phase of melatonin secretion, overnight sleep study, and daytime testing with the MSLT. The laboratory sleep schedule was fixed to each student's average school-night schedule based on the data from the wrist monitor (actigraph).

18   As predicted, the actigraph data showed that students woke up earlier when confronted with the 7:20 a.m. start time, although rising time was on average only about 25 minutes earlier (6:26 a.m. to 6:01 a.m.), not the 65 minutes represented by the school schedule change. Sleep onset times did not change, averaging about 10:40 p.m. in both grades. The average amount of sleep on school nights fell from seven hours and nine minutes to six hours and 50 minutes, a statistically significant amount and probably a meaningful amount when considered as producing an ever cumulating sleep deficit.

19   The amount of sleep these students obtained in ninth grade was below the amount we feel is required for optimal alertness, and the further decline in 10th grade had added impact. One way to examine the impact is to look at the MSLT data from tests that occurred at 9:30 a.m., 10:30 a.m., 12:30 p.m., and 2:30 p.m. If we look at comparable MSLT data from Figure 1, we find an average score of 18.9 minutes for the early pubertal children and 15.5 minutes for the mid- to late pubertal adolescents sleeping on the optimizing 10-hour schedule. The ninth-grade students in this more naturalistic study, by contrast, had an average MSLT speed of falling asleep of 11.4 minutes, and in 10th grade the sleep score

was 8.5 minutes. In clinical terms, these students were in a borderline zone for daytime sleepiness, well below the alert range and below the "normal" range, yet not in the "pathological" range.

20   A closer look at the MSLT test results shows that the students in 10th grade were in the pathological range when tested at 8:30 a.m. (MSLT score = 5.1 minutes). Furthermore, nearly 50% of these 10th-graders showed a reversed sleep pattern on the morning MSLT tests that is similar to the pattern seen in patients with the sleep disorder called narcolepsy—that is, REM sleep occurs before non-REM sleep. The 12 students who showed this "narcoleptic" pattern fell asleep in an average of 3.4 minutes when tested at 8:30 a.m. These students did not have narcolepsy; what they did have was a significant mismatch between their circadian rhythms and the necessity to get up and go to school. The evidence for this mismatch was a later time for the onset of melatonin secretion compared with those who did not have the "narcoleptic" pattern: 9:46 p.m. versus 8:36 p.m. This marker of the circadian timing system indicates that 1) the students' natural time to fall asleep is about 11 p.m. or later (on average) and 2) the abnormally short time to sleep onset on the 8:30 a.m. MSLT and the abnormal occurrence of REM sleep took place because the students were tested at the very nadir of their circadian day. In other words, at 8:30 a.m., these students' brains were far better suited to be asleep than awake!

21   Why were these 12 students so different from the others? We were unable to identify a specific cause. None of the 25 students made an optimal adjustment to the new schedule; none was sleeping even as much as 8¼ hours on school nights, a value we suggest elsewhere might be adequate if not optimal for high school students.[11] A few students maintained a "normal" level of alertness, others were borderline, and still others were in the pathological range. The 12 students whose circadian timing systems moved to a much later timing in 10th grade, however, showed signs associated with marked impairment, particularly in the morning hours.

Consequences, Concerns, and Countermeasures

22   Among the known consequences of insufficient sleep are memory lapses, attentional deficits, depressed mood, and slowed reaction time. Sleep deprivation studies have shown that divergent thinking suffers with inadequate sleep. A few surveys have noted poorer grades in students with inadequate sleep. Many important issues have not yet been well studied. For example, little is known about the consequences of insufficient sleep for relationship formation and maintenance, emotion regulation, delinquency, drug use, and violent behavior. Long-term consequences of insufficient sleep—particularly at critical developmental stages—are utterly unknown.

23   The problem of inadequate sleep affects more segments of our society than adolescents; however, adolescents appear to be particularly vulnerable and face difficult challenges for obtaining sufficient sleep. Even without the pressure of biological changes, if we combine an early school starting time—say 7:30 a.m., which, with a modest commute, makes 6:15 a.m. a viable rising time—with our knowledge that optimal sleep need is 9¼ hours, we are asking that 16-year-olds

go to bed at 9 p.m. Rare is the teenager of the 1990s who will keep such a schedule. School work, sports practices, clubs, volunteer work, and paid employment take precedence. When biological changes are factored in, the ability even to have merely "adequate" sleep is lost. As a consequence, sleepy teens demand that parents provide an extreme form of reveille, challenge teachers to offer maximal classroom entertainment and creativity just to keep them awake, and suffer the consequences of disaffection from school and dissatisfaction with themselves.

24   Can these problems be solved by delaying the starting time for school as adolescents move into the pubertal years? Not entirely. Moving the opening bell to a later time may help many teens with the mismatch between biological time and scholastic time, but it will not provide more hours in the day. It is not difficult to project that a large number of students see a later starting time as permission to stay up later at night studying, working, surfing the net, watching television, and so forth. Today's teens know little about their sleep needs or about the biological timing system. Interestingly, students do know they are sleepy, but they do not have skills to cope with the issue, and many assume— just as adults do—that they are expected to function with an inadequate amount of sleep. This assumption is a physiological fallacy: sleep is not optional. Sleep is biologically obligatory. If students learn about sleep, they have a basis to use a changed school starting time to best advantage. Adding information about sleep to the school curriculum can certainly help.

25   As with other fields of scientific investigation, the knowledge base, the scientific opportunities, and the level of pure excitement in sleep and biological rhythms research have never been greater. This knowledge and excitement can be shared with students at every academic level. Furthermore, sleep and biological rhythms are natural gateways to learning because students are drawn to the topics. Thus, as grammar school students learn about the nutrition pyramid, so too could they learn about the body's sleep requirements and how the biological timing system makes humans day-active rather than night-active. (Did you know that, if you put your hamster in a box with lights that turn on at night and off in the daytime, it will start running on its wheel during the day?)

26   As middle school students are learning about comparative biology, they can be sharing in the excitement of where, when, and how animals sleep. (Did you know that certain dolphins can be half asleep . . . literally? One half of the brain sleeps while the other half is awake! Did you know that mammals stop regulating body temperature in REM sleep? Did you know that you are paralyzed in REM sleep?)

27   High school students can share the excitement in the discoveries about genes that control the biological clock, about the brain mechanisms that control dreaming, about the way sleep creates breathing problems, and about sleep disorders that may affect their family members. (Did you know that snoring may be a sign of a serious sleep disorder afflicting as many as 5% of adults? Did you know that some people act out their dreams at night? Did you know that genes controlling the biological clock in mice and fruit flies are nearly identical?)

Challenges and an Opportunity

28 The challenges are great, and solutions do not come easily. School scheduling is incredibly complex, and accounting for youngsters' sleep needs and biological propensities adds to the complexity. Yet we cannot assume that the system is immutable. Given that the primary focus of education is to maximize human potential, then a new task before us is to ensure that the conditions in which learning takes place address the very biology of our learners.

Notes

1. Mary A. Carskadon, "Determinants of Daytime Sleepiness: Adolescent Development, Extended and Restricted Nocturnal Sleep" (Doctoral dissertation, Stanford University, 1979); idem, "The Second Decade," in Christian Guilleminault, ed., *Sleeping and Waking Disorders: Indications and Techniques* (Menlo Park, Calif.: Addison Wesley, 1982), pp. 99–125; and Mary A. Carskadon, E. John Orav, and William C. Dement, "Evolution of Sleep and Daytime Sleepiness in Adolescents," in Christian Guilleminault and Elio Lugaresi, eds., *Sleep/Wake Disorders: Natural History, Epidemiology, and Long-Term Evolution* (New York: Raven Press, 1983), pp. 201–16.

2. Mary A. Carskadon and William C. Dement, "The Multiple Sleep Latency Test: What Does It Measure?" *Sleep*, vol. 5, 1982, pp. 67–72.

3. Mary A. Carskadon et al., "Pubertal Changes in Daytime Sleepiness," *Sleep*, vol. 2, 1980, pp. 453–60.

4. Carskadon, "Determinants of Daytime Sleepiness."

5. Mary A. Carskadon, "Patterns of Sleep and Sleepiness in Adolescents," *Pediatrician*, vol. 17, 1990, pp. 5–12.

6. Mirian M. M. Andrade and Luiz Menna-Barreto, "Sleep Patterns of High School Students Living in São Paulo, Brazil," in Mary A. Carskadon, ed., *Adolescent Sleep Patterns: Biological, Social, and Psychological Influences* (New York: Cambridge University Press, forthcoming); Kaneyoshi Ishihara, Yukako Honma, and Susumu Miyake, "Investigation of the Children's Version of the Morningness-Eveningness Questionnaire with Primary and Junior High School Pupils in Japan," *Perceptual and Motor Skills*, vol. 71, 1990, pp. 1353–54; Helen M. Bearpark and Patricia T. Michie, "Prevalence of Sleep/Wake Disturbances in Sidney Adolescents," *Sleep Research*, vol. 16, 1987, p. 304; and Inge Strauch and Barbara Meier, "Sleep Need in Adolescents: A Longitudinal Approach," *Sleep*, vol. 11, 1988, pp. 378–86.

7. Alexander A. Borbély, "A Two Process Model of Sleep Regulation," *Human Neurobiology*, vol. 1, 1982, pp. 195–204.

8. Mary A. Carskadon, Cecilia Vieira, and Christine Acebo, "Association Between Puberty and Delayed Phase Preference," *Sleep*, vol. 16, 1993, pp. 258–62.

9. Carskadon et al., "An Approach to Studying Circadian Rhythms."

10. Mary A. Carskadon et al., "Adolescent Sleep Patterns, Circadian Timing, and Sleepiness at a Transition to Early School Days," *Sleep*, in press.

11. Amy R. Wolfson and Mary A. Carskadon, "Sleep Schedules and Daytime Functioning in Adolescents," *Child Development*, vol. 69, 1998, pp. 875–87.

Review Questions

1. What fundamental shift in sleep patterns occurs in the transition to adolescence, and what problems does this shift cause?

2. What did investigators discover when they examined the "axiom" that "the older you are, the less sleep you need"?

3. What behavioral and social factors can affect adolescent sleep?

4. Carskadon presents two "conceptual models of the underlying internal mechanisms that control the length and timing of sleep." What are they and how can they be measured?

5. What, exactly, are the colliding worlds of Carskadon's title?

Discussion and Writing Suggestions

1. Carskadon describes the results of a study measuring the sleepiness of students transitioning to high school (see paragraphs 17–21). For the 12 students who "were far better suited to be asleep than awake," the typical school start time of 8:30 a.m. represented "the very nadir of their circadian day." In a paragraph of (vivid) description, corroborate this insight from personal experience.

2. Is there any sense in which you feel vindicated in your early morning sleepiness by Carskadon's article? Throughout adolescence, adults may have blamed your sleepiness on character flaws—laziness, perhaps. Does the science behind Carskadon's article help you to feel any better about yourself? Write a letter to one such adult accuser explaining why you were not a lazy-good-for-nothing after all!

3. In matters relating to sleepiness/wakefulness, in what ways has your world "collided" with the world of "societal demands"? Collisions often produce casualties. Have there been casualties in your case?

4. Carskadon calls our attention to the problems adolescents may face when their sleep schedules conflict with the scheduling demands of the broader world. She points, as well, to the seemingly intractable causes of this conflict. (See especially paragraphs 22–23.) What do you think of her proposals to minimize, if not avoid, this conflict? Can you offer any proposals of your own?

Sleep Debt and the Mortgaged Mind
William C. Dement and Christopher Vaughan

William Dement, MD, PhD, is one of the founders of modern sleep medicine, universally acknowledged as a pioneer (along with Mary Carskadon, whose work appears earlier in this chapter). A professor and researcher at Stanford University, Dement has authored numerous articles, books, and book chapters on sleep. His particular interest has been the topic of sleep "debt," the focus of the following selection, which appeared originally as a chapter in The Promise of Sleep *(1999), cowritten with Christopher Vaughan.*

1   The night of March 24, 1989, was cold and calm, the air crystalline, as the giant *Exxon Valdez* oil tanker pulled out of Valdez, Alaska, into the tranquil waters of Prince William Sound. In these clearest of possible conditions the ship made a planned turn out of the shipping channel and didn't turn back in time. The huge tanker ran aground, spilling millions of gallons of crude oil into the sound. The cost of the cleanup effort was over $2 billion. The ultimate cost of continuing environmental damage is incalculable. Furthermore, when the civil trial was finally over in the summer of 1995, the Exxon Corporation was assessed an additional $5 billion in punitive damages. Everyone I query in my travels vividly recalls the accident, and most have the impression that it had something to do with the master's alcohol consumption. No one is aware of the true cause of the tragedy. In its final report, the National Transportation Safety Board (NTSB) found that sleep deprivation and sleep debt were direct causes of the accident. This stunning result got a brief mention in the back pages of the newspapers.

2   Out of the vast ocean of knowledge about sleep, there are a few facts that are so important that I will try to burn them into your brain forever. None is more important than the topic of sleep debt. If we can learn to understand sleep indebtedness and manage it, we can improve everyday life as well as avoid many injuries, horribly diminished lives, and premature deaths.

3   The *Exxon Valdez* disaster offers a good example of how sleep debt can create a tragedy and how the true villain—sleep indebtedness—remains concealed. I am sure that I was just as shocked as anyone when I learned about America's worst oil spill. The TV coverage of the dead birds and seals filled me with outrage over the environmental devastation. One of my friends went to Alaska and participated in the cleanup. He brought back photos and a big jar of crude oil. If you haven't been exposed to crude oil, keep away from it. It isn't the purified stuff that goes into your car. It's awful. It stinks to high heaven. You want to vomit.

4   I was among the millions who were following the news, but I had no idea that it would have a special meaning for me a year later. The National Commission on Sleep Disorders Research finally mandated by Congress was convened for the first time in March 1990, and 20 commissioners were assembled in Washington, D.C. After the first meeting I decided to visit a friend, Dr. John Lauber, who had been confirmed by the Senate as one of five members of the National Transportation Safety Board. He told me that the board would very likely identify sleep deprivation as the "direct cause" of the grounding of the *Exxon Valdez*.

5   I had worked with John a few years earlier on a study of the layover sleep of pilots on intercontinental airlines. He was head of human factors research at NASA-Ames and at the beginning of the layover study knew little about "sleep debt." At the end of the study, he was one of the few real experts in the world. Two months after the visit with John he sent me the NTSB's final report.

6   The report noted that on the March night when the *Exxon Valdez* steamed out of Valdez there were ice floes across part of the shipping lane, forcing the ship to turn to avoid them. The captain determined that this maneuver could be done safely if the ship was steered back to the main channel when it was abeam of a well-known landmark, Busby Island. With this plan established, he turned over command to the third mate and left the bridge. Although news reports linked much of what happened next to the captain's alcohol consumption, the captain was off the bridge well before the accident. The direct cause of America's worst oil spill was the behavior of the third mate, who had slept only 6 hours in the previous 48 and was severely sleep deprived.

7   As the *Exxon Valdez* passed Busby Island, the third mate ordered the helm to starboard, but he didn't notice that the autopilot was still on and the ship did not turn. Instead it plowed farther out of the channel. Twice lookouts warned the third mate about the position of lights marking the reef, but he didn't change or check his previous orders. His brain was not interpreting the danger in what they said. Finally he noticed that he was far outside the channel, turned off the autopilot, and tried hard to get the great ship pointed back to safety—too late.

8   For several years I would ask every audience that I addressed if there was anyone in the audience who had not heard the words "*Exxon Valdez*." A hand was never raised. Then I would say, "Who knows what caused the grounding?" Many hands would be raised, and the answer would always be "alcohol." Thus I could never exploit the potential impact of this catastrophe in getting knowledge about sleep into the mainstream, because of the media emphasis on the captain's drinking. When the report finally came out, there was no real interest. Even at the trial, in the summer of 1995, the true cause of the accident received little attention. What everyone ought to be talking about is how to deal with sleep deprivation and how to avoid it in the transportation industry and throughout all components of society, saying over and over again "Look what it caused." But instead, the poor captain has been hounded for nearly a decade.

9   An even more dramatic tragedy was the explosion of the space shuttle *Challenger*. After a year-long investigation, the Rogers Commission declared that in the absence of adequate data on O-ring function at low temperatures the decision to launch the rocket was an error. Those of us who saw this catastrophic event on television over and over and over know the ghastly consequences of that error. But not well known at all is the fact that the Human Factors Subcommittee attributed the error to the severe sleep deprivation of the NASA managers. This conclusion was only included in the committee's final report, which only noted that top managers in such situations are generally the ones who sacrifice the most sleep.

10   Was this the most costly case of sleepiness in history? The parents of any teenager who has died while asleep at the wheel might not agree. Even the most careful drivers are at risk, because we simply do not tell people—not even young

people in the driver-training courses required in many states—how to recognize signs of dangerous sleepiness.

11   Of course, even children are at risk. For example in the past several years I have received many reports of school bus accidents where the driver fell asleep. Unfortunately, it may take another *Exxon Valdez* or *Challenger* before the sleep community can mobilize public opinion to do something about this issue. Thus, I find myself in the bizarre circumstance of simultaneously fearing and at the same time hoping for another highly visible disaster.

12   Just last year I stepped up to the podium to make the danger absolutely clear to my Stanford students. Drowsiness, that feeling when the eyelids are trying to close and we cannot seem to keep them open, is the last step before we fall asleep, not the first. If at this moment we let sleep come, it will arrive instantly. When driving a car, or in any hazardous situation, the first wave of drowsiness should be a dramatic warning. Get out of harm's way instantly! My message to the students is "Drowsiness is red alert!" I delivered and explained this message over and over in my 1997 undergraduate course "Sleep and Dreams," and the students got it. I am confident few will ever drive while drowsy.

13   Everyone can recall a jolt of heart-stopping panic in the face of peril—when we realize a cab seems about to jump the curb we're standing on, or when we lose track of a child in a crowd. The response is instantaneous. We act. We should have a similar response the instant we feel drowsy at the wheel.

Ignorance About Sleepiness

14   . . . I now think of the continuum of sleepiness and alertness as the state upon which all human behavior is acted out. Today we can claim with confidence that where we are on this continuum, from the high peak of optimal alertness to the deep trough of extreme drowsiness, is the single most important determinant of how well we perform. Accordingly, the total absence of this subject from psychology textbooks or any other educational materials is incomprehensible. Although the scientific knowledge has been available for more than two decades, students are still not acquiring crucial knowledge about sleepiness, sleep debt, and sleep deprivation in any of our educational institutions. . . .

15   The feeling of being tired and needing sleep is a basic drive of nature, like hunger. If you don't eat enough, you are driven to eat. If you go long enough without food, you can think of nothing else. Once you get food, you eat until you feel full and then you stop. Thus, the subjective responses of hunger and satiation ensure that you fulfill your overall daily requirement for calories. In essentially the same way, your sleep drive keeps an exact tally of accumulated waking hours. Like bricks in a backpack, accumulated sleep drive is a burden that weighs down on you. Every hour that you are awake adds another brick to the backpack: The brain's sleep load increases until you go to sleep, when the load starts to lighten.

16   In a very real sense all wakefulness is sleep deprivation. As soon as you wake up, the meter starts ticking, calculating how many hours of sleep you will need to pay off that night. Or, to continue the load metaphor, it tallies how many bricks you will have to shed to get back to zero. Generally people need to sleep one hour for every two hours awake, which means that most need around eight

hours of sleep a night. Of course, some people need more and some need less, and a few people seem to need a great deal more or less. From the work we have done, we must conclude that each person has his or her own specific daily sleep requirement. The brain tries to hit this mark, and the further you are from getting the number of hours of sleep you need, the harder your brain tries to force you to get that sleep.

. . .

Sleep Debt: Nature's Loan Shark

17 . . . The brain keeps an exact accounting of how much sleep it is owed. In our first study, we restricted the sleep of 10 volunteers to exactly 5 hours each night for 7 nights and observed that the tendency to fall asleep increased progressively each successive day. For the first time in the history of sleep research, we discovered that the effect of each successive night of partial sleep loss carried over, and the effect appeared to accumulate in a precisely additive fashion. In other words, the strength of the tendency to fall asleep was progressively greater during each successive day with exactly the same amount of sleep each night. For some time Mary [Carskadon] and I referred to this as an increased sleep tendency, and it was clear that the increase did not dissipate without additional rest. How people recover from various levels of sleep deprivation after getting sleep has not been well studied. However, current evidence suggests that the accumulated lost sleep must be paid back at some time, perhaps even hour for hour.

18 We use the term "sleep debt" because accumulated lost sleep is like a monetary debt: It must be paid back. Regardless of how rapidly it can be paid back, the important thing is that the size of the sleep debt and its dangerous effects are definitely directly related to the amount of lost sleep. My guess is that after a period of substantial sleep loss, we can pay back a little and feel a lot better, although the remaining sleep debt is still large. The danger of an unintended sleep episode is still there. Until proven otherwise, it is reasonable and certainly safer to assume that accumulated lost sleep must be paid back hour for hour. Therefore, if you miss 3 hours one night, you must sleep 11 hours the next night (3 plus your normal 8) in order to feel alert throughout the day.

19 Your sleep debt may have accumulated in small increments over many days. For example, during a five-day work week where you needed 8 hours each night and instead got 6, you would build up a sleep debt of 10 hours (5 times 2). From this perspective, sleeping in until noon on Saturday is not enough to pay back the 10 lost hours plus your nightly requirement of 8; you would have to sleep until about 5:00 P.M. to balance the sleep ledger. Of course, most people won't sleep that long, and in fact it is difficult to do because of the alerting process of the biological clock. . . . More likely, you will sleep in an extra hour or two and get up feeling better. But the debt is still there, demanding to be paid. Later that day you'll start feeling the effects of the sleep debt again. And if you borrow more sleep time over subsequent nights, you won't just stay sleepy, you'll get even sleepier. As your debt grows, your energy, mood, and cognition will be undermined.

20   There is another important way that sleep deprivation can occur and sleep debt can accumulate. . . . [S]everal sleep disorders are characterized by very severe and impairing daytime sleepiness. In such patients we typically see hundreds of brief interruptions of sleep in a single night. In spite of this, careful tabulation of the intervening short periods of sleep can add up to what ought to be a satisfactory amount of total sleep.

21   Several groups of sleep researchers have carried out studies on normal volunteers which have clarified this situation. In these studies, subjects were awakened every minute or so throughout entire nights, and the next day's alertness was evaluated using the [Multiple Sleep Latency Test, which measures sleepiness, the speed with which subjects fall asleep]. The nocturnal awakenings were brief, 5 to 10 seconds, and subjects usually returned to sleep immediately. Although there were usually several hundred interruptions, the cumulative total sleep can add up to normal amounts. Nevertheless, daytime sleepiness is markedly increased, as if there had been no sleep at all, or very little.

22   Interrupting sleep every minute or so all night long is a heroic experimental manipulation. I am happy to report that the results of these particular experiments have been very consistent. Accordingly, we may conclude that the restorative value of sleep is severely curtailed if sleep periods are not allowed to continue for at least several minutes. If 10 to 15 minutes of sleep are allowed to occur before an interruption, this effect is greatly lessened. These studies have led to the concept that there are minimal units of restorative sleep. In other words, it is as if the bank that keeps track of sleep debt doesn't accept small deposits.

23   In one of our first studies we evaluated the clinical usefulness of the MSLT by comparing narcoleptics and normal sleepers. The results were fabulous. The MSLT sharply distinguished patients and normals. However, the MSLT scores of a few normal volunteers were in the pathologically sleepy range (1 to 5 minutes). This latter group tended to be college students. For a while we thought that these younger "normals" were in the early stages of the narcoleptic sleep disorder, not yet manifesting the other symptoms. But it was hard to imagine why Stanford University would attract so many budding narcoleptics. We tested a few more students, allowing a baseline normal amount of sleep (8 hours a day) and carefully measuring their sleep tendency day to day with the MSLT. Nearly all of the students appeared to be pathologically sleepy! I should not have been so surprised, because I have been watching students fall asleep in class ever since I was a college student myself.

24   The obvious explanation finally occurred to Mary and me: The students needed more sleep. To prove this we did studies where we extended their nightly hours in bed to 10, and over several days, the MSLT score steadily improved. Now that we know about sleep debt, we can only imagine how many thousands of observations on human behavior have been made over the decades on chronically sleep-deprived subjects whom researchers thought were "normal." Since people are so severely affected by a large sleep debt, its presence can potentially alter the results of almost all research measures, from I.Q. tests to observations of drug side effects. The baseline studies of all human research, regardless of their

nature, now must include measures of daytime sleep tendency, so that the variable degree of chronic sleep loss does not contaminate every study.

25   Despite the fact that "sleep debt" has entered common parlance (some researchers also call it "sleep load" or "sleep tendency"), many people don't fully understand the concept. Again and again I hear people complain that they sleep a full night, even an extra hour or so, and still feel just as sleepy or even sleepier than before. "Well," they think, "I must be sleepy because I am sleeping too much." The fact is that you don't work off a large sleep debt, which is what most of us have, by getting one good night's sleep.

· · ·

Driving Under the Influence of Sleep Debt

26 People *must* learn to pay attention to their own sleep debt and how it is affecting them. Not doing so, and misunderstanding the rules of sleep debt and arousal, can be extremely dangerous. A friend of mine, also a Stanford professor, once participated in a bicycle race that lasted several days and included a number of laps around Lake Tahoe. He got very little sleep at night during the period of the race, but then he slept about nine hours a night for the two nights he stayed at the lake after the race. He woke up on Sunday morning feeling rested, ready to pack up and drive home. But as he was coming down the winding mountain road he began to yawn and his eyelids felt heavy. He told me that he was a little surprised because he thought he had gotten plenty of sleep. If someone had been with him, he probably would have traded places, but it did not occur to him to pull over and take a nap. As he drove on, it became harder and harder to keep his eyes open, and he began to be concerned. At that moment he saw a sign for a restaurant only several miles farther down the road. "Good," he thought, "I'll be able to get some coffee." Right after that he fell asleep, just for a moment, and awoke with a terrible start to find that he had drifted into the oncoming lane. He jerked the wheel to the right, but the road curved to the left, and the car went over a 30-foot ledge. The next thing he knew he was upside down, suspended by his seat belt, the car impaled on a jagged rock that had sliced through the roof and into the empty passenger seat next to him. He sustained serious cuts and bruises, and his right arm was completely paralyzed, but miraculously he was alive.

27   When he told me the story later, he still didn't understand how he could have been so sleepy. "But Bill, I got two full nights of sleep before I left Tahoe." Not knowing about sleep debt, he could not know that a few hours of extra sleep does not alleviate the sleep debt accumulated over the preceding nights or weeks. He was driving alone without the stimulation of conversation, along a route he knew fairly well. In short, there was little to act as a dike against the sea of sleep debt that he had built up. Ironically, his awareness of how terribly drowsy he was feeling may have forestalled sleep in the minutes before the crash. When he saw the sign for the restaurant up ahead and knew that he would soon get coffee, he relaxed and let that worry go. A few moments later he was hurtling off the mountain road. If the idea that drowsiness is supremely dangerous had been burned into his brain, he would have stopped driving no matter how difficult or inconvenient.

Fatal Fatigue: Alcohol and Sleep Debt

28 . . . [O]lder children never feel sleepy during the day. They were the only group we studied in the Stanford Summer Sleep Camp who never fell asleep in the 20 minutes allotted for the individual sleep latency tests. And of course, children are usually not sleep deprived. Putting all our results together, we can state with confidence that if you feel sleepy or drowsy in the daytime, then you must have a sizable sleep debt. Sleep debt is the physical side of the coin, and the feelings of sleepiness or drowsiness are the psychological side. As an analogy, dehydration is the physical side of the coin and the feeling of being thirsty is the psychological side. To carry the analogy a little further, if we have thoroughly quenched our thirst, we cannot immediately feel thirsty. But if we are becoming dehydrated, the desire to drink may be diminished if we are involved in something very interesting or demanding. At some point, of course, thirst becomes overwhelming. Likewise, we cannot feel sleepy in the daytime if we do not have a sleep debt, but we may not feel sleepy if we are doing something that excites us. If we have a very strong tendency to fall asleep and we reduce the stimuli that are keeping us awake, we will very soon begin to feel sleepy and will inevitably fall asleep, intentionally or otherwise.

29   But all those interested in traffic safety and all those who wish to have a long life as well must take note. When a crash is attributed to alcohol, the real culprit, or at least a coconspirator, is often sleep deprivation. In studies that are second to none in importance, the powerful interaction between sleep and alcohol was revealed by the outstanding sleep research team at Henry Ford Hospital Sleep Disorders Center. A group of volunteers slept 10 hours a night for one week, 8 hours a night during a separate week, and on a third schedule simulated a social weekend by getting 5 hours of sleep for 2 nights. In the morning after completing each schedule, all of the volunteers were given either a low dose of alcohol or a placebo. Then their degree of impaired alertness was evaluated utilizing the MSLT and performance tests. When the subjects were given the low dose of alcohol after the 8-hour schedule, they became slightly more sleepy than when given placebo. After the schedule of 2 nights with little sleep, the exact same dose of alcohol the next morning made them severely sleepy, barely able to stay awake. However, the exact same dose of alcohol after 10 hours of sleep every night for a week had no discernible effect. In other words, alcohol may not be a potent sedative by itself, but it becomes very sedating when paired with sleep debt. It is tempting to speculate that all sedatives, particularly sleeping pills, interact with sleep debt. This area deserves much more research. . . .

30   The implications of this are far-reaching. People are well aware of the dangers of drinking and driving, but they don't know that a large sleep debt and even a small amount of alcohol can create a "fatal fatigue." People can be just fine driving after a single drink one day (when they have little sleep debt), yet be a hazard to themselves and others if they have that same drink on a day in which they have a large sleep debt. A fact little known by the public at large is that in nearly every accident linked to alcohol consumption, sleep debt almost certainly plays a major role.

31   In one state traffic agency, researchers are trying very hard to understand traffic accidents designated as alcohol related even though the alcohol in the tissue is far below any level thought to be impairing.

. . .

32   [E]xperiments demonstrate that individuals thought to be completely normal can be carrying a sizable sleep debt, which impairs their mood, energy, and performance. If you haven't already done so, I think it's worthwhile to ask yourself how your sleep debt is affecting you. How often do you think about taking a quick snooze? How often do you rub your eyes and yawn during the day? How often do you feel like you really need some coffee? Each of these is a warning of a sleep debt that you ignore at your peril. I can't overemphasize the dangers of unintended sleep episodes or severe drowsiness. I hope this information can save your life.

33   I know that people often are driven to stay up late and get up early, that the demands of modern life push us to stay up past our biological bedtime. But I also know it's not too onerous to avoid accumulating sleep debt. . . . Studies suggest the likelihood that people can avoid dangerously high sleep debt by adding a relatively small amount of sleep to their normal sleep schedule. People who have lowered their sleep debt usually report that they gain a new sense of well-being. That may just mean not watching the news at night, or putting off some other nonessential pleasure, like the bedtime crossword puzzle. I bet most people would give up many late-night diversions if they could feel truly awake throughout the day—fresh and full of hope, senses wide open, the mind receptive to people and ideas.

Review Questions

1. What was the actual, though little reported, cause of the *Exxon Valdez* disaster?
2. Dement asserts that "Drowsiness is red alert!" What does he mean?
3. What is the "continuum of sleepiness and alertness"? What is its significance?
4. How is sleeping like eating and drinking?
5. What is sleep debt? How is it "carried over"? How is the amount of sleep debt correlated with the dangers posed by sleep debt?
6. Why may a person feel sleepy even after getting a full night's sleep?
7. In what way is sleep debt often a "co-conspirator" in alcohol-related crashes?

Discussion and Writing Suggestions

1. Consider your own sleep habits. Given what you've read in this article, are you currently sleep deprived? Have you ever been? Have you ever noticed in your daily performance of a task the kinds of impairments due to sleep debt that Dement discusses?

2. In the title and throughout the article, Dement uses a metaphor from the banking industry—mortgage—to discuss sleep debt. (This term is sometimes useful to politicians and social commentators—who speak of "mortgaging" our future.) Cite several instances of the use of this metaphor and comment on its effectiveness. To what extent does the metaphor help to convey Dement's central message? In your answer, discuss how a mind can be "mortgaged."

3. Have you ever experienced the sensation of driving drowsy—which Dement says should be a "red alert" to stop your car and rest? In a paragraph, describe the scene: the sensation of drowsiness, the conversation you have with yourself to stay awake, the efforts to fight off sleep (e.g., turning on the radio, opening a window, slapping your face)—and then the nodding head and the startled waking.

4. Do you respond to Dement's raising a "red alert" (paragraph 12) about driving and drowsiness any differently than you would if a parent raised the same alert? Why?

The Pittsburgh Sleep Quality Index
Daniel Buysse

In light of William Dement's cautions on the dangers of sleep debt—and also Mary Carskadon's review of the biological, behavioral, and social forces that converge to rob adolescents of sleep—we offer a tool to assess the quality of your own sleep: the Pittsburgh Sleep Quality Index, or PSQI. Because the test can be self-scored, you can get a numerical indicator of the quality of your own sleep. Daniel J. Buysse, MD, is medical director of the Sleep Evaluation Center in the department of psychiatry at the University of Pittsburgh. A past president of the American Academy of Sleep Medicine, Buysse developed the PSQI with Charles F. Reynolds, III, MD; Timothy H. Monk, PhD; Susan R. Berman; and David J. Kupfer, MD. The authors first presented the PSQI in Psychiatry Research *(May 1989) as a tool "specifically designed to measure sleep quality in clinical populations." Today, the PSQI is a widely used instrument in sleep research.*

Pittsburgh Sleep Quality Index (PSQI)

Name _____ ID # _____ Date _____ Age _____

Instructions:

The following questions relate to your usual sleep habits during the past month *only.* Your answers should indicate the most accurate reply for the *majority* of days and nights in the past month. Please answer all questions.

1. During the past month, when have you usually gone to bed at night?
   USUAL BED TIME _____
2. During the past month, how long (in minutes) has it usually taken you to fall asleep each night?
   NUMBER OF MINUTES _____

3. During the past month, when have you usually gotten up in the morning?

USUAL GETTING UP TIME _____

4. During the past month, how many hours of *actual sleep* did you get at night? (This may be different than the number of hours you spend in bed.)

HOURS OF SLEEP PER NIGHT _____

For each of the remaining questions, check the one best response. Please answer *all* questions.

5. During the past month, how often have you had trouble sleeping because you . . .

(a) Cannot get to sleep within 30 minutes

| Not during the past month _____ | Less than once a week _____ | Once or twice a week _____ | Three or more times a week _____ |

(b) Wake up in the middle of the night or early morning

| Not during the past month _____ | Less than once a week _____ | Once or twice a week _____ | Three or more times a week _____ |

(c) Have to get up to use the bathroom

| Not during the past month _____ | Less than once a week _____ | Once or twice a week _____ | Three or more times a week _____ |

(d) Cannot breathe comfortably

| Not during the past month _____ | Less than once a week _____ | Once or twice a week _____ | Three or more times a week _____ |

(e) Cough or snore loudly

| Not during the past month _____ | Less than once a week _____ | Once or twice a week _____ | Three or more times a week _____ |

(f) Feel too cold

| Not during the past month _____ | Less than once a week _____ | Once or twice a week _____ | Three or more times a week _____ |

(g) Feel too hot

| Not during the past month _____ | Less than once a week _____ | Once or twice a week _____ | Three or more times a week _____ |

(h) Had bad dreams

| Not during the past month _____ | Less than once a week _____ | Once or twice a week _____ | Three or more times a week _____ |

(i) Have pain

| Not during the past month _____ | Less than once a week _____ | Once or twice a week _____ | Three or more times a week _____ |

(j) Other reason(s), please describe _____

_____

How often during the past month have you had trouble sleeping because of this?

| Not during the past month _____ | Less than once a week _____ | Once or twice a week _____ | Three or more times a week _____ |

6. During the past month, how would you rate your sleep quality overall?

Very good _____
Fairly good _____
Fairly bad _____
Very bad _____

7. During the past month, how often have you taken medicine (prescribed or "over the counter") to help you sleep?

| Not during the past month _____ | Less than once a week _____ | Once or twice a week _____ | Three or more times a week _____ |

8. During the past month, how often have you had trouble staying awake while driving, eating meals, or engaging in social activity?

| Not during the past month _____ | Less than once a week _____ | Once or twice a week _____ | Three or more times a week _____ |

9. During the past month, how much of a problem has it been for you to keep up enough enthusiasm to get things done?

    No problem at all _____

    Only a very slight problem _____

    Somewhat of a problem _____

    A very big problem _____

10. Do you have a bed partner or roommate?

    No bed partner or roommate _____

    Partner/roommate in other room _____

    Partner in same room, but not same bed _____

    Partner in same bed _____

If you have a roommate or bed partner, ask him/her how often in the past month you have had . . .

(a) Loud snoring

| Not during the past month _____ | Less than once a week _____ | Once or twice a week _____ | Three or more times a week _____ |

(b) Long pauses between breaths while asleep

| Not during the past month _____ | Less than once a week _____ | Once or twice a week _____ | Three or more times a week _____ |

(c) Legs twitching or jerking while you sleep

| Not during the past month _____ | Less than once a week _____ | Once or twice a week _____ | Three or more times a week _____ |

(d) Episodes of disorientation or confusion during sleep

| Not during the past month _____ | Less than once a week _____ | Once or twice a week _____ | Three or more times a week _____ |

(e) Other restlessness while you sleep; please describe _____

_____

| Not during the past month _____ | Less than once a week _____ | Once or twice a week _____ | Three or more times a week _____ |

Scoring Instructions for the Pittsburgh Sleep Quality Index

The Pittsburgh Sleep Quality Index (PSQI) contains 19 self-rated questions and 5 questions rated by the bed partner or roommate (if one is available). Only self-rated questions are included in the scoring. The 19 self-rated items are combined to form seven "component" scores, each of which has a range of 0–3 points. In all cases, a score of "0" indicates no difficulty, while a score of "3" indicates severe difficulty. The seven component scores are then added to yield one "global" score, with a range of 0–21 points, "0" indicating no difficulty and "21" indicating severe difficulties in all areas.

Scoring proceeds as follows:

Component 1: Subjective sleep quality

Examine question #6, and assign scores as follows:

Response	Component 1 score
"Very good"	0
"Fairly good"	1
"Fairly bad"	2
"Very bad"	3

Component 1 score: _____

Component 2: Sleep latency [amount of time needed to fall asleep]

1. Examine question #2, and assign scores as follows:

Response	Score
≤ 15 minutes	0
16–30 minutes	1
31–60 minutes	2
> 60 minutes	3

Question #2 score: _____

2. Examine question #5a, and assign scores as follows:

Response	Score
Not during the past month	0
Less than once a week	1
Once or twice a week	2
Three or more times a week	3

Question #5a score: _____

3. Add #2 score and #5a score

Sum of #2 and #5a: _____

4. Assign component 2 score as follows:

Sum of #2 and #5a	Component 2 score
0	0
1–2	1
3–4	2
5–6	3

Component 2 score: _____

Component 3 Sleep duration

Examine question #4, and assign scores as follows:

Response	Component 3 score
≥ 7 hours	0
≥ 6 < 7 hours	1
≥ 5 < 6 hours	2
< 5 hours	3

Component 3 score: _____

Component 4: Habitual sleep efficiency

(1) Write the number of hours slept (question #4) here: _____
(2) Calculate the number of hours spent in bed:

Getting up time (question #3): _____
− Bedtime (question #1): _____

Number of hours spent in bed: _____

(3) Calculate habitual sleep efficiency as follows:

(Number of hours slept/Number of hours spent in bed) × 100 = Habitual sleep efficiency (%)
(_____/_____) × 100 = _____%

(4) Assign component 4 score as follows:

Habitual sleep efficiency %	Component 4 score
>85%	0
75–84%	1
65–74%	2
<65%	3

Component 4 score: _____

Component 5: Sleep disturbances

(1) Examine questions #5b–5j, and assign scores for *each* question as follows:

Response	Score
Not during the past month	0
Less than once a week	1
Once or twice a week	2
Three or more times a week	3

#5b score _____

c score _____

d score _____

e score _____

f score _____

g score _____

h score _____

i score _____

j score _____

(2) Add the scores for questions #5b–5j:

Sum of #5b–5j: _____

(3) Assign component 5 score as follows:

Sum of #5b–5j	Component 5 score
0	0
1–9	1
10–18	2
19–27	3

Component 5 score: _____

Component 6: Use of sleeping medication

Examine question #7 and assign scores as follows:

Response	Component 6 score
Not during the past month	0
Less than once a week	1
Once or twice a week	2
Three or more times a week	3

Component 6 score: _____

Component 7: Daytime dysfunction

(1) Examine question #8, and assign scores as follows:

Response	Score
Never	0
Once or twice	1
Once or twice each week	2
Three or more times each week	3

Question #8 score: _____

(2) Examine question #9, and assign scores as follows:

Response	Score
No problem at all	0
Only a very slight problem	1
Somewhat of a problem	2
A very big problem	3

Question #9 score: _____

(3) Add the scores for question #8 and #9:

Sum of #8 and #9: _____

(4) Assign component 7 score as follows:

Sum of #8 and #9	Component 7 score
0	0
1–2	1
3–4	2
5–6	3

Component 7 score: _____

Global PSQI Score

Add the seven component scores together:

Global PSQI Score: _____

Discussion and Writing Suggestions

1. Complete the Pittsburgh Sleep Quality Index and compute your score, which will fall in a scale from 0 to 21 points. The higher your score, the greater your sleep difficulties. Where do you fall in the range?

2. Examine your seven "component" scores, which you will have calculated in computing your overall score. ("Sleep Latency" refers to the ease with which you fall asleep. The other six components are self-explanatory.) Which component(s) does the PSQI indicate are your strongest? Your weakest? Based on your subjective assessment of your own sleep, is the scoring accurate?

3. Did you need a formal test to determine how well you are sleeping? Were you aware that the quality of your sleep could be assessed along seven dimensions?

4. How useful do you find a numerical sleep score, as compared to an impressionistic assessment, such as "I sleep well" or "I'm a poor sleeper"? Why might sleep researchers develop an instrument that yields numerical scores?

5. If you are interested in seeing how an instrument such as the PSQI is created and clinically tested for accuracy, see the article that introduced it to the world in *Psychiatry Research* (Volume 28, No. 2, May 1989). You should be able to locate the article in your school library's electronic database—or via electronic interlibrary loan.

6. If your PSQI score suggests that you have difficulties sleeping, do you see any need to take action—especially in light of the preceding selection by William Dement? What action(s) (if any) might be appropriate?

How Sleep Debt Hurts College Students
June J. Pilcher and Amy S. Walters

The "all-nighter" is a rite of passage among many college students, who—pressed by com-
peting schedules (and, let's be honest, the desire to have fun)—sometimes ignore the need
to sleep, for 24 hours or more, in order to study for an exam or meet a paper deadline.
Propped up by caffeinated beverages the next day, the student may even boast: "It was hard,
but I got it done. I aced that exam." Perhaps not. Sleep researchers June Pilcher, who holds
a PhD in biopsychology and teaches at Clemson University, and Amy Walters, MA, of Bradley
University (when this article was published), report on an experiment that deprived students
of a night's sleep and tested their cognitive functioning the next day. Both the results of these
tests and the students' estimates of their performance may surprise (and deflate) you. This
selection first appeared in the Journal of American College Health *(November 1997).*

A note on the specialized language of statistics: You should be able to understand this arti-
cle whether or not you are familiar with the terms standard deviation, mean, *or* probability
(e.g., p <05). Like all researchers who collect numerical information, Pilcher and Walters run
their data through statistical analyses to determine if their results are significant. For a useful
guide to definitions of statistical terms, see the online "Statistics Glossary," by Valerie J. Easton
and John H. McColl, <http://www.stats.gla.ac.uk/steps/glossary/index.html>. Consult their
"Alphabetical index of all entries."

Abstract. The effects of sleep deprivation on cognitive performance and on psychological variables related to cognitive performance were studied in 44 college
students. Participants completed the Watson-Glaser Critical Thinking
Appraisal after either 24 hours of sleep deprivation or approximately 8 hours
of sleep. After completing the cognitive task, the participants completed 2 questionnaires, one assessing self-reported effort, concentration, and estimated performance, the other assessing off-task cognitions. As expected, sleep-deprived
participants performed significantly worse than the nondeprived participants on
the cognitive task. However, the sleep-deprived participants rated their concentration and effort higher than the nondeprived participants did. In addition,
the sleep-deprived participants rated their estimated performance significantly
higher than the nondeprived participants did. The findings indicate that college students are not aware of the extent to which sleep deprivation negatively affects their ability to complete cognitive tasks.

1 Voluntary sleep deprivation is a common occurrence for many college students,
who often partially deprive themselves of sleep during the week and compensate by increasing their sleep time over the weekend.(n1) This pattern of sleep
deprivation and rebound becomes more pronounced around examination periods, sometimes resulting in 24 to 48 hours of total sleep deprivation. By depriv-
ing themselves of sleep, college students are not only increasing their feelings of
sleepiness during the day, thus decreasing their ability to pay attention in class,
but are also negatively affecting their ability to perform on exams.

2   It is well established that sleep deprivation of 24 hours or more leads to noticeable decrements in performance levels.(n2, n3) The psychological variables behind these decrements, however, are less clear. One theory states that decreases in performance are attributable to a decrease in the ability of the sleep-deprived person to focus the attention and effort necessary to complete the task successfully.(n4, n5) Similarly, a number of early sleep-deprivation studies concluded that the detrimental effects of sleep loss on performance result from periods of inattention called lapses.(n6-n8) Moreover, one early study specifically concluded that sleep loss leads to a decrease in attention to external stimuli.(n9) None of the earlier studies, however, attempted to assess self-reported variables that reflect changes in psychological events or thoughts that may be associated with the observed decrements in performance.

3   The effect of sleep deprivation on psychological variables associated with performance, such as self-reported estimates of attention, effort, and performance, have not been thoroughly investigated. Few studies have examined perceived effort and performance,(n11-n15) and the results from those studies have often been contradictory. For example, some researchers have suggested that sleep deprivation may affect the willingness of the individual to put forth the effort to perform well on a task more than the actual ability of the individual to perform.(n11, n12)

4   By contrast, other researchers have concluded that participants may recognize their decreased performance levels following sleep deprivation and attempt to overcome this decrease by increasing their effort.(n15) However, other studies have shown that a perceived increase in effort does not appear to overcome the detrimental effects of sleep deprivation. In one study,(n13) the participants were given a reward for better performance, which resulted in an increase in perceived effort but no change in actual performance. In addition, studies have shown that increasing amounts of sleep loss do not have a detrimental effect on participants' self-reported motivation levels.(n14, n15) As these results show, the relationships between sleep deprivation and psychological variables associated with performance are not clearly understood.

5   Another method of examining psychological variables that may be associated with the decrease in performance following sleep deprivation is assessment of off-task cognitions. Off-task cognitions are thoughts that are not directed to the completion of the task at hand but that intrude upon concentration. These cognitions can include negative evaluations of one's performance on the task, such as "I don't know how to do this," or completely unrelated thoughts, such as "I wonder what I should have for lunch today." Only one study to date has investigated the effect of sleep deprivation on off-task cognitions,(n10) but the participants in that study were specifically selected for their high baseline levels of off-task cognitions. Conclusions, therefore, could not be drawn about the effect of sleep deprivation on off-task cognitions independent of baseline levels.

6   Sleep-deprived participants' current mood state may provide additional information about the ability of the individual to perform following sleep deprivation. One of the best documented effects of sleep deprivation and one that

would be expected to decrease complex task-solving ability is an increase in self-reported sleepiness and fatigue.(n14, n16, n17)

7   Other specific mood states could also influence successful task completion. For example, if sleep deprivation has a consistent negative effect on tension or anxiety, sleep-deprived participants would be expected to have more difficulty than nondeprived participants in maintaining the necessary attention and effort to complete a complex cognitive task. Although several studies have reported that sleep deprivation decreases positive mood states and increases negative mood states,(n3, n14, n18, n19) relatively few studies have examined the effect of sleep deprivation on specific mood states.

8   Another important consideration is the effect of sleep deprivation on an individual's ability to accurately assess psychological variables, such as concentration, effort, and estimated performance. Research findings have shown that the accuracy of self-reports varies, depending upon experimental characteristics surrounding the task. For example, Johnson and colleagues(n20) found that participants' self-reports of the amount of effort they put into a task corresponded better with performance on a difficult task than on a very easy task. The researchers also found that the amount of reported effort, but not necessarily actual performance, could be increased by giving an external incentive.

9   In addition, Beyer(n21) noted that self-evaluations of performance on longer tasks are more accurate than self-evaluations of performance on shorter tasks. Self-report estimates of performance have also been shown to be altered by feedback on the accuracy of actual performance as the person completes the task.(n22) These findings indicate that self-report data on psychological variables can be manipulated by a variety of experimental conditions. One experimental condition that has not been thoroughly investigated is sleep deprivation.

10   In sum, our current study addressed three specific issues. First, does sleep loss lead to changes in self-reported levels of psychological variables related to actual performance? As measures of psychological variables, we examined self-reported levels of concentration, effort, and estimated performance and self-reported off-task cognitions while the participant completed a complex cognitive task. Because sleep deprivation increases feelings of sleepiness and fatigue, we expected the sleep-deprived individuals to report lower levels of concentration, effort, and estimated performance and higher levels of off-task cognitions if they were capable of accurately assessing these psychological variables.

11   The second aim of our study was to determine whether sleep deprivation significantly alters mood states that may be related to performance. As specific measures of mood, we assessed feelings of tension, depression, anger, vigor, fatigue, and confusion. On the basis of a previous study that used the same mood measures,(n23) we expected sleep-deprived participants to report increased fatigue, confusion, and tension and decreased vigor.

12   The final purpose of our current study was to determine whether sleep deprivation alters people's ability to make an accurate assessment of their concentration, effort, and estimated performance. To investigate this aspect of sleep deprivation, we compared self-reported assessments with actual performance levels.

Method

Participants

13 We solicited study participants from five psychology classes, two 100-level courses, one 200-level course, and two 400-level courses. Of the original 65 volunteers, 44 (26 women and 18 men) completed the study. The mean age of the
respondents, who were given extra credit points as an incentive to participate,
was 20.5 years (SD = 4.37).

Materials

14 We used the Watson-Glaser Critical Thinking Appraisal (WG; The
Psychological Corporation, San Antonio, TX) to measure cognitive performance. We chose the WG because it would be cognitively challenging and similar to normal testing conditions for college students in that it is a linguistic task
that requires mental but no physical effort. The WG contains three portions:
inference, recognition of assumptions, and deduction. To increase the similarity of the task to normal testing conditions for college students, we administered
the test with a 40-minute time limit.

15   We used self-report scales to measure mood, off-task cognitions, effort, concentration, and estimated performance. To assess current mood, we used the
Profile of Mood States (POMS; Educational and Industrial Testing Service, San
Diego, CA). The POMS scale provides a list of 65 words describing current
mood states (see Table 1). The student participants rated each word based on
their current mood.

**TABLE 1   Examples of Self-Report Scale Used in Study of Sleep
Deprivation**

Test/question	Response/scale
Profile of Mood Status	
1. Friendly	Not at all (0) to extremely (4)
2. Tense	Not at all (0) to extremely (4)
3. Angry	Not at all (0) to extremely (4)
Cognitive Interference Questionnaire	
1. I thought about how poorly I was doing.	Never (1) to very often (5)
2. I thought about what the experimenter would think of me.	Never (1) to very often (5)
3. I thought about other activities (eg, assignments, work).	Never (1) to very often (5)
Psychological Variables Questionnaire	
1. How well were you are able to concentrate on the task?	Not at all (1) to extremely (well) (7)
2. How well do you think you performed on this task?	Poorly (1) to extremely well (7)
3. How much effort did this task take?	Very little (1) to very much (7)

Note. These are examples of the types of questions to which participants were asked to respond.

16 We assessed the number of off-task cognitions while the participant completed the WG task, using the Cognitive Interference Questionnaire (CIQ).(n24) The CIQ provides a list of types of thoughts. The participants respond by stating how often they experienced those thoughts while completing the WG task. We developed a short psychological variables questionnaire, using Likert-type scales (1 to 7), to measure self-reported estimates of effort, concentration, and estimated performance. In the written instructions for the questionnaire, participants were told to respond to the questions in relation to the WG task. A complete copy of the psychological variables questionnaire is available from the author on request. Higher numbers on each of the self-report variables represent a greater frequency of that variable. For example, higher numbers on the estimated performance scale indicate a higher level of estimated performance.

Procedures

17 The experiment began at 10 PM on a Friday night and concluded at 11 AM the next morning. Approximately 8 participants were tested each Friday night. All participants were requested in advance not to drink alcoholic beverages or take nonprescription drugs from 10 PM on Thursday night until the conclusion of the experiment. In addition, we asked all participants to get out of bed between 7 AM and 9 AM on Friday morning and not to nap during the day.

18 The experiment commenced with all participants reporting to the sleep laboratory at 10 PM on Friday night. At that time, the students were randomly assigned in a block fashion to either a sleep-deprived (n = 23) or a nondeprived group (n = 21), were given the final set of instructions for the experiment, and signed consent forms. In an effort to create realistic sleep loss and nonsleep loss conditions for college students, we chose to limit the length of sleep deprivation to 24 hours for the sleep-deprived group and to allow the nondeprived group to sleep in their own beds under normal sleeping conditions for approximately 8 hours.

19 After the meeting at the sleep laboratory on the Friday night of the experiment, the members of the nondeprived group were told to go home and sleep approximately 8 hours. They were instructed to go to bed between 11 PM and 1 AM and to get out of bed between 7 AM and 9 AM on Saturday morning. The nondeprived participants were called at 9 AM on Saturday morning to ensure that they were awake, and they were encouraged to eat breakfast before reporting to the testing site at 10 AM.

20 The sleep-deprived group remained awake under the supervision of two research assistants in the sleep laboratory. Participants interacted with each other and with the research assistants, watched movies, played video and board games, or worked on personal projects during the night. They were allowed to bring food to eat during the night, but were asked to limit caffeinated beverages and sugary snacks to two of each. Sleep-deprived participants were escorted to a restaurant for breakfast at about 8 AM on Saturday morning. After breakfast, they were escorted to the testing area at 10:00 AM.

21 Testing took place at the university library in an isolated room of study cubicles, with one person per cubicle. To assess their compliance with instructions, we asked the participants to complete a short questionnaire that included questions on sleep times and items consumed since Thursday night. All participants

then completed the POMS scale, followed by the WG. After finishing the WG, all of the participants completed the questionnaire assessing self-reported effort, concentration, and estimated performance in relation to the WG. The last 18 participants in each of the groups also filled out the CIQ. The entire testing period took less than 1 hour.

Data Analyses

22 The data from the POMS, WG, and CIQ were initially scored according to the directions given for each measure. We calculated six POMS scores (tension-anxiety, depression-dejection, anger-hostility, vigor, fatigue, and confusion-bewilderment), one WG score representing the performance percentile of the individual in relation to other college students, and three CIQ scores (off-task cognitions relevant to task, off-task cognitions irrelevant to task, and general mind wandering). We derived self-reported effort, concentration, and estimated performance from the questions on the psychological variables questionnaire. We averaged self-reported sleep data for the sleep-deprived and the nondeprived groups separately, by group, for Thursday and Friday nights.

23   All statistical analyses were completed on SAS (SAS Institute, Cary, NC). To assess whether sleep deprivation had an effect on actual performance and self-reported estimates of psychological variables and mood states, we performed multiple analysis of variance (MANOVA), by sleep condition, on all variables.

Results

24 All of the student participants reported that they slept approximately 8 hours on Thursday night. The sleep-deprived participants reported sleeping an average of 7.91 hours (SD = 1.26), whereas nondeprived participants reported sleeping an average of 7.79 hours (SD = 0.69). The wake-up times on Friday morning were very similar for both groups. The deprived group reported a mean time of getting out of bed of 8:55 AM (SD = 1.22 hours), and the nondeprived group reported a mean time of getting out of bed time of 8:30 AM (SD = 1.10 hours).

25   On Friday night, nondeprived participants reported sleeping an average of 7.92 hours (SD = 0.51 hours) and a mean time of getting out of bed on Saturday morning of 8:40 AM (SD = 0.73 hours). Two participants, one in each sleep condition, reported taking a nap of less than 30 minutes on Friday. We analyzed the data both with and without the two napping participants included. Because the results from the two analyses were very similar, we report the results from all participants. None of the participants reported using alcohol or nonprescription drugs (except for acetaminophen) between 10 PM on Thursday and 10 AM on Saturday.

26   For means and standard deviations on the WG and the self-report tasks, see Table 2. As expected, the sleep-deprived participants performed significantly worse on the WG than the nondeprived participants did, $F(1,42) = 4.02$, $p < .05$.

TABLE 2   Means and Standard Deviations of Sleep- and Nondeprived Participant Groups

Variables	Sleep-deprived		Nondeprived	
	M	SD	M	SD
Watson-Glaser	24.52	21.29	38.71	25.63[*]
Cognitive Interference Questionnaire				
Distracting task-relevant thoughts	2.36	0.62	2.22	0.53
Distracting task-irrelevant thoughts	1.59	0.70	1.58	0.58
General mind wandering	4.17	1.92	3.72	1.60
Estimated effort	4.03	1.00	3.41	0.70 [*]
Estimated concentration	4.30	1.66	3.28	1.31 [*]
Estimated performance	4.54	1.36	3.36	0.84 [***]
Profile of Mood States				
Tension/anxiety	14.22	7.30	11.19	8.05
Depression/dejection	11.96	12.08	9.86	10.22
Anger/hostility	11.65	9.00	8.00	7.46
Vigor	16.87	6.90	17.86	6.06
Fatigue	12.35	6.80	7.95	5.88 [*]
Confusion/bewilderment	10.65	5.22	5.95	4.10 [**]

Note. Significant differences between groups: [*] $p < .05$; [**] $p < .01$; [***] $p < .001$.

27   Although we expected that sleep-deprived participants would have more difficulty concentrating on the task and, thus, would show an increase in off-task cognitions, none of the CIQ scales was significantly increased in the sleep-deprived group. Furthermore, instead of the expected decrease in self-reported concentration, as measured by the psychological variables questionnaire, the sleep-deprived participants reported higher subjective levels of concentration while completing the task than the nondeprived participants did, $F(1,42) = 5.03, p < .05$.

28   The sleep-deprived participants also estimated that they expended significantly more effort to complete the task than did the nondeprived participants, $F(1,42) = 5.49, p < .05$. Interestingly, although sleep-deprived participants actually performed worse on the WG than the nondeprived participants, the students deprived of sleep reported significantly higher levels of estimated performance than the nondeprived participants did, $F(1,42) = 11.79, p < .001$.

29   The sleep-deprived participants reported higher levels on five of the six POMS scales, but only the increases in the fatigue and confusion scales were significant: fatigue, $F(1,42) = 5.21, p < .05$; confusion, $F(1,42) = 10.88, p < .01$.

Discussion

30 As we expected, the results from our current study indicated that participants who were deprived of sleep for 24 hours performed significantly worse on a complex cognitive task than nondeprived participants. Although they actually per-

formed worse, the sleep-deprived participants reported significantly higher levels of estimated performance, as well as more effort expended on the cognitive task, than the nondeprived participants did. In addition, sleep-deprived participants reported a significantly higher level of self-rated concentration than nondeprived participants did. We found no significant differences in levels of off-task cognitions between the sleep-deprived and nondeprived groups.

31   The apparent contradiction between the self-reported data on effort, concentration, and estimated performance and the actual performance level of sleep-deprived participants is somewhat surprising. It is unlikely that the disagreement between the self-reported variables and actual performance was a result of the type of task used. The Watson-Glaser task should have provided a suitable scenario for accurately assessing psychological variables because more difficult and longer tasks have been shown to result in more accurate self-estimates of both effort and performance.(n20, n21)

32   Several explanations for the disagreement between the self-report data and the actual performance levels are possible. Sleep-deprived participants may have expended more effort to complete the task, but the effort was not sufficient to overcome the performance decrements caused by being deprived of sleep. Furthermore, the increase in effort could have led the sleep-deprived participants to believe that they were performing better and concentrating more than they actually were.

33   An alternative explanation is that sleep deprivation may have negatively affected the degree to which participants recognized internal effort. In turn, this could have led the sleep-deprived participants to believe that they were expending more effort than they actually were, which may also have led to increases in estimated performance and self-rated concentration. Regardless of the mechanism behind the self-report data, the results indicated that our sleep-deprived participants did not realize the extent to which their own performances were affected by sleep loss, and they appeared to be making incorrect assumptions about their ability to concentrate and to provide the necessary effort to complete the task.

34   Interestingly, sleep deprivation did not result in the expected change in reporting off-task cognitions. Although a previous study(n10) found that participants who habitually reported distracting thoughts were more likely to do so when deprived of sleep, it appears that the effect of sleep deprivation on off-task cognitions depends on whether the sleep-deprived person regularly experiences high levels of off-task cognitions. Therefore, reporting off-task cognitions does not appear to be specifically affected by sleep deprivation, independent of baseline levels.

35   A second major finding of this research is that sleep deprivation differentially affected mood states in these college students. The current findings indicate that sleep deprivation significantly affected only the fatigue and confusion subscales on the POMS. The reported increase in fatigue and confusion could have contributed to the significant decrease in actual performance that we observed in the sleep-deprived student participants. It is interesting to note that none of the remaining POMS subscales changed significantly in the sleep-deprived participants, indicating that some mood changes commonly ascribed to sleep deprivation, such as anger, irritability, and anxiety, were not necessarily products of 24 hours of sleep loss.

36   The current findings on mood states are very similar to those reported by Dinges and colleagues.(n23) Sleep-deprived participants in both studies reported significantly more fatigue and confusion than nondeprived participants. Dinges and colleagues reported significantly more tension and significantly less vigor in sleep-deprived participants.

37   Similarly, we noted a trend for more tension and less vigor in the sleep-deprived participants in our study. The most likely reason for the small differences between the two studies is that Dinges and colleagues collected mood data every 2 hours for a 64-hour sleep-deprivation period, whereas we collected mood data only once—immediately before the students' completion of the cognitive task. Furthermore, neither study reported a significant increase in angry or depressed feelings following sleep deprivation, indicating that sleep deprivation does not necessarily increase reports of anger and depression, as is commonly believed.

38   In sum, our findings suggest that college students are not aware of the extent to which sleep deprivation impairs their ability to complete cognitive tasks successfully because they consistently overrate their concentration and effort, as well as their estimated performance. In addition, the current data suggest that 24 hours of sleep deprivation significantly affects only fatigue and confusion and does not have a more general effect on positive or negative mood states. The practical implication of these findings is that many college students are unknowingly sabotaging their own performance by choosing to deprive themselves of sleep [while] they complete complex cognitive tasks.

References

(n1.) Hawkins J, Shaw P. Self-reported sleep quality in college students: A repeated measures approach. Sleep. 1992;15(6):545–549.

(n2.) Dinges DE. The nature of sleepiness: Causes, contexts, and consequences. In: Eating, Sleeping, and Sex. Stunkard A, Baum A, eds. Hillsdale, NJ: Erlbaum; 1988.

(n3.) Pilcher JJ, Huffcutt AI. Effects of sleep deprivation on performance: A meta-analysis. Sleep. 1996;19(4):318–326.

(n4.) Johnson LC. Sleep deprivation and performance. In: Webb WW, ed. Biological Rhythms, Sleep, and Performance. New York: Wiley; 1982.

(n5.) Meddis R. Cognitive dysfunction following loss of sleep. In: Burton E, ed. The Pathology and Psychology of Cognition. London: Methuen; 1982.

(n6.) Williams HL, Lubin A. Speeded addition and sleep loss. J EXP Psychol. 1967;73:313–317.

(n7.) Elkin AL, Murray DJ. The effects of sleep loss on short-term recognition memory. Can J Psychol. 1974;28:192–198.

(n8.) Polzella DJ. Effects of sleep-deprivation on short-term memory and recognition. J Exp Psychol. 1975;104:194–200.

(n9.) Hockey GRJ. Changes in attention allocation in a multicomponent task under loss of sleep. Br J Psychol. 1970;61(4):473–480.

(n10.) Mikulincer M, Babkoff H, Caspy T, Weiss H. The impact of cognitive interference on performance during prolonged sleep loss. Psychol Res. 1990;52:80–86.

(n11.) Kjellberg A. Sleep deprivation and some aspects of performance. Waking Sleeping. 1977;1:139–154.

(n12.) Horne JA. Why We Sleep. New York: Oxford University Press; 1988.

(n13.) Horne JA, Pettitt AN. High incentive effects on vigilance performance during 72 hours of total sleep deprivation. Acta Psychologica. 1985;58:123–139.

(n14.) Mikulincer M, Babkoff H, Caspy T, Sing H. The effects of 72 hours of sleep loss on psychological variables. Br J Psychol. 1989;80:145–162.

(n15.) Dinges DF, Kribbs NB, Steinberg KN, Powell JW. Do we lose the willingness to perform during sleep deprivation? Sleep Res. 1992;21:318.

(n16.) Angus RG, Heslegrave RJ. Effects of sleep loss on sustained cognitive performance during a command and control simulation. Behav Res Methods Instruments Computers. 1985;17:55–67.

(n17.) Linde L, Bergstrom M. The effect of one night without sleep on problem-solving and immediate recall. Psychol Res. 1992;54:127–136.

(n18.) Brendel DH, Reynolds CF III, Jennings JR, et al. Sleep stage physiology, mood, and vigilance responses to total sleep deprivation in healthy 80-year-olds and 20-year-olds. Psychophysiology. 1990;27:677–686.

(n19.) Leung L, Becker CE. Sleep deprivation and house staff performance: Update. J Occup Med. 1992;34:1153–1160.

(n20.) Johnson NE, Saccuzzo DP, Larson GE. Self-reported effort versus actual performance in information processing paradigms. J Gen Psychol. 1995;122(2):195–210.

(n21.) Beyer S. Gender differences in the accuracy of self-evaluations of performance. J Pers Soc Psychol. 1990;59(5):960–970.

(n22.) Critchfield TS. Bias in self-evaluation: Signal probability effects. J Exp Anal Behav. 1994;62:235–250.

(n23.) Dinges DF, Gillen KA, Powell JW, et al. Mood reports during total and partial sleep deprivation: Is anger inevitable? Sleep Res. 1995;24:441.

(n24.) Sarason IG, Sarason B, Keefe D, Hayes B, Shearin EN. Cognitive interference: Situational determinants and traitlike characteristics. J Pers Soc Psychol. 1986;51:215–226.

Discussion and Writing Suggestions

1. Have you ever stayed awake all night to complete schoolwork? How many college students of your acquaintance (or, perhaps, you yourself) believe that it is possible to "pull an all-nighter" without degrading your performance the next day? Does the study by Pilcher and Walters change your opinion? Explain your response.

2. The authors conclude that "college students are not aware of the extent to which sleep deprivation impairs their ability to complete cognitive tasks successfully because they consistently overrate their concentration and effort, as well as their estimated performance. . . . [M]any college students are unknowingly sabotaging their own performance by choosing to deprive themselves of sleep [while] they complete complex cognitive tasks." To what extent do these conclusions describe you?

3. In paragraphs 32–33, the authors present several explanations to account for the discrepancy between students' "self-report data and

[their] actual performance levels" on the cognitive task in the experiment. Which of these explanations seems most plausible? Why?

4. How convincing do you find the results of this study? Can you refute them? Do you find yourself *wanting* to refute them? To the extent that you are convinced, what are the odds you will stop staying awake all night to study for exams or to write papers?

5. Carefully review paragraphs 1–12 to understand how the authors justify the need to conduct their present research. Summarize how they go about making this justification. Focus on how they make their argument, not on the content of their argument.

6. Why does the experimental method lend itself to studying questions related to sleep deprivation and self-reports of concentration, effort, etc.?

7. Would you volunteer for an experiment similar to the one Pilcher and Walters conducted? Why or why not?

Starting Time and School Life
Patricia K. Kubow, Kyla L. Wahlstrom, and Amy Bemis

The Minneapolis Public School system was the first major system in the country to change school starting times to accommodate the sleep needs of adolescents. The effort represents an attempt at social engineering, the use of the best scientific evidence available (in this case, on the phase-delayed sleep of adolescents) to effect a desired change: specifically, better sleep and improved learning for students. As you might imagine, altering the start times of an entire school district was a tremendous logistical undertaking, and inevitable conflicts emerged. In the selection that follows, Patricia Kubow of Bowling Green University and Kyla Wahlstrom of the University of Minnesota Center for Applied Research and Educational Improvement report on some of the birth pangs of the Minneapolis initiative. You might read with a question in mind: Would sleep-deprived students at your former high school have benefited from a delayed start time?

Reflections from Educators and Students

1 With the 1997–98 school year in the Minneapolis Public Schools (MPS) came a change in the starting time for most of the schools in the district. It appears that Minneapolis may be the first major metropolitan school district in the United States to undertake systemwide changes in school starting time based on the current research about adolescents and their sleep needs. The seven high schools changed from a 7:15 a.m. to an 8:40 a.m. start. . . .

2 A study is being conducted by the Center for Applied Research and Educational Improvement (CAREI) at the University of Minnesota in conjunction with the MPS to ascertain the impact of changing school starting times on the educational endeavor and on the community. The findings reveal that

the changes affect the various stakeholders differently and are acutely felt at the personal level.

. . .

Findings from the High Schools

3   The focus group data from the high schools revealed that there were three main areas of concern regarding the change in starting time: its impact on students, its impact on teachers' instructional endeavors, and its impact on teachers' personal lives. Thus we developed a survey questionnaire that sought to gauge the magnitude of concern among teachers about those three areas.

Impact on students as perceived by teachers.

4   Fifty-seven percent of the teachers responding to the written survey reported that a greater number of students were more alert during the first two periods of the day than had been the case with the earlier starting time. In fact, this item generated the most agreement of any question on the survey. Sixteen percent were neutral in their answers, and 27% disagreed. Slightly more than half (51%) of the teachers also agreed or strongly agreed that they saw fewer students sleeping at their desks. Interestingly, the respondents were evenly divided (33% agreed or strongly agreed, 32% neither agreed nor disagreed, 35% disagreed or strongly disagreed) regarding the statement "I see improved student behavior in general." This finding contrasts with the findings from Edina that reported markedly improved student behavior, as evidenced by quieter behavior in the hallways between classes and less lunchroom misbehavior.

5   Teachers were evenly divided in reporting the nature of the comments (positive versus negative) they had heard from students and from parents regarding the later starting time. Twenty-five percent said that they had heard neither positive nor negative comments from students, and 40% said that no comment had been heard from parents. Although practices, extended-day programs, and rehearsals were shortened, students still arrived home at a later hour than they had the previous year, fostering parental concerns about safety and somewhat reducing student participation in after-school activities.

6   Difficulties with students' work schedules were noted by several MPS respondents, who wrote that these teenagers had less time to work or had to work later in the day in order to put in as many hours as they once had. In the study by Wahlstrom and Freeman, 15 employers of suburban high school students were asked about the impact of the later start on their businesses. Fourteen of the 15 employers agreed that there had been no negative impact from the later dismissal, because their businesses did not need the extra help until the schools were dismissed. Minneapolis teachers observed that there appeared to be less involvement in extracurricular activities; Edina teachers did not notice any appreciable decrease in student involvement in after-school activities. Finally, both suburban and city teachers noted that some students seemed more tired at the end of the day, now that class extended an hour later into the afternoon. Additional parent feedback will be gathered in order to more fully understand the impact of the later start on students and families.

Impact on students as reported by students.

7 Minneapolis high school students in the focus groups reported general dissatisfaction with the later start's impact on after-school activities and their own schedules. The data suggest some differentiation between grade levels, with ninth-graders consistently more negative about the later start than older students. Because the after-school schedule was pushed later in the day, students reported that they were more tired, had less time to study and do homework, and had shorter practices or practices at odd hours. For example, a lack of facilities and field lights necessitated morning practices; consequently, some students had to forgo the morning sleep that was to be a benefit of the later school starting time. Moreover, there were often conflicts in the scheduling of activities, forcing students to make tough decisions about which activity to choose and reducing their opportunities to participate in more than one.

8 As did the high school staff members, students expressed concern about having to leave school during the last period to attend practices and games and about middle-schoolers' being unable to participate in senior high athletics. Students explained that the later school starting time sometimes limited the number of hours they could work, reduced their income, and affected the types of jobs available to them. The schedule changes affected not only work, sports, and studying but also opportunities for relaxation and socialization. The good news is that several students reported that they were more alert and efficient during the day, and this enabled them to complete more of their homework at school.

9 Student focus groups in the suburban high school revealed a very different, and generally positive, picture. As in Minneapolis, some students mentioned that athletic practices were moved to an early morning time, which seemed to them to negate the beneficial effects of having a later start. However, the majority of students in the suburban focus groups said that they felt less tired at the end of the day when they did their homework and that the later dismissal had not negatively affected their involvement in after-school activities. Nearly all the students in the focus groups noted that they were feeling more rested and alert for the first hour of class and that they were generally going to bed at the same time as they had been when the starting time was an hour earlier—thus they were, indeed, getting about one hour more of sleep each school night.

Impact on instructional endeavors.

10 By a slight majority, teachers reported that the later start enabled students to come to school more rested and therefore more ready for learning. The tradeoff, however, was that at the end of the day many student athletes needed to be excused from their last hour of class to get to an athletic event on time. One teacher wrote, "Now, I lose one-half of my sixth-hour International Baccalaureate class in the fall to sports' start times." The dilemma was felt by the coaches as well as the classroom teachers: "As a teacher and a coach, I was extremely troubled that I had to excuse my student athletes from class 13 times this spring for track meets. Many of us coaches were very distressed about this situation because it goes against everything we stand for as educators." The majority sentiment about students' missing class because of sports was summed

up in this comment: "Please keep in mind that the primary purpose of schools is to educate, not to run extracurricular sports programs. The coaches will have to adapt." Clearly, this is a critical issue to resolve if the later starting time is to remain in place and benefit all students, not just those who are not involved in athletics.

11   During the focus groups with teachers, the participants noted that fewer students were seeking academic help before and after school. This concern was substantiated by the written survey, in which 50% of the teachers disagreed or strongly disagreed that more students were seeking academic help before school and 60% disagreed or strongly disagreed that more students were seeking academic help after school. Again, this was in direct contrast to the finding in Edina, where teachers reported that with the later start many more students came to school early to get additional help from teachers with their homework or to prepare for a quiz. Whether these findings are related to economics and having access to a car instead of having to rely on a school bus needs to be studied further.

12   During the focus groups, the high school teachers generally agreed that the 8:40 start had a negative impact on the end of the school day, defined as the time period right after lunch through the last academic hour. Because of early dismissals for activities, sports practices, and personal appointments, many students missed the last period. As a result, teachers were unable to cover the desired amount of curriculum, and students missed class discussions, labs, and required assignments. Some students even chose electives rather than required courses because they had to miss their last class so often. This, in turn, created a high demand for certain classes during fifth hour and small classes during sixth hour.

13   The impact of the late starting time on transportation issues and on learning appeared to be vastly different between the city high schools and the suburban high school. Being in the "second tier" of the MPS's three-tiered busing schedule meant that buses arrived late much more often. This was usually because of delays that occurred during the first run for the elementary schools that started at 7:40. One teacher noted, "Tardies are still a problem with the 8:40 start time, with many students late because of late buses. This is very frustrating—almost impossible to teach when you have a continuous stream of late students." Late buses were never mentioned by teachers as an ongoing problem in the suburban district of Edina, whose high school is also in the second tier of a three-tiered transportation schedule. However, it is very important to note that the suburb is about one-seventh the size of the city in terms of square miles, and it was easier to make up time with shorter distances between neighborhoods and schools.

14   Finally, many teachers in the high schools with a later starting time commented on the positive effect the change had had on their own preparation for the instructional day. Faculty or department meetings were being held before school instead of after school, and teachers found that they were fresher for thinking through difficult curriculum issues and had greater energy to be engaged in professional discussions. Two suburban teachers noted that they had time to incorporate the most recent world events into their daily social studies and economics lessons because they had time to go to the Internet each morning before classes began. Will the overall effect of a later start be to improve

instruction and student achievement? That question is being studied at this time, and we may have some answers within the next year.

Impact on teachers' personal lives.

15   The professional and personal lives of teachers are unquestionably interdependent, and the findings from the focus groups highlighted the need to ask more definitively about teachers' personal lives on the written questionnaire. Fifty-one percent of the respondents agreed or strongly agreed with the statement "I have found that the later start time has had a positive impact on my personal schedule before school." Thirty-four percent disagreed or strongly disagreed, and only 14% were neutral. By contrast, 68% disagreed or strongly disagreed with the statement "I have found that the later start time has had a positive impact on my personal schedule after school" (with 49% of that total at the strongly disagree level). Sixteen percent were neutral, and 16% agreed or strongly agreed.

16   Those teachers who experienced a positive personal outcome from the later start cited improved health, more personal family time in the morning, greater alertness in the morning, and time to exercise in the morning before going to work. The fact that they were getting more sleep and were better rested was brought up by 16% of the teachers. One stated, "I did not get more and more exhausted as the year progressed as I formerly did," while another reflected, "I realized in May that in years past I've been totally sleep deprived and acted as such!"

17   The negative outcomes from the later start were a strong theme in the focus groups and were even slightly more prevalent on the written questionnaire. The most often mentioned personal reason for disliking the later starting time was that it resulted in having to drive in heavier traffic both to and from school. Teachers also reported being more tired at the end of the day than in previous years. The combination of personal obligations and teacher fatigue was perceived by Minneapolis faculty members as having decreased teacher supervision of after-school activities.

Overall view of the high school changes.

18   The teachers were asked to complete the statement "My feelings, overall, about the later start are . . . " with one of the following responses: "Hate it," "Don't like it," "Neutral," "Like it," or "Love it." Only slightly more respondents (45%) chose "like it" or "love it" than chose "don't like it" or "hate it" (44%). Only 11% felt neutral. As for the strongest responses, 23% chose "love it," and 15% chose "hate it."

19   Finally, the following question was asked: What would be the ideal starting time for school? Although 44% of respondents had said that they either hated or did not like the new starting time, the responses to this question made it clear that very few (3.5%) wanted to return to the previous starting time of 7:15 a.m. The most popular time for Minneapolis high schools to start, according to these teachers, was 8 a.m. . . . Indeed, almost three-quarters of the teachers surveyed (72.7%) chose a starting time of 8 a.m. or later.

. . .

Conclusion

20 The findings of [this] study raise questions about whether a universal starting time or a flexible one is best for students. It is unlikely that any one schedule could accommodate the needs of all stakeholders. Given this fact, the district could investigate the possibility of creating flexible schedules so as to offer viable options for students, families, and school personnel. Several respondents to the high school teachers' questionnaire spontaneously made such suggestions.

- "I would rather restructure the school day and schedule. Provide more learning (not just credit makeup or remediation) for students after 2 p.m.—especially courses that are interdisciplinary."
- "Flexible starts/endings would be ideal."
- "At the high school, flexible starting time should be an option. Athletes need the early time. Students who work need the early start, morning people like the early start, but others benefit from the later start."
- "I think we should have an early start and a late start. Have school start at 7:15 for those who want to come then and another start at 9:15 for those who like it late. Everyone goes a full six periods, but the early ones get out two hours sooner (or take an extra class). There certainly are enough students and staff who would like both start times."

21 One teacher noted, "The 7:15 a.m. starting time was a death knell for period 1 (and often period 2)." The research on adolescent sleep patterns is indicating that some change in school starting times may be beneficial. . . .

22 Educators who have experienced the change to a later start as positive speak forcefully about its impact. "Even though the change in starting time has affected after-school activities, I feel that the benefits—of having school hours more tuned in to 'teenage clocks'—are significant," said one teacher. Another commented, "If you are involved in any kind of after-school activity, it can be difficult to take care of personal business, but the positives for the kids outweigh this single personal consideration." And finally, a word of caution from a teacher about hasty decisions in any direction: "This change has been a long time in coming—please give it a long trial before making a judgment." The effects on teaching and learning are only beginning to emerge. If we are to know anything of substance, the medical and educational research into this issue and its outcomes must continue for several years to come.

Discussion and Writing Suggestions

1. The experiment in the Minneapolis Public Schools "to undertake systemwide changes in school starting time based on the current research about adolescents and their sleep needs" is an example of social engineering: changes in public policy based on the desire to bring about a particular effect. Based on your reading of this report, what factors make

social engineering a highly complex effort? What aspects of real social settings make unintended consequences likely?

2. There are many stakeholders in the experiment on delayed start times in the Minneapolis Public Schools: students, parents, teachers, administrators, coaches, staff (cafeteria workers, for instance), bus drivers, and others. With so many people affected by *whatever* time school is set to begin, how would you, as a superintendent of schools in your hometown, weigh the competing needs of stakeholders and select an optimal start time? How would you define "optimal"? Whose needs would be paramount? Why?

3. Earlier in this chapter, the noted adolescent sleep researcher Mary Carskadon writes: "Can these problems [associated with sleep-deprived adolescents] be solved by delaying the starting time for school as adolescents move into the pubertal years? Not entirely. Moving the opening bell to a later time may help many teens with the mismatch between biological time and scholastic time, but it will not provide more hours in the day." Your comments? To what extent are their days so crammed with activities that high school students will be left sleep deprived *regardless* of start times?

4. Would a delayed start time have addressed any significant problems at your high school? How might teachers have responded to the later start time? Students? Coaches? Parents?

5. Several of those interviewed in the Minneapolis study supported a "flexible starting time" for high schools. Colleges have essentially adopted this approach by scheduling classes throughout the day (as opposed to having all students begin at a fixed time each morning). Given their flexible schedules, do you think college students are any less sleep deprived than high school students? What implications does your answer hold for the Minnesota experiment and others like it?

6. The authors of this article based their research report on surveys and focus groups, a very different strategy from the lab-based research of Pilcher and Walters (see pages 551–560). Consider both types of research. What can researchers do in a lab that they cannot do in field research via surveys or focus groups? And, vice versa, what is possible with a broad survey approach that is not possible in a lab?

THE MEDICALIZATION OF SLEEP: A CASE STUDY IN CONFLICTING INTERPRETATIONS OF DATA

- **Dramatic Increase in Prescription Sleep Aids Among Young Adults**
  Medco Health Solutions, 17 Oct. 2005

- **Are Your Kids Little Addicts?**
  Kim Painter, *USA Today*, 13 Nov. 2005

- **Doctors Ponder Drugs for Sleepless Nights of Adolescence**
  Mary Duenwald, *New York Times*, 15 Nov. 2005

- **Kids Using Sleeping Pills**
  Rebecca Goldin and Grace Harris, Statistical Assessment Service,
  20 Nov. 2005

Following are four articles on the "medicalization" of sleep among adolescents—that is, the use of prescription drugs to help teenagers get the rest they are not getting on their own. As researchers gain greater understanding of the relationships between brain and blood chemistry and body function, we are witnessing a revolution in medicine's approach to conditions that, in earlier times, may never have warranted a doctor's attention. For instance, years ago a child's inability to focus in school may have triggered parent-teacher conferences, special lesson plans, and (in dire circumstances) expulsion. Today, the same inattention may be labeled "ADD" and merit a prescription for Ritalin. The medicalization of undesirable behavior now extends to sleep—as you likely know from television and magazine ads promising to help you awake refreshed and energetic each morning.

This cluster of readings addresses the increasing popularity of prescription sleep aids among adolescents. The first selection, by Medco Health Solutions (a large managed health care company), reports on a study of prescription drug use among 2.4 million Americans. The USA Today and New York Times articles offer conflicting interpretations of the Medco data. As a researcher in training, be alert to such differences. When you find them, ask: Why the difference? Which is the more accurate—and responsible—use of data?

Compare your analysis of the Medco news coverage with that of the Statistical Assessment Service (STATS) at George Mason University, a watchdog group that assesses "the use and abuse of science and statistics in the media" (see <http://www.stats.org/>). The STATS article studies both the USA Today and the New York Times articles in light of the original Medco data and concludes that one newspaper "mauled the issue entirely." Based on your own close reading, can you tell which one?

Dramatic Increase in Prescription Sleep Aids Among Young Adults
Medco Health Solutions

1   FRANKLIN LAKES, October 17, 2005—For many Americans a good night's sleep is just a pillow away, but the number of people—including children—who find themselves tossing and turning the night away is increasing. A nationwide analysis released today by Medco Health Solutions, Inc. (NYSE:MHS) finds that the most dramatic increases in the use of prescription sleeping aids are among younger adults and school-age children.

2   According to the research, the number of adults aged 20–44 using sleeping medications doubled from 2000 to 2004, and rose by 85 percent for children from 10–19. The increase in spending on these medications was highest for 10–19 year olds—up 223 percent; younger adults showed a 190 percent spending spike over the four-year period. The analysis reviewed prescription drug claims of 2.4 million Americans between 2000 and 2004.

3   "Although the elderly are still the most frequent users of sleeping aids, the evidence found in this study shows that younger adults and children are starting to use these medications with even greater frequency," said Dr. Robert Epstein, chief medical officer for Medco. "With several new medications that treat sleep disorders coming to the marketplace in the next three years, we anticipate that this trend will continue to accelerate."

4   A supplemental analysis of the same patients looked at the concurrent use of both prescription sleeping aid medications and drugs used to treat attention deficit/antihyperactivity disorder (ADHD) during the first six months of 2004. Children ages 10–19 showed the highest dual usage in these two therapeutic categories at 15 percent, followed by the 20–44 age-category at nearly 4 percent.

5   "One of the potential side-effects of drugs to treat ADHD is insomnia. Therefore, for some, the additional use of medications to assist in sleeping is something one might anticipate," said Epstein. "The number of people in our analysis that have concomitant use in these two therapeutic classes is significant and warrants continued research, especially since these two conditions are accelerating at similar rates and among similar demographic audiences."

Additional Research Findings:

- Females are far more likely to use sleeping aids than males. In 2004, there were 37 percent more girls ages 19 and under, 58 percent more women ages 20–64, and 36 percent more women 65 and over taking sleeping medications than their male counterparts.
- In 2004, the highest prevalence of adults under 65 on sleep medications was seen in a portion of the central region of the U.S., which includes Kentucky, Tennessee, Alabama and Mississippi, while higher percentages of children (19 and under) were prescribed sleeping pills in the mountain states including Idaho, Montana, Wyoming, Nevada, Utah, Colorado, Arizona and New Mexico than in any other area of the nation.

- Although adults over 64 have the highest rate of sleeping-medication use, they showed the lowest increase in prevalence from 2000 to 2004—only a 16.5 percent change over that time, 84 percent lower than the increase seen in adults 20–44.

A Sleepless Nation

6   According to the National Institutes of Health (NIH), more than 70 million people in the U.S. may be affected by a sleep problem and, for 60 percent of them, it's a chronic disorder. There are significant gender differences when it comes to sleeping problems, with women being twice as likely as men to have trouble sleeping, which is reflected in the prescription data.

7   Common sleep disorders include insomnia, sleep apnea, and restless leg syndrome. Menopause and perimenopause are also frequently associated with sleep impairment in women. Sleep deprivation and disorders cost the nation $15 billion in health care expenses and $50 billion in lost productivity each year, according to United States Surgeon General.

8   Treatments for sleep disorders include both over-the-counter and prescription medications, as well as behavioral interventions. Americans filled more than 35 million prescriptions for sleeping pills in 2004, spending $2.1 billion on these medications. Although drug therapy may be beneficial for short-term improvement and long-term use may be needed in some cases, the American Academy of Family Physicians cautions that long-term use of many psychotropic or sedative-hypnotic drugs may cause adverse reactions and may actually impair return to normal sleep. A combination of medication and behavioral interventions is often more effective than either approach alone for those with chronic insomnia.

9   A 2003 study published in the *Journal of Pediatrics* found that 75 percent of practitioners surveyed reported recommending a non-prescription sleeping aid and 50 percent had actually prescribed one for their pediatric patients during a six month period. In addition, the study found that the likelihood of prescribing sleep medications was two-to-four times greater for those physicians who treated children with ADHD.

Managing Cost in Sleeping Medication Use

10   Three new sleep medications introduced in 2005 are the first of other additional hypnotics that will be coming to market in the next few years. These new products, some with better data supporting long-term use and improved safety profiles, are expected to address some of the problems associated with older sleep aids and as a result are being approved for longer-term use. These single source products could significantly increase costs of hypnotics. T. Rowe Price Health Sciences Fund predicts that the market for sleep drugs will more than double to $5 billion by 2010.

11   One factor that may help keep costs down despite these new products is that the most popular sleep medication currently on the market (zolpidem) is expected to be available as a generic in late 2006.

12   To help manage the growth in both use and spending associated with hypnotics, Medco provides its clients with a number of cost-saving solutions within
their plan design. The company uses nationally recognized clinical guidelines
and an independent Pharmacy and Therapeutics Committee of medical experts
to determine drug classes that can be used as first-line courses of therapy. In
many cases, there may be lower-cost medications that should be tried first before
moving to newer, more expensive brand-name drugs. Prior authorization rules
can be put in place to assure that the most appropriate treatment is being prescribed to meet the needs of the patient—avoiding waste and cost. Daily dosage
and duration of therapy management can help reduce costs, while providing an
increased level of safety, by helping to ensure that an appropriate and cost-
effective medication dosage or dosage form is prescribed for the correct duration.

Sleeping Medication Analysis—Data Back-up and Actuals [Medco Report 2005]

"Number of young adults (age 20–44) on sleeping medications doubled in four years."

- The prevalence rate of 20–44 year old patients using sleeping medications
  went from 13 per 1,000 patients in 2000 to 27 per 1,000 patients in 2004—
  slightly more than a 100% increase.
- In 2000, the sample size for adults 20–44 was 742,819, and of those, 10,118
  were taking sleeping medications.
- In 2004, the sample size for adults 20–44 was 693,495, and of those, 18,894
  were taking sleeping medications.

Estimated Numbers for Sleeping Aids in USA 2004

Age Gender	Population	Prevalence	Patient Count
0–19 Males	41,285,000	0.19%	77,201
0–19 Females	39,264,000	0.26%	103,693
0–19 All	80,549,000	0.22%	181,050
20–44 Females	51,781,000	3.37%	1,744,465
20–44 Males	52,294,000	2.02%	1,058,431
20–44 All	104,075,000	2.72%	2,835,483
45–64 Females	32,059,000	6.44%	2,063,377
45–64 Males	30,381,000	4.14%	1,257,533
45–64 All	62,440,000	5.33%	3,325,353
65+ Females	20,610,000	7.33%	1,510,855
65+ Males	14,452,000	5.40%	780,389
65+ All	35,061,000	6.40%	2,242,844
Total			8,584,730

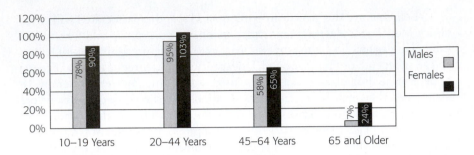

Growth in Use of Sleep Medications by Gender (2000–2004)

"Children 10–19 increased use of sleeping aids by 85 percent."

- The prevalence rate for children 10–19 went from .16% in 2000 to .3% in 2004—an 85% increase.
- In 2000, the sample size for children 10–19 was 340,124, and of those, 554 were taking sleeping medications.
- In 2004, the sample size for children 10–19 was 342,568, and of those, 1,032 were taking sleeping medications.

". . . the increase in spending on these medications was highest for 10–19 year olds—up 223 percent; younger adults showed a 190 percent spending spike over the four year period."

- Total spending for 10–19 year olds in 2000 was $32,141
- Total spending for 10–19 year olds in 2004 was $104,537
- (104,537 – 32,141)/32,141 = 223% increase from 2000 to 2004
- Total spending for 20–44 year olds in 2000 was $1,299,188
- Total spending for 20–44 year olds in 2004 was $3,521,042
- (3,521,042 – 1,299,188)/1,299,188 = 190% increase from 2000 to 2004

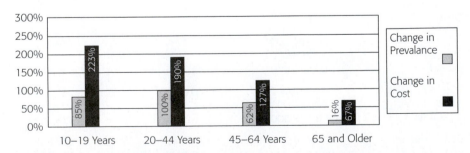

Growth in Sleep Medication Use and Spending (2000–2004)

"Children ages 10–19 showed the highest dual usage in these two therapeutic categories at 15 percent, followed by the 20–44 age category at nearly 4 percent."

- In 2004 (1/1 to 6/30) there were 371 children ages 10–19 on a sleeping medication in our sample size; of these 56 (15.1%) also had concomitant use of an ADHD medication.
- In the 20–44 age category, 8,487 patients were on a prescription for sleeping medication with 317 having concomitant use of an ADHD drug (3.7%).

"Females are far more likely to use sleeping aids than males. In 2004, there were 37 percent more girls ages 19 and under, 58 percent more women ages 20–64, and 36 percent more women 65 and over taking sleeping medications than their male counterparts."

- There were 734 females (0–19) out of 277,933 patients on sleeping meds (.26%) compared to 541 males (0–19) out of 289,313 patients (.19%); 38,963 females (20–64) out of 777,501 (5.01%) compared to 22,855 males (20–64) out of 721,976 (3.17%); and 16,272 females (65+) out of 221,971 (7.33%) compared to 11,224 males (65+) out of 207,857 (5.4%).

"In 2004, the highest prevalence of adults under 65 on sleep medication was seen in a portion of the central region of the U.S., while the higher percentages of children (19 and under) were prescribed sleeping pills in the mountain states . . . "

- Adults ages 20–64 had an overall 5.27% prevalence rate in the East South Central region of the U.S.—women showed a 6.49% prevalence rate and men a 3.99% prevalence rate.
- Children ages 0–19 had an overall prevalence rate of .34% in the Mountain Region, with girls showing a .42% rate and boys a .27% rate.

"Although adults over 64 have the highest rate of sleeping medication use, they showed the lowest increase in prevalence from 2000 to 2004—only a 16.5 percent change over that time, 84 percent lower than the increase seen in adults 20–44."

- In 2004, 6.4% of adults 65+ were taking sleeping medications. In 2000, that number was 5.49%, resulting in only a 16.5% increase over four years. Adults 20–44 showed a 100% increase over the time frame, 84% greater than the 65+ group.

Are Your Kids Little Addicts?
Kim Painter, USA Today

1   As shocking health statistics go, this one is an eye-popper: Prescription sleeping-pill use is up 85% among older children and adolescents. The recent study that includes this information also shows a doubling of use among young adults.

2   So are we raising a generation of pill-dependent insomniacs—overscheduled kids so hyped up on caffeinated sodas, energy drinks and Frappuccinos that they need drugs to fall asleep?

3   Not really. A closer look at the data, and some additional information, suggests the actual number of kids getting sleeping pills is tiny and the reasons complex.

4   The study, from managed-care company Medco Health Solutions, looked at prescription data for 2.4 million customers. Among them were 554 kids ages 10 to 19 getting "hypnotic" medications (drugs classified specifically as sleeping pills) in 2000; four years later, 1,032 kids were getting the drugs—0.3% of the 342,568 kids in the sample. That's 3 kids in 1,000. And the vast majority likely were teens, not children, says Medco's chief medical officer Robert Epstein.

5   Still, experts find any increase troubling—because, they say, the medications included in the study have not been tested on children and teens, and, even if safe, are probably inappropriate for most kids.

6   "I'm not sure why people are prescribing these medications. Sometimes children with neurodevelopmental problems like autism have sleep problems that are very severe and we sometimes prescribe medication for them," says Thomas Anders, president of the American Academy of Child and Adolescent Psychiatry and a researcher in pediatric sleep disorders at the UC-Davis M.I.N.D. Institute. However, Anders says, most specialists don't use hypnotics in children—not even the new ones now heavily marketed to adults. Instead, they use other sedating drugs, often older antidepressants with long pediatric track records.

7   "But we never prescribe and shouldn't prescribe a sleep medication with a child who only has insomnia," he says. That's because insomnia—in children as in adults—is primarily a learned behavior that can be unlearned, specialists say. Behavior-changing techniques like enforcing a sleep schedule and insisting kids fall asleep only in their beds—work for most kids.

8   Judith Owens, a sleep specialist at Hasbro Children's Hospital in Providence, says she recommends that parents try a behavior-changing plan even if they try medication, too. She says newer medications should be studied to find better options for the few children—mostly with disabilities—who truly need them.

9   But she also suspects a lot of kids and teens getting pills aren't chronic insomniacs at all, but instead are kids going on overseas trips or facing other temporary sleep disruptions. Some parents have long coped with extended plane trips by slipping their children sedating antihistamines bought over the counter, she says.

10   After speaking with Anders and Owens, I asked Medco to look again at their data. Sure enough, 61% of the prescriptions in 2004 were never refilled—suggesting they were for one-time, not chronic, use. And Medco found that 39% of kids of all ages taking hypnotics also took some other behavioral drug, and 13% took at least two more. The most common were antidepressants (31%), followed by ADHD drugs (12%) and anti-psychotics (9%). Anti-psychotics are sometimes prescribed for children with autism and bipolar disorder. Antidepressants are used in a wide range of disorders, including anxiety, obsessive-compulsive disorder and autism. Those profiles suggest that many kids getting the pills—for sound reasons or not—have complex health problems, not just insomnia.

Doctors Ponder Drugs for Sleepless Nights of Adolescence
Mary Duenwald, New York Times

1   When is it a good idea for an adolescent to take a sleeping pill? There is reason to suppose the answer may be never.

2   No prescription sleep aids are approved by the Food and Drug Administration for use in people under 18, largely because they have not been well studied in children.

3   But children do take sleeping pills.

4   In 2004, more than 180,000 people under age 20 in the United States—most of them 10 or older—took sleep medications, according to estimates released last month by Medco Health Solutions, a large managed-care company.

5   Although that represents only about one child in 500, Medco found that usage was up by 85 percent since 2000.

6   The numbers reported by Medco were somewhat mysterious: the company's report did not indicate why the pills were prescribed for the patients under 18, or which pills were prescribed for them.

7   That makes some doctors worry that the large increase may reflect a certain amount of unnecessary prescribing.

8   To some extent, not sleeping enough is a normal part of adolescence.

9   Teenagers are generally inclined to stay up late, thanks in part to the stimulation of things like television, homework, instant messaging and soft drinks spiked with caffeine.

10   And adolescents' internal clocks naturally shift ahead, making teenagers more alert in the evening.

11   So doctors say it is important that a child's sleeping problem be thoroughly investigated to learn whether it stems from a medical problem, and whether medication is really necessary.

12   "The last thing we want to suggest is that it's O.K. to throw a medication at something without understanding the problem," said Dr. Judith Owens, the director of the Pediatric Sleep Disorders Clinic at Hasbro Children's Hospital, in Providence, R.I. "Insomnia is a symptom, not a disorder. It's like pain. You're not going to give a patient pain medication without figuring out what's causing the pain."

13   Yet even cautious physicians say there are times when it makes sense to prescribe sleeping pills for children in combination with behavioral strategies in an effort to battle insomnia.

14   "We try not to," said Dr. Helene A. Emsellem, a neurologist and the director of the Center for Sleep and Wake Disorders, in Chevy Chase, Md. "But if you've got a child who's not sleeping and is in school and they have to get up in the morning and they're falling over . . . "

15   Sleeping pills, she said, are helpful "for the short-term treatment of sleep-onset insomnia while you are working on the underlying causes."

16   A 2003 survey of pediatricians, conducted by Dr. Owens, found that the kinds of sleeping pills that were most frequently prescribed for children were

clonidine and other alpha agonists, drugs that were developed as medications for high blood pressure but are also sedating; prescription antihistamines; antidepressants; and benzodiazepines like Valium, older-generation sleeping pills that are also used as muscle relaxants and drugs that are used to fight anxiety.

17 Sleep specialists say newer sleeping pills like Sonata, Ambien and Lunesta may in some cases be better choices for adolescents because they act more narrowly on areas of the brain that regulate sleep.

18 Studies in adults suggest that such new generation medications are not as habit-forming as older sleeping pills can be. And because the newer pills stay active for a shorter time, they are less likely to make people feel dizzy, groggy or hung over the next morning.

19 "Ambien is a Category B drug for pregnancy," Dr. Emsellem said, referring to a class of drugs that is thought to pose no risk to a developing fetus. "No wonder doctors think it might be safe for teenagers."

20 Because teenagers are more likely to have trouble falling asleep than staying asleep all night, shorter-acting drugs, like Sonata and Ambien, may be more appropriate for them than Lunesta, which is longer-lasting, the specialists say.

21 Rozerem, an insomnia medication just approved by the F.D.A. in July for use in adults, may have an even more selective effect on the brain.

22 It is directed at receptors in the suprachiasmatic nucleus, which sets the body's internal clock.

23 And because this clock is thought to shift adolescents' sleep patterns, some doctors suspect that Rozerem may be useful in treating their sleep problems.

24 "We're very interested in its potential," said Dr. David N. Neubauer, the associate director of the Johns Hopkins Sleep Disorders Center in Baltimore. "There just have not been studies done yet to demonstrate how well it would work."

25 The newer prescription drugs may also be better for children in some cases than over-the-counter sleep aids, which, according to Dr. Owens's 2003 survey, 75 percent of pediatricians say they sometimes recommend.

26 Doctors most often suggest products like Benadryl, Nytol and Tylenol PM. These drugs contain antihistamines—typically, diphenhydramine, which can be sedating. But antihistamines taken at bedtime can also leave people feeling drowsy the next day.

27 "Diphenhydramine has been shown to decrease alertness and neural-cognitive performance up to 48 hours," said Dr. Clete A. Kushida, the director of the Stanford University Center for Human Sleep Research.

28 Dr. Owens's survey also found that pediatricians are most likely to turn to sleep medications when [their patients] have some kind of pain, when they have difficulty tolerating travel, or when they have sleeping problems related to conditions like attention-deficit hyperactivity disorder, autism or anxiety disorders.

29 Attention disorder itself can disturb sleep—and so can some of the longer-acting stimulant medications that are used to treat it.

30 The Medco report noted that 15 percent of children taking sleeping pills were also taking medicine for attention disorder.

31 When chronic conditions keep children up at night, doctors are sometimes inclined to prescribe sleeping pills for the sake of the parents.

32 "They're dealing with challenging kids all day long, and then no one's sleeping at night," Dr. Owens said. "It's like the straw that broke the camel's back."

33   In such cases, the medications may be given for months at a time. But when children have severe insomnia alone, it is more likely that they will be given sleeping pills only for a few days or a few weeks.

34   Ideally, that buys some time while the child cuts out caffeinated drinks, finds ways to quiet down before bedtime, establishes a consistent wake time and otherwise makes changes in behavior to get more sleep.

35   How much to prescribe is an open question. "The absurdity of this is that a lot of times we're put in a position of saying, 'Well, I guess we'll just give them half the adult dose,' " Dr. Owens said. "We're sort of flying by the seat of our pants here."

36   Still another question is whether sleeping pills can affect teenagers' still-developing brains.

37   "We need studies," said Mary A. Carskadon, a sleep researcher at Brown Medical School and Bradley Hospital, in Providence, "because we need to know how sleeping pills are affecting learning and memory, much less sleep."

Kids Using Sleeping Pills
Rebecca Goldin and Grace Harris, **Statistical Assessment Service**

1   *USA Today* and the *New York Times* both reported on a recently published Medco Health Solutions study on sleeping medication use. Focusing on the study's findings that adolescent and child usage of prescription sleep medication has increased, the two newspapers published two very different interpretations of the study. *USA Today* admirably avoided shocking headlines, and thoughtfully analyzed the data from the study. In contrast, the *New York Times* lumped together the data on sleeping pills with data on over-the-counter sleeping medications, and data on prescription drugs that are not sleeping medications.

2   The Medco study looked at sleep medication usage from 2000 to 2004 and found that child and adolescent use of prescription sleeping pills increased by 85% over that time period. The number of kids prescribed these pills is small: about 3 in 1000.

3   *USA Today* correctly emphasized that adolescents are not becoming addicts. Not only are the numbers of those taking the pills small, but 61% of prescriptions for sleeping pills for children were never refilled, suggesting that the medication was used once or for a short period. *USA Today* also notes that 39 percent of adolescent users were also taking at least one other behavioral drug. This figure suggests that "many kids getting the pills . . . have complex health problems, not just insomnia."

4   Another important point made by *USA Today* is that doctors sometimes prescribe antidepressants for children rather than sleeping pills, because the antidepressants have a longer (and therefore more reliable) history. As time goes on, it stands to reason that doctors would become more confident that sleeping pills do not carry big risks, and prescribe them more frequently.

5   While we laud *USA Today*'s attempt to keep the risk in perspective, we also note that this conservative interpretation may be underestimating the trend in prescription drug use for young people. If children are already over-medicated (due to overly-aggressive treatment of symptoms that seem like depression, anxiety, ADHD, etc.) as some parties have suggested, then the increase in prescribing sleeping pills may be a symptom of a larger problem: instead of dealing with the problem through behavioral and therapeutic means, we drug our kids. We do not necessarily support this thesis, but the Medco data is certainly consistent with it.

6   In contrast, the *New York Times* mauled the issue entirely. They begin with the statement that it may never be a good idea for an adolescent to take sleeping pills. After citing various statistics, they contradict their own opinion with expert testimony: "Yet even cautious physicians say there are times when it makes sense to prescribe sleeping pills for children in combination with behavioral strategies in an effort to battle insomnia."

7   Sleeping pills-or-not aside, the *New York Times* confuses the data. The Medco study specifically refers to the number of kids 10–19 taking sleeping medications—these are drugs designed to combat sleeping disorders. The *New York Times* throws together an assortment of drugs, from true sleeping pills, to antihistamines, anxiety drugs, and high blood pressure drugs. All of these drugs may aid sleep, but only the sleeping pills were part of the Medco results. For flavor, they also toss in a statistic about the percentage of pediatricians who occasionally prescribe over-the-counter cold medicines as sleeping aids. This information, of course, tells us nothing about how many kids were told to take the aids, nor what the trend is.

8   The reader of the *New York Times* is left with a lot of data adding up to very little information, either on trends or on the proportion of the problem. They are handed on a platter the idea that "sleeping meds are bad news" without any discussion of the risks associated with any of the medications they mention. Indeed, even the cited experts don't seem to concur.

9   The root cause of the increase in usage of sleeping pills among adolescents and children is unclear. Perhaps doctors are becoming more comfortable prescribing better or more time-tested drugs. Perhaps doctors have always been prescribing sleeping aids to children at these rates but had previously been using surrogate medication whose main use is not to aid sleep. While *USA Today* did a great job of dampening hysteria over drug-usage rates, neither newspaper was particularly astute at addressing what the problem with prescription sleep medication really is.

Review Questions

1. What increase does Medco report in the use of sleeping medications among 10- to 19-year-olds? Review Medco's "Sleeping Medication Analysis—Data Back-up and Actuals." What were the actual numbers of 10- to 19-year-olds who were taking prescription sleep aids in 2000 versus those taking them in 2004?

2. Adolescents receiving prescription sleep aids are sometimes prescribed drugs for which other conditions? How might this association account for a rise in the use of prescription sleep aids?

3. How many people in the United States are estimated to have a sleep disorder? What costs are associated with these disorders?

4. Why should children "never" be prescribed sleeping pills for insomnia, according to Thomas Anders in the *USA Today* article?

5. Based on what she learned from interviewing sleep experts, Kim Painter (of *USA Today*) contacted Medco for a clarification of its data. What did she learn? What conclusions can be drawn from the clarified data?

6. The authors of the Statistical Assessment Service review claim that Mary Duenwald's *New York Times* article contradicts itself. How so? Locate the (allegedly) contradictory statements in the *New York Times* article— both the ones cited in the review and any others that you find.

7. According to the Statistical Assessment Service (STATS) review, what is particularly praiseworthy about Kim Painter's coverage of the Medco report in *USA Today?* The STATS review also offers what caution regarding Painter's coverage?

8. In the estimate of the STATS reviewers, both newspapers fall short in their coverage of the Medco report in at least one respect. How so?

Discussion and Writing Suggestions

1. The writers for *USA Today* and the *New York Times* interpret data from the Medco report differently. How so—and with what differing impressions does each article leave you? To what extent did the divergent coverage confuse you, given that you also read the original Medco report?

2. Based on what you've read and heard, have you formed any opinions about the reputations of *USA Today* and the *New York Times* with regard to quality of reporting? To what extent did the conclusions of the STATS review surprise you? What are the implications of the STATS findings for your possible career as a researcher?

3. Reread the last paragraph of the news release. How do the initiatives Medco mentions in this paragraph suggest its priorities as a managed health care provider that earns money (like any other company) by keeping down costs? How sympathetic are you to these initiatives, especially if you or someone you know has been denied drug coverage due to an insurer's rules for specific classes of drugs? What are the issues involved in balancing costs versus patient needs?

4. Both Kim Painter of *USA Today* and Mary Duenwald of the *New York Times* interviewed the same expert in pediatric sleep: Judith Owens of the Pediatric Sleep Disorders Clinic at Hasbro Children's Hospital in Providence, Rhode Island. Based on the reporters' use of information

from these interviews, infer the questions each asked Dr. Owens. Create a list of questions for each reporter.

5. Consider the headline choices for the *USA Today* and the *New York Times* articles, both of which report on the same news release by Medco. What is the logic behind the selection of each headline? To what extent does each headline accurately reflect the content of its story? Do you prefer one headline over the other? Discuss.

6. Study the STATS review as a model of critique. How is the critique structured? How effective is it, in your view, as an example of critique? (For criteria by which to make this judgment, you may want to see the "Guidelines for Writing Critiques" box on page 66 in Chapter 2.)

SYNTHESIS ACTIVITIES

1. Explain the fundamentals of sleep for an audience (perhaps someone like yourself before reading this chapter) who regards sleep as a passive state characterized by the absence of wakefulness. Make clear that sleep is ubiquitous (fruit flies, fish, cats, alligators, and humans all sleep); is an active, not a passive behavior; has an "architecture" that changes over one's life; can be especially troubling for adolescents; and can be delayed or otherwise disrupted in ways that cause sleep debt and associated problems. Refer to the selections by Martin, Ince, the National Sleep Foundation, Dement, Carskadon, and Pilcher and Walters. Refer also to the case study on the medicalization of sleep.

2. Use one or more of the selections in this chapter to analyze the quality of your sleep in a typical week. As part of your analysis, be sure to take (and score) the Pittsburgh Sleep Quality Index. Recall that the purpose of any analysis is to increase understanding of a little-understood phenomenon—in this case, *your* sleep patterns. What principle(s) or definition(s) will you use from the chapter readings to guide your analysis? Follow the general format for writing analyses on page 203.

3. Evaluate the Statistical Assessment Service review "Kids Using Sleeping Pills" as a model critique. Use the "Guidelines for Writing Critiques" box on page 66 as your standard for evaluating how successfully Goldin and Harris evaluate the *USA Today* and the *New York Times* treatments of Medco's report on prescription drugs and adolescent sleep. Understand that you will be writing a critique of a critique.

4. Three selections in this chapter first appeared in journals or books intended for professionals interested in sleep: those by Pilcher and Walters; Carskadon; and Kubow, Wahlstrom, and Bemis. Using

standards of good writing established by your composition instructor and textbooks, evaluate the presentation of one of these three selections. In your critique, focus on the author's or authors' success at communicating a key idea. What are your standards for evaluation: a writer's ability to organize at the global, section, or paragraph level? Sentence style? Word choice? Conciseness? Tone? How many criteria will you use in making your overall assessment? Follow the general format for writing critiques on page 66.

5. In an explanatory synthesis, discuss phase-delayed sleep: whom it affects; its biological, behaviorial, and social causes; its related problems; and its remedies (to the extent they exist). Refer to chapter selections as needed, but be sure to reference Dement; Carskadon; and Kubow, Wahlstrom, and Bemis. Follow the general format for writing syntheses on pages 106–107.

6. Discuss why cramming for an examination (staying awake all night to study or to write a paper) can be a mistake. Your discussion should include an account of sleep debt and its consequences. Refer to chapter selections as needed, but be sure to reference Dement, Carskadon, and Pilcher and Walters. Follow the general format for writing syntheses on pages 106–107.

7. Draw upon the selections in this chapter to create an advertising campaign aimed at promoting good sleep hygiene among college students. The campaign might take the form of a brochure, a poster, a series of e-mails, or a Web site. In your campaign, explain the importance of sleep, particularly for adolescents. Create a separate Works Cited page for the sources you reference in your campaign.

8. Argue for or against the proposition that the health office at your college should set up an educational program to promote good sleep hygiene among students. In developing your argument, refer to the scientific evidence on adolescent sleep needs and sleep debt and its consequences. Among the selections you refer to should be those by the National Sleep Foundation, Dement, Carskadon, and Pilcher and Walters.

9. Argue for or against the proposition that the start time of the high school you attended should be later than it currently is. In your argument, consider the scientific evidence relating to problems associated with phase-delayed sleep. Consider also the complications of coordinating schedules among the various stakeholders in any change of start time: for instance, among students, teachers, parents, coaches, and staff. In your paper, refer to the selections by the National Sleep Foundation, Dement, Carskadon, and Kubow, Wahlstrom, and Bemis.

10. Explain your reactions to the reading selections in this chapter. What you have learned about sleep will inevitably find its way into this paper. But keep the focus on your *reactions* to learning

about one or more of the following: sleep debt and cramming for exams; sleep debt and the dangers of drowsiness while driving; the problems caused when adolescent sleep patterns collide with the scheduling demands of the business and scholastic worlds; the rise in use of sleep medications among adolescents and young adults. Let your interest in the topic dictate the specific focus of your explanation.

RESEARCH ACTIVITIES

1. Sleep specialists do not agree on the purpose of sleep. Investigate theories of why we—as well as other creatures—sleep. The oldest theories—based largely on speculation—date to the times of Aristotle and earlier. In recent decades biologists and physicians have proposed theories based on current scientific research.

2. Research "unihemispheric sleep," the phenomenon that allows certain species (of dolphins and birds, for instance) to put one half of their brain to sleep at a time. Which species exhibit this behavior? Why? What are the mechanisms involved?

3. Discuss references to sleep in one or more artistic works. Macbeth's and Lady Macbeth's troubled sleep following their murder of King Duncan comes to mind. You might consider "The Pains of Sleep" (<http://etext.virginia.edu/stc/ Coleridge/poems/ Pains_of_Sleep.html>), the work of the famous insomniac Samuel Taylor Coleridge. You might consider, as well, cinematic works like the Al Pacino film *Insomnia* (2002), directed by Christopher Nolan, or the unusual dreamlike visions of Richard Linklater in films like *Waking Life* (2001) and *A Scanner Darkly* (2006).

4. Research and write an overview of sleep disorders (there are 84, divided into four general classifications). If you find yourself especially intrigued by one disorder—for instance, sleep apnea, restless leg syndrome, or night terrors—focus your research on that.

5. Investigate sleep specialists' use of the polysomnograph to monitor body functions as patients sleep in a laboratory. What does the polysomnograph measure? How is the patient monitored? How is the polysomnograph read and interpreted? What role does it play in the diagnosis and treatment of sleep disorders?

6. Several authors in this chapter discuss circadian rhythm. Conduct more research into the "internal clock" that determines for us (and other creatures) patterns of wakefulness and sleep. What is this clock? Where is it located? When, in response to what, and how did it evolve?

7. Investigate NASA's interest in the sleep problems of astronauts, a select group whose accelerated daily exposure to patterns of light and dark plays havoc with their sleep. What, precisely, are the

problems? What solutions is NASA devising? (You might also want to investigate the sleep challenges that NASA anticipates for long-distance missions to Mars and beyond.)

8. Investigate sleep researchers' inquiries into sleep deprivation. Begin with a close reading of Pilcher and Walters in this chapter. Consult their reference list, and see especially the pioneering work of William Dement, whose scholarship is also represented in this chapter.

9. Investigate the history or promotion of sleeping aids—medicinal (for instance, opiates, melatonin, and the new prescription drugs), behavioral (what's "counting sheep" all about?), and mechanical (white noise machines, etc.). If one particular area of this research captures your attention (for example, the business aspects of sleeping aids, or the social consequences), pursue that area, rather than preparing a broad overview.

10. The inventor of psychoanalysis, Sigmund Freud, initially made his reputation with his startling theories about the interpretation of dreams. (In Freud's theories, people and objects occurring in dreams were frequently symbolic.) Investigate one or more current theories on the content of the dreams that occur during REM sleep, as discussed, for example, by Susan Ince in the *Harvard Health Letter.* How does the content of dreams correlate with the dreamer's life?

11. Several authors in this chapter discuss the sometimes catastrophic consequences (such as the *Exxon Valdez* disaster) of sleep deprivation. In some cases, insufficient sleep time is built into the job—for example, the duty schedules of some airline flight crews, long-distance truck drivers, or medical interns. Select one such job area, and discuss the particular problems caused by enforced (or voluntary) sleep deprivation. Or discuss recent attempts to address such long-standing problems with policies designed to ensure that people get sufficient sleep so as not to pose a danger to themselves or others.

12 Fairy Tales: A Closer Look at Cinderella

In August 2001, when the crown prince of Norway married a single mother and former waitress, hundreds of thousands of Norwegians cheered, along with an estimated 300 million television viewers worldwide. Observers called it a "Cinderella" tale—and everyone everywhere understood the reference. Mette-Marit Tjessem Hoiby had become a Cinderella figure. But why had the bride's humble beginnings so endeared her to a nation? We can begin to offer answers by examining an ancient and universally known tale in which a young girl—heartsick at the death of her mother, deprived of her father's love, and scorned by her new family—is nonetheless recognized for her inner worth.

"Once upon a time. . . ." Millions of children around the world have listened to these (or similar) words. And, once upon a time, such words were magic archways into a world of entertainment and fantasy for children and their parents. But in our own century, fairy tales have come under the scrutiny of anthropologists, linguists, educators, psychologists, and psychiatrists, as well as literary critics, who have come to see them as a kind of social genetic code—a means by which cultural values are transmitted from one generation to the next. Some people, of course, may scoff at the idea that charming tales like "Cinderella" or "Snow White" are anything other than charming tales, at the idea that fairy tales may really be ways of inculcating young and impressionable children with culturally approved values. But even if they are not aware of it, adults and children use fairy tales in complex and subtle ways. We can, perhaps, best illustrate this by examining variants of "Cinderella."

"Cinderella" appears to be the best-known fairy tale in the world. In 1892, Marian Roalfe Cox published 345 variants of the story, the first systematic study of a single folktale. In her collection, Cox gathered stories from throughout Europe in which elements or motifs of "Cinderella" appeared, often mixed with motifs of other tales. All told, more than 700 variants exist throughout the world—in Europe, Africa, Asia, and North and South America. Scholars debate the extent to which such a wide distribution is explained by population migrations or by some universal quality of imagination that would allow people at different times and places to create essentially the same story. But for whatever reason, folklorists agree that "Cinderella" has appealed to storytellers and listeners everywhere.

The great body of folk literature, including fairy tales, comes to us from an oral tradition. Written literature, produced by a particular author, is preserved through the generations just as the author recorded it. By contrast, oral literature changes with every telling: The childhood game comes to mind in which one child whispers a sentence into the ear of another; by the time the second child repeats the sentence to a third, and the third to a fourth (and so on), the sentence has changed considerably. And so it is with oral literature, with the qualification that these stories are also changed quite consciously when a teller wishes to add or delete material.

Modern students of folk literature find themselves in the position of *reading* as opposed to hearing a tale. The texts we read tend to be of two types, which are at times difficult to distinguish. We might read a faithful transcription of an oral tale or a tale of *literary* origin—a tale that was originally written (as a short story would be), not spoken, but that nonetheless may contain elements of an oral account. In this chapter, we include tales of both oral and literary origin. Jakob and Wilhelm Grimm published their transcription of "Cinderella" in 1812 and Andrew Lang his transcription, " The Seven Foals," in 1890. The version by Charles Perrault (1697) is difficult to classify as the transcription of an oral source, since he may have heard the story originally but appears (according to Bruno Bettelheim) to have "freed it of all content he considered vulgar, and refined its other features to make the product suitable to be told at court." Of unquestionable literary origin are the Walt Disney version of the story, based on Perrault's text and Anne Sexton's poem.

Preceding these variants of "Cinderella," we present a selection that will orient you, we hope, to the experience of reading fairy tales as "literature": a general introduction to the topic by renowned folklorist Stith Thompson. Following the variants are five selections that respond directly to the tale. First, art historian Bonnie Cullen examines how Perrault's "Cinderella" emerged as the canonical, or standard, version. We hear from Bruno Bettelheim, who, employing psychoanalytic theory, finds in "Cinderella" a story of "Sibling Rivalry and Oedipal Conflicts." Law professor Patricia J. Williams then revisits "Cinderella" and wonders whether the story can resonate for girls and women of color. On a lighter note, in "I Am Cinderella's Stepmother and I Know My Rights," Judith Rossner sets the record straight on "Cinderella" from a point of view not typically represented in variants of the tale. The chapter concludes with "Cinderella: *Not* So Morally Superior," Elisabeth Panttaja's surprising analysis that our heroine succeeds not because she is patient or virtuous (the standard moral to the story) but because "she disobeys the stepmother, enlists forbidden helpers, uses magic powers, lies, hides, dissembles, disguises herself, and evades pursuit."

In recent years "Cinderella" has come in for a critical drubbing, as wised-up and often sarcastic commentators reject her rags-to-riches, someday-my-prince-will-come myth as out of date. Feminists, in particular, have objected to a children's story that promotes the idea—both unrealistic and undesirable—that young women should wait for a handsome prince to carry them off to a happily-ever-after marriage in a magnificent castle. (On this point see Anne Sexton's version of "Cinderella," pages 619–621.) Some of these critical commentators regard Cinderella to be just as mercenary a soul as her evil stepsisters or stepmother (see "Cinderella: *Not* So Morally Superior," pages 644–647). Others offer their own surprising countermyths aimed at reversing our sympathies (see "I Am Cinderella's Stepmother and I Know My Rights," pages 640–643).

Such reversals have become a familiar strategy in contemporary story-telling: In the past generation or so, we have seen the old English myth of *Beowulf* presented from the monster's point of view (*Grendel* by John Gardner); *The Wizard of Oz*, from the witch's point of view (*Wicked* by Gregory Maguire); and even Jane Austen's *Pride and Prejudice*—itself a "Cinderella" variant—from the ostensible prince's point of view (*Darcy's Story* by Janet Aylmer). The larger question posed by such revisionists is whether or not the familiar myth continues to resonate with contemporary readers. If it does-n't, they propose that we abandon it, or they offer makeovers to help the myth resonate in our consumer culture. For example, in a recent *New York Times* article, "Love the Riches, Lose the Rags: Younger Fans Embrace Cinderella, Updated as the Material Girl," Jodi Kantor details the ways in which Cinderella and other Disney princesses have become commodified: "Younger girls . . . are watching their movies on special pink-and-blue Cinderella tele-vision and DVD players, dressing their dogs in Cinderella costumes and eating breakfast made in a waffle iron that stamps her image into the batter." Older females can also live the myth: "At the Disney parks, the most popular theme wedding is the Cinderella one. For $2,500 a bride can arrive in a glass coach copied straight from the film, drawn by four ponies."

A note on terminology: "Cinderella," "Jack and the Beanstalk," "Little Red Riding Hood," and the like are commonly referred to as fairy tales, although, strictly speaking, they are not. True fairy tales concern a "class of supernatural beings of diminutive size, who in popular belief are said to possess magical powers and to have great influence for good or evil over the affairs of humans" (*Oxford English Dictionary*). "Cinderella" and the others just mentioned concern no beings of diminutive size, although extraordinary, magical events do occur in the stories. Folklorists would be more apt to call these stories "wonder tales." We retain the traditional "fairy tale," with the proviso that in popular usage the term is misapplied. You may notice that the authors in this chapter use the terms "folktale" and "fairy tale" interchangeably. The expression "folktale" refers to *any* story conceived orally and passed on in an oral tradition. Thus, "folktale" is a generic term that incorporates both fairy tales and wonder tales.

Universality of the Folktale
Stith Thompson

Folklorists travel around the world, to cities and rural areas alike, recording the facts, tradi-tions, and beliefs that characterize ethnic groups. Some folklorists record and compile jokes; others do the same with insults or songs. Still others, like Stith Thompson, devote their careers to studying tales. And, as it turns out, many aspects of stories and storytelling are worth examining. Among them: the art of narrative—how tellers captivate their audiences; the social and religious significance of tale telling; the many types of tales that are told; the many variants, worldwide, of single tales (such as "Cinderella"). In a preface to one of his own books, Thompson raises the broad questions and the underlying assumptions that govern the folklorist's study of tales. We begin this chapter with Thompson's overview to set a context for the variants of "Cinderella" that you will read.

Note the ways that Thompson's approach to fairy tales differs from yours. Perhaps you regard stories such as "Cinderella" as entertainment. Stith Thompson assumes, as you might not, that tales should be objects of study as well.

Stith Thompson (1885–1976) led a distinguished life as an American educator, folklorist, editor, and author. Between 1921 and 1955, he was a professor of folklore and English, and later dean of the Graduate School and Distinguished Service Professor at Indiana University, Bloomington. Five institutions have awarded Thompson honorary doctorates for his work in folklore studies. He published numerous books on the subject, including European Tales Among North American Indians *(1919),* The Types of the Folktales *(1928), and* Tales of the North American Indian *(1929). He is best known for his six-volume* Motif Index of Folk Literature *(1932–1937; 1955–1958, 2nd ed.).*

1   The teller of stories has everywhere and always found eager listeners. Whether his tale is the mere report of a recent happening, a legend of long ago, or an elaborately contrived fiction, men and women have hung upon his words and satisfied their yearnings for information or amusement, for incitement to heroic deeds, for religious edification, or for release from the overpowering monotony of their lives. In villages of central Africa, in outrigger boats on the Pacific, in the Australian bush, and within the shadow of Hawaiian volcanoes, tales of the present and of the mysterious past, of animals and gods and heroes, and of men and women like themselves, hold listeners in their spell or enrich the conversation of daily life. So it is also in Eskimo igloos under the light of seal-oil lamps, in the tropical jungles of Brazil, and by the totem poles of the British Columbian coast. In Japan too, and China and India, the priest and the scholar, the peasant and the artisan all join in their love of a good story and their honor for the man who tells it well.

2   When we confine our view to our own occidental world, we see that for at least three or four thousand years, and doubtless for ages before, the art of the story-teller has been cultivated in every rank of society. Odysseus entertains the court of Alcinous with the marvels of his adventures. Centuries later we find the long-haired page reading nightly from interminable chivalric romances to entertain his lady while her lord is absent on his crusade. Medieval priests illustrate sermons by anecdotes old and new, and only sometimes edifying. The old peasant, now as always, whiles away the winter evening with tales of wonder and adventure and the marvelous workings of fate. Nurses tell children of Goldilocks or the House that Jack Built. Poets write epics and novelists novels. Even now the cinemas and theaters bring their stories directly to the ear and eye through the voices and gestures of actors. And in the smoking-rooms of sleeping cars and steamships and at the banquet table the oral anecdote flourishes in a new age.

3   In the present work we are confining our interest to a relatively narrow scope, the traditional prose tale—the story which has been handed down from generation to generation either in writing or by word of mouth. Such tales are, of course, only one of the many kinds of story material, for, in addition to them,

narrative comes to us in verse as ballads and epics, and in prose as histories, novels, dramas, and short stories. We shall have little to do with the songs of bards, with the ballads of the people, or with poetic narrative in general, though stories themselves refuse to be confined exclusively to either prose or verse forms. But even with verse and all other forms of prose narrative put aside, we shall find that in treating the traditional prose tale—the folktale—our quest will be ambitious enough and will take us to all parts of the earth and to the very beginnings of history.

4   Although the term "folktale" is often used in English to refer to the "household tale" or "fairy tale" (the German *Märchen*), such as "Cinderella" or "Snow White," it is also legitimately employed in a much broader sense to include all forms of prose narrative, written or oral, which have come to be handed down through the years. In this usage the important fact is the traditional nature of the material. In contrast to the modern story writer's striving after originality of plot and treatment, the teller of a folktale is proud of his ability to hand on that which he has received. He usually desires to impress his readers or hearers with the fact that he is bringing them something that has the stamp of good authority, that the tale was heard from some great story-teller or from some aged person who remembered it from old days.

5   So it was until at least the end of the Middle Ages with writers like Chaucer, who carefully quoted authorities for their plots—and sometimes even invented originals so as to dispel the suspicion that some new and unwarranted story was being foisted on the public. Though the individual genius of such writers appears clearly enough, they always depended on authority, not only for their basic theological opinions but also for the plots of their stories. A study of the sources of Chaucer or Boccaccio takes one directly into the stream of traditional narrative.

6   The great written collections of stories characteristic of India, the Near East, the classical world, and Medieval Europe are almost entirely traditional. They copy and recopy. A tale which gains favor in one collection is taken over into others, sometimes intact and sometimes with changes of plot or characterization. The history of such a story, passing it may be from India to Persia and Arabia and Italy and France and finally to England, copied and changed from manuscript to manuscript, is often exceedingly complex. For it goes through the hands of both skilled and bungling narrators and improves or deteriorates at nearly every retelling. However well or poorly such a story may be written down, it always attempts to preserve a tradition, an old tale with the authority of antiquity to give it interest and importance.

7   If use of the term "folktale" to include such literary narratives seems somewhat broad, it can be justified on practical grounds if on no other, for it is impossible to make a complete separation of the written and the oral traditions. Often, indeed, their interrelation is so close and so inextricable as to present one of the most baffling problems the folklore scholar encounters. They differ somewhat in their behavior, it is true, but they are alike in their disregard of originality of plot and of pride of authorship.

8   Nor is complete separation of these two kinds of narrative tradition by any means necessary for their understanding. The study of the oral tale . . . will be valid so long as we realize that stories have frequently been taken down from the

lips of unlettered taletellers and have entered the great literary collections. In contrary fashion, fables of Aesop, anecdotes from Homer, and saints' legends, not to speak of fairy tales read from Perrault or Grimm, have entered the oral stream and all their association with the written or printed page has been forgotten. Frequently a story is taken from the people, recorded in a literary document, carried across continents or preserved through centuries, and then retold to a humble entertainer who adds it to his repertory.

9   It is clear then that the oral story need not always have been oral. But when it once habituates itself to being passed on by word of mouth it undergoes the same treatment as all other tales at the command of the raconteur. It becomes something to tell to an audience, or at least to a listener, not something to read. Its effects are no longer produced indirectly by association with words written or printed on a page, but directly through facial expression and gesture and repetition and recurrent patterns that generations have tested and found effective.

10   This oral art of taletelling is far older than history, and it is not bounded by one continent or one civilization. Stories may differ in subject from place to place, the conditions and purposes of taletelling may change as we move from land to land or from century to century, and yet everywhere it ministers to the same basic social and individual needs. The call for entertainment to fill in the hours of leisure has found most peoples very limited in their resources, and except where modern urban civilization has penetrated deeply they have found the telling of stories one of the most satisfying of pastimes. Curiosity about the past has always brought eager listeners to tales of the long ago which supply the simple man with all he knows of the history of his folk. Legends grow with the telling, and often a great heroic past evolves to gratify vanity and tribal pride. Religion also has played a mighty role everywhere in the encouragement of the narrative art, for the religious mind has tried to understand beginnings and for ages has told stories of ancient days and sacred beings. Often whole cosmologies have unfolded themselves in these legends, and hierarchies of gods and heroes.

11   Worldwide also are many of the structural forms which oral narrative has assumed. The hero tale, the explanatory legend, the animal anecdote—certainly these at least are present everywhere. Other fictional patterns are limited to particular areas of culture and act by their presence or absence as an effective index of the limits of the area concerned. The study of such limitations has not proceeded far, but it constitutes an interesting problem for the student of these oral narrative forms.

12   Even more tangible evidence of the ubiquity and antiquity of the folktale is the great similarity in the content of stories of the most varied peoples. The same tale types and narrative motifs are found scattered over the world in most puzzling fashion. A recognition of these resemblances and an attempt to account for them brings the scholar closer to an understanding of the nature of human culture. He must continually ask himself, "Why do some peoples borrow tales and some lend? How does the tale serve the needs of the social group?" When he adds to his task an appreciation of the aesthetic and practical urge toward storytelling, and some knowledge of the forms and devices, stylistic and histrionic, that belong to this ancient and widely practiced art, he finds that he must bring to his work more talents than one man can easily

possess. Literary critics, anthropologists, historians, psychologists, and aestheticians are all needed if we are to hope to know why folktales are made, how they are invented, what art is used in their telling, how they grow and change and occasionally die.

Review Questions

1. According to Thompson, why do people venerate a good storyteller?
2. For Thompson, what features distinguish a "folktale" from modern types of fiction?
3. How does religion help encourage the existence of folktale art?
4. What is a strong piece of evidence for the great antiquity and universality of folktales?

Discussion and Writing Suggestions

1. Based on Thompson's explanation of the qualities of oral folktales, what do you feel is gained by the increasing replacement of this form of art and entertainment by TV?

2. What do you suppose underlies the apparent human need to tell stories, given that storytelling is practiced in every culture known?

3. Interview older members of your family, asking them about stories they were told as children. As best you can, record a story. Then examine your work. How does it differ from the version you heard? Write an account of your impressions on the differences between an oral and a written rendering of a story. Alternatively, you might record a story and then speculate on what the story might mean in the experiences of the family member who told it to you.

Nine Variants of "Cinderella"

The existence of Chinese, French, German, African, and Native American versions of the popular Cinderella tale, along with 700 other versions worldwide, comes as a surprise to many. Which is the real "Cinderella"? The question is misleading in that each version is "real" for a particular group of people in a particular place and time. Certainly, you can judge among versions and select the most appealing. You can also draw comparisons and contrasts. Indeed, the grouping of the stories that we present here invites comparisons. You might wish to consider a few of the following categories as you read:

- *Cinderella's innocence or guilt, concerning the treatment she receives at the hands of her stepsisters*

- *Cinderella's passive (or active) nature*

- *Sibling rivalry—the relationship of Cinderella with her sisters*

- *The father's role*

- *The rule that Cinderella must return from the ball by midnight*

- *The levels of violence*

- *The presence or absence of the fairy godmother*

- *Cinderella's relationship with the prince*

- *The characterization of the prince*

- *The presence of Cinderella's dead mother*

- *The function of magic*

- *The ending*

Cinderella
Charles Perrault

Charles Perrault (1628–1703) was born in Paris of a prosperous family. He practiced law for a short time and then devoted his attentions to a job in government, in which capacity he was instrumental in promoting the advancement of the arts and sciences and in securing pensions for writers, both French and foreign. Perrault is best known as a writer for his Contes de ma mère l'oye *(Mother Goose Tales), a collection of fairy tales taken from popular folklore. He is widely suspected of having changed these stories in an effort to make them more acceptable to his audience—members of the French court.*

1   Once there was a nobleman who took as his second wife the proudest and haughtiest woman imaginable. She had two daughters of the same character, who took after their mother in everything. On his side, the husband had a daughter who was sweetness itself; she inherited this from her mother, who had been the most kindly of women.

2   No sooner was the wedding over than the stepmother showed her ill-nature. She could not bear the good qualities of the young girl, for they made her own daughters seem even less likable. She gave her the roughest work of the house to do. It was she who washed the dishes and the stairs, who cleaned out Madam's room and the rooms of the two Misses. She slept right at the top of the house, in an attic, on a lumpy mattress, while her sisters slept in panelled rooms where they had the most modern beds and mirrors in which they could see themselves from top to toe. The poor girl bore everything in patience and did not dare to complain to her father. He would only have scolded her, for he was entirely under his wife's thumb.

3   When she had finished her work, she used to go into the chimney-corner and sit down among the cinders, for which reason she was usually known in the house as Cinderbottom. Her younger stepsister, who was not so rude as the other, called her Cinderella. However, Cinderella, in spite of her ragged clothes, was still fifty times as beautiful as her sisters, superbly dressed though they were.

4   One day the King's son gave a ball, to which everyone of good family was invited. Our two young ladies received invitations, for they cut quite a figure in the country. So there they were, both feeling very pleased and very busy choosing the clothes and the hair-styles which would suit them best. More work for Cinderella, for it was she who ironed her sisters' underwear and goffered their linen cuffs. Their only talk was of what they would wear.

5   "I," said the elder, "shall wear my red velvet dress and my collar of English lace."

6   "I," said the younger, "shall wear just my ordinary skirt; but, to make up, I shall put on my gold-embroidered cape and my diamond clasp, which is quite out of the common."

7   The right hairdresser was sent for to supply double-frilled coifs, and patches were bought from the right patch-maker. They called Cinderella to ask her opinion, for she had excellent taste. She made useful suggestions and even offered to do their hair for them. They accepted willingly.

8   While she was doing it, they said to her:

9   "Cinderella, how would you like to go to the ball?"

10   "Oh dear, you are making fun of me. It wouldn't do for me."

11   "You are quite right. It would be a joke. People would laugh if they saw a Cinderbottom at the ball."

12   Anyone else would have done their hair in knots for them, but she had a sweet nature, and she finished it perfectly. For two days they were so excited that they ate almost nothing. They broke a good dozen laces trying to tighten their stays to make their waists slimmer, and they were never away from their mirrors.

13   At last the great day arrived. They set off, and Cinderella watched them until they were out of sight. When she could no longer see them, she began to cry. Her godmother, seeing her all in tears, asked what was the matter.

14   "If only I could . . . If only I could . . . " She was weeping so much that she could not go on.

15   Her godmother, who was a fairy, said to her: "If only you could go to the ball, is that it?"

16   "Alas, yes," said Cinderella with a sigh.

17   "Well," said the godmother, "be a good girl and I'll get you there."

18   She took her into her room and said: "Go into the garden and get me a pumpkin."

19   Cinderella hurried out and cut the best she could find and took it to her godmother, but she could not understand how this pumpkin would get her to the ball. Her godmother hollowed it out, leaving only the rind, and then tapped it with her wand and immediately it turned into a magnificent gilded coach.

20   Then she went to look in her mouse-trap and found six mice all alive in it. She told Cinderella to raise the door of the trap a little, and as each mouse came out she gave it a tap with her wand and immediately it turned into a fine horse. That made a team of six horses, each of fine mouse-coloured grey.

21   While she was wondering how she would make a coachman, Cinderella said to her:

22   "I will go and see whether there is a rat in the rat-trap, we could make a coachman of him."

23   "You are right," said the godmother. "Run and see."

24   Cinderella brought her the rat-trap, in which there were three big rats. The fairy picked out one of them because of his splendid whiskers and, when she had touched him, he turned into a fat coachman, with the finest moustaches in the district.

25   Then she said: "Go into the garden and you will find six lizards behind the watering-can. Bring them to me."

26   As soon as Cinderella had brought them, her godmother changed them into six footmen, who got up behind the coach with their striped liveries, and stood in position there as though they had been doing it all their lives.

27   Then the fairy said to Cinderella:

28   "Well, that's to go to the ball in. Aren't you pleased?"

29   "Yes. But am I to go like this, with my ugly clothes?"

30   Her godmother simply touched her with her wand and her clothes were changed in an instant into a dress of gold and silver cloth, all sparkling with precious stones. Then she gave her a pair of glass slippers, most beautifully made.

31   So equipped, Cinderella got into the coach: but her godmother warned her above all not to be out after midnight, telling her that, if she stayed at the ball a moment later, her coach would turn back into a pumpkin, her horses into mice, her footmen into lizards, and her fine clothes would become rags again.

32   She promised her godmother that she would leave the ball before midnight without fail, and she set out, beside herself with joy.

33   The King's son, on being told that a great princess whom no one knew had arrived, ran out to welcome her. He handed her down from the coach and led her into the hall where his guests were. A sudden silence fell; the dancing stopped, the violins ceased to play, the whole company stood fascinated by the beauty of the unknown princess. Only a low murmur was heard: "Ah, how lovely she is!" The King himself, old as he was, could not take his eyes off her and kept whispering to the Queen that it was a long time since he had seen such a beautiful and charming person. All the ladies were absorbed in noting her clothes and the way her hair was dressed, so as to order the same things for themselves the next morning, provided that fine enough materials could be found, and skillful enough craftsmen.

34   The King's son placed her in the seat of honour, and later led her out to dance. She danced with such grace that she won still more admiration. An excellent supper was served, but the young Prince was too much occupied in gazing at her to eat anything. She went and sat next to her sisters and treated them with great courtesy, offering them oranges and lemons which the Prince had given her. They were astonished, for they did not recognize her.

35   While they were chatting together, Cinderella heard the clock strike a quarter to twelve. She curtsied low to the company and left as quickly as she could.

36   As soon as she reached home, she went to her godmother and, having thanked her, said that she would very much like to go again to the ball on the next night—for the Prince had begged her to come back. She was in the middle

of telling her godmother about all the things that had happened, when the two sisters came knocking at the door. Cinderella went to open it.

37   "How late you are!" she said, rubbing her eyes and yawning and stretching as though she had just woken up (though since they had last seen each other she had felt very far from sleepy).

38   "If you had been at the ball," said one of the sisters, "you would not have felt like yawning. There was a beautiful princess there, really ravishingly beautiful. She was most attentive to us. She gave us oranges and lemons."

39   Cinderella could have hugged herself. She asked them the name of the princess, but they replied that no one knew her, that the King's son was much troubled about it, and that he would give anything in the world to know who she was. Cinderella smiled and said to them:

40   "So she was very beautiful? Well, well, how lucky you are! Couldn't I see her? Please, Miss Javotte, do lend me that yellow dress which you wear about the house."

41   "Really," said Miss Javotte, "what an idea! Lend one's dress like that to a filthy Cinderbottom! I should have to be out of my mind."

42   Cinderella was expecting this refusal and she was very glad when it came, for she would have been in an awkward position if her sister really had lent her her frock.

43   On the next day the two sisters went to the ball, and Cinderella too, but even more splendidly dressed than the first time. The King's son was constantly at her side and wooed her the whole evening. The young girl was enjoying herself so much that she forgot her godmother's warning. She heard the clock striking the first stroke of midnight when she thought that it was still hardly eleven. She rose and slipped away as lightly as a roe-deer. The Prince followed her, but he could not catch her up. One of her glass slippers fell off, and the Prince picked it up with great care.

44   Cinderella reached home quite out of breath, with no coach, no footmen, and wearing her old clothes. Nothing remained of all her finery, except one of her little slippers, the fellow to the one which she had dropped. The guards at the palace gate were asked if they had not seen a princess go out. They answered that they had seen no one go out except a very poorly dressed girl, who looked more like a peasant than a young lady.

45   When the two sisters returned from the ball, Cinderella asked them if they had enjoyed themselves again, and if the beautiful lady had been there. They said that she had, but that she had run away when it struck midnight, and so swiftly that she had lost one of her glass slippers, a lovely little thing. The Prince had picked it up and had done nothing but gaze at it for the rest of the ball, and undoubtedly he was very much in love with the beautiful person to whom it belonged.

46   They were right, for a few days later the King's son had it proclaimed to the sound of trumpets that he would marry the girl whose foot exactly fitted the slipper. They began by trying it on the various princesses, then on the duchesses and on all the ladies of the Court, but with no success. It was brought to the two sisters, who did everything possible to force their feet into the slipper, but they

could not manage it. Cinderella, who was looking on, recognized her own slipper, and said laughing:

47   "Let me see if it would fit me!"

48   Her sisters began to laugh and mock at her. But the gentleman who was trying on the slipper looked closely at Cinderella and, seeing that she was very beautiful, said that her request was perfectly reasonable and that he had instructions to try it on every girl. He made Cinderella sit down and, raising the slipper to her foot, he found that it slid on without difficulty and fitted like a glove.

49   Great was the amazement of the two sisters, but it became greater still when Cinderella drew from her pocket the second little slipper and put it on her other foot. Thereupon the fairy godmother came in and, touching Cinderella's clothes with her wand, made them even more magnificent than on the previous days.

50   Then the two sisters recognized her as the lovely princess whom they had met at the ball. They flung themselves at her feet and begged her forgiveness for all the unkind things which they had done to her. Cinderella raised them up and kissed them, saying that she forgave them with all her heart and asking them to love her always. She was taken to the young Prince in the fine clothes which she was wearing. He thought her more beautiful than ever and a few days later he married her. Cinderella, who was as kind as she was beautiful, invited her two sisters to live in the palace and married them, on the same day, to two great noblemen of the Court.

Ashputtle
Jakob and Wilhelm Grimm

Jakob Grimm (1785–1863) and Wilhelm Grimm (1786–1859) are best known today for the 200 folktales they collected from oral sources and reworked in Kinder- und Hausmärchen *(popularly known as* Grimm's Fairy Tales)*, which has been translated into 70 languages. The techniques Jakob and Wilhelm Grimm used to collect and comment on these tales became a model for other collectors, providing a basis for the science of folklore. Although the Grimm brothers argued for preserving the tales exactly as heard from oral sources, scholars have determined that they sought to "improve" the tales by making them more readable. The result, highly pleasing to lay audiences the world over, nonetheless represents a literary reworking of the original oral sources.*

1   A rich man's wife fell sick and, feeling that her end was near, she called her only daughter to her bedside and said: "Dear child, be good and say your prayers; God will help you, and I shall look down on you from heaven and always be with you." With that she closed her eyes and died. Every day the little girl went out to her mother's grave and wept, and she went on being good and saying her prayers. When winter came, the snow spread a white cloth over the grave, and when spring took it off, the man remarried.

2   His new wife brought two daughters into the house. Their faces were beautiful and lily-white, but their hearts were ugly and black. That was the beginning of a bad time for the poor stepchild. "Why should this silly goose sit in the parlor with us?" they said. "People who want to eat bread must earn it. Get into the kitchen where you belong!" They took away her fine clothes and gave her an old gray dress and wooden shoes to wear. "Look at the haughty princess in her finery!" they cried and, laughing, led her to the kitchen. From then on she had to do all the work, getting up before daybreak, carrying water, lighting fires, cooking and washing. In addition the sisters did everything they could to plague her. They jeered at her and poured peas and lentils into the ashes, so that she had to sit there picking them out. At night, when she was tired out with work, she had no bed to sleep in but had to lie in the ashes by the hearth. And they took to calling her Ashputtle because she always looked dusty and dirty.

3   One day when her father was going to the fair, he asked his two step-daughters what he should bring them. "Beautiful dresses," said one. "Diamonds and pearls," said the other. "And you, Ashputtle. What would you like?" "Father," she said, "break off the first branch that brushes against your hat on your way home, and bring it to me." So he brought beautiful dresses, diamonds, and pearls for his two stepdaughters, and on the way home, as he was riding through a copse, a hazel branch brushed against him and knocked off his hat. So he broke off the branch and took it home with him. When he got home, he gave the stepdaughters what they had asked for, and gave Ashputtle the branch. After thanking him, she went to her mother's grave and planted the hazel sprig over it and cried so hard that her tears fell on the sprig and watered it. It grew and became a beautiful tree. Three times a day Ashputtle went and sat under it and wept and prayed. Each time a little white bird came and perched on the tree, and when Ashputtle made a wish the little bird threw down what she had wished for.

4   Now it so happened that the king arranged for a celebration. It was to go on for three days and all the beautiful girls in the kingdom were invited, in order that his son might choose a bride. When the two stepsisters heard they had been asked, they were delighted. They called Ashputtle and said: "Comb our hair, brush our shoes, and fasten our buckles. We're going to the wedding at the king's palace." Ashputtle obeyed, but she wept, for she too would have liked to go dancing, and she begged her stepmother to let her go. "You little sloven!" said the stepmother. "How can you go to a wedding when you're all dusty and dirty? How can you go dancing when you have neither dress nor shoes?" But when Ashputtle begged and begged, the stepmother finally said: "Here, I've dumped a bowlful of lentils in the ashes. If you can pick them out in two hours, you may go." The girl went out the back door to the garden and cried out: "O tame little doves, O turtledoves, and all the birds under heaven, come and help me put

> the good ones in the pot,
> the bad ones in your crop."

Two little white doves came flying through the kitchen window, and then came the turtledoves, and finally all the birds under heaven came flapping and fluttering and settled down by the ashes. The doves nodded their little heads and started in, peck peck peck peck, and all the others started in, peck peck peck peck, and they sorted out all the good lentils and put them in the bowl. Hardly an hour had passed before they finished and flew away. Then the girl brought the bowl to her stepmother, and she was happy, for she thought she'd be allowed to go to the wedding. But the stepmother said: "No, Ashputtle. You have nothing to wear and you don't know how to dance; the people would only laugh at you." When Ashputtle began to cry, the stepmother said: "If you can pick two bowlfuls of lentils out of the ashes in an hour, you may come." And she thought: "She'll never be able to do it." When she had dumped the two bowlfuls of lentils in the ashes, Ashputtle went out the back door to the garden and cried out: "O tame little doves, O turtledoves, and all the birds under heaven, come and help me put

> the good ones in the pot,
> the bad ones in your crop."

Two little white doves came flying through the kitchen window, and then came the turtledoves, and finally all the birds under heaven came flapping and fluttering and settled down by the ashes. The doves nodded their little heads and started in, peck peck peck peck, and all the others started in, peck peck peck peck, and they sorted out all the good lentils and put them in the bowls. Before half an hour had passed, they had finished and they all flew away. Then the girl brought the bowls to her stepmother, and she was happy, for she thought she'd be allowed to go to the wedding. But her stepmother said: "It's no use. You can't come, because you have nothing to wear and you don't know how to dance. We'd only be ashamed of you." Then she turned her back and hurried away with her two proud daughters.

5   When they had all gone out, Ashputtle went to her mother's grave. She stood under the hazel tree and cried:

> "Shake your branches, little tree,
> Throw gold and silver down on me."

Whereupon the bird tossed down a gold and silver dress and slippers embroidered with silk and silver. Ashputtle slipped into the dress as fast as she could and went to the wedding. Her sisters and stepmother didn't recognize her. She was so beautiful in her golden dress that they thought she must be the daughter of some foreign king. They never dreamed it could be Ashputtle, for they thought she was sitting at home in her filthy rags, picking lentils out of the ashes. The king's son came up to her, took her by the hand and danced with her. He wouldn't dance with anyone else and he never let go her hand. When someone else asked for a dance, he said: "She is my partner."

6   She danced until evening, and then she wanted to go home. The king's son said: "I'll go with you, I'll see you home," for he wanted to find out whom the beautiful girl belonged to. But she got away from him and slipped into the dovecote. The king's son waited until her father arrived, and told him the strange girl

had slipped into the dovecote. The old man thought: "Could it be Ashputtle?" and he sent for an ax and a pick and broke into the dovecote, but there was no one inside. When they went indoors, Ashputtle was lying in the ashes in her filthy clothes and a dim oil lamp was burning on the chimney piece, for Ashputtle had slipped out the back end of the dovecote and run to the hazel tree. There she had taken off her fine clothes and put them on the grave, and the bird had taken them away. Then she had put her gray dress on again, crept into the kitchen and lain down in the ashes.

7   Next day when the festivities started in again and her parents and stepsisters had gone, Ashputtle went to the hazel tree and said:

> *"Shake your branches, little tree,*
> *Throw gold and silver down on me."*

Whereupon the bird threw down a dress that was even more dazzling than the first one. And when she appeared at the wedding, everyone marveled at her beauty. The king's son was waiting for her. He took her by the hand and danced with no one but her. When others came and asked her for a dance, he said: "She is my partner." When evening came, she said she was going home. The king's son followed her, wishing to see which house she went into, but she ran away and disappeared into the garden behind the house, where there was a big beautiful tree with the most wonderful pears growing on it. She climbed among the branches as nimbly as a squirrel and the king's son didn't know what had become of her. He waited until her father arrived and said to him: "The strange girl has got away from me and I think she has climbed up in the pear tree." Her father thought: "Could it be Ashputtle?" He sent for an ax and chopped the tree down, but there was no one in it. When they went into the kitchen, Ashputtle was lying there in the ashes as usual, for she had jumped down on the other side of the tree, brought her fine clothes back to the bird in the hazel tree, and put on her filthy gray dress.

8   On the third day, after her parents and sisters had gone, Ashputtle went back to her mother's grave and said to the tree:

> *"Shake your branches, little tree,*
> *Throw gold and silver down on me."*

Whereupon the bird threw down a dress that was more radiant than either of the others, and the slippers were all gold. When she appeared at the wedding, the people were too amazed to speak. The king's son danced with no one but her, and when someone else asked her for a dance, he said: "She is my partner."

9   When the evening came, Ashputtle wanted to go home, and the king's son said he'd go with her, but she slipped away so quickly that he couldn't follow. But he had thought up a trick. He had arranged to have the whole staircase brushed with pitch, and as she was running down it the pitch pulled her left slipper off. The king's son picked it up, and it was tiny and delicate and all gold. Next morning he went to the father and said: "No girl shall be my wife but the one this golden shoe fits." The sisters were overjoyed, for they had beautiful feet. The eldest took the shoe to her room to try it on and her mother went with her. But the shoe was too

small and she couldn't get her big toe in. So her mother handed her a knife and said: "Cut your toe off. Once you're queen you won't have to walk any more." The girl cut her toe off, forced her foot into the shoe, gritted her teeth against the pain, and went out to the king's son. He accepted her as his bride-to-be, lifted her up on his horse, and rode away with her. But they had to pass the grave. The two doves were sitting in the hazel tree and they cried out:

> *"Roocoo, roocoo,*
> *There's blood in the shoe.*
> *The foot's too long, the foot's too wide,*
> *That's not the proper bride."*

He looked down at her foot and saw the blood spurting. At that he turned his horse around and took the false bride home again. "No," he said, "this isn't the right girl; let her sister try the shoe on." The sister went to her room and managed to get her toes into the shoe, but her heel was too big. So her mother handed her a knife and said: "Cut off a chunk of your heel. Once you're queen you won't have to walk any more." The girl cut off a chunk of her heel, forced her foot into the shoe, gritted her teeth against the pain, and went out to the king's son. He accepted her as his bride-to-be, lifted her up on his horse, and rode away with her. As they passed the hazel tree, the two doves were sitting there, and they cried out:

> *"Roocoo, roocoo,*
> *There's blood in the shoe.*
> *The foot's too long, the foot's too wide,*
> *That's not the proper bride."*

He looked down at her foot and saw that blood was spurting from her shoe and staining her white stocking all red. He turned his horse around and took the false bride home again. "This isn't the right girl, either," he said. "Haven't you got another daughter?" "No," said the man, "there's only a puny little kitchen drudge that my dead wife left me. She couldn't possibly be the bride." "Send her up," said the king's son, but the mother said: "Oh, no, she's much too dirty to be seen." But he insisted and they had to call her. First she washed her face and hands, and when they were clean, she went upstairs and curtseyed to the king's son. He handed her the golden slipper and sat down on a footstool, took her foot out of her heavy wooden shoe, and put it into the slipper. It fitted perfectly. And when she stood up and the king's son looked into her face, he recognized the beautiful girl he had danced with and cried out: "This is my true bride!" The stepmother and the two sisters went pale with fear and rage. But he lifted Ashputtle up on his horse and rode away with her. As they passed the hazel tree, the two white doves called out:

> *"Roocoo, roocoo,*
> *No blood in the shoe.*
> *Her foot is neither long nor wide,*
> *This one is the proper bride."*

Then they flew down and alighted on Ashputtle's shoulders, one on the right and one on the left, and there they sat.

10   On the day of Ashputtle's wedding, the two stepsisters came and tried to ingratiate themselves and share in her happiness. On the way to church the elder was on the right side of the bridal couple and the younger on the left. The doves came along and pecked out one of the elder sister's eyes and one of the younger sister's eyes. Afterward, on the way out, the elder was on the left side and younger on the right, and the doves pecked out both the remaining eyes. So both sisters were punished with blindness to the end of their days for being so wicked and false.

The Cat Cinderella
Giambattista Basile

"One of the first major collections of European folktales taken from oral sources was Giambattista Basile's Il Pentamerone, *published posthumously during the years 1634–1636. Originally entitled* Lo Cunto de li Cunte, *the tale of tales, the work consisted of five sets of ten diversions, or stories. Supposedly each set of narratives represented one day's worth of tale-telling. The sixth diversion of the first day was 'The Cat Cinderella.'*

"Basile (1575–1632) had apparently heard in Naples many of the stories he reported in the Pentamerone. *In any case, the book was published in Neapolitan dialect, which unfortunately made it relatively inaccessible even to readers of other Italian dialects. Not until 1742 was it translated into Bolognese dialect and in 1747 into Italian. It was not translated into German until 1846, when Felix Liebrecht undertook the task. This volume contained an introduction by Jakob Grimm. The Grimm brothers had known of Basile's collection earlier and were quite astonished to find that so many of 'their' German 'Kinder und Hausmärchen' had been reported in Naples nearly two centuries before."* *

1   There was once . . . a Prince who was a widower, and he had a daughter so dear to him that he saw with no other eyes but hers. He gave her an excellent teacher of sewing, who taught her chainwork, openwork, fringes and hems and showed her more love than was possible to describe. The father, however, shortly remarried, and his wife was an evil, malicious, bad-tempered woman who began at once to hate her step-daughter and threw sour looks, wry faces and scowling glances on her enough to make her jump with fright.

2   The poor child was always complaining to her governess of her step-mother's ill-treatment, finishing up with "O would to God that you could be my little mother, who are so kind and loving to me," and she so often repeated this song to her that she put a wasp in her ear and, at last, tempted by the devil, her teacher ended by saying, "If you must follow this madcap idea, I will be a mother

---

* Note: Introduction to "The Cat Cinderella" was written by Alan Dundes.

to you and you shall be the apple of my eye." She was going on with the prologue, when Zezolla (as the girl was called) interrupted her by saying, "Forgive
my taking the words out of your mouth. I know you love me well, mum's the
word, and *sufficit*; teach me the way, for I am new; you write and I will sign."
"Well, then," answered the governess, "listen carefully; keep your ears open and
you shall always enjoy the whitest bread from the finest flour. When your father
leaves the house, tell your step-mother that you would like one of those old
dresses that are kept in the big chest in the closet, to save the one you now have
on. As she always wants to see you in rags and tatters, she will open the chest
and say, 'Hold the lid.' You must hold it while she is rummaging inside and then
suddenly let it fall so that it breaks her neck. After that, you know well that your
father would even coin false money to please you, so when he fondles you, beg
him to take me for his wife, and then you shall be happy and the mistress even
of my life."

3   When Zezolla had heard the plan, every hour seemed a thousand years until
she had carried out her governess's advice in every particular. When the period
of mourning for her step-mother was over, she began to sound her father about
marrying her governess. At first the Prince took it as a joke, but Zezolla so often
struck with the flat that at last she thrust with the point, and he gave way to the
persuasive words of his daughter. He therefore married Carmosina, the governess,
with great celebrations.

4   Now, while this couple were enjoying themselves, Zezolla was standing at a
balcony of her house, when a dove flew on to the wall and said to her, "If ever
you desire anything, send to ask for it from the dove of the fairies of the Island
of Sardinia, and you will at once have it."

5   For five or six days the new step-mother lavished every sort of caress of
Zezolla, making her take the best seat at table, giving her the best tidbits, and
dressing her in the finest clothes. But after a little time the service that Zezolla
had done her was forgotten, and banished from her memory (how sorry is the
mind that has an evil mistress!) and she began to push forward six daughters of
her own that she had kept in hiding till then, and so worked on her husband
that they won his good graces and he let his own daughter slip out of his heart.
So that, a loser to-day and a pauper to-morrow, Zezolla was finally brought to
such a pass that she fell from the *salon* to the kitchen, from the canopy to the
grate, from splendid silks and gold to dish-clouts, from sceptres to spits; not only
did she change her state, but also her name, and was no longer called Zezolla,
but "Cat Cinderella."

6   Now it happened that the Prince was forced to go to Sardinia on important affairs of State, and before he left he asked one by one of his step-daughters, Imperia, Colomba, Fiorella, Diamante, Colombina, and Pascarella, what
they wanted him to bring back for them on his return. One asked for a splendid gown, another for a head-dress, one for cosmetics for the face, and another games to pass the time; one one thing and one another. At last, and almost
to make fun of her, he asked his daughter, "And you! what would you like?"
and she answered, "Nothing, except to commend me to the dove of the
fairies and beg them to send me something; and if you forget, may it be
impossible for you to go forward or back. Bear in mind what I say: thy intent,
thy reward."

7   The Prince went away, transacted his affairs in Sardinia, and bought the things his step-daughters had asked for, but Zezolla went quite out of his mind. But when they were embarked with the sails ready unfurled, it was found impossible to make the vessel leave the harbour: it seemed as if it were detained by a sea-lamprey. The captain of the ship, who was almost in despair, dropped off to sleep with weariness and in his dreams a fairy appeared to him who said; "Do you know why you cannot leave the harbour? Because the Prince who is with you has broken his promise to his daughter, remembering all the others except his own flesh and blood." As soon as he woke up the captain told his dream to the Prince, who was overcome with confusion at his omission. He went to the grotto of the fairies, and commending his daughter to them, begged that they should send her some gift.

8   Behold, out of the grotto there came a young girl, beautiful as a gonfalon, who bade him thank his daughter for her kind remembrances and tell her to be of good cheer for love of her. With these words, she gave him a date tree, a spade and a golden can with a silken napkin; the date tree for planting and the other articles to keep and cultivate it.

9   The Prince, surprised at this present, took leave of the fairy and turned towards his own land. When he arrived, he gave his step-daughters the things they had asked for, and lastly he handed the fairy's present to his own daughter. Zezolla nearly jumped out of her skin with joy and planted the date tree in a fine pot, watering it every day and then drying it with the silken napkin.

10   As a result of these attentions, within four days the date tree grew to the size of a woman, and a fairy came out who said to the girl, "What do you want?" Zezolla answered that she would like sometimes to leave the house without the sisters knowing it. The fairy replied, "Whenever you want this, come to the plant and say:

> O my golden date tree,
> With golden spade, I've dug thee,
> With golden can I've watered thee,
> With golden napkin dried thee,
> Strip thyself and robe thou me.

11   Then when you want to undress, change the last line and say: "Strip thou me and robe thou thee."

12   One day it happened to be a feast-day, and the governess's daughters went out of the house in a procession all fluttering, bedaubed and painted, all ribbons, bells and gewgaws, all flowers and perfumes, roses and posies. Zezolla then ran to the plant and uttered the words the fairy had taught her, and at once she was decked out like a queen, seated on a white horse with twelve smartly attired pages. She too went where the sisters had gone, and though they did not recognize her, they felt their mouths water at the beauty of this lovely dove.

13   As luck would have it, the King came to this same place and was quite bewitched by the extraordinary loveliness of Zezolla. He ordered his most trusty attendant to find out about this fair creature, who she was and where she lived. The servant at once began to dog her footsteps, but she, noticing the trap, threw down a handful of crowns that she had obtained for that purpose from the date

tree. The servant, fired by the desire for these glittering pieces, forgot to follow the palfrey and stopped to pick up the money, whilst she, at a bound, reached the house and quickly undressed in the way the fairy had told her. Those six harpies, her sisters, soon returned, and to vex and mortify her, described at length all the fine things that they had seen at the feast.

14   The servant in the meantime had returned to the King and had told him about the crowns, whereupon the King was furious, and angrily told him that he had sold his pleasure for a few paltry coins and that at the next feast he was at all costs to discover who this lovely girl was and where nested so fair a bird.

15   When the next feast-day came, the sisters went out, all bedecked and bedizened, leaving the despised Zezolla by the hearth. But she at once ran to the date tree and uttered the same words as before, and behold a band of maidens came out, one with the mirror and one with the flask of pumpkin water, one with the curling-tongs and another with the rouge, one with the comb and another with the pins, one with the dresses and one with the necklace and earrings. They all placed themselves round her and made her as beautiful as a sun and then mounted her in a coach with six horses accompanied by footmen and pages in livery. She drove to the same place as before and kindled envy in the hearts of the sisters and flames in the breast of the King.

16   This time too, when she went away, the servant followed her, but so that he should not catch her up, she threw down a handful of pearls and jewels, which this trusty fellow was unable to resist pecking at, since they were not things to let slip. In this way Zezolla had time to reach home and undress herself as usual. The servant, quite stunned, went back to the King, who said, "By the soul of your departed, if you don't find that girl again, I'll give you a most thorough beating and as many kicks on your seat as you have hairs in your beard."

17   On the next feast day, when the sisters had already started off, Zezolla went up to the date tree. She repeated the magic spell and was again magnificently dressed and placed in a golden coach with so many attendants around it that it looked as if she were a courtesan arrested in the public promenade and surrounded by police agents. After having excited the envy and wonder of her sisters, she left, followed by the King's servant, who this time fastened himself to the carriage by double thread. Zezolla, seeing that he was always at her side, cried, "Drive on," and the coach set off at such a gallop that in her agitation she let slip from her foot the richest and prettiest patten you could imagine.

18   The servant, not being able to catch up to the carriage, which was now flying along, picked up the patten and carried it to the King, telling him what had happened. The King took it in his hands and broke out into these words: "If the foundation is so fair, what must be the mansion? Oh, lovely candlestick which holds the candle that consumes me! Oh, tripod of the lovely cauldron in which my life is boiling! Oh, beauteous corks attached to the fishing-line of Love with which he has caught his soul! Behold, I embrace and enfold you, and if I cannot reach the plant, I worship the roots; if I cannot possess the capitals, I kiss the base: you first imprisoned a white foot, now you have ensnared a stricken heart. Through you, she who sways my life was taller by a span and a half; through you, my life grows by that much in sweetness so long as I keep you in my possession."

19   The King having said this called a secretary and ordered out the trumpeters and tantarara, and had it proclaimed that all the women in the land were to

come to a festival and banquet which he had determined to give. On the appointed day, my goodness, what an eating and feasting there was! Where did all the tarts and cakes come from? Where all the stews and rissoles? All the macaroni and graviuoli which were enough to stuff an entire army? The women were all there, of every kind and quality, of high degree and low degree, the rich and the poor, old and young, the well-favoured and the ill-favoured. When they had all thoroughly worked their jaws, the King spoke the proficiat and started to try the patten on his guests, one by one, to see whom it fitted to a hair, so that he could find by the shape of the slipper the one whom he was seeking. But he could find no foot to fit it, so that he was on the point of despair.

20   Nevertheless, he ordered a general silence and said, "Come back to-morrow to fast with me, but as you love me well, do not leave behind a single woman, whoever she may be!" The Prince then said, "I have a daughter, but she always stays to mind the hearth, for she is a sorry, worthless creature, not fit to take her place at the table where you eat." The King answered, "Let her be at the top of the list, for such is my wish."

So they all went away, and came back the next day, and Zezolla came with Carmosina's daughters. As soon as the King saw her, he thought she was the one he wanted, but he hid his thoughts. After the banquet came the trial of the patten. The moment it came near Zezolla's foot, it darted forward of itself to shoe that painted Lover's egg, as the iron flies to the magnet. The King then took Zezolla in his arms and led her to the canopy, where he put a crown on her head and ordered every one to make obeisance to her as to their queen. The sisters, livid with envy and unable to bear the torment of their breaking hearts, crept quietly home to their mother, confessing in spite of themselves that:

He is mad who would oppose the stars.

A Chinese "Cinderella"
Tuan Ch'êng-shih

"The earliest datable version of the Cinderella story anywhere in the world occurs in a Chinese book written about 850–860 A.D." Thus begins Arthur Waley's essay on the Chinese "Cinderella" in the March 1947 edition of Folk-Lore. The recorder of the tale is a man named Tuan Ch'êng-shih, whose father was an important official in Szechwan and who himself held a high post in the office arranging the ceremonies associated with imperial ancestor worship.

1   Among the people of the south there is a tradition that before the Ch'in and Han dynasties there was a cave-master called Wu. The aborigines called the place the Wu cave. He married two wives. One wife died. She had a daughter called Yeh-hsien, who from childhood was intelligent and good at making pottery on the wheel. Her father loved her. After some years the father died, and she was ill-treated by her step-mother, who always made her collect firewood in dangerous places

and draw water from deep pools. She once got a fish about two inches long, with red fins and golden eyes. She put it into a bowl of water. It grew bigger every day, and after she had changed the bowl several times she could find no bowl big enough for it, so she threw it into the back pond. Whatever food was left over from meals she put into the water to feed it. When she came to the pond, the fish always exposed its head and pillowed it on the bank; but when anyone else came, it did not come out. The step-mother knew about this, but when she watched for it, it did not once appear. So she tricked the girl, saying, "Haven't you worked hard! I am going to give you a new dress." She then made the girl change out of her tattered clothing. Afterwards she sent her to get water from another spring and reckoning that it was several hundred leagues, the step-mother at her leisure put on her daughter's clothes, hid a sharp blade up her sleeve, and went to the pond. She called to the fish. The fish at once put its head out, and she chopped it off and killed it. The fish was now more than ten feet long. She served it up and it tasted twice as good as an ordinary fish. She hid the bones under the dung-hill. Next day, when the girl came to the pond, no fish appeared. She howled with grief in the open countryside, and suddenly there appeared a man with his hair loose over his shoulders and coarse clothes. He came down from the sky. He consoled her, saying, "Don't howl! Your step-mother has killed the fish and its bones are under the dung. You go back, take the fish's bones and hide them in your room. Whatever you want, you have only to pray to them for it. It is bound to be grant-ed." The girl followed his advice, and was able to provide herself with gold, pearls, dresses, and food whenever she wanted them.

2   When the time came for the cave-festival, the step-mother went, leaving the girl to keep watch over the fruit-trees in the garden. She waited till the step-mother was some way off, and then went herself, wearing a cloak of stuff spun from kingfisher feathers and shoes of gold. Her step-sister recognized her and said to the step-mother, "That's very like my sister." The step-mother suspected the same thing. The girl was aware of this and went away in such a hurry that she lost one shoe. It was picked up by one of the people of the cave. When the step-mother got home, she found the girl asleep, with her arms around one of the trees in the garden, and thought no more about it.

3   This cave was near to an island in the sea. On this island was a kingdom called T'o-han. Its soldiers had subdued twenty or thirty other islands and it had a coast-line of several thousand leagues. The cave-man sold the shoe in T'o-han, and the ruler of T'o-han got it. He told those about him to put it on; but it was an inch too small even for the one among them that had the smallest foot. He ordered all the women in his kingdom to try it on, but there was not one that it fitted. It was light as down and made no noise even when treading on stone. The king of T'o-han thought the cave-man had got it unlawfully. He put him in prison and tortured him, but did not end by finding out where it had come from. So he threw it down at the wayside. Then they went everywhere* through all the people's houses and arrested them. If there was a woman's shoe, they arrested them and told the king of T'o-han. He thought it strange, searched the inner-rooms and found Yeh-hsien. He made her put on the shoe, and it was true.

---

* Something here seems to have gone slightly wrong with the text. [Waley]

4   Yeh-hsien then came forward, wearing her cloak spun from halcyon feathers and her shoes. She was as beautiful as a heavenly being. She now began to render service to the king, and he took the fish-bones and Yeh-hsien, and brought them back to his country.

5   The step-mother and step-sister were shortly afterwards struck by flying stones, and died. The cave people were sorry for them and buried them in a stone-pit, which was called the Tomb of the Distressed Women. The men of the cave made mating-offerings there; any girl they prayed for there, they got. The king of T'o-han, when he got back to his kingdom, made Yeh-hsien his chief wife. The first year the king was very greedy and by his prayers to the fish-bones got treasures and jade without limit. Next year, there was no response, so the king buried the fish-bones on the seashore. He covered them with a hundred bushels of pearls and bordered them with gold. Later there was a mutiny of some soldiers who had been conscripted and their general opened (the hiding-place) in order to make better provision for his army. One night they (the bones) were washed away by the tide.

6   This story was told me by Li Shih-yuan, who has been in the service of my family a long while. He was himself originally a man from the caves of Yung-chou and remembers many strange things of the South.

The Maiden, the Frog, and the Chief's Son (An African "Cinderella")

The version of the "Cinderella" tale that follows was recorded in the Hausa (West African) language and published, originally, in 1911 by Frank Edgar. The tale remained unavailable to non-speakers of Hausa until 1965, when Neil Skinner (of UCLA) completed an English translation.

1   There was once a man had two wives, and they each had a daughter. And the one wife, together with her daughter, he couldn't abide; but the other, with her daughter, he dearly loved.

2   Well, the day came when the wife that he disliked fell ill, and it so happened that her illness proved fatal, and she died. And her daughter was taken over by the other wife, the one he loved; and she moved into that wife's hut. And there she dwelt, having no mother of her own, just her father. And every day the woman would push her out, to go off to the bush to gather wood. When she returned, she had to pound up the *fura*. Then she had the *tuwo* to pound, and, after that, to stir. And then they wouldn't even let her eat the *tuwo*. All they gave her to eat were the burnt bits at the bottom of the pot. And day after day she continued thus.

3   Now she had an elder brother, and he invited her to come and eat regularly at his home—to which she agreed. But still when she had been to the bush, and

returned home, and wanted a drink of water, they wouldn't let her have one. Nor would they give her proper food—only the coarsest of the grindings and the scrapings from the pot. These she would take, and going with them to a borrow-pit, throw them in. And the frogs would come out and start eating the scrapings. Then, having eaten them up, they would go back into the water; and she too would return home.

4   And so things went on day after day, until the day of the Festival arrived. And on this day, when she went along with the scrapings and coarse grindings, she found a frog squatting here; and realized that he was waiting for her! She got there and threw in the bits of food. Whereupon the frog said, "Maiden, you've always been very kind to us, and now we—but just you come along tomorrow morning. That's the morning of the Festival. Come along then, and we'll be kind to you, in our turn." "Fine," she said, and went off home.

5   Next morning was the Festival, and she was going off to the borrow-pit, just as the frog had told her. But as she was going, her half-sister's mother said to her, "Hey—come here, you good-for-nothing girl! You haven't stirred the *tuwo*, or pounded the *fura*, or fetched the wood or the water." So the girl returned. And the frog spent the whole day waiting for her. But she, having returned to the compound, set off to fetch wood. Then she fetched water, and set about pounding the *tuwo*, and stirred it till it was done and then took it off the fire. And presently she was told to take the scrapings. She did so and went off to the borrow-pit, where she found the frog. "Tut tut, girl!" said he, "I've been waiting for you here since morning, and you never came." "Old fellow," she said, "You see, I'm a slave." "How come?" he asked. "Simple," she said, "My mother died—died leaving me her only daughter. I have an elder brother, but he is married and has a compound of his own. And my father put me in the care of his other wife. And indeed he had never loved my mother. So I was moved into the hut of his other wife. And, as I told you, slavery is my lot. Every morning I have to go off to the bush to get wood. When I get back from that I have to pound the *fura*, and then I pound the *tuwo*, and then start stirring it. And even when I have finished stirring the *tuwo*, I'm not given it to eat—just the scrapings." Says the frog, "Girl, give us your hand." And she held it out to him, and they both leaped into the water.

6   Then he went and picked her up and swallowed her. (And he vomited her up.) "Good people," said he, "Look and tell me, is she straight or crooked?" And they looked and answered, "She is bent to the left." So he picked her up and swallowed her again and then brought her up, and again asked them the same question. "She's quite straight now," they said. "Good," said he.

7   Next he vomited up cloths for her, and bangles, and rings, and a pair of shoes, one of silver, one of gold. "And now," said he, "Off you go to the dancing." So all these things were given to her, and he said to her, "When you get there, and when the dancing is nearly over and the dancers dispersing, you're to leave your golden shoe, the right one, there." And the girl replied to the frog, "Very well, old fellow, I understand," and off she went.

8   Meanwhile the chief's son had caused the young men and girls to dance for his pleasure, and when she reached the space where they were dancing he saw her. "Well!" said the chief's son, "*There's* a maiden for you, if you like. Don't you let her go and join in the dancing—I don't care whose home she comes from. Bring her here!" So the servants of the chief's son went over and came back with her to where he was. He told her to sit down on the couch, and she took her seat there accordingly.

9   They chatted together for some time, till the dancers began to disperse. Then she said to the chief's son, "I must be going home." "Oh, are you off?" said he. "Yes," said she and rose to her feet. "I'll accompany you on your way for a little," said the chief's son, and he did so. But she had left her right shoe behind. Presently she said, "Chief's son, you must go back now," and he did so. And afterwards she too turned and made her way back.

10   And there she found the frog by the edge of the water waiting for her. He took her hand and the two of them jumped into the water. Then he picked her up and swallowed her, and again vomited her up; and there she was just as she had been before, a sorry sight. And taking her ragged things she went off home.

11   When she got there, she said, "Fellow-wife of my mother, I'm not feeling very well." And the other said, "Rascally slut! You have been up to no good— refusing to come home, refusing to fetch water or wood, refusing to pound the *fura* or make the *tuwo*. Very well then! No food for you today!" And so the girl set off to her elder brother's compound, and there ate her food, and so returned home again.

12   But meanwhile, the chief's son had picked up the shoe and said to his father, "Dad, I have seen a girl who wears a pair of shoes, one of gold, one of silver. Look, here's the golden one—she forgot it and left it behind. She's the girl I want to marry. So let all the girls of this town, young and old, be gathered together, and let this shoe be given to them to put on." "Very well," said the chief.

13   And so it was proclaimed, and all the girls, young and old, were collected and gathered together. And the chief's son went and sat there beside the shoe. Each girl came, and each tried on the shoe, but it fitted none of them, none of the girls of the town; until only the girl who had left it was left. Then someone said "Just a minute! There's that girl in so-and-so's compound, whose mother died." "Yes, that's right," said another, "Someone go and fetch her." And someone went and fetched her.

14   But the minute she arrived to try it on, the shoe itself of its own accord, ran across and made her foot get into it. Then said the chief's son, "Right, here's my wife."

15   At this, the other woman—the girl's father's other wife—said, "But the shoe belongs to my daughter; it was she who forgot it at the place of the dancing, not this good-for-nothing slut." But the chief's son insisted that, since he had seen the shoe fit the other girl, as far as he was concerned, she was the one to be taken to his compound in marriage. And so they took her there, and there she spent one night.

16   Next morning she went out of her hut and round behind it, and there saw the frog. She knelt respectfully and said, "Welcome, old fellow, welcome," and

greeted him. Says he, "Tonight we shall be along to bring some things for you."
"Thank you" said she, and he departed.

17   Well, that night, the frog rallied all the other frogs, and all his friends, both great and small came along. And he, their leader, said to them, "See here—my daughter is being married. So I want every one of you to make a contribution." And each of them went and fetched what he could afford, whereupon their leader thanked them all, and then vomited up a silver bed, a brass bed, a copper bed, and an iron bed, and went on vomiting up things for her—such as woollen blankets, and rugs, and satins, and velvets.

18   "Now," said he to the girl, "If your heart is ever troubled, just lie down on this brass bed," and he went on, "And when the chief's son's other wives come to greet you, give them two calabashes of cola-nuts and ten thousand cowrie shells; then, when his concubines come to greet you, give them one calabash of cola-nuts and five thousand cowries." "Very well," said she. Then he said, "And when the concubines come to receive corn for making *tuwo*, say to them, 'There's a hide-bag full, help yourselves.'" "Very well," she said. "And," he went on, "If your father's wife comes along with her daughter and asks you what it is like living in the chief's compound, say 'Living in the chief's compound is a wearisome business—for they measure out corn there with the shell of a Bambara groundnut.'"

19   So there she dwelt, until one day her father's favorite wife brought her daughter along at night, took her into the chief's compound, and brought the other girl out and took her to her own compound. There she said, "Oh! I forgot to get you to tell her all about married life in the chief's compound." "Oh, it's a wearisome business," answered our girl. "How so?" asked the older woman, surprised. "Well, they use the shell of a Bambara groundnut for measuring out corn. Then, if the chief's other wives come to greet you, you answer them with the 'Pf' of contempt. If the concubines come to greet you, you clear your throat, hawk, and spit. And if your husband comes into your hut, you yell at him." "I see," said the other—and her daughter stayed behind the chief's son's compound.

20   Next morning when it was light, the wives came to greet her—and she said "Pf" to them. The concubines came to greet her, and she spat at them. Then when night fell, the chief's son made his way to her hut, and she yelled at him. And he was amazed and went aside, and for two days pondered the matter.

21   Then he had his wives and concubines collected and said to them, "Look, now—I've called you to ask you. They haven't brought me the same girl. How did that one treat all of you?" "Hm—how indeed!" they all exclaimed. "Each morning, when we wives went to greet her, she would give us cola-nuts, two calabashes full, and cowries, ten thousand of them to buy tobacco flowers. And when the concubines went to greet her, she would give them a calabash of cola-nuts, and five thousand cowries to buy tobacco flowers with; and in the evening, for corn for *tuwo*, it would be a whole hide-bag full." "You see?" said he, "As for me, whenever I came to enter her hut, I found her respectfully kneeling. And she wouldn't get up from there, until I had entered and sat down on the bed."

22   "Hey," he called out, "Boys, come over here!" And when they came, he went into her hut and took a sword, and chopped her up into little pieces, and

had them collect them and wrap them up in clothing; and then taken back to her home.

23   And when they got there, they found his true wife lying in the fireplace, and picking her up they took her back to her husband.

24   And next morning when it was light, she picked up a little gourd water-bottle and going around behind her hut, there saw the frog. "Welcome, welcome, old fellow," said she, and went on. "Old fellow, what I should like is to have a well built; and then you, all of you, can come and live in it and be close to me." "All right," said the frog, "You tell your husband." And she did so.

25   And he had a well dug for her, close to her hut. And the frogs came and entered the well and there they lived. That's all. *Kungurus kan kusu.*

Oochigeaskw—The Rough-Faced Girl (A Native American "Cinderella")

The following version of the "Cinderella" tale was told, originally, in the Algonquin language. Native Americans who spoke Algonquian lived in the Eastern Woodlands of what is now the United States and in the northern, semiarctic areas of present-day Canada.

1   There was once a large village of the MicMac Indians of the Eastern Algonquins, built beside a lake. At the far end of the settlement stood a lodge, and in it lived a being who was always invisible. He had a sister who looked after him, and everyone knew that any girl who could see him might marry him. For that reason there were very few girls who did not try, but it was very long before anyone succeeded.

2   This is the way in which the test of sight was carried out: at evening-time, when the Invisible One was due to be returning home, his sister would walk with any girl who might come down to the lakeshore. She, of course, could see her brother, since he was always visible to her. As soon as she saw him, she would say to the girls:

3   "Do you see my brother?"

4   "Yes," they would generally reply—though some of them did say "No."

5   To those who said that they could indeed see him, the sister would say:

6   "Of what is his shoulder strap made?" Some people say that she would enquire:

7   "What is his moose-runner's haul?" or "With what does he draw his sled?"

8   And they would answer:

9   "A strip of rawhide" or "a green flexible branch," or something of that kind.

10   Then she, knowing that they had not told the truth, would say:

11   "Very well, let us return to the wigwam!"

12   When they had gone in, she would tell them not to sit in a certain place, because it belonged to the Invisible One. Then, after they had helped to cook

the supper, they would wait with great curiosity, to see him eat. They could be sure he was a real person, for when he took off his moccasins they became visible, and his sister hung them up. But beyond this they saw nothing of him, not even when they stayed in the place all the night, as many of them did.

13   Now there lived in the village an old man who was a widower, and his three daughters. The youngest girl was very small, weak, and often ill: and yet her sisters, especially the elder, treated her cruelly. The second daughter was kinder, and sometimes took her side: but the wicked sister would burn her hands and feet with hot cinders, and she was covered with scars from this treatment. She was so marked that people called her *Oochigeaskw*, the Rough-Faced Girl.

14   When her father came home and asked why she had such burns, the bad sister would at once say that it was her own fault, for she had disobeyed orders and gone near the fire and fallen into it.

15   These two elder sisters decided one day to try their luck at seeing the Invisible One. So they dressed themselves in their finest clothes, and tried to look their prettiest. They found the Invisible One's sister and took the usual walk by the water.

16   When he came, and when they were asked if they could see him, they answered: "Of course." And when asked about the shoulder strap or sled cord, they answered: "A piece of rawhide."

17   But of course they were lying like the others, and they got nothing for their pains.

18   The next afternoon, when the father returned home, he brought with him many of the pretty little shells from which wampum was made, and they set to work to string them.

19   That day, poor Little Oochigeaskw, who had always gone barefoot, got a pair of her father's moccasins, old ones, and put them into water to soften them so that she could wear them. Then she begged her sisters for a few wampum shells. The elder called her a "little pest," but the younger one gave her some. Now, with no other clothes than her usual rags, the poor little thing went into the woods and got herself some sheets of birch bark, from which she made a dress, and put marks on it for decoration, in the style of long ago. She made a petticoat and a loose gown, a cap, leggings, and a handkerchief. She put on her father's large old moccasins, which were far too big for her, and went forth to try her luck. She would try, she thought, to discover whether she could see the Invisible One.

20   She did not begin very well. As she set off, her sisters shouted and hooted, hissed and yelled, and tried to make her stay. And the loafers around the village, seeing the strange little creature, called out "Shame!"

21   The poor little girl in her strange clothes, with her face all scarred, was an awful sight, but she was kindly received by the sister of the Invisible One. And this was, of course, because this noble lady understood far more about things than simply the mere outside which all the rest of the world knows. As the brown of the evening sky turned to black, the lady took her down to the lake.

22   "Do you see him?" the Invisible One's sister asked.

23   "I do indeed—and he is wonderful!" said Oochigeaskw.

24   The sister asked:

25   "And what is his sled-string?"

26   The little girl said:

27   "It is the Rainbow."

28   "And, my sister, what is his bow-string?"

29   "It is The Spirit's Road—the Milky Way."

30   "So you *have* seen him," said his sister. She took the girl home with her and bathed her. As she did so, all the scars disappeared from her body. Her hair grew again, as it was combed, long, like a blackbird's wing. Her eyes were now like stars: in all the world there was no other such beauty. Then, from her treasures, the lady gave her a wedding garment, and adorned her.

31   Then she told Oochigeaskw to take the *wife's* seat in the wigwam: the one next to where the Invisible One sat, beside the entrance. And when he came in, terrible and beautiful, he smiled and said:

32   "So we are found out!"

33   "Yes," said his sister. And so Oochigeaskw became his wife.

The Seven Foals
Andrew Lang

Andrew Lang's "Cinderella" is notable because its main character is a boy ("Boots" in this edition of the story, "Cinderlad" in others), rather than a girl, who does "little else than lie by the fire and poke about in the ashes." As you read, decide how closely Lang's story follows other variants of "Cinderella" that you have read. Are the elements that make a tale recognizably "Cinderella" present? Andrew Lang (1844–1912) was a Scottish journalist, poet, novelist, translator of classical literature, and literary critic. He also collected folktales and published them as a series of Fairy Books, *each title distinguished by a different color (blue, green, yellow, etc.). "The Seven Foals" appears in the* Red Fairy Book *(1890).*

1   Once on a time there was a poor couple who lived in a wretched hut, far, far away in the forest. How they lived I can't tell, but I'm sure it was from hand to mouth, and hard work even then; but they had three sons, and the youngest of them was Boots, of course, for he did little else than lie by the fire and poke about in the ashes.

2   So one day the eldest lad said he would go out to earn his bread, and he soon got leave, and wandered out into the world. There he walked and walked the whole day, and when evening drew in, he came to a king's palace, and there stood the King out on the steps, and asked whither he was bound.

3   'Oh, I'm going about, looking for a place,' said the lad.

4   'Will you serve me?' asked the King, 'and watch my seven foals. If you can watch them one whole day, and tell me at night what they eat and what they drink, you shall have the Princess to wife, and half my kingdom; but if you can't, I'll cut three red stripes out of your back. Do you hear?'

5   Yes! that was an easy task, the lad thought; he'd do that fast enough, never fear.

6   So next morning, as soon as the first peep of dawn came, the King's coachman let out the seven foals. Away they went, and the lad after them. You may fancy how they tore over hill and dale, through bush and bog. When the lad had run so a long time, he began to get weary, and when he had held on a while longer, he had more than enough of his watching, and just there, he came to a cleft in a rock, where an old hag sat and spun with a distaff. As soon as she saw the lad who was running after the foals till the sweat ran down his brow, this old hag bawled out:

7   'Come here, come here, my pretty fellow, and let me comb your hair.'

8   Yes! the lad was willing enough; so he sat down in the cleft of the rock with the old hag, and laid his head on her lap, and she combed his hair all day whilst he lay there, and stretched his lazy bones.

9   So, when evening drew on, the lad wanted to go away.

10   'I may just as well toddle straight home now,' said he, 'for it's no use my going back to the palace.'

11   'Stop a bit till it's dark,' said the old hag, 'and then the King's foals will pass by here again, and then you can run home with them, and then no one will know that you have lain here all day long, instead of watching the foals.'

12   So, when they came, she gave the lad a flask of water and a clod of turf. Those he was to show to the King, and say that was what his seven foals ate and drank.

13   'Have you watched true and well the whole day, now?' asked the King, when the lad came before him in the evening.

14   'Yes, I should think so,' said the lad.

15   'Then you can tell me what my seven foals eat and drink,' said the King.

16   'Yes!' and so the lad pulled out the flask of water and the clod of turf, which the old hag had given him.

17   'Here you see their meat, and here you see their drink,' said the lad.

18   But then the King saw plain enough how he had watched, and he got so wroth, he ordered his men to chase him away home on the spot; but first they were to cut three red stripes out of his back, and rub salt into them. So when the lad got home again, you may fancy what a temper he was in. He'd gone out once to get a place, he said, but he'd never do so again.

19   Next day the second son said he would go out into the world to try his luck. His father and mother said 'No,' and bade him look at his brother's back; but the lad wouldn't give in; he held to his own, and at last he got leave to go, and set off. So when he had walked the whole day, he, too, came to the King's palace. There stood the King out on the steps, and asked whither he was bound? and when the lad said he was looking about for a place, the King said he might have a place there, and watch his seven foals. But the King laid down the same punishment, and the same reward, as he had settled for his brother. Well, the lad was willing enough; he took the place at once with the King, for he thought he'd soon watch the foals, and tell the King what they ate and drank.

20   So, in the grey of the morning, the coachman let out the seven foals, and off they went again over hill and dale, and the lad after them. But the same thing happened to him as had befallen his brother. When he had run after the

foals a long, long time, till he was both warm and weary, he passed by the cleft in a rock, where an old hag sat and spun with a distaff, and she bawled out to the lad:

21 'Come here, come here, my pretty fellow, and let me comb your hair.'

22 That the lad thought a good offer, so he let the foals run on their way, and sat down in the cleft with the old hag. There he sat, and there he lay, taking his ease, and stretching his lazy bones the whole day.

23 When the foals came back at nightfall, he too got a flask of water and clod of turf from the old hag to show to the King. But when the King asked the lad:

24 'Can you tell me now, what my seven foals eat and drink?' the lad pulled out the flask and the clod, and said:

25 'Here you see their meat, and here you see their drink.'

26 Then the King got wroth again, and ordered them to cut three red stripes out of the lad's back, and rub salt in, and chase him home that very minute. And so when the lad got home, he also told how he had fared, and said, he had gone out once to get a place, but he'd never do so anymore.

27 The third day Boots wanted to set out; he had a great mind to try and watch the seven foals, he said. The others laughed at him, and made game of him, saying:

28 'When we fared so ill, you'll do it better—a fine joke; you look like it—you, who have never done anything but lie there and poke about in the ashes.'

29 'Yes!' said Boots, 'I don't see why I shouldn't go, for I've got it into my head, and can't get it out again.'

30 And so, in spite of all the jeers of the others and the prayers of the old people, there was no help for it, and Boots set out.

31 So after he had walked the whole day, he too came at dusk to the King's palace. There stood the King out on the steps, and asked whither he was bound.

32 'Oh,' said Boots, 'I'm going about seeing if I can hear of a place.'

33 'Whence do you come then?' said the King, for he wanted to know a little more about them before he took anyone into his service.

34 So Boots said whence he came, and how he was brother to those two who had watched the King's seven foals, and ended by asking if he might try to watch them next day.

35 'Oh, stuff!' said the King, for he got quite cross if he even thought of them; 'if you're brother to those two, you're not worth much, I'll be bound. I've had enough of such scamps.'

36 'Well,' said Boots; 'but since I've come so far, I may just as well get leave to try, I too.'

37 'Oh, very well; with all my heart,' said the King, 'if you *will* have your back flayed, you're quite welcome.'

38 'I'd much rather have the Princess," said Boots.

39 So next morning, at grey of dawn, the coachman let out the seven foals again, and away they went over hill and dale, through bush and bog, and Boots behind them. And so, when he too had run a long while, he came to the cleft in the rock, where the old hag sat, spinning at her distaff. So she bawled out to Boots:

40   'Come here, come here, my pretty fellow, and let me comb your hair.'

41   'Don't you wish you may catch me,' said Boots. 'Don't you wish you may
catch me,' as he ran along, leaping and jumping, and holding on by one of the
foals' tails. And when he had got well past the cleft in the rock, the youngest
foal said:

42   'Jump up on my back, my lad, for we've a long way before us still.'

43   So Boots jumped up on his back.

44   So they went on, and on, a long, long way.

45   'Do you see anything now,' said the Foal.

46   'No,' said Boots.

47   So they went on a good bit farther.

48   'Do you see anything now?' asked the Foal.

49   'Oh, no,' said the lad.

50   So when they had gone a great, great way farther—I'm sure I can't tell how
far—the Foal asked again:

51   'Do you see anything now?'

52   'Yes,' said Boots; 'now I see something that looks white—just like a tall, big
birch trunk.'

53   'Yes,' said the Foal; 'we're going into that trunk.'

54   So when they got to the trunk, the eldest foal took and pushed it on one side,
and then they saw a door where it had stood, and inside the door was a little
room, and in the room there was scarce anything but a little fireplace and one
or two benches; but behind the door hung a great rusty sword and a little pitcher.

55   'Can you brandish the sword?' said the Foals; 'try.'

56   So Boots tried, but he couldn't; then they made him take a pull at the pitcher, first once, then twice, and then thrice, and then he could wield it like anything.

57   'Yes,' said the Foals, 'now you may take the sword with you, and with it you
must cut off all our seven heads on your wedding-day, and then we'll be Princes
again as we were before. For we are brothers of that Princess whom you are to
have when you can tell the King what we eat and drink; but an ugly Troll has
thrown this shape over us. Now mind, when you have hewn off our heads, to
take care to lay each head at the tail of the trunk which it belonged to before,
and then the spell will have no more power over us.'

58   Yes! Boots promised all that, and then on they went.

59   And when they had travelled a long, long way, the Foal asked:

60   'Do you see anything?'

61   'No,' said Boots.

62   So they travelled a good bit still.

63   'And now?' asked the Foal.

64   'No, I see nothing,' said Boots.

65   So they travelled many, many miles again, over hill and dale.

66   'Now then,' said the Foal, 'do you see anything now?'

67   'Yes,' said Boots, 'now I see something like a blue stripe, far, far away.'

68   'Yes,' said the Foal, 'that's a river we've got to cross.'

69   Over the river was a long, grand bridge; and when they had got over to the other side, they travelled on a long, long way. At last the Foal asked again, if Boots didn't see anything?

70   Yes, this time he saw something that looked black, far, far away, just as though it were a church steeple.

71   'Yes,' said the Foal, 'that's where we're going to turn in.'

72   So when the foals got into the churchyard, they became men again, and looked like Princes, with such fine clothes that it glistened from them; and so they went into the church, and took the bread and wine from the priest who stood at the altar. And Boots he went in too; but when the priest had laid his hands on the Princes, and given them the blessing, they went out of the church again, then Boots went out too; but he took with him a flask of wine and a wafer. And as soon as ever the seven Princes came out into the churchyard, they were turned into foals again, and so Boots got up on the back of the youngest, and so they all went back the same way that they had come; only they went much, much faster. First they crossed the bridge, next they passed the trunk, and then they passed the old hag, who sat at the cleft and span, and they went by her so fast, that Boots couldn't hear what the old hag screeched after him; but he heard so much as to know she was in an awful rage.

73   It was almost dark when they got back to the palace, and the King himself stood out on the steps and waited for them.

74   'Have you watched well and true the whole day?' said he to Boots.

75   'I've done my best,' answered Boots.

76   'Then you can tell me what my seven foals eat and drink,' said the King.

77   Then Boots pulled out the flask of wine and the wafer, and showed them to the King.

78   'Here you see their meat, and here you see their drink,' said he.

79   'Yes,' said the King, 'you have watched true and well, and you shall have the Princess and half the kingdom.'

80   So they made ready the wedding-feast, and the King said it should be such a grand one, it should be the talk of far and near.

81   But when they sat down to the bridal-feast, the bridegroom got up and went down to the stable, for he said he had forgotten something, and must go to fetch it. And when he got down there, he did as the Foals had said, and hewed their heads off, all seven, the eldest first, and the others after him; and at the same time he took care to lay each head at the tail of the foal to which it belonged; and as he did this, lo! they all became Princes again.

82   So when he went into the bridal hall with the seven Princes, the King was so glad he both kissed Boots and patted him on the back, and his bride was still more glad of him than she had been before.

83   'Half the kingdom you have got already,' said the King, 'and the other half you shall have after my death; for my sons can easily get themselves lands and wealth, now they are Princes again.'

84   And so, like enough, there was mirth and fun at that wedding. I was there too; but there was no one to care for poor me; and so I got nothing but a bit of bread and butter, and I laid it down on the stove, and the bread was burnt and

the butter ran, and so I didn't get even the smallest crumb. Wasn't that a great big shame?

Walt Disney's "Cinderella"
Adapted by Campbell Grant

Walter Elias Disney (1901–1966), winner of 32 Academy Awards, is famous throughout the world for his cartoon animations. After achieving recognition with cartoon shorts populated by such immortals as Mickey Mouse and Donald Duck, he produced the full-length animated film version of Snow White *and the* Seven Dwarfs *in 1937. He followed with other animations, including* Cinderella *(1950), which he adapted from Perrault's version of the tale. A Little Golden Book, the text of which appears here, was then adapted by Campbell Grant from the film.*

1   Once upon a time in a far-away land lived a sweet and pretty girl named Cinderella. She made her home with her mean old stepmother and her two stepsisters, and they made her do all the work in the house.

2   Cinderella cooked and baked. She cleaned and scrubbed. She had no time left for parties and fun.

3   But one day an invitation came from the palace of the king.

4   A great ball was to be given for the prince of the land. And every young girl in the kingdom was invited.

5   "How nice!" thought Cinderella. "I am invited, too."

6   But her mean stepsisters never thought of her. They thought only of themselves, of course. They had all sorts of jobs for Cinderella to do.

7   "Wash this slip. Press this dress. Curl my hair. Find my fan."

8   They both kept shouting, as fast as they could speak.

9   "But I must get ready myself. I'm going, too," said Cinderella.

10   "You!" they hooted. "The Prince's ball for you?"

11   And they kept her busy all day long. She worked in the morning, while her stepsisters slept. She worked all afternoon, while they bathed and dressed. And in the evening she had to help them put on the finishing touches for the ball. She had not one minute to think of herself.

12   Soon the coach was ready at the door. The ugly stepsisters were powdered, pressed, and curled. But there stood Cinderella in her workaday rags.

13   "Why, Cinderella!" said the stepsisters. "You're not dressed for the ball."

14   "No," said Cinderella. "I guess I cannot go."

15   Poor Cinderella sat weeping in the garden.

16   Suddenly a little old woman with a sweet, kind face stood before her. It was her fairy godmother.

17   "Hurry, child!" she said. "You are going to the ball!"

18   Cinderella could hardly believe her eyes! The fairy godmother turned a fat pumpkin into a splendid coach.

19   Next her pet mice became horses, and her dog a fine footman. The barn horse was turned into a coachman.

20   "There, my dear," said the fairy godmother. "Now into the coach with you, and off to the ball you go."

21   "But my dress—" said Cinderella.

22   "Lovely, my dear," the fairy godmother began. Then she really looked at Cinderella's rags.

23   "Oh, good heavens," she said. "You can never go in that." She waved her magic wand.

> *"Salaga doola,*
> *Menchicka boola,*
> *Bibbidi bobbidi boo!" she said.*

24   There stood Cinderella in the loveliest ball dress that ever was. And on her feet were tiny glass slippers!

25   "Oh," cried Cinderella. "How can I ever thank you?"

26   "Just have a wonderful time at the ball, my dear," said her fairy godmother. "But remember, this magic lasts only until midnight. At the stroke of midnight, the spell will be broken. And everything will be as it was before."

27   "I will remember," said Cinderella. "It is more than I ever dreamed of."

28   Then into the magic coach she stepped, and was whirled away to the ball.

29   And such a ball! The king's palace was ablaze with lights. There was music and laughter. And every lady in the land was dressed in her beautiful best.

30   But Cinderella was the loveliest of them all. The prince never left her side, all evening long. They danced every dance. They had supper side by side. And they happily smiled into each other's eyes.

31   But all at once the clock began to strike midnight, Bong Bong Bong—

32   "Oh!" cried Cinderella. "I almost forgot!"

33   And without a word, away she ran, out of the ballroom and down the palace stairs. She lost one glass slipper. But she could not stop.

34   Into her magic coach she stepped, and away it rolled. But as the clock stopped striking, the coach disappeared. And no one knew where she had gone.

35   Next morning all the kingdom was filled with the news. The Grand Duke was going from house to house, with a small glass slipper in his hand. For the prince had said he would marry no one but the girl who could wear that tiny shoe.

36   Every girl in the land tried hard to put it on. The ugly stepsisters tried hardest of all. But not a one could wear the glass shoe.

37   And where was Cinderella? Locked in her room. For the mean old stepmother was taking no chances of letting her try on the slipper. Poor Cinderella! It looked as if the Grand Duke would surely pass her by.

38   But her little friends the mice got the stepmother's key. And they pushed it under Cinderella's door. So down the long stairs she came, as the Duke was just about to leave.

39   "Please!" cried Cinderella. "Please let me try."

40   And of course the slipper fitted, since it was her very own.

41   That was all the Duke needed. Now his long search was done. And so
Cinderella became the prince's bride, and lived happily ever after—and the
little pet mice lived in the palace and were happy ever after, too.

Cinderella
Anne Sexton

Anne Sexton (1928–1974) has been acclaimed as one of America's outstanding contemporary poets. In 1967, she won the Pulitzer Prize for poetry for Live or Die. *She published four other collections of her work, including* Transformations, *in which she recast, with a modern twist, popular European fairy tales such as "Cinderella." Sexton's poetry has appeared in the* New Yorker, Harper's, The Atlantic, *and* Saturday Review. *She received a Robert Frost Fellowship (1959), a scholarship from Radcliffe College's New Institute for Independent Study (1961–1963), a grant from the Ford Foundation (1964), and a Guggenheim Award (1969). In her book* All My Pretty Ones, *Sexton quoted Franz Kafka: "The books we need are the kind that act upon us like a misfortune, that make us suffer like the death of someone we love more than ourselves. A book should serve as the axe for the frozen sea within us." Asked in an interview (by Patricia Marz) about this quotation, Sexton responded: "I think [poetry] should be a shock to the senses. It should almost hurt."*

You always read about it;
the plumber with twelve children
who wins the Irish Sweepstakes.
From toilets to riches.
5   That story.

Or the nursemaid,
some luscious sweet from Denmark
who captures the oldest son's heart.
From diapers to Dior.
10   That story.

Or a milkman who serves the wealthy,
eggs, cream, butter, yogurt, milk,
the white truck like an ambulance
who goes into real estate
15   and makes a pile.
From homogenized to martinis at lunch.

Or the charwoman
who is on the bus when it cracks up
and collects enough from the insurance.
20   From mops to Bonwit Teller.
That story.

Once
the wife of a rich man was on her deathbed
and she said to her daughter Cinderella:
25   Be devout. Be good, Then I will smile
down from heaven in the seam of a cloud.
The man took another wife who had
two daughters, pretty enough
but with hearts like blackjacks.
30   Cinderella was their maid.
She slept on the sooty hearth each night
and walked around looking like Al Jolson.
Her father brought presents home from town,
jewels and gowns for the other women
35   but the twig of a tree for Cinderella.
She planted that twig on her mother's grave
and it grew to a tree where a white dove sat.
Whenever she wished for anything the dove
would drop it like an egg upon the ground.
40   The bird is important, my dears, so heed him.
Next came the ball, as you all know.
It was a marriage market.
The prince was looking for a wife.
All but Cinderella were preparing
45   and gussying up for the big event.
Cinderella begged to go too.
Her stepmother threw a dish of lentils
into the cinders and said: Pick them
up in an hour and you shall go.
50   The white dove brought all his friends;
all the warm wings of the fatherland came,
and picked up the lentils in a jiffy.
No, Cinderella, said the stepmother,
you have no clothes and cannot dance.
55   That's the way with stepmothers.

Cinderella went to the tree at the grave
and cried forth like a gospel singer:
Mama! Mama! My turtledove,
send me to the prince's ball!
60   The bird dropped down a golden dress
and delicate little gold slippers.
Rather a large package for a simple bird.
So she went. Which is no surprise.

Her stepmother and sisters didn't
65   recognize her without her cinder face
and the prince took her hand on the spot
and danced with no other the whole day.

As nightfall came she thought she'd better
get home. The prince walked her home
70 and she disappeared into the pigeon house
and although the prince took an axe and broke
it open she was gone. Back to her cinders.
These events repeated themselves for three days.
However on the third day the prince
75 covered the palace steps with cobbler's wax
and Cinderella's gold shoe stuck upon it.
Now he would find whom the shoe fit
and find his strange dancing girl for keeps.
He went to their house and the two sisters
80 were delighted because they had lovely feet.
The eldest went into a room to try the slipper on
but her big toe got in the way so she simply
sliced it off and put on the slipper.
The prince rode away with her until the white dove
85 told him to look at the blood pouring forth.
That is the way with amputations.
They don't just heal up like a wish.
The other sister cut off her heel
but the blood told as blood will.
90 The prince was getting tired.
He began to feel like a shoe salesman.
But he gave it one last try.
This time Cinderella fit into the shoe
like a love letter into its envelope.

95 At the wedding ceremony
the two sisters came to curry favor
and the white dove pecked their eyes out.
Two hollow spots were left
like soup spoons.

100 Cinderella and the prince
lived, they say, happily ever after,
like two dolls in a museum case
never bothered by diapers or dust,
never arguing over the timing of an egg,
105 never telling the same story twice,
never getting a middle-aged spread,
their darling smiles pasted on for eternity.

Regular Bobbsey Twins.
That story.

The Rise of Perrault's "Cinderella"
Bonnie Cullen

In this next selection, art historian Bonnie Cullen explains how, from among the hundreds of "Cinderellas" throughout the world, Charles Perrault's version came to be what many in the West think of as the canonical, or standard, one. Of the seven variants of "Cinderella" named in this article, six appear earlier in the chapter. A longer version of this article first appeared in The Lion and the Unicorn *(Volume 27, 2003).*

1   Why [did] Perrault's story, above all others, [become the dominant version of "Cinderella"]? Considering its origins, there were many contestants for the dominant tale. "Cinderella" is really a large family of tales first analyzed by folklorists in the nineteenth century. Studying more than 300 related narratives from Europe and Asia, Marian Roalfe Cox identified Cinderella stories according to the presence of certain themes: an abused child, rescue through some reincarnation of the dead mother, recognition, and marriage.

2   The earliest known Cinderella story is actually a literary version from ninth-century China. Already it has the familiar elements. Yeh-hsien (Cinderella) has lost both her father and mother and seeks consolation from a pet fish. Her cruel stepmother eats the fish and buries the bones. A man comes from the sky advising her to find and save the bones—she will get whatever she wishes for.

3   When her stepmother and stepsister leave for a festival, Yeh-hsien follows them in a cloak of kingfisher feathers and gold shoes. She loses a shoe, the shoe is found, and given to a king. A search for the foot small enough to fit the shoe ensues. Yeh-hsien is finally shown to be the rightful owner and marries the king (Ting 4–5).

4   In most early Cinderella tales, the dead mother hovers protectively, reincarnated as a cow, a fish, or a tree. Her relationship with the grieving daughter is as significant as the girl's triumph. Occasionally the protagonist is male.* The shoe is not always the means of identification, although it is extremely common, as is the use of some magic garment (Philip).

5   By the sixteenth century, Cinderella appears in print in the West. One major debut is in Basile's seventeenth-century collection, *Il Pentamerone (Lo cunto de li cunti)*, as the feisty "Gatta Cenerentola" or "Cat Cinderella." Zezolla (Cinderella) kills her wicked stepmother with the help of a governess, but when the governess marries Zezolla's father, the girl is mistreated again. A fairy in a tree supplies magic clothes and a coach for a feast where Zezolla captures a king's heart.

6   In Basile's tale, the dead mother is no longer a significant presence, although she might be vaguely identified with the fairy. While close to some oral versions, his bawdy narrative is full of intricate metaphors and clearly written for an adult audience (Canepa 14–15). The book was published in Neapolitan dialect, which probably limited its dissemination in print (Canepa 12; Opie and Opie

---

* See "The Seven Foals," pages 612–617.

20–21), although Basile's stories may have passed into the oral repertoire and traveled in other languages.

7   During the ancien régime of Louis the XIV, folktales were transformed into a new literary genre, the fairy tale. Narrated as a kind of conversational game in the salons of the *précieuses*, by the end of the century they were being written down (Zipes, *Beauties* 1–9; Warner 167–70). Two distinct versions of "Cinderella" issued from the pens of Charles Perrault and the Countess d'Aulnoy.

8   Marie-Catherine Le Jumel de Barneville, Baronne d'Aulnoy, was a feminist and writer, the first to publish her stories as "fairy tales," or literary versions of popular folktales. Her Cinderella, "Finette Cendron," is both altruistic and spirited. When their parents abandon Finette and her sisters, she engineers daring escapes for all three. They plot against her, but Finette remains loyal. With a godmother's help she finds some magnificent clothing and triumphs at the ball. She loses a shoe and gallops back to claim it, but refuses to marry the prince until her parents' kingdom, which they lost, is restored (d'Aulnoy, *Fairy Tales* 227–45).*

9   Perrault's "Cendrillon" is quite a different lady. He dubs her chief virtue "la bonne grace," i.e., in the face of adversity she is generous, long-suffering, charming and good-humored; the ideal bride, from the gentleman's perspective.

---

* An example of Finette's resourcefulness: Held captive in a castle, Finette devises a plan when a hungry ogre orders her and her two sisters to cook for him and his ogress (instead of eating them straightaway). It is the last request he makes:

> "But," said [the ogre], turning to Finette, "when you have lit the fire, how can you tell if the oven be hot enough?" "My lord," she answered, "I throw butter in, and then I taste it with my tongue." "Very well," he said, "light the fire then." The oven was as big as a stable, for the ogre and ogress ate more bread than two armies. The princess made an enormous fire, which blazed like a furnace; and the ogre, who was standing by, ate a hundred lambs and a hundred sucking pigs while waiting for the new bread. [Finette's sisters] Fleur d'Amour and Belle-de-Nuit kneaded the dough. "Well," said the great ogre, "is the oven hot?" "My lord," replied Finette, "you will see presently." And so saying she threw a thousand pounds of butter into the oven. "I should try it with my tongue," she said, "but I am too little." "I am big enough," said the ogre, and bending down he went so far into the oven that he could not draw back again, so that he was burned to the bones. When the ogress came to the oven she was mightily astonished to find a mountain of cinders instead of her husband.
>
> Fleur d'Amour and Belle-de-Nuit, who saw that she was in great distress, comforted her as they could, but they feared lest her grief should be consoled only too soon, and that regaining her appetite she would put them in a salad, as she had meant to do before. So they said to her: "Take courage, madam; you will find some king or some marquis who will be happy to marry you." At that she smiled a little, showing her teeth, which were longer than your finger. When they saw she was in a good humour, Finette said: "If you would but leave off wearing those horrible bear-skins, and dress a little more fashionably! We could arrange your hair beautifully, and you would be like a star." "Come then," she said, "let us see what you can do; but be sure that if I find any ladies more beautiful than myself I shall hack you into little bits." Thereupon the three princesses took off her cap, and began to comb and curl her hair, entertaining her all the while with their chatter. Then Finette took a hatchet, and with a great blow from behind, severed her head from her body.

For the complete version of d'Aulnoy's "Finette Cendron," go to <http://www.surlalunefairytales.com/authors/aulnoy/1892/finettecendron.html>.

10   A bland protagonist perhaps, but Perrault exhibits his wit. Cendrillon plays her own tricks on the sisters, asking one if she can borrow a dress to see the mysterious princess at the next ball. He also writes tongue-in-cheek. The slipper, evoking female virginity, is made of glass in his tale. Not only is it fragile and extremely pure, but Perrault hints that visual proof will be necessary.

11   Perrault's position as a member of the French Academy may have led him to adopt this tone for tales of the peasant class (Warner 168–70). He also shifts the spotlight to the fairy godmother, giving her a dominant role. In the ancien régime, fairies were equated with powerful women at court (232–34). D'Aulnoy's fairy is sympathetic and dignified, asking Finette to be her lady's maid and comb her hair. Her magic is in providing the necessary items, whether or not she is present. Perrault's elaborate description of rat-and-pumpkin tricks is a spoof: his fairy godmother is a witch.

. . .

12   When literary Cinderellas began to appear in English in the eighteenth century, it was Madame d'Aulnoy's story that took the lead. [An early version of her work appeared] in *A Collection of Novels and Tales, Written by that Celebrated Wit of France, the Countess d'Anois* (1721–22). Perrault's *Contes* did not appear in English until 1729.

13   By the nineteenth century, the tables had turned, apparently. Only seven English editions of d'Aulnoy's tales survive in the British Library; not all contain "Finette." There are over thirty editions of Perrault's "Cinderella" as a separate volume, besides its inclusion with the tales. Perrault's story was also adapted for pantomime and plays.

14   Perrault's version faced new competition, however. Searching for an antidote to bourgeois life—the stale "getting and spending," as Wordsworth put it— Romantics turned to nature. Might not the oral tales of country folk contain some primal wisdom? How closely they transcribed their originals is debated, but the Grimm brothers believed they were collecting rather than writing stories as they prepared their editions of *Die Kinder- und Hausmärchen* in 1812 (Warner 188–93). Their "Cinderella," "Aschenputtel," is indeed close to folk versions such as the Scottish tale, "Rashin Coatie" (Opie and Opie 117–18).

15   Mourning and revenge underlie "Aschenputtel": the heroine plants a tree on her mother's grave and tends it lovingly. A bird in the tree answers her calls for help. She begs for a dress, attends the feast and attracts the prince. The sisters cheat at the slipper test, cutting off parts of their feet, but birds reveal their deceit and at the wedding, peck out the sisters' eyes.

16   "Primal" tales had their opponents. With the first English translation, in volume two of *German Popular Stories* (1826), the brutal eye-pecking disappeared. During the previous century, the market for printed tales had expanded through chapbooks, devoured by a new audience of young readers as well as adults. By the end of the eighteenth century there was a movement in England to sanitize children's literature. Mrs. Trimmer, reviewing children's books for middle-class families; argued that the often brutal tales "excite . . . groundless fears" and "serve no moral purpose" (2: 185–86). This explains the intrusion of religious motifs, such as praying and church architecture, in chapbook illustration from the early nineteenth century, and the relative scarcity of expensive editions at the time.

17   Fairy tales would not go away, however. Those who wanted to imbue them with bourgeois morality faced equally vociferous champions of "pure" tales. "A child," Ruskin wrote, "should not need to chose between right and wrong. It should not be capable of wrong . . . " Innocent, children could be "fortif[ied] . . . against the glacial cold of selfish science" with the "inextinguishable life" of the folk tradition (83). As Zipes points out, arguments about fairy tales became part of the greater "Condition of England" debate on the effects of the Industrial Revolution (*Victorian Fairy Tales* xvi–xxix).

18   In the case of "Cinderella," it was a somewhat revised Perrault that prevailed in Victorian England.

. . .

19   One reason Perrault's tale [did so] was its suitability for a modern audience. During the nineteenth century, the market for literary fairy tales in England was increasingly urban and middleclass. Perrault focuses on the social sphere, rather than the forest. He delineates hairdos, costume, behavior at the ball and reactions to Cendrillon's appearance with the ironic tone of a society reporter.

20   D'Aulnoy's Finette is busy slaying ogres and galloping through the mud, while in "Aschenputtel" there is blood from the sisters' mutilated feet. Romantics like Ruskin favored the rugged terrain of folktales, but as Mrs. Trimmer's remarks indicate, "polite" readers were concerned about "improving" young minds to function effectively in society.

21   More important, perhaps, Perrault's tale prevailed in English because it was the best vehicle for Victorian notions of femininity. D'Aulnoy's heroine liberates herself through female power, both magical and human. Folk Cinderellas like Aschenputtel also take action, advised by incarnations of their lost mothers. Perrault's Cendrillon is the least active, and he shifts the spotlight to her fairy godmother, whose magic is as amusing as it is powerful.

22   Whether or not the oral fairy tale had been a female genre, as Warner argues, by the nineteenth century the fairy tale in print was increasingly dominated by male writers and illustrators in an industry controlled by male publishers. That even some women writers followed the "party line" with canonical Cinderellas shows how powerful a formula it was for the middleclass market of nineteenth-century England.

23   It is interesting to note that Disney's revival of "Cinderella," which repeats the Victorian interpretation of Perrault's story, came out in 1950: a time when women, indispensable in the workforce during the war years, were being urged back home with imagery of ideal wives and mothers. There have been attempts to reclaim the tale in recent years in both print and film. Yet the canonical tale, with its Victorian ideology, persists.

Works Cited

Canepa, Nancy L. *From Court to Forest. Giambattista Basile's Lo Cunto de li Cunti and the Birth of the Literary Fairy Tale*. Detroit: Wayne State UP, 1999.

Cox, Marian Roalfe. *Cinderella; Three Hundred and Forty-five Variants*. Publications of the Folk-lore Society (no. 31). London, 1893.

D'Aulnoy, Marie Catherine Baronne. *The Fairy Tales of Madame D'Aulnoy*. Trans. Annie Macdonnell and Miss Lee. London: Lawrence and Bullen, 1892.

Opie, Iona, and Peter Opie. *The Classic Fairy Tales*. Oxford: Book Club Associates by arrangement with Oxford UP, 1992.

Philip, Neil. *The Cinderella Story*. Harmondsworth: Penguin, 1989.

Ruskin, John. "Fairy Stories." Ed. Lance Salway. *Signal* (May 1972): 81–86.

Ting, Nai-Tung. *The Cinderella Cycle in China and Indo-China*. F. F. Communications no. 213. Helsinki: Suomalainen, 1974.

Trimmer, Sarah. *The Guardian of Education*. 5 vols. London: J. Johnson, 1801–05.

Warner, Marina. *From the Beast to the Blond*. London: Vintage, 1995.

Zipes, Jack David. *Beauties, Beasts and Enchantment: Classic French Fairy Tales*. New York: New American Library, 1989.

———.*Victorian Fairy Tales: The Revolt of the Fairies and Elves*. New York: Methuen, 1987.

Review Questions

1. What are the classic elements of the "Cinderella" tale?

2. What features distinguished the early "Cinderella" folktales from later fairy tale versions? When and where did the transformation from folktale to fairy tale occur?

3. In the nineteenth century, what motivated the Grimm brothers to record their version of "Cinderella" and others like it as an alternative to Perrault's "Cinderella"?

4. How does Perrault's "Cinderella" differ from those of D'Aulnoy and Grimm?

5. How did Perrault's "Cinderella" become "canonical"?

Discussion and Writing Suggestions

1. Of the versions of "Cinderella" presented in this chapter, was Perrault's the most familiar—the one you were/are inclined to call the "real" "Cinderella"? To what extent were you aware of the historical, social, and even political forces at work to make Perrault's "Cinderella" the canonical one?

2. Cullen finds it "interesting to note that Disney's revival of 'Cinderella,' which repeats the Victorian interpretation of Perrault's story, came out in 1950: a time when women, indispensable in the workforce during the war years, were being urged back home with imagery of ideal wives and mothers." What does Cullen's "interesting to note" suggest to you? Do you suppose that Disney was lobbying for a specific economic or social agenda by bringing out his "Cinderella"—both the film and print versions?

3. Read D'Aulnoy's "Finette Cendron" (<http://www.surlalunefairytales. com/authors/aulnoy/1892/finettecendon.html>). Also read Perrault's and Disney's versions of "Cinderella," "Ashputtle," the "Chinese

'Cinderella,'" and "The Cat Cinderella" in this text. In her article, how accurately has Cullen described the differences among these versions?

4. Address the notion of selecting a fairy tale based on its "suitability" for a particular audience. In broad cultural terms, how is suitability determined? How would *you* determine suitability for your children or younger siblings, if the decision of which story to read, or movie or television show to watch, were left to you?

"Cinderella": A Story of Sibling Rivalry and Oedipal Conflicts
Bruno Bettelheim

Having read several variants of "Cinderella," you may have wondered what it is about this story that's prompted people in different parts of the world, at different times, to show interest in a child who's been debased but then rises above her misfortune. Why are people so fascinated with "Cinderella"?

Depending on the people you ask and their perspectives, you'll find this question answered in various ways. As a Freudian psychologist, Bruno Bettelheim believes that the mind is a repository of both conscious and unconscious elements. By definition, we aren't aware of what goes on in our unconscious; nonetheless, what happens there exerts a powerful influence on what we believe and on how we act. This division of the mind into conscious and unconscious parts is true for children no less than for adults. Based on these beliefs about the mind, Bettelheim analyzes "Cinderella" first by pointing to what he calls the story's essential theme: sibling rivalry, or Cinderella's mistreatment at the hands of her stepsisters. Competition among brothers and sisters presents a profound and largely unconscious problem to children, says Bettelheim. By hearing "Cinderella," a story that speaks directly to their unconscious, children are given tools that can help them resolve conflicts. Cinderella resolves her difficulties; children hearing the story can resolve theirs as well: This is the unconscious message of the tale.

To accept this argument, you'd have to agree with the author's reading of "Cinderella" and its hidden meanings; and you'd have to agree with his assumptions concerning the conscious and unconscious mind and the ways in which the unconscious will seize upon the content of a story in order to resolve conflicts. Even if you don't accept Bettelheim's analysis, his essay makes fascinating reading. First, it is internally consistent—that is, he begins with a set of principles and then builds logically upon them, as any good writer will. Second, his analysis demonstrates how a scholarly point of view—a coherent set of assumptions about the way the world (in this case, the mind) works—creates boundaries for a discussion. Change the assumptions and you'll change the analyses that follow from them.

Bettelheim's essay is long and somewhat difficult. While he uses no subheadings, he has divided his work into four sections: paragraphs 2–10 are devoted to sibling rivalry; paragraphs 11–19, to an analysis of "Cinderella's" hidden meanings; paragraphs 20–24, to the psychological makeup of children at the end of their Oedipal period; and paragraphs 25–27, to the reasons "Cinderella," in particular, appeals to children in the Oedipal period.

Bruno Bettelheim, a distinguished psychologist and educator, was born in 1903 in Vienna. He was naturalized as an American citizen in 1939 and served as a professor of psychology at Rockford College and the University of Chicago. Awarded the honor of fellow by several prestigious professional associations, Bettelheim was a prolific writer and contributed articles to numerous popular and professional publications. His list of books includes Love Is Not Enough: The Treatment of Emotionally Disturbed Children *(1950),* The Informed Heart *(1960), and* The Uses of Enchantment *(1975), from which this selection has been excerpted. Bettelheim died in 1990.*

1   By all accounts, "Cinderella" is the best-known fairy tale, and probably also the best-liked. It is quite an old story; when first written down in China during the ninth century A.D., it already had a history. The unrivaled tiny foot size as a mark of extraordinary virtue, distinction, and beauty, and the slipper made of precious material are facets which point to an Eastern, if not necessarily Chinese, origin.* The modern hearer does not connect sexual attractiveness and beauty in general with extreme smallness of the foot, as the ancient Chinese did, in accordance with their practice of binding women's feet.

2   "Cinderella," as we know it, is experienced as a story about the agonies and hopes which form the essential content of sibling rivalry; and about the degraded heroine winning out over her siblings who abused her. Long before Perrault gave "Cinderella" the form in which it is now widely known, "having to live among the ashes" was a symbol of being debased in comparison to one's siblings, irrespective of sex. In Germany, for example, there were stories in which such an ash-boy later becomes king, which parallels Cinderella's fate. "Aschenputtel" is the title of the Brothers Grimm's version of the tale. The term originally designated a lowly, dirty kitchenmaid who must tend to the fireplace ashes.

3   There are many examples in the German language of how being forced to dwell among the ashes was a symbol not just of degradation, but also of sibling rivalry, and of the sibling who finally surpasses the brother or brothers who have debased him. Martin Luther in his *Table Talks* speaks about Cain as the God-forsaken evildoer who is powerful, while pious Abel is forced to be his ash-brother (*Aschebrüdel*), a mere nothing, subject to Cain; in one of Luther's sermons he says that Esau was forced into the role of Jacob's ash-brother. Cain and Abel, Jacob and Esau are Biblical examples of one brother being suppressed or destroyed by the other.

4   The fairy tale replaces sibling relations with relations between step-siblings— perhaps a device to explain and make acceptable an animosity which one wishes would not exist among true siblings. Although sibling rivalry is universal and "natural" in the sense that it is the negative consequence of being a sibling, this same relation also generates equally as much positive feeling between siblings, highlighted in fairy tales such as "Brother and Sister."

5   No other fairy tale renders so well as the "Cinderella" stories the inner experiences of the young child in the throes of sibling rivalry, when he feels hope-

---

* Artistically made slippers of precious material were reported in Egypt from the third century on. The Roman emperor Diocletian in a decree of A.D. 301 set maximum prices for different kinds of footwear, including slippers made of fine Babylonian leather, dyed purple or scarlet, and gilded slippers for women. [Bettelheim]

lessly outclassed by his brothers and sisters. Cinderella is pushed down and degraded by her stepsisters; her interests are sacrificed to theirs by her (step)mother; she is expected to do the dirtiest work and although she performs it well, she receives no credit for it; only more is demanded of her. This is how the child feels when devastated by the miseries of sibling rivalry. Exaggerated though Cinderella's tribulations and degradations may seem to the adult, the child carried away by sibling rivalry feels, "That's me; that's how they mistreat me, or would want to; that's how little they think of me." And there are moments—often long time periods—when for inner reasons a child feels this way even when his position among his siblings may seem to give him no cause for it.

6   When a story corresponds to how the child feels deep down—as no realistic narrative is likely to do—it attains an emotional quality of "truth" for the child. The events of "Cinderella" offer him vivid images that give body to his overwhelming but nevertheless often vague and nondescript emotions; so these episodes seem more convincing to him than his life experiences.

7   The term "sibling rivalry" refers to a most complex constellation of feelings and their causes. With extremely rare exceptions, the emotions aroused in the person subject to sibling rivalry are far out of proportion to what his real situation with his sisters and brothers would justify, seen objectively. While all children at times suffer greatly from sibling rivalry, parents seldom sacrifice one of their children to the others, nor do they condone the other children's persecuting one of them. Difficult as objective judgments are for the young child—nearly impossible when his emotions are aroused—even he in his more rational moments "knows" that he is not treated as badly as Cinderella. But the child often feels mistreated, despite all his "knowledge" to the contrary. That is why he believes in the inherent truth of "Cinderella," and then he also comes to believe in her eventual deliverance and victory. From her triumph he gains the exaggerated hopes for his future which he needs to counteract the extreme misery he experiences when ravaged by sibling rivalry.

8   Despite the name "sibling rivalry," this miserable passion has only incidentally to do with a child's actual brothers and sisters. The real source of it is the child's feelings about his parents. When a child's older brother or sister is more competent than he, this arouses only temporary feelings of jealousy. Another child being given special attention becomes an insult only if the child fears that, in contrast, he is thought little of by his parents, or feels rejected by them. It is because of such an anxiety that one or all of a child's sisters or brothers may become a thorn in his flesh. Fearing that in comparison to them he cannot win his parents' love and esteem is what inflames sibling rivalry. This is indicated in stories by the fact that it matters little whether the siblings actually possess greater competence. The Biblical story of Joseph tells that it is jealousy of parental affection lavished on him which accounts for the destructive behavior of his brothers. Unlike Cinderella's, Joseph's parent does not participate in degrading him, and, on the contrary, refers him to his other children. But Joseph, like Cinderella, is turned into a slave, and, like her, he miraculously escapes and ends by surpassing his siblings.

9   Telling a child who is devastated by sibling rivalry that he will grow up to do as well as his brothers and sisters offers little relief from his present feelings of

dejection. Much as he would like to trust our assurances, most of the time he cannot. A child can see things only with subjective eyes, and comparing himself on this basis to his siblings, he has no confidence that he, on his own, will someday be able to fare as well as they. If he could believe more in himself, he would not feel destroyed by his siblings no matter what they might do to him, since then he could trust that time would bring about a desired reversal of fortune. But since the child cannot, on his own, look forward with confidence to some future day when things will turn out all right for him, he can gain relief only through fantasies of glory—a domination over his siblings—which he hopes will become reality through some fortunate event.

10   Whatever our position within the family, at certain times in our lives we are beset by sibling rivalry in some form or other. Even an only child feels that other children have some great advantages over him, and this makes him intensely jealous. Further, he may suffer from the anxious thought that if he did have a sibling, his parents would prefer this other child to him. "Cinderella" is a fairy tale which makes nearly as strong an appeal to boys as to girls, since children of both sexes suffer equally from sibling rivalry, and have the same desire to be rescued from their lowly position and surpass those who seem superior to them.

11   On the surface, "Cinderella" is as deceptively simple as the story of Little Red Riding Hood, with which it shares greatest popularity. "Cinderella" tells about the agonies of sibling rivalry, of wishes coming true, of the humble being elevated, of true merit being recognized even when hidden under rags, of virtue rewarded and evil punished—a straightforward story. But under this overt content is concealed a welter of complex and largely unconscious material, which details of the story allude to just enough to set our unconscious associations going. This makes a contrast between surface simplicity and underlying complexity which arouses deep interest in the story and explains its appeal to the millions over centuries. To begin gaining an understanding of these hidden meanings, we have to penetrate behind the obvious sources of sibling rivalry discussed so far.

12   As mentioned before, if the child could only believe that it is the infirmities of his age which account for his lowly position, he would not have to suffer so wretchedly from sibling rivalry, because he could trust the future to right matters. When he thinks that his degradation is deserved, he feels his plight is utterly hopeless. Djuna Barnes's perceptive statement about fairy tales—that the child knows something about them which he cannot tell (such as that he likes the idea of Little Red Riding Hood and the wolf being in bed together)—could be extended by dividing fairy tales into two groups: one group where the child responds only unconsciously to the inherent truth of the story and thus cannot tell about it; and another large number of tales where the child preconsciously or even consciously knows what the "truth" of the story consists of and thus could tell about it, but does not want to let on that he knows. Some aspects of "Cinderella" fall into the latter category. Many children believe that Cinderella probably deserves her fate at the beginning of the story, as they feel they would, too; but they don't want anyone to know it. Despite this, she is worthy at the

end to be exalted, as the child hopes he will be too, irrespective of his earlier shortcomings.

13   Every child believes at some period of his life—and this is not only at rare moments—that because of his secret wishes, if not also his clandestine actions, he deserves to be degraded, banned from the presence of others, relegated to a netherworld of smut. He fears this may be so, irrespective of how fortunate his situation may be in reality. He hates and fears those others—such as his siblings—whom he believes to be entirely free of similar evilness, and he fears that they or his parents will discover what he is really like, and then demean him as Cinderella was by her family. Because he wants others—most of all, his parents—to believe in his innocence, he is delighted that "everybody" believes in Cinderella's. This is one of the great attractions of this fairy tale. Since people give credence to Cinderella's goodness, they will also believe in his, so the child hopes. And "Cinderella" nourishes this hope, which is one reason it is such a delightful story.

14   Another aspect which holds large appeal for the child is the vileness of the stepmother and stepsisters. Whatever the shortcomings of a child may be in his own eyes, these pale into insignificance when compared to the stepsisters' and stepmother's falsehood and nastiness. Further, what these stepsisters do to Cinderella justifies whatever nasty thoughts one may have about one's siblings: they are so vile that anything one may wish would happen to them is more than justified. Compared to their behavior, Cinderella is indeed innocent. So the child, on hearing her story, feels he need not feel guilty about his angry thoughts.

15   On a very different level—and reality considerations coexist easily with fantastic exaggerations in the child's mind—as badly as one's parents or siblings seem to treat one, and much as one thinks one suffers because of it, all this is nothing compared to Cinderella's fate. Her story reminds the child at the same time how lucky he is, and how much worse things could be. (Any anxiety about the latter possibility is relieved, as always in fairy tales, by the happy ending.)

16   The behavior of a five-and-a-half-year-old girl, as reported by her father, may illustrate how easily a child may feel that she is a "Cinderella." This little girl had a younger sister of whom she was very jealous. The girl was very fond of "Cinderella," since the story offered her material with which to act out her feelings, and because without the story's imagery she would have been hard pressed to comprehend and express them. This little girl had used to dress very neatly and liked pretty clothes, but she became unkempt and dirty. One day when she was asked to fetch some salt, she said as she was doing so, "Why do you treat me like Cinderella?"

17   Almost speechless, her mother asked her, "Why do you think I treat you like Cinderella?"

18   "Because you make me do all the hardest work in the house!" was the little girl's answer. Having thus drawn her parents into her fantasies, she acted them out more openly, pretending to sweep up all the dirt, etc. She went even further, playing that she prepared her little sister for the ball. But she went the "Cinderella" story one better, based on her unconscious understanding of the

contradictory emotions fused into the "Cinderella" role, because at another moment she told her mother and sister, "You shouldn't be jealous of me just because I am the most beautiful in the family."

19   This shows that behind the surface humility of Cinderella lies the conviction of her superiority to mother and sisters, as if she would think: "You can make me do all the dirty work, and I pretend that I am dirty, but within me I know that you treat me this way because you are jealous of me because I am so much better than you." This conviction is supported by the story's ending, which assures every "Cinderella" that eventually she will be discovered by her prince.

20   Why does the child believe deep within himself that Cinderella deserves her dejected state? This question takes us back to the child's state of mind at the end of the oedipal period.* Before he is caught in oedipal entanglements, the child is convinced that he is lovable, and loved, if all is well within his family relationships. Psychoanalysis describes this stage of complete satisfaction with oneself as "primary narcissism." During this period the child feels certain that he is the center of the universe, so there is no reason to be jealous of anybody.

21   The oedipal disappointments which come at the end of this developmental stage cast deep shadows of doubt on the child's sense of his worthiness. He feels that if he were really as deserving of love as he had thought, then his parents would never be critical of him or disappoint him. The only explanation for parental criticism the child can think of is that there must be some serious flaw in him which accounts for what he experiences as rejection. If his desires remain unsatisfied and his parents disappoint him, there must be something wrong with him or his desires, or both. He cannot yet accept that reasons other than those residing within him could have an impact on his fate. In this oedipal jealousy, wanting to get rid of the parent of the same sex had seemed the most natural thing in the world, but now the child realizes that he cannot have his own way, and that maybe this is so because the desire was wrong. He is no longer so sure that he is preferred to his siblings, and he begins to suspect that this may be due to the fact that *they* are free of any bad thoughts or wrongdoing such as his.

22   All this happens as the child is gradually subjected to ever more critical attitudes as he is being socialized. He is asked to behave in ways which run counter to his natural desires, and he resents this. Still he must obey, which makes him very angry. This anger is directed against those who make demands, most likely his parents; and this is another reason to wish to get rid of them, and still another reason to feel guilty about such wishes. This is why the child also feels that he deserves to be chastised for his feelings, a punishment he believes he can escape only if nobody learns what he is thinking when he is angry. The feeling of being unworthy to be loved by his parents at a time when his desire for their love is very strong leads to the fear of rejection, even when in reality there is

---

* Oedipal: Freud's theory of the Oedipus complex held that at an early stage of development a child wishes to replace the parent of the same sex in order to achieve the exclusive love of the parent of the opposite sex.

none. This rejection fear compounds the anxiety that others are preferred and also maybe preferable—the root of sibling rivalry.

23   Some of the child's pervasive feelings of worthlessness have their origin in his experiences during and around toilet training and all other aspects of his education to become clean, neat, and orderly. Much has been said about how children are made to feel dirty and bad because they are not as clean as their parents want or require them to be. As clean as a child may learn to be, he knows that he would much prefer to give free rein to his tendency to be messy, disorderly, and dirty.

24   At the end of the oedipal period, guilt about desires to be dirty and disorderly becomes compounded by oedipal guilt, because of the child's desire to replace the parent of the same sex in the love of the other parent. The wish to be the love, if not also the sexual partner, of the parent of the other sex, which at the beginning of the oedipal development seemed natural and "innocent," at the end of the period is repressed as bad. But while this wish as such is repressed, guilt about it and about sexual feelings in general is not, and this makes the child feel dirty and worthless.

25   Here again, lack of objective knowledge leads the child to think that he is the only bad one in all these respects—the only child who has such desires. It makes every child identify with Cinderella, who is relegated to sit among the cinders. Since the child has such "dirty" wishes, that is where he also belongs, and where he would end up if his parents knew of his desires. This is why every child needs to believe that even if he were thus degraded, eventually he would be rescued from such degradation and experience the most wonderful exaltation—as Cinderella does.

26   For the child to deal with his feelings of dejection and worthlessness aroused during this time, he desperately needs to gain some grasp on what these feelings of guilt and anxiety are all about. Further, he needs assurance on a conscious and an unconscious level that he will be able to extricate himself from these predicaments. One of the greatest merits of "Cinderella" is that, irrespective of the magic help Cinderella receives, the child understands that essentially it is through her own efforts, and because of the person she is, that Cinderella is able to transcend magnificently her degraded state, despite what appear as insurmountable obstacles. It gives the child confidence that the same will be true for him, because the story relates so well to what has caused both his conscious and his unconscious guilt.

27   Overtly "Cinderella" tells about sibling rivalry in its most extreme form: the jealousy and enmity of the stepsisters, and Cinderella's sufferings because of it. The many other psychological issues touched upon in the story are so covertly alluded to that the child does not become consciously aware of them. In his unconscious, however, the child responds to these significant details which refer to matters and experiences from which he consciously has separated himself, but which nevertheless continue to create vast problems for him.

Review Questions

1. What does living among ashes symbolize, according to Bettelheim?

2. What explanation does Bettelheim give for Cinderella's having stepsisters, not sisters?

3. In what ways are a child's emotions aroused by sibling rivalry?

4. To a child, what is the meaning of Cinderella's triumph?

5. Why is the fantasy solution to sibling rivalry offered by "Cinderella" appropriate for children?

6. Why is Cinderella's goodness important?

7. Why are the stepsisters and stepmother so vile, according to Bettelheim?

8. In paragraphs 20–26, Bettelheim offers a complex explanation of oedipal conflicts and their relation to sibling rivalry and the child's need to be debased, even while feeling superior. Summarize these seven paragraphs, and compare your summary with those of your classmates. Have you agreed on the essential information in this passage?

Discussion and Writing Suggestions

1. One identifying feature of psychoanalysis is the assumption of complex unconscious and subconscious mechanisms in human personality that explain behavior. In this essay, Bettelheim discusses the interior world of a child in ways that the child could never articulate. The features of this world include the following:

   All children experience sibling rivalry.

   The real source of sibling rivalry is the child's parents.

   Sibling rivalry is a miserable passion and a devastating experience.

   Children have a desire to be rescued from sibling rivalry (as opposed to rescuing themselves, perhaps).

   Children experience an Oedipal stage, in which they wish to do away with the parent of the same sex and be intimate with the parent of the opposite sex.

   "Every child believes at some point in his life . . . that because of his secret wishes, if not also his clandestine actions, he deserves to be degraded, banned from the presence of others, relegated to a netherworld of smut."

   To what extent do you agree with these statements? Take one of the statements and respond to it in a four- or five-paragraph essay.

2. A critic of Bettelheim's position, Jack Zipes, argues that Bettelheim distorts fairy tale literature by insisting that the tales have therapeutic value and

speak to children almost as a psychoanalyst might. Ultimately, claims Zipes, Bettelheim's analysis corrupts the story of "Cinderella" and closes down possibilities for interpretation. What is your view of Bettelheim's psychoanalytic approach to fairy tales?

My Best White Friend: Cinderella Revisited
Patricia J. Williams

*Even as make-believe, how viable a story is "Cinderella" for girls and women of color? In the selection that follows, Patricia J. Williams preps herself for "a gala fund-raiser"—a ball—questioning the enterprise at every step. Williams is a graduate of Wellesley College and Harvard Law School and teaches at Columbia University Law School. A prolific writer, she is the author of numerous academic publications, popular books (*The Alchemy of Race and Rights, *1991;* Open House*, 2004), and a regular column for the *Nation*. She was awarded a MacArthur Foundation Fellowship in 2000. This essay first appeared in *The New Yorker *in 1996.*

1   My best white friend is giving me advice on how to get myself up like a trophy-wife-in-waiting. We are obliged to attend a gala fund-raiser for an organization on whose board we both sit. I'm not a wife of any sort at all, and she says she knows why: I'm prickly as all getout, I dress down instead of up, and my hair is "a complete disaster." My best white friend, who is already a trophy wife of considerable social and philanthropic standing, is pressing me to borrow one of her Real Designer gowns and a couple of those heavy gold bracelets that are definitely not something you can buy on the street.

2   I tell her she's missing the point. Cinderella wasn't an over-thirty black professional with an attitude. What sort of Master of the Universe is going to go for that?

3   "You're not a *racist*, are you?" she asks.

4   "How could I be?" I reply, with wounded indignation. "What, being the American Dream personified and all."

5   "Then let's get busy and make you up," she says soothingly, breaking out the little pots of powder, paint, and polish.

6   From the first exfoliant to the last of the cucumber rinse, we fight about my man troubles. From powder base through lip varnish, we fight about hers.

7   You see, part of the problem is that white knights just don't play the same part in my mythical landscape of desire. If poor Cinderella had been black, it would have been a whole different story. I tell my best white friend the kind of stories my mother raised me on: about slave girls who worked their fingers to the bone for their evil half sisters, the "legitimate" daughters of their mutual father, the master of the manse, the owner of them all; about scullery maids whose oil-and-ashes complexions would not wash clean even after multiple waves of the wand. These were the ones who harbored impossible dreams of love for lost mates who had been sold down rivers of tears to oblivion. These were the ones who became runaways.

8   "Just think about it," I say. "The human drama is compact enough so that when my mother was little she knew women who had been slaves, including a couple of runaways. Cinderellas who had burned their masters' beds and then fled for their lives. It doesn't take too much, even across the ages, to read between those lines. Women who invented their own endings, even when they didn't get to live happily or very long thereafter."

9   My best white friend says, "Get a grip. It's just a party."

10   I've called my best white friend my best white friend ever since she started calling me her best black friend. I am her only black friend, as far as I know, a circumstance for which she blames "the class thing." At her end of the social ladder, I am *my* only black friend—a circumstance for which I blame "the race thing."

11   "People should stop putting so much emphasis on color—it doesn't matter whether you're black or white or blue or green," she says from beneath an avocado mask.

12   Lucky for you, I think, even as my own pores are expanding or contracting—I forget which—beneath a cool neon-green sheath.

13   In fact, I have been looking forward to the makeover. M.B.W.F. has a masseuse and a manicurist and colors in her palette like Apres Sun and Burnt Straw, which she swears will match my skin tones more or less.

14   "Why don't they just call it Racial Envy?" I ask, holding up a tube of Deep Copper Kiss.

15   "Now, now, we're all sisters under the makeup," she says cheerfully.

16   "When ever will we be sisters without?" I grumble.

17   I've come this far because she's convinced me that my usual slapdash routine is the equivalent of being "unmade"; and being unmade, she underscores, is a most exclamatory form of unsophistication. "Even Strom Thurmond wears a little pancake when he's in public."

18   M.B.W.F. is somewhat given to hyperbole, but it is awfully hard to bear, the thought of making less of a fashion statement than old Strom. I do draw the line, though. She has a long history of nips, tucks, and liposuction. Once, I tried to suggest how appalled I was, but I'm not good at being graceful when I have a really strong opinion roiling up inside. She dismissed me sweetly. "You can afford to disapprove. You are aging *so* very nicely."

19   There was the slightest pause as I tried to suppress the anxious rise in my voice: "You think I'm aging?"

20   Very gently, she proceeded to point out the flawed and falling features that gave me away to the carefully trained eye, the insistent voyeur. There were the pores. And those puffs beneath my eyes. No, not there—those are the bags under my eyes. The bags aren't so bad, according to her—no deep wrinkling just yet. But keep going—the puffs are just below the bags. Therein lies the facial decay that gives my age away.

21   I had never noticed them before, but for a while after that those puffs just dominated my face. I couldn't look at myself for their explosive insolence—the body's betrayal, obscuring every other feature.

22   I got over it the day we were standing in line by a news rack at the Food Emporium. Gazing at a photo of Princess Diana looking radiantly, elegantly

melancholic on the cover of some women's magazine, M.B.W.F. snapped, "God! Bulimia must work!"

23   This is not the first time M.B.W.F. has shepherded me to social doom. The last time, it was a very glitzy cocktail party where husband material supposedly abounded. I had a long, businesslike conversation with a man she introduced me to, who, I realized as we talked, grew more and more fascinated by me. At first, I was only conscious of winning him over, then I remember becoming aware that there was something funny about his fierce infatuation. I was *surprising* him, I slowly realized. Finally, he came clean: he said that he had never before had a conversation like this with a black person. "I think I'm in love," he blurted in a voice bubbling with fear.

24   "I think not," I consoled him. "It's just the power of your undone expectations, in combination with my being a basically likable person. It's throwing you for a loop. That and the Scotch, which, as you ought to know, is inherently depoliticizing."

25   I remember telling M.B.W.F. about him afterward. She had always thought of him as "that perfect Southern gentleman." The flip side of the Southern gentleman is the kind master, I pointed out. "Bad luck," she said. "It's true, though—he's the one man I wouldn't want to be owned by, if I were you."

26   My best white friend doesn't believe that race is a big social problem anymore. "It's all economics," she insists. "It's how you came to be my friend"—for once, she does not qualify me as black—"the fact that we were both in college together." I feel compelled to remind her that affirmative action is how both of us ended up in the formerly all-male bastion we attended.

27   The odd thing is, we took most of the same classes. She ended up musically proficient, gifted in the art of interior design, fluent in the mother tongue, whatever it might be, of the honored visiting diplomat of the moment. She actively aspired, she says, to be "a cunning little meringue of a male prize."

28   "You," she says to me, "were always more like Gladys Knight."

29   "Come again?" I say.

30   "Ethnic woman warrior, always on that midnight train to someplace else, intent on becoming the highest-paid Aunt Jemima in history."

31   "Ackh," I cough, a sudden strangulation of unmade thoughts fluttering in my windpipe.

32   The night after the cocktail party, I dreamed that I was in a bedroom with a tall, faceless man. I was his breeding slave. I was trying to be very, very good, so that I might one day earn my freedom. He did not trust me. I was always trying to hide some essential part of myself from him, which I would preserve and take with me on that promised day when I was permitted to leave; he felt it as an innate wickedness in me, a darkness that he could not penetrate, a dangerous secret that must be wrested from me. I tried everything I knew to please him; I walked a tightrope of anxious servitude and survivalist withholding. But it was not good enough. One morning, he just reached for a sword and sliced me in half, to see for himself what was inside. A casual flick, and I lay dead on the floor in two dark, unyielding halves; in exasperated disgust, he stepped over my remains and rushed from the room, already late for other business, leaving the cleanup for another slave.

33   "You didn't dream that!" M.B.W.F. says in disbelief.

34   "I did so."

35   "You're making it up," she says. "People don't really have dreams like that."

36   "I do. Aren't I a people, too?"

37   "That's amazing! Tell me another."

38   "O.K., here's a fairy tale for you," I say, and tell her I dreamed I was being held by Sam Malone, the silly, womanizing bartender on "Cheers." He was tall, broad-chested, good-looking, unbelievably strong. My head, my face were pressed against his chest. We were whispering our love for each other. I was moved deeply, my heart was banging, he held me tight and told me that he loved me. I told him that I loved him, too. We kissed so that heaven and earth moved in my heart, I wanted to make love to him fiercely. He put a simple thick gold band on my finger. I turned and, my voice cracking with emotion and barely audible, said, "What's this?" He asked me to marry him. I told him yes, I loved him, yes, yes, I loved him. He told me he loved me, too. I held out my hand and admired the ring in awe. I was the luckiest woman on earth.

39   Suddenly Diane Chambers, Sam's paramour on "Cheers," burst through the door. She was her perky, petulant self, bouncing blond hair and black-green eyes like tarnished copper beads, like lumps of melted metal—eyes that looked carved yet soft, almost brimming. She turned those soft-hard eyes on me and said, "Oh no, Sam, not tonight you promised!"

40   And with that I realized that I was to be consigned to a small room on the other side of the house. Diane followed me as I left, profusely apologetic with explanations: she was sorry, and she didn't mind him being with me once or twice a month, but this was getting ridiculous. I realized that I was Sam's part-time mistress—a member of the household somehow, but having no rights.

41   Then Diane went back into the master bedroom and Sam came in to apologize, to say that there had been a mixup, that it was just this, once, that he'd make it up to me, that he was sorry. And, of course, I forgave him, for there was nothing I wanted more than to relive the moment when he held me tightly and our love was a miracle and I was the only woman he wanted in the world, forever.

42   "Have you thought of going into therapy?" she jokes.

43   "As a matter of fact, I have," I say, sighing and rubbing my temples. "On average, we black women have bigger, better problems than any other women alive. We bear the burden of being seen as pretenders to the thrones of both femininity and masculinity, endlessly mocked by the ambiguously gendered crown-of-thorns imagery of 'queen' Madame Queen, snap queen, welfare queen, quota queen, Queenie Queen, *Queen* Queen Queen. We black women are figured more as stand-ins for men, sort of like reverse drag queens: women pretending to be women but more male than men—bare-breasted, sweat-glistened, plow-pulling, sole supporters of their families. Arnold Schwarzenegger and Sylvester Stallone meet Sojourner Truth, the *Real* Real Thing, the Ace-of-Spades Gender Card Herself, Thelma and Louise knocked up by Wesley Snipes, the ultimate hard-drinking, tobacco-growing-and-aspitting, nut-crushing ball-buster of all time. . . . I mean, think about it—how'd you like to go to the ball dressed like a walking cultural pathology? Wouldn't it make you just a wee bit tense?"

44   "But," she sputters, "but you always seem so *strong!*"

45   We have just about completed our toilette. She looks at my hair as though it were a rude construction of mud and twigs, bright glass beads, and flashy bits of tinfoil. I look at hers for what it is: the high-tech product of many hours of steam rollers, shine enhancers, body spritzers, perms, and about eighteen hundred watts of blow-dried effort. We gaze at each other with the deep disapproval of one gazing into a mirror. It is inconceivable to both of us that we have been friends for as long as we have. We shake our heads in sympathetic unison and sigh.

46   One last thing: it seems we have forgotten about shoes. It turns out that my feet are much too big to fit into any of her sequinned little evening slippers, so I wear my own sensible square-soled pumps. My prosaic feet, like overgrown roots, peek out from beneath the satiny folds of the perfect dress. She looks radiant; I feel dubious. Our chariot and her husband await. As we climb into the limousine, her husband lights up a cigar and holds forth on the reemerging popularity of same. My friend responds charmingly with a remarkably detailed production history of the Biedermeier humidor.

47   I do not envy her. I do not resent her. I do not hold my breath.

Review Questions

1. In paragraph 7 and elsewhere, Williams suggests that "Cinderella" is not a story for an African-American girl (or woman). Why not?

2. Throughout the essay, Williams connects the stories of "Cinderella" with both the American Dream and the narratives of slave women sexually abused in the master's house. Explain these connections.

3. Explain how the cocktail scene in paragraphs 23–24 presents a very un-Cinderella-like moment.

4. Williams's dream of the future and that of her best white friend differ. How so?

5. In the final paragraph, Williams writes that she does not "hold her breath." For what?

Discussion and Writing Suggestions

1. What is the effect on you, as a reader, of Williams's repeated use of "my best white friend" to refer to her, well, best white friend? What does Williams seem to be saying with this repetition?

2. Reread paragraph 8: "The human drama is compact enough so that when my mother was little she knew women who had been slaves, including a couple of runaways. Cinderellas who had burned their masters' beds and then fled for their lives. It doesn't take too much, even across the ages, to read between those lines." As you read between those lines, what did you learn?

3. Characterize the relationship between Williams and her "best white friend." What evidence do you see of the closeness of their friendship? What evidence do you see of strains? How well do they communicate across racial lines?

4. In paragraph 43, Williams suggests how difficult it is "to go to the ball dressed like a walking cultural pathology." This is a difficult, but evocative paragraph that gets to the heart of her essay. What is Williams saying about the identity of black women? Even if she wanted to go to Cinderella's ball and be swept off her feet by a prince, that's pretty much an impossibility. Why?

5. The subtitle of this piece is "Cinderella Revisited." In what way has Williams revisited the fairy tale?

**I Am Cinderella's Stepmother
and I Know My Rights**
Judith Rossner

In the humorous piece that follows, Judith Rossner lets Cinderella's much-maligned step-mother speak for herself, and we learn that she has successfully sued the Disney corporation for bringing out a movie that unfairly characterizes her and her daughters and misrepresents Cinderella as "a saint incapable of thoughts of revenge." Judith Rossner has written many novels, the most well-known being Looking for Mr. Goodbar *(1975). One of her continuing interests, expressed most notably in* Olivia *(1994) and* Perfidia *(1997), has been the psychological entanglements of complex mother-daughter relationships. The following selection appeared originally in the* New York Times *on April 19, 1987. The piece begins with the following disclaimer:*

> I have been asked to verify for those to whom it is not immediately apparent that since the following is a work of fiction . . . "written by" a person who never existed, the events referred to in it could not have taken place.

1   I've been often asked to explain why I never sued the Brothers Grimm or took public exception to the ugly little tale people think is about me and my daughters, yet have chosen to sue Mr. Disney over his loathsome movie. It's fair to guess that if I hadn't won the lawsuit, no one would care a bit about us or about the damages we've sustained. Having succeeded in getting the movie out of circulation, and in discouraging new editions of the story as well, I am besieged by hostile queries and comments, usually masquerading as concern for the storyteller's freedom.

2   First, it's essential to say I didn't look forward to pressing the suit and had hoped the whole matter would simply go away. If the picture the Grimms painted was distorted beyond belief, at least the name Cinderella—a name not bequeathed to my daughter by her parents or used by anyone who ever knew

her—seemed to afford us some protection. Between scholars explicating the text and psychiatrists relating it to the events of our lives, not to speak of reporters investigating us for some gossip magazine, the story has not blown over. In fact, I have felt hostile eyes upon me all the time.

3   One of the defense attorneys claimed it wasn't the restoration of my good name I was after, but only attention. I was jealous, he said, of the unending spotlight on my stepdaughter Cinderella. I can only wish that he be locked in a room with the Grimms for eternity. He deserves the company of two men who constantly rewrite reality to make it bearable to themselves, no matter what havoc they create for those around them.

4   I have never claimed my girls were easy. Their father, my first husband, a remote and undemonstrative man, tended to show affection by lavishing gifts of clothing and jewelry upon them. When he died suddenly, leaving a legacy of debt and an estate in disorder, the girls were denied, not only the token protection of his presence, but also those material compensations he had provided. They became anxious and moody and worried that their prospects for decent marriages had been ruined.

5   At that time, Cinderella—as I shall call her to avoid confusion—was 14. Her father was a man of no particular ability or ambition who had made a good deal of money on a stock-market fluke. When he began to court me he was floundering, incapable of mobilizing himself or controlling his strong-willed daughter. She would not go to school. She had a foul mouth. She would not dress decently for any occasion. And she was filthy.

6   The notion of anyone's being forced to sweep the cinders in a household that can afford help is ludicrous except in certain circumstances. Cinderella spent her waking time at home, sitting at the fire, poking at the cinders and getting covered with ash, which she did not mind in the least! Since she neither kept her own room neat or helped in other household tasks, tending the fireplace seemed a perfect job for her. Nor did she appear to mind! That is one of the ironies of the charming little tale she later told people who relayed it to the people who told the Grimms. She would starve before she'd cook a meal and let her clothing get stiff with dirt before she'd wash it, but tending the fireplace was a task she appeared to enjoy!

7   Allow me to move to the tale of her father's bringing home from town (as requested by them respectively) fine clothing and jewelry for my daughters, the branch of a hazelnut tree for Cinderella. As the Grimms told it, Cinderella planted the branch in memory of her mother and proceeded to weep over it such copious tears as to cause it to sprout into a tree.

8   I promise you that her mother would not have done the same for Cinderella, who, she'd often said, would be the death of her. And her father, if he let her come close, was usually rewarded by a slap in the face. What I am saying is that those tears that watered the hazelnut tree were tears not of mourning but of jealously and guilt. The girl had ample reason for both. One of the qualities that made the Grimms' tale less objectionable to us than Mr. Disney's was that in their own way, the Grimms showed the suffering my girls endured. Those birds that pecked the beans from the fireplace and brought Cinderella the gown, and were thus clearly seen to be in her service, also

pecked out my daughters' eyes. Mr. Disney, of course, gives us a saint incapable of thoughts of revenge, a portrait which, in its deep untruth, is much more unsettling to us.

9   Let us pass on to the matter of the Prince, who and what he was (a Prince, of course), and who he most distinctly was not (a responsible young man). Even if the rumors of drink and seductions and shoplifting were true, time might have turned him into a responsible adult. On the other hand, such escapades would worry any parent and were strikingly similar to our experiences with Cinderella. I've always found it peculiar that people failed to wonder why the Prince should have wanted this one pretty young girl of all the pretty young girls, including my two daughters, who lived in his kingdom.

10   To make a long story short, they were two of a kind. Those same stores in the village that locked the doors when they saw Cinderella approaching (do we need to deal, at all, with the nonsense of fairy godmothers and/or mice who provide her with clothes?) had, obviously, a much greater problem in dealing with our little Prince, who could buy whatever he wanted but chose to rip it off instead. If Cinderella didn't drink it was only because she liked to be in full control of everyone around her; if she was not promiscuous, it was because her filth discouraged advances (though it has always amused me that people swallowed whole the notion of a girl's being unrecognizable because she took a bath, combed her hair and put on a new dress).

11   In any event, my daughters were as eager as all the other young girls in the kingdom to be chosen by the Prince. Even in the modern era, when television has given an idea of the boredom of royalty's daily life, many girls might say they would give an arm or a leg to be a princess. Surely the Grimms knew the difference between using such an expression and actually cutting off one's big toe so one's foot will fit a glass slipper! Just as surely, any sane girl who thought of performing such a lunatic act would have been afraid of losing the Prince upon his discovery that she had a stump where her big toe had been! This is one of the few places where Mr. Disney's story is less objectionable than the Grimms'.

12   Which returns us to the matter of my motive in bringing this suit. Simply put, I owed it to my daughters. As you have seen, I have never claimed they were perfect. But beautiful they were. We knew it, everyone in town knew it, the Grimms knew it! It is the only quality allowed them in a tale that is otherwise a nightmare of caricature. Yet Mr. Disney chose to send them into history via the movies— which are seen in one theatrical showing by more people than read the Grimms' tales in the decade after they were written—as not only unhappy, but hideously ugly! Still, I was reluctant to sue. If I dreaded each release of the movie, I dreaded more the revelation and recrimination trying to stop it would entail.

13   Then video stores began to open near my home. I couldn't pass them without wondering if they stocked The Movie. I'd feel a change in some neighbor and sense she'd seen it and connected me and my girls to the story for the first time. Nightmares made sleep increasingly difficult. I entered therapy with a man I thought was being kind because he felt sorry for me. Finally, I talked to a lawyer who urged that I bring suit, with the results that you know. I FEEL vindicated by the court's decision, almost as pleased that certain bookstores have

ceased to carry the Grimms. I think my life would now be pleasant and "normal" were I not being subjected to all sorts of pressures from disturbed children and misguided parents who are angry when they can't find "Cinderella" at their book or video stores.

14   I'm sick of the argument that a child's imagination conjures stories more frightening than anything in Grimm, and that the stories offer deep consolation for the difficulties of the real world. It is my own feeling that children will be better rather than worse off if confined to a diet of after-school specials and quiz shows. I wish that both had been available when I was raising my girls. They have a variety of problems that might never have arisen had they not been exposed, too young, to the ugly fantasies of the Brothers Grimm.

15   The other day a little girl and her mother got on the elevator in my building and the little girl shrieked "Mommy, is that the witch who killed 'Cinderella'?" Nobody can tell me that this idea came from a child's mind, and when I find out where she got that one, I'll sue him, her or them, too.

Discussion and Writing Suggestions

1. Discuss the ways in which this selection is both a parody and a critique of two versions of "Cinderella." How does Rossner achieve her humor? How does she embed a critique within her humor? Base your answers on particular passages from the selection.

2. The stepmother objects less to the portrait of her family as painted by the brothers Grimm than she does to the one offered by the makers of the Disney animation. Why? (Why did she sue Disney, not Jakob and Wilhelm Grimm?) If you have not done so, read the Disney version of the story (pages 617–619), which parallels the movie, and the version by the brothers Grimm (pages 595–600). What, exactly, is the stepmother's complaint against Disney? Why has the Disney version offended her while the Grimm version has not?

3. What was the "truth" about Cinderella, according to the stepmother? What kind of girl was she when the stepmother first met her? What was she like later, when the Prince entered the picture? In what ways were they "two of a kind"?

4. In paragraph 14, Cinderella's stepmother rejects the claims of analysts like Bettelheim who assert that in themes, plot lines, and tensions, fairy tale literature expresses the complex inner lives of children. On reading or listening to fairy tales, goes the argument, children find a tool that helps them understand their inner turmoil. The stepmother disagrees, saying that as far as her daughters are concerned, the "ugly fantasies of the Brothers Grimm" may well have *caused* inner turmoil, not helped to resolve it. Do you have an opinion on this important point? Insofar as

you can tell, to what extent were fairy tales a psychological boon to you—or a problem?

5. Rossner relates the "Cinderella" story from an unexpected point of view. To what extent do you find the stepmother to be sympathetic in Rossner's telling? Is she any less "wicked" to you in this version?

Cinderella: *Not* So Morally Superior
Elisabeth Panttaja

In this brief analysis of "Cinderella," Elisabeth Panttaja offers what for some will be an unsettling claim: that Cinderella succeeds not because she is more patient or virtuous than her stepsisters or stepmother (the typical moral of the story) but because she is craftier, willing to employ powerful magic to defeat the forces arrayed against her. Nor can it be said from the evidence of the story, according to Panttaja, that the prince or Cinderella love each other. Is this the same "Cinderella" that you grew up with? The article from which this selection was excerpted appeared originally in Western Folklore *in January 1993. Elisabeth Panttaja taught at Tufts University when the article was written.*

1   It is not surprising . . . that modern criticism of "Cinderella" . . . has been so strangely indifferent to the role that Cinderella's mother plays in the story. In our post-Freudian world, Cinderella's mother is imagined as absent despite the fact that she plays a central part in the unfolding of Cinderella's destiny. Indeed, Cinderella's mother's role is far from marginal: the words and actions of Cinderella's mother are of vital importance in narrative sequencing and the overall "moral" of the story. The Grimms' version of "Cinderella" opens significantly with the dying mother's injunction to the soon-to-be-orphaned girl. On her deathbed, the mother gives Cinderella the following advice: "Dear child, be good and pious. Then the dear Lord shall always assist you, and I shall look down from heaven and take care of you." In fairy tales, the opening scene is always of particular importance, since it is here that the tale sets forth the problem which it will then go on to solve. Cinderella's problem is precisely the fact that her mother has died. It is this "lack," the lack of the mother, which Cinderella must overcome in the course of the story. The narrative instantly complicates her task by staging the arrival of a powerful mother and her two daughters, who, in the strength of their unity, hope to vanquish the motherless girl. Thus the story quickly amplifies the mother/daughter theme, rubbing salt, if you will, in Cinderella's wound. For just as Cinderella's powerlessness is a result of her mother's death, so the stepsisters' power is associated with their strong, scheming mother. In short order, then, Cinderella finds herself in need of her mother's good advice, and it is through keeping her mother's advice that she manages to overcome her own social isolation and the plots of her enemies. In the end, Cinderella rises to a position of power and influence, and she accomplishes this, apparently, despite her motherless status.

2   But is she really motherless? Not really, since the twig that she plants on her mother's grave grows into a tree that takes care of her, just as her mother promised to do. The mother, then, is figured in the hazel tree and in the birds that live in its branches. Early in the story, the tree offers solace to the grieving girl; later, it gives her the dresses she needs to attend the ball. Likewise, the two pigeons who live in the tree expose the false brides as they ride away, with bleeding feet, on the prince's horse, and they lead the flock of birds who help Cinderella sort the lentils that the stepmother throws on the hearth. In addition, the fleeing Cinderella is said to find safety in a dovecote and a pear tree ("a beautiful tall tree covered with the most wonderful pears"). Since these places of refuge continue the bird/tree symbolism, it is quite possible that we are meant to see the mother's influence also at work in the rather mysterious way that Cinderella manages to avoid too-early detection. Thus, at every turn in the narrative, the magical power of the mother vies with the forces arrayed against Cinderella, whether they be the selfish designs of the stepmother and stepsisters or the futile attempts of the father and prince to capture and identify her. In the end, the mother, despite death, reigns supreme. Not only does she take her revenge on her daughter's enemies by plucking out the eyes of the stepsisters, but, more importantly, she succeeds in bringing about her daughter's advantageous marriage. The happy ending proves that it is the mother, after all, who has been the power of the story. Cinderella's success resides in the fact that, while apparently motherless, she is in fact well-mothered. In spite of death, the mother/daughter dyad has kept its bonds intact. At its most basic level, the story is about this mother/daughter relationship. It is about the daughter's loyalty to the (good) mother's words and the mother's continuing, magical influence in the (good) daughter's life.

3   Unlike the narratives favored by psychoanalysis, which are about maternal absence and disempowerment, this tale tells a story about a strong mother/daughter relationship that actively shapes events. Cinderella's mother performs a specific social function vis-à-vis her daughter—she assists in her coming out. Her gifts are directed toward a specific goal—to help Cinderella into an advantageous marriage. From this perspective, what is most interesting about Cinderella's mother is her similarity to the stepmother. These two women share the same devotion to their daughters and the same long-term goals: each mother wants to ensure a future of power and prestige for her daughter, and each is willing to resort to extreme measures to achieve her aim. Thus, Cinderella's mother is a paradoxical figure: while her power is associated at the outset with the power of the Christian god and while she seems to instruct Cinderella in the value of long-suffering self-sacrifice, she is also a wily competitor. She plots and schemes, and she wins. She beats the stepmother at the game of marrying off daughters. She does for Cinderella exactly what the wicked stepmother wishes to do for her own daughters—she gets her married to the "right" man.

4   Considering the similarities in their goals and strategies, the idea that Cinderella and her mother are morally superior to the stepsisters and their mother is shot through with contradictions. Throughout the tale, there exists a

structural tension between the character that is drawn thematically (the pious Cinderella) and the character that acts in the narrative (the shrewd, competitive Cinderella). The superficial moral of the story would have us believe that Cinderella's triumph at the ball is a reward for her long-suffering patience. But while Cinderella's piety does play an important role in the forging of her supernatural alliance, it plays almost no role in the important practical business of seducing the prince. Indeed, the battle for the prince's attention is not waged at the level of character at all but at the level of clothes. Cinderella wins the battle because her mother is able, through magic, to provide raiment so stunning that no ordinary dress can compete. Cinderella's triumph at the ball has less to do with her innate goodness and more to do with her loyalty to the dead mother and a string of subversive acts: she disobeys the stepmother, enlists forbidden helpers, uses magic powers, lies, hides, dissembles, disguises herself, and evades pursuit. The brutal ending of the tale, in which Cinderella allows the mother (in the form of two pigeons) to peck out the eyes of the stepsisters, further complicates the story's moral thematics.

5   Just as there is a structural tension between the tale's thematization of Cinderella's goodness and the actual plot, so there is a tension between plot and the alleged theme of romantic love. I say "alleged" here because although modern readers and critics have sought to enshrine romantic love as a central value of the tale, there is actually nothing in the text itself to suggest either that Cinderella loves the prince or that the prince loves her. The prince marries Cinderella because he is enchanted (literally) by the sight of her in her magical clothes. What is interesting about these clothes, at least in the Grimms' version, is that, far from simply enhancing a natural but hidden beauty, they actually create it. In the Grimms' version, Cinderella is described as "deformed," while the sisters are described as "fair," so we can only conclude that the power of Cinderella's clothes is indeed miraculous, since they turn a deformed girl into a woman whose beauty surpasses that of the already fair. Thus, the prince's choice of Cinderella can be explained neither by her piety, which he has never experienced, nor by her own beauty, which does not exist. It is the mother's magic which brings about the desired outcome, an outcome in which the prince has actually very little choice. The prince's oft-repeated statement, "She's my partner," as well as his obsessive tracking down of the true bride, suggests that he is operating under a charm rather than as an autonomous character, and the fact that both these motifs are repeated three times is further evidence that magic, not free choice, is at work here.

6   This is not surprising: the enchantment of a potential marriage partner is one of the most common motifs in fairy tales and mythology. The motif of an enchanted or somehow disguised bride or bridegroom usually appears in tales that depict some kind of unusual marriage, either the marriage of a god or demon to a human (Cupid and Psyche) or the marriage of a poor or ordinary mortal to a member of the deity or the nobility (Beauty and the Beast). The idea, of course, is that one member, by being disguised or by disguising another, can enter into a marriage that he or she would not normally enter into, usually one that crosses class lines. Thus, the enchantment of a prospective bride

or bridegroom has more to do with power and manipulation than it does with romance or affection. Rather than talking about Cinderella's love for the prince, then, it is more accurate to say that Cinderella, in alliance with her mother, bewitches the prince in order to gain the power and prestige that will accrue to her upon her marriage to a member of the nobility.

Review Questions

1. Generally, why is the opening scene of a fairy tale so important? Why is it of particular importance in "Cinderella"?

2. Panttaja claims that, despite death, Cinderella's mother remains very much present in the story. How so?

3. How is Cinderella's mother similar to the stepmother?

4. The claim that Cinderella and her mother are morally superior to the sisters and their mother is "shot through with contradictions." What are these contradictions?

5. Why is romantic love *not* central to winning the prince, according to Panttaja? What (and whose) personal qualities *are* essential?

6. What is often the purpose of a disguise or enchantment in fairy tales?

Discussion and Writing Suggestions

1. Does Panttaja's claim that Cinderella's mother is not absent surprise you? Convince you? Explain.

2. What is your response to the claim that Cinderella is not morally superior to the wicked stepsisters or stepmother? Do you find Panttaja's argument compelling? Do you find yourself resisting it at all?

3. Number the sentences of paragraph 2, and then reread the paragraph and respond to these questions: What is the main point (the topic sentence) and where is it located? How does each sentence advance the main idea of the paragraph? Finally, examine the sequence of sentences. Why does Panttaja place sentences where she does? Having completed the analysis, what is your assessment of the paragraph? How successful is it?

4. If Panttaja is correct in her analysis of "Cinderella," what is the moral of the story? How does this moral compare with the one(s) you more typically associate with the story? Do you prefer one moral to another? Why?

5. Read the Grimm brothers' version of "Cinderella" and compare your reading with Panttaja's. Do you find her use of evidence in support of

her main points persuasive? Have you, reading the same story, reached different conclusions? Explain, if you can, how two people reading one story can reach different conclusions. What does this say about the story? About the people reading it?

Synthesis Activities

1. Along with many other fairy tales, "Cinderella" is a story of transformations—of unrecognized talent and beauty eventually being recognized and valued; of low circumstance rising to good fortune; of haughtiness punished and made humble. So central are transformations to fairy tale literature that Anne Sexton gave that name to her volume of poetry in which she revisited (and ironically reworked) the tales. Preparing to go to her own ball, Patricia J. Williams (along with Sexton) openly distrusts happily-ever-after endings and princes who sweep girls off their feet. In an argument synthesis that draws on these and other sources in this chapter, define the important transformations in "Cinderella." Refer to variants of the story that most appeal to you. Make the central argument of your paper a response to this question: Do you believe in the transformations promised in tales like "Cinderella"?

2. In 1910, Antti Aarne published one of the early classifications of folktale types as an aid to scholars who were collecting tales and needed an efficient means for telling where, and with what changes, similar tales had appeared. In 1927, folklorist Stith Thompson, translating and enlarging Aarne's study, produced a work that is now a standard reference for folklorists the world over. We present the authors' description of type 510 and its two forms, 510A ("Cinderella") and 510B. Use this description as a basis on which to analyze any two versions of "Cinderella," in this chapter, determining the extent to which they conform to the stated pattern. Compare and contrast the versions and decide which, in your view, is more authentic.

   510.   *Cinderella and Cap o' Rushes.*

   I.   *The Persecuted Heroine.* (a) The heroine is abused by her stepmother and stepsisters, or (b) flees in disguise from her father who wants to marry her, or (c) is cast out by him because she has said that she loved him like salt, or (d) is to be killed by a servant.

   II.   *Magic Help.* While she is acting as servant (at home or among strangers) she is advised, provided for, and fed (a) by her dead mother, (b) by a tree on the mother's grave, or (c) by a supernatural being, or (d) by birds, or (e) by a

goat, a sheep, or a cow. When the goat is killed, there springs up from her remains a magic tree.

  III. *Meeting with Prince.* (a) She dances in beautiful clothing several times with a prince who seeks in vain to keep her, or she is seen by him in church. (b) She gives hints of the abuse she has endured, as servant girl, or (c) she is seen in her beautiful clothing in her room or in the church.

  IV. *Proof of Identity.* (a) She is discovered through the slipper-test, or (b) through a ring which she throws into the prince's drink or bakes in his bread. (c) She alone is able to pluck the gold apple desired by the knight.

  V. *Marriage with the Prince.*

  VI. *Value of Salt.* Her father is served unsalted food and thus learns the meaning of her earlier answer.

Two forms of the type follow.

A. *Cinderella.* The two stepsisters. The stepdaughter at the grave of her own mother, who helps her (milks the cow, shakes the apple tree, helps the old man). Threefold visit to church (dance). Slipper-test.

B. *The Dress of Gold, of Silver, and of Stars. (Cap o' Rushes).* Present of the father who wants to marry his own daughter. The maiden as servant of the prince, who throws various objects at her. The threefold visit to the church and the forgotten shoe. Marriage.

3. Speculate on the reasons folktales are made and told. As you develop a theory, rely first on your own hunches regarding the origins and functions of folktale literature. You might want to recall your experiences as a child listening to tales so that you can discuss their effects on you. Rely as well on the variants of "Cinderella," which you should regard as primary sources (just as scholars do). And make use of the critical pieces you've read—Thompson, Bettelheim, Cullen, and Panttaja—selecting pertinent points from each that will help clarify your points. *Remember:* Your own speculation should dominate the paper. Use sources to help you make *your* points.

4. At the conclusion of his article, Stith Thompson writes:

> Literary critics, anthropologists, historians, psychologists, and aestheticians are all needed if we are to hope to know why folktales are made, how they are invented, what art is used in their telling, how they grow and change and occasionally die.

What is your opinion of the critical work you've read on "Cinderella"? Writing from various perspectives, authors in this chapter have analyzed the tale. To what extent have the analyses illuminated (or ruined) "Cinderella" for you? Do you believe that attempts at analysis are inappropriate for a children's story?

In responding to these questions, you might begin with Thompson's quotation and then follow directly with a statement of your thesis. Critique the work of Bettelheim, Cullen, and/or Panttaja as a way of demonstrating which analyses of folktales (if any) seem worthwhile. Throughout, refer directly to the variants of "Cinderella."

5. Review the variants of "Cinderella" and select two you would read to a favorite child. Then justify your decision. Do your selections meet Aarne and Thompson's classification—see Synthesis Activity #2.) You might also justify your choices negatively by *eliminating* certain variants because they don't meet certain criteria (e.g., that the story is overly violent). In concluding the paper, explain how the variants you've selected work as a pair. (Or, perhaps, they *don't* complement each other, which is why you've selected them.)

6. Try writing a version of "Cinderella" and setting it on a college campus. For your version of the story to be an authentic variant, you'll need to retain certain defining features, or motifs. See Aarne and Thompson—Synthesis Activity #2. As you consider the possibilities for your story, recall Thompson's point that the teller of a folktale borrows heavily on earlier versions; the virtue of telling is not in rendering a new story but in retelling an old one and *adapting* it to local conditions and needs. Unless you plan to write a commentary "Cinderella," as Sexton does, you should retain the basic motifs of the old story and add details that will appeal to your particular audience: your classmates. *An option:* Create a reality television show or an Internet blog based on elements of "Cinderella."

7. In her 1981 book *The Cinderella Complex,* Colette Dowling wrote:

> It is the thesis of this book that personal, psychological dependency—the deep wish to be taken care of by others—is the chief force holding women down today. I call this "The Cinderella Complex"—a network of largely repressed attitudes and fears that keep women in a kind of half-light, retreating from the full use of their minds and creativity. Like Cinderella, women today are still waiting for something external to transform their lives.

In an essay, respond to Dowling's thesis. First, in an analysis, test her thesis by applying it to a few of the variants of "Cinderella." Does the thesis hold in each case? Next, respond to her view that "the chief force holding women down today" is psychological dependency, or the need for "something external" (i.e., a Prince) to transform their lives. In your experience, have you observed a Cinderella complex at work?

8. Explain the process by which Cinderella falls in love in these tales. The paper that you write will be an extended comparison-and-contrast in which you observe this process at work in the variants

and then discuss similarities and differences. (In structuring your paper, you'll need to make some choices: Which variants will you discuss and in what order?) At the conclusion of your extended comparison-and-contrast, answer the "So what?" question. Pull your observations together and make a statement about Cinderella's falling in love. At some point, you should raise and respond to Elisabeth Panttaja's assertion that Cinderella does *not*, in fact, fall in love in this tale.

9. Based on your own reading of the tale and on your response to the selection by Rossner, develop a point of view about Cinderella's stepmother. Is she truly wicked? Misunderstood? Worthy of our sympathy? Develop your response into an argument. Refer generously to the story itself.

10. The theories of Freud as applied by Bruno Bettelheim to "Cinderella" leave little room for the folktale's *not* reaching into the private lives of children and speaking to them in a profound way. Bettelheim writes, for instance, that " 'Cinderella' . . . is experienced as a story about the agonies and hopes which form the essential content of sibling rivalry; and about the degraded heroine winning out over her siblings." Such a grand pronouncement would seem to apply to *all* children. Yet the noted law professor and writer Patricia J. Williams suggests that "Cinderella" does not resonate for African-American girls and women for several reasons, primarily the history of abuse of black women at the hands of white "princes" (or slave owners). In light of Williams's essay, do you believe that Bettelheim is correct in claiming a universal psychological appeal for the story? Respond to this question in an argument synthesis that draws on both selections.

11. Many people read the tale as an ideal expression of courtship. Is this your view? What are the romantic legacies of stories like "Cinderella" for relationships today? In developing your answer, how will you account for Elisabeth Panttaja's claim that romantic love has nothing to do with the eventual union of Cinderella and her prince? And how will you account for Patricia J. Williams's observation that images of ideal courtship do not look the same to girls and women of color as they do to white girls and women? Develop your response into an argument.

RESEARCH ACTIVITIES

1. Research the fairy tale literature of your ancestors, both the tales and any critical commentary that you can find on them. Once you have read the material, talk with older members of your family to hear any tales they have to tell. (Seek, especially, oral versions of stories you have already read.) In a paper, discuss the role that fairy tale literature has played, and continues to play, in your family.

2. Locate the book *Morphology of the Folktale* (1958) by Russian folklorist Vladimir Propp. Use the information you find there to analyze the elements of any three fairy tales of your choosing. In a paper, report on your analysis and evaluate the usefulness of Propp's system of classifying the key elements of fairy tale literature.

3. Bruno Bettelheim's *Uses of Enchantment* (1975) generated a great deal of reaction on its publication. Read Bettelheim and locate as many reviews of his work as possible. Based on your own reactions and on your reading of the reviews, write an evaluation in which you address Bettelheim's key assumption that fairy tale literature provides important insights into the psychological life of children.

4. Locate and study multiple versions of any fairy tale other than "Cinderella." Having read the versions, identify—and write your paper on—what you feel are the defining elements that make the tales variants of a single story. See if you can find the tale listed as a "type" in Aarne and Thompson's *The Types of Folk-Tales*. If you wish, argue that one version of the tale is preferable to others.

5. Jack Zipes, author of *Breaking the Magic Spell* (1979), takes the approach that fairy tales are far from innocuous children's stories; rather, they inculcate the unsuspecting with the value systems of the dominant culture. In a research paper, explicitly address the assumption that fairy tales are not morally or politically neutral but, rather, imply a distinct set of values.

6. In anticipation of writing a children's story, decide on an age group that you will address, and then go to a local public library and find several books directed to the same audience. (1) Analyze these books and write a brief paper in which you identify the story elements that seem especially important for your intended audience. (2) Then attempt your own story. (3) When you have finished, answer two questions: What values are implicit in your story? What will children who read or hear the story learn about themselves and their world? Plan to submit your brief analytical paper, your story, and your final comment.

7. Videotape, and then study, several hours of Saturday morning cartoons. Then locate and read a collection of Grimm's fairy tales. In a comparative analysis, examine the cartoons and the fairy tales along any four or five dimensions that you think are important. The point of your comparisons and contrasts will be to determine how well the two types of presentations stack up against each other. Which do you find more entertaining? Illuminating? Ambitious? Useful? (These criteria are suggestions only. You should generate your own criteria as part of your research.)

8. Arrange to read to your favorite young person a series of fairy tales. Based on your understanding of the selections in this chapter,

develop a list of questions concerning the importance or usefulness of fairy tale literature to children. Read to your young friend on several occasions and, if possible, talk about the stories after you read them (or while you are reading). Then write a paper on your experience, answering as many of your initial questions as possible. (Be sure in your paper to provide a profile of the child with whom you worked; to review your selection of stories; and to list the questions you wanted to explore.)

13

New and Improved: Six Decades of Advertising

Possibly the most memorable ad campaign of the twentieth century (dating from the late 1920s) takes the form of a comic strip. A bully kicks sand into the face of a skinny man relaxing on the beach with his girlfriend. Humiliated, the skinny man vows to get even. "Don't bother, little boy!" huffs the scornful girlfriend, who promptly dumps him. At home, the skinny man kicks a chair in frustration, declares that he's sick of being a scarecrow, and says that if Charles Atlas (once a "97-lb. weakling" himself) can give him a "real body," he'll send for his FREE book. In the next frame, the once-skinny man, now transformed into a hunk, thanks to Atlas's "Dynamic Tension" fitness program, admires himself in front of the mirror: "Boy, it didn't take Atlas long to do this for me. Look, how those muscles bulge! . . . That big stiff won't dare insult me now!" Back on the beach, the bully is decked by the once-skinny man, as his adoring girlfriend looks on: "Oh Mac! You are a real man after all!"

Crude? Undoubtedly. But variations of this ad, which made Atlas a multimillionaire, ran for decades (his company is still in business). Like other successful ads, it draws its power from skillful appeals to almost primitive urges—in this particular case, the urge to gain dominance over a rival for the attention of the opposite sex. Of course, effective ads don't always work on such a primal level. Another famous ad of the 1920s appeals to our need to gain respect from others for higher accomplishments than punching out opponents. Headlined "They Laughed When I Sat Down at the Piano—But When I Started to Play. . . !" the text offers a first-person account of a man who sits down to play the piano at a party. As he does so, the guests make good-natured fun of him; but once he began to play, "a tense silence fell on the guests. The laughter died on their lips as if by magic. I played through the first bars of Liszt's immortal 'Liebenstraum.' I heard gasps of amazement. My friends sat breathless—spellbound." For 16 additional paragraphs, the writer goes on to detail the effect of his playing upon the guests and to explain how "You, too, can now *teach yourself* to be an accomplished musician—right at home," by purchasing the program of the U.S. School of Music. Again, the reader is encouraged to send for the free booklet. And by the way, "Forget the old-fashioned idea that you need 'special talent'" to play an instrument.

The ubiquity of advertising is a fact of modern life. In fact, advertising can be traced as far back as ancient Roman times when pictures were inscribed on walls to promote gladiatorial contests. In those days, however, the illiteracy of most of the population and the fact that goods were made by hand and could not be mass produced limited the need for more widespread advertising. One of the first American advertisers was Benjamin Franklin, who pioneered the use of large headlines and made strategic use of white space. But advertising as the mass phenomenon we know is a product of the twentieth century, when the United States became an industrial nation—and particularly of the post–World War II period, when a prosperous economy created our modern consumer society, marked by the middle-class acquisition of goods, the symbols of status, success, style, and social acceptance. Today, we are surrounded not only by a familiar array of billboards, print ads, and broadcast ads, but also by the Internet, which has given us "spam," the generic name for an entire category of digital pitches for debt reduction, low mortgage rates, and enhanced body parts—compared to which the average Buick ad in a glossy magazine reads like great literature.

Advertisements are more than just appeals to buy; they are windows into our psyches and our culture. They reveal our values, our (not-so-hidden) desires, our yearnings for a different lifestyle. For example, the Marlboro man, that quintessence of taciturn cowboy masculinity, at home only in the wide open spaces of Marlboro Country, is a mid-twentieth-century American tribute to (what is perceived as) nineteenth-century American values, popularized in hundreds of westerns. According to James Twitchell, a professor of English and advertising at the University of Florida, "He is what we have for royalty, distilled manhood. . . . The Marlboro Man needs to tell you nothing. He carries no scepter, no gun. He never even speaks. Doesn't need to." He is also the product of a bolt of advertising inspiration: Previously, Marlboro had been marketed—unsuccessfully—as a woman's cigarette. Another example of how ads reveal culture is the memorable campaign for the Volkswagen Beetle in the 1960s. That campaign spoke to the counterculture mentality of the day: Instead of appealing to the traditional automobile customer's desire for luxury, beauty, size, power, and comfort, Volkswagen emphasized how small, funny-looking, bare-bones—but economical and sensible—their cars were. On the other hand, snob appeal—at an affordable price, of course—has generally been a winning strategy. In the 1980s and 1990s Grey Poupon mustard ran a successful campaign of TV commercials featuring one Rolls-Royce pulling up alongside another. A voice from one vehicle asks, "Pardon me; do you have any Grey Poupon?" "But of course!" replies a voice in the other car; and a hand with a jar of mustard reaches out from the window of the second car to pass to the unseen occupant of the first car. This campaign is a perfect illustration of what University of California at Davis history professor Roland Marchand calls the appeal of the democracy of goods: "the wonders of modern mass production and distribution enable . . . everyone to enjoy society's most desirable pleasures, conveniences, or benefits."

So pervasive and influential has advertising become that it has created a significant backlash among social critics. Among the most familiar charges against advertising: It fosters materialism, it psychologically manipulates people to buy things they don't need, it perpetuates gender and racial stereotypes (particularly in its illustrations), it is deceptive, it is offensive, it debases the language, and it is omnipresent—we cannot escape it. Although arguing the truth or falsity of these assertions (more fully covered in the selection by Bovée and Arens, pages 685–690) makes for lively debate, our focus in this chapter is not on the ethics of advertising, but rather on how it works. What makes for successful advertising? How do advertisers—and by advertisers we mean not only manufacturers but also the agencies they hire to produce their advertisements—pull our psychological levers to influence us to buy (or think favorably of) their products? What are the textual and graphic components of an effective advertisement—of an effective advertising campaign? How—if at all—has advertising evolved over the past several decades?

Advertising has seen significant changes in the six decades since the end of World War II. It is unlikely that the comic strip Charles Atlas ad or the verbose "They Laughed When I Sat Down at the Piano" ad would succeed today. Both seem extremely dated. More representative of today's advertising style is the successful milk campaign; each ad features a celebrity such as Bernie Mac or Lauren Bacall with a milk mustache, a headline that says simply "got milk?", and a few short words of text supposedly spoken by the pictured celebrity. But the changes in advertising during the six decades covered in this chapter are more of style than of substance. On the whole, the similarities between an ad produced in the 1950s and one produced today are more significant than the differences. Of course, hair and clothing styles change with the times, message length recedes, and both text and graphics assume a lesser degree of apple-pie social consensus on values. But on the whole, the same psychological appeals, the same principles of headline and graphic design that worked 60 years ago, continue to work today. We choose one automobile over another, for instance, less because our vehicle of choice gets us from point A to point B, than because we invest it—or the advertiser does—with rich psychological and cultural values. In 1957 the French anthropologist and philosopher Roland Barthes wrote (in a review of a French automobile, the Citroën DS), "I think that cars today are almost the exact equivalent of the great Gothic cathedrals: I mean the supreme creation of an era, conceived with passion by unknown artists, and consumed in image if not in usage by a whole population which appropriates them as a purely magical object." It's not known whether Barthes ever considered a career as an advertising copywriter; but he probably would have been a good one.

How advertising works, then, is the subject of the present chapter. By applying a variety of theoretical and practical perspectives to a gallery of six decades of advertisements (and to other ads of your own choosing), you'll be able to practice your analytical skills upon one of the more fascinating areas of American mass culture. The main subjects of your analyses are represented later in this chapter by a portfolio of 42 advertisements that originally appeared in such magazines as *Time, Newsweek, U.S. News and World Report,* and *Sunset.* For ease of comparison and contrast, most of the ads can be classified into a relatively few categories: cigarettes, alcohol, automobiles, and food, with a number of other ads in the "miscellaneous" category. These ads have been selected for their inherent interest, as well as for the variety of tools that have been employed to communicate the message, what some advertisers call the USP—the Unique Selling Proposition.

The first part of the chapter, however, consists of a number of articles or passages from books, each representing an analytical tool, a particular perspective from which one can view individual advertisements. In the first selection, "Advertising's Fifteen Basic Appeals," Jib Fowles offers a psychological perspective. Fowles identifies and discusses the most common needs to which advertisers attempt to appeal. Among these are the need for sex, the need for affiliation with other people, the need for dominance, and the need for autonomy. In "Making the Pitch in Print Advertising," Courtland L. Bovée et al. outline the key elements of the textual component of advertising—including headlines, subheadlines, and body text. In "Elements of Effective Layout," Dorothy Cohen discusses the key components of advertising graphics: balance, proportion, movement, unity, clarity and simplicity, and emphasis. In "The Indictments Against Advertising" Courtland L. Bovée and William F. Arens consider and respond to some of the most frequent charges leveled against Madison Avenue.

Finally, as indicated above, the chapter continues and concludes with "A Portfolio of Advertisements: 1945–2003," a collection of 42 ads for various products published in popular magazines in the United States and Great Britain during the last 60 years.

Charles O'Neill, an independent marketing consultant, has written, "Perhaps, by learning how advertising works, we can become better equipped to sort out content from hype, product values from emotions, and salesmanship from propaganda." We hope that the selections in this chapter will allow you to do just that, as well as to develop a greater understanding of one of the most pervasive components of American mass culture.

Advertising's Fifteen Basic Appeals
Jib Fowles

Our first selection provides what you will likely find the single most useful analytical tool for studying advertisements. Drawing upon studies of numerous ads and upon interviews with subjects conducted by Harvard psychologist Henry A. Murray, Fowles developed a set of 15 basic appeals he believes to be at the heart of American advertising. These appeals, according to Fowles and to Murray, are directed primarily to the "lower brain," to those "unfulfilled urges and motives swirling in the bottom half of [our] minds," rather than to the part of the brain that processes our more rational thoughts and impulses. As you read Fowles's article and his descriptions of the individual appeals, other examples from contemporary print and broadcast ads may occur to you. You may find it useful to jot down these examples for later incorporation into your responses to the discussion and synthesis questions that follow.

Jib Fowles has written numerous articles and books on the popular media, including Mass Advertising as Social Forecast: A Method for Futures Research *(1976),* Why Viewers Watch: A Reappraisal of Television's Effects *(1992),* Advertising and Popular Culture *(1996), and* The Case for Television Violence *(1999). This selection first appeared in* Etc. 39:3 *(1982) and was reprinted in* Advertising and Popular Culture.

Emotional Appeals

1   The nature of effective advertisements was recognized full well by the late media philosopher Marshall McLuhan. In his *Understanding Media,* the first sentence of the section on advertising reads, "The continuous pressure is to create ads more and more in the image of audience motives and desires."

2   By giving form to people's deep-lying desires, and picturing states of being that individuals privately yearn for, advertisers have the best chance of arresting attention and affecting communication. And that is the immediate goal of advertising: to tug at our psychological shirtsleeves and slow us down long enough for a word or two about whatever is being sold. We glance at a picture of a solitary rancher at work, and "Marlboro" slips into our minds.

3   Advertisers (I'm using the term as a shorthand for both the products' manufacturers, who bring the ambition and money to the process, and the advertising agencies, who supply the know-how) are ever more compelled to invoke consumers' drives and longings; this is the "continuous pressure" McLuhan refers to. Over the past century, the American marketplace has grown increasingly congested as more and more products have entered into the frenzied competition after the public's dollars. The economies of other nations are quieter than ours since the volume of goods being hawked does not so greatly exceed demand. In some economies, consumer wares are scarce enough that no advertising at all is necessary. But in the United States, we go to the other extreme. In order to stay in business, an advertiser must strive to cut through the considerable commercial hub-bub by any means available—including the emotional appeals that some observers have held to be abhorrent and underhanded.

4   The use of subconscious appeals is a comment not only on conditions among sellers. As time has gone by, buyers have become stoutly resistant to advertisements. We live in a blizzard of these messages and have learned to turn up our collars and ward off most of them. A study done a few years ago at Harvard University's Graduate School of Business Administration ventured that the average American is exposed to some 500 ads daily from television, newspapers, magazines, radio, billboards, direct mail, and so on. If for no other reason than to preserve one's sanity, a filter must be developed in every mind to lower the number of ads a person is actually aware of—a number this particular study estimated at about seventy-five ads per day. (Of these, only twelve typically produced a reaction—nine positive and three negative, on the average.) To be among the few messages that do manage to gain access to minds, advertisers must be strategic, perhaps even a little underhanded at times.

5   There are assumptions about personality underlying advertisers' efforts to communicate via emotional appeals, and while these assumptions have stood the test of time, they still deserve to be aired. Human beings, it is presumed, walk around with a variety of unfulfilled urges and motives swirling in the

bottom half of their minds. Lusts, ambitions, tendernesses, vulnerabilities—they are constantly bubbling up, seeking resolution. These mental forces energize people, but they are too crude and irregular to be given excessive play in the real world. They must be capped with the competent, sensible behavior that permits individuals to get along well in society. However, this upper layer of mental activity, shot through with caution and rationality, is not receptive to advertising's pitches. Advertisers want to circumvent this shell of consciousness if they can, and latch on to one of the lurching, subconscious drives.

6   In effect, advertisers over the years have blindly felt their way around the underside of the American psyche, and by trial and error have discovered the softest points of entree, the places where their messages have the greatest likelihood of getting by consumers' defenses. As McLuhan says elsewhere, "Gouging away at the surface of public sales resistance, the ad men are constantly breaking through into the *Alice in Wonderland* territory behind the looking glass, which is the world of subrational impulses and appetites."

7   An advertisement communicates by making use of a specially selected image (of a supine female, say, or a curly-haired child, or a celebrity) which is designed to stimulate "subrational impulses and desires" even when they are at ebb, even if they are unacknowledged by their possessor. Some few ads have their emotional appeal in the text, but for the greater number by far the appeal is contained in the artwork. This makes sense, since visual communication better suits more primal levels of the brain. If the viewer of an advertisement actually has the importuned motive, and if the appeal is sufficiently well fashioned to call it up, then the person can be hooked. The product in the ad may then appear to take on the semblance of gratification for the summoned motive. Many ads seem to be saying, "If you have this need, then this product will help satisfy it." It is a primitive equation, but not an ineffective one for selling.

8   Thus, most advertisements appearing in national media can be understood as having two orders of content. The first is the appeal to deep-running drives in the minds of consumers. The second is information regarding the good[s] or service being sold: its name, its manufacturer, its picture, its packaging, its objective attributes, its functions. For example, the reader of a brassiere advertisement sees a partially undraped but blandly unperturbed woman standing in an otherwise commonplace public setting, and may experience certain sensations; the reader also sees the name "Maidenform," a particular brassiere style, and, in tiny print, words about the material, colors, price. Or, the viewer of a television commercial sees a demonstration with four small boxes labeled 650, 650, 650, and 800; something in the viewer's mind catches hold of this, as trivial as thoughtful consideration might reveal it to be. The viewer is also exposed to the name "Anacin," its bottle, and its purpose.

9   Sometimes there is an apparently logical link between an ad's emotional appeal and its product information. It does not violate common sense that Cadillac automobiles be photographed at country clubs, or that Japan Air Lines be associated with Orientalia. But there is no real need for the linkage to have a bit of reason behind it. Is there anything inherent to the connection between Salem cigarettes and mountains, Coke and a smile, Miller Beer and comradeship? The link being forged in minds between product and appeal is a pre-logical one.

10   People involved in the advertising industry do not necessarily talk in the terms being used here. They are stationed at the sending end of this communications channel, and may think they are up to any number of things—Unique Selling Propositions, explosive copywriting, the optimal use of demographics or psychographics, ideal media buys, high recall ratings, or whatever. But when attention shifts to the receiving end of the channel, and focuses on the instant of reception, then commentary becomes much more elemental: an advertising message contains something primary and primitive, an emotional appeal, that in effect is the thin end of the wedge, trying to find its way into a mind. Should this occur, the product information comes along behind.

11   When enough advertisements are examined in this light, it becomes clear that the emotional appeals fall into several distinguishable categories, and that every ad is a variation on one of a limited number of basic appeals. While there may be several ways of classifying these appeals, one particular list of fifteen has proven to be especially valuable.

Advertisements can appeal to:

1. The need for sex
2. The need for affiliation
3. The need to nurture
4. The need for guidance
5. The need to aggress
6. The need to achieve
7. The need to dominate
8. The need for prominence
9. The need for attention
10. The need for autonomy
11. The need to escape
12. The need to feel safe
13. The need for aesthetic sensations
14. The need to satisfy curiosity
15. Physiological needs: food, drink, sleep, etc.

Murray's List

12 Where does this list of advertising's fifteen basic appeals come from? Several years ago, I was involved in a research project which was to have as one segment an objective analysis of the changing appeals made in post-World War II American advertising. A sample of magazine ads would have their appeals coded into the categories of psychological needs they seemed aimed at. For this content analysis to happen, a complete roster of human motives would have to be found.

13   The first thing that came to mind was Abraham Maslow's famous four-part hierarchy of needs. But the briefest look at the range of appeals made in advertising was enough to reveal that they are more varied, and more profane, than Maslow had cared to account for. The search led on to the work of psychologist Henry A. Murray, who together with his colleagues at the Harvard Psychological Clinic has constructed a full taxonomy of needs. As described in *Explorations in Personality*, Murray's team had conducted a lengthy series of in-

depth interviews with a number of subjects in order to derive from scratch what they felt to be the essential variables of personality. Forty-four variables were distinguished by the Harvard group, of which twenty were motives. The need for achievement ("to overcome obstacles and obtain a high standard") was one, for instance; the need to defer was another; the need to aggress was a third; and so forth.

14   Murray's list had served as the groundwork for a number of subsequent projects. Perhaps the best-known of these was David C. McClelland's extensive study of the need for achievement, reported in his *The Achieving Society*. In the process of demonstrating that a people's high need for achievement is predictive of later economic growth, McClelland coded achievement imagery and references out of a nation's folklore, songs, legends, and children's tales.

15   Following McClelland, I too wanted to cull the motivational appeals from a culture's imaginative product—in this case, advertising. To develop categories expressly for this purpose, I took Murray's twenty motives and added to them others he had mentioned in passing in *Explorations in Personality* but not included on the final list. The extended list was tried out on a sample of advertisements, and motives which never seemed to be invoked were dropped. I ended up with eighteen of Murrays' motives, into which 770 print ads were coded. The resulting distribution is included in the 1976 book *Mass Advertising as Social Forecast*.

16   Since that time, the list of appeals has undergone refinements as a result of using it to analyze television commercials. A few more adjustments stemmed from the efforts of students in my advertising classes to decode appeals; tens of term papers surveying thousands of advertisements have caused some inconsistencies in the list to be hammered out. Fundamentally, though, the list remains the creation of Henry Murray. In developing a comprehensive, parsimonious inventory of human motives, he pinpointed the subsurface mental forces that are the least quiescent and most susceptible to advertising's entreaties.

Fifteen Appeals

17   **1. Need for Sex.**   Let's start with sex, because this is the appeal which seems to pop up first whenever the topic of advertising is raised. Whole books have been written about this one alone, to find a large audience of mildly titillated readers. Lately, due to campaigns to sell blue jeans, concern with sex in ads has redoubled.

18   The fascinating thing is not how much sex there is in advertising, but how little. Contrary to impressions, unambiguous sex is rare in these messages. Some of this surprising observation may be a matter of definition: the Jordache ads with the lithe, blouse-less female astride a similarly clad male is clearly an appeal to the audience's sexual drives, but the same cannot be said about Brooke Shields* in the Calvin Klein commercials. Directed at young women and their credit-card carrying mothers, the image of Miss Shields instead invokes the need

---

* Brooke Shields (b. 1965) is a model (at age 3 she was the Ivory Snow baby), as well as a stage (*Grease*), TV, and film actress; her most well-known films are *Pretty Baby* (1978) and *Blue Lagoon* (1980).

to be looked at. Buy Calvins and you'll be the center of much attention, just as Brooke is, the ads imply; they do not primarily inveigle their target audience's need for sexual intercourse.

19   In the content analysis reported in *Mass Advertising as Social Forecast* only two percent of ads were found to pander to this motive. Even *Playboy* ads shy away from sexual appeals: a recent issue contained eighty-three full-page ads, and just four of them (or less than five percent) could be said to have sex on their minds.

20   The reason this appeal is so little used is that it is too blaring and tends to obliterate the product information. Nudity in advertising has the effect of reducing brand recall. The people who do remember the product may do so because they have been made indignant by the ad; this is not the response most advertisers seek.

21   To the extent that sexual imagery is used, it conventionally works better on men than women; typically a female figure is offered up to the male reader. A Black Velvet liquor advertisement displays an attractive woman wearing a tight black outfit, recumbent under the legend, "Feel the Velvet." The figure does not have to be horizontal, however, for the appeal to be present as National Airlines revealed in its "Fly me" campaign. Indeed, there does not even have to be a female in the ad; "Flick my Bic"* was sufficient to convey the idea to many.

22   As a rule, though, advertisers have found sex to be a tricky appeal, to be used sparingly. Less controversial and equally fetching are the appeals to our need for affectionate human contact.

23   **2. Need for Affiliation.**   American mythology upholds autonomous individuals, and social statistics suggest that people are ever more going it alone in their lives, yet the high frequency of affiliative appeals in ads belies this. Or maybe it does not: maybe all the images of companionship are compensation for what Americans privately lack. In any case, the need to associate with others is widely invoked in advertising and is probably the most prevalent appeal. All sorts of goods and services are sold by linking them to our unfulfilled desires to be in good company.

24   According to Henry Murray, the need for affiliation consists of desires "to draw near and enjoyably cooperate or reciprocate with another; to please and win affection of another; to adhere and remain loyal to a friend." The manifestations of this motive can be segmented into several different types of affiliation, beginning with romance.

25   Courtship may be swifter nowadays, but the desire for pair-bonding is far from satiated. Ads reaching for this need commonly depict a youngish male and female engrossed in each other. The head of the male is usually higher than the female's, even at this late date; she may be sitting or leaning while he is standing. They are not touching in the Smirnoff vodka ads, but obviously there is an intimacy, sometimes frolicsome, between them. The couple does touch for

---

* "Flick my Bic" became a famous and successful slogan in advertisements for Bic cigarette lighters during the late 1970s and 1980s. Fowles hints at the not-too-subtle sexual implications of the line.

Martell Cognac when "The moment was Martell." For Wind Song perfume they have touched, and "Your Wind Song stays on his mind."

26   Depending on the audience, the pair does not absolutely have to be young— just together. He gives her a DeBeers diamond, and there is a tear in her laugh lines. She takes Geritol* and preserves herself for him. And numbers of consumers, wanting affection too, follow suit.

27   Warm family feelings are fanned in ads when another generation is added to the pair. Hallmark Cards brings grandparents into the picture, and Johnson and Johnson Baby Powder has Dad, Mom, and baby, all fresh from the bath, encircled in arms and emblazoned with "Share the Feeling." A talc has been fused to familial love.

28   Friendship is yet another form of affiliation pursued by advertisers. Two women confide and drink Maxwell House coffee together; two men walk through the woods smoking Salem cigarettes. Miller Beer promises that afternoon "Miller Time" will be staffed with three or four good buddies. Drink Dr. Pepper, as Mickey Rooney is coaxed to do, and join in with all the other Peppers. Coca-Cola does not even need to portray the friendliness; it has reduced this appeal to "a Coke and a smile."

29   The warmth can be toned down and disguised, but it is the same affiliative need that is being fished for. The blonde has a direct gaze and her friends are firm businessmen in appearance, but with a glass of Old Bushmill you can sit down and fit right in. Or, for something more upbeat, sing along with the Pontiac choirboys.

30   As well as presenting positive images, advertisers can play to the need for affiliation in negative ways, by invoking the fear of rejection. If we don't use Scope, we'll have the "Ugh! Morning Breath" that causes the male and female models to avert their faces. Unless we apply Ultra Brite or Close-Up to our teeth, it's good-bye romance. Our family will be cursed with "House-a-tosis" if we don't take care. Without Dr. Scholl's antiperspirant foot spray, the bowling team will keel over. There go all the guests when the supply of Dorito's nacho cheese chips is exhausted. Still more rejection if our shirts have ring-around-the-collar, if our car needs to be Midasized. But make a few purchases, and we are back in the bosom of human contact.

31   As self-directed as Americans pretend to be, in the last analysis we remain social animals, hungering for the positive, endorsing feelings that only those around us can supply. Advertisers respond, urging us to "Reach out and touch someone," in the hopes our monthly [phone] bills will rise.

32   **3. Need to Nurture.**   Akin to affiliative needs is the need to take care of small, defenseless creatures—children and pets, largely. Reciprocity is of less consequence here, though; it is the giving that counts. Murray uses synonyms like "to feed, help, support, console, protect, comfort, nurse, heal." A strong

---

* The original Geritol (a combination of the words "geriatric" and "tolerance") was an iron tonic and vitamin supplement marketed to people over 40 between 1950 and 1979 with the slogan, "Do you have iron poor, tired blood?" Though today Geritol is the label on a group of health-related products, the name became famous—and, to some extent, funny—as a means of restoring energy and youthful vigor to middle-age and elderly people.

need it is, woven deep into our genetic fabric, for if it did not exist we could not successfully raise up our replacements. When advertisers put forth the image of something diminutive and furry, something that elicits the word "cute" or "precious," then they are trying to trigger this motive. We listen to the child-ish voice singing the Oscar Mayer weiner song, and our next hot-dog purchase is prescribed. Aren't those darling kittens something, and how did this Meow Mix get into our shopping cart?

33   This pitch is often directed at women, as Mother Nature's chief nurturers. "Make me some Kraft macaroni and cheese, please," says the elfin preschooler just in from the snowstorm, and mothers' hearts go out, and Kraft's sales go up. "We're cold, wet, and hungry," whine the husband and kids, and the little woman gets the Manwiches ready. A facsimile of this need can be hit without children or pets: the husband is ill and sleepless in the television commercial, and the wife grudgingly fetches the NyQuil.

34   But it is not women alone who can be touched by this appeal. The father nurses his son Eddie through adolescence while the John Deere lawn tractor sur-vives the years. Another father counts pennies with his young son as the sub-ject of New York Life Insurance comes up. And all over America are businessmen who don't know why they dial Qantas Airlines* when they have to take a trans-Pacific trip; the koala bear knows.

35   **4. Need for Guidance.**   The opposite of the need to nurture is the need to be nurtured: to be protected, shielded, guided. We may be loath to admit it, but the child lingers on inside every adult—and a good thing it does, or we would not be instructable in our advancing years. Who wants a nation of nothing but flinty personalities?

36   Parent-like figures can successfully call up this need. Robert Young[†] recom-mends Sanka coffee, and since we have experienced him for twenty-five years as television father and doctor, we take his word for it. Florence Henderson[‡] as the expert mom knows a lot about the advantages of Wesson oil.

37   The parent-ness of the spokesperson need not be so salient; sometimes pure authoritativeness is better. When Orson Welles[§] scowls and intones, "Paul Masson will sell no wine before its time," we may not know exactly what he means, but we still take direction from him. There is little maternal about

---

* Qantas Airlines is an Australian airline whose ads during the 1980s and 1990s featured a cuddly koala bear standing in for both the airline and the exotic delights of Australia.

[†] Robert Young (1907–1988) acted in movies (including Alfred Hitchcock's *Secret Agent* (1936) and *Crossfire* (1947) and TV (starring in the long-running 1950s series *Father Knows Best* and the 1960s series *Marcus Welby, M.D.*). A classic father figure, in his later career he appeared in ads for Sanka coffee.

[‡] Florence Henderson (b. 1934), acted on Broadway and TV (primarily, in musical and comedy roles). Her most famous TV show was *The Brady Bunch* (1968–74), where she played a mother of three daugh-ters who married a man with three sons.

[§] Orson Welles (1915–1985) was a major American filmmaker and actor whose films include *Citizen Kane* (1941—generally considered the greatest American film of all time), *The Magnificent Ambersons* (1942), *The Lady from Shanghai* (1947), *Macbeth* (1948), and *Touch of Evil* (1958). Toward the end of ⁱs life—to the dismay of many who revered him—the magisterial but financially depleted Welles ̣ame a spokesman for Paul Masson wines.

Brenda Vaccaro* when she speaks up for Tampax, but there is a certainty to her that many accept.

38   A celebrity is not a necessity in making a pitch to the need for guidance, since a fantasy figure can serve just as well. People accede to the Green Giant, or Betty Crocker, or Mr. Goodwrench.[†] Some advertisers can get by with no figure at all: "When E. F. Hutton[‡] talks, people listen."

39   Often it is tradition or custom that advertisers point to and consumers take guidance from. Bits and pieces of American history are used to sell whiskeys like Old Crow, Southern Comfort, Jack Daniel's. We conform to traditional male/female roles and age-old social norms when we purchase Barclay cigarettes, which informs us "The pleasure is back."

40   The product itself, if it has been around for a long time, can constitute a tradition. All those old labels in the ad for Morton salt convince us that we should continue to buy it. Kool-Aid says "You loved it as a kid. You trust it as a mother," hoping to get yet more consumers to go along.

41   Even when the product has no history at all, our need to conform to tradition and to be guided are strong enough that they can be invoked through bogus nostalgia and older actors. Country-Time lemonade sells because consumers want to believe it has a past they can defer to.

42   So far the needs and the ways they can be invoked which have been looked at are largely warm and affiliative; they stand in contrast to the next set of needs, which are much more egoistic and assertive.

43   **5. Need to Aggress.**   The pressures of the real world create strong retaliatory feelings in every functioning human being. Since these impulses can come forth as bursts of anger and violence, their display is normally tabooed. Existing as harbored energy, aggressive drives present a large, tempting target for advertisers. It is not a target to be aimed at thoughtlessly, though, for few manufacturers want their products associated with destructive motives. There is always the danger that, as in the case of sex, if the appeal is too blatant, public opinion will turn against what is being sold.

44   Jack-in-the-Box sought to abruptly alter its marketing by going after older customers and forgetting the younger ones. Their television commercials had a seventy-ish lady command, "Waste him," and the Jack-in-the-Box clown exploded before our eyes. So did public reaction until the commercials were toned down. Print ads for Club cocktails carried the faces of octogenarians under the headline, "Hit me with a Club"; response was contrary enough to bring the campaign to a stop.

---

* Brenda Vaccaro (b. 1939) is a stage, TV, and film actress; her films include *Midnight Cowboy* (1969), *Airport '77* (1977), *Supergirl* (1984), and *The Mirror Has Two Faces* (1996).

[†] Mr. Goodwrench (and the slogan "Looking for Mr. Goodwrench"), personified as an engaging and highly capable auto mechanic, is a product of the General Motors marketing department.

[‡] E. F. Hutton (named after its founder, Edward Francis Hutton) was a major brokerage firm that was brought down in the 1980s by corporate misconduct. Its most famous TV ad portrayed, typically, two well-dressed businesspeople in conversation in a crowded dining room or club room. The first man says to the other, "My broker says. . . . " The second man listens politely and responds, "Well, my broker is E. F. Hutton, and *he* says . . . ," and everyone else in the room strains to overhear the conversation. The tag line: "When E. F. Hutton talks, people listen."

45   Better disguised aggressive appeals are less likely to backfire: Triumph cigarettes has models making a lewd gesture with their uplifted cigarettes, but the individuals are often laughing and usually in close company of others. When Exxon said, "There's a Tiger in your tank," the implausibility of it concealed the invocation of aggressive feelings.

46   Depicted arguments are a common way for advertisers to tap the audience's needs to aggress. Don Rickles* and Lynda Carter† trade gibes, and consumers take sides as the name of Seven-Up is stitched on minds. The Parkay [margarine] tub has a difference of opinion with the user; who can forget it, or who (or what) got the last word in?

47   **6. Need to Achieve.**   This is the drive that energizes people, causing them to strive in their lives and careers. According to Murray, the need for achievement is signalled by the desires "to accomplish something difficult. To overcome obstacles and attain a high standard. To excel one's self. To rival and surpass others." A prominent American trait, it is one that advertisers like to hook on to because it identifies their product with winning and success.

48   The Cutty Sark ad does not disclose that Ted Turner failed at his latest attempt at yachting's America Cup; here he is represented as a champion on the water as well as off in his television enterprises. If we drink this whiskey, we will be victorious alongside Turner. We can also succeed with O. J. Simpson‡ by renting Hertz cars, or with Reggie Jackson§ by bringing home some Panasonic equipment. Cathy Rigby‖ and Stayfree maxipads will put people out front.

49   Sports heroes are the most convenient means to snare consumers' needs to achieve, but they are not the only one. Role models can be established, ones which invite emulation, as with the profiles put forth by Dewar's scotch. Successful, tweedy individuals relate they have "graduated to the flavor of Myer's rum." Or the advertiser can establish a prize: two neighbors play one-on-one

---

* Don Rickles (b. 1926) is a night-club comedian (who has also appeared in TV and films) famous for his caustic wit and for humorously insulting people in the audience.

† Lynda Carter (b. 1951) is an actress whose most famous role was the heroine of the 1976 TV series *Wonder Woman*.

‡ O. J. Simpson (b. 1957) is a famous football player–turned film actor (*The Naked Gun*) and defendant in a notorious murder trial in the 1990s. In a highly controversial decision, Simpson was acquitted of killing his ex-wife Nicole Simpson and her friend Ron Goldman; but in a subsequent civil trial he was found liable for the two deaths. Before the trial, Simpson was well-known for his TV commercials for Hertz rental cars, featuring him sprinting through airports to get to the gate to demonstrate what you *wouldn't* have to do if you rented a car through Hertz.

§ Reggie Jackson (b. 1946), a member of the Baseball Hall of Fame, played as an outfielder between 1967 and 1987. Known as "Mr. October" for his dramatic game-winning at-bats during post-season play, he had more strikeouts (2,597) than any other player. He was the first baseball player to have a candy bar (the "Reggie Bar") named after him, and toward the end of his career was a pitchman for Panasonic televisions.

‖ Cathy Rigby, an Olympian, was the first American gymnast to win a medal (in 1970) at the World Championships. She went on to star in a Broadway revival of the musical *Peter Pan* (surpassing Mary Martin for the greatest number of performances). Subsequently, she became a sportscaster for ABC Sports.

basketball for a Michelob beer in a television commercial, while in a print ad a bottle of Johnnie Walker Black Label has been gilded like a trophy.

50   Any product that advertises itself in superlatives—the best, the first, the finest—is trying to make contact with our needs to succeed. For many consumers, sales and bargains belong in this category of appeals, too; the person who manages to buy something at fifty percent off is seizing an opportunity and coming out ahead of others.

51   **7. Need to Dominate.**   This fundamental need is the craving to be powerful—perhaps omnipotent, as in the Xerox ad where Brother Dominic exhibits heavenly powers and creates miraculous copies. Most of us will settle for being just a regular potentate, though. We drink Budweiser because it is the King of Beers, and here comes the powerful Clydesdales to prove it. A taste of Wolfschmidt vodka and "The spirit of the Czar lives on."

52   The need to dominate and control one's environment is often thought of as being masculine, but as close students of human nature advertisers know, it is not so circumscribed. Women's aspirations for control are suggested in the campaign theme, "I like my men in English Leather, or nothing at all." The females in the Chanel No. 19 ads are "outspoken" and wrestle their men around.

53   Male and female, what we long for is clout; what we get in its place is Mastercard.

54   **8. Need for Prominence.**   Here comes the need to be admired and respected, to enjoy prestige and high social status. These times, it appears, are not so egalitarian after all. Many ads picture the trappings of high position; the Oldsmobile stands before a manorial doorway, the Volvo is parked beside a steeplechase. A book-lined study is the setting for Dewar's 12, and Lenox China is displayed in a dining room chock full of antiques.

55   Beefeater gin represents itself as "The Crown Jewel of England" and uses no illustrations of jewels or things British, for the words are sufficient indicators of distinction. Buy that gin and you will rise up the prestige hierarchy, or achieve the same effect on yourself with Seagram's 7 Crown, which ambiguously describes itself as "classy."

56   Being respected does not have to entail the usual accoutrements of wealth: "Do you know who I am?" the commercials ask, and we learn that the prominent person is not so prominent without his American Express card.

57   **9. Need for Attention.**   The previous need involved being *looked up to,* while this is the need to be *looked at.* The desire to exhibit ourselves in such a way as to make others look at us is a primitive, insuppressible instinct. The clothing and cosmetic industries exist just to serve this need, and this is the way they pitch their wares. Some of this effort is aimed at males, as the ads for Hathaway shirts and Jockey underclothes. But the greater bulk of such appeals is targeted singlemindedly at women.

58   To come back to Brooke Shields: this is where she fits into American marketing. If I buy Calvin Klein jeans, consumers infer, I'll be the object of fascination. The desire for exhibition has been most strikingly played to in a print campaign of many years' duration, that of Maidenform lingerie. The woman exposes herself, and sales surge. "Gentlemen prefer Hanes" the ads dissemble, and women who want eyes upon them know what they should do. Peggy

Fleming* flutters her legs for L'eggs, encouraging females who want to be the star in their own lives to purchase this product.

59   The same appeal works for cosmetics and lotions. For years, the little girl with the exposed backside sold gobs of Coppertone, but now the company has picked up the pace a little: as a female, you are supposed to "Flash 'em a Coppertone tan." Food can be sold the same way, especially to the diet-conscious; Angie Dickinson poses for California avocados and says, "Would this body lie to you?" Our eyes are too fixed on her for us to think to ask if she got that way by eating mounds of guacomole.

60   **10. Need for Autonomy.**   There are several ways to sell credit card services, as has been noted: Mastercard appeals to the need to dominate, and American Express to the need for prominence. When Visa claims, "You can have it the way you want it," yet another primary motive is being beckoned forward—the need to endorse the self. The focus here is upon the independence and integrity of the individual; this need is the antithesis of the need for guidance and is unlike any of the social needs. "If running with the herd isn't your style, try ours," says Rotan-Mosle, and many Americans feel they have finally found the right brokerage firm.

61   The photo is of a red-coated Mountie on his horse, posed on a snow-covered ledge; the copy reads, "Windsor—One Canadian stands alone." This epitome of the solitary and proud individual may work best with male customers, as may Winston's man in the red cap. But one-figure advertisements also strike the strong need for autonomy among American women. As Shelly Hack[†] strides for Charlie perfume, females respond to her obvious pride and flair; she is her own person. The Virginia Slims tale is of people who have come a long way from subservience to independence. Cachet perfume feels it does not need a solo figure to work this appeal, and uses three different faces in its ads; it insists, though, "It's different on every woman who wears it."

62   Like many psychological needs, this one can also be appealed to in a negative fashion, by invoking the loss of independence or self-regard. Guilt and regrets can be stimulated: "Gee, I could have had a V-8." Next time, get one and be good to yourself.

63   **11. Need to Escape.**   An appeal to the need for autonomy often co-occurs with one for the need to escape, since the desire to duck out of our social obligations, to seek rest or adventure, frequently takes the form of one-person flight. The dashing image of a pilot, in fact, is a standard way of quickening this need to get away from it all.

64   Freedom is the pitch here, the freedom that every individual yearns for whenever life becomes too oppressive. Many advertisers like appealing to the need for escape because the sensation of pleasure often accompanies escape, and what nicer emotional nimbus could there be for a product? "You deserve a break today," says McDonald's, and Stouffer's frozen foods chime in, "Set yourself free."

65   For decades men have imaginatively bonded themselves to the Marlboro cowboy who dwells untarnished and unencumbered in Marlboro Country some

---

* Peggy Fleming (b. 1948), an Olympic figure skater, and Gold Medal winner (1968), later became a TV sports commentator and a representative for UNICEF (the United Nations Children's Emergency Fund).

† Shelly Hack (b. 1952) portrayed Tiffany Welles in the 1970s TV show *Charlie's Angels*.

distance from modern life; smokers' aching needs for autonomy and escape are personified by that cowpoke. Many women can identify with the lady ambling through the woods behind the words, "Benson and Hedges and mornings and me."

66   But escape does not have to be solitary. Other Benson and Hedges ads, part of the same campaign, contain two strolling figures. In Salem cigarette advertisements, it can be several people who escape together into the mountaintops. A commercial for Levi's pictured a cloudbank above a city through which ran a whole chain of young people.

67   There are varieties of escape, some wistful like the Boeing "Someday" campaign of dream vacations, some kinetic like the play and parties in soft drink ads. But in every instance, the consumer exposed to the advertisement is invited to momentarily depart his everyday life for a more carefree experience, preferably with the product in hand.

68   **12. Need to Feel Safe.**   Nobody in their right mind wants to be intimidated, menaced, battered, poisoned. We naturally want to do whatever it takes to stave off threats to our well-being, and to our families'. It is the instinct of self-preservation that makes us responsive to the ad of the St. Bernard with the keg of Chivas Regal. We pay attention to the stern talk of Karl Malden* and the plight of the vacationing couples who have lost all their funds in the American Express travelers cheques commercials. We want the omnipresent stag from Hartford Insurance to watch over us too.

69   In the interest of keeping failure and calamity from our lives, we like to see the durability of products demonstrated. Can we ever forget that Timex takes a licking and keeps on ticking? When the American Tourister suitcase bounces all over the highway and the egg inside doesn't break, the need to feel safe has been adroitly plucked.

70   We take precautions to diminish future threats. We buy Volkswagen Rabbits for the extraordinary mileage, and MONY insurance policies to avoid the tragedies depicted in their black-and-white ads of widows and orphans.

71   We are careful about our health. We consume Mazola margarine because it has "corn goodness" backed by the natural food traditions of the American Indians. In the medicine cabinet is Alka-Seltzer, the "home remedy"; having it, we are snug in our little cottage.

72   We want to be safe and secure; buy these products, advertisers are saying, and you'll be safer than you are without them.

73   **13. Need for Aesthetic Sensations.**   There is an undeniable aesthetic component to virtually every ad run in the national media: the photography or filming or drawing is near-perfect, the type style is well chosen, the layout could scarcely be improved upon. Advertisers know there is little chance of good com-

---

* Karl Malden (b. 1912), with his familiar craggy face and outsized nose, was a stage and later a film actor. He was the original Mitch in the Broadway production of Tennessee Williams's *Streetcar Named Desire*, a role he reprised in the 1951 movie version. His films include *On the Waterfront* (1954), *Cheyenne Autumn* (1964), and *Patton* (1970), and he starred in the 1972 TV series *Streets of San Francisco*. Malden became famous to a later generation of viewers as a pitchman for the American Express card, with the slogan, "Don't leave home without it!"

munication occurring if an ad is not visually pleasing. Consumers may not be aware of the extent of their own sensitivity to artwork, but it is undeniably large.

74   Sometimes the aesthetic element is expanded and made into an ad's primary appeal. Charles Jordan shoes may or may not appear in the accompanying avant-grade photographs; Kohler plumbing fixtures catch attention through the high style of their desert settings. Beneath the slightly out of focus photograph, languid and sensuous in tone, General Electric feels called upon to explain, "This is an ad for the hair dryer."

75   This appeal is not limited to female consumers: J&B scotch says "It whispers" and shows a bucolic scene of lake and castle.

76   **14. Need to Satisfy Curiosity.**   It may seem odd to list a need for information among basic motives, but this need can be as primal and compelling as any of the others. Human beings are curious by nature, interested in the world around them, and intrigued by tidbits of knowledge and new developments. Trivia, percentages, observations counter to conventional wisdom—these items all help sell products. Any advertisement in a question-and-answer format is strumming this need.

77   A dog groomer has a question about long distance rates, and Bell Telephone has a chart with all the figures. An ad for Porsche 911 is replete with diagrams and schematics, numbers and arrows. Lo and behold, Anacin pills have 150 more milligrams than its competitors; should we wonder if this is better or worse for us?

78   **15. Physiological Needs.**   To the extent that sex is solely a biological need, we are now coming around full circle, back toward the start of the list. In this final category are clustered appeals to sleeping, eating, drinking. The art of photographing food and drink is so advanced, sometimes these temptations are wondrously caught in the camera's lens: the crab meat in the Red Lobster restaurant ads can start us salivating, the Quarterpounder can almost be smelled, the liquor in the glass glows invitingly. Imbibe, these ads scream.

Styles

79   Some common ingredients of advertisements were not singled out for separate mention in the list of fifteen because they are not appeals in and of themselves. They are stylistic features, influencing the way a basic appeal is presented. The use of humor is one, and the use of celebrities is another. A third is time imagery, past and future, which goes to several purposes.

80   For all of its employment in advertising, humor can be treacherous, because it can get out of hand and smother the product information. Supposedly, this is what Alka-Seltzer discovered with its comic commercials of the late sixties; "I can't believe I ate the whole thing," the sad-faced husband lamented, and the audience cackled so much it forgot the antacid. Or, did not take it seriously.

81   But used carefully, humor can punctuate some of the softer appeals and soften some of the harsher ones. When Emma says to the Fruit-of-the-Loom fruits, "Hi, cuties. Whatcha doing in my laundry basket?" we smile as our curiosity is assuaged along with hers. Bill Cosby gets consumers tickled about the children in his Jell-O commercials, and strokes the need to nurture.

82 An insurance company wants to invoke the need to feel safe, but does not want to leave readers with an unpleasant aftertaste; cartoonist Rowland Wilson creates an avalanche about to crush a gentleman who is saying to another, "My insurance company? New England Life, of course. Why?" The same tactic of humor undercutting threat is used in the cartoon commercials for Safeco when the Pink Panther wanders from one disaster to another. Often humor masks aggression: comedian Bob Hope in the outfit of a boxer promises to knock out the knock-knocks with Texaco; Rodney Dangerfield, who "can't get no respect," invites aggression as the comic relief in Miller Lite commercials.

83 Roughly fifteen percent of all advertisements incorporate a celebrity, almost always from the fields of entertainment or sports. The approach can also prove troublesome for advertisers, for celebrities are human beings too, and fully capable of the most remarkable behavior. If anything distasteful about them emerges, it is likely to reflect on the product. The advertisers making use of Anita Bryant* and Billy Jean King[†] suffered several anxious moments. An untimely death can also react poorly on a product. But advertisers are willing to take risks because celebrities can be such a good link between producers and consumers, performing the social role of introducer.

84 There are several psychological needs these middlemen can play upon. Let's take the product class of cameras and see how different celebrities can hit different needs. The need for guidance can be invoked by Michael Landon, who plays such a wonderful dad on "Little House on the Prairie"; when he says to buy Kodak equipment, many people listen. James Garner for Polaroid cameras is put in a similar authoritative role, so defined by a mocking spouse. The need to achieve is summoned up by Tracy Austin and other tennis stars for Canon AE-1; the advertiser first makes sure we see these athletes playing to win. When Cheryl Tiegs[‡] speaks up for Olympus cameras, it is the need for attention that is being targeted.

85 The past and future, being outside our grasp, are exploited by advertisers as locales for the projection of needs. History can offer up heroes (and call up the need to achieve) or traditions (need for guidance) as well as art objects (need for aesthetic sensations). Nostalgia is a kindly version of personal history and

---

* Anita Bryant (b. 1940), a singer and entertainer (and as Miss Oklahoma, runner-up in the 1958 Miss America competition), became controversial during the late 1970s with her campaigns against homosexuality and AIDS. At the time, she was making ads and TV commercials for Florida orange juice, but was dropped by the sponsor after boycotts by activists.

[†] Billy Jean King (b. 1943) was a championship tennis player in the late 1960s and 1970s. In 1973 she was named *Sports Illustrated*'s "Sportsperson of the Year," the first woman to win this honor. She won four U.S. championships and six Wimbledon's single championships. In 1973, in a much publicized "Battle of the Sexes" match, King won all three sets against the 55-year-old Bobby Riggs (once ranked as the best tennis player in the world), who had claimed that "any half-decent male player could defeat even the best female players."

[‡] Cheryl Tiegs (b. 1947) is a supermodel perhaps best known for her affiliation with the *Sports Illustrated Annual Swimsuit Issue*. A 1978 poster of Tiegs in a pink swimsuit became a cultural icon. Recently, she has entered the business world with an accessory and wig line for Revlon.

is deployed by advertisers to rouse needs for affiliation and for guidance; the need to escape can come in here, too. The same need to escape is sometimes the point of futuristic appeals but picturing the avant-garde can also be a way to get at the need to achieve.

Analyzing Advertisements

86 When analyzing ads yourself for their emotional appeals, it takes a bit of practice to learn to ignore the product information (as well as one's own experience and feelings about the product). But that skill comes soon enough, as does the ability to quickly sort out from all the non-product aspects of an ad the chief element which is the most striking, the most likely to snag attention first and penetrate brains farthest. The key to the appeal, this element usually presents itself centrally and forwardly to the reader or viewer.

87 Another clue: the viewing angle which the audience has on the ad's subjects is informative. If the subjects are photographed or filmed from below and thus are looking down at you much as the Green Giant does, then the need to be guided is a good candidate for the ad's emotional appeal. If, on the other hand, the subjects are shot from above and appear deferential, as is often the case with children or female models, then other needs are being appealed to.

88 To figure out an ad's emotional appeal, it is wise to know (or have a good hunch about) who the targeted consumers are; this can often be inferred from the magazine or television show it appears in. This piece of information is a great help in determining the appeal and in deciding between two different interpretations. For example, if an ad features a partially undressed female, this would typically signal one appeal for readers of *Penthouse* (need for sex) and another for readers of *Cosmopolitan* (need for attention).

89 It would be convenient if every ad made just one appeal, were aimed at just one need. Unfortunately, things are often not that simple. A cigarette ad with a couple at the edge of a polo field is trying to hit both the need for affiliation and the need for prominence; depending on the attitude of the male, dominance could also be an ingredient in this. An ad for Chimere perfume incorporates two photos: in the top one the lady is being commanding at a business luncheon (need to dominate), but in the lower one she is being bussed (need for affiliation). Better ads, however, seem to avoid being too diffused; in the study of post-World War II advertising described earlier, appeals grew more focused as the decades passed. As a rule of thumb, [only twenty percent of ads have one primary appeal,] about sixty percent have two conspicuous appeals; the last twenty percent have three or more. Rather than looking for the greatest number of appeals, decoding ads is most productive when the loudest one or two appeals are discerned, since those are the appeals with the best chance of grabbing people's attention.

90 Finally, analyzing ads does not have to be a solo activity and probably should not be. The greater number of people there are involved, the better chance there is of transcending individual biases and discerning the essential emotional lure built into an advertisement.

Do They or Don't They?

91 Do the emotional appeals made in advertisements add up to the sinister manipulation of consumers?

92   It is clear that these ads work. Attention is caught, communication occurs between producers and consumers, and sales result. It turns out to be difficult to detail the exact relationship between a specific ad and a specific purchase, or even between a campaign and subsequent sales figures, because advertising is only one of a host of influences upon consumption. Yet no one is fooled by this lack of perfect proof; everyone knows that advertising sells. If this were not the case, then tight-fisted American businesses would not spend a total of fifty billion dollars annually on these messages.

93   But before anyone despairs that advertisers have our number to the extent that they can marshal us at will and march us like automatons to the check-out counters, we should recall the resiliency and obduracy of the American consumer. Advertisers may have uncovered the softest spots in minds, but that does not mean they have found truly gaping apertures. There is no evidence that advertising can get people to do things contrary to their self-interests. Despite all the finesse of advertisements, and all the subtle emotional tugs, the public resists the vast majority of the petitions. According to the marketing division of the A. C. Nielsen Company, a whopping seventy-five percent of all new products die within a year in the marketplace, the victims of consumer disinterest which no amount of advertising could overcome. The appeals in advertising may be the most captivating there are to be had, but they are not enough to entrap the wily consumer.

94   The key to understanding the discrepancy between, on the one hand, the fact that advertising truly works, and, on the other, the fact that it hardly works, is to take into account the enormous numbers of people exposed to an ad. Modern-day communications permit an ad to be displayed to millions upon millions of individuals; if the smallest fraction of that audience can be moved to buy the product, then the ad has been successful. When one percent of the people exposed to a television advertising campaign reach for their wallets, that could be one million sales, which may be enough to keep the product in production and the advertisements coming.

95   In arriving at an evenhanded judgment about advertisements and their emotional appeals, it is good to keep in mind that many of the purchases which might be credited to these ads are experienced as genuinely gratifying to the consumer. We sincerely like the goods or service we have bought, and we may even like some of the emotional drapery that an ad suggests comes with it. It has sometimes been noted that the most avid students of advertisements are the people who have just bought the product; they want to steep themselves in the associated imagery. This may be the reason that Americans, when polled, are not negative about advertising and do not disclose any sense of being misused. The volume of advertising may be an irritant, but the product information as well as the imaginative material in ads are partial compensation.

96   A productive understanding is that advertising messages involve costs and benefits at both ends of the communications channel. For those few ads which

do make contact, the consumer surrenders a moment of time, has the lower brain curried, and receives notice of a product; the advertiser has given up money and has increased the chance of sales. In this sort of communications activity, neither party can be said to be the loser.

Review Questions

1. Why is advertising more common in highly industrialized countries like the United States than in countries with "quieter" economies?

2. How are advertisers' attempts to communicate their messages, and to break through customer resistance, keyed to their conception of human psychology, according to Fowles?

3. What are the "two orders of content" of most advertisements, according to Fowles?

4. How is Fowles indebted to Henry Murray?

5. Why must appeals to our need for sex and our need to aggress be handled carefully, according to Fowles?

6. How does the use of humor or the use of celebrities fit into Fowles's scheme?

Discussion and Writing Suggestions

1. In paragraph 4 Fowles cites a study indicating that only a fraction of the advertisements bombarding consumers every day are even noticed, much less acted upon. How do the results of this study square with your own experience? About how many of the commercial messages that you view and hear every day do you actually pay attention to? What kinds of messages draw your attention? What elicits positive reactions? Negative reactions? What kinds of appeals are most successful in making you want to actually purchase the advertised product?

2. What do you think of Fowles's analysis of "advertising's fifteen basic appeals"? Does this classification seem an accurate and useful way of accounting for how most advertising works upon us? Would you drop any of his categories, or perhaps incorporate one set into another set? Has Fowles neglected to consider other appeals that you believe to be equally important? If so, can you think of one or more advertisements that employ such appeals omitted by Fowles?

3. Categorize several of the ads in the ad portfolio later in the chapter (pages 691–737) using Fowles's schema. Explain how the headlines, body text, and graphics support your categorization choices.

4. Fowles asserts that "[c]ontrary to impressions, unambiguous sex is rare in [advertising] messages." This article first appeared in 1982. Does Fowles's statement still seem true today? To what extent do you believe that advertisers in recent years have increased their reliance on overt sexual appeals? Cite examples.

5. Fowles believes that "the need to associate with others [affiliation] . . . is probably the most prevalent appeal" in advertising. To what extent do you agree with this statement? Locate or cite print or broadcast ads that rely on the need for affiliation. How do the graphics and text of these ads work on what Fowles calls "the deep running drives" of our psyches or "the lower brain"?

6. Locate ads that rely upon the converse appeals to nurture and to guidance. Explain how the graphics and text in these ads work upon our human motivations. If possible, further categorize the appeal: for example, are we provided with guidance from a parent figure, some other authority figure, or from the force of tradition?

7. Conduct (perhaps with one or more classmates) your own analysis of a set of contemporary advertisements. Select a single issue of a particular magazine, such as *Time* or the *New Yorker.* Review all of the full-page ads, classifying each according to Fowles's categories. An ad may make more than one appeal (as Fowles points out in paragraph 89), but generally one will be primary. What do your findings show? Which appeals are the most frequent? The least frequent? Which are most effective? Why? You may find it interesting to compare the appeals of advertising in different magazines aimed at different audiences—for example, a general-interest magazine, such as *Newsweek,* compared with a more specialized magazine, such as the *New Republic,* or *People,* or *Glamour,* or *Guns and Ammo.* To what extent do the types of appeals shift with the gender or interests of the target audience?

Making the Pitch in Print Advertising
Courtland L. Bovée, John V. Thill, George P. Dovel, and Marian Burk Wood

No two ads are identical, but the vast majority employ a common set of textual features: headlines, body copy, and slogans. In the following selection, the authors discuss each of these features in turn, explaining their importance in attracting the potential customer's attention and selling the virtues of the product or service offered. You will find this discussion useful in making your own analyses of advertisements.

Courtland L. Bovée is the C. Allen Paul Distinguished Chair at Grossmont College. John V. Thill is CEO of Communication Specialists of America. George P. Dovel is president of the

Dovel Group. Marian Burk Wood is president of Wood and Wood Advertising. This passage originally appeared in the authors' textbook Advertising Excellence *(McGraw-Hill, 1995).*

Copywriters and Copywriting

1   Given the importance of copy, it comes as no surprise that copywriters are key players in the advertising process. In fact, many of the most notable leaders and voices in the industry began their careers as copywriters, including Jane Maas, David Ogilvy, Rosser Reeves, Leo Burnett, and William Bernbach. As a profession, copywriting is somewhat unusual because so many of its top practitioners have been in their jobs for years, even decades (rather than moving up the management ranks as is usual in many professions). Copywriters can either work for agencies or set themselves up as free-lancers, selling their services to agencies and advertisers. Because it presents endless opportunities to be creative, copywriting is one of those rare jobs that can be fresh and challenging year after year.

2   Although successful copywriters share a love of language with novelists, poets, and other writers, copywriting is first and foremost a business function, not an artistic endeavor. The challenge isn't to create works of literary merit, but to meet advertising objectives. This doesn't mean that copywriting isn't an art, however; it's simply art in pursuit of a business goal. Nor is it easy. Such noted literary writers as Stephen Vincent Benét, George Bernard Shaw, and Ernest Hemingway tried to write ad copy and found themselves unable to do it effectively. It's the combined requirements of language skills, business acumen, and an ability to create under the pressure of tight deadlines and format restrictions (such as the limited number of words you have to work with) that make copywriting so challenging—and so endlessly rewarding.

3   Copywriters have many styles and approaches to writing, but most agree on one thing: copywriting is hard work. It can involve a great deal of planning and coordinating with clients, legal staffers, account executives, researchers, and art directors. In addition, it usually entails hammering away at your copy until it's as good as it can be. David Ogilvy talked about doing 19 drafts of a single piece of copy and writing 37 headlines for a Sears ad in order to get 3 possibilities to show to the client. Actually, the chance to write and rewrite that many times is a luxury that most copywriters don't have; they often must produce copy on tight schedules with unforgiving deadlines (such as magazine publication deadlines).

4   The task of copywriting is most often associated with the headlines and copy you see in an ad, but copywriters actually develop a wide variety of other materials, from posters to catalogs to press releases, as well as the words you hear in radio and television commercials.

Print Copy

5   Copywriters are responsible for every word you see in print ads, whether the words are in a catchy headline or in the fine print at the bottom of the page. The three major categories of copy are headlines, body copy, and slogans.

Headlines

6   The *headline*, also called a *heading* or a *head*, constitutes the dominant line or lines of copy in an ad. Headlines are typically set in larger type and appear at the top of the ad, although there are no hard-and-fast rules on headline layout. *Subheads* are secondary headlines, often written to move the reader from the main headline to the body copy. Even if there is a pageful of body copy and only a few words in the headline, the headline is the most important piece of copy for two reasons: First, it serves as the "come-on" to get people to stop turning the page and check out your ad. Second, as much as 80 percent of your audience may not bother to read the body copy, so whatever message these nonreaders carry away from the ad will have to come from the headline.

7   Copywriters can choose from a variety of headline types, each of which performs a particular function.

- *News headlines.* News headlines present information that's new to the audience, such as announcing a new store location, a new product, or lower prices. This approach is common because potential customers are often looking for new solutions, lower prices, and other relevant changes in the marketplace. For example, a newspaper ad from the Silo home electronics chain announced a recent sale using a news headline: "Everything on Sale! 4 Days Only! 5–20% Off Everything!" Headlines like this are typical in local newspaper advertising.

- *Emotional headlines.* The emotional appeal . . . is represented by emotional headlines. The quotation headline "I'm sick of her ruining our lives" was used in an ad for the American Mental Health Fund to echo the frustration some parents feel when they can't understand their teenagers' behavior. Combined with a photo of a sad and withdrawn teenage girl, the headline grabs any parent who has felt such frustration, and the body copy goes on to explain that families shouldn't get mad at people with mental illnesses but should help them get treatment for their conditions.

- *Benefit headlines.* The benefit headline is a statement of the key customer benefit. An ad for Quicken personal finance software used the question-form headline: "How do you know exactly where your money goes and how much you have?" followed by "It's this simple" above a photograph of the product package. The customer benefit is keeping better track of your money, and Quicken is the solution offered.

- *Directive headlines.* Headlines that direct the reader to do something, or at least suggest the reader do something, can motivate consumer action. Such headlines can be a hard sell, such as "Come in now and save," or they can be something more subtle, such as "Just feel the color in these black and whites," the headline in an ad for Ensoniq keyboards.

- *Offbeat and curiosity headlines.* Humor, wordplay, and mystery can be effective ways to draw readers into an ad. An ad promoting vacation travel to Spain used the headline "Si in the dark," with a photo of a lively nighttime scene. The word *Si* is catchy because it first looks like an error, until the reader reads the body copy to learn that the ad is talking about Spain (*si* is Spanish for "yes").

- *Hornblowing headlines.* The hornblowing headline, called "Brag and Boast" heads by the Gallup & Robinson research organization, should be used with care. Customers have seen it all and heard it all, and "We're the greatest" headlines tend to sound arrogant and self-centered. This isn't to say that you can't stress superiority; you just need to do it in a way that takes the customer's needs into account, and the headline must be honest. The headline "Neuberger & Berman Guardian Fund" followed by the subhead "#1 Performing Growth and Income Fund" blows the company's own horn but also conveys an important product benefit. Since investors look for top-performing mutual funds, the information about being number one is relevant.

- *Slogan, label, or logo headlines.* Some headlines show a company's slogan, a product label, or the organization's logo. Powerful slogans like Hallmark's "When you care enough to send the very best" can make great headlines because they click with the reader's emotions. Label and logo headlines can build product and company awareness, but they must be used with care. If the label or logo doesn't make some emotional or logical connection with the reader, the ad probably won't succeed.

8 Headlines often have maximum impact when coupled with a well-chosen graphic element, rather than trying to carry the message with words alone. In fact, the careful combination of the two can increase the audience's involvement with the ad, especially if one of the two says something ironic or unexpected that has to be resolved by considering the other element. A magazine ad for Easter Seals had the headline "After all we did for Pete, he walked out on us." At first, you think the birth-defects organization is complaining. Then you

---

CHECKLIST FOR PRODUCING EXCELLENT COPY

❑ A. Avoid clichés.
- Create fresh, original phrases that vividly convey your message.
- Remember that clever wordplay based on clichés can be quite effective.

❑ B. Watch out for borrowed interest.
- Make sure you don't use inappropriate copy or graphics since they can steal the show from your basic sales message.
- Be sure nothing draws attention from the message.

❑ C. Don't boast.
- Be sure the ad's purpose isn't merely to pat the advertiser on the back.
- Tout success when you must convince nonbuyers that lots of people just like them have purchased your product; this isn't the same as shouting "We're the best!"

see a photo of Pete with new artificial legs, walking away from a medical facility. It's a powerful combination that makes the reader feel good about the things Easter Seals can do for people.

Body Copy

9　The second major category of copy is the *body copy*, which constitutes the words in the main body of the ad, apart from headlines, photo captions, and other blocks of text. The importance of body copy varies from ad to ad, and some ads have little or no body copy. Ads for easy-to-understand products, for instance, often rely on the headline and a visual such as a photograph to get their point across. In contrast, when the selling message needs a lot of supporting detail to be convincing, an ad can be packed full of body copy. Some advertisers have the impression that long body copy should be avoided, but that isn't always the case. The rule to apply here is to use the "right" number of words. You might not need many words in a perfume ad, but you might need a page or two to cover a complex industrial product.

10　As with headlines, body copy can be built around several different formats. *Straight-line copy* is copy that takes off from the headline and develops the selling points for the product. *Narrative copy*, in contrast, tells a story as it persuades; the same selling points may be covered, but in a different context. *Dialog/monolog copy* lets one or two characters in the ad do the selling through what they are saying. *Picture-and-caption copy* relies on photographs or illustrations to tell the story, with support from their accompanying captions.

❏ D. Make it personal, informal, and relevant.
  • Connect with the audience in a way that is personal and comfortable. Pompous, stiff, and overly "businesslike" tends to turn people away.
  • Avoid copy that sounds like it belongs in an ad, with too many overblown adjectives and unsupported claims of superiority.

❏ E. Keep it simple, specific, and concise.
  • Make your case quickly and stick to the point. This will help you get past all the barriers and filters that people put up to help them select which things they'll pay attention to and which they'll ignore.
  • Avoid copy that's confusing, meandering, too long, or too detailed.

❏ F. Give the audience a reason to read, listen, or watch.
  • Offer a solution to your audience's problems.
  • Entertain your audience.
  • Consider any means possible to get your audience to pay attention long enough to get your sales message across.

Slogans

11 The third major category of copy includes *slogans*, or *tag lines*, memorable sayings that convey a selling message. Over the years, Coca-Cola has used such slogans as "Coke is it," "It's the real thing," and "Always Coca-Cola." Slogans are sometimes used as headlines, but not always. Their importance lies in the fact they often become the most memorable result of an advertising campaign. You've probably got a few slogans stuck in your head. Ever heard of "Quality is job number 1," "Don't leave home without it," or "Melts in your mouth, not in your hand"?

12 The Korean automaker Hyundai recently switched back to the slogan "Cars that make sense," which is a great way of expressing its desired positioning as a lower-cost but still reliable alternative to Japanese and U.S. cars. For several years, the company had used "Hyundai. Yes, Hyundai," but "Cars that make sense" has proved to be a much more effective way to define the value it offers consumers.

Review Questions

1. What are the particular challenges of copywriting, as opposed to other types of writing?

2. How do the authors classify the main types of ad headlines?

3. What are the main types of body copy styles, according to the authors?

Discussion and Writing Suggestions

1. Apply the authors' criteria for effective headlines to three or four of the ads in the portfolio (pages 691–737)—or to three or four ads of your own choosing. To what extent do these headlines succeed in attracting attention, engaging the audience, and fulfilling the other requirements of effective headlines?

2. Imagine that you are a copywriter who has been assigned the account for a particular product (your choice). Develop three possible headlines for an advertisement for this product. Incorporate as many as possible of the criteria for effective headlines discussed by the authors (paragraphs 6–8).

3. Classify the *types* of headlines in a given product category in the ad portfolio (pages 691–737). Or classify the types of headlines in full-page ads in a single current magazine. Which type of headline appears to be the most common? Which type appears to be the most effective in gaining your attention and making you want to read the body copy?

4. Classify the *types* of body copy styles in a given product category in the ad portfolio. Or classify the types of body copy styles in full-page ads in a single current magazine. How effective is the copy in selling the virtues of the product or the institution or organization behind the product?

5. Assess the effectiveness of a given ad either in the ad portfolio or in a recent magazine or newspaper. Apply the criteria discussed by the authors in the box labeled "Checklist for Producing Excellent Copy." For example, to what extent is the copy fresh and original? To what extent does the copy make the message "personal, informal, and relevant" to the target audience? To what extent is the message "simple, specific, and concise"?

6. Write your own ad for a product that you like and use frequently. In composing the ad, apply the principles of effective headlines, subheads, body copy, and slogans discussed by the authors. Apply also the principles of "Checklist for Producing Excellent Copy." You will also need to think of (though not necessarily create) an effective graphic for the ad.

Elements of Effective Layout
Dorothy Cohen

In the previous selection, Courtland L. Bovée et al. discuss the chief textual features of print advertising. In the following passage Dorothy Cohen reviews the equally important (and perhaps more important, in terms of seizing the reader's attention) graphic components. Chief among these are balance, proportion, movement, unity, clarity and simplicity, *and* emphasis. *After reading Cohen, you should be well equipped to work on the analysis assignments in this chapter and, more generally, to assess the graphic quality of the ads you regularly encounter in magazines and newspapers.*

This selection originally appeared in Dorothy Cohen's textbook Advertising *(1988).*

1 Fundamentally a good layout should attract attention and interest and should provide some control over the manner in which the advertisement is read. The message to be communicated may be sincere, relevant, and important to the consumer, but because of the competitive "noise" in the communication channel, the opportunity to be heard may depend on the effectiveness of the layout. In addition to attracting attention, the most important requisites for an effective layout are balance, proportion, movement, unity, clarity and simplicity, and emphasis.

Balance
2 Balance is a fundamental law in nature and its application to layout design formulates one of the basic principles of this process. Balance is a matter of weight distribution; in layout it is keyed to the *optical center* of an advertisement, the point which the reader's eye designates as the center of an area. In an advertisement a vertical line which divides the area into right and left halves contains the center; however the optical center is between one-tenth and one-third the distance above the mathematical horizontal center line. . . .

3   In order to provide good artistic composition, the elements in the layout must be in equilibrium. Equilibrium can be achieved through balance, and this

process may be likened to the balancing of a seesaw. The optical center of the advertisement serves as the fulcrum or balancing point, and the elements may be balanced on both sides of this fulcrum through considerations of their size and tonal quality.

4   The simplest way to ensure *formal balance* between the elements to the right and left of the vertical line is to have all masses in the left duplicated on the right in size, weight, and distance from the center. . . . Formal balance imparts feelings of dignity, solidity, refinement, and reserve. It has been used for institutional advertising and suggests conservatism on the part of the advertiser. Its major deficiency is that it may present a static and somewhat unexciting appearance; however, formal balance presents material in an easy-to-follow order and works well for many ads.

5   To understand *informal balance*, think of children of unequal weight balanced on a seesaw; to ensure equilibrium it is necessary to place the smaller child far from the center and the larger child closer to the fulcrum. In informal balance the elements are balanced, but not evenly, because of different sizes and color contrast. This type of a symmetric balance requires care so that the various elements do not create a lopsided or top-heavy appearance. A knowledge or a sense of the composition can help create the feeling of symmetry in what is essentially asymmetric balance.

6   Informal balance presents a fresh, untraditional approach. It creates excitement, a sense of originality, forcefulness, and, to some extent, the element of surprise. Whereas formal balance may depend on the high interest value of the illustration to attract the reader, informal balance may attract attention through the design of the layout. . . .

Proportion

7   Proportion helps develop order and creates a pleasing impression. It is related to balance but is concerned primarily with the division of the space and the emphasis to be accorded each element. Proportion, to the advertising designer, is the relationship between the size of one element in the ad to another, the amount of space between elements, as well as the width of the total ad to its depth. Proportion also involves the tone of the ad: the amount of light area in relation to dark area and the amount of color and noncolor.

8   As a general rule unequal dimensions and distances make the most lively design in advertising. The designer also places the elements on the page so that each element is given space and position in proportion to its importance in the total advertisement and does not look like it stands alone.

Movement

9   If an advertisement is to appear dynamic rather than static, it must contain some movement. *Movement* (also called *sequence*) provides the directional flow for the advertisement, gives it its follow-through, and provides coherence. It guides the

reader's eye from one element to another and makes sure he or she does not miss anything.

10   Motion in layout is generally from left to right and from top to bottom—the direction established through the reading habits of speakers of Western language. The directional impetus should not disturb the natural visual flow but should favor the elements to be stressed, while care should be taken not to direct the reader's eye out of the advertisement. This can be done by the following:

* *Gaze motion* directs the reader's attention by directing the looks of the people or animals in an ad. If a subject is gazing at a unit in the layout, the natural tendency is for the reader to follow the direction of that gaze; if someone is looking directly out of the advertisement, the reader may stop to see who's staring.
* *Structural motion* incorporates the lines of direction and patterns of movement by mechanical means. An obvious way is to use an arrow or a pointed finger. . . .

Unity

11 Another important design principle is the unification of the layout. Although an advertisement is made up of many elements, all of these should be welded into a compact composition. Unity is achieved when the elements tie into one another by using the same basic shapes, sizes, textures, colors, and mood. In addition, the type should have the same character as the art.

12   A *border* surrounding an ad provides a method of achieving unity. Sets of borders may occur within an ad, and, when they are similar in thickness and tone, they provide a sense of unity.

13   Effective use of white space can help to establish unity. . . . *White space* is defined as that part of the advertising space which is not occupied by any other elements; in this definition, white space is not always white in color. White space may be used to feature an important element by setting it off, or to imply luxury and prestige by preventing a crowded appearance. It may be used to direct and control the reader's attention by tying elements together. If white space is used incorrectly, it may cause separation of the elements and create difficulty in viewing the advertisement as a whole.

Clarity and Simplicity

14 The good art director does not permit a layout to become too complicated or tricky. An advertisement should retain its clarity and be easy to read and easy to understand. The reader tends to see the total image of an advertisement; thus it should not appear fussy, contrived, or confusing. Color contrasts, including tones of gray, should be strong enough to be easily deciphered, and the various units should be clear and easy to understand. Type size and design should be selected for ease of reading, and lines of type should be a comfortable reading length. Too many units in an advertisement are distracting; therefore, any elements that can be eliminated without destroying the message should be. One way in which clarity can be achieved is by combining the logo, trademark, tag line, and company name into one compact group.

Emphasis

15 Although varying degrees of emphasis may be given to different elements, one unit should dominate. It is the designer's responsibility to determine how much emphasis is necessary, as well as how it is to be achieved. The important element may be placed in the optical center or removed from the clutter of other elements. Emphasis may also be achieved by contrasts in size, shape, and color, or the use of white space.

Review Questions

1. How does balance in an ad differ from proportion?
2. What two possible types of movement can be incorporated into an advertisement?
3. Cite some of the chief ways of achieving unity in an ad.

Discussion and Writing Suggestions

1. Select an advertisement either in the ad portfolio (pages 691–737) or in a current magazine or newspaper. Analyze the ad in terms of Cohen's discussion of effective layout. How well does the ad employ *balance, proportion, movement, unity, clarity and simplicity,* and *emphasis* to sell the product or communicate the main idea? Which of these elements are most important in accomplishing the task?

2. Cohen writes that "balance is a fundamental law in nature." What do you think she means by this? What natural examples of balance occur to you?

3. Select two ads, one demonstrating what Cohen calls "formal balance," one demonstrating "informal balance." Cohen writes that formal balance "imparts feelings of dignity, solidity, refinement, and reserve" and that it suggests "conservatism on the part of the advertiser." Informal balance, on the other hand, "presents a fresh, untraditional approach" and "creates a sense of originality, forcefulness, and, to some extent, the element of surprise." To what degree do the ads you have selected demonstrate the truth of Cohen's assertions?

4. Find an ad demonstrating unusual use of proportion among its graphic elements. How does the distinctive proportionality help communicate the advertiser's message?

5. Find an ad demonstrating striking use of movement, clarity and simplicity, or emphasis. How does the element you have chosen work to help communicate the ad's message?

6. Find an ad that violates one or more of the graphic principles that Cohen discusses. To what extent do such violations hurt (or even destroy) the ad's effectiveness? How would you fix the problem?

The Indictments Against Advertising
Courtland L. Bovée and William F. Arens

If we were completely rational beings, then advertisements would simply inform us that a particular product or service was available and explain its benefits—if not also its drawbacks. (Some ads still do this: If we wanted to sell a CD, for example, we might just post a "For Sale" notice on a bulletin board, giving the name of the CD and its price.) Since—for better or for worse—we're not completely rational beings, but subject to the sway of powerful emotional appeals (as Jib Fowles explains, in the first selection of this chapter), and since modern advertising is a multibillion-dollar enterprise involving market research, customer psychology, skillful copywriting, and sophisticated graphic arts, the typical magazine or broadcast ad aims to do much more than simply inform us of the availability of consumer products. In addition, the pervasiveness of contemporary advertising means that almost everywhere we turn, we are bombarded with appeals to buy—mostly under the guise of persuading us that buying will somehow improve our lives. The ubiquity and apparent power of advertising (it does work, to some degree, or why would companies continue to advertise?) have inevitably caused a backlash, not only among the general public, but also among social critics, who see advertising—the original spam—as more than just an annoyance, but also as a pernicious influence in contemporary society.

The following selection sums up the chief arguments against advertising and also attempts to respond to these arguments. As you read this passage, think of current ads, either print or broadcast, that may illustrate the points made by the authors.

Courtland L. Bovée is the author or coauthor of several textbooks on business and advertising, including Techniques of Writing Business Letters, Memos, and Reports *(1974),* Advertising Excellence *(1995), and* Contemporary Advertising *(1986), where the following selection first appeared. William F. Arens is coauthor of* Contemporary Advertising.

Social Criticism of Advertising

1   Advertising is the most visible activity of business. What a company may have been doing privately for many years suddenly becomes public the moment it starts to advertise. By publicly inviting people to try their products, companies invite public criticism and attack if their products do not live up to the promised benefits. Defenders of advertising say it is therefore safer to buy advertised than unadvertised products. By putting their names behind the goods, the makers of advertised articles stick their necks out and will try harder to fulfill their promises.

2   Because advertising is so public, it is widely criticized, not only for the role it plays in selling products but also for the way it influences our society. As a selling tool, advertising is attacked for its excesses. Some critics charge that, at its worst, advertising is downright untruthful and, at best, it presents only positive information about products. Others charge that advertising manipulates people psychologically to buy things they can't afford by promising greater sex appeal, improved social status, or other unrealistic expectations. Still others attack advertising for being offensive or in bad taste. Many argue that there is

just too much advertising and that this overwhelming quantity is one reason it has such an impact on our society.

3   As a social influence, advertising is often charged, on the one hand, with contributing to crime and violence and, on the other hand, with making people conform. Critics attack advertising for perpetuating stereotypes of people, for making people want things they don't need and can't afford, and for creating insecurity in order to sell goods. Advertising, they say, debases our language, takes unfair advantage of our children, makes us too materialistic, and encourages wastefulness. Finally, by influencing the media, critics charge, advertising interferes with freedom of the press. . . .

4   Let's examine some of the more common criticisms as they are usually expressed. . . .

Advertising Makes Us Too Materialistic

5   Critics claim that advertising adversely affects our value system because it suggests that the means to a happier life is the acquisition of more things instead of spiritual or intellectual enlightenment. Advertising, they say, encourages people to buy more automobiles, more clothing, and more appliances than they need, all with the promise of greater status, greater social acceptance, and greater sex appeal. For example, they point to the fact that millions of Americans own 20 or more pairs of shoes, several TV sets, and often more than one vehicle.

6   There is no doubt that we are the most materialistic society in the world. So the basic question concerning materialism is this: Is there a relationship between happiness and materialism? Does the acquisition of more goods and services contribute to contentment and the joy of living?

7   Philosophers and social scientists have debated the relationship between affluence and happiness for centuries, but they have reached no concrete conclusions. Defenders of advertising maintain that material comfort is necessary before a person can devote time to higher cultural and spiritual values. Therefore, they say, the stress on material things doesn't rule out spiritual and cultural values. In fact, they believe it may create a greater opportunity for it since the satisfaction of a person's higher desires is more likely when that person's lower, more basic desires have been met. They also like to point out that, through its support of the media, advertising has brought literature, opera, drama, and symphonies to millions who would never have seen them otherwise.

8   In reality, the first responsibility of advertising is to aid its sponsor by informing, persuading, and reminding the sponsor's customers and prospects. Most sponsors are frankly more interested in selling goods and making profits than in bringing about cultural changes or improvements. Sponsors find that advertising is most effective when it accurately reflects the society and the market to which it is targeted. Therefore, when culturally uplifting advertising copy sells goods, advertisers will use it. And some of them do. Likewise, if people want a more cultural approach to advertisements and respond to them, advertisers will probably be delighted to comply because it will be in their own best interest. Ultimately, the bottom line will prevail. The profit and loss in dollars and cents determine the advertising approach.

Advertising Manipulates People Psychologically to Buy Things They Don't Need

9   Advertising is often criticized for its power to make people do irrational things. The following are some suggestions based on variations of this criticism:

1. Advertising should be informative but not persuasive.
2. Advertising should report only factual, functional information.
3. Advertising shouldn't play on people's desires, emotions, fears, or anxieties.
4. Advertising should deal only with people's functional needs for products not their psychological needs for status, appeal, security, sexual attractiveness, or health.

10   Underlying all these criticisms is (1) a belief in the power of advertising to control customers against their will, or (2) an attitude that consumers simply have no freedom of choice when confronted with advertising persuasion.

11   Apologists for advertising point out that persuasion is a fact of life and so is our need to confront persuasion on a daily basis. We see it in every avenue of our existence, not just in advertising. Teachers try to persuade students to study. Students try to persuade teachers to give them better grades. Girlfriends persuade boyfriends; preachers persuade congregations; charities persuade donors; borrowers persuade lenders; stockbrokers persuade investors; kids persuade parents; and advertising persuades people. In short, we are all busy persuading or being persuaded in one way or another.

12   Second, they point out that when we persuade, we usually use a variety of tactics depending on the subject matter and the response of the listener. Sometimes the simple facts of our case are overwhelmingly persuasive. Other times we appeal to some other need or motive of our listener because the facts alone aren't persuasive enough. Should we use emotional appeals in persuasion? If not, say the defenders, then we are all guilty because we all do it.

13   Frankly, all of us have needs and desires beyond the basics of food, clothing, and shelter. One benefit of a free society is that we can choose to what degree we wish to indulge our desires, needs, and fantasies. Some people prefer a simple life without mortgage payments, fancy cars, and trips abroad. Others enjoy the material pleasures of a modern, technological society. There are advertising sponsors at both ends of that spectrum. Food companies offer natural products as well as convenience packaged goods. Shoe companies offer simple sandals as well as formal footwear.

14   Perhaps, if we recognize that advertising is persuasive by definition, then we can become better consumers and critics of advertising. All companies attempt to persuade consumers to try their products. Not all are successful, though. In spite of the fact that advertising techniques have become far more effective and efficient in recent years, there is still no black magic. The final reality is that many more products fail than succeed in the marketplace. . . .

Advertising Is Offensive or in Bad Taste

15   Many people find advertising offensive to their religious convictions, morality, or political perspective. Others find the use of advertising techniques that

emphasize sex, violence, or body functions to be in bad taste. Certainly this is one of the most controversial issues.

16   Taste is highly subjective. Apologists point out that what is good taste to some is bad taste to others. And tastes change. What is considered offensive today may not be offensive in the future. People were outraged when the first advertisement for underarm deodorant was published in the *Ladies Home Journal,* but today no one questions such an advertisement. Some people find liquor ads offensive, while others find them simply informative. There has been some experimentation with advertising birth control products on television. Some feel this advertising supplies badly needed consumer information. Others feel that birth control is not a proper subject for a mass medium.

17   In the not-so-distant past, nudity was rarely seen in print advertisements. Today it is often featured in ads for grooming and personal hygiene products. Where nudity is relevant to the product being advertised, people are less likely to regard it as obscene or offensive.

18   Often the products themselves are not offensive, but the way they are advertised may be open to criticism. Advertising frequently emphasizes the sensational aspects of a product, particularly a book or motion picture. Shock value may be used to gain attention, particularly by inexperienced copywriters. However, this sensationalism is often a reflection of the tastes and interests of the American people. If the advertisements don't attract the people they seek, the advertising campaign will falter and die. The audience, therefore, has the ultimate veto authority by ignoring offensive material.

19   It is unrealistic to assume that advertising, particularly mass advertising, will ever be free of this criticism. But reputable advertisers try to be aware of what the public considers to be tasteful advertising.

Advertising Perpetuates Stereotypes

20 Groups such as the National Organization for Women (NOW) protest that many of today's advertisements do not acknowledge the changing role of women in our society. One feminist says:

> Advertising is an insidious propaganda machine for a male supremacist society. It spews out images of women as sex mates, housekeepers, mothers, and menial workers—images that perhaps reflect the true status of women in society, but which also make it increasingly difficult for women to break out of the sexist stereotypes that imprison them.

21   Consumer charges of ethnic and racial bias and of animal abuse in advertising were made to federal and business regulatory agencies for some time. The targets of these complaints included ads that showed a Japanese gardener at work and floor wax commercials that featured a black scrubwoman. Charges of animal abuse were made against beer commercials in which a dray horse was seen hauling a huge, old-fashioned brewery wagon. While none of these advertisements were illegal, all were objects of consumer efforts to halt their use, even to penalizing the advertisers.

22   Unfortunately, despite the efforts of many, there is still too much bias and sexism in advertising. The proper portrayal of women and minorities is still open to debate, however, and changes with the times.

23   Today it is especially important to portray women realistically, since they make so many important purchasing decisions. An area of vast change is the representation of minorities. Blacks, Hispanics, Italians, Chinese, American Indians, and others are now shown in favorable environments as a result of their upward mobility as well as organized pressure and threats of boycotts. New advertising agencies staffed with minority personnel are succeeding in reaching minority markets. Likewise, advertisers are taking special care to create advertisements that will neither offend nor alienate minority groups.

Advertising Is Deceptive

24 Perhaps the greatest attack on advertising has been and continues to be against the deceptive practices of some advertisers. This area has also received the greatest regulatory scrutiny. . . .

25   Critics define deceptiveness not only as false and misleading statements but also as any false impression conveyed, whether intentional or unintentional. Advertising deception can take a number of forms, and many of these are highly controversial with no hard and fast rules. . . .

26   Advertising must have the confidence of consumers if it is to be effective. Continued deception is self-defeating because, in time, it causes consumers to turn against a product.

27   Advertising puts the advertiser on record for all who care to look. Because of greater scrutiny by consumers and the government, it is in the advertisers' own interest to avoid trouble by being honest. The company that wants to stay in business over the long term knows it can do so only with a reputation for honest dealing.

Defense of Advertising

28 Advertising professionals admit that advertising has often been used irresponsibly over the years. But they like to use the analogy of a high-powered automobile: if a drunk is at the wheel, there's going to be a lot of damage. The problem, though, is the drunk at the wheel, not the car.

29   In other words, they admit that advertising has been and sometimes still is misused. But they believe the abuse that has been heaped on advertising as a marketing tool and as a social influencer is no longer justified and is so excessive as to make all advertising appear bad. In support, they point out that of all the advertising reviewed by the Federal Trade Commission in a typical year, 97 percent is found to be satisfactory. Moreover, they say, the very critics who attack advertising's excesses use advertising techniques themselves to sell their books and further their points of view.

30   Frankly, the sins of the past still haunt advertising today. What was once an unchecked, free-swinging business activity is now a closely scrutinized and heavily regulated profession. The excesses with which advertising has been right-

fully or wrongfully charged have created layer upon layer of laws, regulations, and regulatory bodies. These are used by consumer groups, government, special-interest groups, and even other advertisers to review, check, control, and change advertising.

Review Questions

1. How do defenders of advertising respond to the charge that advertising makes us too materialistic?

2. According to the authors, what are the main rebuttals to the charge that advertising manipulates us to buy things that we don't need?

3. What evidence is cited by those who charge that advertising perpetuates stereotypes?

4. What do the authors see as effective checks on deception in advertising?

Discussion and Writing Suggestions

1. Find an ad, either in the ad portfolio (pages 691–737), or in a newspaper or magazine, that might be charged with debasing our language. What specifically in this ad might provoke such a charge? To what extent could you defend the ad from the charge in the terms described by Bovée and Arens?

2. That advertising makes us more materialistic than we otherwise would be is one of the most common charges leveled against advertising. Find ads, either in the ad portfolio or in magazines or newspapers, that would lend credence to such a charge, and explain your conclusions with specific references to the text and graphics of the ad.

3. In general, to what extent do you think it is a good thing to encourage materialism—that is, to encourage people not only to buy products and services but also to *want* to buy? What specific evidence do you find in contemporary American society of the benefits and problems of materialism?

4. Recall an advertising campaign—either print or broadcast—that seems to support the charge that "advertising manipulates people psychologically to buy things they don't need." What particular features of this advertising campaign are manipulative? To what extent do you believe that the rebuttals to such charges by the "[a]pologists" for the advertisers (paragraph 16) effectively refute this charge? You might consider other social forces, besides advertising, that manipulate people to buy what they don't need.

5. Cite one or more examples of advertisements or advertising campaigns that you believe are in bad taste. What particular features of these ads are distasteful, and why? What evidence do you see that the distasteful campaign has either failed or been successful?

6. Select an ad, either in the ad portfolio or in a newspaper or magazine, that you believe perpetuates racial, gender, or other stereotypes. What features of the text and graphics in the ad encourage and perpetuate such stereotypes? How do you believe that such stereotyping might be considered, and perhaps even intended, by the sponsor of the ad as being necessary or desirable to help sell the product or service?

7. To what extent does the ad portfolio provide evidence of changing attitudes toward racial, gender, sexual, or other stereotyping from 1945 to the present? Discuss particular ads in developing your response.

8. Find an ad—either in the ad portfolio or in a newspaper or magazine, or on TV—that you believe to be deceptive, and explain the nature of the deception. Refer to particular features of the ad's language and/or graphics.

A Portfolio of Advertisements: 1945–2003

The following portfolio offers for your consideration and analysis a selection of 42 full-page advertisements that appeared in American and British magazines between 1945 (shortly after the end of World War II) and 2003. In terms of products represented, the ads fall into several categories—cigarettes, alcohol (beer and liquor), automobiles, food and drink, household cleaners, lotions, and perfumes. The portfolio also includes a few miscellaneous ads for such diverse products as men's hats, telephones, and airlines. These ads originally appeared in such magazines as Time, Newsweek, U.S. News and World Report, Sports Illustrated, Ladies Home Journal, Ebony, *and* Ms. *A number of the ads were researched in the Advertising Archive, an online (and subscription) collection maintained by The Picture Desk <www.picture-desk.com>.*

The advertisements in this portfolio are not representative of all ads that appeared during the last 60 years. We made our selection largely on the basis of how interesting, striking, provocative, and unusual these particular ads appeared to us. Admittedly, the selection process was biased. That said, the ads in this portfolio offer rich possibilities for analysis. With practice, and by applying principles for analysis that you will find in the earlier selections in this chapter, you will be able to "read" into these ads numerous messages about cultural attitudes toward gender relations, romance, smoking, and automobiles. The ads will prompt you to consider why we buy products that we may not need or why we prefer one product over another when the two products are essentially identical. Each advertisement is a window into the culture. Through careful analysis, you will gain insights not only into the era in which the ads were produced but also into shifting cultural attitudes over the last 60 years.

Following the portfolio, we provide two or three specific questions for each ad (pages 738–747), questions designed to stimulate your thinking about the particular ways that the graphics and text are intended to work. As you review the ads, however, you may want to think about the more general questions about advertisements raised by the readings in this chapter:

1. *What appears to be the target audience for the ad? If this ad was produced more than two decades ago, does its same target audience exist today? If so, how would this audience likely react today to the ad?*
2. *What is the primary appeal made by the ad, in terms of Fowles's categories? What, if any, are the secondary appeals?*
3. *What assumptions do the ad's sponsors make about such matters as (1) commonly accepted roles of women and men; (2) the relationship between the sexes; (3) the priorities of men and women?*
4. *What is the chief attention-getting device in the ad?*
5. *How does the headline and body text communicate the ad's essential appeals?*
6. *How do the ad's graphics communicate the ad's essential appeals?*
7. *How do the expressions, clothing, and postures of the models, as well as the physical objects in the illustration, help communicate the ad's message?*
8. *How do the graphic qualities of balance, proportion, movement, unity, clarity and simplicity, and emphasis help communicate the ad's message?*

"...not a creature was stirring..."

(*None, save the doctor going out on a call.*)

You remember how it starts—that beloved old Christmas poem:

'Twas the night before Christmas, when all through the house Not a creature was stirring,—not even a mouse.

Well, that isn't always true for the doctor. Sometimes there's just no rest at all for him—even on Christmas Eve.

Blizzard or heat wave . . . December or July . . . night or day . . . near or far . . . early or late . . . no matter when you call, he comes!

According to a recent nationwide survey:

MORE DOCTORS SMOKE CAMELS THAN ANY OTHER CIGARETTE

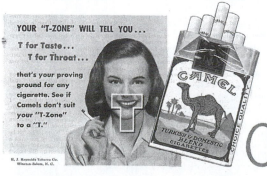

YOUR "T-ZONE" WILL TELL YOU...

T for Taste...
T for Throat...

that's your proving ground for any cigarette. See if Camels don't suit your "T-Zone" to a "T."

R. J. Reynolds Tobacco Co.
Winston-Salem, N. C.

• Not a single branch of medicine was overlooked in this nationwide survey made by three leading independent research organizations. To 113,597 doctors from Canada to Mexico, from the Atlantic to the Pacific went the query — *What cigarette do you smoke, Doctor?*

The brand named most was Camel.

Like anyone else, a doctor smokes for pleasure. He appreciates rich, full flavor and cool mildness just as any other smoker. If you don't happen to be a Camel smoker now, try Camels. Let your "T-Zone" give you the answer.

Camels *Costlier Tobaccos*

Camels, 1947

The Christmas Gift
for Important Men

• Websters are being specially boxed and Christmas wrapped this year. Boxes of 25, as low as $3.75. Give Websters by the box. A luxurious gift to yourself and to men who are used to the best.

• There are five different sizes of Websters. Each is made of 100% long Havana, bound in top-quality Broadleaf and wrapped in finest Connecticut Shadegrown. Boxes of 25 and 50 in all sizes. Wherever fine cigars are smoked.

WEBSTER CIGARS
EXECUTIVE AMERICA'S TOP CIGAR

| Golden Wedding, 15c | Chico, 15c | Queens, 18c | Fancy Tales, 25c | Directors, 35c |
| Box of 25—$3.75 | Box of 25—$3.75 | Box of 25—$4.50 | Box of 25—$6.25 | Box of 25—$8.75 |

A PRODUCT OF THE WEBSTER TOBACCO COMPANY, INC., NEW YORK

Webster Cigars, 1945

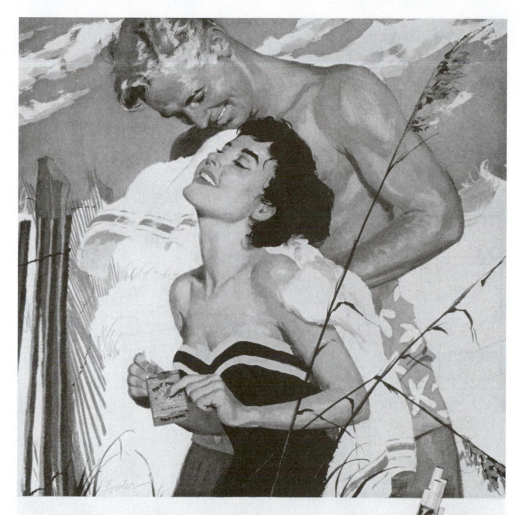

Gently Does It

Gentleness makes good friends in fun-making . . . and in a cigarette, where gentleness is one of the greatest requirements of modern taste. That's why today's Philip Morris, born gentle, refined to special gentleness in the making, makes so many friends among our young smokers. Enjoy the gentle pleasure, the fresh unfiltered flavor, of today's Philip Morris. In the convenient snap-open pack, regular or smart king-size.

. . . gentle for modern taste

Philip Morris, 1950s

Marlboro, 1970s

Camels, 1979

Can you spot the Camel Filters smoker?

©1972 R. J. Reynolds Tobacco Company, Winston-Salem, N. C.

In this picture everybody has a gimmick... almost everybody. Try picking the one who doesn't go along.

1. Nope. He's Lance Boyle. Gimmick: brags about wars he was never in. Yells "bombs away" as he flicks his French cigarette. **2.** Sorry. He's Harvey Dibble. His restaurant specializes in dried prunes. Gimmick: smokes wheat germ cigarettes. **3.** Eunice Trace, Starlet. Gimmick: restoring wholesomeness to movies. (Last film review: "At last, a movie the entire family can walk out on.") **4.** Smokey Stanhope, accountant. Gimmick: a guitar. Unfortunately makes the mistake of playing it. **5.** Right. He's just himself. And he sees through all the gimmicks. That's why he wants an honest, no-nonsense cigarette. Camel Filters. Easy and good tasting. Made from fine tobacco. **6.** Calls himself "Killer." Gimmick: thinks soccer uniform enhances his image. When he puffs out his chest, his pants fall down.

Camel Filters. They're not for everybody (but they could be for you).

20 mg. "tar," 1.4 mg. nicotine av. per cigarette, FTC Report AUG. '72.

Camel Filters, 1970s

More, 1980s

Camel Lights, 1992

Camels, 2000s

Pabst Blue Ribbon, 1940s

America is returning to the genuine—in foods, fashions and tastes. Today's trend to Ballantine <u>light</u> Ale fits right into this modern picture. <u>In all the world, no other beverage brewed has such extra excellence brewed into it.</u> And "Brewer's Gold" is one big reason for Ballantine Ale's deep, rich, genuine flavor.

They all ask for ale **Ballantine** LIGHT **Ale !**

Ballantine Ale, 1950s

ERNEST HEMINGWAY, who has been called the greatest living American writer, is also internationally famous as a deep-sea fisherman. Since publication of *The Sun Also Rises* in 1926, his novels and short stories have enriched the literature of the English language consistently, year after year. His newest book is *The Old Man and the Sea*.

Ballantine Ale, 1953

HOW WOULD YOU put a glass of Ballantine Ale into words?

Here—Ernest Hemingway turns his famous hand to it...

Ernest Hemingway

FINCA VIGIA, SAN FRANCISCO DE PAULA, CUBA

Bob Benchley first introduced me to Ballantine Ale. It has been a good companion ever since.

You have to work hard to deserve to drink it. But I would rather have a bottle of Ballantine Ale than any other drink after fighting a really big fish.

We keep it iced in the bait box with chunks of ice packed around it. And you ought to taste it on a hot day when you have worked a big marlin fast because there were sharks after him.

You are tired all the way through. The fish is landed untouched by sharks and you have a bottle of Ballantine cold in your hand and drink it cool, light, and full-bodied, so it tastes good long after you have swallowed it. That's the test of an ale with me: whether it tastes as good afterwards as when it's going down. Ballantine does.

Ernest Hemingway

More people like it...   More people buy it...   than any other ale...   ...by Four to One!

BALLANTINE  ALE

PURITY BODY FLAVOR

Since 1840

P. Ballantine & Sons, Newark, N.J.

BACARDI. rum is so "mixable"... It's a one-brand bar.

Big, bold highballs, sassy Daiquiris, cool tonics and colas—Bacardi rum is enjoyable always and *all* ways. Extra Special: our man Fernando is pouring very rare Bacardi Añejo rum (Ahn-YAY-ho), one of the fine rums from Bacardi. So incredibly smooth he enjoys it even in a snifter. Try it, too!

*BACARDI IMPORTS, INC., MIAMI, FLA. RUM, 80 PROOF.

Bacardi Rum, 1960s

AT THE PULITZER FOUNTAIN, N.Y.C.

In Fine Whiskey...

FLEISCHMANN'S
is the BIG buy!

The First Taste will tell you why!

BLENDED WHISKEY • 86 AND 90 PROOF • 65% GRAIN NEUTRAL SPIRITS
THE FLEISCHMANN DISTILLING CORPORATION, NEW YORK CITY

Fleischmann's Whiskey, 1964

"I'll have a Hennessy Very Superior Old Pale Reserve Cognac, thank you."

The Taste of Success

Every drop of Hennessy V.S.O.P. Reserve is Grande Fine Champagne Cognac.
It's made solely from grapes grown in La Grande Champagne—the small district in
the Cognac region which is the source of the very greatest Cognac.
What's more, Hennessy is selected from the largest reserves of aged Cognacs in existence.
Enjoy a taste of success today...

Hennessy V.S.O.P. Reserve Cognac

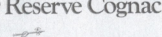

Hennessy V.S.O.P. Grande Fine Champagne Cognac. 80 Proof. ©Schieffelin & Co., N.Y.

Hennessy Cognac, 1968

Smirnoff Vodka, 1970s

Cossack Vodka, 1970s

Now comes Miller time.
Time to head for the best-tasting beer
you can find. Miller High Life.
America's quality beer since 1855.

© 1979 Miller Brewing Co., Milwaukee, Wis.

Miller Beer, 1979

Budweiser Beer, 1990s

Pay-off for Pearl Harbor!

Three years ago, the sneak attack on Pearl Harbor found America unprepared to defend its rights. Yet, even at that early date, Cadillac was in its third year of building aircraft engine parts for military use. Today are look hopefully forward to the time when this important contribution to America's air power will pay off in such a scene as that illustrated above.

For more than five years we have been working toward that end. Back in 1939, we started building precision parts for Allison—America's famous liquid-cooled aircraft engine—used to power such potent fighters as the Lightning, the Warhawk, the Mustang, the Airacobra and the new Kingcobra.

In addition to our work for Allison, which has included more than 57,000,000 man-hours of precision production—we assisted Army Ordnance Engineers in designing the M-5 Light Tank and the M-8 Howitzer motor carriage, and have produced them in quantities. Both are powered by Cadillac engine equipped with Hydra-Matic transmissio

We are now building other weapons whi utilize some of our Cadillac peacetime pr ucts. We can't talk about all of them yet—t we are confident they will prove signific additions to Allied armor.

Every Sunday Afternoon . . . GENERAL MOTORS SYMPHONY OF THE AIR–NBC Network

CADILLAC MOTOR CAR DIVISION  GENERAL MOTORS CORPORATION

LET'S ALL
BACK THE ATTACK
BUY WAR BONDS

Cadillac, 1945

Of all the De Soto cars ever built, 7 out of 10 are still running

8 out of 10 owners say, "De Soto is the most satisfactory car I ever owned"*

*FROM A MAIL SURVEY AMONG THOUSANDS OF OWNERS
OF 1941 AND 1942 DE SOTO CARS

DE SOTO DIVISION OF CHRYSLER CORPORATION

DeSoto
DESIGNED TO ENDURE

De Soto, 1947

"Ford's out Front from a Woman's Angle"

1. **"I don't know** synthetic enamel from a box of my children's paints... but if synthetic enamel is what it takes to make that beautiful, shiny Ford finish, I'm all for it!

2. **"My husband says the brakes** are self-centering and hydraulic—whatever that means! All I know is they're so easy that I can taxi the children all day without tiring out!

3. **"Peter, he's my teen-age son,** tells me that 'Ford is the only car in its price class with a choice of a 100-horsepower V-8 engine or a brilliant new Six.' He says no matter which engine people pick, they're out front with Ford!

6. **"Now here's another thing** women like and that's a blissfully comfortable ride—one that isn't bumpity-bump even on some of our completely forgotten roads."

Listen to the Ford Show starring Dinah Shore on Columbia Network Stations Wednesday Evenings.

4. **"The interior of our Ford is** strictly my department! It's tailored with the dreamiest broadcloth. Such a perfect fit! Mary Jane says women help design Ford interiors. There's certainly a woman's touch there!

5. **"Do you like** lovely silver, beautifully simple and chaste looking? That's what I always think of when I touch those smart Ford door handles and window openers.

There's a *Ford* in your future

Ford, 1947

Worth Its Price

If a motorist wanted to make the move to Cadillac solely for the car's prestige—he would most certainly be justified in doing so. For the Cadillac car has never stood so high in public esteem as it does today—and the rewards which grow out of this unprecedented acceptance comprise the rarest and greatest satisfactions in all motordom.

There is, for instance, *the inescapable feeling of pride* that comes with ownership of so distinguished and beloved a possession . . . the wonderful *sense of wellbeing* that comes from having reached a point of achievement where you can enjoy one of the world's most sought-after manufactured products . . . and the *marvelous feeling of confidence and self-esteem* that is found

CADILLAC MOTOR CAR DIVISION

Cadillac, 1954

in PRESTIGE !

in the respect and admiration universally accorded the owner of a Cadillac car. Those who presently enjoy these unique Cadillac virtues will tell you that they are, in themselves, worth the car's whole purchase price.

Of course, most motorists would hesitate to take such a step purely for their personal edification. But in Cadillac's case, this wonderful prestige is actually a "bonus", so to speak—an extra dividend that comes with every Cadillac car, in addition to its breath-taking styling, its magnificent performance, its superlative luxury and its remarkable economy.

Have you seen and driven the 1954 Cadillac? If you haven't, then you've a truly wonderful adventure awaiting you—and one that you should postpone no longer.

GENERAL MOTORS CORPORATION

This is your reward for the great Dodge advance—the daring new, dramatic new '56 Dodge.

The Magic Touch of Tomorrow!

The *look* of success! The *feel* of success! The *power* of success! They come to you in a dramatically beautiful, dynamically powered new Dodge that introduces the ease and safety of push-button driving –the Magic Touch of Tomorrow! It is a truly great value.

New '56 DODGE

Dodge, 1955

Drive a Riviera home tonight. Who cares if people
think you're younger, richer and more romantic than you really are?

A Riviera has a strange effect on people. Simply looking at one makes your mouth water, your eyes
open wider and your heart beat faster. You grin admiringly when you notice the headlights, tucked
behind shields that open with the touch of the headlight switch. You breathe harder when you
turn loose some of those 325 horsepower. And that's just what happens to the driver. Wait till you see the
awe a Riviera inspires in passersby! Amazing. Also attainable, for considerably less than
you might suspect. (Before you fall headlong for a Riviera, ask yourself if a firmer suspension and
assorted other sporting touches give you a twinge of anticipation. Yes? Ask your dealer about
our new Riviera Gran Sport. The name alone is a hint of what's in it for you.) Check with your Buick dealer
soon. He may convince you you're younger, richer and more romantic than you thought you were.

Wouldn't you really rather have a Buick?

Buick, 1965

Corvette Sting Ray Sport Coupe with eight standard safety features, including outside rearview mirror. Use it always before passing.

The day she flew the coupe

What manner of woman is this, you ask, who stands in the midst of a mountain stream eating a peach?

Actually she's a normal everyday girl except that she and her husband own the Corvette Coupe in the background. (He's at work right now, wondering where he misplaced his car keys.)

The temptation, you see, was over-powering. They'd had the car a whole week now, and not once had he offered to let her drive. His excuse was that this, uh, was a big hairy sports car. Too much for a woman to handle: the trigger-quick steering, the independent rear suspension, the disc brakes—plus the 4-speed transmission and that 425-hp engine they had ordered—egad! He would teach her to drive it some weekend. So he said.

That's why she hid the keys, forcing him to seek public transportation. Sure of his departure, she went to the garage, started the Corvette, and was off for the hills, soon upshifting and downshifting as smoothly as he. His car. Hard to drive. What propaganda!

'66 CORVETTE BY CHEVROLET
Chevrolet Division of General Motors, Detroit, Michigan

Corvette, 1966

Jeep vehicle, 2003

The Turbo engine with the Family Pack.

The Diesel engine with

VOLVO GIVE THEIR BLESSING

When it comes to marriages Volvo like to put on a big spread.

That's why, with the 400 series, we're giving you a wider choice than any other manufacturer. You can pick a bigger engine with standard specification or a smaller engine with the luxury package.

In fact, with a total of five different engine sizes and six different interior packages on offer, you can mix and match as much as you like.'

You could for instance, unite the 1.6 engine with the Luxury Pack, which features air-conditioning and leather upholstery.

With other manufacturers however, you don't get such a happy coupling. You'll find that the luxury package for example, only comes with the larger engine.

Volvo, 1990s

the Business Pack.   The 1.6 engine with the Leather Interior.

TO ALL SORTS OF MARRIAGES.

Volvo's approach (which applies to the 440 hatchback and 460 saloon) means you not only get the car that suits your exact needs, but you decide exactly where your money goes.

And you don't have to wait any longer for

delivery of your specially built car. For information pack call 0800 400 430.

The Volvo 400 series. From £11,175 (w ribbons not included).

THE VOLVO 400 SERIES. A CAR YOU CAN BELIEV

Good School Day Lunches

make healthier, brighter youngsters

Many children do not get adequate lunches! And yet upon proper food depends not only their future health, but today's well-being, cheerfulness—and even report cards!

Lunch should include a hot dish, and be substantial but easy to digest. Good nourishing soup is a big help—and Campbell's Vegetable Soup is just right! Children love it, and it brings them all the sturdy goodness of 15 different garden vegetables combined with a rich, invigorating beef stock. No wonder mothers everywhere agree "It's almost a meal in itself!"

Campbell's VEGETABLE SOUP

LOOK FOR THE RED-AND-WHITE LABEL

A WEEK'S SCHOOL LUNCHES

MONDAY
Campbell's Vegetable Soup
Peanut Butter Sandwich
Orange   Baked Custard   Celery
                Graham Crackers

TUESDAY
Campbell's Tomato Soup
Cottage Cheese and Orange Marmalade Sandwich
Banana   Carrot Sticks
                Molasses Cookies

WEDNESDAY
Campbell's Scotch Broth
Lettuce and Hard-Cooked Egg Salad
Toasted Raisin Bread
Fresh Pear
                Cocoa

THURSDAY
Campbell's Vegetable Soup
Cold Roast Veal Sandwich
Baked Apple   Celery
                     Milk

FRIDAY
Campbell's Cream of Spinach Soup
Toasted Tuna Fish Salad Sandwich
Sliced Tomatoes
Stewed Peaches   Chocolate Milk

Campbell's, 1945

Coca-Cola, 1945

What's for dinner, Duchess?

Prediction: The new wives of 1947 are going to have more fun in the kitchen.

Previous cooking experience is desirable, perhaps, but not essential. There are so many new easy-to-use foods, so many new ways to prepare foods, so many interesting ways to serve foods, cooking will be a novel and exciting adventure.

Further prediction: Cheese dishes will be featured more often on their menus. They'll know that cheese gives tastiness and variety to meals. And cheese, like milk (nature's most nearly perfect food), is rich in protein, calcium, phosphorus, in vitamins A and G.

Yes, we have a personal interest in cheese. For Kraft, pioneer in cheese, is a unit of National Dairy. And what we've said about housewives using more cheese is entirely true.

It's also true that they're learning more about the whys and wherefores of food each year — just as the scientists in our laboratories are learning more about better ways to process, improve and supply it.

These men are backed by the resources of a great organization. They explore every field of dairy products, discover new ones. And the health of America benefits constantly by this National Dairy research.

Dedicated to the wider use and better understanding of dairy products as human food . . . as a base for the development of new products and materials . . . as a source of health and enduring progress on the farms and in the towns and cities of America.

NATIONAL DAIRY
PRODUCTS CORPORATION
AND AFFILIATED COMPANIES

National Dairy Products Corporation, 1947

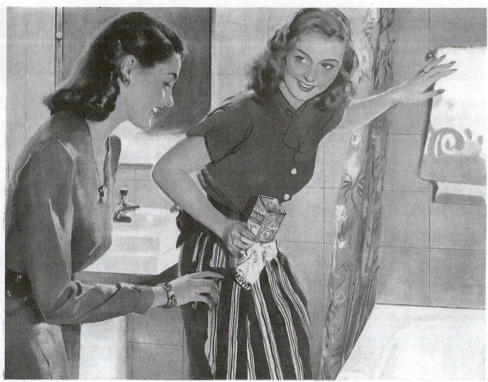

MAY: # Heavens, Ann — wish I could clean up quick as that!

ANN: You could, hon! Just use a cleanser that doesn't leave dirt-catching scratches.

MAY: Goodness! What in the world do scratches have to do with it?

ANN: A lot, silly! Those tiny scratches you get from gritty cleansers hold onto dirt and double your cleaning time.

MAY: Well, you old smartie! I'd never thought of *that* before.

ANN: I hadn't thought of it either—till I discovered Bon Ami! See how fine-textured and white it is. It just *slides* dirt off—and when you rinse it away, it doesn't leave any of that horrid grit in the tub.

MAY: Say no more, darling! From now on there's going to be a new cleaning team in our house —me and Bon Ami!

EASY ON YOUR HANDS, Bon Ami *Powder* is the ideal cleanser for kitchen sinks, as well as bathtubs. Also try Bon Ami *Cake* for cleaner windows, mirrors and windshields.

Bon Ami

THE **SPEEDY** CLEANSER *that* *"hasn't scratched yet!"*

Bon Ami, 1947

This is the story of Annie...

NOW ANNIE WAS...

AS BEAUTIFUL A GIRL...

AS EVER WAS PUT TOGETHER!

WHY, WHEN ANNIE WALKED DOWN THE STREET...
WOW!

YET ANNIE HAD HER BAD MOMENTS...LIKE ANY OTHER GAL.

AND YOU WANT TO KNOW WHY? ANNIE'S HANDS WERE A MESS. ALWAYS ROUGH AND DRY, LIKE SANDPAPER.

AND WHEN A MAN WANTS TO HOLD A GIRL'S HANDS... EVEN A GIRL LIKE ANNIE ...HE DOESN'T WANT TO WEAR GLOVES...

THEN, LUCKILY, FANNIE TOLD ANNIE ABOUT AN ENTIRELY NEW AND DIFFERENT HAND LOTION! THE **BEFOREHAND** LOTION...**TRUSHAY!**

SO ANNIE SMOOTHED CREAMY, FRAGRANT **TRUSHAY** ON HER HANDS BEFORE SHE DID DISHES...BECAUSE **TRUSHAY** GUARDS HANDS EVEN IN HOT, SOAPY WATER!

AND ANNIE PUT **TRUSHAY** ON HER HANDS BEFORE SHE TUBBED HER UNDIES...SO **TRUSHAY'S** SPECIAL "OIL-RICHNESS" COULD HELP PREVENT DRYNESS AND ROUGHNESS.

SO NOW ANNIE IS ABLE TO KEEP HER HANDS SOFT AND SMOOTH AND HOLDABLE... THANKS TO **TRUSHAY'S** WONDERFUL SOFTENING HELP.

TRUSHAY

The "Beforehand" Lotion

PRODUCT OF BRISTOL-MYERS

P. S. Trushay's grand for softening hands at *any* time. Wonderful, too, for rough, dry elbows and heels...as a powder base...before and after exposure to weather. Trushay contains no alcohol, is not sticky. Begin today to use Trushay.

Trushay, 1947

Mrs. Dorian Mehle of Morrisville, Pa., is all three: a housewife, a mother, and a very lovely lady.

"I wash 22,000 dishes a year... but I'm proud of my pretty hands!"

You and Dorian Mehle have something in common. Every year, you wash a stack of dishes a quarter-mile high!

Detergents make your job so much easier. They cut right into grease and grime. They get you through dishwashing in much less time, but while they dissolve grease, they also take away the natural oils and youthful softness of your hands!

Although Dorian hasn't given up detergents her hands are as soft, as smooth, as young-looking as a teenager's. Her secret is no secret at all. It's the world's best-known beauty routine. It's pure, white Jergens Lotion, after every chore.

When you smooth on Jergens Lotion, this liquid formula doesn't just "coat" your hands. It penetrates right away, to help *replace* that softening moisture your skin needs.

Jergens Lotion has two ingredients doctors recommend for softening. Women must be recommending it, too, for more women use it than any other hand care in the world. Dorian's husband is the best testimonial to Jergens Lotion care. Even after years of married life, he still loves to hold her pretty hands!

Use Jergens Lotion like a prescription: three times a day, after every meal!

Now—lotion dispenser FREE of extra cost with $1.00 size. Supply limited.

Use JERGENS LOTION – avoid detergent hands

Jergens Lotion, 1954

President Lee A. Potter Jr., *of the Young Presidents Organization Inc. and Forman, Ford & Co. "To be successful, look the part. That certain look of success attracts the confidence of important men."*

A man's hat speaks eloquently of his personal measure of authority. That's why Disney hats are so often considered part of a businessman's equipment. The rare skill of their handcraftsmanship, the executive character of their styling reflect the critical judgment and taste of the wearer.* Disney's uniquely impressive effect has made these hats the choice of prominent men for 65 years.

*Case in point, THE DISNEY CAPELLO. This marvelously light hat, styled with flattering tapered crown and narrow brim, is fashion at its finest. At fine stores, $20. Many other Disney hats from $10 to $40.
Free! Handsome booklet containing helpful hints by American business leaders. Ask your Disney dealer for "Guide Quotes to Success."

The Hat of Presidents

Disney Hats, 1954

Madam! Suppose you traded jobs with your husband?

You can just bet the first thing he'd ask for would be a telephone in the kitchen.

You wouldn't catch him dashing to another room every time the telephone rang, or he had to make a call.

He doesn't have to do it in his office in town. It would be mighty helpful if you didn't have to do it in your "office" at home.

That's in the kitchen where you do so much of your work. And it's right there that an additional telephone comes in so handy for so many things.

Along with a lot of convenience is that nice feeling of pride in having the best of everything—especially if it is one of those attractive new telephones in color.

P.S. *Additional telephones in kitchen, bedroom and other convenient places around the house cost little. The service charge is just pennies a day.*

Bell Telephone System

Bell Telephone, 1956

Bell Telephone, 1974

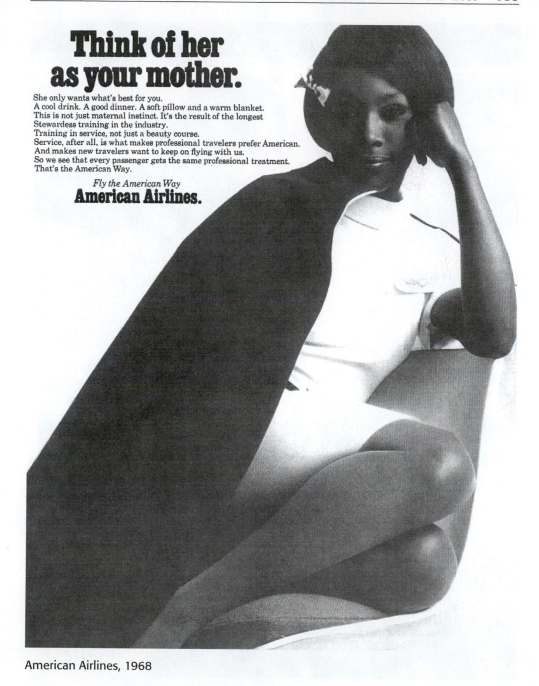

Think of her as your mother.

She only wants what's best for you.
A cool drink. A good dinner. A soft pillow and a warm blanket.
This is not just maternal instinct. It's the result of the longest
Stewardess training in the industry.
Training in service, not just a beauty course.
Service, after all, is what makes professional travelers prefer American.
And makes new travelers want to keep on flying with us.
So we see that every passenger gets the same professional treatment.
That's the American Way.

Fly the American Way
American Airlines.

American Airlines, 1968

Charlie, 1988

Shineaway 17 Lotion, 1980s

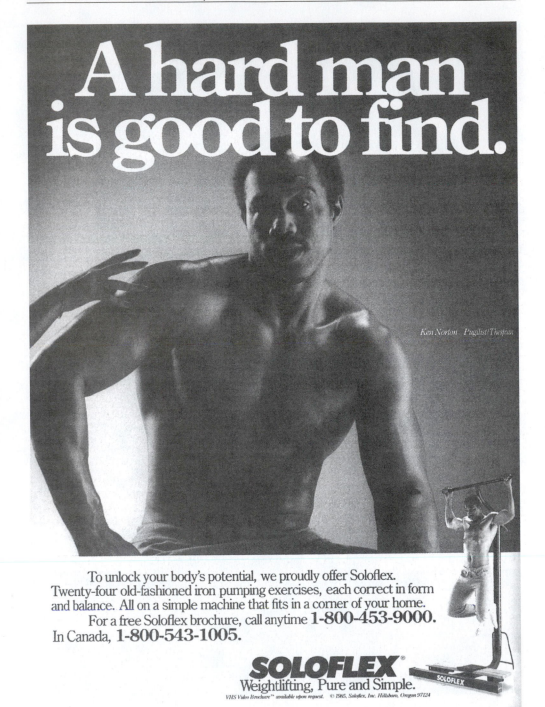

Soloflex, 1985

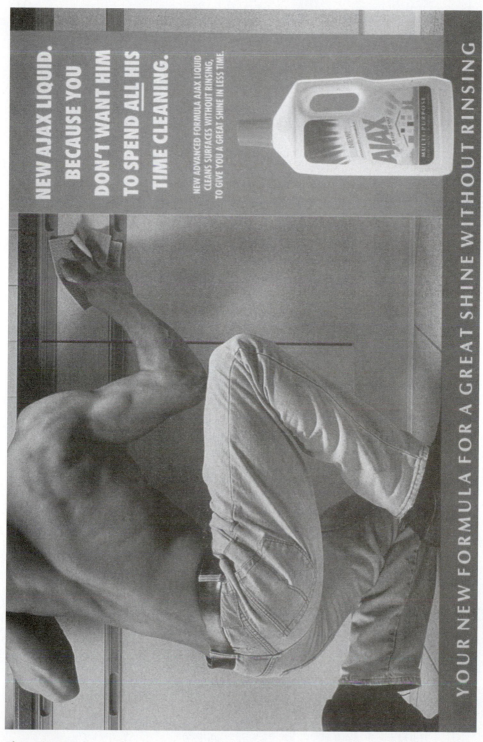

Ajax, 1990s

Discussion and Writing Suggestions

TOBACCO

Camels, 1947 (p. 693)

1. How does the intended appeal of this ad differ most dramatically from a comparable ad today?

2. What kind of psychological appeals are made by the picture in the top half of this ad and the text accompanying it? How does the image of a doctor out on a night call tie in, for selling purposes, with the ad's headline?

Webster Cigars, 1945 (p. 694)

1. How does the dress and general appearance of the people in the ad, as well as the setting depicted, communicate meaning, particularly as it applies to the appeal of the product?

2. To whom is this advertisement addressed? Cite headline and body text, as well as graphics, that support your response. What kind of ads today are addressed to a similar audience?

Philip Morris, 1950s (p. 695)

1. How do the placement, posture, and dress of the models in the ad help create its essential psychological appeal? Why do you suppose (in relation to the selling of cigarettes) the models' eyes are closed?

2. Discuss some of the messages communicated both by the graphic and the text of this ad. Focus in particular on the quality of "gentleness" emphasized in the ad.

Marlboro, 1970s (p. 696)

1. The Marlboro Man has become one of the most famous—and successful—icons of American advertising. What elements of the Marlboro Man (and his setting, Marlboro Country) do you notice, and what role do these elements play in the appeal being made by this ad?

2. This ad appeared during the 1970s. (The popularity of the Marlboro Man extended into the 1980s, however.) To what extent do you think it would have the same appeal today?

3. Comment on the elements of graphic design (balance, proportion, movement, unity, clarity and simplicity, emphasis) that help make this ad effective. Focus particularly on the element of movement.

Camels, 1979 (p. 697)

1. What do the relative positions and postures of the man and the woman in the ad indicate about the ad's basic appeal?

2. What roles do the props—particularly, the motorcycle and the models' outfits—and the setting play in helping to sell the product?

3. How do the design elements in the ad emphasize the product?

4. Compare the graphic elements of this ad to those of the Fleischmann's Whiskey ad (page 707).

Camel Filters, 1970s (p. 698)

1. How do the contrasts in appearance (including posture and facial expressions) between the Camel Filters smoker and the others in the graphic support the essential appeal made by this ad?

2. How does the body text—particularly the thumbnail descriptions of each of the six candidates for Camel Filters smoker—reinforce the ad's intended meaning?

More, 1980s (p. 699)

1. What qualities are conveyed by the couple depicted in the ad? Focus on their dress, posture, and facial expressions. How do these qualities contribute to the appeal of the product?

2. Compare and contrast the effect of this ad with earlier ads depicted for this product (Webster Cigars, Philip Morris) that also show two or more people enjoying tobacco products.

3. Comment on the effectiveness of the graphic elements of this advertisement.

Camel Lights, 1992 (p. 700)

1. During the early 1990s, Joe Camel (depicted here, shooting pool) became one of the most popular and recognized icons of contemporary marketing. The cartoon figure appeared not only on billboards and magazine ads, but also on T-shirts and baseball caps. Joe Camel's appeal, particularly to teenagers, was deemed so pernicious that a group of state attorneys general joined forces in 1997 to force R. J. Reynolds, manufacturer of Camels, to retire the offending dromedary. (The Marlboro Man was targeted in the same settlement, though one of the first models for the Marlboro Man had already died—of lung cancer.) Based on this advertisement, what appears to be the essential elements of Joe Camel's appeal?

2. Contrast this ad with the earlier Camels ads (the man on the motorcycle, the "Can you spot the Camels Filters smoker?" query), as well as the earlier ads for tobacco products, such as Webster Cigars, Philip Morris, and Marlboro. How does the appearance of Joe Camel indicate a major shift of cultural attitudes?

Camels, 2000s (p. 701)

1. This is an example of retro appeal. What elements make it so? What elements mark the ad, on the other hand, as a contemporary one? How does the combination of retro and contemporary elements (including, for example, the posture and attitude of the model) contribute to create a particular type of appeal?

2. Compare and contrast the five Camels ads presented in this section of the portfolio. Focus on the psychological appeals, the cultural values implied in the ads, and the graphic and textual means used to persuade the buyer to smoke Camels.

BEER AND LIQUOR

Pabst Blue Ribbon, 1940s (p. 702)

1. Ads in the 1940s often took comic book form. (See also the 1947 Trushay ad later in this portfolio, page 728.) To what kind of audience is this format most likely to appeal? What are some of the advantages and disadvantages of the comic book format?

2. The problem/solution structure of the narrative in this ad is one of the oldest and still most frequently employed (particularly in TV commercials) in marketing. To what extent does it seem appropriate for the selling of beer? To what extent is it appropriate for other products and services? (Cite examples from contemporary or recent ads.)

3. To what extent do you find examples of outdated social attitudes in this ad?

Ballantine Ale, 1950s (p. 703)

1. This illustration, reminiscent of some of Norman Rockwell's paintings, is typical of many beer and ale ads in the 1950s, which depict a group of well-dressed young adults enjoying their brew at a social event. Comment on the distinctive graphic elements in this ad and speculate as to why these elements are seldom employed in contemporary advertisements for beer and ale. Why, in other words, does this ad seem old-fashioned?

2. Contrast the appeal and graphics of this ad with the ads for Miller and Budweiser later in this portfolio.Contrast the appeal and graphics of this ad with the ads for Miller and Budweiser later in this portfolio.

3. Identify the adjectives in the body text and attempt to correlate them to the graphic in helping to construct the message of the ad.

Ballantine Ale, 1953 (pp. 704–705)

1. You may be surprised to find Ernest Hemingway selling ale. To what extent do you find celebrity endorsements an effective method of marketing? Why do you think that the creators of this ad might have

believed that Hemingway (as opposed, say, to a professional athlete) might be an effective promoter of (or is qualified to address the need for guidance on) Ballantine Ale?

2. Comment on the apparent strategy behind the graphic and textual elements in this ad—particularly, the setting, Hemingway's posture, and his letter.

3. If you are familiar with any of Hemingway's stories or novels, do you notice any similarity of style or subject matter between what you have previously read and Hemingway's testimonial letter to Ballantine Ale?

Bacardi Rum, 1960s (p. 706)

1. What meaning is conveyed by the placement, posture, and expressions of the four models in this ad? How do you think this meaning is intended to help sell the product? (Does the picture remind you of a particular movie hero?)

2. Comment on the significance of the props in the photo.

3. How does the text ("Big, bold highballs, sassy Daiquiris, cool tonics . . .") help reinforce the meaning created by the picture?

Fleischmann's Whiskey, 1964 (p. 707)

1. Comment on (1) the significance of the extra-large bottle of whiskey; (2) the stances of the two models in the ad; (3) the way the headline contributes to the ad's meaning.

2. Compare and contrast the graphic in this ad with that of the 1979 Camels ad earlier in this portfolio (the man on the motorcycle).

Hennessy Cognac, 1968 (p. 708)

1. What is the primary appeal of this ad? How do the woman, the horse, and the headline work to create and reinforce this appeal?

2. Compare and contrast this ad to the Webster Cigars ad in terms of their appeal and their graphics.

Smirnoff Vodka, 1970s (p. 709)

1. What meaning is conveyed by the two figures in this ad? How do the models' postures and the props help reinforce this meaning?

2. How do you interpret the headline? How does the headline—and the subheadline ("You drink it for what it is")—tie in to the meaning created by the photo?

Cossack Vodka, 1970s (p. 710)

1. What is the essential appeal behind this ad?

2. The comic book style of the drawing is reminiscent of the work of Roy Lichtenstein (1923–1997), an American painter who drew inspiration

from advertisements and romance magazines, as well as comic books, to depict and parody artifacts of pop culture. What is the effect of this particular style on creating—and perhaps commenting upon—the message in the text balloon and in the ad in which it appears?

3. How does the text at the bottom of the idea reinforce the message created by the graphic? In particular, how is this message intended to sell the product?

Miller Beer, 1979 (p. 711)

1. To what extent does this 1979 ad embody marketing techniques for beer that are still employed today?

2. Comment on the posture and expressions of the three models depicted in the ad. How do these elements help create the ad's essential appeal?

3. Compare and contrast this ad with the 1950s Ballantine Ale ad earlier in this portfolio (page 703).

Budweiser Beer, 1990s (p. 712)

1. To what extent is this ad based on a similar appeal as the preceding Miller ad? To what extent is it based on other appeals?

2. What's the advantage (in terms of effectiveness of appeal) of using the second person—"you"—in the body text? How does the text attempt to make the connection between the product advertised and the activities of the football players? To what extent do you think that this is an effective ad?

3. Comment on the workings and effectiveness of the graphic design elements in this ad.

AUTOMOBILES

Cadillac, 1945 (p. 713)

1. What is the essential strategy behind portraying a group of military aircraft on a bombing raid in an automobile ad? What, exactly, is this ad selling?

2. Explain how the graphic elements of this ad—and the interplay between the elements of the graphic and the text (headline and body text)—reinforce the ad's basic appeal.

De Soto, 1947 (p. 714)

1. How does the scene portrayed in the illustration help create the basic appeal of this ad? Focus on as many significant individual elements of the illustration as you can.

2. To what extent does the caption (in the illustration) and the headline support the message communicated by the graphic?

3. Explain why both this ad and the preceding Cadillac ad are products of their particular times.

Ford, 1947 (p. 715)

1. Cite and discuss those textual elements in the ad that reflect a traditional conception of the American woman.

2. How do the visual elements of the ad reinforce the assumptions about traditional gender roles reflected in the ad?

Cadillac, 1954 (pp. 716–717)

1. What is the particular marketing strategy behind this ad? Based on the ad's text, compose a memo from the head of marketing to the chief copywriter proposing this particular ad and focusing on the strategy. The memo doesn't have to be cynical or to insult the prospective Cadillac buyers; it should just be straightforward and direct.

2. How do the ad's graphics reinforce the message in the text?

Dodge, 1955 (p. 718)

1. Discuss the multiple appeals of this ad. How are these appeals reflected in the ad's text and graphics? For instance, discuss the angle from which the automobile is photographed.

2. Both this ad and the 1947 Ford ad (page 715) feature one or more women in the graphic. Compare and contrast the use of women in the two ads.

Buick, 1965 (p. 719)

1. Compare and contrast the appeal made in this ad to the appeal made in either the 1947 Ford ad (page 715) or the 1954 Cadillac ad (pages 716–717). Cite particular aspects of the text and graphics to support your comparison.

2. The text of the ad discusses two categories of the "people" mentioned in the first sentence. Discuss how the ad makes different, if related, appeals to these two categories of "people."

3. Discuss, in terms of their overall effect, the placement of the automobile and the woman in the ad, as well as the perspective from which both are viewed.

Corvette, 1966 (p. 720)

1. How do the graphic elements reinforce the message developed in the text of this ad?

2. Comment on the dress and the posture of the model, as these relate to the ad's essential appeal. What's the significance of the woman eating a peach in a mountain stream?

3. The body text in this ad tells a story. What kind of husband-wife dynamic is implied by this story? To what extent do you find similarities

between the implied gender roles in this ad and those in the 1947 Ford ad ("Ford's out Front from a Woman's Angle," page 715)? To what extent do you find differences, ones that may be attributable to the 20 years between the two ads?

Jeep vehicle, 2003 (p. 721)

1. Explain the meaning of the ad's headline.
2. Discuss the graphic, in terms of the ad's headline. Consider the significance of the viewing angle.

Volvo, 1990s (pp. 722–723)

1. What cultural phenomenon is being addressed in the graphic and the headline of this ad? To what extent do you believe that associating Volvo with this phenomenon is an effective way to market this particular automobile?
2. What is the connection between the three apparently ill-matched couples in the illustration and the ad's basic message and appeal?
3. How is humor used to enhance the ad's (and the message's) appeal? That is, how are the couples in the illustration presented as incongruous (if happy)?

FOOD, CLEANSERS, BEAUTY PRODUCTS, AND OTHER

Campbell's, 1945 (p. 724)

1. What kind of appeal is being made in the first two sentences of the body text? How does the graphic in the top half of the ad support this appeal?
2. What kind of marketing strategy is behind the menu in the lower-right portion of the ad?

Coca-Cola, 1945 (p. 725)

1. This ad appeared shortly after the conclusion of World War II. How do the text and the graphics of the ad take advantage of the international mood at the time? Comment on the appearance and arrangement of the men portrayed in the ad.
2. Compare the strategy of this Coca-Cola ad (text and graphics) with that of the 1950s Ballantine ad (page 703).

National Dairy Products Corporation, 1947 (p. 726)

1. How does the couple pictured in the ad illustrate gender expectations of the period? Comment on the dress, postures, and expressions of the models.
2. What, exactly is this ad *selling?* (It is presented more as a news-magazine article than as a conventional advertisement.) How is the

appeal tied to contemporary developments by "scientists" and their "research," particularly as these relate to "the new wives of 1947"?

3. What does the text of this ad imply about the situation of young married couples in postwar households?

Bon Ami, 1947 (p. 727)

1. How do the text and graphics of this ad illustrate a bygone cultural attitude toward gender roles? Notice, in particular, the dress, postures, and expressions of the women pictured, as well as the style of the illustration. Focus also on the wording of the text.

2. In terms of Jib Fowles's categories, what kind of appeal is being made by the Bon Ami ad?

Trushay, 1947 (p. 728)

1. Retell the "story of Annie" in narrative form, in a paragraph. What does Annie's story tell us about gender relations in the 1940s? To what extent have gender relations changed on the particular issue covered by Annie's story?

2. Ads that resembled comic strips were not uncommon 60 years ago. Based on the impact made by this ad today, why do you think the comic strip format might have gone out of fashion?

3. Suppose you are a contemporary copywriter for a hand lotion product. Develop some ideas for an ad or a campaign that might be effective for today's potential customers.

Jergens Lotion, 1954 (p. 729)

1. Compare and contrast the appeals and the strategies of this Jergens Lotion ad and the Trushay ad preceding it. Are the ads intended to appeal to the same target audiences? To what extent are the psychological appeals of the two ads similar? Compare the illustrations of the two ads. How do they differ in basic strategy?

2. The model in the Jergens Lotion ad is immaculately dressed and groomed, and she is sitting among stacks of fine china (as opposed to everyday dishware). What do you think is the marketing strategy behind these graphic choices?

Disney Hats, 1954 (p. 730)

1. Point out specific language in the headline and body that helps create the basic appeal of this ad for Disney hats. How does the illustration— both the man in the hat and the background against which he is posed—reinforce this appeal?

2. Comment on how the connotations and significance of men's headwear have changed—and not changed—over the years or how they help support the appeal of the product advertised. (Notice, for example, the

hat-wearing models in the 1947 Camels ad, the 1954 Cadillac ad, the 1970s Marlboro ad, and the 1992 Camel Lights ad.)

Bell Telephone, 1956 (p. 731)

1. Discuss the attitude toward gender roles implicit in the 1956 Bell ad. How do the graphics, the headline, and the body text reinforce this attitude? What is the significance of the quotation marks around "office" in the final sentence of the third paragraph?

2. Notice that the woman at the desk seems a lot more comfortable and at ease than the man holding the crying baby and the dishes. What does this fact tell us about the attitudes toward gender roles of those who created this ad?

Bell Telephone, 1974 (p. 732)

1. Compare and contrast the 1956 Bell ad with the 1974 Bell ad, in terms of their attitudes toward gender roles. How do the text and graphics reinforce the essential differences?

2. The 1956 Bell ad pictures a woman at a desk (a white-collar job); the 1974 ad pictures a woman working at a telephone pole (a blue-collar job). Would the 1974 ad have the same impact if "Alana MacFarlane" had, like her 1956 counterpart, been pictured at a desk?

3. Like the 1954 Cadillac ad (pages 716–717) the 1974 Bell ad seems more of a public service announcement than a conventional advertisement. Compare and contrast these ads in terms of their messages to-readers.

American Airlines, 1968 (p. 733)

1. Discuss the mixed messages (in terms of appeal) being transmitted by the American Airlines ad. To what extent do you think the apparently conflicting appeals make for an effective ad?

2. Comment on the dress, pose, and expression of the model in the ad, which appeared in *Ebony* magazine. How do these create a different impact than would an illustration, say, of a flight attendant serving a drink or giving a pillow to an airline passenger?

Charlie, 1988 (p. 734)

1. Notice the woman's outfit, as well as her briefcase, in the Charlie ad. How is the appearance of this woman as significant as the appearance of the woman in the Smirnoff Vodka ad (page 709) for the ad's basic message?

2. The Charlie ad and the 1974 Bell ad (page 732) are as different as can be imagined from the Trushay ad. Yet, the Bell and the Charlie ads make quite different appeals. Explain. Consider, for example, how a

woman—or a man—of the late 1940s might respond to the Bell ad, on the one hand, and the Charlie ad, on the other.

Shineaway 17 Lotion, 1980s (p. 735)

1. Account for the postures of the man and the woman, in terms of the essential message and appeal of this ad.
2. Both this and the preceding Charlie ad rely to some extent on sex appeal. Compare and contrast other aspects of these two ads.

Soloflex, 1985 (p. 736)

1. How does the illustration in this ad reinforce the basic appeal of the headline?
2. Ads are frequently criticized for the incongruity between illustration and product being advertised—for example, a scantily clad woman posed provocatively in front of a pickup truck. To what extent does the Soloflex ad present an appropriate fit between graphic and product advertised?

Ajax, 1990s (p. 737)

1. Why do you suppose the model's head is not pictured?
2. How does this ad play off shifting cultural attitudes toward gender roles? Would the ad be more objectionable if it pictured a female in a comparable state of undress?
3. Compare and contrast this ad to earlier ads for cleaners and cleansing lotions, such as Bon Ami and Jergens Lotion.

SYNTHESIS ACTIVITIES

1. Select one *category* of advertisements (cigarettes, alcohol, etc.) represented in the ad portfolio. Compare and contrast the types of appeals underlying these ads, as discussed by Fowles. To what extent do you notice significant shifts of appeal from the 1940s to the present? Which types of appeal seem to you most effective with particular product categories? Is it more likely, for example, that people will buy cigarettes because they want to feel autonomous or because the cigarettes will make them more attractive to the opposite sex?

2. Select a series of ads in different product categories that all appear to rely on the same primary appeal—perhaps the appeal to sex or the appeal to affiliation. Compare and contrast the overall strategies of these ads. Draw upon Fowles and other authors represented in this chapter to develop your ideas. To what extent do your analyses support arguments often made by social critics (and advertising people) that what people are really buying is the image, rather than the product?

3. Discuss how a selection of ads reveals shifting cultural attitudes over the past six decades toward either (a) gender relations; (b) romance between men and women; (c) smoking; (d) automobiles. In the case of (a) or (b) above, the ads don't have to be for the same category of product. In terms of their underlying appeal, in terms of the implicit or explicit messages embodied both in the text and the graphics, how and to what extent do the ads reveal that attitudes of the target audiences have changed over the years?

4. Select a TV commercial or a TV ad campaign (for example, for Sprint phone service) and analyze the commercial(s) in terms of Fowles's categories, as well as the discussions of some of the authors in this chapter. To what extent do the principles discussed by these authors apply to broadcast, as well as to print ads? What are the special requirements of TV advertising?

5. Find a small group of ads that rely upon little or no body copy—just a graphic, perhaps a headline, and the product name. What common features underlie the marketing strategies of such ads? What kinds of appeals do they make? How do their graphic aspects compare? What makes the need for text superfluous?

6. As indicated in the introduction to this chapter, social critics have charged advertising with numerous offenses: "It fosters material-ism, it psychologically manipulates people to buy things they don't need, it perpetuates gender and racial stereotypes (particularly in its illustrations), it is deceptive, it is offensive, it debases the lan-guage." To what extent do some of the advertisements presented in the ad portfolio (and perhaps others of your own choosing) demon-strate the truth of one or more of these charges? In developing your response, draw upon Bovée and Arens as well as some of the ads in the portfolio (or elsewhere).

7. Read the textual content (headlines and body text) of several ads *without* paying attention (if possible) to the graphics. Compare the effectiveness of the headline and body text by themselves with the effectiveness of the ads, *including* the graphic elements. Focusing on a group of related ads (related by product category, by appeal, by decade, etc.), devise an explanation of how graphics work to effectively communicate the appeal and meaning of the products advertised.

8. Many ads employ humor—in the graphics, in the body copy, or both—to sell a product. Examine a group of advertisements that rely on humor to make their appeal and explain how they work. For example, do they play off an incongruity between one element of the ad and another (such as between the headline and the graphic), or between one element of the ad (or the basic message of the ad) and what we know or assume to be the case in the "real world"? Do they employ wordplay or irony? Do they picture people doing funny things (funny because inappropriate or unreal-

istic)? What appeal underlines the humor? Aggression? Sex? Nurturing? Based on your examination and analyses, what appear to be some of the more effective ways of employing humor?

9. Think of a new product that you have just invented. This product, in your opinion, will revolutionize the world of (fill in the blank). Devise an advertisement to announce this product to the world. Consider (or reject) using a celebrity to help sell your product. Select the basic appeal of your product (see Fowles). Then, applying concepts and principles discussed by other authors in this chapter, write the headline, subhead, and body copy for the product. Sketch out (or at least describe) the graphic that will accompany the text. Show your proposed ad to one or more of your classmates, get reactions, and then revise the ad, taking into account your market feedback.

10. Imagine that you own a small business—perhaps an independent coffee shop (not Starbucks, Peet's, or Coffee Bean), a videogame company, or a pedicab service that conveys tourists around a chic beach town. Devise an ad that announces your services and extols its benefits. Apply the principles discussed by Fowles and other writers in this chapter.

11. Write a parody ad—one that would never ordinarily be written— applying the selling principles discussed by Fowles and other authors in this chapter. For example, imagine you are the manager of the Globe Theatre in Elizabethan England and want to sell season tickets to this season's plays, including a couple of new tragedies by your playwright-in-residence, Will Shakespeare. Or imagine that you are trying to sell Remington typewriters in the age of computers (no software glitches!). Or—as long as people are selling bottled water—you have found a way to package and sell air. Advertisers can reportedly sell anything with the right message. Give it your best shot.

12. Based on the reading you have done in this chapter, discuss the extent to which you believe advertisements create needs in consumers, reflect existing needs, or some combination of both. In developing your paper, draw on both particular advertisements and on the more theoretical overviews of advertising developed in the chapter.

13. Select one advertisement and conduct two analyses of it, using two different analytical principles: perhaps one from Fowles's list of 15 emotional appeals and one from Cohen's principles of effective layout. Having conducted your analyses and developed your insights, compare and contrast the strengths and weaknesses of the analytical principles you've employed. Conclude more broadly with a discussion of how a single analytical principle can close down, as well as open up, understanding of an object under study.

14. As you have seen, advertisements change over time, both across product categories and within categories. And yet the advertisements remain a constant, their presence built on the assumption that consumers can be swayed both overtly and covertly in making purchasing decisions. In a paper drawing on the selections in this chapter, develop a theory on why ads change over time. Is it because people's needs have changed and, therefore, new ads are required? (Do the older ads appeal to the same needs as newer ads?) In developing your discussion, you might track the changes over time in one product category.

RESEARCH ACTIVITIES

1. Drawing upon contemporary magazines (or magazines from a given period), select a set of advertisements in a particular product category. Analyze these advertisements according to Fowles's categories, and assess their effectiveness in terms of the discussions of other authors in this chapter.

2. Select a particular product that has been selling for at least 25 years (e.g., Bayer aspirin, Tide detergent, IBM computers, Oldsmobile—as in "This is not your father's Oldsmobile") and trace the history of print advertising for this product over the years. To what extent has the advertising changed over the years? To what extent has the essential sales appeal remained the same? In addition to examining the ads themselves, you may want to research the company and its marketing practices. You will find two business databases particularly useful: ABI/INFORM and the academic version of LexisNexis.

3. One of the landmark campaigns in American advertising was Doyle, Dane, Bernbach's series of ads for the Volkswagen Beetle in the 1960s. In effect a rebellion against standard auto advertising, the VW ads' Unique Selling Proposition was that ugly is beautiful—an appeal that was overwhelmingly successful. Research the VW ad campaign for this period, setting it in the context of the agency's overall marketing strategy.

4. Among the great marketing debacles of recent decades was Coca-Cola's development in 1985 of a new formula for its soft drink that (at least temporarily) replaced the much-beloved old formula. Research this major development in soft drink history, focusing on the marketing of New Coke and the attempt of the Atlanta-based Coca-Coca company to deal with the public reception of its new product.

5. Advertising agencies are hired not only by manufacturers and by service industries; they are also hired by political candidates. In fact, one of the common complaints about American politics is that

candidates for public office are marketed just as if they were bars of soap. Select a particular presidential or gubernatorial election and research the print and broadcast advertising used by the rival candidates. You may want to examine the ads not only of the candidates of the major parties but also the candidates of the smaller parties, such as the Green and the Libertarian parties. How do the appeals and strategies used by product ads compare and contrast with those used in ads for political candidates?

6. Public service ads comprise another major category of advertising (in addition to product and service advertising and political advertising). Such ads have been used to recruit people to military service, to get citizens to buy war bonds, to contribute to charitable causes, to get people to support or oppose strikes, to persuade people to stop using (or not to start using) drugs, to prevent drunk driving, etc. Locate a group of public service ads, describe them, and assess their effectiveness. Draw upon Fowles, Bovée et al., and Cohen in developing your conclusions.

7. Research advertising in American magazines and newspapers before World War II. Focus on a limited number of product lines— for example, soft drinks, soap and beauty products, health-related products. What kind of differences do you see between ads in the first part of the twentieth century and more recent or contemporary advertising for the same types of products? In general, how have the predominant types of appeal used to sell products in the past changed (if they have) with the times? How are the graphics of early ads different from preferred graphics today? How has the body copy changed? (Hint: You may want to be on the alert for ads that make primarily negative appeals—i.e., what may happen to you if you don't use the product advertised.)

14 Has the Jury Reached a Verdict?

WILLIAM ROPER: So now you'd give the Devil benefit of law!

MORE: Yes. What would you do? Cut a great road through the law to get
after the Devil?

ROPER: I'd cut down every law in England to do that!

MORE: Oh? And when the last law was down, and the Devil turned round on
you—where would you hide, Roper, the laws all being flat? This country's
planted thick with laws from coast to coast—man's laws, not God's—and if
you cut them down—and you're just the man to do it—d'you really think
you could stand upright in the winds that would blow then? [*Quietly.*] Yes,
I'd give the Devil benefit of law, for my own safety's sake.

—Robert Bolt, *A Man for All Seasons*

Robert Bolt's hero Thomas More in *A Man for All Seasons* offers one way of looking
at the law, but clearly, many people take a different view of the legal profession. One
of Shakespeare's characters declares, "The first thing we do, let's kill all the lawyers"
(*Henry VI*, Pt II). Never mind that while playing off the public's perennial resentment
of lawyers, Shakespeare intended this line as a sardonic commentary on mob mentality. Still, everyone loves a good lawyer joke. ("Why didn't the shark eat the lawyer
who fell out of his boat? Professional courtesy.") Of course, in these litigious times,
the same people who tell lawyer jokes hurry to get their own after they slip on the
ice in their neighbor's driveway or when they're arrested on a drunk driving charge.

In Bolt's play, Thomas More views the law as civilized society's first line of defense
against chaos and anarchy. Without the law, he argues, we would have no protection against "the winds that would blow" in a lawless society. But even if we don't
accept this exalted view of the law, it's certainly true that all of us, at some points in
our lives, will have dealings with the law (not necessarily as a defendant, we hasten

to add), and that as citizens of society, most of us rely upon the law to protect us against those who would violate our rights and to impose damages upon those who have injured us. (Those who don't rely on the law sometimes rely instead on their own private arsenals to repel invaders and predators.)

If the average citizen is not the plaintiff or the defendant in a court case, then her or his most common direct experience with the law may be as a juror. Chosen at random from a cross section of the population, jurors may be called upon to render a verdict in a civil case (a case of product liability, for example, or negligence, or libel) or in a criminal case (such as robbery or murder). After the lawyers on both sides have presented their witnesses and their evidence, after they have made their arguments and rebutted their opponents, and after the judge has explained the law to the jury in language they can understand, it falls to the jury to apply the law to the facts of the particular case. They must decide whether or not a law has been violated, and if it has, the price the defendant must pay—perhaps a fine, perhaps a jail term, perhaps even the forfeiture of his or her life.

Underlying this chapter is the assumption that you are a jury member (or perhaps a judge) in a particular case. You will be presented with the facts of the case. You will also be presented with the relevant law. It will be your task to study the issues, to render a verdict either for the plaintiff (i.e., the person bringing the lawsuit) or for the defendant (the target of the lawsuit), and—most importantly, for our purposes—to explain your reasoning. Don't worry about becoming tangled in the thickets of the law (and some of these thickets are very dense indeed). We will assume no previous legal knowledge, and for each case we will present enough facts and enough statements about the law to enable you to make an educated judgment, just as if you were a member of a jury.

Don't worry, either, about making the "right" choice. The most important thing is not that you come out on the correct side or even the side that actually prevailed in the end. (Keep in mind that through the appeals process, a higher court can reverse the ruling of a lower court—saying, in effect, that the lower court was wrong.) What is important is that you carefully analyze the case, that you go through the reasoning process systematically and logically, in a manner consistent with the facts. This chapter will therefore provide you with additional opportunities to practice the analysis skills you learned in Chapter 6 of this text.

In one sense, this chapter previews a particular situation in which you might one day find yourself—fulfilling your civic duty as a juror in an actual case. More generally, it will provide you with some interesting cases through which you can practice a very fundamental intellectual task in the academic and professional worlds: the task of applying a general rule or principle to a particular case or circumstance. Obviously, this process of analysis (described in Chapter 6) doesn't happen only in law. As a student in a sociology course, for example, you might show how some principles relating to the ways that individuals obey authority apply in particular cases (for example, the suicides in the Heaven's Gate cult) and even allow you to make certain broad predictions about behavior. As a film student, you might show how the general features of the typical *film noir* operate in particular films such as *The Big Sleep* or *A Touch of Evil*. As a composition student, you may find yourself applying a set of "basic appeals" to a set of advertisements published over the last 60 years (Chapter 13).

Besides exercising your intellectual faculties, you'll see that it's often fascinating to plunge into legal battles. After all, legal cases are, at heart, conflicts, and conflicts are inherently interesting. That's why we like to read books or watch TV shows or movies that are set in the courtroom.

We begin our chapter with "Incident at the Airport," a hypothetical case involving a charge of battery by an old man against a young woman. Next, in "IRAC: How to Argue Your Case," Leonard Tourney and Gina Genova describe the process of developing and organizing legal arguments, focusing particularly on the important IRAC (issue, rule, application, conclusion) technique as it might be applied to the "Incident at the Airport" case.

The rest of the chapter focuses on cases in five broad legal areas: *emotional distress, students' freedom of speech, child custody, homicide,* and *parental responsibility for the destructive acts of their children.* In each of these sections, we begin with an article from a popular periodical that discusses the particular subject in question and may focus on one or more relevant cases. Then we present two or more additional cases, along with the applicable rules, and ask you, the reader—in effect, a jury member—to render fair verdicts, based on the law.

Plaintiffs in emotional distress cases charge that defendants have engaged in "outrageous conduct" that has caused "mental distress, mental suffering, or mental anguish." For example, one plaintiff, whose dog has just died, sues the animal hospital after she opens the casket and finds a cat. In another case, a General Motors employee with a speech impediment sues his employer because his boss has "maliciously and cruelly ridiculed" him.

The freedom of speech cases focus on students who sue their school districts for restricting their First Amendment rights. In one case, a student is disciplined for making an allegedly obscene election speech. In the other, a principal censors a story about student pregnancy slated for publication in the school newspaper.

The child custody cases focus on the "best interest" of the children of divorced parents, as well as on the rights of the parents themselves. In one case, the divorced father disapproves of the living conditions of his children, who reside with his ex-wife and her lover, and sues to get custody. In another case, a noncustodial father sues to force his ex-wife and her child to move back to the county where he lives and works so as not to disrupt his relationship with his son.

The two homicide cases focus on the particular issue of the responsibility of teenagers who remove stop signs, allegedly causing a traffic fatality soon afterward. Two cases, 20 years apart, one in Florida, the other in Utah, feature remarkably similar circumstances, resulting in the teenagers involved being charged with manslaughter.

The final section of the chapter focuses on the responsibility of parents whose children commit destructive acts. In one case, the plaintiff sues the father of a 14-year-old boy who drove away on his unsecured motorcycle and subsequently collided with a young child, causing significant injury. In another case, a rape victim sues the parents of the rapist, a teenager with a history of drug problems and antisocial behavior.

We conclude with a legal glossary that defines key terms used in the chapter.

Each selection of the chapter consists of two key elements. The first element presents the *facts of the case*, as written either by a reporter or by the panel of appeals court judges who ruled upon the case. All of the cases you will read in this chapter are cases that have been appealed by either the plaintiff or the defendant to an appeals court after the original jury verdict. The second element presents the *statements of the law*, statements that you will apply to the facts of the case, just as if you were following the judge's instructions. In some selections, these statements consist of the kinds of instructions that a judge would give to a jury in such cases. In others, they will be the actual statutes that may or may not have been violated. You may also read excerpts from case law—judicial opinions from previous cases dealing with similar issues that may have bearing upon the case you are currently considering.

What you will not find, however, as you consider these cases, is the ultimate outcome. If you know the outcome in advance, you are likely to be unduly swayed in your reasoning, attempting to bring it in line with the arguments of the side that prevailed. As we suggested earlier, which side won is less important for our purposes than the process of logically applying general principles to specific cases. Nevertheless, if you *must* know which side won, ask your instructor; she or he will be able to consult the *Instructor's Manual*.

Occasionally, however, it will be difficult or even impossible to find out which side ultimately won. That's because some cases are sent back by the appeals court to the trial court, and most trial court cases are not published—though photocopied transcripts are available (for a hefty fee) from the clerk of the court—and the more newsworthy cases are covered by reporters. Also, a good many civil cases, after going up and down through the appeals process, are ultimately settled out of court—and frequently, the terms of the settlement are not publicly available.

This chapter offers considerable opportunities for group work. After all, work on a jury is a collective enterprise, and before a jury arrives at a verdict, unanimous or otherwise, its individual members must engage in a good deal of discussion, perhaps even argument. In some cases, your papers may be written collectively by the group; but even when individually written, they could reflect the views of more than one viewpoint. In fact, as you will see in the Tourney and Genova selection, the IRAC format, used widely in legal writing, should include a consideration and a rebuttal of opposing arguments.

A NOTE ON THE AMERICAN LEGAL SYSTEM

According to law professor David Hricik, it is important to indicate what the law is *not*: "Laws are not the same," he emphasizes, "as personal or individual morality." For example, many find the legal practice of abortion to be immoral, just as many find the widely illegal practice of assisted suicide to be morally justified, under certain circumstances. Hricik continues:

> [T]he law is a set of "rules" which create "duties," the breaking of
> which may result in "liability" [or criminal prosecution], usually in the
> form of money damages [or prison terms]. Put at its simplest, "the
> law" is an expression of the social policy that people have a duty to
> follow the rules, and those who don't will incur liability for any harm
> they cause.*

The cases you will consider in this chapter fall into one of two broad categories: *civil* cases and *criminal* cases. Civil cases are essentially lawsuits in
which one party—the *plaintiff*—claims that he or she has been injured in some
way because the defendant has breached his or her legal duty. Examples of
civil offenses include assault, battery, infliction of emotional distress, trespass,
negligence, invasion of privacy, defamation, violation of civil rights, fraud,
breach of contract, and wrongful death. Verdicts in civil cases are one of two
kinds: *liable* or *not liable*. As indicated above, defendants who are found liable
in civil cases often have to pay monetary damages to the plaintiff.

In criminal cases (in our chapter, the homicide cases), the plaintiff is the
state, or "the people." Examples of criminal offenses include burglary, robbery, extortion, rape, arson, kidnapping, and murder. Verdicts in criminal
cases are generally one of two kinds: *guilty* or *not guilty*. Defendants found
guilty in criminal cases may have to pay a fine, go to prison, or in extreme
cases (generally involving murder), be put to death.

The American legal system draws upon two main sources of law: *statutes*
passed by legislatures (Congress, state legislatures, city councils, etc.) and *case
law*. Case law is the sum total of decisions written by judges of federal and
state appeals courts that are used as precedent for current cases. In many
areas of law, case law is considerably more important (and certainly more
voluminous) than statutory law. So in arguing, for example, whether or not a
particular defendant is liable for causing emotional distress, lawyers will turn
not to the "rule book" (or statutes) on emotional distress—since there is no
legislation on emotional distress—but rather to one or more previously decided cases—*precedents*—that exhibit factual elements close to the one they are
trying. If the precedent case resulted in a verdict against the defendant, the
plaintiff's lawyer will likely argue the *similarities* of the facts between the
precedent case and the current case. If, on the other hand, the precedent case
resulted in a verdict for the defendant, the plaintiff's lawyer will likely argue
the essential *differences* of the facts between the two cases.

The losing party in civil and criminal cases may appeal the verdict to a
higher court (except that the state may not appeal a verdict of "not guilty"
in a criminal case). However, they must have some grounds for appeal, other
than that they disagree with the verdict. Their lawyers usually claim that the
trial judge has made one or more legal errors, such as improperly overruling their objection during trial or improperly refusing to allow the introduction of crucial testimony or evidence that would have helped their cases. If
the request for appeal is granted (and most applications for appeal are

---

* David Hricik. *Law School Basics: A Preview of Law School and Legal Reasoning.* Los Angeles: Nova
Press, 2000. 25, 26.

refused), then the case is heard before the appropriate state or federal appellate court. Appellate judges do not hear additional testimony from witnesses or gather additional evidence. The appeals court has none of the traditional
"courtroom drama" of the trial court. The judges on the court render their
judgment on the basis of briefs and oral arguments by the attorneys for the
plaintiff(s) and the defendant(s), and of course the transcript of the trial itself.
The appellate court decision may itself be appealed to the supreme court of
the state or, in federal cases, to the U.S. Supreme Court.

Appellate court rulings are published in legal journals called *reporters*.
These reporters—available in legal libraries and in online legal databases,
such as LexisNexis—are the source of many of the case descriptions and case
law found in this chapter.

A Note on Synthesis Activities

Because of the special nature of legal reasoning, we include synthesis activities, where appropriate, as part of the Discussion and Writing Suggestions following some of the grouped case selections, rather than at the end of the
chapter.

Lawyers synthesize cases as a matter of course, but only when they are
closely related, in order to point out legal precedents. We do include some
closely related cases in this chapter (for example, those involving the pulled
stop signs); but for the most part, the cases we have selected are too factual-
ly different to be usefully synthesized.

Incident at the Airport
Leonard Tourney

*We begin not with an actual case but a "hypothetical." As you read the following set of
"facts," imagine that you are a member of a jury hearing testimony and arguments in the
case of Sommers v. St. John. After reading the narrative, you will be asked to consider the
case, applying the rules governing battery to the relevant facts, deciding upon a verdict, and
providing reasons for your verdict.*

*Leonard Tourney teaches legal writing at the University of California, Santa Barbara. He
has authored several historical mystery novels, including* The Players' Boy is Dead *(1980),*
The Bartholomew Fair Murders *(1986),* Old Saxon Blood *(1988), and* Time's Fool *(2004).*

1   Lisa St. John arrived at Los Angeles International Airport late in the afternoon
after a grueling flight from London via New York and Chicago. She was
exhausted and irritable, ready to chuck her job as a computer consultant for
international corporations. Her mood did not improve when she found that
Frank Mason, her fiancé, was not waiting to pick her us as he had promised. She
had long suspected Frank of being a closet flake just waiting to reveal himself to
her after he and Lisa were married and only an expensive divorce would undo

the damage. The upside of his failure to show was that it gave Lisa cause to break things off. While she waited, she steamed and rehearsed just how she would tell him to marry someone else.

2   The plane had arrived at 4. Frank didn't appear until nearly 7. Lisa had avoided eating so that her blood sugar level would drop. She wanted to feel awful, look awful. Frank deserved what he got: a whining, inconsolable wreck. Then she saw him, and her cup of wrath overflowed. Frank was smiling, carrying a dozen roses and a box that looked very much like Lisa's favorite chocolates. He threw his arms open wide to greet her and in so doing hit Eben Sommers, a 90 year old man waiting to get a plane to Detroit. The blow broke Mr. Sommers' glasses and his nose.

3   "You moron, why don't you watch what you're doing?" Lisa cried, as Frank struggled with the roses, candy, and Mr. Sommers, whom he was trying to help up off the floor. The old man had reminded her of her grandfather who had died a month earlier. Enraged, Lisa kicked at Frank but missed, hitting Mr. Sommers in the leg, breaking his tibia. Mr. Sommers cried out in agony. His cries brought Albert Fenstermocker, a German tourist, to his aid. Fenstermocker, thinking Lisa and Frank were assaulting the old man, began to beat Frank over the head with his cane. Seeing her fiancé assaulted by a perfect stranger, Lisa's feelings changed. She threw herself at Fenstermocker, knocking him to the ground.

Discussion and Writing Suggestion

Eben Sommers sued Lisa St. John for battery. You are a member of the jury that has just heard testimony and considered evidence about the facts of the case, as summarized above. At the conclusion of the trial, the judge gives the jury instructions, which include the following key definitions. Based on these instructions, do you conclude that Lisa is liable to Eben Sommers for battery to Eben Sommers? According to the law, do her actions meet the legal definition of battery?

1. **Battery.**   Battery is a harmful or offensive touching of another that is intentional, unconsented, and unprivileged.

2. **Transfer of Intent.**   In tort law [the law covering the wrongs committed by individuals against one another], if A, intending to strike B, misses B and hits C instead, the intent to strike B is transferred and supplies the necessary intent for the tort against C.

3. **Self-Defense Privilege.**   The right to protect oneself or another from unlawful attack, the law of self-defense justifies an act done in reasonable belief of immediate danger, with use of reasonable force in the absence of more peaceful alternatives.

IRAC: How to Argue Your Case
Leonard Tourney and
Gina Genova

What differentiates legal writing—good legal writing—from writing on other subjects is not such legalistic phrases as "aforesaid," "wherein," "prima facie," or "cease and desist." It is, rather, the systematic application of general rules to specific facts for the purpose of arriving at reasonable, persuasive conclusions. An attorney writing a legal memorandum to her colleagues, or a motion to a judge, or presenting a closing argument to a jury is applying the law to the particular set of circumstances constituting the case at hand. She or he may have an opinion as to the guilt or innocence of the defendant (if the case at hand is a criminal one). But these opinions must be subordinate to the logical conclusions that follow from the careful application of rules to facts.

The selections that follow demonstrate this process of application of rule to fact. We present a hypothetical case—a particular set of facts, only some of which are legally relevant. We then offer a systematic analysis, in outline form, of these facts, based on the applicable laws. Next, we present a legal essay on the case based on our analysis. This example should serve as a useful model for much of your own writing in the subsequent cases presented in this chapter.

Before presenting our case, we should introduce IRAC, a method of presenting arguments on legal cases that has been successfully used by generations of law students. IRAC is an acronym created from the following words:

> ***I**ssue*
> ***R**ule*
> ***A**nalysis (or **A**pplication)*
> ***C**onclusion*

Let's define each of these terms:

*The **Issue** is the central question around which the case turns. It is generally couched in the following form: "Is a defendant who [indicate specifically what the defendant did] guilty of (in a criminal case) or liable for (in a civil case, or lawsuit) [the specific crime/legal wrongdoing (tort) charged]?" For example, "Is the defendant, who was recorded by a police officer as traveling 80 mph in a 55 mph zone, guilty of speeding?" This section is generally one sentence long. (See "A Short Guide to Writing Effective Issue Statements," pages 764–765.)*

*The **Rule** is the primary law (or set of laws) that apply in this case. It is quoted verbatim (and placed within quotation marks) because the letter of the law is crucial. This rule may be a statutory law (such as a section of the criminal code, like arson) or it may be an accepted legal principle based on precedent. This section is frequently one sentence long. Note: Secondary rules—those that define or clarify certain elements or terms of the primary rule (such as "privileged" or "intent")—may also apply to the case. These secondary rules are introduced in the appropriate places in the next section, the analysis.*

*The **Analysis**, the longest section of the essay, is a systematic application of components—or elements of the primary and secondary rules—to those facts of the case that are legally relevant. For example, robbery is defined in the California Penal Code (section 211) as "the felonious taking of personal property in the possession of another, from his person or immediate presence, and against his will, and accomplished by means of force or fear." The separately underlined phrases are individual elements of robbery, and each element* *must be satisfied for the defendant to be found guilty of robbery. In the case of phrases joined by "or" (as in "force or fear"), only one of the two elements need be satisfied.*

In the analysis, it is frequently necessary to bring in additional legal principles that provide definitions or clarifications of key terms in the primary rule. These secondary rules should also be quoted verbatim. For example, the self-defense privilege is a secondary rule that clarifies the conditions under which an attack against another may be legally justified, or "privileged." By "facts of the case that are legally relevant" (in the paragraph above), we mean those facts that can be associated with one or more elements of the rule. For example, the fact that the defendant used a gun to inspire fear would be legally relevant. The fact that the defendant was in a bad mood because he had just been fired from his job is legally irrelevant. In general, it is a good idea to use climactic order in developing your analysis. That is, first dispose of those elements about which there is likely to be little dispute or about which there is little question as to whether they have been satisfied. Then, move on to the elements that require more extended discussion.

It is a good idea to conclude each section of the analysis by indicating in some manner that a particular element of the rule has or has not been satisfied. However, defer the overall conclusion (the guilt or innocence or liability or nonliability of the defendant) for the very end of the essay. Do not conclude guilt or liability prematurely, before you have analyzed all the applicable facts.

Also, do not merely summarize facts in this section, as if they speak for themselves. Analyze them by applying rule to fact.

The **Conclusion** *is the answer to the question that is posed in the issue statement. It is generally no more than a few sentences (and sometimes just one sentence) long.*

To see how this process works, read the selections that follow. First we present an analysis of the "Incident at the Airport" case in outline format, with a systematic application of each element of the rule (in this case, the rule for battery) to the relevant facts of the case. The analysis was written by Gina Genova, who also teaches legal writing at U.C., Santa Barbara, and who practices law in that city. Next, we present a model legal essay based on Genova's analysis, written by Leonard Tourney. Tourney's essay is followed by his "Short Guide to Writing Effective Issue Statements." Finally, we present three problematic model essays (written by Tourney) based on the "Incident at the Airport" scenario. You are invited to discover and discuss the problems.

Pre-Writing Analysis of "Incident at the Airport"
Gina Genova

Issue: Does defendant who inadvertently kicked plaintiff while intending to kick a third party who had accidentally struck the plaintiff commit a battery?

A. *Did Lisa batter Mr. Sommers?*
   1. **Battery** is a <u>harmful OR offensive touching of another</u> that is <u>intentional, unconsented</u> and <u>unprivileged.</u>
      a. *Harmful or offensive*—Lisa kicked Mr. Sommers so hard it broke his tibia and caused him to fall to the ground, his cries of pain so loud they brought Albert Fenstermocker to the scene. Thus, the blow was harmful to another, Mr. S. Because this element can be either harmful OR offensive and we have proven harm, no discussion of offense needs to be made. However, his age makes this act offensive to our

cultural sensibilities as well as to Mr. S personally.

b. *Touching*—Lisa's foot touched Mr. S's tibia, satisfying this element.

c. *Intentional*—After a grueling flight that left her exhausted and irritable, Lisa intentionally missed a meal and "steamed" herself into an "inconsolable wreck" because Frank was late. She let herself get more angered by Frank's flowers and chocolate, and his mishap with Mr. S who reminded her of her recently deceased grandfather. Lisa could have stopped her mounting ire at any of these points or even at her verbal abuse but she went further. Showing a clear intent to welcome her aggravated mental state, unwilling or unable to restrain her rage, she used it to aim a kick at the object of her wrath, Frank. Unfortunately for Mr. S's tibia, her aim was off and her foot found it instead. By all factual accounts, Lisa did not intend to hit Mr. S. This element has not been met.

Is there a rule that allows for this element to be circumvented? Yes.

Transfer of Intent. In tort law, if <u>A, intending to strike B, misses B</u> and <u>strikes C instead</u>, the <u>intent to strike B is transferred</u> and supplies the <u>requisite intent for the tort against C.</u>

1. For this rule to apply, we must decide whether Lisa <u>intended</u> to harm another when she inadvertently struck Mr. S.

2. As analyzed above, Lisa intended to hit Frank when she missed and struck Mr. S instead. She purposely worked herself into a fit and was so "enraged" by Frank that she aimed to kick him. At any time before the kick she could have stopped herself. Frank did arrive with flowers and candy, and a reasonable person might assume he got the pickup time wrong. He also held his arms out to hug her and accidentally hit Mr. S in the nose. She acknowledges this accident with her statement "You moron, why don't you watch what you're doing," implying clumsiness not malice. Instead, she chose to disregard these facts, manifesting clear intent to harm Frank.

3. Because Lisa intended to harm Frank, that intent is transferred to Mr. S, the actual but unintended victim.

d. *Unconsented*—There is no evidence that Mr. S, a total stranger to Lisa and only in the airport to board a flight, asked or allowed Lisa to strike him.

e. *Unprivileged*—There is no evidence that a relational privilege exists between the two strangers: Mr. S, an innocent bystander embarking on a plane, and Lisa arriving on one. Mr. S had nothing to do with the argument between Lisa and Frank nor had he any apparent relationship or contact with either of them prior to this incident to create a privilege. There is, however, the possible applicability of the self-defense privilege—the right to <u>protect oneself</u> or another from <u>unlawful attack</u> and justifies an act done in <u>reasonable belief of immediate danger</u>, with the use of <u>reasonable force</u> in the <u>absence of more peaceful alternatives.</u>

1. *Protect oneself or another*—Lisa was not under attack but she could argue she was protecting another, Mr. S, from Frank.

2. *Unlawful attack*—Since battery is a crime, if Frank battered Mr. S, his actions would constitute an unlawful attack. Thus, we need to work through a quick battery IRAC: Frank hit Mr. S so hard it broke Mr. S's nose and glasses = offensive and harmful; the two were strangers with no apparent consent and no relationship to form a privilege = unconsented; Frank, however, threw his arms wide open to greet Lisa, not to hit Mr. S. The element of intent is missing and nothing in the facts invokes the transfer of intent rule to create liability for battery. We may argue then that this blow was pure accident and did not rise to the level of "unlawful" or an "attack."

3. *Belief of immediate danger*—Lisa's cry "you moron," etc. indicates that she knew Frank's actions were not intentional and she knew that she was not in any danger. It is also unreasonable for her to fear attack from her fiancé since there is no indication that Frank had been abusive to her in the past. Frank also had flowers and candy in his hands, making it difficult for him to attack anything. Finally, Frank, fully loaded with his gifts, "struggled" to help Mr. S up—clearly contradictory to the behavior of an aggressor. Based on all the above, Lisa could not have held any reasonable belief of immediate danger from Frank.

4. *Reasonable force*—Even if Lisa argues her belief of immediate danger, was the force she used commensurate with the threat posed? Frank's blow did break Mr. S's glasses and his nose. She responded with a kick so forceful that it broke Mr. S's tibia, a traditionally strong bone. But the elderly are known to break bones more easily than the rest of the population so, perhaps, her kick was less forceful than Frank's backhand. Also, since she was kicking at Frank and missed, perhaps some of the action's momentum and force was lost. One more thing—she is a female and although we don't know her stature, maybe Frank is a much larger person and thus a bigger threat to her and a feeble 90-year-old, warranting greater force. However, it is more likely that her force was unreasonable given any slight threat she felt from Frank's accidental blow to Mr. S.

5. *Absence of alternatives*—Lisa could easily have stopped at her verbal abuse of Frank. Or she could have merely grabbed his arms or pushed him back down. These alternatives were far more peaceful and readily available to her at the time since Frank was busy picking Mr. S up off the ground with his hands full of gifts for her.

6. Thus, Lisa cannot invoke the privilege of self-defense to avoid liability.

B. *Conclusion:* Lisa committed an unprivileged battery upon Mr. S. Mr. S suffered damages as a result: bodily harm of a broken leg and emotional distress. Mr. S is entitled to compensation for these damages, which are a direct result of the battery. Lisa is therefore civilly liable to Mr. S for the above damages in an amount to be proven at trial.

Model Student Analysis and Commentary:
"Incident at the Airport"
Leonard Tourney

ESSAY	DISCUSSION OF ESSAY
Does defendant who inadvertently kicked plaintiff while intending to kick a third party who had accidentally struck the plaintiff commit a battery?	The issue statement, in one sentence, meets the guidelines in the "Short Guide to Writing Effective Issue Statements" below.
According to the law, "battery is the harmful or offensive touching of another that is intentional, unconsented, and unprivileged."	The primary rule is quoted verbatim.
At LAX, Lisa St. John, defendant, kicked Eben Sommers, plaintiff, breaking his tibia. This constitutes harmful and, surely, offensive touching to which Sommers, a total stranger, did not consent. Ms. St. John was aiming at a third party, her fiancé, Frank Mason, who had accidentally struck Sommers moments before, breaking his nose and glasses.	Only the undisputed relevant facts relating to primary rule are summarized at the outset of the analysis: those dealing with "harmful" or "offensive touching" that is "unconsented."
Nevertheless, according to the rule of transfer of intent, "in tort law, if A, intending to strike B, misses B and hits C instead, the intent to strike B is transferred and supplies the necessary intent for the tort against C." Therefore, Ms. St. John's intent to kick Mason is transferred to the actual victim, Sommers.	Having disposed of the "easy calls," the writer takes up the matter of intent, an element about which there is some question since Lisa did not intend to hit Mr. S. The secondary rule of transfer of intent is quoted and then applied to the facts. Having applied this secondary rule, the writer can now conclude that the element of intent in the primary rule has been satisfied.
But can Ms. St. John invoke the self-defense privilege to shield her from liability? "The right to protect oneself from another from unlawful attack, the law of self-defense justifies an act done in reasonable belief of immediate danger, with use of reasonable force in the absence of more peaceful alternatives."	All that remains to discuss of the primary rule is whether the element of "unprivileged" has been met. To deal with this question, the writer brings in the secondary rule for the only applicable privilege in this case, the self-defense privilege.

Ms. St. John might argue that she kicked Mason to protect Sommers from further harm. But since her statement to Mason asking him to "watch what he was doing" suggests she knew that Mason's striking of Sommers was accidental and therefore not likely to be repeated since he was immediately aware of what he had done, she cannot be said to have acted to protect Sommers from further immediate danger as the law requires. Nor was the force she exerted reasonable. If she had really believed that Mason intended another blow against Sommers, she could have seized Mason's arms or flung herself at him, as she did later when she threw herself at a German tourist assaulting Mason. The kick was excessive force, reckless, given the proximity of bystanders, and more likely motivated by anger against Mason for his tardiness than a desire to protect Sommers.

The writer begins the discussion of privilege by offering a counter-argument that might be offered by the plaintiff: she did act in self-defense to protect plaintiff from harm. The writer then draws upon the facts to rebut this defense.

Having disposed of the question of whether Lisa acted to prevent Mr. Sommers from harm (and thus acted to "protect another"), the writer next turns to another element of the self-defense privilege: whether the force Lisa used was "reasonable." Facts are cited to support the argument that the force was not reasonable, but rather excessive.

Given the evidence, it seems likely that Lisa St. John will be liable to Sommers for battery.

Having addressed all of the elements of the primary and secondary rules, the writer can now conclude that the defendant will likely be held for battery. The conclusion as to Lisa's liability for battery has been delayed until the end, until all analysis has been completed.

A Short Guide to Writing Effective Issue Statements
Leonard Tourney

An issue statement is a single sentence defining exactly and correctly the legal question to be addressed. It must define the point on which the case turns—the question that when answered really makes a difference. Here are some basic rules for formulating such a sentence:

1. Do *not* use personal names in issue statements; instead, refer to parties in the case by legal status (defendant, plaintiff) or by relevant occupational categories (employer, employee, contractor, minor, etc.). An issue statement, while originating in a specific factual situation, is a hypothetical extrapolation. The particular names of the individuals, businesses, or institutions involved are usually immaterial.

2. The issue statement *must* name the specific cause of legal action (i.e., the grounds of the suit or prosecution). Vague references to defendant's wrongdoing, liability, or criminal conduct are not enough.

3. The issue statement *should* provide specific details of the case, especially those relevant to the key elements of the rule. ("Did the defendant commit robbery" is insufficient.) Your issue statement should enable the reader to distinguish your case from other cases involving the same crime or tort.

4. The issue statement should be grammatically correct. This means that the sentence must be grammatically complete: verbs should agree with their subjects, and modifiers such as relative clauses and descriptive phrases should be clearly and correctly linked to the words they modify. An issue statement can be expressed as a question (e.g., one beginning with "Is . . . " or "Does"), or it may be presented as a "Whether" statement ("Whether defendant, who [specific actions] commits (or is guilty of/liable for) [specific offense charged]").

5. An effective issue statement is concise: it does not use unnecessary words, flowery language, or redundant phrases. Good sentences are fat free.

6. Spell and punctuate your issue statement correctly. Avoid unnecessary commas.

7. Use legal terminology correctly. Check your usage with a good legal dictionary. [See the Legal Glossary on pages 826–832.]

8. Revise your issue statement carefully. A good issue statement reflects the quality of your thinking about the case and increases the likelihood that the discussion that follows will have the same qualities.

Problematic Student Responses: "Incident at the Airport"

Here are three additional student responses to the "Incident at the Airport" case. All are problematic. Explain why.

Response B

Here the issue in this case is whether Lisa St. John is liable for battery against Eben Sommers, a 90 year old man, injured at LAX when Lisa returned from a business trip. Battery is the harmful or offensive touching of another that is intentional, unconsented, and unprivileged. Lisa St. John is definitely liable for battery. While she meant to kick her fiancé, she kicked Mr. Sommers instead, causing him harm and offense. Furthermore, he didn't consent to being kicked. The big problem here is transfer of intent. According to that rule, if A, intending to strike B, misses B and hits C instead, the intent to strike B is transferred and supplies the necessary intent for the tort against C. This means that her intent to strike Frank is transferred to Mr. Sommers. Thus, she committed a battery against Eben Sommers.

Response C

Lisa St. John arrived at LAX late in the afternoon. She was mad at her fiancé for being late, so when he greeted her she kicked at him, missing and hitting Eben Sommers, who was this old guy. She broke his tibia in doing so, which was a harmful or offensive touching. It was also unconsented and unprivileged. But was it intended? According to the transfer of intent rule, it was.

The facts speak for themselves. Lisa is guilty of battery.

Response D

Sometimes we aim at one thing and do another, hurting another person in the process. That's basically what happened in this case, the issue of which is if Lisa St. John committed a crime or tort against Eben Sommers.

Lisa St. John committed a battery. She kicked Eben Sommers even though she did not mean to do it, because the transfer of intent rule applies. Thus, she meets all the elements of the following two rules. . . .

OUTRAGEOUS CONDUCT? SOME CASES OF EMOTIONAL DISTRESS

> Against a large part of the frictions and irritations and clashing of temperaments incident to participation in a community life, a certain toughening of the mental hide is a better protection than the law could be. . . . No pressing social need requires that every abusive outburst be converted into a tort; upon the contrary, it would be unfortunate if the law closed all the safety valves through which irascible tempers might legally blow off steam.
>
> —*Calvert Magruder, "Mental and Emotional Disturbance in the Law of Torts" (1936) 49* Harvard Law Review *1033*

In 1990, a Bakersfield, California, couple sued their nineteen-year-old neighbor for shooting hoops in his back yard at night. The pair charged the pro basketball hopeful with infliction of emotional distress. That same year two passengers witnessed a fatal accident in a Palm Springs tramway ride. They themselves were not physically injured, and they did not know the woman who was killed, but they sued the tram company for emotional distress. In 1997 actor Brad Pitt filed an emotional distress suit against *Playgirl* magazine for publishing nude shots of him and his girlfriend Gwyneth Paltrow taken while the couple were vacationing in the French West Indies.

Such cases seem to confirm the public's suspicions that all emotional distress cases are trivial or ridiculous and are filed primarily by greedy clients and their greedy lawyers for the sole purpose of making easy money. But while it's true that numerous emotional distress claims are bogus, it's also true that many people who suffer genuine and severe emotional distress as a direct result of the malice or the negligence of others often have no other recourse than the law if they hope for restitution.

Even the silly claims are often filed by people who have suffered genuine emotional distress. The question is whether anyone who inflicts emotional distress on another should be hauled into court. If we sued everyone who inflicted emotional distress on us, we'd sue our parents for not letting us have our own cell phone, our bratty siblings on general principles, our girlfriends or boyfriends for breaking up with us, our teachers for not giving us A's, our employers for not paying us what we're really worth, and on and on. To be human is to be (at least some of the time) emotionally distressed. So where do we draw the line between legitimate and illegitimate claims?

One important distinction, of course, is between minor and severe emotional distress (sometimes termed "mental anguish"). Another is between distress that has been intentionally inflicted and distress that has been unintentionally or negligently inflicted. For example, a collection agency that threatens a debtor with bodily harm unless he pays up might be liable for intentional infliction of emotional distress, even though the debtor suffers no physical harm. Another person might be liable for unintentional infliction of emotional distress to a parent if his negligence causes an automobile accident in which the parent's child is killed.

Suits for emotional distress are a relatively recent development in the law (although scholars often cite a fourteenth-century case in which a tavern keeper's wife charged emotional distress against an irate customer who had thrown a hatchet at her). And generally, courts have been more inclined to allow lawsuits for intentional than for unintentional infliction of emotional distress. They have argued that emotional distress caused by an act of negligence is usually a side effect of the physical damage (or, to use the legal term, the "impact") caused by that act, and so the defendant should properly be sued for causing this physical damage. According to this line of reasoning, it is more appropriate to sue the defendant for negligently causing death or injury than to sue for the emotional distress occasioned by this death or injury. If a negligent act has caused emotional distress alone, without physical injury, then (the courts have reasoned) its seriousness is difficult to gauge, and, in any case, the negligent defendant can be held only indirectly responsible. By its very nature, emotional distress is more intangible and subjective than physical damage; it is harder to assess and to verify, easier to fake. Many judges are wary of opening the doors to emotional distress claims wider than they already are, for fear of being deluged with cases of "social rudeness" and garden-variety embarrassment, and with the kind of cases cited at the start of this introduction.

In recent years, however, more judges have been willing to allow claims for mental distress unaccompanied by physical damage. Definitions and illustrations of "severe emotional distress" have been incorporated into the law and provided to juries hearing such cases. Distinctions have been drawn between petty annoyances and outrageous behavior, between the trivial and the serious, between the fraudulent and the genuine, between the transitory and the enduring.

In this section of the chapter, we'll explore some of the varieties of emotional distress. The "Discussion and Writing Suggestions" that follow this group of cases provide opportunities to practice your analytic and rhetorical skills. Playing the role of jury member, attorney for the plaintiff, attorney for the defendant, or just average citizen, you'll hone your ability to argue with logic and cogency, and perhaps even with flourish and flair. Draw upon the procedures and sample argument in "IRAC: How to Argue Your Case," preceding, as you develop your own arguments.

Take $2,000 and Call Me in the Morning
Howie Carr

1   A new disease is stalking my home state. It's called Emotional Distress. I learned about ED while perusing the 1994 report of the Massachusetts Commission Against Discrimination (MCAD). Almost everything causes ED. But thank goodness this new malady is treatable—with massive doses of legal tender.

2   Here are some of the people recently cured of Emotional Distress through the dollars prescribed by MCAD:

- A woman, seven months pregnant, applied for a job as a bartender and was turned down. MCAD found her ED-positive.
  Prescription: 15,000 greenbacks.
- A guy who's completely deaf in one ear wanted to be a policeman, but his city would not hire him because he wasn't "capable of performing the essential functions of the job without risk of injury to himself or others."
  Prescription: $25,000 and a job as a cop.
- A female cop in a town north of Boston was told to remain at the police station while her colleagues—"men of imposing size"—went on a drug raid. A commissioner/physician from MCAD diagnosed this as "the kind of stereotypic thinking which the anti-discrimination laws forbid."
  Prescription for this full-blown case of ED: $25,000.

3   Here's my favorite: A paraplegic has a "legal aid dog," which I guess is like a Seeing Eye dog. Trouble is, this hound apparently tends to confuse restaurants with fire hydrants. When the owner of one establishment recognized the canine as the same one that had recently defiled his floor, he told the paraplegic "to leave the dog outside."

Boston Herald 9 Mar. 1995.

4   Now, that's ED. Ruled the MCAD hearing officer: "The exclusion of the legal aid dog based on one incident was discriminatory."

5   Prescription: 5000 pictures of George Washington.

6   You read MCAD's annual report and you don't know whether to laugh or cry. Is *everybody* walking around with a chip on his shoulder? Is *everybody* entitled to *everything*?

7   People file because they have chronic-fatigue syndrome, a sleeping disorder, dyslexia or even "an emotional condition which manifests itself in an extreme need for personal safety." (She got $97,500.) They file because they're black and because they're white. They file because they're from Cape Verde, Haiti or Bombay. Now they've all moved here to Victim Nation, and they've all been struck down by ED.

8   A teen-age mother with a 2-year-old kid got her father to file a grievance against a landlord who didn't want to rent to her. No answer as to why her father wasn't able to find room for his daughter and grandchild to live with him, but he was available to grab some ED cash—all $3000 of it.

9   And there's the guy who is legally blind without glasses and had no driver's license, yet went after a company that wouldn't hire him as an auto mechanic. ED cure: $20,000.

10   I could go on—and on and on—but I'm sick. You guessed it. After reading this report, I've come down with a full-blown case of ED. Who do *I* sue?

The Cat in the Casket

1   On or about January 28, 1978, the plaintiff brought her 15 year old poodle into the defendant's premises for treatment. After examining the dog, the defendant recommended euthanasia and shortly thereafter the dog was put to death. The plaintiff and the defendant agreed that the dog's body would be turned over to Bide-A-Wee, an organization that would arrange a funeral for the dog. The plaintiff alleged that the defendant wrongfully disposed of her dog, failed to turn over the remains of the dog to the plaintiff for the funeral. The plaintiff had arranged for an elaborate funeral for the dog including a head stone, an epitaph, and attendance by plaintiff's two sisters and a friend. A casket was delivered to the funeral which, upon opening the casket, instead of the dog's body, the plaintiff found the body of a dead cat. The plaintiff described during the non-jury trial, her mental distress and anguish, in detail, and indicated that she still feels distress and anguish. The plaintiff sustained no special damages.

2   The question before the court now is two-fold. 1) Is it an actionable tort that was committed? 2) If there is an actionable tort is the plaintiff entitled to damages beyond the market value of the dog?

Corso v. Crawford Dog and Cat Hospital. 415 N.Y.S. 2d 182 (1979).

Judge's Instructions to the Jury: Intentional Infliction of Emotional Distress

1 Ladies and Gentlemen of the Jury:

2 It is now my duty to instruct you on the law that applies to this case. It is your duty to follow the law.

3 As jurors it is your duty to determine the effect and value of the evidence and to decide all questions of fact.

4 You must not be influenced by sympathy, prejudice or passion.

5 The plaintiff _____ seeks to recover damages based upon a claim of intentional infliction of emotional distress.

6 The essential elements of such a claim are:

1. The defendant engaged in outrageous, [unprivileged] conduct;
2. [a. The] defendant intended to cause plaintiff to suffer emotional distress; or
   [b. (1) defendant engaged in the conduct with reckless disregard of the probability of causing plaintiff to suffer emotional distress;
   (2) The plaintiff was present at the time the outrageous conduct occurred; and
   (3) The defendant knew that the plaintiff was present;]
3. The plaintiff suffered severe emotional distress; and
4. Such outrageous . . . conduct of the defendant was a cause of the emotional distress suffered by the plaintiff.

7 The term "emotional distress" means mental distress, mental suffering or mental anguish. It includes all highly unpleasant mental reactions, such as fright, nervousness, grief, anxiety, worry, mortification, shock, humiliation and indignity, as well as physical pain.

8 The word "severe," in the phrase "severe emotional distress," means substantial or enduring as distinguished from trivial or transitory. Severe emotional distress is emotional distress of such substantial quantity or enduring quality that no reasonable person in a civilized society should be expected to endure it.

9 In determining the severity of emotional distress you should consider its intensity and duration.

10 Extreme and outrageous conduct is conduct which goes beyond all possible bounds of decency so as to be regarded as atrocious and utterly intolerable in a civilized community.

11 Extreme and outrageous conduct is not mere insults, indignities, threats, annoyances, petty oppressions or other trivialities. All persons must necessarily be expected and required to be hardened to a certain amount of rough language and to occasional acts that are definitely inconsiderate and unkind.

12 Extreme and outrageous conduct, however, is conduct which would cause an average member of the community to immediately react in outrage.

California Jury Instructions, Civil: Book of Approved Jury Instructions 8th ed. Prepared by the Committee on Standard Jury Instruction Civil, of the Superior Court of Los Angeles County, California. Hon. Stephen M. Lachs, Judge of the Superior Court, Chairman. Compiled and Edited by Paul G. Breckenridge, Jr. St. Paul, MN: West Publishing, 1994.

13   The extreme and outrageous character of a defendant's conduct may arise from defendant's knowledge that a plaintiff is peculiarly susceptible to emotional distress by reason of some physical or mental condition or peculiarity. Conduct may become extreme and outrageous when a defendant proceeds in the face of such knowledge, where it would not be so if defendant did not know.

14   If you find that plaintiff is entitled to a verdict against defendant, you must then award plaintiff damages in an amount that will reasonably compensate plaintiff for all loss or harm, provided that you find it was [or will be] suffered by plaintiff and was caused by the defendant's conduct. The amount of such award shall include:

15   Reasonable compensation for any fears, anxiety and other emotional distress suffered by the plaintiff.

16   . . . In making an award for emotional distress you shall exercise your authority with calm and reasonable judgment and the damages you fix shall be just and reasonable in the light of the evidence.

The Spelling Bee

1   Gavin was a contestant in the 1987 Scripps Howard National Spelling Bee, sponsored in Ventura County by the newspaper, the *Ventura County Star–Free Press*. The contest is open to all students through the eighth grade who are under the age of sixteen. Gavin won competitions at the classroom and school-wide levels. This earned him the chance to compete against other skilled spellers in the county-wide spelling bee. The best speller in the county wins a trip to Washington, D.C. and a place in the national finals. The winner of the national finals is declared the national champion speller.

2   Gavin came in second in the county spelling bee. Being adjudged the second best orthographer in Ventura County is an impressive accomplishment, but pique overcame self-esteem. The spelling contest became a legal contest.

3   We search in vain through the complaint to find a legal theory to support this metamorphosis. Gavin alleges that two other boys, Stephen Chen and Victor Wang, both of whom attended a different school, also competed in the spelling contest. Stephen had originally lost his school-wide competition to Victor. Stephen was asked to spell the word "horsy." He spelled it "h-o-r-s-e-y." The spelling was ruled incorrect. Victor spelled the same word "h-o-r-s-y." He then spelled another word correctly, and was declared the winner.

4   Contest officials, who we trust were not copy editors for the newspaper sponsoring the contest, later discovered that there are two proper spellings of the word "horsy," and that Stephen's spelling was correct after all.

McDonald v. Scripps. 257 Cal. Rptr. 473 (1989).

5   Contest officials asked Stephen and Victor to again compete between themselves in order to declare one winner. Victor, having everything to lose by agreeing to this plan, refused. Contest officials decided to allow both Victor and Stephen to advance to the county-wide spelling bee, where Gavin lost to Stephen.

6   Taking Vince Lombardi's aphorism to heart, "Winning isn't everything, it's the only thing," Gavin filed suit against the *Ventura County Star–Free Press* and the Scripps Howard National Spelling Bee alleging breach of contract, breach of implied covenant of good faith and fair dealing, and intentional and negligent infliction of emotional distress.

7   In his complaint, Gavin asserts that contest officials violated spelling bee rules by allowing Stephen Chen to compete at the county level. He suggests that had Stephen not progressed to the county-wide competition, he, Gavin, would have won. For this leap of faith he seeks compensatory and punitive damages. . . .

8   The third cause of action, paragraph 29, states that plaintiff has suffered humiliation, indignity, mortification, worry, grief, anxiety, fright, mental anguish, and emotional distress, not to mention loss of respect and standing in the community. These terms more appropriately express how attorneys who draft complaints like this should feel.

9   A judge whose prescience is exceeded only by his eloquence said that ". . . Courts of Justice do not pretend to furnish cures for all the miseries of human life. They redress or punish gross violations of duty, but they go no farther; they cannot make men virtuous: and, as the happiness of the world depends upon its virtue, there may be much unhappiness in it which human laws cannot undertake to remove." (*Evans v. Evans* (1790) Consistory Court of London.) Unfortunately, as evidenced by this lawsuit, this cogent insight, although as relevant today as it was nearly 200 years ago, does not always make an impression on today's practitioner.

Shunned by Jehovah's Witnesses

1   Janice Paul was raised as a Jehovah's Witness. Her mother was very active in the Church and, from the age of four, Paul attended church meetings. In 1962, when Paul was 11 years old, her mother married the overseer of the Ephrata, Washington congregation of Jehovah's Witnesses. In 1967, Paul officially joined the Witnesses and was baptized.

2   According to Paul, she was an active member of the congregation, devoting an average of 40 hours per month in door-to-door distribution of the Witnesses' publications. In addition to engaging in evening home bible study, she attended church with her family approximately 20 hours per month. She eventually married another member of the Jehovah's Witnesses.

Paul v. Watchtower Bible and Tract Society. 819 F.2d 895 (1987).

3   In 1975, Paul's parents were "disfellowshiped" from the Church. According to Paul, her parents' expulsion resulted from internal discord within their congregation. The Elders of the Lower Valley Congregation told Paul that she and her husband should not discuss with other members their feeling that her parents had been unjustly disfellowshiped. That advice was underscored by the potential sanction of her own disfellowship were she to challenge the decision.

4   Sometime after the Elders' warning, Paul decided that she no longer wished to belong to the congregation, or to remain affiliated with the Jehovah's Witnesses. In November 1975, Paul wrote a letter to the congregation withdrawing from the Church.

5   The Witnesses are a very close community and have developed an elaborate set of rules governing membership. The Church has four basic categories of membership, non-membership or former membership status; they are: members, non-members, disfellowshiped persons, and disassociated persons. "Disfellowshiped persons" are former members who have been excommunicated from the Church. One consequence of disfellowship is "shunning," a form of ostracism. Members of the Jehovah's Witness community are prohibited—under threat of their own disfellowship—from having any contact with disfellowshiped persons and may not even greet them. Family members who do not live in the same house may conduct necessary family business with disfellowshiped relatives but may not communicate with them on any other subject. Shunning purportedly has its roots in early Christianity and various religious groups in our country engage in the practice including the Amish, the Mennonites, and, of course, the Jehovah's Witnesses.

6   "Disassociated persons" are former members who have voluntarily left the Jehovah's Witness faith. At the time Paul disassociated, there was no express sanction for withdrawing from membership. In fact, because of the close nature of many Jehovah's Witness communities, disassociated persons were still consulted in secular matters, e.g. legal or business advice, although they were no longer members of the Church. In Paul's case, for example, after having moved from the area, she returned for a visit in 1980, saw Church members and was warmly greeted.

7   In September 1981, the Governing Body of Jehovah's Witnesses, acting through the defendants—Watchtower Bible and Tract Society of Pennsylvania, Inc., and the Watchtower Bible and Tract Society of New York, Inc.—issued a new interpretation of the rules governing disassociated persons. The distinction between disfellowshiped and disassociated persons was, for all practical purposes, abolished and disassociated persons were to be treated in the same manner as the disfellowshiped. The September 15, 1981 issue of *The Watchtower*, an official publication of the Church, contained an article entitled "Disfellowshiping—how to view it." The article included the following discussion:

Those Who Disassociate Themselves

. . . Persons who make themselves 'not of our sort' by deliberately rejecting the faith and beliefs of Jehovah's Witnesses should appropriately be viewed and treated as are those who have been disfellowshiped for wrongdoing.

The *Watchtower* article based its announcement on a reading of various passages of the Bible, including 1 John 2:19 and Revelations 19:17–21. The article noted further that "[a]s distinct from some personal 'enemy' or worldly man in authority who opposed Christians, a . . . disassociated person who is trying to promote or justify his apostate thinking or is continuing in his ungodly conduct is certainly not one to whom to wish 'Peace' [understood as a greeting]. (1 Tim. 2:1, 2)." Finally, the article stated that if "a Christian were to throw in his lot with a wrongdoer who . . . has disassociated himself, . . . the Elders . . . would admonish him and, if necessary, 'reprove him with severity.'" (citing, *inter alia*, Matt. 18:18, Gal. 6:1, Titus 1:13).

8   Three years after this announcement in *The Watchtower,* Paul visited her parents, who at that time lived in Soap Lake, Washington. There, she approached a Witness who had been a close childhood friend and was told by this person: "I can't speak to you. You are disfellowshiped." Similarly, in August 1984, Paul returned to the area of her former congregation. She tried to call on some of her friends. These people told Paul that she was to be treated as if she had been disfellowshiped and that they could not speak with her. At one point, she attempted to attend a Tupperware party at the home of a Witness. Paul was informed by the Church members present that the Elders had instructed them not to speak with her.

9   Upset by her shunning by her former friends and co-religionists, Paul, a resident of Alaska, brought suit in Washington State Superior Court alleging common law torts of defamation, invasion of privacy, fraud, and outrageous conduct.

Covert Videotaping

1   On August 10, 1985, Petitioner Dan Boyles, Jr., then seventeen, covertly videotaped nineteen-year-old Respondent Susan Leigh Kerr engaging in sexual intercourse with him. Although not dating steadily, they had known each other a few months and had shared several previous sexual encounters. Kerr testified that she had not had sexual intercourse prior to her relationship with Boyles.

2   Kerr and Boyles, who were both home in Houston for the summer, had made plans to go out on the night of the incident. Before picking Kerr up, Boyles arranged with a friend, Karl Broesche, to use the Broesche house for sexual intercourse with Kerr. Broesche suggested videotaping the activity, and Boyles agreed. Broesche and two friends, Ray Widner and John Paul Tamborello, hid a camera in a bedroom before Kerr and Boyles arrived. After setting up the camera, the three videotaped themselves making crude comments and jokes about the activity that was to follow. They left with the camera running, and the ensuing activities were recorded.

Boyles v. Kerr. 855 S.W.2d 593 (1993).

3   Boyles took possession of the tape shortly after it was made, and subsequently showed it on three occasions, each time at a private residence. Although he showed the tape to only ten friends, gossip about the incident soon spread among many of Kerr and Boyles' friends in Houston. Soon many students at Kerr's school, Southwest Texas State University, and Boyles' school, the University of Texas at Austin, also became aware of the story. Kerr did not learn of the video until December 1985, long after she and Boyles had stopped seeing each other. After she confronted him, Boyles eventually admitted what he had done and surrendered the tape to Kerr. No copies had been made.

4   Kerr alleges that she suffered humiliation and severe emotional distress from the videotape and the gossip surrounding it. At social gatherings, friends and even casual acquaintances would approach her and comment about the video, wanting to know "what [she] was going to do" or "why did [she] do it." The tape stigmatized Kerr with the reputation of "porno queen" among some of her friends, and she claimed that the embarrassment and notoriety affected her academic performance. Kerr also claimed that the incident made it difficult for her to relate to men, although she testified to having had subsequent sexually-active relationships. Eventually, she sought psychological counselling.

5   Kerr sued Boyles, Broesche, Widner and Tamborello, alleging intentional invasion of privacy, negligent invasion of privacy, and negligent (but not intentional) infliction of emotional distress. Before the case was submitted to the jury, however, Kerr dropped all causes of action except for negligent infliction of emotional distress. The jury returned a verdict for Kerr on that claim, assessing $500,000 in actual damages. The jury also found that all defendants were grossly negligent, awarding an additional $500,000 in punitive damages, $350,000 of which was assessed against Boyles. The trial court rendered judgment in accordance with the jury's verdict.

6   Only Boyles appealed to the court of appeals. That court affirmed the judgment against him, concluding that Kerr established negligent infliction of emotional distress under the facts of this case. The court of appeals also affirmed based on negligent invasion of privacy, even though Kerr abandoned this theory prior to submission of the case to the jury and did not brief or argue it as a basis for affirmance in the court of appeals. [Boyles then appealed to the Texas Supreme Court.]

Judge's Instructions to the Jury: Unintentional and Negligent Infliction of Emotional Distress (NIED)

1   The plaintiff _____ seeks to recover damages based upon a claim of negligent infliction of emotional distress.

2   The elements of such a claim are:

   1. The defendant engaged in negligent conduct;
   2. The plaintiff suffered serious emotional distress;

3. The defendant's negligent conduct was a cause of the serious emotional distress.

3   Serious emotional distress is an emotional reaction which is not an abnormal response to the circumstances. It is found where a reasonable person would be unable to cope with the mental distress caused by the circumstances.

The Ridiculed Employee

Facts of the Case

1   The plaintiff, William R. Harris, a 26-year-old, 8-year employee of General Motors Corporation (GM), sued GM and one of its supervisory employees, H. Robert Jones, in the Superior Court of Baltimore City. The declaration alleged that Jones, aware that Harris suffered from a speech impediment which caused him to stutter, and also aware of Harris' sensitivity to this disability, and his insecurity because of it, nevertheless "maliciously and cruelly ridiculed . . . [him] thus causing tremendous nervousness, increasing the physical defect itself and further injuring the mental attitude fostered by the Plaintiff toward his problem and otherwise intentionally inflicting emotional distress." It was also alleged in the declaration that Jones' actions occurred within the course of his employment with GM and that GM ratified Jones' conduct.

2   The evidence at trial showed that Harris stuttered throughout his entire life. While he had little trouble with one-syllable words, he had great difficulty with longer words or sentences, causing him at times to shake his head up and down when attempting to speak.

3   During part of 1975, Harris worked under Jones' supervision at a GM automobile assembly plant. Over a five-month period, between March and August of 1975, Jones approached Harris over 30 times at work and verbally and physically mimicked his stuttering disability. In addition, two or three times a week during this period, Jones approached Harris and told him, in a "smart manner," not to get nervous. As a result of Jones' conduct, Harris was "shaken up" and felt "like going into a hole and hide."

4   On June 2, 1975, Harris asked Jones for a transfer to another department; Jones refused, called Harris a "troublemaker" and chastised him for repeatedly seeking the assistance of his committeeman, a representative who handles employee grievances. On this occasion, Jones, "Shaking his head up and down" to imitate Harris, mimicked his pronunciation of the word "committeeman" which Harris pronounced "mmitteeman." As a result of this incident, Harris filed an employee grievance against Jones, requesting that GM instruct Jones to properly conduct

California Jury Instructions, Civil: Book of Approved Jury Instructions 8th ed. Prepared by the Committee on Standard Jury Instruction Civil, of the Superior Court of Los Angeles County, California. Hon. Stephen M. Lachs, Judge of the Superior Court, Chairman. Compiled and Edited by Paul G. Breckenridge, Jr. St. Paul, MN: West Publishing, 1994.

Harris v. Jones. 380 A.2d 611 (1977).

himself in the future; the grievance was marked as satisfactorily settled after GM so instructed Jones. On another occasion during the five-month period, Harris filed a similar grievance against Jones; it too was marked as satisfactorily settled after GM again instructed Jones to properly conduct himself.

5   Harris had been under the care of a physician for a nervous condition for six years prior to the commencement of Jones' harassment. He admitted that many things made him nervous, including "bosses." Harris testified that Jones' conduct heightened his nervousness and his speech impediment worsened. He saw his physician on one occasion during the five-month period that Jones was mistreating him; the physician prescribed pills for his nerves.

6   Harris admitted that other employees at work mimicked his stuttering. Approximately 3,000 persons were employed on each of two shifts, and Harris acknowledged the presence at the plant of a lot of "tough guys," as well as profanity, name-calling and roughhousing among the employees. He said that a bad day at work caused him to become more nervous than usual. He admitted that he had problems with supervisors other than Jones, that he had been suspended or relieved from work 10 or 12 times, and that after one such dispute, he followed a supervisor home on his motorcycle, for which he was later disciplined.

7   Harris' wife testified that her husband was "in a shell" at the time they were married, approximately seven years prior to the trial. She said that it took her about a year to get him to associate with family and friends and that while he still had a difficult time talking, he thereafter became "calmer." Mrs. Harris testified that beginning in November of 1974, her husband became ill-tempered at home and said that he had problems at work. She said that he was drinking too much at that time, that on one occasion he threw a meat platter at her, that she was afraid of him, and that they separated for a two-week period in November of 1974. Mrs. Harris indicated that her husband's nervous condition got worse in June of 1975. She said that at a christening party held during that month Harris "got to drinking" and they argued.

8   On this evidence, the case was submitted to the jury after the trial court denied the defendants' motions for directed verdicts; the jury awarded Harris $3,500 compensatory damages and $15,000 punitive damages against both Jones and GM. [The verdict was then appealed by the defendants.]

Discussion and Writing Suggestions

1. How would you define emotional distress? Suppose someone did something—either intentionally or unintentionally—that caused you considerable emotional distress. How serious would this distress have to be for you to consider suing that person? Provide examples to clarify your responses.

2. How does Carr communicate his attitudes toward the kind of "ED" cases that he describes? To what extent do you share his attitudes? Do you think that he is being insensitive toward the people he describes? Have you encountered—in your reading or your own experience—other examples of the "disease" he is discussing?

3. If you were on the jury for the "Cat in the Casket" case, would you vote in favor of the plaintiff or in favor of the defendant, the dog and cat hospital? Explain your reasons, drawing upon the legal rules relating to emotional distress. Draw also upon the procedures and sample argument in "IRAC: How to Argue Your Case," on pages 759–765, as you develop your own arguments.

4. Consider the "Cat in the Casket," the "Spelling Bee," and the "Shunned by Jehovah's Witnesses" cases from an ethical, as opposed to a legal, standpoint. In which case is the action at the heart of the lawsuit most reprehensible? Least reprehensible? Why? To what extent might there be plausible justifications (as opposed to reasons) for these actions?

5. Compare and contrast the "Cat in the Casket," the "Spelling Bee," and the "Shunned by Jehovah's Witnesses" cases. Do you think that all three cases have equal merit (or lack of merit), or do you find significant differences among them? Explain, citing examples, and referring to appropriate sections of the "Judge's Instructions to the Jury: Intentional Infliction of Emotional Distress."

6. In the "Covert Videotaping" case, Kerr sued Boyles for *negligent,* rather than *intentional,* infliction of emotional distress. Review the rules for each type of claim. Do you believe that Kerr and her attorneys made the right choice? Explain, citing relevant sections of the law, as they apply to the facts of the case.

7. Boyles's attorneys charged that the real reason Kerr sued for negligent rather than intentional infliction of emotional distress was to get at the "deep pockets" of Boyles's insurance company. They pointed out:

> In Texas, a homeowner's policy covers only accidents or careless conduct and excludes intentional acts. Ms. Kerr's lawyers may have believed that if they obtained a judgment declaring that Boyles' conduct came within the rubric of "negligence" (inadvertence or carelessness), they could tap the homeowners policies owned by the parents of Boyles and the other defendants. Thus, this case has a lot to do with a search for a "deep pocket" who can pay. If the purpose of avoiding damages is to punish the wrongdoer and deter such conduct in the future, then the individuals responsible for these reprehensible actions are the ones who should suffer, not the people of Texas in the form of higher insurance premiums for homeowners.

React and respond to this argument as if you were one of Kerr's attorneys.

8. Assume that you have heard the evidence in "The Ridiculed Employee" case (*Harris v. Jones*) as summarized in the "Facts of the Case." Assume also that you have heard the jury instructions for "Intentional Infliction of Emotional Distress." If you were a member of the jury deliberating on a verdict, how would you vote? Explain your reasoning, specifically referring to the particular facts of the case and to the defini-

tions or explanations of "emotional distress." How do these definitions and explanations either support or fail to support the plaintiff's claim for damages? Emphasize those elements of the case that seemed crucial to you in reaching a determination.

9. Have you (or has someone you know) ever suffered emotional distress of the type that would fit the legal definition of this term? If so, lay out the facts of the case in a manner similar to the narratives in this section. Then, using IRAC format, apply the legal standards for a judgment of emotional distress to the event or events you have described.

10. As an alternate assignment to #9 above, select a character in a story, novel, film, or TV show who has suffered emotional distress. Using IRAC format, write a brief either for the plaintiff or the defendant. For example, could Othello charge Iago with intentional infliction of emotional distress? Could Piggy in *Lord of the Flies* charge Jack and the others?

11. *Group Assignment:* Form a jury, a group consisting of several other members of the class. (It doesn't have to have 12 members.) Choose a foreperson—someone to moderate, not dominate, the discussion and to keep the deliberations on track and keep the main issues in the forefront. Appoint someone to take notes. You may wish to tape-record the discussion.

Deliberate on the case before you (one of those in this section on emotional distress): Study the facts of the case; study the applicable law; apply the law to the facts of the case. Before or while you are developing your own conclusions, take account of other people's arguments. Weigh the merits of these arguments before deciding upon your vote. At the conclusion of discussion, the group will vote on a verdict. (Criminal cases require a unanimous vote; civil cases require a three-quarters majority.) If the jury is badly split, deliberate more in order to reach greater consensus.

After you arrive at a verdict, work with the foreperson as she or he prepares a report, written in IRAC format, that presents your verdict (as a conclusion) and explains the issue and the rule, and also summarizes the main points of the discussion in the "counterargument" and "response" sections.

DO STUDENTS HAVE FREEDOM OF SPEECH?

Congress shall make no law respecting an establishment of religion, or prohibiting the free exercise thereof; or abridging the freedom of speech, or of the press; or of the people peaceably to assemble, and to petition the government for a redress of grievances.

—*First Amendment to the U.S. Constitution*

In 1992, a high school student in Norfolk, Virginia, suspended for wearing a T-shirt proclaiming "Drugs Suck!", sued the school district for violating her

First Amendment rights. (She lost.) A trivial incident, to be sure, light-years removed from the noble language—and intent—of the First Amendment, but it does indicate the pervasive degree to which freedom of speech is taken for granted in American society. Such freedom was not specifically articulated in the original Constitution. But in response to popular demand, a Congress mindful of the abusive restrictions on freedom of speech both in England and in the American colonies insisted on enshrining this democratic right in the Bill of Rights, adopted in 1791. One of the most eloquent defenses of the often controversial First Amendment was articulated by Judge Learned Hand: "[The First Amendment] presupposes that right conclusions are more likely to be gathered out of a multitude of tongues than through any kind of authoritative selection. To many this is, and always will be, folly, but we have staked upon it our all."*

The right to freedom of speech was tested almost immediately in the new American republic with the passage of the Alien and Sedition Acts of 1798. The Sedition Act was used by John Adams's Federalist administration to retaliate against criticism by members of Jefferson's Democratic-Republican party, and the tables were turned with the accession of Jefferson. Although the Alien and Sedition Acts were never tested in court, they were soon thrown out as unconstitutional by Congress, which repaid all fines levied. Since that time, the limits of First Amendment freedoms have been tested many times, particularly during wartime and other periods of heightened national tensions. In the last sixty years, perceived threats of Communist subversion during the cold war; antiwar protests, such as occurred during the Vietnam War; and, more recently, antiwar protests in the aftermath of the invasion of Iraq, have repeatedly raised questions of just how much freedom of speech can be tolerated in a democratic society.

Of course, freedom of speech has never been absolute. The most well-known example of its limits is Supreme Court Justice Oliver Wendell Holmes's remark that freedom of speech does not give one the freedom to falsely shout "fire!" in a crowded theater. Similarly, a person who used a bullhorn to make a political statement in a residential street at 2 A.M. would most likely be charged with disturbing the peace—and would be unsuccessful in claiming First Amendment protection. The First Amendment has always been subject to a balancing of interests: Is the harm done by the speech act greater than the harm that would be done by restricting it? Speech that breaches the peace is often not protected because whatever social value it may have "is clearly outweighed by the social interest in order and morality."

The First Amendment does not give one the right to slander or libel others by knowingly making false statements about them that would harm their reputation. Nor does it give one the right to solicit others to commit crimes or to blackmail them, to disclose state secrets, or to incite people to riot. And a continuing source of controversy is whether the First Amendment allows someone to publish or circulate obscene materials—a particularly difficult

---

* *United States v. Associated Press.* 52 F.Supp. at 372 (1943).

question because the definition of obscenity is so subjective and changeable over time.

The First Amendment does not provide protection for "fighting words"— words that are highly likely to provoke a violent reaction from the person or persons to whom they are directed. However, words that merely annoy or even deeply wound others are protected, as long as they are not likely to result in physical violence. In recent years, many have debated whether "hate speech" should enjoy First Amendment protection—whether, for example, it is constitutional for college administrators to prohibit people from making statements that attack others on the basis of their race, ethnicity, or sexual orientation.

"Symbolic speech" deals with nonverbal acts of communication, such as burning a crucifix, burning an American flag (or, in the 1960s, one's draft card), wearing an armband to protest a war, or wearing a T-shirt saying "Drugs Suck!" to promote an antidrug message.

The readings in this section of the chapter, which focus on the issue of whether students have the same degree of freedom of speech as adults, will allow you to explore some of these issues.

The Obscene Election Speech
Philip Hager

1   There was no mistaking the ominous tone of the announcement over the public address system at Bethel High School [in Tacoma, Washington] in the spring of 1983: "Matt Fraser, please come to the principal's office—immediately."

2   Fraser, a senior honor student and the state's top-ranked debater, soon was headed down the hall for a confrontation with administrators over a speech laden with sexual innuendo he had made before 600 classmates at a student election assembly. He was promptly suspended for making an "indecent" speech that violated a school rule against disruptive conduct.

3   But Fraser, an aspiring law student, decided to make a federal case out of it— and won an appellate court ruling that will be reviewed Monday before the Supreme Court in a pivotal test of student free-speech rights against the authority of school officials to maintain order. The justices' ruling, expected by this summer, could have a broad impact on the students, teachers and administrators in the nation's 22,000 public secondary schools.

Broad Power Cited

4   States generally give school authorities broad power to establish rules and standards for student conduct, and some specifically allow disciplinary action for vulgar or profane language. In California, habitual use of such language is grounds for punishment.

Los Angeles Times 2 Mar. 1986.

Bethel School District v. Fraser. 478 US 675 (1984).

5   In the past, the justices, noting that high school students do not shed free-speech rights "at the schoolhouse gate," have upheld the students' right to wear black armbands in an anti-war protest. But the court also has recognized that authorities must be permitted to promote moral values in the schools and that, in some instances, they can curtail conduct by students that would be fully permissible for adults.

6   The Reagan Administration and a wide-ranging coalition of school administrators have joined Bethel officials in asking the high court to overturn the appellate ruling and grant school authorities the same "reasonable" power to restrict indecent speech that the justices granted them last year to search students for weapons and other contraband.

7   But Fraser, backed by the American Civil Liberties Union and some teacher and student press groups, says that his speech was neither obscene, disrespectful nor disruptive and thus is protected by the First Amendment. A ruling for the school district, he says, could lead to curtailed student speech and press, teaching an "ugly lesson" of suppression instead of constitutional rights.

Text of Speech Made by Student for Nomination
This is the speech Matthew Fraser made in 1983 nominating a fellow student to a class office.

"I know a man who is firm—he's firm in his pants, he's firm in his shirt, his character is firm—but most of all, his belief in you, the students of Bethel, is firm.

"Jeff Kuhlman is a man who takes his point and pounds it in. If necessary, he'll take an issue and nail it to the wall. He doesn't attack things in spurts, he drives hard, pushing and pushing, until finally—he succeeds.

"Jeff is a man who will go to the very end—even to the climax—for each and every one of you.

"So vote for Jeff for ASB vice president—he'll never come between you and the best our high school can be."

---

8   "I think it's really important that the First Amendment actually be in existence in high school," Fraser, now a student at UC Berkeley, said in an interview there. "You can't expect students to learn about it if they're not able to exercise it.

9   "I think it's good for students to challenge authority to find out what the legal boundaries are. But in this case I was nowhere near passing the boundaries."

10   An attorney for the school district, Clifford D. Foster Jr., says the school has a duty to regulate student speech to preserve a stable and civil environment for learning.

11   "We're not a bunch of right-wing Neanderthals," Foster said. "We're not saying he can't express an idea. The issue here is the way he expressed it. That's the only power we're asserting. He could have gone to a park and given the same speech and there'd be no problem. But a school assembly—that's different."

12   For Fraser, the controversy was born almost by accident. On short notice, he was asked to speak in behalf of Jeff Kuhlman, a nominee for student body vice president. He composed a speech filled with sexual metaphors and showed it to three teachers—two of whom recommended against giving it. Both sides agree that he was not specifically warned he would be suspended if he gave it.

13   Fraser went ahead with the speech, drawing hoots, hollers and applause. Some students were seen mimicking sexual gestures during the speech, and the next day one teacher reported that pupils seemed more interested in discussing the speech than in doing class work. Kuhlman, the candidate Fraser nominated, was elected to office.

14   School officials charged Fraser with violating the school's rule against conduct that "materially and substantially interferes with the educational process." He was suspended for three days and told he would not be eligible to be on a forthcoming ballot for graduation speaker.

Elected Class Speaker

15 Fraser made a quick telephone call to the ACLU and later, with his parents' permission, filed a federal civil rights suit against the school district. Meanwhile, he received enough write-in votes to be elected graduation speaker but still was denied the right to speak by school officials.

16   At trial in June, 1983, U.S. District Judge Jack E. Tanner ruled that Fraser's rights had been violated and awarded him the $278 he sought as damages—the equivalent of a teacher's pay for the time he was suspended—and attorneys' fees of $12,750. The judge also issued an injunction allowing him to speak at graduation.

17   Last year a federal appellate panel in San Francisco upheld the decision by a vote of 2 to 1, rejecting the district's claim that it could restrict student speech it considered indecent.

18   "We fear that if school officials had the unbridled discretion to apply a standard as subjective and elusive as 'indecency' . . . it would increase the risk of cementing white, middle-class standards for determining what is acceptable and proper speech and behavior in our public schools," Judge William A. Norris wrote for the court.

19   The appeals court acknowledged that officials could exercise substantial control over the classroom but found that a "voluntary activity" like the election assembly amounted to an "open forum," where the First Amendment protected Fraser from punishment.

20   In their appeal to the Supreme Court (*Bethel vs. Fraser*, 84–1667), the school district's attorneys contend that the assembly was not an open forum but an educational activity, where authorities had a duty to promote community standards of decency and civility. They also denied that the rule they enforced was vague and overly broad or that they should be required to provide students with specific written warnings of potential punishment.

21   The Justice Department, in a "friend of the court" brief supporting the district, contends that the appellate ruling erroneously bars school officials from punishing students for speech that is anything less than legally obscene or physically disruptive. The public schools, in their role of inculcating basic values, should be empowered to prohibit indecent speech just as they bar racial or religious slurs, the department says.

22   The district also is backed in a brief filed by the Pacific Legal Foundation and the National School Safety Center on behalf of several school administration groups and officials. They point to the justices' decision last year holding that students' right to privacy must give way to school officials' power to make rea-

sonable searches to maintain order. In this case, they say, students' right of free speech must give way to reasonable limits to guard against disruption.

Speech Defended

23 Fraser's attorney, Jeffrey T. Haley of Seattle, argues that the speech is not even indecent—let alone obscene—and that Fraser's use of sexual metaphor in a student political assembly should not have been punished by school officials.

24 "Restrictions within the classroom are fine," Haley said. "There's nothing wrong with enforcing good grammar or requiring certain forms of address to teachers. But a voluntary student assembly is different. If students are to be punished for the kind of speech Matt made, they will get a very distorted view of free-speech rights. In our system, we can generally say what we want."

25 The Student Press Law Center, citing the right of students to speak out against school administrators, backs Fraser in the case. So does the National Education Assn., which concludes that the speech presented no threat to teachers or administrators but was merely a non-disruptive expression of opinion on a subject he was fully entitled to discuss.

26 For his part, Fraser retains the suspicion that he was "singled out" for punishment by school authorities because he had criticized administrators in editorials in the student newspaper and in confrontations in student gatherings.

27 "They thought I was a troublemaker," he said. "I think they were happy to finally have an opportunity to suspend me."

28 There was divided feeling at the high school over the incident. Following Fraser's suspension some students put up posters and placards in his support—some of them containing sexual references. But later, when as the result of a court order he gave the graduation address, some in the audience left in protest.

29 The theme of his graduation talk was the importance of standing up for one's rights. But in Fraser's view, his suspension had a "chilling effect," as he puts it, on the willingness of students to speak out against authority.

30 "It's too bad," he said. But, he added with a smile, "They don't recognize how much fun it can be."

The Censored High School Newspaper

1 *Spectrum* was written and edited by the Journalism II class at Hazelwood East. The newspaper was published every three weeks or so during the 1982–1983 school year. More than 4,500 copies of the newspaper were distributed during that year to students, school personnel, and members of the community.

2 The Board of Education allocated funds from its annual budget for the printing of *Spectrum*. These funds were supplemented by proceeds from sales of the

---

Hazelwood School District v. Kuhlmeier. 484 US 260 (1988).

newspaper. The printing expenses during the 1982–1983 school year totaled $4,668.50; revenue from sales was $1,166.84. The other costs associated with the newspaper—such as supplies, textbooks, and a portion of the journalism teacher's salary—were borne entirely by the Board.

3   The Journalism II course was taught by Robert Stergos for most of the 1982–1983 academic year. Stergos left Hazelwood East to take a job in private industry on April 29, 1983, when the May 13 edition of *Spectrum* was nearing completion, and petitioner Emerson took his place as newspaper adviser for the remaining weeks of the term.

4   The practice at Hazelwood East during the spring 1983 semester was for the journalism teacher to submit page proofs of each *Spectrum* issue to Principal Reynolds for his review prior to publication. On May 10, Emerson delivered the proofs of the May 13 edition to Reynolds, who objected to two of the articles scheduled to appear in that edition. One of the stories described three Hazelwood East students' experiences with pregnancy; the other discussed the impact of divorce on students at the school.

5   Reynolds was concerned that, although the pregnancy story used false names "to keep the identity of these girls a secret," the pregnant students still might be identifiable from the text. He also believed that the article's references to sexual activity and birth control were inappropriate for some of the younger students at the school. In addition, Reynolds was concerned that a student identified by name in the divorce story had complained that her father "wasn't spending enough time with my mom, my sister and I" prior to the divorce, "was always out of town on business or out late playing cards with the guys," and "always argued about everything" with her mother. . . . Reynolds believed that the student's parents should have been given an opportunity to respond to these remarks or to consent to their publication. He was unaware that Emerson had deleted the student's name from the final version of the article.

6   Reynolds believed that there was no time to make the necessary changes in the stories before the scheduled press run and that the newspaper would not appear before the end of the school year if printing were delayed to any significant extent. He concluded that his only options under the circumstances were to publish a four-page newspaper instead of the planned six-page newspaper, eliminating the two pages on which the offending stories appeared, or to publish no newspaper at all. Accordingly, he directed Emerson to withhold from publication the two pages containing the stories on pregnancy and divorce. He informed his superiors of the decision, and they concurred.

7   Respondents subsequently commenced this action in the United States District Court for the Eastern District of Missouri seeking a declaration that their First Amendment rights had been violated, injunctive relief, and monetary damages.

Opinion of Justice A

8   The initial paragraph of the pregnancy article declared that "[a]ll names have been changed to keep the identity of these girls a secret." The principal con-

cluded that the students' anonymity was not adequately protected, however, given the other identifying information in the article and the small number of pregnant students at the school. Indeed, a teacher at the school credibly testified that she could positively identify at least one of the girls and possibly all three. It is likely that many students at Hazelwood East would have been at least as successful in identifying the girls. Reynolds therefore could reasonably have feared that the article violated whatever pledge of anonymity had been given to the pregnant students. In addition, he could reasonably have been concerned that the article was not sufficiently sensitive to the privacy interests of the students' boyfriends and parents, who were discussed in the article but who were given no opportunity to consent to its publication or to offer a response. The article did not contain graphic accounts of sexual activity. The girls did comment in the article, however, concerning their sexual histories and their use or nonuse of birth control. It was not unreasonable for the principal to have concluded that such frank talk was inappropriate in a school-sponsored publication distributed to 14-year-old freshmen and presumably taken home to be read by students' even younger brothers and sisters.

9   The student who was quoted by name in the version of the divorce article seen by Principal Reynolds made comments sharply critical of her father. The principal could reasonably have concluded that an individual publicly identified as an inattentive parent—indeed, as one who chose "playing cards with the guys" over home and family—was entitled to an opportunity to defend himself as a matter of journalistic fairness. These concerns were shared by both of *Spectrum*'s faculty advisers for the 1982–1983 school year, who testified that they would not have allowed the article to be printed without deletion of the student's name.

Opinion of Justice B

10   [My fellow justice] relies on bits of testimony to portray the principal's conduct as a pedagogical lesson to Journalism II students who "had not sufficiently mastered those portions of the . . . curriculum that pertained to the treatment of controversial issues and personal attacks, the need to protect the privacy of individuals" . . . and "the legal, moral, and ethical restrictions imposed upon journalists. . . ." In that regard, [he] attempts to justify censorship of the article on teenage pregnancy on the basis of the principal's judgment that (1) "the [pregnant] students' anonymity was not adequately protected," despite the article's use of aliases; and (2) the judgment that "the article was not sufficiently sensitive to the privacy interests of the students' boyfriends and parents. . . ." Similarly, [he] finds in the principal's decision to censor the divorce article a journalistic lesson that the author should have given the father of one student an "opportunity to defend himself" against her charge that (in the Court's words) he "chose 'playing cards with the guys' over home and family. . . ."

11   But the principal never consulted the students before censoring their work. "[T]hey learned of the deletions when the paper was released. . . ." Further, he explained the deletions only in the broadest of generalities. In one meeting called at the behest of seven protesting *Spectrum* staff members (presumably a

fraction of the full class), he characterized the articles as " 'too sensitive' for 'our immature audience of readers,' " and in a later meeting he deemed them simply "inappropriate, personal, sensitive and unsuitable for the newspaper." [My fellow justice's] supposition that the principal intended (or the protestors understood) those generalities as a lesson on the nuances of journalistic responsibility is utterly incredible. If he did, a fact that neither the District Court nor the Court of Appeals found, the lesson was lost on all but the psychic *Spectrum* staffer.

Discussion and Writing Suggestions

1. To what extent do you think the school district was justified in taking disciplinary action against Matt Fraser—that is, suspending him for three days and not allowing him to give the commencement address? To what extent do you think that Fraser's First Amendment rights had been violated? In developing your answer, consider the following points:

   - Should public school administrators and teachers have the right to prohibit "vulgar and obscene language" in classrooms? In assemblies?
   - Did Fraser's speech violate the school's rule prohibiting obscene language?
   - Was his language disruptive to the educational process?
   - To what extent do you believe that Fraser was aware of the rule he had violated and the penalties for violating it?
   - What is the significance, for you, that Fraser showed his speech to three teachers before delivering it?

2. Do you think that Principal Reynolds acted appropriately in the "Censored High School Newspaper" case? Or were the three students who brought suit justified in claiming that their constitutional right to freedom of speech had been violated? Reynolds claimed that he was concerned about the lack of journalistic fairness toward the boyfriends and parents mentioned in the article. Further, he was concerned with protecting the privacy of those mentioned in the article. To what extent were these concerns legitimate? To what extent did they justify pulling the article? Were there alternatives to deleting the article or not publishing the newspaper at all?

3. Compare and contrast the "Obscene Election Speech" case with the "Censored High School Newspaper" case. To what extent are the underlying issues similar? To what extent are they different? How do the differences in the essential facts of each case affect your conclusions about whether or not constitutional protections of freedom of speech apply and about whether or not the schools in each case took the correct actions? What competing social interests had to be balanced, in each case?

4. Write a brief—a legal argument—either supporting or opposing Matt Fraser's suspension in the case of "The Obscene Election Speech." Imagine that you are either Matt Fraser's attorney (if opposing the suspension) or the Bethel School District's (if supporting it). Draw on both the First Amendment and the information in the section introduction (pages 779–781) as well as on your own sense of what is the right thing to do. *Alternatively,* drawing upon these same sources as well as on the opinions of Justices A and B (pages 785–787), write a brief either supporting or opposing the Hazelwood School District in its decision.

WHO GETS THE KIDS? SOME CASES OF CHILD CUSTODY

Custody battles are among the most bitter conflicts fought in the nation's courts—which is ironic, considering that the adversaries generally began their relationship in an atmosphere of love and trust. In many cases, the divorcing couple is able to resolve the issue of child custody through private negotiation, sometimes with the aid of a mediator. But in cases where they cannot agree on which parent gets which kids, one will generally sue the other, and a judge in a family court must resolve the matter. What usually needs to be decided is which parent gets physical custody—that is, with which parent do the children live most of the time?—as well as what kind of visitation rights are awarded to the other parent, and what kind of child support the noncustodial parent must pay. In many cases, a court will rule that a child or children live with one parent part of the week, or the year, and with the other parent the rest of the time. Such arrangements are made, of course, only if both adversaries are ruled fit parents.

During the first half of the last century, courts almost automatically awarded custody to the mother. This preference arose from the assumption that the mother did not work and was available at home to serve as a full-time caregiver for her children. With more women joining the workforce since the 1950s, and with a general movement toward equality of the sexes, awarding custody to the mother no longer became automatic. Judges had to decide whether it would be in the best interest of the child to live with the mother or the father. This "best interest of the child" standard has become the main criterion that determines who gets physical custody. And as indicated in the next section, joint custody arrangements are becoming increasingly common.

What factors go into determining the best interest of the child? The courts look for a stable home environment, where a loving parent takes care of the children's physical and emotional needs: makes sure that they are well fed and housed, sees that they get adequate medical care, ensures that they regularly go to school. The custodial parent has to be financially able to take care of the child (which means, generally, that the parent must be gainfully employed), but otherwise the relative financial conditions of the two parents is not a factor in awarding custody. The parent with custody must also be considered moral-ly fit by the court; this often precludes the awarding of custody to parents who are involved in criminal activities, who take illegal drugs, who drink to excess, or who have serious emotional problems. Sexual behavior or promiscuity (or sexual inclination) in itself does not necessarily bar a parent from being award-ed custody unless the other parent or the state can show that such behavior has led to the parent neglecting the children's needs. The courts will also con-sider the age and sex of each child; judges will often award female children to the mother and male children to the father. Finally, courts may also take into account the children's wishes, but those wishes must be based on sound rea-sons (the child wants to continue going to the same school, for instance, not that the parent doesn't buy the child enough presents).

A significant change in any of the conditions that determined the original settlement (such as a planned out-of-state move by one parent) will often bring the parties back to court, with one arguing that the changed conditions justify a change in custody. And—as is the case in all of the following dis-putes—a losing party who disagrees with the trial court's judgment may appeal to a higher court for a reversal of the original ruling.

Joint Custody Blues
Pamela Paul

1   Nobody said raising kids after a divorce would be easy. But for Chuck Kabat, 38, a father of two from Dedham, Mass., it's a daily test. With his ex-wife Cathy living four blocks away and the two taking turns caring for their kids every few days, Kabat often gets frustrated. "For the first year, I felt completely out of control," he explains. "There were so many things to keep track of: How do I get them to soccer? Where do I find child care? Did they go potty before bedtime?" But the hardest part, even two years after the divorce, is keeping his cool with his ex.

2   "There are days when I want to just scream from the rooftops, 'How did this happen and why?' " Kabat says. "I've become a master at learning how to count to 10 when I get angry. But I don't have much choice except to behave with as much integrity and character as I can, because even though the marriage failed, we can make the divorce succeed, especially where the children are concerned."

3   A lofty goal and one all can agree on: do what's best for the kids. But what about the parents' well-being? Having to cooperate in a shared-custody arrange-ment after an acrimonious split can be exhausting, infuriating and interminably stressful. Yet joint custody is rapidly becoming the norm in the U.S., displacing the old-fashioned model of awarding custody to mothers. The arrangements vary. Joint legal custody means parents make shared decisions over major issues like education and medical treatment regardless of where the children live. Joint

Time 30 Aug. 2004: W7.

physical custody, which is steadily becoming the preferred arrangement in many states, is when kids divide their time between Mom's place and Dad's place, usually with at least a 70%–30% split. While custody laws vary widely by state, the trend in Wisconsin is probably typical: in 1981 joint physical custody was awarded in just 2% of divorce cases involving children; by 1998 the figure was 23%.

4   All around the country, more kids find themselves shuttling between quietly seething—or outwardly warring—parents. Mom has to raise her darling baby boy with her bitterest enemy. Dad has to negotiate ballet pickups and preteen dating policies with an ex he would rather forget. According to Isolina Ricci, author of the groundbreaking book *Mom's House, Dad's House: Making Two Homes for Your Child,* published in 1980, shortly after joint custody entered the legal system 10% to 12% of divorcing parents continue to be hostile after their marriage is over. Today, she says, "learning how to navigate joint custody has become a difficult but necessary rite of passage for many people trying to get past their divorce experience."

5   Often that translates into bickering over who bought the last pair of shoes or who took the kids to McDonald's one too many times. Others fight about more serious matters. Armin Brott's disputes with his ex-wife over religion and lifestyle mean that at Mom's house, his two daughters keep kosher as Orthodox Jews, but they drive on the Sabbath and eat vegetarian while at Dad's. Despite using a mediator, the two have trouble avoiding clashes. At first, says Brott, "all I wanted was for her to disappear into a hole in the ground, but here she is, every other day. I still sometimes have to restrain myself from yelling."

6   "Raising kids with joint custody means you have to stay in constant communication with a person you either a) hate, or b) still love and are therefore crushed, or c) both hate and love," explains Judy Corcoran, co-author of *Joint Custody with a Jerk: Raising a Child with an Uncooperative Ex.* "There's still anger, jealousy, hurt and fear that doesn't disappear just because the marriage ended. And those feelings are constantly reignited with every disagreement and drop-off."

7   Joint custody blues are a sign of the times, a by-product of egalitarian marriages between working moms and involved dads, replacing the old "tender years" policy, in which mothers were routinely awarded primary custody and fathers were relegated to visitation. The reasoning behind joint custody sounds sensible. Divorce is traumatic for kids; why have them suffer the additional pain of losing a parent? Moreover, studies show children do better when two parents are involved. Kids have higher self-esteem, better grades and fewer behavioral problems. Add to that deadbeat-dad prevention: fathers with joint custody are more likely to share the expense of raising kids. Finally, there's the growing fathers' rights movement, which advocates equitable custody laws.

8   For Jamie Ayers, 32, of Pittsburgh, Pa., there was never any question he would participate equally in raising his son Austin, 5. "The generation of fathers before mine didn't do everything they could for their children," he says. "I wanted to take responsibility for bringing a child into this world and be dedicated to raising him." Yet when he and Austin's mom Dawn Williams split up, Williams fought to retain sole custody. "It was incredibly frustrating," Ayers

explains. "She knew it was important for our son to have a father in his life but couldn't emotionally deal with it."

9   Williams defends her behavior. "Austin was only 2, and I thought he needed the consistency of sole custody," she explains. "The courts today aren't interested in what's best for the child; it's all about parents' rights." Besides, she says, letting go of her son every week so he could be with his dad has been excruciating. "I want to know where my child is all the time, that he's eating three meals a day and that he's happy, but I have to go five days without knowing."

10   There may be good reason to worry. Because the shared-physical-custody trend is relatively new, the outcomes of such arrangements are just beginning to be examined. A small 2002 study at Ohio State University involving 59 children and mothers found that kids in joint custody arrangements in which the parents did not get along were likely to feel sad and behave less cooperatively with others. They were also inclined to intervene in parental conflict themselves, something child psychologists strongly discourage.

11   For exes who find it impossible to get along, some psychologists suggest "parallel parenting." That means each household has its own set of rules, and the parents have a minimum of contact and communication. Richard Warshak, author of *Divorce Poison: Protecting the Parent-Child Bond from a Vindictive Ex*, estimates more than half of divorced parents sharing custody follow this path.

12   But even that arrangement won't keep the peace for the angriest exes. Some parents never accept the fifty-fifty split and appeal endlessly to the courts for modifications, says Candice Komar, a family-law attorney in Pittsburgh. "They'll say it's in the best interest of the child to change the custody arrangement," she says. "But the truth is, often it's because joint custody is driving these parents crazy. I've had people consult me because they fight over whether their child wears a spring coat or a winter coat—and I'm not kidding."

13   Parenting experts say legal wrangling is to be avoided if at all possible. Mediators and parent educators can help. So can new programs intended to disarm parents in contentious custody situations. Elizabeth Thayer and Jeffrey Zimmerman founded Parents Equally Allied to Co-Parent Effectively (PEACE) in 1998 to help high-conflict parents who are referred by their weary attorneys. So far, the program has trained more than 400 sets of parents in Connecticut and is expanding to other states. PEACE throws out the psychotherapy model of conflict resolution and approaches custody battles as a business. Get rid of the emotions and anger, Thayer says. Instead, think about the bottom line: What will the kids say about their parents' divorce when they're adults?

14   It's tempting to think that when parents fail to compromise, kids should decide for themselves where to live. Yet most courts try to protect children from having to make such choices, partly because parents will try to manipulate them. In Pittsburgh, Komar doesn't often hear testimony from kids younger than 11. "The first thing out of kids' mouths, whether they talk to the judge in chambers or talk to me," she says, "is, 'Don't make me pick.'"

Unfit Mother? Unfit Father?

1   On August 17, 1953, an interlocutory [temporary] decree of divorce was entered in an action brought by Norma Jeanne Ashwell, appellant herein, against Curtis Lee Ashwell, respondent herein. The decree was granted to Norma upon the ground of extreme cruelty and upon default of Curtis. Custody of the four children of the marriage was given to Norma. The oldest of the children was 6 and the youngest less than 2. During the interlocutory period and on January 19, 1954, Curtis filed a notice of motion to modify the interlocutory decree by taking the custody of the children from Norma and awarding that custody to Curtis. The notice of motion stated that the modification sought would be to the effect that Norma was not a fit and proper person to have custody. . . .

2   Norma gave birth to a fifth child on February 14, 1954 (conceived prior to the interlocutory decree). The father of the child was one Barney Cassella. Norma, the five children and Cassella were living in the same house when the motion to modify the decree was heard. Curtis was a master sergeant in the United States Army, stationed in Sacramento [California]. That county had also been the situs of the domicile of the parties when the decree of divorce was granted. Curtis testified he had visited the children about once a week and a number of times had found them in the charge of a 12-year-old girl. He said they were generally raggedly dressed in dirty clothes and appeared to need a bath; that whenever he visited Barney Cassella was always present; that Norma and the children had, after the decree, moved from a residence in Sacramento and were living in West Sacramento, across the river in Yolo County; that on December 23, 1953, at about 10 P.M. he visited there and Cassella answered the door and was improperly dressed (he did not specify in what the impropriety consisted); that Norma then told him she was pregnant, but denied that Cassella was responsible. Curtis stated to the court that if he obtained custody of the children he intended to get a discharge from the Army and take the children back to Virginia to live with his parents who were living on a farm three miles out of Huddleston; that the home was an average home, with access to schools and churches; that his parents were Mormons; that his mother was 45 years of age and his father 54 years old; that he, Curtis, is a mechanic by trade and had been offered a job in Huddleston and expected to support his children from his earnings. He said he had never seen any improprieties between Norma and Cassella.

3   Barney Cassella testified he was a taxi driver employed in Sacramento and since November 1953 had been living in the same house with Norma and the children; that he rented the house; that before that time he rented an apartment from Mrs. Ashwell in Sacramento; that he had had sexual intercourse with her several times, but not since June of 1953; that he was the father of the child she bore February 14, 1954; that when he moved to West Sacramento it was to a house which he rented which had three bedrooms, one of which was occupied by him and his adult nephew, one by Norma with the new baby and the youngest

Ashwell v. Ashwell. 286 P.2d 983 (1955).

Ashwell child, and the other by the three older children; that he loved Norma and intended to marry her as soon as her divorce became final. Norma testified that Cassella was the father of her last born child; that she and Cassella had had no sexual relations since she became pregnant in June of 1953; that she had not told Curtis at any time that Cassella was not the father of her last born child. In explanation of her conduct she testified that she had been compelled, while living in Sacramento and after her separation from Curtis, to rent an apartment to Cassella, and that the compulsion was from economic necessity; that she was compelled to leave her Sacramento home because Curtis came there at unreasonable hours and abused and insulted her beyond endurance; that she had moved into a house which Cassella rented because she could not afford a place of her own; that she loved Cassella and intended to marry him as soon as her divorce became final; that she had always properly cared for the children; that she loved them and devoted her full time to their care; that they were healthy and happy. She said: "I am living with Mr. Cassella now because of economic necessity. I receive $100.00 a month from him to apply toward the support of myself and my children. I cannot afford to live separate and apart from him at the present time. If my children were taken back to Virginia, I could not afford to go there to visit, and I would probably never see them again." Two women, neighbors to Norma, testified that Norma was a good mother, cared for her children well and that they appeared to be healthy, happy, normal children; that she was conscientious and never neglected or abused her children in any way.

The Torn-Up $5 Bill

1   This is an appeal by a mother who has lost physical custody of her two minor children to their father who successfully convinced the trial judge that the mother had engaged in a longstanding effort to interfere with his visitation rights. . . .

Father's Version

2   Father was, at the time of combined hearings, a 30-year-old painting contractor who lived in Bakersfield with his then present wife (a data support operator) and her son by a previous marriage. A school where the minor children of the parties would attend classes was nearby. When the children were with their father they got along well with his new family.

3   Mother moved to Oakland, California, with the children. Thereafter, Father attempted to exercise his visitation rights on alternate weekends, but by the time of the hearing had missed 16 weekends and 6 holidays, allegedly due to actions of Mother. When she moved, Mother refused to give Father her address, telephone number or the name of the school attended by the children. On three occasions, Father notified Mother that he was making the 700-mile round trip from Bakersfield to Oakland to exercise his visitation rights, but when he

---

Wood v. Wood. 190 Cal. Rptr. 469 (1983).

arrived at her house (the location of which he had learned from the children), no one was home. On some occasions when he telephoned the children, Mother refused to let them speak to him. When he wrote to the children, she would not let them reply unless he enclosed a self-addressed, stamped envelope. He asked her to share in the financial burden of transporting the children between Bakersfield and Oakland, but she refused, and when he once attempted to require her to obey the then existing court order by insisting that she pick up the children at his home in Bakersfield, she told him that he would never see the children again.

4   On three occasions when Father was scheduled to drive to Oakland to pick up the children for visitation, he was told by Mother that she had arranged to take them to a baseball game and he would have to delay his visitation. On one occasion he arranged to have a relative pick up the children at her house in Oakland to attend a birthday party in the Bay Area; she refused, stating that he was required to personally exercise his visitation rights. She later agreed to let the relative pick up the children, but when the relative arrived at her home, no one was there. A $5 bill that Father had mailed to the children to buy a present for the party was returned to him, torn in quarters, in one of the self-addressed, stamped envelopes he was forced to provide. Father believed that Mother was attempting to sever his relationship with his children.

5   Father and his present wife reported earnings for tax purposes of $16,201 in 1978, $23,574 in 1979 and $20,988 in 1980. He felt that $75 per month child support per child was adequate and was unable to pay more at that time.

Mother's Version

6 Mother had primary care of the two minor children of the marriage since their birth and custody of them during the five years since the parties separated. Having become a licensed registered nurse since her divorce, she moved to Oakland to work at a hospital there and to be near her relatives. She owned a home, which she and the children shared with Raul Martinez, a student from Argentina who attended a local college and who babysat the children at night while she worked. She had not remarried.

7   Mother testified that she made the children available for Father's visitation on every appropriate weekend, but he frequently did not come to Oakland—he only came once a month. In the past he had become belligerent in dealing with her, used swear words, and harassed her, such as by calling the hospital where she worked. Someone did tear up a $5 bill he had sent to the children and mailed it back to him.

8   Her gross monthly income excluding child support was at the time of the hearing $1,745.12 and her net monthly income, $1,327.60. She could not afford to transport the children from Bakersfield to Oakland, and $75 per month child support per child was inadequate; she requested $150 per child.

Children's "Testimony"

9 Bryan, a first-grader, and David, a fourth-grader, initially expressed a preference to continue living with their mother and visiting their father. There had been times when their father was supposed to pick them up but their mother wouldn't

let them go with him. Bryan thought they had moved from Bakersfield so that their father wouldn't make any problems. In response to questions by the court the children indicated that they would be willing to live with their father and have visits with their mother.

10   In the course of argument, Mother's counsel, after learning that the trial court proposed to place the children in the custody of Father, suggested to the court that joint physical custody be ordered. The trial court found both parents fit and ordered joint legal custody but expressed a desire that the maximum relationship be maintained by the children with both parents.

11   The court found that for the welfare of the children and to have the maximum beneficial relationship with each parent, greater exposure to the father was desirable, and therefore granted the physical custody of the children to Father, with the visitation rights formerly ordered for him granted to Mother. She was ordered to pick up the children for visitation and Father to pick them up when visitation had concluded. Mother was ordered to pay $75 per child per month child support to Father.

Which Parent Should Move?

1   Pamela Fingert (Pamela) and Michael Fingert (Michael) were married on November 13, 1980, and lived in Ventura County [California]. They separated approximately nine months later when Pamela was pregnant. Michael filed a petition for dissolution of the marriage on December 28, 1981. Their son Joshua was born on February 1, 1982. In January 1983 Pamela and Michael executed a marital settlement agreement in which they agreed to joint legal custody, with actual physical custody to Pamela, and reasonable visitation rights to Michael. The interlocutory decree was entered making orders in accordance with the agreement.

2   During Joshua's first year of life, he and Pamela lived in Ventura. She decided to relocate to Chicago, Illinois, where her family resided. Michael sought and obtained an ex parte restraining order temporarily enjoining Pamela from moving. Pamela changed her plans and relocated to San Diego. The custody order was modified to provide that Pamela was to have physical custody of Joshua except for alternate weekends and certain summer and holiday periods, when the child was to be with Michael. Pamela obtained employment in San Diego in the computer industry and lived there for approximately 18 months. During that period, both Pamela and Michael would drive approximately 100 miles to a half-way point between Ventura and San Diego to exchange Joshua to implement the custody agreement.

3   Pamela accepted a better job which required her to move to San Mateo County. Pamela and Michael, through their attorneys, agreed to an informal

Fingert v. Fingert. 271 Cal Rptr. 389 (1990).

modification of the visitation schedule. Michael had Joshua approximately one week per month. Joshua was met by one of his parents at both ends of his flights between the San Francisco and Los Angeles areas.

4   Pamela's father was ailing and wanted to retire from his small publishing business located in Chicago. He asked Pamela to take over the business. Pamela petitioned the court for permission to move to Chicago to take over this business. This request was denied but the court confirmed the informal arrangement agreed upon by the parents by ordering that Michael would have visitation from the second Friday to the third Saturday of each month and during certain summer and holiday periods. Joshua was now in kindergarten, and the arrangement meant he would attend one school for three weeks and another for one week each month.

5   Pamela became concerned about how this arrangement was affecting Joshua and how it would affect him when he started first grade. In April 1988 she filed a motion to modify the custody order to provide for visitation to Michael consistent with Joshua's school schedule. Pamela's suggestion was that Michael have Joshua on weekends, holidays, and during the summer. The parties were ordered to and did meet with a court mediator and a hearing was eventually set for September 12, 1988, by which time Joshua had already begun first grade in San Mateo County.

6   Michael filed a responsive declaration to Pamela's motion in which he suggested that "the optimum living arrangement for my six-year-old boy is for he and his mother to move back into the County of Ventura, allowing Joshua 50 percent time in each home while being a student at only one school." In the alternative, Michael suggested that Joshua live with him for one year and with Pamela the next.

7   In response Pamela argued that requiring Joshua to move to Ventura would not be in his best interests, that he attended the same school in San Mateo County for three years, he was enrolled in his second year in a Sunday school and had participated on the same soccer team for years and has had the same set of playmates ever since he was three years old. She contended that Joshua's "roots" were in San Mateo County.

8   On September 12, 1988, the court heard testimony from Pamela, Michael and Robert L. Beilin, Ph.D., the director and senior mediator of the family relations department on the Ventura County Superior Court.

9   The court mediator testified that he had met with Pamela and Michael, alone and together, and had spent some time with Joshua. He recommended that because of "the significance of the father and son relationship," Michael should be allowed to continue to see Joshua on a regular basis and that "neither a weekend father arrangement, nor paternal visitation during holidays and vacations was the best situation." He felt that "it would be best if Joshua and [Pamela] moved to Ventura in order to make it easier for [Michael] and Joshua to continue to spend time together regularly." He recommended that the court order Pamela to move back to west Ventura County.

10   Michael testified that he and his son needed to be together because they are father and son and that he and Joshua are very close and their time together is extremely important to them both. Pamela's testimony centered on the ties they had in San Mateo County. She objected to the dislocation in her own life if she

and Joshua were ordered to move to Ventura County as recommended by the mediator.

11   The mediator testified that in considering whether Pamela should move instead of Michael, he was "swayed by the fact [Michael] owned a home and 10 year old business in Ventura and offered to help [Pamela] move to Ventura County whereas [Pamela] had only launched [her business] in the San Francisco bay area in the last year, did not have substantial financial ties there, and was not financially in a position where she could meet [Michael's] offer and assist him in relocating."

12   The trial judge stated that he felt there were "... strong equities both ways" and that he considered granting summer custody to Michael and ordering Joshua to continue to spend the school year with Pamela in Northern California. However, the judge explained that he had faith in the court mediator and would follow his recommendations. He ordered that "[t]he minor's residence shall be in Ventura County and shall not be changed from said county without order of this court or written agreement signed by both parties . . . " and that Michael "financially assist [Pamela] in moving back to West Ventura County at a cost not to exceed $1,000.00 in connection with moving expenses."

13   The court acknowledged that its order would "force [Pamela] to Ventura County or else give up custody of her child." He stated it would not make sense to have Michael move because of Michael's "long-standing roots in business in Ventura and his greater ability financially to help [Pamela] relocate."

The Law on Child Custody

Uniform Marriage and Divorce Act, §402

1   The court shall determine custody in accordance with the best interest of the child. The court shall consider all relevant factors including:

(1) The wishes of the child's parent or parents as to his custody;
(2) The wishes of the child as to his custodian;
(3) The interaction and interrelationship of the child with his parent or parents, his siblings, and any other person who may significantly affect the child's best interest;
(4) The child's adjustment to his home, school and community; and
(5) The mental and physical health of all individuals involved.

The court shall not consider conduct of a proposed custodian that does not affect his relationship to the child.

California Civil Code §4600 (a)

2   The Legislature finds and declares that it is the public policy of this state to assure minor children of frequent and continuing contact with both parents after the parents have separated or dissolved their marriage, and to encourage

parents to share the rights and responsibilities of child rearing in order to effect this policy. In any proceeding where there is at issue the custody of a minor child, the court may, during the pendency of the proceeding or at any time thereafter, make such order for the custody of the child during minority as may seem necessary or proper. If a child is of sufficient age and capacity to reason so as to form an intelligent preference as to custody, the court shall consider and give due weight to the wishes of the child in making an award of custody or modification thereof. In determining the person or persons to whom custody shall be awarded under paragraph (2) or (3) of subdivision (b), the court shall consider and give due weight under Article 1 (commencing with Section 1500) of Chapter 1 of Part 2 of Division 4 of the Probate Code.

California Family Code §3011 (2001): Factors Considered in Determining Best Interest of Child

3 In making a determination of the best interest of the child in a proceeding described in Section 3021, the court shall, among any other factors it finds relevant, consider all of the following:

(a) The health, safety, and welfare of the child.
(b) Any history of abuse by one parent or any other person seeking custody against any of the following:
　(1) Any child to whom he or she is related by blood or affinity or with whom he or she has had a caretaking relationship, no matter how temporary.
　(2) The other parent.
　(3) A parent, current spouse, or cohabitant, of the parent or person seeking custody, or a person with whom the parent or person seeking custody has a dating or engagement relationship.

4 As a prerequisite to the consideration of allegations of abuse, the court may require substantial independent corroboration, including, but not limited to, written reports by law enforcement agencies, child protective services or other social welfare agencies, courts, medical facilities, or other public agencies or private nonprofit organizations providing services to victims of sexual assault or domestic violence. As used in this subdivision, "abuse against a child" means "child abuse" as defined in Section 11165.6 of the Penal Code and abuse against any of the other persons described in paragraph (2) or (3) means "abuse" as defined in Section 6203 of this code.
(c) The nature and amount of contact with both parents, except as provided in Section 3046.
(d) The habitual or continual illegal use of controlled substances or habitual or continual abuse of alcohol by either parent. Before considering these allegations, the court may first require independent corroboration, including, but not limited to, written reports from law enforcement agencies, courts, probation departments, social welfare agencies, medical facilities, rehabilitation facilities, or other public agencies or nonprofit organizations providing drug and alcohol abuse services. As used in this subdivision, "controlled substances" has the same meaning as defined in the California Uniform

Controlled Substances Act, Division 10 (commencing with Section 11000) of the Health and Safety Code.

(e) (1) Where allegations about a parent pursuant to subdivision (b) or (d) have been brought to the attention of the court in the current proceeding, and the court makes an order for sole or joint custody to that parent, the court shall state its reasons in writing or on the record. In these circumstances, the court shall ensure that any order regarding custody or visitation is specific as to time, day, place, and manner of transfer of the child as set forth in subdivision (b) of Section 6323.

(2) The provisions of this subdivision shall not apply if the parties stipulate in writing or on the record regarding custody or visitation.

California Family Code §3020 (2001): Legislative Intent on Child Custody

(a) The Legislature finds and declares that it is the public policy of this state to assure that the health, safety, and welfare of children shall be the court's primary concern in determining the best interest of children when making any orders regarding the physical or legal custody or visitation of children. The Legislature further finds and declares that the perpetration of child abuse or domestic violence in a household where a child resides is detrimental to the child.

(b) The Legislature finds and declares that it is the public policy of this state to assure that children have frequent and continuing contact with both parents after the parents have separated or dissolved their marriage, or ended their relationship, and to encourage parents to share the rights and responsibilities of child rearing in order to effect this policy, except where the contact would not be in the best interest of the child, as provided in Section 3011.

(c) Where the policies set forth in subdivisions (a) and (b) of this section are in conflict, any court's order regarding physical or legal custody or visitation shall be made in a manner that ensures the health, safety, and welfare of the child and the safety of all family members.

California Family Code §3040 (2001): Order of Preference in Granting Custody

(a) Custody should be granted in the following order of preference according to the best interest of the child as provided in Sections 3011 and 3020:

(1) To both parents jointly pursuant to Chapter 4 (commencing with Section 3080) or to either parent. In making an order granting custody to either parent, the court shall consider, among other factors, which parent is more likely to allow the child frequent and continuing contact with the noncustodial parent, consistent with Section 3011 and 3020, and shall not prefer a parent as custodian because of that parent's sex. The court, in its discretion, may require the parents to submit to the court a plan for the implementation of the custody order.

(2) If to neither parent, to the person or persons in whose home the child has been living in a wholesome and stable environment.

(3) To any other person or persons deemed by the court to be suitable and able to provide adequate and proper care and guidance for the child.

(b) This section establishes neither a preference nor a presumption for or against joint legal custody, joint physical custody, or sole custody, but allows the court and the family the widest discretion to choose a parenting plan that is in the best interest of the child.

California Family Code §3041 (2001): Custody Granted to Non-Parent

5 Before making an order granting custody to a person or persons other than a parent, without the consent of the parents, the court shall make a finding that granting custody to a parent would be detrimental to the child and that granting custody to the non-parent is required to serve the best interest of the child. Allegations that parental custody would be detrimental to the child, other than a statement of that ultimate fact, shall not appear in the pleadings. The court may, in its discretion, exclude the public from the hearing on this issue.

Discussion and Writing Suggestions

1. To what extent do the issues discussed by Pamela Paul in "Joint Custody Blues" reflect your own knowledge of the realities of joint custody? Given the often intractable conflicts between the parents, in what ways could the law and the court system better deal with child custody issues to minimize the adverse effects on all parties concerned, but particularly on the kids?

2. In the "Unfit Mother? Unfit Father?" case, should Curtis Lee Ashwell be awarded custody of the four children he had with Norma Jeanne Ashwell? Apply relevant elements of child custody law to this case. To what extent should the following factors be significant in determining who gets custody: (1) Norma's sexual relationship and living arrangements with Cassella before her divorce became final; (2) Curtis's planned move across the country to Virginia; (3) Curtis's Army status; (4) Curtis's testimony about the children being frequently raggedly dressed and dirty when he visited and their being cared for by a 12-year-old babysitter. Take into primary account the best interest of the children.

3. In the "Torn-Up $5 Bill" case, should custody of the children remain, as the trial court judge ruled, with the father? Base your conclusion upon the best interest of the children. Reviewing the three "versions" of the situation—by father, mother, and children—what do you conclude about the actual facts of this case and about which parent was most/least blameworthy in terms of the father's visitations? To what extent should the trial court judge's rulings on custody, child support payments, and visitation arrangements be upheld? To what extent reversed? Apply the relevant laws on child custody to the facts of this case.

4. To what extent do you agree with the trial court judge's decision in the "Which Parent Should Move?" case? Should Pamela be required by the appellate court to either relocate to Ventura or give up custody of

Joshua? Discuss the mediator's recommendation (the one with which the judge agreed) that the father had a home and an established business in Ventura, whereas the mother "had only launched [her business] in the San Francisco bay area in the last year, did not have substantial financial ties there, and was not financially in a position where she could meet [Michael's] offer and assist him in relocating." In light of the relevant laws on child custody, consider whether or not the best interest of the child would be served by awarding the father custody.

THE FELLED STOP SIGNS:
TWO CASES OF HOMICIDE

The following selections deal with two remarkably similar cases, almost 20 years apart. In both cases—the earlier one in Utah, the later one in Florida—teenagers looking for an evening of fun pulled out or pulled down stop signs at intersections. In both cases, their actions resulted in one or more persons killed in automobile crashes. The teens were blameworthy: No one disputed that. But how blameworthy, from a legal standpoint? With what crime should they be charged? To what extent were they directly responsible for the fatalities that occurred? You'll explore these and other issues by reading accounts of the two cases: first, the more recent case, described in an article in the *Los Angeles Times* (as of publication, no appeals ruling had been issued on this case); second, the Facts of the Case section of the earlier case, as described in the ruling of the Utah appellate court. Following these accounts are two statements on the law that will provide guidelines for your deliberations: The first, from statutory law, offers excerpts from the "Homicide" section of the Utah Criminal Code, along with definitions of some key terms. The second, from case law, is a brief distinction (contained in a later legal opinion from an Arizona appellate court in the case of *State v. Fisher*) between "negligent homicide" and "manslaughter."

For Fallen Stop Sign, Vandals Face Life
Mike Clary

1   Tampa, Fla.—It was a clear, dark February night when the fates collided in front of Tim's Cafe at a rural intersection where a stop sign lay face-down by the side of the road.

2   One of the vehicles involved was an eight-ton Mack truck loaded with phosphate. The other was a white Camaro carrying three 18-year-old friends on a one-way ride to eternity. Chances are, police said, they never knew what hit them.

3   Tow trucks and sheriff's deputies were still on the scene a few hours later when a fourth young man named Thomas Miller pulled up. He and a friend had

Los Angeles Times. 11 June 1997.

just finished working the graveyard shift at a welding shop and were heading to Tim's for breakfast.

4   Miller got out of his car to see the wreckage better and, he recalled later, he stood right next to the fallen stop sign.

5   Now, 16 months after that fatal crash, Miller and two friends stand convicted on three counts of manslaughter, guilty of causing three deaths by pulling that stop sign out of the ground days earlier.

6   Although Miller, 20, and his housemates, Nissa Baillie, 21, and her boyfriend, Christopher Cole, 20, admitted taking about 20 road signs during a late-night spree sometime before the fatal crash, they denied tampering with the stop sign in front of Tim's Cafe.

7   But a jury did not believe them.

8   On June 19 Miller, Baillie, and Cole could be sentenced to life in prison in what is believed to be the first case in the United States in which the vandalism of a traffic sign has led to a multiple manslaughter conviction.

9   What has become known as the "stop sign case" has had a wrenching effect on the families of the six young people involved, while sparking a passionate community debate on the nexus of crime and punishment.

10   On one side is Assistant State Atty. Leland Baldwin, who prosecuted the three young people. "I have heard people ask: 'How dare you charge them with manslaughter? This was a prank. It was an unintentional crime,'" she said. "But this was not a prank. These were not young kids. These were young adults. So give me a break."

11   On the other side is Joseph Registrato, chief assistant to the Hillsborough County public defender, which represented Cole and Baillie.

12   "It's one thing to take a car when you're drunk and recklessly kill somebody," Registrato said. "That law is well-understood. But in this case, they may have committed criminal mischief and then later three people died. But others had gone through that intersection and didn't die. So there is a serious question about whether the [fallen] stop sign caused the deaths.

13   "From that they could get life in prison? It's hard to follow the ball here."

Road Sign Theft Called a Commonplace Prank

14 About this there is no debate: The chain of events that led up to that horrific crash in front of Tim's Cafe makes up a cautionary tale of sobering complexity.

15   Joe Episcopo figures at least half the population of America at one time or another has stolen a road sign to hang on a bedroom wall, to win a scavenger hunt or just for kicks.

16   In fact, says Episcopo, a lawyer who represents Miller, road sign theft is so common that, when potential jurors in the case against his client were asked if they had ever taken a sign, half the pool raised a hand and three of those who answered yes ended up being seated on the six-member panel. "Everybody has somebody in their family who takes signs," he said.

17   Indeed, vandalism and theft of road signs is a problem all across the country. After the trial here in the Hillsborough County courthouse was broadcast by Court TV, public officials from as far away as Washington state have been speaking out about the expense and danger resulting from defaced or stolen road signs.

18   In Iowa, a county engineer has announced plans to use the Tampa case as a springboard for a national education campaign on the issue.

19   Dave Krug, Hillsborough County public works department engineer, estimated that 25% of all road signs ever put up in the Tampa area are damaged by vandals, knocked down or stolen. Most road sign vandalism, however, does not result in triple fatalities, attract media attention and provoke heart-wrenching community anguish over wasted lives.

20   Moreover, most sign vandalism does not give rise to the sea of regrets among thousands of people—including at least 11 people who testified in the trial here—who noticed the downed stop sign during the 24 hours preceding the crash and failed to report it.

21   "Well, what did you do?" Baldwin asked of one witness who noticed that the stop sign was down.

22   "We just went back to work, got busy," the witness replied.

Three Target Signs "for a Rush"

23 Miller, Baillie, and Cole lived together in a rented $300-a-month mobile home on a country road less than three miles from the intersection of Keysville and Lithia-Pinecrest roads in eastern Hillsborough County where the fatal crash occurred just before midnight on Feb. 7, 1996.

24   According to interviews they gave to a local television station and Cole's testimony at trial, the three had been shopping at a nearby Wal-Mart, had drunk a couple of beers and were headed home when one of the three suggested that they take a few railroad signs. Cole told a television reporter that they began taking signs "for a rush."

25   Over a period of a couple of hours and a distance of about five miles, they unbolted and pulled up railroad signs, street name signs, a "Dead End" sign, a "Do Not Enter" sign and—from neighboring Polk County—at least one stop sign, tossing all of them in the back of their pickup truck.

26   Was it fun? Cole was asked. "I suppose so, yeah," he replied. "Yeah, it was fun at the time."

Night of Bowling Ends in Collision

27 Kevin Farr, who worked in his family's data processing business, had been bowling with his father, Les, and his two older brothers on the evening of his death. He rolled a 218 in his final league game and, as he left the bowling alley, he shouted at one of his brothers: "Tell Mom I'll be home between 11 o'clock and 12. I don't want her to worry."

28   From the bowling alley Farr drove to the house of Brian Hernandez, his best and oldest friend, and the pair then picked up Randall White. No one seems to know where they were going.

29   June Farr said that the death of the youngest of her four children has condemned her to live day by day. "And day by day takes on a whole new meaning after something like this," she said. "Sometimes it's more like a few minutes at a time."

30   The case against Miller, Cole and Baillie was circumstantial. There were no fingerprints on the stop sign and no eyewitnesses who put them at the scene. But

the fallen stop sign was well within the general area of the thefts to which the three had confessed and prosecutors presented expert testimony that the stop sign appeared to have been pulled from the ground, not run over by a vehicle.

31   The defense also had its own expert witness, a mechanical engineer who testified that the stop sign had been struck by a "lateral force."

Defendants Say They Panicked Next Day

32   Perhaps the most damning evidence against Cole, Miller, and Baillie came from their own statements to police. Ron Bradish, a Sheriff's Department traffic homicide investigator, testified that Cole and Miller admitted that—during their stealing spree—they sometimes would pull signs from the ground and, if a car came by, leave them to pick up later.

33   The day after the fatal crash, the three defendants admitted to police, they panicked. They gathered up most of the stolen signs from inside and outside their mobile home and tossed them off a bridge into nearby Alafia Creek. According to Bradish, Cole said that they got rid of the signs "so no one would think they took the stop sign down at the crash."

34   Held without bail, Cole, Miller, and Baillie are to be sentenced next week after the judge hears from lawyers on both sides, as well as from relatives of the convicted and those who died.

35   While she will not lobby for life sentences, Baldwin says, she will insist on long terms. "I hope this case will be a deterrent, or, at least, somewhat thought-provoking," she said. "Perhaps this is one of the types of cases that have to be tried every generation to remind high school kids and others that vandalism has consequences. And this does have an effect. Just days ago some kids in Leon County [Tallahassee] had a stop sign in a scavenger hunt and the media [publicly] stopped them."

36   Again, Registrato demurs. "This case is useless as a deterrent," he said. "Send these three children to prison for life and the kids in Hillsborough County where it happened won't have a clue about it the next day."

37   Episcopo and Registrato said they have prepared their clients for the worst. Sentencing guidelines call for 28 years to life and Judge Bob Anderson Mitcham has been known to use the suggested maximum as a starting point. Last year he put a man convicted of wounding two Tampa police officers in prison for seven consecutive life terms, ignoring guidelines that called for 14 to 24 years.

38   For June Farr, the sentencing decision seems straightforward. "My child got the maximum penalty and he had no choice in the matter," she said. "They knew exactly what was going to happen. They just didn't know who the victims would be. This was not a prank. Pranks don't kill."

39   To those who would find life in prison too harsh a price to pay for yanking out a stop sign, Farr responds: "They didn't have to go pick out a coffin."

40   Registrato said he would argue that Miller, Cole and Baillie could better atone for their sins and better service society by doing "a couple of years hard time in Florida State Prison and then be required for the next 18 years to go to

high schools twice a month and tell about the consequences of criminal mischief."

41   But Miller, Thomas Miller's father, clings to hope that his son will win a retrial and be found not guilty. He acknowledged that his son, who has a juvenile record for theft, has lied to him before. But this time, Miller said, "Tommy says he didn't take that sign and I believe it with all my heart. We know when he's lying."

42   Whatever the outcome, said Miller, 69, a retired postal worker, he knows that the lives of his family, as well as the other five families involved, are forever changed.

43   "I was in court every day," he said, "sitting in the front row on one side, across from the families of the dead boys. We didn't speak but I felt for them. . . . They lost their children. I understand.

44   "Now they have to understand that I've lost mine. Win or lose, this is a tragedy for both sides."

"Revelry and Mischief" in Utah

1   On the evening of September 24, 1977, a number of young people gathered at the defendant's home in Kearns. During the evening, some of them engaged in drinking alcoholic beverages. At about 10:30 P.M., they left the home, apparently bent on revelry and mischief. When they got to the intersection of 5215 South and 4620 West, defendant [Kelly K. Hallett] and the codefendant Richard Felsch (not a party to this appeal) bent over a stop sign, which faced northbound traffic on 4620 West, until it was in a position parallel to the ground. The group then proceeded north from the intersection, uprooted another stop sign and placed it in the backyard of a Mr. Arlund Pope, one of the state's witnesses. Traveling further on, defendant and his friends bent a bus stop sign over in a similar manner.

2   The following morning, Sunday, September 25, 1977, at approximately 9:00 A.M., one Krista Limacher was driving east on 5215 South with her husband and children, en route to church. As she reached the intersection of 4620 West, the deceased, Betty Jean Carley, drove to the intersection from the south. The stop sign was not visible, since the defendant had bent it over, and Ms. Carley continued into the intersection. The result was that Mrs. Limacher's vehicle struck the deceased's car broadside causing her massive injuries which resulted in her death in the hospital a few hours later.

State of Utah v. Hallett. 619 P.2d 337 (1980).

The Law on Homicide

Utah Criminal Code

Criminal Homicide

Criminal homicide—elements—designations of offenses

(1) (a) A person commits criminal homicide if he intentionally, knowingly, recklessly, with criminal negligence, or acting with a mental state otherwise specified in the statute defining the offense, causes the death of another human being, including an unborn child.

Murder

(1) Criminal homicide constitutes murder if the actor:

   (a) intentionally or knowingly causes the death of another;

   (b) intending to cause serious bodily injury to another commits an act clearly dangerous to human life that causes the death of another;

   (c) acting under circumstances evidencing a depraved indifference to human life engages in conduct which creates a grave risk of death to another and thereby causes the death of another;

   (d) while in the commission, attempted commission, or immediate flight from the commission or attempted commission of aggravated robbery, robbery, rape, object rape, forcible sodomy, or aggravated sexual assault, aggravated arson, arson, aggravated burglary, burglary, aggravated kidnapping, kidnapping, child kidnapping, rape of a child, object rape of a child, sodomy of a child, forcible sexual abuse, sexual abuse of a child, aggravated sexual abuse of a child, or child abuse . . . , when the victim is younger than 14 years of age, causes the death of another person . . . ; or

   (e) recklessly causes the death of a peace officer while in the commission or attempted commission of:

      (i) an assault against a peace officer; or

      (ii) interference with a peace officer if the actor uses force against a peace officer.

(2) Murder is a first degree felony.

Manslaughter

(1) Criminal homicide constitutes manslaughter if the actor:

   (a) recklessly causes the death of another; or

   (b) causes the death of another under the influence of extreme emotional disturbance for which there is a reasonable explanation or excuse; or

   (c) causes the death of another under circumstances where the actor reasonably believes the circumstances provide a legal justification or excuse

---

Utah Code Unannotated, 1996. Vol. 4. Charlottesville, VA: Michie Law Publishers, 1988–96.

for his conduct although the conduct is not legally justifiable or excusable under the existing circumstances.

(2) Under Subsection (1)(b), emotional disturbance does not include a condition resulting from mental illness.

(3) The reasonableness of an explanation or excuse under Subsection (1)(b), or the reasonable belief of the actor under Subsection (1)(c), shall be determined from the viewpoint of a reasonable person under the then existing circumstances.

(4) Manslaughter is a felony of the second degree.

Negligent homicide

(1) Criminal homicide constitutes negligent homicide if the actor, acting with criminal negligence, causes the death of another.

(2) Negligent homicide is a class A misdemeanor.

Definitions

Requirements of criminal conduct and criminal responsibility

No person is guilty of an offense unless his conduct is prohibited by law and:

(1) He acts intentionally, knowingly, recklessly, with criminal negligence, or with a mental state otherwise specified in the statute defining the offense, as the definition of the offense requires; or

(2) His acts constitute an offense involving strict liability.

Definitions of "intentionally, or with intent or willfully"; "knowingly, or with knowledge"; "recklessly, or maliciously"; and "criminal negligence or criminally negligent"

A person engages in conduct:

(1) Intentionally, or with intent or willfully with respect to the nature of his conduct or to a result of his conduct, when it is his conscious objective or desire to engage in the conduct or cause the result.

(2) Knowingly, or with knowledge, with respect to his conduct or to circumstances surrounding his conduct when he is aware of the nature of his conduct or the existing circumstances. A person acts knowingly, or with knowledge, with respect to a result of his conduct when he is aware that his conduct is reasonably certain to cause the result.

(3) Recklessly, or maliciously, with respect to circumstances surrounding his conduct or the result of his conduct when he is aware of but consciously disregards a substantial and unjustifiable risk that the circumstances exist or the result will occur. The risk must be of such a nature and degree that its disregard constitutes a gross deviation from the standard of care that an ordinary person would exercise under all the circumstances as viewed from the actor's standpoint.

(4) With criminal negligence or is criminally negligent with respect to circumstances surrounding his conduct or the result of his conduct when he ought to be aware of a substantial and unjustifiable risk that the circumstances exist or the result will occur. The risk must be of such a nature and degree that the failure to perceive it constitutes a gross deviation from the standard

of care that an ordinary person would exercise in all the circumstances as viewed from the actor's standpoint.

State v. Fisher

Negligent homicide and manslaughter. The general rule is that negligent homicide is a lesser included offense of manslaughter. In *State v. Parker*, 128 Ariz. 107, 624 P.2d 304 (App. 1980) . . . the Court of Appeals determined that the only difference between manslaughter and negligent homicide is an accused's mental state at the time of the incident. See also *State v. Montoya*, Ariz. 155, 608 P.2d 92 (App. 1980). Manslaughter is established where a person, aware of a substantial and unjustifiable risk that his or her conduct will cause the death of another, consciously disregards that risk. Negligent homicide is established where a person fails to perceive the substantial and unjustifiable risk that his or her conduct will cause the death of another. The element of the greater not found in the lesser is awareness of the risk.

Discussion and Writing Suggestions

1. You are either (1) a prosecuting attorney or (2) a defense attorney involved with the "For Fallen Stop Sign, Vandals Face Life" case. In researching precedents, you find the "'Revelry and Mischief in Utah" case. For purposes of preparing either your prosecution or your defense, compare and contrast the circumstances of the two cases. Consider (a) the activities of the respective defendants prior to the action being prosecuted; (b) their motivations; (c) the relationship between the defendants' actions and the automobile accidents that subsequently occurred; (d) the relative blameworthiness of the defendants; (e) with what crime, if any, the defendants should be charged; (f) any other factors you find relevant. Prepare your findings in the form of a memorandum to the District Attorney (if you are prosecuting) or the partners in your law firm (if you are defending).

2. Read the Utah Criminal Code in "The Law on Criminal Homicide," focusing on the distinctions drawn between murder, or manslaughter, or negligent homicide. Should the defendants Hallett and Felsch be charged with murder, or manslaughter, or negligent homicide? In a memo to the District Attorney, justify your decision. To help you with your thinking on this subject, review the definitions provided by the Utah Code of various key phrases ("intentionally, or with intent or willfully," "recklessly, or maliciously," etc.) in the Code. Review also the distinction drawn between "negligent homicide" and "manslaughter" in "The Law on Criminal Homicide."

State v. Fisher. 686 P.2nd2d 750 (1984).

3. In the "'Revelry and Mischief' in Utah" case, Hallett argued that the pulling down of a stop sign did not show the required *intent* to constitute negligent homicide. The Utah statute provides that a person is guilty of negligent homicide if he causes the death of another person

> with criminal negligence or is criminally negligent with respect to circumstances surrounding his conduct or the result of his conduct when he ought to be aware of a substantial and unjustifiable risk that the circumstances exist or the result will occur. The risk must be of such a nature and degree that the failure to perceive it constitutes a gross deviation from the standard of care that an ordinary person would exercise in all the circumstances as viewed from the actor's standpoint.

Based on the evidence before you and the inferences you draw from this evidence, do you believe, beyond a reasonable doubt, that the defendant's conduct met the elements of the above statute? Explain, in terms of the defendant's actions, viewed from his standpoint.

4. In the "'Revelry and Mischief' in Utah" case, Hallett argued that the evidence did not support the conclusion that his acts were the *proximate cause* of Ms. Carley's death. To quote from the court's "Opinion," summarizing this argument,

> [Defendant] starts with a uniformly recognized definition: that proximate cause is the cause which through its natural and foreseeable consequence, unbroken by any sufficient intervening cause, produces the injury which would not have occurred but for that cause. His [argument] here is that there was evidence that as the deceased approached from the south, she was exceeding the speed limit of 25 mph; and that this was subsequent intervening and proximate cause of her own death. This is based upon the fact that a motorist, who was also coming from the south, testified that he was going 25 mph and that Ms. Carley passed him some distance to the south as she approached the intersection.

Considering this argument, do you believe that the defendant's action in pulling down the stop sign was the *proximate* cause of the fatal accident? Explain your reasoning.

5. In separate opinions, two judges of the appellate court hearing the "'Revelry and Mischief' in Utah" case made the following arguments concerning the defendant's degree of responsibility for the fatality:

Maughan's Opinion

[W]here a party by his wrongful conduct creates a condition of peril, his action can properly be found to be the proximate cause of a resulting injury, even though later events which combined to cause the injury may also be classified as negligent, so long as the later act is something which can reasonably be expected to follow in the natural sequence of events. Moreover, when reasonable minds might differ as to whether it was the creation of the dangerous condition (defendant's conduct) which was the proximate cause, or whether it was some subsequent act (such as Ms. Carley's driving), the question is for the trier of the fact [the jury] to determine.

Reflecting upon what has been said above, we [believe] that whether the defendant's act of removing the stop sign was done in merely callous and thoughtless disregard of the safety of others, or with malicious intent, the result, which he should have foreseen, was the same: that it created a situation of peril; and that nothing that transpired thereafter should afford him relief from responsibility for the tragic consequences that did occur.

Hall's Opinion

The evidence produced at trial does not discount beyond a reasonable doubt the possibility that the actions of the decedent on the morning of September 25, 1977, constituted an independent, unforeseeable intervening cause. In this regard, it is to be noted that the evidence produced at trial clearly established that the accident occurred in broad daylight and that the stop sign in question had not been removed from the intersection, but merely bent over into a position where it was still marginally visible. Moreover, the word "Stop" was clearly printed in large block letters on the pavement leading into the intersection. Even if we were to assume, however, that defendant's action in bending the stop sign over erased all indication that vehicles proceeding north on 4620 West were obliged to yield right-of-way, such would render the location of the accident an unmarked intersection. The law requires due care in approaching such intersections, with such reasonable precautions as may be necessary under the circumstances.

Evidence also appearing in the record indicates that decedent was moving at an imprudent speed when she entered the intersection. Although the exact rate of speed is disputed, it is unchallenged that she had, less than a block behind, passed a truck which, itself, was doing the legal speed limit. All parties testified that she made no attempt to slow or brake upon entering the intersection. Under such circumstances, reasonable minds must entertain a reasonable doubt that the defendant's conduct was the sole efficient legal cause of her death. . . .

I would dismiss the charge of negligent homicide.

Which argument do you find more persuasive? Explain your reasoning.

6. Try to enter into the minds of the teenagers in the Florida case. One of these teens told a TV reporter that they pulled out the traffic signs "for a rush." What do you think he meant? Attempt to explain, from his point of view (to bewildered adults), why "it was fun at the time" to pull out traffic signs. What factors do you think contribute to some teenagers finding fun in such antisocial outlets? Suppose, for the sake of argument, that the teens were guilty of negligent homicide. Why would they fail to perceive the "substantial and unjustifiable risk that his or her conduct will cause the death of another"?

7. Almost certainly, you have not been involved in activities with such horrific consequences as those of the defendants in the Florida and Utah
cases. Almost certainly, however, all of us have been involved in actions
that, under certain circumstances, could have resulted in very serious
outcomes. And we must be prepared to deal with those outcomes. To
quote a widespread slogan these days: "Actions have consequences."
How do we go about determining—and dealing with—our responsibility
for the consequences of our actions? To what extent are our conscious
intentions a factor in our personal responsibility? Discuss these issues,
drawing upon one or two specific incidents in your own life—or the life
of someone you know.

8. *Group Assignment:* See Discussion and Writing Suggestion #11 on
page 779 and apply that assignment to one of the cases in this group.

SHOULD WE HOLD PARENTS RESPONSIBLE FOR THE ACTS OF THEIR CHILDREN?

In April 1999, two youths in Littleton, Colorado, went on a shooting rampage
in their high school. Thirteen students and a teacher died, and many more
were wounded before the shooters turned their weapons on themselves.
When police searched the youths' homes, they found in plain view (among
quantities of hate literature) a sawed-off shotgun and pipe bomb ingredients.
In the wake of the tragedy, many people wondered about the responsibilities of the parents of the two young killers: Didn't they see the danger signs?
Didn't they realize that their sons were walking time bombs? To what extent
might they share responsibility for the terrible acts of their children?

The last question has no easy answer, either in a particular case like this or
in a more general social context. Most societies, however, recognize the crucial role of parents in shaping the moral, as well as the emotional and intellectual, development of their children, and our society imposes liability, in
some cases, on parents who are negligent in this area.

Negligence in law is the failure to exercise the standard of care that a reasonably prudent person would have exercised in a given situation. One can
be negligent by doing something that a reasonable person would not do, or
by not doing something that a reasonable person would do. While parents
cannot be found criminally liable for the acts committed by their children,
they can be found civilly liable if their own negligence has made it possible
or easier for their children to harm others. A father who keeps a loaded gun
in an unlocked drawer may be found liable for negligence if his child takes
the gun and uses it, even unintentionally, to shoot someone.

A parent may also be liable for negligence if he or she knows, based on past
experience, that a child's conduct may pose a danger to others and fails to
exercise sufficient control over the child to prevent harm from occurring or
fails to warn the victim of the potential danger. Of course, the plaintiff in a
lawsuit must show that the parent *has* control—both legal control, in terms of

custody, and the ability to deter harmful conduct of the child. Generally, courts do recognize that it is more difficult to control a troubled 17-year-old than a five-year-old.

The cases that follow deal with the liability of parents for acts committed by their children. In these cases the victims or families of the victims have brought lawsuits for negligence against the parents, and they seek damages in the form of financial recompense. (Note that in these cases the children are sometimes referred to as "infants," even though they may be teenagers; this is simply legal terminology for minors.) This section begins with an article on parental liability, "When the Sins of the Child Point to Parents, Law's Grip Is Tenuous," by Kim Murphy and Melissa Healy. Three cases follow. This section also includes statements on the law that concern parental liability for the acts of children.

When the Sins of the Child Point to Parents, Law's Grip Is Tenuous
Kim Murphy and Melissa Healy

1   Should Steven Pfiel's parents have seen the signs of their son's murderous outburst?

2   At 7, he allegedly set fire to a motor home. As a grammar school student in suburban Chicago, he was accused of singing death chants to a classmate. After the student complained, Pfiel admitted to police that he had vandalized the student's home with a knife and had spray-painted satanic symbols on its side. According to friends, Pfiel dropped rocks on cars from over-passes.

3   When he was old enough to drive, he would swerve his car in hopes of picking off small animals.

4   Still, when he turned 17, his birthday gift from his parents was a hunting knife with a serrated, 5-inch blade. And three weeks later, on July 12, 1993, Pfiel used the knife to murder 13-year-old Hillary Norskog, and 17 months later, while awaiting trial, Pfiel beat his brother with a bat, slit his throat and then fled with three of his father's guns.

5   He is now serving a life prison sentence in Illinois, having pleaded guilty to both murders. And Pfiel's parents, a business executive and a stay-at-home mother who volunteered at his school, are facing a lawsuit from Norskog's mother.

6   "There are a whole lot of parents out there who act as if being a parent is just their right and it doesn't come with responsibilities," says Donald Pasulka, the Chicago attorney who brought the suit on behalf of Norskog's family.

7   "We sometimes view the parents as victims," Pasulka said. "When they see the school shootings in Arkansas and Littleton [Colo.] and Kentucky, people

Los Angeles Times 30 Apr. 1999: A1+.

are starting to wake up and say, 'Wait a minute: If you're not going to control your children, we're going to start controlling them—and you.' "

8   Across the country, 25 states have extended some form of legal sanctions against parents whose children commit crimes, although rarely have they been invoked for major crimes.

9   Los Angeles County has prosecuted 40 parents for not sending their children to school under California's 11-year-old parental responsibility law, one of the toughest in the nation. An Oregon woman got a hefty fine under a local ordinance when her son was repeatedly arrested for tobacco, marijuana and curfew violations. In Michigan, a pizza baker was ordered to pay a $300 fine for overlooking the fact that his son had in his bedroom property from a string of burglaries.

Increasing Cases in Civil Courts

10 Increasingly, parents are also being held accountable in civil courts for the wrongdoing of their offspring. The National Center for Victims of Crime has tracked as many as 100 cases in the past decade in which parents like the Pfiels have been sued for negligent care. And the volume is rising sharply, said staff attorney Lisa Ferguson.

11 Parents of school shooters in Jonesboro, Ark., West Paducah, Ky., and Moses Lake, Wash., all face substantial lawsuits from families of the victims—alleging they should have done more to control their children.

12 And President Clinton, as part of a package of proposals unveiled last week, called for making it a felony for parents to knowingly or recklessly allow children to use guns to commit crimes. Illinois last week became the 17th state to pass similar legislation.

13 Yet drawing a firm connection between what children do and what their parents could have done to stop it remains difficult and constitutionally problematic, say lawyers and almost any parent who has tried to tell a teenager: "Don't."

14 In the case of the recent high school shootings in Littleton that left 13 innocent victims dead, authorities have said they are looking at a diary, bomb-making equipment and part of a shotgun found in the home of one of the two teenage assailants, 18-year-old Eric Harris, to help determine whether the parents should face criminal charges.

15 "Parents of children in most states are subject to civil liability when they fail to exercise appropriate control over their children and their children cause harm. But in terms of criminal law, current legal principles provide significant obstacles to any significant prosecution of the parents, and I think for good reason," said Peter Arenella, professor of criminal law at UCLA.

16 "In this country, we believe that people should only be held accountable for their own criminal acts or the criminal acts of others they've encouraged. Clearly, you have here at best parents who were aware of the fact that their children had access to weapons. That doesn't mean they were aware of the possibility that their children would engage in such horrendous acts, much less that they encouraged them," Arenella said.

17   Tom Higgins, head of the Los Angeles County district attorney's juvenile division, suggests that in balancing a child's right to some measure of privacy and a parent's oversight responsibilities, the principle of probable cause ought to play a role.

18   "I don't go searching through my kids' bedroom," Higgins said. "They have drawers, they have boxes. I occasionally go in there to tell them to pick their stuff up off the floor, or wake them up when the alarm goes off. But I don't search my kids' room. So, 'should have known' needs to be prefaced with, is there something in their behavior that should have prompted them to search their kid's room?

19   "And let's just suppose they knew. And let's suppose they said, 'I'm taking that stuff out of your room, and I'm destroying it or I'm calling the cops, make your choice.' If they made the effort, and the kid [responded with] some expletive, what does a parent do? If there were reasonable efforts made and they failed, then I don't think they would fall under a parental accountability law."

Liability Laws Have Proliferated

20   Most states have had statutes on contributing to the delinquency of a minor since the 1950s and 1960s. Occasionally, they are brushed off to prosecute a pimp or an adult who serves alcohol to a minor.

21   But, experts say, specific parental liability laws have proliferated amid a surge in youth crime that has scared Americans and prompted a search for what—or who—is to blame. In pressing their cases, lawmakers and attorneys frequently draw on the argument that, along with their rights to raise children free of government meddling, parents bear the responsibility to provide adequate oversight.

22   In 1988, California amended its statute to target parents who do not "exercise reasonable care, supervision, protection and control" over their children. Penalties can include a year in jail and a $2,500 fine.

23   Although similar laws have been attacked as unconstitutionally vague, the California Supreme Court upheld the law in 1993, overruling lawyers for the American Civil Liberties Union who said it was "unfair to blame poor parents for something that is a failure of our society as a whole."

24   Since then, the revised California law has been used sporadically: against parents who served alcohol to a juvenile who then went out and injured someone in an automobile accident, for example, or parents who left a gun in the house unlocked. Its primary target in Los Angeles has been parents of elementary school children who are chronically absent from school.

25   In recent years, parents of 40,000 truant children have been threatened with prosecution under the law. Only about 40 have had criminal charges filed—the longest jail term was nine months—because most parents opt to send their children to school instead, Higgins said, adding that "in fact, our goal is not court but to turn the behavior around."

26   Oregon, Louisiana, Alabama, Wyoming and Hawaii all adopted laws in recent years threatening parents with fines or prison for negligent parenting, although some have been struck down in the courts. An Oklahoma law requires parents to complete community service or pay a fine of up to $2,000 if their

child possesses a firearm at school. Florida requires parents to pay the cost of their child's criminal prosecution, and in Tennessee, parents must pay the cost of medical exams, treatment and pretrial placement of their children.

Citations Drop after Supervision Ordinance

27 Silverton, Ore., whose 1995 parental supervision ordinance became a model for the state law, has seen its citations under the law go down from 14 the first year to two last year. There has been a 35% reduction in overall juvenile crime during the same period, said Police Chief Rick Lewis. "So the word has gotten out. The parents understand what their role is in their kids' lives."

28   Most of the crimes prosecuted in Silverton involve relatively minor infractions, like marijuana possession and alcohol offenses. Criminal charges against parents in a case like Littleton have been rare or nonexistent, most legal experts said, because of the difficulty in proving criminal recklessness: that a parent knew there was a substantial risk the child was going to commit a crime but did nothing to prevent it.

29   "A criminal charge is kind of like a cake recipe. We have to have a number of elements that go into it, and if we don't have them all, we don't have a crime," said John Knodell, prosecuting attorney in Grant County, Wash. "We've got to show that the parents were more than oblivious, that they actually knew that what they were doing was causing the problem."

30   Knodell is familiar with what it takes to charge a parent with such a crime because he strongly considered charging the parents of Barry Loukaitis, a 14-year-old who, wearing a black trench coat to hide two handguns and a deer rifle, fatally shot two students and a teacher at a Moses Lake junior high school in 1996.

31   His mother, JoAnn Phillips, admitted in testimony at his criminal trial that a month before the killings she told her son that she was going to tie up her ex-husband and his girlfriend and shoot herself as they watched.

32   Barry, she said, a former straight-A student, had been listening to her talk about her marital problems for years but became worried and depressed after she told him of her plan to kill herself.

"Testified That They Were Lousy Parents"

33 Phillips also admitted that she had helped her son buy the trench coat and that she had taken him target shooting not long before the high school attack, Knodell said. Indeed, at least one of the guns used in the shooting had been left in the back of the father's car, he said.

34   "They both testified that they were lousy parents, their lousy parenting was what led Barry to snap and become delusional or aggressive. Dad was absent most of the time," Knodell said. But neither parent had the requisite mental state to support criminal charges, he said.

35   "It had to be more than simple negligence, it had to be criminal recklessness," he said. "There's a difference between moral culpability and legal culpability."

36   Lawyers in civil cases need only prove negligence and by a lesser standard than the proof "beyond a reasonable doubt" required in criminal cases.

37   A Chicago-area family won a $300,000 settlement from the well-to-do parents of 16-year-old David Biro, who broke into a townhome in an affluent suburb and murdered a man and his pregnant wife in 1990. Attorney John Corbett introduced evidence that Biro had previously shot his BB gun out of his bedroom window at passers-by, injuring at least two, and had tried to poison his family by pouring wood alcohol into their milk.

38   A search of the boy's room, according to evidence introduced at trial, turned up two guns, a set of handcuffs, a bag of burglary tools and a bounty of satanic writings.

39   "I don't think they ever went into his room," Corbett said of the parents. "They were pretty much oblivious."

40   A judge in Kentucky last week refused to dismiss a case filed against the parents of Michael Carneal, who pleaded guilty in the shooting deaths of three fellow middle school students in West Paducah in 1997.

41   "People are appreciating the fact that if they're going to stop the violence in the schools, it's going to have to start someplace, and the home is the best place to do that," said Michael Breen, the attorney representing parents of the victims. "What better way to get Mom and Dad to start taking care of what's going on at home than to start putting them in jail?"

42   "The analogy is of a vicious dog," added Bobby McDaniel, who is suing the parents of 12-year-old Andrew Golden and 14-year-old Mitchell Johnson on behalf of three of the five students killed at a Jonesboro, Ark., middle school last year. "An owner of a dog is liable for harm inflicted by the dog if the owner knew, or should have known, the dog would do it.

43   "I believe the law takes the position that a parent cannot say, 'I didn't see this problem, I had no idea, I didn't realize, I looked but I didn't see, I listened but I didn't hear.' The parent must have the responsibility to know, appreciate and understand what their child is doing."

44   But Michael Borders, the Chicago lawyer defending the Pfiels in a case set to go to trial in October, said it is too easy to "flyspeck" a family's history and come out with a pronouncement that "you should have known."

45   "Everybody is all too quick to judge parents after something like this," said Borders, who dismisses virtually all of the charges alleged in the Norskog lawsuit as "rumor and innuendo without a shred of evidence."

"Children Have Their Own Minds"

46   Parents who have never experienced this with their own children "can't appreciate that children have their own minds, make their own decisions, not only on the basis of what they learn at home but from society, that teenagers are notorious for not sharing with their parents what they want to hide," Borders added. "It's a tragedy, but it's not going to be cured by dragging a bunch of parents into court."

47   Indeed, some people caution, holding parents liable for their children's crimes could have the result of further fracturing troubled families. . . .

48   "If parents feel they're going to get prosecuted because their children are planning something or hiding something, and that leads to parents being more intrusive in terms of checking out the children's bureau drawers and their computer and stuff like that, what's that going to do to parent-child trust issues?"

asked Howard Davidson, director of the American Bar Assn.'s Center on Children and the Law. "Do we want to promote parents being snoops and informers against their kids?"

The Law on the Duty of Parent to Control Conduct of Child

Restatement of Torts, § 316. Duty of Parent to Control Conduct of Child

1 A parent is under a duty to exercise reasonable care so to control his minor child as to prevent it from intentionally harming others or from so conducting itself as to create an unreasonable risk of bodily harm to them, if the parent

(a) knows or has reason to know that he has the ability to control his child, and
(b) knows or should know of the necessity and opportunity for exercising such control.

Comment:

2 *a.* While the father as head of the family group is no longer responsible for the actions of all the members of his household or even for those of his minor child, he is responsible for their conduct in so far as he has the ability to control it. This duty is not peculiar to a father. It extends to the mother also in so far as her position as mother gives her an ability to control her child.

3 *b.* The duty of a parent is only to exercise such ability to control his child as he in fact has at the time when he has the opportunity to exercise it and knows the necessity of so doing. The parent is not under a duty so to discipline his child as to make it amenable to parental control when its exercise becomes necessary to the safety of others.

4 *c.* In order that the parent may be liable under the rule stated in this Section, it is not necessary that the actions of the child which he fails to prevent or control are such as to make the child himself subject to liability. The child may be so young as to be incapable of negligence, but this does not absolve the parent from the performance of his duty to exercise reasonable care to control the child's conduct. Indeed, the very youth of the child is likely to give the parent more effective ability to control its actions and to make it more often necessary to exercise it.

Illustration:

1. A is informed that his six-year-old child is shooting at a target in the street with a .22 rifle, in a manner which endangers the safety of those using the street. A fails to take the rifle away from the child, or to take any other action. The child unintentionally shoots B, a pedestrian, in the leg. A is subject to liability to B.

Restatement of the Law, Second: Torts, 2nd. As Adapted and promulgated by the American Law Institute, Washington, D.C. May 25, 1963, and May 22, 1964. St. Paul, MN: West Publishing, 1965.

Case Law: Seifert v. Owen

[Parental liability for acts of children applies:]

(1) where the parent permits the child to have access to an instrument which, because of its nature, use and purposes is so dangerous as to constitute, in the hands of a child, an unreasonable risk to others (Firearms, dynamite, etc.)

(2) where the parent permits the child to have access to an instrumentality which, though not "inherently dangerous," is likely to be put to a dangerous use by a *known* propensity of the child (Matches, baseball bat, bicycle ridden on a busy sidewalk, etc.) and

(3) where the parent fails to restrain the child from vicious conduct imperiling others and the parent knows of the child's propensity toward such conduct (Beating up little children, etc.)

Parental Responsibility: California Civil Code

5   [California] *Civil Code* section 1714.1 subdivision (a): Any act of willful misconduct of a minor which results in injury or death to another person or in any injury to the property of another shall be imputed to the parent or guardian having custody and control of the minor for all purposes of civil damages, and the parent or guardian having custody and control shall be jointly and severally liable with the minor for any damages resulting from the willful misconduct. [¶] The joint and several liability of the parent or guardian having custody and control of a minor under this subdivision shall not exceed ten thousand dollars ($10,000) for each tort of the minor, and in the case of injury to a person, imputed liability shall be further limited to medical, dental and hospital expenses incurred by the injured person, not to exceed ten thousand dollars ($10,000). The liability imposed by this section is in addition to any liability now imposed by law.

6   [California] *Civil Code* section 1714.3: . . . Civil liability for any injury to the person or property of another proximately caused by the discharge of a firearm by a minor under the age of 18 years shall be imputed to a parent or guardian having custody or control of the minor for all purposes of civil damages, and such parent or guardian shall be jointly and severally liable with such minor for any damages resulting from such act, if such parent or guardian either permitted the minor to have the firearm or left the firearm in a place accessible to the minor. [¶] The liability imposed by this section is in addition to any liability now imposed by law. However, no person, or group of persons collectively, shall incur liability under this section in any amount exceeding fifteen thousand dollars ($15,000) for injury to or death of one person as a result of any one occurrence or, subject to the limit as to one person, exceeding thirty thousand dollars ($30,000) for injury to or death of all persons as a result of any one such occurrence.

Seifert v. Owen. 460 P.2d 19 (1969).

The Motorcycle Accident

1   The defendant father [Walter Hicks] purchased, by personal check, a 1976, 250CC Bultaco "trials" motorcycle for his 14-year-old son Walter, Jr., approximately one month prior to the collision. The bill of sale was made out to "Walter Hicks," without the suffix "Jr." According to defendants, Walter Jr. repaid his father from money he had saved and the proceeds from the sale of the fifth motorcycle the boy had owned over a five-year period—a 125CC Power Dyne. Neither defendant could recall if the repayment equalled the cost of the motorcycle. Since the 250CC Bultaco motorcycle was a trials competition bike, it was not equipped with a rear view mirror, horn, or headlight. The motorcycle was neither inspected nor registered and Walter Jr. did not have a motorcycle license. Walter Jr. had participated in trials competition with smaller motorcycles, but the 193-pound, 250CC Bultaco was the largest machine the 14-year-old boy had ever used. The maximum speed the five-gear motorcycle could attain was 35 miles per hour.

2   Walter Hicks placed restrictions on his son's use of the motorcycle because he knew that absent such limitations, the vehicle's use was dangerous to his son and others. Therefore, Walter Jr. was directed not to operate the motorcycle off his father's property unless accompanied by either his father or his older brothers, all of whom owned motorcycles. Walter Jr. admitted that he had violated said restriction on prior occasions and the father admitted that he possessed knowledge of the violations. Furthermore, the father acknowledged that the motorcycle was capable of being locked, chained or otherwise secured at the house, which would have prevented its use off his premises when neither he nor an older son was present. Such measures were not taken and Walter Jr. continued to have unimpeded access to the motorcycle. On the day of the collision Walter Jr. was violating his father's restrictions by operating the motorcycle off his father's premises, without his permission and unaccompanied by an older member of the family.

3   The scene of the accident is a residential neighborhood where many small children are accustomed to playing on the dirt and gravel streets and in the nearby woods. Old Haverstraw Road is the only paved street in the neighborhood, running in a north-south direction. The defendants' residence is located on Chester Avenue, a dirt and gravel road, running east and west. Parallel with and to the south of Chester Avenue is Central Avenue. Central Avenue's road surface is similarly composed of dirt and gravel. Both Chester Avenue and Central Avenue are dead-end streets which intersect with Old Haverstraw Road to the east. A path through the woods, about 200 feet long, connects Chester Avenue with Central Avenue. The wooded path stops at the northern edge of Central Avenue, approximately 250 feet west of the intersection of Central Avenue and Old Haverstraw Road. On the south side of Central Avenue, across from the wooded path, is the Vassallo residence. On the day of the accident a six-inch high sand pile was located a short distance west of the wooded path, in

Costa v. Hicks. 470 N.Y.S. 2nd 627 (1983).

the middle of Central Avenue. A milk truck was parked on the north side of Central Avenue, approximately 20 feet west of the sand pile. West of the parked milk truck was another path through the woods, leading to the residence of Walter Jr's. friend, Doug Bull.

4   Aside from the infant plaintiff (Michael Costa) and defendant Walter Jr., the only eyewitnesses to the accident were Joseph Griffin, then age eight, and Michael's younger brother, Jeffrey Costa, then age five; both testified on behalf of the plaintiffs.

5   According to plaintiffs' eyewitnesses, the infant plaintiff, his brother Jeffrey and Joe Griffin, were standing on the front lawn of the residence of the Plesach family, which is located at the end of Chester Avenue. They observed Walter Jr. riding his motorcycle, "fairly fast," back and forth on Chester Avenue. During these runs, Walter Jr. performed more than one "wheelie," meaning he raised the front wheel off the ground and rode on the rear wheel only. Walter Jr.'s father acknowledged that a "wheelie" was a dangerous maneuver, especially in the vicinity of children. Two other children, under the age of five, were also present on the Plesach's front lawn. The memory of the witnesses as to the number of wheelies performed and whether Walter Jr. performed them at the children's request differed.

6   Subsequently, Walter Jr. proceeded to drive the motorcycle south along the wooded path connecting Chester Avenue with Central Avenue. The children followed. Some discrepancies in the plaintiffs' witnesses' testimony exist as to the events which occurred after the children arrived at the edge of the wooded path, where it exists onto Central Avenue.

7   Joseph Griffin, age 12 at the time of the trial, testified that upon arriving at the edge of the wooded path, where it exits onto Central Avenue, he observed Walter Jr. turning his motorcycle around at the intersection of Central Avenue and Old Haverstraw Road. Walter Jr. then drove west on Central Avenue, passing the witness. After Walter Jr. passed the parked milk truck, he turned his motorcycle around and proceeded east on Central Avenue. Jeffrey Costa was standing in the path of the motorcycle, i.e., the area between the sand pile and the Vassallo's front lawn. The motorcycle was "[c]lose" to and "about to run Jeffrey down," when the infant plaintiff Michael ran off the sand pile and pushed his younger brother out of the way. Michael pushed Jeffrey in the direction of the Vassallo's house. The motorcycle then hit the infant plaintiff.

8   Jeffrey Costa, age nine at the time of the trial, testified that while standing at the edge of the wooded path, he saw Walter Jr. drive past him, going east on Central Avenue, toward Old Haverstraw Road. During this run, Walter Jr. did one "wheelie." When Walter Jr. reached Old Haverstraw Road, he turned around and proceeded to drive to the west end of Central Avenue, passing the children. Walter Jr. stopped at the parked milk truck, turned around and drove east, back toward Old Haverstraw Road. All the boys, including the witness, were standing near the edge of the wooded path, but Jeffrey could not remember his brother Michael's nor Joe Griffin's exact location. The witness recalled that his brother began to run across Central Avenue toward the Vassallo's house

when Walter Jr.'s motorcycle was "stopped" near the milk truck. Jeffrey next saw the motorcycle collide with Michael at the edge of the Vassallo's yard during Walter Jr.'s operation of the motorcycle in an easterly direction, toward Old Haverstraw Road.

9   Michael Costa, the infant plaintiff, age 11 at the time of the trial, testified that while standing on the sand pile on Central Avenue he saw Walter Jr. ride past him on the motorcycle and do wheelies. He did not recall how many times Walter Jr. drove past him, but it was more than once. The last thing he remembered was seeing Walter Jr. drive around the parked milk truck, going west on Central Avenue. He did not see the motorcycle after it went around the milk truck, but he thought "it was on the other side." The next thing he recalled was waking up in a car on the way to the hospital.

10   Walter Hicks Jr., age 18 at the time of trial, a high school graduate and an auto mechanic, presented a different version of the events leading up to the collision. Although he admitted that he twice raised the front wheel of the motorcycle off the ground and dropped it while riding up and down Chester Avenue, he explained that he was not doing wheelies, but was checking the front wheel suspension after having changed the fork oil. He observed a number of children on the Plesach's lawn, but he did not have a conversation with them. He then drove through the wooded path to Central Avenue. He did not see any children following him; the motorcycle was not equipped with a rear view mirror. At the end of the wooded path, he drove west on Central Avenue, past the parked milk truck, to another wooded path which leads to the house of his friend, Doug Bull. He never turned east on Central Avenue to go toward Old Haverstraw Road, nor did he do wheelies on Central Avenue. Upon arriving at Bull's residence, he observed that his friend's van was not in the driveway so he proceeded to drive home, retracting his prior route. When he reached the parked milk truck on Central Avenue, he saw six or seven children playing in the sand pile. He did not slow down, but continued to proceed east along the path which ran between the sand pile and the Vassallo's front lawn, at a speed of approximately 10 to 15 miles per hour. When he was 10 feet from the sand pile, all the children started running in different directions. The infant plaintiff and his brother ran south, toward Vassallo's residence. While applying his back brakes, Walter Jr. turned south, off the path and onto the Vassallo's lawn. On the lawn, at the point approximately 10 feet from the edge of Central Avenue, the left handlebar of the motorcycle collided with the infant plaintiff's forehead. The motorcycle fell to the ground about three feet past the point of impact.

11   Whether defendant Walter Hicks, Jr. exercised reasonable care in operating the motorcycle under the circumstances of this case was dependent upon several factors, not the least important of which was speed.

12   Walter Jr. maintained that he was proceeding at 10 to 15 miles per hour. The credibility of this statement is suspect when evaluated in light of the testimony of plaintiffs' expert that the subject motorcycle was equipped with five gears, which enables it to accelerate to its maximum speed of 35 miles per hour over a shorter period of time and distance than the average motorcycle, and the state-

ment of defendant Walter Jr., in his deposition, that the motorcycle was in fourth gear when the accident happened.

13 . . . The motorcycle was equipped with front and rear brakes, yet Walter Jr. applied only the rear brakes. Although a degree of skill is required to safely apply the front brakes of a motorcycle, he conceded that he had applied the front brakes on occasions prior to the accident. Expert testimony was elicited that the stopping distance could be reduced by half if both brakes were applied. The motorcycle came to rest three feet from the point of impact.

Shouldn't the Parents Have Known?

1   The plaintiff brought this personal injury action against the defendant, John C. Crumpton, Jr. and his parents, the defendants John C. Crumpton and Carol Crumpton, alleging that John, Jr. had raped her during the early morning hours of 28 June 1978. On that date John, Jr. was 17 years old having been born on 19 October 1960. The plaintiff further alleged that the defendants John and Carol Crumpton knew or had reason to know that John, Jr. used drugs and was of a dangerous mental state and disposition which made it foreseeable that he would intentionally injure others unless reasonable steps were taken to supervise and control him. The plaintiff asserted that the defendants John C. Crumpton and Carol Crumpton had a legal duty to exercise reasonable care to control and supervise John, Jr. so as to prevent him from intentionally injuring others. She alleged that they failed to perform this duty, in that they failed to prevent John, Jr. from having access to and using illegal drugs and deadly weapons and failed to prevent him from going abroad alone at night after having used such drugs and after having gained possession of such deadly weapons. She further alleged that, as a proximate result of the negligence of the defendants John and Carol Crumpton, the defendant John C. Crumpton, Jr. broke into her home while under the influence of illegal drugs and repeatedly raped her by force and against her will after using a deadly weapon, a knife, to overcome her resistance. . . .

2   The . . . evidence of the parties established that John Crumpton, Jr. was one of five children of John and Carol Crumpton. John, Jr. was born with a club foot and was found during early childhood to have hypoglycemia, diabetes and ulcerative colitis. During his childhood and early adolescence, his family life was comfortable and secure. He went with his parents and grandparents on regular hunting, fishing and golfing activities as well as on frequent trips to the beach.

3   He began using marijuana and other controlled substances at an early age, however, and was a regular user of various controlled substances by the time he was thirteen years old. His parents were aware of his use of controlled sub-

---

Moore v. Crumpton. 295 S.E.2d 436 (1982).

stances and attempted by various methods to discourage his use of these illegal substances. John, Jr. continued the use of controlled substances, purchasing them at times with the allowance money his parents still gave him on an irregular basis and at times with money he earned from part-time jobs. During this period of his life, John, Jr. frequently argued with his parents and skipped school. He was once arrested for carrying a concealed knife. He also impregnated a young girl and apparently was hospitalized on one occasion for a drug overdose. Prior to the rape of the plaintiff, John, Jr. owned or was in possession of various hunting knives and guns given to him by his parents. Although his parents kept alcoholic beverages in the home, the pint of bourbon which John, Jr. drank on the night of the rape was apparently obtained at a friend's home.

4   During May of 1978, Carol Crumpton and John Crumpton separated and she moved to a new address. By agreement of the couple, Carol Crumpton took their three youngest children to live with her, and John Crumpton had custody of John, Jr. and one other child of the marriage. On 28 June 1978, Carol Crumpton was on vacation at the beach. Sometime prior to that date, John Crumpton completed plans for a vacation for himself and the other child in Hawaii. Before leaving home, he made arrangements for John, Jr. to visit with grandparents in Roxboro. Apparently, after his father left Chapel Hill on vacation, John, Jr. drank a large amount of whiskey, took some type of controlled substances, got "high" and broke into the plaintiff's home on 28 June 1978 and raped her.

5   The forecasts of evidence of the parties also tended to indicate that the defendants John and Carol Crumpton consulted a psychologist when John, Jr. was nine years old due to problems associated with his physical infirmities. They sought the help of school guidance counselors and various mental health professionals when John, Jr. was in junior high school and had developed academic and drug related problems. The parents made frequent attempts to discipline John, Jr. and to reason with him. They sent him to a private high school during the tenth grade in order to provide a change of environment, and he performed well there. They returned him to the private high school for the eleventh grade, but John, Jr. refused to stay and returned home early during that school year. John, Jr. and his parents went to numerous mental health professionals for counseling. In addition to this counseling, John, Jr. was treated by John A. Gorman, Ph.D., a clinical psychologist, and Landrum S. Tucker, M.D., a psychiatrist. Each of these men saw, diagnosed and treated John, Jr. on several occasions. Dr. Tucker saw John, Jr. on five occasions in January and February of 1978 and among other things reviewed his psychological testing. Both Dr. Gorman and Dr. Tucker indicated to the defendants John and Carol Crumpton that John, Jr. was not disposed toward violent or dangerous behavior and that he was not a person who should or could be involuntarily committed. Although both doctors indicated that John, Jr. would require continued treatment, he broke off his counseling with both of them. His parents could not or did not require him to return.

The Teenage Sniper

1   Michael Clark, aged 16, left his home in Long Beach shortly after 8 o'clock on the evening of 24 April 1965, taking without permission a family automobile, credit cards, and his father's 6.5 × 55 millimeter Swedish Mauser military rifle equipped with telescopic sight. About 6 o'clock the following morning he stationed himself near Santa Maria on a hill overlooking Highway 101 and began firing at passing automobiles, as a consequence of which three persons were killed and others seriously wounded. When the police moved in on his position, Michael put the rifle to his head and killed himself.

2   William, Lucille, and Kim Reida, victims of Michael's shooting, brought this action for personal injuries and wrongful death against Michael's estate and against Forest Clark and Joyce Clark, Michael's parents. The complaint charged the parents with negligence in the training, supervision, and control of Michael, and negligence in making firearms available to him. A summary judgment was entered in favor of the Clarks, and the Reidas have appealed.

3   . . . Forest Clark was a Long Beach businessman, a veteran of two wars, an active member of his church, and the father of three children, Michael, 16, another son 15, and a daughter, 10. Michael, a student of average scholastic ability in the eleventh grade at Woodrow Wilson High School, was friendly, quiet, neat, a member of the Boy Scouts, and a member of the Sea Scouts. He liked music, dances, and sports, and he played saxophone in the high school band. He got along well with others, including his brother and sister. He regularly attended church with his family, he did not use alcohol or drugs, he never displayed emotional instability, nor had he ever been in trouble with the school authorities, the police, or the juvenile authorities. According to the father's declaration Michael had never intentionally harmed anyone prior to the shootings. In 1961 Forest Clark purchased a Mauser rifle and converted it into a hunting rifle with telescopic sight. On two occasions, the first on a rifle range and the second on a hunting trip, he showed Michael how to operate the rifle. Together with a sack of steel-jacketed military ammunition, the rifle was stored in the garage in a locked cabinet to which there were two keys, one which was regularly kept in the father's dresser drawer in a location known to Michael, and the other which had disappeared earlier but whose whereabouts were known to the younger son. On the night of Michael's disappearance the father did not know the rifle had been taken, and he did not discover it until the morning of the shootings.

4   Joyce Clark, a housewife and school teacher, declared that to her knowledge her son Michael had been congenial, nonaggressive, and without emotional problems. He never intentionally injured any living thing and she could not explain why he had acted the way he had. She had not known the rifle was missing until after the shootings took place.

Reida v. Lund. 96 Cal. Rptr. 102 (1971).

5   In opposition to the motion plaintiffs filed the declaration of a psychologist, who said he had read the Clark's declarations, the transcript of the coroner's inquest, and newspaper articles about the shootings. On the basis of his reading he concluded: that Michael suffered from schizophrenia, paranoid type; that the symptoms of this disease must have been apparent to the Clarks; that the Clarks knew or should have known that Michael was capable of violent, irrational acts and might use any weapon available to him; that their denials of such knowledge were inconsistent with Michael's behavior at Santa Maria and therefore incredible.

6   Plaintiff's complaint in effect charged two kinds of negligence: (1) failure of the Clarks to train, control, and supervise Michael, and (2) failure of Forest Clark to keep the rifle out of Michael's hands.

Discussion and Writing Suggestions

1. In "The Motorcycle Accident" case, should the plaintiffs, Peter and Michael Costa, be able to recover damages from Walter Hicks, father of Walter Hicks, Jr., who unintentionally ran down young Michael with his motorcycle? (The boy suffered a fractured skull in the accident.)

   Keep in mind that the defendant in this case is not the driver of the motorcycle, but rather, his parent, who is being sued for negligence. Based on the law on parental liability, as outlined in the *Restatement of Torts,* Sec. 316, and on the case law in *Seifert v. Owen* (see page 818), to what extent was the father negligent in failing "to exercise reasonable care so to control his minor child"? Did the father have reason to believe, based on his past experience, that his son might operate the motorcycle off his property, and should he have foreseen that his son might operate it in a way that might be dangerous to others? Cite evidence to support your views. You might also add what the elder Hicks could have done to reduce the possibility of such an accident.

2. You are on the jury of the "Shouldn't the Parents Have Known?" case. How would you vote on the civil liability of John C. Crumpton and Carol Crumpton for negligence in controlling their son, who committed a rape? Consider each parent's liability separately. Apply the standards of the *Restatement of Torts,* Sec. 316 (see page 817). How much did each parent know of John, Jr.'s violent propensities? What steps did each take to control him? To what extent should they have foreseen the crimes that their son committed? You may also want to respond to a larger, but not necessarily legal, question: What could they have done, if anything, to prevent what happened from happening?

3. Based on the facts provided in the "Teenage Sniper" case, discuss the liability of each parent, Forest Clark and Joyce Clark, for "negligence in the training, supervision, and control of Michael, and negligence in making firearms available to him." Apply the standards of the

Restatement of Torts, Sec. 316. Take into account, also, Sections 1714.1 and 1714.3 (see page 818) of the California Civil Code (following the Facts of the Case).

To what extent did the Clarks have foreknowledge of their son's violent propensities? Did Forest Clark take adequate steps to secure his rifle and keep it out of the hands of his son? How do you assess the evidence provided by Michael's psychologist?

4. Based upon your reading and discussion of the cases in this section, what do you think parents can do to prevent the kinds of damages and crimes illustrated here? To what extent should the law be a factor in enforcing parental responsibility to control and supervise their children's activities? To what extent is it a good idea to allow victims and families of victims to sue the parents of minors who injure or kill others? In formulating your response, draw also upon the opening article, "When the Sins of the Child Point to Parents, Law's Grip Is Tenuous."

5. Select one of the cases treated in this group. Imagine that you are representing either the plaintiff or the defendant. Compose either an opening statement or a closing argument for this case. Remember that your audience is the jury. Draw upon the facts of the case in a way that is likely to have the greatest impact upon the jury. Keep in mind, however, that jury members may turn against you—and your client—if they think that you are overly manipulating the facts, being deceptive, making reckless claims, or attempting too crudely to play upon their emotions.

Legal Glossary

Like every other profession (and perhaps more than most), the law has its own special language—a language often so complicated and obscure that even lawyers have difficulty understanding it. Here is a glossary of legal terms that you will encounter while reading this chapter. The definitions, for the most part, are from The Plain Language Law Dictionary, *edited by Robert E. Rothenberg. In some cases (indicated by "[Black's]" after the definition), they are taken from* Black's Law Dictionary: New Pocket Edition, *edited by Bryan A. Garner. In a very few other cases [indicated in brackets], we have provided definitions that do not appear in the dictionaries. Not included here are terms that are defined in the text itself— for example, when a statute or judicial instruction defines what is meant by "public nuisance" or "defective condition" or explains the meaning of "involuntary manslaughter."*

abettor   One who promotes or instigates the performance of a criminal act.

alleged   Claimed; charged.

appeal   The request for a review by a higher court of a verdict or decision made by a lower court.

appellant The party who appeals a case from a lower to a higher court.

appellate court A court with the authority to review the handling and decision of a case tried in a lower court.

appellee The respondent; the party against whom an appeal is taken.

breach A violation.

case A contested issue in a court of law; a controversy presented according to the rules of judicial proceedings.

civil Of or relating to private rights and remedies that are sought by action or suit, as distinct from criminal proceedings. [Black's]

civil law Law dealing with civil [private], rather than criminal matters.

codify A code is a collection of laws; the published statutes governing a certain area, arranged in a systematic manner [thus, to "codify" is to render into law].

common law 1. Law declared by judges in area not controlled by government regulation, ordinances, or statutes. 2. Law originating from usage and custom, rather than from written statutes.

comparative negligence A term that is used in a suit to recover damages, in which the negligence of the defendant is compared to that of the plaintiff. In other words, if the plaintiff was slightly negligent but the defendant was grossly negligent, the plaintiff may be awarded damages. Or, if the plaintiff was grossly negligent and the defendant only slightly negligent, no award may be granted.

compensatory damages The precise loss suffered by a plaintiff, as distinguished from punitive damages, which are over and above the actual losses sustained.

contributory negligence Negligence in which there has been a failure on the part of the plaintiff to exercise ordinary, proper care, thus contributing toward an accident. Such contributory negligence on the part of the plaintiff in a damage suit often constitutes a defense for the defendant.

counsel A lawyer, an attorney, a counsellor. To counsel means to advise.

court A place where justice is administered.

criminal law That branch of the law that deals with crimes and their punishment. In other words, this type of law concerns itself with public wrongs, such as robbery, burglary, forgery, homicide, etc.

culpable At fault; indifferent to others' rights; blamable; worthy of censure.

decedent A person who has died.

decision A judgment or decree issued by a judge or jury; the deciding of a lawsuit; findings of a court.

defendant A person sued in a civil proceeding or accused in a criminal proceeding. [Black's]

deposition The written testimony of a witness, given under oath. Such a statement may be presented in a trial, before a trial, at a hearing, or in response to written questions put to a witness. A deposition is also called an *affidavit* or a *statement under oath.*

directed verdict   A situation in which a judge tells the jury what its verdict must be [because the evidence is so compelling that only one decision can reasonably follow]. [Black's]

discovery   Compulsory disclosure by a party to an action, at another party's request, of facts or documents relevant to the action; the primary discovery devices are interrogatories, depositions, requests for admissions, and requests for production. [Black's]

duty   A legal obligation.

enjoin   To forbid; to issue an injunction, thus restraining someone from carrying out a specific act; a court order demanding that someone not do, or do, something.

evidence   Anything that is brought into court in a trial in an attempt to prove or disprove alleged facts. Evidence includes the introduction of exhibits, records, documents, objects, etc., plus the testimony of witnesses, for the purpose of proving one's case. The jury or judge considers the evidence and decides in favor of one party or the other.

fact   Something that took place; an act; something actual and real; an incident that occurred; an event.

felony   A major crime, as distinguished from a minor one, or misdemeanor. Felonies include robberies, burglaries, felonious assault, murder, etc.

finding of fact   A conclusion reached by a court after due consideration; a determination of the truth after consideration of statements made by the opposing parties in a suit.

findings   The result of the deliberations of a court or jury; the decisions expressed by a judicial authority after consideration of all the facts.

grand jury   A group of citizens whose duties include inquiring into crimes in their area for the purpose of determining the probability of guilt of a party or parties. Should a grand jury conclude that there is a good probability of guilt, it will recommend an indictment of the suspects.

highest court   A court of last resort; a court whose decision is final and cannot be appealed because there is no higher court to consider the matter.

indictment   An accusation by a grand jury, made after thorough investigation, that someone should be tried for a crime. When an indictment is handed down, the accused must stand trial for the alleged offense, but the indictment in itself does not necessarily mean that the accused will be found guilty.

injunction   A restraining order issued by a judge that a person or persons can or cannot do a particular thing. . . . . Injunctions may be temporary or permanent.

interlocutory Temporary; not final or conclusive, as an interlocutory decree of divorce or an interlocutory judgment.

interrogatories A set of written questions presented to a witness in order to obtain his written testimony (deposition) while he is under oath to tell the truth. Interrogatories are part of the right of discovery that a party in a suit has of obtaining facts from his adversary. They often take place prior to the commencement of the trial.

judge A public official, appointed or elected, authorized to hear and often to decide cases brought before a court of law.

judicial Anything related to the administration of justice; anything that has to do with a court of justice.

jurisdiction The power and right to administer justice; the geographic area in which a judge or a court has the right to try and decide a case.

jury A specified number of men and/or women who are chosen and sworn to look into matters of fact and, therefore, to determine and render a decision upon the evidence presented to them.

justice The attempt by judicial means to be fair and to give each party his due, under the law.

law The rules, regulations, ordinances, and statutes, created by the legislative bodies of government, under which people are expected to live.

lawsuit A dispute between two or more parties brought into court for a solution; a suit; a cause; an action.

liability Legal responsibility; the obligation to do or not do something; an obligation to pay a debt; the responsibility to behave in a certain manner.

litigation A lawsuit; a legal action; a suit.

lower court A trial court, or one from which an appeal may be taken, as distinguished from a court from which no appeal can be taken.

malice Hatred; ill will; the intentional carrying out of a hurtful act without cause; hostility of one individual toward another.

negligence Failure to do what a reasonable, careful, conscientious person is expected to do; doing something that a reasonable, careful, conscientious person would not do. *Contributory negligence:* Negligence in which there has been a failure on the part of the plaintiff to exercise ordinary, proper care, thus contributing toward an accident. *Criminal negligence:* Negligence of such a nature that it is punishable as a crime. *Gross negligence:* Conscious disregard of one's duties, resulting in injury or damage to another. Gross negligence exists when an individual, by exercising ordinary good conduct, could have prevented injury or damage. *Ordinary negligence:* Negligence that could have been avoided if only one had exercised ordinary, reasonable, proper care. Ordinary negligence is not wishful or purposeful, but rather "unthinking." *Willful negligence:* Conscious, knowing neglect of duty, with knowledge that such conduct will result in injury or damage to another.

oath   A pledge to tell the truth; a sworn promise to perform a duty; a calling on God to witness a statement.

obligation   Something a person is bound to do or bound not to do; a moral or legal duty. Penalties may be imposed upon people who fail in their obligations.

ordinance   A local law; a law passed by a legislative body of a city or township or other local government; a statute; a rule.

party   1. A person engaged in a lawsuit, either a plaintiff or a defendant. 2. A person who has taken part in a transaction, such as a party to an agreement or contract.

petitioner   One who presents a petition [a written formal request for a particular thing to be done or a certain act to be carried out] to a court seeking relief in a controversial matter. The person against whom the petition is leveled is called a *respondent.*

plaintiff   The party who is bringing a lawsuit against a defendant; the person or persons who are suing.

prejudice, with   Indicates a matter has been settled without possibility of appeal.

proximate cause   The immediate cause of an injury or accident; the legal cause; the real cause; a direct cause. [A cause that directly produces an event and without which the event would not have occurred. [Black's]]

punitive damages   An award to a plaintiff beyond actual possible loss. Such damages are by way of punishing the defendant for his act.

question of fact   The question of truth, such question to be decided after hearing evidence from both sides in a case. It is the judge's or jury's function to decide questions of fact.

question of law   A matter for the courts to decide, based on interpretation of existing laws pertaining to the matter at hand.

reasonable man   Someone who acts with common sense and has the mental capacity of the average, normal, sensible human being, as distinguished from an emotionally unstable, erratic, compulsive individual. In determining whether negligence exists, the court will attempt to decide whether the defendant was a reasonable person.

rebuttal   The presentation of facts to a court demonstrating that testimony given by witnesses is not true.

reckless   Careless; indifferent to the outcome of one's actions; heedless; negligent; acting without due caution.

recovery   The award of money given by a court to the person or persons who win the lawsuit.

redress   The receiving of satisfaction for an injury one has sustained.

requisite   [Required; necessary.]

respondent   A person against whom an appeal is brought.

Restatement of Torts   [A codification of the common law relating to torts (private wrongs) compiled by legal practitioners and scholars; most jurisdictions accept the Restatement as the equivalent of law, even though states have often passed their own laws on matters covered by the Restatements. The first series of Restatements (Restatement First) was begun in 1923; the second (Restatement Second) was begun in 1953. Restatements have been written in many other areas of civil law, such as contracts, property, and trusts.]

restraining order   An order issued by the court without notice to the opposing party, usually granted temporarily to restrain him until the court decides whether an injunction should be ordered. In actuality, a restraining order is a form of an injunction.

reversal   The annulment or voiding of a court's judgment or decision. Such reversal usually results from a higher court overruling a lower court's action or decision.

review   1. To re-examine, consider. 2. The consideration by a higher (appellate) court of a decision made by a lower (inferior) court.

ruling   The outcome of a court's decision either on some point of law or on the case as a whole. [Black's]

statute   A law passed by the legislative branch of a government.

stipulation   An agreement between the opposing parties in a lawsuit in respect to some matter or matters that are connected to the suit. Such stipulations are made in order to avoid delays in the conducting of the trial. Many stipulations consist of the admission of facts to which both parties agree.

summary judgment   A means of obtaining the court's decision without resorting to a formal trial by jury. Such judgments are sought when the opposing parties are in agreement on the facts in the dispute but wish to obtain a ruling as to the question of law that is involved.

testimony   Evidence given under oath by a witness, as distinguished from evidence derived from written documents.

tort   A wrong committed by one person against another; a civil, not a criminal wrong; a wrong not arising out of a contract; a violation of a legal duty that one person has toward another. Every tort is composed of a legal obligation, a breach of that obligation, and damage as a result of the breach of the obligation. *Tort-feasor:* a wrongdoer.

tortious   Hurtful; harmful; wrongful; injurious; in the nature of a tort.

vacate   To cancel; to annul; to set aside.

verdict   The finding or decision of a jury, duly sworn and impaneled, after careful consideration, reported to and accepted by the court.

witness   1. An individual who testifies under oath at a trial, a hearing, or before a legislative body. 2. To see or hear something take place. 3. To be present, and often to sign, a legal document, such as a will or deed.

writ   A formal order of a court, ordering someone who is out of court to do something.

RESEARCH ACTIVITIES

LEGAL RESEARCH

Unless the institution you are attending has a law school, it will likely not have the resources you need to do genuine legal research, except at the secondary source level—i.e., general books and periodical articles dealing with legal matters. If you do not have access to a law school library, but are in or near a city that serves as the county seat, you may be able to use the law library at the county courthouse. The public does have access to these libraries, which should contain the basic tools you need to conduct research—legal encyclopedias and dictionaries; legal periodicals and indexes; style manuals; a set of state, regional, and federal case reporters; and state and federal statutes and codes. Ask a librarian for assistance in using these resources.

Many college libraries will have a set of Supreme Court decisions (in *United States Reports*), even if they do not have collections of state-level cases in regional or state case reporters such as the *Pacific Reporter* or the *California Reports*. Supreme Court cases also are available on the Web; see below. Thus, you should be able to conduct research on cases such as *Roe v. Wade*, 410 U.S. 113 (1973), which reached the Supreme Court. (This citation means volume 410 of *United States Reports*, beginning on page 113. To refer to a statement on a particular page, insert "at" before the page number; thus 410 U.S. at 125).

Legal research has been transformed by the computer revolution, and vast legal databases are now available online through LexisNexis and Westlaw. If you do not have special access to online sources, however, systematic legal research on the Internet is difficult. Some sites offer valuable resources, however. FindLaw <www.findlaw.com>, for example, provides links to various federal, state, and local statutes, as well as to a number of specialized sites on such issues as constitutional law and poverty/legal assistance. Some states have placed their statutes online: For example, you may find complete state penal and civil codes on the World Wide Web at <http://www.findlaw.com/casecode/state/html>.

The FindLaw site also provides a searchable database of all Supreme Court opinions since 1893. And FindLaw offers access to Federal Circuit Court cases and state codes and cases, though only for recent years. Searchability for these cases varies from state to state.

Supreme Court cases:

<http://www.findlaw.com/casecode/supreme.html>

Federal Circuit Court cases:

<http://www.findlaw.com/casecode/courts/index.html>

State codes and cases:

<http://www.findlaw.com/casecode/state.html>

Using an electronic legal database such as LexisNexis or Westlaw is similar to using any other database; you conduct a systematic search, using key terms. If you wanted to conduct research on tobacco cases, and particularly on the issue of the liability of tobacco manufacturers for deaths resulting from their products, your search terms would include the words "tobacco" and "manufacturer" and "death" and "liability" and the appropriate connectors ("and," "or," etc.). Following the search, the system provides citations to all cases, within the time and regional boundaries you specify, that include these terms. If your institution provides access to these legal databases, a librarian should be able to help you to track down relevant cases, statutes, case law, or analyses in legal periodicals.

Some excellent books that teach novice legal researchers how to find cases, statutes, and articles by topic include:

Cohen, Morris, Robert C. Berring, and Kent C. Olson. *How to Find the Law.* 9th ed. St. Paul, MN: Westlaw, 1989. (See also Berring's abridged version of this book, entitled *Finding the Law.*)

Jacobstein, J. Myron, Roy M. Mersky, and Donald J. Dunn. *Fundamentals of Legal Research.* 6th ed. Wesbury, NY: Foundation Press, 1994.

RESEARCH TOPICS

1. Select a particular legal issue dealt with in this chapter (for example, emotional distress or homicide) and research book and periodical indexes to find some interesting recent cases. Use an index to legal periodicals if your school library has one. Select one of these cases and report on its progress. Describe the facts of the case, identify the legal issues involved, describe and analyze the arguments on both sides, and discuss the case's outcome.

2. Using some of the Internet legal sites mentioned above, browse the Web until you find a topic that interests you (for example, tobacco lawsuits). Then, using the hyperlinks, research the topic as fully as you are able, online. (Remember to write down, electronically copy, or bookmark important URLs so that you can easily return to them.) Write a report *on the progress of your research,* rather than on the topic itself. Focus on what you were able to find using Web resources, and what you were unable to find. Explain your frustrations, as well as your high points of discovery. Indicate what other

information—whether available online or in print—you would need to find before being able to complete a report on the topic.

3. Visit the county courthouse (if one is nearby) and sit in for a period of time on one or more trials. Report on your observations. Describe what you have seen and analyze the various aspects of the case or cases: the prosecution and defense lawyers, the defendant, the witnesses, the judge, and the jury. What conclusions, from this limited observation, can you make about the legal process? What recommendations would you make to better achieve justice—or, at least, a higher standard of fairness or efficiency?

4. Research the legal system in a country other than the United States. Based upon your own experience or knowledge and upon what you have learned in this chapter, how does the process of criminal or civil cases in this other country compare to that in the United States? Which aspects of the other country's legal system appear superior to those of the United States? Which seem inferior? In your discussion refer to specific cases tried in the other country's legal system. You may choose to focus partially on offenses (such as criticizing the government) that are not crimes in the United States but are in some other countries; however, focus primarily upon the ways that the other country's legal system *works*.

5. Many feature films focus on courtroom drama and other legal matters. Examples are: *Young Mr. Lincoln* (1939), *Adam's Rib* (1949), *The Caine Mutiny* (1954), *12 Angry Men* (1957), *Witness for the Prosecution* (1957), *Anatomy of a Murder* (1961), *Inherit the Wind* (1960), *Judgment at Nuremberg* (1961), *To Kill a Mockingbird* (1962), *The Paper Chase* (1973), *The Verdict* (1982), *True Believer* (1989), *Class Action* (1991), *A Few Good Men* (1992), *Ghosts of Mississippi* (1996), and *A Civil Action* (1998).

View one or more of these films, and then report on and draw conclusions from your observations. Using inductive reasoning, *infer* points of law and rules of courtroom procedure from what you see. Point out similarities and differences, where appropriate. For example, *The Caine Mutiny* deals (partially) with a court-martial, where the rules of procedure are somewhat different from those in civilian courts. *Judgment at Nuremberg* deals with war crimes tribunals in postwar Germany. *12 Angry Men* deals with jury room deliberations, rather than with the trial itself. *The Paper Chase* deals with a tyrannical law professor attacking the "skullsful of mush" in his students' heads and goading them to "think like a lawyer!"

Credits

CHAPTER 1

Page 8: "The Future of Love: Kiss Romance Goodbye, It's Time for the Real Thing" by Barbara Graham, *UTNE Reader*, November/December 1996. Reprinted by permission of the author. **Page 23:** Reprinted with permission of Simon & Schuster Adult Publishing Group and Gillon Aitken Associates, Ltd., from *In Patagonia* by Bruce Chatwin. Copyright © 1977 by Bruce Chatwin. **Pages 29–32:** "Choosing a Mate in Television Dating Games: The Influence of Setting, Culture, and Gender," Figures 1.1, 1.2, 1.3, Table 1.1 by Amir Hetsroni, from *Sex Roles: A Journal of Research*, January 2000, vol. 42, p. 1, pp. 90–97, published by Springer Netherlands. Reprinted with kind permission from Springer Science and Business Media and the author. **Page 32:** Figure 1, p. 511 from "The (Un)Acceptability of Betrayal: A Study of College Students' Evaluations of Sexual Betrayal by a Romantic Partner and Betrayal of a Friend's Confidence" by S. Shirley Feldman et al., from *Journal of Youth and Adolescence,* 2000, 29:4, published by Springer. Netherlands. Reprinted with kind permission from Springer Science and Business Media and the author. **Page 34:** From "In Vitro Fertilization: From Medical Reproduction to Genetic Diagnosis" by Dietmar Mieth, *Biomedical Ethics: Newsletter of the European Network for Biomedical Ethics 1.1* (1996): 45. Copyright © 1996 by Dietmar Mieth. Reprinted by permission of the author.

CHAPTER 2

Page 54: "We Are Not Created Equal in Every Way" by Joan Ryan from *San Francisco Chronicle*, December 12, 2000. Copyright © 2000 by *San Francisco Chronicle*. Reproduced with permission of *San Francisco Chronicle* via Copyright Clearance Center, Inc.

CHAPTER 3

Page 94: "Scenario for Scandal" by Mark Naison, *Commonweal* (January 2004). Copyright © 2004 Commonweal Foundation. Reprinted by permission.

CHAPTER 4

Page 102: Excerpts from "Private Gets 3 Years for Iraq Prison Abuse" by David S. Cloud, *The New York Times*, September 28, 2005. Copyright © 2005 by The New York Times Co. Reprinted with permission. **Page 103:** Excerpt from "Military Abuse," Globe Editorial, published in *The Boston Globe*, September 28, 2005. Copyright © 2005 by The New York Times Co. Reprinted with permission. **Page 109:** From "The Fuel Subsidy We Need" by Ricardo Bayon. Copyright © 2003 Ricardo Bayon, as first published in *The Atlantic Monthly*. Reprinted by permission of the author. **Page 110:** "Putting the Hindenburg to Rest," by Jim Motavalli, *The New York Times*, June 5, 2005. Copyright © 2005 The New York Times Company. Reprinted with permission. **Page 112:** "Using Fossil Fuels in Energy Process Gets Us Nowhere," *Los Angeles Times*, Nov. 9, 2003 by Jeremy Rifkin, author of *The Hydrogen Economy: The Creation of the World Wide Energy Web and the Redistribution of Power on Earth* (Tarcher/Putnam). Reprinted by permission of the author. **Page 114:** "Lots of Hot Air About Hydrogen" by Joseph J. Romm, originally published in *Los Angeles Times*, March 28, 2004. Reprinted by permission of the author. **Page 139:** From The World Fuel Cell Council e.V. (www.fuelcellworld.org). Reprinted by permission of David Lockie, Fuel Cell Markets Ltd. on behalf of Patrick Trezona, World Fuel Cell Council e.V.

CHAPTER 5

Page 154: "A New Start for National Service" by John McCain and Evan Bayh, *The New York Times*, November 6, 2001. Copyright © 2001 by The New York Times Company. Reprinted by permission. **Page 156:** From "Calls for National Service" by Roger Landrum, from *National Service: Social, Economic, and Military Impacts,* edited by Michael W. Sherraden and Donald J. Eberly (Pergamon Press, 1982). Reprinted by permission of the author. **Page 157:** "Politics and National Service: A Virus Attacks the Volunteer Sector" by Bruce Chapman. Reprinted from *National Service: Pro and Con,* edited by Williamson M. Evers with the permission of the publisher, Hoover Institution Press. Copyright 1990 by the Board of Trustees of the Leland Stanford Junior University.

CHAPTER 6

Page 192: From *The Plug-In Drug, Revised and Updated—25th Anniversary Edition* by Marie Winn, copyright © 1977, 1985, 2002 by Marie Winn Miller. Used by permission of Viking Penguin, a division of Penguin Group (USA) Inc. **Page 194:** "The Coming Apart of a Dorm Society" by Edward Peselman. Reprinted by permission of the author.

CHAPTER 7

Page 217: From "The Curse of Nepotism," published in *The Economist*, January 8, 2004. Copyright © 2004 The Economist Newspaper Ltd. All rights reserved. Reprinted with permission. Further reproduction prohibited. www. economist.com. **Page 218:** "May the Best Man or Woman Win," by Miriam Schulman from *Issues in Ethics*, Vol. 7, No. 3, Fall 1996. Reprinted by permission of the Markkula Center for Applied Ethics at Santa Clara University. **Page 220:** Excerpt from "Legacy Admissions are Defensible Because the Process Can't be 'Fair' " by Debra J. Thomas and Terry Shepard, *Chronicle of Higher Education*, Vol. 49, No. 27, March 14, 2003. Copyright © 2003 by Debra Thomas and Terry Shepard. Reprinted by permission of the authors. **Page 224:** "Time to Bury the Legacy" by Robert DeKoven, originally published in *The San Diego Union-Tribune*, February 12, 2003. Reprinted by permission of the author. **Page 226:** From "Legacies in Black and White: The Racial Composition of the Legacy Pool," by Cameron Howell and Sarah E. Turner, from *Research In Higher Education*, Vol. 45, No. 4, June 2004, published by Springer Netherlands. Reprinted with kind permission from Springer Science and Business Media and the authors. **Page 228:** From "The Social Logic of Ivy League Admissions" by Malcolm Gladwell, originally published in *The New Yorker*, October 10, 2005. Reprinted by permission of the author. **Page 229:** Excerpt from "So Your Dad Went to Harvard: Now What About the Lower Board Scores of White Legacies?" by Mark Megalli from *The Journal of Blacks in Higher Education*, Spring, 1995. Reprinted by permission of *The Journal of Blacks in Higher Education*. **Page 232:** "Preserve Universities' Right to Shape Student Community ('Our View')" from *USA Today*, January 26, 2004. Reprinted with permission. **Page 233:** From *Admissions Confidential* by Rachel Toor, copyright © 2001 by Rachel Toor, and reprinted by permission of St. Martin's Press, LLC. **Page 235:** Pages 182–183, 186–187, 190–191, 193, from *American Business Values, 3rd Edition*, by Gerald Cavanagh, S.J., © 1990. Reprinted by permission of Pearson Education, Inc., Upper Saddle River, NJ.

CHAPTER 8

Page 244: "The Satisfactions of Housewifery and Motherhood in an Age of 'Do-Your-Own-Thing' " by Terry Martin Hekker, originally published in *The New York Times*, Dec. 20, 1977. Reprinted by permission of the author. **Page 246:** "Modern Love: Paradise Lost (Domestic Division)," by Terry Martin Hekker, *The New York Times*, January 1, 2006. Copyright © 2006 The New York Times Company. Reprinted with permission. **Page 250:** "The Radical Idea of Marrying for Love," "From Yoke Mates to Soul Mates," from *Marriage, A History* by Stephanie Coontz, copyright © 2005 by the S.J. Coontz Company. Used by permission of Viking Penguin, a division of Penguin Group (USA) Inc. **Page 263:** Excerpts from "The State of Our Unions: The Social Health of Marriage in America," by David Popenoe and Barbara Dafoe Whitehead, reprinted with permission from *USA Today Magazine*, July 2002. Copyright © 2002 by the Society for the Advancement of Education, Inc. All rights reserved; Excerpts from "The State of Our Unions: The Social Health of Marriage in America - 2005," by David Popenoe and Barbara Dafoe Whitehead, reprinted by permission of the National Marriage Project, Rutgers University. **Page 276:** Pages 8–13 from *Marriages and Families: Diversity and Change, 3rd Edition*, by Mary Ann Schwartz and Barbara Marliene Scott, © 2000. Reprinted by permission of Pearson Education, Inc., Upper Saddle River, NJ. **Page 282:** From *Virtually Normal* by Andrew Sullivan, copyright © 1995 by Andrew Sullivan. Used by permission of Alfred A. Knopf, a division of Random House, Inc. **Page 287:** "…But Not a Very Good Idea, Either" by William J. Bennett, published in *The Washington Post*, May 21, 1996. Reprinted by permission of the author. **Page 290:** "Many Women at Elite Colleges Set Career Path to Motherhood" by Louise Story, *The New York Times*, September 20, 2005. Copyright © 2005 The New York Times Company. Reprinted with permission. **Page 296:** "What Yale Women Want, and Why it is Misguided" by Karen Stabiner, from the *Los Angeles Times*, September 24, 2005. Reprinted by permission of the author. **Page 298:** "Work vs. Family, Complicated by Race" by Lynette Clemetson, *The New York Times*, February 9, 2006. Copyright © 2006 The New York Times Company. Reprinted with permission. **Page 303:** "A Marriage Agreement" by Alix Kates Shulman, first published in 1969 in *Up From Under*, and later reprinted in *Life Magazine*, *Redbook*, and other publications. Copyright © 1969, 1970, 1971 by Alix Kates Shulman. Reprinted by permission of the author. **Page 309:** "How Serfdom Saved the Women's Movement" by

CHAPTER 9

CHAPTER 10

CHAPTER 11

Page 503: From *Counting Sheep* by Paul Martin. Copyright © 2004 by Paul Martin and reprinted by permission of St. Martin's Press, LLC. **Page 512:** Excerpted from the Harvard Health Publications Special Report, "Improving Sleep," © 2005, President and Fellows of Harvard College. For more information visit: www.health.harvard.edu. Harvard Health Publications does not endorse any products or medical procedures. Reprinted by permission. **Page 521:** "America's Sleep Deprived Teens Nodding Off at School, Behind the Wheel, New National Sleep Foundation Poll Finds," press release from March 28, 2006, from the National Sleep Foundation. Used with permission of the National Sleep Foundation. For further information, please visit http://www.sleepfoundation.org. **Page 524:** "Tips for Teens" from *Adolescent Sleep Needs and Patterns: Research Report and Resource Guide*, National Sleep Foundation, 2000. Used with permission of the National Sleep Foundation. **Page 527:** From "When Worlds Collide: Adolescent Need for Sleep Versus Societal Demands" by Mary A. Carskadon, from *Adolescent Sleep Needs and School Starting Times* ed. by Kyla L. Wahlstrom, published by Phi Delta Kappa Educational Foundation, 1999. Reprinted by permission of the author. **Page 537:** From *The Promise of Sleep* by William C. Dement, copyright © 1999 by William C. Dement. Used by permission of Dell Publishing, a division of Random House, Inc. **Page 545:** "Appendix: Pittsburgh Sleep Quality Index (PSQI)" from "The Pittsburgh Sleep Quality Index: A New Instrument for Psychiatric Practice and Research" by Daniel J. Buysse, Charles F. Reynolds III, Timothy H. Monk, Susan R. Berman, and David J. Kupfer, from *Psychiatry Research*, Vol. 28, No.2, May 1989. Reprinted by permission of Daniel Buysse. **Page 551:** "How Sleep Deprivation Affects Psychological Variables Related to College Students' Cognitive Performance" by June J. Pilcher and Amy S. Walters, from *Journal of American College Health*, Vol. 46, issue 3, November, 1997, pp. 121–126. Reprinted with permission of the Helen Dwight Reid Educational Foundation. Published by Heldref Publications, 1319 Eighteenth St., NW, Washington, DC 20036-1802. Copyright © 1997. **Page 561:** Excerpts from "Starting Time and School Life" by Patricia K. Kubow, Kyla L. Wahlstrom, and Amy Bemis, *Phi Delta Kappan*, Vol. 80, Issue 5, January 1999. Reprinted by permission of Patricia Kubow. **Page 569:** "Sleep Deprivation Driving Drug Use and Cost: New Research Finds Increased Use of Prescription Sleeping Aids," from a news release, October 17, 2005, from Medco Health Solutions, Inc. Reprinted by permission of Medco Health Solutions, Inc. **Page 573:** "Are Your Kids Little Addicts?" by Kim Painter, *USA Today*, Nov. 13, 2005. Reprinted with permission. **Page 575:** "Doctors Ponder Drugs for Sleepless Nights of Adolescence" by Mary Duenwald, *The New York Times*, November 15, 2005. Copyright © 2005 The New York Times Company. Reprinted with permission. **Page 577:** "Kids Using Sleeping Pills" by Rebecca Goldin and Grace Harris, from Statistical Assessment Service (STATS) at George Mason University, posted Nov. 20, 2005. Reprinted by permission.

CHAPTER 12

Page 586: "The Universality of the Folktale" from *The Folktale* by Stith Thompson. Copyright 1946 by Henry Holt and Company. Reprinted by permission of Henry Holt and Company, LLC. **Page 591:** "Cinderella" from *Fairy Tales* by Charles Perrault, translated by Geoffrey Brereton (Penguin Books, 1957). Translation copyright © 1957 by Geoffrey Brereton. Reprinted with permission of the Geoffrey Brereton Estate. **Page 595:** From *Grimm's Tales for Young and Old* by Jakob and Wilhelm Grimm, translated by Ralph Manheim, copyright © 1977 by Ralph Manheim. Used by permission of Random House Children's Books, a division of Random House, Inc. **Page 600:** "The Cat Cinderella" from *The Pentamerone of Giambattista Basile*, translated from the Italian of Benedetto Croce, edited and with preface, notes and appendices by N.M. Penzer, published by John Lane, The Bodley Head Ltd., London, 1932. *Note:* Introduction to "The Cat Cinderella" was written by Alan Dundes. **Page 604:** "The Chinese Cinderella Story" by Tuan Cheng-Shih, translated by Arthur Waley, from *Folklore*, vol. 58 (1947). Reprinted by permission of Taylor & Francis Ltd., http://www.tandf.co.uk/journals. **Page 606:** "The Maiden, the Frog, and the Chief's Son" from "Cinderella in Africa" by William Bascom, from *Cinderella: A Folklore Casebook*, edited by Alan Dundes, copyright © 1982 Alan Dundes. Originally published in the *Journal of the Folklore Institute*, 9 (1972), pp. 54–70. Reproduced by permission of Routledge/Taylor & Francis Group, LLC. **Page 610:** "The Algonquin Cinderella" from *World Tales: The Extraordinary Coincidence of Stories Told in All Times, in All Places* by Idries Shah, copyright © 1979 by Technographia, S. A. and Harcourt, Inc. Reprinted by permission of Harcourt, Inc. **Page 617:** Textual excerpts from Walt Disney's *Cinderella* as adapted by Campbell Grant. © Disney Enterprises, Inc. Reprinted by permission of Disney Publishing Worldwide. **Page 619:** "Cinderella," from *Transformations* by Anne Sexton. Copyright © 1971 by Anne Sexton. Reprinted by permission of Houghton Mifflin Company. All rights reserved. **Page 622:** "For Whom the

Index of Authors and Titles

APA In-text Citations in Brief

If you do not mention the author's name in your sentence, provide it and the relevant page numbers in parentheses.

> A good deal of research shows that rather than inducing any lasting changes in a child's behavior, punishment "promotes only momentary compliance" (Berk, 2002, p. 383).

If you mention the author's name and the year of publication in your sentence, omit them from the parenthetical citation.

> According to Berk (2002), a good deal of research shows that rather than inducing any lasting changes in a child's behavior, punishment "promotes only momentary compliance" (p. 383).

Provide page numbers only for direct quotations, not for summaries or paraphrases. If you are not referring to a specific page, simply indicate the date.

> Berk (2002) asserted that many researchers view punishment as a quick fix, not a long-term solution to children's behavior problems.

APA References List in Brief

At the end of the paper, on a separate page titled "References" (no italics or quotation marks), alphabetize sources you have referred to, providing full bibliographic information for each. These are the most common entry types:

Book

Basic entry

> Fahs, A. (2003). *The imagined civil war: Popular literature of the north and south, 1861–1865.* Chapel Hill: University of North Carolina Press.

Selection from an edited book

> Halberstam, D. (2002). Who we are. In S. J. Gould (Ed.), *The best American essays 2002* (pp. 124–136). New York: Houghton Mifflin.

Later edition

Whitten, P. (2001). *Anthropology: Contemporary perspectives* (8th ed.). Boston: Allyn & Bacon.

Article from a Magazine

Davison, P. (2000, May). Girl, seeming to disappear. *Atlantic Monthly,* 108–111.

Article from a Journal Paginated Continuously Through the Annual Volume

Tomlins, C. L. (2003). In a wilderness of tigers: Violence, the discourse of English colonizing, and the refusals of American history. *Theoretical Inquiries in Law, 4,* 505–543.

Article from a Journal Paginated by Issue

O'Mealy, J. H. (1999). Royal family values: The Americanization of Alan Bennett's *The Madness of King George III. Literature/Film Quarterly, 27*(2), 90–97.

Article from a Newspaper

Vise, D. A. (2000, September 6). FBI report gauges school violence indicators. *The Washington Post,* pp. B1, B6.

Article from the Internet

Sheehan, K. B., & Hoy, M. G. (1999). Using e-mail to survey Internet users in the United States: Methodology and assessment. *Journal of Computer-Mediated Communication, 4*(3). Retrieved August 14, 2001, from http://www.ascusc.org/jcmc/vol4/issue3/ sheehan.html

QUICK INDEX: MLA DOCUMENTATION BASICS

MLA In-text Citations in Brief

In your paper, give in-text citations as follows. If you do not mention the author's name in the sentence, provide it, with the relevant page numbers, in parentheses:

> From the beginning, the AIDS antibody test has been "mired in controversy" (Bayer 101).

If you mention the author's name in the sentence, omit it from the citation in parentheses:

> According to Bayer, from the beginning, the AIDS antibody test has been "mired in controversy" (101).

MLA Works Cited List in Brief

At the end of the paper, on a separate page titled "Works Cited," alphabetize the sources you have referred to, providing full bibliographic information for each. These are the most common entry types:

Book

Basic entry

> Fahs, Alice. The Imagined Civil War: Popular Literature of the North and South, 1861—1865. Chapel Hill: U of North Carolina, P, 2003.

Selection from an edited book

> Hardy, Melissa. "The Heifer." The Best American Short Stories 2002. Ed. Sue Miller. Boston: Houghton, 2002. 97—115.

Later edition

> Whitten, Phillip. Anthropology: Contemporary Perspectives. 8th ed. Boston: Allyn, 2001.

Article from a Magazine

    Davison, Peter. "Girl, Seeming to Disappear."
        Atlantic Monthly May 2000: 108–11.

Article from a Periodical Paginated Continuously Through the Annual Volume

    Haan, Sarah C. "The 'Persuasion Route' of the
        Law: Advertising and Legal Persuasion."
        Columbia Law Review 100 (2000): 1281–1326.

Article from a Periodical Paginated by Issue

    O'Mealy, Joseph H. "Royal Family Values: The
        Americanization of Alan Bennett's The
        Madness of King George III." Literature/Film
        Quarterly 27.2 (1999): 90–97.

Article from a Newspaper

    Vise, David A. "FBI Report Gauges School Violence
        Indicators." Washington Post 6 Sept. 2000:
        B1+.

Article from the Internet

    Epstein, Paul. "The Imitation of Athena in the
        Lysistrata of Aristophanes." Animus 7
        (2002). 16 July 2003. 8 Aug. 2004
        <http://www.swgc.mun.ca/animus/
        current/epstein7.htm>.

CHECKLIST FOR WRITING SUMMARIES

- **Read the passage carefully.** Determine its structure. Identify the author's purpose in writing.
- **Reread.** *Label* each section or stage of thought. *Highlight* key ideas and terms.
- **Write one-sentence summaries** of each stage of thought.
- **Write a thesis:** a one- or two-sentence summary of the entire passage.
- **Write the first draft** of your summary.
- **Check your summary** against the original passage.
- **Revise** your summary.

CHECKLIST FOR WRITING CRITIQUES

- **Introduce** both the passage being critiqued and the author.
- **Summarize** the author's main points, making sure to state the author's purpose for writing.
- **Evaluate** the validity of the presentation.
- **Respond** to the presentation: agree and/or disagree.
- **Conclude** with your overall assessment.